KU-068-310

Contents

Food and drink
colour section
following p.264

Outdoor adventure
colour section
following p.536

◄◄ Cappadocia ◄ Temple of Apollo, Side

Introduction to

Turkey

With its unique mix of the exotic and the familiar, visiting Turkey can be a mesmerizing experience. More than the "bridge between East and West" of tourist-brochure cliché, the country combines influences from the Middle East and the Mediterranean, the Balkans and central Asia. Invaded and settled from every direction since the start of recorded history, its contradictions and fascinations persist. Mosques coexist with churches, Roman theatres and temples crumble not far from ancient Hittite cities and dervish ceremonies or gypsy festivals are as much a part of the social landscape as classical music concerts or avidly attended football matches.

Another facet of Turkey that makes it such a rewarding place to travel is the **Turkish people**, whose reputation for friendliness and hospitality is richly deserved; indeed you risk causing offence by declining invitations and find yourself making friends through the simplest of transactions. Of course at the big resorts and tourist spots this can simply be the pretext to selling you something, but in most of the country the warmth and generosity is genuine – all the more amazing when much recent Turkish history saw outsiders mainly bringing trouble in their wake.

Politically modern Turkey was a grand experiment, largely the creation of one man – **Kemal Atatürk**. Endowed with fervent patriotism and superhuman

The **Rough Guide** to

Turkey

written and researched by

Marc Dubin and Terry Richardson

with additional contributions from
**Katie Parla, Tristan Rutherford,
Kathryn Tomasetti and Martin Zatko**

ROUGH
GUIDES

www.roughguides.com

energy he salvaged the Turkish state from the wreckage of the Ottoman Empire and defined it as a modern, secular nation – his statue gazes down from public squares across the land. While the country's secular status remains intact for now, most of the inhabitants are at least nominally **Muslim** and Turkey's heritage as home to the caliphate and numerous dervish orders, plus contemporary Islamist movements, still often deflects its moral compass south and east rather than northwest.

In spite of official efforts to enforce a uniform Turkish identity, the population is remarkably heterogeneous. When the Ottoman Empire imploded, large numbers of Muslim Slavs, Kurds, Greeks, Albanians, Crimean Tatars, Azeris, Daghestanlis, Abkhazians and Circassians – to name only the most numerous non-Turkic groups

▶ Sunrise in İstanbul

Fact file

• Turkey's **total area** is a vast 814,578 sq km (97 percent in Asia, 3 percent in Europe). A 8333-kilometre **coastline** is lapped by four seas: the Mediterranean, the Aegean, the Marmara and the Black Sea. Numerous **peaks** exceed 3000m, the highest being 5165-metre Ararat (Ağrı Dağı). Largest of many **lakes** is Lake Van (3713 sq km) in the far southeast. The three longest **rivers** wholly in Turkey – the Kızılırmak, Yeşilırmak and Sakarya – flow into the Black Sea.

• The **population** of over 70 million is 98 percent Muslim (Sunni or Alevî), with dwindling **religious minorities** of the Armenian Apostolic or Catholic, Greek Orthodox, Syrian Orthodox and Jewish faiths. Besides standard Turkish, two dialects of Kurdish are widely spoken; other **languages** heard include Arabic, Laz, Circassian, Albanian, Macedonian, Bulgarian, Romany and Greek. Well over half the inhabitants live in **cities**; the four largest are İstanbul, Ankara (the capital), İzmir and Adana.

• Since 1922 Turkey has been a **republic**. The single-chamber **Grand National Assembly** (Büyük Meclis) in Ankara has 550 seats, and the **president** is elected by this parliament. Both, however, are answerable to a **National Security Council** dominated by elements of the armed forces.

• Since 1950 the Turkish **economy** has often been in crisis, with inflation devaluing the currency. The most important foreign-exchange earners are tourism, clothing and food.

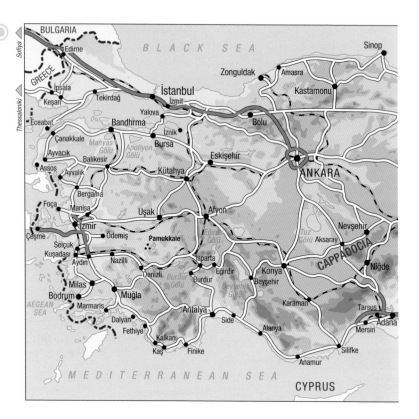

– streamed into Anatolia, the safest refuge in an age of anti-Ottoman nationalism. This process has continued in recent years from formerly Soviet or Eastern Bloc territories, so that the **diversity** endures, constituting one of the surprises of travel in Turkey. Another obvious aspect is the **youthfulness** of the country: more than half the population is under 30, something borne out in the legions of young people working in coastal resorts, and

▼ Fairy chimneys, Cappadocia

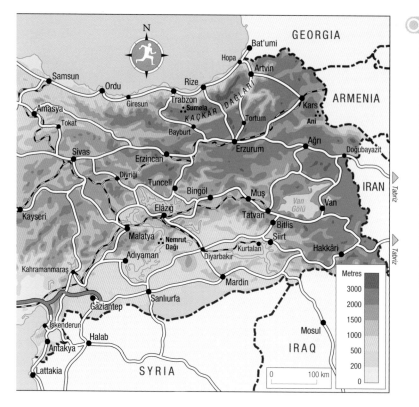

the shoals of school kids surging through city streets. This brings with it a palpable dynamism but also its fair share of problems, not least high youth unemployment and disparate educational opportunities.

In terms of physical attractions, a huge part of Turkey's appeal lies in its **archeological sites**, a legacy of the bewildering succession of states – Hittite, Urartian, Phrygian, Hellenistic, Roman, Byzantine, Armeno-Georgian – that held sway here before the twelfth century. From grand Classical cities to hilltop fortresses and remote churches, some still produce exciting new finds today. There is also, of course, a vast number of graceful **Islamic monuments** dating from the eleventh century onwards, as well as intriguing city **bazaars**, still hanging on despite the new wave of chain stores and shopping malls. Modern architecture is less pleasing – an ugliness manifest at most **coastal resorts**, where it can be hard to find a beach that matches the tourist-board hype. Indeed it's **inland** Turkey – Asiatic expanses of mountain, steppe, lake, even cloud-forest – that may leave a more vivid memory, especially when accented by some crumbling *kervansaray*, mosque or castle.

7

Turkish identify: east or west?

Turkey is keen to be accepted on equal terms by the West. Long the only NATO member in the Middle East and uniquely among Muslim countries on good terms with Israel, it is a major recipient of US military aid. Since late 2005 Turkey has also been a candidate for **EU membership**, the potential culmination of a modernization process begun during the nineteenth century.

Yet staggering disparities in development and income levels persist, one of several issues worrying potential EU partners. İstanbul boasts clubs as expensive and exclusive as any in New York or London, while town-centre shops across western Anatolia are full of imported luxury goods, but in much of the chronically underdeveloped eastern interior, standards and modes of living have scarcely changed from a century ago. It's still debatable whether Westernization has struck deep roots in Turkish culture, or rather extends no further than a mobile-phone- and credit-card-equipped urban elite.

Where to go

Western Turkey is both the more economically developed and far more visited part of the country. **İstanbul**, straddling the straits linking the Black and Marmara seas, is touted as Turkish mystique par excellence, and understandably so: it would take weeks to even scratch the surface of the old imperial capital, still the country's cultural and commercial hub. Flanking it on opposite sides of the Sea of Marmara are the two prior seats of the Ottoman Empire, **Bursa** and **Edirne**, each with their monumental attractions and regal atmosphere. Beyond the Dardanelles and its World War I battlefield cemeteries lie Turkey's two **Aegean islands**, Gökçeada and Bozcaada, popular for their excellent beaches, lingering Greek-ethnic identity and (except in midsummer) tranquillity.

Further south, the Classical character of the **North Aegean** is epitomized by olive-swathed landscapes around Bergama and Ayvalık, the region's star attractions. The old Ottoman princely training-ground of Manisa and ancient Sardis at the foot of Bozdağ also make a fine pair, although İzmir is merely the functional introduction to the **Central and Southern Aegean**, a magnet for travellers since the eighteenth century. Celebrated Ephesus overshadows in visitors' imaginations the equally deserving ancient Ionian sites of Priene and Didyma, or the intriguing ruins of Aphrodisias and Labranda in old Caria. Don't overlook evocative hill towns like Şirince or Birgi, still existing in something of an Ottoman time-warp. Also inland are tranquil, islet-dotted Bafa Gölü, the architectural showcase town of Muğla and the circus-like but compelling geological oddity of Pamukkale, its travertine formations abutting Roman Hierapolis. Be warned that the coast itself is heavily developed, though its star resorts – of which Datça is perhaps the quietest and Bodrum the most characterful – make comfortable bases.

Beyond the huge natural harbour at Marmaris, the Aegean gradually becomes the Mediterranean, the shore increasingly convoluted and piney. Coastal cruises are popular and easily arranged in brazen Marmaris or more manageable Fethiye, principal town of the **Turquoise Coast**. Two of Turkey's finest beaches sprawl at Dalyan and Patara, near the eerie tombs of the Lycians, the fiercely independent locals of old. Further east, Kaş and Kalkan are busy resorts, good for resting up between explorations of the mountainous hinterland. Beyond relatively untouched Çıralı beach, at ancient Olympos, sprawling Antalya is Turkey's fastest-growing city, at the beginning of the **Mediterranean Coast** proper. This is graced by extensive sands and archeological sites – most notably Perge, Side and Aspendos – though its western parts get swamped in season. Once past castle-topped Alanya, however, tourist numbers diminish, and numerous points of interest between Silifke and Adana include Roman Uzuncaburç plus the romantic offshore fortress at Kızkalesi. Further east, Arab-influenced Antakya is the heart of the **Hatay**, culturally part of Syria.

▶ Outdoor eating, İstanbul

Storks

Between April and September, storks are a common sight across Turkey, which forms a stopover between the birds' winter quarters in Africa and their summer habitat in the Balkans and central Europe. The clattering of the birds' beaks is an equally common sound. Storks mate for life, and the breeding pairs – of which around 30,000 are believed to visit Turkey – often return to the same nest year after year to raise new chicks. They are considered lucky in both Christian and Islamic belief, and rarely harmed, being dubbed "pilgrim birds" in Turkish; some municipalities even go so far as to build special platforms to augment the stork's favourite nesting perches which range from chimneys and minarets to utility poles.

Inland in **South Central Anatolia**, the rock-hewn churches, subterranean cities and tuff-pinnacle landscapes of Cappadocia await you. The dry, salubrious climate, excellent local wine, artistic and architectural treasures, plus horse-riding or hot-air ballooning opportunities could occupy you for ten days, including a stop in Kayseri – with its bazaar and tombs – on the way north. En route to or from the coast, you might also pause at historic Eğirdir or Beyşehir – fronting two of the numerous lakes that spangle the region – or in Konya, renowned for both its Selçuk architecture and associations with the Mevlevî dervishes.

Ankara, Turkey's capital, is a planned city whose contrived Western feel gives concrete (in all senses) indication of the priorities of the Turkish Republic; it also features the outstanding Museum of Anatolian Civilizations. Highlights of surrounding **North Central Anatolia** include the bizarre, isolated temple of Aezani, near Kütahya; the Ottoman museum-town of Safranbolu; exquisitely decorated early Turkish monuments in Divriği; and remarkable Hittite sites at Hattuşaş and Alacahöyük. If you're travelling north to the Black Sea, pause in the Yeşilırmak valley towns of Sivas, Tokat and Amasya, each with its quota of early Turkish monuments. The **Black Sea** shore itself is surprisingly devoid of architectural interest other than a chain of Byzantine-Genoese castles, but the lush landscape goes some way to compensate. The oldest, most interesting towns are Sinop, the northernmost point of Anatolia, and Amasra, the latter easily reached from Safranbolu. East of Sinop, a four-lane highway brings you to fabled Trabzon, once the seat of a Byzantine sub-empire and today convenient for Aya Sofya and Sumela monasteries.

The Ankara–Sivas route poises you for the trip along the Euphrates River into the "back half" of Turkey. First stop in **Northeastern Anatolia** is likely to be Erzurum, highest and bleakest major city of Turkey, from where you can head on to visit the temperate, church-studded valleys of southern medieval Georgia or go trekking in the Kaçkar mountains – Turkey's most popular hiking area – walling off the area from the Black Sea. Kars is mainly visited for the sake of nearby Ani, the ruined medieval Armenian capital, and various other Armenian monuments in the area – though many of these require some resourcefulness to seek out.

South of here, the **Euphrates and Tigris Basin** have a real Middle Eastern flavour in all senses. Booming Gaziantep, the region's gateway, offers a world-class collection of Roman mosaics, an atmospheric old quarter and Turkey's spiciest cuisine. Further east, biblical Urfa is distinguished by its colourful bazaar and sacred pool, while cosmopolitan, hilltop Mardin overlooks the vast Mesopotamian Plain. The major local attraction, however, living up to its tourist-poster hype, is a dawn or sunset trip to Nemrut Dağı's colossal ancient statues. Between Mardin and Nemrut Dağı, teeming, ethnically Kurdish Diyarbakır nestles inside medieval basalt walls. The terrain becomes increasingly mountainous as you head towards the Iranian frontier, an area dominated by the unearthly blue, alkaline expanse of **Lake Van**. Urartian, Selçuk and Armenian monuments abound within sight of the water, in particular the exquisite, restored Armenian church on picturesque Akdamar

▲ Lycian ruins, Kekova

islet. The east-shore city of Van is notable for its massive camel-shaped rock punctured with ancient tombs. Beyond Van looms the fairy-tale Kurdish castle of Hoşap, while just outside of Doğubeyazit, another isolated folly, the İşak Paşa Sarayı, stands at the very end of Turkey.

When to go

Among coastal areas, **İstanbul** and the **Sea of Marmara** shores have a relatively damp, Balkan climate, with muggy summers and cool, rainy (though seldom snowy) winters. These areas get crowded between late June and early September. Also busy in summer are the popular **Aegean and Mediterranean coasts** which can be uncomfortably hot during July and August, especially between İzmir and Antakya, where the heat is tempered only slightly by offshore breezes. Perhaps the best time to visit these regions is spring or autumn, when the weather is gentler and the crowds thinner. Late October and early November feature the **pastırma yazı** or "Indian summer", an idyllic time here. Indeed, even during winter, the Turquoise and Mediterranean coasts are – except for rainy periods in January and February – still fairly pleasant, and beyond Alanya up to the Hatay, winters can be positively balmy, though you may not be able to brave the water. The **Black Sea** is something of an anomaly, with exceptionally mild winters for so far north, and rain likely during the nine coolest months of the year, lingering as mist and subtropical humidity during summer.

Cut off from the coast by mountains, **Central Anatolia** is mostly semi-arid steppe, with a bracing climate – warm but not unpleasant in summer, cool and

▲ Mount Barla, Central Anatolia

Camels

Most **camels** in Turkey are simply tourist attractions, used for pleasure rides or as photographic props in places like Pamukkale and Side. It wasn't always so, however. Camel caravans once crisscrossed most of Anatolia, transporting gemstones, spices and woven finery. Before the Balkan Wars of 1912–13, they extended northwest as far as Bosnia, beyond which the beasts

fell ill due to the damp central European climate. One quintessentially Turkish use of camels is for sport, more specifically **camel wrestling**. The bizarre sight of male camels in rut, butting and leaning on each other (their mouths are bound to prevent biting) draws vast crowds across the western Aegean region and there's even a camel wrestling league. In Muslim folklore the perceived haughty demeanour of the animals is attributed to their knowledge of the hundredth, mystical epithet of Allah – humans only know the conventional ninety-nine.

fairly dry in winter, which lasts approximately from late November to late March. Cappadocia in particular makes a colourful, quiet treat during spring and autumn – or even in December, when its rock formations dusted with snow are especially beautiful. As you travel east, into **Northeast Anatolia** and around **Lake Van**, the altitude increases and conditions become deeply snowy between October and April, making late spring and summer by far the best (in some cases the only practical) time to visit. In the lower **Euphrates and Tigris Basin**, a more pronounced Middle Eastern influence exerts itself, with winters no worse than in central Anatolia but torrid summers – and without the compensation of a nearby beach.

Average midday temperatures in °C &°F

	Jan	Feb	Mar	Apr	May	Jun	Jul	Aug	Sep	Oct	Nov	Dec
İstanbul												
Av temp (°C)/(°F)	6/43	6/43	7/45	12/54	17/63	21/70	24/75	24/75	20/68	16/61	12/54	8/47
Antalya												
Av temp (°C)/(°F)	11/52	12/54	13/56	17/63	21/70	23/77	29/84	29/84	25/77	21/70	16/61	12/54
Ankara												
Av temp (°C)/(°F)	1/34	1/34	5/41	12/54	17/63	20/68	24/75	24/75	19/66	13/56	8/47	3/37
Trabzon												
Av temp (°C)/(°F)	8/47	8/47	9/48	12/54	16/61	20/68	23/73	24/75	20/68	17/63	14/57	10/50
Diyarbakır												
Av temp (°C)/(°F)	2/35	4/39	9/48	14/57	20/68	26/79	31/88	31/88	25/77	18/65	10/50	5/41

30

things not to miss

It's not possible to see everything Turkey has to offer in one trip – and we don't suggest you try. What follows is a selective and subjective taste of the country's highlights: outstanding buildings and historic sites, natural wonders and exciting activities. They're all arranged in five colour-coded categories to help you find the very best things to see, do and experience. All entries have a page reference to take you straight into the Guide, where you can find out more.

14

01 Roman theatre at Aspendos Page **398** • The largest and best-preserved Classical theatre in Anatolia – if you can, visit during the summertime opera and ballet festival held here.

02 **Nemrut Dağı** Page **633** • This mountain-top temple-tomb complex, its megalomania sharply at odds with the harsh surroundings, is the outlandish legacy of an obscure, first-century BC kingdom.

03 **Gallipoli cemeteries and memorials** Page **200** • Moving and unexpectedly beautiful legacy of one of the fiercest campaigns of World War I.

04 **Museum of Anatolian Civilizations, Ankara**

Page **507** • Housing finds of all native cultures from the Stone Age to about 700 BC, this superb museum is the capital's one must.

05 **Acropolis of ancient Pergamon** Page **224** • Pergamon was one of the chief Roman cities of Anatolia, and extensive ruins remain; shown here is the restored Trajan temple.

06 **Hot-air ballooning over Cappadocia** Page **468** • A lighter-than-air float gives you an unrivalled perspective on the "fairy chimneys" and other aspects of the landscape.

07 **Ani ruins** Page **608** • Medieval Armenian capital in a superb setting at the border of modern Turkey, scattered with fine churches and monasteries.

ΠΛΛΑΧΗΑΣ

08 Byzantine frescoes, Cappadocia Page **473** • About 150 of Cappadocia's rock-hewn churches contain fine examples of early Christian frescoes, mostly from the tenth and eleventh centuries.

09 Selimiye Camii, Edirne Page **164** • This sixteenth-century mosque is the masterwork of the greatest Ottoman architect, Mimar Sinan.

10 Cruising the southwest coast Page **291** • The deeply indented coastline between Bodrum and Finike is the venue for multi-day cruises on a *gulet*, or traditional wooden motor-schooner.

11 **Aya Sofya, İstanbul** Page **94** • The seemingly unsupported dome of Aya Sofya, built during the sixth century as a Byzantine church, is one of the architectural marvels of the world.

12 **Lycian Way long-distance path** Page **325** • This marked, well-documented path passes through some of the most scenic portions of the Turquoise Coast, with sections suitable for all abilities.

13 **Hittite capital of Hattuşa** Page **527** • The second-millennium BC capital of the Hittites still impresses, with perimeter walls extending to six kilometres.

14 **Orthodox monastery of Sumela** Page **565** • Dramatically built into the side of the Pontic mountains, this Byzantine monastery harbours excellent if damaged frescoes.

15 **Oil-wrestling** Page **166** • Although a popular sport across Turkey, the best time to see olive-oil-coated contestants get to grips with each other is during Edirne's Kırkpınar Festival.

16 Patara beach Page **345** • This unspoilt beach, one of the longest in the Mediterranean, is the perfect coda to a visit of the nearby, eponymous ancient city.

17 Ancient Ephesus Page **261** • This ancient city where Saint Paul addressed one of his epistles, is the best preserved of its kind in the Eastern Mediterranean.

18 Shopping in a bazaar Page **107** • You may not get the bargain of a lifetime but you can't beat the banter and the range of products, especially at İstanbul's Grand Bazaar.

19 **Kariye Museum, İstanbul** Page **117** • Arguably the finest collection of mosaics and frescoes in Turkey, adorning a late-Byzantine church.

20 **Mardin** Page **645** • Medieval houses, historic mosques, Syrian Orthodox churches and boutique hotels mingle in the hilltop eyrie of Mardin, high above the sweeping Mesopotamian plain.

21 **Visiting a hamam** Page **54** • One of the traditional sensual comforts of Turkey, *hamams* are a wonderfully relaxing (and cleansing) way to round off a day's sightseeing.

22 **Kaçkar Dağları** Page **595** • Lying just inland from the Black Sea, this glacially sculpted granite mountain range, spangled with dozens of lakes, is Turkey's premier trekking venue.

23 **Gözleme** Page **44** • A delicious snack of paper-thin dough stuffed with everything from spinach and sheep's cheese to lamb; watching their concoction is part of the fun.

24 **Outdoor restaurants** Page **132** • The Ottomans introduced the concept of dining alfresco to Europe, and outdoor restaurants or *meyhanes* do a roaring trade in warmer weather.

25 Safranbolu
Page **520** •
Admirably preserved Ottoman town of exquisite half-timbered mansions and restored public buildings nestled in a ravine.

26 Lake Van Page **658** • The cobalt blue expanse of Lake Van, Turkey's largest, is most scenic in late spring or early summer.

27 Whirling dervishes Page **457** • Members of a sect founded by the Konya-based Sufi mystic Celaleddin Rumi conduct "turning" ceremonies to effect union with God.

28 İşak Paşa Sarayı

Page **678** • Strategically astride the Silk Route, this architecturally eclectic seventeenth-century palace is one of eastern Turkey's most emblematic sites.

29 Churches of the Georgian valleys

Page 582 • Numerous medieval-Georgian churches northeast of Erzurum are among the most striking monuments in northeastern Anatolia.

30 Gaziantep Archeological Museum

Page 621 • A fabulous collection of mosaics from ancient Zeugma, a Hellenistic/Roman frontier city now under the waters of a reservoir on the nearby Euphrates.

Basics

Basics

Getting there

There are a wide choice of flights to Turkey from the UK (fewer from Ireland) taking between three and a half to five hours depending on your start and end point. Just two carriers fly direct to Turkey from North America, so most North Americans reach Turkey via a European gateway airport. Many travellers from Australia and New Zealand use a Round-the-World (RTW) ticket that includes İstanbul, though there are advantageous return flights from Sydney. Driving to Turkey from Europe (perhaps with a ferry hop from Italy or Greece as the final stage) can be expensive and time-consuming, but once inside the country having a car can prove worthwhile.

Airfares from Europe and North America are highest during Easter week and from June to early September; fares drop between April/ May and late September/October – and you'll get the best prices between November to March (excluding Christmas and New Year, when seats are at a premium). Australian and New Zealand fares are lowest from mid-January to the end of February and October/November; peak season is mid-May to August, plus December to mid-January.

Flights from the UK and Ireland

You can **fly direct from the UK** to İstanbul (both airports), İzmir, Bodrum, Dalaman and Antalya. Reaching any other destination in Turkey involves a change of flights in İstanbul, though if you're flying with Turkish Airlines you can get a discounted **domestic connecting flight** to most of the internal airports which they serve. At busy times, it may be worth considering cheaper, **indirect (ie one-stop) flights** with other European airlines such as Swiss, Air France or Lufthansa (which serves several Turkish airports direct from Germany).

Direct, scheduled flights are provided by Turkish Airways (THY), British Airways (BA) and Cyprus Turkish Airways (KTHY). THY links London (Stansted or Heathrow) with İstanbul (Atatürk or Sabiha Gökçen) several times daily year-round, with the Stansted–Sahiba Gökçen route comparing well price-wise to the "no-frills" airlines. There are three daily departures from Heathrow to Atatürk, with prices across the year hovering around the £200 mark. BA has two to three daily services from Heathrow at comparable fares. THY also has daily services from Birmingham and Manchester to İstanbul. Domestic fares from İstanbul to Mediterranean resorts start at 39TL (€18) with either THY or competitors such as Sunexpress (see p.40 for more on domestic flights). KTHY (only bookable direct or through specialist agents) offers useful direct flights to the southwest coast year-round out of several UK airports, though on-board standards aren't up to those of BA or THY. To the following year-round services (Stansted–Antalya, 4 weekly; Heathrow or Stansted–İzmir, 3 weekly; and Manchester–Antalya, 1 weekly) are added in summer once weekly each Stansted–Dalaman, Stansted–Bodrum, Heathrow–Antalya and Birmingham–Dalaman. Winter fares can be as low as £150 return, rising to about £260 in summer.

Budget and charter flights

Among **budget airlines**, easyJet flies from London (Luton and/or Gatwick) to İstanbul Sahiba Gökçen most days all year, as well as from Gatwick to Dalaman (April–Oct only). Advance low-season fares can be under £40 each way, though in peak season or at short notice they're hardly different from "real" airlines. Pegasus links Stansted to İstanbul Sahiba Gökçen daily all year, with fares likely to be a bit higher than easyJet. Jet2 serves Dalaman from Leeds Bradford, Manchester, East Midlands and Newcastle (summer only, from about £60 each way).

Six steps to a better kind of travel

At Rough Guides we are passionately committed to travel. We feel strongly that only through travelling do we truly come to understand the world we live in and the people we share it with – plus tourism has brought a great deal of **benefit** to developing economies around the world over the last few decades. But the extraordinary growth in tourism has also damaged some places irreparably, and of course **climate change** is exacerbated by most forms of transport, especially flying. This means that now more than ever it's important to **travel thoughtfully** and **responsibly**, with respect for the cultures you're visiting – not only to derive the most benefit from your trip but also to preserve the best bits of the planet for everyone to enjoy. At Rough Guides we feel there are six main areas in which you can make a difference:

- Consider what you're contributing to the **local economy**, and how much the services you use do the same, whether it's through employing local workers and guides or sourcing locally grown produce and local services.
- Consider the **environment** on holiday as well as at home. Water is scarce in many developing destinations, and the biodiversity of local flora and fauna can be adversely affected by tourism. Try to patronize businesses that take account of this.
- Travel with a purpose, not just to tick off experiences. Consider **spending longer** in a place, and getting to know it and its people.
- Give thought to how often you **fly**. Try to avoid short hops by air and more harmful night flights.
- Consider **alternatives to flying**, travelling instead by bus, train, boat and even by bike or on foot where possible.
- Make your trips "**climate neutral**" via a reputable carbon offset scheme. All Rough Guide flights are offset, and every year we donate money to a variety of charities devoted to combating the effects of climate change.

The widest choice of **charter flights** to Turkish coastal resorts are offered by Thomas Cook and Thomson. With Thomas Cook, you can choose different departure and return airports, flexible dates and even book one-ways. There are now year-round charters to Antalya and Dalaman, while those serving İzmir and Bodrum usually operate from late April/early May to late October. In peak season these flights are often scarcely cheaper than scheduled services – £300 London–Dalaman is not unheard of – but you do avoid having to change planes in İstanbul. In winter, tickets can be picked up for under £100 return from almost anywhere in the UK to Dalaman or Antalya.

Flights from Ireland

From Belfast, there are no direct scheduled services to Turkey, and stopping routes will likely cost over €400; get yourself to mainland Britain first. **From Dublin**, matters are better, with daily direct services all year on THY to İstanbul Atatürk (from €225 return off season). Alternatively, take a budget Ryanair or similar flight to the UK (Stansted is a major hub of KTHY), and then on to Turkey.

Flights from the US and Canada

No matter where you're flying from, İstanbul will be the cheapest gateway airport. For the best value, pick up a bargain transatlantic fare to Europe, then arrange the final Turkey-bound leg of the journey yourself; onward flights from the UK are detailed on p.27.

Turkish Airways (THY) is the sole carrier flying direct year-round from North America, with daily flights from New York (JFK) to İstanbul, and several weekly out of Chicago. **Delta Airlines** is the only other airline offering a direct service (April–Nov), from

New York JFK to İstanbul. All other flights route through **European hubs** such as London, Paris, Frankfurt, Milan and Zürich. THY is often a bit cheaper, from US$700–900 round trip low season compared to Delta's US$850 or so. At the opposite end of the spectrum, count on well over US$1600 for peak season travel from the west coast.

Despite many domestic competitors, THY still has the most comprehensive selection of **connecting flights** within Turkey, a major incentive for booking with them at least part of the way. THY normally charges an add-on fare for these cities when the domestic leg is purchased as part of an international itinerary, but specialists might be able to book you straight through (or with a stop in İstanbul) for less.

The only direct flights from **Canada** are on THY from Toronto to İstanbul three days per week all year; fares vary from C$800 to just C$1000 depending on the season. Otherwise several airlines fly to İstanbul via major European hubs. From **Vancouver** to İstanbul indirect flights via American or European hubs can be found from C$1300 to C$1400 year-round.

Flights from Australia, New Zealand and South Africa

There are no direct flights from Australia or New Zealand to Turkey. However, several weekly scheduled flights will get you there after either a plane change or short layover in Asia or the Middle East. Fares from **Sydney** range from A$1700 (low season) to A$2600 (high season), with the likes of Korean Air, Malaysian Airlines, Singapore Airlines and Gulf Air. **From New Zealand**, flights tend to be pricey, involving two or three stops – you're probably better off getting cheaply to Australia and arranging onward travel from there. **Round-the-world tickets** including Turkey could be worth considering for a long trip taking in many destinations; several free stopovers are allowed, with fares starting at A$2000/NZ$2500. From **South Africa**, routes (out of Johannesburg only) are mostly via one of the Gulf states, and return fares on the likes of Emirates vary from ZAR6000 to ZAR10,000 depending on the time of year.

Trains

Travelling to Turkey **by rail** is both slow and expensive, and only makes sense if you want to visit other countries en route (try the excellent ⓦwww.seat61.com for detailed planning). The most direct route **from the UK** begins with the Eurostar (ⓦwww.eurostar.com) service from London St Pancras International to Paris, then an overnight sleeper to Munich or Vienna, followed by a morning departure to Budapest, and finally two more nights aboard a sleeper to İstanbul (including a change in Bucharest), making a total minimum journey of three days and nights. The return trip is likely to set you back between £540–610, depending on class of trains selected and whether you have a rail pass (see below). An alternative strategy, potentially cheaper, is to get to Italy by train and then proceed by ferry to Greece (48hr journey time) or even all the way to Turkey (see p.30).

The "Global" **InterRail pass** (ⓦwww .interrailnet.com) required to reach Turkey may save a bit of money, especially if you're under 26. These are valid for unlimited travel (except for Eurostar) and fees apply for express train reservations. For North Americans, Australians and New Zealanders (not eligible to buy InterRail passes), a standard **Eurail pass** (ⓦwww.eurail.com) is unlikely to pay for itself, whether going to, or travelling in, Turkey.

By car from Europe

You can **drive from the UK** to Turkey in three to four days. However, this allows little time for stopping and sleeping, and most will prefer to do this more slowly, taking in a few places en route. For customs formalities and car insurance cover once in Turkey, see "Getting around", p.34.

The all-land itinerary goes via Belgium, Germany, Austria, Hungary, Romania and Bulgaria, though a more relaxing if less direct route is through France, Italy and Greece. You can cut driving time even more by using a ferry from Italy, direct to Turkey; there are also short-hop ferry or catamaran services from various Greek islands to the Turkish Aegean coast.

Ferries

Ferries run from both Ancona and Brindisi in Italy to Çeşme, near İzmir. **Marmara Lines** (⚈www.marmaralines.com) has services from early May to late October, departing Ancona on Saturday evening. A one-way Pullman seat in high season is €160 and an average-sized car €260, with twenty-percent round-trip reductions. **MedEuropeanSeaways (Mesline)** operates a service between mid-June and mid-September from Brindisi to Çeşme (departs Brindisi Sat and Wed); they have no website but Genoa-based ⚈www.cemar.it may prove useful.

Ferries and catamarans from Greece

Many travellers take the short-hop ferries or catamarans over from the Greek islands of Lésvos, Híos, Sámos, Kós, Kastellorizo/Meis, Sými, and Rhodes to the respective Turkish ports of Ayvalık, Foça, Çeşme, Kuşadası, Datça, Bodrum, Kaş, Marmaris and Fethiye. Services are daily in season (early May to early Oct) and, except for the Fethiye-, Foça- and Datça-based services, they still run after a fashion in winter, but you may have to wait five to seven days between departures. Although they've dipped slightly in recent years, fares are still overpriced for the distances involved; full details of every service are given at the end of chapters 3, 4 and 5. At the time of writing **car-shuttle services** serve all of the above Turkish ports except Foça, Fethiye, Kaş and to a degree Kuşadası, which only has one semi-reliable service weekly. ⚈www.feribot.net is useful if not infallible.

Airlines, agents and operators

Airlines

Air France ⚈www.airfrance.com
BA ⚈www.ba.com
easyJet ⚈www.easyjet.com
Delta ⚈www.delta.com
Emirates ⚈www.emirates.com
Gulf Air ⚈www.gulfair.com
Jet2 ⚈www.jet2.com
Korean Air ⚈www.koreanair.com
KTHY ⚈www.kthy.net
Lufthansa ⚈www.lufthansa.com

Malaysia Airlines ⚈www.malaysiaairlines.com
Pegasus ⚈www.flypgs.com
Ryanair ⚈www.ryanair.com
Singapore Airlines ⚈www.singaporeair.com
Swiss ⚈www.swiss.com
ThomasCook ⚈www.flythomascook.com
Thomson ⚈www.thomsonfly.com
Turkish Airways ⚈www.thy.com

Agents and operators

Alternative Travel UK ☎020/7249 9800, ⚈www.alternativeturkey.com. Specialist Turkish travel agency, good for Cyprus Turkish Airlines flights to coastal resorts.
Avro UK ☎0161/209 4259, ⚈www.avro.co.uk. Seat-only sales of charter flights to Antalya and Dalaman from various regional airports.
Flightcentre US ☎1-866 WORLD-51, ⚈www.flightcentre.us; Canada ☎1-888 WORLD-02, ⚈www.flightcentre.ca; Australia ☎13 31 33, ⚈www.flightcentre.com.au; New Zealand ☎0800/243 544, ⚈www.flightcentre.co.nz. Rock-bottom fares worldwide.
North South Travel UK ☎01245/608291, ⚈www.northsouthtravel.co.uk. Friendly, competitive flight agency, offering discounted fares – profits are used to support projects in the developing world
STA Travel UK ☎0870/160 0599, ⚈www.statravel.co.uk; US ☎1-800/781-4040, ⚈www.statravel.com; Australia ☎1300/733 035, ⚈www.statravel.com.au; New Zealand ☎0800/474 400, ⚈www.statravel.co.nz. Specialists in low-cost flights for students and under-26s.
Trailfinders UK ☎020/7938 3939, ⚈www.trailfinders.com; Republic of Ireland ☎01/677 7888, ⚈www.trailfinders.ie; Australia ☎1300/780 212, ⚈www.trailfinders.com.au. One of the best-informed and most efficient agents for independent travellers.
Turkish Tursan Travel US ☎212/888-1180. Turkish specialist consolidator, based in New York.

Package tours and special-interest holidays

Scores of companies in the UK offer some sort of Turkish **package deal**. Most of these target İstanbul and the coast between Çeşme and Alanya, but most outfits also feature fly-drive plans. Coastal yachting (*gulet*) packages are available from May to October, while winter breaks are increasing in popularity. Inland holidays concentrate on Cappadocia, while special-interest programmes include trekking, bird-spotting,

yoga retreats, whitewater rafting and battlefield tours.

Three- or four-night İstanbul city breaks start at around £130 off season for three-star bed-and-breakfast accommodation (including flights and transfers). The main price factor is the departure airport, the cheapest relying on easyJet's Luton– or Gatwick–İstanbul (Sahiba Gökçen) runs.

Prices for a cheap-and-cheerful, two-week **beach package** start at around £300 per person (double occupancy) in low season, including flights; using a four-star hotel will set you back £550–800. Quality self-catering villas tend to cost £700–1100 per person for one/two week(s), flight included, increasing to £1100–1800 at peak periods. **Fly-drive**-only deals weigh in at around £450 per person for four adults travelling for two weeks in high season, around £550 if there are only two of you.

A ten-night, eleven-day **yachting or cruising** holiday will cost £900–1050 per person (double occupancy basis) depending on season, booked in the UK through an agent, less if arranged in Turkey directly with skippers. **Cycling/hiking** trips vary from £250–300 for 7 to 8 days along the Lycian Coast arranged locally, to £500–550 for a higher-quality adventure booked in the UK. **Specialist holidays**, relying on the services of expert natural history/archeological guides, are priciest of all, from £1100 (1 week) to over £1900 (2 weeks). All these figures exclude flights.

The best of the US-based cultural or adventure tours don't come cheap either – expect to pay at least US$5100 for a 13-day land-and-sea combo (inevitably with a couple of days in İstanbul at the start and end). The price will include all meals (excluding drinks), guides and ground transport, but not flights.

General tour operators

Anatolian Sky ☎0121/764 350, ⊛www.anatoliansky.co.uk. Mid-range to upmarket hotels and apartments on the southwest coast (particularly Kalkan, Dalyan, Akyaka, the Loryma peninsula, Antalya and Ölüdeniz), classic hotels in İstanbul, and a tailor-made programme.

Cachet Travel ☎020/8847 8700, ⊛www.cachet-travel.co.uk. Small selection of villas and hotels along the Turquoise Coast, plus guided, low-season

special-interest tours, and select İstanbul/Cappadocia hotels.

Exclusive Escapes ☎020/8605 3500, ⊛www.exclusiveescapes.co.uk. Perhaps the best portfolio of properties (both boutique hotels and villas) along the Turquoise Coast, as well as points west to Datça, Cappadocia and İstanbul. Noted for a high level of customer service, which extends to dedicated check-in counters at airports.

Tapestry Holidays ☎020/8995 7787, ⊛www.tapestryholidays.com. Limited but carefully selected portfolio of hotels and villas along the Turquoise Coast, as well as boutique hotels in Cappadocia and İstanbul.

Turkish Collection (Ilios Travel) ☎01444/225633, ⊛www.iliostravel.com. Top-quality (and thus pricey) villas-with-pool on the Bodrum and Datça peninsulas, plus somewhat more conventional accommodation at Akyaka, Kalkan and Kaş.

Sailing and yachting

Cavurali ☎0090 542/595 7377, ⊛www.cavurali.com. Turkish-American guide Enver Lucas and his father-in-law Tosun Sezen, both with years of local experience, offer bespoke sailing (and scuba) itineraries along the Turquoise Coast in a *gulet*-dive boat.

Day Dreams ☎01884/849200, ⊛www.turkishcruises.co.uk. Large fleet of *gulets* or schooners hosting "house parties" for singles and couples; also makes on-land arrangements in unusual areas like Kazdağı.

Nautilus Yachting ☎01732/867445, ⊛www.nautilus-yachting.co.uk. Bare-boat charters out of Marmaris, Bodrum, Fethiye and Göcek, plus set flotilla itineraries from Bodrum or Fethiye.

Setsail ☎01787/310445, ⊛www.setsail.co.uk. Flotilla holidays from Göcek and Marmaris; also bare-boat charter.

Sunsail ☎0844/463 6495, ⊛www.sunsail.co.uk. Flotilla holidays out of Göcek, Orhaniye and Turgutreis, taking in the Turquoise Coast and the peninsulas between Bodrum and Marmaris.

SCIC ☎020/8510 9292, ⊛www.tussockcruising.com. Bodrum-area-based fleet of three wooden *gulets* specially adapted so that you actually travel under sail power rather than (as normally on such craft) with merely decorative rigging.

Trekking and adventure operators

Adrift ☎01488/71152, ⊛www.adrift.co.uk. Whitewater rafting on the Çoruh River from late May to late July; one-week programme.

Exodus Travel ☎020/8675 5550, ⊛www.exodus.co.uk. Strong on mountain biking and hiking along the Lycian Coast; also more conventional itineraries, staying in small hotels and village houses.

Explore Worldwide ☎01252/760 000, ⓦwww
.explore.co.uk. Selection of 8- or 15-day trips,
mostly in Cappadocia, the east and Lycia (including a
cruising section).

The Imaginative Traveller ☎01473/667337,
ⓦwww.imaginative-traveller.com. Vast assortment
of 7 to 19-day tours, many pitched at families, taking
in all the Turkish highlights plus some lesser-known
spots, make this about the best overland group-tour
operator for Turkey.

Special-interest holidays

Andante Travels UK ☎01722/713 800, ⓦwww
.andantetravels.co.uk. Upmarket tours to Turkey's
major (and many minor) archeological and historical
sites, led by distinguished professors or other experts
in their fields.

Cultural Folk Tours US ☎1-800/935-8875,
ⓦculturalfolktours.com. US-based company
offering up to nine annual tours (accompanied by
company founder and Turkish musician Bora Ozkok)
which give a real insight into seldom-visited regions
of the country.

Geographic Expeditions US ☎1-800/777-8183,
ⓦwww.geoex.com. Offers Aegean Odyssey (taking
in some Greek islands as well), or 16-day walk-
plus-*gulet*-cruises off the Turquoise Coast; four-day
Cappadocia add-on available.

Gölköy Centre UK ☎020/8699 1900, ⓦwww
.yogaturkey.co.uk. Yoga retreat on Bodrum
peninsula offering week-long courses, also
encompassing shiatsu and assorted "personal
growth" themes, from May to October; budget
£415–495 per person per week, including full board
and activities but not flights.

Greentours UK ☎01298/83563, ⓦwww
.greentours.co.uk. Offers three annual, one- or
two-week natural-history holidays (emphasis on
wildflowers), typically inland from the Turquoise or
Mediterranean coasts. Enthusiastic English or Turkish
guides know their subjects in incredible detail.

Holt's Battlefield Tours UK ☎01293/865000,
ⓦwww.holts.co.uk. One-week tour of Gallipoli and
the Dardanelles, in autumn (thus avoiding Anzac Day
mayhem).

Huzur Vadisi ⓦwww.huzurvadisi.com. One-week
yoga programmes from May to October at a secluded

complex with felt yurts or nomad dwellings set around
a renovated farmhouse and pool, 10km inland of
Göcek. From £450 a week, including full board and
activities but not flights.

Mythic Travel US ☎831/688-6550, ⓦwww
.mythic-travel.com. Distinctly New Age company
offering "Magic Carpets" as opposed to tours with
themed tags like "Mary and the Divine Feminine",
"Jewish Life" and "Sufi Solstice".

Wilderness Travel US ☎1-800/368-2794,
ⓦwww.wildernesstravel.com. Offers three tours in
western Turkey, including a 16-dayer incorporating an
11-day cruise using the same personnel and itinerary
as Geographic Expeditions.

World Expeditions Australia, five city branches;
New Zealand ☎0800/350354, ⓦwww
.worldexpeditions.com.au. Probably the most
interesting Antipodean adventure operator for Turkey:
its 20-day "Turkey Panorama", including five days'
trekking and three days' cruising, is one of a half-
dozen itineraries.

Getting around

Most of Turkey is well covered by public transport including long-distance buses, minibuses, domestic flights and ferries. The train network is sketchy, many routes slow and booking a headache – but it's the cheapest and safest form of domestic travel. Late booking is the norm but book well in advance for major public holidays – especially for flights and trains. Car rental rates tend to be high by European standards, but there are out-of-season bargains. "Travel details" at the end of each chapter rounds up all the relevant routes and schedules.

By train

Turkey's train network is run by **Turkish State Railways** (TCDD; Ⓦ www.tcdd.gov.tr). Trains are best used to span the distances between the three main cities (İstanbul, Ankara and İzmir) and more provincial centres such as Konya, Kayseri, Erzerum and Diyarbakır. Most trains are slow because the mountainous terrain of much of Turkey has resulted in circuitous routes. As a result, journeys can sometimes take double that by road. The advantages are additional comfort at comparable or lower prices than the bus, and the chance to unwind and watch the scenery unfold at leisure. To get accurate schedule **information**, go to the station in person, scan the placards and then confirm departures with staff.

There are several choices of **seats** available on most routes, including first-class, reclining Pullman seats; first-class standard seats (usually in a six-seater compartment) and second-class seats (generally in an eight-seater compartment). For long distances, though, it's advisable to get a **sleeper**. Cheapest are *küşetli* (couchettes), with either four or six bunks in a compartment depending on the route, and two-bedded *yataklı* (sleeping-cars) with a basin, soap, towel and air conditioning. All *yataklı* beds come with sheets, pillows and blankets provided, as do *örtülü küşetli* beds; for standard *küşetli* beds you'll need to bring your own bedding. For maximum privacy, and for women travelling without male companions, it's probably best to book a *yataklı* berth to avoid having to share. There are always (usually helpful but tip expected) porters on hand to make up beds. Note that all beds fold away in the day to convert the compartment into a seating area.

All long-distance services should have a licensed *büfe* wagon which offers simple meals at surprisingly reasonable prices, but it's as well to check in advance (note that most wayside stations will have snacks of some sort on offer). On major train routes it's essential to **reserve ahead**, but unfortunately this cannot be done earlier than two weeks in advance – and it's almost impossible to arrange sleeper facilities from a station that's not your start point. It's theoretically possible to book online but the English version of TCDD's website is so difficult to use that you'd be brave to risk it (rail site Ⓦ www.seat61.com has a step-by-step guide on this).

Fares and passes

To give some idea of **prices**, a pullman seat for the mammoth 38hr, 1,424km journey from İstanbul to Kars (close to the Armenian border) costs 45TL, while a bed in a two-berth *yataklı* compartment costs 75TL. An economy seat on the *Yüksek Hızlı Tren* (High-Speed Train) between İstanbul and Ankara costs 40TL for the 423km, 5hr 30min journey. Buying a return ticket brings the fare down by twenty percent while foreign **students** (with appropriate ID) and children also get twenty percent off. InterRail passes (see p.29) are valid, though a better bet for Turkey-only travel is the one-month **TrenTur** card (available at major stations) which costs 150TL a month for unlimited second-class travel or 500TL for any class of sleeping car.

By long-distance bus

Long-distance buses are a key part of the Turkish travel experience and, despite competition from domestic flights and relatively high road accident rates (see p.36 for more), look set to remain so. Bus journeys are almost always accompanied by loud Turkish music or film soundtracks. Partial compensation for this are the attendants dishing out drinking water and cologne for freshening up. Every ninety minutes there will be a fifteen-minute **rest stop** (*mola*) for tea, as well as less frequent half-hour pauses for meals at purpose-built roadside cafeterias. Many of the better companies serve free coffee/tea/soft drinks and cakes on board.

There's no comprehensive national bus **timetable**, although individual companies often provide their own. **Prices** vary considerably between top- and bottom-drawer companies, though convenience of departure and on-board service are equally important criteria. If in doubt, inspect the vehicle out in the loading bay (*peron* in Turkish) and ask at the ticket office how long the trip will take. It's worth bearing in mind that long-haul journeys (over 10hr) generally take place at night, and that because of rest stops buses never cover more than 60km an hour on average. As a broad example of fares, İstanbul–Antalya (a 450km trip) costs around 40TL with a standard bus company, 75TL with a premium company. Antalya–Nevşehir (for Cappadocia) is around 45TL for the 540km journey.

Buying tickets

Most bus companies have ticket booths both at the **otogars** (bus terminals) and in the city centre. Touts at *otogars* will try to escort you direct to their company's booth. When buying tickets, ask to see the **seating plan** so that you can choose window or aisle, a front seat (better views) or avoid certain less comfortable seats, such as those above the wheels and immediately behind the central door, which have less legroom. Unacquainted women and men are not usually allowed to sit next to each other, and you may be asked to switch your assigned seat to accommodate this convention. If you buy your ticket at a sales office in the centre you should ask about free *servis* (service) **transfer buses** to the *otogar*, especially if (as most now are) it's located a few kilometres out of town. These buses will often also take passengers from *otogars* into town centres, but this is a more erratic system. The country's two **premium coach companies** are Ulusoy and Varan. Their seats are more comfortable than most and they don't segregate single passengers by sex. Kamil Koç and Pamukkale are two of the best standard outfits, in that order of preference.

By dolmuş

A **dolmuş** (literally "stuffed") refers to a car or small van (*minibüs* in Turkish) which runs along set routes, picking passengers up (give a normal taxi hand signal) and dropping them off along the way (just say *inecek var* or *müsait bir yerde* to be set down). On busy **urban routes** it's better to take the dolmuş from the start of its run, at a stand marked by a blue sign with a black-on-white-field "D", sometimes with the destination indicated – though usually you'll have to ask to learn the eventual destination, or look at the dolmuş' windscreen placard. The **fare** is invariably a flat rate (usually 1.5TL) making it very good value for cross-city journeys, not so great for a one-stop hop. In some cities (eg Antalya) dolmuşes have been banned because pulling in at random is both dangerous and slows traffic. The locals, confusingly, still refer to the midibuses that replaced them, and stop only at fixed points, as dolmuşes.

Intertown and village services are always provided by twelve- or fifteen-seater minibuses, and in these instances the term "dolmuş" is seldom used. For the remotest villages there will only be two services a day: to the nearest large town in the morning and back to the village in mid-afternoon. Generally, though, minibuses run constantly between 7 or 8am and 7pm in summer, stopping at sunset in winter or extending until 10 or 11pm (or even later) near popular resorts.

By city bus and taxi

In larger towns the main means of transport are the **city buses** which take pre-purchased tickets available from kiosks near the main terminals, newsagents, or from kerbside touts (at slightly inflated prices); in some cities it's possible to pay on the bus. Yellow city **taxis** are everywhere, with ranks at appropriate places. Hailing one in the street is the best way to get a cab, but in suburban areas there are useful street-corner telephones from which you can call one; sometimes there is just a buzzer – press and wait for a cab to turn up. City cabs all have working, digital-display meters and **fares** are reasonable. Each town sets its own rates, which includes the minimum charge and a unit charge for the distance covered. The daily rate is called "*gündüz*" and flashes up on the meter, the night rate (which flashes up as "*gece*") between midnight and 6am, is fifty percent higher – make sure you don't get charged the night rate for a daytime journey. In 2009 İstanbul removed the higher night tariff, with cabs charging an initial 2.5TL, then 1.4TL per kilometre, with an additional charge for keeping a cab waiting more than five minutes.

By car

The excellent intercity bus network makes travel between major centres easy, but having a **car** allows you to visit many off-the-beaten-track sites. But be warned – the standard of driving in Turkey is often both poor and aggressive and the enforcement of traffic rules inconsistent and arbitrary, all factors which have lead to the country's high **road accident rate** with over 6,000 fatalities per year. Driving during public holidays, especially the religious Şeker and Kurban *bayram*s, and an hour or so prior to the *iftar* (fast-breaking meal) during Ramadan, is especially dangerous.

Rules of the road

You **drive on the right**, and yield to those approaching from the right, even on the numerous roundabouts. **Speed limits** are 50km/h within towns (40km/h if towing a trailer or caravan); open road limits are 90km/h for cars, 80km/h for vans (70km/h if towing something); motorways (*otoyol* in Turkish), 120km/h for cars, 100km/h for vans and small trucks. **Drink-driving laws** are in line with those of the European Union – 50mg of alcohol per 100ml of blood and drink-driving carries a fine of 480TL. Front seat belts are mandatory and it's a fineable offence not to buckle up.

Traffic control points at the approaches to major cities are common. You'll probably be waved through simply upon showing your foreign ID, especially if it's a rental car. Make sure the rental company provides the insurance certificate, the pollution compliance certificate (*eksoz muayene tasdiknamesi*) and the vehicle registration, or certified copies thereof.

Speeding fines, levied on a sliding scale according to how far above the limit you were, are heavy, with penalties of 200–300TL commonplace (though there's a considerable "discount" if the fine is paid within 10 days). Usually you'll be given a ticket, which you then take to a designated bank to pay. Jumping red lights or turning illegally also carry stiff fines.

If you have an accident serious enough to immobilize you and/or cause major damage to other people's property, the traffic police will appear and administer alcohol tests to all drivers, results of which must also be submitted along with an official **accident report** (*kaza raporu*) in order to claim insurance cover. It's an offence to move a vehicle involved in a car crash before the police show up.

Heed the signposted **no-parking zones**, especially in resorts, as towing is common and although the fines are not too heavy the hassle of finding the pound and negotiating language barriers is considerable. Generally, it's wisest to patronize the covered (*katlı*) or open *otoparks*. In open car parks you may well be required to leave your keys so the attendant can move your car. If you leave your car in the street in some towns and cities, you may return to find a chit on your windscreen (typically 4–5TL), to be paid to the roving attendant.

Road conditions

Ordinary **main roads** are often danger-ously narrow and road-markings unclear. There's usually a hard-shoulder area to the right of the driving lane, and often slower moving vehicles pull into this to allow impatient drivers to overtake. Be very wary

Road signs

Dur	Stop	*Düşük banket*	Abrupt verge/shoulder
Tek yön	One way	*Şehir merkezi*	City centre
Çıkmaz sokak	Dead end/ cul-de-sac	*Park yapılmaz/ edilmez*	No parking
Yol kapalı	Road closed	*Araç giremez*	No entry
Yol boyunca	Road narrows	*Araçınız çekilir*	Your car will be towed
Tırmanma şeridi	Overtaking lane		
Araç çıkabılır	Vehicles exiting	*Giremez*	No entry
Yaya geçidi	Pedestrian crossing	*Askeri bölge*	Military zone
Yol yapımı	Roadworks	*Heyelan bölgesi, heyelanlı bölge*	Landslide zone
Bozuk satıh	Rough surface		

of doing this, especially at night, as you might find yourself ploughing into pedestrians or parked/broken-down vehicles. With continual road improvements being made countrywide, roadworks are often a (sometimes dangerous) nuisance – especially in the southeast region. Sizeable archeological sites are usually marked by large white-on-brown-field signs, but side roads to minor sites or villages are often poorly signposted.

Typical **hazards** include drivers overtaking right, left and centre, failure to signal and huge trucks. Small-town driving hazards include suicidal pedestrians, horsecarts, speeding scooters and motorcycles (often with the entire family astride one vehicle) and tractors.

Toll highways, marked with white-on-green signs are well worth the modest fees (2–6TL) to use. The main ones include İstanbul–Ankara, İstanbul–Edirne; Adana–Gaziantep; Adana–Pozantı through the Cilician Gates; İzmir–Çeşme; and İzmir–Denizli.

Night driving is best not attempted by beginners – be prepared for unlit vehicles, glare from undipped lights, speeding intercity coaches and trucks and, in rural areas, flocks of sheep and goats and unlit tractors. Warning triangles are obligatory, make sure you put it on the road behind your vehicle following a flat, breakdown or accident, and ensure your hire car has one.

Fuel and repairs

Filling stations are commonplace and open long hours, so it's difficult to run out of fuel.

Fuel costs are very high owing to high taxes and even diesel (*mazot or dizel*) is 2.8TL per litre. Petrol (*benzin*), available in four-star (*süper*) and lead-free (*kurşunsuz*) grades, goes for around 3.4TL per litre. Rental cars generally use unleaded, but in some remote eastern areas it may be difficult to find.

In western Turkey, roadside **rest-stop culture** conforming to Italian or French notions has arrived in a big way. You can eat, pray, patch a tyre, phone home, shop at mini-marts and, sometimes, even sleep at what amount to small hamlets (essentially the descendants of the medieval *kervansarays*) in the middle of nowhere. In the east you'll find more basic amenities.

Credit and debit cards (Visa Electron, Visa and MasterCard but also American Express) are widely honoured for fuel purchases in much of Turkey (chip-and-PIN protocol is the norm), but carry cash in more remote rural areas and the east.

Car **repair workshops** are located in industrial zones called *sanayis* at town outskirts. To repair a punctured tyre (a common event in Turkey) head to a *lastıkçı* (tyre workshop); a new tyre for a small car is about 90TL. Always check that the spare and toolkit are sound and complete before leaving the rental agency.

Car rental

To rent a car you need to be at least 21 with a **driving licence** held for at least one year. Your home country licence should be enough but it is very helpful, especially at traffic-control points, to be able to show an international driver's permit (IDP). On the

Aegean and Mediterranean coast advance online bookings can get rates as low as 50TL/€24 per day in low season (Nov–March) but you'll be lucky to get a high season multi-day rate in the same region for less than 73TL/€35 – this is assuming you use a Turkish firm. Walk-in day rates from major multinational chains are likely to be 94TL/45 minimum. Car hire in out of the way (for the average tourist) places such as Trabzon and Van is generally more expensive, expect to pay at least €35 per day with a local company, 104TL/€49 with a major chain.

Some rental companies allow rental in one town and drop off in another – at a premium. The international players like Hertz have outlets at many of Turkey's airports as well as downtown/resort offices; local outfits (some of whom also offer advance, online booking services), may not have an office in the airport but with advance booking will bring the car to the airport and have someone meet you outside arrivals. Be warned, tanks are often near empty so you need to fill up right away.

When checking any car out, agency staff should make a thorough note of any **blemishes** on the vehicle – go around the vehicle with them when they do this as you may be liable for scratches and dents not noted at the time of hire. Basic **insurance** is usually included, but CDW (Collision Damage Waiver) is not, and given typical driving conditions taking this out is virtually mandatory. Along with KDV (Value Added Tax), all these extras can push up the final total considerably. Rental insurance never covers smashed windscreens or ripped tyres.

By bicycle and motorcycle

Touring Turkey by **bicycle** is perfectly possible for experienced cyclists, so long as you avoid the hottest months, the busiest roads and don't expect any kind of deference from motorists. Be prepared to do your own repairs as the (admittedly ingenious) local mechanics are not used to working on state-of-the art bikes, although the home-grown mountain bike industry has progressed in leaps and bounds in recent years. Indeed, unless you're passing through Turkey or are a real bicycle freak, it's worth considering buying a bike locally, as that way the spares and repairs will be less problematic. Reasonable bikes start from 300TL. In cities, lock your bike; in rural areas theft is not likely to be a problem, the curious stares of incredulous locals could be. **Bike-rental facilities** are few and far between in Turkey; a notable exception is Cappadocia, particularly Göreme (see p.468).

Given Turkey's road conditions only confident, experienced **motorcyclists** should consider driving here. Plenty of bikers do, however, particularly from Italy, and many more visitors risk a day or two on a **scooter** in resort areas. In larger resorts and big cities there will be at least one motorbike **rental agency**, or a car-rental company which also rents out motor-scooters and mopeds (*mobilet*). You'll need an appropriate driving licence, and most companies insist that it has been held for at least a year. As with cars, always check the bike for scratches and dents before renting it. Helmets are mandatory, despite the endless numbers of helmet-less riders you'll see.

By ferry

Turkey's domestic **ferry network** is confined to İstanbul and the Sea of Marmara. İstanbul Deniz Ötobüsleri (🕸 www.ido.com.tr) operates both ferries and (the faster and more expensive) sea-buses along the Bosphorus, between European and Asian sides of the same strait, and to the Princess Islands. Longer runs across the Sea of Marmara to Yalova (for Termal & İznik), Mudanya (for Bursa), and Bandırma (for the Aegean coast) are the preserve of sea-buses. Any of the trans-Marmara car-ferry links save time compared to the dreary, circuitous road journey, but are relatively expensive with a vehicle.

Private companies offer services from Taşucu, Mersin and Alanya to Girne in Northern Cyprus, and a state-owned ferry still plies between Mersin and Famagusta. Details of these are given in the relevant town accounts.

By plane

Travel by air may be unkind to the environment but it is becoming increasingly the norm in what is a very big country, and makes sense for those on a tight schedule or who wish to visit far-flung places like Van or Erzurum. Turkish Airways (Türk Hava Yolları or THY; ⓣ0212/225 0566, ⓦwww.thy.com), the semi-privatized state-run airline, still offers the most comprehensive domestic flight network. However, it faces stiff competition from private airlines, and has set up its own budget wing, Anadolujet (ⓣ444 2538, ⓦwww.anadolujet.com.tr) which covers many of the same domestic routes as its parent, with Ankara as the hub. Sunexpress (ⓣ444 0797, ⓦwww.sunexpress.com), which has direct flights from the Mediterranean gateway resort of Antalya to Adana, Bursa, Dalaman, Diyarbakir, Erzerum, İstanbul, İzmir, Samsun, Trabzon and Van, was set up jointly by THY and Lufthansa. The private airlines are Onur Air (ⓣ0212/663 2300, ⓦwww.onurair.com.tr), Atlasjet (ⓣ444 0387, ⓦwww.atlasjet.com) and Pegasus ⓣ444 0737 (ⓦwww.flypgs.com). Onur Air offers direct flights from İstanbul to Adana, Antalya, Diyarbakır, Erzerum, Gaziantep, İzmir, Kayseri, Kars, Malatya, Samsun and Trabzon. Atlasjet covers the same destinations plus Nevşehir, Sivas and Van, Pegasus covers Adana, Ankara, Antalya, Trabzon and Van.

Fares with THY can be reasonable – for example, promotional one-way fares from İstanbul to Antalya (tax inclusive) are 39TL, though more usual prices are from 69TL. THY also offers variable student, youth and family discounts. Fares with Atlas, Onur, Pegasus and Sunexpress also start from as low as 39TL (occasionally less if there's a special offer) one way and are very good value. On the downside, last-minute cancellations (by text message in Turkish) are not unknown, particularly with Sunexpress. You're told to appear at the airport an hour and a half before your departure but an hour is usually adequate leeway for completing security procedures.

Accommodation

Finding a bed for the night is generally not a problem in Turkey, except in high season at the busier coastal resorts and larger towns. Lists of hotels, motels and guesthouses (*pansiyon*s) are published by local tourist offices, and we've listed the best options throughout the Guide. Prices, while good value by most Western European standards, are no longer rock-bottom, and can be downright expensive in İstanbul. To some extent facilities have improved correspondingly, though not surprisingly you often get less for your money in the big tourist resorts, and little choice between fleapits or four-star luxury in relatively untouristed towns of the interior. However, with the Turkish economy as it is, backpackers can often afford to go mid-range, and those on mid-range budgets can sometimes secure rooms at the best hotels available east of Cappadocia.

Rooms are generally on the small side by European standards with dim lighting and rarely enough power points. In the newer, three- to five-star establishment **single rooms** generally go for just over half the price of a double, since proprietors are well used to lone (male) business travellers. Rooms with **en-suite bathrooms** are generally about 25 percent more than unplumbed ones; triples are also usually available, costing about thirty percent more than a double.

To avoid **noise**, pick a room away from main thoroughfares or mosque minarets or one with double-glazing. You won't cause offence by asking to see another room, and never agree on a price for a room without seeing it first. Though break-ins aren't the norm in Turkey, **security** should be at least a token consideration. Another possible source of noise is from prostitutes and their clients; although we try not to list any hotels used in this way owners feeling the economic pinch may be tempted to turn a blind-eye to boost profits – especially off season.

Hot water (*sıcak su*) is not always reliable, even in starred hotels, as the solar-powered systems ubiquitous in coastal resorts struggle to cope with demand – check to see if there's an electric back up. Plumbers quite frequently pipe the taps up the wrong way round, so check that the tap that should be the hot one is not the cold! Bathtubs and sinks seldom have plugs, so bring a universal plug from home.

Especially on the south and southwest coast, **air conditioning** (a/c) is almost always found in most establishments of category ❹ and above – and in quite a few below. **Double beds** for couples are becoming more popular; the magic words are *Fransiz yatak* ("French" bed). Incidentally, in some conservative rural areas, hotel management may refuse to let a heterosexual couple share a room unless there is documentary evidence that they are married. A law exists to this effect, so it's no use arguing the toss.

Lift/elevator buttons can be a source of potential confusion. "Ç" stands for "call", a lit-up "K" means the car is already on your floor; an illuminated "M" means "in use"; "Z"

The trouble with touts

Accommodation **touts** can be incredibly persistent in the coastal resorts and other touristy areas, often descending on weary travellers fresh off the bus. If you take your chances with them, rather than our recommendations, note that certain outfits have generated serious complaints, ranging from dangerous wiring to extortion and even false imprisonment. Nevşehir, Eğirdir, Selçuk, Kuşadası and a few other bus stations are often frequented by touts – but note that some are just genuine *pansiyon* owners/workers.

Accommodation price codes

All hotels, motels and *pansiyon*s have been categorized according to the **price codes** outlined below. These represent the minimum you can expect to pay for a double room in high season. For backpackers' hostels, trekkers' lodges and coastal "treehouses", where guests are charged per person, actual prices are given. For band ❸ and up breakfast (see p.44) is included in the price.

Price range categories are given in euros and TL, though you'll usually be quoted in euros for places in categories ❻ and up (and for many İstanbul hotels).

It's worth bargaining for any standard of accommodation at slack times. The walk-in price of hotels in bands ❺–❾ is invariably much higher than pre-booking as part of a package, so it's worth reserving in advance.

❶ €19 (40TL) and under Budget hotels in untouristed areas with shared bathrooms.

❷ €20–28 (41–60TL) Basic en-suite *pansiyon*s and more salubrious hotels inland.

❸ €29–38 (61–80TL) Establishments in touristed areas, sometimes with roof terraces, a bar and/or small pool.

❹ €39–57 (81–120TL) Good-value two-star hotels and *pansiyon*s in resorts. Air conditioning/heating makes an appearance.

❺ €58–80 (121–170TL) Comfortable three-star hotels and *pansiyon*s.

❻ €81–110 (171–230TL) Four-star hotels, smaller holiday villages, and some boutique hotels.

❼ €111–140 (231–300TL) More exclusive four-star and boutique hotels.

❽ €141–190 (301–400TL) Five-star hotels with all the facilities you'd expect – plus some of the best boutique hotels.

❾ €191 (401TL) and over Restored palaces, and the most luxurious boutique/character hotels in upscale areas of İstanbul and trendy coastal resorts.

stands for ground floor whilst "A" means the mezzanine floor.

Hotels

Turkish hotels are graded on a scale of one to five stars by the Ministry of Tourism; there is also a lower tier of unstarred establishments rated by municipalities. At the **four- and five-star** level you're talking international-standard mod cons and prices, flat-screen TVs, air conditioning, etc. **Two- or three-star** outfits are more basic; no tubs in bathrooms and more spartan breakfasts. Boutique hotels are popping up all over the place, especially in restored old mansions in places such as Amasya, Cappadocia, Gaziantep, İstanbul, Urfa, and Safranbolu. However, the term is overused to market any accommodation that has been done up in a minimalist or modernist style.

The **unrated hotels** licensed by municipalities can be virtually as good as the lower end of the one-star class, sometimes with en-suite bathrooms, televisions and phones. Others though, at the very bottom end of the market will have a basin in the

room but shared showers and (squat) toilet down the hall. Most solo female travellers will feel uncomfortable in unstarred, and even many one- and two-star hotels, especially in less touristed parts of the interior.

Particularly when it comes to family-run pensions, you may well find that the proprietor has links with similar establish-ments in other towns; often he/she will offer to call ahead to arrange both a stay and a transfer from the *otogar* for you. This informal network is a good way of avoiding the hassle with touts and a late-night search for a comfy bed.

Pansiyons and apartments

Often the most pleasant places to stay are **pansiyons** (pensions), small guesthouses common in touristy areas. Try to avoid the touts (see box, p.41) and look for little signs with the legend *Boş oda var* ("Empty rooms free"). *Pansiyon*s usually have en-suite facilities, and many feature common gardens or terraces where breakfast (usually 7–10TL a head when not included in the room price) is served. Rooms tend to be spartan but clean, furnished in one-star hotel mode and always with two sheets (*çarşafs*) on the bed. Hot water is always available, though with solar-powered systems not always when you want it, and many now have air conditioning, often for a supplement. Prices are often rigidly controlled by the local tourist authorities, set according to the establishment's rating.

Self-catering apartments are becoming widespread in coastal resorts, and are mostly pitched at vacationing Turks or foreigners arriving on pre-arranged packages. Some are available to walk-in trade – local tourist offices maintain lists – and apart from the weekly price the major (negotiable) outlay will be for the large gas bottle feeding the stove. Ensure, too, that kitchens are equipped well enough to make them truly self-catering.

Hostels, lodges and treehouses

There's only a handful of internationally affiliated, foreigner-pitched hostels in the country, but this gap has been amply filled by **backpackers' hostels**, found most notably in İstanbul, Çanakkale, Selçuk, Köyceğiz and Fethiye. Basically 1970s *pansiyons* which have been adapted to feature multi-bedded rooms, laundry and internet facilities, self-catering kitchen, tours and lively bars, they can be fair value – costs vary from €10–12 a head in a large dorm, considerably more for a double room.

In recent years a large number of **trekkers' lodges** have sprung up in the foothills of the Kaçkar mountains, especially on the south slope, and along the Lycian Way. These generally offer a choice between communal sleeping on mattresses arrayed on a wooden terrace, or more enclosed double to quadruple, non en-suite rooms – strangely, cooking facilities may often be absent. Costs are comparable to the backpackers' hostels.

Found principally on the southwestern coast between Antalya and Fethiye are the so-called **"treehouses"**, often ramshackle collections of elevated shacks or even just open platforms made of rough timber. Some have dorm rooms while an increasing number are designed for two people and have doors, windows, electricity, air conditioning and, rarely, en-suite facilities.

Campsites

In areas frequently visited by independent travellers, *pansiyons* and hostels with gardens will often allow **camping**. Charges run from a couple of euros to €7 per head in a well-appointed site at a major resort; you may also be charged to park your vehicle – anything from €2 to €7, depending on the site and season. The most appealing campsites are those run by the **Ministry of Forestry**, open April to October inclusive; look for brown wooden signs with yellow lettering. There are 20 of them in shady groves at strategic locations (mostly coastal) across the west of the country, and they make an ideal choice if you have your own transport, especially a combi-van or car and caravan. **Camping rough** is not illegal, but hardly anybody does it except when trekking in the mountains, and, since you can expect a visit from curious police or even nosier villagers, it's not really a choice for those who like privacy.

Food and drink

At its finest, Turkish food is among the best in the world – indeed it is sometimes ranked alongside French and Chinese as one of the three classic cuisines – with many venerable dishes descended from Ottoman palace cuisine. The quality of produce is reliably exceptional with most ingredients available locally. Prices aren't going to break the bank, with three-course meals starting at around 14TL (€6.5/£5.80). However, you'll pay more (often considerably more) at resorts, where standards have often sadly declined. Unadventurous travellers can get stuck in a kebab rut, berating the monotony of the cuisine; in fact, all but the strictest vegetarians should find enough variety to satisfy them.

Places to eat and specialities are summarized below, but for a full **menu reader**, turn to p.745. Generic "Mediterranean" restaurants and burger/pizza chains, needing no translation, are almost everywhere.

Breakfast

The so-called "Turkish" **breakfast** (*kahvaltı*) served at modest hotels and *pansiyon*s is invariably a pile of spongy white bread slices with a pat of margarine, a slice or two of processed cheese and (beef) mortadella, a dab of pre-packed jam and a couple of olives. Only tea is likely to be available in quantity; extras such as *sahanda yumurtalar* (fried eggs) will probably be charged for. In the better hotels and top-end *pansiyon*s you can expect a variety of breads and pastries, fresh fruit slices, a choice of olive and cheese types, and an array of cold and hot meats, plus eggs in various styles.

You can breakfast better on a budget by using street-carts or *büfes* (snack cafés), the source of **börek**, a rich, flaky, layered pastry containing bits of mince or cheese. Alternatives include a simple **simit** (bread rings speckled with sesame seeds) or a bowl of **çorba** (soup) with a lemon wedge.

Street food

With breakfast over, vendors hawk **lahmacun**, small, round pizzas with a thin meat-based topping. Unlike in Britain, **kebabs** (*kebap* in Turkish) are not generally considered takeaway food unless wrapped in *dürüm*, a paratha-like bread; more often you'll find *döner* or *köfte* in takeaway stalls,

served on a baguette or hamburger bun. A **sandwich** (*sandviç*) is a baguette chunk with various fillings (often *kokoreç* – stuffed lamb offal – or fish). In coastal cities deep-fried **mussels** (*midye tava*) are often available, as are *midye dolması* (mussels stuffed with rice, pine nuts and allspice) – though these are best avoided during summer, especially if sold unrefrigerated by street vendors.

Unlike *lahmacun*, flat bread stuffed with various toppings – **pide** – is served to diners in a *pideci* or *pide salonu* from 11am onwards. The big advantage of this dish is that it's always made to order: typical styles are *kaşarlı* or *peynirli* (with cheese), *yumurtalı* (with egg), *kıymalı* (with mince), and *sucuklu* (with sausage).

Other specialities worth seeking out are **mantı** – the traditional Central Asian, meat-filled ravioli, served drenched in yoghurt and spice-reddened oil – or **gözleme**, a stuffed-crêpe-like delicacy. At **kuru yemiş** stalls, also known as *leblebeci*s, nuts and dried fruit are sold by weight – typically in 100g shots. Aside from the usual offerings, keep an eye out for increasingly rare *cezeriye*, a sweetmeat made of carrot juice, honey and nuts; the east Anatolian snack of **peştil** (dried fruit), most commonly apricot and peach, pressed into sheets; and **tatlı sucuk**, a fruit, nut and molasses roll (not to be confused with meat *sucuk* or sausage).

Restaurants

A "**restoran**", denoting anything from a motorway-bus pit stop to a white-tablecloth affair, will provide *ızgara yemek* or meat dishes grilled to order. A **çorbacı** is a soup kitchen; **kebapçıs** and **köftecıs** specialize in kebab and *köfte* respectively, with limited side dishes – usually just salad, yoghurt and a few desserts. A **lokanta** is a restaurant emphasizing *hazır yemek*, pre-cooked dishes kept warm in a steam-tray. Here also can be found *sulu yemek*, "watery food" – hearty meat chunks swimming in broth or sauce. Despite their often clinical appearance, the best *lokanta*s may well provide your most memorable taste of Turkish cooking. **İskembe salonus** are aimed at revellers emerging from clubs or taverns in the early hours, and open until 5 or 6am. Their stock-in-trade is tripe soup laced liberally with garlic oil, vinegar and red pepper flakes, an effective hangover cure. They also sell *piliç* (small chickens), often seen spit-roasting in the window.

At an **ocakbaşı**, the grill and its hood occupy centre-stage, as diners watch their meat being prepared. Even more interactive is the **kendin pişir kendin ye** (cook-it-and-eat-it-yourself) establishment, where a *mangal* (barbecue with coals), a specified quantity of raw meat, plus *kekik* (oregano) and *kimyon* (cumin) are brought to your outdoor/indoor table. Such places are excellent value, and you get to inspect the state of the meat; they may also offer *tandır kebap*, a side of oven-roasted lamb or goat.

Most budget-priced restaurants are **alcohol-free** (*içkisiz*); any **licensed** place (marked *içkili*) is likely to be more expensive. A possible exception is a **meyhane** (tavern), where eating is on a barely equal footing to tippling. In the fancier İstanbul ones, though, food – often unusual delicacies – can be very good and not always drastically overpriced. In Ankara and İstanbul (especially in Beyoğlu and Kumkapı) groups of "respectable" Turkish women attend such establishments, though elsewhere unaccompanied foreign woman may baulk at patronizing *meyhane*s, and some will seem dodgy to Western men too. That said, any foreign men or couples bold enough to visit the more decorous *meyhane*s will be treated with utmost courtesy.

Prices vary widely according to the type of establishment: from 2.5–3TL per item at a simple boozeless soup kitchen up to 15–20TL at the flashier resort restaurants and big-city establishments. **Portions**, especially in *meyhane*s, tend to be tiny, so if you're a big eater you may need to order two ostensibly main courses. Having your plate whisked away before you're done with it is irritatingly common – not so much a ploy to hurry you along, but from the Turkish custom of never leaving a guest with an "empty" or "dirty" plate before them. *Kalsın* ("may it remain") is the term to stop this practice in mid-air.

Dishes and specialities

The most common **soups** (*çorbas*) are *mercimek* (lentil), *ezo gelin* (a thick rice and vegetable broth – an appetizing breakfast), or *işkembe* (tripe). *Çoban* (shepherd's) *salatası* means the ubiquitous, micro-chopped cucumber, tomato, onion, pepper and parsley **salad** (approach the peppers with caution); *yeşil* (green) salad, usually just some *marul* (lettuce), is less often available. The more European *mevsim salatası* ("seasonal" salad) – perhaps tomato slices, watercress, red cabbage and lettuce hearts sprinkled with cheese and drenched in

Waiter tricks to beware of

Fancy, and not so fancy, places will try to levy both a *küver* (cover charge) *and* either a *garsoniye* ("waiter" charge) or *servis ücreti* (service charge, either typically ten percent), though if it's not documented in writing on the menu, technically you don't have to pay this. At places without **menus** (common), you'll need to ascertain prices beforehand and review bills carefully when finished. Waiting staff are adept at bringing you items (pickles, garlic bread, *çiğ börek*, mini-*meze*, bottled water, etc) that you haven't specifically ordered – but which you will definitely pay for unless announced by the magic words *ıkramızdır* (with our compliments). All these little tricks deployed together can bump an apparently reasonable bill up by nearly a third.

dressing – makes a welcome change from "shepherd's" salad.

Meze and vegetable dishes

In any *içkili restoran* or *meyhane*, you'll find the **meze** (appetizers) for which Turkey is justly famous. They are also the best dishes for vegetarians, since many are meat-free, while the variety of vegetables and pulses used will sustain your dietary needs.

The most common platters include *patlıcan salatası* (aubergine mash), *piyaz* (white haricot vinaigrette), *semizotu* (purslane weed, usually in yoghurt), *mücver* (courgette croquettes), *sigara böreği* (tightly rolled cheese pastries), *imam bayıldı* (cold baked aubergine with onion and tomato) and *dolma* (any stuffed vegetable, but typically peppers or tomatoes). Note that during Ramadan, *meze* may be unavailable as few chefs reckon it worth their while to prepare them for after-dark consmption.

In *hazır yemek* restaurants, *kuru fasulye* (haricot bean soup), *taze fasulye* (French beans), *sebze turlu* (vegetable stew) and *nohut* (chickpeas) are the principal **vegetable dishes**. Although no meat may be visible, they're almost always made with lamb or chicken broth; even bulgur and rice may be cooked in meat stock. Vegetarians might ask *İçinde et suyu var mı?* (Does it contain meat stock?).

Bread and cheese

Bread is edible hot out of the oven, but otherwise is spongily stale, mainly for scooping up puréed *meze*. Flat, unadorned *pide* is served with soup, during Ramadan and at *kebapcıs*; *kepekli* (wholemeal) or *çavdar* (rye bread; only from a *fırın* or bakery) afford relief in larger towns. In villages, cooked *yufka* – the basis of *börek* pastry – makes a welcome respite, as does *bazlama* (similar to an Indian paratha).

Many people return from Turkey having sampled only *beyaz peynir* (like Greek feta) at breakfast but other Turkish **cheeses** deserve mention. *Dil peynir* ("tongue" cheese), a hard, salty cheese comprised of mozzarella-like filaments, and the plaited *oğru peynir*, can both be grilled or fried like Cypriot halloúmi. *Tulum peynir* is a strong,

salty, almost granular goat's cheese cured in a goatskin; it is used as *börek* stuffing, although together with walnuts, it makes a very popular *meze*. *Otlu peynir* from the Van area is cured with herbs; cow's-milk *kaşar*, especially *eski* (aged) *kaşar* from the Kars region, is also highly esteemed.

Meat dishes

Grilled meat dishes – normally served simply with a few *pide* slices and raw vegetable garnish – include several variations on the stereotypical kebab. *Adana kebap* is spicy, with sprinkled purple sumac herb betraying Arab influence; *İskender kebap*, best sampled in Bursa, is heavy on the flat bread and yoghurt; while *kiremit kebap* appears on a hot clay tray. If you've any appetite, order *bir buçuk* (a portion and a half – adequate) or *çift* (double portion – generous). A *karışık ızgara* (mixed grill) is always good value. Chicken (*piliç* or *tavuk*) is widely available and usually cheaper than other meats, served as *şiş*, *pırzola* (grilled breast), or *kanat* (grilled wings). Offal is popular, particularly *böbrek* (kidney), *yürek* (heart), *ciğer* (liver), and *koç yumurtası* (ram's egg) or *billur* (crystal) – the last two euphemisms for testicle.

More elaborate **meat-and-veg combinations** include *mussaka* (inferior to the Greek rendition), *karnıyarık* (a much better Turkish variation), *güveç* (clay-pot fricassee), *tas kebap* (stew), *hunkar beğendi* (lamb, puréed eggplant and cheese), *saray kebap* (beef stew topped with béchamel sauce and oven-browned), *macar kebap* (fine veal chunks in a spicy sauce with tomatoes and wine) and *saç kavurma*, an inland speciality of meat, vegetables and spices fried up in a *saç* (the Turkish wok).

Fish and seafood

Fish and seafood is good, if usually pricey, and sold by weight more often than by item (40–45TL per kilo in remote spots, more than double that in flash resorts), though per-portion prices of about 15–20TL prevail for less bijoux species. Choose with an eye to what's in season (as opposed to farmed, frozen and imported), and don't turn your nose up at humbler varieties, which will likely be fresher. Budget mainstays include *sardalya* (grilled sardines), *palamut* (autumn tuna), *akya* (*liche* in French; no English name), and *sarıgöz* (black bream). *Çipura* (gilt-head bream) and *levrek* (sea bass), when suspiciously cheap, are almost invariably farmed. Fish is invariably served simply, with just a garnish of spring onion (*soğan*) and rocket (*roka*).

Desserts and sweets

Turkish chefs pander shamelessly to the sweet-toothed, who will find a huge range of sugary treats at a **pastane** (sweet shop).

Turkish Delight and baklava

The best-known Turkish sweet, *lokum* or **"Turkish Delight"**, is available from most *pastane*s and the more touristy shops. It's basically solidified sugar and pectin, flavoured (most commonly) with rosewater, sometimes pistachios, sprinkled with powdered sugar – and laced with far too many chemical additives. There are also numerous kinds of **helva**, including the tahini-paste chew synonymous with the concoction in the West, although in Turkey the term usually means any variation on the basic theme of baked flour or starch, butter, sugar and flavoured water.

Of the syrup-soaked **baklava**-type items – all permutations of a sugar, flour, nut and butter mix – the best is *antep fıstıklı sarması* (pistachio-filled *baklava*) – pricey at 3–4TL per serving; other *baklava* tend to be *cevizli* (walnut-filled), and slightly cheaper. *Künefe* – the "shredded wheat" filaments of *kadayif* perched atop white cheese, baked and then soaked in syrup – has become an ubiquitous dessert in kebab and *lahmacun* places; both *baklava* and *künefe* are often served, luxuriously if not exactly healthily, with large dollops of ice cream.

Puddings, ice cream and fruit

Less sweet and healthier are the **milk-based** dishes, popular everywhere. *Süpangile* ("süp" for short, a corruption of *soupe d'Anglais*) is an incredibly dense, rich chocolate pudding with sponge or a biscuit embedded inside. More modest are *keşkül* (vanilla and nut-crumble custard), and *sütlaç*

(rice pudding) – one dessert that's consistently available in ordinary restaurants. The most complicated dish is *tavukgöğsü*, a cinnamon-topped morsel made from hyper-boiled and strained chicken breast, semolina starch and milk. *Kazandibi* (literally "bottom of the pot") is *tavukgöğsü* residue with a dark crust on the bottom – not to be confused with *fırın sütlaç*, which is actually *sütlaç* pudding with a scorched top baked in a clay dish.

If you coincide with the Islamic month of Muharrem, you'll be able to sample *aşure*, a devotional dish of Turkey's Alevî and Bektaşi communities (also available in many *pastane*s year-round). A sort of rosewater jelly laced with pulses, wheat berries, raisins and nuts, it supposedly contains forty ingredients, after a legend which claims that after the Ark's forty-day sail on the Flood, and the first sighting of dry land, Noah commanded that a stew be made of the forty remaining kinds of food on board.

Traditional Turkish ice cream (*dondurma*) is an excellent summer treat, provided it's genuine *Maraşlı döşme* (whipped in the Kahraman Maraş tradition – a bit like Italian gelato), not factory-produced rubbish. The outlandishly costumed *dondurma* street-sellers of yore have been overtaken by upmarket parlours selling every conceivable flavour; the best chain of these is Mado, with high prices but equally high quality.

Summer fruit (*meyve*), generally means *kavun* (Persian melon, honeydew) or *karpuz* (watermelon). Autumn choices include *kabak tatlısı* (candied squash with walnut chunks and *kaymak*, or clotted cream) or *ayva tatlısı* (stewed quince served with nuts or dried fruit, topped with *kaymak* and dusted with grated pistachio).

Tea and coffee

Tea is the national drink and an essential social lubricant – you'll most likely be offered some within twenty minutes of arrival. It's prepared in the *çaydanlık* or *demlik*, a double-boiler apparatus, with a larger water chamber underneath the smaller receptacle containing dry leaves, to which a small quantity of hot water is added. After a suitable (or unsuitably long) wait the tea is decanted into tiny tulip-shaped glasses, then diluted with more water to taste: *açık* is weak, *demli* or *koyu* steeped. Sugar comes as cubes on the side; milk is never added. If you're frustrated by the usual tiny glass at breakfast, ask for a *düble çay* (a "double tea", served in a juice glass).

Herbal **teas** are also popular, particularly *ıhlamur* (linden flower), *kuşburnu* (rose hip), *papatya* (camomile) and *ada çay* ("island" tea), an infusion of a sage common in coastal areas. The much-touted **apple tea** (*elma çay*) contains chemicals and not a trace of apple essence.

Coffee is not as commonly drunk in Turkey, though instant is increasingly popular, available in several brands besides the inevitable Nescafé. It's much stronger, however, than Anglo-Saxon formulas, more in line with German tastes. The traditional, fine-ground Turkish coffee is preferable, brewed up *sade* (without sugar), *orta şekerli* (medium sweet) or *çok şekerli* (very sweet). Only in the largest towns and more cosmopolitan resorts will you find Western notions (and Western pricings) of coffee, such as filtered or cappuccino. For extended tea- or coffee-drinking sessions, retire to a **çay bahçesi** (tea garden), which may also serve ice cream and soft drinks.

Soft drinks

Fruit juice (*meyva suyu*) can be excellent if it comes as pulp in a bottle, most often as *kayısı* (apricot), *şeftali* (peach) and *vişne* (sour cherry); thin, preservative-spiked cardboard-packaged juice-drinks are distinctly less thrilling. Of late there's a veritable craze for fresh-squeezed, pricey *karadut suyu* (red mulberry juice) and *nar suyu* (pomegranate juice).

Bottled **spring water** (*memba suyu*), or fizzy **mineral water** (*maden suyu*) are restaurant staples, but in some establishments chilled, potable tap water in a glass bottle or a jug is routinely provided, for which there should be no extra charge. *Meşrubat* is the generic term for all types of carbonated **soft drinks**.

Certain beverages accompany particular kinds of food or appear at set seasons. *Sıcak süt* (hot milk) is the traditional complement to *börek*, though in winter it's fortified with *salep*, made from the ground tubers of a phenomenally expensive wild orchid (*Orchis mascula*) gathered in coastal hills near İzmir. **Salep** is a good safeguard against colds (and also reputedly an aphrodisiac), though most packages sold are heavily adulterated with powdered milk, starch and sugar – only in the İzmir bazaar will you find the real thing (which incidentally it's illegal to export). **Ayran** (chilled, watered-down yoghurt) is always on offer at *pideci*s and *kebapcı*s, an excellent accompaniment to spicy meat. In autumn and winter, stalls sell **boza**, a delicious, mildly fermented millet drink. Similarly tangy is **şıra**, a lightly alcoholic grape juice acceptable to religious Muslims and available in late summer and autumn.

Alcoholic drinks

Since the accession of the nominally Islamist AK Parti in 2002, there's good and bad news concerning **alcoholic drinks** (*içkiler*) in Turkey. These are still available theoretically without restriction in resorts – even within 200m of a mosque, normally a no-no – though booze has vanished from all municipally owned concessions in the many AK-run towns, and you will have some thirsty moments in conservative interior towns such as Afyon, Konya, Erzerum or Diyarbakır. The ruling party has also slapped a twenty percent tax on all alcohol, pushing prices (beer aside) up significantly. The bright spot has been the sale and break-up of Tekel (the state alcohol-producing monopoly) and resulting increased competition and quality amongst distilled spirits.

Beer

Beer (*bira*) comes principally in returnable bottles but also in cans (expensive) and on draught (*fıcı bira*; cheaper). Prices vary widely, from 2TL per bottle in a shop to 6TL in a mid-range bar, with even higher prices prevailing in trendier clubs – 4–5TL is typical at restaurants. The most popular domestic brand is Efes Pilsen (5 percent ABV); it's normally sold as a half-litre bottle, though also exists as 33cl bottles or cans of "Lite" (low alcohol), "Dark" (6.1 percent), and "Xtra" (7.5 percent). The main international brands are Tuborg and Carlsberg, both brewed locally. Gusta is a dark, locally brewed wheat beer which makes a nice change. Imported bottled beers are also available in the largest cities, at a price. There are very few relatively civilized beer **pubs** as opposed to the **beer hall** (*birahane*), imitation German-style establishments, which often have a distinctly macho atmosphere.

Wine

Wine (*şarap*) comes from vineyards scattered across western Anatolia between Cappadocia, the Euphrates Valley, Thrace and the Aegean. Fine wine now has a local audience, with expensive imported labels available in most upmarket town-centre or hotel restaurants and the bigger supermarkets. Local wines are also now better distributed, resulting in a huge variety in trendy resorts, though quality remains inconsistent. Red wine is *kırmızı*, white *beyaz*, rose *roze*. In shops, count on paying 8–18TL per bottle of basic to mid-range wine, or as much as 25TL for a bottle from some obscure, self-styled boutique winery that may be scarcely better than the major players. In restaurants, it will be double that – if you're not keen on shelling out for a bottle of an unknown quantity, most places sell a few labels by the glass (*kade'le* in Turkish) for 6–8TL.

The market is dominated by two large vintners: Doluca (try their Antik premium labels, or Moskado Sek) and Kavaklıdere (whose Çankaya white, Angora red and Lâl rose are commendable). Kavaklıdere also produces a sparkling white, İnci Damalası, the closest thing to local champagne. Other smaller, regional brands to watch for include Turasan, Narbağ, and Peribacası (Cappadocia). Feyzi Kutman red in particular is superb, though rarely found outside the largest centres; another affordable Aegean producer worth sampling is Sevilen, which makes organic reds – Merlot and Cabernet – at premium prices, good whites and a palatable, MOR label, Tellibağ. Similarly confined to their areas of production are Majestik red, available only around İzmir, cheap-and-cheerful wines from Şirince, plus the vintners of Bozcaada, covered in detail on p.209.

Rakı and other spirits

The Turkish national aperitif is **rakı**, not unlike Greek ouzo but stronger (45–48 percent alcohol), usually drunk over ice and topped up with bottled water. The *meyhane* routine of an evening is for a group to order a big bottle of *rakı*, a bucket of ice and a few bottles of water, and then slowly drink themselves under the table between bites of seafood *meze* or nibbles of *çerez* – the generic term for pumpkin seeds, chickpeas, almonds etc, served on tiny plates. Since the Tekel was broken up, private distilleries of varying quality have proliferated, the best (and priciest) being Efe, particularly its green-label line. However, Burgaz brand is often better value and nearly as good (again in green-label variety). Tekirdağ, especially its "gold series", is also recommendable. Sadly, most of the time only the ex-Tekel Yeni is available at most establishments, with a double *rakı* in a *meyhane* running 6–8TL. Shop carefully for souvenir bottles – prices vary from 27TL for a 70cl bottle of Burgaz in an expensive resort to just 37TL for a full litre of Efe in a megastore.

Stronger **spirits** – *cin* (gin), *votka* (vodka) and *kanyak* (cognac) – exist as imported labels or cheaper but often nastier *yerli* (locally produced) variants. Domestically produced, rather cloying **liqueurs** may be given on the house as a *digestif*.

 # Health

No special inoculations are required for Turkey, although the cautious might want typhoid and tetanus jabs, particularly for eastern Anatolia. Some visitors also get injections against hepatitis A, for which the risk is possibly greater in İstanbul than in rural areas. Malaria is a seasonal (April–July) problem between Adana and Mardin (in Chapter 11), especially in areas irrigated by the Southeastern Anatolia Project. However, for brief visits you shouldn't need prophylactic drugs. For up-to-date advice consult a travel clinic.

Stomach upsets and drinking water

Many people experience bouts of **diarrhoea**, especially on longer stays. If you do get struck down note that Lomotil or Imodium (trade names for diphenoxylate), are easily available in Turkey. They allow you to travel without constantly running to the bathroom, but do not kill the bug that ails you. Buscopan, also sold locally, is particularly good for stomach cramps while Ge-Oral powder dissolved in pure water is an effective rehydration remedy. **Turkish tap water** is heavily chlorinated and usually drinkable, though not exactly delectable (some restaurants may serve it chilled and minimally filtered). In İstanbul, however, it is absolutely to be avoided in favour of bottled water. **Rural springs** are labelled *içilir*, *içilbelir* or *içme suyu* (all meaning "potable"), or *içilmez* (not drinkable).

Particularly during the hot summer months, serious **food poisoning** is a possibility – even in the biggest cities and resorts, and especially in southeastern Turkey. In restaurants, avoid dishes that look as if they have been standing around and make sure meat and fish are well grilled. Don't, whatever you do, eat stuffed mussels in summer. If you're struck down, let the bug run its course and drink lots of fluids; eating plain white rice and yoghurt also helps. Stubborn cases will need a course of antibiotics or Flagyl (metronidazole), the latter effective against giardia and protozoans as well as certain bacteria; pharmacists (see opposite) are trained to recognize symptoms and you don't need a prescription.

Bites and stings

Mosquitoes are often a problem, and since no good topical repellents are available locally, you should bring your own. At night mozzies are dispatched with locally sold incense coils (*spiral tütsü*) or an *Esem Mat*, a small, electrified tray that slowly vaporizes an odourless disc. A mosquito net is a *çibindirik*, provision of which by hotels and *pansiyons* in heavily infested areas is almost standard.

Jellyfish are an occasional hazard along the Aegean shore; more ubiquitous are **sea urchins**, whose spines easily detach if trodden on; the splinters must be removed to prevent infection. **Snakes** and **scorpions** can lurk among the stones at archeological sites, and in nooks and crannies of ground-floor accommodation. There are two kinds of vipers (*engerek* in Turkish): the deadly, metre-long Ottoman viper, fortunately rare, and the smaller, more common and less dangerous asp viper. Neither is particularly aggressive unless disturbed; both are most commonly seen during mild spring days.

Certain **ticks** in Turkey carry the Crimean-Congo haemorragic fever (**CCHF**) virus, with hundreds of cases (and fatalities in two figures) annually, though the danger seems confined to rural areas of several provinces between Ankara and the Black Sea.

Although rare (one to two cases per year) **rabies** is another potential danger. Be wary of any animal that bites, scratches or licks you, particularly if it's behaving erratically. If you do suspect you have been bitten by a rabid animal, wash the wound thoroughly (preferably with iodine) and seek medical attention immediately. Farmland is often patrolled by giant Sivas-Kangal sheepdogs, though these are rarely aggressive unless their flock is closely approached.

Medical treatment

Minor complaints can be dealt with at a **pharmacy** (*eczane*); even the smallest town will have one. Turkish pharmacists may know some English or German, and dispense medicines that would ordinarily require a prescription abroad. Prices for locally produced (as opposed to imported) medicines are low, but it may be difficult to find exact equivalents to your home prescription. *Nöbet(ci)* or **night-duty pharmacies** are often found near hospitals; a duty roster is posted in Turkish in every chemist's front window.

For more serious conditions go to one of the **public clinics** (*sağlık ocağı*), or a **hospital** (*hastane*), indicated by a blue street sign with a large white "H" on it. Hospitals are either public (*Devlet Hastane* or *SSK Hastanesi*) or private (*Özel Hastane*); the latter are (usually) preferable in terms of cleanliness and standard of care, and since all foreigners must pay for treatment, you may as well get the best available. Fees are lower than in northern Europe and North America but still substantial enough to make insurance cover essential (there are no reciprocal healthcare arrangements between Turkey and the EU). The medical faculties of major universities – eg İstanbul, İzmir, Edirne and Bursa – also have teaching hospitals infinitely better than the state hospitals, but less expensive than the private ones. Admission desks of private hospitals can also recommend their affiliated doctors if you don't want or need to be an in-patient. If you're too ill to move, but must summon a doctor, hotel-room visits will cost about €50, with perhaps another €25 for medication delivered from a local pharmacy. If you're on a **package tour**, the better companies will have arrangements with competent, English-speaking doctors and dentists in or near the resort. In a medical **emergency** summon an ambulance by dialling ☏112.

Contraception and female hygeine

International brands of **birth control** pills (*doğum kontrol hapıları*) are sold at pharmacies. **Condoms** (*preservatif*) are sold in most pharmacies and also supermarkets like Gima and Migros; don't buy off street-carts, where stock may be tampered with or expired. **Tampons** are available from pharmacies and supermarkets at UK prices; Orkid is the adequate domestic brand of "sanitary towel".

Culture and etiquette

Many Turks, even in remote areas, have lived and worked abroad (mainly in Germany) or at tourist resorts in Turkey, and are used to foreign ways. But traditional customs matter, and although you're unlikely to cause offence through a social gaffe, it's best to be aware of prevailing customs. Also, many Turks are devout (or at least conservative) Muslims, so you should adhere to local dress codes – particularly away from resorts and when visiting mosques. For more on the Turkish art of bargaining see p.59.

Invitations and meals

Hospitality (*misafirperverlik*) is a pillar of rural Turkish culture, so you're unlikely to leave the country without at least one invitation to **drink tea**, either in a *çayhane* (teahouse) or someone's home. If you really can't spare the time, mime "thanks" by placing one hand on your chest and pointing with the other to your watch and then in the direction you're headed. If you do stop, remember that drinking only one glass may be interpreted as casting aspersions on their tea. If offered a full meal, decline the first offer – if it's sincere it will be repeated at least twice and custom demands that you accept the third offer.

Being **invited for a meal** at a Turkish home is both an honour and an obligation. Always remove your shoes at the door. In urban, middle-class homes you'll sit at a table and eat with cutlery. In village houses, however, the meal is usually served at a low table with cushions on the floor; hide your feet under the table or a dropcloth provided for the purpose. (Feet, shod or not, are considered unclean and should never be pointed at anyone.) When scooping food with bread sections from a communal bowl, **use your right hand** – the left is reserved for bodily hygeine. If you use toothpicks provided at restaurants, cover your mouth while doing so.

Dress and body language

Turkey remains a conservative country concerning dress. **Beachwear** should be confined to the beach, while strolling shirtless around resort streets is ultra-offensive (though plenty of foreign men do it). Tight clothing, halter tops, skimpy shorts and the like should also be avoided away from heavily touristed areas. **Nude sunbathing** is not acceptable anywhere though at any major Mediterranean/Aegean resort discreet topless sunning takes place.

If you venture much off the tourist track, accept that being **stared at** is part of the experience and not considered rude. In some parts of the southeast, you may be mobbed by small children wishing to guide you around the local ruins and/or beg for pens, sweets or money.

Turks employ a variety of not immediately obvious **body language**. Clicking the tongue against the roof of the mouth and simultaneously raising the eyebrows and chin means "no" or "there isn't any"; those economical of movement will rely on their eyebrows alone. By contrast, wagging the head rapidly from side to side means "Explain, I don't understand", while a single, obliquely inclined nod means "yes".

Black and Asian travellers

In remoter areas, **black and Asian people** may find themselves something of a curiosity, and may receive unsolicited comments – ranging from *Arap!* (a Black!) to the notionally more appreciative *çok güzel* (very pretty!). Turkey is in fact one of the least racist countries around the Mediterranean. Many black footballers from Africa and South America play in Turkish teams and you may also notice the country's black minority group, termed "Afro Turks", particularly around İzmir.

Female travellers

While many **female travellers** encounter little more than some flirtatious banter while travelling in Turkey, a minority experience unwanted attention and more serious harrassment in both resorts and rural areas. The key to avoiding trouble is to be aware of your surroundings, dress and behaviour and how it might be interpreted. If travelling alone, it's best to stick to mid-range hotels (particularly in the interior) and schedule transport to arrive during daylight hours. That said, the back-streets of most Turkish towns are a lot safer at night than those of many Western cities. This is partly due to heavy police presence; do not hesitate to ask them for help. Away from the main resorts, **unaccompanied women** are a rare sight at night; when heading out for an evening, try to go as part of a group, preferably mixed-sex, otherwise as an all-female group, which may, however, get some unwelcome attention. In restaurants, unaccompanied women may be directed to the *aile salonu* (family parlour), usually upstairs, rather than be served with other diners. While **public drunkenness** is unacceptable for both genders, this is especially true for women.

Turkish women have over the years devised successful tactics to protect themselves from **harassment** – specifically, avoiding eye contact with men and looking as confident and purposeful as possible. When all else fails, the best way of neutralizing harassment is to make a public scene. You won't elicit any sympathy by swearing in

Turkish, but the words *Ayıp* ("Shame!") or *Beni rahatsız ediyorsun* ("You're disturbing me"), spoken very loudly, generally have the desired effect – passers-by or fellow passengers will deal with the situation for you. *Defol* ("Piss off!") and *Bırak beni* ("Leave me alone") are stronger retorts. In general, Turkish men back down when confronted and cases of violent sexual harassment are very rare.

Prostitution

Prostitution is thriving in Turkey, both in legal, state-controlled brothels and, illegally, on the streets and in certain bars and dubious hotels. Many prostitutes working here illegally are from Russia and former Soviet-bloc countries such as Moldova or Ukraine, and are known locally as "Natashas". Female travellers may be mistaken for prostitutes by local men assuming that any foreign woman out unaccompanied at night must be on the game. If you wander through **seedy districts** such as Laleli/Aksaray in İstanbul, or stumble across known pick-up points on major highways, expect to be followed by kerb-crawlers; it's usually enough to explain that you're not a *natasha*. This Guide

doesn't recommend hotels used for prostitution but management and clientele can change, so keep your antennae primed.

Gay and lesbian travellers

Turkish society has always been deeply ambivalent about male **homosexuality**, since the days of a rampantly bisexual Ottoman culture, when transvestite dancers and entertainers were the norm. That said, public attitudes are generally intolerant or closeted. The only place with a recognized gay scene is İstanbul, though the more liberal towns of Antalya and Izmir and the resorts of Bodrum, Marmaris and Alanya are considered gay friendly.

Homosexual acts between adults over 18 are legal, but existing laws against "spreading homosexual information" in print – ie advocating the lifestyle – are sporadically enforced, "Gay Pride" festivals have been forcibly cancelled, and police have raided İstanbul's numerous gay bars on occasion, forcing customers to submit to STD testing. Things have worsened under the current government, with increased cases of police harassment, censorship of gay websites and

Women in Turkey

Acceptable behaviour and roles for **women** vary widely by class and region. In İstanbul and along the heavily touristed coastline, social freedom approximates that in Western Europe; in more traditional areas females act conservatively, with headscarves in abundance.

Turkish women have long held **jobs** in the professions and civil service as well as in the tourist sector in hotels and for airlines. You will also see female police but rarely encounter them working in bazaars, restaurants and bars. Recently, fast-food chains and supermarkets have offered more job opportunities. In rural areas, women rarely have access to formal employment and work the land. **Literacy rates** for girls are also significantly lower in rural areas despite primary education being compulsory.

In villages parents still choose wives for their sons; in cities more Western attitudes prevail and couples even live together unmarried. Abortion is available on demand; contraceptives are readily obtainable; and a baby can be registered to unmarried parents. The annual birth rate is typically under two children per woman, though there's a huge disparity between eastern and western Turkey. The law gives men considerable say over their children, though divorce law is fairly equitable.

Sadly Turkey is also known for hundreds of annual **"honour" killings**, particularly in Kurdish areas. These occur for actual or suspected adultery, pregnancy out of wedlock or dating someone disapproved of by the family. While in the past this crime was carried out by a male relative, lately women have been forced to commit suicide instead.

hate crimes – including periodic murders of transexuals – being left uninvestigated.

There are currently two gay activist groups locally: a chapter of the gay-rights group **Lambda** (W www.lambdaistanbul.org), and an "alternative" gay/lesbian/transsexual group, **Kaos** (W www.kaosgl.com), both with English news pages.

Mosques

Despite Turkey's avowedly secular constitution, at least half the population are conservative/observant Muslims, something to remember when visiting a **mosque**. Most of those likely to be of interest to a foreigner (and many more besides) post the following entry rules by the door:

Hamams (Turkish baths)

The **hamam** (Turkish bath) once played a pivotal role in hygiene, social discourse and religious life (they were often part of a mosque complex) in Turkey, but as the standard of living has increased, its importance has diminished. As an exercise in nostalgia, however, it's well worth visiting one – İstanbul in particular boasts many historic hamams worth experiencing for their architecture alone – and, of course, they make for a very relaxing end to a day of slogging around the sights.

Most Turkish towns (except for some coastal resorts formerly populated by Orthodox Christians) have at least one hamam, usually signposted; otherwise look for the distinctive external profile of the roof domes. Ordinary hamams **charge** 8–10TL basic admission, the price normally indicated by the front desk; hamams in coastal tourist resorts and İstanbul can be far more expensive (15–25TL), with an optional massage adding to the cost. Baths are either for men or women, or **sexually segregated** on a schedule, with women usually allotted more restricted hours, usually midweek during the day.

Hamam etiquette

On entering, leave your **valuables** in a small locking drawer, keeping the key (usually on a wrist thong) with you for the duration. Bring soap and shampoo as it's not always sold in the foyer. Men are supplied with a *peştamal*, a thin, wraparound sarong; women generally enter in knickers but not bra; both sexes get *takunya*, awkward wooden clogs, and later a *havlu* (towel). Leave your clothes in the changing cubicle (*camekan* in Turkish).

The *hararet* or **main bath chamber** ranges from plain to ornate, though any decent hamam will be marble-clad at least up to chest height. Two or more *halvets*, semi-private corner rooms with two or three *kurnas* (basins) each, lead off from the main chamber. The internal temperature varies from tryingly hot to barely lukewarm, depending on how well run the baths are. Unless with a friend, it's one customer to a set of taps and basin; refrain from making a big soapy mess in the basin, which is meant for mixing pure water to ideal temperature. Use the scoop-dishes provided to sluice yourself. It's considered good etiquette to clean your marble slab with a few scoopfuls of water before leaving.

At the heart of the hamam is the *göbek taşı* or "navel stone", a raised platform positioned over the furnaces that heat the premises. The *göbek taşı* will be piping hot and covered with prostrate figures absorbing the heat. It's also the venue for (very) vigorous massages from the *tellâk* or masseur/masseuse. A *kese* (abrasive mitt) session from the same person, in which dead skin and grime are scrubbed away, will probably suit more people. Terms for the *tellâks'* services should be displayed in the foyer. Few hamams have a masseuse, so female visitors will have to think very carefully before accepting a massage from a masseur – though this is far from unknown. Scrubs and massages are charged extra, so make sure you know what you'll be paying. Upon return to your cubicle with its reclining couch(es) you'll be offered tea, soft drinks or mineral water – charged extra as per a posted price placard. Except in heavily touristed establishments, **tips** apart from the listed fees are not required or expected.

• Cover your head (women) and shoulders/ upper arms (both sexes)
• No shorts or miniskirts
• Take off your shoes before entering
Many mosques now provide a plastic bag to slip your shoes into and carry them around with you. Alternatively, place your footwear on the shelves provided.

In very devout cities such as Konya or Şanlıurfa, avoid coinciding with noon prayers – particularly those on Friday, the most important session of the week. Once inside, you're free to wander around and admire the mosque – but photography is often forbidden. Keep quiet as there are often people praying or reciting the Koran outside of prayer times. Upkeep of the building is down to charity, so you may want (or occasionally be requested) to contribute to the collection box. The call to prayer echoes out five times daily: sunrise, midday, late afternoon, sunset and after dark.

Smoking

With over forty percent of the adult popula-tion (around 25 million) indulging the nicotine habit, the old saying "smokes like a Turk" is a fairly accurate assessment. Yet things are beginning to change. **Smoking was banned** on public transport and in airports, bus terminals and train stations back in 1997, and much to everyone's surprise, the law is more or less adhered to. In July 2009, it was prohibited in all public buildings, and all enclosed public spaces including bars,

cafés, restaurants and clubs. There was of course a major outcry, largely from the owners of *kahvehanes* (the basic, invariably all-male, tea-and-coffee dens), some of whom claim their profits dropped fifty percent overnight. At the time of writing nobody, including the authorities, seemed clear on whether puffing on a herbal *nargile* counts as smoking.

Toilets

Western-style toilets are now common in many hotels, restaurants, cafés and bars across the country. The only difference you're likely to notice is a small pipe fitted at the rear rim of the basin – which serves the same purpose as a bidet. The tap to turn it on is usually located on the wall behind the loo. The waste bins provided are for used toilet paper – blockages are not uncommon.

In rural areas (and less touristed parts of major cities), however, traditional **squat toilets** are still the norm, especially those attached to service stations, basic eateries and mosques. Mosque loos are often the only "public" toilet you'll be able to find in remote parts of big cities or in smaller towns. There's always a tap and plastic jug next to the toilet for washing the unmentionables but few provide paper, so carry some around with you. An attendant at the entrance will divest you of between 50 kuruş and a lira on your way out and, in return, give you a tissue and splash of cologne on your hands.

Festivals

Celebrations in Turkey comprise religious festivals, observed throughout the Islamic world on dates determined by the Muslim Hijra calendar, and annual cultural or harvest extravaganzas held in various cities and resorts across the country.

Religious festivals

The most important religious festival is **Ramadan** (*Ramazan* in Turkish), the Muslim month of daylight abstention from food,

water, tobacco and sexual relations. Otherwise, life carries on as normal despite the fact that half the population is fasting from sunrise to sunset. Some restaurants close for the duration or severely curtail their menus, others discreetly hide their salons behind curtains, but at most establishments you will be served with surprisingly good grace. The Koran allows pregnant and nursing mothers, the infirm and travellers to be excused from obligatory fasting; immediately after dark there's an orgy of eating (the *iftar yemeği*) by the famished in places public and private and restaurants will be sold out of everything within an hour of sunset.

Kadir Gecesi (The Eve of Power), when Mohammed is supposed to have received the Koran from Allah, takes place between the 27th and 28th days of the month of Ramadan. Mosques – brilliantly illuminated for the whole month – are full all night, as it's believed that prayers at this time have special efficacy. On **Arife**, the last day of Ramadan, it is customary to go to the cemeteries and pay respects to departed ancestors; many rural restaurants close that evening. The three-day *Şeker Bayramı* (Sugar Holiday) immediately follows Ramadan, celebrated by family reunions and the giving of presents and sweets to children, and restrained general partying in restaurants; on *Arife* eve you will have to book well in advance for tables at better establishments.

The four-day **Kurban Bayramı** (Festival of the Sacrifice), in which the sacrificial offering of a sheep represents Abraham's son Ishmael (a Koranic version of the Old Testament story) is marked by the massive slaughter of sheep. Only wealthy families can afford to buy a whole animal, so part of the meat is distributed to the poor of the neighbourhood.

During the *Şeker* and *Kurban festivals* **travel** becomes almost impossible – without advance planning you won't get a seat on any long-distance coach, train or plane. If you're driving, note that the already high accident rate on Turkey's roads soars in these national holidays. Many shops and all banks, museums and government offices close during these periods (although corner grocery stores and most resort shops stay open) and when the festivals occur close to a national secular holiday, the whole country effectively grinds to a halt for up to a week.

Religious festival dates

As the Islamic calendar is lunar, the **dates** of the four important religious festivals drift backwards eleven days each year (twelve in a leap year) relative to the Gregorian calendar. Future dates of festivals given on Islamic websites are provisional, owing to factors such as when the moon is sighted and the international dateline.

Şeker Bayramı

10–12 Sept, 2010
31 Aug–2 Sept, 2011
19–21 Aug, 2012
8–10 Aug, 2013

Kurban Bayramı

16–20 Nov, 2010
6–10 Nov, 2011
26–30 Oct, 2012
15–18 Oct, 2013

Cultural festivals

Cultural festivals are most interesting in cities and resorts with the resources to attract internationally renowned acts. Almost every town will have some yearly bash, though many are of limited interest to outsiders. We've highlighted the best below, with fuller descriptions in the Guide.

Folk-dance festivals provide an opportunity to see some of Turkey's best dance troupes perform a sample of the varied repertoire of Turkish dances in traditional costumes. There's a full festival calendar for İstanbul on p.138, in addition to the summary below.

January

Camel wrestling at Selçuk, last two weekends, though bouts (between two male camels in rut) occur throughout Aydın province from December onwards.

April

İstanbul International Film Festival Full-length features and documentaries.

May

İstanbul International Theatre Festival Even-numbered years; dance and workshops as well as theatre performances.

Takava Gypsy Festival at Kırklareli, featuring bonfires; around May 5–6.

Ephesus Festival The ancient theatre hosts folk dancing plus more conventional acts.

Hıdırellez Gypsy festival at Edirne, May 5–6, with music and dance.

June–July

Oil wrestling (Yağlı güreş) near Edirne, late June or early July (see p.166).

Kafkasör Festival at Artvin, late June, features bullfighting between young beasts.

Pir Abdal Musa in Tekke village near Elmalı, early June; rites honouring the second most important Alevî saint after Hacı Bektaş Veli.

İstanbul International Classical Music Festival Performances often in historic venues by top soloists and orchestras.

International İzmir Festival Pop festival with many international names performing at Ephesus theatre and Çeşme castle.

Aspendos Opera and Ballet Festival The Mediterranean Coast's big highbrow event.

İstanbul Jazz Festival Jazz as well as rock acts (see p.138); early July.

August

Chef's Contest at Mengen (Bolu province) – the region purportedly produces the country's best cooks.

Hacı Bektaş Veli Commemoration at Hacıbektaş village, latter half of August. Bektaşis and their affiliates, the Alevîs, meet for a weekend of ritual singing and dancing.

September–October

Bodrum Festival Centred on the castle there, stressing ballet and opera; early Sept.

İstanbul Biennial Art exhibition held odd-numbered years; dozens of projects lasting into November.

Akbank Jazz Festival İstanbul More traditional programme than the July event.

Altın Portakal ("Golden Orange") Film Festival Antalya; a major fixture on the international festival circuit.

Grape Harvest/Wine Festival Ürgüp, Cappadocia features some of the better local winery products.

Watermelon Festival in Diyarbakır, showcases the region's most outsized fruit; mid- to late September.

Tourism and Handicrafts Festival in Avanos, promotes the town's distinctive pottery.

December

Mevlâna Festival at Konya, 10–17 of month; Whirling dervish performances at the home of the order (see also p.457).

The media

Newspapers and magazines were forbidden in Turkey until the mid-nineteenth century; now there are over forty titles, representing the full gamut of public tastes. The airwaves were government-controlled until the late 1980s, but the advent of satellite dishes and overseas transmitters has seen a huge growth in TV and radio stations of variable quality.

Turkish-language publications

Three titles – Sabah, Hürriyet and Milliyet – dominate the **newspaper** market. Politically left of these stands Radikal, although another title, Taraf, is far more radical than Radikal and frequently incurs establishment ire. Cumhuriyet, founded as the mouthpiece of the Turkish republic in 1924, mixes conservative nationalism with old-style socialism. Turkey's liberal-Islamist papers, Yeni Şafak and Zaman, give generally intelligent and thoughtful coverage. Satirical weekly **comic strips** have a long history in Turkey. Look out for the distinctive artwork of L-Manyak, Le Man, Penguen and Uykusuz.

English-language publications

The longest-running English-language **newspaper**, available in major cities and resorts, is the *Hürriyet Daily News*. Poor translation sometimes makes it a turgid read though it's useful for its daily listings – mainly for İstanbul, Ankara and İzmir. *Today's Zaman* is backed by the controversial Islamic scholar/businessman Fetullah Gülen. It's more professional, glossier and reads better than the *HDN*. The *Daily News* follows the secular/nationalist line and *Today's Zaman* is liberal/Islamic. Both have online versions at Ⓦwww.hurrriyetdailynews.com and www.todayszaman.com respectively.

Time Out Istanbul, the local imprint of the London listings magazine, with an eighty-page English edition (5TL), is by far the best what's-on listings magazine available. Bimonthly *Cornucopia* (20TL) is an upmarket glossy, covering everything from history and travel to carpets and property renovation.

Television

Turkish channels include the four **state-owned TRT** (Turkish Radio and Television) channels, with a mix of films, panel discussions, classical Turkish music shows and soaps. TRT-6, launched in 2009, broke a long-held Republican taboo by broadcasting in Kurdish. The most watched **private channels** include Show, Star, ATV and Kanal D. For Turkish pop the MTV-style Kral and Power Turk lead the way, whilst Dream has a mix of Turkish and Western sounds.

The nation's leading digital company, Digiturk, has a number of English-language channels including CNBC-e and E2, both of which concentrate on re-runs of US TV shows and films. BBC Entertainment offers a mix of BBC comedies, dramas and soaps, whilst CNN, BBC World and Al Jazeera are best for news. Most high-end hotels subscribe to the Digiturk package screening these channels.

Digiturk also shows Turkish Premier League **football** on its Lig TV channel. English Premier League matches are shown on Spormax – many bars, and cafés subscribe to these and often have big screens.

Web censorship

Don't bank on watching YouTube while you're here. It was first closed in 2007 for featuring a clip insulting to the nation's founder, Mustafa Kemal Atatürk, a crime (along with the rather vague offence of "insulting Turkishness") under Turkish law. Although soon back online, it was blocked again in January 2008 and was still blocked at the time of writing. Many other sites have been banned by the courts for the same reasons. So if the website you're after comes up with the message *"Bu siteye erişim engellenmiştir"* ("This site has been disabled"), you'll know why.

Radio

Frequency-crowding means even popular channels are almost impossible to pick up without interference. Of the four **public radio stations**, Radyo Üç (The Third Programme or TRT-3), most commonly found at 88.2, 94 and 99MHz, broadcasts the highest proportion of Western music. NTV Radiyo (102.8) has the news in English at 6pm daily.

For Western music try Açık Radyo (FM 94.9) for rock, jazz and soul. Alternatively search out FM (99.5), Kiss FM (90.3) and Metro FM (97.2). For Turkish music, the best stations are Kral (92.0) and Best FM (98.4).

Cinema

With the exception of İstanbul's Beyoğlu district, which has some period-pieces dating back to the 1920s, most cinemas are in shopping malls. **Films** are shown in the original language with Turkish subtitles, though kid-orientated films are dubbed into Turkish. There are often five screenings daily, generally at 11.30am or noon, then at around 3pm, 6pm, 9pm and usually midnight. **Tickets** in provincial cities cost between 7–10TL, with reduced prices (5TL) one or more days midweek; some of the plusher İstanbul cinemas charge up to 15TL. Films have a fifteen-minute interval.

Shopping

Few people return from Turkey without some kind of souvenir; whether it's a cheap-and-cheerful pack of local herbs and spices or an expensive carpet depends on the budget of the traveller and the skill of the salesman. The best selection of good-quality wares is to be found in the major tourist centres: İstanbul, Cappadocia, Bursa and the coastal resorts. You won't find a bargain at the production centres themselves as wholesalers and collectors have been there long before you.

How to bargain

Bargaining is a way of life in Turkey; whether you love it or hate it depends on your character. In general it's acceptable to haggle over the price of souvenirs, which often lack price tags, meaning the vendor is able to adjust his asking price to what he thinks you are willing/able to pay. This applies to everything from expensive items such as carpets or kilims through to cheaper items like *lokum* (Turkish Delight) and spices. As a guideline, begin at a figure lower than whatever you are prepared to pay, say half the shopkeeper's starting price. Once a price has been agreed on, you are ethically committed to buy, so don't commence haggling unless you are reasonably sure you want the item.

"Assistance" from touts, whether in İstanbul, major resorts or even provincial towns, will automatically bump up the price thirty to fifty percent, as they will be getting a commission. Also, be prepared to hand over between three and seven percent extra if paying by credit card; your bargaining position is strongest with crisp, bunched notes, either foreign or TL.

Don't bargain for bus, rail or air tickets, or for fruit or vegetables at street markets.

Bazaars, shops, and markets

There are several types of traditional bazaar in Turkey, which continue to coexist with the modern American/European-style shopping malls that dominate the wealthier districts of large cities.

Covered bazaars are found in larger towns like İstanbul, Bursa and Şanlıurfa.

Essentially medieval Ottoman shopping malls, they comprised several *bedesten*s at which particular types of goods were sold, linked by covered arcades also originally assigned to a particular trade – though strict segregation has long since broken down.

Surrounding these covered bazaars are large areas of **small shops**, open-air extensions of the covered areas and governed by the same rules: each shop is a separate unit with an owner and apprentices, and successful businesses are not allowed to expand or merge.

Weekly or twice-weekly **street markets** are held in most towns and all cities, similar to those in northern Europe and selling cheap clothes, household utensils and most importantly fruit, vegetables, cheese, yoghurt, olives, nuts and the like. More exotic are the semi-permanent **flea markets** (*bit pazarı*, literally "louse markets"), ranging in quality from street stalls where old clothes are sold and resold among the homeless, to lanes of shops where you can buy second-hand clothes, furniture or occasionally an antique of real aesthetic or monetary value.

In many cities, particularly in İstanbul, everyday shopping is increasingly done in Western-style department stores, shopping malls and supermarkets – at least by the middle classes.

Carpets and kilims

Turkish carpets and **kilims** (flat-weave rugs) are renowned for their quality and have a very long history (the designs on many kilims have their origins in the Neolitihic period). Be warned, though, that they are no longer necessarily cheaper in Turkey than overseas, and some dealers reckon there are now more old kilims and carpets outside the country than in it.

Most visitors will find themselves in a carpet shop at some point in their visit – willingly or unwillingly. It's very easy to be drawn into buying something you don't really want at a price you can barely afford once you've been smooth-talked and drip-fed with copious quantities of apple tea. However, It's still possible to get a good deal and enjoy the process (see our tips below).

Carpets

Turkish carpets are single-sided, and knotted with a pile. They are either all-wool, wool pile on cotton warps and wefts, all-silk or – easily mistaken for silk – a glossy mercerised cotton pile on cotton warps and wefts. Needless to say, the higher the silk content, the more expensive the rug, with new, hand-woven wool carpets starting from around €150 per square metre, with pure silk ones starting at €540. Turkish carpets are made using the double-knot technique, making them more durable than their single-knot Persian counterparts. The most famous Turkish carpets are Hereke, named after their town of origin. Pure silk, they have an extremely high-knot density.

Larger Hereke take up to four years to weave and cost around €1,010 per square metre, with prime examples going for tens of thousands of euros. Silk carpets woven in the Central Anatolian province of Kayseri are usually a third cheaper. Other key carpet maufacturing areas are Bergama, Uşak and Milas – all near the Aegean coast. Be warned – any carpets which seem suspiciously cheap, especially silk ones, are almost certainly Chinese, not Turkish.

Kilims

A **kilim** is a pile-less, flat-woven wool rug. The better-quality ones are double-sided (that is, the pattern should look much the same top or bottom). A cicim is a kilim with additional, raised designs stitched onto it. Traditionally woven by nomadic Anatolian tribal groupings such as the Turcomans and Kurds, kilims are generally much more affordable than carpets. Prices for newly woven examples (invariably woven by women and sold by men) start from around €30 per square metre, whereas a rare antique kilim can fetch thousands of euros. The vast majority of kilims are heavily patterned with geometric motifs – invariably stylized birds, animals, flowers or other

Capet and kilim buying tips

- Do some research, preferably before you leave home (check out some of the books reviewed on p.735).
- Avoid buying in the first shop you visit, and look around several. You can always go back – preferably the next day, when you've had time to think about it.
- Don't be embarrassed at how many carpets the dealer is laying out for you – that's his (or usually his lowly assistant's) job.
- Ask as many questions as you can – this will test the dealer's worth, and could give you some interesting historical background should you make a purchase.
- Check the pieces for flaws, marks and the density of weave – hand-woven wool is preferable to machine as it is stronger and the rug will last for longer.
- Natural dyes such as tobacco and saffron are the most highly prized and less likely to fade. You should be able to tell by opening up a section of the pile with your fingers. If the tint at the bottom of the pile is different to that at the top it is a chemical dye.
- Even in the most reputable shop bargaining is essential. Whatever you do, don't engage in the process if you've no intention of buying.
- You'll probably get a better deal for cash – this will also help overcome the temptation to credit-card splurge.
- Most important of all, only buy the piece if you really like it and are sure it'll look the part back home – any other considerations such as future appreciation are mere distractions.

images from the natural world which formed the backdrop to the nomads' lives. Originally they were used as floor coverings, tent partitions and blankets or, stitched together, as storage/saddlebags and bolsters.

Clothes

Turkish designs are beginning to match the quality of local fabrics such as Bursa silk and Angora wool. Nowadays you will pay near-Western prices for genuine locally designed items at reputable shops – local brands are aggressively protected from counterfeiting, if necessary by police raids.

However, many visitors find it hard resist the allure of the cheap **fake designer clothing** available everywhere, with all the usual suspects (Armani, Diesel, Louis Vuitton et al) the victims. Genuine international designer wear is priced little differently to elsewhere.

Jewellery

Both in terms of design, quality and price, Turkey is a great country to buy **jewellery**. Gold and silver are sold by weight – with little regard for the disparate level of craftsmanship involved – as are semi-precious stones. At the time of writing silver was 0.9TL per gram, gold 47TL. One particularly intricate method is *telkârî* or wire filigree, most of which comes from eastern Turkey, particularly Diyarbakır and Mardin. Gold in particular can be very good value and is so pure (22 carat) that *telkârî* bangles bend easily. Also remember that sterling silver items should bear a hallmark.

Leather goods

Leather is still big business in Turkey. The industry was originally based in western Anatolia where alum deposits and acorn-derived tannin aided the tanning process. Today, İzmir and İstanbul still have the largest workshops, though the retail business also booms on the Mediterranean coast, particularly in Antalya and Alanya. Jackets are the most obvious purchase, the prices of which vary from around €70 from a downmarket outlet to well over €350 from a branded "designer" shop such as Matraş, Desa or Derimod. Shoes are less good value and women's sizes rarely go over 40.

Miscellaneous souvenirs

A *tavla takimi* or backgammon set is a good **souvenir** of Turkish popular culture. Mother-of-pearl inlaid sets are the most expensive, but as fakes abound be wary and if in doubt go for one of the plain, wood-inlay sets. Copperware is still spun and hammered in the traditional way in some Turkish towns, notably Gaziantep in the southeast. The most popular items are lidded jugs, large serving trays and bowls. *Mavi boncuk* (blue bead) key rings, lintel ornaments and animal collars are sold all over the place to ward off *nazar* (the evil eye).

Meerschaum **pipes** carved from *lületaşı* stone quarried near Eskişehir, are available in all tourist areas. Less common are Karagöz puppets, representing the popular folk characters Karagöz and Hacıvat, preferably made from camel skin in Bursa. Towelling and silk goods, the best of which come from Bursa, are also good buys, as are the pure cotton *peştamal*s (the usually striped cotton wraps used in Turkish baths), bathrobes and tablecloths woven in Denizli. Kütahya **ceramics** may not be the finest ever produced in Turkey, but the vases, bowls, plates and, in particular, tiles, churned out in this western Anatolian town are attractive enough and reasonable value as decorative items. Revived İznik ware is a cut above, and discussed fully on p.176. For more contemporary ceramics try the nationwide store Paşabahçe.

Musical instruments

Traditional Turkish **musical instruments** are sold all over the country. The most easily portable are the *ney*, the Mevlevî flute made from a length of calamus reed, the *davul* or drum, and the *saz*, the long-necked Turkish lute. Rock and jazz musicians might like to score, a bit cheaper than abroad, a set of cymbals from one of two world-famous brands – İstanbul and Zildjian – both made by İstanbul-based or İstanbul-origin Armenian companies

If you've any interest in local recordings it's worth listening to a cross section of Turkish styles and making a purchase (CDs go for 10–15TL) or two. See p.724 for a discography of recommended items.

Antiques and smuggling: a warning

Under Turkish law it is an offence to buy, sell, attempt to export or even possess genuine antiquities (which includes fossils). Exact age limits are not specified, suggesting that decisions by customs officials are subjective, though a principal measure of antiquity is rarity. At popular archeological sites like Ephesus, you may be offered "antiques" by hawkers though these are invariably fake.

In the case of **carpets** handled by established dealers, you run a very slight risk of investing a lot of money in a supposed "collector's item" that turns out to be collectable only by the Turkish Republic. If you're apprehensive about a proposed purchase, ask the dealer to prepare both a *fatura* (invoice) recording the exact purchase price – also necessary to satisfy customs – and a declaration stating that the item is not an antiquity. Expect a heavy fine and possibly imprisonment if you transgress these laws.

Spices and foodstuffs

Acknowledging the slight risk of having certain goods confiscated on return to the European Union or North America, locally produced **spices, condiments and foodstuffs** make for a compact, lightweight souvenir purchase. Low-grade saffron (*zafran*), the stamen of a particular kind of crocus, is still gathered in northern Anatolia. Sumac (*sumak*) is a ground-up purple leaf for sprinkling on barbecued meats and salad onions, much encountered in districts with an Arab heritage. Pine nuts (*dolmalık fıstığı* or *çam fıstığı*), gathered in the coastal mountains, are excellent and, especially if purchased in northwest Turkey, are considerably cheaper than in Europe. *Pekmez* (molasses of grape, mulberry or carob pods) is phenomenally nutritious and makes a splendid ice cream, muesli or yoghurt topping. Olive oil, most famously from Gemlik, is a worthwhile purchase, as are the olives it's made from. Olive oil soaps are also popular, especially Defne Sabunı, a laurel-scented olive-oil soap from Antakya. Both hot and sweet peppers are made into concentrated pastes (*salçalar*), while dried aubergine/eggplant and pepper shells are convenient for stuffing. *Nar eksisi* is a sour sweet pomegranate syrup widely used as a salad dressing or meat marinade. Turkish Delight (*lokum*) is a perennial favourite and comes in a bewildering variety of flavours.

Sports and outdoor activities

Whether you want to stand alongside some of the most passionate football fans in the world, hike a long-distance trail, climb up or ski down a mighty peak, raft the rapids of a mountain torrent, or paraglide over/dive beneath the warm waters of the Mediterranean, Turkey is the place to do it.

Football

Football is hugely popular in Turkey, with most Turks professing allegiance to one of the "Big Three" İstanbul sides Galatasaray, Beşiktaş or Fenerbahçe (for more information and ticketing see p.125). The one exception is the Black Sea coastal town of Trabzon, whose citizens support their local team, Trabzonspor – a club which ranks up there with the İstanbul big boys.

Turkey has produced plenty of home-grown footballing talent (some now playing in England, Germany and Spain) and many Turkish teams now include international players, particularly from Africa and South America. The managers of the İstanbul giants are often recruited from abroad (with mixed results; Spain's successful national coach Arragones lasted only a year at Fenerbahçe). Although the teams qualifying for the European Cup usually fall at the first hurdle, Galatasaray became the first Turkish team to win the UEFA Cup (in 2000; beating Arsenal 4–1 on penalties).

Matches are usually on weekend evenings between September and May. Obtaining **tickets** for provincial teams is usually both cheap and easy, with tickets available at the ground on match day for as little as 10TL, but prices rise sevenfold or more when one of the İstanbul "giants" is in town. Many bars show games on big screens, and can be very atmospheric, especially for derby games.

Football violence is not uncommon here (in 2000, two English Leeds United fans were stabbed to death in İstanbul during running street-fighting with Galatasaray fans) though it's unlikely the average foreigner will get caught up in trouble. While a losing team occasionally gets attacked by its own supporters, more likely you'll witness delirious celebrations, with flag-waving fans leaning on the horns of cruising cars embroiled in massive traffic jams.

Hiking and mountaineering

The small (though increasing) number of Turkish **hikers** means foreign visitors have virtually free-rein in this most mountainous of countries. The absence of decent maps (with a few exceptions) makes hiking a real adventure here, but the unspoilt quality of the countryside, the hospitality of rural Turks, the fascination of the *yaylas* (summer pastures) and the friendliness of other mountaineers more than compensate.

The alpine **Kaçkar Dağları**, paralleling the Black Sea, are the most rewarding mountains in Turkey for trekking and a number of companies organize expeditions there. Next up in interest are the **Toros**

(Taurus) ranges, which form a long chain extending from central Turkey to above the main Turquoise Coast resort areas. The southwestern terminus of this range boasts the wonderful way-marked **Lycian Way** long-distance trail and the nearby but more challenging St Paul Trail

Aside from this, high-altitude **mountaineering** in Turkey consists mostly of climbing the volcanos of the central plateau. Serious trekkers may not find these mountains quite as interesting as the more conventional ranges, but all offer superb views from their summits. Most famous is 5137m **Ağrı Dağ** (Ararat) on the eastern borders of Turkey, though this requires a special permit (see p.680) because of its sensitive location. By contrast, Erciyes and Hasan Dağı near Cappadocia are excellent for winter ascents, without any of the expense or bureaucracy prevalent at Ararat. **Süphan Dağı** (4058m) Turkey's second highest volcanic peak, stands in splendid isolation north of Lake Van. Unfortunately the magnificent Cilo–Sat mountains south of Lake Van are sometimes a battleground between the Kurdish separatists and Turkish security forces so are currently closed to outsiders.

Hiking equipment and safety

Alpine huts are nonexistent, so you'll need to carry full camping gear to trek in the mountains. It's best to bring your own as only İstanbul and Ankara have European-standard mountaineering shops. **Water** can be a problem in the limestone strata of the Toros and on the volcanos, detailed **maps** are very difficult to obtain (see p.64) and **trails** (when present) are seldom marked.

Rescue services are no match for those in more developed mountain areas in Europe and the US, but things are improving. The local *jandarma* (see p.67) will turn out in an emergency, and AKUT (Search and Rescue Association; @www.akut.org.tr) have established some eight centres across western, southern and central Turkey (though not yet in the popular Kaçkar range).

See the *Outdoor adventure* colour section for more on Turkey's sporting activities.

You'll find details on specific hiking routes through the Kaçkar Dağları and a selection of walks on Bursa's Uludağ and along the Turquoise Coast, in the Guide, but if you're daunted at the prospect of going alone, contact one of the adventure-travel companies listed in the "Getting there" section on p.32. The various guides to mountaineering and trekking in Turkey are reviewed on p.736.

Trekking maps

Except for the Lycian Way, Kaçkar mountains and St Paul Trail; see p.325, p.595 & p.450), it is virtually impossible to obtain large-scale topographical maps of specific areas for **trekking** (though usable enough maps for the most popular trekking areas can be found in *Trekking in Turkey* (o/p). The only (medium-scale) maps available are 1:250,000 topographic sheets from the Turkish Mapping Ministry (*Harita Genel Müdürlügü* ☎0312/595 2072) in the Dikmen district of Ankara. You will need to speak reasonable Turkish to get them in the door – it's best to have a local get them on your behalf. Omni Resources in the US (☎910/227-8300, ⊛www.omnimap .com) stock 1980s-vintage, 1:50,000 Soviet topographic maps for the entire country although given their cost – nearly $2000 for the full, 162-sheet set (or $50 per single sheet) – they are only really aimed at well-funded expeditions.

Skiing

Few foreigners come to Turkey specifically to **ski** but it is growing in popularity and if you are travelling around the country between December and April it's well worth considering a day or more on the piste. If you're willing to forego doorstep skiing, it's surprisingly easy and cheap to do it based in towns like Erzurum or Bursa that are near to resorts. The Turkish State Meteorological Service gives information on snow heights at the various resorts (⊛www.meteor.gov.tr).

Best known of Turkey's ski resorts is **Uludağ**, above Bursa, with easy and intermediate runs, but the slopes are prone to mist and snow turns slushy after February. The **Saklıkent** complex in the Beydarlağı near Antalya would seem potentially ideal for an early spring sea-cum-ski holiday, but snow cover tends to be thin and runs limited. Close

by is much better **Davraz**, near İsparta. Snow conditions here are more reliable and there is plentiful accommodation in the nearby lakeside town of Eğirdir as well as at the resort. Roughly midway between İstanbul and Ankara, near Bolu, **Kartalkaya** is better than any of the foregoing, despite a modest top altitude of 2223m; facilities now nearly match those of Uludağ, plus there are several red and black runs and, most importantly, in recent years there has been plentiful snow. The longest season and best snow conditions are usually at **Palandöken**, near Erzurum, where the top lift goes over 3000m and the Turkish Olympic team trains; there are three chairlifts, one T-bar and a three-kilometre-long gondola car to service a mix of blue and red runs. At **Tekir Yaylası** on Erciyes Dağı near Kayseri, the season is nearly as long, the snow almost as powdery, and the top lift is 2770m (one to 3100m is planned), though thus far runs are only green and red grade, served by two chairlifts and two T-bars. **Sarıkamış**, near Kars has two chairlifts and one T-bar to service a handful of runs (mostly red and blue grade); top lift is 2634m.

Watersports and other activities

Waterskiing and its offspring, parasailing, are available at most medium to large resorts; the even more exciting thrill of kite-surfing is centred on Alaçatı, near Çeşme (see p.249), whilst wind surfers head for the Bodrum peninsula (see p.238).

For information on other activities including scuba-diving and rock climbing, canyoning, paragliding and ballooning see the *Outdoor adventure travel* colour section.

Birdwatching

Turkey stands astride several major bird migration routes and possesses some very bird-friendly habitat (see p.411, p.425 & p.494 for site specific information). On an active birdwatching holiday you could expect to tick off nearly three hundred different species. For a database of bird species and distribution in Turkey, as reported by local and foreign birdwatchers see ⊛www.kusbank.org.

Travelling with children

Turks adore children and Turkish families tend to take their children with them wherever they go, thinking nothing of letting them run around restaurants until the early hours. In this sense, the country is a great place to visit with kids. And, of course, the coastal resorts offer a generally calm, warm sea and have pools, beaches (and sometimes water-parks) aplenty. On the down side, the number of play areas and children's attractions lags far behind Western Europe.

Turks have an uninhibited Mediterranean attitude toward children. Don't be surprised to find your child receive an affectionate pinch on the cheek by a passer-by, often accompanied by the word *maşallah*, which serves both to praise your offspring and ward off the evil eye, whilst waiters will sometimes unselfconsciously pick a kid up and waltz them off into the kitchen to show their workmates, often accompanied by cries all around of "how sweet" ("çok tatlı").

With a few honourable exceptions (eg Miniatürk and the Rahmi M. Koç Industrial Museum in İstanbul), there are few **attractions** aimed specifically at younger children, and few museums have kid-friendly displays or activities. And for buggy-pushing parents, the uneven surfaces and metre-high kerbs of the average Turkish pavement (where there is one) are a nightmare. For older kids there are plenty of outdoor activities on offer – kayaking and windsurfing at some coastal resorts, for example, and white water rafting, mountain biking and canyoning in the hinterland.

Turkish **food** should appeal to most kids – what's *köfte* but a (very) tasty burger, *pide* a pizza without the tomato paste, and *gözleme* a stuffed pancake? Maraş ice cream is just as delicious as Italian gelato and comes in myriad flavours. In general, restaurants are relaxed and very welcoming to families – just don't expect highchairs. Disposable nappies are widely available from supermarkets and the larger *bakkal*s, as are formula/baby foods.

Travel essentials

Archeological sites

Major **archeological sites** are generally open daily from 8.30am to 6.30pm in summer, but the exact times are listed in the Guide. Winter opeming hours are generally shorter. Some smaller archeological sites are only guarded during the day and left unfenced, permitting (in theory) a free wander around in the evening though, in the wake of antiquities theft (see p.62) this could feasibly result in you being picked up by the *jandarma*. Others are staffed until dark by a solitary warden, who may have enough English to give you a guided tour, for which he will probably expect a tip.

Don't pay **entrance fees** unless the wardens can produce a ticket, and keep it with you for the duration of your visit and even afterwards, as some sites (eg, Patara and Olympos in Chapter 5) straddle the route to a good beach and the ticket is valid for a week (sparing you repayment if you re-cross the area).

Beaches

Except near major cities where sea water is often polluted, Turkish **beaches** are safe to swim at, though be prepared for occasional mountains of rubbish piled at the back of the beach. Tar can also be a problem on south-coast beaches facing Mediterranean shipping lanes; if you get tar on your feet scrub it off with olive oil rather than chemical solvents. All beaches are free in theory, though luxury compounds straddling routes to the sand will control access in various ways. Never pay a fee for a beach-lounger or umbrella unless the seller provides you with a ticket.

Costs

Turkey is no longer the cheap destination it was, with **prices** in the heavily touristed areas comparable to many places in Europe. Exercise a little restraint, however, be prepared to live life at least occasionally at the local level (many Turks somehow survive on 600TL a month) and you can still enjoy a great-value trip here.

Stay in a "treehouse" or backpackers' inn, eat in local workers' cafés or restaurants, travel around by train or bus, avoid alcohol and the most expensive sites and you could get by on 50–60TL (£20–25/$35–40) a day. If that doesn't sound like much fun, double that and you could stay in a modest hotel, see the sights and have a beer or two with your evening meal. Equally, a night out on the town in İstanbul or one of the flasher coastal resorts could easily set you back over 100TL (£40/$70), and if you intend seeing a lot of what is a very big country transport costs could be a considerable drain on your budget (though travellers often

mitigate this by taking overnight buses and thus save on accommodation).

The more expensive tourist sites such as Ephesus, the Tokapı Palace and Aya Sofya are a hefty 20TL (£8/$13.50), but there are many more sites varying between 3TL and 15TL. Unfortunately since the introduction of the *Müze Kart* (Museum Card) scheme, which gives Turkish citizens admission to all state-run museums for a mere 20TL per annum, there are no longer any discounts for students who are not Turkish citizens – even for those in the country on an exchange programme.

Crime and personal safety

Turkey's **crime rate** remains lower than most of Europe and North America, although pickpocketing and purse-snatching are becoming more common in İstanbul (see p.80) and other major cities. Violent street crime is fortunately rare. Keep your wits about you and an eye on your belongings just as you would anywhere else, and make sure your passport is secure at all times, and you shouldn't have any problems. Except for well-known "red-light" districts, and some eastern towns, female travellers (see p.52 for more) are probably safer on their own than in other European countries.

As well as the usual warnings on drugs, note that exporting antiquities (see p.62) is illegal. It is also an offence to **insult Atatürk or Turkey** which can result in a prison sentence. Never deface, degrade, or tear up currency or the flag; drunkenness will likely be considered an aggravating, not a mitigating, factor. Also, do not take **photographs** near the numerous, well-marked military zones.

KDV: Turkish VAT

The Turkish variety of VAT (*Katma Değer Vergisi* or **KDV**), ranging from 8 to 23 percent depending on the commodity, is included in the price of virtually all goods and services (except car rental, where the eighteeen-percent figure is usually quoted separately). Look for the notice *Fiyatlarımız KDV Dahildir* (VAT included in our prices) if you think someone's trying to do you for it twice. There's a VAT refund scheme for large souvenir purchases made by those living outside Turkey, but it's such a rigmarole to get that it's probably not worth pursuing; if you insist, ask the shop to provide a *KDV İade Özel Fatura* (Special VAT Refund Invoice), assuming that it participates – very few do, and they tend to be the most expensive shops.

The police, army and gendarmerie

Turkey's police service is split into several groups. The blue-uniformed **Polis** are the everyday security force in cities and towns with populations over 2000; the white-capped **Trafik Polis** (traffic police) are a branch of this service. İstanbul and several other large towns have a rapid-response squad of red-and-black-uniformed motorbike police known as the *yunus* (dolphin) *polis*; they are generally courteous and helpful to tourists and may speak some English. In the towns you're also likely to see the **Belediye Zabıtası**, the navy-clad market police, who patrol the markets and bazaars to ensure that tradesmen aren't ripping off customers, but who seem to ignore the huge number of shops selling pirated DVDs and the like – approach them directly if you have reason for complaint. You're unlikely to come across plain-clothes police unless you wander off the beaten track in the ethnically Kurdish southeast (see below).

In most rural areas, law enforcement is in the hands of the **jandarma** or gendarmerie, a division of the regular army charged with law-enforcement duties. Gendarmes, despite their military affiliation, are often kitted out not in fatigues but well-tailored gear, modelled on the French uniform, to make them appear less threatening; most of them are conscripts who will be courteous and helpful if approached.

Security and restricted areas

There is a noticeable security presence in the Kurdish-dominated southeast of the country (chapters 11 and 12 of the Guide), with attacks on Turkish security forces by the PKK (Kurdish Workers Party) continuing, albeit sporadically, at the time of writing. Security is tightest along the Iraqi and Iranian borders, particularly south of Hakkari and around Siirt, in the mountains south of Lake Van and in the rural hinterland of Diyarbakır. Although checkpoints on main roads are being slowly phased out, you may be stopped if you attempt to travel to off-the-beaten track sites and/or villages, and your presence may attract the attention of the *jandarma* (and quite possibly the plain-clothes secret police, who generally stand out a mile from the locals). This may involve, at most, a rather tedious, though polite, interrogation. Lone males especially may find themselves suspected of being journalists with Kurdish/Armenian sympathies. Avoid talking politics with anyone unless you are absolutely sure you can trust them and, if you are questioned, keep calm, smile a lot, and emphasize wherever possible that you are a *turist* (tourist). Of more concern to the average visitor are the violent pro-Kurdish street demonstrations which break out from time to time in southeastern cities such as Diyarbakır and Van. For more information on the Kurdish problem see Contexts p.712.

Electricity

Turkey operates on 220 volts, 50 Hz. Most European appliances should work so long as you have an adaptor for European-style two-pin plugs. American appliances will need a transformer as well as an adaptor.

Entry requirementes

Ninety-day **tourist visas** (available at ports of entry for a fee) are issued to citizens of the UK (£10), Ireland (€10), the US (US$20), Canada (Can$60) and Australia (Aus$20). South Africans are granted 30 days only. New Zealanders currently do not require a visa. Tourist visas are valid for multiple entries into Turkey – if you leave on a day-trip, to Greece or Bulgaria say, you should not have to pay for a new visa on your return. Everyone, regardless of nationality, should have at least six months validity on their passport.

Once inside the country, you can **extend your visa** once only, for a further three months, by applying to the Foreigners' Department (*Yabancı Bürosu*) of the Security Division (*Emniyet Müdürlüğü*) in any provincial capital. Do this well before your time expires, as it may take several weeks to process. Generally its easier to nip across the border to a Greek island, Bulgaria or Northern Cyprus every three months and re-enter Turkey to obtain a new three-month stamp. For the latest information on visas check with the Turkish Ministry of Foreign Affairs at ⓦwww.mfa.gov.tr.

Turkish embassies and consulates abroad

Australia 60 Mugga Way, Red Hill, Canberra ACT 2603 ⓉⓉ 02/6295 0227.
Canada 197 Wurtemburg St, Ottawa, ON K1N 8L9 ⓉⓉ 613/789-4044.
Ireland 11 Clyde Rd, Ballsbridge, Dublin 4 ⓉⓉ 01/668 5240.
New Zealand 15–17 Murphy St, Level 8, Wellington ⓉⓉ 04/472 1290.
South Africa 1067 Church St, Hatfield 0181, Pretoria ⓉⓉ 012/342-5063.
UK 43 Belgrave Square, London SW1X 8PA ⓉⓉ 020/7393 0202.
US 2525 Masschusetts Ave NW, Washington, DC 20008 ⓉⓉ 202/612-6700.

Customs and border inspections

As Turkey is not yet an EU member, **duty-free limits** – and sales – for alcohol and tobacco are still prevalent. Limits are posted clearly at İstanbul's airports, and apply for all frontiers.

Few people get stopped departing Turkey, but the guards may be on the lookout for **antiquities** and **fossils**. Penalties for trying to smuggle these out include long jail sentences, plus a large fine. What actually constitutes an antiquity is rather vague (see p.62), but it's best not to take any chances.

Insurance

It is essential to take out an **insurance policy** before travelling to cover against illness or injury, as well as theft or loss. Some all-risks homeowners' or renters' insurance policies may cover your possessions when overseas, and many private medical schemes (such as BUPA and WPA) offer coverage extensions for abroad.

Rough Guides offers its own insurance policy, detailed in the box below. Most policies exclude so-called **dangerous sports** unless an extra premium is paid: in Turkey this can mean scuba-diving, whitewater rafting, paragliding, windsurfing and trekking, though probably not kayaking or jeep safaris. Travel agents and package operators may require travel insurance when you book a holiday – you're not obliged to take theirs, though you have to sign a declaration saying that you already have another policy. Similarly, many no-frills airlines make a tidy sum from selling you unnecessary insurance at the time of ticket booking – beware, and opt out.

Internet

Many hotels, pensions and even hostels in tourist areas have **internet access** – often both terminals and wi-fi signal, as do an ever-increasing number of cafés. In more remote places in the interior, and the east of the country, only the more expensive hotels have wi-fi. Rates in internet cafés tend to be 2TL per hour. The Turkish-character keyboard you'll probably be faced with may cause some confusion. The "@" sign is made by simultaneously pressing the "ALT" and "q" keys. More frustrating is the the dotless "ı" (confusingly enough found right where you'll be expecting the conventional "i") – the Western "i" is located second key from right, middle row.

Mail

Post offices are easily spotted by their bold black-on-yellow **PTT** (Posta, Telegraf,

Telefon) signs. Stamps are only available from the PTT, whose website (Ⓦwww.ptt .gov.tr) has a (not necessarily up-to-date) English-language listing of services and prices. Post offices are generally open Mon–Fri 8.30am–5.30pm and until noon on Saturday. Airmail (*uçakla*) rates to Europe are 0.90TL for postcards, 1TL for letters up to 20g, 19TL for 2kg, the maximum weight for letters. Delivery to Europe or North America can take seven to ten days. A pricier express (*acele*) service is also available, which cuts delivery times to the EU to about three days. When sending airmail, it's best to give your stamped letter/card to the clerk behind the counter, who will ensure it gets put in the right place; otherwise, place it in the relevant slot if one is available (*yurtdışı* for abroad; *yurtiçi* for elsewhere in Turkey).

Maps

Maps of Turkey are notoriously poor quality owing to the lack of survey-based cartography. The best **foreign-produced touring maps**, accurately showing many smaller villages, are those published by Kartographischer Verlag Reinhard Ryborsch (1:500,000; Frankfurt, Germany), which cover the entire country in seven maps. They are sporadically available online, but both original and pirated versions are sold at better bookshops in İstanbul, Ankara and big resorts. Reasonable second choices, easier to obtain, include Insight *Turkey West* (1:800,000), easy to read and with up-to-date motorway tracings, and Reise Know-How's 1:700 000 *Mediterranean Coast and Cyprus*, which despite the title covers the entire southern and western third of the country with passable accuracy.

In terms of **Turkish-produced touring maps**, the 1:400,000 atlas produced by *Atlas* magazine is highly accurate if sadly difficult to read owing to murky printing – but still a useful 20TL investment. The best regional touring maps are Sabri Aydal's 1:250,000 products for Cappadocia, Lycia, Pamphylia and Pisidia, available from local bookshops and museums.

İstanbul, Ankara, Antalya, Bursa and İzmir (as well as overseas) tourist offices stock reasonable, free **city street plans**, although the İstanbul one is restricted to the centre and lacks detail. Sketch plans from provincial tourist offices vary widely in quality.

Amongst **Turkish-produced city maps**, Keskin Colour's 1:8,500 "İstanbul Street Plan" is clear and accurate, though misses out most of the Asian side of the city. The most detailed A–Z-style atlas for the European side, ideal for out-of-the-way monuments, is Mepmedya's 1:7500 "İstanbul Avrupa Yakası", though it's pricey (50TL) and heavy; İki Nokta's "Sokak Sokak Avrupa" is the alternative. All these are sold in town and (Mepmedya excepted) far cheaper than anything produced abroad.

For **trekking maps** see p.64.

Money

Turkey's currency is the **Türk Lirası** or **TL** for short, subdivided into 100 kuruş. At the time of writing the **exchange rate** was around 2.10TL to the euro, 2.40TL to the pound and 1.5TL to the US dollar. As recently as 2004 hyperinflation meant that millions of lira were needed to purchase the smallest everyday item. In 2005 the government introduced the Yeni Türk Lirası (New Turkish Lira), abbreviated as YTL, and knocked all the zeroes off. In January 2009, it was the turn of the "Y" to go, and the currency reverted to its old name. Despite the changes, many Turks still talk in millions, which can be confusing when you are asked "bir milyon" or one million lira for a glass of tea. **Coins** are in denominations of 5, 10, 25 and 50 kuruş, as well as 1 lira, whilst **notes** come in denominations of 5, 10, 20, 50, 100 and 200 lira.

Rates for foreign currency are always better inside Turkey, so try not to buy much lira at home. Conversely, don't leave Turkey with unspent lira, as you won't get a decent exchange rate for them outside the country. It's wise to bring a fair wad of **hard currency** with you (euros are best, though dollars and sterling are often accepted), as you can often use it to pay directly for souvenirs or accommodation (prices for both are frequently quoted in euros). **Travellers' cheques** are, frankly, not worth the bother as exchange offices (see p.70) and some banks refuse them, whilst those that do accept them charge a hefty commission on transactions and the bureaucracy is tedious.

Changing money

The best exchange rate is usually given by **state-owned banks** (try Ziraat Bankası or Halk Bankası), but queues can be long. **Döviz**, or exchange houses, are common in Turkey's cities and resorts. They buy and sell foreign currency of most sorts instantly, and have the convenience of long opening hours (usually 9/10am–8/10pm) and short or nonexistent queues. Some, however, charge commission (though they usually waive it if you make a fuss, as locals never pay it), and the rate given is not as high as in the banks.

Remember to keep all foreign-exchange slips with you until departure, if only to prove the value of purchases made in case of queries by customs.

Credit/debit cards and ATMs

Credit cards are now widely used in hotels, shops, restaurants, travel agencies and entertainment venues and with no commission (though many hotels and shops offer discounts for cash rather than credit-card payments). Don't expect, however, to use your card in basic eating-places or small corner shops. Swipe readers plus **chip-and-PIN** protocol are now the norm in most of Turkey – if you don't know your PIN, you probably won't be able to use it.

The simplest way to get hold of money in Turkey is to use the widespread **ATM** network. Most bank ATMs will accept any debit cards that are part of the Cirrus, Maestro or Visa/Plus systems. Screen prompts are given in English on request. You can also normally get cash advances (in TL only) at any bank displaying the appropriate sign. It's safest to use ATMs attached to banks during normal working hours so help can be summoned if your card is eaten (not uncommon). Turkish ATMs sometimes "time out" without disgorging cash, whilst your home bank may still debit your account – leaving you to argue the toss with them. ATM fraud is rife in Turkey – make sure you are not overlooked when keying in your PIN.

You can also use Visa or MasterCard to get cash from ATMs, though American Express holders are currently restricted to those of Akbank and Vakıf.

Opening hours and public holidays

Office workers keep conventional Monday to Friday 9am to 6pm schedules, with a full lunch hour; civil servants (including tourist offices and museum staff) in theory work 8.30am to 5.30pm, but in practice hours can be much more erratic – don't expect to get official business attended to the same day after 2.30pm. Most state **banks** are open Monday to Friday, 8.30am to noon and 1.30 to 5pm. Private banks such as Garanti Bankası and Köç operate throughout the day.

Ordinary **shops**, including large department stores and mall outlets, are open continuously from 8.30 or 9am until 7 or 8pm (sometimes even later in many major cities and resorts). Craftsmen and bazaar stallholders often work from 9am to 8 or 9pm, Monday to Saturday, with only short breaks for meals, tea or prayers. Even on Sunday the tradesmen's area may not be completely shut down – though don't count on this.

Museums are generally open from 8.30 or 9am until 5.30 or 6pm, except Mondays, though for some smaller museums you may have to find the *bekçi* (caretaker) and ask him to open up (for archeological sites see p.65). All tourist sites and museums are closed on the mornings of public holidays (see below), while İstanbul's palaces usually shut on Mondays and Thursdays.

Public holidays

Secular **public holidays** are generally marked by processions of schoolchildren or the military, or by some demonstration of national strength and dignity, such as a sports display. Banks and government offices will normally be closed on these days (exceptions given below). See p.56 for religious holidays.

Jan 1 *Yılbaşı* – New Year's Day.

April 23 *Ulusal Egemenlik ve Çocuk Bayramı* – Independence Day, celebrating the first meeting of the new Republican parliament in Ankara, and Children's Day.

May 19 *Gençlik ve Spor Günü* – Youth and Sports Day, also Atatürk's birthday.

May 29 İstanbul's capture by Mehmet the Conqueror in 1453 (İstanbul only).

July 1 *Denizcilik Günü* – Navy Day (banks and offices open).
Aug 26 *Silahlı Kuvvetler Günü* – Armed Forces Day (banks and offices open).
Aug 30 *Zafer Bayramı* – Celebration of the Turkish victory over the Greek forces at Dumlupınar in 1922.
Sept 9 *Kurtuluş Günü* – Liberation Day, with parades and speeches marking the end of the Independence War (İzmir only).
Oct 29 *Cumhuriyet Bayramı* – commemorates the proclamation of the Republic by Atatürk in 1923.
Nov 10 Anniversary of Atatürk's death in 1938. Observed at 9.05am (the time of his demise), when the whole country stops whatever it's doing and maintains a respectful silence for a minute. It's worth being on a Bosphorus ferry then, when all the engines are turned off, and the boats drift and sound their foghorns mournfully.

Phones

Most fixed-line **telecom services** are provided by TT (Türk Telekom); its website (ⓦ www.turktelekom.com.tr) has an English-language page listing all services and tariffs. The best place to make phone calls is from either a PTT (post office) or a TT (Türk Telekom) centre. Inside, or just adjacent, there is usually a row of card (*köntürlü* or *smartkart*) call boxes (TTs are blue-and-turquoise), and/or a *kontürlü* (metered, clerk-attended) phone, the latter sometimes in a closed booth. **Public phones** are to be found in squares and parks, outside many public buildings and at train stations and ferry terminals. The standard Turkish phone replies are the Frenchified *Allo* or the more local *Buyurun* (literally, "Avail yourself/at your service").

"Smart" **phonecards** are available from PTT or TT centres; when using these wait for the number of units remaining to appear on the screen before dialling and be aware that you will have little warning of being cut off. They are bought in units of 50 (3.75TL), 100 (7.50TL), 200 (15TL) and 350 (19TL). A steadily increasing number of phones have also been adapted to accept foreign **credit cards**. **Metered booths** inside PTTs or TTs, or at street kiosks or shops (look for signs reading *kontürlü telefon bulunur*) work out more expensive than cards, but are certainly far cheaper than hotels, and also tend to be quieter (plus you won't be cut off). Their

disadvantage is that you can't see the meter ticking over, and instances of overcharging are not unknown.

Overseas calls

Overseas call rates are 0.25TL per minute to Europe or North America. Try not to make anything other than local calls from a hotel room – there's usually a minimum 100 percent surcharge on phonecard rates. For extended chat overseas, it's best to buy an international phonecard. Best is the Alocard, available from PTT branches and usable in public phones. Reveal the 12-digit pin by scratching; then call the domestic access number, followed by the destination number. Rates are very low – for example, a 10TL card allows 2hrs chat to the UK. The cards can also be used for domestic calls, giving 140 minutes of calling time.

Turkey uses a system of eleven-digit **phone numbers** nationwide, consisting of four-digit area or mobile-provider codes (all starting with "0") plus a seven-digit subscriber number. To call a number in Turkey **from overseas**, dial your country's international access code, then 90 for Turkey, then the area or mobile code minus the initial zero, and finally the subscriber number. To call home **from Turkey**, dial ☏ 00 followed by the relevant international dialling code (see list on p.72), then the area code (without the initial zero if there is one) then the number.

Mobile phones

Most European **mobile phones** will connect on arrival with one of the three Turkish networks: Turkcell (best coverage), Avea and Vodafone; US mobiles will not work here. If you're staying longer than a week and intend calling home (or within Turkey) frequently, it may be worth purchasing a **local SIM card** and pay-as-you-go package. These are available from shops advertising *kontürlü* SIM cards. Typically, calls cost 0.9TL/min to Europe and North America, while an SMS message to the UK costs around 0.3TL. Unfortunately foreign phones using Turkish SIMs may be detected after two or three weeks and the number blocked. It's theoretically possible to re-register your phone and unblock it, but this doesn't always work. Travellers here for a substantial period may find it worthwhile buying a cheap Turkish secondhand mobile (60TL is standard for a bottom-of-the-range Nokia).

Time

Turkey is two hours ahead of GMT in winter; as in Europe, daylight saving is observed between March and October – clocks change at 2am of the last Sunday in each month.

Tourist information

Most Turkish towns of any size will have a *Turizm Danışma Bürosu* or **tourist office** of some sort, often lodged inside the *Belediye* (city hall) in the smaller places. However, outside the larger cities and obvious tourist destinations there's often little hard information to be had, and world-weary staff may dismiss you with a selection of useless brochures. Lists of accommodation are sometimes kept at the busier offices; personnel, however, will generally not make bookings. On the other hand, staff in out-of-the-way places can be embarrassingly helpful. It's best to have a specific question – about bus schedules,

festival ticket availability or museum opening hours – although in remote regions there is no guarantee that there will be anyone who can speak English.

Tourist offices generally adhere to a standard opening schedule of 8.30am to 12.30pm and 1.30 to 5.30pm, Monday to Friday. Between May and September in big-name resorts and large cities, these hours extend well into the evening and through much of the weekend. In winter, by contrast, many tourist offices in out-of-the-way spots will be shut most of the time.

Turkish information offices abroad

Overseas Turkish tourist offices (often the embassy's Information Office) will provide a few very basic maps and glossy brochures. For more information check ⓦwww .goturkey.com.

UK 29–30 St James's St, London SW1A 1HB ☎020/78397778, ⓦwww.gototurkey.co.uk.
US 821 United Nations Plaza, New York, NY 10017 ☎212/687-2194; 2525 Massachusetts Ave NW, Washington, DC 20008 ☎202/612-6800; 5055 Wilshire Blvd, Suite 850, Los Angeles CA 90036 ☎323/937-8066, ⓦwww .tourismturkey.org.

Useful websites

ⓦ**www.biletix.com** An online booking service for arts, cultural, music and sports events (mainly in İstanbul and Ankara), in both English and Turkish.
ⓦ**www.goturkey.com** Turkey's official tourist information site.
ⓦ**www.mymerhaba.com** Intended for long-term residents, and strongest on İstanbul, but nonetheless an authoritative, wide-ranging site with news of upcoming events and ticket-booking functions.
ⓦ**www.trekkinginturkey.com** Well researched information on major trekking areas and long-distance routes, with links to relevant outdoor-activity-type sites.
ⓦ**www.turkeycentral.com** Useful information portal with links to huge range of sites from scuba-diving operators to estate agents.
ⓦ**www.turkeytravelplanner.com** This somewhat American-orientated site has loads of practical tips for journey planning, and also many links to vetted service providers.

Guide

Guide

1

İstanbul and around

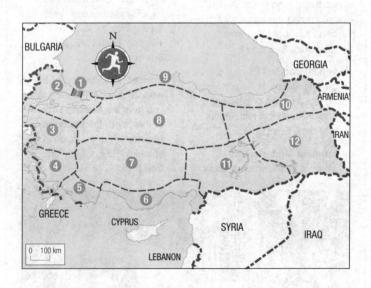

CHAPTER 1 # Highlights

* **Aya Sofya** Now a fascinating museum, the Church of the Divine Wisdom is the ultimate expression of Byzantine architecture. See p.94

* **Topkapı Palace** Contemplate the majesty of the Ottoman sultanate in the fine buildings, gilded pavilions and immaculate gardens. See p.96

* **Kariye Museum** Frescoes portraying the life of Christ are among the most evocative of all İstanbul's Byzantine treasures. See p.117

* **İstiklâl Caddesi** İstanbul's busiest and most elegant street boasts a wealth of palaces, churches, shops, restaurants and bars. See p.122

* **İstanbul Modern** Bold attempt to showcase (mainly Turkish) contemporary art in a converted warehouse with stunning views over the Bosphorus. See p.123

* **Nevizade Sokak** Soak up the atmosphere in one of the numerous traditional fish restaurants or bars along one of the city's liveliest streets. See p.132

* **Cruise the Bosphorus** Float past sumptuous villas, imposing fortresses, timeworn fishing villages and two intercontinental bridges. See p.147

* **Princes' Islands** One of the world's cheapest cruises takes you from the heaving streets of the city to the tranquillity of these historic islands in the sparkling Sea of Marmara. See p.151

▲ Tram on İstiklâl Caddesi

İstanbul and around

İ **STANBUL**, uniquely amongst the world's cities, stands astride two continents, Europe and Asia. As if its spectacular geographical location were not enough, it can also boast of being the only city to have played capital to consecutive **Christian and Islamic empires**, a role which has shaped the region's history for over 2500 years and bequeathed to İstanbul a staggering wealth of attractions; these range from the masterpiece Byzantine church of **Aya Sofya** to the formidable **city walls** and the domes and minarets of the **Ottoman mosques** and **palaces** which dominate the city skyline.

Although no longer its capital, the city remains the vibrant economic, cultural and intellectual heart of modern Turkey, a bustling, go-ahead city where east really does meet west. In conservative districts such as Fatih bearded men sporting

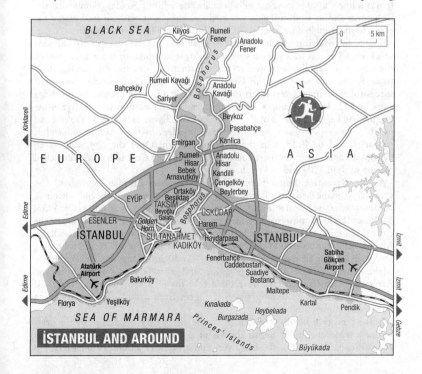

İSTANBUL AND AROUND

skullcaps and baggy *shalwar*-style trousers devoutly heed the call to prayer while women wouldn't dream of leaving the house with their heads uncovered. Yet across the water, in the tidal wave of humanity sweeping down İstiklâl Caddesi (Independence Street) are young Turkish men and women in designer jeans and trainers who have never been to the mosque in their lives. In business districts such as Şişli commuters arrive via the metro to work in high-rise office blocks, shop in state-of-the-art malls – and at weekends can be out clubbing until 6am.

Whether yours is the İstanbul of the Blue Mosque and the Topkapı Palace, or the Beyoğlu nightclubs and swish rooftop cocktail bars, the city takes time to get to know. Three to four days is enough to see the major historical sights in **Sultan-ahmet** and take a ferry trip out for the afternoon on the **Bosphorus**. But plan on staying a week, or even two, if you want to explore fully the backstreets of the **Old City** and the outlying suburbs and islands.

Some history

In 2008, while digging the Yenikapı metro station, archeologists uncovered a Neolithic settlement dating back to circa 6500 BC. But in popular tradition the city was founded in the seventh century BC by **Byzas, from Megra in Greece** – hence the original name of Byzantium. Over the next thousand years Byzantium became an important centre of trade and commerce, though it was not until the early fourth century AD that it would reach the pinnacle of its wealth, power and prestige. For more than 350 years, it had been part of the Roman province of Asia. On Diocletian's retirement in 305, Licinius and **Constantine** fought for control of the empire. Constantine finally defeated his rival on the hills above Chrysopolis (Üsküdar) and chose Byzantium as the site for the new **capital of the Roman Empire** in 330 BC. It was a fine choice – its seven hills (a deliberate echo of Rome) commanded the Bosphorus and its landward side was easily defensible. It was also well placed for access to the troublesome frontiers of both Europe and the Persian Empire.

In 395, the **division of the Roman Empire** between the two sons of Theodosius I left what was now named **Constantinople** as capital of the eastern part of the empire. It rapidly developed its own distinctive character, dissociating itself from Rome and adopting the Greek language and **Christianity**. Long and successful government was interrupted briefly, in Justinian's reign, by the Nika riots in 532. Half a century later, however, the dissolution of the Byzantine Empire had begun, as waves of Persians, Avars and Slavs attacked from the east and north. The empire was overrun by Arab invaders in the seventh and eighth centuries, and by Bulgars in the ninth and tenth. Only the city walls saved Constantinople, and even these could not keep out the **Crusaders**, who breached the sea walls in 1204 and sacked the city.

As the Byzantine Empire declined, the **Ottoman Empire** expanded. The Ottomans established first Bursa, then Edirne, as their capital, and Ottoman territory effectively surrounded the city long before it was taken. In 1453, **Mehmet II (the Conqueror)** – also known as Fatih Sultan Mehmet – besieged the city. It fell after seven weeks and, following the capture and subsequent pillage, Mehmet II began to rebuild the city, beginning with a new palace and following with the Mosque of the Conqueror (Fatih Camii) and many smaller complexes. Mehmet was tolerant of other religions, and actively encouraged Greek and Armenian Christians to take up residence in the city. His successor Beyazit II continued this policy, settling Jewish refugees from Spain into the city in an attempt to improve the economy.

In the century following the Conquest, the victory was reinforced by the great military achievements of **Selim the Grim** and by the reign of **Süleyman the Magnificent** (1520–66), "the Lawgiver" and greatest of all Ottoman leaders. His attempted conquest of Europe was only thwarted at the gates of Vienna, and the wealth gained in his military conquests funded the work of **Mimar Sinan**, the finest Ottoman architect.

A century after the death of Süleyman, the empire began to show signs of **decay**. Territorial losses abroad combined with corruption at home, which insinuated its way into the very heart of the empire, Topkapı Palace itself. Newly crowned sultans emerged, often insane, from the institution known as the Cage (see p.97), while others spent time in the harem rather than on the battlefield, consorting with women who increasingly became involved in grand-scale political intrigue.

As Ottoman territory was lost to the West, succeeding sultans became interested in Western institutional models. A short-lived parliament of 1876 was dissolved after a year by Abdülhamid II, but the **forces of reform** led to his deposition in 1909. The end of World War I saw İstanbul occupied by Allied, mainly British, troops as the victors procrastinated over how best to manage the rump of the once great empire. After the War of Independence, Atatürk's declaration of the **Republic** in 1923 and the creation of a new capital in Ankara effectively solved the problem.

İstanbul today

The **population** of Greater İstanbul has increased twelvefold since the establishment of the Turkish Republic. Today, estimates vary from 15–25 million which now constitutes close to 25 percent of the entire country. Needless to say this rapid urban growth has left the city with more than its fair share of problems, from horrendous traffic congestion to housing and water shortages and rising crime rates. Of more concern to visitors, perhaps, is the degradation of many of the sites they have come to see, so much so that UNESCO has threatened to revoke the city's "World Heritage" status and place it on the "In Danger" list. The boost of being nominated a **European capital of Culture** for 2010 should focus the minds of the relevant officials and ensure that the city preserves its unique heritage.

But much has been done, and continues to be done, to improve the infrastructure of one of the world's leading cities. A government-backed housing scheme has begun to offer quality, affordable housing to low-income families in order to eventually replace the shanty-dwellings that have long ringed the suburbs. The gigantic **Marmaray transport project** will see the European and Asian sides of the city linked by a rail tunnel under the Bosphorus by 2011, and there are plans to link the metro systems either side of the Golden Horn. The Horn itself, once heavily polluted, has been cleaned up and both anglers and cormorants can now be seen successfully fishing in its waters.

Orientation

İstanbul is divided in two by the **Bosphorus**, the narrow 30km strait separating Europe from Asia and linking the Black Sea and the Sea of Marmara. Feeding into the southern end of the strait from the European side is the **Golden Horn**, a 7km-long inlet of water that empties into the mouth of the Bosphorus. The city effectively has two **centres**, separated by the Golden Horn but both situated on the European side of the Bosphorus. The Old City, centred on the **Sultanahmet district**, is the historical core of the city and home to the main sights, while **Taksim** and **Beyoğlu** across the Horn are the fulcrum of the modern city. The two can easily be made out from the water, distinguished respectively by the landmarks of the Topkapı Palace and the modern *Marmara Hotel*.

City crimewatch

İstanbul is undoubtedly far safer than most European or North American cities, and cases of mugging and assault against tourists are rare. Having said this, the crime rate is soaring (thirty percent up according to recent statistics), due in part to the increasing disparity between rich and poor.

For the average visitor, pickpocketing is the main cause for concern: be particularly careful around Sirkeci station, the Eminönü waterfront, the Galata Bridge, and around Taksim (especially at night). You should also be careful on **public transport**, particularly when it is crowded. If you feel anyone is harassing or attempting to pickpocket you, try calling out *imdat!* meaning "help!" and contact the tourist police (see p.147).

A little way west of Sultanahmet is the massive Grand Bazaar (**Kapalı Çarşı**), the focal point of a disparate area stretching from the shores of the Sea of Maramara in the south up to the hill overlooking the Golden Horn to the north. Above is the commanding presence of the impressive **Süleymaniye Camii**. Some 6km west of the Old City, stretching between the Sea of Marmara and the Golden Horn, are the remarkably intact Byzantine **land walls**.

From Sultanahmet and Eminönü, you're most likely to cross the Golden Horn by the Galata bridge, entering the port area of **Karaköy**, then heading up the steep hill to the ancient **Galata** district. Near the northern end of Galata bridge is the **Tünel**, the French-built underground funicular railway, which chugs up to **Beyoğlu**, the city's elegant nineteenth-century European quarter. From the upper Tünel station, an antique tram runs the length of Beyoğlu's pedestrianized boulevard, **İstiklâl Caddesi**, to **Taksim Square**, the twin focal points of the modern city's best hotels, bars, clubs and restaurants.

North of Taksim, and on the metro line, are the city's newest business districts of Harbiye, Etiler, Nişantaşi and Şişli, location of many airline offices and embassies. Downhill from Taksim, on the Bosphorus shore, lie Tophane, **Beşiktaş** and **Ortaköy**, inner-city districts with scenic waterside locations and a number of historic palaces and parks. Across the straits, in Asia, the main centres of **Üsküdar, Haydarpaşa and Kadıköy** form part of İstanbul's commuter belt, but also have a few architectural attractions and decent shops, restaurants and clubs.

Arrival and information

İstanbul's main **points of arrival** by air are Atatürk airport on the European side of the Bosphorus, or Sabiha Gökçen airport across the strait in Asia. Most buses come into Esenler bus station, in the suburbs on the European side, trains into centrally located Sirkeci station. There are taxis and public transport from any of these transport hubs to the main accommodation areas in Sultanahmet or Taksim/Beyoğlu. For all **departure information**, see "Listings", p.154.

By air

İstanbul's **Atatürk airport** (Atatürk Hava Limanı; ⓦ www.atatürkairport.com) is 12km west of the centre at Yeşilköy, near the Sea of Marmara. It has two adjacent terminals, a kilometre apart: international (*dışhatları*) and domestic (*içhatları*). The Havaş **bus service** runs from both the international and the domestic terminals to the THY (Turkish Airlines) office on the north side of Taksim Square (every 30min 5am–11pm; 10TL); journey time into İstanbul is around forty minutes.

The only scheduled stop is at Aksaray, 200m from Yenikapı train station, from where you can take a municipal train to Cankurtan station (for Sultanahmet) or walk up the hill to the Aksaray tram stop for trams into Sultanahmet or Eminönü.

Much cheaper, the **light railway** or *hafif metro* (see also "City transport", p.84) runs from Atatürk airport to the city centre. The first train is at 6am, the last at 12.40am, with departures every ten minutes at peak times. To reach it follow signs for "Hafif Metro/Rapid Transit". Buy two *jetons* (1.50TL each) from the kiosk. Get off at Zeytinburnu and follow the signs a short distance to the Zeytinburnu tram stop (this is where you need the second *jeton*). The tram runs to Sultanahmet and across the Golden Horn, via the Galata bridge, to Kabataş. For Sultanahmet get off at the Sultanahmet tram stop, for Beyoğlu continue to the Karaköy stop just over the Galata bridge, and either walk or take the Tünel funicular train up to the southern end of İstiklâl Caddesi.

Alternatively, a **taxi** from the airport to Sultanahmet or Taksim should cost around 35–40TL (fifty percent more between midnight and 6am). Many hotels can arrange airport taxi collections (on request) for 30TL.

From **Sabiha Gökçen** airport (ⓦ www.sgairport.com), near Pendik on the Asian side of the city, shuttle buses run every hour, on the hour, into Taksim Square (12TL) taking around an hour. Alternatively catch the green #E10 bus for the 45-minute journey to Kadıköy (3TL). The bus terminates right opposite the Turyol ferry, which will whisk you across the Bosphorus to either Eminönü (for Sultanahmet) or Karaköy (for Beyoğlu) for 1.5TL – alternatively there's an IDO ferry a short walk south (NB there are no ferry services between midnight and 6am).

By train

İstanbul has two main-line **train stations**, one in Europe at Sirkeci, the other, at Haydarpaşa, across the Bosphorus in Asia. The two are linked by ferry.

Two daily trains from Western Europe arrive at **Sirkeci train station**, (☎0212/527 0051), located 250m above Eminönü ferry terminal. At Sirkeci it's easy to find a taxi, or catch the tram from outside the station directly uphill to Sultanahmet, or out to Yusufpaşa, where you can change onto the light railway (Aksaray stop) to reach the main intercity bus station at Esenler.

Trains from Asian Turkey arrive at **Haydarpaşa train station** (☎0216/348 8020), 1km north of Kadıköy. Ferries across the Bosphorus (frequently between 6.30am and 11.50pm) to Eminönü (for Sultanahmet) leave from in front of the station, and arrive directly below Sirkeci station – or continue across the Golden Horn to Karaköy (for Beyoğlu).

By bus

There are two major **otogars** (bus stations) in İstanbul: Esenler is 10km northwest of the centre; Harem is on the Asian side between Üsküdar and Kadıköy. Most national bus services stop at both, regardless of destination, and both are open 24 hours.

Esenler bus station is well organized and some 150 companies have numbered ticket stands here. Most run free service buses to and from Taksim, or can arrange for you to travel on one run by another company. To get to Sultanahmet from Esenler, take the light railway (every 15min, 6am–midnight) from the station in the centre of the *otogar* to Aksaray and switch to the tram to Sultanahmet. After midnight, your only option is to take a taxi into town (around 20TL). Travelling from the city centre to Esenler by light railway, remember to get off at Otogar, not Esenler station. There's a (free) shuttle service from Taksim or Sultanahmet to Esenler (usually an hour before departure) for tickets booked through a travel agent or bus company's city offices.

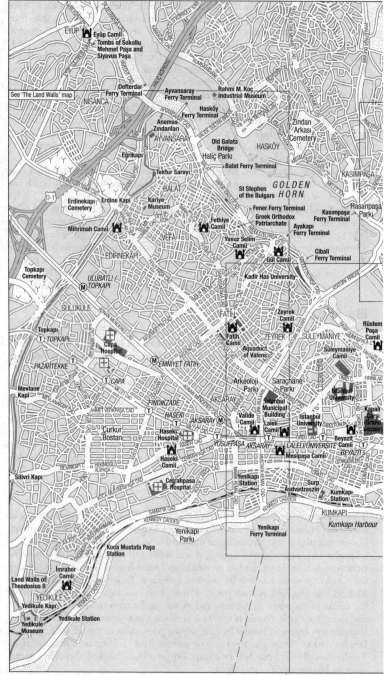

EYÜP
Eyüp Camii
Tombs of Sokollu
Mehmet Paşa and
Siyavus Paşa

Defterdar
Ferry Terminal
See 'The Land Walls' map
NİSANCA

Ayvansaray
Ferry Terminal
Rahmi M. Koç
Industrial Museum

Anemas
Zindanları
Hasköy
Ferry Terminal
Zindan
Arkası
Cemetery

AYVANSARAY
KASIMPAŞA

Eğrikapı
Old Galata
Bridge
HASKÖY

Haliç Parkı

Tektur Sarayı
Balat Ferry Terminal

BALAT
St Stephen
of the Bulgars
GOLDEN
HORN

Erdinekapı
Cemetery
Erdine Kapı
Kariye
Museum
Fener Ferry Terminal
Hasanpaşa
Parkı

Greek Orthodox
Patriarchate
Kasımpaşa
Ferry Terminal

Mihrimah Camii
Fethiye
Camii
Ayakapı
Ferry Terminal

VEFA
Yavuz Selim
Camii
Cibali
Ferry Terminal

EDİRNEKAPI
Gül Camii

Topkapı
Cemetery
Kadir Has University

ULUBATLI /
TOPKAPI

SULUKULE
FATİH
Zeyrek
Camii
Rüstem
Paşa
Camii

Topkapı
TOPKAPI
Çapa
Hospital
ZEYREK
SÜLEYMANİYE

PAZARTEKKE
Fatih
Camii
Süleymaniye
Camii

EMNİYET FATİH
Aquaduct
of Valens
İstanbul
University

CAPA
Kapalı
Çarsı
(Grand
Bazaar)

FINDIKZADE
Arkeoloji
Parkı
Saraçhane
Parkı

HASEK
AKSARAY
İstanbul
Municipal
Building
İstanbul
University
Beyazıt
Camii

Çurkur
Bostan
Haseki
Hospital
Valide
Camii
Laleli
Camii
BEYAZIT

YUSUFPAŞA
AKSARAY
LALELİ / ÜNİVERSİTE

Haseki
Camii
Mesipaşa Camii

Cerrahpaşa
Hospital
Yenikapı
Station
Surp
Asdvadzaszin
Kumkapı
Station

Silivri Kapı
KUMKAPI

Kumkapı Harbour

Yenikapı
Parkı

Koca Mustafa Paşa
Station
Yenikapı
Ferry Terminal

Imrahor
Camii

Land Walls of
Theodosius II
YEDİKULE

Yedikule Kapı

Yedikule Station

Yedikule
Museum

▼ *Yalova (Termal & İznik) & Güzuelyalı (for Bursa)*

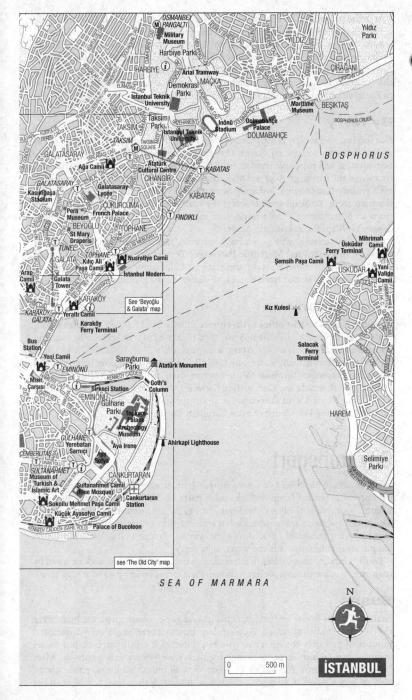

İSTANBUL

0   500 m

N

SEA OF MARMARA

BOSPHORUS

Yıldız Parkı

ÇIRAĞAN

BEŞİKTAŞ

Maritime Museum

BOSPHORUS CRUISE

YILDIZ

Military Museum

OSMANBEY
PANGALTI

Harbiye Parkı

HARBIYE

Arial Tramway

Demokrasi Parkı

MAÇKA

İstanbul Teknik University

Taksim Parkı

TAKSIM

İstanbul Teknik University

İnönü Stadium

Dolmabahçe Palace

DOLMABAHÇE

TAKSIM SQUARE

Atatürk Cultural Centre

CİHANGİR

KABATAŞ

KABATAŞ

GALATASARAY

Ağa Camii

Galatasaray Lycée

Kasımpaşa Stadium

GALATASARAY

Pera Museum

French Palace

ÇUKURCUMA

FINDIKLI

BEYOĞLU

St Mary Draperis

TOPHANE

TÜNEL

GALATA

TOPHANE

Kılıç Ali Paşa Camii

Nusretiye Camii

Arap Camii

Galata Tower

İstanbul Modern

KARAKÖY

Yeraltı Camii

See 'Beyoğlu & Galata' map

KARAKÖY
GALATA

Karaköy Ferry Terminal

Mihrimah Camii

Üsküdar Ferry Terminal

Şemsih Paşa Camii

ÜSKÜDAR

Yeni Vafide Camii

Kız Kulesi

Salacak Ferry Terminal

HAREM

Bus Station

Yeni Camii

EMİNÖNÜ

Sarayburnu Parkı

Atatürk Monument

Mısır Çarşısı

Sirkeci Station

Goth's Column

EMİNÖNÜ

Gülhane Parkı

Topkapı Palace

Archeology Museum

Ahirkapi Lighthouse

GÜLHANE

Yerebatan Sarnıçı

Aya Irene

Aya Sofya

ÇEMBERLİTAŞ

DIVAN YOLU C

SULTANAHMET

Museum of Turkish & Islamic Art

CANKURTARAN

Sultanahmet Camii (Blue Mosque)

Cankurtaran Station

Sokollu Mehmet Paşa Camii

Küçük Ayasofya Camii

Palace of Bucoleon

KENNEDY CADDESİ (SAHİL YOLU)

Selimiye Parkı

see 'The Old City' map

Arriving in İstanbul by bus from Asia, it's worth disembarking at **Harem**, saving a tedious journey to Esenler through terrible traffic snarl-ups. From Harem, regular ferries cross the Bosphorus to Eminönü (every hour, daily 6.20am–midnight) and there are private boats running to Beşiktaş and Kabataş. Dolmuşes run every few minutes to Kadıköy and to Üsküdar, leaving from the south side of the complex, beyond the ticket offices. From either of these suburbs, ferries cross to Eminönü, or from Üsküdar to Beşiktaş for Taksim.

By ferry

Car ferries, operated by IDO (İstanbul Deniz Otobüsleri; enquiries on ☎0212/444 4436, ⓦwww.ido.com.tr), cross the Bosphorus from Harem to Eminönü. **Sea-bus**, car and passenger services from Yalova, Bandırma (on the İzmir–İstanbul route) and the islands of Avşa and Marmara arrive at the **Yenikapı ferry terminal**, off Kennedy Caddesi in Kumkapı, just south of Aksaray. From here, simply catch the train from Yenikapı station across the road from the ferry terminal; it's two stops to Sultanahmet (Cankurtaran station) or three to Sirkeci. Frequent buses depart Yenikapı for Taksim via Aksaray.

Cruise-ship arrivals will go through customs and immigration procedures at **Karaköy International Maritime Passenger Terminal**, across the Galata bridge from Eminönü. From here take the tram to Sultanahmet, or the Tünel up to Beyoğlu; or the funicular from Kabataş to Taksim Square; alternatively, take a taxi.

Information

The most helpful **tourist office** in the city is on Divan Yolu Caddesi, in Sultanahmet, near the Hippodrome (daily 9am–5pm; ☎0212/518 8754). Others can be found in the international arrivals area of **Atatürk airport** (daily 24hr; ☎0212/573 4136); in **Sirkeci train station** (daily 9am–5pm; ☎0212/511 5888); at **Karaköy International Maritime Passenger Terminal** (Mon–Sat 9am–5pm; ☎0212/249 5776); and in the **Hilton Hotel arcade** on Cumhuriyet Caddesi (Mon–Sat 9am–5pm; ☎0212/233 0592). Each hands out an abundance of city maps and leaflets and the staff have an excellent working knowledge of most European languages.

City transport

İstanbul has a wide choice of means of transport, from ferry to high-speed tram. The newly extended tramway links most parts of the city that you're likely to want to visit, while the bus system is daunting, but manageable on certain routes. The municipal trains are ramshackle but efficient, while taxis and dolmuşes (shared taxis) are very reasonably priced. A great way to explore a city that, historically, has put its best face towards the water, is by ferry.

Traffic jams are unavoidable in İstanbul, so where possible either walk or travel by tram, metro, suburban train or ferry, though these can all be jam-packed at peak times.

Buses

İstanbul's **buses** (*otobus* in Turkish) come in a range of colours, with the bulk being the red-and-white or green municipality buses. There are also a substantial number of privately run, green or pale-blue buses. For information on bus routes and numbers (which seem to change regularly) see ⓦwww.iett.gov.tr/en. Most buses run daily from 6.30am to 11.30pm. For all municipal buses, either use an *akbil* or buy a ticket in advance, which you deposit in the metal box next to the

Akbils – automatic travel passes

An *akbil* (automatic travel pass) is worth considering if you're staying for a few days or more. After paying an initial, refundable, deposit of 6TL, these can be "charged" to whatever value you require at kiosks at Sultanahmet, Eminönü, Sirkeci, Aksaray, Taksim and the Tünel, or at the automatic terminals in main *otogars*. The passes are accepted on all municipal and some private buses, sea-buses, ferries, trains (for local journeys only), the light railway and the tram. All either have *akbil* machines or turnstiles; press the *akbil* against the receptor and the appropriate journey cost (including a small discount) is deducted. Weekly and monthly passes are also available, but as you need a photo ID card these are probably only of interest to long-stayers.

driver on boarding. On privately run buses, the conductor will accept cash, and some companies accept *akbils*.

Tickets are sold at *otogar* ticket kiosks next to main bus, tram or metro stops (regular ticket 1.5TL). Touts at most main stops also sell them for a small mark-up. Buy a good supply when you get the chance, since you can walk for miles trying to find a ticket kiosk in suburban areas: better still, use an *akbil*.

On the European side **main bus terminals** are at Eminönü, Taksim Square, Beşiktaş and Aksaray, and on the Asian side at Üsküdar and Kadıköy. **From Eminönü** bus station (three tram stops down the hill from Sultanahmet) there are buses to Taksim, west-bound services to Aksaray and Topkapı, and services to the Bosphorus shore through Beşiktaş, Ortaköy and Arnavutköy to Bebek where you'll have to change to continue on through the suburbs as far as the village of Rumeli Kavağı. Buses **from Taksim Square** head through Mecidiyeköy to the northern suburbs, down along the Bosphorus through Beşiktaş, Ortaköy and Aranvutköy, and across the Horn to Topkapı and Aksaray.

Useful routes include: #12 and #14 Kadıköy to Üsküdar; #22 Kabataş up the Bosphorus to Beşiktaş, Ortaköy, Kuruçeşme, Arnavutköy, Bebek, Emirgan and İstinye; #25/A Levent Metro, Maslak, Sariyer and Rumeli Kavağı; #28T Edirnekapı to Beşiktaş via Fatih, Eminönü, Karaköy, Tophane and Kabataş; #38E Eminönü to Edirne Kapı (city land walls) via Unkapanı/Atatürk Bridge and Fatih; #40 Taksim up the Bosphorus including Beşiktaş, Kuruçeşme, Arnavutköy, Bebek, Emirgan, İstinye, Tarabya and Sariyer; #42T Taksim to Beşiktaş, Ortaköy, Emirgan and Tarabya; #54HT Taksim to upper Golden Horn (for Miniatürk, Rami Koç Museum and Santralistanbul).

Trains

The **municipal train network** – operated by Türkiye Cumhuriyeti Devlet Demiryolları (TCDD) – consists of one line on either side of the Bosphorus. The currently rather ramshackle lines will be unrecognizable after the completion of the ongoing work to link the two via a tunnel under the Sea of Marmara (p.86).

Suburban or *banliyö* trains are frequent and cheap, though crowded at morning and evening rush hours; daily hours of operation are 6am to midnight. One line runs **from Haydarpaşa** (enquiries on ☎0212/336 0475) out to Göztepe and Bostancı, and along the Gulf of İzmit to Gebze; the other, **from Sirkeci** (☎0212/527 0051), runs to Halkala, along the shores of the Sea of Marmara, stopping at Kumkapı (known for its fish restaurants), Yenkapı (for the sea-bus ferry terminal) and Yedikule fortress. Journeys cost the same flat **fare** (1.50TL) and *akbils* are accepted on local lines. At Sirkeci, you buy a *jeton* (metal token) from the kiosk (insert it at the turnstile), but Haydarpaşa still uses tickets, again available from kiosks.

The Marmaray Project

In the autumn of 2008, the laying of sections of tubing forming a tunnel under the Bosphorus was completed and an underwater link between European and Asian İstanbul, an idea that first hit the drawing board back in the Ottoman period, finally became a reality. Set to open in 2011, the tunnel will form part of a line stretching some 76km, and will link the city's two international airports, Atatürk and Sabiha Gökçen. The section from Yenikapı to Sirkeci will be underground, as will the new Sirkeci station and its counterpart across the Bosphorus in Üsküdar. Work has been delayed by the unearthing of many important archeological finds during construction, notably a massive Byzantine harbour, complete with ships, at Yenikapı.

There is also a one-stop underground funicular train line, between Karaköy and İstiklâl Caddesi in Beyoğlu, known as the **Tünel** (every 15min, daily 8am–9pm); use an *akbil* or *jeton* (1.30TL), available at the kiosks on entry.

Trams

The **main tram** service runs from Zeytinburnu via Topkapı Gate to Aksaray, Laleli, Beyazit, Cemberlitaş, Sultanahmet, downhill to Eminönü, and across the Galata bridge to Karaköy (for Beyoğlu/Galata) Tophane, Findıklı and Kabataş (where it connects with the funicular to Taksim Square and the ferryboat terminal for boats to the Princes' Islands). Trams are frequent and operate from 6am to midnight. Approaching trams signal their arrival with a bell and passengers must wait on the concrete platforms, placed at regular intervals along the tracks. Note that the tram stops are marked, confusingly, by the same "M" sign as the light railway/*hafif metro*. *Jeton*s (1.50TL) can be bought at booths next to the platforms and are deposited in turnstiles on entry, or you can use an *akbil*.

The **antique tram** (with ticket collectors in appropriately antiquated uniforms) runs between the Tünel station, at the Beyoğlu end of İstiklâl Caddesi, for 1.5km to Taksim Square (every 15min, daily 9am–9pm; 1.30TL). Tickets can be purchased from kiosks at either end of the route or at the one fixed stop halfway at Galatasaray School; *akbil*s are also accepted.

The light railway and metro

Once the building of a tunnel underneath the Golden Horn has been completed, the light railway will connect the whole of the European side of İstanbul. At present the service is limited to a line on each side of the Horn. The **southern line** runs west from Aksaray via the intercity *otogar* near Esenler, to Atatürk airport. Although it's called a metro, only small sections of this line run underground. On the **northern side** of the Golden Horn, the Şişhane (at the southern end of İstiklâl Caddesi) to Levent 4 section is truly underground, and runs to Levent 4 via Taksim Square, Osmanbey, Şişli, Gayrettepe and Levent. Trains leave every fifteen minutes (Mon–Thurs 6am–12.30am, Fri & Sat 6.30am–1am, Sun 6.30am–12.30am); **tickets** (1.50TL) are inserted in turnstiles on entry, or use an *akbil*.

Dolmuşes and minibuses

Dolmuşes are shared taxis running on fixed routes, departing only when full ("dolmuş" means "full"). Minibus services on longer routes tend to run along main arteries and depart according to a schedule known only to their drivers. Both dolmuşes and minibuses display their destination in the window. A flat fare (fixed by the municipality) is levied: watch what Turkish passengers are paying – usually a little more than a municipality bus – shout your destination to the driver and pay accordingly, passing the money via other passengers. Dolmuş and minibus stands at points of origin are denoted with a signposted "D".

Taxis

Taxis are ubiquitous, with over 19,000 legal **taksici** (taxi drivers) in the city. They are invariably painted yellow. Fares are reasonable: a theoretical rate of just under 10TL per 5km, with an extra toll when crossing either of the Bosphorus bridges. All taxis are equipped with meters, but check that the driver switches it on to avoid arguments later. Be careful that you're not charged either ten times what's shown on it, or the night rate (an extra fifty percent that should only be levied between midnight and 6am). Older meters have two small lights marked *gündüz* (day) and *gece* (night); on newer meters, the rate flashes up alternately with the running cost.

Ferries, sea-buses and sea taxis

Ferries are a quick and exciting way to travel around the city, particularly between Europe and Asia – though as most are essentially for commuters, can be very crowded at peak times. On the busiest routes – such as Eminönü to Kadıköy or Üsküdar – there are generally three to five ferries an hour between 6am and midnight; all have a flat fare of 1.5TL each way. Faster **sea-buses** (*deniz otobüsleri*) run on longer routes, fares are 7TL for the Princes' Islands and 15TL to Yalova on the south shore of the Sea of Marmara. For both ferries and sea-buses, buy a *jeton* and deposit it at the turnstile on entry, or use your *akbil*. The main ferry company is the efficient **İDO** (*İstanbul Deniz Otobüsleri*; enquiries on ⊕0212/444 4436, ⊛www.ido.com.tr), with seasonal timetables available from the ferry terminals. Some routes are also served by small, privately run ferries, many under the umbrella of the cooperative **Turyol**. Most Turyol boats leave from a terminal just west of the Galata bridge in Eminönü, for a wide range of destinations; tickets are sold at kiosks on the quayside.

At the main **City Ferry Terminal** at Eminönü – between Sirkeci train station and the Galata bridge –is a line of ferry quays or terminals (*iskelesi* in Turkish). Each terminal is clearly marked with the name of the end destination, which include (on the Asian side) Harem (frequent departures from 8am–9.30pm for car and passenger ferries); Üsküdar (frequent departures from 6.35am–11.30pm) and Kadıköy (frequent departures from 7.40am–9pm). Ferries from Boğaz İskelesi run up the Bosphorus to Rumeli Kavağı (see Bosphorus Tours, below). On the west side of Galata bridge is Yemiş İskelesi, for ferries up the Golden Horn to Eyüp via Kasımpaşa, Fener and Balat (roughly hourly 7.45am–9pm).

Frequent İDO ferry routes go from Karaköy (on the other side of the Galata bridge) to Haydarpaşa and Kadıköy (6.10am–midnight) and from Beşiktaş to Kadıköy or Üsküdar (roughly every hour 8am–9pm). For the Princes' Islands see p.151. Less frequent are ferries up (and across) the Bosphorus from Eminönü.

Timetables are available from all ferry/sea-bus terminals and at ⊛www.ido .com.tr under "*tarife bilgileri*". Sea buses also operate further afield, from İstanbul to Bandırma and Yalova on the opposite shore of the Marmara (see p.154).

Water taxis (*deniz taksi*) are massively oversubscribed, and you have to book well in advance. Theoretically, you call ⊕0212/444 4436, give your name and your pick-up, drop-off points and a water taxi will collect you from one of the 27 designated docks, which include the Princes' Islands as well as numerous stops on both sides of the Bosphorus as far up as Rumeli Kavağı. It's a shared fare system, and the initial 15TL fare, plus 10TL per nautical mile travelled, is not too expensive if there are several passengers. Night fares are double. For more information, see ⊛www.deniztaksi.com.tr.

The Bosphorus Tour

From Boğaz İskelesi İDO operates the popular daily **Bosphorus Tour** (*Boğaz Hatti*), a cruise to Rumeli Kavağı and Anadolu Kavağı, the most distant villages up the Bosphorus on the European and Asian sides respectively. Trips depart daily during summer (June–Oct) at 10.35am, noon and 1.35pm, and return from Anadolu Kavağı at 3pm, 4.15pm and 5pm (7pm at weekends), crisscrossing from one side to the other. The rest of the year there is just one departure at 10.35am, returning at 3pm. The return journey costs 20TL and takes about an hour and a half each way, with stops at Beşiktaş, Kanlıca, Emirgan, Yeniköy, Sariyer, Rumeli Kavağı and Anadolu Kavağı. You can jump off in any of these places, but you pay again to re-board, alternatively you could catch a bus back from either Rumeli or Anadolu Kavağı as there is a new, 13TL one-way option. There is also a summer/Saturday-only night cruise (20TL return) departing Eminönü at 7.15pm, returning for 10.30pm.

Accommodation

With new hotels opening on a seemingly daily basis, it's nearly always possible to find a decent room with a modicum of advance planning. Be aware, however, that during major conferences and international events (such as the Formula 1 Grand Prix) prices in many establishments will be higher and the choice less. Where you stay depends on your interests. For nightlife head across the Golden Horn to Beyoğlu, to be on the doorstep of the major historical sites it makes more sense to base yourself in or around Sultanahmet. Virtually all but the most basic İstanbul hotels have wi-fi.

Many hotels offer discounts for cash or booking through their **website**, though some, fed-up with "no-show" internet bookers, require payment upfront – which means you're stuck with the room even if on arrival you find it doesn't match up to your expectations. Hotels in the major tourist and business areas tend to quote in euros, smaller hotels still use the TL, but all should accept payment in either currency.

Sultanahmet

Some of the city's best small hotels, *pansiyon*s and hostels are in **Sultanahmet**, the historic heart of touristic İstanbul, within a few minutes' walk of the Blue Mosque, Topkapı Palace and Aya Sofya. Those around the **Hippodrome** are particularly well placed to give a sense of history. A high concentration of accommodation is to be found in and around **Akbıyık Caddesi and Cankurtaran**, while the hotels off **Divan Yolu Caddesi** have the advantage of being handy for the tram. All the places reviewed below are marked on the Sultanahmet map on p.95.

Around the Hippodrome

Alzer At Meydanı 72 ☎ 0212/516 6262, ⊛ www .alzerhotel.com. Not the most characterful of the area's hotels, but the extremely comfortable rooms have cable TV, a/c, central heating and safe box; the roof terrace has stunning views over walnut trees to the Blue Mosque and the sea. Rooms at the back overlooking the Hippodrome are dearer. Good value. ❻

Deniz Konak Cayıroğlu Sok 14 ☎ 0212/518 9595, ⊛ www.denizkonakhotel.com. Perched on a small cliff overlooking Kennedy Cad and the Sea of Marmara, this well-run, homely place has more of a seaside feel than the average Sultanahmet hotel. Hardwood floors, tasteful kilims, well-appointed bathrooms (some with tubs), flat-screen TVs, a/c and central heating make for a comfy stay. Rooms overlooking the sea are dearer but the cosy rooftop breakfast room has great sea vistas for all, and views up to the Blue Mosque. ❸

🏃 **İbrahim Pasha Hotel** Terzihane Sok 5 Adliye Yani ℡0212/518 0394, ⓦwww.ibrahimpasha.com. This lovely townhouse, once the guesthouse for the İbrahim Paşa Sarayı (now the Museum of Turkish & Islamic Art), is arguably the most tasteful boutique hotel in Sultanhamet, successfully blending a stylish modern interior with Ottoman antiques. The rooms are uncluttered and very comfortable and, owing to its side-street location, quiet. Views from the roof terrace across the domes and minarets of Sultanhamet and down to the Sea of Marmara are superb, and the freshly prepared breakfast (with latte and espresso on tap) in the cosy and charming downstairs breakfast room a delight. ❼

Turkoman Hotel Asmalı Çeşme Sok, Adliye Yana 2 ℡0212/516 2956, ⓦwww.turkomanhotel.com. Converted house in nineteenth-century Turkish style, right on the Hippodrome and opposite the Egyptian obelisk, with fine views of the Blue Mosque from the roof terrace. Each attractive room is named after one of the old Turkoman tribes, and has a brass bed and wooden floors. Free airport transfers. ❺

Around Topkapı Palace

Ayasofya Pansiyonlar Soğukçeşme Sok ℡0212/513 3660, Ⓔayapans@escourtnet.com. A row of pastel-coloured houses reconstructed in nineteenth-century style, in a peaceful cobbled street tucked away behind the back wall of the Aya Sofya. The setting is fantastic and lit up theatrically at night, but the rooms are rather simply furnished, perhaps in an attempt to match the period feel. ❾

Around Divan Yolu Caddesi

Kybele Hotel Yerebatan Cad 35 ℡0212/511 7766, ⓦwww.kybelehotel.com. Atmospheric, unusual, late nineteenth-century rendered brick building, colourfully painted. Inside are over 3000 multi-hued antique-style light fittings and some great original Bakelite radios. The spacious rooms sport marbled wallpaper and old wood flooring. Breakfast is served in a courtyard full of candelabras, cushions, empty bottles and other knick-knacks. Friendly staff. ❻

🏃 **Nomade Hotel** Ticarethane Sok 15 ℡0212/511 1296, ⓦwww.hotelnomade.com. Described as "ethnic trendy" by the French designer responsible for its chic interior, this hotel has white-floored rooms finished in bold colours, with rich coordinating fabrics and blonde-wood modernist furniture. The charming and sophisticated twin sisters who run it ensure excellent service. There's a great roof terrace, too. ❻

Ottoman Hotel Imperial Caferiye Sok 6/1 ℡0212/513 6151, ⓦwww.ottomanhotelimperial.com. Hard to believe this well-positioned, tastefully refurbished hotel was once the Yücelt Hostel, mainstay of the young and impecunious heading out to India in the 1970s (and apparently came back). The best rooms, at a premium, have views over the Cafer Ağa Medresesi, big tubs, plasma TVs – all have tea-and-coffee making facilities and wifi. ❼

Sultanahmet (Cankurtaran)

Alp Hotel Akbıyık Cad, Adliye Sok 4 ℡0212/517 9570, ⓦwww.alpguesthouse.com. This fine establishment, with a dark-wood exterior, is situated down a quiet lane. The smallish rooms are immaculately furnished, some with four-poster beds, and have a/c, wooden floors and tidy bathrooms. The pretty breakfast terrace commands views of palaces, mosques and the sea. ❺

🏃 **Apricot Hotel** Amiral Tafdil Sok 18 ℡0212/638 1658, ⓦwww.apricothotel.com. Set in a quiet backstreet running parallel to busy Akbıyık Cad, this small hotel has an intimate atmosphere. Rooms vary in size and are painted in soothing apricot tones; some have balconies. Bathrooms either have big tubs, fancy showers or jacuzzis. Owner Hakan, a professional tour guide, is a fount of knowledge about the city. Double-glazing, a/c and cable TV are standard. Hakan also has three stylish apartments nearby, in a restored townhouse overlooking the Sea of Marmara. ❹

🏃 **Bauhaus Hostel** Bayramfırını Sok 11–13 ℡0212/638 6534, ⓦwww.travelinistanbul.com. With a mix of dorm bunks (€12 depending on number of bunks per room) and doubles from €40, this is a homely, clean and friendly option. There's a nice roof terrace, a kilim-cushioned sitting area and free internet use, but breakfast is extra. Good value. ❹

Big Apple Bayram Fırını Sok 12 ℡0212/517 7931. Good value, cheerful hostel sporting a large lobby with billiard table (free) and well-kitted-out dorms (25TL) with wooden floors, and bunk beds with new mattresses. Shared, clean, separate toilet and shower on each floor. You can use the kitchen, and there's a nice covered terrace and a small roof terrace, both with decent outlooks.

🏃 **Empress Zoe** Akbıyık Cad, Adliye Sok 10 ℡0212/518 2504, ⓦwww.emzoe.com. Owned by American Ann Nevans, who has decorated throughout with her personal touch – the nineteen rooms are in dark wood with richly coloured textiles, accessed by a narrow spiral staircase. Part of the basement walls belong to the

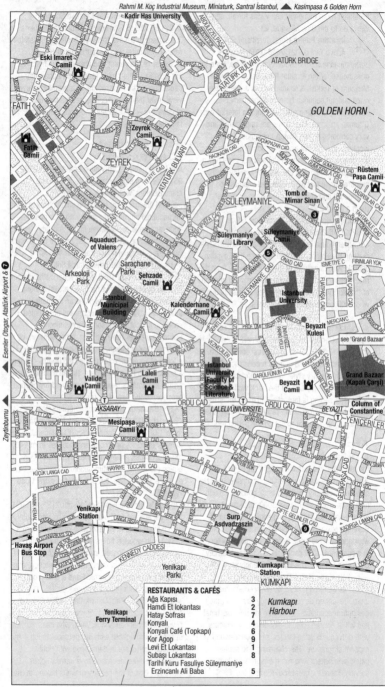

Rahmi M. Koç Industrial Museum, Miniaturk, Santral İstanbul, ▲ Kasımpaşa & Golden Horn

Kadir Has University

Eski İmaret Camii

FATİH

Fatih Camii

Zeyrek Camii

ZEYREK

GOLDEN HORN

ATATÜRK BRIDGE

Rüstem Paşa Camii

SÜLEYMANIYE

Tomb of Mimar Sinan

Aquaduct of Valens

Saraçhane Parkı

Süleymaniye Library

Süleymaniye Camii

Arkeoloji Park

Şehzade Camii

İstanbul Municipal Building

Kalenderhane Camii

İstanbul University

Beyazit Kulesi

see 'Grand Bazaar'

Grand Bazaar (Kapalı Çarşı)

İstanbul University (Faculty of Science & Literature)

Valide Camii

Laleli Camii

Beyazit Camii

Column of Constantine

AKSARAY

ORDU CAD

LALELİ/ÜNİVERSİTE

ORDU CAD

BEYAZIT

YENİÇERİLER

Mesipaşa Camii

Yenikapı Station

Surp Asdvadzasin

Havaş Airport Bus Stop

Kumkapı Station

KENNEDY CADDESİ

KUMKAPI

Yenikapı Parkı

Kumkapı Harbour

Yenikapı Ferry Terminal

RESTAURANTS & CAFÉS

Ağa Kapısı	3
Hamdi Et lokantası	2
Hatay Sofrası	7
Konyalı	4
Konyali Café (Topkapı)	6
Kor Agop	9
Levi Et Lokantası	1
Subaşı Lokantası	8
Tarihi Kuru Fasuliye Süleymaniye Erzincanlı Ali Baba	5

▼ Yalova (Termal & İznik) & Güzuelyalı (for Bursa)

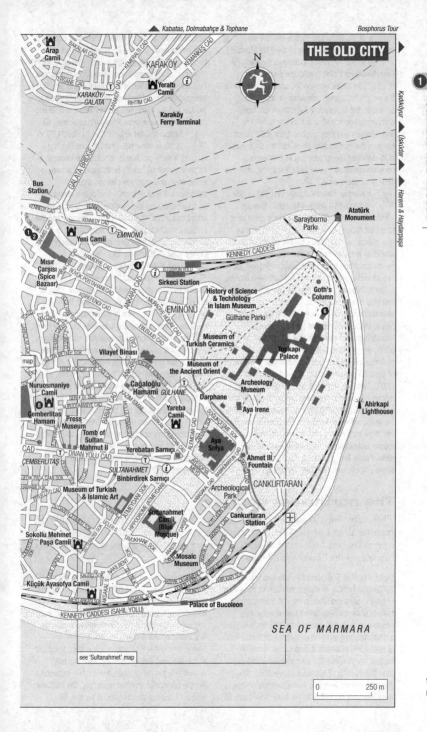

THE OLD CITY

N

Arap Camii

KARAKÖY

Yeraltı Camii

Karaköy Ferry Terminal

Kadıköy ▶
Üsküdar ▶
Harem & Haydarpaşa ▶

Sarayburnu Parkı

Atatürk Monument

Bus Station

KENNEDY CAD

EMINÖNÜ

Yeni Camii

KENNEDY CADDESİ

Mısır Çarşısı (Spice Bazaar)

Sirkeci Station

EMINÖNÜ

History of Science & Technology in Islam Museum

Goth's Column

Gülhane Parkı

Museum of Turkish Ceramics

Topkapı Palace

Vilayet Binası

Museum of the Ancient Orient

Cağaloğlu Hamamı

GÜLHANE

Darphane

Archeology Museum

Nuruosmaniye Camii

Yareba Camii

Aya Irene

Ahirkapi Lighthouse

Çemberlitaş Hamam

Press Museum

Tomb of Sultan Mahmut II

Yerebatan Sarnıçı

Aya Sofya

DIVAN YOLU CAD

Ahmet III Fountain

CANKURTARAN

ÇEMBERLITAŞ

SULTANAHMET

Binbirdirek Sarnıçı

Archeological Park

Museum of Turkish & Islamic Art

Sultanahmet Camii (Blue Mosque)

Cankurtaran Station

Sokollu Mehmet Paşa Camii

Mosaic Museum

Küçük Ayasofya Camii

KENNEDY CADDESİ (SAHİL YOLU)

Palace of Bucoleon

SEA OF MARMARA

see 'Sultanahmet' map

0   250 m

remains of the Byzantine Palace and the sun terrace has panoramic views of the Blue Mosque and Aya Sofya. Ten percent discount for cash. ❻

Four Seasons Hotel Tevfikhane Sok 1 ☏0212/638 8200, ⓦwww.fourseasons.com. Until the early 1980s, this formidable building still served as the Sultanahmet Prison before being completely renovated as a five-star hotel. The watchtowers and exercise court are still evident beneath the flowers and vines, but the 54 beautiful high-ceilinged rooms (starting at €400) are unrecognizable as former cells. Excellent, attentive service as you'd expect. ❾

Hanedan Hotel Kakbıyık Cad, Adliye Sok 3 ☏0212/516 4869–418 1564, ⓦwww .hanedanhotel.com. Tucked away on a quiet side street off Akbıyık Cad, this friendly hotel, run by four friends, is great value for the quality of accommodation and service. The dark-wood floors in the rooms are offset by the pale plain walls, and the overall feel is one of unfussy comfort. New fittings in the bathrooms gleam, and a/c, central heating and safe box are standard. There's a roof terrace with stunning views over the Aya Sofya and the Sea of Marmara. Discount for long stays. ❺

Istanbul Hostel Kutlugün Sok 35 ☏0212/516 9380, ⓦwww.istanbulhostel.net. All round, probably the best of İstanbul's hostels, in the heart of the backpacker quarter, with 64 dorm beds (20TL), two double rooms, and spotless, shared, marble bathrooms. The beds are good quality and comfy. The cosy cellar-bar has big-screen satellite TV, video, a fireplace and internet access, and there are more bars on the roof terrace, as well as regular entertainment from belly dancers. ❸

Hotel Poem Terbıyık Sok 12 ☏0212/638 9744, ⓦwww.hotelpoem.com. Very friendly family-run establishment, in two adjoining nineteenth-century wooden mansion-houses. Rooms are named after famous Turkish poets or their poems (you can stay in "Nirvana") and have a/c and immaculate bathrooms. The downstairs terrace is shaded by walnut and fig trees, while the roof terrace has panoramic views of the Aya Sofya and the sea. Rooms with a sea view cost twenty percent extra. Free internet access. ❺

Sultan Hostel Akbıyık Cad 21 ☏0212/516 9260, ⓦwww.sultanhostel.com. Big, but relaxed, friendly place and very popular because of its spotless rooms, comfy beds sporting gleaming white linen, and regularly cleaned shared bathrooms. A spot in the six-bed dorms offers the best value, though the en-suite doubles or twins aren't bad either. The staff are very friendly and the restaurant, which spills out onto the street, is incredibly popular with both guests and passers-by. Dorms from 25TL, rooms ❸

Side Hotel & Pension Utangaç Sok 20 ☏0212/517 2282, ⓦwww.sidehotel.com. Owned by three charismatic brothers, this place is bright, spacious and friendly and resists the pressure to go all modern or faux-Ottoman. Pricier en-suite rooms (a/c) on the hotel side, cheaper ones with shared bathroom in the pension, both sharing the extensive breakfast terraces, which have great views of the Princes' Islands. Pension ❹, hotel ❺

Yeşil Ev Kabasakal Cad 5 ☏0212 517 6785, ⓦwww.turing.org.tr. On a leafy cobbled street between Aya Sofya and the Blue Mosque. Built in the style of the house that originally occupied the site, *Yeşil Ev* ("Green House") is furnished in period (mid-nineteenth-century) style, with wood-panelled ceilings and antique rugs. There's a fine garden restaurant with a central marble fountain open to nonresidents. ❾

The northwest quarter

There are only a couple of options worth considering in this atmospheric, traditional area of the Old City, but their proximity to some of the city's most interesting yet little-visited sights is a major plus. The places listed below are marked on the "Land Walls" map on p.115.

Hotel Daphnis Sadrazam Ali Paşa Cad 26 ☏0212/531 4858, ⓦwww.hoteldaphnis.com. This charming boutique hotel, contrived from a small terrace of century-old Greek townhouses, is situated close to the shore of the Golden Horn, just a short distance from Fener's Greek Orthodox Patriachate – which means it gets its fair share of visitors from Greece. It's less messed about with than the majority of boutique conversions, though the front rooms, with fine views over the Golden Horn, are very noisy due to the busy main road. ❻

Kariye Hotel Kariye Camii Sok 6, Erdirne Kapı ☏0212/534 8414, ⓦwww.kariyeotel .com. Situated right next door to the Kariye Museum and a stone's throw from the Theodosian land walls, this carefully restored nineteenth-century mansion is a model of restraint and elegance. There are ceiling fans rather than a/c, which is quite sufficient in this elevated, tree-shaded location. The only downside is the rather small, shower-only bathrooms, but the wonderful attached restaurant, the *Asithane* (see p.133), more than makes up for this. ❻

Beyoğlu, Taksim and the waterfront

The heart of **Beyoğlu**, the former European quarter, is undoubtedly **İstiklâl Caddesi** – lined with gorgeous nineteenth-century townhouses and arcades, it's İstanbul's premier entertainment area, home to the city's densest concentration of restaurants, bars and clubs. **Tepebaşı**, a mixed commercial/tourist district just west of İstiklâl Caddesi's southern end, gives easy access to İstiklâl but has a number of charms of its own, from trendy rooftop bars and restaurants to the impressive Pera Museum. There are also a couple of options close to the **Galata Tower**. **Cihangir**, on the northern side of Sıraselviler Caddesi, is an affluent yet bohemian backwater with splendid views of the Bosphorus.

At the northeastern end of İstiklâl Caddesi, the business district of **Taksim** has a wide range of hotels aimed largely at business travellers and tour groups. Rates here are usually higher than in other areas, but bargains can be found. All the places reviewed below are marked on the "Beyoğlu and Galata" map on pp.120–121.

Tepebaşı, İstiklâl Caddesi and Galata

Suite Home İstiklal İstiklâl Cad 45 ☎0212/245 0772, ⊛www.istanbulsuite.com. In the heart of the action near the Taksim end of this buzzing street, this upmarket hotel offers a range of doubles (some with balcony views) and suites. Decor is simple and modern without being too minimalist, and there's a pleasant garden restaurant. Prices drop considerably for longer stays and there's another branch in nearby, trendy Cihangir. ⑥

Büyük Londra Oteli Meşrutiyet Cad 117, Tepebaşı ☎0212/249 1025, ⊛www.londrahotel.net. Palatial, mid-nineteenth-century townhouse. Many of the rooms are timeworn and cluttered with battered period furniture, which gives the hotel its retro-bohemian charm. Others that have been modernized have inevitably lost their raffishness. Ernest Hemingway stayed here in 1922 when he was a journalist covering the Turkish War of Independence, as did Alexander Hacke when shooting the definitive film of the city's music scene, *İstanbul: Crossing the Bridge*. ⑨

Hotel Devman Asmalımescit Sok 52 ☎0212/245 6212, ⊛www.devmanhotel .com. Modern hotel in the arty nineteenth-century backstreets off İstiklâl Cad, with spotless blue-tiled bathrooms with power shower, firm beds and a passable open-buffet breakfast. Good value for the location and right next to the nightlife – try to bag a room at the rear to avoid the worst of the noise of carousing diners and music from the bars. ③

Galata Residence Bankalar Cad, Hacı Ali Sok 27, Galata ☎0212/292 4841, ⊛www .galataresidence.com. Period apartments in a beautifully restored late nineteenth-century building, once the home of a wealthy Jewish family. There are seven two-bed apartments (€75) and twice as many four-bed apartments (€120). It's not as designer-flash as some of the newer places, but extremely comfortable and well located, and the ceiling fans keep things cool enough on hot summer nights. Weekly and monthly lets are considerably cheaper. There's also a roof-terrace Greek-style fish restaurant (closed July & Aug).

Hotel Silviya Asmalımescit Sok 54 ☎0212/292 7749, ☏243 6115. Not quite as good value as the next door *Hotel Devman*, this is a nonetheless good backup option. Spacious, carpeted rooms painted a soothing green, and spotless bathrooms with decent-quality fittings. The nominal breakfast is taken in the small ground-floor TV room. Good situation for sampling the vibrant nightlife around and good value. ③

Triada Residence İstiklâl Cad, Meşelik Sok 4 ☎0212/251 0101 ⊛www.triada .com.tr. Small (approx 50 square metres) but stylish apartments in a lovely turn-of-the-century townhouse on a quiet side street opposite Aya Triada church. A/c, laminate floors, American-style kitchen and neat bathrooms. There's even a shared sauna. ⑥

World House Hostel Galipdede Cad 85 ☎0212/293 5520, ⊛www.worldhouse istanbul.com. If you're looking for the cheapest possible accommodation in Beyoğlu, then this is the place, with a spot in an eight-bed dorm at 20TL – including breakfast. The doubles, though, are as expensive as those in nearby budget hotels. Clean, light, high-ceilinged rooms, it has friendly staff and a wonderful location between the Galata Tower and the Tünel end of İstiklâl Cad. Despite the nearby 24hr entertainment, it's quiet, too – bar the prayer call from the adjacent mosque. Dorms €12, rooms ④

1

Villa Zurich Akarsu Yokuşu Cad 44–46 ⓣ 0212/293 0604, ⓕ 249 0232. Delightful, good-value hotel offering large, well-equipped doubles with satellite TV, a/c and a baby-sitting service. Rooms with a stunning panorama of the Bosphorus are €80, city-view rooms are €55. The rooftop terrace has the best views of all, and serves as the breakfast salon, and in the evening a very well-regarded fish restaurant (full meal including drinks €25–40). ❹

Sultanahmet

Most short-stay visitors spend all their time in **Sultanahmet**, home of İstanbul's main sightseeing attractions: the church of **Aya Sofya**, the greatest legacy of the Byzantine Empire; the **Topkapı Palace**, heart of the Ottoman Empire and the massive **Sultanahmet Camii** (Blue Mosque). Here also are the ancient **Hippodrome**, the **Museum of Turkish and Islamic Art** (housed in the former Palace of İbrahim Paşa), the eerily-lit **Yerebatan Sarnıçı**, a fascinating Byzantine underground cistern and the **Grand Bazaar** (Kapalı Çarşı), the largest covered bazaar in the world. The monumental architecture, attractive parks and gardens, street-side cafes, and the benefits of a relatively traffic-free main road (courtesy of the tramline) combine to make this area pleasant for both sightseeing and staying – but beware of **hustlers**, particularly of the carpet-selling variety.

Aya Sofya

For almost a thousand years **Aya Sofya**, or Haghia Sophia (daily except Mon 9am–7pm, upper galleries close at 6.30pm; 20TL), was the largest enclosed space in the world, designed to impress the strength and wealth of the Byzantine emperors upon their own subjects and visiting foreign dignitaries alike. Superbly located between the Topkapı Palace and Sultanahmet Camii on the ancient acropolis, the first hill of İstanbul, the church dominated the city skyline for a millennium, until the domes and minarets of the city's mosques began to challenge its eminence in the sixteenth century.

Some history

Aya Sofya, "the Church of the Divine Wisdom", is the third church of this name to stand on the site. Commissioned in the sixth century by Emperor Justinian after its predecessor had been razed to the ground in 532, its architects were **Anthemius of Tralles** and **Isidore of Miletus**. Prior to their pioneering design, most churches followed the pattern of the rectangular, pitch-roofed Roman basilica or meeting hall. **Anthemius and Isidore** were to create a building of a type and scale hitherto unknown to the Byzantine world, and no imitation was attempted until the sixteenth century. The mighty thirty-metre **dome** was unprecedented, and the sheer dimensions of the structure meant that the architects had no sure way of knowing that their plans would succeed. Constructed in five years, the building survived several earthquakes before, some twenty years later, the central dome collapsed. During reconstruction the height of the external buttresses and the dome was increased, and some of the windows blocked, resulting in an interior much gloomier than originally intended.

In 1204 it was ransacked by Catholic soldiers during the **Fourth Crusade**. Mules were brought in to help carry off silver and gilt carvings and a prostitute was seated on the throne of the patriarch. In 1452, far too late, the Byzantine Church reluctantly accepted union with the Catholics in the hope that Western powers would come to the aid of Constantinople against the Turks. On May 29, 1453,

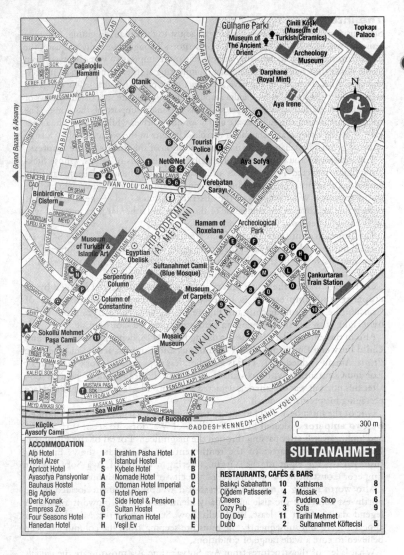

SULTANAHMET

ACCOMMODATION			
Alp Hotel	I	İbrahim Pasha Hotel	K
Hotel Alzer	P	İstanbul Hostel	M
Apricot Hotel	S	Kybele Hotel	B
Ayasofya Pansiyonlar	A	Nomade Hotel	D
Bauhaus Hostel	Q	Ottoman Hotel Imperial	C
Big Apple	Q	Hotel Poem	O
Deriz Konak	T	Side Hotel & Pension	J
Empress Zoe	G	Sultan Hostel	L
Four Seasons Hotel	F	Turkoman Hotel	N
Hanedan Hotel	H	Yeşil Ev	E

RESTAURANTS, CAFÉS & BARS			
Balıkçi Sabahattın	10	Kathisma	8
Çiğdem Patisserie	4	Mosaik	1
Cheers	7	Pudding Shop	6
Cozy Pub	3	Sofa	9
Doy Doy	11	Tarihi Mehmet	
Dubb	2	Sultanahmet Köftecisi	5

those who had said they would rather see the turban of a Turk than the hat of a cardinal in the streets of Constantinople got their way when the city was captured. **Mehmet the Conqueror** rode to the church of Aya Sofya and stopped the looting that was taking place. He had the building cleared of relics and he said his first prayer there on the following Friday; this former bastion of the Byzantine Christian Empire was now a mosque.

Extensive restorations were carried out on the mosaics in the mid-nineteenth century by the Swiss **Fossati brothers**, but due to Muslim sensitivities the mosaics were later covered over again. The building functioned as a **mosque** until 1932, and in 1934 it was opened as a **museum**.

The interior

Stepping inside Aya Sofya, eyes blinking to adjust to the subdued lighting, inspires a sense of awe in even the least spiritual of visitors. Though essentially a square, the nave, surmounted by its heavenly cupola (far more impressive when viewed from inside rather than outside) is rectangular, culminating at its eastern end in an impressive apse. At each corner of the nave are semicircular niches (exedrae). The **galleries**, which follow the line of these exedrae around the building, are supported by rows of columns and by four piers, which double as the main support of the dome. The columns supporting the galleries are green antique marble, while those in the upper gallery of the exedrae are Thessalian marble. Upstairs in the western gallery a large circle of green Thessalian marble marks the position of the **throne of the empress**.

The interior of the church was originally lit by legions of lamps, whose flickering light reflected in the pieces of glass or gold which had been carefully embedded at minutely disparate angles, giving an appearance of movement and life to the **mosaics**. What remains of the **abstract mosaics**, and of the large areas of plain gold that covered the underside of the dome and other large expanses of wall and ceiling, dates from the sixth century.

The **figurative mosaics**, dating from after the Iconoclastic era (726–843), are located in the narthex, the nave, the upper gallery and the vestibule. Some of the most impressive are in the south gallery where there's a comparatively well-lit mosaic depicting Christ, the Virgin and St John the Baptist.

On the east wall of the south gallery is a fine **mosaic of Christ flanked by an emperor and empress**. It is believed that the two figures are those of Constantine IX Monomachus and Empress Zoë, who ruled Byzantium in her own right with her sister Theodora before she married Constantine.

Also in the south gallery is a mosaic dating from 1118, depicting the **Virgin and Child between Emperor John II Comnenus and Empress Irene**, and their son Prince Alexius, added later. This is a livelier, less conventional work than that of Zoë and Constantine, with faces full of expression: Prince Alexius, who died soon after this portrait was executed, is depicted as a wan and sickly youth, his lined face presaging his premature death.

One of the most beautiful mosaics in the church is a **Virgin and Child flanked by two emperors**, located in the Vestibule of Warriors. To see it turn around and look upwards after passing through the magnificent **Portal of the Emperor**. Dated to the last quarter of the tenth century, the mosaic shows Emperor Justinian, to the right of the Virgin, offering a model of Aya Sofya, while Emperor Constantine offers a model of the city of Constantinople.

Also worth noting is the famous brass-clad **weeping column**, located in the northwest corner of the aisle and usually identifiable by the crowd it attracts. A legend dating from at least 1200 tells how St Gregory the Miracle-worker appeared here and subsequently the moisture seeping from the column has been believed to cure a wide range of conditions.

What is left of the structures from Aya Sofya's time as a **mosque** are the *mihrab*, set in the south wall of the apse, the *mimber* (pulpit), the sultan's loge (a raised kiosk allowing the sultan to worship hidden from prying eyes), and most strikingly, the enormous wooden plaques that bear sacred Islamic names of God, the Prophet Mohammed and the first four caliphs. These and the inscription on the dome by the calligrapher Azzet Efendi all date from the time of the restoration by the Fossati brothers.

Topkapı Palace

Commandingly located on the very tip of the promontory on which the Old City of İstanbul is set is the **Topkapı Palace** (daily except Tues 9am–7pm; 20TL). The symbolic and political centre of the Ottoman Empire for nearly four centuries, its sheer opulence defies its origins in the tented encampments of nomadic Turkic warriors. Originally known as *Sarayı Cedid*, or New Palace, Topkapı was built between 1459 and 1465 as the seat of government of the newly installed Ottoman regime. Similar to the Alhambra of Granada and just as unmissable, the palace consists of a collection of buildings arranged around a series of courtyards and attractive gardens.

The first courtyard and Aya Irene
The first courtyard, the palace's service area, entered from the street through Mehmet the Conqueror's **Bab-ı Hümayün**, the great defensive imperial gate opposite the fountain of Ahmet III, was always open to the general public. The **palace bakeries** are behind a wall to the right of the courtyard and the buildings of the **imperial mint and outer treasury** are behind the wall north of the church of Aya Irene. In front of Aya Irene were located the quarters of the straw-weavers and carriers of silver pitchers, around a central courtyard in which the palace firewood was stored.

Today, **Aya Irene**, "the Church of the Divine Peace", is only opened for large groups by special request at the Directorate of Aya Sofya, located at the entrance of Aya Sofya, It is also open for concerts, especially in the summer İstanbul music festival. The original church was one of the oldest in the city, but it was rebuilt along with Aya Sofya after being burnt down in the Nika riots of 532.

Ortakapı, the second courtyard and the Divan
To reach the **second courtyard** you pass through the **Bab-üs Selam**, "the Gate of Salutations", otherwise known as the **Ortakapı**, or middle gate (where the entry fee is collected). Entering through Ortakapı, with the gateway to the third courtyard straight ahead of you, the Privy Stables of Mehmet II (closed to the public) are on your immediate left, while beyond them are the buildings of the Divan and the Inner Treasury and the entrance to the Harem. Opposite the Divan, on the right side of the courtyard, is the kitchen area.

The gardens between the paths radiating from the Ortakapı are planted with ancient cypresses and plane trees, rose bushes and lawns. Originally they would also have been resplendent with peacocks, gazelles and fountains. Running water, considered to have almost mystical properties by Muslims, was supplied in great quantity to the palace from the Byzantine cistern of Yerebatan Sarnıçı (see p.103). This **second courtyard** would have been the scene of pageantry during state ceremonies, when the sultan would occupy his throne beneath the Bab-üs Saadet, "the Gate of Felicity".

The Cage

The Cage or *Kafes* was the suite of rooms of the Harem where possible successors to the throne were kept incarcerated. The practice was adopted by Ahmet I as an alternative to the fratricide that had been institutionalized in the Ottoman Empire since the rule of Beyazit II. After the death of their father, the younger princes would be kept under house arrest along with deaf mutes and a harem of concubines, while their eldest brother acceded to the throne. They remained here until such time as they were called upon to take power themselves. The concubines never left the Cage unless they became pregnant in which case they were immediately drowned. The decline of the Ottoman Empire has in part been attributed to the institution of the Cage, as sultans who spent any length of time there emerged crazed, avaricious and debauched. The most infamous victim was "İbrahim the Mad" (see p.100).

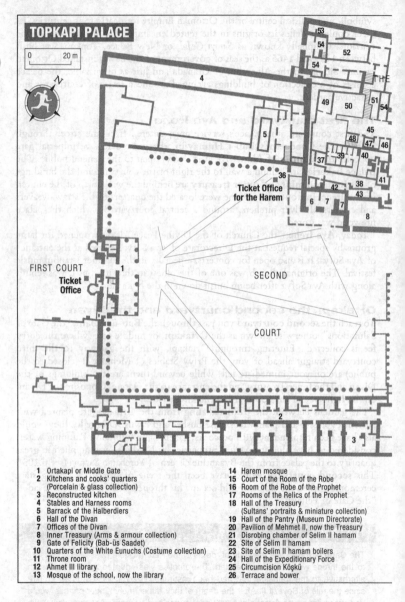

TOPKAPI PALACE

0   20 m

FIRST COURT

Ticket Office

Ticket Office for the Harem

SECOND COURT

1. Ortakapi or Middle Gate
2. Kitchens and cooks' quarters (Porcelain & glass collection)
3. Reconstructed kitchen
4. Stables and Harness rooms
5. Barrack of the Halberdiers
6. Hall of the Divan
7. Offices of the Divan
8. Inner Treasury (Arms & armour collection)
9. Gate of Felicity (Bab-üs Saadet)
10. Quarters of the White Eunuchs (Costume collection)
11. Throne room
12. Ahmet III library
13. Mosque of the school, now the library
14. Harem mosque
15. Court of the Room of the Robe
16. Room of the Robe of the Prophet
17. Rooms of the Relics of the Prophet
18. Hall of the Treasury (Sultans' portraits & miniature collection)
19. Hall of the Pantry (Museum Directorate)
20. Pavilion of Mehmet II, now the Treasury
21. Disrobing chamber of Selim II hamam
22. Site of Selim II hamam
23. Site of Selim II hamam boilers
24. Hall of the Expeditionary Force
25. Circumcision Köşkü
26. Terrace and bower

Entering the buildings of the **Divan**, to the left of the courtyard, is a metal grille in the Council Chamber (the first room on the left), called "the Eye of the Sultan". Through this he could observe the proceedings of the Divan, where the eminent imperial councillors sat in session and which took its name from the couch running around the three walls of the room. The building dates essentially from the reign of Mehmet the Conqueror, and the Council Chamber was restored to its sixteenth-century appearance in 1945, with some of the original İznik tiles and

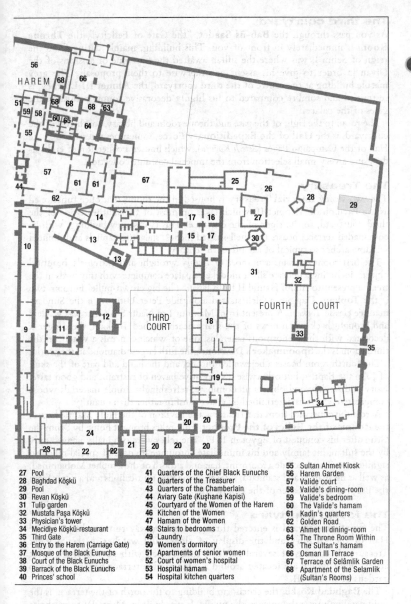

27 Pool	41 Quarters of the Chief Black Eunuchs	55 Sultan Ahmet Kiosk
28 Baghdad Köşkü	42 Quarters of the Treasurer	56 Harem Garden
29 Pool	43 Quarters of the Chamberlain	57 Valide court
30 Revan Köşkü	44 Aviary Gate (Kuşhane Kapisi)	58 Valide's dining-room
31 Tulip garden	45 Courtyard of the Women of the Harem	59 Valide's bedroom
32 Mustafa Paşa Köşkü	46 Kitchen of the Women	60 The Valide's hamam
33 Physician's tower	47 Hamam of the Women	61 Kadin's quarters
34 Mecidiye Köşkü-restaurant	48 Stairs to bedrooms	62 Golden Road
35 Third Gate	49 Laundry	63 Ahmet III dining-room
36 Entry to the Harem (Carriage Gate)	50 Women's dormitory	64 The Throne Room Within
37 Mosque of the Black Eunuchs	51 Apartments of senior women	65 The Sultan's hamam
38 Court of the Black Eunuchs	52 Court of women's hospital	66 Osman III Terrace
39 Barrack of the Black Eunuchs	53 Hospital hamam	67 Terrace of Selâmlik Garden
40 Princes' school	54 Hospital kitchen quarters	68 Apartment of the Selamlik (Sultan's Rooms)

arabesque painting. Next to the Divan is another building from Mehmet the Conqueror's original palace, the **Inner Treasury**, a six-domed hall with displays of Ottoman and European **armour**.

Across the courtyard are the **palace kitchens and cooks' quarters**, with their magnificent rows of chimneys. The ten kitchens, which had a staff of 1500, all served different purposes, including two just to make sweets and *helva*.

The third courtyard

As you pass through the **Bab-üs Saadet**, "the Gate of Felicity", the **Throne Room** is immediately in front of you. This building, mainly dating from the reign of Selim I, was where the sultan awaited the outcome of sessions of the Divan in order to give his assent or otherwise to their proposals. The grey marble building at the centre of the third courtyard, the **Ahmet III Library**, is restrained and sombre compared to his highly decorative fountain outside the gates of the palace.

The room to the right of the gate and throne room and library, southwest of the courtyard, is the **Hall of the Expeditionary Force**, sometimes referred to as the Hall of the Campaign Pages (*Seferli Koğuşu*), which houses a collection of embroidery and a very small selection from the imperial costume collection.

The Treasury

The two-storey **Imperial Treasury** is housed in the rooms that once functioned as the Pavilion of Mehmet II, which takes up most of the southeast side of the third courtyard, to the right of the entrance. This two-storey building, with its colonnaded terrace, boasts the shell-shaped niches, stalactite capitals and pointed window arches so typical of the fifteenth century.

The first room contains a number of highly wrought and extremely beautiful objects, including a delicate silver model of a palace complete with tiny birds in the trees, a present to Abdül Hamid II from Japan. The big crowd-puller in room two is the **Topkapı Dagger**, which starred alongside Peter Ustinov in the Sunday-matinée classic *Topkapi*. A present from Mahmut I to Nadir Shah that was waylaid and brought back when news of the shah's death reached Topkapı, the dagger is decorated with three enormous emeralds, one of which conceals a watch. In the third room is the **Spoonmaker's Diamond**, the fifth largest diamond in the world.

The fourth room boasts a bejewelled throne, and the hand and part of the skull of John the Baptist, but otherwise it's a relative haven of restraint and good taste. Ivory and sandalwood objects predominate, refreshingly simple materials whose comparative worth is determined by craftsmanship rather than quantity.

Across the courtyard from the Treasury, the Pavilion of the Holy Mantle houses the **Rooms of the Relics of the Prophet**, holy relics brought home by Selim the Grim after his conquest of Egypt in 1517. The relics were originally viewed only by the sultan, his family and his immediate entourage on days of special religious significance. They include a footprint, hair and a tooth of the Prophet Mohammed, as well as his mantle and standard, swords of the first four caliphs and a letter from the Prophet to the leader of the Coptic tribe.

The fourth courtyard

The **fourth courtyard** is entered through a passageway running between the Hall of the Treasury and the display of clocks and watches in the Silahdar Treasury. It consists of several gardens, each graced with pavilions, the most attractive of which are located around a wide marble terrace beyond the tulip gardens of Ahmet III.

The **Baghdad Köşkü**, the cruciform building to the north of the terrace, is the only pavilion presently open to the public. It was built by Murat IV to celebrate the conquest of Baghdad in 1638. The exterior and cool, dark interior are tiled in blue, turquoise and white, and the shutters and cupboard doors are inlaid with tortoiseshell and mother-of-pearl. If you think this is redolent of unseemly excess, take a look at the attractive pool and marble fountain on the terrace, scene of debauched revels among İbrahim I and the women of his harem. Deli İbrahim, or **İbrahim the Mad**, emerged dangerously insane from 22 years in the Cage, his reign culminating in a fit of sexual jealousy when he ordered death by drowning in the Bosphorus for the 280 concubines of his harem – only one of them lived to tell the tale, picked up by a passing French ship and taken to Paris.

The **Circumcision Köşkü**, in the Portico of Columns above the terrace, also dates from the reign of İbrahim the Mad. The exterior is covered in prime-period İznik tiles of the sixteenth and early seventeenth centuries. At the other end of the Portico of Columns is the **Revan Köşkü**, built to commemorate the capture of Erivan in the Caucasus by Mehmet IV.

The **Mecidiye Köşkü** – the last building to be erected at Topkapı – commands the best view of any of the Topkapı pavilions. It's been opened as the expensive *Konyali* café (see p.130) and on a clear day from its garden terrace you can identify most of the buildings on the Asian shore of the Bosphorus.

The Harem

It is well worth visiting the **Harem** (daily except Tues 10am–4pm, 15TL) as many visitors (put off by the steep extra entrance fee) give it a miss, often leaving it relatively uncrowded. The word "harem" means "forbidden" in Arabic; in Turkish it refers to a suite of apartments in a palace or private residence where the head of the household lived with his wives, odalisques (female slaves) and children. Situated on the north side of the Second Court, it consisted of over four hundred rooms, centred on the suites of the sultan and his mother, the Valide Sultan.

The Harem was connected to the outside world by means of the **Carriage Gate**, so called because the odalisques would have entered their carriages here when they went on outings. To the left of the Carriage Gate as you enter the Harem is the Barracks of the Halberdiers of the Long Tresses, who carried logs and other loads into the Harem. The Halberdiers, who also served as imperial guardsmen, were only employed at certain hours and even then they were blinkered. The Carriage Gate and the Aviary Gate were both guarded by black eunuchs, who were responsible for running the Harem.

The **Court of the Black Eunuchs**, dates mainly from a rebuilding programme begun after the great fire of 1665, which damaged most of the Harem as well as the Divan. The tiles in the eunuchs' quarters date from the seventeenth century, suggesting that the originals were destroyed in the fire. The *Altın Yol* or **Golden**

The women of the harem

The **women of the harem** were so shrouded in mystery that they became a source of great fascination for the world in general. Many were imported from Georgia and Caucasia for their looks, or were prisoners of war, captured in Hungary, Poland or Venice. Upon entering the harem, they would become the charges of the *haznedar usta*, who would teach them how to behave towards the sultan and the other palace inhabitants. The conditions in which the majority of these women lived were dangerously unhygienic and many of them died of disease, or from the cold of an İstanbul winter. The women who were chosen to enter the bedchamber of the sultan, however, were promoted to the rank of imperial odalisque, given slaves to serve them, and pleasant accommodation. If they bore a child, they would be promoted to the rank of favourite or wife, with their own apartments. If the sultan subsequently lost affection for one of these women, he could give her in marriage to one of his courtiers.

Most renowned of the harem women was Haseki Hürrem, or **Roxelana** as she was known in the West, wife of Süleyman the Magnificent. Prior to their marriage, it was unusual for a sultan to marry at all, let alone to choose a wife from among his concubines. This was the beginning of a new age of harem intrigue, in which women began to take more control over affairs of state, often referred to as the "Rule of the Harem".

Road ran the entire length of the Harem, from the quarters of the Black Eunuchs to the fourth courtyard. Strategically located at the beginning of the Golden Road were the **apartments of the Valide Sultan**, also rebuilt after 1665. They include a particularly lovely domed dining room.

Beyond the Valide Sultan's apartments are the apartments and reception rooms of the *selâmlik*, the sultan's own rooms. The largest and grandest of them is the **Hünkar Sofrası**, the Imperial Hall, where the sultan entertained visitors. Another important room in this section is a masterwork of the architect Sinan: the **bedchamber of Murat III**, covered in sixteenth-century İznik tiles.

The northernmost rooms of the Harem are supported by immense piers and vaults, providing capacious basements that were used as dormitories and store-rooms. Below the bedchamber is a large indoor **swimming pool**, with taps for hot and cold water, where Murat is supposed to have thrown gold to women who pleased him. Next to the bedchamber is the light and airy **library of Ahmet I**, with windows overlooking both the Bosphorus and the Golden Horn; beyond this is the **dining room of Ahmet III**, whose walls are covered in wood panelling painted with bowls of fruit and flowers, typical of the extravagant tulip-loving sultan.

It's usual to depart from the Harem by way of the **Aviary Gate**, or Kuşhane Kapısı, into the Third Court.

Gulhane Parkı and around

Gulhane Parkı surrounds Topkapı Palace on all sides and was once the extended gardens of the sultans. It is now a public park with a relaxed atmosphere. Among the attractions is the recently opened (2008) **History of Science and Technology in Islam Museum** (Islam Bilim ve Teknoloji Tarihi Müzesi; daily except Mon 9am–5pm; 5TL) a generally successful attempt to show, using carefully constructed replicas of everything from astronomical observatories to medical equipment, the contribution scientists and inventors from the Islamic world made to civilization between the eighth and sixteenth centuries.

The Darphane

Located next to Gulhane Parkı, though also entered from the first courtyard of Topkapı Palace, the **Darphane** (Royal Mint; Wed–Sun 9.30am–5.30pm; free; Ⓦ www.tarihvakfi.org.tr) was moved to this site in 1715, although there is evidence that coins were struck hereabouts as early as the sixteenth century. Most of the current buildings date from the 1830s and the reign of Mahmut II. The monetary reforms introduced by Abdülmecit between 1839 and 1861 saw the introduction of modern steam-powered machinery to improve the quality of coins produced.

The Archeology Museum complex

The Archeology Museum complex, which includes the Museum of the Ancient Orient and Çinili Köşk (see opposite; all daily except Mon 8.30am–7pm; combined entry 10TL), can be entered either through Gulhane Parkı or from the first courtyard of the Topkapı Palace. The **Archeology Museum** itself (Arkeoloji Müzesi) is centred on a marvellous collection of sarcophogi from Sidon housed in the two rooms to the left of the entrance on the ground floor. The most famous is the so-called **Alexander Sarcophagus** from the late fourth century. Covered with scenes of what is presumed to be Alexander the Great hunting and in battle, it cannot be Alexander's tomb as he is known to have been buried in Alexandria. It is ascribed variously by different sources to a ruler of the Seleucid dynasty or to the Phoenician Prince Abdolonyme.

Upstairs exhibits include some of the fascinating finds made by Schliemann and Dorpfeld at **Troy**, including some beautiful gold jewellery. Well worth visiting in these upper rooms is the **"İstanbul through the Ages"** exhibition, which traces the history of the city from archaic to Ottoman times, and includes the chain used by the Byzantines to block entry to the strategically crucial Golden Horn. Down in the basement, but beautifully presented, are finds from the oft-neglected **Byzantine period**, with some lavishly carved capitals the pick of the exhibits.

The Museum of the Ancient Orient

The **Museum of the Ancient Orient** (Eskı Şark Eserleri Müzesi) contains a small but dazzling collection of Anatolian, Egyptian and Mesopotamian artefacts. These include the oldest peace treaty known to mankind, the **Treaty of Kadesh** (1280–1269 BC), which was signed when a battle fought between Pharaoh Ramses II and the Hittite king Muvatellish, ended in a stalemate. The copy of the treaty on display in the museum was uncovered during excavations at the site of the Hittite capital of Hattuşa (see p.527), and includes a ceasefire agreement and pledges of a mutual exchange of political refugees. A copy of the treaty decorates the entrance to the UN building in New York.

The blue-and-yellow **animal relief** in the corridor beyond the first room dates from the reign of Nebuchadnezzar (604–562 BC), the last hero-king of Babylonia, where it would have lined the processional way in Babylon. Other exhibits were taken from the palace-museum of Nebuchadnezzar, located at the Ishtar Gate. Another massive relief, in Room 8, depicts the **Hittite king Urpalla** presenting gifts of grapes and grain to a vegetation god, who is three times his own size. This is a plaster copy of a relief found at İvriz Kaya near Konya, dating from the eighth century BC.

Çinili Köşk

The graceful **Çinili Köşk** or Tiled Pavilion – a few metres north of the Museum of the Ancient Orient – was built in 1472 as a kind of grandstand, from which the sultan could watch sporting activities such as wrestling or polo. It now houses the **Museum of Turkish Ceramics**, displaying tiles of equal quality to those in Topkapı Palace and İstanbul's older mosques, along with well-written explanations of the different periods in the history of Turkish ceramics.

Yerebatan Sarnıçı

The **Yerebatan Sarnıçı** (daily 9am–6.30pm; 10TL), the "Sunken Palace" – also known as the Basilica Cistern, was once an integral part of the Old City's water supply. It's one of several underground cisterns, this one buried under the very core of Sultanahmet and is the first to have been extensively excavated.

Probably built by the Emperor Constantine in the fourth century, and enlarged by Justinian in the sixth, the cistern was supplied by aqueducts with water from the Belgrade Forest. It in turn supplied the Great Palace and later Topkapı Palace. The cistern fell into disuse after the Ottoman conquest, but was rediscovered in 1545 by the Frenchman **Petrus Gyllius**. His interest was aroused when he found fresh fish being sold in the streets nearby, and he enquired at some local houses. The residents let him on their "secret" – wells sunk through into the cistern and boats kept on the water from which they could fish its depths.

Restored in 1987, the cistern is now **beautifully lit** and access made easier by specially constructed walkways. The largest covered cistern in the city, at 140m by 70m, Yerebatan held 80,000 cubic metres of water. The small brick **domes** are supported by 336 columns, many of which have Corinthian capitals. Two of the columns are supported by **Medusa heads**, clearly relics of an earlier building.

The Hippodrome

The arena of the **Hippodrome**, formerly the cultural focus of the Byzantine Empire, is now a long, narrow municipal park known as At Meydanı, or Square of Horses, a reference to the chariot races held here in Roman times. Attractively flanked by the Palace of İbrahim Paşa on one side and the Blue Mosque to the other, it is usually thronged with tourists posing in front of the **Egyptian Obelisk**. Originally 60m tall, though only the upper third survived shipment from Egypt in the fourth century, the obelisk was commissioned to commemorate the campaigns of Thutmos III in Egypt during the sixteenth century BC, but the scenes on its base commemorate its erection in Constantinople under the direction of Theodosius I. Among the figures depicted are dancing maidens with musicians, Theodosius and his family watching a chariot race (south side) and a group of captives kneeling to pay homage to Theodosius (west side).

The **Serpentine Column** comes from the Temple of Apollo at Delphi, where it was dedicated to the god by the 31 Greek cities that defeated the Persians at Plataea in 479 BC. The column was brought to Constantinople by Constantine the Great. The three intertwining bronze serpents originally had heads, which splayed out in three directions from the column itself.

The third ancient monument on the *spina* is a huge lump of masonry, a 32-metre-high column of little or no decorative or practical worth. The origins of this so-called **Column of Constantine** are uncertain, but an inscription records that it was already decayed when Constantine restored it.

Sultanahmet Camii: the Blue Mosque

On the southeastern side of the Hippodrome is the monumental **Sultanahmet Camii**, or Blue Mosque. With its six minarets, imposing bulk and commanding position on the skyline of old İstanbul, it is one of the most famous and visited monuments in the city. Viewed from the all-important approach from the Topkapı Palace, it is a striking mass of shallow domes, half-domes and domed turrets, but its most striking profile is from the Sea of Marmara where, elevated above the hillside, it totally dominates its surroundings.

Before construction began under architect Mehmet Ağa, in 1609, objections were raised to the plan of a mosque with six minarets on the grounds that it would be unholy to rival the six minarets of the mosque at Mecca. More importantly, it would be a drain on state resources already in a parlous state following a succession of (unsuccessful) wars with Austria and Persia. But Sultanahmet I, after whom the mosque is named, was determined to try and outdo his predecessors even if it meant bankrupting his empire – he even helped dig the foundations himself.

There are two entrances to the mosque's prayer hall; at the side facing the Aya Sofya (always very busy) or (despite the notices asking you to do otherwise) through the large beautifully proportioned **courtyard** to the northwest – itself best entered through the graceful main (southwest) portal. Make sure you are suitably covered (limbs for men and women, heads for women) and take off your shoes and put them in the plastic bag provided.

Inside, four **"elephant foot" pillars** (so called because of their size) of five metres in diameter impose their disproportionate dimensions on the interior – particularly the dome which is smaller and shallower than that of Sinan's İstanbul masterpiece, the nearby Süleymaniye Camii. The name "Blue Mosque" derives from the mass (over 20,000) of predominantly **blue İznik tiles** which adorn the interior, though much of the "blue" is, in fact, stencilled paintwork. The glass in the numerous arched windows was originally mainly coloured Venetian bottle glass, but this has now been replaced by poor-quality modern windows.

▲ Sultanahmet Camii, the Blue Mosque

At the northeast corner of the Sultanahmet complex is the richly decorated and elegant **royal pavilion**, approached by ramp and giving access to the sultan's loge inside the mosque – the ramp meant that the sultan could ride his horse right up to the door of his chambers. The royal pavilion now houses a **Museum of Carpets** (Halı Müzesi; Tues–Sat 9am–4pm; 2TL), which traces the history of Turkish carpets through the ages and includes some ancient, priceless pieces.

Outside the precinct wall to the northwest of the mosque is the *türbe* or **tomb of Sultan Ahmet** (Tues–Sat 9am–4pm; free), decorated, like the mosque, with seventeenth-century İznik tiles. Buried here along with the sultan are his wife and three of his sons, two of whom (Osman II and Murat IV) ruled in their turn.

Between May 1 and September 30 (on alternate evenings) there is a free **sound and light show** conducted from the small seating area in the park between the Blue Mosque and Aya Sofya. The show starts at 7.30pm; beware that it attracts plenty of hustlers.

The Museum of Turkish and Islamic Art

The attractive **İbrahim Paşa Sarayı** (Palace of İbrahim Paşa), on the eastern side of the Hippodrome, is now the **Museum of Turkish and Islamic Art** (Türk ve İslam Eserleri Müzesi; daily except Mon 9am–4.30pm; 10TL), containing one of the best-exhibited collections of Islamic artefacts in the world. The main concentration of **exhibits** deals with Selçuk, Mamluk and Ottoman Turkish art, though there are also several important Timurid and Persian works on display. The **Selçuk Turks**, precursors of the Ottomans, are represented by some beautiful wall tiles and fine woodcarvings. Other impressive exhibits include sixteenth-century Persian miniatures and the tiny Sancak Korans, meant for hanging on the standard of the Ottoman imperial army in a jihad (holy war), so that the word of God would precede the troops into battle.

The **Great Hall** of the palace houses a collection of **Turkish carpets** that is among the finest in the world. These range from tattered remains dating from the thirteenth century to carpets that once adorned İstanbul's palaces, some weighing in at thousands of kilograms. On the basement floor, there is an ethnography section, with everything from the black goat-hair tents of the *Yörük* tribes of Anatolia, to a re-creation of the interior of a late-Ottoman wooden house in Bursa.

The Hamam of Roxelana

The double-domed building between the Sultanahmet Camii and Aya Sofya is the **Hamam of Roxelana** (Haseki Hürrem Sultan Hamami; daily except Tues 9.30am–5pm; free). Built by Mimar Sinan in 1556, it replaced the Byzantine baths of Zeuxippus on the same site and was named in honour of Süleyman's wife, Roxelana. The 75-metre-long hamam used to serve the worshippers at the mosque of Aya Sofya. The hamam, now restored with stained-glass windows, has kept the original marble fountains in the changing rooms, and now serves as a (pricey) showroom for traditional handwoven carpets and kilims.

Sokollu Mehmet Paşa Camii

The little-visited **Sokollu Mehmet Paşa Camii** (usually open at prayer times only, but the *imam* may be around to unlock it during the day) is one of the most attractive mosques in the city. A short walk downhill from the Hippodrome, it is one of Mimar Sinan's later buildings (1571) and was commissioned by Sokollu Mehmet Paşa, the last grand vizier of Süleyman the Magnificent.

The **interior** of the mosque is distinguished by the height of its dome and the impressive display of **İznik tiles** on its east wall. These are from the best period of Turkish ceramics: the white is pure, the green vivid and the red intense. Calligraphic inscriptions are set against a jungle of enormous carnations and tulips, and the designs and colours are echoed all around the mosque and in the conical cap of the *mimber*, the tiling of which is unique in İstanbul.

Küçük Ayasofya Camii

Located some 500m below the Blue Mosque, downhill on Küçük Ayasofya Caddesi is the oft-overlooked, recently restored **Küçük Ayasofya Camii**, the "small mosque of Aya Sofya" (entry 7am–dusk; donations expected). Built as a church between 527 and 536 it is thought to precede its much larger namesake up the hill. It was originally named after two Roman soldiers, **Sergius** and **Bacchus**, who were martyred for their faith and later became the patron saints of Christians in the Roman army, but was renamed because of its resemblance to Aya Sofya. The church was converted into a mosque comparatively early in the sixteenth century during the reign of Beyazit II.

Like most Byzantine churches of this era, its **exterior** is austere brick, and only inside can the satisfying proportions be properly appreciated. It is basically an octagon with semicircular niches at its diagonals, inscribed in a rectangle, but both these shapes are extremely irregular. A delicately carved frieze honouring Justinian, Theodora and St Sergius runs around the architrave under the gallery, and numerous columns sport ornate Byzantine captials.

The Palace of Bucoleon and the Great Palace

About halfway between Küçük Ayasofya Camii and the Cankurtaran train station is the facade of the **Palace of Bucoleon**, a seaside annexe to the **Great Palace of the Byzantine emperors**. It was part of a larger complex known as The Great Palace, which covered around five square kilometres from Sultanahmet to the sea walls. In 1204 the palace was taken over by the Crusaders, who ransacked the complex for its gold, silver and other valuables – an act of vandalism from which it never recovered.

It's easy to miss what's left of the **Palace of Bucoleon**, especially if you pass at speed along Kennedy Caddesi. It is draped in beautiful red vine and set back from the road with a little park in front. Three enormous marble-framed windows set high in the wall offer glimpses of the remains of a vaulted room behind. Further sections of the palace exist under land currently belonging to the *Four Seasons Hotel* (see p.92), at the time of writing in the process of being turned into an **Archeological Park**.

The Mosaic Museum

The other substantial reminders of the Great Palace are the mosaics displayed in the **Mosaic Museum** (Büyüksaray Mozaik Müzesi; daily except Mon 9am–4.30pm; 8TL. It can be reached by running the gauntlet of salespeople in the **Arasta Çarşısı** – a renovated street-bazaar selling tourist gifts, whose seventeeth-century shops were originally built to pay for the upkeep of the nearby Sultanahmet Camii.

The building has been constructed so that some of the mosaics, probably dating from Justinian's rebuilding programme of the sixth century, can be viewed from a catwalk as well as at floor level. Among them are portrayals of animals in their natural habitats, and domestic scenes. These include a vivid illustration of an elephant locking a lion in a deadly embrace with its trunk and two children being led on the back of a camel.

The Grand Bazaar and around

The Ottoman-era **Grand Bazaar** gets more than its fair share of souvenir-hungry visitors. But the area around it is relatively little explored, which is a shame as there are some very worthwhile attractions, from the historic **Cembirlitaş Hamamı**, arguably the best Turkish baths in the country, to the city's very best mosque, the hilltop **Süleymaniye Camii**. Throw in the gritty districts of **Aksaray** and **Laleli**, half a kilometre west of the bazaar, notable for the ornate Baroque **Laleli Camii**, and it's easy to see how you can spend a day in this area alone. It's easy enough to walk to this district from Sultanahmet, or take a tram to the Beyazit, Laleli or Aksaray stops depending on your proposed itinerary.

The Grand Bazaar: Kapalı Çarşı

With sixty-six streets and alleys, over four thousand shops, numerous storehouses, moneychangers and banks, a mosque, post office, police station, private security guards and its own health centre, İstanbul's **Grand Bazaar** (Kapalı Çarşı: Mon–Sat 9am–7pm) is said to be the largest **covered bazaar** in the world. In Ottoman times it was based around two *bedestens* (a domed building where foreign trade took place and valuable goods stored): the İç Bedesten probably dates from the time of the Conquest, while the Sandal Bedesten was added in the sixteenth century. The bazaar extends much further than this however, sprawling into the streets that lead down to the Golden Horn. This whole area was once controlled by strict laws laid down by the trade guilds, thus reducing competition between traders. Each shop could support just one owner and his apprentice, and successful merchants were not allowed to expand their businesses. Similar unwritten laws control market forces among traders in the covered bazaar even today.

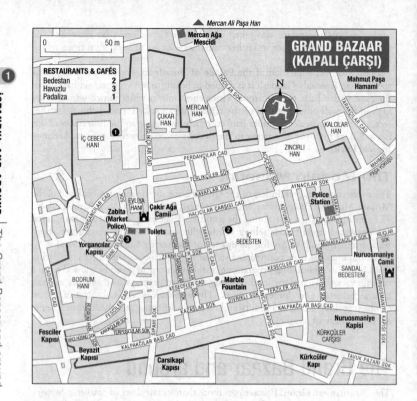

▲ Mercan Ali Paşa Han

GRAND BAZAAR (KAPALI ÇARŞI)

RESTAURANTS & CAFÉS

Bedestan	2
Havuzlu	3
Padaliza	1

Visiting the bazaar

The best time to visit is during the week as Saturday sees it becoming far too crowded with local shoppers. Expect to get lost as most streets are either poorly marked or their signs are hidden beneath goods hung up on display. However, try finding Kavaflar Sok for **shoes**, Terlikçiler Sok for **slippers**, Kalpakçılar Başı and Kuyumcular *caddesi*s for **gold**, and Tavuk Pazarı Sok, Kürkçüler Sok, Perdahçılar Caddesi and Bodrum Han for **leather clothing**. Carpet-sellers are just about everywhere, with more expensive collector's pieces on sale on Halıcılar Çarşısı, Takkeciler and Keseciler *caddesi*s, and cheaper ones in the tiny Rubiye Han or İç Cebeci Han. **Ceramics** and leather and kilim **bags** can be found along Yağlıkçılar Caddesi, just off it in Çukur Han, and also along Keseciler Caddesi. For details of specific shops, see p.141.

The old bazaar (or İç Bedesten), located at the centre of the maze, was traditionally reserved for the most precious wares because it could be locked at night. You'll still find some silver and gold on sale, but these days the emphasis is more on reproduction brass ship-fittings, fake scrimshaw and souvenirs.

There are a number of decent **cafés** in the bazaar (see p.131) where you can unwind and avoid the constant importuning of traders.

East of the Grand Bazaar

Heading back towards Sultanahmet from the south exits of the Grand Bazaar follow Yeniçeriler Caddesi, which becomes **Divan Yolu**, a major thoroughfare that gained its name because it was the principal approach to the Divan.

First point of interest is the the the **Gazi Atık Ali Paşa Camii**, one of the oldest mosques in the city, built in 1496 by the eunuch Atık âli Paşa, who rose to the rank of grand vizier under Sultan Beyazit II. A little further east is the **Çembirlitaş** ("the hooped stone"), a burnt column of masonry, also known as the **Column of Constantine**. Erected by Constantine the Great in 330 AD, it commemorated the city's dedication as capital of the Roman Empire. The column is currently scaffolded and covered, awaiting restoration. Across Vezirhanı Caddesi from the column is the four-hundred-year-old **Çemberlitaş Hamamı** (daily 6am–midnight; 29TL, 46TL with massage; ⓦ www.cemberlitashamami.com.tr), founded in the sixteenth century by Nur Banu, one of the most powerful of the Valide Sultans. Architecturally it's arguably the finest Ottoman hamam in İstanbul, and well used to dealing with novice visitors.

The baths and column also mark the southern end of Vezirhanı Caddesi, turn north up here to reach the **Nuruosmaniye Camii**, just outside the bazaar to the east. Begun by Mahmut I in 1748 and finished seven years later by Osman III, this mosque was the first and most impressive of the city's Baroque mosques.

The Süleymaniye complex

Built by the renowned architect **Mimar Sinan** (see below) in honour of his most illustrious patron, Süleyman the Magnificent, the Süleymaniye complex, some 300m northwest of the Grand Bazaar, is arguably his greatest achievement. Completed in just seven years the mosque and its satellite buildings achieves a perfection of form and a monumentality of appearance that set it apart from other Ottoman architecture

On the university side of the complex is the **Süleymaniye Library** (Mon–Sat 8.30am–5pm), housed in the Evvel and Sani *medreses*. These buildings, mirror images of each other, are situated around shady garden courtyards. Süleyman established the library in an effort to bring together collections of books and mauscripts scattered throughout the city. On the north side of the complex, on Mimar Sinan Caddesi, is the **Türbe (tomb) of Mimar Sinan** himself.

Otherwise, the buildings of the complex served the usual functions. On Şıfahane Sokak is the *imaret* (soup kitchen), which despite its ornate design was constructed as a public kitchen supplying food for the local poor, a *kervansaray* (hotel) and a

Mimar Sinan, master builder

Many of the finest works of Ottoman civil and religious architecture throughout Turkey can be traced to **Mimar Sinan** (1489–1588), who served as court architect to three sultans – Süleyman the Magnificent, Selim II and Murat III. Probably born the son of Greek or Armenian Christian parents, he was conscripted into the janissaries in 1513. As a military engineer, he travelled the length and breadth of southeastern Europe and the Middle East, giving him the opportunity to become familiar with the best Islamic – and Christian – monumental architecture there. His bridges, siegeworks, harbours and even ships, earned him the admiration of his superiors. Sultan Süleyman appointed him court architect in April 1536. In 1548 he completed his first major religious commission, İstanbul's Şehzade Camii, and shortly thereafter embarked on a rapid succession of ambitious projects in and around the capital, including the waterworks leading from the Belgrade Forest and the Süleymaniye Camii. Competing with the Süleymaniye as his masterpiece was the Selimiye Camii, constructed between 1569–75 in the former imperial capital of Edirne (see p.160). Despite temptations to luxury he lived and died modestly, being buried in a simple tomb he made for himself in his garden in the grounds of the Süleymaniye Camii – the last of more than five hundred constructions by Sinan, large and small, throughout the empire.

mektep (primary school). The **Süleymaniye hamam**, built by Sinan in 1557, is on the corner of Mimar Sinan Caddesi and Dökmeciler Hamamı Sokak (daily 6.30am–midnight; 60TL for a massage, scrub and return transfer to a hotel in the Old City; ⓦ www.suleymaniyehamami.com). Legend has it that the great architect took all his baths here from 1557 to 1588.

The mosque itself, the **Süleymaniye Camii**, is preceded by a rectangular courtyard, whose portico stands on columns of porphyry, Marmara marble and pink Egyptian granite, and by four tapering minarets. The doorway into the mosque is high and narrow, its wooden doors inlaid with ebony, mother-of-pearl and ivory. Move inside, and the sense of light and space is staggering – the dome 53m high (twice its diameter), surmounts a perfect square of 26.5m while the double panes of 200 windows ensure a softly filtered light. In the adjacent **cemetery** (daily 5.30am–8pm) are located the tombs of Süleyman the Magnificent and of Haseki Hürrem, or Roxelana, his powerful wife.

The Aqueduct of Valens

The magnificent **Aqueduct of Valens** spans Atatürk Bulvarı around 300m southwest of the Süleymaniye complex, here reaching a height of 18.5m. The aqueduct was originally built during the late fourth-century waterworks programme carried out by the Emperor Valens, and was part of a distribution network that included reservoirs in the Belgrade Forest and various cisterns located around the city centre. It was in use right up to the end of the nineteenth century, having been kept in good repair by successive rulers, who maintained a constant supply of water to the city in the face of both drought and siege.

Beyazit Meydanı and İstanbul University

Just west of the Grand Bazaar is **Beyazit Meydanı**, the main square of Beyazit, marking the principal approach to İstanbul University. Just off the square is the famous **Sahaflar Çarşısı**, the secondhand-booksellers' market (though most of the books on sale now are new), which dates back to the Byzantine era.

The Ottomans were uneasy with human pictorial representation and used calligraphy for artistic expression. On the west side of the square the tradition is reflected in a small **Museum of Calligraphy**, closed for restoration at the time of writing. To the east of the square, **Beyazit Camii**, completed in 1506, is the oldest surviving imperial mosque in the city. It has a sombre courtyard full of richly coloured marble, including twenty columns of verd antique, red granite and porphyry. Inside, the building is a perfect square of exactly the same proportions as the courtyard (although the aisles make it feel elongated).

İstanbul University commands an impressive position at the crown of one of the city's seven hills. The fire tower located in the grounds, Beyazit Kulesi, is a landmark all over the city. The university has been a centre of **political activity** of the Left, the Right and Muslim fundamentalists, with occasional demonstrations, lock-ins and even violence on the campus. Apart from the monumental gateway, where you enter the campus, the most impressive building on the site is a small *Koşk*, to the right of the entrance, which has a Baroque interior.

Aksaray, Laleli and its mosque

The area south and west of the **Laleli Camii** complex (situated on Ordu Caddesi between the Laleli and Aksaray tram stops) is full of Eastern Europeans and Turkic peoples from the states of Central Asia, the shops are full of fake designer bags, clothes and shoes. On the plus side, the prostitution the district was once notorious for is confined to the southwest of the area, and there are a number of restaurants (see p.133), originally catering to migrants from elsewhere in Turkey, offering regional specialties.

The Laleli **mosque** was founded by Mustafa III, whose octagonal tomb is located at the southeast gate. It's full of Baroque elements including a grand staircase and ramps (one of which the reigning sultan would have used to ride up to his loge), and the detail, for example in the window grilles of the tomb and in the carved eaves of the *sebil* (drinking fountain). Inside, a mass of pillars dominates, especially to the west, where the columns beneath the main dome seem to crowd those supporting the galleries into the walls.

North of Sultanahmet: Eminönü

Heading north from Sultanahmet brings you to the waterfront district of **Eminönü**. Once the maritime gateway to the city, it remains one of the largest and most convenient transport hubs, where buses, ferries, trams and trains converge, the latter at the grand **Sirkeci station**, once the last stop on the famed Orient Express. Sights within this district include the **Cağaloğlu hamam** and the landmark **Yeni Cami** complex which includes the ornate Ottoman-era **Spice Bazaar**.

Cağaloğlu Hamamı

The **Cağaloğlu Hamamı** is located on Kazım Ismail Gürkan Caddesi (daily: men 8am–10pm, women 8am–8.30pm; 24TL for self-service bath, 54TL for bath and scrub, 72TL for bath, scrub and massage; ⓦwww.cagalogluhamami.com.tr); the women's entrance to the hamam is around the corner on Cağaloğlu Hamam Sok. The most popular baths this side of town, they are famous for their beautiful *hararet*s or steam rooms – open cruciform chambers with windowed domes supported by a circle of columns. The baths were built in 1741 by Mahmut I to pay for the upkeep of his library in Aya Sofya, and the arches, basins and taps of the hot room, as well as the entries to the private cubicles, are all magnificently Baroque. Florence Nightingale is said to have bathed here and the hamam has appeared in several movies, including *Indiana Jones and the Temple of Doom*.

Yeni Cami and Spice Bazaar

The **Yeni Cami**, or "new mosque", is a familiar city landmark, sited across the busy road from Eminönü's bustling waterfront. The last of İstanbul's imperial mosques to be built, it was erected for the Valide Sultan, Safiye, mother of Mehmet III and one of the most powerful of the Valide Sultans. who effectively ruled the whole empire through the weakness of her son. It was built on a seemingly inappropriate site, in a slum neighbourhood inhabited by a sect of Jews called the Karaites, who were relocated across the Horn to Hasköy. Work was then hindered by court politics and it took some sixty years to complete the building, in 1663.

The most intriguing part of the Yeni Cami mosque complex is the **Spice Bazaar** (daily 9am–7pm), known in Turkish as the **Mısır Çarşısı** or "Egyptian Bazaar", which has been the city's premier spice outlet for several centuries. Completed a few years before Yeni Cami, the L-shaped bazaar was endowed with customs duties from Cairo (which explains its name); it has 88 vaulted rooms and chambers above the entryways at the ends of the halls. Far more manageable than the Grand Bazaar, it sells a good range of herbs, spices, Turkish Delight and quack aphrodisiacs – most of which are available (cheaper) in the tiny shops outside.

The Golden Horn

The **Golden Horn** (*Halic* or estuary in Turkish) is one of the finest natural harbours in the world and its fortunes have been closely linked with those of the city. On two separate occasions, capture of the Horn proved to be the turning point of crucial military campaigns. The first occasion, in 1203–04, was when the Crusaders took the Horn and proceeded to besiege the city for ten months, until they breached the walls separating the inlet from the city. The second was a spectacular *tour de force* by Mehmet the Conqueror, who was prevented from entering the Horn by a chain fastened across it and so carried his ships overland at night and launched them into the inlet from its northern shore. Mehmet then constructed a pontoon across the top of the Horn over which he transported his army and cannons in preparation for the siege of the land walls, which were finally breached in 1453. For the Ottoman Empire, the Horn was a vital harbour, supplying the Genoese, Venetian and Jewish trading colonies on its northern shore.

Rüstem Paşa Camii

One of the most attractive of İstanbul's smaller mosques is **Rüstem Paşa Camii**, a short walk west of the spice bazaar. Built for Süleyman the Magnificent's grand vizier Rüstem Paşa in 1561, it is decorated inside and out by some of the finest İznik **tiles** in Turkey. Designs covering the walls, piers and pillars, and decorating the *mihrab* and *mimber*, include famous panels of tulips and carnations and geometric patterns. Built by Sinan on an awkward site, the mosque is easy to miss as you wander the streets below. At ground level on the Golden Horn side an arcade of shops occupies the vaults, from where a flight of steps leads up to the mosque's terrace. Through an attractive entrance portal is a wide courtyard and a tiled double portico along the west wall.

The northwest quarter

One of the least visited but most fascinating areas of the Old City, the **northwest quarter** is bounded on the west by the major thoroughfare of Fevzi Paşa Caddesi, to the north by the land walls of Theodosius, the Golden Horn to the east and on the south by traffic-choked Atatürk Bulvarı. Once home to a cosmopolitan population of Muslims, Christians and Jews it's now a devoutly Muslim area, particularly in the district of **Fatih** where you will notice many women in chadors and bearded men in *şalvar* pants, long baggy shirts and skullcaps (dress appropriately).

The most notable sights are a former Byzantine church, now the **Zeyrek Camii**, two notable Ottoman mosques, the **Fatih** and **Yavuz Selim**, the magnificent Byzantine mosaics in the **Fethiye Camii**, and the spiritual centre of the Orthodox Christian world, the **Greek Patriarchate**. A spiritual centre of a different order awaits a couple of kilometres up the Golden Horn from the Patriarchate, the **Eyüp** area, sacred to Muslims worldwide as it boasts the tomb of Eyüp Ensari, standard-bearer of the Prophet Mohammed.

To get here take a ferry up the Golden Horn to Fener or Balat from either Eminönü or Karköy, or a #99 (for the Atatürk Bridge) or #38/E (for the Zeyrek Camii) bus from Eminönü – or walk up from the Laleli or Aksaray tram stops.

Zeyrek Camii

In the heart of Zeyrek nestles **Zeyrek Camii**, the former Church of the Pantocrator, built in the twelfth century and converted into a mosque at the time of the conquest. To reach it take İtfaiye Caddesi northwards, then turn left on to İbadethane Arkası Sokak.

The building is officially open only at prayer times, though you may be able to persuade the *imam* to open the door for you (his house is up the stone steps behind the wooden door, next to the mosque). It originally consisted of two churches and a connecting chapel, built between 1118 and 1136 by John II Comnenus and Empress Irene. The chapel was built as a mausoleum for the Comnenus dynasty and continued to be used as such by the Paleologus dynasty.

The **mosque**, which occupies the south church, is also in an advanced state of dilapidation and it's difficult to believe that it was once an imperial mausoleum.

Fatih Camii

A little over 300m east of the Zeyrek Camii is the **Fatih Camii**, the "Mosque of the Conqueror". Begun in 1463 but not completed until 1470, it was much rebuilt following a devastating earthquake in 1766. The **inner courtyard** contains green antique marble and highly polished porphyry columns supporting a domed portico, while an eighteenth-century fountain is surrounded by four enormous poplar trees. The architect was supposedly executed because the dome wasn't as large as that of Aya Sofya. The rather drab **interior** is rarely empty, even outside prayer times.

The **tombs** of Mehmet II and of one of his wives, Gülbahar (Wed–Sun 9am–4.30pm), are situated to the east of the mosque. The originals were destroyed in the earthquake, and while Gülbahar's tomb is probably a replica of the original, the *türbe* of the Conqueror is sumptuous Baroque.

Yavuz Selim Camii

Twenty minutes' walk northeast through the backstreets of Fatih brings you to the **Yavuz Selim Camii** (also known as the Selimiye). Building probably commenced in the reign of Selim the Grim, but was completed by Süleyman. The exterior is austere, fittingly so for this cruel ruler, with just a large dome atop a square room fronted by a walled courtyard. Inside, however, this simple, restrained building emerges as one of the most attractive of all the imperial mosques. A central fountain is surrounded by tall cypress trees, the floor of the portico is paved with a floral design, while its columns are a variety of marbles and granites.

The **domed rooms** to the north and south of the mosque – which served as hostels for travelling dervishes – are characteristic of early Ottoman architecture. The paintwork designs in the mosque are reminiscent of the delicacy of Turkish carpets or ceramics. The **tomb of Selim the Grim** (daily except Tues 9.30am–4.30pm), beside the mosque, retains two beautiful tiled panels on either side of the door.

Fethiye Camii

Attractively set on a terrace overlooking the Golden Horn half a kilometre northwest of the Yavuz Selim Camii is the **Fethiye Camii**, formerly the **Church of Theotokos Pammakaristos**. Built in the twelfth century, the church conforms to the usual cross in a square design, its large central dome enhanced by four smaller, subsidiary domes. Despite the Ottoman conquest of Constantinople in 1453, it remained a Christian place of worship; indeed, between 1456 and 1587 it served as the seat of the Greek Orthodox Patriarch (now situated very nearby, in the district of Fener). It was finally converted into a mosque in 1573, when it was renamed the Fethiye Camii or "Mosque of the Conquest". The southwest wing is now a museum (daily except Wed 9am–4.30pm; 2TL), with superb examples of the renaissance of Byzantine art, including a **mosaic** in the dome of Christ Pantocrator, encircled by the twelve prophets of the Old Testament.

The Greek Orthodox Patriarchate

The **Greek Orthodox Patriarchate** (daily 9am–5pm; free), north of the Yavuz Selim Camii almost on the shores of the Golden Horn, has been the spiritual centre of the Orthodox world since 1599. It remains so today – despite the fact that the Greek Orthodox community in the city is now so meagre (around 2,500) and that a Turkish court controversially ruled that the authority of the Patriarch (currently Bartholomew I) was confined solely to Turkey's remaining Greek Orthodox Christians, rather than to the Orthodox Christian community worldwide. Greek tourists still flock to the nineteenth-century **Church of St George** (which stands in the compound of the Patriarchate) on Sunday mornings in the tourist season – especially for the Easter Sunday Mass.

Along the land walls

Theodosius II's **land walls** are among the most fascinating Byzantine remains in Turkey. Well-preserved remnants can still be found along the whole of their 6.5km length, though purists (and UNESCO) decry the fact that much of the recent work done on the walls looks like new-build rather than restoration.

The land walls were named after Theodosius II, and construction started in 413 AD. Stretching from the Marmara to Tekfur Saray, 2km further out than the previous walls of Constantine, they were built to accommodate the city's expanding population. All citizens, regardless of rank, were required to help in the rebuilding following their collapse in the earthquake of 447 and the imminent threat of attack by Attila the Hun. The completed construction consisted of the original wall, 5m thick and 12m high, plus an outer wall of 2m by 8.5m, and a 20-metre-wide moat, all of which proved sufficient to repel Atilla's assault.

A **walk along the walls** takes a little over two hours, though a full day will allow time to fully enjoy it and the adjacent sites. Most of the outer wall and its 96 towers are still standing; access is restricted on some of the restored sections, though elsewhere there's the chance to scramble along the crumbling edifice. There are still plenty of run-down **slums** in this area meaning it's best avoided at night (especially Topkapı).

There are three obvious **sites** (which can also be visited independently). The **Yedikule fortifications**, towards the southern terminus of the walls, are best reached by walking up from the suburban train station at Yedikule. The **Kariye Museum**, a former Byzantine church containing some of the best-preserved mosaics and frescoes in the world, just in from Edirnekapı and around 750m north of the Golden Horn, is easily accessed from the Ulubatlı metro stop, the **Mihrimah Camii** likewise. To reach the north end of the walls (for the Kariye Museum) take the ferry from Eminönü to Ayvansaray İskelesı on the Golden Horn, just before the Haliç bridge. For Eyüp, take the #99 bus from Eminönü, or the much less frequent ferry from Eminönü to the Eyüp ferry landing.

Yedikule and around

Yedikule (Seven Towers) around 5km from the west of Sultanahmet is an attractive quarter, full of churches since it is a centre of Rum Orthodoxy, the last remaining descendants of the Byzantine Greeks. The most impressive single site here is the **Yedikule Museum** (Yedikule Müzesi; daily except Mon 9am–6pm; 5TL), a massive fortification astride the line of the walls, situated to the southwest of İmrahor Camii on Yedikule Meydanı Sokak, Yedikule Caddesi.

Eyüp

Miniatürk & Santral İstanbul

Ayvansaray İskelesi

Rahmi M. Koç Industrial Museum

Hasköy İskelesi

BOSPHORUS BRIDGE ROAD

YENİMAHALLE SOK

AYVANSARAY

Eğrikapı

İvaz Efendi Camii

HASKÖY

Balat İskelesi

SIVACLAR CAD

Tekfur Saray

BALAT

RAMI-EDIRNEKAPI CAD

Church of St Stephen of the Bulgars

Golden Horn

Bus Station at Esenler

Kariye Museum

FENER

Fethiye Camii

Fener İskelesi

Ayakapi İskelesi

Edirnekapı Cemetery

Mihrimah Camii

FETHIYE CAD

Greek Orthodox Patriarchate

Cibali İskelesi

Vefa Stadium

FEVZI PAŞA CAD

Yavuz Selim Camii

EDİRNEKAPI

TOPKAPI-EDIRNEKAPI CAD

City Walls of Theodosius II

ULUBATLI/TOPKAPI

Topkapı Cemetery

ADNAN MENDERES BUL

YAVUZ SELIM CAD

BOSPHORUS BRIDGE ROAD

SÜLÜKULE

Topkapı

TOPKAPI CAD

Fatih Camii

Ahmet Paşa Camii

TOPKAPI

FATİH

TOPKAPI-EDIRNEKAPI YOLU

MACARKARDEŞLER CAD

Çapa Hospital

AKDENIZ CAD

Aqueduct of Valens

ATATÜRK BUL

Cemetery

Şehzade Camii

MEVLANA-TOPKAPI YOLU

Mevlanakapı

TURGUT ÖZAL CAD

Tashan Covered Bazaar

MEVLANIKAPI CAD

AHMET VEFIK PAŞA CAD

AKSARAY

Valide Camii

ORDU CAD

SILIVRIKAPI-MEVLANAKAPI YOLU

Haseki Camii

Haseki Hospital

Laleli Camii

Sultanahmet

BOLUKLU YOLU

Silivri Kapı

NAMIK KEMAL CAD

MUSTAFA KEMAL CAD

Cerrahpaşa Hospital

KOCA MUSTAFA PAŞA CAD

Koca Mustafa Paşa Camii

Yenikapı Train Station

KENNEDY CAD

Yenikapı Ferry Terminal

Belgrat Kapı

Kocamustafapaşa Train Station

BELGRATKAPISI DEMIRHANE YOLU

İmrahor Camii

IMBRAHOR CAD

YEDİKULE

BEY CAD

Yedikule Kapı

Land Walls of Theodosius II

Yedikule Museum

Yedikule Train Station

Airport & Galleria Shopping Mall

Marble Tower

SEA OF MARMARA

N

THE LAND WALLS

0   400 m

RESTAURANTS

| Asithane | A |
| Develi | 1 |

ACCOMMODATION

| Hotel Daphnis | B |
| Kariye Hotel | A |

1

The so-called **Golden Gate**, constructed by Theodosius I in 390, is made from stone and was used by important visitors of state and of conquering emperors to enter the city. The other five towers of the Yedikule fortifications were added by Mehmet the Conqueror, and with their twelve-metre-high curtain walls they form the enclave that can be seen today. Despite its design this was never actually used as a castle, but two of the towers served as prisons and others were used as treasuries and offices for the collection of revenue of the *Vakıf* or pious foundation.

The two **prison towers** are those immediately to the left of the entrance: the "tower with inscriptions" and the tower on the north side of the Golden Gate. The inscriptions around the outside of the first of these were carved into the walls by prisoners. Many of these were foreign ambassadors on some hapless errand. The prison in the second tower doubled as an execution chamber: the wooden gallows and "well of blood", into which heads would roll, are still to be seen, and the odd instrument of torture can be found lying about outside in the courtyard.

The public gateways

North along the walls, the first of the public gateways is the **Yedikule Kapı**, with its Byzantine eagle cut in the blackened marble overhead. The land in and around the first section between Yedikule and **Belgrat Kapı** is in use as market gardens. **Belgrat Kapı** was a military gate, different from a public gateway in that there was no bridge crossing the moat beyond the outer walls. It was named for the captives who were settled in this area by Süleyman the Magnificent after his capture of Belgrade in 1521. The walls here, which are floodlit at night, have been substantially renovated and it's now one of the best places to walk along the parapet. North from Belgrat Kapı to **Silivri Kapı** the walls are largely untouched, though the sections around Silivri Kapı itself have been extensively renovated. There is more restoration work at the **Mevlanakapı**, and also some interesting inscriptions on the outer wall.

Topkapı and Edirnekapı

A road system dominates the outer side of the 1km Mevlanakapı–Topkapı section of wall and a pleasant pavement has been constructed along the moat. Just south of Topkapı the walls have been destroyed to make way for the enormous thoroughfare of Turgut Özal Caddesi, complete with its central tram track. Beyond it is the **Topkapı** (the "Gate of the Cannonball"), named after the most powerful cannon of Mehmet the Conqueror (see below), some of whose enormous stone cannonballs have been placed around the inside of the gate.

Between Topkapı and Edirnekapı there is a pronounced valley, formerly the route of the Lycus River, now taken by Vatan Caddesi. At this point the walls are at their least defensible, since the higher ground outside gives the advantage to attackers. The famed **Orban cannon** of Mehmet the Conqueror was trained on this part of the walls during the siege of 1453, hence their ruinous state. It was here, too, that Constantine XI rode into the midst of the Turkish army after he realized that all hope of holding out was gone.

The gate of **Edirnekapı** takes its name from the route to modern Edirne. The sixteenth-century **Mihrimah Camii** is a little to the left of the *otogar* you see today as you face the walls. Mihrimah, the favourite daughter of Süleyman the Magnificent, had a passion for architecture as great as that of her husband Rüstem Paşa, and the couple commissioned many of Sinan's early works. Situated on the highest of İstanbul's seven hills, it's further raised on a platform and can be seen from all over the city.

The Kariye Museum

The **Kariye Museum** (Kariye Müzesi; daily except Wed 9am–6pm; 15TL), formerly the church of St Saviour in Chora, is decorated with a superbly preserved series of **frescoes and mosaics** portraying the life and miracles of Christ. It's arguably the most evocative of all the city's Byzantine treasures, thought to have been built in the early twelfth century on the site of a much older church far from the centre: hence "in Chora", meaning "in the country". Between 1316 and 1321 the statesman and scholar Theodore Metochites rebuilt the central dome and added the narthexes and mortuary chapel.

The mosaics

Inside the church, the most prominent of the mosaics is that of **Christ Pantocrator**, bearing the inscription "Jesus Christ, the Land of the Living". Opposite is a depiction of the Virgin and angels, with the inscription "Mother of God, the Dwelling Place of the Uncontainable". The third in the series is located in the inner narthex and depicts Metochites offering a model of the building to a seated Christ. Sts Peter and Paul are portrayed on either side of the door leading to the nave, and to the right of the door are Christ with his Mother and two benefactors, Isaac (who built the original church) and the figure of a nun.

In the two domes of the inner narthex are medallions of **Christ Pantocrator** and the Virgin and Child, and in the fluting of the domes, a series of notable figures – starting with Adam – from the **Genealogy of Christ**. The **Cycle of the Blessed Virgin** is located in the first three bays of the inner narthex. Episodes depicted here include the first seven steps of the Virgin; the Virgin caressed by her parents, with two beautiful peacocks in the background; the Virgin presented as an attendant at the temple, the Virgin receiving a skein of purple wool, as proof of her royal blood; Joseph taking the Virgin to his house, in which is also depicted one of Joseph's sons by his first wife; and Joseph returning from a trip to find his wife pregnant.

The next cycle, found in the arched apertures of the outer narthex, depicts the **Infancy of Christ**. The mosaics can be followed clockwise, starting with Joseph dreaming, the Virgin and two companions, and the journey to Bethlehem. Apart from well-known scenes such as the Journey of the Magi and the Nativity, there are depictions in the seventh bay of the Flight into Egypt. In the sixth bay is the Slaughter of the Innocents, complete with babies impaled on spikes.

The **Cycle of Christ's Ministry** fills the vaults of the outer narthex and parts of the south bay of the inner narthex. It includes wonderful scenes of the Temptation of Christ, with dramatic dialogue (Matthew 4: 3–10) that could almost be in speech bubbles, beginning "Devil: If thou be the Son of God, command that these stones be made bread. Christ: It is written, Man shall not live by bread alone, but by every word that proceedeth out of the mouth of God."

The frescoes

In the nave, the main frescoes echo the mosaics, featuring the death of the Virgin, over the door and, to the right of this, another depiction of Christ. The best known of all the works in the church, however, are the frescoes in the **funerary chapel** to the south of the nave.

The most spectacular of the frescoes is the **Resurrection**, also known as the Harrowing of Hell. This depicts Christ trampling the gates of Hell underfoot and forcibly dragging Adam and Eve from their tombs. A black Satan lies among the broken fetters at his feet, bound at the ankles, wrists and neck. To the left of the painting, animated onlookers include John the Baptist, David and Solomon, while to the right Abel is standing in his mother's tomb; behind him is another group of the righteous.

Other frescoes in the chapel, in the vault of the east bay, depict the **Second Coming**, and in the east half of the domical vault Christ sits in judgement.

Eyüp

Eyüp is one of the holiest places in Islam, its mosque being the site of the tomb of Eyüp Ensari (674–678), the Prophet Mohammed's standard-bearer who was killed in the first Arab siege of Constantinople. Muslims come here from all over the Islamic world on pilgrimage. Try not to visit on Fridays, out of respect for conservative worshippers.

Originally built by Mehmet the Conqueror in honour of Eyüp Ensari, the mosque was destroyed by an earthquake in the eighteenth century. Its Baroque replacement, filled with light, gold, pale stone and white marble, was completed in 1800 and later used in the investiture ceremonies of the Ottoman sultans. The **tomb of Eyüp Ensari** (Tues–Sun 9.30am–4.30pm), with its tile panels from many different periods, is more compelling than the mosque.

There are a number of other important tombs in the Eyüp district. The **tombs of Sokollu Mehmet Paşa and Siyavus Paşa** (Tues–Sun 9.30am–4.30pm), stand opposite each other on either side of Camii Kebir Caddesi, five minutes' walk from Eyüp Camii towards the Golden Horn. Both are works of Sinan, the former is notable for its stained glass, some of which is original.

The hills above the mosque are covered in plain modern stones interspersed with beautiful Ottoman tombs. This is the **Eyüp cemetery**, most beautiful at sunset with an arresting view of the Golden Horn. It's a twenty-minute walk from Eyüp Camii to reach the romantic *Pierre Loti Café* (daily 8am–midnight) overlooking the Horn, or take the new cable car (1.5TL) from the shores of the Golden Horn.

The mosque is most easily reached by boat up the Golden Horn from Eminönü – it's the last **ferry** stop before the Horn peters out into two small streams, and the mosque and tomb are about a ten-minute walk from the ferry terminal on Camii Kebir Caddesi. Or catch the #39/A or #99 **bus** from Eminönü.

Beyoğlu and Galata

The district of **Beyoğlu**, across the Golden Horn from Eminönü, is the beating heart of modern İstanbul, particularly along İstiklâl Caddesi. The locals head here in droves to shop, wine and dine, take in a film, club, gig or gallery – or simply promenade. So, too, do an ever-increasing number of visitors, many of whom base themselves here to take advantage of the nightlife. At the northern end of İstiklâl Caddesi is massive **Taksim Square**, regarded as a symbol of the secular Turkish Republic and home to numerous hotels and convenient bus and metro terminals. Crossing the Galata bridge from the Old City, the first place you come to is the gritty port area of **Karaköy**, now swamped with cruise liners. Further inland is **Galata** proper, once a Genoese city state within İstanbul and now an up and coming district full of bars and restaurants.

The Galata bridge and Karaköy

The **Galata Köprüsü** (Galata bridge) lacks grace, but its stunning location and supreme importance in linking the old and new İstanbuls together more than make up for its lack of architectural merit. There's a walkway either side of the bridge close to water level, backed by a myriad of lively cafés, bars and restaurants. The tram rumbles across the upper level, and the bridge's guardrails are invisible behind a solid wall of expectant anglers. To discover more about this landmark bridge and the myriad of people whose lives revolve around it, read Geert Mak's thoroughly entertaining "The Bridge" (see p.733).

At the northern end of the bridge is the rough-and-ready port area of **Karaköy**, from where you can either walk up to Galata/Beyoğlu on the steep Yüksek Kaldırım Caddesi, past the Galata Tower, or take the **Tünel** underground train/funicular (daily 9am–9pm; 1.2TL). Karaköy's port and Ottoman shipyard was once enclosed within the walls of the Castle of Galata. In 1446 the Byzantines stretched a great chain across the mouth of the Horn to prevent enemy ships from entering. Originally constructed around 580, the subterranean keep of the castle is thought to be preserved as the **Yeraltı Cami**, or "Underground Mosque", on Kemankeş Caddesi. At the far end of the port area is another mosque, the **Kiliç Ali Paşa Camii**, constructed in 1580 by Sinan, and essentially a smaller copy of Aya Sofya.

The Zülfaris Synagogue on Meydanı Perçemli Sokak, to the west of the bridge, is home to the **Jewish Museum** (Mon & Thurs 10am–4pm, Fri & Sun 10am–2pm; 5TL). Its small but fascinating display includes documents and photographs donated by local Jewish families, chronicling Turkish Jews since they first came to the country over seven hundred years ago.

The Galata Tower and around

In 1261 the area of **Galata**, north of Karaöy was granted to the **Genoese** by Byzantine emperor Michael Paleologus. This was a reward for their supporting his attempts to drive out the Crusaders. Built by the Genoese in 1349, the **Galata Tower** (Galata Kulesi; daily 9am–8pm; 10TL) sits on the site of a former tower constructed by Justinian in 528. Originally known as the Tower of Christ, it stood at the apex of the several sets of fortifications that surrounded the Genoese city-state. It has had a number of functions over the centuries, including a jail, a fire tower and even a springboard for early adventurers attempting to fly. Nowadays, there's a restaurant on the top floor. At 61m high, the tower's **viewing gallery** – reached by elevator – offers magnificent panoramas of the city and views across the Sea of Marmara and Golden Horn.

A short walk south of the tower, at Galata Külesi Sok 61, is the **British prison**. Under the capitulations granted by the Ottomans, Western powers had the right to try their citizens under their own law, so consulates possessed their own court-houses and prisons. The court originated in the 1600s, but the current building dates from 1904 and today houses the *Galata House* restaurant-café. Around 300m further south on Yanık Kapı (or "Burned Gate") Sokak, is the only remaining Genoese **city gate**. Somewhat the worse for wear, it still boasts a marble slab bearing the Cross of St George. With its tall square tower and pyramidal roof the **Arap Camii** was, under the Genoese, the largest church in Galata. It was converted into a mosque to serve the needs of the Moorish community that settled here in the early sixteenth century following their expulsion from Spain.

Beyoğlu

The district of **Pera** (Greek for "beyond" or "across"), now known as **Beyoğlu**, lies to the north and uphill from Galata. By the mid-nineteenth century Pera was the area of choice for the main European powers to build their ambassadorial palaces, and it is this imported **architecture** that still dominates today. The completion of the Orient Express Railway in 1889 encouraged an influx of tourists, catered for in luxurious hotels like the splendid *Pera Palas*.

The **nightlife** of the quarter was notoriously riotous even in the seventeenth century, and by the nineteenth and early twentieth centuries, the area had become

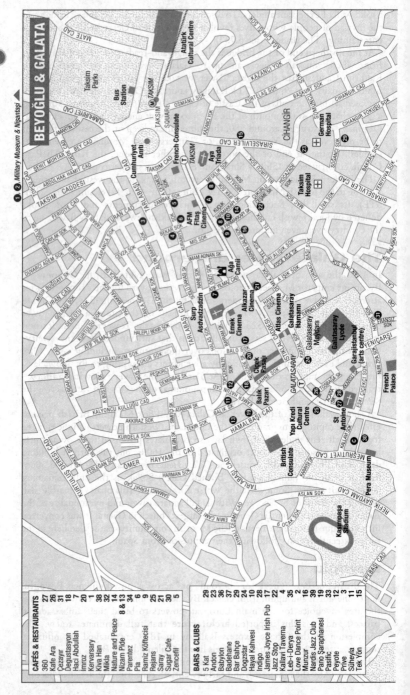

BEYOĞLU & GALATA

① ② Military Museum & Nişantaşı ▲

CAFÉS & RESTAURANTS	
360	27
Kafe Ara	26
Çezayir	31
Degustasyon	18
Haci Abdullah	7
Imroz	20
Kervansary	1
Kiva Han	32
Mikla	38
Nature and Peace	14
Nizam Pide	8 & 13
Parentez	34
Pia	9
Ramiz Köftecisi	6
Rejans	25
Saray	21
Sugar Cafe	30
Zencefil	5

BARS & CLUBS	
5 Kat	29
Andon	23
Babylon	36
Badehane	37
Bar Bahçe	29
Dogzstar	24
Hayal Kahvesi	10
Indigo	28
James Joyce Irish Pub	17
Jazz Stop	22
Kallavi Taverna	4
Leb-i-Derya	35
Love Dance Point	2
Munzur	16
Nardis Jazz Club	39
Pano Şaraphanesi	19
Pasific	33
Peyote	12
Prive	3
Süheyla	11
Tek Yön	15

120

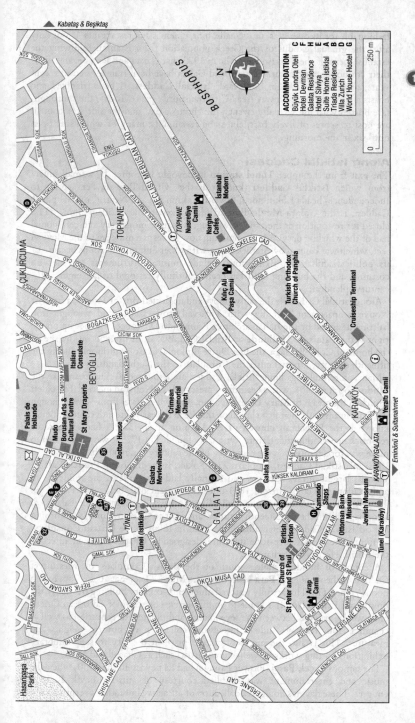

ACCOMMODATION

Büyük Londra Oteli	C
Hotel Devman	F
Galata Residence	H
Hotel Silviya	E
Suite Home Istiklal	A
Triada Residence	B
Villa Zurich	D
World House Hostel	G

0   250 m

fashionable for its operettas, music halls, inns, cinemas and restaurants. It was only after the gradual exodus of the Greek population from İstanbul following the establishment of the Turkish Republic in 1923 that Galata and Pera began to lose their cosmopolitan flavour. Beyoğlu and Galata have been transformed in recent years, and Beyoğlu's main boulevard, **İstiklâl Caddesi**, is pedestrianized and boasts a cute antique tramway (see "City transport", p.84). Today, the thoroughfare bustles with life virtually twenty-four hours a day, and the side streets off it are host to scores of lively bars, clubs and restaurants, many of which stay open until six in the morning.

Along İstiklâl Caddesi

The exit from the upper **Tünel station** in Beyoğlu is fronted by a small square from which **İstiklâl Caddesi** (known as the "Grand Rue de Pera" prior to Independence) heads 1.5km north towards Taksim Square. Nearby, on Galipdede Caddesi, is the **Galata Mevlevihanesi** (daily except Tues 9.30am–5pm; 5TL), closed for restoration at the time of writing. A former monastery and ceremonial hall of the whirling dervishes, the building now serves as a museum to the Mevlevî sect, which was banned by Atatürk along with other Sufi organizations because of its political affiliations. Exhibitions include musical instruments and dervish costumes and the building itself has been beautifully restored to late eighteenth-century splendour.

Along İstiklâl Caddesi is the sadly empty and neglected **Botter House**, a fine Art Nouveau apartment building with a carved stone facade and wrought-iron balcony designed by the Italian architect Raimondo D'Aronco. Further up on the right is the **Palais de Hollande** at İstiklâl Cad 393. Built in 1858 on the site of the home of Cornelis Haga, the first Dutch diplomat in Constantinople during the fifteenth century, it now houses the Consulate to the Netherlands.

Many other buildings lining İstiklâl Caddesi are also typically European, like the **Mudo** shop at no. 401, with a beautifully preserved Art Nouveau interior. The oldest church in the area is **St Mary Draperis** at no. 429, which dates from 1789, although the Franciscans built their first church on the site in the early fifteenth century. Better known is the Franciscan **church of St Antoine** at no. 325, a fine example of red-brick neo-Gothic architecture. Originally founded in 1725 it was demolished to make way for a tramway at the beginning of the century and rebuilt in 1913.

Just off İstiklâl Caddesi, on Nuru Ziya Sokak, is the imposing **French Palace**, with its large central courtyard and formally laid-out gardens, the residence of ambassadors and consuls from 1831 until the present day. Below the Palace, on Tom Tom Kaptan Sokak, stands the **Italian Consulate**, originally the Palazzo di Venezia, built in the seventeenth century, and host to Casanova in 1744. Turning left off İstiklâl Caddesi, Hamalbaşı Sok, leads in 100m to the **British Consulate**, an impressive Renaissance-style structure, designed by Charles Barry, architect of the British Houses of Parliament.

A couple of hundred metres south of the British Consulate, on Meşrütiyet Caddesi, is the wonderful **Pera Museum** (Pera Müzesi:Tues–Sat 10am–7pm & Sun noon–7pm; 7TL). This artfully restored nineteenth-century building (formerly the prestigious Bristol Hotel) is home to an impressive collection of European Orientalist works, painted between the seventeenth and nineteenth centuries, as well as ceramics from Küthaya and an interesting collection of historic weights and measures. This is also the most convenient place in the city to see temporary exhibitions hosting works by well-known artists such as Chagall and Miró.

The famous **Çiçek Pasaj** (Flower Passage) had its heyday in the 1930s when the music and entertainment was supplied courtesy of anti-Bolshevik Russian émigrés. These days it's home to a collection of attractive but rather overpriced and touristy restaurants. Far better is **Nevizade Sokak**, a street dedicated to fish restaurants (all with outside tables), and incredibly lively bars and clubs and, further south near the Tünel entrance, the similar but trendier streets around **Asmalımescit Sokak**.

Taksim Square and around

Taksim in Turkish means "distribution" and the low **stone reservoir** on the south side is the building from which Taksim Square takes its name. The reservoir was constructed in 1732 to distribute water brought from the Belgrade Forest by aqueduct. Steps on the north side of the square above the main bus terminal lead up to the pleasant **Taksim Parkı**, with its bench-lined paths and open-air tea gardens.

The **Atatürk Cultural Centre** (Atatürk Kültür Merkezi or AKM; see p.140) is to the east of the square and is one of the leading venues for İstanbul's various international festivals. It is also home to the State Opera and Ballet, the Symphony Orchestra and the State Theatre Company, but was closed for restoration at the time of writing.

A further 1.5km north along Cumhuriyet Caddesi is the **Military Museum** (Askeri Müzesi; Wed–Sun 9am–5pm; 3TL), housed in the military academy where Atatürk received some of his training. Inside, there is a comprehensive collection of memorabilia proudly displayed and labelled in English. The most striking exhibits are the cotton- and silk-embroidered tents used by campaigning sultans and a rich collection of Ottoman armour and weaponry. In summer a marching band plays outside between 3 and 4pm. To get there, walk or catch a bus north along Cumhuriyet Caddesi to the İstanbul Radyoevi (radio building).

Tophane, Beşiktaş and Ortaköy

Heading northeast along the Bosphorus waterfront from the Galata bridge are three areas of interest to visitors. First up is Tophane, around a kilometre from the Galata bridge but easily reached by the tram, notable mainly for the presence of the city's leading gallery, **İstanbul Modern**. Beyond it is Besiktaş, where the grandiose **Dolmabahçe Palace** presides over the Bosphorus. Still further along is Ortaköy, a trendy suburb which retains some of its former fishing-village charm beneath the towering Bosphorus suspension bridge.

Tophane

Tophane is a mixed area of run-down dockland dotted with venerable Ottoman buildings, most notable of which are the **Kılıç Paşa Camii** dating from 1780, and the more recent **Nusretiye Camii** (1822). The district is also home to the city's contemporary art collection, **İstanbul Modern** (Tues–Sun 10am–6pm; 7TL, free on Thurs 10am–2pm), in a revamped warehouse on the edge of the Bosphorus, just in front of the Nusretiye Camii. The museum's interior is all big, blank white walls and an exposed ventilation system, with picture windows giving views across the Bosphorus to the Topkapı Palace. The collection includes the best of modern Turkish art, as well as some intriguing video installations from foreign artists. There's a reference library, a cinema showing arts and independent movies, and a trendy café with a terrace right on the edge of the Bosphorus.

To reach the museum from Sultanahmet, take the tramway to the stop just west of Nusretiye Camii, from where it's a three-minute walk.

▲ Inside İstanbul Modern

Beşiktaş

Most visitors to the district of **Beşiktaş** are here to see the Dolmabahçe Palace, successor to Topkapı as the residence of the Ottoman sultans. However, it's worth aiming to spend a few more hours in the neighbourhood if you can, to visit the city's excellent Maritime Museum, as well as Yıldız Parkı and palace. It's also home to one of İstanbul's three major football teams (see box opposite).

Concrete shopping centres and a sprawling fruit and vegetable market cluster around the main shore road and **ferry terminal**, in front of which stands the **bus station**. To get here take bus #25/T or #40 from Taksim or #28 or #28/T from Eminönü.

Dolmabahçe Palace

The **Dolmabahçe Palace** (daily except Mon & Thurs 9am–4pm; *Selâmlik* 15TL, Harem 10TL) is the largest and most sumptuous of all the palaces on the Bosphorus, with an impressive 600m waterside frontage. Built in the nineteenth century by various members of the Balian family, it's an excessive display of ostentatious wealth. Indeed, critics see the palace's wholesale adoption of Western architectural forms as a last-ditch effort to muster some respect for a crumbling and defeated empire.

Sultan Abdul mecid ordered the construction of a new palace to replace Topkapı as the imperial residence of the Ottoman sultans. It was built by Armenian architect Karabet Balian and his son Nikoğos between 1843 and 1856 in as ostentatious manner as possible, with copious use of gold. The palace is divided into **selâmlik** and **harem** by the 36-metre-high **throne room** (double the height of the rest of the rooms), held up by 56 elaborate columns. The ceremonies conducted here were accompanied by an orchestra playing European marches and watched by women of the harem through the *kafes*, grilles behind which women were kept

Fever pitch

İstanbul's three leading football teams **Beşiktaş**, **Fenerbahçe** and **Galatasaray** receive fanatical support – match times remain one of the few occasions when the city streets fall silent – and dominate the Turkish league. There are sporadic outbreaks of football violence here, but the chances of a foreigner getting caught up in it are slim. There are two Turkish daily newspapers, *Fotomaç* and *Fanatik*, devoted almost entirely to the three İstanbul heavyweights, and matches (Aug–May) are staggered over each weekend in season so television coverage of the three doesn't clash.

Beşiktaş (℡0212/236 7202, 🌐www.bjk.com.tr) play at the most convenient and attractive ground of the three, İnönü Stadium on Kadırgalar Cad, between Taksim and Beşiktaş, opposite the Dolmabahçe Palace; walk down the hill, or take bus #23/B from Taksim Square or #30 from Sultanahmet or Eminönü. The wealthiest club, Fenerbahçe (℡0216/449 5667, 🌐www.fenerbahce.org), play at the 52,000 capacity Şükrü Saracoğlu Stadyium on Bağdat Cad in Kızıltoprak on the Asian side of the Bosphorus; take a ferry to Kadıköy, then a dolmuş marked "Cadde Bostan". Galatasaray (℡0212/251 5707, 🌐www.galatasaray.org.com) play at the Ali Sami Yen Stadyumu in Mecidiyeköy; catch any bus marked "Mecidiyeköy" from near the *McDonalds* in Taksim Square. Tickets are sold at the stadiums two days before a match. For regular fixtures tickets start from 30TL for Beşiktaş and Galatsaray, from 45TL for Fenerbahçe. Tickets are also available online from Biletix (🌐www.biletix.com) and Biletix outlets. For information in English see 🌐www.budgetairlinefootball.co.uk.

hidden even in the days of reform. The four-tonne chandelier in the throne room, one of the largest ever made, with 750 bulbs, was a present from Queen Victoria. Atatürk, the founder of the Turkish Republic, died here in his private apartment in 1938.

In the east wing of the palace, the former apartments of the heir to the throne house the **Museum of Fine Arts** (Resim ve Heykel Müzesi; Wed–Sun 10am–4pm; free), usually entered from the Kaymakamlık building, which used to house the palace staff, around 300m further along the main road from the Dolmabahçe entrance.

The Maritime Museum

Back towards the ferry landing in Beşiktaş is the interesting **Maritime Museum** (Deniz Müzesi; daily except Wed & Thurs 9am–12.30pm & 1.30–5pm; 3TL). The collection is divided between two buildings, the one facing the water housing seagoing craft, the other the maritime history of the Ottoman Empire and the Turkish Republic. Most of the labels are in Turkish but the best of the exhibits – such as the enormous wooden figureheads depicting tigers and swans, and the display of items from Atatürk's yacht, the *Savarona* – need little explanation. Next door, the exhibition continues with a collection of caïques, which were used to row the sultans to and from their homes along the Bosphorus. The oarsmen – the *Bostanci* – reputedly barked like dogs whilst they rowed so as not to overhear the sultans talking.

Çırağan Palace

A ten-minute walk east along busy Çırağan Caddesi, the grand **Çırağan Palace**, with 300m of marble facade facing the shore, was built when Sultan Abdulmecid decided to move his official residence from Dolmabahçe in 1855. It was completed in 1874, during the reign of Abdülaziz, and it was here that Abdülaziz was either murdered or committed suicide – the cause of death was never established. Murat V was later imprisoned here after being deposed by his brother. Following a period of abandonment, Çırağan housed the Turkish parliament for two years in 1908, before a fire reduced it to a blackened shell in 1910. It was restored in 1991 to its present magnificence as İstanbul's foremost luxury hotel, the *Çırağan Palace & Kempinski Hotel*. The *Gazebo* restaurant provides a magnificent setting for a traditional afternoon tea, while *Tuğra* is the place for a grand Ottoman night out.

Yıldız Parkı

Opposite the Çırağan Sarayı on Çırağan Caddesi is the public entrance to **Yıldız Parkı** (daily dawn–dusk; free), a vast wooded area dotted with mansions, pavilions, lakes and gardens, which was the centre of the Ottoman Empire for thirty years during the reign of Abdülhamid II. Its superb hillside location makes Yıldız Parkı one of the most popular places in İstanbul for city-dwellers thirsting for fresh air and open spaces: on public holidays the park is always crowded. Of the many buildings in the park, only the Yıldız Palace Museum and the Şale Köşkü are open to the public, though it's easy enough to wander around the outside of the other pavilions, each with marvellous terraces and panoramic views of the Bosphorus.

The most important surviving building in the park is the **Şale Köşkü** (daily except Mon & Thurs 9.30am–5pm; Oct–Feb closes 4pm; guided tours obligatory, 4TL, camera 6TL). The first of the pavilion's three separate sections was modelled on a Swiss chalet, while the second and third sections were built to receive Kaiser Wilhelm II on his first and second state visits, in 1889 and 1898. The most impressive room, the Ceremonial Hall, takes up the greater part of the third section, with a Hereke carpet so big (approximately 400 square metres) that part of a wall was knocked down to install it.

In the same complex, the **Yıldız Palace Museum** (Yıldız Sarayı Müzesi; daily except Mon 9.30pm–6pm; 5TL) is housed in Abdülhamid's converted carpentry workshop, and exhibits items and furniture from throughout the palace. Whilst not in their original grand settings in the pavilions, there are some exquisite porcelain pieces, giant vases and more of the joinery produced by the sultan himself.

Ortaköy

Ortaköy is 1km from Beşiktaş, past Yıldız Parkı and the Çırağan Palace. This former Bosphorus backwater was traditionally an area of tolerance – a mosque, church and synagogue have existed side by side for centuries – though its erstwhile character has been hijacked by flash nightclubs, trendy eateries, and the overwhelming presence of the Bosphorus bridge just to the north. To get to Ortaköy take a #40 **bus** from Taksim, the #30 from Eminönü or take the tram from the Old City to Kabataş, then the #22/E to Ortaköy; or you can take a bus or **ferry** to Beşiktaş and walk (about 15min).

When Ortaköy was just a tiny fishing village, university students and teachers used to gather here to sip tea and discuss weighty topics. It's a time remembered in the name of the Sunday *entel*, or "intellectual", **market**, a crowded affair held on the waterfront square, which sells all kinds of arts and crafts. There are also daily market stalls selling trendy silver jewellery and sunglasses on the waterfront, or **Ortaköy boardwalk** as it's rather pretentiously known. This is also the location of the attractive, Baroque **Büyük Mecidiye Camii**, built in 1855, and some of the liveliest teahouses on the Bosphorus.

The Golden Horn: north shore

Heading northwest from Beyoğlu, along the newly spruced-up north shore of the once heavily polluted **Golden Horn**, are three sights well worth a look, especially if you're fed-up with historic buildings and/or have kids in tow: the **Rahmi M. Koç Industrial Museum**, Turkey's landmark buildings done to scale at **Miniatürk** and the trendy exhibition centre of **Santralistanbul**, in a refurbished old power station.

The Rahmi M. Koç Industrial Museum

Formerly home to a substantial Jewish community **Hasköy**, a couple of kilometres up the Golden Horn from Karaköy, was also the location of an Ottoman naval shipyard and royal park. Today it's noted for the excellent **Rahmi M. Koç Industrial Museum** at Hasköy Cad 27 (Tues–Fri 10am–5pm, Sat & Sun 10am–7pm; 10TL, kids 5TL; ⓦwww.rmk-museum.org.tr), an old factory restored by by Rahmi M. Koç, one of Turkey's most famous – and wealthiest – industrialists, to house his private collection of models, machines, vehicles and toys. Upstairs, the starboard main engine of the *Kalender* steam ferry, made in Newcastle-upon-Tyne in 1911 is the main exhibit. Downstairs are a number of old bikes, from penny-farthings to an early Royal Enfield motorbike – and much else besides. The in-house *Café du Levant* (closed Mon) in the museum grounds is a good French bistro. Another section of the museum, fronting the Golden Horn, has a moored submarine (entrance an extra 4.5TL) and a number of great vintage vehicles, plus another pricey restaurant, the *Halat*.

Catch **bus** #47/A from Eminönü, or the #54/H from Taksim. Alternatively, take the Eyüp-bound **ferry** from Eminönü and get off at Kasımpaşa ferry terminal, a short walk away from the museum.

Miniatürk

Upstream of Hasköy in dull Sütlüce, on the north side of the monumental Haliç Bridge, is one of those attractions you'll either love or hate: **Miniatürk** (May–Oct Mon–Fri 9am–7pm, Sat & Sun 9am–9pm; Nov–April daily 9am–9pm; 10TL, under-9s free; ⓦwww.miniaturk.com). On display here are over a hundred 1:25 scale models of some of Turkey's most impressive sights, spaced out along a 1.8-kilometre-signed route. Forty-five of them are of attractions in İstanbul – from the relatively obscure (how about Sirkeci Post Office) through to the most famous (the Blue Mosque et al) – another 45 cover sights in Anatolia, including the Library of Celsus at Ephesus and Atatürk's mausoleum, the Anıtkabir, in Ankara, and there are also fifteen from former Ottoman dominions. Not all the well-detailed models are buildings – if you've ever wanted to see Cappadocia's fairy chimneys or the travertine cascades of Pamukkale in miniature, then this is the place to see them. To reach Miniatürk, take bus #47/A from Eminönü or the #54/H from Taksim.

Santralistanbul

Set in the attractively landscaped campus of Bilgi University, built on reclaimed industrial land at the head of the Golden Horn, **Santralıstanbul** is a striking symbol of the new İstanbul. The major point of interest is the Museum of Energy (Tues–Sun 10am–8pm; free; ⓦwww.santalistanbul.org), housed, appropriately enough, in an old power station. Between 1914 and its closure in 1983, this plant, the Silahtarağa, was the only electricity generating station in İstanbul. The interior is now a successful mix of the carefully preserved innards of the power plant and hi-tech wizardry. To the left of the entrance is an impressive exhibition space, which has hosted events ranging from retrospectives of contemporary Turkish art to the headscarf issue. The campus also has a trendy bar, *Otto Santral*, and hosts the annual "One Love" alt-music festival (see p.138).

A free shuttle-bus runs from outside the AKM building on Taksim Square until 8pm; after that, you'll have to take the #47/A or #54/H bus and taxi-it back to the centre.

Asian İstanbul

The best single reason to head across to the **Asian shore** of the city is to experience the ferry ride. The views from the Bosphorus are superb, with domes and minarets dominating the skyline of the Old City, skyscrapers the business districts beyond Beyoğlu – and where else in the world can you cruise from one continent to another for less than a euro? The three Asian neighbourhoods, **Üsküdar**, **Haydarpaşa** and **Kadıköy** all have some interesting sites, including some exquiste Ottoman mosques and a British war cemetery – not to mention a handful of eating places of some repute.

Üsküdar

Üsküdar has some fine Islamic architecture, with the most obvious mosque being **İskele** or **Mihrimah Camii**, opposite the ferry landing on İskele Meydanı. This sits on a high platform, fronted by an immense covered porch. Designed by Mimar Sinan and built in 1547–48, this is the only Ottoman mosque with three semi-domes (rather than two or four), a result of the requirements of a difficult site against the hillside behind. Directly across the square is the **Yeni Valide Camii**. Built between 1708 and 1710 by Ahmet III in honour of his mother, it is most easily identified by the Valide Sultan's green, birdcage-like tomb, whose meshed roof was designed to keep birds out while allowing rain in to water the garden tomb below.

One of the most attractive mosques in Üsküdar is the **Çinili Cami**, or Tiled Mosque, which dates from 1640. To get there on foot, take Hakimiyet-i Milliye Caddesi out of the centre and turn left into Çavuşdere Caddesi; after passing Çavuşdere fruit and veg market, continue to climb the same street and you'll see the mosque on your right. The tiles are mainly blues and turquoise, but there's a rare shade of green to be found in the *mihrab*. Below the mosque, in the same street, is the beautifully restored **Çinili Hamamı** (men 8am–10pm, women 8am–8pm; 30TL), which retains its original central marble stones for massage and acres of marble revetments.

The **Atık Valide Külliyesi** is just a short walk from Çinili Cami: go back down Çavuşdere Caddesi and turn left into Çinili Hamam Sokak and you'll find the mosque on the right. Dating from 1583, the complex is a work of the master architect Mimar Sinan, built for Nur Banu, wife of Selim II and mother of Murat III. The mosque courtyard is very beautiful, and inside fine İznik tiles cover the *mihrab*.

To the south of Üsküdar on an island in the Bosphorus, is the small white **Kız Kulesi** (Maiden's Tower), also known as Leander's Tower. Many myths are associated with it: in one a princess, who was prophesied to die from a snake bite, came here to escape her fate, only to succumb to it when a serpent was delivered to her retreat in a basket of fruit. The tower also featured in the 1999 James Bond film, *The World Is Not Enough*. It's now a **museum** (daily except Mon noon–7pm; free), doubling as an expensive restaurant in the evening. It can be reached from Salacak (on the main coast road between Üsküdar and Harem) by **boat** (7.15am–1.30am; every 20min) or from Kabataş, departing 7pm, returning at 11.15pm.

Üsküdar's main square is set to become the exit point of the Marmaray rail tunnel linking the European and Asian sides of the city but until its completion (scheduled for 2011) you'll need to take a ferry from Eminönü. Buses run from Üsküdar up the Bosphorus, as far as Anadolu Kavağı, leaving from in front of İskele Camii on Paşa Liman Caddesi.

Haydarpaşa

South of Üsküdar and across the bay from Kadıköy is Haydarpaşa, whose serried ranks of enormous nineteenth- and early twentieth- century buildings make quite an impact as you approach by ferry. The main-line **Haydarpaşa train station**, jutting out into the Bosphorus, was completed in 1908 by a German architect as part of Germany's grandiose plans for a Berlin to Baghdad railway, the palace-like building was presented to Sultan Abdül Hamit II by Kaiser Wilhelm II. The stained glass is particularly impressive, and it's well worth a look even if you are not heading into Asian Turkey by rail. You can reach it directly by ferry from Eminönü or Karaköy, or it's a ten-minute walk from Kadıköy ferry terminal.

Directly north of the station, between the sea and Tıbbiye Caddesi, is the Marmara University and the **British War Cemetery** (daily 7am–7pm), a beautifully kept spot sheltering the dead of the Crimean War and the two world wars. To find it, turn off Tıbbiye Caddesi into Burhan Felek Caddesi, between the university building and the military hospital. A few minutes' walk northeast of the university, along Kavak Iskele Caddesi, is the imposing **Selimiye Barracks**. Its northwest wing was used as a hospital by the British during the Crimean War (1854–56). **Florence Nightingale** lived and worked in the northern tower, now a **museum** (Mon–Fri 9am–5pm; appointment only). Her famous lamp is on show and you can see the rooms where she lived and worked. To visit you must fax a photocopy of the ID page of your passport, desired visiting time and date and telephone number to the museum's military guardians ☏0216/553 1009 or 310 7929 at least 24 hours in advance.

Ferries to Haydarapaşa depart regularly from Eminönü and Karaköy; all continue the short way to terminate at Kadıköy (see below).

Kadıköy

The suburb of **Kadıköy** was, in the nineteenth century, a popular residential area for wealthy Greeks, Armenians and foreign businesspeople. Now it is a lively place, with good shops, restaurants, bars and cinemas and well worth a quick explore. There's little in the way of sights as such, but look out for the evidence of its cosmopolitan Christian past in the nineteenth-century churches of Aya Eufemia (Greek Orthodox), Surp Takvor (Armenian Apostolic) and Surp Levon (Armenian Orthodox), all in the maze of narrow streets southeast of the waterfront. Further behind the waterfront is the home of Turkey's wealthiest football club, Fenerbahçe.

Eating

İstanbul is home to Turkey's best restaurants, including several that lavish time and skill on old Ottoman cuisine, and, thanks to the lengthy coastline, fish is a firm menu favourite. Snacks are ubiquitous, with kebab stands, pastry shops, fast-food outlets and cafés across the city catering to locals, workers and tourists alike.

Restaurants around tourist honey-pot Sultanahmet tend to be of poorer quality and are more expensive than elsewhere in the city.

Workers' **cafés** and *lokanta*s open as early as 6am and serve until 4pm; other cafés generally open daily between 9am and 9pm. **Restaurants** open for lunch and dinner, with last orders at 10 or 11pm, with more popular areas (such as Nevizade Sokak) and live music venues staying open until the early hours. In the more commercial districts, eateries follow the shops and close on a Sunday. **Credit cards** are widely accepted in all but the smallest restaurants. We've included telephone numbers for places where it's wise to **reserve a table**.

Cafés and restaurants are located on the relevant **maps**: Sultanahmet (p.95); Eminönü, the Grand Bazaar and around (including Kumkapı) on the Old City map (pp.90–91); Land Walls and around on the Land Walls map (p.115) and Galata, Beyoğlu and Taksim on the map on pp.120–121.

Cafés and budget eating

Today's İstanbul has a wide range of **cafés**, ranging from sophisticated continental cafés serving trendy coffees and imported alcoholic drinks to simple *lokanta*s dishing up cheap-and-cheerful stews from *bains-maris*.

Budget options include *lokanta*-style buffets (where what you see is what you get), and *pide* or *kebap salonu* for cheap and filling meat- and bread-based staples. Barrow-boys all over the city offer *simit*s and other bread-type snacks, fishermen in Karaköy and Eminönü serve dubious fish sandwiches off their boats, while sizzling tangles of sheep innards (*kokoreç*), stuffed mussels (*midye dolması*) and *pilaf* rice are sold from booths and pushcarts in the more salubrious areas. **Prices** vary depending on the establishment and location, but range from 0.50TL for a *simit* to 2TL or so for a takeaway chicken *durum* (slivers of döner chicken and salad in a flat-bread wrap). A café latte or similar, by contrast, will likely set you back at least 6TL.

Sultanahmet

Çiğdem Patisserie Divan Yolu Cad 62. For over forty years, the *Çiğdem* has been offering a good selection of both Turkish and non-Turkish pastries and sweets – plus fresh juices, coffee and tea. The *baklava* and *sutlaç* (rice pudding) are both reliable.

Doy Doy Sıfa Hamamı Sok 13. A backpacker's favourite with a well-deserved reputation for cheap and well-prepared kebabs, *pide* and *sulu yemek*. Try the unusual *fıstıklı fırın beyti* (oven-cooked kebab with pistachios). Dining is on four floors, including a roof terrace with great views of the harbour and a night-time light show over the Blue Mosque. No alcohol.

The Pudding Shop (Lale Restaurant) Divan You Cad 6. This Sultanahmet institution first opened its doors in 1957, and in the late 1960s became the meeting place for hippies and other travellers overlanding to India. Times have changed but *The Pudding Shop* is still dishing up its signature rice pudding along with a wide array of traditional Turkish dishes. The food's not outstanding, but it's well located right on Divan Yolu, serves alcohol and has a unique place in the history of baby-boom-generation travel.

Sofa Mimarmehmet Ağa Sok 32, off Akbeyik Cad. A world away from most of the places on Akbeyik Cad, this casual and relaxing place is run by the laid-back bearded Sayfullah (also the chef). It serves up a good mix of Western grub such as pizza, salad bowls and sandwiches, and Turkish fare, including *köfte*, kebab and grilled fish. Mains from 8–18TL. There's a happy hour, outside of which small beers go for 5TL – not the cheapest hereabouts but worth the extra for the ambience.

Tarihi Sultanahmet Köftecisi Divan Yolu 4. Longest established of the three *köfte* specialists at this end of Divan Yolu, and well frequented by Turkish celebrities (check out the framed newspaper clippings and thank-you letters on the tiled walls). A plate of tasty meatballs, pickled peppers, fresh bread and a spicy tomato-sauce dip will set you back a bargain 8TL.

North of Sultanahmet

Konyalı Ankara Cad 233, Sirkeci. Excellent pastry and cake shop opposite the train station, open by 7am and frequented by the quarter's office workers, who eat their breakfast standing at the marble-topped counters. An affordable 6TL for coffee and pastry. Closed Sun.

Grand Bazaar and around

Ağa Kapısı Nazir Izzet Efendi Sok 11. Tucked away on a dead-end street just below the Süleymaniye Camii and frequented mainly by local traders, young headscarved women students (it's unlicensed) and their lecturers, the Ağa Kapısı has the picture window beyond compare, giving a stunning panoramic view down over the Galata bridge, the mouth of the Golden Horn and the Bosphorus beyond. Try the *gözleme* (a kind of paratha stuffed with goat's cheese) and a glass of tea, traditional Turkish style, or splash out on Ottoman-style sherbet drinks.

Bedesten Café Cevahir Bedesteni 143–151, Kapalı Çarşı. This is the best café in the Grand Bazaar, an oasis of peace and tranquillity away from the main thoroughfares (look out for the two giant *alem* – the crescent- and star-topped finials that adorn mosque domes and minarets – and an even bigger portrait of Atatürk). The food is quality, with delicacies such as scrambled omelette *menemen* (8TL) or a full Turkish breakfast. Lunch mains include Turkish ravioli (*mantı*) in garlic and yoghurt sauce (13TL), and there's a great selection of cakes.

Subaşı Lokantasi Nuruosmaniye Cad 48, Çarşı Kapı. Behind Nuruosmaniye Camii, just inside the main entrance of the Grand Bazaar, this spit-and-sawdust place serves excellent lunchtime food to the market traders. Go early (noon–1pm), as it gets packed and food may run out. Mains are between 6 and 12TL a portion depending on the amount of meat in them – try the stuffed peppers or delicious *karnı yarık* (mince-topped aubergine).

Süleymaniye Erzincanlı Ali Baba Siddik Sami Onar Cad 11. In the gorgeous Süleymaniye Camii complex, with tables set out on the precinct between the mosque and *medrese* behind, this simple place serves up some of the tastiest beans in town (and they're not out of a can) for a bargain 5TL.

Beyoğlu

Kafe Ara Tosbağa Sokak8/A, off Yeniçarşı Cad, Beyoğlu. Great place tucked away just off Galatasaray Meydani, with a raft of tables out in the alley and a lovely dark-wood bistro-style interior lined with black-and-white photography by Ara Güler. A large, tulip-shaped glass of Turkish tea is a reasonable 2.5TL, big bowls of salad 10–15TL.

Kiva Han Galata Külesi Meyfanı 4. The emphasis at this small bistro, in the spruced-up square at the feet of the Galata Tower, is on Anatolian home-cooking, with speciality dishes from places as far apart as Trabzon and İzmir and Kars and Gazinatep. Veggie options from 6–10TL, meat-based mains 8–18TL.

Nizam Pide İstiklâl Cad, Büyükparmakkapı Sok. Offers excellent *pide*s (5TL and up). A second branch on Kalyoncu Kulluğu Cad, behind Nevizade Sok in the fish market, has framed articles from Turkish newspapers proclaiming it to be one of the top ten *pide* outlets in Turkey.

Pia İstiklâl Cad, Bekar Sok 7. Pleasant split-level café attracting a trendy clientele. It's a popular pre- and post-cinema hangout, with a good selection of English-language magazines to browse through, and decent pasta. Mains from 8–18TL.

Ramiz Köfteci İstiklâl Cad. Now a modish chain, the original place opened in provincial Akşehir back in 1928. It mixes the traditional (delicious *köfte*) with the contemporary (a serve-yourself salad bar). Salad plates are 5TL (40 varieties), *köfte* 7TL.

Saray İstiklâl Cad 102–104, Beyoğlu ☎ 0212/292 3434. Daily 8am–11pm. Established in 1935, the emphasis is on classic Turkish desserts such as *fırın sütlaç* (baked rice-pudding), *irmik helvası* (semolina with nuts) and baklava-type sweets, including wonderful *fıstık sarma* (pistachios packed in a syrup-drenched pastry roll) – cakes cost 5TL and up – though it also serves soups and grills.

Asian İstanbul

Baylan Muvakkithane Cad 19, Kadiköy. This famous patisserie is a must for nostalgia freaks, with its 1950s dark-wood and chrome frontage. The trellis-shaded garden area is popular with mums and their offspring, many of whom tuck into traditional ice creams or plates of pastel-coloured macaroons. Evidence of the Christian Armenian origins of the café are the liqueur chocolates on sale here.

Restaurants

Generally the Old City, including **Sultanahmet**, can't compare with the city's Beyoğlu entertainment hub for variety or quality, but there are a few exceptions. **Kumkapı**, south of Laleli, off the coast road, Kennedy Caddesi, boasts over fifty fish restaurants. It's a popular spot on a balmy summer evening, with candlelit tables spilling out on to the narrow, traffic-free streets. Restaurants in **Beyoğlu**, Galata and Taksim cater for theatre- and cinema-goers and young people filling up before a night out, as well as for those who want to spend all evening over a meal

▲ Outdoor restaurants along Nevizade Sokak

and a bottle of *rakı*. The most lively spot is undoubtedly **Nevizade Sokak** where restaurants serve *mezes*, kebabs and fish, accompanied by the sound of serenading street musicians. Otherwise you can try your luck in the cobbled streets around the ferry terminal in **Ortaköy**, where there are numerous trendy options rubbing shoulders with older, more traditional places, or across the Bosphorus in **Üsküdar** or **Kadıköy**.

Expect to pay more for extras, such as live music or to dine on a terrace overlooking the Bosphorus, while fish is always pricier than meat. **Main courses** start from 5TL at a cheap restaurant frequented by locals, though run up to 60TL or more at a swish restaurant with all the trimmings. **Set meals** at 50–70TL represent the best value, with a wide choice of *mezes* followed by a substantial main course, Turkish desserts and, usually, half a bottle of wine or *rakı*.

Sultanahmet

Balıkçı Sabahattin Seyit Hasan Koyu Sok 1, Cankurtan ☎ 0212/458 1824 Fish restaurant by Cankurtan station, five minutes' walk but a world away from the tourist joints up the hill. It's not cheap (it's the in-place for moneyed locals) but about as atmospheric as you can get, with vine-shaded tables set out in a narrow alley in summer, and a wood-floored dining room in an old wooden house in winter. Starters begin at 5TL, mains around 30TL and up, with every kind of locally caught fish on the menu.

Dubb İncili Çavuş Sok A funky spot with one Indian and two Turkish chefs serving up authentic Subcontinent dishes in a chic yet ethnic setting. The rooms, spread over several floors, are small, and there's a roof terrace and tables on the street. Delicious samosa and pakora go for 6–8TL, vegetable curries 15TL. Owner Mehmet and his

Japanese wife have now opened *Dubb Ethnic* on Mimar Ağa Cad 25, just off Akbıyık Cad, with ethnic cuisine from Turkey to Japan. It's superb food, immaculately presented, though not cheap (mains 20TL and up).

Kathisma Restaurant Yeni Akbıyık Cad 26. A bit pricier than the average on this very touristy street, but it's worth it for the well-prepared fish and meat dishes (or vegetarian options such as the spinach with pistachios), extensive wine list, excellent sweets and relaxed ambience of the bare-brick dining room, terrace – or tables on the street in summer.

Mosaik Restaurant Divan Yolu Cad, İncili Çavuş Sok 1. A well-established restaurant in a nicely restored, late nineteenth-century house, all wooden floors, kilims and subdued lighting. The tables out on the quiet side street are great in the warmer months, and there's a cosy downstairs bar (with small beers at 7TL). Serves a range of less common Turkish dishes, including Armenian, Greek and Kurdish specialities.

Grand Bazaar and around

🏃 **Hatay Sofrası** Ahmediye Cad 44/A, Aksaray. This spotless emporium may not suit those in search of a romantic dinner, but it does serve up some of the best and most unusual dishes in İstanbul. The hummus is served warm and liberally sprinkled with pistachios, and the dip *muhammara* (a spicy mix of breadcrumbs, walnuts, tomato and hot pepper) is delicious; the whole chicken roasted in salt (*tuzda tavuk*) needs to be ordered a couple of hours ahead. To get here take the tram to the Aksaray stop, from where it's a 500m walk along Vatan Cad.

Havuzlu Gani Çelebi Sok 3, Kapalı Çarşı. See map, p.108. Appealing Grand Bazaar restaurant, with Ottoman-style decor and white tablecloths on dark-wood tables laid out beneath a barrel-vaulted ceiling. Offers a good range of kebabs (the Iskender is recommended) and *hazır yemek* (steam-tray food) dishes. Brisk service, tasty food and reasonable prices (kebabs around 10TL). No alcohol.

Kör Agop Ördekli Bakkal 7–9 ☎0212/517 2334. Third-generation Armenian-owned fish restaurant, one of the oldest in town (since 1938) and hugely popular. Offers a standard selection of seasonal fish, *meze*s and salads, accompanied by a *fasil* band in the evening. Not cheap, at about 50TL a head, but a reliable night out.

Padaliza Off Yağlıkcılar Cad, Kapalı Çarşı. The best-value eating establishment in the Grand Bazaar, in a beautifully restored, exposed-brick, barrel-vaulted han. The waiters are white-shirted, black-tied and black-trousered but are friendly rather than formal, and dish up delicious stuffed vegetables (5TL) and a variety of kebabs, including *kağıt kebabı*, cubes of lamb and vegetables oven-baked in greased-paper for 10TL. There are some tables in the bustling alley outside.

North of Sultanahmet

🏃 **Hamdi Et Lokantası** Kalçin Sok 17 Tahmis Cad, Eminonu. The uninspiring facade of this five-floor joint fronting the square in Eminönü belies the quality of the food on offer inside. Tender, charcoal-grilled kebabs of various kinds form the mainstay of the menu, but it's also a good place to try *lahmacun*, a thin chapati-type bread smeared with spicy mincemeat. The clientele is a mix of local shopkeepers, businessmen and tourists – try to get a seat at the terrace, which offers great views over the Golden Horn. Mains from 10TL, though *lahmacun* is only 3TL (two suffice most people for a meal). No alcohol.

Levi Et Lokantası Tahmis Kalçın Sok, Çavuşbaşı Han 23/6. If you want to sample kosher Sephardic food, prepared mainly for İstanbul's Jewish community and a growing number of Jewish tourists, then this small restaurant, overlooking the the square to the west of the Mısır Çarşısı, is the place to come. Unusual dishes (mains 12–18TL) include *ağristada* (meatballs in béchamel sauce), *patlican reynada* (aubergine and mince fritters) and *armide de domat* (a purée of rice and tomatoes). The (Muslim) owner is very friendly. Wine served.

The Land Walls and around

🏃 **Asithane** Kariye Hotel, Kariye Camii Sok 18 ☎0212/534 8414. Garden-restaurant next door to the Kariye Museum. It's expensive, but you may feel like splashing out for good service and food in such a peaceful (if distant) location. The menu is described as nouvelle Ottoman cuisine – plenty of meat- and fruit-based stews from 13TL, or try the *hükar beğendi* (tender lamb with aubergine purée). Meals served on a lovely terrace swamped by roses, accompanied by classical Turkish music.

🏃 **Develi** Gümüş Yüzük Sok 7, Samatya. Out of the way but easy enough to reach on the suburban train line from either Sirkeci or Cankur-taran – get off at the Kocamustafapaşa stop. Posh (and unusually, licensed) joint serving up the best food from Gaziantep in Turkey's southeast. Great variety of kebabs from 12TL, but best are the starters (hummus with pastrami) and baklava-type desserts. Nice roof terrace overlooking a quaint square with the Sea of Marmara beyond.

Beyoğlu and Galata

Cezayir Hayriye Cad 16 ☎0212/245 9980. This stylish restaurant sprang up before the boom in minimalist chic, and is no worse for that. Set in a beautifully restored turn-of-the-twentieth-century townhouse, it is soothingly atmospheric, with stripped-pine doors, space-enhancing mirrors, chandeliers and other refreshingly anti-modernist features. The food (modern Mediterranean/Turkish) is generally good, too. Best bet for a reasonable night out is one of the fixed menus – the cheapest option is for two drinks to be included 45TL.

Degustasyon Sahne Sok 41, Balık Pazarı ☎0212/292 0667. Lively *meyhane* run by Nazim, Turkish TV's star chef. Dishes mix Turkish and inter-national flavours, such as the chicken soya stir-fry, and set menus are 24TL (meat) or 32TL (fish). Lesser-known Turkish wines available, plus a selection of imports from Bulgaria and Georgia. There are cheaper options in the surrounding fish market, but a lot of thought has been put into this menu.

Hacı Abdullah İstiklâl Cad, Sakızağacı Cad 17 ℡0212/293 8561. One of the best traditional restaurants in town sports a high-ceilinged atrium salon at the back. Main courses from 12TL – try the *hunkar beğendili kebap* (beef stew on a bed of aubergine and cheese purée) and the *ayva tatlı* (stewed quince with clotted cream). Strictly no alcohol served.

🏃 **İmroz** Nevizade Sok 24. This Greek-owned İstanbul institution has been dishing up reasonably priced fish dishes (mains around 14TL) since 1942. Spread over three floors, it is perhaps the liveliest of the fish restaurants in the Balık Pazarı area.

Nature and Peace İstiklâl Cad, Büyükparmakkapı Sok 21. Earthy vegetarian restaurant on a lively street, where specialities include green lentil balls, falafels and nettle soup, from around 7TL a dish. Some chicken dishes served, too; the only alcohol available is wine.

🏃 **Parentez** Sofyalı/Jurnal Sok 1, Tünel. Small bistro that stands out from the many decent (and trendy) eating places around here. The food is international in style, ingredients are top-notch and the preparation immaculate. Big salad bowls from 12TL, steaks, pastas etc more, a glass of decent wine a reasonable 8.5TL.

Rejans İstiklâl Cad, Emir Nevruz Sok 17 ℡0212/243 3882. This famous establishment was founded by White Russians in the 1930s and thrives on its nostalgic reputation. It's somewhat shabby and staid, but, considering the quality of the food, not too expensive. Main courses (barbecued salmon, grilled quail) start from 13TL, accompanied by the excellent lemon vodka. Lunches noon–2pm; dinner 7–10pm.

Zencefil Kurabiye Sok 3. The ever-changing menu includes vegetarian versions of various Turkish dishes from as little as 6TL plus some chicken and fish specials, great salads, home-made breads, herbal teas and local wines. Closed Sun.

Ortaköy

Banyan Salhane Sok 3, off Muallim Naci Cad. Asian cuisine is the theme here, everything from Indian to Vietnamese, which makes it stand out from most café-restaurants in the city. The views of Ortaköy mosque and the Bosphorus Bridge from the pretty terrace are stunning, but you pay for them, with most mains over 40TL.

House Café Salhane Sok 1, off Muallim Naci Cad. The food is largely aimed at young, affluent and Westernized Turks, with (admittedly upmarket) burgers and pizza a couple of menu staples – along with an expensive (40TL) Sunday brunch. Outfoor eating here has its charms, though, especially if you can grab one of the tables right on the edge of the Bosphorus. Now has branches near Tünel and on İstiklâl Cad.

Asian İstanbul

🏃 **Çiya Sofrası & Kebabçi** Güneşlibahçe Sok 43, Kadıköy A very well-regarded place on a pleasant pedestrianized street. "Çiya" means "mountain" in Kurdish, though the inspiration for the food here comes from many different corners of this vast country (try the *perde pilaf*, a delicately spiced and pan-crusted rice dish from the far southeast), though many stick to the excellent serve-yourself salad bar. The *Çiya Kebabçı* opposite boasts a huge oven ideal for *lahmacun* and the house Çiya kebab is tender meat coated with crushed pistachio and walnut, rolled in a thin unleavened bread.

Kanaat Selmanipak Cad 25, Üsküdar. One of the city's more famous *lokantas*, established in 1933, featuring copies of İznik-tile panels from the Selimiye Camii in Edirne and a copper chimney-piece. Meals are reasonably cheap at about 11TL a head; no alcohol served.

Yanyalı Fehmi Lokantası Yağlıka İsmail Sok 1, off Soğütlüçeşme Cad, Kadıköy. Established back in 1919 by refugees from Greece, this well-run place serves up some of the best food on the Asian side of the Bosphorus – and there's an incredible variety to choose from, with twenty types of soup alone, including non-standards such as okra or spinach. The *çömlek* kebab – meat, aubergine, beans, peppers, onion and garlic oven-cooked in a clay pot – is delicious (10TL). Desserts include *kabak tatlısı* (candied courgette), delicious when, as here, it's done well. No alcohol.

Nightlife

With such a youthful population, a booming economy and relentless Westernization, it is not surprising that İstanbul is establishing a major reputation for **clubbing**. The best **bars** and **clubs** are in Beyoğlu, Taksim, Ortaköy and the richer Bosphorus suburbs such as Kadıköy. For a more traditional night out, head to a **meyhane** (tavern), where a traditional *fasil* band might accompany your food

İstanbul listings

The monthly magazine *Time Out İstanbul* (ensure you buy the English-language version) is available from newsstands all over the city for 5TL. It is the best source of listings and features on what to do and see in the city. Other English-language publications include the bimonthly *İstanbul: The Guide*, available in hotel lobbies or bookshops for 5TL, also with listings and city features. *Cornucopia*, a glossy bimonthly covering the Ottoman arts scene, auctions, galleries and exhibitions, is available from bookshops that stock foreign newspapers and publications.

and bottle of *rakı*. Alternatively, try a **Türkü bar**, where you can drink and listen to the plaintive sounds of Anatolian folk music. Both *meyhanes* and Türkü bars are enjoying something of a revival of late, but if you want something more familiar there are countless café-bars and modern nightclubs as well.

Bars

İstanbul, away from conservative Islamic areas like Fatih and Eyüp, takes drinkers in its stride and you'll find bars ranging from the dangerously seedy to the chic and overpriced. **Sultanahmet**'s bars are dull in comparison to buzzing **Beyoğlu**, where drinking goes on well into the early hours. There's a variety of bars along the lively streets leading off **İstiklâl Caddesi**, at the Taksim Square end – from jazz joints to student-bars, sophisticated rooftop cafés to throbbing basement rock-bars. (All Beyoğlu bars are marked on the map on pp.120–121.) **Kadıköy** on the Asian side of the **Bosphorus**, boasts a number of drinking haunts. To reach Kadıköy's studenty/arty Kadife Sokak, walk or take a taxi from the Kadıköy ferry terminal south down Moda Caddesi, until it turns into Doktor Esat Işık Caddesi – Kadife Sokak is on the left.

The line between İstanbul's bars and cafés tends to blur, with most open during the day to serve food and coffee, becoming more alcoholic as the evening progresses. A cover charge is often introduced between 10pm and 2am if there is live music.

Sultanahmet

Cheers Akbıyık Cad 20. It's been around on busy Akbıyık Cad long enough to know what it's doing – knocking out reasonably priced beer to a mix of impecunious backpackers and strays from the street's posher establishments. It often gets lively, particularly when there's big-screen sport to be watched.

Cozy Pub Divan Yolu Cad 66. Modern, Western-style pub that appeals to tourists – hence the high prices. Outside tables are not a bad place to watch the world go by on the Divan Yolu Cad.

Beyoğlu

Badehane General Yazgan Sok 5. If you're not in the big-money, rooftop-drinking league, this is one of the best places in Beyoğlu. Small and cosy in winter, it spills out onto the alley in a big way in the summer. Crowded with students and alternative types, it serves cheap beer; people-watching and occasional live bands (usually winter only) provide the entertainment.

James Joyce Irish Pub Balo Sok 26. Housed in a wonderfully ornate nineteenth-century apartment block, the focal point is the lively pub, but this is a rambling place with rooms for regular live acts, internet access etc.

Leb-i-Derya Kumbaracı Yokuşu 115/7. A great place for an early-evening (or early-morning) drink, with fabulous Bosphorus views and chilled-out sounds. There's also a decent food menu if you're peckish – but it's not cheap (11TL a small beer) and you may be turned away if you look scruffy.

Pano Şaraphanesi İstiklâl Cad, Hamalbaşı Cad 26, Galatasaray. Beautifully restored century-old Greek wine bar, on the opposite corner to the British Consulate. Beer, local wine and good-value food available (*meze* 3.5TL, pasta dishes 9TL and steaks 16TL). The owners also run *Cumhuriyet Meyhane*, another historical drinking den, just round the corner in the Fish Market.

Pasific Sofyalı Sok. Small, friendly bar with a good selection of rock music and well-priced beer

(5TL for draught). Also does shots for 4TL if that's your thing. It's a struggle to find a seat on the alleyway tables in summer, though the *Kino Garden* next door is run jointly with *Pasific* and has a garden out back.

Asian İstanbul

Isis Kadife Sok 26, Caferağa Mah. Kadıköy three-storey townhouse that's a café by day and bar-disco at night. Cutting-edge music and good food, plus a garden open during the summer months.

Karaga Kadife Sok 16, Kadıköy. Self-consciously cool venue on the trendiest street in Asian İstanbul, this grungy/arty place is set in a tall, narrow nineteenth-century townhouse. Part pub (the lower floors) and part art gallery (top floor), it also has a large, pleasant garden out back. Beer is cheap (6TL) for a big Efes, and there's a reasonable snack-type menu.

Clubs and live music

İstanbul's best clubs are bang up to date in terms of design, lighting and atmosphere, while **live music** – jazz, rock, alternative, blues, R&B and even reggae – is plentiful around the backstreets of Beyoğlu. Expect to spend no less than you would in London, New York or Sydney on a night out. Most places have entry charges (anything from 10TL to 60TL) and tend to be open from around 9pm until 2 or 4am.

Local and visiting foreign bands also play at a welter of annual **festivals** – including two jazz festivals, a rock festival, an international music festival, plus separate dance and techno and blues events. See the festival calendar on p.138 for more details.

Beyoğlu and around

Babylon Şehbender Sok 3, Asmalımescit ☎0212/292 7368, ⊕www.babylon-ist.com. Tues–Thurs 9.30pm–2am, Fri & Sat 10pm–3am. Set in a modest-sized but atmospheric bare-brick vault, this is İstanbul's premier live music club, with a regular programme of local and foreign groups playing jazz, world and electronica. Drinks are expensive (10TL for a small beer, 12TL for a glass of local wine) and ticket prices vary wildly according to the act (booking office across the street daily noon–6pm, or from Biletix); performances usually start around 10pm. In summer, the action moves to the Aegean coast near İzmir.

Dogzstar Kartal Sok 3, İstiklâl Cad ☎0532/747 7494. Daily 6pm–5am. Run by dedicated alternative-music fanatic Taylan, who aims to support Turkish bands of all kinds – from psychobilly to electro-punk, and you can see the results at the regular live gigs (entry fee varies). Spread over three floors, with great views from the terrace, it's free midweek, with a 5TL cover charge at weekends.

Hayal Kahvesi, Büyükparmakkapı Sok 19. Attractive brick-and-wood joint with occasionally good blues and rock every night from 11pm. Fridays see ageing but deservedly popular Turkish rockers Bulutsuz Özlemi take the stage. In summer, the scene moves to Çubuklu Hayal Kahvesi in Burunbahçe on the Asian side of the Bosphorus.

Indigo Akarsu Sok 1/2, off İstiklâl Cad. The venue of choice for lovers of the latest in electronica, it's small, packed and intimate. Sees sets from both local and foreign DJs – naturally enough, the bigger names tend to play Fri and Sat. In summer, the beats skip to the resort of Bodrum.

Jazz Stop Tel Sok 2, off Büyükparmakkapı Sok. Stylish bare-brick basement club with steep cover charge – one of İstanbul's leading venues for jazz and flamenco. Owned by the band members of the local jazz group Moğollar, who perform regularly. Performances start about 11pm. Mon–Sat 4.30pm–4am.

Mojo İstiklâl Cad, Büyükparmakkapı Sok 26. Ultra-modern basement club, recently revamped, with live music most nights – best when the blues bands turn up. Has seen sets by Turkey's leading rock/punksters, Duman. Daily 9pm–4am.

Nardis Jazz Club Galata Kulesi Sok 14, Galata. Run by a couple of enthusiasts, this small, intimate venue is a great introduction to the city's jazz scene, with performances by both local and international artists. The emphasis is on the mainstream, but modern, fusion and ethnic get an airing from time to time. Advance booking recommended.

Peyote Kameriye Sok 4, Balık Pazarı. Daily 10pm–4am. This is the city's best place for alternative/indie types looking for an "underground" scene. The owners are in a band themselves, and they give stage space to upcoming rivals from across the metropolis. There's a lively roof terrace with an eclectic mix of music, live bands play on the second floor, whilst the first floor is given over to electronica. Beers are a reasonable 6TL and the (variable) entry charge not too steep.

Ortaköy

Crystal Muallim Naci Cad 65 ℡ 0212/229 7152. Thurs–Sat midnight–5.30am. The steep 35TL admission (Fri & Sat only) includes one free drink, but this is probably the best place for techno, house and other assorted dance sounds in the city, at least for the twenty- to thirty-something crowd who flock here – youngsters may well give the accolade to *Indigo* (see opposite). The well-scuffed dancefloor says it all about the quality of foreign and local DJs who spin their stuff here.

Reina Muallim Naci Cad 120. Summer drinking outside until dawn for the bright young things who manage to get through the door. There are dancefloors, video screens and bars all directly overlooking the Bosphorus, and overpriced sushi – early birds get 30 percent off drinks between 6 and 8pm. June–Sept only, daily 6pm–4am.

Gay bars and clubs

İstanbul is the country's **gay** capital, with the scene centred on Taksim and Beyoğlu. For information on the gay scene check out Ⓦwww.istanbulgay.com, which gives a run down of the best gay bars and clubs (including guided cruises of the best venues) and gay-friendly hotels, reviews the sauna cruising scene and has a section on lesbian İstanbul. Otherwise the weekly *Time Out İstanbul* reviews gay and lesbian venues.

Cafés

Sugar Café Sakalsalim Çıkmazı 7, off İstiklâl Cad, Beyoğlu. Low-key meeting and hangout joint off the busy main drag, somewhere to decide what you're going to do later on.

Bars and clubs

Bar Bahçe Soğancı Sok 7, off Sıraselviler Cad, Beyoğlu In the same building as *5.Kat* but on the first floor, this place has an excellent reputation amongst İstanbul's gay sophisticates. It's modestly sized, but there's a decent dancefloor, a couple of bars, good house music and regular parties and other events – with a mixed crowd of mainly affluent punters.

Love Dance Point Cumhuriyet Cad 349, Harbiye. Glitzy, hi-tech and spacious club opposite the Military Museum with free admission Wed, 25TL cover Fri & Sat including one drink. DJs spin a wide range of sounds, from techno to Turkish pop. A proper club rather than a glorified café/bar, it also holds regular parties.

Prive Tarlabasi Bul 28, Taksim. Daily 11pm–5am. Gay-only dance club, with a devoted following due to its reputation as a pick-up place. The mix of electro and Turkish music will appeal to most punters. Really gets going after 1am. Entry Fri & Sat only (20TL including a drink). This street has a bad reputation in the city – and not just amongst straights – so take care if you decide to venture out here.

Tek Yön Siraselviler Cad. Very popular, possibly because it's so mainstream, and plenty of foreigners get through the doors. Friendly staff who perform occasional drag shows.

Arts, entertainment and festivals

İstanbul hosts a decent variety of annual cultural **festivals** and matches other European cities for the breadth of its **arts scene**. State-subsidized theatre, opera and ballet make performances affordable for all and there's something going on almost every night at various venues around the city. Music features heavily over the summer months when international festivals draw musicians from all over the world.

Tickets for many cultural events, as well as sporting events, can be purchased online from **Biletix** (℡ 0216/556 9800, Ⓦwww.biletix.com.), whose website is in both Turkish and English. There are also many Biletix outlets around the city, the most useful of which is the Ada bookstore on İstiklâl Caddesi.

The most important modern art event in the city is the **International İstanbul Biennial**, organized by IKSV, the İstanbul Foundation for Culture and Arts (Ⓦwww.iksv.org). The biennials (held on odd-numbered years) are themed and use different venues across the city, from historic buildings such as the Topkapı Palace to urban-chic industrial warehouses.

Film

There are hundreds of **cinemas** (*sinema*) all over İstanbul showing mainly Hollywood releases with Turkish subtitles. Many of the modern complexes are situated in large shopping malls, with the best old-style cinemas in Beyoğlu, once the centre of domestic film production. Most still have a fifteen-minute coffee and cigarette interval. Tickets cost around 10TL, but most cinemas have one or more day(s) midweek where tickets are discounted. The annual **International Film Festival** (mid-April to May) takes place mainly at cinemas in Beyoğlu.

AFM Fitaş İstiklâl Cad 24–26, Beyoğlu ☎0212/292 1111, ⓦwww.afm.com.tr. A popular ten-screen cinema not far from Taksim Square, showing the newest films. The smartest of the cinemas in Beyoğlu, but lacking in character.
Alkazar İstiklâl Cad 179, Beyoğlu ☎0212/293 2466. Three screens on three floors, this former

music hall rivals the Emek as the most interesting place to watch a film in the city. Shows a mix of standard Hollywood fare and some art-house films if you're lucky.
Emek Yeşilçam Sok 5, İstiklâl Cad, Beyoğlu ☎0212/293 8439. This palatial auditorium (875 seats) built in the 1920s is a popular venue during the International Film Festival.

İstanbul's festivals

The annual festival calendar is pretty full – at least between April and October, when most of the best events take place. The highlights are detailed below; for more information, consult the city tourist offices or the İstanbul Foundation for Culture and Arts (see "Theatres and concert halls", opposite).

April

International Film Festival Turkish, European and Hollywood movies premiere at İstanbul's cinemas, mainly in Beyoğlu, plus the best of the non-English-speaking world's releases from the previous year and new prints of classic films – visiting celebrities add glitz and glamour. 2009 saw over 200 films screened. Midweek tickets are usually a bargain.

Tulip Festival Week-long festival honouring the national flower, including concerts, arts events and competitions at different locations around the city, and a final showing of the hundred best tulips. Over three million bulbs flower across the city, planted by the municipality.

May

Conquest Celebrations Week-long celebration of the Ottoman conquest of old Constantinople (May 29, 1453) – concerts by the Ottoman Mehter military band, fancy-dress processions and fireworks.

International Puppet Festival A celebration of Turkish Shadow Theatre, or *karagöz* – silent puppets perform behind a two-dimensional screen.

International Theatre Festival The year's best Turkish plays (both local avant-garde and established theatre groups) and performances by visiting foreign theatres. Biennial event (next up in 2010).

June/July

Efes Pilsen One Love Moderately alternative city-centre weekend-long festival (2009's was held at Santralistanbul) with plenty of DJ-led dance sets and performances from international bands such as Röyksopp and Klaxons, plus assorted home-grown acts.

The International Music Festival This hugely successful festival was launched in 1973 to celebrate Turkey's fifty years of independence and brings top-notch orchestras and soloists from all over the world to perform in such atmospheric venues as the church of Aya Irene.

Kanyon, Mars Kanyon Mall, Büydere Cad 185, Levent ☎ 0212/353 0814, ⓦ www.marssinema .com. Unsurprisingly given its location in this ultramodern shopping mall, the ticket prices are above average, but probably worth it if you want the comfiest seats and best picture and sound quality in town.

Şafak Yeniçeriler Cad, Çemberlitaş ☎ 0212/516 2660, ⓦ www.ozenfilm.com.tr. The closest cinema to Sultanahmet, buried in the bowels of a shopping centre, with seven screens showing the latest Western and Turkish releases.

Theatres and concert halls

There are regular **classical music**, **ballet** and **opera** performances in İstanbul, held at Taksim's Atatürk Cultural Centre (under restoration at the time of writing) and at other venues across the city. The main annual event is the **International Music Festival** during June and July, which includes jazz, classical and world music concerts, as well as performances by the İstanbul State Symphony Orchestra. **Theatre** is popular, but it's mostly Turkish plays that are performed on the thirty or so stages in the city. Information on all music and theatre events, and on the

July/August
International Jazz Festival Two weeks of gigs and jamming sessions from world-class performers (with the definition of jazz stretched to include rock artists such as Lou Reed and Marianne Faithful).

Rumeli Hisarı Fortress Concerts Nightly summer concerts within the walls of this Ottoman fortification overlooking the Bosphorus – a varied programme from classical to rock.

Rock N' Coke ⓦ www.rockncoke.com. A weekend of Western and Turkish rock, in 2009 held on the Asian side of the Bosphorus at the Grand Prix circuit, İstanbul Park. Headliners in 2009 were the Prodigy and Linkin' Park.

September
Electronica Music Festival Venues change from year to year, as do sponsors and therefore names. In 2008 held in Parkorman, north of the city, with David Guetta and Dorfmeister.

İstanbul Arts Fair A week-long fair selling the work of some fifty or so İstanbul galleries and visiting foreign artists – paintings, sculptures, pottery and fabrics.

International İstanbul Biennial Multimedia contemporary arts festival that usually runs mid-September to the first week in November. Held odd years, next up in 2011.

October/Novemeber
Akbank International Jazz Festival Two-week festival concentrating on traditional jazz, with performers such as Dave Holland and Henry Threadgill. Events include film screenings, informal jamming sessions and drum workshops. Varied venues include the Byzantine church of Aya Irene and the Babylon Performance Centre in Beyoğlu.

Efes Pilsen Blues Festival Two-day late-night blues festival – a showcase of new local talent and famous foreign bands.

Filmeki Week-long film festival brings the pick of the crop from Cannes, Sundance and Berlin to İstanbul, hosted by the Emek Sineması.

various cultural festivals, is available from the **İstanbul Foundation for Culture and Arts**, İstiklâl Cad 146, Beyoğlu ☎0212/334 0700, ⊛www.iksv.org.

Atatürk Cultural Centre (AKM) Taksim Square; Theatre ☎0212/251 5600; Opera & Ballet ☎0212/243 2011; Symphony Orchestra ☎0212/243 1068. Multi-purpose venue shared by the Symphony Orchestra, State Theatre Company, and State Opera and Ballet. Leading venue during the various international festivals and has regular performances of classical music, opera and ballet.
Borusan Arts and Cultural Centre İstiklâl Cad 421, Tünel, Beyoğlu ☎0212/292 0655, ⊛www.borusansanat.com. Home to the Borusan Philharmonic Orchestra, one of Turkey's most successful private orchestras, which performs two monthly concerts (tickets 16–24TL). Also boasts one of the country's most extensive CD libraries.
Cemal Reşit Rey (CRR) Darülbedai Cad 1, Harbiye ☎0212/231 5497, ⊛www.crrks.org. Chamber music, classical, jazz and Turkish music, plus regular performances by visiting international orchestras. Venue for the International Music

Festival in June and the CRR Piano Festival in December. Daily performances (season Oct–May; 8–16TL) at 8pm; no credit cards.
Garajistanbul Kaymakan Reşit Bey Sok 11, off Yeniciler Cad, Beyoğlu ☎0212/244 4499, ⊛www.garajistanbul.com. Trendy, stripped-down performing-arts venue in a former underground car park just off Galatasaray Meydanı. This is as cutting-edge as it gets in İstanbul, with workshops, films and art projects, modern dance, theatre and other performances. With seating limited to 250, it's worth booking for most things. Closed July & Aug.
Süreyya Opera Bahariye Cad 29, Kadıköy ☎0216/346 1531, ⊛www.sureyyaoperasi.org. Set in a gorgeous, beautifully restored opera house built in 1924, this is a delightfully intimate place to watch opera, ballet and classical music and a rare oasis of culture on the Asian side of the Bosphorus. The season runs from October through to May. Tickets online from ⊛www.dobgm.gov.tr.

Turkish music and Cabaret

A night of **traditional Turkish music** in a friendly bar-restaurant is not to be missed. Most venues offer either a kind of Türkü (folk) music, usually played on a *bağlama* (long-necked stringed lute), or *fasıl*, generally played by gypsy bands and heavy on the violin with *ud* (lute), *darabuka* (drum) and maybe a *zurna* (clarinet). In bars featuring livelier music, you'll be expected to dance. As well as the places around Beyoğlu listed below, most of the fish restaurants in Kumkapı on the Sultanahmet side of the Horn have live *fasıl* music in the evenings. Expect to pay 50–80TL per head for a meal and a couple of drinks (sometimes included in the charge) in a restaurant that provides traditional live music.

Cabaret is probably the most expensive and least authentic way to develop a feel for the Orient. Stick to the more established venues, some of the best of which are reviewed below, otherwise you may be overcharged for anything you eat or drink and belly dancers expect to be given generous amounts of money (stuffed in their bras) by foreign tourists. Unless otherwise stated, the cabaret venues have daily **performances**, with dinner served at 7.45pm, the show running from 8.30pm to around midnight.

Fasıl and Türkü venues

Andon Sıraselviler Cad 89. Popular with İstanbul's fashionable set, with five overwhelming floors, each with their own personality: the first floor Pera bar has music mixed by the city's top DJs; the second floor has a Wine House with local and imported wines and cheese; live Turkish music and belly dancing features in the Müdavim Bar on the third floor while the fourth-floor *meyhane* features 101 types of *meze* accompanied by *fasıl* music; capping it all off are the stunning views from the fifth-floor roof-terrace restaurant. A fixed-price

menu of 60TL includes unlimited local alcoholic drinks; booking advised. On Fri and Sat, the 20TL admission charge includes one drink.
Kallavi Taverna Kurabiye Sok 16, Beyoğlu. Small, traditional restaurant, recently moved to this location. Fixed menu of 60TL includes 10 starters, 4 entrées, a main and fruit, plus unlimited local drinks. Live *fasıl* music most nights. It's very popular with the locals; there's another branch at Şefik Bey Sok, Kadıköy. Closed Sun.
Munzur Hasnün Galip Sok 9, off İstiklâl Cad. The Munzur mountains, away to the east in the

heartland of Turkey's Kurdish Alevî population (the Alevî have spawned the nation's best *bağlama* players), are the inspiration for this no-frills but lively Türkü bar. The food is OK, the drinks not too pricey, and when things get going there's plenty of linked bodies dancing around the tables.

Süheyla Kalyoncu Kulluğu Sok 45, off Nevizade Sok. Friendly late-night *lokanta* behind the Balik Pazarı. The house band members are a talented lot and have been knocking out both *fasil* and Türkü classics for the last fifteen years – the sets usually begin around 9.30pm. The fixed menu is a reasonable 70TL, including local drinks, and much merriment is assured when things get into full swing. Booking advised weekends.

Cabaret venues

Kervansaray Cumhuriyet Cad 30, Harbiye ☎0212/247 1630, ⓦ www.kervansaray.com.tr. Not far from the *Hilton*, it's a huge, pillared, chandeliered hall where you won't feel comfortable unless you dress up a bit. It's expensive at 105TL a head including food and two complimentary drinks (80TL without food), but the club has a good reputation for its floor show, which includes Oriental and folk dancers.

Orient House *President Hotel*, Tiyatro Cad 27, Beyazit ⓦ www.orienthouseistanbul.com. Traditional Turkish and folk music, plus belly dancing. A four-course meal with wine and show is 120TL a head (without food 80TL).

Turkish Cultural Dance Theatre Fırat Culture Centre, Divan Yolu, Sultanahmet. Presents Dances of Colours from ten different regions of Turkey, including belly dancing and Whirling Dervishes, in an a/c auditorium next to the Çemberlitaş tram stop. This is purely theatre, with no dinner or the other trappings of a club. Twice-weekly shows (30TL) on Tues at 5.15pm and Fri at 7pm.

Shopping

Shopping in İstanbul is an experience. Whether it is a pleasant one or not depends on your ability to ignore the hustlers when you're not in the mood, and to bargain hard when you are. Don't miss the Grand Bazaar (Kapalı Çarşı, see p.107), a hive of over four thousand little shops. Scattered around the city are a number of equally interesting shopping districts – **İstiklâl Caddesi** for clothes, **Nişantaşı** for upmarket international fashion; and the Spice Bazaar (Mısır Çarşısı) for spices and sweets. Out of the centre, **shopping malls** have taken off in a big way, good for homeware and clothes, and thankfully prices are fixed.

Opening hours for most shops are Monday to Saturday 10am to 7pm, though the modern shopping malls stay open daily until 10pm. Supermarkets and hypermarkets open 9am to 10pm every day but smaller food shops close much earlier. The covered bazaar opens Monday to Saturday 9am to 7pm and is credit-card friendly, as are all shops except the smallest of grocers (*bakals*) or kiosks.

Antiques and bric-a-brac

If you're expecting to find bargain **antiques**, you'll probably be disappointed – the average Istanbullu may care little for the old and worn, but in a city of over 15 million those that do are enough to ensure buoyant prices. Bear in mind that you're supposed to have clearance from the Museums Directorate to take anything out of the country that's over one hundred years old (see p.62). The best place for twentieth-century items up to 1980s retro stuff are the streets leading down from İstiklâl Caddesi in Çukurcuma.

Atrium Tünel Geçiti 7, İs Han building, off İstiklâl Cad, Beyoğlu. Pricier than the places down in Çukurcuma but with a good selection of miniatures, ceramics, maps and prints.

Kato Export Halıcılar Cad 55, Kapalı Çarşı. Ottoman copper and Byzantine icons from the eighteenth and nineteenth centuries.

Levant Corner of Ağa Hamam Cad & Turancıbaşı Cad, off İstiklâl Cad, Beyoğlu. Eclectic range of wares in a funky shop occupying a nice corner plot where Turnacabaşı Cad becomes Ağ a Hamam Cad. From Greek Orthodox icons to 1950s tin toys and Erickson phones to kitsch figurines.

Leyla Altıpatlar Sok 10, Çukurcuma. This well-established shop stocks all manner of antique clothing, from the late nineteenth century to the 1960s, plus all sorts of cloth-related items – including embroidered cushions and throws – collected by enthusiast Leyla Seyhanlı.
Müstamel Eşya Evi Turancıbaşı Cad 38/1, off İstiklâl Cad, Beyoğlu. Spread over two floors, this

retro-orientated shop run by friendly, architect-trained Aslıhan Kendiroğlu, concentrates on the 1950s to the 1970s, from bakelite phones to chrome light-fixtures and Furniture to clothes.
Selim Mumcu Yenicarşı Cad 7/C, off İstiklâl Cad, Beyoğlu. Mainly secondhand books, but also does a nice line in tin toys and old (1960s and onwards) cinema posters.

Books, maps and prints

The most traditional place for books in the city is **Sahaflar Çarşısı** (old book market) at Beyazit, between the Grand Bazaar and Beyazit Camii, which stocks numerous new titles on both İstanbul and Turkey in general – in English – as well as some secondhand books. For the widest range of books **Beyoğlu** is the best bet, either on or just off İstiklâl Caddesi; there are also a number of secondhand booksellers around here.

Galeri Kayseri Divan Yolu Cad 58, Sultanahmet. The biggest distributor of English-language books in Turkey, with a vast range of books on Ottoman history and all other imaginable Turkish topics.
Greenhouse Bookshop Café Moda Cad 28, Kadıköy. Best bookshop on the Asian shore, managed by an English woman and stocking an excellent range of books in English, including an extensive children's department.
Homer Yeni Çarşşı Cad 28, Beyoğlu. A wonderful selection of anything archeological, historical and

cultural written on Turkey, and has even been known to stock the odd *Rough Guide*.
Pandora İstiklâl Cad, Büyükparmakkapı Sok 3, Beyoğlu. Excellent selection of foreign-language books on three storeys; carries some gay literature and will order books on request.
Robinson Crusoe İstiklâl Cad 389, Tünel, Beyoğlu. Reasonably priced, extensive collection of English-, French-, and German-language books, and a number of guides and maps.

Clothes

Many Western high-street stores produce their clothes in Turkey, and a number of outlets across the city specialize in seconds and production overruns at bargain prices. **Fakes** abound, so check thoroughly before purchasing. The best places to look are the arcades off İstiklâl Caddesi. **Turkish stores** (with multiple branches) to watch out for include: Beymen, Damat Tween, Homestore, Karaca, La Luna, Mudo City, Mudo, and Yargıcı. Vakko is one of the most reputable fashion chains in İstanbul; Vakkorama is its youth-market offshoot.

Bargain clothes

Atlas Pasajı Off İstiklâl Cad 209, Beyoğlu. This trendy and historic arcade behind the Atlas Cinema has bargain clothing – plus a number of alternative/street-style clothes outlets, funky jewellery shops, piercing places and CD/DVD shops, plus an amazing selection of original film posters in a couple of the basement stores.
Beyoz İş Merkezi İstiklâl Cad 331–369. Three floors of bargain end-of-line and seconds clothing, with the odd genuine bargain for the persistent.
Terkoz Çıkmaz Beyoğlu. A side street off İstiklâl Cad; next to the Paşabahçe glass store, down towards Tünel. Open daily and crammed with stalls selling overruns bearing British, French and German high-street names.

High-street and designer clothes

Beyman Akmerkez Shopping Mall, Etiler. Quality chain store for tailored men and women's suits, dress shirts, silk ties and scarves and other accessories for the well-turned-out executive.
Crash Sahkulu Sok 1/A, off Galip Dede Cad, Galata Small alternative outlet in up-and-coming Galata, with a good range of individually designed ts, hoodies, shorts, etc – and some secondhand retro stuff as well
Mavi İstiklâl Cad 117, Beyoğlu; and in all shopping malls. Gap-inspired jeans label, good-quality denimwear, T-shirts (including a good-range of "cool" İstanbul designs), sweat tops and funky bags.

Roll Turnacıbaşı Sok 13/1, off İstiklâl Cad, Beyoğlu. Outlet of choice for indie types who want cutting-edge street fashion. Much of their output is generic, but look out for the range of tongue-in-cheek T's emblazoned with "legendary" Turkish cars such as the Murat 124 and the Anadol. Also stocks secondhand retro-style clothing.

Vakko İstiklâl Cad 123–125, Beyoğlu; Akmerkez Shopping Mall, Etiler, and other branches; ⓦwww.vakko.com.tr. Classy fifty-year-old Turkish fashion label renowned for its sense of style and use of fine fabrics. The clothes don't come cheap

though, and you have to dress up a bit simply to get in the flagship store on İstiklâl Cad where you may come under some scrutiny from the rather snooty assistants. Vakkorama is the younger version aimed at wealthy teenagers. At the **Vakko Sales Store**, at Seylülislam Hayri Cad in Eminönü, items can be picked up for a quarter of the regular price.

Yargıcı Akmerkez Shopping Mall, Etiler, and other branches. Turkey's answer to Marks & Spencers – well-made and reasonably priced clothing from work suits to sportswear and underwear.

Carpets and kilims

Turkish carpets and **kilims** are world famous, and with the best selection to be found in İstanbul, it's not surprising that buying one is high on many people's lists. For buying tips and background information see Basics p.60. The below dealers are all based in the Grand Bazaar (Mon–Sat 9am–7pm).

Adnan & Hasan Halıcılar Cad 89–92. A wide range of modern and antique kilims and carpets from a reputable dealership, established in 1978. Ushak and Hereke carpets vie for shop space with Anatolian and Caucasian kilims.

Ethnicon Takkeciler Sok 58–60. Fixed-prices for kilims made in the traditional way (with natural dyes and no child labour) but with contemporary (often large, geometric blocks of colour) styling.

Galeri Şirvan Halıcılar Cad 50–54. Internationally known dealer Erol Kazancı specializes in older pieces, so don't expect anything cheap, but he does have a good reputation and also stocks some modern stuff.

Şişko Osman Zincirli Han. Arguably the most knowledgeable dealer in the Grand Bazaar, reputable Şişko ("Fat") Osman's family origins are in the east of Turkey, but he has been flogging top-quality rugs to all-comers (including the rich and famous) here for many years. Over sixty percent of his clients are Turks, which gives some idea of the quality of the (mainly) dowry pieces on offer here. His kilims range from €400–€2500 and carpets €500–2500 – excluding the more expensive genuine period pieces, some dating back to the eighteenth century, stocked in one of his four adjacent shops.

Food and spices

İstanbul is a great place to stock up on **herbs** and **spices**, most obviously in the splendid Mısır Çarşısı (Spice Bazaar). **Dried fruits** are also great value and delicious (see also p.62). Two specialities to look out for are *nar ekşisi*, the viscous pomegranate syrup used so liberally in many Turkish salads, sold in small bottles and *pekmez,* a sweet topping for yoghurt, usually made from either grapes or mulberries. **Turkish coffee** (*Türk kahvesi*) is about as traditional a Turkish product as you can get, though you'll need to buy a small pan known as a *kahve tenceresi* if you want to make it properly back home. Then, of course, in all its glutinous splendour, there is *lokum*; known in the west as Turkish Delight.

Ali Muhidin Haci BekirBalı Hamidiye Cad 83, Eminönü. Founded in 1777, this is the best place in the city to buy Turkish Delight (choose from over twenty varieties) and more unusual delicacies such as *fındıklı ezmesi* (hazelnut marzipan). The interior is wonderful, with an eye-catching array of sugary treats displayed on period wooden shelves and in glass-fronted cabinets.

Güllüoğlu Mumhane Cad 171, Karaköy. Arguably the best baklava in the city, delicious, buttery and

nut-filled. If you're looking to take some home, this is the place to buy it – not only is it the best, but it's not so syrupy as other brands and therefore less likely to leak over your hand-luggage.

Kurukahveci Mehmet Efendi Tamis Sok 66, Eminönü. There are always big queues outside this wonderful paean to the aromatic coffee bean. Started in 1871, it's now housed in a rare (for this city) and impressive Art Deco building to the west of the Spice Bazaar. Sells beans and powder for Turkish

and filter coffees, plus *sahlep*, the ground-orchid-root drink so popular in İstanbul in the winter.
Malatya Pazarı İstiklâl Cad 375, Beyoğlu. Malatya, in the far east of Turkey, is famous for its apricots, and you can sample the dried product here. Some come in gift packs stuffed with pistachios and walnuts, plus there's a wide range of nuts, sweets and spices.

Mısır Çarşısı Eminönü. To choose between the myriad purveyors of different spice, herb, herbal tea, Turkish Delight, nut and dried-fruit in the historic Spice Bazaar would be meaningless. Don't buy this kind of stuff in the Grand Bazaar, get it here – and don't be afraid to try a bit before parting with your cash.

Gifts and handicrafts

See Basics p.61 for a rundown of classic Turkish **souvenirs** worth getting hold of. In their own way just as authentic as the traditional Ottoman crafts are the modern twists on old designs sold in upmarket household goods stores such as Paşabahçe – especially glassware.

Abdulla Halıcılar Cad 53, Kapalı Çarşı. Restrained design is the key to this chic store selling handmade olive oil-based soaps, bath wraps (*peştemal*), bed linen, fluffy towels and the like – it tweaks traditional products to fit the tastes of the city's new elite and Western visitors alike.
Deli Kızın Yeri Halıcılar Cad 82, Kapalı Çarşı. In the Grand Bazaar, "Crazy Lady's Place" sells a vast amount of junk and collectibles, including limited-edition clothes, wall-hangings, scarves, Christmas decorations and unusual objects from Turkish artists. Linda is the "Crazy (American) Lady".
İstanbul Handicrafts Centre Kabasakal Cad 5, Sultanahmet. Restored *medrese* – an extension to

the *Yeşil Ev Hotel* – where artists and craftsmen keep alive traditional skills such as ebru marbling, calligraphy, lace-making and embroidery.
Mudo Pera İstiklâl 401, Beyoğlu. Worth going in just to see the gorgeous Art Nouveau interior, this long-established outlet has a range of upmarket giftware as well as quality clothing.
Paşabahçe İstiklâl 314, Beyoğlu. Sells a range of well-designed wares that add the finishing touches to the homes of many middle- and upper-class İstanbullus – from cruet sets to juicers, dinner services to clocks. Some of its glass products, made up the Bosphorus in its Beykoz factory, are worth looking out for.

Leather

For background on buying **leather** see p.61. Note that you run less chance of getting ripped off if you shop at one of the classier outlets listed below than in the Grand Bazaar.

Derimod Akmerkez Mall, Nisbetiye Cad, Etiler. Excellent-quality leather goods – coats, jackets, bags, shoes and other accessories. Classic rather than cutting-edge, but then most people don't want to make a short-lived fashion mistake at these prices.
Derishow Yeşil Çimen Sok 17, Beşiktaş. also at Akmerkez Mall; Bağdat Cad 381, Suadiye; and Akkavak Sok 18, Nişantaşı. Derishow is noted for its fine-quality leather goods.
Desa Abdi İpekçi Cad 5, also at İstiklâl Cad 140, Beyoğlu; and Akmerkez, Capitol and Galleria shopping malls. Top-quality Turkish designs.

Koç Deri Kürküçüler Cad 22/46, Kapalı Çarşı. Established in 1960, this specialist leather shop in the Grand Bazaar runs up stuff for the likes of Armani and Dolce&Gabbana. Needless to say, it's not cheap, but it does have a good reputation – your wallet may be considerably lighter after a purchase, but you won't have been "done".
Matraş Akmerkez Mall, Nisbetiye Cad, Etiler. Everything in leather from this quality Turkish store, including wallets, handbags, belts and briefcases.

Music and musical instruments

Turkish music aside, you'll find a good general selection of world music, classical, pop and jazz in the **music shops** listed below and in the many outlets on İstiklâl Caddesi and in the shopping malls. International CDs are often pricier than elsewhere in Europe, as there's no real discounting, but Turkish CDs are considerably cheaper. Traditional musical instruments are on sale in the Grand Bazaar, though prices are much better at any one of the myriad instrument shops on and around Galipdede Caddesi, near the upper Tünel station in Beyoğlu.

D & R Kanyon Mall. Chain that stocks a decent range of traditional and contemporary Turkish sounds, as well as foreign CDs, DVDs, computer accessories, books, magazines and games. Other branches across the city.
Lale Plak Galipdede Cad 1, Tünel, Beyoğlu. Funky old-style music store, the best place for traditional Turkish music CDs but even more so for jazz. The

staff know their stuff – aided, no doubt, by the continuity of a business that's been going for nigh on fifty years.
Naturel Müzik Galipdede Cad 103/B, Beyoğlu. A good choice on "music alley", stocked with reasonably priced quality guitars, *bağlama*, *saz*, *ud*, *darasbuka* and other traditional Turkish instruments.

Shopping malls

Looked at in a positive way, an American-style **mall** is just a modern version of a bazaar – and whilst their food courts may boast a *McDonald's* or *Burger King*, there are far more outlets knocking out traditional Turkish fare such as *pide*, *lahmacun* and *köfte*.

Cevahir Büyükdere Cad 22, Şişli. Conveniently located close to Levent metro, this is said to be the largest mall in Europe. Set over six storeys, it's very popular with Istanbullus, and boasts the inevitable multiplex.
City's Mall Teşvikiye Cad 162, Nişantaşı. Upmarket addition to the city's mall scene, well designed, with sleek Art Deco lines. It's exclusive and mainly fashion-orientated – think Louis Vuitton,

Dolce&Gabbana, Paul Gaultier and the like. There's an attached luxury multi-screen cinema and a few posh eateries.
Kanyon Büyükdere Cad 185, Levent. Take the metro to Levent for this "open air" canyon-shaped, four-storey, state-of-the-art shopping mall. Features most popular Western consumer chains and has an extremely plush cinema.

Street markets

For a lively atmosphere it's worth heading out to one of the city's famous **street markets**. Most now concentrate on fresh fruit, vegetables, olives, cheese and other foodstuffs – along with cheap (often fake designer-ware) clothing and household essentials.

Çarşamba Pazarı Fatih. Held every Wednesday and occupying the narrow streets close to Fatih Cami, this is the most authentic of the city's markets, but better for fruit, vegetables and the like than bargain clothing.
Örtaköy On the waterfront, next to the ferry terminal. The daily market sells mainly arty crafts and upmarket souvenirs, though there are some

antiques and retro items to be found. The best day to go is Sunday.
Salı Pazarı Kadıköy. Held on Tuesdays, Fridays and Sundays, this large market has the typical mix of fresh produce and cheap clothing, with Sundays seeing the stallholders knocking out bric-a-brac and antiques.

Listings

Airlines Most airlines have their offices around Taksim Square, Elmadağ and the business districts of Şişli/Levent further north. THY (Turkish Airlines; ☎444 0849, ⊕www.turkishairlines.com), is the semi-privatized state carrier offering the widest range of domestic and international flights. Anadolujet (☎444 2538, ⊕www.anadolujet.com.tr), Atlas Jet (☎444 3387, ⊕www.atlasjet.com),

Pegasus Airlines (☎444 0737, ⊕www.flypgs.com), Onur Air (☎0212/233 3800, ⊕www.onurair.com.tr) and Sunexpress (☎444 0797, ⊕www.sune xpresss.com) also run domestic flights (see "Travel details", p.154), Pegasus and Sunexpress also have some international flights. For international services, contact: Air France ☎0212/310 1919; Alitalia ☎0212/315 1900; Balkan Bulgarian Airlines

℡0212/245 2456; British Airways ℡0212/317 6600; El-Al ℡0212/246 5303; Emirates Airlines ℡0212/315 4545; KLM ℡0212/310 1900; Kuwait Airlines ℡0212/240 4081; Lufthansa ℡0212/315 3434; Northern Cyprus–Turkish Airlines ℡0212/274 6932; Olympic Airways ℡0212/247 3701; Qantas ℡0212/240 3532; Singapore Airlines ℡0212/232 3706; Swiss ℡0212/349 9900.

Airport Atatürk airport (℡0212/465 5555, ⓦwww .ataturkairport.com): Havaş (℡0212/465 4700) runs buses to the airport from Cumhuriyet Cad, Taksim, near the THY office, picking up at Tepebaşı and Aksaray; departures every 30min on the hour (daily 4am–1am; 10TL), journey time 30–40min, depending on traffic. Sabiha Gökçen airport (℡0216/585 5000, ⓦwww.sgairport.com) has Havaş buses running hourly, on the hour, to Taksim from 4am–1am for 12TL, journey time around 1hr. A number of travel agents on Divan Yolu Cad, as well as most hotels in Sultanahmet, Beyoğlu and Taksim, can arrange an airport transfer.

Banks and exchange Exchange offices (*döviz*) around Eminönü, Sultanahmet and Taksim, and on most main city thoroughfares, change cash. Many ask for commission, but if you change a decent amount and ask they will usually do it for free; open daily from 9am to 8pm (sometimes later in peak season). There are also exchange offices at the airport (24hr), Esenler *otogar* (daily 8.30am–11pm) and Sirkeci station (daily 9am–5pm). Opening hours for banks are Mon–Fri 9am–12.30pm & 1.30–5pm, though the larger branches of Garanti Bankası stay open through lunch; major banks have ATMs, some of which also dispense euros. Bank rates are generally better than *döviz*, especially at the Ziraat Bankası.

Bus companies All the following are based at Esenler *otogar*. Barış (bay 37 ℡0212/658 0595), for northeast Anatolia; Has Diyarbakir (℡444 1121) for southeast Anatolia; Kamil Koç (bays 144–146 ℡0212/658 2000, ⓦwww.kamilkoc.com.tr), to Ankara and southern resorts; Mersin (bay 8 ℡0212/658 3535), for the east; Metro (bays 51–52 ℡444 3455, ⓦwww.metroturizm.com.tr) for the Black Sea coast; Göreme Turizm (℡0212/658 1213) Nevtur (℡444/5050) or Nevşehir Seyahat (℡444 5050), for Cappadocia; Özkaymak (℡0212/658 0475, ⓦwww.ozkaymak .com.tr) for Konya and the southwest Mediterranean; Pamukkale (bays 41–42 ℡0212/658 2222, ⓦwww.pammukkaleturizm.com.tr), to the west and southern coasts; Ulusoy (bay 127 ℡444 1818, ⓦwww.ulusoy.com.tr), to major cities and the Black Sea coast; Varan (bays 1–2 ℡444 8999, ⓦwww.varan.com.tr), for western and southern destinations including nonstop luxury services to

Ankara, İzmir and south-coast resorts. Also, see "Travel details" at the end of the chapter.

Car rental Avis, Atatürk airport ℡0212/465 3455, Sabiha Gökçen airport ℡0216/585 5154 and Abdülhakhamit Cad, İnal Apt 72/A, Elmadağ ℡0212/297 9610, ⓦwww.avis.com.tr; Europcar, Atatürk airport ℡0212/465 3695, and Topçu Cad 1, Taksim ℡0212/254 7710; Hertz, Atatürk airport ℡0212/465 5999, Sabiha Gökçen airport ℡0216/588 0141 or Ye dikuyular Cad 4/1, Elmadağ ℡0212/225 6404.

Consulates Australia, Asker Ocağı Cad 15, Elmadağ, Şişli ℡0212/243 1333; Canada, İstiklâl Cad 373/5 ℡0212/251 9838; New Zealand, Yesilçimen Sok 75, Ihlamur ℡0212/327 2211; South Africa (Honorary Consul) Alarko Centre, Musallim Naci Cad 113–115, Ortaköy ℡0212/260 378; UK, Meşrutiyet Cad 34, Tepebaşı, Beyoğlu ℡0212/293 7540; US Kaplıcalar Mevkii Sok 2, İstinye ℡0212/335 9000.

Dentists Alternatives to the practices in the German and American hospitals (see Hospitals below) both with English-speaking staff, are Prodent-Can Ergene, Valikonağı Cad 109/5, Nişantaşi ℡0212/230 4635 and Reha Sezgin, Halaskargazi Cad 48/9, Harbiye ℡0212/240 3322.

Emergencies Ambulance ℡112; Fire ℡110; Police ℡155.

Hamams Most central, and the most frequented by tourists, are the Çemberlitaş Hamam (see p.109) near the Grand Bazaar, the nearby Cağaloğlu Hamam) and the Galatasaray Hamam on Turnacıbaşı Sok, Beyoğlu (daily: men 8am–8pm, women 8am–8pm; bath 24TL, massage 13TL extra).

Hospitals The Taksim First Aid Hospital (Taksim İlkyardim Hastanesi) at Sıraselviler Cad 112, Taksim ℡0212/252 4300, is state-run and deals with emergencies only; patients are often referred on to one of the hospitals listed below. For emergencies, as well as regular doctor's appointments, private foreign hospitals are better, though more expensive than the state hospitals, which are understaffed and overcrowded. One of the city's best equipped is the American Hospital (Amerikan Hastanesi), Güzelbahçe Sok 20, Nişantaşı (℡0212/311 2000, ⓦwww.ameikanhastanesi.com.tr). The German Hospital, at Sıraselviler Cad 119, Taksim (℡0212/293 2150, ⓦwww.almanhastanesi.com .tr), also has a dental and eye clinic.

Internet access Many İstanbul hotels and hostels have wi-fi and/or an internet terminal for guests to use, plus there are internet cafés all over town. Well-located places include Otanik Internet Café, Alayköşkü Cad 2, Cağaloğlu (Sultanahmet) and Robin Hood, off İstiklâl Cad on Yeni Çarşı Cad 24 (Beyoğlu).

Left luggage Left-luggage offices (*Emanet* in Turkish) can be found at Atatürk airport (open 24hr, 15TL standard size bags, 20TL large bags), Esenler and Harem *otogar*s and Sirkeci and Haydarpaşa train stations also have left-luggage facilities.

Pharmacies Pharmacies (*Eczane*) are found everywhere and Turkish pharmacists are qualified to give injections, take blood pressure and treat minor wounds. In each İstanbul neighbourhood they take turns in providing a 24hr service called *Nöbetçi*. At night, the *Nöbetçi* rota is posted on the window of the other pharmacies.

Police Reports of theft or loss should be made to the Tourist Police, located in a prominent blue wooden building at Yerebatan Cad 6, Sultanahmet (℡0212/527 4503); there are English-speaking officers on the premises 24hr a day. Any commercial misdealings should be reported to the *Zabita* (market police) offices found all over town, including a handy one in Sultanahmet, at the far end of the Hippodrome.

Post offices The main post office (PTT) is on Büyük Posthane Cad in Sirkeci, not far from the train station (8.30am–5.30pm for full postal services, 24hr section for stamps and phone-calls). Other branch offices – including that at Cumhuriyet Cad in Taksim Square, are open daily 8.30am–12.30pm and 1.30–5pm. Smaller branch offices are usually open Mon–Fri 8am–3pm. Address poste restante (general delivery) mail to Büyük PTT, Büyük Posthane Cad, Sirkeci.

Swimming pools For a substantial fee (45TL up to well over a 100TL at weekends) you can use the pools in the major hotels including; *Ceylan Intercontinental* Asker Ocağı Cad 1, Taksim, which has the great advantage of being centrally located in Taksim, with a large, heated outdoor pool and pool bar. The *Cırağan Palace Hotel Kempinski* Cırağan Cad 32, Beşiktaş indoor and outdoor pools in one of the city's most expensive hotels. The *Enka Sports Club* Sadi Gülcelik Spor Merkezi, İstinye has a multi-purpose gym (and a swimming pool and tennis courts) but is inconveniently located in this Bosphorus suburb, the *Hilton* on Cumhuriyet Cad, Harbiye has a fitness centre as well, whilst the monstrous *Ritz Carlton* on Asker Ocağı Cad in Elmadağ has indoor and outdoor lap pools, and stunning views over the Bosphorus and the rest of the city.

Telephones İstanbul has two phone-number prefixes, one for Europe, one for Asia, which must be used when calling the opposite shore; Europe ℡0212, Asia ℡0216. Local and international calls can be made from any public booth, at the PTTs (post offices) or TT (Türk Telekom) centres. Useful clusters of booths can be found in Sultanahmet, Taksim Square and Sirkeci train station. Most accept "Smart" phonecards, which can be bought at PTT counters, newsagent kiosks and shops.

Travel agents Travel agents are concentrated along Divan Yolu Cad in Sultanahmet and Cumhuriyet Cad in Taksim. Most can book destinations anywhere in Turkey, and arrange hotel stays, car rental and transfers to the airport or bus station: try Pasifik, Divan Yolu Cad 34, (℡0212/512 3050, ⊚www.pasifiktravel.com) or, better, Turista Travel, Divan Yolu Cad 16, (℡0212/518 6570, ⊚www.turistatravel.com. For budget tours, bus tickets and backpacker travel, contact Backpackers Travel, Yeni Akbiyik Cad 22, Sultanahmet (℡0212/638 6343, ⊚www .backpackerstravel.com).

Along the Bosphorus

The 30km strait known as the **Bosphorus** divides Europe and Asia and connects the Marmara and Black seas, its width varying from 660m to 4.5km. Its name derives from the Greek myth of Io, lover of Zeus, whom the god transformed into a cow to conceal her from his jealous wife Hera. She plunged into the straits to escape a gadfly, hence Bosphorus, or "Ford of the Cow".

Around 80,000 cargo ships, oil tankers and ocean liners pass through the strait each year, while for residents and visitors alike the Bosphorus remains İstanbul's most important transport artery. The passenger ferries and sea-buses that weave their way up and down from shore to shore provide one of the city's real highlights: along the way are imperial palaces and ancient fortresses interspersed with small fishing villages and wooden *yalı*s (waterside mansions). Despite its pollution the Bosphorus is also full of fish – from swordfish to *hamsi* (a small fish belonging to the anchovy family).

It's possible to explore the Bosphorus by ferry and bus under your own steam (make sure you have an IDO ferry timetable and buy plenty of *jetonlar* for the ferries and buses in advance) but most people prefer the ease of the **Bosphorus Tour** (see p.88). To ensure a good outside seat in summer, arrive at least half an hour before departure.

The European shore

The **European shore** is very built-up to the second Bosphorus bridge. The villages turned sunburbs of Arnavutköy and Bebek, popular haunts of the rich, are pretty enough when viewed from a boat. Further north, the fish restaurants in the villages of Sariyer and Rumeli Kavağı make pleasant destinations for lunch or dinner. West of Sariyer is the Belgrade Forest, offering quiet, rural surroundings in İstanbul's nearest tract of woodland. There are several ferry options on the European side or catch the very useful **#25/E bus**, which runs from the Kabataş tram terminal along the coast to Rumeli Kavağı.

From Ortaköy the coast road runs north under the kilometre-long **Atatürk bridge**, completed in 1973. A couple of kilometres beyond it is **Arnavutköy**, famous for its line of *yalıs*, wooden waterfront mansions with their boat moorings carved out beneath them. A fifteen-minute walk further up the strait is affluent **BEBEK**. Both suburbs have a number of trendy eateries. If you arrive by boat, to the left of the jetty is Bebek's most famous building, the peeling, waterfront **Hıdıv Sarayı** (Khedive's Palace), an Art Nouveau-style mansion belonging to the Egyptian consulate.

A fifteen-minute walk along the promenade north of Bebek, is the impressive **fortress of Rumeli Hisarı** (Tues–Sun 9am–4.30pm; 3TL). Grander than its counterpart, Andalou Hisarı, across the strait, this Ottoman fortress was constructed in four months in 1452, before the Ottoman conquest of the city. It houses a small open-air theatre, providing a summer-evening venue for concerts and plays, particularly during the International Music Festival (see p.138). The fortress lies in the shadow of the second Bosphorus bridge, the **Fatih Sultan Mehmet bridge**. Completed in 1988, it's amongst the world's longest suspension bridges (1090m), and spans the Bosphorus at the point where King Darius of Persia crossed the straits by pontoon bridge in 512 BC.

From Emirgan to Rumeli Kavaği

EMIRGAN is notable for its fine park and the excellent **Sakip Sabancı Museum** (Sakip Sabancı Müzesi: Tues, Fri & Sun 10am–6pm, Wed 10am–10pm, Sat 10am–7pm; 10TL). Located in a beautifully restored 1920s villa just behind the waterfront, the museum boasts some exquisite examples of Ottoman calligraphy and hosts a varied and prestigious number of temporary exhibitions, which have included Picasso and Dali. A couple of kilometres further up the Bosphorus is swanky Yeniköy (a stop on the Bosphorus Tour), the most expensive place on the İstanbul Monopoly board, and Büyükdere, with public transport links to the Belgrade Forest. Also a stop on the Bosphorus Cruise is Sariyer, around 5km north of Yeniköy, worth visiting for the **Sadberk Hanım Museum**, Büyükdere Cad 27–29 (Sadberk Hanım Müzesi; daily except Wed 10am–5pm; 7TL), with its beautifully displayed assortment of archeological and ethnographical objects. It's 300m south of the Sariyer jetty; bus **#25/E** to Sariyer from Kabataş, the **#25/T** from Taksim and **#40/B** from Beşiktaş pass by.

The last village on the European Bosphorus shore is **RUMELI KAVAĞİ**, a 2km dolmuş or short ferry ride from Sariyer. Nicer than Sariyer, with more of a village feel, it's no more than a string of houses, with some simple **fish restaurants** clustered around its ferry terminal. The easiest way to get here is on the Bosphorus Tour, when restaurant owners expectantly await the arrival of the ferry. There is a local ferry connecting Rumeli Kavağı with Anadolu Kavağı on the opposite Asian shore, and with Sariyer.

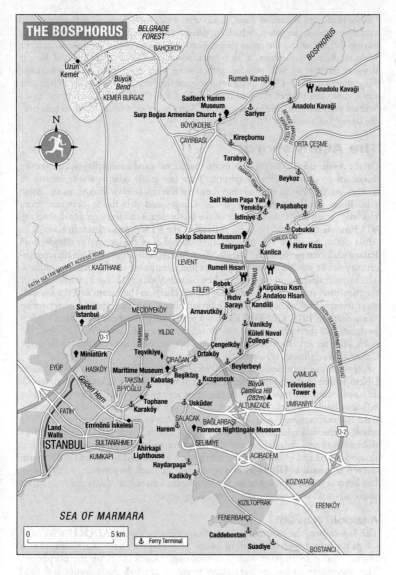

THE BOSPHORUS

BELGRADE FOREST

BAHÇEKÖY

BOSPHORUS

Üzün Kemer

Büyük Bend

KEMER BURGAZ

Rumeli Kavaği

Anadolu Kavaği

Anadolu Kavaği

Sadberk Hanım Museum

Surp Boğas Armenian Church

Sariyer

BÜYÜKDERE

ORTA ÇEŞME

ÇAYIRBAŞI

Kireçburnu

Tarabya

Beykoz

TARABYA-YENİKÖY CAD

PAŞABAHÇE CAD

Sait Halım Paşa Yalı

Yeniköy

Paşabahçe

İstiniye

Çubuklu

KANLICA CAD

Sakip Sabancı Museum

Emirgan

Hıdıv Kıssı

Kanlica

O-2

LEVENT

Rumeli Hısarı

FATİH SULTAN MEHMET ACCESS ROAD

KAĞITHANE

BOSPHORUS

Bebek

Küçüksu Kısrı

ETİLER

Hıdıv Sarayı

Andalou Hısarı

Kandilli

FATİH SULTAN MEHMET ACCESS ROAD

Santral İstanbul

MECİDİYEKÖY

Arnavutköy

Vaniköy

Küleli Naval College

O-1

YILDIZ

CUMHURİYET CAD

Çengelköy

Miniatürk

Teşvikiye

Ortaköy

EYÜP

HASKÖY

ÇIRAĞAN

Beylerbeyi

ÇAMLICA

Maritime Museum

Beşiktaş

Kuzguncuk

Büyük Çamlica Hill (282m)▲

Television Tower

Golden Horn

TAKSİM

Kabataş

ALTUNİZADE

UMRANİYE

BFYOĞLU

FATİH

Tophane

Karaköy

Üsküdar

O-2

Land Walls

Eminönü İskelesi

SALACAK

BAĞLARBAŞI

İSTANBUL

SULTANAHMET

Harem

Florence Nightingale Museum

ACIBADEM

KUMKAPI

Ahirkapi Lighthouse

SELİMİYE

Haydarpaşa

KOZYATAĞI

Kadiköy

ERENKÖY

KIZILTOPRAK

SEA OF MARMARA

FENERBAHÇE

0   5 km

Caddebostan

Ferry Terminal

Suadiye

BOSTANCI

Belgrade Forest

Several kilometres west of Sariyer, off the main road to Kılyos in the Istranca hills, **Belgrade Forest** (Belgrad Ormanları) was originally a hunting preserve of the Ottomans. The pine, oak and beech forest is now a popular retreat from the city. It's most easily reached by car though determined non-drivers can take a dolmuş from Sırmacılar Sok in the suburb of Büyükdere, on the Bosphorus, to the village of **BAHÇEKÖY**, on the east side of the forest. From here it is a 1.5km walk to **Büyük Bend reservoir** and the largest picnic ground in the forest, where there's a tea garden and an exercise area in the trees.

A sophisticated system of dams, reservoirs, water towers and aqueducts is still in evidence around the forest, which supplied İstanbul with most of its fresh water during Byzantine and Ottoman times. The most impressive of the aqueducts is the *Uzun* or **Long Aqueduct**, a 1km walk south of Büyük Bend beyond Kemer Burgaz. Its tiers of tall, pointed arches were built by Sinan for Süleyman the Magnificent in 1563. Close to the reservoir are the remains of Belgrade village; the name came about after the capture of Belgrade in 1521, when a community of Serbian well-diggers, prisoners of war of Süleyman, were settled here to take over the upkeep of the water-supply system.

The Asian shore

On the **Asian side** of the Bosphorus are vast suburbs and small villages, all virtually unknown to tourists. The Bosphorus Tour (see p.88) calls in at the suburb of Kanlıca on the way to its final stop Anadolu Kavağı, the last village on the Asian side. Buses run here (stopping at the villages and suburbs in between) from Üsküdar's main bus station in front of the İskele Camii and ferry terminal, with the #15 running from Üsküdar as far as Beykoz, the #15/A onto Anadolu Kavağı.

Just 500m north of the first (Atatürk) Bosphorus bridge, is the **Beylerbeyi Palace** (daily except Mon & Thurs 9.30am–5pm; guided tours 8TL), a nineteenth-century white marble summer residence and guesthouse of the Ottoman sultans. The interior decoration was designed by Sultan Abdülaziz himself, while some of the furniture, including the matching dining chairs in the harem and the *selâmlik*, was carved by Sultan Abdülhamid II during his six years of imprisonment here up to his death in 1918. **ÇENGELKÖY** is a pretty village, a short walk from Beylerbeyi, around the next bend of the Bosphorus. Its main landmark building, the *kuleli*, once served as a hospital under the direction of Florence Nightingale in the Crimean War, though it's currently closed to the public.

A ten-minute bus ride from Çengelköy is **Küçüksu Kasrı**, sometimes known as Göksu Palace (daily except Mon & Thurs 9.30am–4pm; 4TL), which takes both its names from the two nearby streams that empty into the Bosphorus. Built by Nikoğos Balian, son of the architect of Dolmabahçe, its exterior is highly ornate – the Rococo carving is best seen from the Bosphorus, the intended approach. The whole of the palace interior is decorated with lace and carpets from Hereke, lit by Bohemian crystal chandeliers and the floors are mahogany, inlaid with rose- and almond-wood and ebony. On the north bank of the Göksu stands the Ottoman fortress of **Anadolu Hisarı** (always open; free), beneath the towering Fatih bridge. Just beyond is **Kanlıca**, a stop on the Bosphorus Cruise but of interest only for its yoghurt, usually served sprinkled with icing sugar.

Anadolu Kavağı

The last call on the Bosphorus Tour from Eminönü is **ANADOLU KAVAĞİ**, where the boat stops for a couple of hours. The village has a distinct, if dilapidated, charm – balconied houses with boat-mooring stations overlook the Bosphorus. The waterfront and main street have some decent **fish restaurants** and food stands, which is just as well as the longest stop on the Bosphorus Cruise is here. Sprawling across an overgrown hilltop above the town, is the Byzantine **fortress** (always open; free) from which the village takes its name. It affords excellent views of the Bosphorus, and, approaching from above you'll see various Greek inscriptions and even the imperial logo of the Paleologus dynasty (a cross with the letter "b" in each corner, which stands for "King of Kings, who Kings it over Kings"). To get to the fortress, take Mirşah Hamam Sokak from the dock and walk uphill for half an hour. From the jetty back in the village, catch bus #15, then #15/A, back to Üsküdar.

The Princes' Islands

The romantic **Princes' Islands**, with their charming waterfront villages, *fin-de-siécle* architecture, wooded hills and rocky coves, have always been a favourite retreat from the mainland. Set in the Sea of Marmara between 15km and 30km southeast of the city, the islands are easily accessible by ferry from İstanbul and can be very crowded in summer, especially at weekends. Cars are banned on the islands, so **transport** is either by foot, phaeton (horse-drawn carriage), bike or donkey. Their proximity to the city make them an easy, enjoyable and very cheap day-trip, but if you do wish to overnight you'll find accommodation both over-priced and, especially on summer weekends, hard to come by.

Some history

The copper mines of Chalkitis (**Heybeliada**) were famed in antiquity, but though long since exhausted they are still visible near Çam Limanı. In the Byzantine era, numerous convents and monasteries were built on the islands, which soon became luxurious prisons for banished emperors, empresses and princes (often after they had been blinded). The islands were neglected by the conquering Ottoman Turks and became a place of refuge for Greek, Armenian and Jewish communities.

In 1846 a ferry service was established and the islands became popular with Pera's wealthy merchants and bankers, becoming İstanbul's favourite summer resort after the establishment of the Republic in 1923. Mosques began to appear in the villages, and hotels and apartment buildings soon followed. A Turkish naval college was established on Heybeliada and Atatürk's private yacht was moored here as a training ship.

Sivriada, uninhabited and unvisitable, gained public notoriety in 1911 when all the stray dogs in İstanbul were rounded up, shipped out there and left to starve; while **Yassıada** is best known as a prison island, used for the detention of political prisoners.

Getting there

IDO **ferries** run from the Adalar terminal in Kabataş, at the end of the tramline, to Büyükada, Heybeliada and Burgazada (summer 17 daily Mon–Sat from 6.50am, Sunday 17 daily from 7.30am; winter 9 daily Mon–Sat from 6.50am, 3TL o/w). Journey time to Büyükada around 1 hour 30 minutes. There is also a quicker **sea-bus** (*deniz otobüs*) service from Kabataş to Büyükada, Heybeliada and Burgazada (12 daily, much less frequently in winter; 25–45min; 7TL each way). Make sure you arrive early as queues can be massive.

Island hopping among the four larger islands – Büyükada, Heybeliada, Burgazada and Kınalıada – is easy, but check ferry times at the dock as the service is notoriously changeable. An *akbil* or a handful of *jeton*s makes island hopping easier.

Büyükada

Büyükada (the "Great Island", the original *Prinkipo*, or "Prince's Island", in Greek) is the largest of the islands and has long been inhabited by minorities. Leon Trotsky lived here from 1929 to 1933, spending most of his time at **İzzet Paşa Köşkü**, an attractive wooden mansion on Çankaya Caddesi. Large mansions like the one Trostsky lived in tend to have beautiful gardens full of magnolia, mimosa and jasmine, and in the surrounding pine forests myrtle, lilac and rock roses grow wild, so the scents of the island on a summer's evening are one of its most memorable aspects.

The island consists of two hills, both surmounted by monasteries. The southern-most, **Yüce Tepe**, is the location of the **Monastery of St George**, probably on the site of a twelfth-century building. In Byzantine times the monastery was used as an insane asylum and iron rings set into the floor of the chapels were used for restraining the inmates. Next to it is a decent **café** with superb views. To reach the monastery, take a phaeton to the small park on the main road that goes over the hill, from where a steep path leads up several hundred metres to the monastery. Alternatively, take a donkey from the stables at the bottom of this path.

The monastery on the northern hill, İsa Tepe, is a nineteenth-century building. Three families still inhabit the precincts and there are services in the chapel on Sundays. The adjacent **café** is famous for its wine; at one time this was produced at the monastery itself.

Practicalities

Ferries and **sea-buses** dock at two adjacent terminals on Büyük İskele Caddesi in Büyükada's main town, from where the main square and most of the hotels, restaurants and shops are just a short walk away. With motor vehicles banned, there are **bike rental** shops (15TL per day) everywhere. **Phaeton** (horse-and-carriage) tours (for up to four people; short tour 35TL, long tour 40TL) leave from the phaeton park off the main square on Isa Çelebi Sokak, 50m above the ferry terminal. **Donkey rides** (about 8TL per ride) up the hills start from a little park found just up Kadayoran Caddesi from the centre of town.

Accommodation is uniformly expensive, though the chance to stay in a grand restored mansion may be appealing. There are lots of good fish **restaurants** along the shore to the left of the ferry terminal. One street back from the shore road, İskele Caddesi has a selection of cheaper **cafés**, selling all the usual Turkish dishes.

Accommodation

Büyükada Princess İskele Meyd ☏216/382 1628, ⓦwww.buyukadaprincess.com. Offers neatly furnished a/c rooms with TV and minibar in a nineteenth-century building with pool. Prices may be negotiable, and drop anyway at the beginning and end of the season by up to twenty percent. ❺

Hotel Splendid Nisan Cad 23 ☏216/382 6950, ⓦwww.splendidhotel.com. Dating from 1908, and once host to Edward VIII and Wallis Simpson, it has serious *fin-de-siècle* grandeur, with cupolas, balconies, a good restaurant, excellent service and a garden with a swimming pool. ❼

Eating and drinking

Alibaba Restaurant Gülistan Cad 20. Period waterfront restaurant to the left of the jetty, frequented by Atatürk in the 1930s. It's a friendly place with white tablecloths. Farmed-fish meals from 15TL, sea-caught fish from 70TL a kilo, and the usual selection of *meze*. Alcohol served.

Yücetepe Kır Gazino Aya Yorgi, Yüce Tepe. Excellent restaurant with beautiful views from its location atop Yüce Tepe. The food is freshly prepared and hearty, with deep-fried, cheese-filled *börek* one of the highlights. The home-made chips are delicious. A satisfying lunch with a beer will set you back 15–20TL.

Heybeliada

Heybeliada, the "Island of the Saddlebag", has managed to retain much of its village identity. The main point of interest is the nineteenth-century, hill-top **Greek Orthodox School of Theology**, the Aya Triada Manastiri. It's a pleasant fifteen-minute walk through pine forest (or take a phaeton; see "Practicalities", below), but getting inside the compound is by appointment only (☏0216/351 8563; Mon–Sat 10am–noon & 2–4pm; free). You'll need to prove scholarship credentials to view the library of 230,000 books, including an important collection of Byzantine manuscripts. The building is set in beautiful grounds, and encloses a pretty, eight-hundred-year-old church, with a stunning gilt iconostasis.

Other buildings you might come across during a stroll around the island include the **Heybeliada Sanatorium**, a private home for TB sufferers located off Çam Limanı Yolu on the south side of the island. The **Naval High School** (Deniz Harp

Okulu), on the east side of the island, along the coast road from the main jetty, was originally the Naval War Academy, situated here since 1852. There is also a further Orthodox church, that of **Aya Nikola**, a prominent red-and-cream building with a curious clocktower, just behind the waterfront in the town centre.

There are several **beaches** around the island, though swimming in the polluted waters is at your own risk.

Practicalities

Ferries and **sea-buses** arrive at Heybeliada ferry terminal on the main quayside of Rıhtım Caddesi. Walking and cycling are good ways to enjoy Heybeliada, its pine forests and hills making for scenic rides and rambles; there's **bike rental** near the quayside at İmralı Sok 3. Phaeton **tours of the island** are also available (short tours for 25TL, longer ones 30TL).

The island is more low-key and **accommodation** is cheaper than neighbouring Büyükada, though booking in advance is recommended, particularly at weekends. The **restaurants** cater to locals all year round and consequently there are plenty to choose from – generally good, simple and cheap, offering standard *lokanta*, kebab and *pide* fare; most are situated on Ayyıldız Caddesi.

Merit Halki Palas Refah Şehitler Cad 88 ①0216/351 0025, ⑩www.merithotels.com. Nineteenth-century villa, restored in dubious taste by the Merit Hotel group as the only five-star hotel on the islands, incorporating gymnasium, jacuzzi and outdoor pool. ❼

Özdemir Pansiyon Ayyıldız Cad 41 ①0216/351 1866, ⑩www.adalar-ozdemirpansiyon.com. Cheapest option on the island, with tiny chalet-type en-suite rooms with a shower over squat loos, plus larger rooms in the main block. Both are comfortable enough. Note that prices rise by fifty percent on Friday and Saturday nights. No breakfast. ❹

Prenset Pansiyon Ayyıldız Cad 74 ①216/351 9388, ⑩www.halkiprenset.com. This converted apartment building with wood-trimmed exterior offers reasonable value, despite most rooms not having views. Friendly management, comfortable rooms with immaculate modern bathrooms, and central heating in winter. Prices, which include breakfast, rise fifty percent at weekends. ❻

Burgazada and Kınalıada

The other two islands served by public ferry are Burgazada and Kınalıada, both small and relatively unspoilt, though holiday homes now outnumber those of permanent residents. In winter the villages around their jetties are practically ghost towns.

Burgazada has a fascinating small **museum** (Tues–Fri 10am–noon & 2–5pm, Sat 10am–noon; free) at Burgaz Çayırı Sok 15, on the other side of the square from the church of St John the Baptist (the dome of which is the town's most prominent landmark). The museum is dedicated to the novelist **Sait Faik** (often described as the Turkish Mark Twain), who lived here, and the house has been so carefully preserved that you feel you're trespassing. In the writer's bedroom a pair of pyjamas is neatly folded on the bed, with a towel on the rack beside it. You get an immediate impression of the man, whose exceptional character is evidenced by the simple bohemian style of furnishings in his island home.

Kınalıada, "Henna Island", takes its name from the red colouring of its eastern cliffs; in Greek it was known as *Proti*, since it's the nearest of the islands to the mainland. Like Heybeliada, Kınalıada's history is notable for exiles, including Romanus IV Diogenes, deposed after his disastrous defeat at the Battle of Manzikert by the Selçuk Turks. Today, its population is seventy percent Armenian. The island is rather bare and barren and is probably the least impressive of all as it is covered in houses. However, it's a favourite for swimming and its beaches are less polluted by sewage than those of the other three islands.

Travel details

Buses

The main bus terminals are at **Esenler** on the European side, and **Harem** on the Asian side. See "Arrival" (p.81) for more information on each station and "Listings", p.146, for company contact details).

Black Sea coast (served by Ulusoy, Dağıştanlı, Metro, Birçik, Barış): Artvin (1 daily; 22hr); Hopa (3 daily; 19hr); Rize (4 daily; 19hr); Samsun (4 daily; 9hr); Trabzon (9 daily; 18hr).

Cappadocia (served by Göreme Turizm, NevTur and Nevşehir Seyahat): Avanos (5 daily; 11hr); Göreme (5 daily; 11hr); Nevşehir (5 daily; 11hr); Ürgüp (5 daily; 11hr 30min).

Eastern Turkey (served by Mersin): Antakya (2 daily; 17hr); Antep (4 daily; 20hr); Diyarbakır (3 daily; 19hr); Doğubeyazit (1 daily; 24hr); Erzurum (3 daily; 24hr); Gaziantep (several daily; 16hr); Konya (7 daily; 10hr); Mardin (1 daily; 22hr); Urfa (1 daily; 21hr).

Mediterranean and Aegean coasts (served by Varan, Ulusoy, Pamukkale, Kamil Koç): Adana (several daily; 14hr); Alanya (12 daily; 15hr); Antakya (2 daily; 17hr); Antalya (several in the evening from 6pm; 12hr); Ayvalık (hourly; 8hr); Bodrum (hourly; 12hr); Datça (1 daily; 17hr); Fethiye (3 daily in the evening; 14hr); İzmir (hourly; 10hr); Kuşadası (5 daily; 9hr); Marmaris (4 daily; 13hr); Side (several in the evening from 6pm; 14hr).

Western Turkey (served by Kamil Koç, Pamukkale, Varan, Uludar Hakiki Koç): Ankara (several hourly; 5-6hr); Bandırma (hourly; 5hr); Bursa (hourly; 3hr); Çanakkale (hourly; 5hr 30min); Denizli (daily; 10hr); Edirne (hourly; 2hr 30min); Kütahya (6 daily; 5hr 30min).

Out of Turkey Bulgaria (with Avar, Alpar and Metro): Sofya (several daily; 12hr). Georgia (Mahmudoğlu): Tiflis (daily; 30hr). Greece (with Ulusoy and Varan): Athens (2 weekly; 22hr 30min); Thessaloniki (2 weekly; 12hr 30min). Russia (with Ortadoğu): Moscow (2 weekly; 36hr).

Trains

Most train services to the rest of Turkey depart from **Haydarpaşa** (☎0216/336 4470 or 337 9911) on the Asian side. International trains to Europe, and local trains to Turkey's European peninsula, depart from **Sirkeci** (☎0212/527 0050 or 527 0051) on the European side.

Haydarpaşa station to: Adana (3 weekly; 18hr 50min); Afyon (3 daily; 13hr 30min); Ankara (3 daily; 8hr 35min; regular train to Eskişehir/fast train onto Ankara; 4 daily, 5hr 30min); Denizli (daily; 14hr 45min; Erzurum (daily; 31hr); Eskişehir (3 daily; 3hr 45min); Gaziantep (3 weekly; 38hr 40min); Halep (weekly; 17hr 20min, sleeper 95TL); Kars (daily; 36hr); Kayseri (3 weekly; 21hr); Konya (daily; 13hr); Tatvan (3 weekly; 39hr 45min); Tehran (weekly; 68hr; sleeper 99TL).

Sirkeci station to: Budapest (1 daily at 11am; 33hr); via Sofya (13hr 40min; Pullman 45TL, sleeper 63TL) and Bucharest (18hr; Pullman 83TL, sleeper 125TL) – change at Budapest for onward services to Prague, Venice and Vienna; Thessaloniki (1 daily at 9pm; 12hr 33min; sleeper €48; connections to Athens at 10.21pm; sleeper €73); Edirne (2 daily at 3.50pm; 6hr 10min).

Ferries

The main **ferry boat services** (☎0212/444 4436, ⊛www.ido.com.tr) are from Yenikapı (see p.84).

Yenikapı to: Bandırma (*hızlı feribotları* 4 daily, more at weekends; 2hr; many connect with the train to İzmir; *deniz otobüsleri* 2 weekly); Güzelyalı (for Bursa) (*hızlı feribotları* at least 2 daily; *deniz otobüsleri* 6 weekly mid-June to end Aug); Marmara islands (*deniz otobüsleri*; mid- to end June & early to mid-Sept 2 daily; July & Aug 6 daily; 2hr 35min to Marmara, 3hr to Avşa); Yalova (*hızlı feribotları* at least 7 daily; 1hr; *deniz otobüsleri* 1 daily).

Flights

Domestic flights depart from either Atatürk airport on the European side or (fewer) from Sabiha Gökcen airport on the Asian side. See "Listings", p.145, for airline contact details and "By plane" on p.40 for more information on the carriers.

Atatürk or Sabiha Gökçen airport to: Adana (at least 17 daily; 1hr 30min); Ankara (at least 25 daily; 1hr 5min); Antalya (at least 20 daily; 1hr 5min); Bodrum (at least 11 daily; 1hr); Dalaman (at least 6 daily; 1hr 10min); Denizli (2 daily; 1hr 10min); Diyarbakır (at least 10 daily; 1hr 45min); Erzurum (at least 4 daily; 1hr 50min); Gaziantep (at least 6 daily; 1hr 40min); İzmir (at least 18 daily; 1hr); Kars (direct 2 daily; 2hr; via Ankara 3 daily; at least 3hr 25min); Kayseri (at least 4 daily; 1hr 25min); Konya (3 daily; 1hr 15min); Malatya (at least 4 daily; 1hr 30min); Mardin (1 daily direct; 2hr; 3 daily via Ankara; at least 4hr 10min); Samsun (at least 6 daily; 1hr 15min); Şanlıurfa (2 daily; 1hr 50min); Trabzon (at least 10 daily; 1hr 35min); Van (at least 4 daily; 2hr 5min).

Around the Sea of Marmara

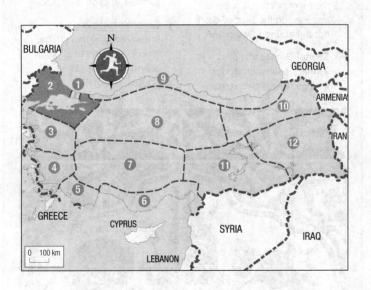

CHAPTER 2 # Highlights

* **Selimiye Camii** The master-piece of architect Mimar Sinan, considered to be the finest mosque in Turkey. See p.164

* **Kırkpınar festival** Wrestlers slicked down head-to-toe in olive oil battle it out every July in a 650-year-old tournament at Edirne. See p.166

* **Beaches at Kıyıköy** Despite their proximity to İstanbul, the most pristine, unspoilt beaches on the Black Sea, if not the country. See p.169

* **Termal** Get steamy at Termal's near-scalding hot springs, where people have taken the waters since Roman times. See p.173

* **İznik** Sleepy lakeside town nestled in an olive-mantled valley, famous for its sixteenth-century tile craft, now revived. See p.174

* **Bursa's Koza Hanı** Centrepiece of Bursa's covered bazaar, occupied by silk-breeders at the early summer auction. See p.183

* **Cumalıkızık** A finely preserved Ottoman village, its cobbled streets full of charmingly dilapidated houses. See p.189

▲ İznik tile design

Around the Sea of Marmara

Despite their proximity to İstanbul, the shores and hinterland of the **Sea of Marmara** are neglected by most foreign travellers. This is not altogether surprising – here Turkey is at its most Balkan and, at first glance, least exotic – but there are good reasons to visit: above all the exquisite early Ottoman centres of **Edirne** and **Bursa**. If your appetite is whetted for more of the same, historic **Lüleburgaz** and **İznik** make good postscripts to the former imperial capitals.

While most of the Thracian coast is disappointing, and the Marmara islands are of little interest with scrappy beaches, there are two bright spots – the beach-and-fortress town of **Kıyıköy** on the Black Sea, and the Saros Gulf resort of **Erikli**. To cross the Sea of Marmara, the port of **Tekirdağ** has potentially useful ferries to the southern shore, while **Gelibolu**, on the eponymous peninsula, is linked by ro-ro craft to Lapseki opposite.

For evocative inland scenery in the southern Marmara, **Uluabat Gölü** and **Manyas Gölü** are shallow lakes that support a dwindling fishing community and a bird sanctuary respectively. The **Uludağ** range above Bursa proves popular with skiers in winter and hikers in summer, while **Cumalıkızık** at the base of the mountain is one of the region's showcase villages.

Before the wars and population exchanges of the early twentieth century, much of the local population was Greek (or Bulgarian) Orthodox, with substantial Jewish and Armenian communities in all the larger towns. On the establishment of the Turkish Republic, massive immigration – both internal and from abroad – changed the mix. The result remains an ethnic stew that includes people of Çerkez (Circassian), Artvinli and Greek Muslim descent, as well as a large settled Romany population, but consists predominantly of **Pomak**, **Bosnian** and **Macedonian Muslims**, plus **Bulgarian Turks**. All these groups had, in fact, been trickling in for decades before 1923, as Austro-Hungarian or Orthodox nationalist victories in the Balkans made their previous homes inhospitable to Turks or Slavic Muslims. This trend was reinforced following the 1989 disturbances in Bulgaria, when hundreds of thousands of ethnic Turks fled to Turkey, though many of the new arrivals subsequently returned to post-Communist Bulgaria.

AROUND THE SEA OF MARMARA

0   50 km

N

Bolu & Ankara

BLACK SEA

istanbul

SEA OF MARMARA

THRACE

BULGARIA

GREECE

Sofia

Svilengrad

Malko Tărnovo (Bulgaria)

Kapikule

Kastaniés

Pazarkule

Edirne

Havsa

Kırklareli

Vize

Kıyıköy

Saray

Çerkezköy

Çorlu

Lüleburgaz

Babaeski

Uzunköprü

Tekirdağ

Kumbağ

Hasköy

Şarköy

Bolayır

Keşan

İpsala

Kışı

Pythio

Meriç Çayı

Ergene Çayı

Medidiye

Enikli

İbrice Limanı

Bakir Koyu

22-53

Gelibolu

Eceabat

Çanakkale

The Dardanelles

Saros Gulf

Gelibolu (Gallipoli) Peninsula

Istranca

E 80

E 84/D 110

D 100

E 87

D 555

E 84/D 110

Şile

E 800

E 80

Gebze

Pendik

Darıca

Hereke

Karamürsel

Topçular

Yalova

İzmit

Adapazarı (Sakarya)

Bilecik

İznik

İznik Gölü

Yenişehir

İnegöl

Orhangazi

Gemlik

Cumalıkızık

Uludağ (2543m)

Bursa

Mudanya

Kumyaka

Zeytinbağı (Trilye)

Gölyazı

Uluabat Gölü

Armutlu

Termal

Çınarcık

Marmara Adası

Kapıdağı Peninsula

BIRD PARADISE/ KUŞ CENNETİ

Bandırma

Erdek

Paşalimanı Adası

Avşa Adası

Gönen

Manyas Gölü

Gönen Çayı

Biga

Biga Çayı

Lapseki

E 90

E 90

Malko Tărnovo (Bulgaria)

Ankara & Kütahya

Balıkesir & İzmir

İzmir

Thessaloníki

Thrace

Thrace (Trakya in Turkish), the historic territory bounded by the rivers Danube and Nestos and the Aegean, Marmara and Black seas, is today divided roughly equally among Turkey, Greece and Bulgaria. In ancient times it was home to warlike tribes, whose bizarre religions and unruly habits presented a continual headache for rulers bent on subduing them. Contemporary life is decidedly less colourful, and until the late 1960s nearly all of Thrace was a military security zone, strictly off-limits to foreigners. Most of the area is now unrestricted, though all the towns remain heavily garrisoned.

The flatter terrain of southern Thrace has long since been denuded of trees, while much of the coast has fallen prey to estates of concrete holiday-homes – seasonal barbecue pads for İstanbul's workers. Inland is staunchly agricultural and in summer a sea of yellow sunflowers, grown for oil, spreads for miles. Further west, in the wetter lands around Üzünköprü, rice is predominant; to the north, the rolling Istranca hills with their dense forests of oak and conifers hide itinerant charcoal burners and myriad fish-farms raising rainbow trout. Across the whole region opencast mines extract sand and gravel from the prehistoric sea bed that once covered Thrace.

The E80 motorway from İstanbul to the main Thracian town of **Edirne** runs parallel to the route of the Roman and Byzantine **Via Egnatia**, which later became the medieval route to the Ottoman holdings in Europe, and is now the D100 highway. Many towns along this road began life as Roman staging posts, a role continued under the Ottomans who endowed all of them with a civic monument or two. Few spots have much to detain you, though keep an eye out for various fine **old bridges**, which like the road itself may be Ottoman reworkings of Roman or Byzantine originals. The best of these is the quadruple Büyükçekmece span, crossing the neck of an estuary west of İstanbul and built by the great architect Mimar Sinan in 1563.

Edirne

More than just the quintessential border town, **EDIRNE** – 230km northwest of İstanbul – is one of the best-preserved Ottoman cities and makes an impressive, easily digestible introduction to Turkey. It's a lively, attractive place of almost 140,000 people, occupying a rise overlooking the mingling of the Tunca, Arda and Meriç rivers, very near the Greek and Bulgarian frontiers. The life of the place is derived from day-tripping foreign shoppers, discerning tourists and students from the University of Thrace. **Downtown**, teeming bazaars and elegant domestic architecture vie for attention with a clutch of striking Ottoman monuments. The best of these, crowning the town's central hillock and sufficient reason alone for a visit, is the **Selimiye Camii**, masterpiece of the imperial architect Mimar Sinan.

Some history

There has always been a settlement of some kind at this strategic point and its military importance has destined it to be captured – and sometimes sacked for good measure – repeatedly over the centuries. Thracian Uscudama became Hellenistic Oresteia, but the city really entered history as **Hadrianopolis**, designated the capital of Roman Thrace by Emperor Hadrian. Under the Byzantines it retained its significance, not least as a forward base en route to the Balkans – or, more ominously from the Byzantine point of view, first stop on the way to attempts on the imperial capital itself. Unsuccessful besiegers of Constantinople habitually vented their frustration on Hadrianopolis as they retreated, and a handful of emperors met their end here in pitched battles with Thracian "barbarians" of one sort or another.

In 1361 Hadrianopolis surrendered to the besieging Murat I and the provisional **Ottoman capital** was effectively transferred here from Bursa. A century later, Mehmet the Conqueror trained his troops and tested his artillery here in preparation for the march on Constantinople; indeed the Ottoman court was not completely moved to the Bosphorus until 1458. Because of its excellent opportunities for hunting and falconry, Edirne, as the Turks renamed it, remained a favourite haunt of numerous sultans for three more centuries, earning the title *Der-I Saadet* or "Gate of Contentment" – during which there were enough victory celebrations, circumcision ceremonies and marriages to rival Constantinople.

Decline set in after a 1751 **earthquake**, while during each of the **Russo-Turkish wars** of 1829 and 1878–1879 the city was occupied and pillaged by Tsarist troops. Worse followed, when the Bulgarians (with Serbian aid) besieged Odrin – as they called, and still call, the city – for 143 days from November 3, 1912 before taking it, thus ending the First Balkan War. The Greeks, as one of the victorious World War I Allies, annexed "**Adrianópoli**" along with the rest of Turkish Thrace from 1920 to 1922 and Turkish sovereignty over the city was only

Thrace border crossings

The Turkish–Greek and Turkish–Bulgarian frontier posts nearest Edirne are **open 24 hours**. For EU nationals and citizens of the US, Canada, Australia and New Zealand, there are no restrictions on travel between Greece and Turkey, or Bulgaria and Turkey, and no advance visas are necessary. South Africans do not need an advance visa to enter Turkey, however they do to enter Greece and Bulgaria. The Bulgarian consulate at Talat Paşa Cad 31 (Mon–Fri 9am–noon; ☎0284/214 0617) in Edirne can issue tourist visas, though the Greek consulate in Edirne, Kocasinan Mahallesi, İkinci Sok 13 (☎0284/235 5804), is unlikely to be able to help. South African nationals should apply for a Schengen Zone visa for Greece in their home country before travelling.

Turkey–Bulgaria

The vast **Bulgarian–Turkish border** complex straddles the busy E80 expressway at **Kapıkule**, 18km northwest of Edirne (and 320km south of Sofia, Bulgaria's capital).

Minibuses from Edirne to Kapıkule (5TL) ply the route every thirty minutes from 6.30am to 9pm, leaving from stops along Londra Asfaltı near the tourist office, while a **taxi** will set you back 30TL. There are no facilities in the nearest Bulgarian village, Kapitan Andreevo, but two reasonable hotels in **Svilengrad**, the first proper town 9km beyond.

Balkan Express trains depart daily at 3am from Edirne, 4am from Kapıkule for Svilengrad, Sofia and Belgrade. The **Bosphor Express** (same train, different wagons) leaves Edirne and Kapıkule at the same time, bound for Veliko Türnovo, Bucharest and (with a change) Budapest. Expect an hour's delay near the frontier whilst Bulgarian customs officials comb the train.

Turkey–Greece

The Turkish frontier post of **Pazarkule**, separated from the Greek one at Kastaniés by a kilometre-wide no-man's-land, is 8km west of Edirne and 2km beyond the last Turkish village of **Karaağaç**.

confirmed by the 1923 **Treaty of Lausanne**. Bulgarian, Latin Catholic and Greek Orthodox churches remain, along with elegant houses and a ruined synagogue in the former Jewish quarter, as evidence of the pre-1912, multicultural city which was half Greek, Bulgarian, Armenian and Jewish.

Arrival and information

Buses from elsewhere in Turkey arrive at Edirne's **otogar**, just over 8km southeast of the centre; minibuses or urban bus #5 will drop you in the centre near the tourist office. The **train station**, a more likely entry point from abroad, is 4km out in the same direction; from here, infrequent city buses (#3), private minibuses or taxis head for the centre. If you're coming directly from the **Greek or Bulgarian highway border posts**, see "Thrace Border crossings", below. **Drivers** will find most of Edirne patrolled by wardens selling **parking** chits, with some of the only free spaces in the far west of the old quarter, Kaleiçi. Street spaces have a notional limit of three hours, so you may have to use off-street car parks.

The main **tourist office** is at Londra Asfaltı 76 (Mon–Fri 9am–5pm, may close later in summer; ℡0284/225 5260); there's also a booth at the Bulgarian (Kapıkule) frontier gate (daily 8.30am–5pm; ℡0284/238 2019). Both supply tourism ministry brochures and an excellent **map** of Edirne – the latter also sometimes stocked by local hotels.

AROUND THE SEA OF MARMARA | Edirne

Minibuses **to Karaağaç** depart regularly from behind the Rüstempaşa Kervansarayı, but you must walk the final 2km from Karaağaç to Pazarkule. If heavily laden, it's easier to take a taxi (€10/20TL) directly from Edirne **to Pazarkule**. Once through the Turkish post, you'll have to take a Greek taxi to the **Kastaniés** post, as you're not allowed to walk across; this applies coming from Greece too – budget €4/8TL per car for the one-kilometre gap. From Kastaniés, on the Greek side, three trains daily (5.58am, 11.40am, 5.56pm), and about as many buses, make the 2hr 30min run down to Alexandhroúpoli, the first major Greek city.

The main, far busier Turkish–Greek road crossing **between İpsala and Kípi** in Greece lies just off the E90/110 highway, 31km west of Keşan, itself 115km south of Edirne. The two posts here are open 24 hours, but as at Pazarkule–Kastaniés, there's a 500-metre-wide military zone that you're not allowed to cross on foot. During daylight hours at least, it's fairly easy to arrange a ride over in either direction with a truck, though drivers will routinely refuse to take you further. From Kípi, 1500m beyond the actual frontier, there are several buses daily further into Greece; at the Turkish immigration post there are only taxis available to take you the 8km to İpsala. You might very well forego all this, as there's a **through Greek bus service** between Keşan's *otogar* and Alexandhroúpoli in each direction run by the KTEL (Greek bus co-op) of Évrou province.

The sole **Turkey–Greece rail link** goes from **Uzunköprü** (whose station is 6km north of town at the end of the new bridge) to **Pýthio** just over the border formed by the **Meriç/Évros River** and its wetlands. The high-standard, sleeper-only **Dostluk/ Filia (Friendship) Express** leaves İstanbul at 9pm, passing through Uzunköprü station at 1.40am (passports are stamped here), continuing to Pýthio where there's a brief halt for passport controls before continuing to Alexandhroúpoli and Thessaloníki. There's also an evening/midnight express in the reverse direction, passing through Pýthio and Uzunköprü (passengers disembark to buy visas) just before 4am. The slower daytime train runs unreliably; when it does, it passes through Uzunköprü bound for Greece at about 2pm, in the opposite direction out of Greece at 4.40pm.

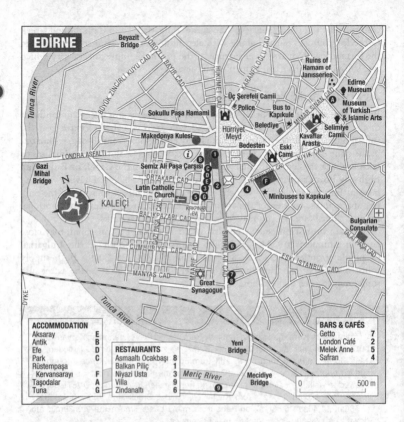

ACCOMMODATION
Aksaray	E
Antik	B
Efe	D
Park	C
Rüstempaşa Kervansarayı	F
Taşodalar	A
Tuna	G

RESTAURANTS
Asmaaltı Ocakbaşı	8
Balkan Piliç	1
Niyazi Usta	3
Villa	9
Zindanaltı	6

BARS & CAFÉS
Getto	7
London Café	2
Melek Anne	5
Safran	4

Edirne's main annual event is the three-day, early-summer **Kırkpınar festival** (see box, p.166), featuring oil-wrestling and preceded by a couple of days of folkloric exhibitions: for more information, visit the **Kırkpınar Evi** in the old town or check ⓦwww.kirkpinar.com or www.turkishwrestling.com.

Accommodation

Accommodation can be tight in Edirne. During the main Turkish holidays and the Kırkpınar festival you'll need to book at least a month in advance. Most places demand rack rates at or near coastal-resort prices, as Edirne's location brings it sufficient, comparatively undemanding, custom. At slow times, however, bargaining usually achieves discounts of about a third. The cheaper central options line **Maarif Caddesi**, though there are a few serious dives here worth avoiding, and all are beset by **traffic noise** – get a rear-facing room if possible. **Parking** here is heavily controlled – hoteliers may (or may not) have a few private spaces or be willing to intercede for you with the (mostly gypsy) wardens.

Hotels and pansiyons

Aksaray Alipaşa Ortakapı Cad 9, corner of Maarif Cad ☎0284/212 6035. This *pansiyon* in a converted old mansion was refurbished in 2009, but it's still as basic as you'd want to be in its mix of en-suite and cheaper, waterless, rooms. ②–③

Antik Maarif Cad 6 ☎0284/225 1555, ⓦwww.edirneantikhotel.com. Three creaky floors' worth of large, plush, slightly chintz decor en-suite rooms in this sympathetically converted mansion with its own garden restaurant. ⑤

Efe Maarif Cad 13 ☎0284/213 6166, ⓦwww
.efehotel.com. Salubrious, if somewhat overpriced
hotel where the cheerful well-appointed rooms vary
– those at the back are almost suite-sized, with
double beds and fridges – plus an English-style,
winter pub on the ground floor. **❺**
Park Maarif Cad 7 ☎0284/213 5276. Not quite as
spruce as the *Efe*, with its bland-modern room
decor and well-worn 1980s common areas, though
the ground-floor restaurant is more contemporary.
Good value if you can bargain them down a
category. **❺**
Rüstempaşa Kervansarayı İki Kapılı Han Cad 57
☎0284/215 6119, ⓦwww.edirnekervansarayhotel
.com. Restored sixteenth-century *kervansaray*
whose cool, cell-like rooms are wrapped around a
pleasant courtyard. Street noise is minimal as its
substantial walls (with tiny windows) are quite
soundproof: the bathrooms were revamped in
2007, but the room decor is painfully spartan. **❻**
but, with bargaining it's easy to get for **❺**

🏃 **Taşodalar** Hamam Sok 3, behind Selimiye
Camii ☎0284/213 1404, ⓦwww.tasodalar
.com. Edirne's newest boutique hotel, this
conversion of a fifteenth-century building is much

the best choice for families (there's a quad room)
and for drivers (with its private, secure car park).
The nine rooms have dark-wood floors and trim
throughout, though the decor – a mix of genuine
antiques and kitsch – is in variable taste to say the
least. The upstairs rooms look towards the mosque
– the best of these is no. 109 with its bay window
– and there's a peaceful tea garden/restaurant at
the back. Can usually get up to 30 percent off the
rack rates of **❻–❼**
Tuna Maarif Cad 17 ☎0284/214 3340, ⓦwww
.edirnetunahotel.net. Unassuming hotel with excellent-value en-suite, medium-sized rooms, though
the terrible breakfast will have you hightailing it
across the street to *Melek Anne*'s (see p.168). **❹**

Campsites
Fifi Mocamp 9km along the D100 towards
İstanbul ☎0284/235 7908. Established campsite
with en-suite motel rooms (**❸**), forty caravan
places and a pool.
Ömür Camping Just off the D100 on the D020
towards Kırklareli ☎0284/226 0037. A nice rural
spot with space for fifty caravans and a large
swimming pool.

The City

You can tour Edirne's main sights on foot, but as the Ottoman monuments are
widely scattered you'll need a full day to do it. Many lie to the north and west of
town, deliberately rusticated by the early sultans to provide a nucleus for future
suburbs. Because of the depopulation suffered by the city since the 1700s, urban
growth never caught up with some of them, which have a rather forlorn atmosphere. Still, if the weather's fine, walking there is a pleasure, especially since you'll
follow the willow-shaded banks of the **Tunca River** for some distance. Public
transport doesn't serve the more far-flung sites, so your own wheels or a taxi are
the other options.

Eski Cami and the Bedesten
The logical starting point is **Eski Cami**, the oldest mosque in town, with recycled
Roman columns out front. This boxy structure, topped by nine vaults arranged
three-square and supported by four square pillars, is a more elaborate version of
Bursa's Ulu Cami. Emir Süleyman, son of the luckless Beyazit I, began it in 1403,
but it was his younger brother Mehmet I – the only one of three brothers left alive
after a bloody succession struggle – who dedicated it eleven years later. The
mosque is famous for its giant calligraphic inscriptions inside.

Just across the way Mehmet I constructed the **Bedesten**, Edirne's first covered
market, a portion of whose rents helped maintain the nearby mosque. The
barn-like structure with its fourteen vaulted chambers – again indebted to a Bursa
prototype – was restored in the 1980s, but shops with tatty wares and cheap tiles
underfoot let the interior down.

Semiz Ali Paşa Çarşısı and Kaleiçi
The other main covered bazaar in Edirne is the nearby, six-gated **Semiz Ali Paşa
Çarşısı**, at the top of **Saraçlar Caddesi**, the liveliest, mostly pedestrianized

modern commercial street. The multi-domed bazaar was constructed by Mimar Sinan in 1568 at the behest of Semiz Ali, one of the most able and congenial grand viziers. A massive 1992 fire gutted many of its 130 shops, but renovations were administered with care – and the building far outshines the mostly dull merchandise sold inside.

Just opposite the north entrance looms the **Makedonya Kulesi** (Macedonia Tower), sole remnant of the town's extensive Roman/Byzantine city walls; the Ottomans, in a burst of confidence after expanding the limits of empire far beyond Edirne, demolished the rest. The tower was partially restored around the millennium, and you pass through the ground floor to a viewing platform overlooking some of Roman Hadrianopolis, excavated in 2003 (no entry).

West and south of the Semiz Ali market sprawls the **Kaleiçi** district, a rectangular grid of streets dating from Byzantine times and lined with much-interrupted terraces of ornate eighteenth- and nineteenth-century townhouses. The best streets for strolling are Maarif Caddesi, its parallel Gazi Paşa Caddesi, and their linking perpendicular Cumhuriyet Caddesi, once the heart of the **Jewish quarter**, where house dedication dates (in the Hebraic calendar) go up to 1912. The now utterly derelict synagogue at the bottom of Maarif Caddesi was built in 1906 to replace thirteen others destroyed by fire: when first built, it was the largest in the Balkans – an indication of the then huge community size. But within a few decades the new frontiers, populist pogroms (unusual in Turkey) and official harassment had impelled local Jews to flee to Europe, İstanbul or Israel.

Üç Şerefeli Cami and the Sokullu Paşa Hamamı

North of Semiz Ali and Hürriyet Meydanı stands the **Üç Şerefeli Cami**, which replaced the Eski Cami as Edirne's Friday mosque in 1447. Ten years in the making, its conceptual daring represented the pinnacle of Ottoman religious architecture until overshadowed by the Selimiye Camii a short time later. The mosque's name – "three-balconied" – derives from the three galleries for the muezzin on the tallest of the four whimsically idiosyncratic **minarets** with different bases; the second highest has two balconies, the others one, and each of the multiple balconies is reached by a separate stairway within the minaret. The **courtyard**, too, was an innovation, centred on a *sadırvan* and ringed by porphyry and marble columns pilfered from Roman buildings. The mosque's experimental nature is further confirmed by its **interior**, much wider than it is deep and covered by a main dome 24m in diameter, with four flanking domes. It was the largest that the Turks had built at the time and, to impart a sense of space, the architect relied on just two freestanding columns, with the other four recessed into front and back walls to form a hexagon.

Right across from the mosque is the sixteenth-century **Sokullu Paşa Hamamı** (daily 7am–10pm), built by Mimar Sinan with separate wings for men and women.

Selimiye Camii and nearby museums

The masterly **Selimiye Camii**, one of Turkey's finest mosques, was designed by the 80-year-old Mimar Sinan (see box, p.109) in 1569 at the command of Selim II. The work of a confident craftsman at the height of his powers, it's visible from some distance away on the Thracian plain.

You can approach the Selimiye across the central park, Dilaver Bey, then through the **Kavaflar Arasta** (Cobbler's Arcade), built by Sinan's pupil Davut and still used as a covered market, full of household goods and cheap clothing; every day, under the market's prayer dome, the shopkeepers promise to conduct their business

▲ Selimiye Camii

honestly. The mosque **courtyard**, approached from the *arasta* up a flight of stone steps, is surrounded by a colonnaded portico with arches in alternating red and white stone, ancient columns and domes of varying size above the arcades. Its delicately fashioned *şadırvan* (ablutions fountain) is the finest in the city. Each of the four identical, slender **minarets** has three balconies – Sinan's nod to his predecessors – and, at 71m, are the second tallest in the world after those in Mecca. The detailed carved portal once graced the Ulu Cami in Birgi and was transported here in pieces, then reassembled.

But it is the celestial **interior** (no photos), specifically the dome, which impresses most. Planned expressly to surpass that of Aya Sofya in İstanbul, it manages this – at 31.5m in diameter – by a bare few centimetres, thus achieving Sinan's lifetime ambition. Held aloft by eight mammoth but surprisingly unobtrusive twelve-sided pillars, the cupola floats 44m above the floor, covered in calligraphy proclaiming the glory of Allah. Immediately below the dome the muezzin's platform, supported on twelve columns, is an ideal place from which to contemplate the proportions of the mosque. The water of the small marble drinking fountain beneath symbolizes life, under the dome of eternity. The most ornate stone carving is reserved for the *mihrab* and *mimber*, backed by fine İznik faïence illuminated by sunlight streaming in through the many windows allowed by the pillar support scheme.

An associated *medrese*, at the eastern corner of the mosque precinct, is now the **Museum of Turkish and Islamic Arts** (Türk İslam Eserleri Müzesi; Tues–Sun 9am–5pm; 3TL), consisting of fifteen rooms around a courtyard. The rooms display assorted wooden, ceramic and martial knick-knacks from the province, including one gallery dedicated to oil-wrestling.

The main **Edirne Museum** (Tues–Sun 9am–5pm; free) – the modern building northeast of the mosque – has a good, archeological section (partly labelled in English) with bronze, glass and ceramic relics from ancient Aenos at the mouth of the Meriç as well as Hadrianopolis. There's also a Turkish-only ethnographic section featuring carpet-weaving and colourful village bridal-wear, the rule at weddings before the bland white confectionery was adopted from the West.

Oil-wrestling

Oil-wrestling (*yağlı güreş*) is popular throughout Turkey, but reaches the pinnacle of acclaim at the doyenne of tournaments, the annual **Kırkpınar festival**, staged early each summer on Sarayiçi islet outside Edirne. The preferred date is the first week of July, but the event is moved back into June if it conflicts with Ramadan or either of the two major *bayram*s following it.

The wrestling matches have been held annually, except in times of war or Edirne's occupation, for over six centuries. Despite the less than atmospheric environment of the modern stadium that now hosts the wrestling, tradition still permeates the event. The contestants – up to a thousand – dress only in leather knickers called *kisbet* and are slicked down head-to-toe in diluted olive oil. Wrestlers are classed by height and ability, not by weight, from toddlers up to the *pehlivan* (full-size) category. Warm-up exercises, the *peşrev*, are highly stereotyped and accompanied by the *davul* (deep-toned drum) and *zurna* (single-reed Islamic oboe). The competitors and the actual matches are solemnly introduced by the *cazgır* (master of ceremonies), usually a former champion.

The bouts, several of which take place simultaneously, can last anything from a few minutes to nearly an hour, until one competitor collapses or has his back pinned to the grass. Referees keep a lookout for the limited number of illegal moves or holds and victors advance more or less immediately to the next round until only the *başpehlivan* (champion) remains. Despite the small prize purse donated by the *Kırkpınar ağaları* – the local worthies who put on the whole show – a champion should derive ample benefit from appearance and endorsement fees, plus the furious on- and off-site betting. Gladiators tend mainly to be villagers from across Turkey who have won regional titles, starry-eyed with the prospect of fame and escape from a rural poverty rut.

In addition to providing the music of the *peşrev*, the local Romany population descends in force during Kırkpınar, setting up a combination circus-carnival on the outskirts of town. They also observe the ancient pan-Balkan **spring festival** (**Hıdırellez**) in the fields around the stadium during the first week of May. The Romany King lights a bonfire on the evening of May 5, a torch relays the flame to other nearby bonfires, and a dish of meat and rice is given to the gathered picnickers. The next morning, young Romany girls are paraded through the streets on horseback around the Muradiye Camii (focus of a Romany *mahalle*) to the accompaniment of *davul* and *zurna*, wearing their own or their mothers' wedding dresses.

Muradiye Camii

Further northeast of the centre, the **Muradiye Camii** (admission only at prayer times) is an easy ten-minute, down-then-up walk along Mimar Sinan Caddesi from the Selimiye Camii. According to legend Celaleddin Rumi, founder of the Mevlevî dervish order, appeared in a dream to the pious Murat II at some date between 1426 and 1435, urging him to build a sanctuary for the Mevlevîs in Edirne. The result is this pleasing, T-shaped *zaviye* (dervish convent) crouched on a hill looking north over vegetable patches and the Tunca River; the grassy entry court lends a final bucolic touch. The interior is distinguished by the best İznik tiles outside Bursa: the *mihrab* and walls up to eye level are solid with them. Higher surfaces once bore calligraphic frescoes, but these have probably been missing since the catastrophic earthquake of 1751. The dervishes initially congregated in the *eyvan*s, the ends of the T's cross-stroke; Murat later housed them in a separate *tekke* in the garden.

Along the Tunca River

Although the bigger river, the **Meriç** has only one major bridge over it, the graceful **Mecidiye**, erected 1842–47 and now effectively Edirne's municipal logo.

By contrast, the narrower **Tunca River** is spanned by a half-dozen fifteenth- or sixteenth-century bridges, better suited to pedestrians and horse-carts than the motor vehicles that trundle across them. The best way to see the spans is to stroll along the riverbank parallel to the dykes and water meadows on the right bank. A good place to start is at the pair furthest upstream, the fifteenth-century **Saray (Kanûni)** and **Fatih bridges**, which join the respective left and right banks of the Tunca with the river-island of **Sarayiçi**. The island takes its name from the *saray* or royal palace which once stood here but was blown up by the Ottomans in 1877 to prevent the munitions stored inside from falling into Russian hands. Beside the resulting ruins is the concrete stadium that hosts the Kırkpınar wrestling matches. Following the riverbank west and downstream, past the **Saraçhane bridge**, brings you, after twenty minutes, to the double-staged **Beyazit bridge**, across another small island in the Tunca, and its extension **Yalnızgöz** ("one-eyed" after its single hump) **bridge**.

Across these two on the far bank is the vast **İkinci Beyazit Külliyesi**, built 1484–88 by Hayrettin, court architect to Beyazit II. Within a single irregular boundary wall, beneath a hundred domes, are assembled a mosque, food storehouse, bakery, *imaret*, dervish hostel, medical school and insane asylum. Unfortunately, most of the buildings are closed to the public these days, though the *imam* or his son may give you a short tour (essentially peering frustratedly through windows and gates). Except for its handsome courtyard and the sultan's loge inside, the **mosque** itself is disappointing; more interesting is the **medical school** in the furthest northwest corner of the complex. This was conveniently linked to the *timarhane*, or madhouse, built around an open garden, which in turn leads to the magnificent **darüşşifa** (therapy centre). This hexagonal, domed structure consists of a circular central space with six *eyvan*s opening onto it; the inmates were brought here regularly, so that musicians could play to soothe the more intractable cases. Strange five-sided rooms with fireplaces open off three of the *eyvan*s. The *darüşşifa* now houses the fairly dull **Sağlık Müzesi** (Museum of Health; daily 9am–6pm; 10TL), a collection of old medical equipment and photographs.

Another fifteen minutes' walk south along the river brings you to the **Gazi Mihal bridge**, an Ottoman refurbishment of a thirteenth-century Byzantine span. Gazi Mihal was a Christian nobleman who became an enthusiastic convert to Islam – hence the epithet *Gazi*, "Warrior for the Faith". From here, it's an easy 700-metre stroll back into town.

Eating and drinking

The local speciality is **ciğer tava**, deep-fried slivers of calf's liver with tomato onion and hot chilli garnish. Most of Edirne's **restaurants** are undistinguished and licensed places are scarce in the centre – we've indicated all known ones. Similarly, despite the large student contingent, **nightlife** is limited to a few venues along Saraçlar Caddesi, especially towards the old Jewish bazaar at the south end, and the area along Karaağaç Yolu between the two river bridges, known as *Bülbül Adası* – "Nightingale Island".

Restaurants

Asmaaltı Ocakbaşı Saraçlar Cad 149. Occupying two floors of an attractively restored old industrial building, this is the only licensed meat-grill downtown, thus a bit bumped up in price – allow 20TL minimum a head.

Balkan Piliç Saraçlar Cad 14. Plenty of wholesome *lokanta* fare – not just chicken but enticing vegetable dishes and good roast lamb – served on two floors.

Niyazi Usta Alipaşa Ortakapı Cad 9. The best regarded of several *ciğerci*s (liver purveyors) in this area, worth a slight price premium for their expert rendition of *ciğer tava*. The salubrious surroundings stretch over two floors, festooned with photos of founder Niyazi and various celebrities. Closes 9.30pm, though an annexe at no. 5 may stay open later; unlicensed.

Villa 1.5km south of town along Karaağaç Yolu, on the Meriç River. Licensed restaurant specializing in meat and *meze*, plus sometimes *yayın* (catfish). Open all year, but their *raison d'être* is a summer outdoor terrace overlooking the river and its elegant, honey-coloured bridge. You pay extra, of course, for the view – typically around 23TL a head.

Zindanaltı Meyhanesi Saraçlar Cad 127. About the only central *meyhane*, arrayed over three floors, with the usual *meze*s and grills, plus a roof terrace.

Bars & cafés

Getto Saraçlar Cad 143. Straightforward booze-and-music bar – the only one downtown – whose name recalls the Jewish history of the area.

London Café Saraçlar Cad 74. This two-storey affair serves proper European coffees, a range of imported alcoholic drinks and Western snack food like pasta, burgers and sandwiches, indoors or out at pavement tables.

Melek Anne Maarif Cad 18. The walled, tree-studded courtyard is the highlight here at this snack-café operating out of an old house. Dishes include *mantı*, *menemen*, *gözleme*, *katmer* and the like. Open 9am–10pm.

Safran Saraçlar Cad 46. The best central outlet for milk-based sweets like *kazandibi*, with seating on two upstairs floors.

South of Edirne: to the Saros Gulf

There's little reason to stop at any point along the E87 highway as it heads south from **Havsa**, the junction 27km southeast of Edirne. This road does, however, connect two transit towns to/from Greece, **Uzunköprü** and **Keşan**, the latter also being a jump-off point for Turkey's northernmost Aegean resorts, on the Gulf of Saros.

UZUNKÖPRÜ (Long Bridge; formerly called Plotinopolis), 64km south of Edirne, gets its current name from the 1400m-long, 174-arched **Ottoman bridge** over the Ergene River's water meadows at the north end of town. A remarkable feat of engineering from 1426–43, the bridge remains entirely intact despite being situated in an earthquake zone. It's long been a notorious traffic bottleneck with heavy lorries and buses posing a far more immediate threat than earth tremors, but a new, four-lane bridge, which ends just south of the train station 2km east, should open in 2010.

A further 53km south, the next major town is **KEŞAN**, a nondescript place that you needn't even enter since the *otogar* – with frequent connections to İstanbul, Edirne, Çanakkale and İpsala, for the Greece-bound – is on the ring road at the northwest outskirts.

İbrice Limanı

Some 5km south of Keşan, the 22-53 road heads 28km south to the central junction at **Mecidiye** village. Continuing straight ahead for around 6km brings you to **İBRİCE LİMANI** on the **Saros Körfezi** (Saros Gulf). Little more than one fish **restaurant** and a few **scuba-dive** boats, this port is home to four diving schools in season, as the gulf is a popular spot for beginners and provides experienced divers with access to a dozen nearby sites. PADI- and/or CMAS-certified **dive schools** here include Yalçın Dalış Merkezi (℡0532/737 2333, ⓦwww.yacindalis.com); TADOK (℡0536/477 4710); and Mavi Tutku Dalış Merkezi (℡0532/374 4245).

The best beach for non-divers is at **Bakirkoyu**, 3km east of the harbour, while the closest **accommodation** is 3km back towards Mecidiye at 🏠 *Sığınak* (℡0284/783 4310, ⓦwww.siginak.com; all year; ❻, half-board only), ten rustic wood-and-stone bungalows and rooms tucked away in the Thracian maquis, with a pleasant fireplace-lounge in the main building. The half-board basis is a blessing as you're in the middle of nowhere – and you can sample the proprietors' own wine.

Erikli

Bearing right at the crossroads in Mecidiye leads, after 6km, to the more mainstream resort of **ERİKLİ**, the only developed one on the gulf coast. It's a bit tatty at the inland edges, but the glorious, broad and long (over 1.5km) **beach** compensates. Only in July and August does it get really busy and, with transport, it makes an excellent first or last stop en route from or to Greece. There are just two **hotels**, both on the beach – rooms at the İşçimen (℡0284/737 3148, ⓦwww .iscimenhotel.com.tr; all year; ⑨) have 1970s decor and tiny bathrooms, so make sure you get one of the sea-view ones. The low-rise *Erikli* (℡0284/737 3565, ⓦwww.eriklihotel.com; ⑥), is slightly pricier but in a better location towards the eastern end of the beach; both hotels have beach clubs thumping away in season, and windsurfing is available. Independent **restaurants** are scarce; the *Elisa*, one block inland from the *İşçimen*, is cheapish and cheerful, with three TVs blaring, two pet rabbits and mostly pizza and grilled meat on offer.

Lüleburgaz

If you've become a Sinan-ophile, you can visit another of his substantial creations, which dominates the centre of **LÜLEBURGAZ**, 79km southeast of Edirne on the D100. The **Sokollu Mehmet Paşa Külliyesi**, originally commissioned by the governor of Rumeli in 1549, wasn't completed until 1569, during Sokollu's term as grand vizier. What you see today is an imposing mosque and *medrese* abutted by a covered bazaar and guarded by two isolated towers. The mosque proper is peculiar, possessing only one minaret; where the others might be, three stubby turret-like towers jut instead. The *medrese*, still used as a Koranic academy, is arrayed around the mosque courtyard, entered by two tiny arcades on the east and west sides; in the middle of the vast space stands a late Ottoman *şadırvan*. The mosque's portico, built to square with the *medrese*, is far more impressive than the interior, and most visitors will soon drift out of the north gate to the **market promenade**, whose shops are still intact and in use. Just outside the gate, a huge dome with a stork's nest on top shades the centre of the bazaar.

Beyond, there was once a massive *kervansaray*, equal in size to the mosque complex. All of it has vanished save for a lone tower, balanced by another, the **Dar-ül-Kura**, at the south edge of the entire precinct, beyond the mosque's *mihrab*. The former **hamam**, across the street from the complex, is now chock-a-block with tiny **restaurants** in its outer bays, though the main dome has collapsed.

Kıyıköy

KIYIKÖY occupies an idyllic location overlooking the Black Sea, flanked on both sides by slow-moving rivers, full of terrapins and rented canoes, and lushly forested spurs of the Istranca hills. It was fortified by the Byzantines around the sixth century, though most of what is still standing dates from the thirteenth and fourteenth centuries. Kıyıköy's pre-1923 Greek population was replaced by Balkan Muslims, but many inhabitants still use the former name, "Midye" – a corruption of Medea – after the locally harvested mussels. Today, gently crumbling half-timbered houses line the backstreets and fishing nets hang everywhere.

The main approach to the walled **citadel** is via the narrow south gate, sadly restored with pink cement bricks. The west gate opens onto what used to be the town's **agora**, now housing a pair of tea gardens and offering superb views to the west. From here a road leads downhill and 300m up the Kazandere River to the impressive **Aya Nikola Manastırı** – an elaborate structure carved into the rock of the hillside, complete with colonnaded aisles, barrel vaulting and a semicircular apse of tiered seats where the clergy once sat. On the northeast side of the village it's possible to see the part-brick **tunnel**, constructed to allow safe passage down to the harbour in time of siege – the only deep-water anchorage on this part of the coast. A fifteen-minute walk west of the village takes you to 2km of pristine **sandy beach**, backed by low cliffs oozing fossils, though some of the landscape inland is blighted by campers' rubbish and semi-permanent tents. Several more almost empty beaches – indeed, some of the most beautiful and undeveloped in Turkey – lie east of Kıyıköy, near where the Pabuçdere meets the sea.

Practicalities

The village is too tiny to have its own *otogar* and direct **buses from İstanbul** (two daily in summer, one in winter; 3hr) drop you right outside the citadel's south gate. There are more frequent buses from İstanbul to **Saray**, a sleepy town 29km southwest of Kıyıköy, from where hourly minibuses depart for Kıyıköy. The closest **ATMs** are in Vize, 30km west, so come prepared.

The best **accommodation** is at the comfortable, professionally managed *Endorfina* (⌾0288/388 6364, ⓦwww.hotelendorfina.com; ❺), above the monastery, with a wood-decked pool and good attached seafood restaurant. Failing that, there are numerous, basic *pansiyons* with shared bathroom and sometimes kitchen facilities, though many fill up from early July to early September. Among these, try the *Hulya* (⌾0288/388 6016; ❷), signposted west of the south gate, with three-, four- and five-bed rooms; the *Midye* (⌾0288/388 6472; ❷) just east of the square on Cumhuriyet Caddesi; or the *Palaz Pansiyon* (⌾0288/388 6177; ❷), outside town on the Saray road, with views of cow-filled fields and the beach.

Kıyıköy is noted for its local, seasonal fish, with several good, if pricey, **restaurants** attracting day-trippers from İstanbul. Try the cliff-top *Yakamoz*, northwest of the centre, or closer to the harbour, the *Köşk* on Güneş Sokağı, run by a father-and-son team, with just ten tables and a fireplace.

The North Marmara coast

West of İstanbul, the city's straggling suburbs stretch up to the junction of the Edirne-bound D100 and the E84/D110 to Keşan and İpsala. Some 60km beyond this fork, the E84/D110 bypasses the port of **Tekirdağ**, the largest port on the **north Marmara coast**. Southwest of here, an almost impossible to find coastal route consists of 22km of steep dirt track between the scruffy Turkish resorts of **Kumbağ** and **Hasköy** (Güzelköy), where rolling, vine-covered hills appear. Most people however, take the faster, if less aesthetic and hair-raisingly dangerous E84/ D110 to the turning of the D555 south to **Şarköy**, largest of the several resorts on this coast. Little more than a weekend bolt hole with a grubby beach and small fishing anchorage, it makes a decent lunch stop en route to **Gelibolu**, the last port before the Dardanelles.

Tekirdağ

With a hilly setting at the head of a gently curving bay, **TEKIRDAĞ** – the ancient and medieval Rodosto – is a fairly pleasant town, with a few remaining, dilapidated wooden houses, a clutch of museums and a ferry service across the Sea of Marmara.

The town's best-known attraction – certainly for numbers of visiting Hungarians – is the **Rákóczi Museum** (Rakoczi Müzesi; Tues–Sun 9am–noon & 1–5pm; 5TL), easily found by going west along the seafront boulevard from the *eski iskele* (old jetty) and then uphill inland. Transylvanian Prince Ferenc Rákóczi (1676–1735) was leader of an unsuccessful 1703–11 revolt against the Austrian Habsburgs; in 1719, Sultan Ahmet III granted him asylum – or rather, internal exile – here, away from the political hotbed of the capital. Rákóczi spent the last fifteen years of his life in this seventeenth-century house, now the property of the Hungarian government. Declared a museum in 1932, it was meticulously restored in 1981–82: the interior, especially the elegant top-floor dining/reception room with its lattice ceiling, stained glass and painted cabinets, far outshines the rather thin exhibits comprising paraphernalia of Rákóczi's insurgent army.

The only other points of mild interest are the **Tekirdağ Müzesi** (Tekirdağ Museum; Tues–Sun 9am–noon & 1–5pm; 3TL) at Barbaros Cad 1, a short walk east from the Rákóczi Museum, with archeological finds from the province, and, further downhill, the **Namik Kemal Evi** (Namik Kemal House; Mon–Sat 9.30am–5pm; free), a two-storey wooden house museum honouring the province's most famous journalist and Young Ottoman (1840–88), though again the building outshines the contents.

Practicalities

From the *eski iskele* down on the shorefront boulevard, afternoon **ferries** ply to Eredek on the far side of the Sea of Marmara, via some of its inhabited islands; the evening ferry goes from the *yeni liman* (new port) just over 1km west. These ro-ro craft are not really meant for foot passengers, but can save drivers a long and pricey journey around the Marmara: see "Travel details", p.190, for costs and timings.

You're unlikely to want to stay, but if need be, there are a couple of **hotels** directly inland from the *eski iskele*, of which the hillside *Rodosto* (℡0282/263 3701, Ⓦwww.rodostohotel.com.tr; ❷), slightly set back from the noisy boulevard, is the best value. Immediately below it is a row of **restaurants** specializing in the local savoury, pellet-shaped meatballs *Tekirdağ köfteleri*; try them at the *Ali Baba* which serves a generous portion of ten *köfte* (7TL) and is open 24 hours a day. Regrettably, none of the restaurants is licensed so you can't sample the renowned **local wine** or **rakı**, the latter reckoned Turkey's best because of the good water available just inland – head for a bottle shop instead.

Gelibolu

Strategically sited at the northern entrance of the Dardanelles, **GELIBOLU** is a moderately inviting, if often windy, medium-sized town. Founded by the ancient Greeks as Kallipolis, it served as the Anglo-French headquarters during the Crimean War, and still has an important naval base. It's too far, around 50km, from the Gallipoli battlefields (see p.200) to be a practical base – the days of inebriated Antipodeans stumbling off a bus here, thinking they'd arrived at the World War I sites, are over.

At the heart of town stands a colourful, square **fishing harbour**, ringed by cafés and restaurants, its two pools separated by a broad stone **tower**, all that remains of the fortifications of Byzantine Kallipolis. The fortress was held by an army of rebelling Catalan mercenaries for seven years in the early fourteenth century and later fell to the Ottomans (1354), who rebuilt and expanded it. Today, the tower houses the **Piri Reis Museum** (Piri Reis Müzesi; Fri–Wed 8.30am–noon & 1–5pm; free), dedicated to the legendary sixteenth-century Turkish cartographer, who prepared navigation charts of the Mediterranean and was the first man to accurately map the American coastline. The only other points of interest are a few sturdy but otherwise unremarkable Ottoman tombs, inland from the port and around **Hamzakoy**, the resort district in the north of town, with its long, coarse-sand beach.

Practicalities

The **ferry jetty** for services to Lapseki (see "Travel details", p.192 for journey times and frequencies) is right at the inner harbour entrance, while the **otogar** is 600m out on the Eceabat road, though a few minibuses to Eceabat or Çanakkale may pass by the harbour.

You're unlikely to want **to stay** in Gelibolu, but if you do, the only passable choices are the *Hotel Oya* on Miralay Şeflik Aker Cad 7, about 100m southeast of the tower and then up left at an angle (℡0286/566 0392; **❸**), or the more modern, light-pink *Hamzakoy*, at the southern end of the eponymous beach (℡0286/566 8080, ⓦwww.hamzakoy.8m.com; **❹**), with its own beach-bar and licensed restaurant.

When eating out, don't miss the locally caught **fish**, particularly *mezgit* (whitebait), *kanat* (baby bluefish) and mackerel, as well as grilled *sardalya* (sardines), the canned variety being the town's main commerce. The harbour pool is surrounded by half a dozen **restaurants** suitable for lunch – *Yelkenci* tucked into the corner is honest and reliable for fair-sized portions of seasonal fish, *meze* and alcohol.

The Southern Marmara

The **southern shoreline** of the Sea of Marmara is sparsely populated west of Erdek, while to the east sprawl polluted dormitory-communities for İstanbul. Many of these were devastated by the **earthquake** of August 17, 1999, which killed an estimated 30,000 people – victims of rogue builders who ignored building regulations yet miraculously managed to pass official inspections. Since then, hastily constructed apartment-blocks have rehoused the tens of thousands who sheltered in makeshift tent-camps after the quake.

Fortunately, **İznik**, historically the most interesting town in the region, suffered little damage. Important as a centre of Christianity and, briefly, capital of the Nicaean Empire, it has several interesting monuments and a revitalized tile-making industry. To the south, **Bursa**, once one of Turkey's most attractive cities, has succumbed to rapid growth since the 1980s, bringing greater wealth but destroying much of its colourful provincial atmosphere.

Fast ferry services (both cars and foot passengers) from İstanbul provide the best access to the region, far preferable to the buses which follow a congested five-hour route along the gulf shore via İzmit. Boats from İstanbul's Yenikapı terminal serve **Yalova**, **Mudanya** and **Bandırma**; for schedules and prices, see "Travel details", p.192. In July and August, it's advisable to pre-book tickets. Using these services (plus buses to İznik and Bursa, or your own vehicle), you could see all the local sights over three to four days.

Southern Marmara ports and resorts

There are few compelling attractions in and around the **coastal ports** of Yalova and Zeytindağı. They like to call themselves resorts – which they are for some locals – but this is mostly a rocky coastline, with inland contours softened by the ubiquitous olive groves and conifer forest. **Yalova** itself is the main transport hub, but there's no need to hang around longer than it takes to catch one of the dolmuşes from the ferry terminal to the new *otogar* at the southern edge of town, where onward services depart at least hourly for Termal, Bursa and İznik.

Termal

The hot springs at **TERMAL** lie 12km southwest of Yalova, or just a dolmuş ride inland from Çınarcık, itself served by a summer sea-bus service from Istanbul. Although patronized by Byzantine and Roman emperors, Termal's springs only became fashionable again in the 1890s, and most of the spa's Ottoman *belle époque* buildings date from that era.

There are several separate bathing centres, of which the **Kurşunlu Banyo** in the central park (Mon–Wed, Fri–Sat 8am–10.30pm, closes earlier Thurs & Sun; 12TL) is the most popular. The water is supposedly beneficial for rheumatism and skin diseases, but temperatures reach 65°C, so the best time to take the plunge is in winter. Otherwise, there's an **open-air pool** nearby at a more manageable 38°C.

The spa resort is dominated by two luxury **hotels** (with a third under construction), of which the nineteenth-century *Çınar* is smaller and with more Olde Worlde charm; both the *Çınar* and its sister hotel the *Çamlık*, can be booked on ☏0226/675 7400, ⓦwww.yalovatermal.com; both ❺. A cheaper alternative can be found nearby in the idyllic village of **Üvezpınar**, on one of the surrounding hills: the *Dinana* (☏0226/675 7668; ❹) is family-run and clean, with pleasant balconied rooms overlooking the forested mountains, and a restaurant serving simple meals. Üvezpınar is a two-kilometre hike up the road leading from the *jandarma* station to the left of the entrance to Termal, or up steps leading from within the resort itself.

Mudanya and Zeytinbaği (Trilye)

MUDANYA is the closest port to Bursa, though with fewer ferries from İstanbul than Yalova (see "Travel details", p.192); mini buses to Bursa and Çanakkale connect with arriving boats. Now rather unappealing, the town's major moment in history was when the provisional armistice between Turkey and the Allies was signed on October 11, 1922, in a wooden waterside mansion, now a small (missable) museum to the event. Mudanya boasts one excellent **hotel**: the *Montania*, Eski İstasyon Caddesi (☏0224/544 6000, ⓦwww.montaniahotel.com; ❼), a renovated 150-year-old train station on the seaside esplanade. It has indoor and outdoor pools, a hamam and well-equipped rooms, some with sea views.

Pleasant, laid-back **ZEYTINBAĞI**, 10km west of Mudanya and connected to it by regular buses, was the Greek Triglia, and Ottoman Trilye, the latter name still much used locally. Its main sights are the central, well-preserved, thirteenth-century **Byzantine church** known as the Fatih Camii, and large numbers of ornate mansions from the town's time as a largely Greek Orthodox community. Two other ruined churches just outside town date from the eighth century. Once you've seen these, you can get a good fish meal by the little anchorage.

İznik

It's hard to believe that **İZNİK** (ancient Nicaea) today a backwater among fruit orchards and olive groves at the east end of the eponymous lake, was once a seat of empire and scene of desperate battles. But looking around the fertile valley, you can understand the attraction for imperial powers needing a fortified base near the sea-lanes of the Marmara. Most people visit İznik as a long day out of İstanbul or Bursa, staying a night at most. This is enough time to sample the town's monuments, and pick up a souvenir or two from the local ceramics workshops. In its heyday in the sixteenth century, İznik produced Turkey's best tiles, and the tradition has been recently revived here.

Some history

Founded by Alexander's general Antigonos in 316 BC, İznik was seized and enlarged fifteen years later by his rival Lysimakhos, who named it **Nicaea** after his late wife. He also gave Nicaea its first set of walls and the grid plan typical of Hellenistic towns; both are still evident. When the Bithynian kingdom succeeded Lysimakhos, Nicaea alternated with nearby Nicomedia as its capital until

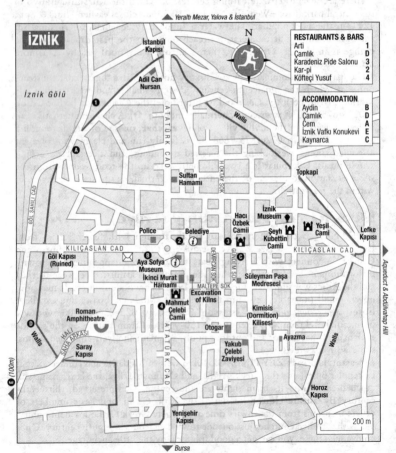

▲ Yeraltı Mezar, Yalova & İstanbul

İZNİK

İstanbul Kapısı

İznik Gölü

RESTAURANTS & BARS
Arti	1
Çamlık	D
Karadeniz Pide Salonu	3
Kar-pi	2
Köfteci Yusuf	4

ACCOMMODATION
Aydın	B
Çamlık	D
Cem	A
İznik Vafkı Konukevi	E
Kaynarca	C

Adil Can Nursan

ATATÜRK CAD

Walls

GÖL SAHİLİ CAD

Sultan Hamamı

H. OKTAY SOK

Topkapi

Hacı Özbek Camii

İznik Museum

Yeşil Camii

Lefke Kapısı

Police

Belediye

Şeyh Kubettin Camii

KILIÇASLAN CAD

KILIÇASLAN CAD

Göl Kapısı (Ruined)

Aya Sofya Museum

İkinci Murat Hamamı

DEMİRCAN SOK

GÜNDEM SOK

Süleyman Paşa Medresesi

Aqueduct & Abdülvahap Hili

MALTEPE SOK

Excavation of Kilns

Mahmut Çelebi Camii

Kimisis (Dormition) Kilisesi

Roman Amphitheatre

ATATÜRK CAD

Otogar

Ayazma

Walls

HALİ SAHA ARKASI

Saray Kapısı

Yakub Çelebi Zaviyesi

Walls

E (100m)

Horoz Kapısı

Yenişehir Kapısı

0   200 m

▼ Bursa

bequeathed to Rome in 74 BC. Under the Roman emperors the city prospered as capital of the province and it continued to flourish during the Byzantine era.

Nicaea played a pivotal role in early Christianity, hosting two important **ecumenical councils**. The first, convened by Constantine the Great in 325 AD, resulted in the condemnation of the Arian heresy – which maintained that Christ's nature was inferior to God the Father's – and the promulgation of the Nicene Creed, affirming Christ's divine nature, which is still central to Christian belief. The seventh council (the second to be held here) was presided over by Empress Irene in 787 AD; this time the Iconoclast controversy was settled by the pronouncement, widely misunderstood in the West, that icons had their proper place in the church so long as they were revered and not worshipped.

Nicaea's much-repaired walls seldom repelled invaders and in 1081 the Selçuks took the city, only to be evicted by a combined force of Byzantines and Crusaders sixteen years later. The fall of Constantinople to the Fourth Crusade in 1204 propelled Nicaea into the spotlight once more, for the Byzantine heir to the throne Theodore Laskaris retreated here and made this the base of the improbably successful **Nicaean Empire**. The Laskarid dynasty added a second circuit of walls before returning to Constantinople in 1261, but these again failed to deter the besieging Ottomans, who, led by Orhan Gazi, the victor of Bursa, broke through in March 1331.

Renamed İznik, the city embarked on a golden age of sorts, interrupted briefly by the pillaging of Tamerlane in 1402. Virtually all the surviving monuments predate the Mongol sacking, but the most enduring contribution to art and architecture – the celebrated **İznik tiles and pottery** – first appeared during the reign of Çelebi Mehmet I, who brought skilled potters from Persia to begin the local industry. This received another boost in 1514 when Selim the Grim took Tabriz and sent more craftsmen west as war booty; by the end of the sixteenth century ceramic production was at its height, with more than three hundred functioning kilns. It was to be a brief flowering, since within another hundred years war and politics had scattered most of the artisans. By the mid-eighteenth century the local industry had packed up completely, with products from nearby Kütahya serving as inferior substitutes. İznik began a long, steady decline, hastened by near-total devastation during the 1920–22 war.

Arrival, information and accommodation

İznik's tiny **otogar** is on Çelebi Sokağı, in the southeast quarter. **Drivers** and **cyclists** should note that the northern-shore road from Orhangazi is far wider, faster and safer than the narrow, twisty southern-shore one. The unlabelled **tourist office** is on the ground floor of the *Belediye* on Kılıçaslan Caddesi (Mon–Fri 8.30am–noon & 1–5.30pm; ☏0224/757 1933); there's also a seasonal wooden information booth by Aya Sofya. **Rooms** are at a premium between late June and early September, especially at weekends, when reservations are recommended.

Hotels and guesthouses

Aydın Kılıçaslan Cad 64 ☏0224/757 7650, ⓦwww.iznikhotelaydin.com. Opposite the police station, the front rooms of this mid-range hotel have balconies overlooking the street, though the decor and bathrooms are dated. Breakfast is in the ground-floor *pastane*. ❸

Çamlık Göl Sahili Yolu 11 ☏0224/757 1362, ⓦwww.iznik-camlikmotel.com. Lakeside motel with rooms of varying sizes, decorated in bland 1980s style, though there are good orthopedic beds and the bathrooms have been revamped. Rooms with lake-view balconies suffer more road noise. ❹

Cem Göl Sahili Yolu 34 ☏0224/757 1687, ⓦwww.cemotel.com. Well-run lakeside hotel, with cheery tan-and-earth-tone decor, renovated bathrooms sporting small tubs, mosaic-paved stairs and a competent ground-floor restaurant, the *Antik*. Set back a bit in a gap of the walls, so quieter then the *Çamlık*. ❹, lake view ❺

İznik Vafkı Konukevi Vakıf Sok 13 ℡ 0224/757 6025, ⓦ www.iznik.com. The upstairs guesthouse of the tile foundation (see p.176) is, unsurprisingly, adorned with colourful, intricate tiles. Rooms are simple but comfortable and quiet, though often booked out by special-interest groups. ❺

Kaynarca Gündem Sok 1 ℡ 0224/757 1753, ⓦ www.kaynarca.s5.com. İznik's best budget option, run by English-speaking Ali and his charming family, with dorm beds (20TL), as well as en-suite rooms with satellite TV; breakfast (5TL extra) is served on the rooftop terrace and there's a s/c kitchen. ❷

The Town

With its regular street plan, İznik is easy to navigate (though drivers will encounter numerous one-way streets). The main north–south boulevard **Atatürk Caddesi** and its east–west counterpart **Kılıçaslan Caddesi** link four of the seven ancient gates, dividing the town into unequal quadrants. Only enthusiasts will want to walk the entire perimeter of the double **walls**, now missing most of their hundred original watchtowers, but two of the seven portals are worth some time. Heavy traffic has been rerouted through modern breaches in the fortifications to prevent vibration damage to the original openings, now restricted to tractors and pedestrians.

The **lake** provides decent swimming in summer, though the shoreline near the town is uninviting; you really need a car to reach the best beaches at its far western end, between Gölyaka and Orhangazi.

The southeast quadrant

The pricey **Aya Sofya Museum** (Aya Sofya Müzesi; Tues–Sun 8.30am–noon & 1–5pm; 7TL), on İznik's central roundabout, is housed in the Byzantine Church of Holy Wisdom, founded by Justinian. The present building was built after an earthquake in 1065 and, as the cathedral of the provisional Byzantine capital, hosted the coronations of the four Nicaean emperors. The Ottomans converted it to a mosque directly on taking the city and Mimar Sinan restored it, but the premises were already half-ruined when razed to the ground in 1922. A 2006–2008 restoration programme raised the walls to their former height and added a roof, but inside there's little to see except some damaged floor mosaics and a faint **fresco** of Christ, John the Baptist and Mary, at ground level behind a glass panel to the left as you enter.

İznik tiles

You can watch **İznik tiles** being made at the **İznik Vafkı**, or İznik Foundation, at Vakıf Sok 13, in the southwest quadrant (ⓦ www.iznik.com), which was established in 1993 to restart production using traditional methods. Tiles of extremely high quality, and correspondingly high price – around 100TL for a 20cm x 10cm border piece – can be bought here. However, there are also numerous other local **workshops** (atölyes) around town, which give bulk discounts bringing the **price** down to a more affordable 20TL for a 10cm x 10cm tile. Be aware, however, that most workshops primarily take orders for domestic customers, and are likely to have only one or two items of each particular design – those showing up on spec hoping to decorate an entire kitchen or bathroom are apt to be disappointed. About the best, reasonably priced, one-stop shop is Adil Can Nursan Sanat Atölyesi, just inside the İstanbul Kapısı. Other quality (as opposed to kitsch) shops cluster along Demircan Sokağı and inside the Süleyman Paşa Medresesi.

The toughest, best, most waterproof – and most expensive – tiles are not ceramic-based but made primarily from locally quarried, finely ground **quartz.** Quartz-rich tiles are air-porous, have good acoustic qualities (thus their use in mosques), and make good insulators, as they contract slightly in winter and expand in summer.

Two blocks south, opposite the fifteenth-century **İkinci Murat Hamamı** (men only daily 6am–midnight; women only Mon, Thurs & Sat afternoons), you'll see the excavations of the medieval İznik **kilns** (closed to the public); finds from the excavations are on display in the local museum (see below).

Four blocks east of the kilns, stands the **Süleyman Paşa Medresesi**, the oldest (1332) Ottoman *medrese* in Turkey and the first one with an open courtyard surrounded by eleven chambers and nineteen domes; today it's a tile bazaar (see p.176). Three blocks south is the fourteenth-century **Yakub Çelebi Zaviyesi**, founded by the luckless prince slain by his brother Beyazit I at Kosovo in 1389 (see p.187). A block to the east, nothing but foundations remain of the **Kimisis Kilisesi** (Church of the Assumption), the presumed burial place of Theodore Laskaris, destroyed in 1922.

The northeast quadrant

Ambling east along Kılıçaslan Caddesi you'll soon reach a vast landscaped park to the north, dotted with İznik's most famous monuments. The **Yeşil Cami** or Green Mosque, erected toward the end of the fourteenth century, is a small gem of a building, its highlight the fantastic marble relief on the portico. Tufted with a stubby minaret that looks back to Selçuk models, the mosque takes its name from the green İznik tiles that once adorned this minaret; they've long since been replaced by mediocre, tri-coloured Kütahya work.

Across the park sprawls the **Nilüfer Hatun İmareti**, commissioned by Murat I in 1388 in honour of his mother. The daughter of a Byzantine noble, Nilüfer Hatun was married off to Orhan Gazi to consolidate a Byzantine–Ottoman alliance. Her ability was soon recognized by Orhan, who appointed her regent during his frequent absences. The T-form building, with a huge main dome flanked by two smaller ones, is more accurately called a *zaviye* than a mere soup kitchen, and is one of the few that doubled as a mosque. It was originally the meeting place of the Ahi brotherhood, a guild drawn from the ranks of skilled craftsmen that also acted as a community welfare and benevolent society. Today the *imaret* contains the **İznik Museum** (Tues–Sun 8am–noon & 1–5pm; 3TL), where you can see genuine İznik pottery, including fourteenth-century tile fragments excavated from the town's kilns. Other exhibits include a bronze dancing Roman-era Pan, some Byzantine gold jewellery and, standing out among the nondescript marble clutter, a sarcophagus in near-mint condition.

The walls and beyond

Closest gate to the Yeşil Cami is the eastern **Lefke Kapısı**, a three-ply affair incorporating two towers erected by Roman Emperor Hadrian between the two courses of walls. You can get up on the ramparts here for a stroll, as it is at the northerly **İstanbul Kapısı**, the best preserved of the gates. It's also triple-layered, with the middle one a triumphal arch celebrating Hadrian's visit in 123 AD: the innermost gate is decorated by two stone-carved **masks**, probably taken from the city's Roman theatre. Other traces of Roman Nicaea are evident in the south-western quarter, including the so-called **Senatus Court** by the lakeshore, outside the **Saray Kapısı**, and the all-but-vanished **Roman theatre**, just inside the gate.

If time permits, you might walk or drive past a Roman aqueduct to the obvious **Abdülvahap hill** 2.5km east of the Lefke Kapısı for comprehensive views over İznik and its surroundings – a popular summer excursion for locals at sunset. The less compelling tomb on top is that of Abdülvahap, a semi-legendary character of the eighth-century Arab raids.

Six kilometres north of İznik in **Elbeyli** village is the **Yeraltı Mezar**, a late Roman or early Byzantine subterranean tomb. Its single chamber with three grave cavities is covered in excellent frescoes, including a pair of peacocks. Staff at İznik Museum (see above) have keys to the site and, for a small fee, will take you to the tomb after the museum closes, though you'll need your own car or taxi.

Eating and drinking

Maple-canopied Kılıçaslan Caddesi has a few unlicensed **restaurants** of the *pide*-and-*köfte* variety, though most visitors choose to eat at licensed places by the lakeshore, which may serve the excellent local grilled or fried *yayın* (catfish). **Tea gardens** and *dondurma* parlours overlook the lake too, as does the town's only central **bar**.

Artı Göl Sahili Yolu. Small garden/lake-view bar serving affordable beers – the only place in town to get a drink outside the licensed restaurants.

Çamlık Motel Göl Sahili Yolu 11. The nicest setting of the waterside restaurants, though staff can be rather brusque. Expect to pay a minimum of 20TL a head for a main course, *mezes* and a beer.

Karadeniz Pide Salon Kılıçaslan Cad. Fresh and cheap *pides* washed down with *ayran* served on the ground floor of this atmospheric, 1935 building.

Kar-pi Kılıçaslan Cad, on the corner of Atatürk Cad. Undeniably handy a/c outfit trading in *köfte* and *pide*.

Köfteçi Yusuf Atatürk Cad 75. Main branch of a small local chain that's a quick-serving, friendly (though unlicensed) carnivore heaven – not just *köfte* on offer but chicken wings, kidneys, *şiş* and the like. A limited range of salads (such as *piyaz*) and desserts rounds off the menu; seating on two levels, with an open terrace.

Bursa

Draped ribbon-like along the leafy lower slopes of Uludağ, which towers more than 2000m above it, and overlooking a fertile plain, **BURSA** does more justice to its setting than any other Turkish city apart from İstanbul. Gathered here are some of the country's finest early Ottoman monuments, set within neighbourhoods that, despite being hemmed in by concrete tower-blocks, remain appealing.

An explosion of the population to almost two million, means that the city overall is no longer exactly elegant as it straggles for some 20km either side of the E90 highway. Silk and textile manufacture, plus the local thermal spas, were for centuries the most important enterprises; they're now outstripped by automobile manufacture (both Renault and Tofaş have plants here), canneries and bottlers processing the rich harvest of the plain, and the presence of Uludağ University. Vast numbers of settlers from Artvin province have been attracted by job opportunities at the various factories, while the students provide a necessary leavening in what might otherwise be a uniformly conservative community. Some of this atmosphere derives from Bursa's role as first capital of the Ottoman Empire and burial place of the first six sultans, their piety as well as authority emanating from the mosques, social-welfare foundations and tombs built at their command.

Bursa is sometimes touted as a long day out from İstanbul, but it really merits at least one and preferably two nights' stay. Central Bursa is particularly good for walking around, whether through the hive of the bazaars, the linear parks of the Hisar district or the anachronistic peace of the Muradiye quarter.

Some history

Although the area had been settled at least a millennium previously, the first city was founded early in the second century BC by King Prusias I of ancient Bithynia, who in typical Hellenistic fashion named the town **Proussa** after himself. Legend claims that Hannibal helped him pick the location of the acropolis, today's Hisar.

Overshadowed by nearby Nicomedia (modern İzmit) and Nicaea (İznik), the city stagnated until the **Romans**, attracted by its natural hot springs, began spending lavish amounts on public baths and made it capital of their province of Mysia. Justinian introduced silkworm culture and Byzantine Proussa flourished until Arab raids of the seventh and eighth centuries, and the subsequent tug-of-war for sovereignty between the Selçuks and Greeks, precipitated its decline. During and after the Latin interlude in Constantinople (1204–61), the Byzantines reconsolidated their hold on Proussa, but not for long.

The dawn of the fourteenth century saw a small band of nomadic Turks, led by **Osman Gazi**, camped outside the walls of Proussa. After more than a decade of siege, the city capitulated in 1326 to Osman's son, Orhan, and the **Ottomans** ceased to be a wandering tribe of marauders. Orhan marked the acquisition of a capital and the organization of an infant state by styling himself sultan and giving the city its present name. Bursa then embarked on a second golden age: the silk industry was expanded and the city, outgrowing the confines of the citadel, was graced with monuments.

In the years following Orhan's death in 1362 the imperial capital was gradually moved to Edirne, but Bursa's place in history, and in the hearts of the Ottomans, was ensured; succeeding sultans continued to add buildings, and to be laid to rest here, for another hundred years. Disastrous fires and earthquakes in the 1800s, and the 1919–22 War of Independence, only slightly diminished the city's splendour.

Arrival, orientation and information

Bursa's position at the foot of the mountain has dictated an elongated layout, with most of the major boulevards running from east to west, changing their names several times as they go. The **airport**, served by flights from Antalya, Trabzon and Erzerum, lies 43km east near Yenişehir; there's no bus service, so you'll have to rent a car, or take a taxi into town. The **otogar** (with a 24hr left-luggage service) lies 10km north of town on the Yalova road; from here, bus #38 serves the centre, #96 serves Çekirge suburb, while service buses may ferry visitors straight to Heykel (also known as Cumhuriyet Alanı), the focal point of the city. Bursa's main **tourist office** (Mon–Fri 8am–noon & 1–5.30pm, also same hours on Sat & Sun in high season; ☎0224/220 1848) is a 200-metre walk from Heykel, in a row of shops under the north side of Atatürk Caddesi, opposite Orhan Gazi Camii; here, you can pick up a reasonable city map.

Bursa's main lengthwise thoroughfare begins life just east of Heykel as **Namazgah Caddesi**, below the district of **Yeşil** and its namesake mosque and tomb. West of the Setbaşı bridge it becomes **Atatürk Caddesi** as it skirts the city's central bazaar and hotel district before changing its name again to **Cemal Nadir Caddesi** right below **Hisar**, the nucleus of the Byzantine settlement. After being fed more traffic by Haşim İşcan Caddesi, the boulevard metamorphoses into **Altıparmak Caddesi**, and then into **Çekirge Caddesi** as it heads west past the Kültür Parkı towards the thermal resort of **Çekirge**, 4km west of the centre.

City transport

While Bursa is narrow, it's sufficiently long enough for you to consider **public transport** to reach the outlying attractions. The two most useful **city bus** routes are the #2/A (connecting Emir Sultan in the east of town with Çekirge to the west) and the #3/A (linking Heykel with the Uludağ *teleferik*); tickets (1.50TL) for all buses must be pre-purchased at kiosks or shops displaying the BuKart logo. More useful are Bursa's multicoloured **dolmuşes**, with major terminals near Koza Parkı and Heykel, plus other pick-up/set-down points marked with a large "D" sign; fares start from 1.25TL. You are unlikely to need the single-line, east–west **metro**, which links various remote suburbs with points well north of the centre. **Drivers** will find parking a nightmare – there are never central street spaces to be had, and car parks are expensive. Resign yourself to parking some way out and walking to the sights.

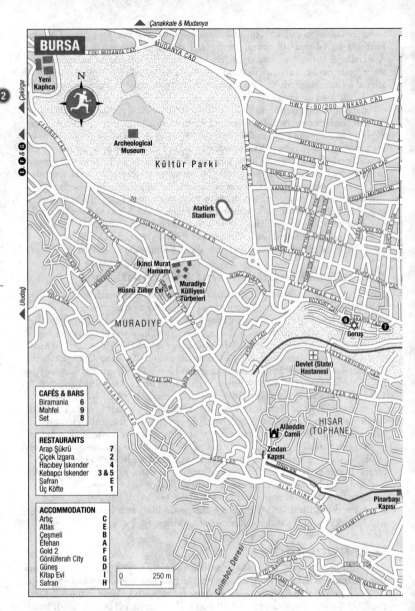

▲ Çanakkale & Mudanya

BURSA

ESKI MUDANYA CAD. MUDANYA CAD.

Çekirge ◄

ÇEKİRGE CAD.

E, F & G ◄

Uludağ ◄

Yeni
Kaplıca

N

Archeological
Museum

Kültür Parkı

HWY E-90/200 ANKARA CAD.

KIBRIS ŞEHİTLER CAD.

USLU SOK.

MERİNOŞLU SOK.

STADYUM CAD.

DARMSTAD CAD.

İLKBAHAR CAD.

SÜMER SOK.

KARAOSMAN SOK.

Atatürk
Stadium

BEŞİKÇİLER CAD.   ÇEKİRGE CAD.

HAMZABEY CAD.

BİLADİYE CAD.

MİRZABEYOĞLU SOK.

YAVLA SOK.

İkinci Murat
Hamamı

Hüsnü Züber Evi

Muradiye
Külliyesi
Türbeleri

MURADİYE

KÖŞK CAD.

KIZLAR CAD.

SAVUR SOK.

ORHANELİ CAD.

İKİNCİ MURAT CAD.

DEĞİRMEN CAD.

BURSALI TAHİR CAD.

ALİPARMAK CAD.

BOZKURT CAD.

AŞIBEY CAD.

HASTALARYURDU CAD.

İLK BAHAR CAD.

BURSALI TAHİR CAD.

ÇİÇEK SOK.

6 ★

Geruş

7

Devlet (State)
Hastanesi

ORTAPAZAR CAD.

HİSAR
(TOPHANE)

CAFÉS & BARS
Biramania   **6**
Mahfel   **9**
Set   **8**

Alâeddin
Camii

Zindan
Kapısı

FERAH SOK.

ALACAHIRKA CAD.

Pınarbaşı
Kapısı

RESTAURANTS
Arap Şükrü   **7**
Çiçek İzgara   **2**
Hacıbey İskender **4**
Kebapçı İskender **3 & 5**
Safran   **E**
Üç Köfte   **1**

HAVRAN YERİ CAD.

KÖŞK CAD.

ACCOMMODATION
Artıç   **C**
Atlas   **E**
Çeşmeli   **B**
Efehan   **A**
Gold 2   **F**
Gönlüferah City **G**
Güneş   **D**
Kitap Evi   **I**
Safran   **H**

0   250 m

Cilimboz Deresi

SEYDİ NASIR CAD.

KESTANELİK CAD.

ESKİYOL SOK.

SEYDİ NASIR CAD.

Accommodation

There's usually no shortage of reasonably priced **hotel** beds in Bursa, as it's off the backpackers' trail and often visited as a day-trip from İstanbul. Wealthier foreigners gravitate towards the luxurious spa-hotels at **Çekirge**, which also has a cluster of modest establishments, around the Birinci Murat Camii. However, the flow of hot water to individual Çekirge establishments (and to some extent the

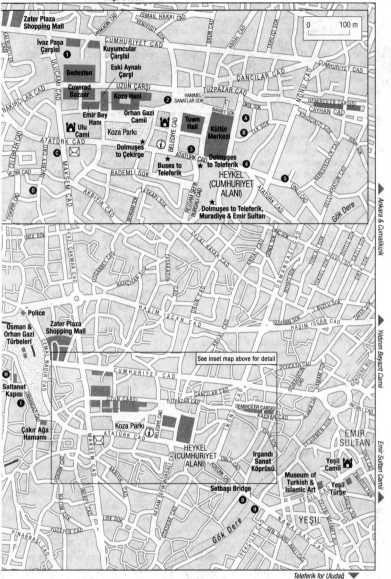

main baths) is currently interrupted (see p.187). If you're mostly interested in monumental Bursa, then staying in the bazaar or Hisar districts makes more sense.

Bazaar

Artıç Atatürk Cad, Ulu Cami Karşısı 95 ☎0224/223 5505, ⓦwww.artichotel.com. Set slightly back from the boulevard, this standard businessman's hotel

has good-value if bland, carpeted rooms with all the usual amenities and a bird's-eye view of the mosque domes from its modern breakfast salon; it's worth paying the extra for a suite. ❺, suites ❻.

Çeşmeli Gümüşçeken Cad 6 ⓉⒹ&Ⓕ 0224/224 1511. Salubrious, extremely welcoming hotel run entirely by women. Rooms, though en suite and a/c, have resolutely 1980s-style decor; buffet breakfast included. ❹

Efehan Gümüşçeken Cad 34 Ⓣ 0224/225 2260, Ⓦ www.efehan.com.tr. Despite its rather grim exterior, this three-star hotel has good-taste rooms with newish bathrooms; ask for a top-floor one with mountain views. There's an on-site restaurant and parking nearby. ❺

Güneş İnebey Cad 75 Ⓣ 0224/224 1404. Clean and friendly family-run *pansiyon*, with centrally heated (though waterless) laminate-floor rooms in a converted Ottoman house. ❷

Hisar

🏃 Kitap Evi Burç Üstü 21, in from Saltanat Kapısı Ⓣ 0224/225 4160, Ⓦ www.kitapevi .com.tr. Bursa's only boutique-style hotel, with eclectically decorated, themed rooms (some old-fashioned, some contemporary in design) and suites with dark-wood floors and (often) freestanding baths. The front rooms (and the roof suite) have glorious city views but some noise; quieter units face the rear-garden breakfast café/restaurant. Limited street parking. ❺, suites ❻

Safran Ortapazar Cad, Arka Sok 4, inside Saltanat Kapısı Ⓣ 0224/224 7216. Converted wooden-house hotel with atmospheric common areas. The a/c

rooms themselves, however, are blandly modern and a bit overpriced. There's limited parking, but a decent in-house restaurant (see p.188), good breakfasts and friendly, helpful staff compensate for this. Limited parking. ❺

Çekirge

Atlas Hamamlar Cad 29 Ⓣ 0224/234 4100, Ⓦ www.atlasotel.com. Reproduction Art Nouveau common areas complement the well-kept rooms with flat-screen TVs, designer bathrooms and modern furnishings; the best ones face the garden courtyard. At the moment the marble basement hamam is not functioning. ❹

Gold 2 Brinici Murat Cami Aralığı Ⓣ 0224/235 6030, Ⓦ www.hotelgold.com.tr. This much-altered 220-year-old building is one of Bursa's quietest hotels, with lavender wallpaper and laminate floors throughout, a creaky lift, pleasant breakfast/bar area, and some parking out front. Some top-floor rooms have balconies (no. 401 has a view of the mosque domes). ❹

Gönlüferah City (ex-*Dilmen*) Murat Cad 20 Ⓣ 0224/233 9500, Ⓦ www.gonluferahcity.com. Four-star hotel whose plain rooms have medium-dark veneer trim and marble sinks – ask for a rear-facing one. Its main selling points are the terrace restaurant, and secure parking. That said, not bad value in these spa-less times at ❺

The City

There's no need to tour Bursa's most significant monuments in chronological order, though many of the oldest ones cluster just outside **Hisar**. The central sites, together with those of **Yeşil** and **Muradiye** districts, can be seen in a single full day.

Central sites

Just across from the main tourist office stands the **Orhan Gazi Camii**, whose 1336 foundation makes it the second-oldest mosque in Bursa, though it has been destroyed and re-built twice since. Originally built as a *zaviye* for dervishes, this is the earliest example of the T-form mosque with *eyvan*s flanking the main prayer hall. **Karagöz puppets**, the painted camel-leather props used in the Turkish national shadow-play, supposedly represent workers who were involved in building the Orhan Gazi Camii. According to legend, the antics of Karagöz and his sidekick Hacıvat so entertained their fellow workmen that Orhan had them beheaded to end the distraction. Later, missing the comedians and repenting of his deed, he arranged to immortalize the pair in the art form that now bears the name of Karagöz.

Just west of Orhan Gazi, the compact **Koza Parkı**, with its fountains, benches, strolling crowds and street-level cafés, is the real heart of Bursa. On its far side looms the tawny limestone **Ulu Cami**, built between 1396 and 1399 by Yıldırım Beyazit I, from the proceeds of booty won from the Crusaders at Macedonian Nikopolis. Before the battle Yıldırım (Thunderbolt) had vowed to construct twenty mosques if victorious. The present building of twenty domes supported by twelve freestanding pillars was his rather loose interpretation of this promise,

Bursa silk and the cocoon auction

Highlight of the bazaar's year is the **cocoon auction** of late June and early July, when silk-breeders from around the province gather to hawk their valuable produce. Then, the courtyard floor of the Koza Hanı becomes a lake of white torpedoes the size of a songbird's egg; the moth, when it hatches, is a beautiful creature with giant onyx eyes and feathery antennae, though this rarely happens as the cocoons are boiled to kill the grub inside and the fibre then spun. You can watch the melee from the upper arcades or, if you're careful, the merchants don't mind you walking the floor.

During the 1700s Bursa's silk trade declined due to French and Italian competition, but has since experienced a tentative revival. However, the quality of contemporary fabric cannot compare to museum pieces from the early Ottoman heyday, and most of the better designs use imported material, which is better quality than the Turkish. If you're buying silk here, make sure the label says *ipek* (silk) and not *ithal ipek* (artificial silk).

but it was still the largest and most ambitious Ottoman mosque of its time. The interior is dominated by a huge *şadırvan* pool in the centre, whose dome oculus (now glassed over) was once open to the elements, and an intricate walnut pulpit pieced together, it's claimed, without nails or glue.

From the north porch you can descend to the two-storeyed **Emir (Bey) Hanı**, originally a dependency of the Orhan Gazi Camii and now home to various offices and shops. A fountain plays next to teahouse tables under the trees in the courtyard. Beyond the Emir Hanı begins Bursa's **covered bazaar**, whose assorted galleries and lesser *hans* sell clothes, silk goods, towels, bolts of cloth and furniture, all Bursa province specialities. The nearby **bedesten** is given over to the sale and warehousing of jewellery and precious metals.

The centrepiece of the bazaar is the **Koza Hanı**, or "Silk-Cocoon Hall", flanking Koza Parkı. Built in 1490, when Bursa was the final stop on the Silk Route from China, it's still filled with silk and brocade merchants (plus a few jewellery stores). On the lower level, in the middle of a cobbled courtyard, a minuscule **mescit** (small mosque) perches directly over its *şadırvan*, while a subsidiary court bulges asymmetrically to the east; there are teahouses in both. Abutting the Koza Hanı to the west, though without access from it, is the **Eski Aynalı Çarşı**, formerly the **Bey Hamamı** of the Orhan Gazi complex (note the domes and skylights), which sells more tourist-orientated goods than the surrounding bazaars.

Another area of the bazaar that has kept its traditions intact despite quakes and blazes is the **Demirciler Çarşısı**, the ironmongers' market. This is just the other side of İnönü Caddesi, best crossed by the pedestrian underpass at Okçular Caddesi. Stall upon stall of blacksmiths and braziers attract photographers, but be advised that some expect a few lira for posing. Further south, the pedestrianized **Irgandı Sanat Köprüsü** (Irgandı Artisanry Bridge) is a feeble attempt to ape Florence's Ponte Vecchio bridge with its rows of faux-Ottoman cafés and tourist shops over the **Gök Dere**, one of two streams that tumble through Bursa, forming an approximate eastern boundary for the centre.

Yeşil

Across the Gök Dere, it's only a few minutes' walk up to **Yeşil**, as the eastern neighbourhood around the eponymous mosque and tomb is known. Designed by architect Hacı İvaz atop a slight rise, the **Yeşil Cami** was begun in 1413 by Çelebi Mehmet I, victor of the civil war caused by the death of Beyazit I. Although unfinished – work ceased in 1424, three years after Mehmet himself died – and despite catastrophic damage from two nineteenth-century earth tremors, it's the most spectacular of Bursa's imperial mosques. The incomplete entrance, faced in a light marble, lacks a portico and, beside the stalactite vaulting and relief calligraphy, you can see the supports for arches never built.

Next you'll pass through a foyer supported by pilfered Byzantine columns to reach the **interior**, a variation on the T-plan usually reserved for dervish *zaviye*s. A fine *şadırvan* occupies the centre of the "T", but your eye is monopolized by the hundreds of mostly blue and green **tiles** that line not just the dazzling *mihrab* but every available vertical surface up to 5m in height, particularly two recesses flanking the entryway. Tucked above the foyer, and only accessible with permission from the imam, is the **imperial loge**, the most extravagantly decorated chamber of all. Several artisans from Tabriz participated in the tiling of Yeşil Cami but the loge is attributed to a certain Al-Majnun, which means "madman" (due to the effects of excessive hashish-smoking) in Arabic.

On the same knoll as the mosque, across the pedestrian precinct, the **Yeşil Türbe** (daily 9am–1pm & 2–6pm; free) contains the sarcophagus of Çelebi Mehmet I and his assorted offspring. Inside, the walls and Mehmet's tomb glisten with the glorious original Tabriz material, while the battered exterior is currently being restored with new İznik tiles.

The immediate environs of the two monuments swarm with tour groups; the resulting competition has restrained prices at most of the nearby cafés, but also led to a clutch of garishly repainted old houses being glutted with souvenir dross. For genuine antique dealers, head over to the lane (İkinci Müze Sokağı) flanking the *medrese* downhill. This now contains Bursa's **Museum of Turkish and Islamic Art** (Türk ve İslam Eserleri Müzesi; daily except Mon 9am–1pm & 2–6pm; free), set around a pleasant courtyard with fountain, trees and picnic tables. Its collection includes poorly labelled İznik ware, dervish paraphernalia, Beykoz glass and antiquarian manuscripts, though some rooms may be closed if the museum is short-staffed.

East of Yeşil: to Yıldırım Beyazit Camii

A 300-metre walk east of Yeşil leads to the **Emir Sultan Camii**, amid extensive graveyards where every religious Bursan hopes to be buried. The mosque was originally endowed by a Bokharan dervish and trusted adviser to three sultans beginning with Beyazit I, then rebuilt from earthquake ruins in the Ottoman Baroque style during the early 1800s; it was further restored in 1990, leaving little of the original essence. The pious, however, seem to harbour no doubts, coming in strength to worship at the tombs of the saint and his family.

If you're short of time, Emir Sultan Camii is the obvious site to omit: climb down steps through the graveyard instead and cross the urban lowlands to the **Yıldırım Beyazit Camii**, perched on a small hillock at the northeastern edge of the city centre. Coming directly from downtown, this is a substantial hike, so you might want to take a dolmuş (marked "Heykel–Beyazit Yıldırım" or the more common "Heykel–Fakülte"), which passes 200m below the mosque. Completed by Beyazit I between 1390 and 1395, the mosque features a handsome, five-arched portico defined by square columns. The interior is unremarkable except for a gravity-defying arch bisecting the prayer hall, its lower supports apparently tapering away to end in stalactite moulding. The only other note of whimsy in this spare building is the use of elaborate niches out on the porch.

The associated **medrese**, exceptionally long and narrow because of its sloping site, huddles just downhill; today it houses a medical clinic. The **türbe** (tomb) of the luckless Beyazit, supposedly kept in an iron cage by the rampaging Tamerlane until his death in 1403, is usually locked. Perhaps the mosque custodians fear a revival of the Ottoman inclination to abuse the tomb of the most ignominiously defeated sultan.

Hisar (Tophane)

Bursa's original nucleus, **Hisar**, also known as Tophane, retains clusters of dilapi-dated Ottoman housing within its warren of narrow lanes, and some courses of medieval wall along its perimeter, including the Sultanat Gate on the east. From where Atatürk Caddesi becomes Cemal Nadir Caddesi, just before the modern **Zafer Plaza** shopping mall with its landmark glass pyramid, you can climb up to Hisar's plateau via pedestrian ramps negotiating the ancient walls. Alternatively, Orhangazi Caddesi allows access to vehicles.

Where Orhangazi stops climbing, the **Osman and Orhan Gazi Türbeleri** stand at the edge of the fortified acropolis that they conquered. The tombs – post-earthquake restorations in gaudy late Ottoman style – are on the site of a Byzantine church that has long since disappeared. More impressive is the view from the cliff-top **park** sprawling around the tombs and adjacent clocktower, with reasonable cafés at the head of walkways down to Cemal Nadir and Altıparmak *caddesi*s, the latter home to many of the city's posher shops and cinemas.

Near the southernmost extreme of the citadel, exit at the **Pınarbaşı Kapısı**, lowest point in the circuit of walls and the spot where Orhan's forces finally entered the city in 1326. Head west from here, parallel to the walls, re-entering at the **Zindan Kapısı**, inside of which is the simple, box-like **Alâeddin Camii**, erected within a decade of the conquest and so the earliest mosque in Bursa.

More directly, follow signs pointing west to Muradiye district, along Ortapazar and Hasta Yurdu *caddesi*s, passing another generous swathe of park studded with teahouses. The furthest ones overlook Muradiye, and from the final café and course of wall, obvious stairs descend to the **Cılımboz Deresi**, the second major stream to furrow the city.

Muradiye

Bursa's best-preserved medieval dwellings line the streets of **Muradiye**, at their liveliest during the Tuesday **street market**. You can get frequent dolmuşes here from Heykel, marked "Muradiye".

The **Muradiye Külliyesi** is easy enough to find and is definitely the place to capture the early Ottoman spirit – there are a few low-key trinket-sellers but little

▲ Decorated dome of Cem Sultan's tomb

pressure to buy and no coachloads to shatter the calm. The mosque complex, begun in 1424 by Murat II, was the last imperial foundation in Bursa, though the tombs for which Muradiye is famous were added piecemeal over the next century or so. The **mosque** is similar in plan to Orhan Gazi, but more impressive with its profuse tiling low on the walls, calligraphy higher up and two domes.

The ten **royal tombs** (daily 8.30am–5.30pm, may close earlier winter; free), are set in lovingly tended gardens – you may have to ask the keeper in the booth by the entrance to unlock them. The first tomb encountered is that of **Şehzade Ahmet** and his brother Şehinşah, both murdered in 1513 by their cousin Selim I to preclude any succession disputes. The luxury of the two-tone blue İznik tiles within contrasts sharply with the adjacent austerity of **Murat II's tomb**, where Roman columns inside and a wooden canopy out front are the only superfluities. Murat, as much contemplative mystic as warrior-sultan, was the only Ottoman ruler ever to abdicate voluntarily, though pressures of state forced him to leave his dervish order and return to the throne after just two years. He was the last sultan to be interred at Bursa and one of the few lying here who died in his bed; in accordance with his wishes, both the coffin and the dome were originally open to the sky "so that the rain of heaven might wash my face like any pauper's".

Next along is the tomb of **Şehzade Mustafa**, Süleyman the Magnificent's unjustly murdered heir; perhaps indicative of his father's remorse, the tomb is done up in extravagantly floral İznik tiles, with a top border of calligraphy. Nearby stands the tomb of **Cem Sultan**, his brother Mustafa and two of Beyazit II's sons, decorated with a riot of abstract, botanical and calligraphic paint strokes up to the dome, with turquoise tiles below. Cem, the cultured favourite son of Mehmet the Conqueror, was one of the Ottoman Empire's most interesting might-have-beens. Following Mehmet's death in 1481, he lost a brief dynastic struggle with the successful claimant, brother Beyazit II, and fled abroad. For fourteen years he wandered, seeking sponsorship of his cause from Christian benefactors who in all cases became his jailers: first the Knights of St John at Bodrum and Rhodes, later the papacy. At one point it seemed that he would command a Crusader army organized to retake Istanbul, but all such plans came to nothing for the simple reason that Beyazit anticipated his opponents' moves and each time bribed them handsomely to desist, making Cem a lucrative prisoner indeed. His usefulness as a pawn exhausted, Cem was probably poisoned in Italy by Pope Alexander VI in 1495, leaving reams of poems aching with nostalgia and homesickness.

A minute's walk uphill from the Muradiye Külliyesi is the **Hüsnü Züber Evi** at Uzunyol Sok 3 (Tues–Sun 10am–noon & 1–5pm; 3TL). This former Ottoman guesthouse, built in 1836, sports a typical overhanging upper storey, wooden roof and garden courtyard. It now houses a collection of carved wooden musical instruments, spoons and farming utensils, many made by the former owner Hüsnü Züber. The main exhibit, however, is the house itself, one of the few of its era to have been well restored and opened to the public.

Kültür Parkı

From Muradiye it's a short walk down to Çekirge Caddesi and the southeast gate of the **Kültür Parkı** (token admission charge when entry booths are staffed; 3TL parking fee), where courting couples stroll along regimented plantations and broad driveways. Inside there's a popular tea garden, a small boating lake and a few overpriced, licensed restaurants.

Near the centre of the park is the city's **Archeological Museum** (Arkeoloji Müzesi; Tues–Sun 8.30am–12.30pm & 1.30–5pm; 5TL). Inside, exhibits in the right-hand gallery vary from the macabre (a Byzantine ossuary with a skull peeking out) to the homely (a Roman cavalryman figurine), but the adjacent hall featuring metal jewellery from all over Anatolia – watch chains, breastplates, belts, buckles, bracelets, anklets, chokers – steals the show. The left wing houses miscellaneous small antiquities, the best of which are the Roman glass items and Byzantine and Roman bronzes. Oil lamps, pottery, a token amount of gold and far too many ceramic figurines complete these poorly labelled collections.

Çekirge

The thermal centre of **Çekirge** ("Grasshopper" – presumably a reference to the natural soundtrack of a summer evening), is another twenty minutes' walk or so along Çekirge Caddesi from the southwest side of Kültür Parkı. Buses (including the #2/A), as well as dolmuşes (marked "Çekirge"), shuttle to and from stops on Atatürk Caddesi.

The main reason to visit Çekirge has traditionally been its hot springs though in 2009, the waters from the surrounding mountainside stopped running; it is not known whether this is a permanent state of affairs. Just west of the Parkı Park is the **Yeni Kaplıca** (New Spa; daily 6am–10pm; 8TL admission), where the water usually flows out at a whopping 84°C. The spa dates from the mid-sixteenth century and has a women's section, though it is nothing like as splendid as the men's with its huge, deep central pool. According to legend, Süleyman the Magnificent was cured of gout after a dip in the Byzantine baths here and had his vizier Rüstem Paşa overhaul them. Fragments of mosaic paving stud the floor and the walls are lined with once-exquisite but now blurred İznik tiles. The two other spas are the rather grim **Kkaynarca baths** for women only and the **Karamustafa spa** (54°C at source) for families.

The **Eski Kaplıca** (Old Baths; daily 7am–10.30pm; 8TL), huddled at the far end of Çekirge Caddesi, next to the *Kervansaray Bursa Hotel*, are Bursa's most ancient baths (and much the nicest public bath for women). Byzantine rulers Justinian and Theodora first improved a Roman spa on the site and Murat I had a go at the structure in the late fourteenth century. Huge but shallow keyhole-shaped pools dominate the *hararetler* (hot rooms) of the men's and women's sections, whose domes are supported by eight Byzantine columns. Scalding (45°C) water pours into the notch of the keyhole, the temperature still so hot in the main basin that you'll soon be gasping out in the cool room, seeking relief at the fountain in the middle.

On a hillock just west of the thermal centre stands the **Hüdavendigar (Birinci) Murat Camii**, which with its five-arched portico and alternating bands of brick and stone seems more like a Byzantine church from Ravenna or Macedonia. Indeed tradition asserts that the architect and builders were Christians, who dallied twenty years at the task because Murat I, whose pompous epithet literally means "Creator of the Universe", was continually off at war and unable to supervise the work. The interior plan, consisting of a first-floor *medrese* above a highly modified, T-type *zaviye* at ground level, is unique in Islam. Unfortunately, the upper storey is rarely open for visits.

In the much-modified **türbe** across the street lies Murat himself, complete apart from his entrails, which were removed by the embalmers before the body began its long journey back from Serbia in 1389. In June of that year Murat was in the process of winning his greatest triumph over the Serbian king Lazar and his allies at the **Battle of Kosovo**, in the former Yugoslavia, when he was stabbed to death in his tent by Miloš Obilić, a Serbian noble who had feigned desertion. Murat's son Beyazit, later styled as Yıldırım, immediately had his brother Yakub strangled and, once in sole command, crushed the Christian armies. Beyazit's acts had two far-reaching consequences: the Balkans remained under Ottoman control until early in the twentieth century, and a gruesome precedent of fratricide was established for subsequent Ottoman coronations.

Eating, drinking and entertainment

Bursa's **cuisine** is solidly meat-oriented and served in a largely alcohol-free environment. The most famous local recipes are *İskender kebabı* (essentially *döner kebap* soaked in a rich butter, tomato and yoghurt sauce) and *İnegöl köftesi* (rich little pellets of mince sometimes laced with cheese, when they're known as *kaşarlı köfte*). The city is also famous for its *kestane şekeri* (candied chestnuts), sold ubiquitously within a 50km radius. If you're sick of Turkish sponge-bread, look out for Bursan *kepekli* (whole bran) loaves at any bakery.

For licensed restaurants, head to the pedestrianized **Sakarya Caddesi** between Altıparmak Caddesi and the walls of Hisar above – the former fish market and main commercial street of the **Jewish quarter** (the **Geruş synagogue**, one of three in town, still exists at no. 61) is now an atmospheric place for an outdoor fish dinner on a summer's evening. The lively **bars** which used to cluster along Sakarya and its continuation Bozkurt Caddesi have mostly vanished, to be replaced by unlicensed tea houses where a young clientele gather to play backgammon and scrabble.

Bursa has relatively few nocturnal or weekend events and the student contingent is responsible for any concerts that take place. The **Kültür Merkezi** (Cultural Centre) on Atatürk Caddesi (℡0224/223 4461) hosts temporary art exhibitions and occasional concerts. The Kültür Parkı's **open-air theatre** is the main venue (tickets 15–25TL) for musical performances of the annual **Uluslarası Bursa Festival** (June–July; ⓦwww.bursafestivali.org), mostly showcasing popular Turkish acts but also with a token roster of foreign performers.

Restaurants

Arap Şükrü Sakarya Cad 6 & 27, Tophane. The sons of the original Arap Şükrü have grouped into two competing eateries (*Çetin* & *Ahmet*) straddling the east end of this pedestrianized lane. Both have near-identical menus of good fish dishes (starting from 20TL a portion), *meze*s (4–6TL) brought out on a tray to choose from, and beer, wine or *rakı* to wash it down, served at tables on both sides of the cobbled street or indoors.

Çiçek İzgara Belediye Cad 15. Popular mid town venue for lunch and dinner overlooking a leafy square, this upstairs spot is beginning to rest on its laurels – you're paying as much for the linen tablecloths and waiter service as for the signature dish *kaşarlı köfte* (10TL). Closed Sun.

Hacibey İskender Taşkapı Sok 4, off Atatürk Cad. This tiny, two-storey establishment near Heykel claims to be the original *İskender* salon, with decor of old wood, fake Ottoman tiles and photos of Olde Bursa. Indeed, their *İskender* is excellent, though you pay extra for the ambience.

Kebapçı İskender Unlu Cad 7A, Heykel. Another fake Ottoman building, and another claimant to be the inventor of the namesake dish – and that's all they serve, not even salads. Always packed, even though it's moderately expensive (17TL and up for smallish portions). There's an annexe on Atatürk Cad, near the Kültür Merkezi.

Safran Restaurant *Safran Hotel*, Ortapazar Cad, Arka Sok 4, Hisar. Chic little à la carte restaurant whose menu includes cold and hot *meze*s, meat and mushroom stews, good salads, and heavenly sweets such as *kaymaklı ayva tatlısı* (quince with clotted cream). Expect to pay 25–30TL a head for a three-course meal, drinks extra.

Üç Köfte Hacı İvaz Paşa Çarşısı 3, in the north of the covered bazaar. The name means "three (İnegöl-style) meatballs", which is what you get at this long-established spot, served up three times so the food on your plate is always piping hot. Lunch only, closed Sun.

Cafés and bars

Biramania Sarkarya Cad 63. As the name implies, beer specialists – and the only place you can get alcohol without food on this street.

Mahfel Namazgah Cad 2, southeast side of Setbaşı bridge. Supposedly Bursa's oldest café, serving slightly pricey Western snack fare but lovely, reasonably priced, puddings. Some evenings, there's live music on its riverside terrace.

Set Café Setbaşı bridge, Namazgah Cad, Heykel. Reasonably priced café-bar on a recessed terrace below street level, which attracts a lively student crowd. Enjoy a beer looking downstream to the next bridge, or on one of the four levels indoors.

Listings

Books Adım (Haşet) Kitapçılık, at Altıparmak Cad 50, has a limited stock of English-language titles and foreign magazines.

Car rental Aktif, Çekirge Cad 139 ☎0224/233 0444; Alize, Çekirge Cad 224 ☎0224/220 9344; Avis, Çekirge Cad 143 ☎0224/236 5133; Europcar, Çekirge Cad 57 ☎0224/223 2321. Most can arrange to deliver to Bursa/Yenişehir airport.

Consulate UK (honorary consulate), Resam Şefik Bursalı Sok, Başak Cad ☎0224/220 0436.

Hamams See p.187, or try the central, historic Çakır Ağa, located just below Hisar on Cemal Nadir Cad (men and women; 6am–midnight); or İkinci Murat, next to the Muradiye tomb complex (Fri & Sun men only, all other days women only; 10am–6pm).

Hospitals Devlet (State) Hastanesi, Hasta Yurdu Cad, Hisar ☎0224/220 0020; and Üniversite Hastanesi, P. Tezok Cad, Hastane Sok, Çekirge ☎0224/442 8400.

Around Bursa

Immediately around Bursa are a couple of worthwhile targets for half-day or even overnight outings. The rural Ottoman village of **Cumalıkızık** was picturesque enough to serve as the location for a popular 2000–05 Turkish TV serial, which greatly enhanced its tourism potential, while the mountain resort of **Uludağ** constitutes a year-round attraction, offering skiing or hiking according to season or just a general high-altitude escape.

Further afield, the 120-kilometre route west from Bursa towards Bandırma port is enlivened by two large but shallow lakes, the largest inland bodies of water in the historical region of Mysia. The first, 36km from central Bursa, is **Uluabat Gölü**, home to the appealing village of **Gölyazı** built atop the ancient settlement of Apollonia, while the second lake, **Manyas Gölü**, 19km southeast of Bandırma, supports an acclaimed bird sanctuary.

Cumalıkızık

The showcase village of **CUMALIKIZIK** lies 17km east, then south of Bursa on the Ankara road; city bus #22 (every 90min) goes there from Atatürk Caddesi. The first records of the village mosque and hamam date from 1685, but the place is thought to be at least three centuries older. Set on the lower slopes of Uludağ, Cumalıkızık's cobbled streets are full of traditional dwellings, some restored and painted, others leaning brokenly into each other. Villagers once made a living from harvesting chestnuts, but a blight annihilated the local trees; now, raspberries and blackberries are grown instead, but there's still not enough work to halt the usual flight of the young to the city.

Buses drop you at the village square, dominated by two enormous plane trees, from which radiates a network of narrow alleys often only wide enough for pedestrians and pack animals. The ground and first floors of the village houses harbour the storerooms and stables, while the living quarters with their latticed bay windows are upstairs under tiled eaves. Many of the surviving double-front doors sport large-headed nails, wrought-iron strips and massive handles.

Cumalıkızık's time in front of the cameras encouraged the setting up of two places to stay in the village, both in coverted old houses: the six-roomed *Mavi Boncuk* (☎0224/373 0955, ⊛www.cumalikizik-maviboncuk.com; ❹) with its half-timbered upper storey is slightly smarter than the eight-room *Konak Pansiyon* (☎0224/372/4869; ❸).

Uludağ

Presiding over Bursa, 2543-metre-high **Uludağ** (or "Great Mountain") is a dramatic, often cloud-cloaked massif, its northern reaches dropping precipitously into the city. In ancient times it was known as the Mount Olympos of Mysia, one of nearly twenty peaks around the Aegean so named (Olympos was possibly a generic Phoenician or Doric word for "mountain"), and in mythology it was the seat from which the gods watched the battle of Troy. Early in the Christian era the range became a refuge for monks and hermits, replaced after the Ottoman conquest by Muslim dervishes.

These days the scent of grilling meat has displaced the odour of sanctity, since Bursans cram the alpine campsites and picnic grounds to the gills on any holiday or weekend. Getting there is definitely half the fun if you opt for the **cable car** (*teleferik*), which links the Teleferüç borough of Bursa with the **Sarıalan** picnic grounds at 1635m, where a cluster of *et mangal*s and *kendin pişin kendin ye* (cook-it-yourself establishments) await your custom.

Much of the dense middle-altitude forest has been designated a **national park**, though there are only a few kilometres of marked hiking trails. In fact, the best part of the mountain lies outside the park to the east, where a few hours' walking will bring you to some glacial **lakes** in a wild, rocky setting just below the highest summit. The best months for a visit are May and June, when the wildflowers are blooming, or September and October, when the mist is less dense. However, due to the nearby Sea of Marmara, the high ridges trap moist marine air, and whiteouts or violent storms can blow up during most months of the year. **Skiing** is possible from December to March, though it's better earlier in the season than later. At around 1800m, there's a dense cluster of hotels known as **Oteller**, most with their own ski lift (day-passes 15TL), and you can rent skis and ski clothes on the spot.

Practicalities

To reach the lower cable-car terminus, take a dolmuş labelled "Teleferik" from the corner of Ressam Şefik Bursalı and Atatürk *caddesi*s. The wobbly **teleferik** gondolas make the trip up from Teleferüç to Sarıalan every 45 minutes (daily 8am–9.30pm in summer, stops at 4.30pm in winter; 8TL return), but are cancelled in high winds; the journey takes about thirty minutes, with a pause part way up at

---

Hiking around Uludağ

From the top of Oteller, a jeep-track leads within ninety minutes' walk to a **tungsten mine**. From behind the mine's guardhouse, an obvious path slips up onto the broad, barren watershed ridge, just below the secondary summit of **Zirve** (2496m); follow this trail for a further ninety minutes to a fork. The right-hand path leads to the **main peak** (2543m), though the cairned left-hand choice is more rewarding, descending slightly to overlook the first of Uludağ's lakes, **Aynalıgöl**, reachable by its own side trail a half-hour beyond the junction.

There are campsites here but none at **Karagöl**, the second and most famous lake, fifteen minutes southeast of Aynalıgöl, sunk in a deep chasm and speckled with ice floes. **Kilimligöl**, the third substantial lake, is tucked away on a plateau southeast of Karagöl and offers more good high-altitude camping. There are two smaller, nameless tarns, difficult to find in the crags above Aynalıgöl.

Returning to Oteller, as long as the weather is good you can stay with the ridge rather than revisiting the tungsten works, passing below the ruined hut on Zirve to meet a faint trail. This soon vanishes and thereafter it's cross-country downhill along the watershed as far as **Cennetkaya**, a knoll above the hotels, served by a marked trail. High above the trees, crowds and jeep tracks, you just might strike lucky and glimpse patches of the distant Sea of Marmara to the north.

Kadıyayla. Try to avoid travelling mid-afternoon, when students make the ascent after school, or at weekends when hour-long queues are the norm. At Sarıalan, there's a fleet of dolmuşes waiting to take you to Oteller. Alternatively, **dolmuşes** from Bursa's Orhangazi Caddesi go all the way to Oteller, along 32km of paved, twisty road, though you'll need a minimum of six passengers (7TL per person).

You follow the same route in your own vehicle, the road veering off above Çekirge and climbing rapidly through successive vegetation zones. Staff at the **Karabelen national park gate**, 20km into the park, charge 5TL per car and sometimes have **information** to hand out. The final stretch of road, from just below the gate to Oteller, is very rough cobble, designed to prevent drivers from skidding – or speeding – so allow nearly an hour for the trip. In bad weather conditions you will be advised to put chains on your wheels and may not be allowed to make the journey without them.

There's little to distinguish the many resorts at the road's end in Oteller: a good resource for winter **accommodation** is Ⓦwww.uludaghotels.com, which details all the area's hotels, even the more modest ones. While summer rates can dip as low as ❹, during the ski season you can expect to pay up to ❽ (full board). With some 7500 hotel beds in the area, you're unlikely to need to **camp**, which is just as well since the national park campsites are squalid and always full in summer.

Uluabat Gölü and Gölyazı

Built mostly on an island now lashed by a causeway to the shore of **Uluabat Gölü**, **GÖLYAZI** is an atmospheric community of storks' nests and a few surviving half-timbered houses daubed with rust-tint or ochre paint. Bits of Roman and Byzantine **Apollonia** have unconcernedly been pressed into domestic service, with extensive courses of wall ringing the island's shoreline. In the smaller mainland neighbourhood, the huge **Ayos Yorgos** Greek church, large enough for a few hundred parishioners, is currently being restored. The lake itself, speckled with nine islets, is only two metres deep, murky and not suitable for swimming, though it does attract numerous water birds. Appearances could lead you to pronounce Gölyazı the quintessential fishing village: there's a daily (11am) **fish auction** at the island end of the causeway, while women mending nets and rowboats are much in evidence. This conceals the fact, however, that pesticide and fertilizer runoff from the surrounding farmland, as well as the proliferation of introduced carp, is constantly diminishing the native catch.

Minibus #5/G links Gölyazı with Bursa's Küçük Sanayı metro station; drivers should look out for an inconspicuous sign, about 31km west of Bursa, indicating the five-kilometre side road to the village. There's no reliable **accommodation**, but there are various **tea houses** on either side of the causeway, plus a good **restaurant** on the island side, the licensed *Pehlivan*: a wooden cabin overhanging the water, it serves reasonably priced *yayın* (catfish) and *turna* (pike), plus decent mixed-*meze* platters for 6TL.

Transiting Bandırma

Bandırma itself – pretty much flattened during battles in 1922 – is a definite finalist in the Turkey's-ugliest-town sweepstakes, and you're unlikely to spend much time here. However, given its status as a major transit-point you may well need to cross from one terminal to another. The main **otogar** is on the southern outskirts of town, 1800m inland from the **ferry port** (with services to and from İstanbul) and its adjoining **train station** (for trains to and from İzmir). It's an uphill walk to the *otogar*, so you can either take a taxi or city buses labelled "Garaj/600 Evler", which depart from a marquee 200m east of the ferry terminal.

Manyas Gölü

Manyas Gölü is remarkable for its 64-hectare bird sanctuary astride a stream delta and swamps at the northeast corner of the lake. The **Bird Paradise National Park** (Kuş Cenneti Milli Parkı; daily 7am–5.30pm; 3TL) contains a small visitor centre full of dioramas, labelled in Turkish, and stocked with stuffed geese, orioles, spoonbills, herons, pelicans, ducks, egrets and owls. More interesting, though, is the wooden **observation tower** (bring your own binoculars), from where you can view pelicans (white and Dalmatian, nesting in May), smew-duck, spoonbills, spotted eagles and night herons, with cormorants and grey herons also common. The best months to visit are October – during the first rains, and various species' southward migrations – and April–May, when the swamps are at their fullest and the birds are flying north. During these migrations, up to three million birds of some 266 species stop by.

There's no **public transport** to the sanctuary, so you'll need your own vehicle: from Bandırma, it's 14km along the Balıkesir highway and then 5km on the signposted side road. There are no facilities in the park grounds, the closest being a simple **restaurant** with a couple of *pansiyon* rooms by the roadside at **Eski Sığırcı** village, 1.5km before the gate.

Travel details

Trains

Bandırma to: İzmir (1–2 daily; 5hr 30min). Morning ferries from İstanbul dovetail well (30min layover) with onward train; midday ferries entail a longer wait (up to 2hr).
Edirne to: İstanbul (2–3 daily; 5hr–6hr). For international services out of Edirne, see p.160.

Buses and dolmuşes

Bandırma to: Bursa (approx hourly; 2hr); Çanakkale (hourly; 3hr); İzmir (7 daily; 6hr).
Bursa to: Ankara (hourly; 6hr); Çanakkale (hourly; 5hr 15min); Gölyazı (10 Mon–Sat, 6 Sun; 40min); İstanbul, with ferry transfer (hourly; 3hr); İzmir via Balıkesir and often Ayvalık (hourly; 7hr); Kütahya (4 daily; 3hr); Mudanya (every 30min; 30min); Yalova (every 30min; 1hr).
Edirne to: Çanakkale (5 daily; 4hr); İstanbul (every 30min; 2hr 30min); Keşan (every 20min; 2hr 30min); Kapıkule (every 30min; 25min); Lüleburgaz (every 30min; 1hr).
Gelibolu to: Eceabat (hourly; 40min); Kilitbahir (hourly; 50min).
İznik to: Bursa (every 30min; 1hr 30min); Yalova (hourly; 1hr).

Short-hop ferries

Gelibolu to: Lapseki, car ferry (hourly 8am–1am, less often at night; 24TL cars, 2TL foot passengers; 30min).

Long-haul ferries and sea-buses

Services are frequent in summer (June–Aug), tail off in shoulder seasons (May & Sept) and are sharply reduced during winter (Oct–April). Routes between İstanbul (Yenikapı terminal) or Pendik and Bandırma, Mudanya (cited as 'Bursa' on schedules) or Yalova are handled by İDO (@ www.ido.com.tr). The only firm information for the Tekirdağ–Bandırma/Erdek ro-ro ferries is to be had at the quayside.
Bandırma to: İstanbul (summer 4–5 daily, winter 2–3 daily; mix of fast car ferries and sea-buses; 30TL foot passenger, 120TL car; 2hr).
Mudanya to: İstanbul (at least 2 daily early morning and early evening; foot passenger 20TL, car 80TL; 1hr 45min).
Tekirdağ to: Bandırma (April–Oct 1 daily at 7pm; 4hr 30min); Erdek (April–Oct 2 daily at 3pm & 5pm, via Marmara islands; 90TL car; 5hr 30min).
Yalova to: İstanbul (May–Oct 5 ferries & 1 sea-bus daily, Nov–April 2–3 daily; foot passenger 13TL, car 65TL; 1hr 10min); Pendik (11 ferries & 2 sea-buses daily; 6TL foot passenger, 50TL car; 45min).

The North Aegean

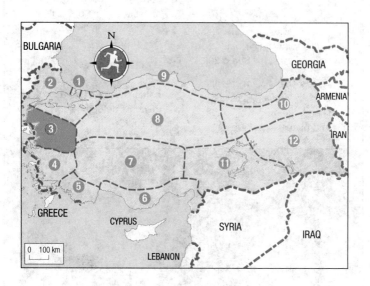

CHAPTER 3 # Highlights

* **Battlefield sites and cemeteries** The Gelibolu (Gallipoli) peninsula was the scene of a major Allied defeat during World War I, commemorated each April on Anzac Day. **See p.200**

* **Gökçeada** Turkey's largest island is a scenic, rugged place, with idyllic beaches and a lingering ethnic-Greek presence. **See p.206**

* **Bozcaada (Tenedos)** Small, popular island with an elegant harbour town, fine wines and decent beaches. **See p.208**

* **Assos** The ancient site offers stunning views of Lésvos island: the medieval village and picturesque harbour downhill are built of the same volcanic stone. **See p.213**

* **Ayvalık and Cunda** Relax in these adjacent, former Greek olive-oil-processing ports, with their intriguing mix of derelict and restored Ottoman houses. **See p.217**

* **Ancient Pergamon** Both the acropolis, with its sweeping views and restored temple, and the Asklepion downhill constitute some of the finest Roman ruins in the Aegean. **See p.224**

* **Sardis** With an evocative Artemis temple and restored baths, these remote ruins reward a detour inland. **See p.231**

▲ Artemis temple, Sardis

The North Aegean

T urkey's **North Aegean** sees far fewer visitors than the coastline further south. While there are some excellent sandy beaches, the lower sea temperature and lack of a major airport have protected the region from widespread development. Most summer visitors are Turks and, while tourism is inevitably important to the local economy, even in August visitor numbers don't match those at the country's more renowned destinations. Away from the few resorts, farming, fishing and (close to İzmir) heavy industry provide the main livelihoods.

In this area, the territory of ancient Aeolia, civilization bloomed under the Phrygians, who arrived in Anatolia during the thirteenth century BC. Later, Greek colonists established coastal settlements, leaving the region rich in Classical and Hellenistic remains. Although the sparse ruins of **Troy** don't quite live up to their literary and legendary reputation, ancient **Assos** and **Pergamon** (modern **Bergama**) display more tangible reminders of the power and wealth of the greater Greek cultural sphere. Less visited are the recently excavated ruins of **Alexandria Troas**, and the isolated Lydian city of **Sardis**, ancient capital of King Croesus, huddled at the foot of impressive mountains.

Coming from İstanbul or anywhere else in northwestern Turkey, the most obvious entry point is **Çanakkale** – useful as a base for both the ruins at Troy and the **World War I battlefields** on the **Gelibolu (Gallipoli) peninsula**. Offshore, the fine Turkish Aegean islands of **Gökçeada** and **Bozcaada** provide an easy escape from Çanakkale. The road south from Çanakkale is justifiably marked as scenic on most maps, with much of the route wooded and gently hilly, giving way to a coastal strip backed by the mountains of the **Kazdağı** range that conceal idyllic villages like **Yeşilyurt** and **Adatepe**. Further south, the best stretches of beach lie near **Ayvalık-Cunda** – the area's longest-established resort – though there are also pleasant sands below **Assos**, at **Çandarlı** and north of **Foça**.

In general there's less to see **inland**, with a mountainous landscape and a few predominantly industrial cities. However, the **İzmir–Bandırma railway** provides an alternative approach to the region, passing through unremarkable Balıkesir (from where there are frequent buses to Ayvalık), Soma (a short bus ride away from Bergama) and **Manisa** – the only town worthy of any prolonged attention.

Çanakkale

While blessed with a superb setting on the Dardanelles straits, **ÇANAKKALE** has little to detain you except for the few traces of a multicultural past that can be found in its compact old quarter, and a busy seafront that's home to a replica of the **Trojan**

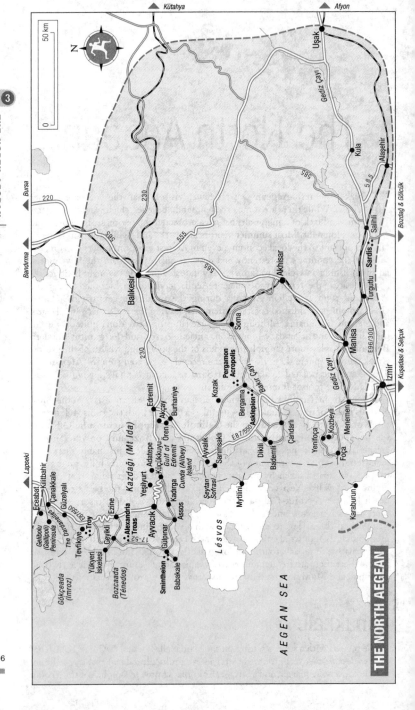

THE NORTH AEGEAN

horse used in the 2004 film *Troy*. Most people, however, use the town as a popular base for visiting the World War I battlefields at Gallipoli on the European side of the Dardanelles, as well as the ruins of Troy. Çanakkale is also the starting point for seasonal sea-buses to the Turkish Aegean islands of Gökçeada and Bozcaada.

The **Dardanelles** (Çanakkale Boğazı in Turkish) have defined Çanakkale's history and its place in myth. The area's Classical name, **Hellespont**, derives from Helle, who, while escaping from her wicked stepmother on the back of a winged ram, fell into the swift-moving channel and drowned. From Abydos on the Asian side, the youth Leander used to swim to Sestos on the European shore for trysts with his lover Hero, until one night he too perished in the currents; in despair Hero drowned herself as well. Byron narrowly escaped being added to the list of victims on his swim in the opposite direction in 1810.

In 480 BC Xerxes' Persian hordes crossed these waters on their way to Greece; and in 411 and 405 BC the last two naval battles of the Peloponnesian War took place in the straits, the latter engagement ending in decisive defeat for the Athenian fleet. Twenty centuries later Mehmet the Conqueror constructed the elaborate fortresses of Kilitbahir and Çimenlik Kale opposite each other to tighten the stranglehold being applied to doomed Constantinople. In March 1915, an Allied fleet attempting to force the Dardanelles and attack İstanbul was repulsed by Turkish shore batteries, with severe losses, prompting the even bloodier land campaign usually known as Gallipoli. These days the straits are still heavily militarized, and modern Çanakkale is very much a navy town.

Arrival and information

Ferries from Eceabat on the Gelibolu peninsula or from Gökçeada dock at the base of Cumhuriyet Bulvarı, which roughly splits the town in two; those from Kilitbahir dock a block southwest. Most of what there is to see or do in Çanakkale, except for the archeological museum, lies within walking distance of here. The **airport** is 2km southeast of town; shuttle buses serve flights to and from İstanbul.

The **otogar**, with buses to Bursa, Edirne and all north Aegean destinations, is out on Atatürk Caddesi, a fifteen-minute walk from the central seafront. However, many buses pass straight through town to cross the straits, and travellers may find it more convenient to board at the ferry docks. Bus companies also provide free shuttles to the *otogar* from their respective offices near the tourist office. **Dolmuşes** to Troy run from the riverside terminal shown on the map on p.198.

The **tourist office** on Cumhuriyet Meydanı (June–Sept daily 8am–noon & 1–7pm, Oct–May Mon–Fri 8am–noon & 1–5pm; ☎0286/217 1187), next to the main dock, gives out an excellent, free, pocket-sized city guide, which can also be picked up at some of the smarter hotels.

Accommodation

Except around Anzac Day, April 25, you'll have little trouble finding a room or a bed, or getting a hefty discount from peak rates. Just south of the tourist office and main ferry landing, the **Saat Kulesi** (clocktower) marks the entrance to a warren of old-town lanes, home to various inexpensive *pansiyon*s and mid-range hotels. More upmarket hotels can be found across Cumhuriyet Meydanı or along the waterfront.

Akol Hotel Kordon Boyu ☎0286/217 9456, ⓦwww.hotelakol.com. Multistorey, four-star, seafront hotel offering a decent level of luxury – albeit rather impersonal – in its good-sized rooms (some with sea views), two restaurants and rooftop bar. ⓖ

Anzac Hotel Saat Kulesi Meyd 8, opposite the clocktower ☎0286/217 7777, ⓦwww .anzachotel.com. Well-run, three-star hotel whose rather grim exterior belies cheerful earth-tone rooms with LCD TVs and big bathrooms. There's also an on-site restaurant

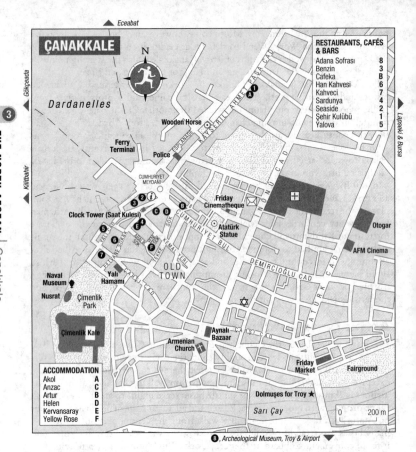

▲ Eceabat

N

Dardanelles

Wooden Horse

Ferry
Terminal

Police

CUMHURIYET
MEYDANI

Clock Tower (Saat Kulesi)

Friday
Cinematheque

Atatürk
Statue

Otogar

AFM Cinema

OLD
TOWN

DEMIRCIOĞLU CAD

Naval
Museum

Yalı
Hamamı

Nusrat

Çimenlik
Park

Çimenlik Kale

Aynalı
Bazaar

Armenian
Church

Friday
Market

Fairground

Dolmuşes for Troy ★

Sarı Çay

0   200 m

RESTAURANTS, CAFÉS & BARS

Adana Sofrası	8
Benzin	3
Cafeka	B
Han Kahvesi	6
Kahveci	7
Sardunya	4
Seaside	2
Şehir Kulübü	1
Yalova	5

ACCOMMODATION

Akol	A
Anzac	C
Artur	B
Helen	D
Kervansaray	E
Yellow Rose	F

Gökçeada

Kilitbahir

Lapseki & Bursa

⑧, Archeological Museum, Troy & Airport ▼

and separate café decorated with mirror art, and private parking. ⑤

Artur Hotel Cumhuriyet Meyd 28 ☏0286/213 2000, ⓦwww.hotelartur.com. The brown, cream and ochre decor of the rooms at this three-star hotel don't quite match the lobby in splendour, but the bathrooms are modern and fair-sized, and there are some superior suites (without balcony, however). Recommended ground-floor restaurant (see opposite). ⑤

Helen Hotel Cumhuriyet Meyd 57 ☏0286/212 1818, ⓦwww.helenhotel.com. A good-value, mid-range hotel. The rooms are somewhat stuffy and balcony-less, but the bathrooms are decent and there's a pleasant breakfast mezzanine. Off-street parking. ④

Kervansaray Fetvane Sok 13 ☏0286/217 8192, ⓦwww.anzachotel.com /kervansaray.htm. Justifiably popular hotel in a

1903 judge's mansion with a later rear annexe, co-managed with the *Anzac*. The mansion rooms are boutique-style with mock belle-époque furnishings, though the front ones suffer from street noise – ask for 206 or 207 facing the lovely central garden. Other than their parquet floors, the annexe rooms are less distinguished, perched above the area where the above-average breakfast is served. There's also a rather nautical garden suite. ⑤

Yellow Rose Pension Aslan Abla Sok 5, 150m from clocktower ☏0286/217 3343, ⓦwww .yellowrose.4mg.com. Much the more pleasant and quieter of Çanakkale's two backpacker hostels, with top-floor dorms (15TL) and basic but en-suite doubles (②) lower down. There's a carp pond in the breakfast area, ping-pong in the garden, internet access, a laundry service and battlefield tours on offer.

The Town

The name Çanakkale means "Pottery Castle", after the garish local ceramics that find their way into the ethnographic section of every Turkish museum. The main nod to local style is the well-restored old **bazaar** beyond the clocktower, with its ornate shops – especially the 1889-built **Yalı Hanı** – and houses, evidence of the town's polyglot profile before 1923: until Cretan Muslims arrived as part of the population exchanges, Çanakkale (like İzmir) had significant Greek, Jewish and Armenian populations, and even foreign consuls – the Italian one donated the clocktower in 1897. The elegant 1880s **synagogue** in the backstreets can be visited (8am–noon & 1–5pm), as can the functioning **Yalı Hamamı** (6am–midnight; men and women), though the **Armenian church** is usually shut.

Beyond the bazaar, **Çimenlik Park** contains Sultan Mehmet II's **Çimenlik Kale** (closed to the public) and an assortment of torpedoes and artillery from various countries. It's also home to the **Naval Museum** (Deniz Müzesi; daily except Mon & Thurs 9am–noon & 1.30–5pm; 3TL), with more military paraphernalia, plus photos of Seddülbahir in ruins after Allied shelling and Atatürk's funeral. Back on the park esplanade is a replica of the minelayer **Nusrat**, which stymied the Allied fleet in March 1915 by re-mining at night zones that the French and British had swept clean by day.

Almost 2km from the town centre, the **Archeological Museum** (Arkeoloji Müzesi; daily: summer 8am–6.45pm; winter 8am–5.30pm; may close at 1pm on Sun & hols; 5TL) can be reached by any Atatürk Caddesi dolmuş labelled "Kepez" or "Güzelyalı". The poorly arranged collection is strong on brass implements, delicate glass and glazed pottery, gold and jewellery, unfired lamps and Hellenistic figurines from the nearby Bozcaada and Dardanos tumuli. The highlights, however, are two exquisite **sarcophagi**: the late Archaic "Polyxena", in perfect condition, with a procession on one side and the sacrifice (in grisly detail) of Priam's daughter on the other, and the fourth-century BC "Altıkulaç", more damaged but showing a finely detailed boar hunt and battle scene with a mounted warrior spearing a victim.

Eating, drinking and nightlife

Restaurants and **cafés** line the quayside both north and south of the main ferry terminal, offering a variety of dishes, with seafood, unsurprisingly, prominent – however, touting is common, and heading a few steps inland will get you better value. A major university town since 1992, Çanakkale has a lively student **nightlife**, especially along Fetvane Sokağı running south from the clocktower. Bars there change regularly – just choose the current fave according to the soundtrack and the crowd. The AFM **cinema** in the Carrefour shopping centre by the *otogar* shows mainstream releases in English; there's also a Friday-night cinematheque in the Belediye İş Merkezi, behind the Atatürk statue.

Restaurants

Adana Sofrası Barış Kordonu, corner Yeni Kordon 1. That rare beast: an upmarket, licensed *kebap* place in a quiet spot with sea views. A good lunch option after taking in the nearby archeological museum.
Cafeka Cumhuriyet Meyd 28. An elegant indoor dining space beneath the *Artur Hotel* with a surprisingly affordable Mediterranean bistro-style menu. As the name suggests, coffee is the highlight. Licensed.
Sardunya Fetvane Sok 11. The most popular of several similar *ev yemekleri* (home-style cooking) places on this lane, where for a set price (about 10TL, including a non-alcoholic drink) you fill your own salad plate and staff top up a bigger platter with stews of the day. Sit on the vine-shaded patio out back, or in the old house in cooler weather. Closes 8.30pm.
Seaside Eski Balikhane Sok 3. A designer interior, with hovering waiters, sculpted vegetables and a Western soundtrack: the menu is Med bistro style, and better for pizza and salads than seafood. Expect to pay around 25TL a head before booze.

Şehir Kulübü Kordon Boyu, opposite yacht marina. One of the less expensive waterfront places, with a standard seafood-grill *meze* menu.

Yalova Eski Balikhane Sok 31. A range of unusual *mezes* and seafood served upstairs or in the ground-floor conservatory of this historic building, but fish prices (typically 75TL/kilo) are the city's highest.

Bars and cafés

Benzin Eski Balikhane Sok 11. Probably the liveliest of the waterfront bars; also does light snacks.

Han Kahvesi Fetvane Sok 28. The courtyard of the historic Yalı Hanı is the place for a well-priced tea, coffee, soft drink, beer or *nargile* (hookah) at any hour; there's live music a few nights a week, when prices climb slightly and the student contingent attends in force. Coming events on ⊛www.yalihani.com (Turkish only).

Kahveci Çarşı Cad 14. Just three outside tables opposite the Yalı Camii, for proper European cappuccinos and espressos – at European prices.

The Gelibolu peninsula

Burdened with a grim military history but endowed with some fine scenery and beaches, the slender **Gelibolu (Gallipoli) peninsula** – roughly 60km in length and between 4km and 18km wide – forms the northwest side of the **Dardanelles**, the straits connecting the Aegean with the Sea of Marmara. Site of the 1915 **Gallipoli landings**, the peninsula contains a sobering series of memorials and cemeteries, both Allied and Turkish.

The **World War I battlefields and cemeteries** scattered around the Gelibolu peninsula are a moving sight, the past violence made all the more poignant by the present beauty of the landscape. The whole area is now either fertile rolling country, or cloaked in thick scrub and pine forest alive with birds, making it difficult to imagine the carnage of 1915. Much of the flatter land is farmed, and ploughing still turns up pieces of rusting equipment, fragments of shrapnel, human bones and even unexploded munitions. The entire area southwest of Eceabat and Kabatepe is a **national historical park**, which means no camping, picnicking, fire-lighting, foliage-plucking or second-home development beyond the few existing villages. The Allied cemeteries and memorials were built in the early 1920s, mostly designed by Scottish architect Sir John Burnet; they replaced and consolidated the makeshift graveyards of 1915, though over half the deceased were never found or identified – thus the massive cenotaphs. Since the ascendance of the AK Party in 2002, the battlefields and cemeteries have also become conspicuously popular with Turkish visitors – up to two million annually – who arrive on massive pilgrimages organized by AK-run municipalities, especially in May and late September. These religious tourists specifically venerate the Turkish fallen as *şehitler*, or martyrs for Islam – in pointed contrast to the secularist narrative spun around the eight-month Gallipoli campaign, which made famous a previously unknown lieutenant-colonel, Mustafa Kemal, later Atatürk.

Visiting the battlefields and cemeteries

Whether visiting the battlefields independently, or on a tour, **Çanakkale**, or **Eceabat** in the south of the peninsula, are the best places to base yourself. Modern Gelibolu town (see p.171) at the northern end of the peninsula is too remote to be of much practical use as a base.

The numerous open-air sites have **no admission fees** or fixed opening hours. Even with your own transport, you'll need a day – two for enthusiasts – to see the major cemeteries and cenotaphs. You'll also want time to wander a little, take in the natural beauty and, in season, swim. Outside the villages of Eceabat and Seddülbahir there are few amenities, so lunch stops must be carefully planned.

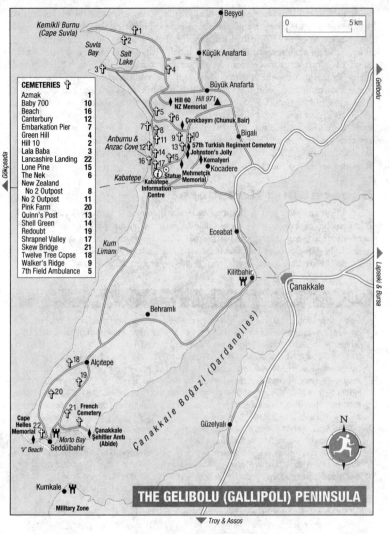

Independent visits to the sites can also be made using a combination of minibus rides and walking. **Minibuses** run from Eceabat to Kabatepe dock via the Kabatepe Information Centre/Museum, and from Eceabat to Kilitbahir. From the information centre, you can walk around the main sites just north within a couple of hours. At Kilitbahir, minibuses meet the Çanakkale car ferries in summer and take passengers to Seddülbahir via Alçıtepe, from where you can tour the surrounding cemeteries and memorials on foot. It's also usually possible to **rent mountain bikes** in Eceabat, but some roads are steep, and secondary tracks can be rough and muddy in winter.

Guided tours

There's little to choose between the many mainstream companies that offer **guided tours** of the battlefields – all are supposed to have licensed, English-speaking guides with a thorough knowledge of the sites. Tours all cost the same (50TL per head), are the same length (5hr; in the afternoon) and visit identical sites, usually preceded by a screening of the 1987 documentary, *The Fatal Shore* and/or Peter Weir's 1981 film *Gallipoli*, and sometimes a picnic lunch. Itineraries, with a strong Anzac emphasis, don't stray much from a core area just north of the park boundary and visit – in this order – the Kabatepe Museum, several beach cemeteries nearby, the Lone Pine cemetery, Johnston's Jolly, the Turkish 57th Regiment cemetery, The Nek and Çonkbayırı hill. By far the best of the conventional tours is run by *Crowded House* in Ecebat (see), who also offer (for 25TL) a morning's add-on of snorkelling over the *Milo*, an Allied ship scuttled in Suvla Bay. If you have your own transport, consider hiring the best **private guide** to the battlefields, Kenan Çelik (ⓦwww .kcelik.com, ⓣ0532/738 6675), an instructor at Çanakkale's university, who leads full- and multi-day tours as well as the usual itineraries.

Eceabat and Kocadere

Forty kilometres south of Gelibolu and diagonally opposite Çanakkale, **ECEABAT** is a scruffy, cheerless place, but without your own transport makes the most convenient base for touring the battlefields. Most **buses** arrive at their ticket offices behind the jetty, where **car ferries** arrive regularly from Çanakkale. There's a **PTT** on the street leading north from the jetty, and an ATM on the jetty *meydan*.

The Gallipoli Campaign

Soon after World War I began, the Allies realized that Russia could not be supplied by sea, nor a Balkan front opened against the Central Powers, unless Ottoman Turkey was eliminated. **Winston Churchill**, then First Lord of the Admiralty, decided that the quickest way to accomplish this would be to force the Dardanelles with a fleet and bombard İstanbul into submission. A combined **Anglo-French armada** made several, repulsed attempts on the straits during November 1914, before returning in earnest on March 18, 1915, when they reached 10km up the waterway before striking numerous Turkish mines, losing several vessels and hundreds of crew.

The Allied fleet retreated and regrouped on the Greek island of Límnos to prepare an amphibious assault on Turkish positions along the peninsula. The plan involved an Anglo-French landing at Cape Helles, Seddülbahir and Morto Bay at the mouth of the straits, and a simultaneous **Anzac** (Australia-New Zealand Army Corps) assault at Kabatepe beach, 13km north. The Australians landed first at dawn on April 25, 1915, with the British and French landing an hour afterwards, followed by the New Zealanders later in the day.

This hare-brained scheme ran into trouble immediately. Anglo-French brigades at the southernmost cape were pinned down by Turkish fire and the French contingent was virtually annihilated; after two days they had only penetrated 6.5km inland, just before Krithia (Alçıtepe) village, and never got any further. The fate of the Anzac landing was even more horrific: owing to a drifting signal buoy, the Aussies and Kiwis disembarked not on the broad sands of Kabatepe, with gentle terrain inland, but at a cramped cove by Arıburnu, 2km north, overlooked by Turkish-held cliffs. Despite heavy casualties (around 2000 on the first day alone), the Ans advanced inland, as the Turks initially retreated. The next day, they threatened the Turkish stronghold of Çonkbayırı, where lieutenant-colonel **Mustafa Kemal** told his poorly equipped, illiterate troops: "I am not ordering you to attack, I am ordering you to die." Turkish reinforcements soon arrived, and the Anzac force never made it further than 800m inland.

Accommodation is not usually a problem, other than around Anzac Day. The best budget option by far is the well-run *Crowded House* (℡0286/814 1565, Ⓦwww.crowdedhousegallipoli.com), just inland from the ferry plaza, with salubrious doubles (❷), six-bunk dorms (20TL), a book swop and on-site café. Alternatively, try the waterside *Aqua Boss Hotel* (℡0286/814 2458, Ⓦwww .heyboss.com; ❸), 800m south of the jetty, with attractive stone walls, renovated bathrooms and galleried, sea-facing family quads, or *TJs Hotel* (℡0286/814 2458, Ⓦwww.anzacgallipolitours.com), behind the jetty, with a mix of doubles (❸) and dorm bunks (15TL), plus a popular roof bar.

Several **restaurants** serve steam-tray dishes along the waterfront south of the jetty; the *Meydan* is as good as any. For fish, head to the licensed *Liman*, at the far southern end of the strip across the road out.

If you have transport, a better place to stay is in tranquil **KOCADERE** village, 7km north, just off the Kabatepe road, at the Belgian/Turkish-run 🏕 *Gallipoli Houses* (℡0286 814 2650, Ⓦwww.gallipoli.com.tr; ❻, suites ❼ half-board only). State-of-the-art rooms are distributed over a restored main house (with roof terrace) and new-built garden units: all the rooms have terraces or balconies, wood cabinetry, insect screens, rain showers and terracotta tiles for underfloor heating. The evening meals are a highlight, marrying Turkish *mezes* with continental mains and an excellent regional wine-and-*rakı* cellar; advance booking is essential, especially in May and autumn.

A supplementary British landing occurred at northerly Cape Suvla, followed by ferocious assaults on the summit in the middle of August, which the Turks repulsed. Otherwise the confrontation consisted of stagnant trench warfare, with neither side having sufficient artillery to gain a decisive advantage. Finally, in November 1915, the Allies gave up, with the last troops leaving Seddülbahir on January 9, 1916. Churchill's career went into temporary eclipse, while that of Mustafa Kemal was only just beginning.

The reasons for the **Allied defeat** are many. In addition to the chanciness of the basic strategy, the incompetence of the Allied commanders – who often counter-manded each other's orders or failed to press advantages with reinforcements – was significant. Much credit for the successful **Turkish resistance** goes to Mustafa Kemal, later known as **Atatürk**, whose role in the two Turkish victories at Çonkbayırı is legendary (countrywide, he's depicted hunched over in silhouette, patrolling that ridge). Enjoying a charmed life, he narrowly escaped death on several occasions and, aside from his tactical skills, succeeded – by threats, persuasion or example – in rekindling morale among often outgunned and outnumbered Ottoman infantrymen.

At various times, half a million men were deployed at Gallipoli; of these over fifty percent were killed, wounded or missing. Allied deaths totalled around 46,000 while the Turkish dead are estimated at 86,000. Fatal **casualties** among the AnzacS in particular – around 11,500 – were severe compared to the island-nations' popula-tions, but would be dwarfed by the 48,000 or so Anzacs killed on the western front later in the war. Some claims (and a major thesis of Peter Weir's *Gallipoli*) that the Allied top brass regarded only Anzac "colonials" as expendable cannon fodder don't bear scrutiny; two Irish battalions suffered over fifty percent casualties on the first day and the 42nd Manchester Division was almost completely wiped out. However, this baptism by blood had several long-term effects: a sense of Australia and New Zealand having come of age as sovereign countries; the designation of April 25 as Anzac Day, a solemn holiday in Australia and New Zealand; and a healthy antipodean scepticism about joining international adventures – though both countries were press-ganged by the US into sending troops to Vietnam.

Kilitbahir

The tiny village of **KILITBAHIR**, 5km south of Eceabat, is dwarfed by Sultan Mehmet's massive, irregularly shaped **castle** (Tues–Sun 8.30am–noon & 1.30–7pm; 3TL), with a lobed, triangular keep and six unguarded stairways leading up to the curtain walls. Climb them at your own risk – a 40-year-old Turk fell to his death in 2008. On its seaward side, you can visit the **Namazgah Tabyası** (Tues–Sun 8.30am–noon & 1.30–7pm; 3TL), a series of half-subterranean bunkers and shore batteries built in the 1890s.

Kilitbahir has a few shoreline **tea houses** and **snack bars** but no accommodation. **Ferries** ply the narrowest (1300m) point of the Dardanelles to Çanakkale every thirty minutes – the fastest (8min) and (for drivers) cheapest crossing (see "Travel details", p.232).

The west coast sites

The first logical stop is at the **Kabatepe Information Centre and Museum** (daily 9am–1pm & 2–6pm; 3TL), 9km northwest of Eceabat, which contains a well-labelled selection of archive photos, maps, weapons, trenching tools, uniforms, mess-kits, personal effects – such as touching letters home – and a few human remains, including a Turkish skull with a bullet lodged in it.

The first sites along the coast road north of the Centre are the **Beach**, **Shrapnel Valley** and **Shell Green** cemeteries – the latter 300m inland up a steep track, suitable only for 4WD vehicles. These are followed by **Anzac Cove** and **Arıburnu**, site of the first, bungled Anzac landing and location of the dawn service on Anzac Day. At both, memorials bear Atatürk's famous conciliatory quotation concerning the Allied dead, which begins: "Heroes who shed their blood and lost their lives! You are now lying in the soil of a friendly country. Therefore rest in peace." Looking inland, you'll see the murderous badlands – including the eroded pinnacle overhead nicknamed "The Sphinx" by the hapless Australians – that gave the defenders such an advantage. Beyond Anzac Cove, the terrain flattens out and the four other cemeteries (Canterbury,

---

Anzac Day

Anzac Day, April 25, is the busiest day of the year on the peninsula, when up to 10,000 Australians and New Zealanders arrive to commemorate the Allied defeat. In the days leading up to the 25th, Eceabat and Çanakkale fill with visitors: tours can be organized locally or from just about any travel agent in İstanbul, while all UK-based overland companies include Anzac Day in their itineraries.

The day begins with the 5.30am **Dawn Service** at Anzac Cove, though most people show up much earlier to camp out, as the police close all roads around the grave sites to traffic from 3am. The service used to be relatively informal, but since the late 1990s antipodean diplomats and government ministers attend and the ceremony now features official speeches, prayers and a member of the Australian or New Zealand forces playing a poignant "Last Post" at sunrise. An hour's breakfast break follows before the rest of the morning's ceremonies resume – **wreath-laying** at the British, French and Turkish memorials, and more services at the Australian memorial at Lone Pine and the New Zealand memorial at Chunuk Bair.

For most people, being at Gallipoli on Anzac Day is a solemn affair – many are here to commemorate ancestors who lost their lives during World War I. However, there have been a few violent confrontations between drunken backpackers and right-wing Turks in the past. As a result, alcohol is now strictly banned at the Dawn Service – and indeed, all year round at any of the cemeteries or memorials.

No. 2 Outpost, New Zealand No. 2 Outpost and Embarkation Pier) are more dispersed.

Good dirt tracks lead north from Arıburnu to the beaches and salt lake at **Cape Suvla**, today renamed Kemikli Burnu ("bone-strewn headland"), location of four more cemeteries of August casualties, mostly English, Scottish, Welsh and Irish.

Central inland sites

From Anzac Cove, most visitors return to the Kabatepe Information Centre, then head uphill along the one-way road that roughly follows what was the front line, to the former strongholds (now cemeteries) scattered around **Çonkbayırı** hill. To the left of this road is **Shrapnel Valley** – the single, perilous supply line that ran up-valley from what is now the Beach Cemetery to the trenches. Along the road, you'll pass a massive **statue** depicting a purported incident from the first day of landings – a Turk carrying a wounded Australian officer back to his lines – supposedly witnessed by another officer who later became Lord Casey, 1965–70 Governor-General of Australia. However, the incident isn't mentioned in Casey's detailed memoirs and he wasn't even at that sector of the lines, so the statue is best viewed as an allegory of the chivalry which (sometimes) prevailed in the campaign.

Just beyond is **Lone Pine** (Kanlı Sırt), lowest strategic position on the ridge and the largest graveyard-cum-memorial to those buried unmarked or at sea. Action here was considered a sideshow to the main August 6–9 offensive further up Çonkbayırı; a total of 28,000 men died in four days at both points. Just up from Lone Pine is the **Mehmetcik memorial** to the Turkish soldiers who perished, and at **Johnston's Jolly** (named after an artillery officer who liked to "jolly the Turks up" with his gun) is a heavily eroded section of **trench** beneath the pine trees. Most of the trenches on display are actually reconstructions, with the original ones hidden and little visited; British/Anzac ones followed a zigzag course, while Turkish ones adopted the German dogtooth pattern. All along the ridge, trenches of the opposing sides lay within a few metres of each other, with the modern road corresponding to the no-man's-land in between.

Further along, on the right, is the **57th Turkish Regiment cemetery**, whose men Mustafa Kemal ordered to their deaths, thus buying time for reinforcements to arrive. Here is made clear the religious aspect of the campaign for contemporary Turks, with an inscription eulogizing martyrdom and a small open-air prayer area. Just beyond, a left fork leads to **The Nek** – scene of the futile charge and massacre of the Australian Light Horse Brigade at the conclusion of Peter Weir's *Gallipoli*. To the right the main road continues uphill past **Baby 700** cemetery – marking the furthest Allied advance on April 25 – and to the massive New Zealand memorial obelisk and the five-monolith Turkish memorial atop **Çonkbayırı** hill (Chunuk Bair). An inscription chronicles Kemal's organization of successful resistance to the August Allied attacks, and marks the spot where Atatürk's pocket-watch stopped a fragment of shrapnel, thus saving his life.

To the southern cape

KABATEPE port, boarding point for the car-ferry to the Turkish Aegean island of Gökçeada (see p.206), lies 1km southwest of the Kabatepe Information Centre. There's a fair **beach** to the north of the harbour – intended site of the Anzac landing – another just south at a forestry picnic grounds (3TL admission), and a third one 5km south at **Kum Limanı**. This is the best of the trio with warm, clean, calm sea, but access is straddled by the grounds of the *Kum Hotel* (℡0286/814 1455, 🖰www.hotelkum.com; ❺), which charges nonresidents for use of the beach. The **hotel** is the smartest on the peninsula, other than *Gallipoli*

Houses (see p.203), but also accepts caravans and camper vans (not tents) in a basic attached **campsite**.

A further 9km south, the village of **ALÇITEPE** village has two private **war museums** and not much else; beyond here lie six scattered British cemeteries, consequences of the landing at Cape Helles. This appears 8km further, adorned by the huge British **Cape Helles Memorial**. The views from here are magnificent, with abundant **Ottoman fortifications** hinting at the age-old importance of the place. Tucked between the medieval bulwarks is the **V Beach** of the Allied expedition, behind which lies the biggest of the local British cemeteries.

Just uphill, the village of **SEDÜLLBAHIR** has one **restaurant** and several basic **pansiyons**, of which the *Helles Panorama*, on the Cape Helles road (T0286/862 0035, W www.hellespanorama.com; ❸), is the most pleasant; it has lovely gardens, at the edge of the village, though none of the rooms are en suite.

A southeasterly turning just before Seddülbahir leads to the striking **French Cemetery**, above the sandy Morto Bay, with its massive ossuaries, rows of black metal crosses (with North and West African troops disproportionately represented), and memorial to the sailors of the *Bouvet*, sunk on March 18, 1915. At the end of this road looms the unmissable Çanakkale Şehitler Anıtı, or **Çanakkale Martyrs' Memorial**, which resembles a stark, tetrahedral footstool and commemorates all the Ottoman dead.

The Turkish Aegean islands

Strategically straddling the Dardanelles, **Gökçeada** and **Bozcaada** were the only Aegean islands to revert to Turkey after the 1923 Treaty of Lausanne, which concluded the Greek-Turkish war. Under the terms of the agreement, the islands' Greek Orthodox inhabitants were exempt from that year's population exchange, but after 1937 both islands were re-militarized (access to foreigners was banned until 1987), and the Turkish authorities began to assert their sovereignty more forcefully. Although a formal population exchange was never instigated, most of the islands' Greek population had left by 1974, to be replaced by Turkish settlers.

Both islands have **good beaches**: the smaller Bozcaada is fashionable with weekenders from İstanbul, thus expensive, while the larger Gökçeada is cheaper and more dramatic, with less-developed tourism.

Gökçeada (İmroz)

Hovering just northwest of the Dardanelles, **GÖKÇEADA** (known as İmroz until 1970) is tantalizingly visible from the Gelibolu battlefields. Scenic, fertile and volcanic, with healthy pine and kermes oak forests in the west and pure springs to drink from, it's big enough to make bringing your own vehicle a must, as sparse local dolmuş services only serve the populated northwest.

İmroz was taken by Greece in the 1912–13 Balkan Wars, and during the Gallipoli campaign served as British commander Sir Ian Hamilton's headquarters, and as an important way-station between Límnos and the battlefields. Today its main claim to fame is its superb, organic produce, especially olive oil, tomato jam, honey and cheese. Its summer tourist trade comprises some Romanians and Bulgarians, but mostly consists of thousands of returned Greek islanders (see box opposite) and their descendants, especially around the main Orthodox *panayır* (festival) of August 14–16, when beds are at a premium.

Gökçeada is easily accessible by **car-ferry** from Kabatepe and sea-bus from Çanakkale (see "Travel details" for frequencies and prices). In August, or any

The Greeks of Gökçeada

After reverting to Turkish sovereignty in 1923, the island's population of 7000 **Orthodox Greeks** (down from over 9000 in 1912) was more or less left to itself for forty years, save for a couple of hundred gendarmes and officials. But when the Cyprus conflict re-erupted in 1964, the Turkish government decided to "claim" the island more pointedly by garrisoning troops, imposing Turkish place-names, closing all Greek-language schools, settling Turkish civilians from the mainland and establishing an open prison, whose inmates terrorized the locals. These measures had the desired effect: today there are only about 250 full-time ethnic Greek residents.

Since the 1990s thaw in relations between Greece and Turkey, however, many Greek islanders have returned seasonally to renovate their previously abandoned houses and keep at least some of the many churches functioning. But the older generation remains wary, dependent as they are on the good will of the authorities and resentful that their children, born elsewhere, don't qualify for Turkish citizenship and thus can't own real estate in this military zone.

summer weekend, car-space must be booked hours in advance, and south winds may cancel services. The island has three **ATMs** and one **petrol pump**, but these can all conceivably run dry in summer, so come prepared.

Gökçeada Merkez and the northeast

Boats dock at **Kuzu Limani** (Áyios Kírykos), 6km from the island's small inland capital, known as **GÖKÇEADA MERKEZ** (Panayiá). Grim modern architecture on the main drag contrasts with island vernacular in the backstreets, especially in the hillside district of Çınarlı. There's a seasonal wooden **tourist information booth** on the central roundabout (daily 10.30am–7pm). Few will opt for the noisy main-drag **hotels** – head instead to Çınarlı, where *Taşkin* (℡0286/887 3266, Ⓦwww.taskinotel.com; ❸), has rear rooms facing open countryside, with big modern bathrooms and small balconies. There are several unlicensed *sulu yemek* **restaurants** along the main street, or sample *pide* and *kebap* at the friendly, cheap and licensed *Ada*, at the start of the road west. A pricier alternative is the central *Hamam* seafood restaurant, in a restored Turkish baths.

From the central roundabout, a road leads north to the turning for ridge-top **ESKİ BADMLİ** (Glykí) with its seasonal Greek population, single café and a comfortable **hotel**, *Masi* (℡0286/887 4619, Ⓦwww.gokceadamasi.com; ❻, sea view ❼) with a pool and restaurant. At the end of the road on the north shore, **KALEKÖY LİMANI** is home to much of the island's **accommodation**, though its port beach – mostly swallowed by an ugly new quay – is an off-limits military zone. The best of several places along its single street is *Kale* (℡0286/887 3438; ❹), with a busy restaurant, though the most unusual **food** can be found at ⌖ *Meyhane Son Vapur*, with good-quality *mezes* and seafood at moderate prices for the location.

Immediately uphill huddles **YUKARI KALEKÖY** (Kástro), with a ruined Byzantine-Genoese castle and the island's former cathedral, **Ayía Marína**, now derelict, but set for renovation. Of its three **pansiyons** the *Yakamoz* (℡0286/887 2057; ❹), has basic rooms and the island's best views stretching north to Greek Samothráki, as well as a good-value terrace **restaurant**.

Western hill villages

Most of the island's remaining Greek Orthodox population lives 3km west of Merkez at **ZEYTİNLİ** (Áyii Theodhóri), where many of the central **cafés** are Greek-run and specialize in *dibek kahvesi* – coffee ground in a giant mortar and pestle. Of these, *Panayot Usta* is the tops for *muhallebi* with a side of ice cream. The only **accommodation** is further uphill at *Zeytindali* (☎0286/887 3707, ⓦwww .zeytindali.com; ⑥), a superbly restored old inn with a decent ground-floor **restaurant**. More interesting, perhaps, is the annexe of *Son Vapur* at the village entrance, or the bucolic *Çakır'ın Yeri*, at the start of the slip road to Zeytinli, a *kendin pişin kendin ye* restaurant serving up fish and meat.

Exclusively Orthodox-inhabited, **TEPEKÖY** (Agrídhia), 7km west, is the focus of the mid-August **festival**, observed here with a fervour now lacking in much of metropolitan Greece. The village is also home to one of the best local **tavernas**, featuring well-priced mains and *mezes* served by a Greek retired here from İstanbul. He also makes most of the island's (rather rough-and-ready) wine from *kundúra* or *kalambáki* grapes, and rents rooms upstairs (☎0286/887 4247, ⓦwww .barbayorgo.com; Easter to early Sept; ③).

Some 15km west of Merkez, **DEREKÖY** (Skhinoúdhi) was once Turkey's largest village, with 1900 houses, shops, craftsmen and even a cinema. A vast communal laundry-hall by the main church hints at its former population of 5500, though today it's all but abandoned, save for fifty full-time inhabitants. At the village's western edge, a track leads 7km north to **Marmaros** pebble cove, with a 38-metre **waterfall** 1km inland. There's a vehicle barrier just below Dereköy, for which the fire station has the key.

The south coast beaches

Arguably the best (and closest) of several south-coast **beaches**, just 10km from Gökçeada Merkez, is **Aydıncık**, 1500m of sugary blonde sand lapped by pristine, warm water. The salt lake just inland is a major habitat for migratory birds, especially flamingos, and the entire area is supposedly a protected reserve – though this hasn't prevented some tourist development. Local windsurfing conditions are the best in the north Aegean; accordingly several windsurfing schools cluster on the beach. All have **accommodation**, the most luxurious being the *Gökçeada Windsurf Club* (☎0286/898 1016, ⓦwww.surfgokceada.com; April–Oct; ⑥), whose stone-clad bungalows have contemporary earth-tone decor and big bathrooms. More basic rooms can be found next door at *Çelik Pansiyon* (☎0286/898 1011; ④), which has a decent **restaurant** that's open out of peak season. The nearby *Şen* **campsite** (☎0286/898 1020), popular with camper vans, also has bungalows (③).

A paved road heads west from here, mostly hugging the coast, for about 15km to the long, unsigned **Kapıkaya** beach (no amenities); another 5km leads to the marked (1km) side road to **Lazkoyu** (Ayía Káli), a 400-metre, eminently scenic, protected sandy bay with just a summer snack-shack. Beyond here, there's no public access to any beaches until **Yuvalı**, a further 9km, and even here you must patronize the beach restaurants of the sprawling *Mavi Su Resort* (☎0286/897 6246, ⓦwww .mavisuresort.com; April–Oct; ⑤), a family-friendly resort with well-appointed doubles and quad bungalows. The final beach, 3km west of little **Uğurlu** (Livoúnia) fishing port, is **Gizli Liman**, with no facilities but fine sand and a pine-grove backdrop. From Uğurlu a paved road leads back to the western hill villages.

Bozcaada (Tenedos)

Only seven nautical miles from the Turkish mainland, the island of **BOZCAADA** (Tenedos) was historically about one fifth Muslim, as evidenced by the odd medieval mosque or two. Less militarized and more architecturally homogeneous than its neighbour, it remains temptingly convenient to Turkish holiday-makers and second-home buyers, and can be quite overrun in summer, when you'll need to book accommodation in advance. Its interior consists of gently undulating

Bozcaada wines

A favourable, breezy climate and volcanic soil mean that **Bozcaada wines** have long been esteemed. Traditional grape varieties found only here and on Gökçeada are the whites Vasilaki and Çavuş, and the reds Karalahna, Kuntra (Kundúra in Greek) and Karasakız. The white grapes are extremely sweet, so need to be fermented to almost 13 percent alcohol. Local red wines tend to be rather tannic owing to the practice of leaving the entire grape in the vats throughout the fermentation process. There are currently six vintners on the island, of which Talay, Corvus and Çamlıbağ have the best reputation; all three have well-signed **tasting boutiques** in the Greek quarter. Corvus is the most prestigious, but also overpriced; at the other outlets you can get decent-quality wines from 10TL a bottle. The Talay tastery even has its own wine bar upstairs, with cheese and charcuterie platters accompanying wine by the glass.

countryside covered in vineyards producing notable **wine** (see box above) and tufted with a few pine groves.

Ferry access is from **Geyikli (Yükyeri) İskelesi**, a tiny port 70km southwest of Çanakkale. Direct dolmuşes from Çanakkale's *otogar* connect with the ferry departures; those coming from the south should aim for Ezine, then Geyikli proper. If you just miss a boat, there's an excellent beach just north of the jetty to while away a couple of hours. Advance booking is recommended for cars in high season, when Bozcaada's two ATMs and two fuel pumps can run out, so come prepared.

The town

Ferries dock at the lone settlement of **BOZCAADA**, built mostly on a grid plan along a slight slope. It's surprisingly elegant, with cobbled streets and a good number of preserved old houses with overhanging upper floors. The former Greek quarter extended east and north from the church to the sea; nowadays just twenty elderly Orthodox inhabitants remain resident. Dominating the little fishing port and ferry jetty is a giant **castle** (daily 10am–1pm & 2–6pm; 1.5TL), one of the largest citadels in the Aegean, successively expanded by Byzantine, Genoese, Venetian and Turkish occupiers, and most recently restored in the 1970s. The only other formal sight is a **History Museum** in the Greek quarter (May–Sept 10am–8pm, 5TL), a rather steep admission charge for a collection of local memorabilia labelled in Turkish only.

Accommodation

Bozcaada is usually packed to the gills from July to early September, when booking in advance is essential. Parking is a problem in town – the only free car parks are behind the castle, and between *Ege* and *Kale*.

Armagrandi Dolaplı Sok 4–6, off road to the beaches ☎0286/697 8424, ⒲www.armagrandi .com. An old wine warehouse sympathetically converted to a stunning boutique hotel, with exposed ceiling beams and stone pointing even in the bathrooms, with some rooms skylit in the absence of windows. Art adorns the ground floor, and there's limited parking out back. Open all year. ❻

Ege Mektep Sok, behind castle ☎0286/697 8189, ⒲www.egehotel.com. In the partially restored nineteenth-century Greek school, this hotel has well-appointed rooms over three floors – the top-floor ones are smaller but have balconies

facing the castle. There's a pleasant garden bar, though breakfast is disappointing. Open all year; some private parking. ❺

Gümüş At the far end of the central park, well signed inland from fishing port ☎0286 697 8252, ⒲www.gumusotel.com.tr. A budget (for Bozcaada) hotel with two wings: the somewhat ramshackle old one, a former government building, and a newer adjacent annexe, both en suite and perfectly acceptable. Open all year. ❹

Kaikias On the north shore behind the castle ☎0286/697 0250, ⒲www.kaikias.com. Old masonry fragments, nautical Greek antiques, faded hall frescoes and distressed wood floors make this rambling boutique hotel seem older than its 2001 origins. Rooms are large, with vaulted ceilings and marble-clad bathrooms, and there's street parking nearby, but it's a little overpriced at ⑥

Kale At the top of Greek quarter, beyond *Ege* ☏ 0286/697 8617, ⓦ www.kalepansiyon.net. One of the island's few professionally run *pansiyon*s, with obsessively clean, wooden-floor, en-suite rooms: they don't have balconies but most have views of the castle. Proprietress Pakize sells home-made jam and serves breakfast at a shaded terrace opposite. Some parking adjacent. ④

🏃 **Katina** Yirmi Eylül Cad, Kısa Sok, 100m south of church ☏ 0286/697 0242, ⓦ www .katinaas.com. Designer hotel occupying two old houses, with every room (and bathroom)

individually decorated. Breakfast is served at tables in the lane under the vines, or at the cosy café opposite. April–Oct. ⑥

Panorama By the giant antenna on the ridge south of town ☏ 0286/697 0217, ⓦ www.panoramaotel .com. A very welcoming family runs this quiet, new inn of six plush rooms. Four of them look out over the *jandarma* camp and sea; the other two, and the lovely breakfast garden, face town. Parking; April–Oct. ⑥

Rengigül Atatürk Cad, below the church ☏ 0286/ 677 8171, ⓦ www.rengigul.net. This *pansiyon* installed in an 1876-vintage townhouse has guestrooms (only one en suite) idiosyncratically decorated with antiques, artwork and curios by its artist owner; breakfast is served in the walled rear garden. ⑤

Eating, drinking and nightlife

Half a dozen **restaurants** line the harbour, trading mostly in seafood and *mezes*, with another cluster of more creative eateries on the castle side of the old Greek quarter. All the usual bill-padding ploys (see p.45) are rife here, as well as other local tricks, such as offering "fresh, sea-caught" fish at a reasonable price, then substituting frozen or farmed fare. Two reliable waterfront restaurants are *Tenedos* and *Şehir*, both serving decent food, with the latter also staying open off season. A bright spot in the Greek quarter is *Salkım*, at Çınarçarşı Cad 20 (☏ 0286/697 0540), a ten-table bistro serving smallish portions of local dishes such as sardines wrapped in grape leaves. Of the **cafés**, Australian-run *Lisa's* (March–Dec), just inland from the middle of the quay does breakfasts, home-cooked desserts, snacks and drinks, as well as hosting occasional exhibits by island-resident artists. Alternatively, try *Ada* between the central park and the jetty, known for its red-poppy-based drink, more traditional dishes and a useful website (ⓦ www .bozcaada.info). The most durable **nightspot** is *Polente* between the park and the quay (motto: "Life is a Cabernet"), playing a variety of cutting-edge music (including even Greek) to a youngish clientele.

Around the island

Bozcaada is small enough that you can get around using the local **minibuses** (summer only, from the base of the jetty), which loop past some fine south-coast **beaches**. In season, two outlets in town rent out **scooters** and **mountain bikes**.

Heading southwest out of town on the right-hand road, you'll reach, after 6km, the island's most developed beach, **Ayazma**, with watersports, sunbeds and four restaurants just inland. The next bay west, **Sulubahçe**, has good broad sand but no parking or facilities, other than a **campsite** well inland. Beyond here, **Habbelle** is more cramped, with a single snack bar/sunbed franchise. Inland from Ayazma and its abandoned, eponymous monastery, another paved road leads southeast past secluded, sandy **Beylik** cove, and then above small **Aqvaryum** bay, tucked scenically to one side of the **Mermer Burnu** cape. Once past **Tuzburnu** with its lighthouse and sandy if exposed bay, the road swings north on its way back to the port. In **Tekirbahçe** district 2km before town, there's another **accommodation** option: the basic, stone-clad *Güler Pansiyon* (☏ 0286/697 8454; ④), beautifully situated behind a small, sandy beach, with only vines – used by the owners to make their own wine – between it and the sea.

Troy

Although by no means Turkey's most spectacular archeological site, **Troy** – thanks to Homer – is probably the most celebrated. Known as Truva or Troia in Turkish, the remains of the ancient city lie 30km south of Çanakkale, 5km west of the main road. If you show up without expectations and use your imagination, you may well be impressed. Modern excavation work has greatly clarified the site, so that nonspecialists can now grasp the basic layout and the different settlement periods.

Some history

Until 1871 Troy was generally thought to have existed in legend only. The Troad plain, where the ruins lie, was known to be associated with the Troy that Homer wrote about in the *Iliad*, but all traces of the city had vanished completely. In 1871 **Heinrich Schliemann**, a successful German/American businessman turned amateur archeologist, obtained permission from the Ottoman government to start digging on a hill called Hisarlık, where earlier excavators had already found the remains of a Classical temple and signs of further, older ruins.

Schliemann's sloppy trenching work resulted in considerable damage to the site, only rectified by the first professional archeologist to work at Troy, Carl Blegen, who began excavations in 1932. Schliemann was also responsible for removing the so-called **Treasure of Priam**, a large cache of copper, silver and gold vessels, plus some fine jewellery, which he smuggled to Berlin where it was displayed until 1941. The hoard disappeared during the Red Army's sacking of the city in May 1945, resurfacing spectacularly in Moscow in 1993: it's now exhibited in the Pushkin Museum there. Legal wrangles to determine ownership are ongoing between Germany and the Russian Federation – with Turkey putting in a claim too.

Whatever Schliemann's shortcomings, his unsystematic excavations did uncover nine distinct layers of consecutive urban developments spanning four millennia. The oldest, **Troy I**, dates to about 3600 BC and was followed by four similar settlements. Either **Troy VI** or **VII** is thought to have been **the city described by Homer**: the former is known to have been destroyed by an earthquake in about 1275 BC, while the latter shows signs of having been wiped out by fire about a quarter of a century later, around the time historians estimate the Trojan War to have taken place. **Troy VIII**, which thrived from 700 to 300 BC, was a Greek foundation, while much of the final layer of development, **Troy IX** (300 BC to 300 AD), was built during the heyday of the Roman Empire.

Although there's no way of proving that the **Trojan War** did take place, there's a fair amount of circumstantial evidence suggesting that the city was the scene of some kind of armed conflict, even if it wasn't the ten-year struggle described in the *Iliad*. It's possible that Homer's epic is based on a number of wars fought between Mycenaean Greeks and the inhabitants of Troy, who were by turns trading partners and commercial rivals.

The site

The **site entrance** (daily: May–Sept 8am–7pm; Oct–April 8am–5pm; 15TL) is by the car and coach park. Here and at nearby shops you can buy a map/guide, *A Tour of Troia* by Dr Manfred Korfmann, the archeologist who, between 1988 and his death in 2005, oversaw the site's excavation.

Just beyond the gate stands a 1970s reconstruction of the Homeric **wooden horse**. You can climb a ladder up into the horse's belly and look out of windows cut into its flanks (which presumably didn't feature in the original design). A few paces west, the city ruins cloak an outcrop overlooking the Troad plain, which extends about 8km to the sea. A circular trail takes you around the site, with twelve explanatory panels going some way to bringing the ruins to life. Standing on what's left of the ramparts and looking across the plain, it's not too difficult to imagine a besieging army, legendary or otherwise, camped below.

Most impressive of the extant remains are the **east wall and gate** from Troy VI (1700–1275 BC), of which 330m remain, curving around the eastern and southern flanks of the city. The inward-leaning walls, 6m high and over 4m thick, would have been surmounted by an additional brick section. A ramp paved with flat stones from Troy II (2500–2300 BC), which would have led to the citadel entrance, also stands out, as does the nearby partially reconstructed **Megaron Building** (protected beneath a giant canvas roof) from the same era, the bricks of which were turned a bright red when Troy II was destroyed by fire. Schliemann erroneously used the evidence of this fire to conclude that this had been Homer's Troy and that the hoard he discovered here made up "Priam's treasure".

The most important monument of Greco-Roman Troy VIII–IX, or Ilium, is the Doric **temple of Athena**, rebuilt by Alexander the Great's general, Lysimakhos, after Alexander himself had visited the temple and left his armour as a gift. The most famous relief from the temple, depicting Apollo astride four pawing stallions, is now in Berlin. Troy was an important religious centre during Greek and Roman times, and another **sanctuary to the Samothracian deities** can be seen near the westernmost point of the site, outside the walls. East of this are a Greco-Roman odeion and bouleuterion (council hall).

Practicalities

Çanakkale is the most sensible base for seeing Troy. **Dolmuşes** run hourly (9.30am–7pm; 30min) from the open-air terminal by the river bridge in Çanakkale to **TEVFIKIYE** village just outside the site entrance. If you're moving on further south, return with the Troy–Çanakkale minibus to the main road, where you can flag down a passing long-haul bus. **Accommodation** in Tevfikiye includes the *Hisarlık Hotel* (☎0286/283 0026; ❸) near the minibus stop, with a restaurant and guided tours offered, or the hospitable *Varol Pansiyon* in the village centre (☎0286/283 0828; ❸), with a self-catering kitchen.

Alexandria Troas

The **ruins of Alexandria Troas**, an ancient city founded by Alexander the Great's general Antigonos I, in 300 BC, lie around 30km south of Troy and 2km south of Dalyan village. Currently being excavated by archeologists from the University of Münster, the site (unenclosed; free) consists of mostly Roman ruins surrounded by 8km of **city wall**; a sacred way linked it to the Apollo Smintheion sanctuary (see opposite), while another **avenue lined with shops** (now uncovered) served the ancient harbour at Dalyan. The modern road roughly bisects the city; just west of this are the site's most obvious features, including the **agora temple**, its columns and reliefs set aside for restoration; a huge structure of unknown function; and a partly dug-up **odeion** with two massive arched entrances. On the other side of the road are a **basilica** and one of several **baths**, with clay piping exposed. If the warden is present and you can understand Turkish, a free guided tour is available: if not, you can wander the site at will.

Smintheion sanctuary and Babakale

The minor coastal road south of Alexandria Troas passes tiny agricultural villages and a hot springs at Tuzla before reaching, after 32km, the curious ancient temple of **Apollo Smintheion**. You're best off going by bike or car as there's only scanty dolmuş service from Ezine, or Ayvacık via Behramkale (Assos), with some services continuing the final 9km southwest to **Babakale**. Coming west along the 25km from Behramkale, the road threads harsher, hillier terrain marked by attractive, stone-built villages.

The Smintheion Sanctuary

Signposted at the western edge of Gülpınar village (no tourist facilities), the shrine of **Apollo Smintheion** is dedicated to one of the more bizarre manifestations of the god, as Slayer of Mice – coins have even been found depicting Apollo treading on a mouse. When the original Cretan colonists here were besieged by mice, they remembered an oracle advising them to settle where they were overrun by the "sons of earth". This they took to mean the rodents, so founded the ancient town of Khryse nearby.

The surviving Hellenistic, Ionic **temple** (daily 8am–5pm; 5TL) has been partly restored and some columns re-erected, though its southwest corner has been reclad in garish new stone. The Efes beer brewery has funded the renovation as well as the ongoing excavations (no photos allowed) at adjacent **Khryse**, which have so far exposed a square **reservoir** in the sacred precinct, an arcaded **baths** complex just below and part of the **Sacred Way** from Alexandria Troas.

A one-roomed **museum** at the site entrance (open on request) displays **temple pediment reliefs** depicting scenes from the *Iliad*, including an early episode where Achilles kidnaps the priestess of the temple here, only to have Agamemnon appropriate her. Apollo duly inflicts a plague on the Greeks for this outrage, alleviated only upon the return of the girl to her father, the temple priest. Sadly, the reliefs are quite damaged except for the mourning of Patroklos.

Babakale

The working fishing port of **BABAKALE** (ancient Lekton) marks the westernmost point of Asia. It's a low-key place, though this may change once its harbour improvements designed to attract yachts are completed. The only local sandy **beach**, with sunbeds and a snack bar, is 4.5km before Babakale at **Akliman**, overlooked by a few holiday villas.

Babakale is dominated by a fine eighteenth-century Ottoman **castle** (always open; free), one of the last of its type built. The "baba" of the name refers to a dervish saint whose tomb is in the graveyard beside the castle. More interesting, however, are the medieval **mosque**, a couple of carved marble **çeşmes** (fountains) and a derelict **hamam** in the backstreets. Babakale has a couple of **hotels** above the harbour – the best is the *Uran* (T0286/747 0218; ❸), whose simple restaurant offers some of the freshest and most reasonably priced fish along this coast.

Assos and around

Situated on and around the eponymous ancient Greek city, **ASSOS**, 25km south of Ayvacık, is a charmingly preserved late-medieval village, with a central core of old houses built in the attractive local volcanic stone. **Assos acropolis** perches above it, spreading down the seaward side of the bluff towards the Aegean. Modern Assos consists of the village of **Behramkale**, wrapped around the landward side of the hill, and the tiny settlement of former warehouses and fishing cottages grouped around the **harbour** below. Further along the coast, 4km east of Assos port, extends the fine shingle beach of **Kadırga**.

Several **dolmuşes** a day serve Assos from the Friday market-town of Ayvacık, 17km north, as well as from Küçükkuyu to the east. The fare from Ayvacık is 3TL per person, but vehicles won't leave with fewer than eight passengers, so at quiet times, if there are few of you, it may be worth paying extra to avoid a long wait. The journey from Ayvacık threads through hilly countryside covered with olive trees and vallonea oak, whose acorns yield tannin used in leather production, the main business of Assos until the early 1900s. The final approach passes a fourteenth-century, humpback **Ottoman bridge**, built with ancient masonry, ending in the square at the village entrance.

Assos acropolis and Behramkale

Assos dates from about 950 BC, when Greek colonists from Mithymna on neighbouring Lesbos (modern Lésvos) established a settlement, later dedicating a huge temple to Athena in 530 BC. Hermias, a eunuch disciple of Plato, ruled here two centuries later, attempting to put Plato's theories of the ideal city-state into practice. From 348 to 345 BC Aristotle lived in Assos as Hermias' guest before crossing to Lesbos, just before the Persians arrived and put Hermias to death. St Paul also passed through en route to Lesbos during his third evangelical journey (c.55 AD; Acts 20:13–14). The site was rediscovered and initially excavated in 1880–83 by a 25-year-old American, Francis Bacon, who was sponsored by the Antiquarian Society of Boston.

From the town square it's a short, steep uphill walk to the single-domed **Murat Hüdavendigar Camii** (closed), an austere, square-plan fourteenth-century mosque. Just beyond is the enclosed acropolis site (open daylight hours; 5TL), where the iconic **Temple of Athena** provides sweeping views across the straits to Greek Lésvos. During the 1980s the temple's Doric columns were re-erected using inappropriate concrete, but remedial work is now underway to replace this with masoned stone from the original quarries. The rest of ancient Assos is a ruined jumble sloping away from the temple summit, enclosed by impressive, partly intact **city walls** accented with towers. The sarcophagi of the **necropolis** (unenclosed) can be visited on the way down from the village to the harbour.

Practicalities

Popular with the İstanbul literati, Assos is anything but cheap – on summer weekends advance booking of **accommodation** is essential, although midweek, and in May or September, you can still find rooms at realistic prices. The acropolis and port attract numerous coach tours, but few stay overnight. **Restaurant** options are fairly limited: *Köyüm* in the centre specializes in *mantı*, whilst *Kale* halfway up to the acropolis also offers grills and *deniz bürülce*. There's also an **ATM** and the only **pharmacy** in the region.

Accommodation

Assosyal East end of the village ℡0286/721 7046, ⊛www.assosyal.com. New boutique inn, whose room interiors contrast sharply with the stone exterior of the three wings. Breakfast is taken on the north-facing conservatory-terrace, also a restaurant. Half-board available. ⑥

Biber Evi By the lower square ℡0286/721 7410, ⊛www.biberevi.com. Behramkale's top lodgings, named for the twenty species of peppers (*biber*) growing in its garden. There are three rooms in the main house (built in 1860) – the best has a fireplace – and three more modest ones in the annexe. Outside is a popular winter fireplace-lounge-bar with terrace. Host Lütfi is a fount of local lore and offers excellent meals (half-board obligatory in season) and proper European coffee. ⑥, half-board ⑤.

Dolunay By the lower square Ⓣ 0286/721 7172. Six cosy, veneer-floored rooms facing a pleasant courtyard (though the en-suite bathrooms are basic), below a simple restaurant. ❸

Eris East end of the village Ⓣ 0286/721 7080, ⓦwww.erispansiyon.com. Hospitable American Emily offers three plain but tasteful rooms with valley views, a book swap, communal terrace and flexible-menu breakfasts. Often closed Jan–March. ❹

Old Bridge House By the old bridge Ⓣ 0286/721 7100, ⓦwww.oldbridgehouse.com.tr. Recently renovated, this two-wing boutique hotel has wooden floors, handmade furniture – and wonky hydromassage showers. There are village views from the upstairs rooms, though breakfasts are only average. ⑥

Tekin At the village entrance Ⓣ 0286/721 7099. Simple but serviceable en-suite rooms at Behramkale's budget option, with an on-site restaurant and a communal balcony upstairs. ❷

Assos harbour (İskele)

Dolmuşes from Ayvacık usually continue to **Assos harbour (İskele)**, where they wait for return custom, though the twenty-minute walk down is worthwhile for the views. Drivers must park in the car park on the final curve before the descent to the sea (about a five-minute walk away) as there's almost no parking at the bottom. Despite the tempting anchorage, there's little yacht traffic here and crossing to Greece is illegal – something enforced by the quayside *jandarma* post. The few hundred metres of waterfront, lined by massive, stone-clad buildings and ending in a small pebble beach, is very picturesque, and can be idyllic out of season, though summer weekends see it overflowing with busloads of tour groups.

Most waterfront properties are **hotels**: the first you come to is the good-value ⚑ *Yıldız Saray* (Ⓣ 0286/721 7025, ⓦwww.assosyildizsarayotel.com; ⑤), its eight upstairs rooms with modern bathrooms and sea views, and some with fireplaces. About the only budget choice, at the eastern end of the waterfront, is the *Çakır Pansiyon* (Ⓣ0286/721 7148; ❸), with simple, small doubles. The best luxury option is the *Nazlıhan* (Ⓣ0286/721 7385; ❼), a converted acorn warehouse on the right as you reach the waterfront, with three grades of boutique-style room, though only eight face the sea. Around and beyond the *Çakır* are several rough-and-ready **campsites** with snack bars.

All the hotels have more formal **restaurants**, of which the most reliable for fresh fish and reasonable prices is the *Yıldız Saray*, while the diner at *Çakır* serves good-value if simple fare. **Nightlife** is provided by the sole bar, *Uzun Ev*, hosting live acoustic Turkish music some evenings.

Kadirga

About 45 minutes east of İskele on foot – the path around the headland starts just beyond the last campsite – lies the beach resort of **KADIRGA**; it's also accessible by the paved road (4km) signposted from Behramkale. The beach here – nearly 2km of fine shingle – is the best in the area, with currents keeping the water clean. Of the half-dozen **accommodation** choices here try the *Yıldız Saray*, affiliated to its namesake in İskele (Ⓣ0286/721 7025, ⓦwww.assosyildizsarayotel.com; ⑥ half-board only), with veneer-floored, 2008-built bungalows and a large pool.

Well worth knowing about, and not shown on most maps, is the **shore road** heading 21km east from Kadırga to Küçükkuyu (see below). While narrow, it is entirely paved, served by the occasional dolmuş, and allows you to bypass the tortuous mountain curves of the main inland route. En route, the professional *Assos Terrace Motel* 4km beyond Kadırga (Ⓣ0286/764 0285; ❺ half-board only) has all sea-view rooms, swimming off a jetty and a terrace diner.

Along the Gulf of Edremit

From Ayvacık, the E87/550 Çanakkale–İzmir road descends in curves through pine-forested hills, allowing occasional glimpses over the **Gulf of Edremit**. The highway straightens out at **Küçükkuyu**, the only real coastal town and gateway to the two traditional villages of **Yeşilyurt** and **Adatepe** in the foothills of the Kazdağı range (the ancient Mount Ida). Beyond here, the road leads past a dreary succession of Turkish-dominated resorts and second-home complexes to the inland county town of **Edremit**, where there's a faint chance you might have to change buses. At Burhaniye, 18km south of Edremit, a side road leads 5km west to the old-fashioned resort of **Ören**, with an excellent, long, west-facing sandy beach.

Küçükkuyu and Yeşilyurt

The small fishing and olive-oil town of **KÜÇÜKKUYU**, 29km southeast of Ayvacık, still has a fleet at anchor, though the local organic olive-oil production is threatened by proposed highly polluting gold prospecting on the slopes of Kazdağ. There are some atmospheric backstreets to wander, though you're unlikely to stay longer than it takes to have a seafood **meal** on the port quay. *Alp Balık Evi*, on the left as you face the water, has its own fish supplier and a good reputation.

For a more characterful base, head for either of two nearby inland villages, though you'll need your own transport. The houses of **YEŞİLYURT**, 3km west on the E87/550 and then 1km inland, are built in yellowish stone and straggle down a slope amidst lush vegetation, peeking at the sea from their pirate-proof location. **Accommodation** options here include the central *Bam Teli Yol Konağı*, (T0286/752 5200, Wwww.yolkonagi.com; ❾), a converted old house just uphill from an exquisite late-medieval mosque. The more design-conscious *Taş Teras Otel* (T0286/752 6666, Wwww.tasteras.com; ❼) at the bottom of the village has sea views and six rooms, four with their own terraces. Next door, *Manici Kasrı* (T0286/752 1731, Wwww.manicikasri.com; ❽ half-board only), has variable, large and rather lush rooms, plus Olde Worlde common areas with a fireplace, beamed ceilings and a terrace restaurant. The only independent **restaurant** is the slightly pricy *Han*, next to the mosque, which offers unusual dishes like *otlu börek* and *giritli tatlısı*.

Adatepe

Exquisitely preserved **ADATEPE** lies just over 4km northeast of Küçükkuyu; look carefully on the main highway for the small sign indicating the village and its "**Zeus Altarı**", a fifteen-minute marked walk from the approach road. This is merely a carved rock platform with a cistern, though the views from the top of the steps are superb. Adatepe has appeared in TV serials and (unlike Yeşilyurt) enjoys statutory protection for its architecture, with some stone houses all but sprouting from volcanic boulders. Again unlike Yeşilyurt, it was ethnically mixed from the 1850s, when in the wake of a killing frost, cash-strapped olive-oil magnates paid their Greek workers with a grant of fields and building plots in the lower quarter, though the Orthodox church on the plane-tree plaza, with its three **snack bars**, was destroyed after 1923. The only **accommodation** is at welcoming 🦋 *Hünnap Han* (T0286/752 6581, Wwww.hunnaphan.com; ❼ half-board only), named after the jujube tree in its serene walled main garden. Stone and wood-trim rooms occupy a rambling, main *konak*, dating from 1750, with the *Taş Ev* annexe (sleeping 8) for groups, and a second annexe (*Palmiye*) downhill.

Ayvalık and around

AYVALİK, 56km south of Edremit, has long been popular with Turkish and European visitors thanks to its charming old quarter of picturesque, Greek houses. Unlike resorts to the south that are dominated by the holiday trade, the town has retained a fishing fleet and olive-based commerce, as well as lively markets and (since 1998) a prestigious classical music academy. The closest good beaches are at the mainstream resort of **Sarımsaklı**, with some remoter, rockier ones on **Cunda island**, both easily reached from town. Ayvalık is also convenient for day-trips to ancient Pergamon, and the Greek island of Lésvos opposite, served by regular ferry.

Due to its excellent anchorages, the area has been inhabited since ancient times, but today's Ayvalık began as the **Ottoman Greek settlement** of Kydoníes during the early 1700s. Both Turkish and Greek names refer to the local quince orchards, now vanished. In the 1790s, the town was effectively granted autonomy by Grand Vizier Cezayırlı Hasan Paşa, who, as an Ottoman admiral, had been rescued in 1771 by the Greeks of Ayvalık following a disastrous defeat by the Russian navy. The town soon became the most prosperous and imposing on the Aegean coast after İzmir, boasting an academy, a publishing house and around twenty Orthodox churches, many of which still remain, albeit converted into mosques after 1923. Ironically, most of the people resettled here were Greek-speaking Muslims from Crete and Mytilini (Lésvos), and many of Ayvalık's older inhabitants still speak Greek.

Arrival, information and boat trips

Most southbound **buses** heading south will drop you 5km northeast of town at the Ayvalık highway junction, from where you'll have to get a taxi into town. The **otogar** is 1.5km north of the town centre, though any city bus labelled "Çamlık" will take you into town, as will most *servis* vehicles of the major companies. Buses from İzmir usually pass through the central seafront İskele Meydanı. Just south of this is a summer-only tourist information booth; the main **tourist office** is just past the marina, about 1km southwest (℡0266/312 2122; Mon–Fri 8am–noon &

▲ View over Ayvalık and the Gulf of Edremit

1–5pm). The morning **ferry from Lésvos** (see "Travel Details, p.232) arrives at a new passenger terminal 1800m north of the centre, opposite the lone ticket agency, Jale (℡0266/312 2740). **Car-rental agencies**, all in the centre, include: Avis, Talatpaşa Cad 67/B (℡0266/312 2456); Duke, İskele Meydanc, (℡0266/312 3794); and Europcar, Gümrük Cad 41/B (℡0266/312 3446).

Boats to Cunda leave from the main quay (see p.221 for details), as do **day-trips** around the numerous local islets (out at 10am, return 4.30pm; 15TL). There are also several **scuba-dive outfitters** along the main quay, with the Ayvalık area noted for its deep-growing red coral, submerged archeological artefacts and cave. Two reputable operators are Körfez (Ⓦ www.korfezdiving.com) and 300 Bar (Ⓦ www.300bar.com.tr), both CMAS- and PADI-affiliated.

Accommodation

Central **accommodation** clusters in two areas: just in from the waterfront either side of the old, closed-down customs house, and in the hilly backstreets behind the bazaar, where numbers of *pansiyon*s – mostly non-en suite – are installed in restored Greek mansions. Incidentally, save for noted exceptions, Ayvalık lodging is a nightmare for parking, and drivers may be better off staying on Cunda (see p.221) and taking the shuttle-ferry to town.

Mansion-pansiyons

Annette's House Neşe Sok 12 ℡0542/663 3193, Ⓦ www.annetteshouse.com. Comprising five linked houses by the Thursday market, with a top-floor quad suite and a good ratio of bathrooms to the other, tasteful white-decor rooms. Delicious breakfasts are served by the German owner in the plant-filled garden. Parking possible except Thurs ❷, en suite ❸
Bonjour Mareşal Çakmak Cad, Çeşme Sok 5 ℡0266/312 8085. Occupies a grand mansion with painted ceilings; there are four rooms and two bathrooms in the main house, plus one en suite behind the courtyard where breakfast is served. ❹
Şato Mareşal Çakmak Cad 100, behind *Taksiyarhis* ℡0266/312 2351. Five rooms (and two bathrooms) in the original old house with a Lésvos-view terrace and s/c kitchen, plus five more en suites being readied by friendly hosts Cemal and Fatma in a nearby annexe. ❸, annexe rooms ❹
🏃 **Taksiyarhis** Mareşal Çakmak Cad 71 ℡0266/312 1494, Ⓦ www.taksiyarhis pension.com. One of the most characterful pensions on the Aegean coast, occupying two knocked-together Greek houses, immediately behind the eponymous church. Each a/c room is harmoniously decorated by owner Yasemin, plus there are two terraces (breakfast on the top one is a major highlight) and a s/c kitchen. Room-to-bath ratio about 1:3. Booking essential in summer. ❹

The waterfront

Ayvalık Palas Gümrük Meyd ℡0266/312 1064, Ⓦ www.ayvalikpalashotel.com. Rather bland, carpeted rooms, the best with sea-view balconies. The large on-site restaurant gets it a third (undeserved) star. ❺
Kaptan Balıkhane Sok 7 ℡0266/312 8834, Ⓦ www.kaptanotelayvalik.com. Some of these serviceable if slightly dated hotel rooms have a/c, sea views and/or balconies. Breakfast is served on a seaside terrace; limited parking. ❺
🏃 **Sızma Han** Gümrük Cad, İkinci Sok 49 ℡0266/312 7700, Ⓦ www.butiksizmahan .com. Beautifully renovated olive-oil press from 1908, enthusiastically managed by owner Mustafa; the competent, seafood-strong seaside terrace restaurant features Sevilen wines. Rooms are low-key modern with veneer floors and furniture, but exposed stone pointing. The lounge-with-fireplace is a focal point; limited street parking. Booking is mandatory at peak times, heavily discounted rates otherwise. ❻

The Town

Central Ayvalık – almost uniquely in the Aegean – is pretty much a perfectly preserved Ottoman market town, though with few of the traditional trades left.

Riotously painted horse-carts still clatter through the cobbled **bazaar**, emanating from a *meydan* to the south where the animals and their drivers wait for commissions. Ayvalık is also famous for its dairy products, *kepekli* (wholegrain)

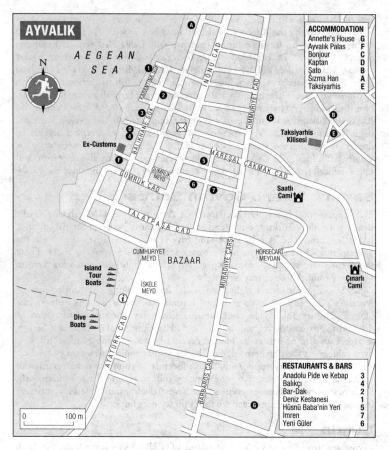

AYVALIK

AEGEAN SEA

N

ACCOMMODATION	
Annette's House	G
Ayvalık Palas	F
Bonjour	C
Kaptan	D
Şato	B
Sızma Han	A
Taksiyarhis	E

İNÖNÜ CAD

CUMHURİYET CAD

TARANTİNO SOK

BALIKHANE SOK

Ex-Customs

Taksiyarhis
Kilisesi

MAREŞAL ÇAKMAK CAD

GÜMRÜK CAD

GÜMRÜK
MEYD

TALATPAŞA CAD

Saatlı
Cami

CUMHURİYET
MEYD

BAZAAR

MURADİYE ÇARŞI

HORSECART
MEYDAN

Çınarlı
Cami

Island
Tour
Boats

İSKELE
MEYD

Dive
Boats

ATATÜRK CAD

BARBAROS CAD

0	100 m

RESTAURANTS & BARS	
Anadolu Pide ve Kebap	3
Balıkçı	4
Bar-Dak	2
Deniz Kestanesi	1
Hüsnü Baba'nin Yeri	5
İmren	7
Yeni Güler	6

bread, olive products (including oil and green soap) and seafood, peddled at the daily **fish market** down by the yacht marina. Thursday is the special **market day** for produce from the surrounding villages, with its epicentre at two *meydan*s either side of *Annette's House pansiyon*.

There are few specific sights other than converted nineteenth-century churches punctuating the warren of inland streets: use the minarets as landmarks and surrender to the pleasure of wandering under numerous wrought-iron window grilles and past ornately carved doorways. The most conspicuous church, Áyios Ioánnis, is now the **Saatlı Cami**, named after its clocktower. Just northeast and uphill stands unconverted **Taksiyarhis Kilisesi** – it's been closed for years, allegedly awaiting conversion to a museum. Also awaiting refurbishment is **Faneroméni**, near the fish market, alias Ayazma after the sacred spring on the site. East of the horse cart square looms the **Çınarlı Cami** (formerly Áyios Yeóryios) misnamed in that not one of its courtyard trees is a plane (*çınar* in Turkish).

Eating and drinking

Ayvalık's **restaurant** scene isn't quite as varied as its accommodation. The obvious fish restaurants just seaward of İskele Meydanı are mostly dubious and overpriced, and the bazaar is surprisingly devoid of eateries. The best-value seafood can be found at *Balıkçı*, by the *Kaptan Otel* at Balıkhane Sok 7, with live *fasıl* music some nights. A notch up in presentation (and price) is *Deniz Kestanesi* on Karantina Sokağı – allow 40TL per head before booze. About the last surviving bazaar *meyhane* is *Hüsnü Baba'nin Yeri*, Cumhuriyet Caddesi, Birinci Sok 12–14 (inland from Bellona Furniture), tops for *mezes* and cheap fishy titbits cooked on a two-burner stove – there's no written menu, so confirm all prices in advance. Non-fish-eaters gravitate to *Anadolu Pide ve Kebap*, in a restored stone building on Balıkhane Sokağı. A bit further north on the opposite side is *Bar-Dak*, the main **nightlife** option with Western music, a young crowd and reasonably priced drinks. If you have a sweet tooth, head for the almost adjacent bakeries on Talatpaşa Caddes, *Yeni Güler* (mastic and wholemeal biscuits, also *dondurma*) and *İmren* (famous for its *lor tatlısı* based on ricotta cheese), both going since the 1920s.

Sarimsakli and Şeytan Sofrası

The longest local beach lies 7km south of Ayvalık at **SARIMSAKLI** ("Garlic Beach"), a mainly Turkish resort reached by frequent dolmuşes from just south of İskele Meydanı. The 3km or so of sand here is attractive, rather more so at the western end where development is set back some distance from the water. There are all the resort trappings you'd expect, but with a slightly downmarket flavour, and few would choose to stay overnight.

Just before Sarımsaklı a right turn leads, initially along the south shore of Ayvalık's giant bay, 3km to a flattish summit known as **Şeytan Sofrası** (the "Devil's Dinner Table"). In clear weather this rocky outcrop affords views of dozens of surrounding volcanic islands, including Cunda and more distant Lésvos, and perhaps also of otherwise hidden beaches below, accessible only with your own vehicle. At the northern edge of the headland people throw money for luck into a small rock cavity, supposedly Satan's footprint. Prominent too are numerous votive rags tied onto bushes by the country folk to placate the presiding spirit, Satan or otherwise. Summer evenings see huge crowds (often bussed in) gathering for the sunset, and parking near the top is pretty near impossible.

Cunda

Across the bay from Ayvalık, the island of **CUNDA** – known as Yonda in Ottoman times and now officially **Alibey Adası** – constitutes either a good day-trip destination or an overnight halt. It's a marginally quieter, less grand version of Ayvalık old town, with a lively main harbour and slightly scruffy backstreets lined by restored stone houses – remnants of life before 1923, when Cunda was known as Moskhonísi to its Greek Orthodox inhabitants. After the Christians were sent to Greece, the island was resettled with Cretan Muslims from around Haniá, and you'll find that most older people speak Cretan Greek as a matter of course. Since the 1990s Cunda has become popular with affluent İstanbulites bent on owning an Aegean retreat though the dense ranks of tatty trinket and ice-cream stalls along the quay clash somewhat with its twee image.

Halfway up the slope from the waterfront stands the derelict Orthodox **Taksiyarhis Cathedral**, its interior scaffolded and off-limits for safety reasons. The church was heavily damaged in the local 1944 earthquake, and the rumoured restoration has yet to materialize. At the top of the hill, a chapel and adjacent windmill have been converted by the Koç Foundation into a worthwhile café with stunning views.

Northern Cunda, known as **Patriça**, is supposedly a protected nature reserve – though this hasn't completely stopped villa construction – and has some relatively deserted beaches. A dirt road goes to them, while boat tours from Ayvalık harbour visit two derelict **Greek monasteries** (Áyios Yórgis and Áyios Dhimítrios tou Sélina) accessible only by sea.

Practicalities

In season, small **bus-boats** leave for Cunda at least hourly (3TL; 30min) from Ayvalık's main quay. Alternatively, there's a circuitous **city-bus** from İskele Meydanı across the causeway linking Cunda to the mainland. From Cunda's harbour, most things are only a short walk away.

Accommodation options are scattered across the town – the further inland you go, the quieter, and easier to park, it becomes. *Ayışığı Pansiyon* at Selamet Cad 33, near Taksiyarhis (℡0266/327 2130, ❺), is a typical mid-range restored establishment; the mock-traditional, new-built *Albayrak Taş Konak*, just below the windmill chapel at Şafak Sok 15 (℡0266/327 3031, ⓦwww.otelalbayrak.com; ❺), is more ambitious, with bay views from the front rooms and the breakfast terrace. *Zehra Teyze'nin Evi* (℡0266/327 2285, ⓦwww.cundaevi.com; ❺), the former priest's house in the grounds of Taksiyarhis, exploits its position with overpriced en-suite rooms. Some 3km southwest of town, **campsite** *Ada* (℡0266/327 1211, ⓦwww.adacamping.com; April–Nov) has its own sandy beach and bungalows (❹), but is mostly populated by caravans.

The cheap local **seafood speciality** is *papalina* (fried sprat). Among the half-dozen waterfront **restaurants**, *Ada* (way to the left as you face the sea) offers the best value, with consistent cooking from a lady chef and loyal staff. The more central *Taş Kahve* is an evergreen café, open all day and into the night.

The old road to Bergama

The **old road from Ayvalık to Bergama** (55km) begins 8km north of town and, with a vehicle (allow over an hour) or bike is an eminently worthwhile alternative to the quicker but monotonous coastal highway. The first half of the route takes you through the magnificent stone pine forests of the **Kozak plateau**, source of many of the pine nuts on sale in Turkey's bazaars. Facilities en route are limited to several pure roadside springs, and – in **KOZAK** village, next to a freestanding ancient tomb – the *Çınar Restaurant* specializing in trout.

Bergama

Although possible as a day-trip destination from Ayvalık, **BERGAMA**, site of the **ancient city of Pergamon**, rates an overnight in its own right. The stunning acropolis is the main attraction, but two lesser sights and the town's medieval quarter may detain you further. Bergama seems unpromising at first: the long approach to the centre passes nondescript modern buildings, with the two parts of ancient Pergamon some distance from town.

Some history

Pergamon first gained prominence as the base of Lysimakhos, one of Alexander the Great's successors. He left considerable treasure with his eunuch-steward Philetaeros, who inherited it when Lysimakhos was killed in 281 BC. Philetaeros passed these riches on to his nephew Eumenes I founder of the Pergamene dynasty but the city did not achieve true greatness until the reign of **Eumenes II** (197–159 BC) who built its gymnasium, the Altar of Zeus, library, theatre and acropolis wall. Eumenes' brother Attalos II ruled until 138 BC, followed by the five-year reign of Pergamon's last king, the cruel but scholarly

Attalos III, who perversely left the kingdom in his will to the **Romans**. Under them Pergamon grew to be a renowned artistic and commercial centre of 150,000 people, but after the arrival of the Goths in 262 AD, the city declined as it was claimed by successive invaders before falling into ruin.

The German engineer **Carl Humann** rediscovered ancient Pergamon in 1871, when some locals showed him a strange mosaic that turned out to be part of the relief from the Altar of Zeus. Humann bought the mosaic, and began excavating the acropolis. Work was completed by 1886, but unfortunately most of the finds were carted off to Germany, including the Altar of Zeus reliefs, now in the Pergamon Museum in Berlin.

In 1998 a second significant archeological site, the Roman spa and asklepion of **Allianoi**, was discovered 19km east of Pergamon. However, it had only been partly excavated before the Yortanlı irrigation dam was built: despite domestic and international protest (see ⓦwww.allianoi.org for details), the site looks set to be submerged beneath 17m of water.

Arrival, orientation and information

The **acropolis** of the Pergamene dynasty towers over modern Bergama, while just west of town is the **Asklepion** or ancient healing spa. The **old town** (site of most cheap accommodation) lies at the foot of the acropolis, while the **otogar**, linked to the centre by dolmuşes, is 6km south near the junction of the E87/550 highway. The last direct minibus back to **Ayvalık**, departs from the *otogar* at 5pm; if you miss it, you'll have to use indirect services via Dikili (which run until 8pm).

When **leaving Bergama**, you can easily connect with trains to Bandırma and the fast ferry to İstanbul by taking a bus to Soma, 45km away (a short taxi ride links Soma's train and bus stations) – by far the easiest and cheapest way of getting to İstanbul. So-called "direct" night buses tend to be slow and expensive.

At Bergama's *otogar*, disembarking passengers are likely to be approached by a **taxi driver** offering to ferry you around the ruins for the extortionate sum of 50–60TL (a bit less out of season). If there are a few of you, or you're in a hurry, this might make sense, but otherwise it's a bit of a racket, limiting you to one hour at the acropolis (you really need two), ten minutes at the Red Basilica and half an hour at the Asklepion. The main **taxi stand** in central Bergama is by two mosques and the functioning **Çarşı Hamamı**.

Bergama's **tourist office** is near the Archeological Museum (Mon–Fri 8.30am–noon & 1–5.30pm; ☎0232/631 2851), though all it offers are the usual tourism-ministry brochures and a feeble town map.

Accommodation

All of Bergama's **hotels** are conspicuous on the way into town along İzmir Caddesi, while the best budget **pansiyons** are located in the old town or by the approaches to the Asklepion. The hotels are neither wildly inspiring nor convenient, and with your own transport you may well prefer to stay in Çandarlı (see p.226) or Ayvalık.

Akropolis Guest House Kayalık Sok 3, base of the road up to the ancient city ☎0232/631 2621, ⓦwww.akropolisguesthouse.com. Two converted stone buildings around a pleasant courtyard with a small plunge-pool contain nine somewhat dark standard rooms and three airier deluxe suites: the latter are worth the extra sum for the views and more light. There's also a well-priced restaurant on site. ❸, suites ❹

Böblingen Pension Asklepion Cad 2 ☎0232/633 2153, ⓦboblingenpansiyon.com. About as far out of town as non-drivers are likely to want to be, with friendly family management and decent, if slightly dated rooms. ❷

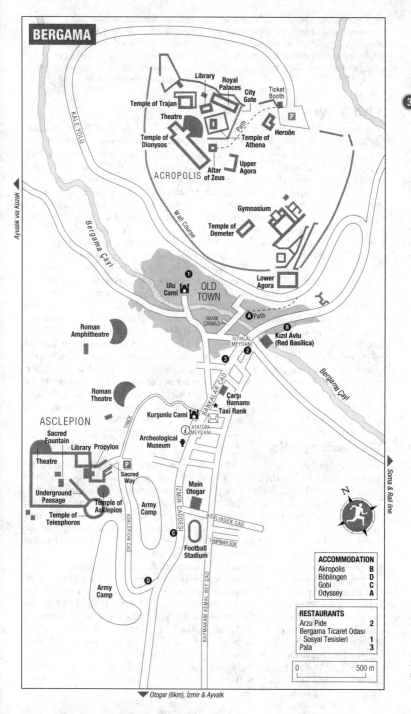

BERGAMA

Ayvalık via Kozak

KALE YOLU

Bergama Çayı

Wall Course

Temple of Trajan

Library

Royal Palaces

City Gate

Ticket Booth

Theatre

Path

P

Heroön

Temple of Dionysos

Temple of Athena

ACROPOLIS

Altar of Zeus

Upper Agora

Gymnasium

Temple of Demeter

Lower Agora

Ulu Cami

OLD TOWN

Roman Amphitheatre

IMAM ÇIKMAZI

İSTİKLAL MEYDANI

Kızıl Avlu (Red Basilica)

BANKALAR CAD

Bergama Çayı

Çarşı Hamamı

Taxi Rank

Roman Theatre

ASCLEPION

TRACK

Kurşunlu Cami

ATATÜRK MEYDANI

Archeological Museum

Sacred Fountain

Library

Propylon

P

Sacred Way

İZMİR CADDESİ

Main Otogar

Theatre

Underground Passage

Temple of Asklepios

Temple of Telesphoros

Army Camp

ASKLEPION CAD

BÖBLINGEN CAD

TANPINAR SOK

Army Camp

Football Stadium

KAYMAKAM KEMAL BEY CAD

Soma & Rail line

N

ACCOMMODATION
Akropolis	B
Böblingen	D
Gobi	C
Odyssey	A

RESTAURANTS
Arzu Pide	2
Bergama Ticaret Odası Sosyal Tesisleri	1
Pala	3

0   500 m

Otogar (6km), İzmir & Ayvalk

Gobi Pension Atatürk Bul 18 ℡ 0232/633 2518, ⓦ www.gobipension.com. Dull 1960s architecture and some street noise is more than made up for by a warm welcome, overall cleanliness, newish (mostly en-suite) bathrooms and good home-style cooking. ❷

Odyssey Guesthouse Abacıhan Sok 13 ℡ 0232/631 3501, ⓦ www.odysseyguesthouse.com. Two linked old Greek houses, with a roof terrace, s/c kitchen, separate reference libraries and a very helpful managing couple. One house has en-suite, high-ceilinged rooms (❸), one doesn't (❷).

The Town

The foremost attraction in Bergama itself is the **Kızıl Avlu** or "Red Basilica" (daily 8.30am–5.30pm; 5TL), a huge red-brick edifice on the river below the acropolis. Originally built as a second-century AD temple to the Egyptian gods Serapis, Harpokrates and Isis, it was used as a basilica by the Byzantines – who merely built a smaller church within the confines. Pergamon was one of the Seven Churches of the Apocalypse addressed by St John the Divine, who referred to it in Revelation 2:13 as "the throne of Satan", perhaps a nod to the still-extant Egyptian cult. It's now a crumbling ruin containing a mosque in one of its towers, with the ancient **Selinos River** (today the Bergama Çayı) passing underneath the basilica via two tunnels. Just downstream you'll see a handsome Ottoman bridge, built in 1384, with two equally well-preserved Roman bridges upstream.

The area uphill from the basilica, north of the river, is the town's **old quarter**, a jumble of Ottoman buildings, antique and carpet shops, mosques and maze-like streets. The antique stalls are full of very beautiful, overpriced copperware – too many coach tours have had their effect. Similarly, the reputation of Bergama carpets has been besmirched by too much synthetic dye and machine-weaving – beware.

Back on İzmir Caddesi, the **Archeological Museum** (Arkeoloji Müzesi; Tues–Sun 8.30am–noon & 1–5.30pm; 5TL), has a large collection of locally unearthed relics, including a statue of Hadrian from the Asklepion. Many of the fourth-century BC statues display a more naturalistic technique, incorporating accentuated body shape and muscle tone which allowed a wider range of expressions to be shown. First developed in Pergamon, this style influenced later European Baroque style. Also of interest is an impressively complete Roman mosaic of Medusa, and a large figurine of Aphrodite holding an oyster shell, found at Allianoi (see p.222).

The acropolis

The **acropolis** (daily: 8.30am–5.30pm; July–Aug until 6.30pm; 20TL) is readily accessible on foot from the old town – though this is one attraction you may want to reach by taxi (15TL), at least going uphill, since the path can be difficult to find. The trail begins on the far side of the second bridge upstream from the Kızıl Avlu, angling obliquely up to the road; cross here and follow a fairly steep incline into the lower agora. Try not to walk up along the main road, which is steep and not particularly direct, doubling back on itself for about 5km. Taxis will drop you at the site car park and ticket booth, from where a ramp leads to the former **city gate**, though this has almost completely disappeared.

A path leads southwest to the huge, square **Altar of Zeus**, standing in the shade of two large stone pines. Built during the reign of Eumenes II to commemorate his father's victory over the Gauls, the altar was decorated with reliefs depicting the battle between the Titans and the gods, symbolizing the triumph of order over chaos (and, presumably, that of Attalos I over the Gauls). Even today its former splendour is apparent, if much diminished by the removal of the reliefs to Berlin. The main approach stairway was on the west, though this is now the most deteriorated side.

Directly northeast of and exactly parallel to the Altar of Zeus, on the next terrace up, lie the sparse remains of the third-century BC **Temple of Athena**. Only some

Pergamon's library and the birth of the modern book

Founded by Eumenes II and enlarged by Attalos II, both fanatical collectors of books, **Pergamon's Library** grew to contain 200,000 titles – volumes by Aristotle and Theophrastos were paid for with their weight in gold. Eventually the Egyptian Ptolemies, alarmed at this growing rival to their own library in Alexandria, banned the export of papyrus, on which all scrolls were written – and of which they were sole producers – thus attempting to stem the library's expansion. In response the Pergamene dynasty revived the old practice of writing on specially treated animal skins – parchment – which led quickly to the invention of the **codex** or paged book, since parchment couldn't be rolled up like papyrus. The words "parchment" and the more archaic "pergamene" are both actually derived from "Pergamon". The library was appropriated by Mark Antony, who gave it to Cleopatra as a gift, and many of its works survived in Alexandria until destroyed by the Arabs in the seventh century.

of its stepped foundations survive *in situ*, although the entrance gate, with its inscribed dedication "King Eumenes to Athena the Bearer of Victories", has been reconstructed in Berlin. The scanty north stoa of the temple once housed Pergamon's famous **Library**, which at its peak rivalled Alexandria's (see box above).

From the Temple of Athena a narrow staircase leads down to the spectacular Hellenistic **theatre**, cut into the hillside and with a capacity for 10,000 spectators. The wooden stage was removed after each performance – the holes into which the supporting posts were driven can still be seen on the stage terrace – to allow free access to the **Temple of Dionysos**, built on the same terrace.

Still further north and uphill looms the Corinthian **Temple of Trajan**, where both Trajan and Hadrian were revered during Roman times – their busts were also taken to Berlin. German archeologists have re-erected some of the temple columns, plus much of the stoa that surrounded the shrine on three sides. The north architrave is lined with Medusa heads, two of them modern recastings.

Behind the temple are the remains of barracks and the highest reaches of the city's **perimeter wall**. Nearby yawns a cistern once fed by an **aqueduct**, traces of which are still visible running parallel to a modern one on the hillside to the northwest. Finally, as you begin your descent back down towards the main entrance, you'll pass – east of the library and Athena temple – the extensive but jumbled ruins of the **royal palaces**.

Just south of the Altar of Zeus lies a terrace, formerly the **upper agora** of Pergamon. There isn't much to see today, other than Carl Humann's grave, at what was once the commercial and social focus of the city. An ancient street descends between houses and the **Temple of Demeter**, where the local variant of the Eleusinian Mysteries was enacted. Across the way lies the **gymnasium**, arranged over three terraces, where the city's youth were educated. The upper level, with its palaestra and lecture hall, was for young men, the middle was used by the adolescents, while the lower served as a playground for small boys. From the **lower agora**, the path back down to town is indicated by circular blue waymarks.

The Asklepion

Bergama's other significant archeological site is the **Asklepion** (daily 8.30am–5.30pm; July–Aug until 6.30pm; 15TL, plus parking fee), the ancient, sacred therapeutic centre. The main road there, about 2km long, begins in front of the *Böblingen Pension* (see p.222) and passes through a large, clearly marked military zone, closed to traffic at dusk – don't take photographs outside of the site itself.

Healing methods at all *asklepia* combined the ritualistic and the practical. Patients were required to sleep in the temple so that Asklepios, semi-divine son of Apollo and god of healing, might appear in their dreams to suggest diagnosis and treatment. However, special diets, bathing in hot or cold water and exercise also figured in the therapeutic regimes. **Galen** (129–202 AD), the greatest physician of antiquity, whose theories dominated medicine until the sixteenth century, was born and worked here as well as in Rome.

Much of what can be seen here today dates from the reign of **Hadrian** (117–38 AD), when the Pergamene Asklepion functioned much like a nineteenth-century spa. Some came to be cured of specific ailments, but for others a prolonged visit was part of the social life of the wealthy and leisured.

The site

From the site entrance, a long, colonnaded **sacred way** originally lined with shops leads to the **propylon**, or monumental entrance gate, rebuilt in the third century AD, after an earthquake seriously damaged it in the previous century. North of the propylon is the square **library**, which also housed the statue of Hadrian now in the local museum.

South of the propylon lies the circular **Temple of Asklepios** (150 AD), modelled on Rome's Pantheon. Although only foundations remain today, when intact its graceful dome was 24m across, with an oculus for light and air to penetrate. The broad, open area to the west was originally enclosed by colonnaded stoas; at the western end of the re-erected, mostly Ionic northern colonnade is an over-restored **theatre** which seated 3500 and entertained towns-people as well as patients. At the centre of the open area, the **sacred fountain** – one of three in the Asklepion – still trickles weakly radioactive water. Nearby, an 80-metre-long underground passage leads to the **Temple of Telesphoros** (the lesser deity of Accomplishment), originally a two-storey circular building where patients slept while awaiting dream diagnoses. The lower, vaulted level survives in good repair.

Eating

If offered meals or half-board at your hotel, you should seriously consider this, as Bergama's **restaurant** scene is limited, with many of its eateries too far out of town to be of any use to those without transport. Worthwhile central options include the busy *Pala* on Kasapoğlu Caddesi, at the corner of İzmir Caddesi, whose speciality is *köfte*, and the keenly priced, popular *Arzu Pide* on İstiklâl Meydanı, serving soups and grills as well as six varieties of *pide*, though it's beset by traffic-noise. Almost the only licensed outfit is *Bergama Ticaret Odası Sosyal Tesisleri* which serves moderately priced grills and *mezes* in a restored Greek school 150m uphill from the Ulu Cami.

Çandarlı

Some 35km southwest of Bergama across a volcanic landscape, the small port resort of **ÇANDARLI** covers a headland that was formerly the site of ancient Pitane, the northernmost Aeolian city. Of this nothing remains other than some recycled masonry visible in the well-restored, fourteenth-century **Genoese fortress** (closed to the public), one of many such forts dotting the northwestern Turkish coast and the Greek islands opposite, a legacy of the days when the military and commercial might of Genoa dominated the North Aegean.

With its two sandy **beaches** – the easterly one facing south, and the more popular western one looking towards the Foça and Karaburun peninsulas – Çandarlı is not a bad place to retreat for a day or two, with a laid-back atmosphere absent from some larger resort towns. Everyday life centres on the east side of the peninsula, where frequent **buses** from İzmir, and regular **minibuses** from Bergama, arrive near the main *meydan* (market day is Friday). A short walk from here through lanes lined with a few old Greek houses leads to all the resort facilities, concentrated along the usually pedestrianized esplanade behind the west beach.

Accommodation is concentrated at the north end of this esplanade. The three best rooms at the *Senger Motel* (℡0232/673 3117; ❸) have sea views, balconies or both, though their colour scheme is decidedly eclectic; they've also a family quad on the roof, and a downstairs restaurant. The *Emirgan Hotel* further north (℡0232/673 2500; May–Sept; ❷), right on the sand, is preferable, with cool, minimalist, veneer-floored rooms, an on-site, normally priced restaurant and parking (a problem here) possible outside. The same friendly family manages the *Samyeli Otel* near the *Senger* (℡0232/673 3428, Ⓦwww.otelsamyeli.com; all year; ❸), with slightly more comfortable rooms. Among fairly touristy, predictable seafood **restaurants** along the esplanade, exceptions at the north end include *Hoca'nin Yeri*, serving good, inexpensive *pide* with soup, and *Pitaneon* next to the *Samyeli*, a popular café doing snacks as well. Around the castle, there are only ice-cream stalls and tea gardens, as well as a live music **bar**, *Villa Papatya*.

Foça and around

FOÇA – 65km southwest of Çandarlı – is the modern successor of ancient **Phokaea**, founded around 1000 BC by Ionian colonists. Great seafarers, the Phokaeans plied the Mediterranean as far as the Straits of Gibraltar, founding numerous colonies, including (around 600 BC) Massalia, now Marseilles. The Byzantines ceded the town to the Genoese, who restored its castle and managed to stay until the Ottomans seized it in the 1400s.

The name *Phokaea* is derived from the ancient Greek for "seal", a reference either to the suggestively shaped islets offshore, or to the real animals that live in the local waters – the municipal seal depicts one of the creatures half-emerged from the water. There's still a handful of Mediterranean **monk seals** about, monitored and protected by the Turkish Underwater Research Foundation, though you're most unlikely to see any on one of the day boat trips offered. Frankly you'd need to *be* a seal to really enjoy the sea here which, thanks to strong currents and a sharp drop-off, is notoriously chilly much of the year. The other restraint on local development has been the pervasive military presence: Foça has an important naval base, and much of the nearby coastline is out of bounds. None of this has stopped Foça becoming a favourite second-home venue for İzmir and Manisa folk; the town accommodates both them and short-term tourists graciously, making a worthwhile stopover.

Arrival, information and transport

The town lies 26km west of the E87/550 highway at Buruncuk. Any long-haul bus will leave you at the turning for Foça, there are regular onward **dolmuşes**. There are also half-hourly direct buses from İzmir, which arrive just south of the seafront main square behind Büyükdeniz, near the **tourist office** (May–Sept Mon–Fri 8.30am–noon & 1.30–5.30pm, Sat 10am–5.30pm; Oct–April Mon–Fri 8.30am–5.30pm; ℡0232/812 1222) and the main taxi rank. A pedestrianized street leads north past the **PTT**, *Foça Rent A Car* (℡0232/812 2496) and several **ATM**s to the head of Küçükdeniz bay.

Accommodation

The choicest **pansiyons** and **hotels** are on or around Reha Midilli Caddesi in Küçükdeniz. Driving in from the main highway, turn right at the edge-of-town junction, signed toward Yenifoça, and then left – don't attempt to drive through the town-centre bazaar.

Amphora Ismetpaşa Mahallesi, 206 Sok ☎0537/ 219 6604. Just three comfortable, carpeted suites in this restored building, not to be confused with the adjacent *Grand Amphora*. ❹

Foçantique Reha Midilli Cad 154 ☎0232/812 4313, ⓦwww.focantiquehotel.com. Foça's first boutique hotel is a restored old garden-house whose small rooms have exposed stonework and rather average bathrooms (except for one with a converted hamam). There's a modern extension at the front with a sea view bar/breakfast area and an apartment to rent upstairs. Open all year. ❼, apartment. ❾

🏃 **Foça Konak** Reha Midilli Cad 140, corner of 149 Sok ☎0532/617 2035 or 232/812 3809. Foça's top boutique hotel, opened in late 2009, installed in a former Orthodox priest's mansion. The two upstairs rooms in the main house preserve high ceilings and the original wood cabinetry, while three more rooms occupy stone buildings in the back garden with its lawn-bar and small spa-pool. ❼

Huzur North end of Küçükdeniz ☎0232/812 1203. Rather basic if en-suite *pansiyon* rooms, some

pricier ones have a sea view; there's also a waterside breakfast terrace. ❸

🏃 **Iyon** Ismetpaşa Mahallesi, 198 Sok 8 ☎0232/812 1415, ⓦwww.iyonpansiyon .com. Welcoming, well-run *pansiyon* with a choice of more basic rooms in a restored Greek house at the front (❷) or more spacious, comfortable ones in the rear garden annexe (❸). Breakfast and drinks are served on the raised front deck, a block back from the sea. Parking possible nearby.

Leon Mersinaki Bay, Yeşiltepe, just north of town ☎0232/812 2960, ⓦwww.otelleon.com. It may be a 1970s architectural monstrosity, but the hotel's position – on its own lido and beach, with sailing club – is five-star, and it's excellent value, even if you choose to eat most meals elsewhere. Limited parking; full board only. ❺

Sempatik Hotel Güneş 163 Sok 10, on the corner of the shore road ☎0232/812 1915, ⓦwww .sempatikhotelgunes.com. All the somewhat bland rooms here have balconies and decent showers; open all year. ❹

The Town

Today little remains visible of **ancient Phocaea**; the most striking remnant, 8km before modern Foça just north of the main road, is the **Taş Ev**, an unusual eighth-century BC tomb cut from the rock, squatting beside an Ottoman bridge and a modern cemetery. A small, much later **ancient theatre** marks the east entry to Foça, while some mosaic pavements from a Roman villa, including a well-preserved portrayal of four Bacchus heads and birds, have been unearthed about 150m southwest of the theatre.

The oldest intact structure in Foça itself is the waterfront **Beşkapılar fortress** (open for art exhibitions), originally Byzantine but much modified by successive occupiers. More authentic are various pre-1923 Greek fishermen's cottages and a few more opulent Ottoman mansions lining the cobbled backstreets. Two interesting, fifteenth-century mosques bracket Beşkapılar: the unheralded but beautiful **Fatih Camii**, and the **Kayalar Camii**, at the summit of the castle enclosure, sporting a distinctly lighthouse-like minaret.

The castle headland lends Foça an interesting layout, splitting the bay into two smaller harbours: the northerly, more picturesque **Küçükdeniz** where most of the action takes place along seafront Reha Midilli Caddesi; and the southerly, rather bleak **Büyükdeniz**, of interest only as the point where ferries from Lésvos dock and the fishing fleet is anchored. Neither bay has a decent beach, though that doesn't stop bathers from establishing themselves on the slightly grubby shingle or launching themselves from platforms at Küçükdeniz.

Boat trips (May–Sept daily 10.30am–6pm; 20TL a head) run from Küçükdeniz to some of the small islets northwest of Foça; most craft follow similar itineraries, with three stops during the day for swimming, and lunch included.

Eating and drinking

The pedestrianized plaza at the head of Küçükdeniz harbour is crammed with identikit seafood **restaurants**, none that exciting. Much the best fish in town can be found at ⌖ *Fokai* (all year), behind the castle overlooking Büyükdeniz at 121 Sok 8, with fresh and farmed fare clearly distinguished, good presentation and a discerning Turkish clientele. In the warren of bazaar lanes east of the seafront plaza, *Foça Meyhane* has affordable prices for unusual *mezes* like *istifnos* (a type of leafy green vegetable) and tongue, while just around the corner *Çarşı Lokantası* (noon–8pm) serves well-priced home-cooked dishes in a cheerful environment, with popular outdoor tables. Finally, *Nazmi Usta* on Küçükdeniz esplanade is the best of several local *dondurma* outlets, serving dozens of flavours including mastic gum. Adjacent to *Foça Meyhane*, some noisy music bars provide the town's **nightlife**.

Northeast to Yenifoça

Along the scenic 25km of road northeast to Yenifoça are some excellent **beaches** not restricted by the military – but they are either only accessible on foot, or by paying hefty fees to the **campsites** which own them (Turks pay 5–10TL, foreigners 10–15TL), for example *People* (5km out) and *Kosova* (7km along). The best sand is at *Acar Kamping* (after 10km), but some 700m before that, paths from the roadside lead down beneath some high-voltage power lines to a succession of idyllic coves opposite an islet. Alternatively, *Mambo Beach Club*, 5km before Yenifoça, usually allows free access to the beach if you patronize their snack bar.

YENİFOÇA itself has a core of well-restored old Greek houses but the town's coarse-sand beach is crowded, grubby and exposed to north winds. The popularity of second homes here means that short-term accommodation is limited to the seafront *Naz* (☎0232/814 6619; ❹), whose restrained rooms belie its cheerful kitsch common areas, and the smaller *Selena* just off the bazaar (☎0232/814 9191; ❸), although parking is difficult here. The bazaar is the place to head for affordable *çorba*, *pide* and grills; the cluster of seafood **restaurants** at the east end of the quay looks tempting but often resorts to the usual bill-inflating tricks (see p.45).

With your own transport, you're better off heading 2km further east, then 6km inland to ungentrified **KOZBEYLİ**. Once the mixed Ottoman village of Kuzubey, its old houses cluster around a much-prized fountain and central *meydan* whose café is famous for its *dibek kahvesi*. Next door ⌖ *Selluka Yemek Evi* has a limited, well-priced menu of *mantı* (mince-stuffed ravioli), *pilaf* with mushrooms and pistachios, and *sütlaç*. **Bus** #45 calls here, plying between Menemen and Yenifoça.

Manisa

Spilling out from the foot of the Manisa Dağı range, **MANISA** (the ancient Magnesia ad Sipylus) lies 38km east of Menemen along the E87/550 highway, and is easily reached from there or from İzmir, also 38km away. Most of the historic centre was torched by the Greek army during its 1922 retreat, but a few fine Selçuk and Ottoman monuments survive.

The area was settled early in the first millennium BC, by veterans of the Trojan War according to legend, and the ancient town was an important Roman centre. For a short time during the thirteenth century Manisa was capital of the Byzantine Empire, after the sacking of Constantinople by the Fourth Crusade. In 1313 the city was captured by Selçuk chieftain Saruhan Bey, from whose rule date the earliest of Manisa's surviving monuments. Later, the Ottomans sent heirs to the throne here to serve an apprenticeship as local governors, in order to ready them for the rigours of İstanbul palace life.

The Town

Dominating the well-signed Sultan Meydanı, the **Sultan Camii** was built in 1522 for Ayşe Hafize, mother of Süleyman the Magnificent, who lived here with her son while he was serving as governor. A rectangular mosque, much wider than it is deep, its single central dome is flanked by two pairs of satellite domes. Late Ottoman Baroque paint decoration and a tiny wood-railed pulpit on the west enliven the porch – actually a *son cemaat yeri* (latecomers' praying place). Of the surrounding complex, that included a *medrese* and mental hospital, only the hamam continues in its original function.

Every year around the spring equinox, the *Mesir Macunu Şenlikleri* **Power-Gum Festival** – now well into its fifth century – takes place around the Sultan Camii, to commemorate local doctor Merkez Efendi's concoction of a special resin to cure Ayşe Hafize of an unspecified ailment. The gum, or *mesir macunu*, containing 41 herbs and spices, is scattered from the minaret by the muezzin to crowds who use the paste as a remedy against aches, pains and snake or insect bites.

Opposite the Sultan Camii stands the **Saruhan Bey Türbesi** (closed), the tomb of Saruhan Bey, who took Manisa from the Byzantines in 1313. His army is said to have attacked Sandıkkale citadel while driving a flock of goats with candles on their horns before them to give the impression that a huge army was attacking; the defenders panicked and the castle fell.

Barely 100m further east along Murat Caddesi stands the **Muradiye Camii**, built for the future Murat III in 1583–85 while he was governor here. The interior, with its stained-glass windows and relatively restrained decoration, is impressive: the carved wooden *mimber*, or pulpit, and the sultan's loge are particularly fine. Unusually, a large women's gallery runs the full length of the cross-stroke of the reverse-T ground plan. Next door, housed in a former *imaret* (soup kitchen), Manisa's **museum** (Tues–Sun 9am–5pm; 2TL) features an interesting collection of archeological and ethnological exhibits, including items retrieved from Sardis.

On a natural, landscaped terrace 250m above the museum stands Manisa's oldest surviving mosque, the **Ulu Cami**, built atop a Byzantine church in 1366 by Işak Çelebi, Saruhan Bey's grandson. The spectacular view north over town rewards the steep climb from the centre. Entering the open-roofed courtyard via the ornate portal, you confront the glory of the place, a forest of varied **antique columns**, some "double" and others carrying Byzantine capitals, presumably recycled from the church that once stood here. More interior columns support a large central dome by means of pointed arches.

Practicalities

From the **otogar**, walk south towards the mountains for about ten minutes to reach **Sekiz Eylül (Doğu) Caddesi** and its continuation Mustafa Kemal Caddesi, the town's main commercial street. The **train station**, with regular services from İzmir, lies fifteen minutes north, along Atatürk Bulvarı.

Accommodation in Manisa leaves much to be desired and fills with local university students between mid-September and June. About the only central hotel is the *Arma* at Sekiz Eylül Cad 14 (℡0236/231 1980, ❹), with its own restaurant and rather faded rooms. The best place to eat in town is at the well-signed, restored **Yenihan**, about four blocks north of the museum along Dumlupınar Caddesi, where there are several (unlicensed) courtyard **restaurants**. The traditional local autumn dessert is stewed quince in *pekmez* (grape molasses), the latter courtesy of regional vineyards.

Sardis

Ancient **Sardis** (Sart in Turkish) lies 65km east of Manisa, at the northern foot of Bozdağ. The route there follows the Gediz river valley, the world's number-one producer of sultanas, with vineyards dominating the landscape. Sardis became incredibly wealthy thanks to the gold flecks that were washed down from Mount Tmolos (now Bozdağ) and caught in sheepskins by the locals. According to legend, the source of this wealth was Phrygian king **Midas**, whose touch turned everything to gold. Unable to eat, his curse was lifted when the gods bid him wash his hands in the River Paktolos, which flowed down to Sardis from the south.

Unsurprisingly perhaps given this abundance of gold, the Lydians invented coinage under Sardis's most celebrated king, **Croesus**. During his rule (560–546 BC) the kingdom's wealth attracted the attention of the Persians under Cyrus. The Delphic oracle ambiguously advised a worried Croesus that should he attack first a great empire would be destroyed. Croesus went to war and was defeated, and after a two-week siege Sardis fell; taken prisoner by Cyrus, Croesus was burnt alive, though some accounts have him rescued from the pyre by a providential rainstorm.

As a Persian city, Sardis was sacked during the Ionian revolt of 499 BC. It revived under Alexander the Great, but was destroyed by an earthquake in 17 AD. The Romans rebuilt it, and Sardis ranked as one of the Seven Churches of Asia addressed by St John in Revelation 3:1–6, though this didn't spare Byzantine Sardis from conquest by Saruhan and destruction at the hands of Tamerlane in 1401. The city only came to light again between 1904 and 1914, when American archeologists began excavating here.

The sites

There are two clusters of ruins, both easily reached on foot from the main road, though the uphill one is a hot walk in summer. The **first site**, essentially the gymnasium and synagogue (daily 8am–6pm, closes 5pm in winter; 3TL), lies just north of the road on the eastern edge of Sartmustafa. Entry is via a partially revealed, marble-paved **Roman avenue**, which passes various shops, though low walls with discernible doorways are all that remain.

A break in the shopping mall leads into the restored **synagogue**, its walls covered with copies of the original coloured stonework, now housed in the Manisa Museum; the extensive floor mosaics are, however, original. Adjacent to the synagogue is the third-century AD **gymnasium and bath complex**, once the city's most prominent building. Its **Marble Court**, the entry from the palaestra to the baths, has been spectacularly restored approximately to its condition when first built in 211 AD. The walls behind the columns would have had marble revetments and the podia would have supported statues, forming a splendid multistoreyed facade implying association with some imperial cult. Behind the court are the remains of a plunge-pool and rest area.

From the Sartmustafa village teahouses, a paved lane – marked with a brown sign on the far side of the highway, west of the synagogue – leads 1200m south from the main road to the other site, the **Temple of Artemis** (daily 8am–7pm, closes at 5pm in winter; same admission ticket). The temple, once among the four largest in Asia Minor, was built by Croesus, destroyed by Greek raiders during the Ionian revolt and later rebuilt by Alexander the Great. Today fifteen massive Ionic columns remain standing, though only two are completely intact. However, enough of the foundations remain to suggest just how large the building, constructed to rival the temples of Ephesus, Samos and Didyma, used to be. By the two complete columns huddle the remains of a small Byzantine church. More than anything, it's the beauty of the setting, enclosed by wooded and vined hills and accented by weird Cappadocia-like pinnacles, that leaves a lasting impression.

Practicalities

Sardis is accessible on Salihli dolmuşes **from Manisa**, or the Salihli bus **from İzmir**, both of which drop you on the main highway, at the turn-off for Sartmustafa. The train is less practical as only one daily combination – the early-afternoon Manisa–Alaşehir service, and the evening Uşak–İzmir service – allows enough time at the sites, and the derelict station (buy a return ticket at the start) is inconveniently located 1500m north, in the large village of Sartmahmut.

The nearest **accommodation** to Sardis is in dreary **SALİHLİ**, 8 km east on the İzmir–Afyon road, where you'll find the comfortable two-star *Berrak*, Belediye Sok 59 (℡0236/713 1452, ⓦwww.berrakotel.com; ❸), near the *otogar*. Accessible with your own transport **BOZDAĞ** village, on the forested north side of the eponymous mountain, makes for a more inspiring stay. Famous for its mineral water, it has a few small *pansiyons* and – overhead – an improbable beginners' **ski centre** (ⓦwww.bozdagkayak.com), with a top point of 2157m and a fancy hotel.

Travel details

Trains

Balıkesir to: Bandırma (Nov–March 1 daily, April–Oct 2 daily; 2hr); Kütahya (2–3 daily; 4hr).
Manisa to: Balıkesir (3 daily; 2hr 30min); İzmir (5 daily; 1hr 45min).

Buses and dolmuşes

Ayvalık to: Balıkesir (hourly; 2hr); Bergama, some via Dikili (11 daily; 1hr); Bursa (10 daily; 4hr 30min); Çanakkale (hourly; 3hr 30min); İstanbul (10 daily; 8hr); İzmir (every 30min; 2hr 30min).
Bergama to: İstanbul (2 daily; 10hr); İzmir (every 30min; 1hr 45min); Soma (hourly; 1hr).
Çanakkale to: Ayvacık (hourly; 1hr 30min); Ayvalık (hourly; 3hr 30min); Bursa (hourly; 4hr 30min); Edirne (5 daily; 4hr 30min); İstanbul (hourly via Thrace; 5hr 30min); İzmir (hourly; 5hr 30min); Lapseki (every 30min; 45min); Yükyeri İskelesi via Geyikli (timed to meet the Bozcaada ferry; 1hr).
Foça to: İzmir (hourly; 1hr 15min).
Manisa to: İzmir (every 10min; 1hr); Salihli via Sart/Sardis (every 30min; 1hr 20min).

Ferries

All services between Gökçeada, Bozcaada and the mainland are run by Gestaş (ⓦwww.gdu.com.tr, ℡0286/444 0752). The Çanakkale–Eceabat car-ferry ticket is valid to continue the same day from Kabatepe to Gökçeada, and vice versa.
Ayvalık to: Lésvos, Greece (May to mid-Oct daily at 6pm, 18 Oct–April 2 weekly; 1hr 30min; €40 single, €50 return; cars €60 one way, €80 return).
Çanakkale to: Bozcaada (late June to early Sept Wed, Fri & Sun, returns at 9pm; 1hr 15min; 10TL); Eceabat (hourly 7am–1am, 3 & 5am; 30min); Gökçeada (mid-June to mid-Sept 5 weekly, not Wed/Sun, at 9am, returns 8–9pm; rest of year 3–4 weekly; 1hr 15min; 10TL, sea-bus, no cars); Kilitbahir (every 30min; 8min).
Eceabat to: Çanakkale, car ferry (on the hour 6am–midnight, then 2am & 4am; 30min; 3TL foot passenger, 23TL car and driver).
Foça to: Karaburun (June–Sept Tues, Wed, Sat, Sun 2 daily; 1hr; 8TL single, 15TL return); Lésvos, Greece (June–Sept Tues, Wed, Fri, Sun 6pm; 2hr; €20 one way, €35 return).
Kabatepe to: Gökçeada (late June to early Sept 5 daily 8.30am–8.30pm; early June & late Sept 3 daily 10am–7pm; rest of year 1–2 daily; 1hr 20min; 2TL foot passenger, 20TL car and driver).
Kilitbahir to: Çanakkale (according to traffic, 6am–11pm; 8min; 3TL foot passenger, 16.5TL car and driver).
Yükyeri (Geyikli) İskelesi to: Bozcaada (June–Sept 7 daily 9am–9pm, plus midnight service Fri–Sun; return 7 daily 7.30am–8pm plus weekends at midnight; Oct–May 3 daily 10am–7pm; 30min).

Flights

Çanakkale to: İstanbul (Wed, Fri, Sun early evening on THY; 1hr).

The central and southern Aegean

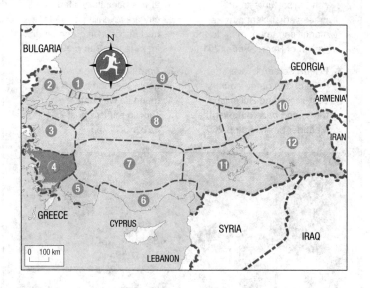

CHAPTER 4 # Highlights

* **Altınkum, Çeşme** Altınkum's remote, sunbaked coves conceal arguably some of the best beaches on the Aegean coast. See p.249

* **Şirince** A beautiful hillside village surrounded by vineyards a short drive from Selçuk. See p.259

* **Ephesus** Hot, crowded and exhausting but you simply can't miss Turkey's best-preserved ancient city – a magnificent monument to the wealth of Rome. See p.261

* **Priene** Scramble over the ruins of one of the country's best-preserved Hellenistic towns and gaze out over the Meander basin. See p.265

* **Heracleia ad Latmos** Former monastic village on Lake Bafa, which had a compelling hold on the imaginations of the Romantic poets. See p.272

* **Bodrum** Spend a few days sampling the nightlife at Turkey's most fashionable and sophisticated beach-resort. See p.275

* **Aphrodisias** New excavations at this beautifully sited Roman city are revealing a site to rival Ephesus in grandeur and importance. See p.300

* **Pamukkale** Visit the geological oddity that has found its way onto every Turkish tourism poster. See p.303

▲ Ruins of Heracleia at Lake Bafa

The central and southern Aegean

The Turkish **central and southern Aegean coast** and its hinterland have seen foreign tourism longer than any other part of the country. The territory between modern İzmir and Marmaris corresponds to the bulk of ancient **Ionia**, and just about all of old **Caria**, and contains a concentration of Classical Greek, Hellenistic and Roman antiquities unrivalled in Turkey. **Ephesus** is usually first on everyone's list of dutiful pilgrimages, but the under-stated charms of exquisitely positioned sites such as **Priene** and **Labranda** have at least as much appeal, if not more.

The landscape can be compelling, most memorably at the eerie lake of **Bafa Gölü**, towering **Samsun Dağı** and the oasis-speckled **Bodrum peninsula**. Towns, however – not least sprawling **İzmir** – tend to be functional places, best hurried through en route to more appealing destinations. But there are some pleasant surprises inland, particularly **Muğla**, **Birgi** and **Şirince**, the first two unselfconscious Ottoman museum-towns, the last a well-preserved former Greek village still just the right side of tweeness.

Despite the tourist-brochure hype, most coastal beaches are average at best. Worse still, of the various resort towns on the so-called "Turkish Riviera", only **Bodrum** and **Çeşme** retain a small measure of intrinsic charm. Costa-style tourism has been embraced with a vengeance and even the shortest and most mediocre sandy stretch is dwarfed by ranks of holiday apartments aimed at the rapidly growing domestic market. However, head off the beaten track to **Alaçatı**, **Datça**, **Ören**, and the **Hisarönü** peninsula, and unspoilt seaside villages, clear seas and shabby-chic guesthouses are yours for the taking.

It takes determination, a good map and, in some places, your own vehicle to get the best out of this coast. **Public transport** in the region is excellent and very cost-effective along well-travelled routes, but connections to less obvious places can be frustratingly difficult. The area is well served by **international flights** to İzmir and, in particular, Bodrum, which is now the main gateway to the Aegean resorts. Five of the eight international **ferry/hydrofoil links** with neighbouring Greek islands are found here too, making a visit to or from Greece feasible. The Turkish authorities rarely cause problems for holders of charter tickets who wish to do this.

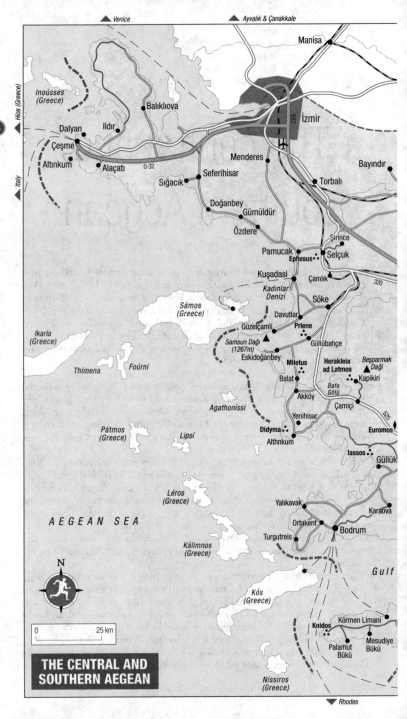

▲ Venice   ▲ Ayvalık & Çanakkale

Manisa

İzmir

◄ Inoússes (Greece)

Balıklıova

◄ Híos (Greece)

Dalyan   Ildır

Çeşme

Altınkum   Alaçatı   0-32

◄ Italy

Menderes   Bayındır

Seferihisar   Torbalı

Sığacık

Doğanbey

Gümüldür

Özdere

Şirince

Pamucak   Selçuk

Ephesus

Kuşadasi   Çamlık

Kadınlar Denizi   Söke

Sámos (Greece)   Davutlar

Güzelçamli   Priene

Samsun Dağı (1267m)   Güllübahçe

Ikaría (Greece)

Eskidoğanbey   Herakleia ad Latmos   Beşparmak Dağı

Miletus

Thimena   Foúrni   Balat   Kapikiri

Bafa Gölü

Akköy   Çamiçi

Agathoníssi

Yenihisar   Euromos

Pátmos (Greece)   Lipsí   Didyma

Althnkum   Iassos

Güllük

Léros (Greece)

Yalıkavak   Karaova

AEGEAN SEA   Ortakent   Bodrum

Kálimnos (Greece)   Turgutreis

Gulf

N

Kós (Greece)

Knidos   Körmen Limani

0   25 km   Palamut Bükü   Mesudiye Bükü

THE CENTRAL AND SOUTHERN AEGEAN

Níssiros (Greece)

▼ Rhodes

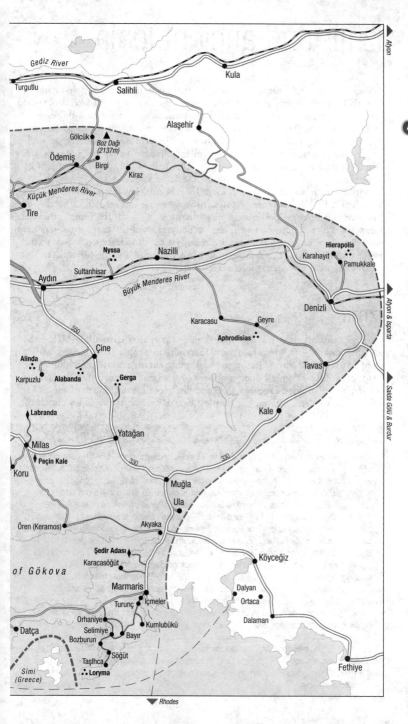

İzmir and ancient Ionia

For most travellers, **İzmir** is an obstacle on the way to more enticing destinations. But it's definitely worth having a look around: the city's setting and ethnological museum are unique, the seafront has been spruced up and there's a burgeoning café-bar and club scene. İzmir might also serve as a base for day-trips or short overnight jaunts, either to nearby **Çeşme** and its peninsula – with some well-preserved villages, fine beaches and excellent dining – or to the valley of the **Küçük Menderes River**, where a pair of untouristed old towns give a hint of what the whole of Turkey was like just a few decades ago.

South of İzmir the territory of Ancient Ionia begins. The main show of the area is undoubtedly the ensemble of ruins that span numerous eras: most notably at **Ephesus** and Priene – perhaps the most dramatic site of all the Ionian cities; at sprawling Miletus, further south; and at Didyma, with its gargantuan temple. **Kuşadası**, is an unabashedly utilitarian resort yet serves well for excursions to the major antiquities and the nearby national park around ancient Mount Mycale. Nearby Selçuk is a prettier, more relaxed, base.

İzmir

Turkey's third largest city and its second biggest port after İstanbul, **İZMİR** – the ancient Smyrna – is home to almost four million people. It is blessed with a comparatively mild climate (summer aside) and an enviable position, straddling the head of a fifty-kilometre-long gulf fed by several streams and flanked by mountains on all sides. Despite a long and illustrious history, much of the city is relentlessly modern, although a bustling bazaar district, parks and a clutch of

Ancient Ionia

The **Ionian coast** was first colonized by Greek-speakers in the twelfth century BC and the culture reached its zenith during the seventh and sixth centuries BC when it was at the forefront of the newly emergent sciences, philosophy and the arts. Enormous advantages accrued to those who chose to settle here: an amenable climate, fertile, well-watered terrain, and a strategic location between the Aegean – with its many fine harbours – and inland Anatolia. Local development was only temporarily hampered by the Persian invasions, Alexander the Great's contrary campaigns, and the chaos following his death, and under the Romans and the Byzantines the region perked up again. Indeed, urban life here might have continued indefinitely were it not for the inexorably receding coastline – thanks to the two silt-bearing rivers of Küçük and Büyük Menderes. By mid-Byzantine times virtually all of the Ionian cities had been abandoned, and with the declaration of Christianity as the state religion, religious centres and oracles met a similar fate.

Today's inhabitants have found the silver lining to the cloud of the advancing deltas, cashing in on the rich soil brought down from the hills. Vast tracts of cotton, tobacco, sesame and grain benefit from irrigation works, while groves of pine, olive and cypress, which need no such encouragement, adorn the hills and wilder reaches. And the sea, though more distant than in former times, still beckons when tramping the ruins palls. Indeed, tourism is now threatening to outstrip agriculture as a means of making a living.

grand old buildings are remnants of a glorious past. The pedestrianized seashore boulevards are home to most of the city's museums and cultural attractions, plus a lively, liberal area of bars and restaurants.

Some history

The possibilities of the site suggested themselves as long ago as the third millennium BC, when aboriginal **Anatolians** settled at Tepekule, a hill in the modern northern suburb of Bayraklı (excavated but only of interest to hardcore archeologists). Around 600 BC, Lydian raids sent Tepekule into a long decline; it was recovering tentatively when **Alexander the Great** appeared in 334 BC. Spurred by a timely dream corroborated by the oracle of Apollo at Claros, Alexander decreed the foundation of a new, better-fortified settlement on Mount Pagos, the flat-topped hill today adorned with the Kadifekale. His generals, Antigonus and Lysimachus, carried out Alexander's plan after his death, by which time the city bore the name – Smyrna – familiar to the West for centuries after.

Roman rule endowed the city with numerous impressive buildings, although **Arab** raids of the seventh century AD triggered several centuries of turbulence. **Selçuk** Turks held the city for two decades prior to 1097, when the **Byzantines** recaptured it. The thirteenth-century Latin tenure in Constantinople provoked another era of disruption at Smyrna, with Crusaders, Genoese, Tamerlane's Mongols and minor Turkish emirs jockeying for position. Order was re-established in 1415 by Mehmet I, who finally incorporated the town into the **Ottoman Empire**, his successors repulsing repeated Venetian efforts to retake it.

Following the defeat of the Ottoman Empire in **World War I**, Greece was given an indefinite mandate over İzmir and its hinterland. Foolishly, a huge Greek expeditionary force pressed inland, inciting the resistance of the Turkish nationalists under Atatürk. The climactic defeat in the two-year-long struggle against Greece and her nominal French and Italian allies was the entry into Smyrna of the Turkish army on September 9, 1922. The secular republic not having yet been proclaimed, the **reconquest of the city** took on the character of a successfully concluded jihad, or holy Muslim war, with three days of murder and plunder. Almost seventy percent of the city burned to the ground and thousands of non-Muslims died. A quarter of a million refugees huddled at the quayside while British, American, French and Italian vessels stood idly by and refused to grant them safe passage until the third day.

Arrival and information

Flights arrive at **Adnan Menderes airport** (ⓦ www.adnanmenderesairport.com), 18km southeast of the city. From here, use either the shuttle train (7.15am–8.15pm; 2TL; 30min) from the airport to Basmane train station downtown, or the Havaş airport bus (hourly departures, 3.30am–11.30pm; 10TL; 50min), which will deposit you in front of the *Swissôtel Grand Efes* on Gaziosmanpaşa Bulvarı. The hourly city bus #202 (4TL) follows a similar route from the airport, terminating in Cumhuriyet Meydanı. **Taxis** are around 35TL to downtown İzmir, 90TL to Selçuk, 120TL to the centre of Kuşadası.

Long-distance trains also pull in at **Basmane**; if you're coming on a train, and only want to transfer to a bus for Ephesus or Kuşadası, head for the cluster of bus-company offices in 9 Eylül Meydanı, just north of Basmane, which provide a free shuttle-bus service to the main *otogar*.

The main *otogar*, known as **büyük otogar**, is 8km northeast of the centre. If you've got much luggage, it's best to take a taxi (35TL) into the centre. Otherwise, use one of the bus-company's free shuttles, which will drop you at 9 Eylül Meydanı. City buses numbered #601–609 link the *otogar* with Konak Bus

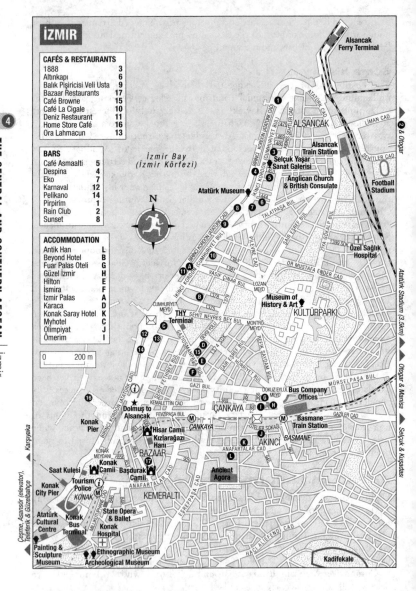

İZMIR

CAFÉS & RESTAURANTS

1888	3
Altınkapı	6
Balık Pişiricisi Veli Usta	9
Bazaar Restaurants	17
Café Browne	15
Café La Cigale	10
Deniz Restaurant	11
Home Store Café	16
Ora Lahmacun	13

BARS

Café Asmaalti	5
Despina	4
Eko	7
Karnaval	12
Pelikano	14
Pirpirim	1
Rain Club	2
Sunset	8

ACCOMMODATION

Antik Han	L
Beyond Hotel	B
Fuar Palas Oteli	G
Güzel İzmir	H
Hilton	E
İsmira	F
İzmir Palas	A
Karaca	D
Konak Saray Hotel	K
Myhotel	C
Olimpiyat	J
Ömerim	I

0   200 m

İzmir Bay
(İzmir Körfezi)

Terminal, the heart of the city's transport system, and stop at Basmane station en route. The #54 will also take you to Basmane and on to Konak.

Arriving from anywhere on the Çeşme peninsula, buses halt at either the main *otogar* or at scrubby car-park terminal in the coastal suburb of **Üçkuyular**, 6km southwest of downtown. From there, cross the road and take any red-and-white urban bus labelled "Konak", or hail a taxi for approximately 20TL.

There's a **tourist office** in the airport arrivals hall (daily: Nov–March 8am–5pm; April–Oct 8.30am–8.30pm; ☎0232/274 2214), and a **central bureau** at 1344 Sok 2,

Pasaport district, across from the Borsa (Mon–Sat 8.30am–5.30pm; ☎0232/483 5117). The offices don't book, but only suggest, **accommodation** (mid-range and up), and have been known to run out of their very useful free, city plan.

City transport

Walking is much the quickest and easiest way of exploring the city. You are rarely better off taking a bus due to the level of city traffic. The underground **Metro** line (daily 6am–midnight; 2TL) through the southern part of the city does provide a useful (and quick) transport link between Basmane Station (accommodation) and the Konak district (attractions). Most of the municipality's numbered bus routes start from **Konak Bus Terminal** at Konak Meydanı.

Accommodation

At most times of the year, it should be easy to find somewhere to stay, though street noise (particularly from car horns) is a nearly universal problem. Be sure to book in advance if you plan to stay overnight during the annual International İzmir Festival (see p.245), between early June and mid-July, as most hotels fill up quickly.

The main area for budget hotels is **Akıncı** (also called Yenigün), which straddles Fevzipaşa Bulvarı immediately in front of Basmane train station. The zone to the south, between Fevzipaşa Bulvarı and Anafartalar Caddesi, is best to avoid as it's home to the city's grimmest hotels. The hotels on the north side of Fevzipaşa, in an area called **Çankaya**, centred around the pedestrianized 1369 Sokak are quieter and more appealing. But for out-and-out luxury, you'll have to head for the streets around the seafront **Cumhuriyet Meydanı**.

Akıncı

Antik Han Anafartalar Cad 600 ☎0232/489 2750, ⓦwww.otelantikhan.com. A real find – this renovated old house on one of the bazaar's busiest streets (it can get a bit noisy) has large, modern rooms, all with TV and ceiling fans, arranged around a lovely lemon tree in the courtyard. ⑥

Konak Saray Hotel Anafartalar Cad 635 ☎0232/483 7755, ⓦwww.konaksarayhotel.com. Brand-new hotel with friendly owners plus wi-fi and modern design touches throughout. All rooms are en suite, with a/c and satellite TV. ⑤

Olimpiyat 945 Sok 2 ☎0232/425 1269. The cheapest acceptable option in the area; old-fashioned and faded, but reasonably maintained. Some of the forty small rooms only have washbasins, some come with TV. No breakfast. ③

Çankaya

Fuar Palas Oteli 1368 Sok 11 ☎0232/446 7020, ⓦwww.fuarpalas.com. Friendly management, with clean, bright rooms overlooking Eylül Meydanı square, and wi-fi throughout. ④

Güzel İzmir 1368 Sok 8 ☎0232/484 6693, ⓦwww.guzelizmirhotel.com. One of the better-value mid-range hotels, though the single rooms with en suites are tiny. ④

Ömerim Hotel 1366 Sok ☎0232/445 9898, ⓦwww.grandzeybekhotels.com. Nicest of four large hotels under the same management. Large, grandiose, marble lobby and staircase, and accommodating staff, a/c rooms come with TV and minibar. ⑤

Around Cumhuriyet Meydanı

Beyond Hotel 1376 Sok 5 ☎0232/463 60585, ⓦwww.hotelbeyond.com. Contemporary boutique choice, offering rooms and suites in six colours (choose your mood), boudoir-esque decor and a pillow menu. ⑧

Hilton Gaziosmanpaşa Bul 7 ☎0232/497 6060, ⓦwww.izmir.hilton.com. Apparently the tallest building on the Aegean coast, the 381-room *Hilton* has grand rooms (including executive floors), indoor swimming pool, fitness centre, sauna, solarium and massage. ⑧

Hotel İsmira Gaziosmanpaşa Bul 28 ☎0232/445 6060, ⓦwww.hotelismira.com. Garish pink three-star choice opposite the *Hilton*, offering 72 generic but comfortable rooms, a decent buffet restaurant, a bar and gym. ⑥

İzmir Palas Atatürk Bul 2 ☎0232/421 5583, ⓦwww.izmirpalas.com.tr. Older, three-star standby with a good seafront location and the excellent *Deniz Restaurant* on site; you should be able to bargain the price down. ❼

Karaca 1379 Sok 55, Sevgi Yolu ☎0232/489 1940, ⊛www.otelkaraca.com.tr. Large, modern hotel, with slick, bilingual staff. Large rooms, bristling with mod cons. Parking available. ❼

Myhotel Cumhuriyet Bul 132 ☎0232/445 3837, ⊛www.myhotel.com.tr. İzmir's original boutique hotel opened in 2006. All 30 rooms have a/c, wi-fi and flat-screen TVs; rates include their very tasty buffet breakfast. ❼

The City

İzmir cannot really be said to have a single centre. Among several possible contenders, the pedestrianized **Konak** area might win by default, simply because it's the spot where visitors will spend much of their time. North and east of Konak lies the **agora** – İzmir's most impressive ancient site – and the **Kadifekale**, or castle. **Cumhuriyet Meydanı**, another traditional orientation point, lies less than a kilometre northeast of Konak. Beyond the square, the prettified, café-lined **Birinci Kordon** seaside boulevard runs north along the western edge of Alsancak, passing the **Atatürk Museum** en route.

For good views head for the **Asansör (free)**, located in the heart of İzmir's old Jewish quarter, just off Mithatpaşa Caddesi, about a fifteen-minute walk southwest from the cultural centre. Constructed in 1907 in a fifty-metre-high brick tower, this elevator originally served as a quick route to and from the mansions perched on the hill above. The lift has since been completely refurbished; at the top is the highly recommended *Asansör Restaurant & Café*, from where you can look down on narrow streets of crumbling houses and out over the bay.

İzmir's museums

The **Archeological Museum** (Arkeoloji Müzesi; daily except Mon 8.30am–5.30pm; 8TL) set in the Turgutreis Parkı in Konak, features an excellent collection of finds from all over İzmir province and beyond. The ground floor is largely given over to statuary and friezes of all eras, while the top floor focuses on smaller objects, with an emphasis on Bronze Age and archaic pottery – more exciting than it sounds, particularly the so-called "orientalized" terracotta and bestiary amphorae from Gryneion and Pitane (Çandarlı).

The **Ethnographic Museum** (Efnografya Müzesi; daily except Mon 8.30am–5pm; 8TL), immediately across from the archeological museum, was built

---

Afro-Turks

Many travellers to western Turkey, and İzmir in particular, are surprised by the sight of **Africans** who are obviously not visitors. Often termed *Arap* or "Arabs" by other Turks, they are in fact descendants of the large numbers of Sudanese, Somalis, Algerians and Egyptians who were brought to Anatolia during the Ottoman Empire. Many arrived as slaves, forced to work in the tobacco and cotton fields or as household servants, particularly wet-nurses. Although slavery was formally abolished by Sultan Abdülmecid, many of these domestic slaves chose to remain in the families with whom they had grown up, in some cases establishing close ties. Others were given free land after the founding of the Republic.

Today there are about 20,000 **Afro-Turks** (as they prefer to be known) in the western Aegean provinces, most of whom live in the mountains between İzmir and Mersin. Speaking fluent Turkish and devoutly Muslim, they are often proud of their Turkish heritage though intermarriage is rare with other Turks. In recent years efforts have been made by the community to re-establish traditional festivals associated with Afro-Turkish culture such as the Dana Bayramı or Calf Festival.

originally as a hospital in 1831. Exhibits on the lower floor concentrate on the two types of traditional İzmir house, the wooden Turkish residence and the more substantial "Levantine" (Christian and Jewish merchants) house.

If time is short, the **Painting and Sculpture Museum** (Resim ve Heykel Müzesi; Tues–Sat 10am–5pm; free) is one to miss. Its lower level hosts changing exhibits, while the two upstairs galleries contain almost two hundred works by Turkish artists, some awful, some decent and most stylistically derivative renderings of pastoral or populist themes reminiscent of Socialist Realism.

One of several substantial buildings that escaped the 1922 destruction is the home of the **Atatürk Museum** (Atatürk Müzesi; daily except Mon 9am–noon & 1–5.15pm; free), at Atatürk Cad 248, occupying the building where the premier stayed on his visits to İzmir. Room-by-stately-room tours of the first floor are of little interest to foreign visitors – apart, perhaps, from the Comments room where you can read Winston Churchill's uniquely negative appraisal of the statesman.

Alsancak and the Kültür Parkı

The Atatürk Museum marks the approximate southern margin of **Alsancak**. Just inland, particularly on 1453, 1469, 1482, 1481 and 1480 *sokak*s, plus the east side of İkinci Kordon, are found entire intact terraces of sumptuous eighteenth- and nineteenth-century **mansions** that once belonged to European merchants, who knew the area as Punta (a term still used). One mansion, at Cumhuriyet Bul 252, now houses the **Selçuk Yaşar Sanat Galerisi** (Mon–Fri 10.30am–6pm, Sat noon–6pm; free), a privately run gallery hosting temporary exhibitions of modern Turkish painting.

Returning from Alsancak to the city centre, you'll pass by or through the **Kültür Parkı** (daily 8am–midnight), a forty-hectare lozenge built on the ruins of the pre-1922 Greek quarter. The park's **Museum of History and Art** (Tarih ve Sanat Müzesi; daily except Mon 8.30am–5.30pm; 3TL) is likely to be of most interest to foreigners. Spread over three buildings, the museum's collection includes a mix of

▲ Nineteenth-century mansions in the Alsancak quarter

archeological finds, with particular emphasis on sculpture, ceramics and coins. The park is also home to a parachute tower, a mini-golf course and funfair, a zoo, an artificial lake, an open-air theatre, plus a dozen *gazino* nightspots and tea/beer gardens.

The agora

The only surviving pre-Ottoman monument in the flatlands is the **agora** (daily 8.30am–noon & 1–5.30pm; 3TL), the most accessible of İzmir's ancient sites. From Anafartalar Caddesi turn south onto Eşrefpaşa Caddesi, then east onto 816 Sokak to the entrance; brown signs confirm the way.

The agora probably dates back to the early second century BC, but what you see now are the remains of a later reconstruction, financed during the reign of the Roman Emperor Marcus Aurelius, after the catastrophic earthquake of 178 AD. It's an impressive site, with water still coursing through ancient ducts and channels. Principal structures include a **colonnade** of fourteen Corinthian columns on the west side and the remains of reputedly the second-largest basilica in the Roman world. Currently under restoration, the basilica's lower floor is well preserved, with traces of frescos remaining on the walls. Rising just southeast of the agora, the **Kadifekale**, or "Velvet Castle" (always open; free), visible by night as by day thanks to skilful floodlighting, is only worth visiting for the views over the city.

Eating

The budget eateries within sight of Basmane station have tables on the street and offer the usual range of kebabs, *pide* and stews. There's a far better selection of inexpensive outfits in the **bazaar**, although its warren of streets can be confusing. Head just north of Hisar Camii – with tables clustered around two fountains, the vine-shaded square is picturesque, chaotic and cheap, all at the same time. Try *Orkide* for *kokoreç*, *Cin ali* for kebabs or *Meşhur Hisar* for wraps and jacket potatoes. Most of the bazaar restaurants close by 7.30pm.

Meals eaten close to the Birinci Kordon **waterfront** represent a definite step up in quality and price, though the best hunting-ground by far is among the restored inland mansions of **Alsancak**; restaurants, café-bars, bars and fast-food outlets abound along Kıbrıs Şehitler Caddesi and its side streets.

Between Konak and Alsancak

Café Browne 1379 Sok. On a quiet lane with outdoor seating, serving an excellent range of lunchtime veggie options.

Home Store Café Konak Pier Alışveriş Merkezi ☎0232/441 5593. Swish terrace at the tip of Konak Pier, perfect for an aperitif and a plate of sushi at sunset.

Ora Lahmacun Akdeniz Cad. Popular with students who crowd its pavement tables, this small restaurant-bar makes a lively lunchtime or early-evening pit stop.

Birinci Kordon and Alsancak

1888 İkinci Kordon (Cumhuriyet Bul) 248 ☎0232/421 6690, ⊛www.1888restaurant.com. Exquisitely prepared Turkish and Mediterranean seafood served in a restored nineteenth-century mansion and its fragrant private garden.

Altınkapı 1444 Sok 14/A ☎0232/422 5687. Good for *döner* and *tavuk* (chicken) grills. It's long established, with popular outdoor seating on the pedestrianized street. They also have a good fish restaurant next door.

Balık Pişiricisi Veli Usta Birinci Kordon 212/A ☎0232/464 2705. Deservedly popular seafood restaurant – you'll have to get there early evening to guarantee a seat. Try their speciality, grilled sole kebabs (17TL).

Café La Cigale Fransız Kültür Merkezi, Cumhuriyet Bul 152 ☎0232/421 4780. In the French Cultural Institute's leafy gardens. Tasty (Turkish) buffet lunch (9TL), plus occasional live music on weekends.

Deniz Restaurant İzmir Palas Hotel, Atatürk Bul ☎0232/422 0601. Somewhat pricey local favourite offering a sophisticated range of seafood dishes, including stuffed squid (9TL) or mixed *Deniz* appetizers (25TL). Reservations essential at weekends.

Drinking, nightlife and entertainment

Clustered around the Konak Meydanı are a number of bars offering live Turkish music and dancing. But it's upper **Alsancak** that has blossomed as the district for trendy **nightlife**, with assorted bars and clubs tucked inland along pedestrianized side streets invisible from Birinci Kordon. It should be stressed that ownership and themes of each establishment tend to roll over on roughly a two-year cycle, so specific recommendations are subject to change.

A good place to start the evening is at the *Café Asmaalti* on 1453 Sokak, with backgammon boards, *nargile* pipes and beer. From here, it's a good idea just to wander and see what looks lively. Sokaks 1482 and 1480, in particular, are home to dozens of often transitory bars in restored old houses, some of which offer live Turkish music later in the evening. *Eko*, on the corner of Pilevne Bulvarı and Cumhuriyet Caddesi, is popular with expats, and the young and trendy, many of whom will probably end up at the large outdoor *Rain Club* on the north side of the city.

The cafés, **bars** and upmarket teahouses lining the shore on **Birinci Kordon** (Atatürk Caddesi) are ideal for a drink and a snack while watching the sunset. The best include *Pirpirim*, with live traditional *fasıl* music, *Despina* and the appropriately named *Sunset* (like many of the local bars, it sells 2.5-litre "tubes" of beer, complete with tap, for 17TL) to the north of Cumhuriyet Meydanı, and *Karnaval* and *Pelikano*, to the south, both of which have seafront seating.

The **Atatürk Cultural Centre** at Mithatpaşa Cad 92 (Atatürk Kültür Merkezi; ☏0232/483 8520) is home to the local symphony orchestra, which plays regularly on Fridays and Saturdays and hosts occasional concerts by soloists. More varied is the programme offered by the **State Opera and Ballet** (Devlet Opera ve Balesi; ☏0232/489 0474, ⓦwww.dobgm.gov.tr), housed in a wonderful Ottoman Art Deco specimen on Milli Kütüphane Caddesi, which encompasses everything from chamber music to pop and jazz. Other **classical music concerts** are held at Dokuz Eylül University's Sabanci Cultural Centre, Mithatpaşa Caddesi (☏0232/441 9009), while with the onset of the hot weather, events move to the open-air theatre in the **Kültür Parkı**.

Listings

Airlines THY (Turkish Airlines), Cumhuriyet Bulv. Mahmut Rıza İş Merkezi ☏0232/484 1220. Other airlines include: British Airways ☏0232/441 3829; KTHY (Cyprus Turkish Airways) ☏0232/421 4472; and Lufthansa ☏0232/298 7272.

Airport Adnan Menderes airport, flight enquiries: domestic ☏0232/274 2626, international ☏0232/455 0000. The Havaş airport bus (ⓦwww.havas.com.tr; hourly departures, 3.30am–11.30pm; 10TL; 50–60min) runs from in front of the Swissotel Grand Efes Izmir on

Gaziosmanpaşa Bul. Alternatively, city bus #202 follows approximately the same route (4TL) from Cumhuriyet Meydanı. Some airline companies may provide a bus transfer; ask in advance.

Books Remzi Kitabevi, Konak Pier; D&R, 175 Cumhuriyet Bul (sells English magazines).

Car rental Avis, Şair Eşref Bul 18/D ☏0232/441 4417; Budget, Şair Eşref Bul 22/1 ☏0232/482 0505; DeCar, Airport ☏0232/274 1779; Europcar, Airport ☏0232/274 2163; Hertz, 1377 Sok 8 ☏0232/464 3440.

The International İzmir Festival

Linchpin of the summer season is the International İzmir Festival, running from mid-June to early July. It's something of a misnomer since many events take place at various restored venues at Ephesus or Çeşme castle. Tickets run to 20–100TL a head, but fifty percent student discounts are available and the acts featured are often world-class – past names have included the Moscow Ballet, Paco Peña and Ravi Shankar. Get this year's programme at ⓦwww.iksev.org; ticket vendors are also listed online.

Consulates UK, 1442 Sok 49, an annexe of the Anglican church ℡ 0232/463 5151, 🌐 ukinturkey .fco.gov.uk; US, 1387 Sok, Mustafa Bey Cad ℡ 0232/464 8755, 🌐 turkey.usembassy.gov.
Hamam The cleanest and most secure is Hoşgör, on an alley inland from Mithatpaşa Cad 10, opposite Karataş Lisesi (daily: men 8–11am & 5pm–midnight; women 11am–5pm; 15TL).
Hospitals The most central state hospitals are Alsancak Devlet Hastanesi on Ali Çetinkaya Bul (℡ 0232/463 6465), and the Konak Hospital (with dental section), across from the ethnographic and archeological museums (℡ 0232/483 2191). Much better are the American Hospital, 1375 Sok (℡ 0212/444 3777) and the Özel Sağlık Hastanesi on 1399 Sok (℡ 0232/463 7700).
Pharmacies Near Basmane, there's Merkez Eczane, 9 Eylül Meyd 5 ℡ 0232/483 2467; also try Kent Eczane, Fevzi Paşa Bul 174/C ℡ 0232/484 2149.

Police 1207 Sok, Basmane ℡ 0232/446 1456; Konak ℡ 0232/489 0500.
Post office Main PTT office is at Cumhuriyet Meyd (Mon–Sat 8am–8pm, Sun 8.30am–5pm); for less bureaucracy, United Parcel Service, Akdeniz Cad 8/K (office hours), also provides cost-effective air delivery to North America and the UK.
Shopping Traditional Turkish musical instruments are best bought from Bağdat Saz Evi, Kızlarağası Hanı 19/P/22. The best *nargile*s (waterpipes) on the Aegean can be found at Ilhan Etike, inside the Kızlarağası Hanı (near Bağdat Saz Evi), or at Mehmet & Osman Kaya, 856 Sok 7/C, in Kemeraltı. The Turkish Ministry of Culture has a shop, Dösim, next to the PTT at Cumhuriyet Bul 115/A, selling high-quality reproductions of Turkish and Ottoman crafts: kilims, silver jewellery and copperware.

Çeşme and its peninsula

The claw-like mass of land extending west from İzmir terminates near **Çeşme**, most low-key of the central Aegean's main coastal resorts. It's a one-hour ride from İzmir along the 80km highway, and makes a decent base for the few attractions within shouting distance of town – most notably **ancient Erythrae**, the hip town of **Alaçatı** and **Altınkum** beach.

The immediate environs of Çeşme are green and hilly, with added colour from the deeply aquamarine sea and the white of the electricity-generating windmills on the approach to the peninsula. The **climate** here is noticeably drier, cooler and healthier than anywhere nearby on the Turkish coast, especially in comparison with occasionally hellish İzmir or muggy Kuşadası. These conditions, combined with the presence of several thermal springs, have made the peninsula a popular resort for over a century.

Çeşme

A picturesque, often sleepy town of old Greek houses wrapped around a Genoese castle, **ÇEŞME** ("drinking fountain" in Turkish) doubtless takes its name from the many Ottoman fountains, some still functioning, scattered around its streets. Despite guarding the mouth of the İzmir Gulf, it has figured little in recent history other than as the site of a sea battle on July 5, 1770, when the Russian fleet annihilated the Ottoman navy in the straits here.

Arrival and information

Coming by ferry **from Híos** (Greece), you arrive at the jetty in front of the castle. The larger ferries **from Italy** (Bari, Brindisi and Ancona) use the ferry dock across the bay. For ticket agencies, see "Listings", p.248. Çeşme's small **otogar** is 1km south of the town centre, although local buses and dolmuşes serving most nearby destinations including İzmir, Dalyan, Ilıca and Alaçatı, stop at the eastern end of İnkilap Caddesi.

The helpful **tourist office** (May–Sept Mon–Fri 8.30am–7pm, Sat & Sun 9am–noon & 1–5pm; Oct–April daily 8.30am–noon & 1–5pm; ℡ 0232/712 6653), by the Customs Office near the quayside, dispenses the usual brochures and town plans.

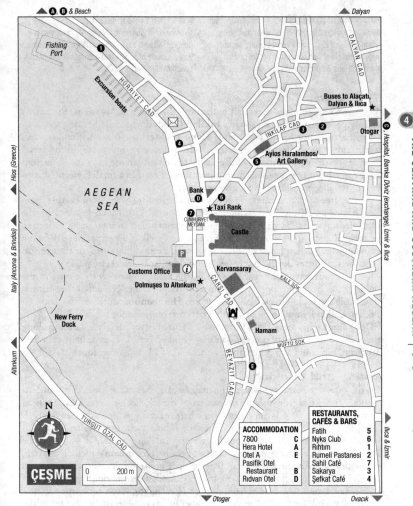

Map labels:

A, B & Beach

Dalyan

Fishing Port

DALYAN CAD

Excursion boats

HÜRRIYET CAD

Buses to Alaçatı, Dalyan & Ilıca

INKILAP CAD

Otogar

Hospital, Banka Döviz (exchange), İzmir & Ilıca

Hios (Greece)

AEGEAN SEA

Ayios Haralambos/ Art Gallery

Bank

Taxi Rank

CUMHURIYET MEYDANI

Castle

Italy (Ancona & Brindisi)

Altınkum

Customs Office

Dolmuşes to Altınkum

Kervansaray

KALE SOK

ÇARŞI CAD

Hamam

MÜFTÜ SOK

BEYAZIT CAD

Ilıca & İzmir

New Ferry Dock

N

TURGUT ÖZAL CAD

ÇEŞME   0   200 m

Otogar

Ovacık

ACCOMMODATION

7800	C
Hera Hotel	A
Otel A	E
Pasifik Otel Restaurant	B
Rıdvan Otel	D

RESTAURANTS, CAFÉS & BARS

Fatih	5
Nyks Club	6
Rihtim	1
Rumeli Pastanesi	2
Sahil Café	7
Sakarya	3
Şefkat Café	4

Accommodation

Çeşme's popularity as a summer bolt hole for residents of İzmir means there's a plethora of budget and moderately priced accommodation. The most desirable places to stay line the waterfront to the left of the castle, as you face it. Alternatively, drop by the kiosk (☎ 0232/712 6176) at İnkilap Caddesi's bus stop, where staff will help you book a *pansiyon* or home stay (doubles 40TL; summer months only).

7800 Boyalık, 5km northeast of Çeşme ☎ 0232/712 0087, ⓦ www.7800cesme.com. Ultra-modern spa hotel, with luxurious, spacious rooms right on the beach. You'll really need your own transport to stay. ❽
Hera Hotel 16 Eylül Mah 4 ☎ 0232/712 6177, ⓦ www.heracesme.com. This family-run pension, north of the town centre, has a

beautiful seafront garden bar and clean, bright rooms. ❺
Otel A Çarşı Cad 24 ☎ 0232/712 6881, ⓦ www .hotela.8k.com. Designed and built by its English-teaching owners, this has bright and immaculately kept en-suite doubles, a sun deck and sea views. The plush interior wouldn't look out of place in a 1970s design catalogue. ❹

Pasifik Otel Restaurant 16 Eylül Mah, Tekke Plajı Mevkii 16 ☏0232/712 2700, ⓦwww.pasifikotel .com. Adjacent to Çeşme's most popular beach, with an excellent fish restaurant on the ground floor. Half-board options available. ❻

Rıdvan Otel By the harbour ☏0232/712 6336, ⓦwww.ridvanotel.com. Five-storey hotel with a/c doubles, all with balconies overlooking the square. Rates include transport and entrance to the hotel's beach club in Ayayorgi. ❻

The Town

The town's three main streets all radiate off **Cumhuriyet Meydanı**, the town's largely pedestrianized main square. **İnkilap Caddesi**, the main bazaar thoroughfare heads off north and east, while **Çarşı Caddesi**, its continuation, saunters south along the waterfront past the castle, *kervansaray* and most of the travel agencies before veering slightly inland. The town's **esplanade** hugs the waterfront to the north passing the small fishing port until it reaches a small crescent-shaped beach. It's all very pleasant, in a low-key way.

You are free to clamber about every perilous inch of the waterfront **castle** (Tues–Sun summer 8.30am–7pm, winter 8.30am–5pm; 3TL). Much repaired by the Ottomans, it's now home to a small museum containing an interesting collection of archeological finds from nearby Erythrae, as well as a permanent exhibition detailing the Russian battle of 1770. The castle's crumbling open-air theatre also hosts performances during the **International İzmir Festival** (see p.245).

The **kervansaray**, a few paces south of the castle and currently closed to the public, dates from the reign of Süleyman the Magnificent. The only other distraction is the huge old Greek basilica of **Ayios Haralambos**, north of the castle on İnkilap Caddesi, now home to a daily crafts market (see door for details).

Daily **boat trips** leave from just north of Cumhuriyet Meydanı, heading along the coast to local beauty spots and nearby Donkey Island. They usually set off at 10.30am, returning at 5.30pm and cost around 25TL, including lunch.

Eating and drinking

Of the quayside **restaurants** near the main square, *Sahil Café's* mix of traditional Turkish dishes and fresh fish are the tastiest of the lot. For a quieter location, head up the seafront to family-run *Şefkat Café*, where tea and a *gözleme* won't set you back more than 5TL. At *Rıhtım*, overlooking the fishing port, good-value set menus include sea bream and bass. About halfway up İnkilap Caddesi, at no. 44, is the *Rumeli Pastanesi*, a local legend, with some of the best **ice cream** – including *sakızlı*, or mastic-resin-flavoured – on the Aegean; their home-made fruit preserves (*reçel*) are also on sale. Nearby *Sakarya* is a friendly, modest *lokanta* offering good-value steam-tray dishes, while *Fatih*, behind Ayios Haralambos, serves up crispy *pide*.

A stroll up İnkilap Caddesi reveals a number of **bars** and small discos. One of the newer spots is *Nyks Club* on Cumhuriyet Meydanı, a stone's throw from the castle, with frequent happy hours, late nights and local DJs.

Listings

Car rental Uzun Rent-a-car, 16 Eylül Mah, 3010 Sok 3 (☏0232/712 0928), is about the cheapest; they also rent motorbikes, perfectly adequate for exploring the peninsula.
Ferries Ertürk (☏0232/712 6768, ⓦwww.erturk .com.tr), opposite the tourist office, runs a morning and evening ferry to Híos and a weekly ferry to Ancona; Marmara Lines (ⓦwww.marmaralines.com) to Ancona is represented by Reca, Turgut Özal Bul 13/D (☏0232/712 2223). There are also occasional ferries for Brindisi, although these were suspended at the time of writing (see p.308 for times).
Hamam Belediye Hamamı on Çarşı Cad, 200m down from the *kervansaray*.
Hospitals Devlet Hastanesi (☏0232/712 0777), at the very top of İnkilap Cad, past Dalyan turning.
Police Within the Customs Office building, behind the tourist office ☏0232/712 6093.
Post office The PTT (daily 8am–midnight) is on the waterfront, 300m north of the ferry dock.

Around Çeşme

For warm, sheltered swimming on largely undeveloped sand beaches, make for the coast **south of Çeşme**. Regular dolmuşes leave from south of Çeşme's tourist office every 15min or so (those for Alaçatı picking up passengers at the eastern end of İnkilap Caddesi), the latest returning around dusk.

Alaçatı

ALAÇATİ, 9km southeast of Çeşme, is one of the region's most upmarket resorts, favoured with İstanbul's cosmopolitan elite. Formerly a somewhat isolated Greek village, its resurgence began when one of the town's charming old stone houses was turned into a swish designer hotel, the *Tas Otel*. This proved so popular that, within a few years, it had spawned over a dozen equally stylish and tasteful imitators, not to mention a similar number of gourmet restaurants. Strict building regulations have meant that, in the centre of town at least, this rapid growth has had little effect on the character of the place, and it's still architecturally stunning. Its old lanes and cobbled streets, particularly on the main thoroughfare, Kemalpaşa Caddesi, are dotted with antique shops, art galleries and snazzy boutiques selling designer goods.

The town's 300-metre-long sandy **beach** is 4km south. Most visitors head here to take advantage of the unique windsurfing and kiteboarding conditions; the strong, reliable "Meltemi" wind, combined with shallow water and lack of waves makes the bay ideal for learners. Both Kite Turkey (ⓦwww.kite-turkey.com; ten-hour courses from €300) and Myga Surf City (ⓦwww.surf-turkey.com; windsurfing lessons from €45 per hour) work with all levels, and can supply all gear needed. The **dolmuşes** from Çeşme run on here every 45 minutes or so.

Accommodation

Incirliev Yeni Mecidiye Mah, 3074 Mahmut Hoca Sok 3 ⓣ0232/716 0353, ⓦwww.incirliev.com. A haven of peace, centred around the garden's giant olive tree. Modern rooms sport lovely, traditional decor. ❻

Naciye Teyze Cemaliye Cad 6 ⓣ0232/716 8970, ⓦwww.naciyeteyze.com. A tad overpriced, but exceptionally friendly. Scrumptious breakfasts served in the shady garden. ❻

Sailors Otel Kemalpaşa Cad 66 ⓣ0232/716 8765, ⓦwww.sailorsotel.com. The best *pansiyon* in town, with spacious wooden-floored, white-and-blue-painted doubles. ❼

🏃 **Tas Otel** Kemalpaşa Cad 132 ⓣ0232/716 7772, ⓦwww.tasotel.com. Lovingly restored 1890s building with eight large, stylish rooms, all with balconies and a/c, plus swimming pool. Guests are invited to help with the olive harvest in the autumn. ❽

Ümit Ev Otel Yeni Mecidiye Mah, 3058 Sok 24 ⓣ0232/716 8133, ⓦwww.umitevotel.com. Simple rooms surrounding an organic garden (used to supply ingredients for breakfast), located on one of Alaçatı's backstreets. ❼

Eating and drinking

Café Agrilia Kemalpaşa Cad 75 ⓣ0232/716 8594. Boasting a wide-ranging Mediterranean menu, served up in their lovely rustic dining room, formerly a tobacco factory.

🏃 **Ferdi Baba** Şifne waterfront ⓣ0232/717 2145. For a fabulous fish blowout, head north out of town to Şifne's stretch of seafront terraces. The seafood – try the stuffed squid or the octopus kebabs – is as exquisite as the location.

Sudan Café Hacı Memiş Mah, Mithatpaşa Cad 22 ⓣ0232/716 7797, ⓦwww.su-dan-cafe.com. South of the main drag but well worth seeking out. A contemporary menu pairs Turkish classics with exotic flavours; the starters, particularly the home-made broad bean houmous, are delicious.

Tuval Restaurant Kemalpaşa Cad 81 ⓣ0232/716 9917. Delicious but pricey; join the elegant diners squeezed into the tables along the town's central pedestrianized street.

Yusuf Usta Atatürk Cad, Zeytinci İş Merkezi 1 ⓣ0232/716 8823, ⓦwww.alacatiyusufusta.com. Excellent budget pick for tasty, traditional Turkish cooking.

Altınkum

The best local beaches are those along **ALTINKUM**, a series of sunbaked coves 9km southwest of Çeşme, beyond the seaside township of Çiftlik.

Altınkum is easily reached by dolmuş, and between June and September the service continues a kilometre or so from the bus stand at the first cove to the **central cove**, stopping opposite the tiny *jandarma* outpost. This is probably the best beach between Bozcaada and the Turquoise Coast, where multi-hued water laps hundreds of metres of sand and dunes. *Okan's Place* (☎0532/394 0131; summer only) rents out very basic bungalows (◐), which can attract the odd bug during the summer. The attached beach club and **restaurant** are popular at weekends, the latter serving assorted fish (15TL), spicy *menemen* and veggies from the on-site organic garden. Five minutes' walk westward along the beach, *Ramo's Café* (☎0536/713 3415) is a friendly stop for kebabs and ice-cold beer; Ramo also has a few tents available (❷). If you have your own wheels, this area of the beach is accessible along a direct, signposted road from Çiftlik (bear left at the north edge of town).

Dalyan

DALYAN, 4km north of Çeşme, built on the west shore of an almost completely landlocked harbour, is a popular location for wealthy Turks to berth their yachts. There are, however, few short-term places to stay, and even less in the way of sandy beach, so for most, the clutch of superb fish restaurants, appealingly set by the narrow channel to the open sea, will be the extent of Dalyan's interest. The *Körfez, Köşem* and *Dalyan Deniz Restaurant* offer (not particularly cheap) *meze* and seafood with outside seating and fine views over the harbour. **Dolmuşes** from Çeşme (every 45min or when full) drop you at the small fisherman statue that acts as the main square for the village, where less pricey options include the *Levant'in Yeri* and *Sülo Nun Yeri*.

The Küçük Menderes valley

With a spare day, the inland towns and villages of the **Küçük Menderes valley**, southeast of İzmir, can be visited by public transport, as connections from both İzmir and Selçuk are good. To reach Birgi village, the lake at Gölcük or the conservative town of Tire, you first have to travel via the undistinguished market town of **Ödemiş** – 80km southeast of İzmir (buses every two hours from İzmir's *büyük otogar*, 3hr; five daily trains from Basmane, 2hr). From Ödemiş *otogar* there are hourly services to Birgi and Tire.

Birgi

A sleepy community of half-timbered houses lining both slopes of a narrow valley at the foot of Boz Dağ, **BIRGI**, 9km east of Ödemiş, is an excellent example of what small-town Turkey looked like before the wars and cement mania of the twentieth century.

The main thing to see is the **Aydınoğlu Mehmet Bey Camii**, also called the Ulu Cami, an engaging fourteenth-century mosque on the site of an earlier church. It's across the ravine from the Çakırağa Konaği (see below), a little way upstream. A sculpted lion has been incorporated into the exterior walls; inside it's an understated masterpiece, with the tiled *mihrab* and a single arch betraying a Selçuk influence. Most impressive, though, are the carved hardwood *mimber* and shutters, some of them replacements for those carted off to the Selimiye Camii in Edirne. The sloping wooden roof is supported by a forest of Roman columns, the whole effect more like Spanish Andalucia than Turkey.

Birgi's houses – ensembles of wood and either brick, stone, lath-and-plaster or half-timbered mud – run the gamut from the simple to the sumptuous. Many are dilapidated, but the restored eighteenth-century **Çakırağa Konağı** (Tues–Sun

9am–noon & 1–6pm; 3TL) mansion operates as a museum and has some explanatory panels in English. Birgi has little **accommodation**: by far the best is *Birgi Çınaraltı Pansiyon* (℡0232/531 5358, ⓦwww.birgicinaralti.com; ⓖ), which offers charming rooms and delicious home-cooked meals.

Tire

Thirty kilometres across the valley floor from Ödemış, **TIRE**, clustered at the base of Güme Dağı, is an altogether different proposition. Much fought over by Byzantines and Selçuks, it eventually became one of the Aydınoğlu clan's first important strongholds, and the conservatism and religious fervour of the inhabitants is still apparent (and disparaged by secular Turks). If you've had an overdose of the touristed coast, Tire makes the perfect antidote – though being stared at may be part of the experience.

The **old quarter** with its rickety houses is uphill from the main traffic roundabout in the northwest of town; you might have a look at the map posted outside the **museum**, but the best strategy is just to wander around. First, find the **Yeşil Imaret Zaviyesi**, also known as the Yahşi Bey Camii, built in 1442 by a general of Murat II as the core of a dervish community. An unusual scallop-shell half-dome looms over the *mihrab*, as does stalactite vaulting over the front door. No other monument cries out for attention – your main impression will be of a staggering number (reputedly 37) of indifferently restored Ottoman mosques, and older *türbes* or tombs, including two by the *otogar*.

Tire's atmosphere is, however, considerably enlivened by a large Gypsy presence from the surrounding villages, most in evidence at the weekly **Tuesday market**, reputedly the best in the Aegean region.

Kuşadası

KUŞADASİ may be brash and mercenary but it holds a perennial charm for groups of mostly boozy Brits, Irish and Australians. In just three decades its population has swelled ten fold and the scrappy, bustling conurbation now extends several kilometres along the coast and inland. The town is many people's first taste of Turkey: efficient ferry services link it with the Greek island of Sámos, while the resort is an obligatory port of call for Aegean cruise ships, which disgorge vast crowds in summer, who delight the local souvenir merchants after a visit to the ruins of Ephesus just inland.

Despite the noisy nightlife, the reasons to stay in Kuşadası are manifold. There are excellent connections to nearby attractions and adjacent beaches, and the accommodation stock is great value. If beer-guzzling holiday-makers leave you cold, you might prefer Selçuk as a base from which to explore the fascinating hinterland.

Arrival and information

Arriving by **ferry** from Sámos, you'll exit customs directly onto Liman Caddesi, and walk right past the resolutely unhelpful **tourist office** at no. 13 (June–Sept daily 8am–5pm; Oct–May Mon–Fri 8am–5pm; ℡0256/614 1103).

The **long-distance otogar**, where you're dropped if coming from the south, is over a kilometre out, past the end of Kahramanlar Caddesi on the ring road (*çevre yolu*) to Söke. **Local dolmuşes**, labelled "Şehir Içi", travel from here to the centre of town, stopping at the corner of Atatürk and İnönü bulvarıs, where you can also pick up services to the northern Tusan beach and its southern annexe of Kadınlar Denizi.

THE CENTRAL AND SOUTHERN AEGEAN

▲ Selçuk & İzmir

KUŞADASI

250 m
0

◄ Tusan & Pamucak

◄ Sámos (Greece)

◄ Crete (Greece) & Ancona (Italy)

► Otogar & Dolmuş Terminal (350m)

► Kadınlar Denizi (2km)

Yacht Marina

Friday Market Area

Covered Car Park

Minibuses to Ladies' Beach, Ephesus, Long Beach, Milli Parkı & Selçuk ★

Bus stop for Tusan & Pamucak ★

See inset above

Main Harbour

N

A E G E A N   S E A

GÜVERCİN ADASI (Pigeon Island)

Excursion boats

Taxi Rank ★

Beach

Yılancı Burnu

Inset map

ISMET İNÖNÜ BUL

Covered Car Park

Medieval Wall

Hanım Camii

Kale Hamamı

Tower

THY

Customs & Immigration ★

Taxi Rank ★

Kale Camii

Bank

Mailbox

Kervansaray

Belediye Hamam

Kale

Barbaros Bul

50 m
0

ACCOMMODATION
Anzac Golden Bed	I
Caravanserail Hotel	G
Cennet Pansiyon	D
Köken Otel	C
Liman Otel	F
Önder	B
Sezgin Hotel	H
Villa Konak	E
Yat Kamping	A

RESTAURANTS
Avlu	5
Balıkçılar	3
Castle	7
Dejezar	1
Holiday Inn	2
Öz Urfa Kebapçısı	6
Paşa	4

If you're bound for İzmir airport most long-distance buses pass within 700m from the terminal proper; ask to be let off at *havalimanı kavşağı* ("airport junction"), and allow an hour and a half for the trip. Taxis usually wait to transfer you the final distance from the junction to the airport and charge around 8TL per car. A taxi between Kuşadası and İzmir airport will cost €60; Bodrum airport €85.

Drivers have a choice of **car parks** in the centre of town, which cost around 5TL for up to three hours, 10TL for the entire day.

Accommodation

The best area for great-value accommodation is southeast of the Kale – the core of the town – uphill from Barbaros Hayrettin Bulvarı, particularly the upper reaches of Yıldırım, Aslanlar and Kıbrıs *caddesi*s, although it's a steep climb if you're carrying luggage. There are a number of sea-view establishments scattered along the entire length of the shore road, although these are much noisier and not half as friendly.

A number of dodgy establishments are touted from the *otogar* or the pier. The following hotels and *pansiyon*s are all clean and highly recommended.

Kıbrıs Caddesi and Kale

Caravanserail Hotel Kale ☎0256/614 4115, Ⓦwww.kusadasihotels.com. Occupying much of the *Öküz Mehmet Paşa Kervansarayı*, this elegant show-stopper is built around an elegant courtyard-cum-restaurant. Rooms boast period furniture, parquet floors and lofty ceilings. ❼

Liman Otel Kıbrıs Cad, Buyral Sok 4 ☎0256/614 77 70, Ⓦwww.limanhotel.com. Exceptionally friendly service, fair-sized rooms with a/c and tiled bathrooms, in a small, modern building. Central but relatively calm; ask for a sea-facing room. ❹

Yıldırım, Aslanlar and Kahramanlar caddesis

Anzac Golden Bed Aslanlar Cad, Uğurlu Sok 1 ☎0256/614 8708, Ⓦwww.anzacgoldenbed.com. Signposted from Yıldırım Cad, this quiet, laid-back, *pansiyon* is nicely decorated with kilims and home furnishings, plus a well-used bbq area. Good views from both the balconied rooms and the rooftop breakfast terrace. Book ahead. ❹

Cennet Pansiyon Yıldırım Cad 69 ☎0256/614 4893, Ⓦwww.cennetpension.com. A haven of peace with a garden containing 200-plus pot plants. Ably run for two decades by the kindly Ahmed, this *pansiyon* also boasts a sea-view roof terrace. ❹

Sezgin Hotel Aslanlar Cad 68 ☎0256/614 4225, Ⓦwww.sezginhotel.com. Another well-run

backpacker favourite with a leafy garden, large pool, satellite TV, internet facilities, €10 dorm beds, basic double rooms and a wide range of other services including airport pick-up and discounts for the Turkish baths. ❸

Villa Konak Yıldırım Cad 55 ☎0256/614 6318, Ⓦwww.villakonakhotel.com. Lovely converted old house with delightful rambling gardens, thick with magnolia and citrus trees. The large, stylish bedrooms are decorated with an assortment of antiques. Entertainment includes a sturdy old pool table and a hammock. ❺

On the seafront

Köken Otel İstiklâl Cad 5 ☎0256/614 3243. Set back just inland from noisy Atatürk Bul, this intimate two-star has balconied rooms with sea views and a roadside breakfast garden. ❹

Campsites

Önder Atatürk Bul 74, behind the Yacht Marina ☎0256/618 1590. Popular, tree-dappled place with good facilities, including tennis courts, kids' play park, swimming pool and restaurant. Open all year. Simple chalet-style double rooms also available.

Yat Kamping Atatürk Bul 76 ☎0256/618 1516, Ⓦwww.campingturkey.com. Just north of *Önder* campsite and offering much the same facilities – tents for hire, a caravan area, a swimming pool, simple double rooms, a restaurant and laundry service.

The Town

Liman Caddesi runs 200m from the ferry port up to the sixteenth-century **Öküz Mehmet Paşa Kervansaray**, restored as a luxury hotel (see above) where themed "Turkish Nights" concerts are held. To the right is the Orient Bazaar shopping centre, while to the left is Atatürk Bulvarı, the main harbour promenade lined with beach cafés on one side, restaurants and hotels on the other. Barbaros Hayrettin Bulvarı is a pedestrian precinct beginning next to the *kervansaray* and homing in on a little **stone tower**, a remnant of the town's medieval walls. To the left as you ascend lies the **Kale district**, huddled inside the rest of the walls, with a namesake mosque and some fine traditional houses that help lend the town what little appeal it has – most of these have been done up as restaurants and bars. Bearing left down Sağlık Caddesi takes you along the rear of Kale, where bits of old wall (including the landscaped stretch parallel to Hacivat Sokak) are visible; bearing right leads up towards some of Kuşadası's more desirable *pansiyons*, scattered among a near locals-only neighbourhood of handsome old dwellings.

Out across the causeway, **Güvercin Adası** (daily 8am–8pm) presents a series of landscaped terraces within its fortifications, dotted with tea gardens and snack bars – a leafy respite from the bustle of town. Swimming off the islet is rocky; for the closest decent sand, head 500m further south to the small beach north of **Yılancı Burnu**, or patronize one of the **day-trips** offered by excursion boats moored along the causeway. Most offer a similar itinerary, leaving at 9.30am, visiting three isolated beaches and returning by 4.30pm. The price hovers around 25TL including lunch; chat with the skippers first before you make your choice.

The beaches

Heading 3km southwest out of town, Kuşadası's most famous beach **Kadınlar Denizi** (also signposted Ladies' Beach) is rather scrappy but is nevertheless very popular in summer. Dolmuşes (labelled "Ladies' Beach") trundle south along the seafront past Güvercin Adası, and continue on to **Paradise Beach**, just one cove further along, which is smaller and quieter with fewer bars.

Bar-lined Tusan beach, a long stretch of hard-packed sand, 5km to the north of town, is probably more worthwhile. This area is also home to two of the largest **water-parks** in Turkey, Adaland (℡0256/618 1252, ⓦwww.adaland.com) and Aquafantasy (℡0232/893 1111, ⓦwww.aquafantasy.com), both of which have all the chutes, slides and wave pools you could possibly want. Both are open from around 9am until dusk. All run free shuttles and all Kuşadası–Selçuk minibuses pass by. Prices start at around €20; double or triple for additional entrance to the aquarium or sea world areas.

Much the best beach in the area – although the sea can be rough on windy days – is **Pamucak**, at the mouth of the Küçük Menderes River, 15km north of town, a little way off the route to Selçuk. The Pamucak-signed dolmuş from Kuşadası's Atatürk Bulvarı (every half-hour) stops at the northern end of the beach.

Eating

The vast majority of **restaurants** here are aimed squarely at the package holiday/ cruise-liner brigade – and are nothing to write home about. Good value is offered by the family-friendly establishments located in the Kale area; more rowdy are the restaurants and bars that line Atatürk Bulvarı. The good news is that authentic local cuisine can be found, and it tends to be cheaper than the foreign fare aimed at tourists. The vast majority of places are licensed.

Kale area

Avlu Cephane Sok 15/A. You'll do no better for traditional Turkish food than this ever-popular place with rear-courtyard seating. It serves low-priced grilled lamb and steam-tray specialities for around 5TL.

Balıkçılar Overlooking customs port. Step up from the main square by the ferry port to the first-floor terrace. Servings of harbour-fresh sea bass, sardines, calamari and anchovies assure its popularity.

Castle Kaleiçi Camikebir Mahallesi Tuna Sok 35. A touch touristy, but a divine location underneath a leafy trellis in the middle of the Kale. The seemingly endless menu is strong on soups and meats, with a long list of beers, wines and *rakı* to accompany.

Öz Urfa Kebapçısı Cephane Sok 9. Well regarded locally for its authentic Turkish dishes; particularly geared towards grilled lamb and chicken. Expect to pay 10TL per dish.

Paşa Cephane Sok 21. Entertaining family affair set within the confines of a picturesque courtyard. Recommended for its seafood and very cheap *meze*s.

Atatürk Bulvarı and around

Dejezar Atatürk Bul 84. Rowdy, fun and popular with British holiday-makers. An excellent array of mostly Turkish wines is backed up by well-executed meaty main courses.

Holiday Inn Restaurant Kahramanlar Cad. Popular with discerning locals and tourists alike, this eastern Turkish outfit – far removed from the hotel chain of the same name – has made a name for itself with its array of kebabs.

Drinking and nightlife

After-dark activity in Kuşadası is distributed over perhaps three dozen **bars**, clumped into distinct groups: a number of arty, genteel bars of the Kale district; their more energetic neighbours, featuring live music sung in either Turkish or English; and Irish/British pubs with karaoke gear and house music, culminating in the downmarket, foreigner-dominated Barlar Sokak area. If you pace the streets named below, guided by the cranked-up sound systems, you'll certainly find something to suit.

The most durable of the **Kale** watering holes, and congenial environments for meeting educated Turks on holiday, include the perennially popular *She*, at the corner of Bahar and Sakarya *sokak*s. *Dubliners* and *San* on Sakarya Sokak offer karaoke and occasional live bands. Several decent bars in the same zone include the appropriately named *Another Bar*. More sophisticated nightspots group around the marina, including trendy *Aura Moonlight* at Atatürk Bul 118. Pull up a beanbag poolside at *Kevam*, one of several chilled bar-cum-*nargile* joints next door.

Listings

Books English-language newspapers and magazines – including the likes of *OK!*, *The Mirror* and *The Daily Mail* – can be found around town.

Car rental Offices (including Avis and Europcar) cluster along İnönü and Atatürk buls; standard walk-in rates of around €70 a day can be bargained down to €40–50 at slack times.

Ferries The main agency for the 8.30am Turkish boat and the 5pm Greek boat to Sámos, is Azim Tours, Güvercinada Cad (☎0256/614 1553, ⓦwww.azimtours.com), although any travel agent in town will be able to sell you a ticket. A one-way costs €30; return €35.

Hamams Kale Hamamı, behind the Kale Camii, is very touristy, Belediye Hamam on Yıldırım Cad slightly less so. Both open daily 9am–8pm and cost 30TL.

Hospital The state hospital is at Atatürk Bul 32 (☎0256/613 1616), near the park; the newly built all-private Universal Hospital Kuşadası is on İstiklâl Cad by the *Köken Otel*.

Laundry Öven Laundry, Yıldırım Cad 29 opposite the Belediye Hamam.

Post office The PTT is on Barbaros Hayrettin Bul (Mon–Sat 8am–5pm).

Tours and travel agencies *The Sezgin* (see "Accommodation" above) and several backpacker places offer day-tours to Ephesus, Pamukkale and combined trips to Didyma, Miletus and Priene. Other recommended travel agents include Anker Travel, Ismet İnönü Bul 14 (☎0256/612 4598, ⓦwww.ankertravel.com). Akdeniz Travel, Atatürk Bul 26 next to the Avis office is recommended for plane tickets.

Dilek Yarımadası Milli Parkı

The imposing outline of **Samsun Dağı**, otherwise known as Dilek Dağı (the ancient Mount Mycale), dominates the skyline south of Kuşadası and may inspire notions of a visit. Regular dolmuşes (8am–dusk; 1hr) make light work of the 28km trip to the national park established around the mountain.

The **Dilek Yarımadası Milli Parkı** (spring & autumn daily 8am–5pm; summer daily 8am–6.30pm; winter closed; 5TL, cars 10TL) was set aside in 1966 for, among other reasons, the protection of its thick forest and diverse fauna, which is said to include rare lynx, jackal and wild cats. However, you are unlikely to see any of the species in question as much of the 28,000-acre park is an off-limits military zone. The most visited portion of the unrestricted zone consists of a ten-kilometre stretch of mostly paved road beyond the entrance and four good, but often windswept, beaches along it – **İçmeler** (hard sand shaded by plane trees), just beyond the gate; **Aydınlık Koyu** (pebbles); **Kavaklı Burun** (pebbles); and the last and prettiest one, **Karasu** (700m of pea gravel). Each beach has its own small snack bar or drinks kiosk operating in high season.

Best access to the **summit ridge** east of 1237-metre Samsun Dağı (Dilek Tepesi) is via a trail from **ESKIDOĞANBEY**, a village to the south. This is an all-day outing, best done in spring or autumn to avoid the heat. Chances of wildlife-spotting, particularly badgers, jackals and birds of prey, are probably better here than within the confines of the national park on the other side of the mountain. Since the closure of most short-term accommodation in Eskidoğanbey, walkers tend to take an early dolmuş to one or other of the trailheads, hike over the mountain, and take an evening dolmuş back to Söke or Kuşadası from the walk's endpoint. There are no facilities for staying overnight in the park, though it does provide WCs, barbecue areas and a small café.

Selçuk and around

A laid-back farming town only two decades ago, **SELÇUK** has been catapulted into the limelight of premier-league tourism by its proximity to the ruins of Ephesus. The flavour of tourism here, though, is markedly different from that at nearby Kuşadası; its less prestigious inland location, good-value accommodation and ecclesiastical connections (not least, the burial place of St John the Evangelist) make it a haven for a mix of both backpackers and religious tours.

Although evidence of settlement as early as 2000 BC has been found atop Ayasoluk hill, the town only really flourished as a Byzantine enterprise during the fifth century AD, after the harbour of adjacent Ephesus had completely silted up. Despite being the site of key events in the life of Sts Paul, John and (supposedly) the Virgin, local Christianity was mostly restricted to the village of Kirkince, now Şirince (see p.259).

Arrival and information

At the base of the castle hill and across the busy E24/550 highway (known as Atatürk Caddesi in town), Cengiz Topel Caddesi leads east through a pedestrian precinct to the **train station**, from where there are four daily connections to İzmir and Denizli, and one each to Afyon and Söke. Along the way you'll pass the **PTT** and several of the town's restaurants and bars. Following Atatürk Caddesi a bit further south brings you to the **otogar**.

On the western side of Atatürk Caddesi, on the corner of the central park and Uğur Mumcu Caddesi (or Love Street as the sign proclaims), the **tourist office** (May–Sept Mon–Fri 8.30am–noon & 1–5.30pm, Sat & Sun 9am–noon & 1–5pm; Oct–April Mon–Fri 9am–noon & 1–5.30pm; ☎0232/892 6328) has limited handouts but will cheerfully assist with information. Note that *pansiyon* promoters have been known to mob bus arrivals, sometimes boarding them at the town limits to deliver their sales pitch. Subsequent hustles are more refined, and may include the time-honoured offer of a lift to Ephesus and loan of a site

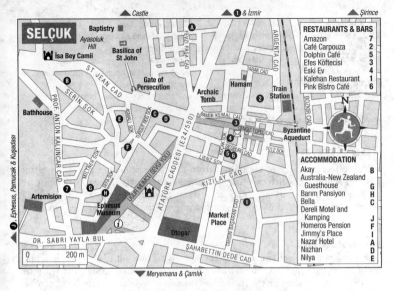

SELÇUK

RESTAURANTS & BARS	
Amazon	7
Café Carpouza	2
Dolphin Café	5
Efes Köftecisi	3
Eski Ev	4
Kalehan Restaurant	1
Pink Bistro Café	6

ACCOMMODATION	
Akay	B
Australia-New Zealand Guesthouse	G
Barım Pansiyon	H
Bella	C
Dereli Motel and Kamping	J
Homeros Pension	F
Jimmy's Place	I
Nazar Hotel	A
Nazhan	D
Nilya	E

guidebook – bracketed by "coincidental" stopovers at a relative's carpet shop for tea and a "chat".

Accommodation

Most places to stay cluster around the central pedestrianized zone or just west of Atatürk Caddesi, near the museum, with additional desirable establishments scattered on and at the base of Ayasoluk hill. Note that most hotels will offer free transport to Ephesus, as well as collection from the ferry in Kuşadası.

Around the museum

Hotel Akay Serin Sok 3 ☎0232/892 3172, ⊛www.hotelakay.com. Affordable boutique-style two-star choice spread over two properties with standard and superior rooms, all with balconies overlooking a garden. Fine views of the mosque, castle and basilica from its cushioned rooftop restaurant and bar. Swimming pool. ❹

Australia-New Zealand Guesthouse 1064 Sok 12 ☎0232/892 6050, ⊛www.anzguesthouse.com. Run by the ebullient Harry, a returned Turkish-Australian, this *pansiyon* is proud of its rug- and cushion-covered courtyard and snug rooftop bar, where nightly barbecues are served. Dorms (€7.5TL) available. Breakfast not included. ❸

Barım Pansiyon 1045 Sok 34 ☎0232/892 6923, ⊛www.barimpension.com. Restored, rambling old house complete with lush courtyard/garden. Rooms have traditional Turkish decor and stone-clad walls, with modern fixtures and fittings. ❸

Homeros Pension Asmalı Sok 17 ☎0232/892 3995, ⊛www.homerospension.com. Split over two adjoining buildings this family-run pension has a choice of

rooms, all nicely furnished by their carpenter son Derviş. Fine sunsets from the roof terrace. ❸

Nilya 1051 Sok 7 ☎0232/892 9081, ⊛www.nilya.com. Set behind high walls, this is a lovely, tranquil hideaway with charmingly cluttered kilim-strewn rooms (all with bathrooms and ceiling fans) laid out around a peaceful, tree-lined courtyard. Excellent breakfasts. ❻

East of Atatürk Caddesi

Hotel Bella St Jean Cad 7 ☎0232/892 3944, ⊛www.hotelbella.com. An ever-popular favourite near the basilica gate, owned by old friends Erdal and Nazmi. Good value, with beautifully decorated rooms, plus eye-level views of local stork nests from the rooftop restaurant. ❹

Jimmy's Place (formerly "Artemis Guest House") Atatürk Mah 1016 Sok 19 ☎0232/892 1982, ⊛www.jimmysplaceephesus.com. Near the central market and run by an irrepressible, well-travelled Turk, *Jimmy's* offers standard, superior and luxury en-suite rooms, plus a hotel pool down the road. Standard rooms ❸, luxury rooms ❹

Nazar Hotel İsabey Mah 2019 Sok 34 ☎0232/892 2222, ⓦwww.nazarhotel.com. Good-value, family-run place with thirteen clean, attractively furnished rooms, a courtyard and pool area, and a good rooftop restaurant. ❹

Nazhan 1044 Sok 2 ☎0232/892 8731, ⓦwww.nazhan.net. A delightful small house packed with antiques and bric-a-brac, chosen by Nazhan and Kemal when they escaped the rat race of İstanbul. ❹

Dereli Motel and Kamping Pamucak beach, 7km west of Selçuk ☎0232/893 1205, ⓦwww.dereli-ephesus.com. Large campsite set amongst palm trees, right on the beach; you could almost be in Thailand. Can arrange pick-up from *otogar* though the Pamucak dolmuş drops at entrance. Open all year. (site for two ❷)

The Town

Selçuk offers a variety of antiquities from diverse eras (not least in its excellent Ephesus Museum), which can easily be toured in a single day. The town's sights are numerous and interesting enough to warrant another night's stay after visiting Ephesus, especially if you also plan on heading out to the shrine at Meryemana or the hill-village of Şirince.

Ayasoluk Hill

The focal point of settlement in every era, **Ayasoluk** hill (daily 8am–6.30pm; 5TL) is the first spot you should head for. Enter the site through the **Gate of Persecution**, so called by the Byzantines because of a relief of Achilles in combat that once adorned it, mistakenly thought to depict a martyrdom of Christians in the amphitheatre of nearby Ephesus.

St John the Evangelist came to Ephesus in the middle of the first century. He died here around 100 AD and was buried on Ayasoluk Hill, whose name is thought to be a corruption of "Ayios Theologos" ("Divine Theologian"). The sixth-century Byzantine emperor Justinian decided to replace two earlier churches sheltering John's tomb with a basilica worthy of the saint's reputation, and until destruction by Tamerlane's Mongols in 1402, it was one of the largest and most ornate Byzantine churches in existence.

Today, various colonnades and walls of the **Basilica of St John** have been re-erected. The purported tomb of the evangelist is marked by a slab on the former site of the altar. Beside the nave is the **Baptistry**, where fundamentalist tourists may pose in the act of dunking for friends' cameras. The restored **Byzantine castle** on top of the hill is currently under lengthy renovation following the partial collapse of one of its walls, and due to reopen in 2012.

The Ephesus Museum

The **Ephesus Museum** (Efes Müzesi; daily 8.30am–6.30pm, winter closes at 5pm; 5TL) is permanently packed with visitors, but is well worth setting aside the time to visit. Its galleries of finds are arranged thematically rather than chronologically which helps to present the ancient city as a living space rather than just a repository of artefacts, although be aware that the labelling is often vague. The first three halls contain some of the most famous bronze and ceramic objects in the collection, including effigies of the phallic god Priapus, a bust of the Greek dramatist Menander, Eros riding a dolphin and various excellent miniatures from the Roman terrace houses at Ephesus. Beyond here, there is a large courtyard, containing sarcophagi, column capitals and stelae.

Continuing through the main galleries, you'll enter a hall devoted to tomb finds and mortuary practices. Just beyond this is the famous **Artemis room**, with two renditions of the goddess studded with multiple bull's testicles (not breasts, as is commonly believed) and tiny figurines of real and mythical beasts, honouring her role as mistress of animals.

The Artemision

Beyond the museum, 200m along the road toward Ephesus and to the right, are the scanty remains of the **Artemision**, or the sanctuary of Artemis (daily 8.30am–5.30pm; free). The archaic temple here replaced three predecessors dedicated to Cybele, and was itself burned down in 356 BC by Herostratus, a lunatic who (correctly) reckoned his name would be immortalized by the act. The massive Hellenistic replacement was considered to be one of the Seven Wonders of the Ancient World, though this is hard to believe today: the Goths sacked it in 263 AD and the Byzantines subsequently carted off most of the remaining masonry to Ayasoluk and Constantinople, leaving just a lone column (re-erected in modern times) amid battered foundation blocks.

İsa Bey Camii

The **İsa Bey Camii** is the most distinguished of the various Selçuk monuments, the style that gives the town its name. It's a late fourteenth-century Aydınoğlu mosque and it represents a transition between Selçuk and Ottoman styles, with its innovative courtyard – where most of the congregation would worship – and stalactite vaulting over the entrance. Inside the main hall, you'll see a high, gabled roof supported by Roman columns and some fine tile-work in the south dome. Just south of the mosque are the fenced-off remains of a fourteenth-century **bath-house**, which can be seen from Prof A Kaluncur Caddesi.

Eating, drinking and entertainment

Virtually all Selçuk's **restaurants** are found in the town centre, and tend to be rather similar, although they are not nearly so exploitative as some in nearby Kuşadası. Good-value establishments along and around the pedestrianized Cengiz Topel Caddesi include *Efes Köftecisi*, which serves up good, simple and cheap steam-tray specials, and the relatively elegant *Eski Ev*, offering good Turkish home-cooking in a leafy courtyard. It's not every restaurant that can offer views of one of the Seven Wonders of the Ancient World, but *Amazon*, on Prof A Kaluncur Caddesi, a stylish, modern dining room just down the road from the İsa Bey Camii, can oblige from its pavement tables. Otherwise, several of the town's hotels – most notably the *Kalehan* – operate decent dining rooms that are open to the public.

After-hours tippling takes place at several noisy **pubs** near Cengiz Topel Caddesi. The *Pink Bistro Café* and *Dolphin Café* have tables spilling out onto Siegburg Caddesi and are good for late-night carousing, while *Café Carpouza*, on the far side of the aqueduct, serves up cocktails until 1am at tables dotted around their vast garden.

Around Selçuk

The main draw in the region is the ancient city of Ephesus, not to be missed if you are staying in Selçuk. However, a few other local diversions are worth considering, including the evocative village of **Şirince**, nestled in the hills 8km to the east. It's increasingly becoming a weekend bolt hole for wealthy Turks and makes for an easily attainable day-trip. **Meryemana**, on the other hand, only of any real interest to those on a biblical tour, requires your own transport or a taxi.

Şirince

ŞIRINCE, a well-preserved, originally Greek-built hill-village, situated 8km east of and above Selçuk, is surrounded by lush orchards and vineyards – you can taste the wines and buy them at the many wine shops here. Laden with pesky hawkers in season, it's a much more pleasant and relaxed place outside summer and genuinely lives up to its reputation as one of the region's most idyllic villages.

▲ Şirince village

At the edge of Şirince stands a late nineteenth-century **church**, with a pebble-mosaic floor, plaster-relief work on the ceiling and wooden vaulting. Nearer the middle of the village there's a larger stone **basilica** dating from 1839 and restored as an art gallery. But the main point of a visit is the idyllic scenery and the handsome domestic architecture, which, since the late 1980s, has attracted wealthy urban Turks in search of characterful vacation homes.

Regular **dolmuşes** leave from Selçuk's *otogar* and drop you in the centre of the Şirince village, where nothing is more than a few minutes' walk away. You could stay overnight here, though **accommodation** prices are relatively high: the *Nişanyan Evleri* (T0232/898 3208, W www.nisanyan.com; ❽) is a restored mansion with serene views and superb singles and doubles, five minutes up on the eastern slopes at the end of a dirt track above the town. Travel-writer owner Sevan also has a number of apartments in the village (❼), some with *kerevet*s (built-in wooden beds) and designer bathrooms.

There are half a dozen **restaurants** clustered around the main square at the east end of the village's single-lane bazaar. Alternatively, the ✲ *Artemis Restaurant* enjoys a spectacular setting in a former school overlooking the valley at the entrance to the village, and offers an excellent Turkish menu (mains are 10–15TL), as well as a wide range of local wines.

Meryemana

Eight kilometres southwest of Selçuk, beyond Ephesus and just below the summit of Bülbül Dağı, stands **Meryemana** (dawn–dusk; 10TL, plus car-park fees), a monument to piety and faith. Though most Orthodox theologians maintain that the Virgin Mary died and was buried in Jerusalem, another school of thought holds that the mother of Jesus accompanied St John the Evangelist when he left Palestine in the middle of the first century on his way to Ephesus.

The site is enclosed within a municipal park and subject to a generous dose of commercialism – though the dense forest and fountain are pleasant enough. The **house** itself, now a chapel aligned unusually southwest to northeast, probably dates from early Byzantine times, though its foundations may indeed be first-century. It overlooks a beautiful wooded valley and two terraces where a spring gushes forth; nearby, tree branches are festooned with the votive rag-scraps left by Muslim pilgrims, for whom *Meryemana* (Mother Mary) is also a saint.

The site is accessible only by private car or taxi (or, if you're really determined, on foot, but it's a good hour's walk). If you want to come, it makes sense to combine a visit with a day at Ephesus, whose upper entrance is 5km to the north; see p.262 for details.

Çamlık Open-Air Rail Museum

Some 12km south of Selçuk on the main highway to Aydın, the village of **ÇAMLİK** is the site of the **Çamlık Open-Air Rail Museum** (Buharlı Lokomotif Müzesi; open daily; 2TL), 50m southwest of the road after the village-limits sign. The museum occupies the sidings of a former train-works and exhibits include more than two dozen steam locomotives, many pre-World War I; the majority are German-made but there are also British, American, Czech, French and Swedish models. A particularly scenic, if slow, way of reaching the museum is by taking one of the three daily Selçuk–Aydın trains, and getting off at Çamlık station. The museum itself is a further 1km walk away in the town's former station.

Ephesus

With the exception of Pompeii, **Ephesus** (Efes in Turkish) is the largest and best-preserved ancient city around the Mediterranean; and, after the Sultanahmet district of İstanbul, it's the most visited tourist attraction in Turkey. The ruins are mobbed for much of the year, although with a little planning and initiative it's possible to tour the site in relative peace. You'll need two to three partly shady hours to see Ephesus, as well as a bottle of water – the acres of stone act as a grill in the heat of the day, and the water sold from the kiosks at either gate is expensive.

Some history

Legends relate that Ephesus was founded by **Androclus**, son of King Kodrus of Athens having been advised by an oracle to settle at a place indicated by a fish and a wild boar. Androclus and his entourage arrived here to find natives roasting fish by the sea; embers from the fire set a bush ablaze, out of which charged a pig, and the city was on its way. The imported worship of Artemis melded easily with that of the indigenous **Cybele**, and the Ephesus of 1000 BC was built on the north slope of Mount Pion (Panayır Dağı), very close to the temple of the goddess.

Alexander the Great, on his visit in 334 BC, offered to fund the completion of the latest version of the Artemis shrine, but the city fathers tactfully demurred, saying that one deity should not support another. Following Alexander's death his lieutenant **Lysimachus** moved the city to its present location – necessary because the sea had already receded considerably – and provided it with its first **walls**, traces of which are still visible on Panayır Dağı and Mount Koressos (Bülbül Dağı) to the south.

In subsequent centuries, Ephesus changed allegiance frequently and backed various revolts against Roman rule. Yet it never suffered for this lack of principle: during the Roman imperial period it was designated the **capital of Asia** and ornamented with magnificent public buildings – the ones on view today – by a succession of emperors. Ephesus's quarter-million population was swelled substantially at times by the right of sanctuary linked to the sacred precinct of Artemis, allowing shelter to large numbers of criminals. Of a somewhat less lurid cast was the more stable, mixed population of Jews, Romans, and Egyptian and Anatolian cultists.

Despite, or perhaps because of, this, **Christianity** took root early and quickly at Ephesus. St John the Evangelist arrived in the mid-first century, and **St Paul** spent the years 51–53 AD in the city, proselytizing foremost among the Jewish community. As usual, Paul managed to foment controversy even in this cosmopolitan environment, apparently being imprisoned for some time – in a tower bearing his name near the west end of the walls – and later provoking the famous silversmiths' riot, described in Acts 19:23–20:1.

Under the Byzantines, Ephesus was the venue for two of the **councils of the Church**, including one in 431 AD at which the Nestorian heresy (see p.675) was anathematized. However, the general tenor of the Byzantine era was one of decline, owing to the abandoning of Artemis-worship following the establishment of state Christianity, Arab raids and (worst of all) the final silting up of the harbour. The population began to siphon off to the nearby hill crowned by the tomb and church of St John, future nucleus of the town of Selçuk, and by the time the Selçuks themselves appeared the process was virtually complete.

Arrival

Approaching Ephesus **from Kuşadası**, get the dolmuş to drop you at the *nearest* junction, from where it's another easy kilometre to the lower entrance and ticket office. **From Selçuk**, most of the hotels offer free transport, or a taxi costs around 8TL. Alternatively, you could walk the 3km: the first 2km of the walk along a mulberry-shaded lane paralleling the busy highway are rather pleasant, the final 1km along a narrow hill with no pavement, less so. There is also a second, **upper entrance** on the southeastern side of Ephesus, on the way to Meryemana (see p.260) – a more sensible route in summer since it enables you to walk downhill through the site (tour buses tend to drop their clients here, retrieving them at the lower gate). Visiting Meryemana first by **taxi from Selçuk** will allow you to use the upper gate: 40TL (per car) should include a half-hour wait at "Mary's house", then a final drop-off at the top of the Ephesus site.

The site

The first hint of the city, well before you reach the lower entrance of **Ephesus** (daily 8am–6.30pm; winter closes 5.30pm; last ticket 30min before closing; 20TL, plus car-park fees) with souvenir stalls and tour buses, is the rather eroded (and pilfered) remains of the **Vedius gymnasium** and the **stadium**, funded by Nero. Once past the entry gate, take a sharp right along a path signed "Meryem Kilisesi", which leads to **St Mary's church**, an absurdly elongated hotchpotch constructed between the second and fourth centuries AD. The building, originally a Roman warehouse, was the venue of the ecumenical council in 431 AD; its baptistry is in good condition. An alternative, recommended in summer, is to start at the top entrance (same opening times and price) and work downhill, although you will be walking with the crowds in this direction. Whatever the season, a hat and a bottle of water are a must. Multilingual audio guides are available from both entrances.

The Arcadian Way and the theatre

Best approached from the church, the **harbour baths** and **gymnasium** are prominent, but overgrown and difficult to explore. Along their western edge, trees and bushes fringe the splendid **Arcadian Way**, named after the fifth-century Byzantine emperor Arcadius who renovated it. Currently roped-off and the site of regular faux-gladiator performances, it's not too difficult to imagine an era when

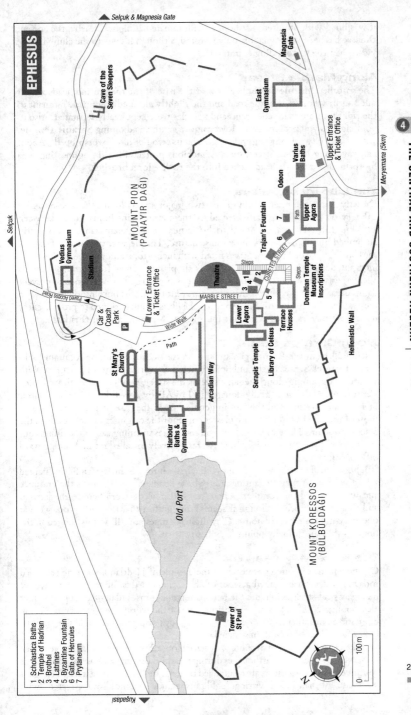

EPHESUS

1 Scholastica Baths
2 Temple of Hadrian
3 Brothel
4 Latrines
5 Byzantine Fountain
6 Gate of Hercules
7 Prytaneum

▲ Selçuk & Magnesia Gate

▲ Selçuk

▼ Kuşadası

▼ Meryemana (5km)

MOUNT PION (PANAYIR DAĞI)

Cave of the Seven Sleepers

Vedius Gymnasium

Stadium

East Gymnasium

Magnesia Gate

Varius Baths

Upper Entrance & Ticket Office

Odeon

Upper Agora

Trajan's Fountain

CURETES STREET

Path

Lower Entrance & Ticket Office

Car & Coach Park

Paved Access Road

Theatre

Steps

MARBLE STREET

Wide Walk

Path

Lower Agora

Steps

Domitian Temple

Museum of Inscriptions

St Mary's Church

Serapis Temple

Terrace Houses

Library of Celsus

Hellenistic Wall

Arcadian Way

Harbour Baths & Gymnasium

Old Port

Tower of St Paul

MOUNT KORESSOS (BÜLBÜLDAĞI)

0   100 m

N

it was lined with hundreds of shops and illuminated at night. Nearby, the ancient **theatre** has been somewhat brutally restored, although it's worth the climb for the views over the surrounding countryside.

Along Marble Street

The so-called **Marble Street** begins near the base of the theatre and heads almost due south; wheel-ruts in the road and the slightly elevated colonnade remnant to the right indicate that pedestrians and vehicles were kept neatly separated. Also to your right as you proceed is the **lower agora**, with an adjoining **Serapis Temple**, where the city's many Egyptian merchants would have worshipped. About halfway along Marble Street, metal stanchions protect alleged "signposting" – a footprint and a female head etched into the rock – for a **brothel**.

The Library of Celsus

Directly across the intersection of the two major streets looms the awe-inspiring **Library of Celsus**, originally erected by the consul Gaius Julius Aquila between 110 and 135 AD as a memorial to his father Celsus Polemaeanus, who is still entombed under the west wall of the structure. The elegant, two-storey facade is the classic image of Ephesus. It was fitted with niches for statues of the four personified intellectual virtues, today filled with plaster copies (the originals are in Vienna). Inside, twelve thousand scrolls were stored in galleries designed to prevent damp damage – a precaution that didn't prevent the Goths burning them all when they sacked the area in 262 AD. Abutting the library, and designed to provide entry to the lower agora, is the restored triple **gate of Mazaeus and Mithridates**.

Along Curetes Street

Just uphill from the Roman city's main intersection, a Byzantine fountain looks across **Curetes Street** to the public **latrines**, a favourite photo opportunity with visitors. Continuing along the same side of the street, you'll come to the so-called **Temple of Hadrian**, actually donated in 118 AD by a wealthy citizen in honour of Hadrian, Artemis and the city in general. As in the case of the library facade, most of the relief works here are plaster copies of the originals, which reside in the Selçuk museum. The two small heads on the arches spanning the four columns out front are of Tyche and possibly Medusa, respectively installed for luck and to ward off evil influences.

Behind and above the temple sprawl the first-century **Scholastica baths**, named after the fifth-century Byzantine lady whose headless statue adorns the entrance and who restored the complex. There was direct access from here to the latrines and thence the brothel, though it seems from graffiti that the baths, too, were at one stage used as a bawdy house. Clay drainage pipes are still visibly lodged in the floor, as they are at many points in Ephesus.

The terrace houses

On the far side of Curetes Street from the Temple of Hadrian lies a huge patterned **mosaic**, which once fronted a series of shops. Behind this, housed in a protective plexiglass-and-steel shelter, are the famous **terrace houses** (daily 8am–6pm; winter closes 5pm; 15TL): 62 rooms comprising one of the world's best-preserved Roman domestic environments. Oddly, many tour groups skip this incredible site – all the better for you to enjoy it unobstructed.

Broken down into seven dwellings, Terrace House 2 was buried, and thus very well preserved, by a series of earthquakes during the third century AD. Excavation teams continue to work as visitors are channelled through the complex via transparent glass walkways. At the time of writing, highlights include a basilica "wall-papered" with

Turkish food and drink

The amazing variety of Turkish food and drink is a direct link to its multilayered history. Here you'll find everything from rustic central Asian country cooking such as gözleme (stuffed pancakes) and mantı ("Turkish ravioli"), to the highly refined, Arab-inspired cuisine of the Ottoman court. This section focuses on some key dishes and drinks to look out for. For more background, see p.44.

Seafood

Turks, given their long coastline, have always adored seafood, even shrimp, squid and mussels which in strict Islamic observance are *haram* (forbidden). Residents of the eastern Black Sea are even nicknamed *hamsi*s (anchovies) after their favourite food. But the main focus of fishy interest is the Bosphorus strait linking the Black Sea and Mediterranean (via the intervening Sea of Marmara and Dardanelles), routes for seasonal migrations of eagerly awaited species. Late autumn sees fish head southwest from the Black Sea on the primary Bosphorus current. Most famous are bluefish (*lüfer*), with five aliases depending on size; sardine (*sardalya*); small bonito (*palamut*) and large (*torik*) – the source of *lakerda*, marinated white-fleshed slices that's a premium *meze*. Having spawned in the warmer Mediterranean, such species return to the Black Sea in spring, sparking off a second round of gastronomic indulgence. There are also many fish which stay put and are available

Street vendor selling mussels ▲

Meze ▼

Meze

Up to thirty kinds of **meze** (from the Arabic *mezza*, "taste" or "sample") may be featured at licensed restaurants or *meyhane*s. They're the stars of Turkish cuisine, comprising a tempting array of rich purées, vinaigrettes and the olive-oil fried then chilled vegetarian dishes known as *zeytin yağlılar*. Most meze appear cold straight out of the display case, but those incorporating filo pastry – the various böreks – are served hot to order. Some platters, such as marinated red beans or rock samphire, are very simple, while others, such as *içli köfte* (bulgur-nut and mince rissoles) or dishes incorporating the versatile aubergine, are fiddly to make, mobilizing much of the chef's creativity.

most of the year, but they don't compare in popular affection and (in bumper years) sheer visibility to the migrators.

Inland, you'll find **freshwater species** such as catfish (*yayın*) and trout (*alabalık*, often farmed) served up at lake- and riverside restaurants – some of the best are found in Eğirdir.

Coffee vs tea

The Ottomans introduced **coffee** – along with the notion of the coffeehouse – to the West during the 1600s. At first religious authorities proscribed the drink as a stimulant forbidden by the Koran, and coffeehouses themselves were intermittently banned as hotbeds of sedition and vice. But they had became a fixture of İstanbul society by the mid-1500s, with early travellers admiring their egalitarian sociability.

The Ottoman method of preparing coffee, still used, involved combining finely ground roasted beans with water and sugar to taste in a *cezve* (long-handled, tapering small pot). The mixture is allowed to rise twice without actually boiling, then the resultant froth, liquid and *telve* (sediment, never drunk) decanted into little cups.

With the formation of the republic, coffee began to fall out of favour. After the Ottoman Arabian territories were lost, **tea-growing** along the Black Sea was heavily subsidized and coffee was taxed beyond the reach of most. Strong black tea – as anyone strolling through a bazaar soon learns – is now the ritual hot drink of choice, though its pedigree can hardly compare to Indian or Sri Lankan tea, and if steeped too long (as is often the case) can be undrinkable. However, since 2000 the price of coffee has fallen and its popularity begun to recover in the land that introduced it to the wider world.

▲ Tea served in a classic tulip-shaped glass

▼ Coffee served with Turkish Delight

▼ Spices on sale at the bazaar

Wine

Anatolia is among the oldest, if not *the* oldest grape-growing region on earth. Some experts believe that **wine** was first made here six thousand years ago, and that viniculture spread west to Greece and Italy. After the Ottoman Muslim conquest, wine-making became the speciality of the Armenian and Greek Christian minorities; indeed, late in the nineteenth century, when phylloxera devastated Europe's vineyards, the Ottoman Empire was briefly among the world's largest wine exporters. The turbulent decade of 1912–1922 and subsequent departure of most Christians sharply curtailed wine production until republican authorities began encouraging this "civilized, western" activity. But for decades Turkey failed to realize its wine-producing potential.

Today, things have changed for the better and private **wineries** with foreign-trained oenologists make quality labels comparable to others around the Mediterranean (see p.49 for the best brands). Local vintners are lucky to rely on almost a thousand indigenous grape varieties. With very little bottled for export, they make one of the best discoveries of a trip to Turkey.

Vineyards, Cappadocia ▲

Helva ▼

Helva

The first recipe for **helva**, the quintessential Turkish sweet made from flour, butter, sugar and sometimes milk or starch, was recorded in 1473 and hasn't changed since. *Helva* (from Arabic *hulv*, "sweet" or "gentle"), symbolizing happiness and prosperity, marked holy days, weddings, funerals and even the conclusion of hostilities. The sweet often appeared part-way through imperial banquets and entire evenings were spent sampling different types. Away from the palace, prosperous commoners served it late in the evening, just before coffee.

thin sheets of marble in Dwelling 6, underfloor heating in Dwelling 5 and the mosaics and murals in the Room of the Nine Muses in Dwelling 3.

To the upper entrance

Returning to Curetes Street, you pass **Trajan's Fountain**, whose ornamentation has been removed to the museum, and then the street splits just above the **Hydreion** (another fountain) and the **Gate of Hercules**, where a remaining column relief depicts the hero wrapped in the skin of the Nemean lion. Bearing right at the junction takes you to the **Domitian Temple**, of which only the lower floor of the complex is left intact.

The main thoroughfare skirts the large, overgrown **upper agora**, which lies opposite the civic heart of the Roman community – the **prytaneum**. This housed the inextinguishable sacred flame of Ephesus and two of the Artemis statues in the Selçuk museum, in spite of Hestia (Vesta) being the presiding goddess; it also served as the reception area for official guests.

The adjacent **odeon**, once the local parliament, has been as insensitively restored as the main theatre, though presumably the 27 rows of seats are the original number. The **Varius baths** mark the end of the paved Roman street-system, and also the location of the upper site entrance. Beyond the gate huddles the massive **east gymnasium**, next to which the **Magnesia Gate** signals the true edge of the old city. The asphalt road here leads 5km south to Meryemana (see p.260), but you'd best hop into one of the waiting taxis – it's too steep and car-infested a walk to be enjoyable.

Priene

Priene is a much less visited site than Ephesus, hence all the lizards scampering around the ruins, and its isolation gives it a lonely, faded grandeur that Ephesus lacks. Perched on a series of pine terraces graded into the south flank of Samsun Dağı, 35km south of Kuşadası, the compact but exquisite site enjoys a situation that bears comparison with that of Delphi in Greece.

Some history

Thought its original settlement was elsewhere in the Meander basin; the townspeople, following the receding shoreline – now just visible to the west – re-founded the city on its present site during the fourth century BC, just in time for Alexander to stop in and finance the cost of the principal temple of Athena. The Panionion sanctuary, cult centre of the league of Ionian cities, had always lain in Priene's territory, just the other side of Samsun Dağı; as a result its priest was usually chosen from Priene, whose secular officials also presided over the regular meetings of the confederacy. Under Roman – and later Byzantine – rule, however, the city enjoyed little patronage from the emperors, with the result that Priene represents the best-preserved Hellenistic townscape in Ionia, without any of the usual later additions. The town was laid out by Hippodamus, an architect from nearby Miletus, who favoured a grid pattern made up of various *insulae* (rectangular units), each measuring roughly 42m by 35m. Within each rectangle stood four private dwellings; a public building had its own *insula*, sometimes two.

Arrival and accommodation

Priene's **site** lies a few hundred metres west of the village of Güllübahçe. **All-in tours** can be arranged from Selçuk hotels and hostels, and are a good idea if time is limited. The tour usually includes a reasonable guide with a 9.30am pick-up from your hotel, a lunch stop and a 5pm return. The itinerary is open to alteration but often starts at Priene moving on to Didyma (p.269) and saving the shadeless Miletus (see opposite) until last. Prices average around €30 but it's worth shopping around as they do vary enormously.

Dolmuş services to Priene require a change of vehicle at Söke, 24km southeast of Kuşadası and 44km south of Selçuk. Making connections is pretty hassle-free: you'll be deposited right next to vehicles leaving for Priene, Miletus and Didyma. The hourly **dolmuşes from Söke** take twenty minutes to reach the very spread-out village of **Güllübahçe**, scattered 200m to 700m east of the ruins.

There are only a couple of small **pensions** in the village, including the *Priene Pansiyon* (℡0256/547 1725; ❹), which offers reasonable en-suite rooms as well as camping space but requires advance booking in high season. Of the handful of **restaurants and cafés**, the best is *Vila Sultan*, at the far west end of the village below the site car park, which serves up *köfte*, kebabs and sandwiches at shady tables near a small fountain.

The site

From the entrance (daily 9am–7pm, winter closes 5.30pm; 3TL), it's a good steep walk up the hill to the northeast gate into the city. The first easily distinguished civic monument, more or less in the centre of the site, just south of the central street, is the square **bouleuterion** or council chamber, the most intact in Turkey, consisting of seats on three sides enclosing the speakers' area, together with a sacrificial altar.

Just east of the bouleuterion are the scantier remains of the **prytaneion**, or town administration offices, with traces of a dining area for the highest municipal officials. On the next terrace down lie the **Temple of Zeus**, the **agora** and the **sacred stoa**, once graced by outer and inner series of Doric and Ionic columns, though nothing is left above knee level of any of these. The commanding views, however, suggest that this was the heart of public life in the city.

Clearly visible below, reached by way of a stairway from the agora, are the **gymnasium** and **stadium**, with nearby **bathing basins**, complete with gutters and lion-head spouts, for use after athletics. On the west side of the stadium there are a few sets of **starting blocks** for foot races; spectators watched from the north side of the 190m-by-20m area, where some seats are still discernible.

Heading west down a gentle slope off the central street brings you into the midst of the densest surviving residential district in Priene, where thick walls stand up to 1.5 metres in some places. The city's **west gate** marks the end of both the main street and the blocks of houses.

North of the central street

The city's most conspicuous monument, the **Temple of Athena Polias**, stands two terraces above the main residential street. The temple took more than two centuries to complete and, in its time, was considered the epitome of Ionic perfection; a manual written by its designer Pytheos was still considered standard reading in Roman times. Directly north of the Athena temple, reached by a faint trail through the pines, is the scant remains of the **Sanctuary of Demeter and Kore**.

The **theatre**, a little way southeast, is by contrast in an excellent state of preservation, its layout and seating (for 5000, Priene's entire population) unchanged from the Hellenistic original. Most prominent are five larger-than-average marble thrones for the municipal dignitaries. The stage buildings were extensively modified during the second century AD – virtually the only Roman tampering with Priene's public buildings. Just behind them are the remains of a **Byzantine basilica**, entrance and columns clearly visible.

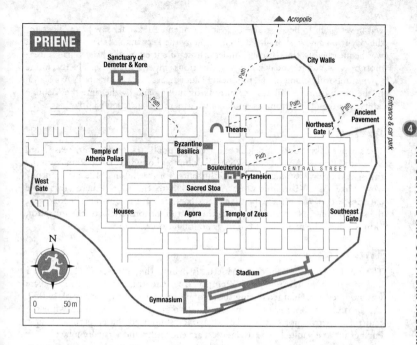

If you're keen on scrambling and the weather is not too hot, take the path beginning above the theatre to the **acropolis**; allow an extra hour and a half for the round trip. The mandatory exit from the site is back out the **main (northeast) gate**.

Miletus

The position of **Miletus** (Milet in Turkish), on an eminently defendable promontory jutting out into the ancient Gulf of Latmos, once outshone that of Priene. However, its modern setting, marooned in the seasonal marshes of the Büyük Menderes, leaves little to bear witness to the town's long and colourful past, although the massive theatre, visible from some distance away, pays some tribute to its former glories. Up close, the site is a confusing juxtaposition of widely scattered relics from different eras, often disguised by weeds, mud or water, depending on the season.

Some history

Miletus is at least as old as Ephesus and far older than Priene; German archeologists working locally since the 1890s have uncovered remnants of a Creto-Mycenaean settlement from the sixteenth century BC. Ionian invaders made their first appearance during the eleventh century, and by the seventh century BC Miletus was in the first flush of a heyday that was to last more than two hundred years.

While not strong enough to completely avoid Persian domination, Miletus did manage to secure favourable terms as an equal, and even took the opportunity to appropriate the nearby oracle of Didyma. But with Athenian instigation, the city was unwisely persuaded to take command of the abortive Ionian revolt against the Persians between 500 and 494 BC leading to being largely destroyed. Within fifty years Miletus was rebuilt some distance to the northeast of its original site, but it was never again to be as great – or as independent. Alexander saw fit to "liberate" the city from a new, short-lived occupation by the Persians and their allies. Later it was bequeathed to the Romans, under whose rule it enjoyed a brief renaissance – most of what you see today is a legacy of various emperors' largesse. The Byzantine town stubbornly clung to life, producing Isidorus, architect of Istanbul's Aya Sofya. In the ninth century Miletus was already dwindling and by the time the Menteşe emirs, and then the Ottomans, took control, there was little left to prize.

Arrival

The site lies 45km south of Selçuk and access by public transport is fairly easy from Söke (see "Priene: Arrival" on p.265): all dolmuşes bound for Balat (2km from the ruins), Akköy or Altınkum run past Güllübahçe (for Priene) and Milet; the journey from Söke takes 40 minutes. At Akköy, 6km to the south, there are simple **eateries**; otherwise some expensive snack bars cater for a tour-bus clientele near the site entrance. Note that following the theft of various artefacts, the **museum**, 1km south of the main ticket booth, is no longer open.

The site

The most obvious attraction at Miletus is behind the entrance (daily: summer 8.30am–7pm; winter 8.30am–5.30pm; 3TL): a **theatre**, whose Hellenistic base was modified and enlarged during the second century AD to a capacity of 15,000. On the orchestra floor is a stone block with two griffins carved in relief, while the centre front row sports two pillars that once supported the emperor's canopy. Further up, the vaulted exit passageways are enormous and virtually intact.

An eighth-century **Byzantine castle** and some contemporaneous ramparts surmount the theatre, giving a marvellous 360-degree view over the flood plain,

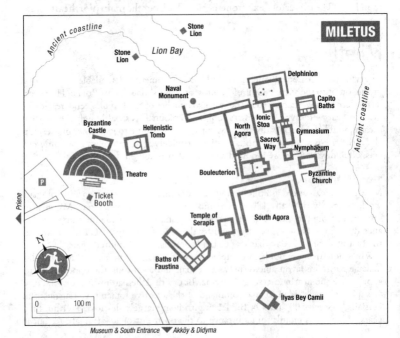

Museum & South Entrance ▼ *Akköy & Didyma*

and the chance to get your bearings on the rest of the site. Visible on the plain a kilometre or so to the west is a scrubby hill, formerly the **Island of Lade**.

Descending east of the walls, a round base marks the remains of the **naval monument**, commemorating an unknown victory of the first century BC, that once overlooked the most impressive of Miletus's four harbours, the "Lion Bay", so called for the two **stone lions** that guarded the entrance – now mostly embedded into the marsh silt.

The end of the tongue-shaped bay was lined by a colonnade that extended east to the sixth-century **Delphinion**, dedicated to Apollo Delphinius, patron of sailors, ships and ports. Not surprisingly in such a maritime community, it was the most important religious establishment in town. Today you can still see the foundations of altars or semicircular benches and the enclosing colonnade.

Both the Delphinion and the nearby **Selçuk baths** stand at the north end of a handsomely paved **Sacred Way**, which in its time linked Miletus with Didyma. On the same side of the pavement as you walk south stands a first-century AD **Ionic stoa**, which partly shields the enormous **Capito baths** and a **gymnasium** of the same era. The most satisfying monument east of the Sacred Way is the **nymphaeum**, the largest public fountain of Miletus, once extremely ornate but now standing at barely half its original height. Just to the south are the ruins of a sixth-century **Byzantine church**, while the Roman **Baths of Faustina** (Marcus Aurelius's wife), west of here at the foot of the theatre hill, are distinctive for their good state of repair.

About 200m to the south and marked by dense vegetation, the early fifteenth-century **İlyas Bey Camii**, built by that Menteşe emir to give thanks for his safe return from captivity by Tamerlane, lost its minaret in the 1958 earthquake that levelled nearby Balat. It otherwise fared well, retaining its fine carved-marble *mihrab*, stalactite vaulting and Arabic inscriptions. The entrance is particularly enchanting, with a carved marble screen flanking the door and triple bicoloured arches just outside.

Didyma

By the time you reach **Didyma** (Didim in Turkish) site fatigue might be beginning to set in. However, the oracular sanctuary of Apollo, though half-ruined and besieged throughout the middle of the day by swarms of tour groups, rarely fails to impress. The best time to visit – and the hour when, having worked their way through either Priene or Miletus or both, many people tend to show up – is late afternoon or early evening, when the masonry glows in the sunset. It's also possible to combine a visit to the ruins with hitting the nearby beach at **Altınkum** (not to be confused with the resort of the same name near İzmir), just 5km to the south. A gently sloping beach with no surf, it's ideal for children, although the packed-out sand and large British package presence means it's definitely not for everyone.

Some history

An oracle and shrine of some sort apparently existed at Didyma long before the arrival of the Ionian settlers in the eleventh century BC – the name itself is an ancient Anatolian word – but the imported **cult of Apollo** quickly appropriated whatever previous oracle, centred on a sacred well and laurel tree, had worked here. Didyma remained a sacred precinct, under the jurisdiction of a clan of priests originally from Delphi, and was never a town as such, though it eventually became a dependency of nearby Miletus. Every four years the sanctuary was also the venue for the Didymeia, a festival of music and drama as well as athletics.

The archaic shrine, begun during the eighth century BC, was finished within two hundred years, and though similar in design to the current structure, it was half the size. After their defeat of the Ionian revolt in 494 BC, the Persians destroyed this first temple and plundered its treasures, including the cult statue of Apollo. The oracle puttered along in reduced circumstances until Alexander appeared on the scene, when the cult statue was retrieved from Persia and a new temple (the one existing today) commissioned.

Despite continuing subsidy from the Romans, work continued at a snail's pace for more than five centuries and the building was never actually completed – not entirely surprising when you consider the formidable engineering problems presented. In the end Christianity put paid to the oracle, and when the edict of Theodosius in 385 AD proscribed all pagan practices, construction ceased for good, after which a medieval earthquake toppled most of the columns. At its zenith Didyma was approached not only from Miletus but also from Panormos, a cove 6km west, via a sacred way whose final stretches were lined with statuary. Neither pavement nor statues are visible today, the latter having been spirited away to the British Museum in 1858.

Arrival and accommodation

Hourly **dolmuşes** and full-size buses cover the route between Söke and Altınkum beach via **Didim village**, the modern name for Didyma. It's a fifty-minute ride to the village; ask to be dropped off at the junction 200m from the ruins, otherwise buses will continue on to the *otogar*, 2km out of Didim village to the west. The **restaurants** across from the archeological zone tend to be overpriced; for a good feed at reasonable prices, head up to the road towards **Yenihisar**.

The best of the limited nearby accommodation is the comfortable, characterful *Medusa House* (☎0256/811 0063, ⓦwww.medusahouse.com; ❼): run by a German–Turkish couple, it features rustic rooms in a restored old building with a lovely rambling garden.

The site

Entry to the **site** (daily 9am–7pm, closes 5.30pm winter; 3TL) is now by way of a gate to the north of the enclosure. At the bottom of the steps look out for the **Medusa head**, which fell from a Roman-era architrave and is now the unofficial logo of the place, repeated ad infinitum on posters and cards all over Turkey.

Pilgrims would first visit a **well** below the resting place of the Medusa head and purify themselves, then approach a still-prominent **circular altar** to offer a sacrifice before proceeding to the **shrine** itself. Even in ruins this is still intimidatingly large – the surviving column stumps alone are considerably taller than a man, and in its nearly complete state it must have inspired reverence. The effect was accentuated by the shrine's position on a steep, stepped base and enclosure in a virtual forest of 108 Ionic **columns** – though only three of these stand to their original height. The remaining twelve stumps supported the roof of the entry porch, reached by a steep flight of steps, where supplicants would deliver their queries to the priest of Apollo, who would reappear after a suitable interval on a terrace some six feet higher to deliver the prophetess's oracular pronouncement. Questions ranged from the personal to matters of state; prophecies were recorded and stored for posterity on the premises.

The cult statue of Apollo, his sacred laurel and the sacred well were formerly enclosed in a miniature shrine of which only traces remain – though the **well** itself is still obvious, roped off to prevent accidents. As at Delphi in Greece, prophecies were formulated by a priestess, who either (accounts disagree) drank from, bathed in or inhaled potent vapours from the waters. Her subsequent ravings were rephrased more delicately to those waiting out front: petitioners did not normally enter the inner sanctum, except to watch the goings-on of the Didymeia from a monumental stairway providing access to the terrace from the interior.

The southern Aegean

South of the main Ionian sites the southern Aegean begins with reminders of another ancient civilization, the **Carians**, a purportedly barbarous people indigenous to the area (a rarity in Anatolia) who spoke a language distantly related to Greek. **Bafa Gölü** (or Lake Bafa) and ancient **Heracleia ad Latmos** on its northeast shore make a suitably dramatic introduction to this once isolated and mysterious region. The nearest substantial town is **Milas**, from where the ancient sites of **Euromos**, **Labranda**, and **Iassos** provide tempting excursions.

South of Milas, on the Gulf of Gökova, **Ören** is a rare treat: an attractive coastal resort that has not yet been steamrollered by modern tourism. Most visitors bypass Ören in favour of **Bodrum** and its peninsula, very much the big tourist event on this coast. Here the tentacles of development creep over almost every available parcel of surrounding land – though what attracted outsiders to the area in the first place still shines through on occasion.

Moving on, **Muğla** makes for a pleasant stopover if you're passing through. Further south, **Marmaris** is another big – and rather overblown – resort, from which the **Loryma (Hisarönü) peninsula** beyond, bereft of a sandy shoreline but blessed with magnificent scenery, offers the closest escape. As a compromise, **Datça** and its surroundings might fit the bill, with some remote beaches nearby more rewarding than the much-touted ruins of ancient **Knidos**.

Bafa Gölü and Mount Latmos

Bafa Gölü (Lake Bafa), one of the most entrancing spectacles in southwestern Turkey, was created when silt deposited by the Büyük Menderes River sealed off the Latmos Gulf from the sea. The barren, weirdly sculpted pinnacles of ancient **Mount Latmos** (Beşparmak Dağı) still loom over the northeast shore, visible from a great distance west. Numerous islets dot the 100-square-kilometre lake, most of them sporting some sort of fortified Byzantine religious establishment, dating from the lake's days as an important monastic centre between the seventh and fourteenth centuries.

Bafa's west end was previously connected to the sea via canals and the Büyük Menderes (now permanently severed). As a result, the water is faintly brackish and fish species include *levrek* (bass), *kefal* (grey mullet), *yayın* (catfish) and *yılan balığı* (eel). Although locals track their depleting levels, stocks are still high enough to support the arrival throughout the year of more than two hundred species of migratory wildfowl, including the endangered crested pelican, of which there are believed to be less than two thousand left in the world.

Heracleia ad Latmos

Across Lake Bafa, most easily seen from the *Cerinin Yeri pansiyon*-restaurant, is a patch of irregular shoreline with a modern village, Kapıkırı, whose lights twinkle at the base of Mount Latmos by night. This is the site of **Heracleia ad Latmos** (Heraklia in Turkish) one of Turkey's most evocatively situated ancient cities.

A settlement of Carian origin had existed here long before the arrival of the Ionians, and Carian habits died hard, though Latmos – as it was then known – had far better geographical communication with Ionia than with the rest of Caria. Late in the Hellenistic period the city's location was moved a kilometre or so west, and the name changed to Heracleia, but despite adornment with numerous monuments and an enormous wall it was never a place of great importance. Miletus, at the head of the gulf, monopolized most trade and already the inlet was beginning to close up.

Heracleia owes its fame, and an enduring hold on the romantic imagination, to a legend associated not with the town itself but with Mount Latmos behind. **Endymion** was a handsome shepherd who, while asleep in a cave on the mountain, was noticed by Selene, the moon goddess. She made love with him as he slept and in time, so the story goes, bore Endymion fifty daughters without their sire ever waking once. Endymion was reluctant for all this to stop and begged Zeus, who was also fond of him, to be allowed to dream forever; his wish was granted and, as a character in Mary Lee Settle's *Blood Ties* flippantly observed, thus became the only known demigod of the wet dream.

The site

Arriving by car, you can park your vehicle next to one of the pensions (see "Practicalities", below). Alternatively, there's a parking area about 300m up the hill. The site is not enclosed, though you'll have to pay 8TL **admission** if you're not staying overnight.

The crudely signposted **bouleuterion** lies 100m to the east of the first parking area, though only the retaining wall and some rows of benches are left of the second-century BC structure. The **Roman baths** visible in the valley below, and a crumbled but appealing **Roman theatre** off in the olives beyond, can be reached via an unmarked trail starting between the first and second parking areas. The path up to the **hermits' caves** on Mount Latmos begins at the rear of the second parking area. Stout boots are advisable, as is a cool day in early spring or late autumn – for a place still so close to the sea, Heracleia can be surprisingly hot and airless. Similar cautions apply for those who want to trace the course of the **Hellenistic walls**, the city's most imposing and conspicuous relics, supposedly built by Lysimachus in the late third century BC.

The *Agora Pansiyon*'s restaurant looks south over the **Hellenistic agora**, now an open, grassy square; the downhill side of its south edge stands intact to two storeys, complete with windows. From the grounds you've a fine view west over the lake and assorted castle-crowned promontories. A box-like Hellenistic **Temple of Athena** perches on a hill west of the agora; less conspicuous is an inscription to Athena, left of the entrance.

From the agora a wide, walled-in path descends toward the shore and the final quota of recognizable monuments at Heracleia. Most obvious is the peninsula – or, in wet years, island – studded with **Byzantine walls** and a **church**. A stone causeway half-buried in the beach here allowed entrance in what must have been drier medieval times. Follow the shore southwest, and across the way you should be able to spot the tentatively identified Hellenistic **Sanctuary of Endymion**, oriented unusually northeast to southwest. Five column stumps front the structure, which has a rounded rear wall – a ready-made apse for later Christians – with sections of rock incorporated into the masonry.

Practicalities

Bus services past Lake Bafa are frequent, but Söke–Milas dolmuşes (every 30min) are more flexible than the big coaches in terms of stopping. The southern shore of Bafa, which the main highway follows, is the location of a few combination **campsite-pansiyon-restaurants**, best thought of as a serene setting for lunch (at least for those in their own vehicle). Heading east, the most acceptable of these are the basic *Ceri'nin Yeri Pansiyon* (℡0252/510 1011, ⓦwww.bafaceri.com; ❹), with a restaurant menu that varies with the day's catch, and the *Club Natura Oliva* (℡0252/519 1073, ⓦwww.clubnatura.com; ❻), a German-owned establishment with thirty very large, if somewhat spartan rooms, in nine houses, all with balconies overlooking the lake. There's also a restaurant serving a wide range of dishes (doused in their own olive oil), and guided hikes of the local area are also offered.

Swimming is best from the far side of the monastery-capped islet, which in dry years is joined to *Ceri's* restaurant by a muddy spit. On the islet, some flattish rocks offer a weed-free corridor out onto the lake, or dive instead off the end of the wooden jetty.

The most common access to Heracleia is by **boat** from *Ceri'nin Yeri*. Tours generally take around half a day, and prices vary according to the number of people in your group.

Alternatively, drive east to Çamiçi village (6km beyond *Ceri'nin Yeri*) and then turn left at the signpost ("Herakleia"). The eight-kilometre paved road leads to the modern village of **KAPIKIRI**, built higgledy-piggledy among the ruins. Scattered in and around Kapıkırı are a few simple **pansiyons** and **restaurants**; most are open from March to October. *Selene's*, near the waterfront (℡0252/543 5221, ⓦwww.bafalake .com; ❺), offers basic rooms and a lakeside restaurant. The *Agora Pansiyon* (℡0252/543 5445, ⓦwww.herakleia.com; half-board obligatory ❼) has doubles, bungalows and a rooftop restaurant arranged around their organic garden: they can also organize guided hikes to nearby cave paintings and boat trips on the lake.

Milas and around

A small, initially nondescript town of some 35,000 people, **MILAS** – or **Mylasa**, as it was formerly known – was an important Carian centre (its original location was at the nearby hill of **Peçin Kale**). While it's unlikely that most foreigners would want to stay the night here, there are a few sights of interest, should you need to fill a few hours between buses.

An elaborate early Roman tomb known as the **Gümüşkesen** (literally "cuts-silver") is the most obviously impressive relic of ancient Mylasa. The way there is poorly marked from the town centre, but the monument is easy enough to find by heading 500m west along Kadıağa Caddesi, which soon becomes the slightly sloping Gümüşkesen Caddesi. There are no formal visiting hours nor an admission fee to the landscaped site, which lies in a slight depression south of Hıdırlık hill. Milas's lively tradesmen's **bazaar** covers the western slopes of Hisarbaşı hill, which has been the focus of settlement in every era. Once past the warren of alleys perpendicular to the main Cumhuriyet Caddesi, veer up to the summit and the late Ottoman **Belen Camii**. Immediately to its right stands the eighteenth-century **Çöllühanı**, one of the last semi-functioning, unrestored *kervansarays* in western Turkey.

The original site of ancient Mylasa on the hill of **Peçin Kale** (*Beçin Kale* in local dialect and signposting), 5km east of Milas, lies just off the road leading southeast to the Gulf of Gökova. Mylasa's shift to its current position during the fourth century BC means that the hill is actually more interesting for its **castle** (daily except Thurs 8.30am–5.30pm; 3TL) an unmistakable fortified bluff, originally Byzantine but adapted by the Menteşe emirs during the fourteenth century. About 400m south from the castle, the main Menteşe buildings are clearly marked, including the unusual two-storeyed **Kızıl Han**, and the fourteenth-century **Orhan Bey Camii**. Bearing right takes you to the **medrese and türbe of Ahmet Gazi**, from the same era – tombs of a Menteşe governor and his wife that are venerated as those of minor Islamic saints, with coloured rags and candles. Take any Ören-bound dolmuş from town (every 45min) and ask to be dropped at the *Beçin Kale* turn-off.

Practicalities

Milas's **otogar** is way out on the northern edge of town, near the junction for Labranda. You'll be left here unless you've come from Güllük or Ören, whose dolmuşes have a separate **terminal** close to the town centre. Getting into the centre from the *otogar*, take either a dolmuş marked "Şehir İçi" or the complimentary shuttle run by the big companies. The drop-off/pick-up point is the pavement south of the *Köşem* restaurant and city park; there's no fixed rank – just wait around. The Havaş bus to **Milas airport** stops at the roundabout at the end of Atatürk Bulvarı and is geared to the times of THY internal flights.

The only central, savoury budget **accommodation** you'll find is the *Yazar Otel* (℡0252/512 4203; ❷) on Kadıağa Caddesi close to the bazaar and Halk bank; it has comfortable rooms with TV and minibar. The surprisingly large *Sürücü Otel* on Atatürk Bulvarı (opposite the Atatürk statue; ℡0252/512 4001, ⓦwww .surucuotel.com; ❸) is a few hundred metres out of the centre and also good value if a little lacking in character; its attached restaurant and café are frequented by students from the nearby university.

Euromos and Labranda

A short distance northwest of Milas lie two impressive Carian ruins: **Euromos** (daily except Sat 8.30am–5.30pm; 8TL), which is easily reached from Milas by taking a dolmuş towards Selimiye (every twenty minutes between 7am and 7pm); and isolated **Labranda** (daily except Tues 8.30am–5.30pm; 8TL) for which you'll really need your own vehicle to visit, as dolmuşes only take you halfway. A treat for dedicated ruin enthusiasts, the former boasts a Corinthian Temple of Zeus, while the latter's sanctuary of Zeus is arguably the most beautifully set, and least visited, archeological zone of ancient Caria.

Iassos

Set on a headland almost completely surrounded by the Gulf of Asim, 15km east of Milas, the ancient site of **Iassos** certainly has a dramatic location although its ruins, dating mostly from the Roman Imperial period of the second century AD, are only mildly diverting. The real reason to make a trip here is the delicious seafood caught nearby and served in the restaurants of the modern village of Kıyıkızlacık.

On entering Kıyıkızlacık, next to the ruins, you first pass a Roman mausoleum, arguably more interesting than anything within the city walls and now in service as the site **museum** (erratic hours; 4TL). Inside, the star exhibit is a Corinthian temple-tomb resting on a stepped platform. The main highlights of the **site** itself (daily except Wed; 4TL admission when staff present) are the well-preserved Roman **bouleuterion**, with four rows of seats and a Roman **villa** with murals and mosaics. The meagre hillside **theatre**, of which only the cavea walls and stumps of the stage building remain offers fine views over the northeast harbour. The hilltop **castle** was a medieval foundation of the Knights of St John, and after the Turkish conquest the place was known as Asimkalesi (Asim's Castle), Asim being a local *ağa* (feudal lord).

Practicalities

There's an hourly dolmuş service to Kıyıkızlacık **from Milas**, 15km to the east. The turning is 8km west of Milas – a pretty drive, first across a plain planted with cotton, then through pine- and olive-studded hills.

In Kıyıkızlacık village, four or five **restaurants** specialize in fish, in particular the cheap and excellent local *çipura* (gilthead bream), and there are a few summer-season **pansiyons** up the hill, overlooking the rather murky fishing and yacht harbour.

Ören

ÖREN is an endangered Turkish species – a coastal resort that's not completely overdeveloped. It's one of the few sizable villages on the north coast of the Gulf of Gökova, and owes its pre-tourism history to the narrow, fertile, alluvial plain adjacent, and the lignite deposits in the mountains behind.

The **upper village**, on the east bank of a canyon mouth exiting the hills, is an appealingly homogenous settlement, scattered among the ruins of **ancient Keramos**. You can easily make out sections of wall, arches and a boat slip, dating from the time when the sea (now 1km distant) lapped the edge of town. The **resort area** down on the coast has little in the way of relics, save for sections of column carted off from the main site by *pansiyon* owners for use as decoration. The **beach** is a more than acceptable kilometre of coarse sand, gravel and pebbles, backed by handsome pine-tufted cliffs; in clear weather you can spy the Datça peninsula opposite. Once there was a working harbour at the east end of the town, but what's left of the jetty now serves a few fishing boats and the occasional wandering yacht.

Dolmuşes from Milas take an hour to reach Ören. Having passed through the upper village you'll be dropped at the beach. Should you plan on **staying**, the best mid-range option is the *Hotel Alnata* (☏0252/532 2813, ⓦwww.alnata.com .tr; ⑥), at the west end of the beach, with large, stylish rooms, a garden and pool. The *Kerme* (☏0252/532 2065; ⑤), with a rudimentary **campsite**, simple wooden cottages and attached seafood and kebab restaurant down on the shore is another good choice.

Bodrum

In the eyes of its devotees, **BODRUM**, with its low-rise whitewashed houses and subtropical gardens, is the longest established, most attractive and most versatile Turkish resort – a quality outfit in comparison to its Aegean rivals, Marmaris and Kuşadası. However, the town's recent attempts to be all things to all tourists have made it more difficult to tell the difference, while the controlled development within the municipality – height limits and a preservation code are in force – has resulted in exploitation of the nearby peninsula, until recently little disturbed. The airport at Milas enables easy access for both tourists and İstanbul-based weekenders, the latter's fondness for the peninsula inflating prices in general.

The Bodrum area has long attracted large numbers of Britons, both the moneyed yacht set and the charter-flight trade, and most of the big UK package-tour operators are active here. If you want waterborne distractions laid on by day and some of the most sophisticated nightlife in Turkey (complete with imported DJs), then Bodrum town, and Gümbet in particular, will probably suit. If you're after a coastal tranquillity with plenty of local character, then peninsular outposts such as Gümüşlük and Akyarlar more closely answer to the description.

Some history

Bodrum, originally known as **Halikarnassos**, was colonized by Dorians from the Peloponnese during the eleventh century BC. They mingled with the existing Carian population, settling on the small island of Zephysia, which in later ages became a peninsula and the location of the medieval castle. During the fifth century BC, **Halikarnassos'** most famous son **Herodotus** chronicled the city's fortunes in his acclaimed *Histories*.

Mausolus (377–353 BC), leader of the **Hecatomnid satraps** dynasty, soon increased the power and wealth of what had already become a semi-independent principality. An admirer of Greek civilization, Mausolus spared no effort to Hellenize his cities, and was working on a suitably self-aggrandizing tomb at the time of his death – thereby giving us the word "mausoleum". **Artemisia II**, his sister and wife, completed the massive structure, which came to be regarded as one of the Seven Wonders of the Ancient World. Like her ancestor Artemisia I, she distinguished herself in warfare, inflicting a humiliating defeat on the Rhodians, who were tricked into allowing her entire fleet into their port.

In 334 BC the rampaging Alexander's arrival coincided with a bitter succession feud between Artemisia's heirs. The Macedonian armies wreaked such havoc that the city never fully recovered. After a period of little importance under the Roman and Byzantine empires, and brief shuffling among Selçuk, Menteşe and Ottoman occupiers, the **Knights of St John** slipped over from Rhodes in 1402 and erected the castle that is now Bodrum's most prominent landmark. Urgently needing to replace the fortress at Smyrna destroyed by the Mongols, the Knights engaged the best military engineers of the era to construct their new stronghold on the promontory. The name *bodrum*, meaning "cellar" or "dungeon" in Turkish, probably pays tribute to the stronghold's subterranean defences. After Süleyman the Magnificent compelled the Knights to depart in 1523, the castle's history was virtually synonymous with that of the town until the twentieth century.

Arrival, orientation and information

International and domestic **ferries** (from Marmaris, Datça, Dalyan, Kós and Rhodes) dock at the jetty west of the castle. Buses drop you at the **otogar**, 500m up Cevat Şakir Caddesi, which links Şehir Meydanı with the main peninsular highway and divides the town roughly in two. Havaş buses run to and from the Milas/Bodrum **airport** (ⓌÿÞwww.bodrum-airport.com), located 35km northeast of town. Otherwise the only other option is taking a taxi, which costs around 75TL.

Cevat Şakir's approximate pedestrianized continuation, Kale Caddesi, defines one edge of the bazaar, huddling in the shadow of the medieval castle. Kale Caddesi ends at İskele Meydanı, officially known as Barış Meydanı and home to the **tourist office** (Mon–Sat 9am–5.30pm; ℡0252/316 1091).

Northwest of Cevat Şakir Caddesi is the service-oriented side of town. Travel, yacht and car rental agencies (the latter also clustered around the *otogar*) line Neyzen Tevfik Caddesi, which continues westwards from Şehir Meydanı. Its most important side streets, especially when hunting for accommodation, are Menekşe Çıkmazı and Türkkuyusu Caddesi.

Driving is difficult in Bodrum, made all the more so by a strict, counter-clockwise one-way system. **Parking** is even more frustrating: shelling out for car-park fees

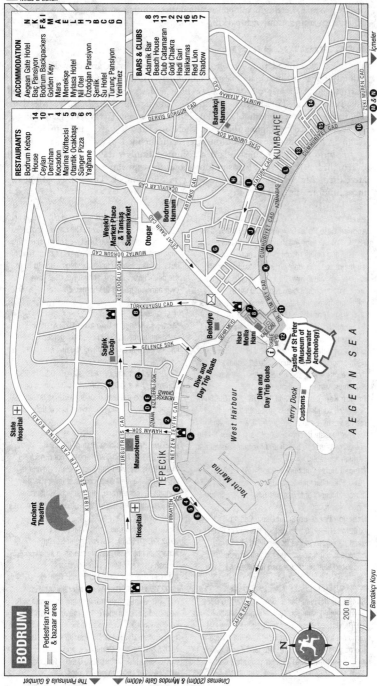

BODRUM

Pedestrian zone
& bazaar area

RESTAURANTS

Bodrum Kebap House	14
Ceylan	10
Denizhan	1
Kocadon	4
Marina Köftecisi	5
Otantik Ocakbaşı	9
Sünger Pizza	6
Yağhane	3

ACCOMMODATION

Aegean Gate Hotel	N
Baç Pansiyon	K
Bodrum Backpackers	F & I
Golden Key	M
Mars	A
Menekşe	E
Mylasa Hotel	L
Nil Otel	H
Özdoğan Pansiyon	J
Şenlik	B
Su Hotel	C
Turung Pansiyon	G
Yenilmez	D

BARS & CLUBS

Adamik Bar	8
Beach House	13
Club Catamaran	11
Gold Chakra	2
Hadi Gari	12
Halikarnas	16
Red Lion	15
Shadow	7

Milas & Güllük

İçmeler

ZEKİ MÜREN CAD

M & N

DERVİŞ GÖRGÜN CAD

Bardakçı Hamam

KUMBAHÇE

MÜMTAZ ATAMAN CAD

DERE UMURCA SOK

CUMHURİYET CAD

ÜÇKUYULAR CAD

ARTEMİS CAD

Bodrum Hamam

Otogar

Weekly Market Place & Tansaş Supermarket

ÇESME SAKİR CAD

MÜMTAZ GÖRGÜN CAD

AZMAKBAŞI

ATATÜRK CAD

CAFER PAŞA SOK

KILCIOĞLU SOK

TÜRKKUYUSU CAD

Sağlık Ocağı

State Hospital

KIBRIS ŞEHİTLERİ CAD (RİNG ROAD)

Ancient Theatre

Hospital

TURGUTREİS CAD

Mausoleum

TEPECİK

NEYZEN TEVFİK CAD

HAMAM SOK

FIRKATEYN SOK

DZMAN

MENEKŞE ÇIKMAZI

KIZILDERELİ SOK

Yacht Marina

GELENCE SOK

Belediye

ŞEHİR MEYD

Haci Molla Hani

KALE CAD

İSKELE MEYD

Castle of St Peter (Museum of Underwater Archeology)

West Harbour

Dive and Day Trip Boats

Dive and Day Trip Boats

Ferry Dock

Customs

AEGEAN SEA

N

0   200 m

The Peninsula & Gümbet

Cinemas (200m) & Myndos Gate (400m)

Bardakçı Koyu

CUMHURİYET CAD

ZEKİ MÜREN CAD

or, even worse, getting a vehicle out of impoundment is disheartening, so we've noted accommodation with parking space.

Accommodation

The best accommodation is concentrated in three main areas: in **Kumbahçe Mahalle**, near the beach and bars of Cumhuriyet Caddesi; in the calmer **Tepecik** district, along or just off Neyzen Tevfik Caddesi; and on the convenient and usually peaceful **Türkkuyusu Caddesi**, winding up from Belediye Meydanı. There are also several desirable locales along, or just off, **Turgutreis Caddesi**.

Prices tend to be higher than elsewhere in Turkey, particularly in July and August, when advance reservations are recommended. Beware the touts at the *otogar*, who often ply substandard accommodation to travellers fresh from an overnight bus ride. Out of season most hotels (except those with central heating) are closed. Air conditioning is a necessity in midsummer. Thankfully all but the most humble *pansiyon*s have it.

Kumbahçe Mahalle

Aegean Gate Hotel Güvercin Sok 2 ☏ 0252/313 7853, Ⓦ www.aegeangatehotel.com A wildly popular and highly recommended option, half a kilometre past the *Halikarnas* nightclub, boasting stupendous views over Bodrum bay. It's centred around an enchanting swimming pool: the minimum two-night stay is an enforced luxury. ⑥

🧗 **Baç Pansiyon** Cumhuriyet Cad 14 ☏ 0252/313 1602. This luxurious, but surprisingly affordable, decade-old boutique hotel is located right in the heart of the action. The stylish rooms are all double-glazed, cutting out much of the noise, and those at the rear have balconies with views of the castle. ⑤

Golden Key Şalvarağa Sok 18 ☏ 0252/313 0304, Ⓦ www.goldenkeyhotels.com. Small luxury hotel at the far eastern end of the seafront with seven lavishly furnished rooms, all with sea views. It also has its own private beach and excellent restaurant. Parking available. ⑧

Mylasa Hotel Cumhuriyet Cad 34 ☏ 0252/316 1846. Friendlier, quieter and better value than the surrounding options with a simple, 1970s, interior. Open year-round. ④

Özdoğan Pansiyon Sanat Okulu Cad 11 ☏ 0252/316 2220. The pick of the row of three quiet *pansiyon*s in this flower-filled alley. No breakfast, but it does have a small terrace bedecked with plastic garden furniture. ④

Türkkuyusu Caddesi

Şenlik Türkkuyusu Cad 115/A ☏ 0252/316 6382, Ⓦ www.senlikpansiyon.com. A slightly shabby 1970s-vintage *pansiyon* with a giant communal terrace, shaded by lush vines. There's a choice of rooms with or without en-suite facilities. ③

🧗 **Su Hotel** 1201 Sok off Turgutreis Cad ☏ 0252/316 6906, Ⓦ www.suhotel.net.

A large well-equipped complex laid out around one of the biggest pools in town. The cheery multi-coloured rooms all have balconies overlooking the central courtyard where there's a cute bar. The hotel is inaccessible to cars (which helps to keep the noise levels down), although it does have its own parking around the corner. ⑦

Tepecik

Menekşe Menekşe Çıkmazı ☏ 0252/316 5890. Good-value rooms set in peaceful gardens. There's limited parking (and stroking the numerous pets is free!). ④

Yenilmez Menekşe Çıkmazı 30 ☏ 0252/316 2520. Central, quiet, modern *pansiyon* with a nice garden; a good option if the next-door *Menekşe* is full. Breakfast in the shady courtyard is a delight. ④

Turgutreis Caddesi

Bodrum Backpackers Atatürk Cad 31 ☏ 0252/313 2762, Ⓦ www.bodrumbackpackers .net. Big, noisy, well-run backpackers' favourite offering clean, well-kept dorms, a few private doubles, a roof terrace, internet access, laundry service and a bar, the latter a great place to meet other travellers. ①

Mars Turgutreis Cad, İmbat Çıkmazı 20 ☏ 0252/316 6559, Ⓦ www.marsotel.com. A tranquil hotel with simple rooms, a small pool, Turkish bath and lively poolside bar. ④

Nil Otel Omurça Mah. Üçkuyular Cad. No:16 ☏ 0252/316 8068, Ⓦ www.nilotel.com. Family-run with a magnificent courtyard complete with pool and patio furniture. Rooms are clean but very basic. ④

Turunç Pansiyon 1923 Sokak off Atatürk Cad ☏ 0252/316 5333. Brand new and clean as a whistle, if a little uninspired. Calm – for Bodrum – with entirely en-suite guestrooms. ④

The Town

The castle neatly divides the town into two contrasting halves: to the west is the more genteel area that surrounds the spruced-up yacht marina, with its upmarket hotels and restaurants; while to the east is the town's party zone where you'll find the highest concentration of bars and restaurants. Immediately to the north of the castle lies the **bazaar**, most of which is pedestrianized along its two main thorough-fares of Kale and Dr Alim Bey caddesi; traffic enters the dense warren of streets to the southeast via Atatürk Caddesi, 200m inland. East of the spot called **Azmakbaşı** (Creek Mouth), Alim Bey becomes Cumhuriyet Caddesi (the two roads are jointly referred to locally as **Uzunyol** – Long Street), which overlooks a thin strip of beach: despite its somewhat scrubby appearance, it's packed to bursting with sunbathers during the day and shoreline diners in the evening.

▲ Bodrum's Castle of St Peter

The Castle of St Peter

Sitting on a promontory splitting the inner and outer harbours, Bodrum's main landmark is the **Castle of St Peter**, now home to the town's cultural centrepiece, the **Museum of Underwater Archaeology** (Tues–Sun 9am–5pm; 10TL). Despite the commercialization of the grounds, the museum is well worth visiting, with its array of towers, courtyards and dungeons, as well as separate museums displaying underwater finds from various wrecks.

The castle was built by the Knights of St John in 1406, over a small Selçuk fortress. More walls and moats were added over succeeding decades along with water cisterns to guarantee self-sufficiency in the event of siege. The finishing touches had just been applied in 1522 when Süleyman's capture of the Knights' headquarters on Rhodes made their position here untenable. Bodrum's castle was subsequently neglected until the nineteenth century, when the chapel was converted to a mosque, the keep to a prison, and a hamam installed. The castle was damaged by shells during World War I and was not properly refurbished until the 1960s, when it was converted into a museum.

Visiting the castle

Initial entrance is through the **west gate**, looking on to the water. Once inside the west moat, you'll notice bits of ancient masonry from the mausoleum incorporated into the walls, as well as some of the 249 Christian coats of arms.

Stairs lead up to the seaward fortifications and then into the **lower courtyard**. To the right, the **chapel** houses a fascinating reconstruction of a seventh-century Byzantine ship, whose remains were excavated off Yassıada. The display, incorporating the salvaged hull, shows how such ships were loaded with cargoes of amphorae. A building at the base of the **Italian Tower** holds a small glass collection, mostly Roman and early Islamic work.

There's a more substantial display in the so-called **Glass Wreck Hall** (Tues–Fri 10am–noon & 2–4pm; 5TL separate admission), which houses a Byzantine shipwreck and cargo found 33m down at Serçe Limanı in 1973. Dating from 1025, this was a peacetime trading vessel plying between Fatimid and Byzantine territories. The craft – tubby and flat-bottomed to permit entry to the Mediterranean's many shallow straits – is displayed in a climate-controlled environment, though only twenty percent of the original timbers are preserved. The rest is a mock-up, loaded with a fraction of the cargo: two tonnes of raw coloured glass. Also displayed are the personal effects of the passengers and crew, including gaming pieces, tools and grooming items. All told, it's a well-labelled and well-lit exhibit, worth the extra expense if you can coincide with the restricted opening hours.

The **Uluburun Wreck Hall** (Tues–Fri 10am–noon & 2–4pm; free) on the east side of the castle precinct houses the local Bronze Age and Mycenaean collection. It features artefacts recovered from three Aegean wrecks, including finds from the Uluburun site near Kaş.

On the next level up, the linked Italian and French towers are now home to a gift shop. Just beyond, the **Carian Princess Hall** (same hours as the Glass Wreck Hall; 5TL separate admission) contains artefacts from an ancient tomb found miraculously unlooted during hotel-building works in 1989. The sarcophagus, with its skeleton of a Carian noblewoman who died in the fourth century BC, is on view, along with a scant number of gold tomb finds, which were almost certainly imported, as the metal is not found locally.

The English Tower, upper courtyard and dungeon

Although financed and built by English Knights during the 15th century, the **English Tower**, at the southeast corner of the castle precinct, now appears a bald

Boat trips and cruises around Bodrum

It's almost impossible to miss the touts for **boat trips** in Bodrum and, if you're not planning to tour the area by land, they are worth taking advantage of. Most of the craft are concentrated on the west harbour, and a typical day out starts around 10.30am and finishes around 4pm, costing roughly 25TL per person (including lunch). Itineraries vary little, with most boats visiting the following attractions.

First stop is the Akvaryum, a snorkellers' venue in the Ada Boğazı (Island Strait): the fish, however, have been frightened off by the crowds of humans and motor noise, and are now seldom seen. Next halt is usually Kara Ada, a sizable island southeast of town, where you bathe in some hot springs issuing from a cave at the island's margin. The final moorings are often Kızıl Burnu (Red Bay) and Tavşan Burnu (Rabbit Bay, devoid of rabbits). Note that boats can range from sleepy 15-person *gulets* to wild party barges squeezing in 70 passengers: choose wisely.

If you're up for something a little more upscale, opt to hire your own (fully staffed) boat. Most set cruises hug the scenic Gökova gulf coast en route to Marmaris, though individual itineraries are catered for. Akustik Travel and Yachting (Ⓦwww.travel bodrum.com) is a long-running outfit offering personalized yacht tours, while S&J Travel & Yachting (Ⓦwww.sjyachting.com) specializes in custom-itinerary *gulet* hire.

---

attempt to pander to Bodrum's major foreign constituency. Inside is a themed cafeteria, around which assorted standards of the Order of St John and of their Muslim adversaries compete for wall space with an incongruous array of medieval armour and weapons. Many visitors attempt to decipher extensive swathes of Latin graffiti incised into the window jambs by bored Knights.

Finish your tour by crossing the **upper courtyard**, landscaped like much of the castle grounds with native flora, to the **German Tower**, with an exhibition of Ottoman royal *tuğras* (seals), and the **Snake Tower** – named for the serpent relief plaque over the entrance.

East of these, it's possible to make a long, dead-end detour, to the Knights' former **dungeon**, adorned with dangling chains and bathed in lurid red light. In case you missed the point, an original Latin inscription over the door reads "Here God does not exist".

The Mausoleum and ancient theatre

A ten-minute walk northwest of the castle, the remains of the **Mausoleum** (daily except Mon in winter 9am–5pm; 4TL) can be found along Turgutreis Caddesi. Designed by Pytheos, architect of the Athena temple at Priene, the complete structure measured 39m by 33m at its base and stood nearly 60m high. A colonnade surmounted the burial vault and supported a stepped pyramidal roof bearing a chariot (now in the British Museum) with effigies of Mausolus and his sister-wife Artemisia. Despite diligent work by archeologists, little is left of the original mausoleum. Visitors can examine the precinct wall, assorted column fragments and some subterranean vaults probably belonging to an earlier burial chamber. In a shed east of the foundation cavity are exhibited plans and models, as well as copies of the original friezes in England.

By way of contrast the **ancient theatre**, just above the main highway bounding Bodrum to the north, has been almost overzealously restored. Begun by Mausolus, it was modified in the Roman era and originally seated 13,000, though it has a present capacity of about half that. The so-called **Myndos Gate**, west of the junction of Turgutreis and Cafer Paşa caddesis, is the best surviving section of Mausolus's ambitious city wall, though remains of five towers are spread round the town.

Eating

Eating out in Bodrum can be pricey, especially if you're close to the water or in a chichi restaurant. Dismal fast-food joints offering British food abound, although if you know where to look, the dining scene can herald more than a couple of pleasant surprises.

A good place to start is the vine-covered **Meyhanelar Caddesi** in the bazaar where a number of small restaurants vie to offer you the traditional Turkish experience. Anywhere else, especially overlooking either bay, you can expect a jump up in price. Near the harbour, there is a cluster of upmarket restaurants boasting a high standard of cuisine; better value are the "meal deal" restaurants just east of here that offer a beer, salad, grilled fish, chips and sides for around TL15.

Bodrum Kebap House Atatürk Cad 90. Offering an authentic range of kebabs, as well as grilled chicken and *köfte*. Squeeze in among the locals; typically 15TL a head.

Ceylan Cumhuriyet Cad, 112 ☏0252/313 3637. Elegantly understated waterside eatery with glitzy tableware, exciting array of *meze* and solid wine list.

Denizhan Turgut Reis Yolu ☏0252/363 7674. West of town, past the antique theatre, this spot is well worth the trip if you fancy spoiling yourself. Dishes are based around a lavish selection of kebabs.

Kocadon Saray Sok ☏0252/316 3705. Traditional Ottoman cuisine served up in an elegant cobbled courtyard. Stick with the *meze* for 10–12TL unless you want to break the bank.

Marina Köftecisi Neyzen Tevfik Cad 214 ☏0252/313 5593. Lively kebab and *köfte* joint with heaps

of outdoor seating and bargain prices.

Otantik Ocakbaşı Atatürk Cad 12/B ☏0252/313 0058. Excellent *meze*, wood-fired *pide* and grilled meats dished up on a breezy outdoor terrace. Licensed.

Sünger Pizza Neyzen Tevfik Cad 218. Cheap, cheerful and popular pizza restaurant, with excellent views from its rooftop; justifiably packed with yachties and locals most evenings. Delivery service available.

Yağhane Neyzen Tevlik Cad 170 ☏0252/313 2732. The burning torches outside this former olive-oil factory make this refined restaurant easy to spot: the distinguished old building is festooned with bougainvillea and the menu thick with French influences. A two-course meal without wine costs around 30TL.

Drinking, nightlife and entertainment

There must be over sixty places to drink and dance in Bodrum, most of them lining Dr Alim Bey Caddesi (where many of the bars on the seaward side lead straight through to a waterfront area) and its continuation, Cumhuriyet Caddesi. All get packed and sweaty on a summer night, with the busiest hours from 11pm to 3am. Many locals are seasonal establishments, consisting of just a bar with a small dancefloor, and few have cover charges, though drink prices are high.

Visitors seeking evening entertainment outside the clubbing scene would do well to plan a visit during April, when Bodrum hosts its new annual Rocks Fest (Ⓦwww.bodrumrocksfest.com), or during August for the town's yearly Ballet Festival (Ⓦwww.bodrumballetfestival.org).

Bars and clubs

The ultimate experience is *Halikarnas* (☏0252/316 8000, Ⓦwww.halikarnas.com .tr), an outdoor club at the eastern end of Cumhuriyet Caddesi. A 30TL cover charge (35TL on Friday and Saturday) and proper dress sees you in with the beautiful people, up to 5000 of them on the mammoth dancefloor. At the western end of Alim Bey, near the tourist office, stands *Hadi Gari* (☏0252/316 0048, Ⓦwww.hadigari.com.tr), another acclaimed disco-club with four different bars and space for 2000 revellers.

Between these two super-clubs are a glut of similar bars dotted along Cumhuriyet Caddesi including *Beach House* and *Red Lion*, all offering happy hours and last season's chart hits. Just inside the bazaar on Banka Sokak is *Shadow*, a live rock bar, and the more chilled *Adamik Bar*. More upscale are the late-night joints just west along Neyzen Tevfik Caddesi, including the exclusive *Gold Chakra*.

Bodrum's latest blowout is *Club Catamaran* (☎0252/316 3600, ⓦwww.club catamaran.com), a disco-boat which leaves port at 10pm and glams it up on the ocean waves until dawn.

Listings

4

Airlines THY (Turkish Airlines), Kıbrıs Şehitleri Cad 82/2/22 ☎0252/317 1203. THY ticket-holders can book here for the shuttle bus to Milas airport; Havaş buses (ⓦwww.havas.com.tr) run between the Milas airport and Bodrum's *otogar* (17TL), and are timed to correspond with flights.

Car rental Avis, Neyzen Tevfik Cad 66/A ☎0252/316 2333, and at Milas airport domestic terminal ☎0252/523 0201, international terminal ☎0252/523 0203; Budget, at Milas airport ☎0252/523 0271; Europcar, Neyzen Tevfik Cad 224 ☎0252/313 0885, and at Milas airport ☎0252/559 0214; and Hertz, Neyzen Tevfik Cad 232 ☎0252/318 1053.

Consulate Honorary British Consulate, Cafer Paşa Cad 2. Emsan Evleri No:7 ☎0252/313 0021, ⓦukinturkey.fco.gov.uk.

Diving Most of the long-running outfits listed below offer courses, tours and servicing, including Aquapro, ☎0252/313 8212, ⓦwww.aquapro-turkey.com. In the west harbour, dive boats offer a full day out, usually including gear rental and lunch for €45.

Ferries and hydrofoils There are domestic services to Marmaris, Dalyan and Datça as well as the short hops to Kós and to Rhodes in Greece; see "Travel details" at the end of this chapter for schedules and prices. Buy tickets from: Bodrum

Express (Kale Cad 18 ☎0252/316 1087, ⓦwww.bodrumexpresslines.com) for hydrofoils; and Bodrum Ferryboat Association (outside Customs on the jetty ☎0252/316 0882, ⓦwww .bodrumferryboat.com) for ferries.

Hamam Bodrum Hamam (ⓦwww.bodrumhamami .com.tr) on Cevat Şakir Cad opposite the *otogar* (daily segregated bathing 6am–midnight) and Bardakçi Hamam on Dere Umurca Sok (daily 8am–8pm; later in summer according to demand).

Hospitals The English-speaking Karia Medical Centre, Kıbrıs Şehitler Cad 97 (☎0252/313 6233), and Medicare, Hamam Sok 4 (☎0252/316 7051), both promise 24hr, seven-day attention. The City Hospital (Devlet Hastanesi; ☎0252/313 1420) is on Elmadağ Cad.

Laundry Mavi, Turgutreis Cad, Davutlar Sok 3.

Newspapers Books are hard to come by, but English-language newspapers can be purchased at the kiosk at the eastern end of Şehir Meydanı.

Pharmacies Eczane Oasis, Oasis Alışveriş Merkezi ☎0252/317 0507.

Police Dr Alim Bey Cad ☎0252/316 1216; Emergency ☎0252/316 1004.

Post office PTT at Cevat Şakir Cad.

Supermarkets Migros, near the turning for Gümbet; Tansaş, by the *otogar.*

Around the peninsula

There is more of interest and beauty in the rest of the **Bodrum peninsula**, and no matter how long or short your stay, time spent exploring it is well worthwhile. The north side of the peninsula tends to be greener, with patches of pine forest; the south, studded with tall crags, is more arid, with a sandier coast.

The population was largely Greek Orthodox before 1923 and villages often still have a vaguely Hellenic feel, with ruined churches, windmills and old stone houses. In recent years, waves of new villas have smothered much of the coast; though, having run out of cash, many of the building projects remain eerily abandoned. An exotic touch is lent by the ubiquitous, white-domed *gümbets* (cisterns) and by the camel caravans – not mere tourist photo ops, but working draught animals, especially during the off season.

There is also a relatively high concentration of serviceable **beaches**, with Bitez, Ortakent, Yalıkavak and Türkbükü, among others, currently holding Blue Flag status for cleanliness. Virtually every resort of any importance is served by **dolmuş** from Bodrum's *otogar* (see "Travel details" at the end of the chapter for schedules). The account of the coastline that follows covers the south, west and north shores in a clockwise direction from Bodrum.

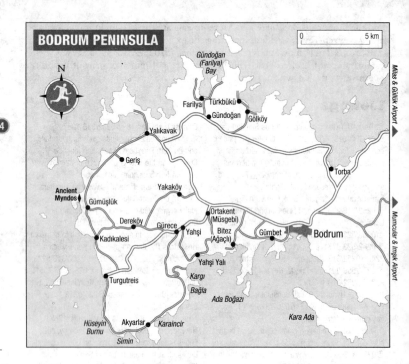

Gümbet

Roughly 2km west of Bodrum on the peninsula's south shore, **GÜMBET** is the closest proper resort to the town – indeed, almost a suburb – and its 600-metre, tamarisk-lined, gritty beach is usually packed, with parasailing, ringo-ing and waterskiing taking place offshore. Development here is exclusively package-oriented with large hotels and *pansiyon*s – a hundred of them on the gradual slope behind, with more springing up – catering for the rowdy, mainly English, 18 to 30 crowd that has effectively claimed this bay. The nightlife is as transient as its clientele and rivals Bodrum in the number of bars and clubs, if not in the quality of its clientele – a taxi fare back to town will set you back 12–25TL depending how early in the morning it is.

Bitez

BİTEZ (Ağaçlı), the next cove west, 10km from Bodrum, is a little more upmarket, and (along with Farilya) seems to have adopted Gümbet's former role as a watersport and windsurfing centre. There are a number of reasonable watering holes for the yachties sailing or cruising through, but the beach is tiny, even after artificial supplementing. Of the thirty-plus **hotels** here, the well-designed, four-star *Okaliptüs* (℡0252/363 7780, ⓦwww.okaliptus.com.tr; ❻), nestled in a grove of tangerine trees with its own small stretch of beach and pool, is probably the pick of the bunch.

Kargı, Bağla and Karaincir

Beyond Yahşi, a turning flanked with hotel signs at Gürece leads high above **Kargı**. The beach and bay are sandy and gently sloping, overlooked by the ubiquitous villas and a handful of fish restaurants.

Bağla, the next cove on, initially seems off-putting, with a water tank resembling an airport control-tower planted amidst the villas that cover the cape. But if you've arrived with your own transport, persevere by going straight past the old Greek chapel to the beachfront parking space, rather than following signs to the fee-parking at a pair of mediocre restaurants. The sand here is the softest in the vicinity of Bodrum.

Karaincir, the next bay with public access, is nearly as good – 600m of sand guarded by a pair of headlands that marks the most westerly point visited by the Bodrum excursion boats. Canoes and windsurfing boards can be rented, and while mid-beach is completely crowded out by sunbeds and umbrellas, the south end of the strand inexplicably remains in its wild, natural state. Of the few simple **motels** up by the main road, the *Bizimtepe* (☎0252/393 6343, ⊛www.hotelbizimtepe .com) is recommended, with either air-conditioned doubles (⑤) or four-person apartments (€50) available.

Akyarlar and beyond

Surrounded by eucalyptus trees, **AKYARLAR** (the former Greek port of Kefalouka), 30km from Bodrum, is more of an actual village – albeit one surrounded by estates of concrete villas – with a stone jetty, yacht harbour and mosque. The often breezy conditions here make it cooler and more comfortable in summer than sweaty Bodrum. Akyarlar's beach is small and hard-packed, mostly given over to windsurfing, but with both Karaincir and, in the opposite direction, the sandy cove at **Simin** – below the *Simin Hotel* – within walking distance, this is no great loss.

More to the point, Akyarlar is your passport to good local eating, with cuisine and a clientele far more Turkish, and prices far lower, than anywhere east of here. For **accommodation**, the *Babadan* (☎0252/393 6002; ④), with simple rooms, some with sea views, and the *Candan* (☎0252/393 6035; ②) offer the best value.

Turgutreıs

Once the road rounds the point to skirt the peninsula's west shore, the wind becomes stronger and the sand disappears, with nothing aside from villas until **TURGUTREİS**, the peninsula's second largest town. Frequent dolmuşes ply the route between here and Bodrum, 20km east. As a primarily all-inclusive resort, this is not the best place to experience authentic local culture, although its Saturday market does attract locals from far and wide. The town itself is a grid of streets packed with over a hundred hotels that leads down to a cobbled esplanade and a small exposed beach; nearby, the new yacht marina aims to lift the town's image in a more upmarket direction. Of the **hotels**, the *Four Seas Apart Hotel* (Şevket Sabancı Cad 7069 Sok 40 ☎0252/382 8228, ⊛www.fourseasapart.com) is centrally located, offering both rooms (④) and self-catering apartments (⑤) that sleep up to four.

Kadıkalesi

The side road starting by the Turgutreis *otogar* leads north to better things, through a fertile landscape of the tangerine groves for which the region is famous. After 4km you reach **KADİKALESI**, with its long, partly protected sand beach and unbeatable views over to assorted islets. The old Greek church on the hill is the most intact around Bodrum, but of the village's namesake "judge's castle" there seems to be no trace. As with Turgutreis, there is little **accommodation** available that's not all-inclusive. Friendly *Hotel Blue Bodrum Beach* (☎0252/382 2017, ⊛www.bodrum -turkey.com/clubblue; full board only ⑦) boasts a swimming pool in addition to simple sea-facing rooms. The beach is overlooked by a couple of fish restaurants.

Gümüşlük

If you've had a bellyful of villa complexes, then sleepy **GÜMÜŞLÜK**, 2km past Kadıkalesi or 6km along a direct road from a turning at Gürece, is a refreshing change. Easily the nicest spot on the peninsula (40min by dolmuş from Bodrum), it partly occupies the site of **ancient Myndos**, so most new development has been prohibited by the archeological service. Yachties are drawn here by the excellent deep anchorage between the headland and Tavşan Adası (Rabbit Island); snorkellers should check out the submerged mosaics that surround the island. The half-kilometre-long sand and gravel **beach** extending south of the island is less protected but still attractive, with watersports gear for rent. The actual village of Gümüşlük lies 2km inland, from where you can climb to an abandoned ridge-top monastery.

Among a handful of low-key **pansiyons**, those that cater well to independent travellers include the family-run *Hera Pansiyon* (℡0252/394 3065; ❹). *Mandalinci Myndos Hotel* (℡0252/394 3151, ⓦwww.mandalincimyndos.com; ❻) rents beachfront studios and cottages, many with private gardens.

A dozen waterfront **restaurants** are expensive, but of a good standard, specializing in *meze*, fish and seafood. *Yakamoz* may be the strip's finest: in business for over a decade, a private boat supplies their fresh catch twice daily. The nearby *Batı* does meat as well as fish, and has its own *pide* oven. On the northern road out of town, *Limon* (ⓦwww.limongumusluk.com) serves up home-grown produce in a bucolic garden setting.

Yalıkavak

In general, the northwest corner of the peninsula, served by a loop road out of Ortakent (or the narrower coastal route from Gümüşlük) tends to be overcrowded, with poor swimming and a relative lack of facilities. The trip over to **YALIKAVAK**, however – 20km from Bodrum – with glimpses of sea from a windmill-studded ridge, makes for one of the area's prettiest drives. Formerly an important sponge-fishing port, Yalıkavak has been somewhat gentrified, the town's commercial neighbourhood now developed into a full-blown resort, which is packed out during the summer months. Its scrappy shorefront windmill marks the edge of the town's pedestrian zone, and vehicles can get little further than the small *otogar*.

There are just a handful of **hotels** along the town's stretch of coast; the simple seaside *Cüneydi Pansion* (℡0252/385 4077, ⓦwww.pansiyon.cuneydi.com; ❹) is family-run, with a tranquil garden. The hills above the town are home to one of the region's swishest establishments with fabulous views over the coast: the ⅌ *Lavanta* (℡0252/385 2167; ⓦwww.lavanta.com; ❽) has luxury suites and a top-notch restaurant set in pristine gardens. The town's best **restaurants**, favoured by the odd Turkish celeb, huddle around the marina; plebs can dine on similar fare at central *Ali Baba*, where ultra-fresh fish weighs in at around a reasonable 10TL a head.

Gündoğan

GÜNDOĞAN (also known as Farilya), three bays east and surrounded by pine forest, is a laid-back, smaller version of Yalıkavak. The long, mostly narrow but serviceable beach, divided by a small harbour, is little impinged upon by the surrounding villas. On the waterfront, *Café Sail Loft* (ⓦwww.gravity.com .tr) takes advantage of the bay's constant breeze, renting windsurfing boards. Restaurants and bars (mostly indifferent) intersperse **accommodation** options along the beach. Of these, the most reasonably priced is the *Gürkaya* (℡0252/387 8352; ❺), while *Butik Han* (℡0252/387 9465, ⓦwww.butikhanotel.com; ❻) has air-conditioned rooms, a swimming pool and its own beach bar.

For a taste of the local Ottoman heritage, you can walk a kilometre inland to **Gündoğan village** proper, where there's a ruined monastery to climb to. Along the way, stop at tiny *Aspava* (across from Migros on the main road), where three generations of the Başkan family serve up excellent home-made *gözleme*.

Türkbükü

The turning for **TÜRKBÜKÜ**, 1km further east, is easy to miss. Aka the St Tropez of the peninsula, this trendy town has lost what little beach it had following enlargement of the quay – everyone swims from platforms. The clientele is overwhelmingly from the İstanbul moneyed and media set, who often come ashore from their yachts at anchor – the indented local coast and island provide shelter for far more craft than at Gümüşlük. Much of the **accommodation** here is unashamedly luxurious and expensive: for those with their own transport, pick of the high-end options is *Ev Hotel* (☎0252/377 6070, ⓦwww.evhotels.com .tr; ❽), whose snow-white, designer apartments are set on a hill overlooking the bay. At the eastern edge of town, the beachfront *Eda Motel* (☎0252/377 5030; ❻) offers basic rooms and a very good fish restaurant. Looping westwards along the shore's perfect curve, restaurants become both swankier and more expensive. Otherwise, the only points of cultural interest in Türkbükü are a ruined church and some partially collapsed rock-tombs.

Muğla and around

Muğla, capital of the province and containing several of the biggest resorts on the Aegean, is something of a showcase town and an exception to the Turkish rule of blocky urban architecture. It's also the closest town to **Akyaka**, the first coastal settlement you encounter at the bottom of the winding grade descending south from Muğla's plateau.

Muğla

MUĞLA's well-planned modern quarter incorporates spacious tree-lined boulevards and accommodates some hillside **Ottoman neighbourhoods** that are among the finest in Turkey. The **bazaar**, encompassing a grid of neat alleys nestling at the base of the old residential slope to the north, is divided roughly by trade. South of the bazaar is the **Ulu Cami**, built in the fourteenth century by the Menteşeoğlu emir, İbrahim Bey. The serene **Yağcılar Hanı**, a restored *kervansaray* located on Kursunlu Caddesi, contains carpet shops and çay stalls, while a second restored *kervansaray*, **Konakaltı Hanı**, on General Mustafa Muğlali Caddesi, is in use as an art gallery. Meanwhile, the town's **museum**, on Yatağan Eskiser Caddesi (daily except Mon 8.30am–noon 1–5pm; 3TL ☎0252/214 6948), houses a collection of locally found dinosaur fossils, including prehistoric rhino, giraffe, horse and elephant.

Practicalities

The large **otogar** lies 400m southwest of the centre on Zübeyde Hanim Caddesi. Muğla's **tourist office**, Cumhuriyet Bul 24 (summer Mon–Fri 8am–7pm; winter Mon–Fri 8am–noon & 1–5.30pm; ☎0252/214 1261), is a fifteen-minute walk from the *otogar*, and willingly provides pamphlets and maps.

As Muğla is not exactly deluged with tourists, **accommodation**, although scarce, shouldn't be a problem. The quietest and least expensive mid-range option is the *Otel Saray* (☎0252/214 1594, ⓦwww.muglasaray.com; ❹), facing the produce market but calm at night, with comfortable rooms with baths and balconies. **Eating out** in Muğla is fairly basic, with plenty of average *lokanta*, kebab and *pide* options. The *Sabah Lokantasi*, opposite the *Otel Saray*, is licensed and serves *meyhane* fare at pleasant outdoor seating opposite a fountain.

Akyaka

Situtated at the very head of the Gulf of Gökova, with steep Sakara Tepe looming overhead, scenic **AKYAKA** (Gökova) has always been popular with Turkish holiday-makers but is now attracting a small number of foreign tourists. The town is arrayed along a pleasant grid of streets on a slight slope amidst dense pine forest; private villas are interspersed between *pansiyon*s and small hotels, most built attractively in a sort of mock-Ottoman-*köşk* architectural style mandated by a local preservation code. Although Akyaka's town **beach** consists of hard-packed sand, merely suitable for getting into the clear waters of the gulf, there's a much better gravel beach 2.5km west of town, beyond the old jetty.

Dolmuşes (marked "Gökova") ply regularly to and from Muğla (30km to the north) and Marmaris (37km south), a thirty-minute journey from either. At the top end of the **accommodation** range, the three-star *Yücelen* (℡0252/248 5108, ⓦwww.yucelen.com.tr; ➐), just inland in the village centre, also manages bungalows, and can organize days out cycling, rafting or kitesurfing. The *Server Apartments* (℡0252/243 5497, ⓦwww.gokova-akyaka.com ➎), on Gökova Caddesi, rent large 4–5-person apartments with self-catering kitchens.

Marmaris

Along with Kuşadası and Bodrum, **MARMARIS** is the third of Turkey's less-than-holy trinity of hugely overdeveloped Aegean resorts. Development has dwarfed the old village core of shops and *lokanta*s lining narrow, bazaar-like streets, an intricate warren contrasting strongly with the European-style marina and waterfront. According to legend, the place was named when Süleyman the Magnificent, not finding the castle here to his liking, was heard to mutter "*Mimari as*" ("hang the architect"), later corrupted to "Marmaris" – a command that ought perhaps still to apply to the designers of the seemingly endless apartments and hotels.

Marmaris's **Netsel Yacht Marina**, tucked away at the far end of town, is one of Turkey's largest and is the main base for most yacht charter organizations operating on the Turquoise Coast. Proximity to Dalaman airport also means that both foreign and domestic tourists pour in nonstop during the warmer months, and – the Netsel Marina aside – the town remains very much a package resort.

Marmaris's **history** has been determined above all by the stunning local topography: a deep, fjord-like inlet surrounded by pine-cloaked hills. This did not seem to spur ancient Physcus, the original Dorian colony, to any growth or importance, but Süleyman comfortably assembled a force of 200,000 here in 1522, when launching the successful siege of the Knights of St John's base in Rhodes. Shortly after this campaign Süleyman endowed the old town nucleus with the tiny castle and a *han*. In 1798 Nelson's entire fleet sheltered here before setting out to defeat Napoleon's armada at the Battle of Aboukir Bay in Egypt.

Arrival and information

Marmaris's **otogar** is 2km outside the town centre on the Muğla road. The Havaş **airport bus** from Dalaman airport leaves you in front of the *otogar*, from which a regular dolmuş service runs down the main Ulusal Egemenlik Caddesi, stopping outside the huge Tansaş shopping centre; most of the town's **dolmuş** services start

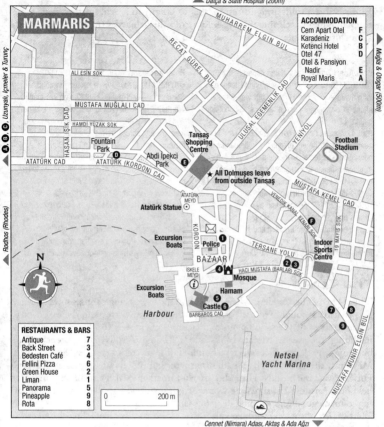

Datça & State Hospital (200m)

MARMARIS

MUHARREM ELGIN BUL

RECAT GÜREL BUL

ALİ ESİN SOK

HAMDİ YÜZAK SOK

HASAN IŞIK CAD

ULUSAL EGEMENLİK CAD

YENİYOL

Tansaş Shopping Centre

Football Stadium

ATATÜRK CAD

ATATÜRK (KORDON) CAD

Abdi İpekci Park

★ All Dolmuşes leave from outside Tansaş

ATATÜRK MEYD

MUSTAFA KEMEL CAD

Atatürk Statue ⊙

Atatürk Statue

VENEDİK KANAL KENARI SOK

19 MAYIS SOK

Excursion Boats

KORDON

Police

TERSANE YOLU

Indoor Sports Centre

BAZAAR

İSKELE MEYD

HACI MUSTAFA (BARLARI) SOK

Excursion Boats

ℹ

Mosque

Hamam

Castle

Harbour

BARBAROS CAD

Netsel Yacht Marina

MUSTAFA MÜNİR ELGİN BUL

ACCOMMODATION
Cem Apart Otel	F
Karadeniz	C
Ketenci Hotel	B
Otel 47	D
Otel & Pansiyon Nadir	E
Royal Maris	A

N

RESTAURANTS & BARS
Antique	7
Back Street	3
Bedesten Café	4
Fellini Pizza	6
Green House	2
Liman	1
Panorama	5
Pineapple	9
Rota	8

0   200 m

Cennet (Nimara) Adası, Aktaş & Ada Ağzı

Uzunyalı, İçmeler & Turunç

Rodhos (Rhodes)

Muğla & Otogar (500m)

THE CENTRAL AND SOUTHERN AEGEAN | Marmaris

4

from here. A taxi from the airport will set you back 140TL. Drivers should note that no **parking** is allowed anywhere along the Kordon, but the Tansaş supermarket has a large multistorey car park which is free if you produce a receipt for shopping (otherwise 15TL a day).

Arriving by **ferry** from the Greek island of Rhodes or **hydrofoil** from Bodrum, you dock by İskele Meydanı, on one side of which stands the extraordinarily knowledgeable **tourist office** (summer daily 9am–6pm; winter Mon–Fri 9am–noon & 1–5pm; ☎0252/412 1035), dispensing town plans, as well as information about bus schedules and accommodation. This is also a good place for details of the current **boat charter** prices (see box, p.291). **Boat-taxis** to İçmeler and Turunç leave from in front of the tourist office (7.5TL per person one way, or 15TL and 20TL per boat, respectively).

Accommodation

Although there are very few *pansiyon*s or small hotels in Marmaris, some apartment-hotels have sprung up in the area inland from the marina, while a handful of basic establishments survive in the **town centre**. Good value for money can be had out at the west end of the Kordon, close to where **Kemal Seyfettin**

Elgin Bulvarı splits away to run parallel to **Uzunyalı** beach. Further west, some three hundred hotels line the five-kilometre palm-fringed strip, with the luxury, all-inclusive complexes clustering at the far end.

Town centre

Cem Apart Otel Venedik Kanal Kenari Sok 25/12 ☎0252/413 1725. Self-catering units (sleep four) with averagely furnished rooms but well-fitted kitchens, arranged around a rather small pool and sauna. ❺

Otel 47 Atatürk Cad 10 ☎0252/412 4747. A huge seafront establishment bristling with balconies and communal sun terraces. It caters for Turks, not foreigners, hence the wonderful (and completely non-English) breakfasts and modest room rates. ❹

Otel & Pansiyon Nadir Kemerati Mahalesi ☎0252/412 1167. Friendly and as cheap as the town's accommodation gets, with clean simple rooms, en-suite bathrooms, a/c and TV, many with balconies. For bargain hunters their *pansiyon* rooms next door are cheaper still. ❹

West of the centre

Hotel Karadeniz Atatürk Cad (Kordon) 68 ☎0252/412 3614, ⊛www.karadenizhotel.com. Comfortable, well-run hotel (200m off our map) offering all the usual amenities. Rooms are large and bright, but the best aspect is its convenient location, just across from the beach. ❹

Ketenci Hotel Kemal Seyettin Elgin Bul ☎0252/412 6395. Its 1980s style may be faded – read piano bar, kidney-shaped pool and gloriously dated rooms – but the *Ketenci* still offers a touch of sea-view luxury at affordable prices. ❺

Royal Maris Hotel Kenan Evren Bul ☎0252/412 8383, ⊛www.royalmarishotel.com. Extremely slick beachside option (400m off our map) with sumptuous rooftop pool and bar, hamam and indoor pool, plus ultramodern guestrooms. ❼

The Town

Ulusal Egemenlik Caddesi, where you'll find the town's huge Tansaş supermarket, cuts Marmaris roughly in half, and the maze of narrow streets to the east of it is home to most of the monuments and facilities of interest to the average tourist, including the castle, bazaar, banks and PTT. Numerous travel agencies and bus-company ticket offices cluster a hundred or so metres to either side of **Atatürk Meydanı**, the seashore plaza at the southern end of Ulusal Egemenlik Bulvarı. Further west the weekly **Thursday market** (marked Açık Pazar on city maps) is held near Anadolu Lisesi, where women from surrounding villages sell a range of home-made goodies, including delicious jams.

Little is left of the sleepy fishing village that Marmaris was a mere three decades ago. The **bazaar**, including its diminutive *kervansaray*, now rivals that at Kuşadası in its array of glitzy kitsch on offer, and only the **Kaleiçi** district, the warren of streets at the base of the tiny castle, offers a pleasant wander. The **castle** itself (daily 8.30am–noon & 1–6.30pm; 3TL) is open as a fully stocked museum with clearly annotated displays of local finds; it also serves as a venue for events during the May festival.

In any case, you don't come to Marmaris for cultural edification, and you swim off the polluted **Kordon beach** at your peril – though this doesn't seem to deter the hundreds of bathers who use it daily. It's far better to take a dolmuş (regular services from Ulusal Egemenlik Bulvarı) or boat-taxi (see opposite) out to **İçmeler**, 9km west of Marmaris, whose old village core survives precariously at the far edge of the recently developed resort. Here the sand is coarse but cleaner than at Kordon, as is the sea.

Eating

Getting a decent meal at a reasonable price is something of a challenge in Marmaris. In town, the **restaurants** around the bazaar tend to offer fast food and English dishes. Simple pizzerias and other spots serving snacky meals abound along the Kordon and further west. East of the castle, the waterfront spots along Barbaros Caddesi change names, management and cuisine frequently – here, a meal with wine will run to around 35TL a head.

Antique Netsel Yacht Marina ☎0252/413 2955. Nautically themed restaurant offering Turkish and Italian dishes for about 45TL per person.
Bedesten Café Below the mosque in the bazaar. Lovely courtyard oasis for coffee and a *nargile* (waterpipe). With a choice of chairs or traditional cushions, and a trickling fountain, it's an "ethnic" kind of place aimed at tourists, but is at its best at night when the daytime awning is drawn back to reveal a star-studded view.
Fellini Pizza Barbaros Cad 71 ☎0252/413 0826. Popular, no-nonsense pizzeria, particularly recommended for its vegetarian options.

Liman Restaurat İsmetpaşa Cad ☎0252/413 6336. Excellent, locals-only fish and seafood restaurant, located in the bazaar.
Pineapple Netsel Yacht Marina ☎0252/412 0976. Ever-popular dressy Turkish/English eatery, famous for its oven-roasted lamb (22.5TL). With an attached English pub upstairs, things can get a bit noisy.
Rota Restaurant Behind Netsel Yacht Marina. Upscale kebabs and grilled meats (10–15TL), served just off the marina's main quay.

Coastal charters and boat excursions

Chartering either a motor schooner (*gulet*) or a smaller yacht out of Marmaris will allow you to explore the convoluted coast from Bodrum as far as Kaş. Especially out of high season, the daily cost isn't necessarily prohibitive – no more than renting a medium-sized car, for example – and in the case of a *gulet*, a knowledgeable crew will be included. Virtually all the shore described in this chapter and the next is accessible by boat, and there are also many other hidden anchorages.

You can pre-book a yacht charter through specialist holiday operators (see Basics for details), or you can make arrangements on the spot; though prices are always quoted in euros or US dollars, it's possible to pay in Turkish lira. Substantial deposits are required – usually fifty percent of the total price.

The best option for individual travellers or small groups is a cabin charter. Several companies set aside one schooner whose berths are let out individually. The craft departs on a particular day of the week with a fixed itinerary of three to seven days. Prices depend on demand but in April, May and October are around €350 per person per week, including all food and watersports equipment – excellent value. From June to September the cost jumps to over €420.

If you can assemble a large group, and have more time at your disposal, consider a standard charter of a twenty-metre motor schooner. A group of twelve, for example, will pay around €30 each daily during May or October, not including food or sporting equipment, and around €40 from June to September. Companies often offer to supply food from about €25 per person per day, though you'd spend about the same eating two meals a day on shore. Probably the best strategy is to dine in restaurants at your evening mooring and to keep the galley stocked for breakfast and snacks. If you tip the crew appropriately they're usually happy to shop for you. One of the oldest and more reliable charter agencies in Marmaris is Yeşil Marmaris, Barbaros Cad 118 (☎0252/412 6486, ⓦwww.yesilmarmaris.com).

For the greatest degree of independence, so-called "bareboat yacht" charter is the answer. Prices range from €1100 for the smallest boat in the off season, to €5800 for the largest in high season. This assumes that at least one of your party is a certified skipper; otherwise count on at least €120 a day extra (plus food costs) to engage one. For bareboat yachts, one of the larger local operators is Offshore Sailing at the Albatros Marina, 3km east of Netsel Marina (☎0252/412 8889, ⓦwww.offshore-sailing.net).

Those looking for a tamer taste of the sea can opt for a day excursion aboard a *gület*, which depart from the southern end of Kordon Caddesi and the castle peninsula. Trips usually visit highlights of the inner bay, heading to a fish farm on the north side of Cennet Adası, caves on its south shore, then completing the day with a visit to Kumlubükü or Turunç coves (see p.294). The price of around 15TL per person includes a full lunch (no drinks). Boats leave around 10.30am, returning between 5 and 6pm, during the summer season.

Drinking, nightlife and entertainment

Most of Marmaris's tippling takes place along **Hacı Mustafa Sokağı** (or Barlar Sok), which in recent years has become a fully fledged "Bar Street" along the lines of those in Kuşadası and Bodrum. More than two dozen **bars and clubs** here feature increasingly sophisticated designer profiles and various sorts of (usually live) music, often in spacious inner courtyards. Names change yearly, if not more often, though *Green House* and *Back Street* (not to be confused with *Back Street Garden* down the road) remain favourites. Up above, behind the castle, the *Panorama* bar offers the best views.

An annual **yachting and arts festival** (ⓦ www.marmarisfestival.com) takes place mid-May, and there's a large **yacht race** during late October or early November. For further details contact the Marmaris Yacht Club (ⓦ www.miyc.org).

Listings

Airport Havaş buses to the Dalaman airport, 90km east, depart from the Marmaris *otogar* 3hr before flights. (ⓦ www.havas.com.tr; 25TL).

Bike/jeep rental and tours Best Motor, Kemal Elgin Bul opposite the *Balim Otel* (ⓣ 0252/412 9436) rents bikes, mopeds, motorbikes and jeeps; Yoshimoto (ⓣ 0252/417 6237, ⓦ www.yoshimoto .de) organizes guided motorbike safaris throughout Turkey, starting at €1380.

Books Arkadaş Kitap, in front of the Sabaci High School on Kordon, has a selection of books in English, French and Russian; Sahaf, 33 Sok opposite the *Star Restaurant*, stocks secondhand English novels by the hundreds. Most kiosks, including the one in front of Tansaş, sell English daily newspapers.

Buses The main bus companies – Varan, Ulusoy, Pamukkale, Kamil Koç, Hakiki Koç – all have offices in or around Tansaş shopping centre at the Kordon Cad end of Ulusal Egemenlik Bul, and all run courtesy buses to the *otogar* to connect with their company's major routes.

Car rental Airtour, Kenan Evren Bul, Ulker Sok 18/A ⓣ 0252/412 8073; Avis, Atatürk Cad 30 ⓣ 0252/412 2638; Europcar, Yunus Nadı Cad 126 ⓣ 0252/417 4588; LeMar, Kenan Evren Bul 6 ⓣ 0252/412 3222.

Consulate Honorary British Consulate, c/o Yeşil Marmaris Tourism & Yachting, Barbaros Cad 118, near the marina ⓣ 0252/412 6486, ⓦ ukinturkey .fco.gov.uk.

Ferries and hydrofoils From April to Oct there's a twice-weekly domestic hydrofoil to Bodrum via

Gökova Bay and daily hops to Rhodes in Greece; there's also a twice-weekly car ferry; see "Travel details" at the end of this chapter for schedules and prices. Authorized agents include Yeşil Marmaris, Barbaros Cad 118 (ⓣ 0252/412 6486, ⓦ www.yesilmarmaris.com).

Hamam There's an old one in the rear of the bazaar at Eski Cami Arkası 3 (daily 8am–11pm for both sexes; entrance, scrub and massage 35TL), and the newer touristic Armutalan Hamam, off the Datça road, 1km north of the town centre (ⓦ www .hamamcilarltd.com; daily 9am–10pm; various packages €12–28).

Hospitals The state hospital is at the junction of Yunus Nadı Cad and the Datça road ⓣ 0252/413 1029; Ahu Hetman private hospital is in Hatipirimi suburb, 167 Sok ⓣ 0252/413 1415.

Laundry Marin laundry is located in the street behind the Netsel Yacht Marina.

Pharmacies The most central ones are: Fulya Eczanesi, Kemeraltı Mah 53/3 ⓣ 0252/412 9314; and Galenos Eczanesi, Ulusal Egemenlik Cad 81 Sok 3 ⓣ 0252/413 0419.

Police On Kordon Cad, next to the government house ⓣ 0252/412 2813.

Post office PTT is within the bazaar on 49 Sok (mail services until 6pm, outdoor phones 24hr).

Rafting Alternatif Turizm, Çamlık Sok 10/1 (ⓣ 0252/417 2720, ⓦ www.alternatifraft.com), offers regular springtime whitewater-rafting trips on the Dalaman River, plus river and sea kayaking, and tailor-made Turkey-wide outdoor-sports packages.

The Hisarönü (Rhodian) peninsula

In ancient times the peninsula extending from the head of the Gulf of Gökova to a promontory between the Greek islands of Sími and Rhodes was known as the **Rhodian Peraea** – the mainland territory of the three united city-states of

Rhodes, which controlled the area for eight centuries. Despite this, there is little evidence of the long tenure. The peninsula was (and still is) something of a backwater, today known as the **Hisarönü peninsula**. Up to now, yachts have been the principal means of getting around this irregular landmass and, although a proper road was completed in 1989, the difficulty of access has so far kept development to a minimum.

North: the Gökova gulf shore

The pristine shores of the **Gulf of Gökova** are tailor-made for exploration by yacht or by boat tour. In Marmaris you'll notice signs pitching an excursion to "Cleopatra's Isle". This is actually **Sedir Adası** (Cedar Island), an islet near the head of the Gulf of Gökova, which still sports extensive fortifications and a theatre from its time as Cedreae, a city of the Peraea. More evocative, however, is its alleged role as a trysting place of Cleopatra and Mark Antony, and the legend concerning the island's beach – the main goal of the day-trips; the sand was supposedly brought from Africa at Mark Antony's behest, and indeed analysis has shown that the grains are not from local strata.

Boat tours depart between 10 and 11am from **Çamli İskelesı**, 6km down a side road beginning 12km north of Marmaris, reachable either via a tour-operator's shuttle bus or the hourly dolmuş from Marmaris, and return at 4 or 5pm. As well as the obvious jaunt to Sedir Adası, boat trips also leave from here to **İNGİLİZLİMANI**, a beautiful inlet reachable only by sea. It got its name from ("English Harbour") from a World War II incident when a British ship sought shelter from pursuing Germans in these nominally neutral waters.

South to Bozburun

Overland access to the bulk of the **Hisarönü peninsula** is by way of a paved road, which branches south from the main Datça-bound highway, 21km west of Marmaris, and describes a loop back to Marmaris via Selimiye, Bayar, Turunç and Içmeler. **Dolmuşes** from Marmaris leave several times daily for Orhaniye, and there are three daily buses to Bozburun, including up to six daily direct dolmuş services in high summer.

Orhaniye and Selimiye

ORHANİYE, 9km off the main highway, is visited mostly for its yacht anchorage. The beach here is confined to muddy, sumpy shallows, though further out in the bay lurks a celebrated curiosity: a long, narrow, submerged sandspit known as **Kızkumu** (Maiden's Sand) extends halfway across the bay that gives anyone who walks on it the appearance of "walking on water". There are two small **hotels** and a mere half-dozen *pansiyons* of note here, including the clean *Palmiye Motel* (☎0252/487 1134; ❹).

SELİMİYE, 9km further south, is the next coastal village where visitors tend to stop, again mostly by yacht. The remains of an Ottoman fort overlook the port here, at the head of an all-but-landlocked arm of the giant Delikyol bay. Numerous quayside restaurants are aimed mostly at the passing boat trade, as are the pleasant *pansiyons* that have sprouted since the road was paved. Recommended alongside the cheaper **accommodation** options are the *Beyaz Güvercin* (☎0252/446 4274, ⓦwww.beyazguvercin.com; ❻) and the classy French-owned *Terrasses de Selimiye* (☎0252/446 4367, ⓦwww.selimiyepension.com; ❻), which boasts a Franco-Turkish restaurant and infinity pool.

Bozburun and beyond

BOZBURUN, 7km over the hill from Selimiye, slumbers in dusty heat six months of the year, but its setting, on a convoluted gulf with a fat islet astride its mouth and the Greek island of Sími beyond, is startling. The place is unlikely to go the way of Datça (see opposite), since there is precious little level land for villas, even less fresh water and absolutely no sand beaches. Nonetheless Bozburun has long been an "in" resort for various eccentrics – ex-journalists turned bartenders, recording executives turned restaurant proprietors, diehard Turkish hippies – who collect in this most isolated corner of coastal Turkey.

Accommodation prospects are a delight, and get more sophisticated and more expensive the further south you walk from the little village centre. *Suna Pansiyon* (☎0252/456 2119; ④) sits alongside several other great *pansiyon*s and offers doubles with bathroom and kitchen access, plus a wonderful sun terrace. A few minutes along is *Pembe Yunus* (the name translates as "Pink Dolphin"; ☎0252/456 2154; half-board obligatory ⑥) a buzzy alternative with a superb fish restaurant, ever popular with Istanbul-based couples. At the end of the quay is the *Otel Mete* (☎0252/456 2099; ⓦwww.otelmete.com; half-board obligatory ④), an inexpensive family-friendly spot, complete with hammocks and a sunlounger-covered sea terrace. Its vine-shaded upmarket cousin *Hotel Aphrodite* (☎0252/456 2268, ⓦwww.hotelaphrodite.net; half-board obligatory ⑥), 100m further along a coastal path, will appeal to the more discerning traveller. Of the ten or so quayside restaurants back in town the *Möwe Bar* (twice-frequented by Bill Gates as the waiter will no doubt assert) and *Fisherman's Restaurant* are by far the best.

In cool weather you could walk east one valley to **SÖĞÜT**, essentially a farming oasis with a minimal shore settlement boasting a few restaurants and a couple of *pansiyon*s. The dolmuş serving Söğüt terminates at **TAŞLICA**, a hilltop village girded by almonds and olives sprouting from what's otherwise a stone desert. From the square where the dolmuş minibus leaves you, a three- to four-hour trail leads south to ancient **Loryma**, where a Rhodian-built fort overlooks the magnificent harbour of **Bozukkale** – which in turn holds several restaurants. If you don't want to walk back the same way, you just might be able to hitch a boat ride out from here.

The east coast of the Hisarönü peninsula

From Selimiye, the main loop road climbs inland to **BAYİR**, a mountain village spread across an amphitheatre of rocky terraces, whose distinctive feature is a 2000-year-old tree on its main square. A side road leads the 3km down from here to **Çiftlik** bay, a once-isolated beach now dominated by a huge holiday village. Occasional dolmuşes do brave the route from Turunç, but their infrequent times make having your own transport the only practical option.

Turunç

The main route curls north back towards Marmaris, with another spur road leading down to **TURUNÇ**, which, since the late 1980s, has been transformed from a few farms and two ramshackle restaurants into an exclusive package-holiday venue. It's stunningly beautiful, boasting a 500-metre beach of coarse sand, backed by impressive, pine-tufted cliffs. These are now dotted with hotels and villas, some of whose residents commute to sea level using cogwheel chairlifts.

The few **hotels** are package only, but two solid options are the *Diplomat Hotel* (☎0252/476 7145, ⓦwww.diplomathotel.com.tr; ⑥) and the *Zeybek Hotel* (☎0252/476 7014, ⓦwww.zeybekhotel.com; ⑥), both complete with beach frontage and swimming pool. A handful of cheaper pensions lie back from the beach.

A spur road heads south, past ancient **Amos** (only Hellenistic walls and theatre remain) to **Kumlubükü**, another large bay with decent amenities. Along with Çiftlik bay, 4km southwest of here by rough tracks or paths, it's the only really big patch of sand on the whole peninsula.

The Datça peninsula

Once past the turning for Bozburun, the main highway west of Marmaris ventures out onto the elongated, narrow **Datça (Reşadiye) peninsula**. There are glimpses through pine gullies of the sea on both sides, and the road is fairly narrow and twisting and it's inadvisable to use it at night. On the way to **Datça** town are several great **campsites** including *Aktur* **camping** (T 0252/724 6836, W www .akturcamping.com), 18km before Datça behind a large, sandy beach.

Beyond Datça the peninsula broadens considerably, and the scenery – almond or olive groves around somnolent, back-of-beyond villages at the base of pine-speckled mountains – is quite unlike that which came before. Towards **ancient Knidos**, the ancient site on the western cape, of the 32km of road beyond **Reşadiye** village the 24km to Yazıköy are paved, but the last 4km are rough and ready.

Datça

Too built-up and commercialized to be the backpackers' haven it once was, **DATÇA** is still much calmer than either Bodrum or Marmaris. It's essentially the shore annexe of inland Reşadiye village, but under the ministrations of visiting yachtspeople and tour operators it has outgrown its parent. Partly due to the basic accommodation on offer, as well as the difficulty of access, prices are noticeably lower than in Bodrum or Marmaris.

Life in and around Datça mostly boils down to a matter of picking your swimming or sunbathing spot. The **east beach** of hard-packed sand, known locally as Kumluk, is oversubscribed but has some shade. The less crowded **west beach**, mixed pebble and sand and called Taşlık, is acceptable and gets better the further you get from the anchored yachts.

Arrival and information

Apart from its setting, Datça's most striking feature is its layout: a single, kilometre-long high street meandering between two sheltered bays separated by a hillock and then a narrow isthmus, finally terminating at a cape. Along the way in you pass – more or less in this order – the **PTT**, most of the main **banks**, the tiny tourist office, a traffic circle dominated by a large tree, with **taxi rank** and **bazaar** grounds (Sat) adjacent, and **travel agencies**. The **tourist office** (Mon–Sat 8.30am–7pm; T 0252/712 3163) is hidden away in a large cream-coloured government building on the high street. It can supply maps and lists of accommodation for the whole peninsula.

The hourly **buses** to and from Marmaris stop at the Pamukkale bus company office, just back from the harbour. Datça also has a small *otogar* on the outskirts of town, near the *jandarma* post; if you end up here **taxis** and service buses will compete to take you into town, but it's only a fifteen-minute walk. Except in high season, few of the big bus companies reach Datça, and you might be best off taking a short-hop dolmuş to either Marmaris or Muğla, from where there will be more frequent onward departures.

Ferries and hydrofoils from Bodrum arrive at Körmen Limani, 9km to the north; your ticket includes a shuttle-bus service into Datça. It's worth taking the boat at least in one direction to avoid duplicating the wild bus journey in from the east. From Körmen Limani there are once-a-week direct return ferries to the Greek islands of Rhodes (Sat) and Sími (Sat) (see p.308). You'll also find small charter boats in Datça offering trips to Knidos (about 20TL) and Koytur (about 35TL).

The local **boat trips** advertised on the west harbour make a good day out. Groups generally depart between 9 and 9.30am, returning between 5 and 6pm. Standard stops include Palamut Bükü, Domuz Çukuru, Mesudiye Bükü and ancient Knidos – most of which are detailed below. The going price per person, excluding lunch (usually in a restaurant at Palamut Bükü) and allowing three swim stops, is around 20TL, which compares well, for example, with the price of taking a taxi to Knidos.

Accommodation, eating and drinking

The most obvious location for desirable accommodation is the hillock separating the two bays, where there are several *pansiyon*s to choose from, including the *Huzur* (℡0252/712 3364; ❹) with an attractive terrace. *Yılmaz Pansiyon* (℡0252/712 3188; ❷), close to the beach strip, is much cheaper. For a touch of Ottoman style in homely surroundings *Datça Turk Evi* (℡0252 712 2129, ⓦwww.datcaturkevi .com; ❻) is a four-roomed boutique hideaway. Top of the range is the exclusive *Mehmet Ali Aga Mansion* (℡0212 599 0350, ⓦwww.kocaev.com; ❾), with its own beach, pool and two centuries of history.

Possibly the smartest choice in town is the *Villa Tokur* (℡0252/712 8728, ⓦwww.hoteltokur.com; ❻), up **on the hill** with unparalleled views of the beach, run by a Turkish–German family, with pool and nicely tended garden. The small, friendly **campsite**, *Ilıca Kamping* (℡0252/712 3400; open all year), perfectly located at the far end of the beach, is an ideal spot to relax, with a good restaurant, bar, and serene views, plus simple and upmarket bungalows (❸ and ❻) and room for several dozen tents.

Various cafés overlooking the east beach offer full **breakfast** for as little as 5TL. Othwerwise, Datça's **restaurants** rank highly in terms of price and quality. The most frantic activity you'll find in Datça is after dark at the handful of small **music pubs** and **bars** along the west harbour and beyond on the west beach.

Eskidatça

Two kilometres from Datça, back on the road towards Marmaris, a left turn takes you along a minor paved road to the original hamlet, **ESKIDATÇA**. The cobbled road leading into the hamlet passes the teahouse before splitting into two, up-and downhill. The sleepy maze of alleys – used mainly by cows – and ancient stone-built farmhouses have lately become a haven for artists and writers, who have renovated many of the dilapidated country homes. One such example is now the *Antik Bar and Restaurant*, with a walled garden, while *Eski Datça Evleri* serves as an agent for several old townhouses (℡0252 712 2129, ⓦwww.eskidatcaevleri.com; ❻).

West to Knidos

Some 9km west of Datça signs point down the five-kilometre side road to the pretty shore hamlet of **MESUDIYE BÜKÜ**. There is an occasional dolmuş to Mesudiye from Datça, leaving from the traffic circle. Accommodation prices here are slightly cheaper than in Datça, but, for better or for worse, not much happens after dark. Both the seafront *Hoppala* (☎0252/728 0148, ⓦwww.hoppala.com .tr; ③) and the relatively new *Olive Garden Hotel* (☎0252/728 0056, ⓦwww .olivegardenhotel.com; ⑤) are heavenly.

HAYİT BÜKÜ, one cove east with the necessary road-fork left well marked, hasn't such a good beach, but the bay itself is well protected by a scenic, claw-like headland to the west. Accordingly, the place sees lots of boat traffic and there's a large dock, a few restaurants and some relatively upmarket **guesthouses** – such as *Ogün's Pansiyon* (☎0252/728 0023, ⓦwww.ogunplace.com; ⑤).

Nine kilometres of rough coast road link Mesudiye with **PALAMUT BÜKÜ**, a fairly tricky prospect without your own transport. The stark setting is balanced by a kilometre-long beach of tiny pebbles lapped by brisk, clear water, with an islet offshore. Of a handful of **pansiyons**, mostly occupied for weeks on end by Turkish families, one of the most appealing is the *Bük* (☎0252/725 5136; ④), at the far eastern end of the bay.

Knidos

Out on windlashed Tekir Burnu (the Cape Krio of antiquity), **Knidos** (Cnidus) was one of the most fabled and prosperous cities of antiquity. With its strategic location astride the main shipping lanes of the Mediterranean it was a cosmopolitan city, and illustrious personalities hailing from here were legion. However, the city was most notorious for an inanimate object, the cult statue of Aphrodite by Praxiteles, the first large-scale, freestanding nude of a woman (modelled by the famous Athenian courtesan, Phryne). This adorned the new city from its earliest days and became, even more than the menacing winds, Knidos's chief source of revenue.

The catch is that very little remains of this former greatness, and it's probably not worth punishing any vehicle for the full distance from Datça to see it. A short halt on a **boat trip** (see opposite) is all that the site will merit for most visitors. You could take a **taxi from Datça**, but this will cost at least 50TL, and give you only an hour at the ruins.

Arriving by boat you dock in the south bay, backed by restaurants and a police post. Leave vehicles at the small **car park**; a nearby sign requests that, although the site is unenclosed, you should observe the official **visiting hours** of 8.30am to 7pm and pay admission – 8TL – if the keeper is manning his booth.

The site

Most of Knidos's partially labelled public buildings were on the mainland side and of these the **Hellenistic theatre**, overlooking the south anchorage, is the best preserved. A military watchtower on the ex-island confirms that most of it is off-limits; visit instead the two **Byzantine basilicas**, one huge with extensive mosaics, overlooking the north harbour. Hellenistic Knidos was laid out in a grid pattern, though the hilly site necessitated extensive terracing, retaining walls and stairways. Clambering along these, you can take a self-guided tour by following arrow-signs to the agora (by the north port), the bouleuterion, a Corinthian temple, a purported sundial and an unidentified mosaic floor. Of the Aphrodite shrine, on the very highest terrace, there remains only the circular foundation of either an altar or perhaps the tholos (round portico) where the image of the goddess was displayed.

Inland to Pamukkale

Away from the coastal regions, the major settlements in ancient Caria tended to be concentrated along the upper reaches of the Meander River, now the Büyük Menderes, and its tributaries, particularly the Marsyas – today's Çine Çayı – see box below. **Aydın**, a small, bustling city easily reached from Kuşadası, is the base of choice for visiting the archeological sites of the Çine valley, most notably **Nyssa** and **Alinda**. Further east, **Aphrodisias**, on a high plateau south of the Büyük Menderes, is similarly isolated, but buses are more obliging since it's fast becoming the archeological rival of Ephesus in the southwest Aegean.

Still further inland, the functional city of **Denizli** has transport connections in every direction, most obviously with **Hierapolis/Pamukkale**, an ancient site cum geological wonder that's the star of every other Turkish tourist poster ever produced.

Aydın and around

AYDİN started life as Tralles, the distinguished ancient town founded, according to legend, by colonists from the Greek Argive and Thrace; the site of the original settlement was a plateau northwest of today's city. Unfortunately Aydın's biggest attraction remains off-limits, as the site of **ancient Tralles** lies in a military zone at the northern end of Serbetçi Caddesi, 1km north of town. Visitors can make do with **İçgözler** ("three eyes"), three arches that were part of Tralles' second-century gymnasium, situated on a small hillock just outside the military zone.

On Gazi Bulvarı, next to the sports centre, lies Aydın's **museum** (daily except Mon 8am–noon & 1.30–5pm; 3TL): exceptional pieces include a bust of Athena and a statue of Nike. The grounds house an extensive range of larger finds from Tralles, including column capitals and parts of recovered statues.

The only additional buildings of note are two mosques: the eighteenth-century **Süleyman Bey Camii**, across from the pleasant, mosaic-paved central park, and the seventeenth-century **Şemsi Çelebi Camii** on İstasyon Meydanı. Otherwise, there's little to see except the bizarre fig sculpture about 100m west of the *otogar* – Aydın is famous for its figs (and olives) and you'll see dried figs on sale almost everywhere.

Practicalities

The **otogar** is 700m south of the centre on the main highway, just west of a large roundabout and the **tourist office** (Mon–Fri 8am–noon & 1.30–5pm; ☏0256/213

The myth of Marsyas

The Çine River's original name, **Marsyas**, commemorates a legend concerning the satyr Marsyas, a devotee of the mother-goddess Cybele. Upon finding a deer-bone flute discarded by Athena, he became entranced by its sound as he played in Cybele's processions, and was so bold as to challenge Apollo to a musical contest. The god accepted on condition that the winner could impose the punishment of his choice on the loser. Marsyas lost; Apollo tied him to a pine tree near the source of the stream that would bear his name, and flayed him alive.

5006), which offers regional (although no city) maps. Adnan Menderes Bulvarı shoots straight up to the heart of town, where the **train station** (services from İzmir and Denizli) and **PTT** face each other, just west of the city's central square. Hükümet Bulvarı, Menderes's narrower continuation, climbs past the bulk of the hotels and restaurants before intersecting Gazi Bulvarı, Aydın's main east–west thoroughfare and home to the **dolmuş station**.

Accommodation is neither inspiring, nor particularly cheap. The best of the basic choices is found at the newly renovated *Özlü*, Adnan Menderes Bul 71 (℗0256/225 3371, ⓦwww.hotelozlu.com; ❺), where en-suite rooms have satellite TV.

You'll find most of the **eating** options tucked in the backstreets around the bazaar, west of Hükümet Caddesi. On Hükümet itself, the *Dede Lokantası* serves up excellent *pide*, as well as vegetables in olive oil and large *çöp* kebabs.

Nyssa

Awash in a sea of orange groves in the hills above the Büyük Menderes valley, ancient **Nyssa** is rarely visited – and except for its theatre, bouleuterion and unusual layout, there is little to interest non-specialist visitors. Originally founded by Peloponnesians, the city flourished from the first century BC until the third century AD, and subsequently remained an important Byzantine community.

The archeological zone lies 2km above **Sultanhisar**, the modern successor to Nyssa, 32km east of Aydın and astride major bus and rail routes; dolmuşes run here every thirty minutes from Aydın. Sultanhisar has simple eateries, but no public transport up to the ruins themselves.

The site

The paved access road from the ticket office (always open; 3TL during daylight hours ℗0256/351 2726) leads into a small car park flanked by picnic tables. Just north of here lies an excellently preserved **Roman theatre** with a capacity of well over 5000 – a structure that is slowly being taken over by wild olives sprouting amidst the seats. The paved road continues another 300m uphill to the start of the 200-metre walk to the **bouleuterion**, where twelve semicircular rows of seats face out onto an area graced with a ceremonial basin and mosaics. A path just to the east of the theatre descends to the mouth of an enormous, 115-metre-long **tunnel** burrowing under the car park: in addition to functioning as a simple storm drain, it could be used to fill the stadium with water for mock naval battles.

To the west of the access road, reached by another path beginning 100m north of the guard post, stand the remains of some **baths** (adjoining the theatre) and a **library**, alleged in many sources to be the most important in Asia Minor after the one in Ephesus – hard to believe from today's muddled, two-storey building, lost in more olives.

Alinda

Alinda, the best of the ancient ruins in the Çine valley, south of Aydın, crowns a huge bluff that dominates the area, and is closely linked with a colourful episode in the life of Alexander the Great. **Ada**, the sister of King Mausolus of Halicarnassus (see p.276), after losing the battle for succession to the Hecatomnid throne during the middle of the fourth century, was exiled to Alinda, then a mere fortress, where she awaited an opportunity to reverse her fortunes. A few years later, upon the arrival of Alexander, Ada offered to surrender Alinda in exchange for his aid in regaining her royal position. Her proposal was accepted, and Alexander holed up in Alinda for some time, preparing their combined – and eventually successful – siege of Halicarnassus. During this period they became close friends, and it seems that Ada even adopted Alexander as her son. After their victory Ada was left to rule over most of Caria, but she was the last of the remarkable Hecatomnid line; little of consequence occurred locally after her death.

The site

From the little square where the dolmuşes stop, follow the signs 400m up a dirt track to the unfenced **site** (always open; 3TL charged during daylight hours) and car park. Close by, the oldest houses of Karpuzlu merge into ancient masonry just below the monstrous **market building**; like so much Carian stonework, they bear a strange resemblance to Inca construction half a world away. Cross the open agora behind to some courses of wall, where an obvious serpentine path leads up to the well-preserved **theatre**. Further north up the hill, an impressive, two-storey **Hellenistic watchtower** surveys a patchwork of fields and trees, with rings of mountains up to 50km distant. Walk west along the neck of the ridge, past the foundations of **acropolis houses**, until you reach a gap in the **city walls**; just beyond are a couple of specimens from Alinda's extensive **necropolis**.

The site lies 28km off the main highway, a total of 58km from Aydın. Direct dolmuşes head to **KARPUZLU**, the fair-sized town at the base of the ruins. Or you can use an Aydın–Çine dolmuş (departing across the road from Aydın tourist office, and from the *otogar*) and change vehicles in Çine town; infrequent dolmuşes also depart from here for the more remote ruins of Alabanda.

Aphrodisias

Situated on a high plateau over 600m above sea level, ringed by mountains and watered by a tributary of the Büyük Menderes, **Aphrodisias** is among the most isolated and beautifully set of Turkey's major archeological sites. Acres of marble peek out from among the poplars and other vegetation that cloaks the remains of one of imperial Rome's most cultured Asian cities. Late-afternoon visits have the bonus of often dramatic cloud formations, spawned by the elevation, and the attendant dappled lighting.

Some history

Aphrodisias was one of the earliest occupied sites in Anatolia. Neolithic and Bronze Age mounds have been found here, and there has been some sort of **fertility cult** here for just as long. The Assyrian goddess of love and war, Nin, became meshed with the Semitic Ishtar, with the Hellenic Aphrodite eventually assuming the goddesses' combined attributes.

Despite a strategic position near the meeting point of ancient Caria, Lydia and Phrygia, and its proximity to major trade routes, for many centuries Aphrodisias remained only a shrine. However, during the second century BC, its citizens were rewarded for their support of the Romans during the Mithridatic revolt. Imperial favour bestowed, various emperors patronized the burgeoning city. Aphrodisias became particularly renowned for its school of sculpture, sourcing high-grade marble from nearby quarries, and local works soon adorned every corner of the empire, including Rome itself.

Perhaps because of this fixation with graven images, paganism lingered here for almost two centuries after Theodosius banned the old religions. The reputation of its Aphrodite love cult had served to protect Aphrodisias since its inception, but by the fourth century AD, two earthquakes and sundry raids began to take their toll, and decline was the dominant theme of Byzantine

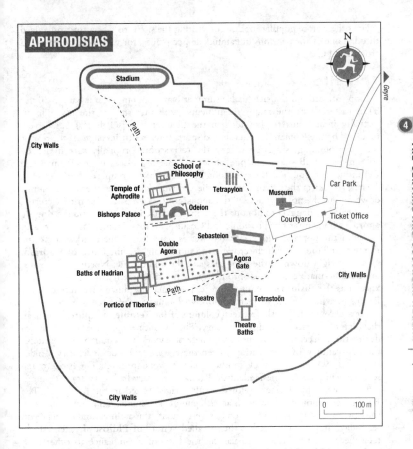

times. The town was abandoned completely during the thirteenth century, its former glories recalled only by the Ottoman village of Geyre – a corruption of "Caria" – among the ruins.

First French, then Italian researchers poked rather desultorily below the surface early last century, but it is only since 1961 that work by a New York University team under Dr Kenan Erim (who died in 1990 and is buried on the site) has permitted a fuller understanding of the site. The intention is to render Aphrodisias on a par with Ephesus and the eventual results will certainly be spectacular, though for now some of the site's more interesting areas remain off-limits.

Arrival and tours

Aphrodisias is situated 13km southeast of **KARACASU**, the nearest sizable town, which lies 25km from the E24/320 highway between Aydın and Denizli. From the highway, you'll need to change transport at **NAZILLI**, whose *otogar* sits just north of the highway on the west edge of town. If coming by train, exit Nazilli station and turn right onto the main town thoroughfare, or follow the tracks southwest – they pass very near the bus stand. **Dolmuşes to Karacasu** depart from the rear of the Nazilli *otogar*; during warmer months the route may extend to Geyre, the village next to the ruins.

The other, more popular, option for visiting the site is to take a **tour** organized through one of the pensions in Pamukkale (see p.305), for which the going rate is around 30TL.

The site

A loop path around the **site** (daily: summer 8am–6.30pm; winter 8am–5.30pm; 8TL) passes all of the major monuments, with first stop at the magnificent, virtually intact **theatre**. Founded in the first century BC, it was extensively modified by the Romans for their blood sports three centuries later. At the rear of the stage building is a large square, the **tetrastoön**, originally surrounded by colonnades on all sides, and one of several meeting places in the Roman and Byzantine city. South of the tetrastoön lies a large baths complex.

The path skirts the north flank of the theatre, right under the hill's summit; down and to the north you'll see the **Sebasteion** – two parallel porticoes erected in the first century AD to honour the deified Roman emperors – and the **double agora**, two squares ringed by Ionic and Corinthian stoas. Numerous columns still vie with the poplars, and the whole area is bounded to the southwest by the **Portico of Tiberius**, which separates the agora from the fine **Baths of Hadrian**, preserved right down to the floor tiles and the odd mosaic. North of the baths, several blue-marble columns sprout from a multi-roomed structure commonly known as the **Bishop's Palace**, from its presumed use during Byzantine times. East of here huddles the Roman **odeion**, with nine rows of seats.

A few paces to the north, fourteen columns of the **Temple of Aphrodite** are all that's left of the city's principal sanctuary. The Byzantines converted it to a basilica during the fifth century, so considerable detective work was required to re-establish the first-century BC foundations. Even these were laid atop at least two older structures, with evidence of mother-goddess worship extending back to the seventh century BC. The Hellenistic/Roman sanctuary had forty Ionic columns arranged eight by thirteen, with the cult image erected in the main hall. The Byzantines removed the columns at each end of the temple, fashioning an apse to the east, an atrium and baptistry on the west, and it's this architectural pastiche you see today. Immediately north is the so-called **School of Philosophy**, tentatively identified, like the bishop's palace, on the basis of resemblance to other such structures elsewhere.

The northernmost feature of the site, 200m off the main path, is the 30,000-seat **stadium**, one of the largest and best preserved in Anatolia, where a version of Delphi's Pythian Games were held, with sporting, musical and dramatic events.

Returning to the main loop trail, the last thing you'll notice before exiting onto the museum square is the re-erected **tetrapylon**, a monumental gateway with two double rows of four columns, half of them fluted, supporting pediments with intricate reliefs. This second-century AD edifice is thought to mark the intersection of a major north–south street with a sacred way heading toward the Aphrodite shrine.

The museum

An earthquake in 1956 damaged the old village of Geyre, giving the authorities a timely pretext to relocate the villagers 1.5km to the north and begin excavations. The old village square is now flanked by the archeologists' quarters and by the attractive **museum** (closed Mon), whose collection consists almost entirely of sculpture recovered from the ruins.

Given that Aphrodisias met most of the demand for effigies under the empire, even what remains after the loss of originals and the spiriting away of works to city museums is considerable. The museum was partially closed for renovation at the time of writing; when it reopens highlights should still include the "Aphrodite Hall", containing statuary related to the cult, with a rendition of the goddess, much defaced by Christian zealots, occupying the position of honour, and in the "Penthesileia Hall", a joyous satyr carrying the child Dionysos in his arms.

Pamukkale and around

As you approach the UNESCO World Heritage Site of **Pamukkale** from Denizli, a long white smudge along the hills to the north suggests a landslide or mine. Getting closer, this clarifies into the edge of a plateau, more than 100m above the valley and edged in white **travertine terraces**. The Turks have dubbed this geological fairyland *Pamukkale*, or "Cotton Castle".

Deriving from a bubbling spring at the foot of Çal Dağı, this stunning natural wonder has been created over millennia. As thermal water surges over the edge of the plateau and cools, carbon dioxide is given off and hard chalk (travertine) accumulates as a solidified waterfall, slowly advancing southwest. Seen at sunset, subtle hues of ochre, purple and pink are reflected in the water, replacing the dazzling white of midday. The spring itself emerges in what was once the centre of the ancient city of **Hierapolis**, whose blissfully located ruins would merit a stop even if they weren't coupled with the incredible natural phenomenon of the terraces.

The hotels here at one time siphoned off the precious mineral waters for their own heated pools; the waterflow is now strictly rotated in order to preserve the site and allow more diminished deposits to "regrow". Present restrictions mean that visitors can dip into but a handful of the pools on the southern edge of the terraces.

▲ Travertine terraces at Pamukkale

Some history

The therapeutic properties and bizarre appearance of the hot springs were known about for thousands of years before an actual town was founded here by one of the Pergamene kings during the second century BC. After incorporation into the Roman Empire in 129 BC, development proceeded apace. Hierapolis seems to have enjoyed considerable imperial favour, especially after catastrophic earthquakes in 17 AD and 60 AD. No fewer than three emperors paid personal visits, stimulating local emperor-worship alongside the veneration of Apollo and his mother Leto, who was venerated in the guise of Cybele.

The presence of a flourishing Jewish community aided the rapid and early establishment of Christianity here. Hierapolis is mentioned in Paul's Epistle to the (neighbouring) Colossians, and Philip the Apostle was martyred here, along with his seven sons. However, as at Aphrodisias, paganism lingered well into the sixth century, until a zealous bishop supervised the destruction of the remaining ancient worship sites and the establishment of nearly one hundred churches, several of which are still visible.

Hierapolis slid into obscurity in late Byzantine times, nudged along by Arab and Turcoman raids. After the Selçuks arrived in the 1100s, the city was abandoned, not to figure much in the Western imagination until Italian excavations began in 1957.

Pamukkale Köyü

PAMUKKALE KÖYÜ, a once-sleepy village at the base of the cliff, is where most foreign travellers stay. In recent years, the village has acquired a rash of carpet shops, hustlers and poor restaurants in its centre. Despite all this, it's still a rural settlement; beyond the main drag, little outward change is evident. For nocturnal peace, it's better to stay on the settlement's outskirts, southwest of the road leading up to the south gate of the ruins.

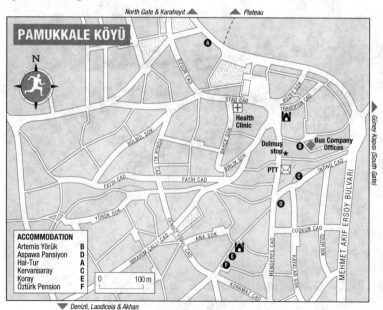

North Gate & Karahayıt ▲   ▲ Plateau

PAMUKKALE KÖYÜ

N

Health Clinic

Dolmuş stop ★

Bus Company Offices

PTT

Güney Kapısı (South Gate) ▶

ACCOMMODATION
Artemis Yörük	B
Aspawa Pansiyon	D
Hal-Tur	B
Kervansaray	C
Koray	A
Öztürk Pension	E
	F

0   100 m

▼ Denizli, Laodiceia & Akhan

Arrival and information

Most travellers arrive from **Denizli**, 20km to the south. Four daily trains (suspended at the time of writing but due to be reinstated shortly) ply the route from İzmir, stopping at Selçuk along the way; the Denizli *otogar* is also well serviced by **long-distance buses**. **Dolmuşes** labelled "Pamukkale/Karahayat" set off from a rank near the *otogar's* post office (7am–11.30pm, earlier in the cooler months; 2TL). A **taxi from Denizli** will set you back around 15TL per car-load; if you've booked in advance, many of the recommended *pansiyons* are able to fetch you for free.

Note that although several bus companies have ticket offices in Pamukkale Köyü, buses are really minibus shuttles to the Denizli *otogar*, from where you'll pick up your **connection**.

Accommodation and eating

Pamukkale Köyü's 1990s accommodation explosion has naturally abated; substandard outfits have folded as day tourists bus in to visit to the nearby site. Still, be prepared for the tenacious attentions of the local accommodation **touts** both in Denizli and in Pamukkale Köyü. An advance telephone call to one of the establishments mentioned below, and an assertive word to the touts, should solve any problems. In any case, it's well worth arranging a room in advance as the various establishments may offer to fetch you from Denizli. Most lodgings in the village are open all year and advertise the presence of a mineral water **swimming pool**, although this is a summertime pleasure only. **Eating out**, the situation is almost uniformly mediocre. You'll usually get better value from your *pansiyon*, almost all of which have an on-site restaurant.

Artemis Yörük Hotel Atatürk Cad ☎0258/272 2674, ⓦ www.artemisyorukhotel.com. Very good budget option in the middle of town, although can be noisy. Rooms sleep up to five, and surround a central pool and barbecue pit. ➋

Aspawa Pansiyon Menderes Cad ☎0258/272 2094, ⓦ www.aspawapension.com. With an off-street mineral pool, a choice of single, double or triple rooms, particularly good breakfasts and satellite TV. ➋

Hotel Hal-Tur Mehmet Akif Ersoy Bul 45 ☎0258/272 2723. One of the most prestigious hotels in the village, directly opposite the terraces, with immaculate a/c rooms, satellite TV and wi-fi. There's a swimming pool and attached restaurant. ➍

Hotel Kervansaray İnönü Cad ☎0258/272 2209, ⓦ www.kervansaraypension.com. A long-standing favourite, about 200m up the main street, owned by the welcoming Kaya family. Many of the centrally heated rooms overlook creek greenery, and there's a pool and a rooftop café-restaurant (though this is closed in winter). ➍

Koray Hotel Fevzi Çakmak, Pamuk Mah 27 ☎0258/272 2222, ⓦ www.otelkoray.com. Popular, small hotel built around a pool and leafy garden, with a good restaurant; half-board options available. ➌

Öztürk Pension Fevzi Çakmak, Pamuk Mah 31 ☎0258/272 2838, ⓦ www.ozturkhotel.com. A quiet off-street location, enclosing a small pool-garden and lovely vine-covered breakfast terrace. Managed by a friendly family. ➌

Hierapolis and the travertines

The combined site of ancient **Hierapolis** and the **travertines** (ⓦ www.pamukkale .org.tr; daily 24hr; 20TL, though admission is only charged during daylight hours) has three entrances. The first, the signposted "Güney Kapısı" or **South Gate**, is at the end of a 2km road describing a lazy loop up from the village. Here you'll find the visitor centre, plus a ticket booth and car park, followed by a long, shadeless walk to the ruins and terraces. Most tour buses use the **North Gate** (where's there's another ticket booth and visitor centre) for access to the central car parks next to the museum; if you park at the North Gate, regular shuttle buses (2TL) will drop you outside the Thermal Baths.

There's also a quite conspicuous **path** up to the plateau (a fifteen-minute hike), from just before the point where the Karahayıt-bound road curls north out of the village. Intended originally to allow the villagers to enjoy the springs, you can also pay to enter the site at the base and walk up – though most people prefer to come down this way. The 500m section of calcium deposits takes you through a collection of thermal pools, where visitors are welcome to wallow. Shoes are forbidden along the entire tract, although for the most part, the calcium surface makes for smooth and pleasant navigation.

If you want to take a proper bath in the springs, visit the **Pamukkale Thermal Baths** (daily 8am–7pm; 23TL admission for two hours) up on the plateau, which encloses the sacred pool of the ancients, with mineral water bubbling from its bottom at 36°C. Changing rooms are to the right as you enter; come as early or late as possible, as midday is the province of large tour groups.

On your way to the pool you'll pass the **tourist office** (daily except Mon 9am–noon & 1.30–7.30pm; ☎0258/264 3971), principally useful for its map of the site, and the **museum** (daily except Mon 9am–12.30pm & 1.30–5.15pm; 3TL), housed in the restored second-century AD baths. Its gardens, visible without a ticket, are beautifully laid out. Indoors, the collection consists primarily of statuary, sarcophagi, masonry fragments and smaller knick-knacks recovered during excavations at Hierapolis. Behind the museum is a large sixth-century **basilica**, probably the Byzantine-era cathedral, with two aisles sandwiching the nave.

Hierapolis

Access to the **eastern area** of ancient Hierapolis is via a narrow road winding up between the central car park and the museum. The first gate – little more than an open passageway – in the roadside fence gives access to a **nymphaeum**, or fountain-house, the **Temple of Apollo** and the adjacent **Plutonium**. The Apollo shrine in its present, scanty form dates from the third century AD, though built on a second-century BC foundation. The grotto of the Plutonium, dedicated to the god of the underworld, is today a small, partly paved cavity beyond which you can hear rushing water and an ominous hissing – the emission of a highly toxic gas, probably a mixture of sulphurous compounds and carbon dioxide. In ancient times the eunuch priests of Cybele were reputedly able to descend into the chasm with no ill effect; today, a formidable metal cage-grille keeps daredevils out. Before this was installed, two Germans died attempting to brave the cave.

The next feature is the well-preserved **Roman theatre**, dating from the second century AD, including stage buildings and their elaborate reliefs. During the **International Pamukkale Song Festival** (Ⓦwww.turkcevizyon .com; late June) performances are

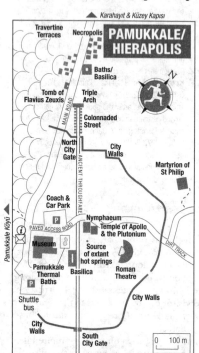

held here: the 46 rows of seats can still hold up to 7000 spectators comfortably, as compared to the former capacity of 10,000.

Return to the dirt track and follow it further east past a stretch of the **city walls**, turning left onto a smaller path and eventually halting before the **Martyrion of St Philip**, built in honour of the apostle, martyred here in 80 AD. This fifth-century structure, comprising many rectangular cells converging on a central octagonal chamber, was almost certainly not Philip's tomb, nor even a church, but probably the venue for festivals and processions on the saint's day.

Arguably the most interesting part of the city is the **colonnaded street**, which once extended for almost 1km from a gate 400m southeast of the sacred pool to another breach in the north wall. This thoroughfare, parallel to the plateau's edge, unevenly bisected the grid plan of the Hellenistic city and terminated at each end in monumental portals a few paces outside the walls. Only the northerly one, a **triple arch** flanked by towers and dedicated to the Emperor Domitian in 84 AD, still stands.

North of Domitian's triple arch, on the east side of the road, stands the squat bulk of some second-century AD baths, converted 200 years later into a **basilica**. Slightly closer to the archway, west of the asphalt, is the elaborate **Tomb of Flavius Zeuxis**, a prominent Hierapolitan merchant – the first of more than a thousand tombs of all shapes and sizes constituting the **necropolis**, the largest in Asia Minor and extending for nearly 2km along the road. The more sumptuous ones bear epitaphs or inscriptions warning grave-robbers of punishments awaiting those caught, and there are forecourts with benches for visits by the deceased's relatives.

Travel details

Trains

Denizli to: İzmir Basmane (4 daily, via Selçuk; 5hr).
İzmir (Basmane) to: Afyon (1 daily; 13hr); Denizli (4 daily, via Aydın & Nazilli; 5hr); Manisa–Balıkesir–Bandırma (2 daily; 5hr 30min; ferry connection at Bandırma for İstanbul); Manisa–Balıkesir–Kütahya–Ankara (3 daily, with sleepers; 11–13hr); Ödemiş (5 daily; 2hr); Selçuk (4 daily; 1hr); Söke (1 daily, via Selçuk; 2hr 45min); Tire (1 daily; 1hr 45min).
Selçuk to: Denizli (2 daily, via Aydın; 4hr); İzmir Basmane (4 daily; 1hr).

Buses and dolmuşes

The schedules below are for the summer season; out of season (Nov–April), the number of buses and minibuses drops drastically.
Aydın to: Alinda (hourly; 1hr); Çine (15 daily; 35min); Denizli (hourly; 1hr 30min); Fethiye (hourly; 4hr); İzmir (every 30min; 2hr); Konya (4 daily; 9hr); Marmaris (hourly; 2hr 30min); Nazilli (every 30min; 45min); Sultanhisar (every 30min; 30min).
Bodrum to: Ankara (4 daily; 11hr); Denizli (5 daily; 5hr); Fethiye (6 daily; 5hr); İstanbul (20 daily; 12hr);

İzmir (hourly; 3hr 30min); Marmaris (hourly; 3hr 15min); Muğla (hourly; 2hr 30min); Ortakent (every 30min; 20min).
Datça to: Ankara (3 daily; 12hr); İstanbul (5 daily; 16hr); Marmaris (9 daily; 2hr).
Denizli to: Antalya (14 daily; 5hr); Bodrum (6 daily; 4hr 30min); Konya (several daily; 7hr 15min); İstanbul (15 daily; 10hr); İzmir (hourly; 4hr); Marmaris (8 daily; 3hr 30min).
İzmir to: Afyon (5 daily; 5hr); Ankara (hourly; 8hr 30min); Antalya (hourly; 7hr); Aydın (every 30min; 2hr); Bodrum (hourly; 3hr 30min); Bursa (hourly; 7hr); Çanakkale (5 daily; 6hr); Çeşme (every 20min; 1hr); Datça (6 daily; 5hr 15min); Denizli (hourly; 4hr); Edirne (6 daily; 12hr); Fethiye (15 daily; 6hr); İstanbul (hourly; 9hr); Kuşadası (every 30min; 2hr); Marmaris (hourly; 3hr 30min); Selçuk (every 20min; 1hr).
Kuşadası to: Aydın (hourly; 1hr 30min); Antalya (2 daily; 8hr); Bodrum (4 daily; 2hr); İstanbul (12 daily; 9hr); İzmir (every 30min; 2hr); Selçuk (every 20min; 30min).
Marmaris to: Akyaka (every 30min; 30min); Ankara (14 daily; 11hr); Antalya (5 daily; 6hr); Bodrum (hourly; 3hr 15min); Bozburun (3–6 daily;

1hr); Datça (9 daily; 2hr); Denizli (8 daily; 3hr 30min); Fethiye (hourly; 3hr); İstanbul (9 daily; 13hr); İzmir (hourly; 3hr 30min).
Nazilli to: Geyre (6–7 daily; 50min); İstanbul (9 daily; 12hr).
Selçuk to: İstanbul (5 daily; 10hr); Kuşadası (every 20min; 30min); Tire (every 20min; 40min).

Domestic ferries and hydrofoils

All schedules are valid during the May–October season only. The first service is operated by Bodrum Express Lines, which quotes prices exclusively in euros, though you can pay in Turkish lira. The Datça service is run by Bodrum Ferryboat Association.
Bodrum–Marmaris 4 weekly; 1hr 15min; €25 one way, €30 day return.
Datça–Bodrum 2 daily; 2hr; 25TL one way, 40TL open return, 70TL for a small car.

Ferries and hydrofoils to the Greek islands

Turkish vessels normally leave in the morning – usually between 8 and 10am – returning from Greece between 4.30 and 5.30pm, depending on the time of year; Greek craft arrive between 9 and 10am and return between 4 and 5pm. For a morning boat, bring your passport to ticket agencies the evening before so that your name is recorded on a passenger manifest; for an afternoon boat it should be enough to hand over your papers two hours before sailing time. In high season the boats occasionally sell out, and schedules are subject to alteration depending on demand and season.

Fares are overpriced for the distances involved due to port taxes at both ends. The following prices do not include the cost of Turkish visas required by various nationalities. All the ferries below quote prices in euros, though you can pay in Turkish lira.
Bodrum–Kós May–Oct 6–12 weekly, 3 weekly in midwinter; 1hr; €28 one way or day return.
Bodrum–Rhodes June–Sept twice weekly; 2hr 15min; €60 one way or day return.
Çeşme–Híos June–Sept daily; Nov–April 1 weekly; 45min; €40 one way or day return.
Didim–Kós June–Sept 4 weekly; 1hr 15min; €40 one way or day return.
Körmen Limani–Rhodes May–Sept 1 weekly; 1hr; €30 one way or day return.
Körmen Limani–Sími May–Sept 1 weekly; 1hr; €25 one way or day return.
Kuşadası–Sámos Twice daily May to late Oct, 1 weekly in midwinter; 1hr 30min; €30 one way or day return.
Marmaris–Rhodes Daily May–Oct, 1 or 2 weekly in midwinter; 50min; €50 one-way, €60 day return.

Ferries to Italy

Çeşme–Ancona mid-May to mid-Oct weekly, usually Wed or Thurs; 57hr; €165 single (€55 port tax); small car €195 (€65 port tax).

Flights

Bodrum (Milas) to: İstanbul (6–14 daily); Antalya (5–16 daily).
Denizli (Çardak airport) to: İstanbul (2 daily).
İzmir to: Ankara (28 daily); Antalya (27 daily); Dalaman (8 daily); İstanbul (21 daily).

The Turquoise Coast

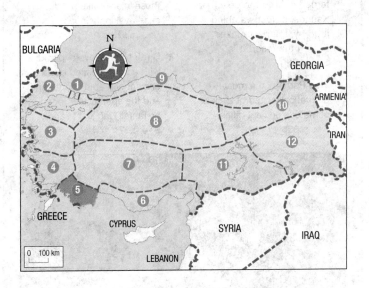

CHAPTER 5 # Highlights

* **Kaya Köyü** Abandoned Greek Orthodox village near Fethiye, a moving relic of the 1923 population exchange. See p.320

* **The Lycian Way** This long-distance trail – linking coves, ruins and mountain wilderness – is ideal in low season. See p.325

* **Dalyan river life** Being ferried on it to the beach and Kaunos, or just watching it go by, the river makes Dalyan the resort it is. See p.328

* **Tlos** Perhaps the most dramatically sited of Lycia's numerous ancient cities. See p.336

* **Patara** Roman ruins behind an enormous sandy beach, among the Mediterranean's longest. See p.348

* **Kaş** Set opposite the Greek islet of Kastellórizo, this is one of the most congenial resorts on this coast. See p.351

* **Kekova** Eerie seascapes and submerged ruins at these inlets make an ideal sea-kayaking venue. See p.361

* **Çıralı** Nature-lovers' paradise with a turtle-nesting beach, an ancient city at the south end and the spectacular foothills of Tahtalı Dağ just inland. See p.374

▲ Lycian ruins near Kekova

5

The Turquoise Coast

Turkey's southwesternmost shore, noted for its fine beaches and stunning scenery, has long been dubbed "**the Turquoise Coast**" in tourist-board speak, after the hues of its horizons and the sea. It's dominated by the Baba, Akdağ and Bey mountains, which drop precipitously to the main coastal highway which often skims just above the water. Along here, and some way inland, lay ancient **Lycia**, whose independent people bequeathed a legacy of distinctive rock tombs to Turkish tourism.

Until the late 1970s there was no continuous paved road through here, and most seaside settlements were reachable only by boat. Many attractive coves and islets are still inaccessible to vehicles, with yachting and *gulet* trips accordingly popular. But local roads have vastly improved since then, reaching hitherto isolated bays such as Kekova, Adrasan and Çıralı. However, the impact of development has been minimized by restricted building height and special protection regimes for nearby archeological sites and wildlife habitats, and touting in the streets and at *otogar*s is not yet at the level of Kuşadası, Selçuk or Pamukkale.

The usually excellent **Highway 400** links Marmaris and Antalya, via most sights along the way, offering occasional views. A bypass between Kalkan and Dalaman, including a 2009-opened tunnel (toll 3TL) at Göcek, has sharply reduced local travel times (eg, Fethiye to Patara in 1hr). The coast is best approached via **Dalaman airport**, to which there are regular direct international flights most of the year, as well as domestic flights from Istanbul.

At the far west of the region, **Dalyan** is noted for its sandy beach – a sea-turtle nesting ground – and the ruins of **Kaunos**, as well as being an attractive small resort in itself, though now – as everywhere on this coast – holiday-home sales nearly match conventional tourism as a money-spinner. East of here, **Fethiye** is the Turquoise Coast's oldest resort and largest town; along with **Ölüdeniz** lagoon, it's handy for some of the area's numerous and spectacularly sited Lycian ruins such as **Oenoanda**, **Kadyanda** and **Tlos**, in dramatic mountainous locations. Further southeast, **Patara** abuts one of Turkey's best beaches, making it easy to combine sea and sun with cultural forays to the **Letoön** sanctuary, **Pınara**, **Sidyma** and **Xanthos**. Other convenient bases are the nearby resorts of **Kalkan** and **Kaş**, smaller than Fethiye and pitched at rather different clienteles.

Further east, **Finike** is the next major town: rather a washout as a resort unless you're a yachtie, though the starting point for a precipitous inland route past ancient **Arykanda** to **Elmalı**. The mountain air and marvellous scenery repay the trip, especially if a return loop to the coast is made via **Gömbe**, jumping-off point for the alpine attractions of **Akdağ**.

Beyond Finike, the scenery becomes increasingly impressive as you enter conifer forests on the slopes of **Tahtalı Dağ**, officially designated a national park, before

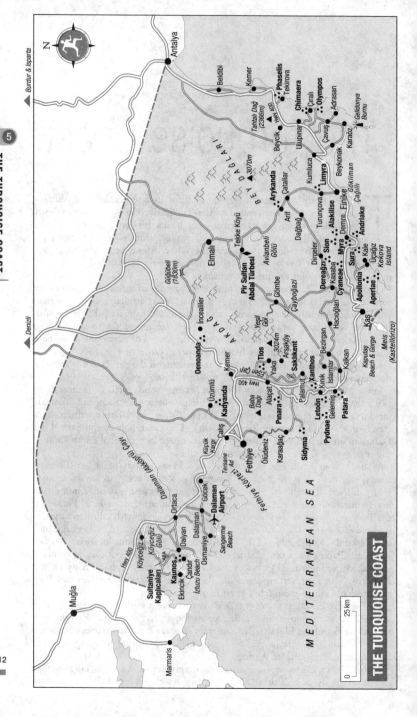

THE TURQUOISE COAST

0   25 km

passing ancient **Olympos** – plus more good beaches at **Adrasan** and **Çıralı** – and ancient **Phaselis**. Thereafter, however, a string of functional (indeed dreary) purpose-built resorts dominated by German and Russian holiday-makers lines the approach to Antalya.

Some history

Mountainous, rugged **Lycia** (*Likya* in Turkish) lies south of a line drawn roughly between Antalya and Köyceğiz Gölü. At the core of the territory, the Bey Dağları and Akdağ, each exceeding 3000m elevation, isolate it from the rest of Anatolia. Relatively secure in their mountain fastness, the fiercely independent ancient Lycians – probably an indigenous, pre-Hittite people – organized their main cities and conurbations of smaller towns as the democratic **Lycian Federation**, with 23 voting units. This elected municipal and federal officials and, until imperial Rome assumed control, made decisions of state. Homer's *Iliad* mentions the Lycians as allies of the Trojans; later, in the sixth century BC, the region was subdued by the Persian general Harpagos, but then largely left to govern itself.

From 454 BC, after the Athenian general Kimon had expelled the Persians from the Mediterranean coast, the Lycians became members of the Athens-dominated Delian League. The League ceased to exist after the Peloponnesian War and Lycia again fell under Persian domination. Alexander the Great arrived in 333 BC and, after conquering Halikarnassos, easily secured the region's surrender; following his death Lycia was ruled by Alexander's general, Ptolemy, also king of Egypt. Under Ptolemaic rule in the third century BC Greek displaced the native Lycian language and Lycian cities adopted Greek constitutions. The Ptolemies were defeated by Antiokhos III in 197 BC, himself bested in 189 BC by the Romans, who handed the kingdom over to the Rhodians. The Lycians bitterly resented Rhodian control and succeeded in 167 BC in having this administrative relegation revoked.

Thereafter, the Lycians enjoyed over two centuries of semi-independence under a revived federation, resisting the Pontic king Mithridates in 88 BC and being subsequently rewarded by Rome for their loyalty. During the Roman civil wars, Lycian reluctance to assist Brutus caused the destruction of Xanthos, and in 43 AD it was joined to Pamphylia in a larger Roman province. **Roman imperial rule** saw Lycia reach its maximum ancient population of 200,000, a figure not again equalled until the twentieth century, and the cities were graced by the Roman civic architecture constituting most of the ruins on view today.

During the fourth century the province was divided by Diocletian and a period of Byzantine-supervised decline followed, abetted by Arab raids in the seventh and eighth centuries. From then on, the area's history resembled that of the rest of western Anatolia, where, after Selçuk Turk sovereignty during the eleventh and twelfth centuries, and an interlude of minor emirates, a more durable Anatolian Muslim state was installed by the **Ottomans**. They continued a pattern of moving nomadic Turkic tribes into the Lycian uplands, leaving the coast to pirates and local chieftains, until in the eighteenth century the sultan ordered its settlement by more tractable, productive Greek Orthodox colonists from the offshore islands.

Fethiye

FETHIYE is the fulcrum of the Turquoise Coast, and a hub of its property industry, though it remains a lively market town of nearly 70,000, expanding north along the coastal plain here. The transport and marketing of oranges and tomatoes is also significant. Fethiye occupies the site of ancient **Telmessos**, and

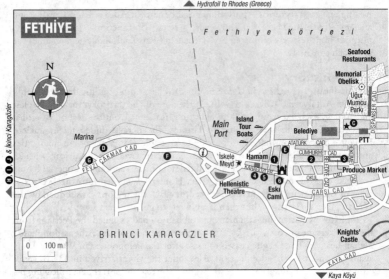

Little is known about early **Telmessos**, except that it wasn't originally part of the Lycian Federation and, in the fourth century BC, actually resisted it. A Lycian ruler later subdued the Telmessans, and during the Roman imperial era it was part of the Federation, if unique in having good relations with Rhodes. During the eighth century, the city's name changed to **Anastasiopolis** in honour of a Byzantine emperor. This became **Makri** in the following century (*Meğri* in Turkish), and – after the expulsion of the predominantly Greek Orthodox population – Fethiye during the 1930s, in honour of Fethi Bey, a pioneering pilot and World War I casualty. A small Jewish community remained here well into Republican times, until dying out or emigrating to Israel by the 1950s. Little remains of the medieval town, partly because it suffered two immense **earthquakes** in 1857 and 1957, which toppled most buildings, their rubble compacted under the present quay and shoreline boulevard.

Arrival, transport and information

The **otogar** is over 2km east of the town centre at the junction with the Ölüdeniz road. Short-haul **dolmuşes** run almost constantly from here to the accommodation district of Karagözler, sparing you a 3km walk, or shelling out for a taxi. Other dolmuşes to Ölüdeniz, Göcek, Faralya, Saklıkent and Kaya arrive and leave from the **minibus garage**, about 500m east of the central market area, south of Çarşı Caddesi on 136 Sokağı. The main **taxi ranks** are near the PTT, and in front of the ancient amphitheatre. Seasonal **hydrofoils** to Rhodes dock at the main jetty.

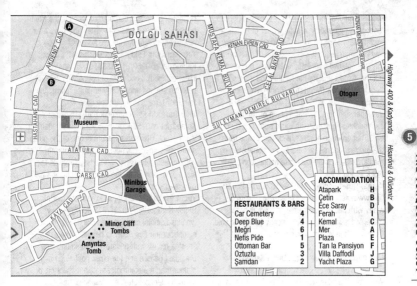

ACCOMMODATION	
Atapark	H
Çetin	B
Ece Saray	D
Ferah	I
Kemal	C
Mer	A
Plaza	E
Tan la Pansiyon	F
Villa Daffodil	J
Yacht Plaza	G

RESTAURANTS & BARS	
Car Cemetery	4
Deep Blue	4
Meğri	6
Nefis Pide	1
Ottoman Bar	5
Oztuzlu	3
Şamdan	2

Drivers are forced to adhere to a central one-way system: westbound on **Atatürk Caddesi**, the main road leading toward the harbour, lined with most services and official buildings, and eastbound mostly along inland **Çarşı Caddesi**, which threads through the heart of the commercial district. **Parking** can be a nightmare: you'll have to either park out near the museum, buy a ticket either from a parking warden or pay-and-display machines, or use one of the handful of fee-paying *otopark*s.

The **tourist office** (May–Sept daily 9am–noon & 1–5.30pm; Oct–April Mon–Sat same hours; ⓣ0252/614 1527), near the harbour at İskele Meydanı 1, is pretty useless.

Accommodation

Fethiye has lodging for all tastes and budgets; unlike other coastal resorts, you should find something even in high summer, though perhaps after considerable trudging or phoning around. Unless otherwise stated, recommended accommodation is open (or claims to be open) year-round.

Divided into Birinci (First) and İkinci (Second), the quiet, desirable **Karagözler** neighbourhood supports the oldest cluster of hotels and *pansiyon*s in Fethiye, with most premises enjoying a bay view. The only drawback is remoteness from transport terminals and restaurants, though parking your own vehicle is easier than in the centre. Fethiye's **bazaar area**, extending roughly two blocks to either side of Çarşı Caddesi, can be noisy even at night; accordingly there are very few accommodation options left there. A few paces toward the **water**, and then north along the shoreline of **Dolgu Sahası** district, are some quieter choices.

Atapark Hotel Shore road, İkinci Karagözler ⓣ0252/612 4081, ⓦwww.atahotels.com. The second best hotel in town after *Ece Saray*, with hamam, fitness centre, good if pricey restaurant and a small pool, though only the larger, pastel-coloured sea-view rooms are worth the money. ❺
Çetin Pansiyon 510 Sok no. 6, Dolgu Sahası ⓣ0252/614 6156, ⓦwww.cetinpansiyon.com.

Oblique sea views and a ground-floor terrace-bar at this welcoming *pansiyon*, run by brothers Şaban and Ramazan, more or less opposite the DSİ (Water Board) building. Rooms without breakfast or a/c are cheaper. ❷

Ece Saray Marina quay, Birinci Karagözler ⓣ0252/612 5005, ⓦwww.ecesaray.net. Indisputably the top lodging in central Fethiye, this mock-traditional low-rise hotel occupies impeccably landscaped grounds in a quiet corner of the shore esplanade. The plush rooms all enjoy a sea view, and common facilities include a spa, fitness centre, infinity pool, two bar/restaurants and a private marina. Good value for the facilities on offer. ❾

Ferah Pansiyon (Monica's Place) 16 Sok 21, İkinci Karagözler ☎0252/614 2816, ⊛www .ferahpension.com. Part of a chain of Turkish backpackers' hostels, with dorm beds (15 TL) or basic but en-suite doubles, pick-up service from the *otogar*s, internet access and optional evening meals. Some sea view, despite its location one block inland. ❷

Kemal Hotel Behind the PTT ☎0252/614 5010, ⊛www.hotelkemal.com. Cheerful, a/c rooms, many with sea views; doubles are small but balconied, suites larger but balcony-less. That said, its main virtue is a convenient and fairly quiet location. ❹

Mer Pansiyon Akdeniz Cad, Dolgu Sahası ☎0252/614 1177, ⊛www.merpansiyon.com. Welcoming, Danish–Turkish-run outfit with pleasant breakfast salon and carpeted a/c rooms, the front ones with sea-view balcony. They also have a large apartment to rent on Şövalye Adası. ❸

Tan Pansiyon Eski Karagözler Cad 41, Birinci Karagözler ☎0252/614 1584, ⓔtanpansiyon @hotmail.com. Good budget option with self-catering kitchen and mostly en-suite rooms; the four roof-terrace units are the best. ❷

Villa Daffodil Fevzi Çakmak Cad 115, İkinci Karagözler ☎0252/614 9595, ⊛www.villadaffodil .com. Mock-Ottoman structure in one of the quieter shoreline corners, its pool, on-site restaurant, hamam and landscaped grounds, as well as fair-sized pine- and white-tile rooms, making it a prime mid-range option. ❹

Yacht Plaza Hotel Opposite the yacht marina, Birinci Karagözler ☎0252/612 5067, ⊛www .yachtplazahotel.com. Aspires like its grander neighbour the *Ece Saray* to be a self-contained seaside resort, with private jetty, lush bay-side breakfast garden and fair-sized pool. Rooms are plainer than the common areas, but cheery and perfectly serviceable. ❹

The Town

The remains of ancient **Telmessos** are obvious as soon as you arrive. Above the bazaar, striking in their proximity to town, are a number of Lycian rock tombs. Most notable – and worth a closer inspection, despite swarms of children offering to guide you there unnecessarily – is the **Amyntas Tomb** (daily 8.30am–sunset; 8TL), so called because of the Greek inscription *Amyntou tou Ermagiou* (Amyntas son of Hermagios) on the wall of the tomb. To get there, take any lane leading south from Kaya Caddesi (cars can make it up) which give onto 115 Sokağı running along the base of the fenced-in archeological area. The tomb porch consists of two Ionic columns surmounted by a triangular pediment, carved in imitation of a temple facade – right down to the bronze nails on the doorframes – giving an excellent impression of what wooden temple porches would have looked like. The tomb would have been entered through the bottom right-hand panel of the doorway, but this was broken by grave robbers long ago.

Behind the main quay sprawls the conspicuous Hellenistic **theatre**, excavated only since 1994. Much of its masonry was carted away after the 1957 earthquake for construction material, so it's rather frayed at the edges. Benefit concerts are sometimes staged to raise funds for further restoration, though the process is completely stalled at present.

There's little else to see in Fethiye, other than the so-called **Knight's Castle**, on the hillside behind the bazaar. The path to the castle leads off Çarşı Caddesi through backstreets, affording good views of the town on the way. The fortress is attributed to the Knights of St John, but a variety of architectural styles suggests handiwork on the part of Lycians, Greeks, Romans, Byzantines and Turks. The Gypsy shantytown formerly around the walls has been cleared for a future park, though as with the theatre, funds are lacking for further works.

Tucked away inconspicuously amongst various schools, Fethiye's **museum** (set to open in 2010) is poorly labelled, dark and small – issues hopefully addressed in the overhaul – but worth a visit for its troves of coins, jewellery, statue fragments

Boat tours and cruises

The standard-issue, multi-island, one-day **boat tours** cost about €12/25TL per person; just turn up at the quayside for daily departures between May and October, usually leaving at around 10am and returning at 6pm. However, these one-day trips take in a set repertoire of relatively spoilt islands, with little time at each; it's far better to charter your own crewed boat to stop at just one or two selected islands. If you've more time, sign on for one of the **cabin cruises** which depart at least five days a week in season. Four-night, three-day itineraries head either west to Marmaris via Göcek and Ekincik (less popular but more scenic), or more commonly four-day cruises run east, with overnights near or at Gemiler Adası, Kalkan and Kekova before a final minibus shuttle from Andriake to the backpacker lodges at Olympos: allow €165–210 per person, including full board and drink (excluding alcohol). Paying a bit over the cheapest option, and boarding only owner-operated craft, is recommended to ensure quality; also make sure you check the craft carefully before paying, and talk to returning clients – complaints about everything from blocked toilets to abusive, non-English-speaking crew to hidden extra charges are common. Two Fethiye **outfitters** which have generated positive feedback are Big Backpackers (℡0252/614 1981 or 0532/235 2978, ⊛www.bigbackpackers.com) and the well-established, Australian/Turkish-run Before Lunch (℡0535/636 0076, ⊛www.beforelunch.com), which runs six- and nine-cabin boats and is noted for its good meals – they're accordingly at the high end of the price range.

and pottery. Its most compelling exhibit is a stele found at the Letoön (see p.341), dating from 358 BC; its trilingual (Lycian, Greek and Aramaic) text was vital in deciphering the Lycian language. The votive "Stele of Promise" to the god Kakasbos is an example of a custom particular to northern Lycia. Highlight of the small ethnographic section is a nineteenth-century Greek carved door.

Finally, another huge stele – or rather nocturnally illuminated **obelisk** – of a different sort dominates waterfront Uğur Mumcu Parkı. A pet project of the MHP (Nationalist)-run municipality, it was erected in 2001 to honour locals killed during the long-running PKK insurrection. Local outcry converted it to a general servicemen's memorial for all recent conflicts.

Eating and drinking

One of the best options for eating in Fethiye is to head for the central courtyard of the **fish and produce market**, and buy the fish of your choice (best selection before 7pm) from the central stalls, then take it to be cooked at one of several *meyhanes* around the perimeter (€2.50/5TL basic fee); however, exorbitantly priced drinks and accompanying *meze* are the norm here, so maybe carry on into the vegetable section and eat your fish at the *Oztulu* diner there. That said, the market square is a lovely, traffic-free environment with views up to the castle, but if you want to eat fish by the sea, the only option is a row of seafood **restaurants** behind Uğur Mumcu Parkı, though they aren't nearly as good value as the central market. Alternatively, the long-running doyenne of local eateries, *Meğri*, Çarşı Cad 30 (supposedly 24-hour), is acceptable for home-style Turkish dishes and puddings, though avoid its blatantly touristy and overpriced annexe at Likya Sok 8–9. Less expensive, alcohol-free meals can be had at *Şamdan*, 96 Sok 7, with a good range of grills, *hazır yemek* and puddings (closes by 8pm), or at the ever-popular *Nefis Pide* at Eski Cami Sok 9, which also serves a range of excellent kebabs and meat dishes at indoor/outdoor tables.

Most of Fethiye's **drinking bars** are in the old bazaar along with a smattering of live Turkish music venues (Fri/Sat only). A well-established favourite is *Car*

Cemetery Bar at the south end of Hamam Sokağı, with the almost adjacent *Deep Blue* getting good marks for conviviality and staying open until 3am. Nearby on Karagözler Sokağı, the *Ottoman Bar* offer *nargile*s as well as drinks and dancing.

Listings

Airline THY is represented centrally by Fetur, Atatürk Cad 72 ☎ 0252/614 2443; service bus to Dalaman airport for THY flights provided.

Books Natur-el, near the Hayal Cinema and PTT, has a limited stock of foreign-language books.

Car rental Hi-Car, at the yacht marina ☎ 0252/614 7434; Intercity, Atatürk Cad 106 ☎ 0252/612 2281, ⊛ www.fethiyerentacar.com; Oscar, Dispanser Sok 23A ☎ 0252/612 7778, ⊛ www .oscarrentacar.com.

Hamam At Hamam Sok 2 (daily 7am–midnight); usually lukewarm and touristy, not a particularly good introduction to Turkish baths despite the purported sixteenth-century vintage of the building.

Hydrofoil From late May to early October, hydrofoils run almost daily directly to Rhodes in Greece (journey time 1hr 30min); current price about €85 return. For exact schedules see "Travel details" at the end of the chapter, and contact designated agent Yeşil Dalyan (see below).

Motorbike rental Abalı, just behind the theatre roundabout ☎ 0252/612 8812.

Post office Main PTT is on Atatürk Cad (Mon–Sat 8am–midnight, Sun 9am–7pm).

Scuba-diving Though sadly lacking in fish, the gulf offers reasonable visibility, coral and other invertebrates, walls and caves, as well as submerged ruins. Two outfits to try are Dolphin Diving Centre,

its boat moored on the quay behind the post office (☎ 0535/717 3130, ⊛ www.dolphindiving.com.tr), or Diver's Delight, Dispanser Sok 25/B, Cumhuriyet Mahallesi, near the memorial obelisk (☎ 0252/612 1099, ⊛ www.diversdelight.com). Two-dive day rates start at £35, while PADI four-day courses cost £265, and CMAS two-star certification £250.

Shopping Fethiye's above-cited central food market is located between Cumhuriyet Cad and Tütün Sok – adjacent is a district with plenty of fake (plus a few real) designer clothes and perfume; safflower marketed as saffron and adulterated honey (plus the odd pickpocket) abound too. Main market day is Tuesday, when local villagers flood into town with their produce; peak hours 10.30am–1pm. The place to hunt for carpets, leather goods, and jewellery is Paspatur district, especially to either side of Hamam Sok. Supermarket chains Tansaş and Carrefour have small branches just inland from Atatürk Cad, near the PTT.

Travel agents Lama Tours by the hamam (☎ 0252/614 4964), and Labranda Tourism, Atatürk Cad opposite Belediye (☎ 0252/612 0323), handle tickets for all airlines; Yeşil Dalyan at Fevzi Çakmak Cad 168 opposite the main jetty (☎ 0252/612 4015), is the sole outlet for hydrofoil tickets to Rhodes.

Around Fethiye

Easily reached on a day-trip are a variety of attractions: the appealingly remote ancient city of **Kadyanda**, the huge abandoned village of **Kaya Köyü**, and a handful of popular if variable coastal havens such as **Aya Nikola** and **Gemiler**. Most of these sites are well served by public transport, and a few can even be reached on foot from Fethiye.

Kadyanda

Under an hour's drive north of Fethiye, the ruined mountain-top city of **Kadyanda** dates back at least 2500 years, but has only seen tourists since the mid-1990s. It's accessible on a broad, well-marked road from a roundabout on the bypass highway, northeast of Fethiye, and the initial, paved 16km to **ÜZÜMLÜ** (served by frequent public transport) are quickly covered. This attractive village has made little of its proximity to the ruins, other than a basic **restaurant** opposite the mosque and a low-key trade in its fine *dastar* cloth. At the crossroads here, turn left at the usual black-on-yellow sign, then proceed 3.5km more on a narrow paved road to just beyond the summit of a pass with a view of Akdağ. Now bear

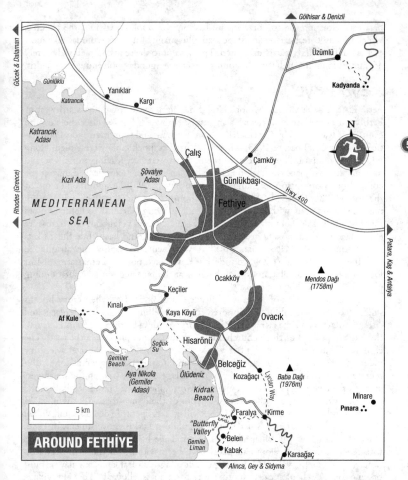

right, following another "Kadyanda" sign, to negotiate over 5km of improved dirt track to a small car park in the pines below the site. The old direct **path from Üzümlü** (90min up, 1hr down), short-cutting all but the last 2km of the road, is waymarked in red and white.

At **the site** (unfenced, always open; 8TL if warden present), an arrow points you towards a self-guided tour along a loop path. First bear south, past numerous vaulted tombs of the **necropolis**, then keep close to bits of the **city wall** on the left, followed by a climb to a false summit with a long, partly preserved **agora**, and views of Fethiye. At the true top of things awaits the site's highlight: a long, narrow **stadium**, with seven rows of seats surviving. Steps in the seats lead up to a huge jumble of masonry, all that's left of a **temple** to an unknown deity. On the opposite side of the stadium stand substantial **Roman baths**, with their polygonal masonry and entry archway. At the northeast edge of the stadium, a flat expanse is pierced by the mouth of a deep cistern that supplied the city with water – one of many, so beware holes in the ground.

Finally the path angles south to the best-preserved stretch of **city wall**, punctuated by windows and affording fine views of distant ridges and forested valleys in between. Crossing the top of a square bastion, you look down into the **theatre**, which retains its rear-facing and stage wall, plus many of its seats – though like most of Kadyanda it's only partly excavated. The descent to the road completes a leisurely 45-minute walk through superb mountain scenery – good reason enough for a visit.

Kaya Köyü

Eerie **KAYA KÖYÜ**, Asia Minor's largest medieval ghost town, lies southwest of Fethiye, near the site of ancient Karmylassos. Known as **Levissi** after the eleventh century, it was settled by Greek Orthodox Christians and supported a local population of over 3000 before 1923, when its Christian inhabitants were exiled, along with more than a million others, to metropolitan Greece, leaving a dramatic and moving site that places in stark relief the human suffering experienced during the compulsory **population exchange** (see Contexts, p.698). Despite the horrors of the 1919–1922 Greco–Turkish war, relations between Christian and Muslim remained good here, with local "Turks" accompanying "Greeks" to Fethiye to bid them farewell. Tales abound of Christians entrusting their neighbours with treasure chests against their possible return; they never did come back, but the caskets remain unopened. Macedonian Muslims were sent to occupy the abandoned buildings but most didn't stay, considering Kaya's land poor and emigrating. Most locals now live in Keçiler and Kınalı hamlets at the far fringes of the surrounding plateau, overlooked by the ruins.

All you can see now of Kaya is a hillside (admission 8TL, when entry booths staffed) covered with about six hundred ruined dwellings – all with fireplaces and cisterns intact – and the attractive **Panayia Pyrgiotissa** basilica (or Kato Panayia), the most important of three churches here, about 200m uphill from the road. The church, dated 1888 by a scandalously deteriorated floor mosaic but over a century older, retains some of its marble altar screen and murals, but its general dereliction merely serves to highlight the plight of the village. A grisly item in the southwest corner of the church precinct is a **charnel house** piled with human leg bones; the departing Orthodox took the exhumed skulls of their ancestors with them.

As with other remote, abandoned Greek villages, proper title deeds for individual Kaya properties were never issued by the Republican Turkish government. In 1988, mass acquisition of the village houses for package-holiday accommodation was threatened, though development plans have been withdrawn and a preservation order slapped on the valley. Only five percent of agricultural land area may be built on and only archeologically approved restoration is allowed. The old village remains the focus of Greco–Turkish **reconciliation festivals**, with its Orthodox diaspora visiting regularly from Greece; Orthodox Patriarch Vartholomeos himself stayed here in 2000. Kaya has again been in the spotlight since Louis de Bernières disguised it as Eskibahçe, the setting for most of his 2003 epic *Birds Without Wings* (see "Books", p.737).

Practicalities

A paved nine-kilometre road – plus a cobbled **path**, still two-thirds intact, which significantly short-cuts it – climb up from behind the castle in Fethiye towards Kaya Köyü (about two hours' walk). By **dolmuş** from the main terminal it's a fifteen-kilometre journey, taking a roundabout route via the resorts of Ovacık and Hisarönü, whose tendrils end around 3km east of the village.

There are various **accommodation** options in Kaya's satellite hamlets. An excellent posh choice in Keçiler, on the valley's north slope, is *Misafir Evi* (T0252/618 0162, Wwww.kayamisafirevi.com; B&B, half board available), a boutique hotel with a well-regarded, all-year restaurant, nine tasteful, wood-trimmed rooms and a large pool. In the same hamlet stand four high-standard

▲ The abandoned village of Kaya Köyü

two-bedroom villas arrayed around a pool (UK ☎0044 118 932 1866, ⓦwww
.turkeyvillas.com); these cost from £600 per week each, with help finding flights
and hire cars available. One of the best-value establishments, about 1500m from
Kaya's central teahouse, at the east edge of Kınalı hamlet, is friendly, family-run
🏕 *Village Garden* (☎0252/618 0259; ❸), comprising four lovely new studios or
one-bed apartments and a fair-priced on-site restaurant balancing meat, seafood
and their own vegetables on its menu. In Kınalı itself, 2km west of Kaya, a trio
of exquisitely refurbished old houses sleeping four can be booked through
Exclusive Escapes (see p.32).

Central Kaya has about a dozen **cafés** and **restaurants** but few are particularly
memorable. *Bülent'in Yeri*, on the through-road near the colonnaded cistern, is
good for a quick snack of budget-priced *saç böreği*. Best of the more ambitious
eateries is *Sarnıç* (open most of the year), with quality live music some nights and
an informal museum of local finds inside what was once a prominent merchant's
house. For a superlative carnivorous feed, head for 🏕 *Cin Bal*, well-signposted at
the eastern edge of the village, where whole hung sheep form much of the indoor
decor; summer seating (book weekends on ☎0252/618 0066) is in the attractive
outdoor garden, while the winter hall – often packed with locals – is kept cosy by
each table having its own grill-fireplace. This is a *kendin pişin kendin ye* place,
where you buy superb lamb by the kilo and then cook it yourself at tableside.
Good if limited *mezes*, vegetable garnish and reasonably priced drink complete
the experience.

Kaya is becoming something of a high-quality **activity centre**. There's English-
run **horseriding** at Perma Ranch (☎0252/618 0182, ⓦwww.permaranch.co.uk)
on the eastern outskirts, and 7 Capes Sea Kayaking has its HQ in Kınalı hamlet
(☎0252/618 0390, ⓦwww.sevencapes.com), offering well-priced **sea-kayaking**
tours along the coast as far south as the eponymous Seven Capes (Yedi Burunlar).

Af Kule, Gemiler and Aya Nikola

About 1km beyond Kınalı, there's a marked turning west for the isolated ruined monastery of **Af Kule**; it's 1km to the road's end, where you bear up and right onto the broad, obvious donkey-track. Blue-paint arrows and red dots lead you west–northwest onto a ridge, 25 minutes from the asphalt road, before the path plunges down five minutes more in zigzags to the roofless but otherwise intact monastery on its terrace. Wedged into the cliff behind are a couple of chapels; stone steps lead to the higher hermitage which, though now bare, is well worth the ascent.

Isolated **Gemiler** beach lies 8km southwest of Kaya Köyü along a paved road not served by any public transport. Despite what you may read elsewhere, it is not possible to walk directly from Kaya to Gemiler – the intervening terrain is steep and dangerous. Instead, first proceed past Kınalı, and then use the paint-blob-marked trail down from the top of the gully, 200m past the point where the road starts its descent.

Gemiler's only amenities are three semi-legal **snack-shacks** to the right – worth avoiding owing to numerous reports of creative billing – and the municipally run canteen on the left with posted prices for light snacks and drinks. The beach itself (not always clean) is divided up by small jetties and sunbed concessions (you pay 2.50TL to park as well); the water offshore can be murky, but offers decent snorkelling in autumn.

Just offshore at Gemiler looms a prime destination for local boat and sea-kayak trips: **Aya Nikola (Gemiler) Adası** (8TL if warden present), on which stand prominent remains including a few rock tombs, a seventh-century Byzantine monastery and a later, ruined hamlet complete with church. Gemiler's environs, along with Ölüdeniz, were used as a location for *The Odyssey* (1997), starring Greta Scacchi and Isabella Rossellini. Without a boat, all you can do is walk from Kaya Köyü to Soğuk Su cove directly opposite Gemiler island, over the saddle with the little white chapel, in about forty minutes – see box opposite for other hikes.

Ocakköy, Ovacık and Hisarönü

South of Fethiye extend a string of functional dormitory-resorts that, despite arid inland settings, sprouted from nothing in the late 1980s and now get the lion's share of tourist overnights in the Fethiye area, with water pumped up a pipeline from around Fethiye.

The main road initially southeast out of Fethiye climbs to a pass, where a signposted track leads west to an abandoned Ottoman shepherd's hamlet, **OCAKKÖY**, once the winter quarters for Ovacık (see below). The ex-hamlet has metamorphosed into *Ocakköy* (☎0252/616 6157, ⓦwww.ocak-koy.com; ❺ cottage, ❹ rooms/apts), some thirty individually styled, self-catering, restored stone cottages dotting the hillside, plus conventional rooms or apartments around three swimming pools. The cottages enjoy commanding views to Baba Dağı, the ancient Mount Antikragos, and make for a wonderfully peaceful stay, barring the occasional disco-thump from Hisarönü. The resort actively caters for disabled clients, and kids, with a crèche and designated family pool. All units are available from mid-April through October, though at other times you can secure a cottage on a self-catering basis, as there's no restaurant service in winter; heat is provided by the working fireplaces.

Just beyond the pass, straggly, linear **OVACİK** seems to consist entirely of estate agencies, villas and about a hundred *pansiyon*s and small hotels dominated by budget-tour operators – surprisingly, in view of its inland, roadside location and

A walk from Kaya Köyü to Ölüdeniz

This mostly downhill walk takes you from Kaya village to the northwest shore of the lagoon in about ninety minutes, with another thirty minutes separating you from the main dolmuş stop. The route begins in Kaya from the easterly Yukarı Kilise (aka Taksiarhis), and is fairly well marked by red-and-yellow blazes; ignore blue or rust-red paint blobs leading you over the pass with a windmill, chapel and Turkish flag. The proper path climbs somewhat faintly to a plateau within fifteen minutes, then levels out through pine woods for another twenty minutes, before reaching fine overviews of Aya Nikola and Soğuk Su, and a stretch of well-engineered, cobbled, descending path. This ends at some charcoal-burners' flats, with a less distinct path to a large rectangular cistern just beyond, before the head of a ravine. Here the trail appears to split; the left-hand option is easier going. Just under an hour along both routes converge before you reach an obvious pass with some pine-studded rocks on the right, affording the first eyeful of the lagoon. From here you've an uncomplicated, if sharp, drop to the first sunbed concession on the shore.

the modest endowments of many establishments. One would love to know what the locals make of the prominent pork butcher's on the bypass road, right opposite an "erotic shop" with relatively demure lingerie on display. Folk party in **HİSARÖNÜ**, which (with as many more lodgings) notionally lies 1km along the side road to Kaya and Gemiler. It has effectively merged with Ovacık and offers all dubious resort delights, from pulsing sound systems to tattoo parlours.

About the highest standard **accommodation** here, well south of the noise, is the four-star *Montana Pine Resort* (℡0252/616 7108, ⓦwww.montanapine.com; ❻; closed Nov–March). It's a sympathetically designed complex, with large rooms or suites and good bathrooms, decent buffet breakfasts and three pools. Given the quick-buck nature of Hisarönü, few **restaurants** – mostly mediocre, identikit places serving "pub grub" priced in pounds or euros – stay in business for long; **bars** have names like *Delboy's* or *Codswallop*. If you're based at Kaya Köyü or Ölüdeniz, Hisarönü's main utility is the presence of bank **ATMs** and competitive **car rental**; Explora (℡0252/616 6890, ⓦwww.exploraturkey.com) is particularly recommended.

Ölüdeniz and beyond

Ölüdeniz, the "Dead Sea" 12km south of Fethiye (frequent **dolmuşes**, 15min journey until late at night) is the azure lagoon (dawn to dusk; admission to the fenced national park 3.5TL per person, 12TL saloon car, 6TL scooter) featuring on every second Turkish travel poster. Its warm, if occasionally turbid, waters make for pleasant swimming even in April or May, or a spin in a rented kayak or pedalo (motorized sports are only allowed in the open sea). However, the environs of this once-pristine lagoon rank as one of the country's most popular resorts, and its beaches – both the spit enclosing the inlet and the more exposed strand of **Belceğiz** – reach saturation level on summer weekends.

At such times, it's perhaps worth avoiding Ölüdeniz altogether in favour of the **Kıdrak** forestry-department beach (not staffed 2009, but expect admission and parking fee), 3km east of Belceğiz beside the all-inclusive *Club Lykia World* (no walk-ins). Kıdrak is cleaner and far less commercialized than Belceğiz, with just a small snack bar and seasonal sunbed/umbrella concession (there's also natural shade in the pines).

Both Belceğiz and Kıdrak serve as landing venues for **paragliders**, kitted out by several beachfront outfits for a hefty €85–100 and taken to a point near the summit of 1976-metre Baba Dağı for launching (April–Nov) – best visibility is in autumn. Despite rates inflated by payoffs to the forest service, this is reputedly the second best spot worldwide to indulge: Sky Sports (℡0252/617 0511, ⓦwww.skysports-turkey.com) is the most heavily publicized and longest established outfit.

A range of **boat trips** to remote coves, islets like Gemiler and Byzantine ruins is also on offer, though beware limp lunches, bored guides and stops missed out or rushed. The cheapest (3 daily dolmuş boats, 11am–6pm; 12TL return) and most popular destination is the beach and limestone canyon just inland dubbed **Butterfly Valley** (*Kelebek Vadisi*) after the many species that flutter about during the right seasons. There's also a waterfall (5TL admission; 20min inland) and the beach itself, which is frequented by an uneasy mix of day-trippers sipping overpriced beers at the café and New Age patrons attending regular yoga, Indian dance and healing seminars whilst staying at the basic tent-or-bungalow accommodation here (ⓦthebutterflyvalley.blogspot.com).

Accommodation

Most accommodation clusters behind Belceğiz beach with its broad, landscaped pedestrian promenade. Of the rough-and-ready **bungalow-campsites** that welcomed the hippie vanguard here during the late 1970s, none survive; the next generation of such clientele is obliged to patronize four **tent/bungalow/caravan sites** along the north shore of the lagoon. First encountered, and best, is *Sugar Beach Club* (℡0252/617 0048, ⓦwww.thesugarbeachclub.com), with three grades of wooden bungalows (80–125TL). In the former orchards behind Belceğiz and on the slopes flanking the road in are perhaps forty **hotels**, mostly in thrall to package companies, though there are worthwhile exceptions.

Jade Residence Mid-promenade, Belceğiz ℡0252/617 0690, ⓦwww.jade-residence.com. Near-identical rooms to the loosely affiliated *Oyster*, perhaps a tad quieter, with a similarly generous buffet breakfast and jacuzzi on the deck of the smaller pool. Open all year. ➐

Oyster Residences Mid-promenade, Belceğiz, adjacent to preceding ℡0252/617 0765, ⓦwww.oysterresidences.com; 26 popular, large, wooden-floored rooms done up in quality textiles, arranged around a fair-sized pool with wooden decking; also direct beach access. ➐

Paradise Garden halfway back to Ovacık ℡0252/617 0545, ⓦwww.paradisegardenhotel .com. Best of the hillside hotels, set in vast grounds, with variably sized if low-ceilinged and balcony-less rooms. It's a longish walk through fifteen acres of garden to the main pool, but that's quite stunning when you get there. ➏

Seyir Beach Hotel Right behind far end of the Belceğiz promenade ℡0252/617 0058, ⓦwww .seyirhotel.com. One of the best-value outfits with easy (for the area) parking: its terracotta and wood-trim units sleep two to four. ➍

Eating, drinking and nightlife

Eating out in the Ölüdeniz area is generally bland, forgettable and unusually exorbitantly priced for Turkey. A sterling exception is the durable, fair-priced *Kumsal Pide* (all year), attached to the recommended *Seyir Beach Hotel*, where the *mezes* are above average in quality and size, and a large *pide* easily feeds two; it has a **bowling alley** in the basement, surely the only one for miles. A posher option worth the money is *Secret Garden*, hidden away in Belceğiz's back lanes, featuring *tandır kebap* and sea bass baked in a salt crust; booking suggested on ℡0252/617 0231. The most obvious beachfront **nightlife** spots are *Help Bar* and its nearby upstairs rival, the *Buzz Beach Bar*.

Beyond Ölüdeniz: hamlets along the Lycian Way

South of Kıdrak lies some of the least exploited coastline in Turkey: the **Yediburun** (Seven Capes) headlands, with several isolated villages just inland. Since the early 1980s dirt (and a few paved) roads have been opened to most of them, though for many points the **Lycian Way** trail remains the most straightforward method of access. Below, we cover the first section of the route between Faralya and Kabak, at the current end of the dirt-road system, though directions are given in reverse order to those in the Lycian Way guidebook – ie, *from* Kabak. This allows for a lightly laden, half-day **walk** back to Faralya, though in 2009 side trails were marked allowing a (very) long-day circuit taking in Kirme, Karaağaç and Alınca villages up in the mountains as well. Up to six daily minibuses from Fethiye go as far as Kabak, a half-hour journey beyond Ölüdeniz careering partly along the edge of the Kelebek Vadisi.

Kabak and Gemile Liman

The bus will drop you off at the turnaround in **KABAK**, where the lower alternative of the east-bound Lycian Way descends within half an hour to the

The Lycian Way

Inaugurated in early 2000, the **Lycian Way** is a long-distance trail running parallel to much of the Turquoise Coast, taking five weeks in theory to complete – though it's expected that walkers will sample it in stages rather than tackling the whole trail at one go. It begins above Ölüdeniz and ends just shy of Antalya, taking in choice mountain landscapes and seascapes en route, with many optional detours to Roman or Byzantine ruins not found in conventional guidebooks. Some of the wildest sections are between Kabak and Gavurağili, above the Yediburun coast (discussed below), and between Kaş and Üçağız. Elevation en route varies from sea level to 1800m on the saddle of Tahtalı Dağ. October (pleasantly warm) or April and May (when water is plentiful and the days long) are the best walking seasons along most of the way, with summer out of the question except in the highest mountain stages.

The route iteslf ranges from rough boulder-strewn trails to brief stretches of asphalt, by way of forested paths, cobbled or revetted Byzantine/Ottoman roads and tractor-tracks. While the entire distance is marked with the conventional red-and-white blazes used in Europe, plus occasional metal signs giving distances to the next key destination, waymarks can be absent when you need them most. Continual bulldozing of existing footpath stretches into jeep tracks is a major problem – such that the notional initial section between Hisarönü and Kirme has now ceased to exist, with most hikers starting at Faralya – and periodic maintenance (and where necessary re-routing) barely keeps pace with fast-growing scrub and rockfalls. An unofficial "add-on" route, the *Likya Yolları*, runs from Hisarönü to Fethiye via Kaya, whilst loop side trails and alternate routes are being marked in different colour schemes. Kate Clow, who marked the original Lycian Way, also adapted the Turkish military's ordnance survey 1:50,000 maps, so a reasonably accurate guide-booklet-with-map called *The Lycian Way* is available, which indicates points for water, camping and (often obsoletely) overnighting indoors. Hard-wearing and waterproof, the map often saves the day, as trail descriptions can be frustratingly vague (though waymarking was completely redone in 2009); also be aware that timings in the text are for those with a full pack, so deduct about 25 percent when doing sections as day-hikes. The English-language version is sold at select bookshops, newsstands and travel agencies all along the coast as well as from online book retailers. A website, ⊛ www.lycianway.com, offers updates on route conditions and a user forum.

sand-and-pebble beach of **Gemile Liman**, beyond the reach of most boat tours. En route it passes through or near several recommended **trekkers' lodges** (out of ten in the valley): *Olive Garden* (℡0252/642 1083; 30–35TL per person half board only), seven bungalows with the best views and congenial locally born management; *Full Moon* (℡0252/642 1081, ⓦwww.fullmooncamp.com; all year; 35TL per person half board only) at the end of the road, with a large hillside pool if you're not up for the drop to the beach, 13 non-en-suite hillside chalets, meals at the popular bar area, and a proprietor who looks after trekkers and the local trails; part-American-run *Reflections Camp* below the *Full Moon* (℡0252/642 1020, ⓦwww.reflectionscamp.com; May–Oct; 40TL half board only), justifying the slight price premium with a high ratio of toilets (4) to chalets (9) and recycling its trash and grey water; plus *Turan's Camp* (℡0252/642 1227, ⓦwww .turancamping.com), with 17 bungalows in grades from basic (40TL half board per person) to en suite with balcony (80TL half board per person), with relatively elaborate cooking, yoga programmes and a small plunge-pool.

Begin hiking from Kabak with a steady ascent north through fields and open woodland to a track; bear right and carry on, with little altitude change, past high grain fields (and no shade) before dropping to a powerful spring in a canyon draining past **Belen** hamlet (not shown on the Lycian Way map). Next, turn right and up onto the resumed path, climbing to the last saddle between Belen and Faralya village. From this pass you've a brief, sharp drop to the road again, along a gorgeous forest path with cobbled surface. Turn right and continue along the road through the Hisar *mahalle* of Faralya.

Faralya to Kirme

FARALYA (officially Uzunyurt), set magnificently partway up the slopes of Baba Dağı, has views across to Rhodes on clear days. From the "centre" a non-vehicle lane leads downhill to *George House* (℡0252/642 1102, ⓦwww.georgehouse.net.tc; 30TL per person half board only), with a pool, tent space, a dorm, several 2008-improved chalets and excellent, mostly vegetarian food. Some 500m further along the main road there's more **accommodation** at *Gül Pansiyon* (℡0252/642 1145; ❷ B&B), which also does slightly pricey trout meals. You're more likely to get a meal or bed on spec at either of these places than at the area's most prestigious accommodation, just up the resumption of the trail proper: ⚒ *Değirmen/Die Wassermühle* (℡0252/642 1245, ⓦwww.natur-reisen.de; closed late Oct to March), where you'll be lulled to sleep by the sound of mill-race water. Seven comfortable apartments (❼ half board only) and two conventional rooms (❻ half board only) are grouped around a restaurant (meals usually for guests only), the restored mill and a stone-crafted swimming pool; minimum one-week stays are preferred.

All three establishments are perched just above "Butterfly Valley", through which a difficult, non-Lycian Way trail (with rope and pegs for safety at the scrambly bits) drops to the eponymous beach in 45 minutes (allow 1hr return). The Lycian Way itself continues sharply uphill and north from *Değirmen*, leaving the stream canyon after twenty minutes to become a steadily broadening forest track to a fountain. Some 45 minutes from Faralya, having passed fields, a goat-pen and a second cistern-spring, the path resumes as far as the central mosque of **Kirme** village (no facilities), flanked to the east and north by pine-flecked cliffs but open to the south. From here, it's recommended that you complete the long day-loop via Karaağaç and Alınca back to Kabak, on a marked path short-cutting the road from Kirme to Karaağaç. The official Lycian Way towards the northwest was ruined in spring 2009 by the blasting of a road from near the *Montana Pine Resort* to Kozağaç, and there is no longer any reason to follow this route on foot.

Göcek

Stunningly set at the northwest corner of the Gulf of Fethiye, **GÖCEK** is an obligatory stop on yacht or *gulet* tours thanks to its four marinas and busy boat-repair yard. It has become very trendy amongst both foreigners and Turks, with the late President Özal himself vacationing here on occasion (the main street is now named after him) and some very high-end apartment complexes fronting the bay. While there's no beach to speak of, the passing boat trade means an aston-ishing concentration of facilities for such a small place: supermarkets, laundries, yacht chandleries and posh souvenir shops along, or just off, the main inland commercial street, largely pedestrianized. The meticulously landscaped, lawn-fringed shore esplanade is car-free too, and venue for one of the best-attended evening promenades on this coast. The nearest proper beaches lie some 10km east at Küçük Kargı. Here two bays, pebbly **Günlüklü** and sandy, protected **Katrancı** (both 2.50TL entrance, 10TL per car) have forest backdrops, basic snack bars and no-frills campsites.

Regular **dolmuşes** link Fethiye with Göcek, leaving you at the main car park just off the inland shopping street. If you're seized by the urge to stay – and it does makes a convenient last overnight before a flight home from Dalaman – you have various **pansiyons** to choose from, plus several **hotels** or apart-hotels. Basic *pansiyons* include the air-conditioned *Ünlü* (℡0252/645 1170; ❸), the nearby, plain *Tufan's* (℡0252/645 1334; ❷) and the *Başak* by the canal (℡0252/645 1024; ❷), with a big communal veranda; all overlook the less busy, west end of the quayside. For a better standard, go for the *Yonca Resort* (℡0252/645 2255, ⓦwww.yoncaresort.com; ❻) well inland, an intimate, antique-furnished eight-room inn with a small pool in the garden.

Many local **restaurants** now cater exclusively for the trendy set with obligatory service charges and miniature portions – trends accentuated the closer you get to the Port Göcek Marina. If you're going to drop a wad, best do it at the far west end of the esplanade, where *Café Bunka* – an annexe of the Japanese Culture Centre in İstanbul – must be one of the few sushi bars on the Turkish coast. *Özcan* is considered tops for traditional Turkish *meze*, while just inland in the pedestrian zone, ⚔*Antep Sofrası* (aka *Kebap Hospital*) specializes in quality kebabs and *lahmacun* at affordable prices – they've now seaside seating as well.

Among **bars**, the most civilized – if expensive – is *Dr Jazz*, with poster decor and a jazz soundtrack; *Del Marinn*, by the fish pond at the base of the central jetty, is more popular. Alternatively, *Café West* serves good breakfast and other light meals, while nearby *Blue* metamorphoses from an expensive eatery to a lively bar after-hours.

Dalaman and Sarıgerme

The first real town west of Fethiye is bleak, grid-planned **Dalaman**, home to the Turquoise Coast's main airport, an open prison and little else. **Dalaman airport** (flight enquiries ℡0252/792 5291) has round-the-clock banking facilities, as well as three **car rental** booths: Avis (℡0252/792 5118), Budget (℡0252/792 5150) and Europcar (℡0252/792 5117). Domestic and international flights arrive at separate terminals. There are no public-transport links from the airport, so barring a transfer coach or rental car you'll have to take a taxi (15TL) 6km into town, with its central *otogar*. If you're arriving on a domestic flight, it's well worth coinciding with the Havaş coaches to Fethiye or Marmaris.

With both Göcek (see p.327) and Dalyan (see p.328) so close, there's no real reason to make Dalaman's acquaintance, though you may wish to patronize a remarkable (if clinical decor) **restaurant** right by the prison gate, run by low-risk convicts. The menu's strictly roast chicken, salad and rice, at rock-bottom prices with friendly service.

The sole other local attraction is **Sarıgerme** beach, 15km southwest of Dalaman; there's a more direct side road from Highway 400, just east of Ortaca, marked with typical black-on-yellow signs. While not quite so long as İztuzu beach near Dalyan, it's as scenic, fringed at its western, developed end with pines and offering sweeping views east toward the mountains above Fethiye. Just offshore, **Baba Adası**, capped by a crumbling, tree-obscured stone pyramid thought to be an ancient lighthouse, only partly protects the beach from prevailing southwesterly winds that make Sarıgerme ideal for sailing sports. The water is often cleaner than at İztuzu, though colder too owing to freshwater springs that dribble into the sea near the westernmost cove.

Several enormous, all-inclusive luxury complexes are set well back from the sand, since Sarıgerme is a loggerhead-turtle-nesting beach, though newer construction on the ridge overhead makes a mockery of official guidelines for such protected areas. Cars are banned from the landscaped park just behind Sardeç Halk Plajı (4TL admission), and parking is difficult. But sunbeds and umbrellas are abundant (mostly linked to the hotels), as well as watersports at three outlets (again run by hotels but open to all). Aside from a drinks stall and rudimentary snack cantina in the park, there's no food available – come prepared. For a proper, unregimented *halk plajı*, fork left at the village roundabout towards Ortaca Belediye beach, with much better parking (fee required) and limitless sand.

Dalyan and around

Westbound buses from Dalaman continue to Ortaca, from where plentiful minibuses make the twenty-minute journey to the growing town of **Dalyan**, 13km off Highway 400 and a good base for the surrounding attractions: the ancient site of **Kaunos** across the river, **İztuzu beach** at the river mouth, the beautiful freshwater lake of **Köyceğiz** with its shoreline hot springs, and the remote bay of **Ekincik**.

Dalyan

DALYAN first achieved international prominence in 1986, when a major controversy erupted over a proposed luxury hotel on nearby İztuzu beach, a hatching ground for **loggerhead turtles**. Conservationists succeeded in halting the scheme, and now the beach is statutorily protected between May and October, when eggs are laid. In the wake of this campaign, the town hoped to syle itself as ecologically correct, but its mess of identikit eateries, trinket shops, t-shirt vendors and loud bars has proved little different from other mainstream resorts. You'll notice the turtle motif everywhere from the turtle statue in the main square to restaurants and *pansiyons* being named after the creatures. Second-home sales have burgeoned locally, and the town centre is now crammed with estate agents, DIY shops and a large Migros supermarket.

Otherwise life in Dalyan revolves around the **Dalyan Çayı**, flowing past the village between Köyceğiz lake and the sea. Many choice *pansiyons* line the river's east bank, and the boats that putt-putt up and down it are the preferred means of

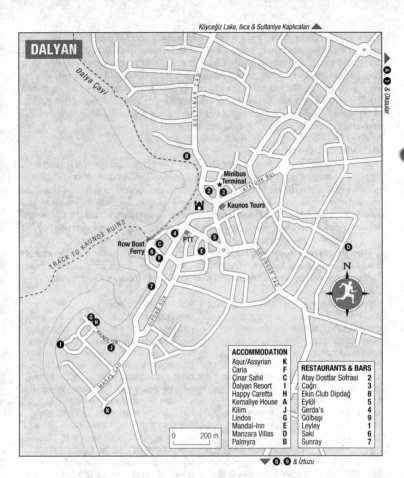

ACCOMMODATION

Asur/Assyrian	K
Caria	F
Çinar Sahil	C
Dalyan Resort	I
Happy Caretta	H
Kemaliye House	A
Kilim	J
Lindos	G
Mandal-Inn	E
Manzara Villas	D
Palmyra	B

RESTAURANTS & BARS

Atay Dostlar Sofrasi	2
Cağrı	3
Ekin Club Dipdağ	8
Eylül	5
Gerda's	4
Gölbaşı	9
Leyley	1
Saki	6
Sunray	7

0   200 m

▼ ⑧, ⑨ & İztuzu

transport to the major local sites. Craft heading downstream pass a series of spectacular fourth-century BC **"temple" tombs** in the west-bank cliffs. Landlubbers can contemplate these tombs over a tea or ice cream at the Kral Bahçesi parkland just opposite, looking out too for hedgehogs in the riverside grass, less heralded than turtles but more easily spotted.

Arrival, information and transport

Regular **dolmuşes** from Ortaca – there's little other service – arrive at the central minibus yard, near the mosque and taxi stand. There's currently no tourist office, but Ⓦ www.dalyanonline.net is a useful resource. **Dolmuş boats** to the river end of İztuzu beach (7.50TL return; 40min) depart from Kordon Boyu, opposite the mosque. In season, most have left by 10.30am, though there may be one more at 2pm. They return every half-hour or so between 3pm and sunset. Otherwise, peak-season **minibuses** ply half-hourly along the 13km road to the east end of the strand. Many of the riverside *pansiyons* and hotels also have their own small motor-boats providing morning service to the beach for a nominal fee.

Renting a **mountain bike** is another possible transport strategy, at least in the cooler months; they're available at better hotels and certain travel agents for under

10TL a day. The best **bike ride** is to İztuzu beach: there's one nasty hill en route, with *ayran* and *gözleme* stalls to pause at for refreshment in the village of Gökbel. This land route is recommended at least once, as you loop around the Sulungur lake and get glimpses of marsh and mountain not possible amid the claustrophobic reed beds of the Dalyan Çayı. The unpublicized **rowboat ferry** (3.5TL round trip), its jetty inside the Kral Bahçesi, allows access to ancient Kaunos (see p.332). Alternatively, bikes and scooters are rented on the far bank, with various local attractions accessible on both paved and dirt roads.

Accommodation

The most desirable *pansiyon*s **line or overlook the river**, though you'll have little hope of a vacancy in high season without calling well in advance. **Maraş Caddesi**, which heads from the middle of town to a dead end nearly 2km south, passes en route the junction with **Kaunos Sokağı**, home to several garden-set *pansiyon*s and hotels, with breakfast served at waterside terraces. Drivers should take the signposted **İztuzu road from the centre**, and then bear right at the second junction, to get around a one-way system and nocturnal street closures for pedestrians.

Mosquitoes are a major plague everywhere, though repellents or vaporization mats are widely sold should your accommodation not provide these or window screens. Unless stated otherwise, establishments close from November to about Easter.

River-view establishments

Asur Otel/Assyrian Hotel South end of Maraş Cad ☎0252/284 3232, ⓦwww.asurotel.com. Well-landscaped complex, with a lawn-garden down to the river, popular with tour companies. Award-winning architecture and pleasant, if small and slightly dark hexagonal rooms, some with double beds and all with a/c, contemporary bathrooms, and river or mountain views. An annexe of one-, two- or three-bedroom apartments (⑤–⑥) in the same style is available 150m inland. ⑤

Caria Hotel Yalı Sok 9, off Maraş Cad ☎0252/284 2075, ⓦwww.hotelcaria.com. Under new Anglo (Susie)-Turkish (Ali) management from 2009, this has Dalyan's best roof-terrace, complementing partly a/c (otherwise fan) 1980s-vintage terrazzo-floored rooms, many with river views. Nocturnal boat trips, bbqs, airport pic-kup on request, limited parking. ⑤ B&B.

Çınar Sahil Pansiyon Yalı Sok 14 ☎0252/284 2117. Set in a small citrus grove and perhaps the best budget choice with clean, airy one-, two- or three-bedded rooms and a rooftop breakfast terrace (plus ground-level restaurant). ②

Palmyra Hotel North of the central park; follow Kordon Boyu ☎0252/284 20 96, ⓦwww.dalyan hotelpalmyra.com. Medium-sized rooms overhauled with mini-fridges, terracotta floors, hardwood beds, plasma TV, new bathrooms and balconies with oblique river views, pitched (unusually for Dalyan) at Turkish groups as well as walk-ins. The usual roof terrace, street parking 100m away. ④

Kaunos Sokağı

Dalyan Resort ☎0252/284 5499, ⓦwww.dalyan resort.com. This self-contained complex is bidding to challenge the *Asur* as the town's top digs, with four grades of units from standard to VIP suites in good taste with travertine tiles much in evidence, airy domed restaurant, rental canoes and hamam with mud therapy offered. It's predictably popular with package operators but open all year. ⑤

Happy Caretta Hotel ☎0252/284 2109, ⓦwww .happycaretta.com. You'll appreciate the thick walls of this older building which keep the 14 rooms cool, though there's also a/c; it's worth extra for one of the four more spacious deluxe triples. Cosy upstairs lounge with fireplace for winter (it's open all year); evening meals on request; kind managing family (proprietress İlknur speaks English). ④

Kilim Hotel ☎0252/284 2253, ⓦwww.kilimhotel .com. Anglo (Becky)-Turkish (Emrah)-managed, well-overhauled 1980s hotel with, stall-showered rooms, half with balconies and/or a/c, plus a new six-room riverside annexe opposite, where breakfast is served. There's a poolside lawn under palm trees, regular bbqs and snacks on request. ③

Lindos Pansiyon ☎0252/284 2005, ⓦwww.lindospension.com. Well-appointed rooms with rare double beds and proper stall showers, as well as a family quad (④) and three upstairs balconied units. Pleasant library-lounge for cool weather, free canoes available, and genial management by English-speaking Levent Sünger. İztuzu-bound boats can be flagged down here. Late March to end Oct. ③

Elsewhere

Kemaliye House 7km towards Ortaca ☎ 0252/692
3613, ⓦ www.yabanci.com/house.html. Sympathetically renovated rural house sleeping six set in
large gardens, with a pool. Run by local travel
agent Alison Hawkes, who can also arrange flights.
All year; £40–100 per night, but minimum 3-night
stay, 1 week (£270–650) preferred.

Mandal-Inn Hotel Rodoğlu Yaşar Sünger Sok
☎ 0252/284 2286, ⓦ www.mandalinnhotel.com. A
large family team keep this cosy, tour-free hotel
with lovingly tended landscaping and a pleasant if
small pool-bar area, on a quiet leafy lane inland
from the post office. Rooms are good standard,
with new baths, if a bit garishly coloured. Airport
pick-up, street parking possible. ➍

Manzara Villas Eastern edge of town off İztuzu
road, 1km from centre; ring Döndü for directions on
☎ 0543/322 9800, 0252/284 4465, in UK
☎ 01304/375093, ⓦ www.manzara.co.uk. Three
well-designed six-person villas around a pool-
garden, with a view of the "Sleeping Giant"
mountain, make an excellent self-catering choice
for families, though good breakfasts are available.
Genial owner Clare Baker's UK office can provide
help in securing flights and car rental. £500–600
per week in high season (ten percent discount for
Rough Guide readers).

Eating and drinking

As a rule, town-centre **restaurants** in Dalyan are steeply priced, bland and anglicized – touts yell "spaghetti!" and bread comes with pots of butter, pub-style. So
it's fairly futile to expect much Turkish culinary authenticity or generous portion
size; with some sterling exceptions, you're better off dining a bit out of town
proper. Local **café** options are humdrum except for *Gerda's Waffles*, a little outdoor
booth doing coffee and cakes as well, under trees near the PTT. **Nightlife** along
the upper pedestrianized reaches of Maraş Caddesi is fairly self-evident; as bar
format and ownership changes almost yearly, just choose according to the noise
level and the crowd. One of the more durable ones is *Sunray*, on the river side of
this street, with live music most summer nights.

Centre

Atay Dostlar Sofrası Opposite the central
mosque. Inexpensive, licensed *hazır yemek* place
with grilled dishes as well.

Çağrı Pide Entrance to the minibus square,
hidden behind ATMs and palm trees. Well-
priced grills and a few competent *meze*s besides
pide; licensed.

Eylül in grid of pedestrianized bazaar lanes near
the Belediye. Tops for home-style steam-tray food
and regional *köfte*; open 24hr.

Saki on the riverbank, near rowboat jetty. The best
traditional Turkish *meze* in town, specializing in
vegetarian recipes as well as meat-based dishes.
Open April–Oct.

Out of town

Ekin Club Dipdağ 5.5km along İztuzu road.
Reasonable value for *gözleme*, grills or farmed fish
with garnish, served in an idyllic lakeside setting at
a mix of conventional tables and *Yörük* platforms.

Gölbaşı 4km along the İztuzu road. Cheapish
grilled meals in a lovely waterside setting, as well
as breakfast with fresh pomegranate juice (charged
extra) from surrounding plantations. Open all year.

LeyLey Okçular, 6km out towards Ortaca. Popular
with middle-class Turks for its authentic if small-
portioned dishes, with efficient liveried waiting staff
scurrying around tables overlooking an illuminated
artificial lake. Open all year; ☎ 0252/284 4669 for
free shuttle.

Tours and activities

The most popular local outing is the **day-tour** offered by the motorboat co-op
(really a cartel) based on the quayside. These excursions – usually departing by
10.30am – take in thermal springs on Köyceğiz lake, Kaunos ruins and the beach,
and are passable value at about 25TL a head (assuming 8–10 passengers), but a bit
rushed for a return by 6pm. Sadly, **custom-renting** of a whole boat may be
unaffordable for all but larger groups, with prices ranging from 90TL (just
Kaunos) to 170TL (anything further afield). Skippers seem to imagine that punters
remain unaware that hire cars cost about 70TL per day, or that the 3.50TL
rowboat-ferry exists. Riverside *pansiyon*s may take you on **evening boat trips** to
spy water snakes, and freshwater terrapins surfacing for air.

Kaunos Tours (℡0252/284 2816, ⓦwww.kaunostours.com) **rents cars** and organizes **adventure trips** – canyoning, scuba-diving, horseriding, mountain biking, sea-kayaking and rafting on the Dalaman Çayı (aka Akköpru Çayı) – though much of this is subcontracted to Alternatif Turizm in Marmaris. Most excursion days are £25 except for rafting which is £35, including lunch and transfers.

Kaunos

Excavations at ancient **Kaunos** began in 1967 and still take place each summer under the aegis of Başkent University. While the ruins are far from spectacular, they're well labelled with CGI reconstructions, and the site is one of the more underrated minor attractions on this coast, alive with herons and storks in summer, flamingos in winter, plus terrapins, tortoises, snakes and lizards in all seasons.

Arriving by **tour boat**, you disembark either at the fish weir or at another jetty at the base of the outcrop supporting Kaunos's acropolis. The fish caught (*dalyan* means weir) are mostly grey mullet and bass, and a Kaunos ancient inscription suggests they've been part of the local diet since ancient times. From either landing point it's a seven-minute walk up to the fenced **site** (daily dawn to dusk; 8TL when warden present).

It's nearly as easy (and cheaper) to walk to Kaunos, using the **rowboat-ferry** from Dalyan (see p.330), which lands just under the cliff-hewn temple tombs on the west bank, fifteen minutes shy of the ruins. One can also **drive to Kaunos** from Köyceğiz via the Sultaniye baths and Çandır village – but the road beyond Sultaniye, while paved, is potholed, meandering and indirect, with no parking by the upper site entrance.

Some history

Although Kaunos was a ninth-century BC Carian foundation, it exhibited Lycian cultural traits, not least the compulsion to adorn nearby cliffs with rock tombs. Kaunos was also closely allied to the principal Lycian city of Xanthos, and when the Persian Harpagos attempted to conquer the region in the sixth century BC, these two cities were the only ones to resist. Kaunos began to acquire a Greek character under the Hellenizing Carian ruler Mausolus. Subsequently, the city passed to the Ptolemies; then to the Rhodians; and finally, after fierce resistance to Rhodes, under indirect Roman imperial administration.

Besides its fish, Kaunos was noted for its figs, and the prevalence of malaria among its inhabitants; excessive fig consumption was erroneously deemed the cause, rather than the anopheles mosquitoes which, until 1948, infested the surrounding swamps. Another insidious problem was the silting up of its harbour, which continually threatened the city's commerce. The Mediterranean originally came right up to the foot of the acropolis hill, surrounding Kaunos on all sides apart from an isthmus of land to the north. But the Dalyan Çayı has since deposited over 5km of silt, leaving an expanse of marshy delta in its wake.

The site

Much of Kaunos is yet to be unearthed, despite the long-running excavations. North of the city extend well-preserved stretches of **defensive wall**, some constructed by Mausolus early in the fourth century BC. Just below the **acropolis** with its medieval and Hellenistic fortified area, the second-century BC **theatre** is the most impressive building here. Resting against the hillside to the southeast, in the Greek fashion it's greater than a semicircle and retains two of its original arched entrances; in 2008 a **nymphaeum** was uncovered next to one archway. Between here and the Byzantine church, a **temple to Apollo** has been identified.

▲ Kuanos ruins viewed from the river

Northwest of the theatre and Apollo temple, closer to the upper ticket booth, the **Byzantine basilica** and the city's **Roman baths** are also in excellent condition. A cobble-paved street leads downhill from the baths to an ancient **Doric temple**, consisting most obviously of an attractive circular structure, possibly an altar, sacred pool or podium, flanked by bits of re-erected colonnade. A path continues to the **agora**, on the lowest level, graced by a restored **fountain-house** at the end of a long **stoa**. The ancient **harbour** below is now the Sülüklü Gölü, or "Lake of the Leeches"; the entrance could be barred by a chain in times of danger.

İztuzu beach

Tourism and turtles have been made to coexist uneasily on the hard-packed sand of **İztuzu beach**, extending southeast from the mouth of the Dalyan Çayı. You should remain wary of easily trampled-on **turtle nests**; turtle tracks – scrapings where the creatures have hauled themselves up onto the beach to lay their eggs – are visible in the sand during June and July. The marshes immediately behind are often alive with other wildlife too, of the sort seen at Kaunos, and the approach road is lined with flowering oleander bushes, as well as trees deformed by high winter winds.

Whether you go to the road's end (May–Oct car park 5TL, season pass 50TL; barrier, 1km before booth, shuts at dusk) or the river-mouth end of İztuzu beach (2TL admission), you face lack of shade (unless you rent an umbrella) and poor eating options. There are only two identical snack kiosks at either end of the beach, their fare pricey and limited to crisps, ice cream, *gözleme* and *sandviç*, so it's best to bring some food. Umbrellas, whose masts damage the turtle nests, are not permitted from a line of squat marker-stakes down to the sea, and all access to the beach is banned between 8pm and 8am in summer. During the day the entire 3.5km-long beach is open to the public (it takes about 30min to jog it from end to end); owing to wind exposure the water can be choppy and murky, but the gently shelving seabed makes İztuzu excellent for children. Alternatively, you could be ferried across the river mouth to a smaller, more peaceful beach shaded by some pines (swimming in the current-laced river mouth is discouraged).

Ilıca and Sultaniye Kaplıcaları

Ten minutes upriver by boat from Dalyan in the direction of Köyceğiz are the **Ilıca thermal baths** (40°C), a series of open-air mud pools (5TL). However, the total area is small, and in season gets packed with tour groups – best go at an odd hour, or have your skipper take you to a remoter set of hot springs, further upstream on the lakeshore itself.

These, the **Köyceğiz Sultaniye Kaplıcaları**, are also accessible by a paved, eighteen-kilometre road from Köyceğiz (see below); follow signposting for Ekincik on the west side of Köyceğiz town, and then veer left to follow signs for Çandır and the Sultaniye Kaplıcaları. The **main baths** themselves (4TL), housed in a conspicuous white-domed structure right on the lakeshore, are claimed to be open around the clock despite nominal posted hours of 6am to 10pm. However, 10.30am to 8pm is set aside for *tur* (ie mixed bathing), while at other times there are roughly alternating hours for men and women. The dome shelters a large round pool with a naturally rocky, uneven bottom, from which the water wells up at 39–41°C; it's best appreciated at night or during the cooler months. Ancient masonry at the pool rim is evidence that the baths have been present in some form at least since Roman times. Around the domed structure are scattered a number of **open-air pools** (also 4TL): one hot (beside the bar), one cold, and one muddy-bottomed (beside the snack-café). The closest accommodation is at Sultaniye village, 2km distant.

Köyceğiz

KÖYCEĞİZ, 23km north of Dalyan, is a laid-back market town eclipsed touristically by its rival across the lake. Its economy is based largely on cotton, olives, lake fishing, logging and citrus cultivation, though its position on the scenic **Köyceğiz Gölü** – once a bay open to the sea – allows it a resort function, albeit one pitched largely at Turks. The centre has a certain charm, with scattered 1920s–30s buildings, an atmospheric bazaar lane lined by *pide salonları* and *hazır* *yemek* kitchens – some open long hours – plus a well-attended lakeshore promenade on warm nights: bikes, prams, pedestrians. The shallow lake itself is threatened by the illegal practice of burning reed beds and then filling in the charred remains as new farmland.

Practicalities

Besides far lower costs than in Dalyan, there are better **transport** connections from Köyceğiz, with a proper *otogar* out towards the main highway, 2km from the lakeshore. Boat tours are available on the quay, though days out are two hours longer compared to Dalyan: typical travel times are 45 minutes to the Sultaniye Kaplıcaları, 1 hour 20 minutes to Kaunos, while moonlight cruises are popular.

Much the best of three **central lakefront hotels** is the welcoming *Alila* (☏0252/262 1150, ✉omeroflaz38@mynet.com; all year; ❸), whose plain but serviceable rooms in varied sizes (including family suites sleeping five) with small balconies mostly face the lake, plus an outstanding ground-floor restaurant (see below). Alternatively, choose from among a handful of establishments **west of the centre**, listed in the order you encounter them. First there's backpackers' favourite *Tango Pension* one block back from the water (☏0252/262 2501, ⓦwww .tangopension.com; open all year; ❷), with minimalist en-suite rooms or six-bed dorms (20TL), garden bar, organized activities and free bikes; next is the older, less noisy but bare-bulb basic *Fulya Pansiyon* on the same street (☏0252/262 2301; ❷) and boasting a fine roof terrace; then, the slightly more elaborate rooms of the waterside *Flora Hotel*, Cengiz Topel Cad 110 (☏0252/262 4976, ⓦwww .florahotel.info; ❹), with a lakefront terrace and free airport transfers, favoured by a sporty clientele into rafting, trekking or biking; finally the nearby, waterside *Panorama Plaza Hotel* at Cengiz Topel Cad 69 (☏0252/262 3773, ⓦwww .panorama-plaza.net; ❹ B&B) has high-standard rooms (featuring large, fancy bathrooms and tiny balconies with lake views), a large pool with restaurant, and watersports.

Besides the market-lane eateries, much the best lakeshore restaurant is attached to the 🍴 *Alila*; owner Ömer's kitchen produces unusual *meze*s to die for, like stewed artichokes, yogurt with coriander greens and caper shoot marinated in sour pomegranate syrup, while mains are generous. A few steps west are almost adjacent *Coliba* and *Thera*, with lake views over a narrow park; *Thera* does fair-priced fish and meat grills plus cold *meze*s, though the cooking's not a patch on the *Alila*.

Ekincik

Idyllic **Ekincik** lies 38km southwest of Köyceğiz, the road there mostly paved and wide except when traversing Hamit Köy. There are several daily minibuses from Köyceğiz, but most visitors arrive either on their own yachts, or with craft of the motorboat co-op based here. As part of the conservation measures instituted at İztuzu, boats were forbidden to anchor the night at the river mouth there, and Ekincik was chosen both as a yacht anchorage and as a base for shuttling yachties to the Kaunos ruins. This, and the road in, have spurred limited development in the *ova mahalle* of very scattered **EKINCIK** village, in the form of a cluster of beachfront **hotels**. Best and most aesthetic of these is the *Ekincik* (☏0252/266 0203, ⓦwww.hotelekincik.com; ❻ half board only) at mid-beach with easy parking, where the smallish rooms arrayed around a garden court have mock-Japanese furnishings. Inland, but still with sweeping sea views (especially from the rooftop restaurant), top choice is the *Akdeniz* (☏0252/266 0255, ⓦwww .akdenizotel.com; ❹ B&B), with large if eccentrically laid-out rooms and kindly resident proprietors who may open off season. Next door is the *Ekincik Pansiyon* (℡0252/266 0179, ⓦwww.ekincikpansiyon.com; ❹), of similar pine furniture and white-tile standard.

The tan-sand **beach** itself is superb, another turtle-egg-laying venue, though access is complicated by private property barring the way; the *halk plajı* at the west side of the bay offers guaranteed public access (for a fee). There's good snorkelling and scuba-diving at **Maden İskelesi**, on the far eastern end of the beach near a system of submarine caves. Another favourite local activity is the walk to or from **Çandır village**, on a mostly preserved old trail affording spectacular sea views, which takes under three hours. The only catch is getting back to your start-point, done either by retracing your steps, getting an expensive ride with the boatmen's co-operative or signing on with an organized excursion.

The Xanthos valley

East of Fethiye lies the heart of Lycia, home to several archeological sites, including the ancient citadel-cities of **Tlos** and **Pınara**, on opposite sides of the **Xanthos river valley**. Tlos had the geographical advantage, lying above a rich, open flood plain and sheltered to the east by the Massikytos range (today's Akdağ); Pınara's surrounding hilly terrain was difficult to cultivate. Even remoter and less fertile is mysterious **Sidyma**, up on the ridge separating the valley from the Mediterranean. All these cities were unearthed by the English traveller Charles Fellows between 1838 and 1842, contemporaneous with his work – or rather pillaging – at **Xanthos**, though he seems to have left unmolested the nearby religious sanctuary of **Letoön** and the naval fortress of **Pydnae**.

The road between Fethiye and Kalkan, mostly following the valley of the ancient Xanthos River (now the Eşen Çayı), threads an immensely fertile area, known for its cotton, tomatoes and other market-garden crops. Plans for a local airport have never been realized and this, in tandem with archeological restrictions, has kept growth at **Patara**, the main resort here, modest by Turkish coastal standards. Between Tlos and Patara, the magnificent river gorge of **Saklıkent** is easily reached by dolmuş or with your own vehicle, though it's become something of a tourist circus. Isolated-ruins buffs can instead visit the unpromoted, unspoilt Lycian city of **Oenoanda**, high in the mountains north of Tlos.

Tlos

Among the most ancient and important Lycian cities, **Tlos** stands beside modern Asarkale village. Fourteenth-century BC Hittite records refer to it as "Dalawa in the Lukka lands", and the local discovery of a bronze hatchet dating from the second millennium BC confirms the long heritage of the place. However, little else is known about its history.

The ruins themselves, while reasonably abundant, are often densely overgrown or even farmed, so precise identification of buildings is debatable. The setting beside modern Asarkale village is undeniably impressive, a high rocky promontory giving excellent views of the Xanthos valley. The acropolis bluff is dominated by an Ottoman Turkish fortress, once home to a nineteenth-century brigand and local chieftain, Kanlı ("Bloody") Ali Ağa, who killed his own wayward daughter to uphold the family's honour. Now used as a football pitch and pasture, it has obliterated all earlier remains on the summit. On its northeast side, the acropolis ends in almost sheer cliffs; the eastern slope bears traces of the Lycian city wall.

There's patchy **public transport** the full distance to Tlos, provided by Saklıkent-bound minibuses from Fethiye, which occasionally detour to the site. Tlos is, however, firmly established on the organized-excursion circuit, so you shouldn't have to hire a private taxi. Under your own steam, **from Fethiye** veer left 22km out of town towards Korkuteli, and once over the Koca Çayı bridge, bear immediately right onto the marked side road to both Tlos and Saklıkent. Some 8.5km along, turn left (east) onto a paved minor road festooned with copious signposting for restaurants and inns; it's 4km up here to the base of the acropolis hill. In spring the route up, with snow-streaked Akdağ as a backdrop for the purple of flowering Judas trees, is memorably beautiful. Coming **from Patara**, at Alaçat take the eastbound road marked "Saklıkent 15km"; at a T-junction in Kadıköy, with "Saklıkent" signposted opposite a mini-market for the right turning, bear left (north) instead, following a "Tloss" sign, for just over 2km until another "Tloss" sign points up the 4km of final approach.

The site

Entry to **the main site** (unenclosed; admission 8TL when staff present) is via the still intact northeastern city gate, next to the guard's portakabin. Cobbled stairs climb to the main **necropolis** with its freestanding sarcophagi and complex of rock-cut house-tombs, one of which was discovered intact in October 2005 yielding treasure kept at the Fethiye museum. If, however, you walk along a lower, level path from the gate, outside the city walls, you reach a second group of rock tombs; dip below and right of these along a zigzagging trail to reach the temple-style **Tomb of Bellerophon**, at the hill's northern base. Its facade was hewn with columns supporting a pediment, and three carved doors. On the porch's left wall is a relief representing mythical hero Bellerophon (from whom one of Tlos' ancient ruling families claimed descent), riding Pegasus, while facing them over the door is a lion symbolically standing guard. It's a fifteen-minute scramble down requiring good shoes, with a ladder ascent at the end, and both figures have been worn down by vandals and the elements.

Between the east slope of the acropolis hill and the curving onward road is a large, seasonally cultivated open space, thought to be the **agora**. Close to the base of the hill are traces of seats, part of a stadium which lay parallel to the marketplace. The opposite side of the agora is flanked by a long, arcaded building identified as the **market hall**.

Well beyond this, reached by a broad path off the eastbound road, lie the **baths**, where the sound of running water in nearby ditches lends credence to its identification. This atmospheric vantage point is perhaps the best bit of Tlos: three complete **chambers**, one with an apsidal projection known as **Yedi Kapı** (Seven Gates), after its seven intact windows, which provide a romantic view of the Xanthos valley. Sadly, it's closed indefinitely for excavations meant to uncover the fine marble floor, which have also revealed a large, possibly Christian, cemetery.

Just north of the modern through-road stands a magnificent second-century AD **theatre**, with 34 rows of seats remaining. The stage building has a number of finely carved blocks – including one with an eagle beside a garlanded youth – and its northern section still stands to nearly full height, vying with the backdrop of mountains.

Practicalities

From the theatre, the onward road continues 3km uphill to several trout restaurants in the village of **YAKA**. Of these the most famous is the *Yaka Park*, formerly a watermill, where at the bar your drink is chilled in a sluice through which your potential dinner swims by. However, too many tours have had an effect, and two or three changeable competitors in the area may have the edge in terms of quality and service.

You can **stay** overnight locally at the ⚶ *Mountain Lodge* (☎0252/638 2515, ⓦwww.themountainlodge.co.uk; closed Nov 15–Dec 15 & Jan 15–Feb 15), just under 2km down the road from the ruins entrance. Choose between well-appointed, carpeted, beam-ceilinged en suites in the garden annexe (❹), or four air-conditioned luxury units (❺) in the wing overlooking the pool and bar. Engaging owner Melahat prepares fine set evening meals (half board from ❺) in an area thin on non-trout-based cuisine, served in the wood-beamed and stone pub-restaurant. She also organizes treks in the area and is knowledgeable about local flora.

Oenoanda

Ancient **Oenoanda**, about 50km northeast of Tlos, was among the northernmost and highest (1350–1450m elevation) of the Lycian cities. Set in wild, forested countryside, it's almost unpublicized but, as an example of how all local sites were before tourism, thoroughly rewards the effort involved in reaching it (own transport essential).

Oenoanda was the birthplace of Diogenes the second-century AD Epicurean philosopher; to him is attributed antiquity's longest inscriptionary discourse, scattered in fragments across the site. Oenoanda was first surveyed by British archeologists in 1996 and is set for more vigorous future excavations. With luck, digs will reassemble Diogenes' text to its full estimated length of 60m, and firmly identify structures. Until then, the site remains a romantic, overgrown maze of tumbled lintels, statue bases, columns, cistern mouths and buried arches, frequented only by squirrels and the occasional hunter or shepherd.

The site

To **reach Oenoanda**, leave Highway 400 at the Kemer river bridge, keeping straight onto Highway 350, signed for Korkuteli. Some 34km later, bear right (east) onto a side road marked for Seki and Elmalı; a fine Ottoman bridge in the Seki Çayı by the modern asphalt is the most durable indicator. Turn south after 1100m onto a more minor road (the sign is rusted over); 800m down this, veer right at an unmarked fork to proceed 1.5km further to İncealiler village. Turn right at the phone box and standard archeological-service sign – do not follow the river further upstream – and park by the **coffeehouse**. Head up the main pedestrian thoroughfare among village houses, then near the top of the grade, bear right at heaped boulders onto a narrower track which soon dwindles to a path. Continue west towards the escarpment in front of you, where the first freestanding **tombs** poke up. The path describes a broad arc south around the top of a stream valley, forging through low scrub.

Some 45 minutes from the coffeehouse, the trail fizzles out at polygonal masonry of the massive south-to-north **aqueduct** that supplied the city, whose site-bluff inclines gently to the south but is quite sheer on all other sides. Slip through a gap in the aqueduct, with necropolis tombs flung about on every side, and veer right along the ridge towards Oenoanda's massive Hellenistic **city wall**, with an arched window; the way through is left of this, by a strong hexagonal **tower** with archers' loopholes. Some fifteen minutes' walk north from here, keeping just east of the ridge line, brings you to the large flat paved **agora**; just beyond stand tentatively identified **baths**, with a surviving apse and dividing arch. Just northeast, a gate in the **Roman wall**, longer but much lower than the Hellenistic one, opens onto a vast flat area, provisionally dubbed an **"esplanade"**, flanked by traces of stoas. Northwest of the presumed baths, a **nymphaeum** or small **palace** with a three-arched facade precedes the partly preserved **theatre**, its fifteen or so rows of seats taking in fine views of Akdağ.

Saklıkent

Back on the country road below Tlos, heading south, the gauntlet of *saç böreği*, *gözleme* and fried-trout stalls confirms you're en route to the hugely popular **Saklıkent gorge**, the most dramatic geological formation in the Xanthos valley. After 9km, bear left for just over 3km to the gorge mouth, 44km from Fethiye. There's a regular minibus service in season, on vehicles marked "Kayadibi/ Saklıkent" at Fethiye's dolmuş *otogar*.

The mouth of the gorge is deceptively modest; to reach it leave the road bridge for a 150-metre pedestrian **walkway** (open during daylight hours; 8TL) spiked into the canyon walls, ending at the **Gökçesu/Ulupınar springs**, which erupt at great pressure from the base of towering cliffs, exiting the narrows to mingle eventually with the Eşen Çayı. It's a magical place, seemingly channelling all the water this side of Akdağ, though less impressive if you coincide with a coached-in tour group.

The water-sculpted chasm extends 18km upstream, though further progress for all except rock-climbers is blocked after about 2km by a boulder slide. If you want to explore up to that point, it's initially a **wading** exercise – take submersible shoes, or rent a pair here. The entire length of the gorge was first descended in 1993 by a **canyoning** expedition which took eighteen hours, bivouacking halfway and abseiling down several dry waterfalls. This trip is now offered on a custom basis, during summer only, by BT in Kaş (see p.354).

With your own vehicle, it's easy to continue from the gorge mouth down the unsignposted but paved road to Xanthos, the Letoön or Patara (all described later in the chapter); proceed over the road bridge past several trout restaurants and the treehouse-format *Saklıkent Gorge Club* (℡0252/659 0074, Ⓦwww.saklikentgorge .com; dorm beds €12, doubles ❸; half board available), which arranges rafting and tubing. After twelve lonely kilometres, initially along the river's left bank, you reach Palamut village; bear right at the fork immediately beyond Çavdır, the next village, and, 6km past Palamut, join Highway 400 through the Xanthos valley. Bearing left leads to Patara; cross the highway and continue on the narrower road to reach Xanthos after 1km.

Pınara

Some 46km southeast of Fethiye on Highway 400, you'll see the well-marked turning west (right) for ancient **Pınara**. Practically nothing is known about this city other than that it may have been founded as an annexe of Xanthos. Later, however, Pınara – meaning "something round" in Lycian, presumably because of the shape of the original, upper acropolis – became one of the region's larger cities, minting its own coins and earning three votes in the Federation.

It's just over 3km along the side road to the edge of Minare village (one café, one restaurant, no public transport), from where 2.2km more of signposted but steep track leads to the edge of the ruins. Approaching the site, the **cliff** on which the city was first founded practically blocks out the horizon – indeed it's worth the trip up just to see this towering mass, its east face covered in rectangular openings, either tombs or food-storage cubicles. These can now only be reached by experienced rock-climbers and it's hard to fathom how they were originally cut.

The site

Most of Pınara's ruins (unenclosed; admission 8TL when guard present) are on the lower acropolis hill, east of the cliff, where the city was relocated after defence became less critical. The **lower acropolis** is densely overgrown with pines and most buildings unidentifiable, though the access track reaches a point almost level with it.

Pınara's **tombs** are its most interesting feature, especially a group on the west bank of the seasonal stream that passes the site. On the east side of the lower acropolis hill (follow arrows on metal signs), the so-called **Royal Tomb** sports detailed if well-worn carvings on its porch of walled cities with battlements, gates, houses and tombs; a frieze survives above, showing people and animals in a peaceable scene – perhaps a religious festival. Inside is a single bench set high off the ground, suggesting that this was the tomb of just one, probably royal, person.

On the same side of this hill but higher up, reached by a direct path north from the Royal Tomb, there's a house-tomb with an arched roof topped by a pair of stone **ox horns** for warding off evil spirits. This stands near the summit of the lower acropolis, at the eastern edge of the presumed **agora**. Just north of the horned tomb, the massive foundations of a **temple** to an unknown god overlook the theatre (see below). Hairpinning back south, a level path threads between the pigeonholed cliff and the lower acropolis, first past a ruinous but engaging **odeion**, then through a chaos of walls, uprights, heart-shaped column sections and tombs clogging the flattish heart of the city.

At the far south end of this little plateau, two sarcophagi flank a man-made terrace and a sharp drop to the stream valley. Above an apsed church here juts a strange **tower**, probably a guardhouse intended to control access to the upper citadel, and a fine vantage point for making sense of the jumbled town. From the terrace, the path descends sharply to the canyon floor, passing more tombs and a permanent spring – which moves downstream as the year progresses – en route to the car park.

Northeast of the town, accessible along a marked side track from the main track passing the base of the lower acropolis, is the well-preserved **theatre**, backing into a hill and looking towards the "Swiss cheese" cliff; small but handsome, and never modified by the Romans (on-site signage to the contrary), it gives an idea of Pınara's modest population.

Sidyma

Sidyma is the remotest of the area's ancient cities – indeed, sited halfway up the ancient Mount Kragos (the modern coastal peak of Avlankara Tepesi), scarcely in the Xanthos valley at all. It's a rewarding, understated site in a striking landscape astride the Lycian Way. Like most local sites, Sidyma was only "rediscovered" by Europeans during the mid-nineteenth century, and has never been properly excavated.

From Highway 400 take the turning marked for Eşen and "Sidyma, 13km", just north of a side road for Kumlova and Letoön. Proceed 6km to a junction, and turn left (south); it's just over 2km to the first buildings of **Dodurga** village, and another 3km to the road's end in Dodurga's Asar Mahallesi, where two mulberry trees flank the ruins of the agora and a Lycian Way metal signpost. Trekking southeast on the **Lycian Way**, it's a day and a half's march from Kabak to Sidyma, via Alınca.

The site

Asar Mahallesi's mosque occupies the site of the baths, and reuses pillars from the agora's stoa. Indeed the principal charm of Sidyma is how ancient masonry crops up everywhere: incorporated into house corners, used as livestock troughs, sprouting incongruously in dooryards next to satellite dishes. An exceedingly ruined **castle**, garrisoned into Byzantine times, sits on a hill to the north; scattered in the fields to the east, and requiring some scrambling over walls to reach, lies the

necropolis, comprising a variety of tomb types, though most have angular gabled roofs rather than the "Gothic" vaulted ones seen elsewhere. Near the centre of the agricultural plain is a group of remarkable, contiguous tombs: one has ceiling panels carved with rosettes and human faces, while the adjacent tomb sports a relief of Eros on its lid and Medusas at the ends (a motif repeated elsewhere). Another spectacular cluster, including a two-storeyed one, covers the low ridge beyond the fields. In the middle of the necropolis stands an enormous, fairly intact, square structure – probably a Roman imperial **heroön** or temple-tomb – with a walled-up doorway on the north side.

Practicalities

The closest tourist facilities are in hillside **ALINCA**, reached by returning to the junction and heading west through Boğaziçi, then northwest. Just off the Lycian Way at the top of the village stands the *Dervish Lodge* (☏0252/679 1142, ⓦwww.dervishlodge.com), with views to die for and accommodation ranging from nomad yurts (❷ HB) to standard doubles in stone huts (❹ HB). Much further off the trail is *Black Tree Farm* (☏0252/617 0045, ⓦwww.blacktree.net; closed Nov–March) in **KARAAĞAÇ**, 3.5km beyond, occupying extensive grounds, 1100m up, with rare Baba Dağı cedars nearby and a zoo's worth of animals on site. Accommodation comprises a restored trekkers' lodge (16 beds at 20TL a head) and nine newer cottages built in local stone and pine (£280/week for one-bedroom, £380/week for three-bedroom). There's a swimming pool, tennis courts and restaurant-bar serving simple lunches. A marked, non-Lycian Way trail links Karaağaç with Kirme, allowing the completion of circular hikes from Faralya (see p.326).

The Letoön

The Letoön, shrine of the goddess **Leto**, was the official religious sanctuary, oracle and festival venue of the Lycian Federation, and extensive remaining ruins attest its importance. The site lies 16km south **of Pınara** along the old road (less on the new highway), the turning marked with a "Kumluova, Karadere, Letoön 10" sign. Driving **from Patara**, leave Highway 400 at the Kınık/Xanthos exit; clear Kınık and cross the Eşençay bridge; then descend into pines and take a hairpin left at a "Letoön 4" marker. There's a **dolmuş from Fethiye** to Kumluova, the village beside the site; from the village centre it's 500m to the Letoön.

Some mythology and history

In legend, the nymph Leto was loved by Zeus and thus jealously pursued by his wife Hera. Wandering in search of a place to give birth to her divine twins Apollo and Artemis, Leto approached a fountain to slake her thirst, only to be driven away by local herdsmen. Leto was then led to drink at the Xanthos River by wolves, and so changed the name of the country to Lycia, *lykos* being Greek for wolf. After giving birth, she returned to the spring – on the site of the existing Letoön, and forever after sacred to the goddess – to punish the insolent herdsmen by transforming them into frogs.

The name Leto may derive from the Lycian *lada* (woman), and the Anatolian mother-goddess, Cybele, was probably worshipped here previously. Another similarity between the two goddesses is a link with incestuous mother-son unions, thought to have been common in Lycian society. Most famous of all the prophecies supposedly delivered at the Letoön was that Alexander the Great would destroy the Persian Empire. Following the demise of the Lycian Federation, the sanctuary became Christianized, and wasn't abandoned until the Arab raids of the seventh century. The Letoön was initially rediscovered by Fellows in 1840, although French-conducted digs didn't begin until 1962, since when it has been systematically uncovered and labelled. The latest phase of excavations has partially reconstructed the main temple here, but lack of official cooperation means that little work has taken place since 2006.

The site

Since excavations of the site (daily: summer 8am–7.30pm; winter 8.30am–5pm; 8TL) began, the remains of three temples and a nymphaeum have been uncovered, as well as various **inscriptions**. One stipulates conditions of entry to the sanctuary, including a strict dress-code prohibiting rich jewellery, ostentatious clothing or elaborate hairstyles.

The low ruins of three **temples** occupy the centre of the site, beyond the relatively uninteresting (and waterlogged) agora. The westernmost temple, straight ahead coming from the site gate, bears a dedication to Leto. Once surrounded by a single Doric colonnade with decorative half-columns around the interior walls, it's of third-century BC vintage. Three columns on the north side of the structure plus the cella walls have been reconstructed; though the masonry seems jarringly garish it was, in fact, sourced from the original marble quarry near modern Finike. The central temple, partly carved out of the rock, is a fourth-century BC structure, identified by a dedication to Artemis. The easternmost temple was similar to the Leto temple; the reproduction **mosaic** on the floor – the original is now in the Fethiye museum – depicts a lyre, bow and quiver with a stylized flower in the centre. This suggests a joint dedication to Artemis and Apollo, the region's most revered deities, since the bow and quiver symbolized Artemis, and the lyre Apollo. The architecture and mosaic technique date the temple to the second and first centuries BC.

Southwest beyond the temples extends a rectangular **nymphaeum** flanked by two semicircular recesses with statue niches. This is abutted by another semicircular paved basin 27m in diameter, now permanently flooded by the high local water-table and full of ducks, terrapins and Leto's croaking victims (see p.341). A **church** was built over the nymphaeum in the fourth century, but destroyed by Arab invaders in the seventh, so that only its foundations and apse are now discernible. The notable stork mosaic on its floor is, alas, headless, though currently exposed to view.

Returning towards the car park, you'll reach a large, well-preserved Hellenistic **theatre**, entered through a vaulted passage. Sixteen plaques, adorned by comic and tragic relief **masks**, decorate the perilously collapsing northeast entrance to this passage; nearby sits an interesting Roman **tomb** with a carved representation of its toga-clad occupant.

Pydnae

Dolmuşes from Kumluova village (labelled "Kumluova–Karadere") run 8km southwest to the end of the paved road, where the ancient **fortress of Pydnae** is obvious on the right, on the far bank of the Özlen Çayı. To reach the fortress, continue to the end of the onward mud-and-sand track (and final dolmuş stop) that leads to the good beach (grass-roofed snack-shack) at the stream mouth. Cross the rickety footbridge here, and then follow a sand-, then jeep-track around greenhouses to pick up Lycian Way markers from the first curve, from which a path leads to – and through – the fortress gate within twenty minutes.

Pydnae was a small, third-century BC port on the larger, deeper bay which existed here before the Özlen stream silted it up. It was in fact the only safe anchorage for Xanthos and Letoön, since even in ancient times the coast from here to Patara was marshland. The irregularly shaped precinct is built of almost perfectly preserved **polygonal masonry**, with steps leading up to the walls at various points and, every so often, square towers with loopholes for archers. The most recent structure inside is a Byzantine **church**, its arched apsidal window overlooking the reedy marshes where fleets once anchored.

Xanthos

The remains of hilltop **Xanthos**, with their breathtaking views of the Xanthos River – now the Eşen Çayı – and its valley, are among the most fascinating in Lycia. The city was first made familiar in 1842, when Charles Fellows carried off the majority of its art works, just four decades after the Elgin marbles had been similarly pillaged. It took two months to strip the site and load the loot onto the HMS *Beacon* for shipment to London. The most important artefact, the fourth-century Nereid Monument, a beautifully decorated Ionic temple on a high podium, is now in the British Museum, along with other items. However, enough was left behind here to still require a two-hour visit. Afternoons are scorchingly hot even by Lycian standards – go earlier or later in the day.

Dolmuşes between Fethiye and Patara will drop you at Kınık, less than 2km beyond the southerly Letoön turn-off, from where it's a twenty-minute uphill walk. Alternatively, Xanthos features regularly in the repertoire of **organized excursions**, usually in tandem with the Letoön.

Some history

Xanthos is linked in legend with Bellerophon and Pegasus (see p.373); King Iobates – who initially set impossible tasks for Bellerophon and later offered him a share in his kingdom – ruled here, and Xanthos was the birthplace of Bellerophon's grandson, Glaukos, cited in the *Iliad* as "from the whirling waters of the Xanthos".

The earliest archeological finds here date to the eighth century BC, but the city enters history in 540 BC during the conquest of Lycia by the Persian Harpagos, who besieged Xanthos. The Xanthians' response was the first local holocaust, making a funeral pyre of their families with their household goods. The women and children died in the flames while the men perished fighting, the only survivors being out of town at the time.

Xanthos subsequently shared the fate of all Lycia, with Alexander following the Persians, in turn succeeded by his general Antigonos and then by Antiokhos III. After Antiokhos's defeat, Xanthos was given to Rhodes along with the rest of Lycia. The second Xanthian holocaust occurred in 42 BC during the Roman civil war, when Brutus's forces surrounded the city, prompting the citizens again to make funeral pyres of their possessions and immolate themselves. Xanthos prospered anew in Roman imperial times, and under Byzantine rule the city walls were renovated and a monastery built.

The site

The **site** is unfenced (except for the theatre area), but officially open 8am to 7.30pm in summer, 8.30am to 5pm in winter; the warden at the car-park café/souvenir stall will collect 6TL admission, plus parking fees.

Beside the access road from Kınık stand the monumental **Arch of Vespasian** and an adjoining **Hellenistic gateway**, the latter bearing an inscription of Antiokhos III dedicating the city to Leto, Apollo and Artemis. East of the road, the former location of the **Nereid Monument** is marked by a plaque.

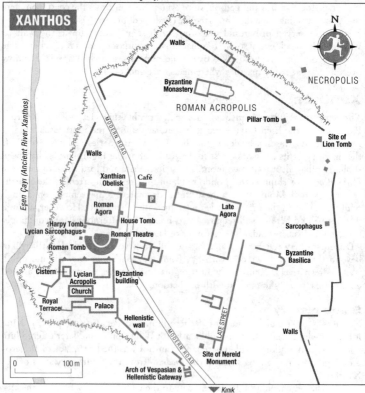

XANTHOS

N

NECROPOLIS

Walls

Byzantine
Monastery

ROMAN ACROPOLIS

Pillar Tomb

Site of
Lion Tomb

Esen Çayı (Ancient River Xanthos)

MODERN ROAD

Walls

Xanthian
Obelisk   Café

Roman
Agora   P

House Tomb

Harpy Tomb
Lycian Sarcophagus

Roman Theatre

Roman Tomb

Late
Agora

Sarcophagus

Byzantine
Basilica

Cistern   Lycian
Acropolis   Byzantine
building

Church

Royal   Palace
Terrace

Hellenistic
wall

LATE STREET

Walls

MODERN ROAD

Site of Nereid
Monument

0   100 m

Arch of Vespasian &
Hellenistic Gateway

The **Roman theatre**, near the summit of the access road, was built on the site of an earlier Greek structure and is pretty complete, missing only the upper seats, which were incorporated into the Byzantine city wall. Behind the theatre, overlooking the valley, lies the **Lycian acropolis**, in whose far southeastern corner are the square remains of what's probably an early Xanthian royal palace destroyed by Harpagos. Beneath protective sand, patches of sophisticated mosaic indicate Roman or Byzantine use of the acropolis; there are also water channels everywhere underfoot plus a huge cistern, suggesting an advanced plumbing system and a preoccupation with outlasting sieges.

In front of the theatre to the north looms the **Harpy Tomb**, once topped with a marble chamber removed by Fellows, now replaced by a cement cast reproduction. The paired bird-women figures on the north and south sides are identified as harpies, or – more likely – sirens, carrying the souls of the dead (represented as children) to the Isles of the Blessed. Other reliefs portray unidentified seated figures receiving gifts, except for the west face where they are regarding opium poppies. Beside the Harpy Tomb a third-century BC **Lycian sarcophagus** stands on a pillar; traces of a corpse and pottery were found inside, along with a sixth-century BC relief – brought from elsewhere – depicting funeral games.

Just northeast of the Roman agora, the so-called **Xanthian Obelisk** is in fact another pillar tomb, labelled as the "Inscribed Pillar" and covered on all four sides by the longest known Lycian inscription, 250 lines including twelve lines of Greek verse. Since the Lycian language hasn't been completely deciphered, interpretation of the inscription is based on this verse, which glorifies a champion local wrestler.

East of the car park, then south through the "**late**" **agora** lies a **Byzantine basilica**, fenced off but easy enough to enter – beware unauthorized guides offering incomprehensible and overpriced "tours". The basilica features extensive abstract **mosaics** – the best in western Turkey – and a synthronon in the semicircular apse. On the **Roman acropolis** to the north are various freestanding **sarcophagi**, and above, cut into the hillside, picturesque **tombs** mainly of the Lycian house (as opposed to temple) type. A well-preserved early **Byzantine monastery**, with washbasins along one side of its courtyard, stands further north.

Patara and Gelemiş

Patara was the principal port of Lycia, famed for its oracle of Apollo, and as the fourth-century AD birthplace of St Nicholas, Bishop of Myra (aka Santa Claus). Today, however, the area is better known for its huge sandy **beach**, served by *pansiyon*s, bars and restaurants in the village of **Gelemiş** over 2km inland (see Ⓦwww.patara-info.com for more).

The beach is a summertime turtle-nesting area, off-limits after dark (May–Oct), while in winter the lagoon behind attracts considerable bird life. Conservationists backed by the Ministry of the Environment have managed to exclude villas from the cape at the southeast end of the strand, while the area's protected archeological status has halted most new building at Gelemiş. Plans for a local airport have been shelved, with a change of venue to near Demre if tourist numbers (and the world economy) ever revive sufficiently. Horseriding and walking in the hills to the east are now promoted, using both the Lycian Way and other trails, as well as **canoeing** on the Eşen Çayı (organized by two agencies in Gelemiş; 40TL per person, Ⓦwww.pataracanoeing.com).

Gelemiş lies 3.5km south of Highway 400, down a conspicuously signposted side road passing a prominent rock outcrop. **Minibuses**, stopping in the centre near the PTT, arrive every half-hour from Kalkan – from Fethiye there are around fifteen a day – and many of these continue past the ruins of Patara to the beach at the road's end. Long-haul buses only call at the junction with the main road.

Some history

Legend ascribes Greek origins to Patara, but in fact the city was originally Lycian, borne out by coins and inscriptions sporting an un-Hellenic PTTRA. The city was famous for its temple and oracle of Apollo, supposedly rivalling Delphi's for accuracy, because Apollo supposedly spent the winter months in the Xanthos valley. However, no verifiable traces of this temple have ever been found.

Patara served as a naval base during the wars between Alexander's successors. Later, in 42 BC, Brutus threatened the Patarans with a fate similar to that of the Xanthians (see p.343) if they didn't submit, giving them a day to decide. He released the women hostages in the hope that they would lessen the resolve of their menfolk. When this didn't work, Brutus freed all the remaining hostages, thereby endearing himself to the Patarans, who subsequently surrendered. Whatever his tactics, his chief motive was suggested by the fact that he exacted no other punishments, but merely confiscated the city's gold and silver.

Gelemiş

GELEMIŞ essentially consists of a busy T-junction, with a main, crescent-shaped neighbourhood threaded by a single twisting high street extending west, and then uphill. Before 1950, the entire area was malarial – a municipal truck still sprays pesticide on spring nights – and the nomadic *Yörüks* who wintered here spent the hottest months up in the healthier mountain village of İslamlar, near Gömbe. Subsequently, a lake northeast of Highway 400 (still shown on many maps) was drained by a canal, and the Patara swamp shrunk by eucalyptus plantations.

It's worth noting, however, that Gelemiş is under perennial threat from a currently dormant Ministry of Culture proposal to evacuate and demolish the entire village, part of a policy of "cleaning up" the environs of archeological sites. The ministry relented in 2001, but the villagers have since been trying to retrospectively legalize all construction and tidy up Gelemiş with new paving and the like.

Accommodation here is a buyers' market as Gelemiş has excess capacity, with package allotments absent. The most desirable premises are either on the ridge east of the T-junction (though sadly a 2008 fire removed all its forest), or on the western hillside. It's possible to walk from the latter neighbourhood past the swamp flanking Patara ruins to the beach in about twenty minutes, but you arrive on an unamenitied part of the dunes, so this route is best for an interesting alternate return to the village at day's end.

Local cuisine tends to be sustaining rather than *haute*. The most reliable **restaurants** are those attached to the *Akay*, the *Golden*, the *Flower* and the *St Nicholas* pansiyons, especially the latter, more sophisticated (and expensive) than the norm for Gelemiş, but with nice touches to the presentation. Best among very few stand-alone eateries is *Tlos* (*Bolu'lu Osman Usta*) near the T-junction, with big platters of hearty fare. If standard Turkish hotel **breakfasts** don't start the day well for you, try the two unusually tasty *gözleme* stalls next to the *Golden Pansiyon*. On the "high street" are a pair of well-established **bars**: *Medusa*, whose proprietor Pamir and French wife lend a cosmopolitan touch, and nearby *Gypsy*, with occasional live Turkish music.

Accommodation

Akay ℡0242/843 5055, ⓦwww .pataraakaypension.com. Kazim and Ayşe provide keen management and good cooking; rooms – best facing away from the approach road – are plain but brand new, with orthopedic mattresses. ❷.

Ferah Hotel ℡0242/843 5180, ⓦwww .ferahhotel.com. On the western hill, with unusually large, a/c rooms with redone baths; pool with travertine terrace, pleasant garden restaurant. ❷

Flower Pension ℡0242/843 5164, ⓦwww .pataraflowerpension.com. The first noteworthy *pansiyon* along the approach to the village from Highway 400, again with renewed bathrooms. Ayşe cooks up mean meals (and breakfast) on the terrace overlooking a lush garden. ❷

Golden Lighthouse Hotel ℡0242/843 5107, ⓦwww.pataragoldenlighthouse.com. North edge of centre, above mosque. Quiet yet central, this 2008-renovated hotel has large airy rooms with plain white decor, a/c and new baths and an unusually large pool. ❹

Golden Pansiyon ℡0242/843 5162, ⓦwww .pataragoldenpension.com. Mayor Arif Otlu caters to budget travellers with fairly large rooms (some balconied, all double-glazed and a/c). The dead-central restaurant here, exhibiting consistent quality, sometimes has trout or ocean fish on the menu. Open all year. ❷

Lumière ℡0242/843 5091, ⓦwww .pataralumierehotel.com. Downhill but set well back from the through-road, close to the T-junction, this offers variable-sized, pastel-decor rooms with kilims, a/c and stall showers, plus a pool-terrace restaurant and cushioned "chillout" bar. Open all year. ❷ B&B

Merhaba Hotel ℡0242/843 5199, ⓦwww .merhabapatara.com. Up on the easterly ridge, just before the archeological zone, these large (fitting 4–5 comfortably) apartments score for sunset and sea views (most reliably from the rooftop restaurant) and peaceful environment. Minimum one-week stay (€350), discounts for longer.

Patara Delfin ℡0242/843 5120, ⓦwww .pataradelfinhotel.com. A mix of doubles, triples and a few pricier apartments, partway down the east ridge, with a large pool, limited parking and half board available at *St Nicholas* restaurant. Credit cards taken. ❷ B&B

🏃 **Patara View Point Hotel** ☎0242/843 5184 or 0533/350 0347, ⓦwww.pataraviewpoint .com. Muzaffer Otlu's and Anne-Louise Thomson's hotel has an unbeatable setting on the easterly ridge. The rooms have mosquito nets, balconies and heating/a/c; there's a shuttle to the beach, a pool-bar where breakfast is served and a Turkish-style night-time terrace with fireplace. Good-value weekly rates. Credit cards accepted with slight surcharge. Open March–Nov. ❹ B&B

Patara

At the southern edge of Gelemiş village, a gate and ticket booth controls vehicle access to both beach and **archeological site** (daily: May–Oct 7.30am–7.30pm; Nov–April 8am–5.30pm; 5TL good 1 week, if ticket date-stamped and your name recorded) beyond. Although the ruins are unfenced, you are not allowed in outside the official opening times.

Much of Patara – especially numerous badly overgrown, polygonal-masonry walls – remains unexcavated (though this is slowly changing). Just a few paths link individual ruins, and there are no facilities or shade – bring water, stout shoes and a head covering during summer.

Two kilometres from the village, the city's entrance is marked by a triple-arched, first-century AD **Roman gateway**, almost completely intact. On a little hill just west, a head of Apollo has been found, prompting speculation that his temple was nearby. Outside the gate, a **necropolis** is being excavated by a team from Antalya's Akdeniz University.

South of the hill sits a **baths complex**, similar to Yedi Kapı at Tlos, with arches and five rectangular apsidal windows; an exotic touch is lent to nearby foundations of either a **basilica** or an extension of the baths by a palm grove sprouting up from the flooring and almost totally obscuring it. West of these, tacked onto the longest surviving stretch of **city walls** – and difficult to reach – is an attractive second-century **temple**. While too modest to be the famous local Apollo shrine, it has a richly decorated seven-metre-high doorframe – its lintel on the point of collapse – leading into a single chamber. Further south, reached by a different track, are more **baths** built by Emperor Vespasian (69–79 AD), impressing mainly by their squat bulk. Just west of these lies a large **paved** main agora or a processional street, with its north end submerged by the high local water-table, and a growing number of re-erected columns.

The **theatre** sits southwest of these baths, under the brow of the acropolis hill and best reached by yet another track heading off the main road, just before the beach car park. The cavea has been cleaned of sand to reveal eighteen rows of seats up to the diazoma (dividing walkway) and a dozen more beyond. The stage building is slowly being reassembled; a Greek inscription outside ascribes its erection to a woman, Vilia Prokla, and her father, both citizens of Patara. Funding for it was approved by the Lycian Federation's assembly, which apparently met in the **bouleuterion** (locked but views through the gate) between the theatre and the agora, with a horseshoe array of seating.

South of the theatre a reasonable path climbs uphill to the city's **acropolis**. At the top lurks an unusual rectangular pit, some ten metres across, with a pillar (for measuring water level) rearing out of the bottom and badly damaged stairs down its side. This was almost certainly a **cistern**, and not the **lighthouse** as originally supposed; that is the square, arched tower, its top collapsed, on the west side of the hill, which still has a fine view over the sea, beach and brackish swamp that was once the **harbour**. The latter silted up gradually in the Middle Ages and was subsequently abandoned, separated today from the beach by 300-metre-wide dunes. On the far side of the swamp, across the dunes, are the bulky remains of **Hadrian's granary**.

The beach

Patara's fine white-sand **beach** ranks as one of the longest continuous strands in the Mediterranean: 9km from the access road to the mouth of the Eşen Çayı, then 6km further to the end. Rather than making the hot, half-hour stroll out from the centre of Gelemiş in summer, most people take a **beach dolmuş** or transport laid on by the hotels. Parking (free) at the road's end is limited, as the archeological authorities have refused permission to expand the space. The villagers have wrested control of the lone wood-built café-restaurant-sunbed concession from a private mafia, and the food is now affordable and decent, with local youth employed and all proceeds going to the community chest.

In season the immediate vicinity of the beach entrance gets crowded, but walking northwest past the dunes brings you to plenty of solitary spots – and a few unharassed colonies of nudists. Spring and autumn swimming is delightful, but in summer the exposed shoreline can be battered by a considerable surf (at least by Mediterranean standards).

Kalkan and around

The former Greek Orthodox village of Kalamaki, now **KALKAN**, tumbles down a steep slope some 13km beyond the Patara turn-off. Tourism and property sales, now the town's *raison d'être*, are fairly new phenomena: until the late 1970s both Kalkan and neighbouring Kaş eked out a living from charcoal-burning and olives. In the 1980s it developed a rather bohemian atmosphere, contrasting with often oppressive conditions in Turkish cities after the 1980 coup. Today its population of 4000 includes some 1500 expats, two thirds of which are British, and the small boutique hotels which used to be Kalkan's lifeblood have mostly been converted into apartments and second homes. The surviving package-holiday trade dominates most of the remaining short-stay accommodation, and ensures that Kalkan remains more exclusive (and considerably more twee) than nearby Kaş.

Once you accept this pervasive social profile and the lack of a sandy beach, Kalkan makes a good base for exploring Patara and the Xanthos valley, while **excursions** east or inland might occupy another day or so. These can be accomplished either with your own vehicle (several **car rental** outlets), **taxis** or short-haul minibuses from near the PTT, or long-haul coaches from the **otogar** at the very top of town, by the roundabout on the 2007-completed bypass road.

Accommodation

A handful of surviving *pansiyon*s occupy converted old buildings lining the central grid of lanes – **Yalıboyu district** – that drops from **Hasan Altan Sokağı** down to the harbour, merging east into **Dereboyu** towards the ravine. There's also a district of newer, purpose-built hotels extending 1.5km west along **Kalamar Yolu**, which heads towards Kalamar Bay. Most such establishments are block-booked by tour operators; larger rooms, and swimming pools, offset the disadvantage of a hefty walk into town. The closest recommendable accommodation actually on **Kalkan Bay** is 1.5km out of town, on either shoreline. Unless otherwise indicated, all lodging is open Easter to early November.

Balıkçıhan Pansiyon Dereboyu ravine, 100m behind Kömürlük beach ☎0242/844 3075. Four tranquil, a/c suites (including three galleried family units), overlooking the ravine and sea. ⑤

Caretta Caretta Pansiyon 1.5km out of town on west bayshore – the last building. ☎0242/844 3435, ⑩www.kalkancaretta.com. Cult *pansiyon*-restaurant with a loyal Turkish and UK following, suffused with the character of owner and chef Gönül Kocabaş. Rooms have quirky decor in cheerful pastels, with stone floors and terraces – best is the rooftop "penthouse". The menu includes Gönül's famous *gül böreği* and homé-style entrées; there's a swimming pool with stunning views. ❹

Meldi Hotel 800m along Kalamar Yolu, seaward side ☏ 0242/844 2541, ⓦ www.meldihotel.com. Fair-sized rooms, all with up-to-date bathrooms and small balconies, either with garden or mountain views; breakfast is served next to the decent-sized pool. May–Oct; airport transfer included for stays of a week or longer. ❺

Stone House Waterfront, east end, Yalıboyu ☏ 0242/844 3076, ⓦ www.korsankalkan.com. Three large, well-appointed rooms plus a self-catering apartment in this restored house, below an affiliated seafood restaurant. ❹

Türk Evi (Eski Ev) Near top of lane heading up from Süleyman Yılmaz Cad, Yalıboyu ☏ 0242/844 3129, ⓦ www.kalkanturkevi.com. Wonderfully refurbished old house with welcoming common areas and rooms with kilims and some with fireplaces. Open in winter by arrangement (there's no other heating); the old road into town passes just up the hill, for easy car access. Discounts for long stays; otherwise ❸–❹ B&B

Viewpoint Villas 1km along Kalamar Yolu, uphill side ☏ 0242/844 3642, ⓦ www.viewpoint villaskalkan.com. Six villas arranged around a pool

and equipped to a very high standard – jacuzzi, full kitchen, fireplace in sitting room, etc – each sleeping 4–5. £600–650/week per villa in high season, discounts for 2 occupants.

Villa Mahal 1.5km east of town, east bay shore ☏ 0242/844 3268, ⓦ www .villamahal.com. Although there is road access, a free boat shuttle from the harbour is the best way to approach Kalkan's most exclusive lodging. A segmented veranda wraps itself around ten irregularly shaped standard rooms, some with huge bathrooms and private massage rooms. Steps descend past an infinity pool to the sea and lido – one of the few in Kalkan directly linked to accommodation, though open to the public for the sake of its popular restaurant. There's also a pool suite and two detached cottages furnished in the same designer-minimalist decor, with the multi-terrace setting among olive trees guaranteeing privacy. Friday evening bbq. May–Oct. ❽

White House Near top of lane leading up from east end of waterfront, Dereboyu ☏ 0242/844 3738 or 0532/443 0012, ⓦ www.kalkanwhite house.co.uk. Turkish–English-run *pansiyon* with large, airy, pine- and white-tile rooms ranging from singles to quads. Although only four of the ten have balconies, the roof terrace is one of the best in town. An adjoining old house is set to be restored as an annexe. ❹

Eating and drinking

Restaurants are scattered fairly evenly across town, though bars tend to cluster either just above the seafront or along Hasan Altan Sokağı, which after dark becomes the main pedestrianized drag into the village centre. Meal prices, however, are stratospheric for Turkey – 45–70TL a head, plus drink – often for bland British comfort-food and pseudo-curries, with *küver* and "service charge" (often in small print) levied at the more pretentious spots. The usual resort trick of heading inland for better deals doesn't always apply here – indeed, the diner of the *Caretta Caretta Pansiyon* (see above) provides some of the best value.

Among central **waterfront restaurants**, the longest established and most consistent are *Deniz (Palanin Yeri)* and adjacent *Korsan Meze* near the east end of the quay, the latter with imaginative *mezes*. **Uphill around the PTT**, *Ali Baba* is popular at lunchtime, and locally patronized, as is *Çatı*, directly uphill from the PTT on the old town-entry road. *Bar BQ*, at the start of the Kalamar road, is a very reasonable (for Kalkan) licensed all-rounder, while *Iso's Kitchen*, Süleyman Yılmaz Cad 39 in Yalıboyu, is a bit dearer but more atmospheric. Some of Kalkan's best food is 3.5km east of town at ⚹ *Kuru'nin Yeri* (all year), one of three eateries here, doling out inexpensive, home-style dishes like *mantı*, *nohutlu et*, *şakşuka* and corn bread. The town's top **café** is *Del Mar*, just inland from mid-quay, with own-made cakes, juices, teas and many varieties of coffee; simpler is quiet *Fener*, at the quay's east end by the lighthouse. Evergreen **bars** include high-decibel *Yalı*, at the top of Yalıboyu, ideal for a pre-dinner drink, and *Yacht Point* down on the quay, with varying music.

Local beaches

The artificially supplemented **pebble beach** called **Kömürlük** at the east edge of town is pleasant enough, the water quite clean and chilled by freshwater seeps, with one spring spilling onto the beach itself from just inland. Although bigger than it looks from afar, it still gets hopelessly full in summer, when you'll probably want to use the swimming platforms or **lidos** flanking the bay – reasonably priced shuttle boats take you to them. The only other bona fide beach within walking distance is a coarse-pebble one well southwest on the coast, which the Lycian Way visits on its way to Gelemiş.

The 27km of road east from Kalkan to Kaş follows a harsh karstic coastline, the terrain stained red from traces of metallic ores, with the Greek isles of Kastellórizo and Rhó increasingly visible out to sea. Just under 6km along you cross the **Kaputaş Gorge**, a deep canyon slashing back into the cliffs. Steps from the roadside parking area – where there's a *jandarma* post, and signs warning you not to leave valuables in cars (break-ins are rife when the *jandarma* aren't patrolling) – take you down to **Kaputaş beach**, a 150-metre-long expanse of pebble and blonde sand that is normally pretty packed, given the mediocre quality of beaches closer to Kalkan or Kaş. Kaputaş has served as the backdrop for innumerable TV advert shoots, and unless there's been a southerly storm the water is crystalline. The closest reliable facility is Ali Taylı's welcoming *Ada Fish Restaurant*, 700m east of Kaputaş overlooking the Sidek peninsula and its Byzantine ruins, doing a roaring trade thanks to the fresh and very reasonably priced fish bought in daily at 8am.

Between Kaputaş and *Ada* yawns the **Mavi Mağara**, claimed the second largest sea-cave in the Med, with blue-light effects inside. Despite signage on the road overhead, it's only accessible by sea – a very long swim from Kaputaş, or (more likely) as part of a boat trip – though Kalkan skippers can be reluctant to include it in itineraries.

Scuba-diving near Kalkan

Most of the twenty-odd local **dive sites** lie a 25 to 40 minute boat ride away, many of them around the islets at the mouth of the bay. Of these, beginners dive the shallows at the north tip of **Yılan Adası** (Snake Island), and almost entire perimeter of the remoter Heybeli; another excellent novice or second-dive-of-day venue is **Frank Wall** on the east side of the bay, with spectacular rock pinnacles and plenty of fish. More advanced divers are taken to an even more dramatic wall between 20m and 50m at the south tip of "Snake", alive with barracuda, grouper and myriad smaller fish, to reefs off Heybeli and Öksüz or to sand-bottom **caves** on the mainland with their entrances at 25m. The most spectacular calm-weather dive site, for intermediate and advanced divers, is **Sakarya Reef**, southeast of Kalkan off İnce Burun. Here, in 15m of water, are the mangled remains of the *Duchess of York*, a North Sea trawler built in Hull in 1893 and apparently scuttled for an insurance payout sometime after 1930. However, more interesting is the newer, larger Turkish-built *Sakarya* nearby, wrecked in the 1940s, broken into three sections at depths of 35–60m, retaining teak-plank decking, intact winches and a vast cargo of lead ballast. Except in the caves, fed by chilly fresh water, **water temperatures** are a comfortable 18–30°C; the sea warms up abruptly in late May or early June with a current change, and stays warm into November. **Visibility** is typically 25–30m.

The two locally based dive operators are Dolphin Scuba Team working off its boat in Kalkan's main port (☎0242/844 2242 or 0542/627 9757, ☜www.dolphinscubateam .com), and **Kalkan Diving/Aquasports**, at the Kalamar Beach Club (☎844 2361 or 0532/553 2006, ☜wwwkalkandiving.com). **Prices** are competitive, with two-dive mornings from £34/€40, and a PADI Open Water course from £170/€210.

Inland: İslamlar and Bezirgan

Two inland mountain settlements near Kalkan make ideal day-trip destinations – or idyllic overnight bases. The closest is **İSLAMLAR**, 6km north of old Highway 400 at Akbel, 8km in all from Kalkan; to get there take the Elmalı road from the town-edge roundabout, then the first unsigned left, then right at the top of the grade. The old name of Bodamya – Ottoman Greek for "rivers" – is still in use, and the village is indeed alive to the sound of falling water, used to power mills and nurture various trout-farm **restaurants**. The posh options, taking credit cards, are *Mahmut's* (all year), worth it for the grilled-vegetable and rocket side garnish and decent service, and *Değirmen* with a seasonally working mill in the basement grinding locally grown sesame seeds, which you can have served with *pekmez* or grape molasses. Budget favourites are *Pınarbaşı* and *Çiftlik*, the latter tucked inconspicuously behind *Değirmen*, doing good *kızartma* vegetables and a garnish of olives, peppers and *yufka* with large trout. Local accommodation is largely the preserve of the more upmarket package companies.

Continuing above İslamlar, about 5km along you hit the main Kalkan–Gömbe road; bear right (southeast) for a pleasant loop back to Kalkan via the upland *ova* (plateau) of **BEZİRGAN**, famous in the past for its horses, but today devoted to barley, sesame, chickpeas and orchard crops. The fertile plain was once a prehistoric lake, drained finally by an ingenious Roman tunnel, and there's a sprinkling of Lycian rock tombs and an ancient citadel on the hillside. At the northwest edge of the two-*mahalle* village is Turkish Erol and Scottish Pauline's well-signposted, excellent, 150-year-old village-house **inn**, *Owlsland* (T0242/837 5214 or 0535/940 1715, Wwww.owlsland.com; closed Dec–Feb; B&B, HB), named after the Scops and little owls resident in the nearby almond trees. It lies about 600m off the Lycian Way, making it a logical stop on the trek; Erol is a mean cook and you're well advised to have half-board. At 720m elevation, you'll need the woodstoves in the minimally restored but en-suite rooms during spring or autumn.

By studying the Lycian Way map, you can fashion a **loop walk** with the *ova* as pivot; only 1.6km separates the two intersections of the path with the ascending road from Kalkan, and indeed this circular walk is offered as an organized outing. On your own, take a minibus from Kalkan's top roundabout to Bezirgan – there are two daily from Kınık bound for Gömbe – and then walk back to Kalkan in about three hours.

The main road **north from Bezirgan** makes a lovely drive, passing great stands of *katran* ("Lebanon" cedar) and the Akyazı *ova*, comprising the flood plain of the Koca Çayı, which eventually becomes the Saklıkent Gorge, with the 3000m-elevation ridge of Akdağ closing the skyline to the northwest. You link up with the Kaş–Gömbe route just past Sütleğen.

Kaş

Tourism has utterly transformed **KAŞ**. What was a sleepy fishing village before the mid-1980s is today a holiday metropolis, whose permanent population of about 7000 is well outnumbered by the vacationers on whom locals depend for a living. Attitudes have inevitably hardened – the *otogar* is well patrolled by accommodation touts – though residential tourism is not as big as at Dalyan or Kalkan. Kaş remains more youth-oriented and more cosmopolitan; aspiring İstanbul or Ankara yuppies flock here, and it's still a fixture on the foreign backpackers' trail. The village, until 1923 a Greek-populated shipping port, has always had an appealing setting, nestling in a curving bay – *kaş* means "eyebrow" or "something curved" – with a backdrop of vertical, 500-metre-high cliffs peppered with rock tombs, and startling, head-on views of Kastellórizo (Meis).

A major halting point on "Blue Cruise" itineraries, **yacht and gulet culture** is as important here as at Kalkan – with day-trips available for the less well-heeled. Set for completion in 2010, a new yacht marina is being built at Bucak Limanı (formerly Vathy), the long fjord west of town, wedged between Highway 400 and the Çukurbağ peninsula, which extends 5km southwest of Kaş. A two-level road system (upper lane westbound, sea level eastbound) is being graded above it, with a new, as yet unfinalized traffic plan to enter town.

Beaches are hardly stellar, which together with the lack of a really convenient airport has spared the town the full impact of modern tourism. However, it gets lively at night, since shops stay open until 1am in season – and the various bars much later. Kaş makes a handy base from which to reach Kekova and nearby Patara, and various types of **adventure activities** are practised in the environs. The modern town is built atop ancient **Antiphellos**, whose remaining ruins speckle the streets and cover the base of the Çukurbağ peninsula.

Arrival, information and transport

All buses and dolmuşes arrive at the **otogar** at the top inland end of Atatürk Bulvarı (alias Elmalı Caddesi). The **tourist office** is at waterfront Cumhuriyet Meydanı 5 (May–Oct Mon–Fri 8.30am–noon & 1–7pm, Sat & Sun 10am–noon & 1–7pm; Nov–April Mon–Fri 9am–noon & 1–5pm; ☎0242/836 1238), stocking glossy brochures plus hotel lists, though rather short on any other information. Central Kaş is small enough to get around on foot, with **parking** (charged for) largely limited to the harbour quay, and behind the old market square. There's a public **shuttle service** around the Çukurbağ peninsula's loop road, provided by at least hourly (to midnight in summer) minibuses labelled "Yarımada-Şehiriçi".

Accommodation

Because of Kaş's nocturnal rhythms, it's worth hunting a bit out of the centre for calm, views and privacy. The highest concentration of desirable hotels and *pansiyon*s within the town limits lies east of the centre, above **Küçük Çakıl**; an enclave of budget lodgings lies west of Atatürk Bulvarı, along **Necip Bey Caddesi** (alias Hastane Caddesi) and around the hilltop **Yeni Cami**, formerly a Greek church. The **Çukurbağ peninsula** has acquired a crop of multi-starred hotels, but few deserve their rating. Most in-town accommodation is open all year, whilst Çukurbağ establishments close from November to April. Given summer temperatures, all are air-conditioned unless stated otherwise.

Necip Bey Caddesi and around Yeni Cami

Gülşen Pansiyon Necip Bey Cad 21 ☎0242/836 1171. Basic but en-suite and partly a/c affair on several floors; lucky balconied rooms face the sea, as does the very pleasant waterside garden and breakfast area. ❸

Hideaway Hotel Eski Kilise Arkası 7 ☎0242/836 1887, ⓦwww.hotelhideaway .com. The most salubrious mid-range option in town. Rooms have new tiled baths plus marble and wood trim; third-floor view rooms are white and airy. Common areas include a small plunge pool, internet corner, a TV-lounge-cum-library, and a

stunning rooftop restaurant with home-style cooking and fair bar prices. Ahmet (Turkish) and Marie (Belgian) are your very engaging, multilingual hosts. Credit cards accepted; all year. ❹

Kale Otel Kilise Mevkii ☎0242/836 4074. Four-building complex popular with German package tourists, though walk-ins welcome; pastel-hued rooms have marble, wood and white-tile decor. The sea view from the back garden is unobstructed, and there's an affiliated restaurant (*Leymona*) by the water. ❺ standard, ❻ suite.

Meltem Pansiyon Meltem Sok, between Elmalı Cad and Yeni Cami ☎0242/836 1855, ⓦwww .kasmeltempansion.com. One of six *pansiyon*s

KAŞ

MEDITERRANEAN SEA

Friday Market, ◀ *Fethiye & Kaputaş Beach* ◀ **Otogar** ▲ Ⓐ *& Antalya*

Campsite & Çukurbağ Peninsula ▲ Ⓔ Ⓕ Ⓖ

Büyük Çakıl Plajı & Path to Limanağzı ▶

Küçük Çakıl Lidos

ACCOMMODATION

Aquarius	F
Arpia	G
Begonvil	J
Club Phellos	I
Deniz Feneri	E
Gardenia	K
Gülşen	H
Hideaway	C
Kale	D
Maki	L
Medusa	M
Meltem	B
Oreo	A

RESTAURANTS

Bahçe	10
Bahçe Fish	13
Chez Evy	7
Kaşım	11
Natur-el	1
Oba	9
Sepkin	12
Sempati	17
Sultan Garden	5
Tekirdağ Köftecisi	5

BARS & CAFÉS

Café Galerie	2
Echo	14
Effendi	16
Hideaway	8
Hi-Jazz	4
Mavi/Blue	15
Red Point	6

Lycian Rock Tombs

Doric Tomb

Lion Tomb

Stairs

LIKYA CAD

ÇUKURBAĞLI (İBRAHİM SERİN) CAD

ZÜMRÜT SOK

SÜLEYMAN TOPÇU

UZUN ÇARŞI

SÜLEYMAN SANDIKÇI SOK

HÜKÜMET CAD

CUMHURİYET MEYD

BAHÇE SOK

Old Market Square

ATATÜRK BULV (ELMALI) CAD

MELTEM SOK

GÜL SOK

SÜLEYMAN YILDIRIM CAD

NECİP BEY (HASTANE) CAD

Yeni Cami

Theatre

Harbour Mosque

Hellenistic Temple

Swimming Platform

Harbour

Tour boats

WC & drinking water

Hükümet Konağı

Jandarma

Taxi Rank

DOĞRU YOL CAD

0   50 m

clustered on this street, and just uphill on Recep Bilgin Cad. This gets the thumbs-up from readers for a warm welcome, sizable en-suite rooms in brown-tile and light-pine trim and decent breakfasts on the airy roof terrace. ❸

Oreo Hotel Yaka Mahallesi, north of the town centre ☎0242/836 2220 or 836 3737. Good-standard hotel managed by BT Travel (see below), and apt to be occupied by sporty types. Over half of the rooms have sea views, there's a big pool and adjacent shady garden for breakfast, and good suppers are available by arrangement, next to a roaring fire in the cooler months. Open March–Dec. ❹

Küçük Çakıl

Begonvil Hotel Koza Sok, about halfway along ☎0242/836 3079, ⓦwww.hotelbegonvil.com. Boutique hotel with old-photo decor, side-facing at the end of a terrace, with small to medium-size, cheerful rooms with tile-mosaic and wrought-iron touches; all but three have a sea view from small balconies, and some have double beds, though bathrooms could stand re-doing. Buffet breakfast taken in the courtyard. ❹

Club Phellos Hotel Doğruyol Sok 4 ☎0242/836 1953, ⓦwww.hotelclubphellos.com.tr. The best-standard town-centre hotel: medium-sized rooms have sea/island views, terracotta floors and (usually) mini-bathtubs. Facilities include a large outdoor pool, hamam/fitness centre, some children's facilities and adequate parking (a major issue in peak season). ❺

Gardenia Küçük Çakıl shore road ☎0242/836 1618, ⓦwww.gardenia hotel-kas.com. Boutique hotel with just 11 quite different rooms and suites over four storeys (beware, no lift) with Philippe Starck decor and marble floors, somewhat at odds with the garish art in the common areas. Proprietors Ömer and Nevin speak American English. Buffet breakfast to 11am; no children under 12. Prices vary: ❺ (rear), ❻ (oblique or full sea view), ❽ suite.

Maki Hotel Koza Sok, east end ☎0242/836 3480, ⓦwww.kasmakihotel.com. Quiet, cul-de-sac hotel spread over two premises: the "old" wing above private parking and the pool garden has fair-sized blue-tiled rooms (including suite-like triples) with good baths, while the newer wing has a lift,

Scuba-diving around Kaş

The Mediterranean around Kaş has arguably the best visibility (up to 30m) and greatest variety of sea life along the entire Turkish coast. Fish you're likely to see – especially in spring or late summer – include grouper, barracuda, amberjack, garfish and ray; smaller common species include cardinal fish, damselfish, parrotfish, flying fish, ornate wrasse, breams and pandora.

There are notionally about ten dive operators here, many operating out of Küçük Çakıl hotel basements, but in terms of boat comfort, safety standards, equipment condition and thorough instruction, only three companies stand out: Sun Diving inside Kaş Camping (☎0242/836 2637, ⓦwww.turkey-diving.com/divecenter-sundiving.html), Anemone at Uzun Çarsı Sok 16 (☎0242/836 3651, ⓦwww.anemonedc-kas.com) and BT Diving, Çukurbağlı Cad 10 (☎0242/836 3737, ⓦwww.bt-turkey.com). It's quite common to dive only in the morning or afternoon, thus prices are per dive rather than per day. The recommended operators advertise single dives at about €22, making this the least expensive place to dive in Turkey. A PADI Open Water course costs €270, Advanced Open Water €180, plus €40 for course materials.

Dive sites

There are nearly sixty dive sites in the area, many along the Çukurbağ peninsula, with most others around the islets at the marine frontier with Kastellórizo. Beginners visit a tunnel at 15m and a shoreline cave fed by an icy freshwater spring in Bayındır Limanı, or "Stone Edge" or Güvercin Adası off the Çukurbağ peninsula. Moderately experienced divers are taken to "Canyon", where they drop through the namesake formation past a reasonably intact Greek cotton-carrying freighter that ran aground here in the 1960s. This was later dynamited to remove the navigational hazard, with its stern in 35m of water. Next there's a traverse of a big-wall dropoff, and then a return north with prevailing currents via a tunnel system. Only advanced divers can visit a wrecked World War II bomber shot down between Kaş and Kastellórizo, resting nearly intact in 65m of water at "Flying Fish", just beyond "Canyon".

beige-tile new baths and big balconies. ④ old wing, ⑤ new wing.

Medusa Hotel Küçük Çakıl shore road ☎0242/836 1440, ⓦwww.medusahotels.com/kas.htm. Well-equipped, well-run three-star hotel with a pool and lido, though standard rooms – some with double beds, 2006-revamped baths and island views – are rather small. Four-person family suites on the roof offer a bit more space. Rooms ⑤, suites ⑥

Çukurbağ peninsula

Aquarius South-shore loop road, about 3.5km out. ☎0242/836 1896, ⓦwww.aquariusotel.com. Discrete, Tardis-like hotel in lush landscaping, consisting of two wings of smallish but cheery rooms with veneer floors and average baths around a large kidney-shaped pool. But the main selling point is the best lido on the peninsula, right opposite Meis, with 1 of 2 on-site restaurants. ⑤ B&B

Arpia North-shore loop road, 7km out of town ☎0242/836 2642, ⓔarpia@bt-turkey.com. Rooms (including a deluxe grade) have been overhauled, but the place really scores for its sunset views, private lido and poolside restaurant (better-than-average breakfast and open buffet supper).

Bookable direct or through the BT agency in town (see "Listings"). Easter to mid-Nov. ④

Deniz Feneri North leg of loop road, 8km out ☎0242/836 2741. Luxury hotel comprising just a dozen minimalist-to-austere units, doubles to family suites – many round-fronted – perched over garden terraces tumbling down to a 150-metre lido and a good (but expensive) waterside restaurant. At reception level there's an infinity pool, hamam and area for (excellent) breakfasts. English co-management from Gillian, and attentive staff. Sunset views, though one faces Bucak and the open sea rather than Meis. Payment must be via Exclusive Escapes (see p.32) for minimum of three nights, effectively ⑨.

Camping

Kaş Kamping Necip Bey Cad, 1km west of town, past the theatre ☎0242/836 1050. Long a favoured halt on the Hippie Trail across Asia, this campsite is perennially for sale, but while it survives as is, there's a swimming platform, lively bar-restaurant, popular caravan space and newish A-frame cabins (②) for the tentless, as well as an on-site diving school.

Ancient Antiphellos

Ancient **Antiphellos** was the harbour of ancient Phellos, inland near modern Çukurbağ village and one of the few Lycian cities with a Greek name (*phellos* means "cork oak"). Excavations have dated the settlement to about the fourth century BC, although Antiphellos only gained importance in Hellenistic times, when increased seagoing commerce meant it thrived while Phellos withered. By the Roman era, it was famed particularly for its exceptionally soft sponges.

The remains of Antiphellos are few and scattered, but what's visible is quite impressive. Some 500m west along Necip Bey Caddesi sits a small, almost complete Hellenistic **theatre** with 26 rows of seats, well used by those watching the sunset. Above and behind here, 100m northeast on a hilltop, stands a unique **Doric tomb**, the so-called *Kesme Mezar*, also almost completely intact. Its single chamber forms a slightly tapering cube cut from the rock on which it stands; inside, the bench at the back is decorated by a frieze of small female figures performing a dance.

The most interesting of the sarcophagi to have survived is the **Lion Tomb** at the top of the Uzun Çarşı. This towering structure has two burial chambers, the lower one forming a base for the Lycian sarcophagus above it. On the side of the lower chamber is an undeciphered Lycian inscription in the same poetic form as the Xanthian obelisk, possibly an epitaph. The tomb's name derives from the lifting bosses for the Gothic-style lid, in the shape of lions' heads resting their chins on their paws.

Local beaches

Considering that Kaş is a major Turkish resort, local natural beaches are surprisingly poor; the only good pebble one on Bucak Limanı is **Akçagerme**, 3km west, with an inexpensive snack bar run by the tourism school. In town itself, **Küçük Çakıl** has been pretty much taken over by the hotels above it, who have installed snack-bar and sunbed concessions and fitted the shoreline with flagstone or wood-deck lidos – though the public is welcome to patronize the facilities. **Büyük Çakıl**, just over 1km east of town, is a small (60m wide), shingle-and-sand cove with a handful of snack bars that gets crowded. For more space, take a water dolmuş (hourly low season, every 20min peak times; 10TL return) to **Limanağzı**, the next, large bay to the southeast, with three tavernas and sunbeds behind each of three swimming areas. Leaving town to the west, the **Çukurbağ peninsula** gives good views of the Greek island Kastellórizo, and is lapped by clear, aquamarine water, but again has no beaches other than two pebble coves either side of the isthmus, which are threatened by plans to open a channel here to "ventilate" bilge waste from the new marina. On the peninsula, there are only hotel-built lidos where you can reach the water unmenaced by ubiquitous sea urchins.

Boat tours and Kastellórizo

Boatmen at the harbour offer standard full-day tours (depart 10am, return 6pm) to either **Kekova** (make sure these do not begin with a land transfer to Üçağız!) or to **Patara** (from 50TL per person, including lunch). **Custom tours** in a boat taking six to eight people start at 300TL a day in low season, reaching 600–650TL in a busy year at peak season.

Day-, night-cruise or one-way trips to **Kastellórizo** have been greatly facilitated by the 2008 designation of that islet as an offical Greek port of entry. Two Kaş companies currently provide a mid-morning service (but never weekends when Turkish customs is closed), the more reliable (and likely to survive) being Meis Express (☎0242/836 1725, ⓦwww.meisexpress.com). There's a "taverna run" on Wednesday night, and there may be an extra, unpublicized Greek boat to Kastellórizo on Friday and Monday afternoons. You'll need to surrender your passport to customs the night before; returning to Kaş from Kastellórizo, no fresh visa fee is payable as long as time remains on your existing multiple-entry visa. For prices and frequencies, see "Travel details", p.377.

▲ Uzun Çarşı, Kaş

Kastellórizo – and its race

The picturesque port **Kastellórizo**, called Meis in Turkish after the Greek alternate name (Meyísti), lies just over three nautical miles off the Turkish coast. It is among the smallest inhabited islands of the Greek Dodecanese archipelago, a haven for yachties and a favourite venue for renewing three-month Turkish tourist visas. You'll find complete coverage in *The Rough Guide to the Greek Islands*, but it's worth saying that there are at least two weekly onward boats to Rhodes most of the year, plus several inexpensive weekly flights on a small aircraft. If you just miss a departure, a day or two on Meis will be well spent, with affordable seafood, walking opportunities and adequate nightlife.

Kaş and Meis have since 2006 hosted an annual, late-June, port-to-port **swimming and kayak race** in the interests of peace and friendship between Greece and Turkey, winked at thus far by both customs authorities as passport controls for all concerned are dispensed with. Winning times on the Meis to Kaş course (7.1km) are typically 1hr 40min for swimmers, 38 minutes for kayakers.

Eating, drinking and nightlife

There are many excellent **restaurants** in Kaş, though few actually face the water-front, and some that do are prone to scams and rip-offs – two in particular to avoid are *Smiley's* and *Mercan*. A varied, crowded, sometimes high-decibel **nightlife and café society** – easily the best on the Turquoise Coast – makes Kaş for many visitors.

Restaurants

Bahçe Uzun Çarşı, top of. The broadest range of cold and hot *meze*s in town, served in the garden (*bahçe* in Turkish). Mains in comparison are almost incidental, though their *ayva tatlısı* is a fitting finale. Nearby is their seafood annexe (booking needed in season on ☎0242/836 2779), with slow service but top *meze*s like *levrek marin* (marinated sea bass fillet) and fluffy squid rings. Both open May to early Nov.

Chez Evy Terzi Sok 2, off Zümrüt Sok ☎0242/836 1253. A worthwhile splurge (60TL each, plus any wine) sees French country recipes meet Turkish flavours. The result is happier and more generous than you'd expect – the fillet in pepper sauce and (in autumn) wild boar are to die for – while Evy herself, who used to cook for the rich and famous on their private mega-yachts, is one of the characters of Kaş. Booking for garden seating is necessary in season; otherwise wait for a table, or have a nightcap, in the rustic bar. Supper only; open much of the year.

Kaşım Öztürk Sok 15. The best of several on this inland pedestrian lane, with a mix of affordable *hazır yemek*, grills and puddings; unlicensed, but very popular at lunch.

Natur-el Gürsoy Sok, off Uzun Çarşı ☎0242/836 2834. Besides Turkish snacks such as *mantı* and *su böreği*, there's an ambitious – if not uniformly successful – range of mains such as *hunkâr beğendi* (lamb in aubergine and cheese sauce) and

cevizli nar tavuk (chicken in walnut and pomegranate sauce). Both outdoor seating and a lovely interior upstairs for the cooler months. Friendly, low-key service; booking suggested.

Oba Çukurbağlı Cad 8, near the PTT. Licensed old-house diner that's ace for simple home-style soups and *sulu yemek*, though portions are on the small side; equally pleasant garden or indoor seating.

Seçkin Atatürk Bul 2, behind Harbour Mosque. Budget-priced, unlicensed outfit pitched mainly at locals, this does *döner kebap* and *hazır yemek* by day, plus *işkembe* (tripe) and *paça* (trotter) soups as hangover tonics after midnight (when it's busiest). It also serves great traditional desserts like *kabak tatlısı* topped with *kaymak* or *dondurma* at any hour. Indoor, garden and pavement seating; open 24hr.

Sempati Gürsoy Sok. This has long had a reputation for excellent meat dishes accompanied by a few *meze*s such as *arnavut ciğer* and *mücver*, plus several varieties of *rakı*.

Sultan Garden Hükümet Cad, opposite Coast Guard. The most romantic outdoor seaside venue (book summer on ☎0242/836 3762), with unusual *meze*s like *paçanga böreği* and a good line in lamb dishes; allow 50TL a head, plus wine. May–Oct, though small conservatory may operate in winter.

Tekirdağ Köftecisi Zümrüt Sok. Serving that homely meat dish, *piyaz*, *şakşuka* and not much else at lovely lane seating; fairly economical for Kaş. Also desserts and coffee.

Bars and cafés

Café Galerie Çukurbağlı Cad 12. Just three tables inside, and six out, but all likely to be occupied owing to superior Austrian-style coffees and cakes – at Austrian prices. May–Sept.

Echo Gürsoy Sok, just in from harbour. Ground-floor café with affordable light snacks wedded to an upstairs view bar with live music two nights weekly, acid jazz/house/funk soundtrack otherwise.

Effendi The quay, start of Hükümet Cad. Natural meeting point with a more secluded upstairs lounge, dishing out waffles, coffees, fruit juice and booze; there's live music (rock, blues) two to three nights per week.

Hideway Cumhuriyet Cad 16/A officially, actually in a lane off the old market square. Easily the coolest garden bar/café in town

(open only May–Nov); vintage rock and blues soundtrack, divan and table seating, romantic lighting and ever-popular (if somewhat pricey) Sunday breakfast.

Hi-Jazz Zümrüt Sok 3. The designated local jazz venue, though the long-standing proprietor has rented it out, so expect a programming change.

Mavi/Blue Cumhuriyet Meydanı. The oldest bar-café in town: three decades ago it was a coffeehouse where retired fishermen played backgammon, now it's musical, young and trendy from mid-afternoon until morning.

Red Point Club Süleyman Topçu Sok. Kaş's premier after-hours dance club in an old barn, packed solid after midnight despite a fairly spacious dancefloor for the sake of DJ-spun rock and soul. Tables out in the lane during summer.

Listings

Books and music Merdiven on İlkokul Sok 4/B has used paperbacks and a few new dictionaries and guidebooks. Dem Müzik Evi on Bahçe Sok near the PTT keeps a good selection of the best Turkish folk, *özgun* and devotional music.

Paragliding The cliffs above Kaş are beginning to rival Ölüdeniz as a paragliding venue, though you'll pay €100 a pop here as well.

Shopping The Uzun Çarşı (Long Market) is precisely that – an uninterrupted bazaar of antique and designer clothing shops with stock (and prices) matching European city-centre malls. Turkish towelling and bathrobes are currently big; besides overseas labels produced under licence, you can have garments custom-tailored from local hand-woven fabrics peddled at the shabby but lively Friday market, at the edge of town en route to Bucak Limanı. The antique shops are all of similar quality, with few worth singling out: carpets, jewellery, metal antiques and kitsch knick-knacks. Off Uzun Çarşı, an exception is Old Curiosity Shop on Lise Sok near the old market square,

stocking a museum-like collection of unique objects in all sizes at fair prices. Finally, Kaş has the only "supermarkets" between Fethiye and Kemer near Antalya, opposite the *otogar*: Gen-Pa and a mini-Migros.

Taxis Ranks in the old market square, and base of the jetty.

Travel agents British/Turkish-run BT Adventure & Diving/Bougainville Travel, Çukurbağlı (officially İbrahim Serin) Cad 10 (℡0242/836 3737, www .bt-turkey.com), is the foremost adventure-travel agency in the area for diving, mountain treks, canyoning and sea-kayaking, but also offering more conventional excursions. Dragoman, Uzun Çarşı 15 (℡0242/836 3614, www.dragoman-turkey.com), offers similar-quality outings (including yoga and wine tasting, or sea-level "coasteering") but is more Francophone-orientated.

Water Delicious and potable, straight from the mountains around Gömbe, available free at taps by the Harbour Mosque; the Saklıkent pipeline water is considered only fit to wash in.

Canyoning above Kaş

Most **canyoning** outings here focus on one of two stream canyons: Hacıoğlan Çayı or Kıbrıs Çayı. The former traverse, starting near Hacıoğlan village east of Bezirgan, makes a good beginners' spring expedition of 6hr, finishing at Dereköy, with plenty of easy slides and long swims as well as one 20-ft abseil about two-thirds of the way along. In summer the action shifts to the latter canyon, which retains water all year (too much, in fact, during spring), and while shorter takes the same time to emerge at Beldibi, with two abseils and two zip-wire transits. The Kaputaş gorge is another potential venue, though there is rarely enough water in it. Days out typically cost €45 with the recommended agencies (see "Listings", above).

North of Kaş: Akdağ and Yeşil Göl

When sea-level pleasures at Kaş pall, especially in broiling weather, there's escape in the cool heights of the **Akdağ range**, which soars to over 3000m in the space of 20km. The standard start-point for excursions into the mountains, reachable by minibus, is **Gömbe**, a small town 60km north of Kaş on the road to Elmalı. This provides access to **Yeşil Göl**, Lycia's only alpine lake, and also serves as a staging point for anyone intending to climb **Akdağ summit** itself, three hours above **Yeşil Göl**.

Gömbe

The ninety-minute ride up from Kaş is graced by extensive pine forests, yielding to apple orchards as you approach **GÖMBE**. Few commercial maps show the huge **Çayboğazı reservoir** which has re-routed any approach from the south – drivers can avoid the circuitous bypass road by going right over the dam-top road. Gömbe is famous for a June festival of the local Tahtacıs, and a farmers' fair the latter half of August.

Around the main Belediye square are three simple but adequate **restaurants**, all with similar bean-soup and *köfte* menus – the *Şafak* is licensed, but the *Çörekçi* is friendlier and more savoury – a few *dondurma* parlours on summer evenings, plus three **pansiyons**, mostly on the hillside south of the square. Of these, fanciest is the en-suite *Paşa* (☏0242/831 5208; ❷), though the nearly adjacent *Akın* (☏0242/831 4117; ❶) is adequate and clean, with shared bathrooms.

Yeşil Göl and Akdağ

Most people come to Gömbe to visit **Yeşil Göl** (Green Lake), a short distance west and the only permanent body of water on generally arid, karstic Akdağ. Tucked into the mountain's east flank at about 1850m elevation, Yeşil Göl is a large, clean and fairly deep tarn at its best between April and June; the earlier in spring you show up, the finer the **wildflower** displays. The southern lakeshore has enough (slightly sloping) turf for a handful of tents, should you wish to **camp**.

To reach the lake, it's best to drive (2WD vehicles passable with care, but preferably 4WD), though the following directions apply equally to hikers. Leave the square heading north and turn left immediately after crossing the river bridge, then take the second paved right, and begin climbing in zigzags to the Çukurbağ Köyü mosque. Turn left here and keep parallel to an aqueduct, asking if necessary for the track to "Subaşı Yayla".

Exactly 6.2km above the bridge, half an hour's low-gear driving around ruts, boulders and treefalls, just above the highest gnarled junipers, you'll reach a widening in the track beside a vigorous stream, near the start of the aqueduct. Some 500m past this widening is another parking place, flanked by a brick privy; immediately beyond a landslide blocks the track. Down in the stream ravine a cement pedestrian bridge gives the only safe access to the far bank, where faint paths lead up to a non-vehicular track, blocked off by boulders at its turn-off from your original track. On foot, follow this rougher track past some rudimentary shepherds' huts and corrals; immediately after this, leave the track for proper paths over a gentle saddle that emerges abruptly at an overlook for the lake (maximum 30min from the privy).

Climbing Akdağ

If you intend to **climb Akdağ peak** (3024m), retrace your steps to the main motorable track and proceed west; after about ten minutes you pass a quadruple-spouted spring. After a few bends, now high above the stream-bed, you adopt the true right bank of the watercourse. When you reach a tributary coming from the south, veer to follow it, keeping to the true left bank. The summit ridge should be ahead, on your right; soon you should pick up a distinct, cairned path that leads all the way to the top, 2hr 30min one way with a daypack, from the spring. The **summit cairn** contains a "guestbook" to sign, and the views over snow-flecked badlands are superb. An ice axe is useful until June or July (depending on the preceding winter), and you'll need adequate water in any season.

To do a complete **traverse of the range**, you'll have to schedule an overnight stop somewhere on the mountain. The classic descent is to **Arsaköy** (with a basic inn and two places to eat) on the west flank of Akdağ, from where a wonderful cobbled path descends for a couple of hours towards Saklıkent before disappearing under a bulldozer track.

Dereağzı

About 30km northeast of Kaş, imposing ruins at **Dereağzı** – an enormous, half -intact Byzantine cathedral, and a strong Byzantine castle built atop earlier fortifications – are worthy destinations for those with transport. The latter guarded a strategic narrows (Dereağzı means "valley mouth") in the easiest route for shipping grain and cedar wood to Andriake (see p.361) from the rich uplands of Elmalı and Kasaba.

To get there, take the road to Gömbe and turn east at Kasaba village, following signs to Çatallar, and then proceed just over 8km to Dirgenler. At a crossroads here with a blue metal bus shelter, a sign points left to three villages; go right instead onto a gravel track. After 2.8km, you reach the head of a gorge, with some rock tombs visible, and a small pumping station in a concrete shed; here the Kasaba plateau begins draining towards the sea. The abrupt, roughly triangular hill on your right is in fact covered by the ruins of a castle, barely noticeable from afar.

The monuments

From just before the pumping station, faint goat paths angle southwest to become the old Byzantine path – still the only way up – leading within twenty minutes to the overgrown **main gate** in the northwest-facing wall. Once up and in, you fully appreciate the amazing site, not unlike those of the Cathar castles of Languedoc: the southwest to northeast ridge is essentially a knife-edge, and the entire fortified hill is lapped by two rivers, the Kasaba (Tokluca) and the Karadağ, which mingle at the hill's southeast base to form the Demre Çayı.

The ancient Lycians first built a castle here during the sixth to fifth centuries BC, using polygonal, unmortared masonry, or occasionally even hewing into the rock. After eighth-century AD Arab raids, the Byzantines improved and enlarged it over two hundred years, using a mortared-rubble technique, and adding six triangular or rectangular **bastions and towers** still visible on the lowest, northwest wall, the castle's weakest side. American surveys from 1974 to 1981 revealed two more inner layers of defence as one proceeds to the summit, complete with a **church**, plus dozens of **cisterns** and water-collecting channels.

From the water-pumping station, walk northwest on a riverbank track along the Karadağ (aka Boğluca) to a point just opposite the huge, knoll-top **cathedral** where channels in the marsh narrow enough for you to cross. Contemporary with the castle reconstruction, this was clearly funded from Constantinople, given its size and rich marble decoration (now in Antalya's archeological museum, leaving the brick-and-rubble core). It has two unusual, freestanding hexagonal structures, one at the apse end and one where the narthex presumably was. The cathedral served quite a large town, which disappeared within two centuries of its foundation; neither the Byzantine nor Lycian name for Dereağzı is known, since no identifying inscriptions or coins have been found.

Down in the Karadağ gorge, most of the area's Lycian **rock tombs and sarcophagi** sit on the east bank of the stream, near the passage of an **ancient road** with numerous steps. This road can still be trekked along for about 5km, though since the bulldozing of a dirt track through the gorge there's less enjoyment to be derived from this. From the pumping station, drivers can make a circuit back to the coast by following this fairly smooth track downstream **along the Demre Çayı**; it's 23km, the last 7km paved, and passable to cars except perhaps at high water in spring (there's one river ford).

The Kekova region

Some of the most beautifully situated ruins on the Turquoise Coast are in the **Kekova** area, named for the eponymous offshore island. It's a stretch of rocky shore littered with remains of Lycian settlements, some now submerged under the translucent waters of the calm, shallow, almost landlocked gulf here. Land access – both by road and by the Lycian Way – has improved considerably, so the region is no longer the exclusive preserve of boat and yacht tours. Many monuments are easily visited by boat-tour from **Üçağız** on the inlet shore – the main activity at this beachless place – while inland lie the neglected remains of **Apollonia**, a dependency of coastal Aperlae, and the substantial ruins of **Cyaneae**.

Üçağız

The region's central village is **ÜÇAĞIZ**, 38km from Kaş and connected to Highway 400 by a surfaced, twenty-kilometre road. Thus its quiet days are past: carpet, antique and jewellery shops have sprouted, boat-trip touts swarm around you on arrival (or pretend to be hitchhikers on the road in), and you've little hope of finding one of the hundred-odd beds unoccupied in July or August. Most of the surroundings have been designated as an archeological site, which protects Üçağız from unseemly concrete expansion; indeed, some illegal buildings have been demolished. And its essential village identity has yet to be completely supplanted – out of season the place is still idyllic.

There's just one daily **dolmuş** from Demre, geared to villagers', not tourists', needs (out at around 5pm, back at 8am). Üçağız's **pansiyons** are simple, but often overpriced considering the remote location and lack of a beach. Although fresh water has been piped in from Gömbe, hot showers can still be erratic. The best, most secluded places lie at the west end of the village. The stone-clad *Kekova* (℡0242/874 2259, Ⓦwww.kekovapansiyon.com; ❹) has relatively palatial air-conditioned rooms and a shared wraparound balcony. Just beyond, the ⚚ *Ekin Hotel* (℡0242/874 2064 or 0534/936 7783, Ⓦwww.ekinpensioncom) sports a pleasant garden, clean, airy rooms in the original building (❷) and a newer extension at the back (❸) housing suites, with all-important insect screens plus air conditioning; it's well run by cultured brothers Ali and Yusuf. None of the several waterside **restaurants** offer especially good value: the most tolerable and durable is *Liman Marina* (aka *İbrahim's*), where drinks and *meze*s are affordable, though mains are expensive.

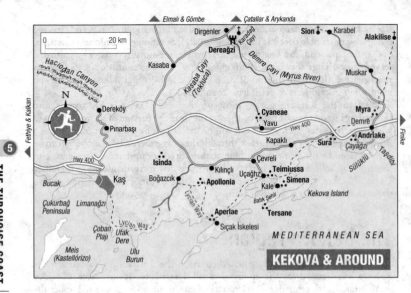

KEKOVA & AROUND

Around Üçağız

Üçağız translates as "three mouths" in Turkish, as does the old Greek name of Tristomo. The three apertures in question are the straits at each end of the island opposite, plus the entry to the lake-like gulf, at whose rear the village is situated. Several small islands, quarried in ancient times to near sea level, dot the bay. Until the road was built, the Lycian remains around Üçağız were visited by few apart from hardy goats and archeologists. Teimiussa – and if you like walking, Simena and Aperlae – can be reached on foot from the village, though most (especially in summer) will opt for a boat excursion. Destinations and prices are fairly standard: €9–10 per boat to take in nearby Kale (Simena) and Kekova island on a two-hour tour; €25 to Aperlae ruins; just under €7 for a one-way shuttle to Kale (the walk back takes 45min over rocky terrain).

Kekova island

The most romantically situated local ruins are those submerged along the northern coast of **Kekova island**, known as Batık Şehir (Sunken City) locally, and not yet identified with any ancient city. The underwater remains of stairs, pavements,

Sea-kayaking around Kekova

BT Adventure and Dragoman in Kaş (see p.358) remain the principal organizers of sea-kayaking day-tours in the Kekova area, a wonderful, low-impact way of appreciating the eerie seascapes. They have the further advantage of allowing you to approach the shoreline, and the Batık Şehir in particular, much closer than the glass-bottomed cruise boats do, and also of using narrow, shallow channels off-limits to larger craft. As long as your head is covered and you bring enough water, you'll tolerate all but the hottest summer days, even wrapped inside a life vest. Trips may begin with a motorized tow from Üçağız to the starting point of your choice, for example Tersane; outings can be as long or short as stamina allows. Per-person rates, including a transfer from Kaş to Üçağız and a picnic lunch, are approximately €30.

house walls and a long quay wall can all be seen; however snorkelling or even just swimming are banned to prevent the removal of antiquities from the area, and most boatmen won't approach the rocky shoreline (the best view is from a kayak; see box, p.362). Near the southwest tip of the island, at the spot called Tersane (Dockyard), looms the apse of a long-vanished church, in whose shadow bathers spread their towels on a fine-shingle beach; unhappily, much of the apse collapsed during a particularly violent storm in 1996.

Teimiussa

The acropolis and necropolis of ancient **Teimiussa** lie just east of Üçağız; nothing is really known about its history, but inscriptions indicate occupation in the fourth century BC. The site, apparently a settlement without walls and few or no public buildings, consists mainly of scattered rock tombs; some have semicircular benches cut into their bases – convenient for pondering mortality as you stare out to sea, and used by the ancients when visiting their deceased relatives with *nekrodeipna* (food for the dead). On the hill above squats a house-sized fort or tower, while at sea level there's a tiny, rock-cut landing stage.

Kale and Simena

A ruined castle of the Knights of St John, visible on the horizon – and the village of **KALE** below it – are a ten-minute boat ride, or a longer kayak-paddle or walk from Üçağız. The secluded village is the haunt of Rahmi Koç, scion of a wealthy industrialist family, who donated a school while restoring an old house here as a holiday retreat. Even for lesser mortals, Kale makes a lovely place to stay – it's another protected archeological zone, with no new buildings permitted – though some rustic-looking **pansiyons**, overlooking the sea and a marooned sarcophagus, are pricey for what you get. The best three are the *Kale Pansiyon* (℡0242/874 2111, ℻874 2110; ❹), occasionally taken up by British package agencies; *Nesrin's Bademli Ev* (℡0242/874 2170; ❹), a charming, three-unit inn with fireplaces in the wood-and-stone rooms, and, just uphill from this, the *Mehtap Pansiyon* (℡0242/874 2146, ⓦwww.mehtappansiyon.com; all year; ❹), with ten plain but air-conditioned, wood-floored rooms. It also has **camping** space available and good suppers served on the terrace. Most of the half-dozen waterfront **restaurants**, which have had a long and jading acquaintance with the tour-boat trade, offer a set-price, fill-your-plate *meze* buffet.

The climb to ancient **Simena's acropolis** (unenclosed; 8TL when warden present) is steep but brief, worth it both for the views as well as for the medieval **castle** itself, whose ramparts are in good condition, partly resting on ancient foundations. Inside the Knights' castle is a fifteen-metre-wide **theatre** carved into the living rock, large enough for perhaps two hundred people; on the eastern slopes of the hill, off the path, stand some well-preserved **sarcophagi**. Brace yourself for being followed by children peddling printed headscarves, and village women pressing oregano into your hands or offering guiding services.

Cyaneae

East of the Üçağız turning, Highway 400 enters wild, inhospitable countryside, amenable only to the herds of sheep and goats grazing it. In antiquity, however, this region was scattered with small settlements, the most interesting nowadays being **Cyaneae** (Kyaneai in Turkish signage), 23km from Kaş above **Yavu** village. The name Cyaneae/Kyaneai derives from the ancient Greek for "dark blue" – also the origin of the word cyanide – but it's uncertain why the place was so named. The Lycian and Roman sarcophagi here are the most numerous of any local site, and the main reason to visit. Cyaneae was the most important Roman town

West along the Lycian Way: Aperlae & Apollonia

Ancient **Aperlae** lies on the far side of a peninsula southwest of Üçağız, astride the Lycian Way. Access most comfortably involves a forty-minute boat ride to a landing stage (2 restaurants), followed by a half-hour walk. Remote Aperlae is practically deserted, though there's a cluster of modern houses at Sıçak İskelesı, beside the ruins. The **city walls** are fairly well preserved, enclosing a rectangular area with the sea lapping the southern side; the **necropolis**, typically, lies almost entirely outside the walls. As at Kekova, subsidence has submerged the harbour quarter, but swimming and snorkelling here are unrestricted. If you follow the line of the old **quay**, now in 1–2m of water and indented at 15-metre intervals for the mooring of ships, you'll see heaps of pottery shards, amphora necks, terracotta tiles and shell-middens from the ancient murex-dye industry, all encrusted together. There are also building foundations divided by narrow **streets**, with some intact pavement near the shore.

If Aperlae is neglected, unexcavated **Apollonia** is even more so. It can be reached on foot, either from Boğazcık, by a spur from the Lycian Way, or from Aperlae (2hr 15min), or partway by a two-kilometre track from the modern village of **Kılınçlı** (alias Sıçak) on the Üçağız-bound road. You may share the path from Aperlae with a camel or two – road construction in this archeologically rich area has been forbidden, and working (as opposed to tourist-attraction) camels are the most efficient transport for shepherds on the Sıçak peninsula.

Apollonia is remarkable for its superb **necropolis**, which spikes the lower northeast slope of the hill on which the city is found, facing Kılınçlı. There is one conventional sarcophagus with extravagant Gothic-type details, but most distinctive are a half-dozen or so **pillar tombs**, considered the ur-burial method of the ancient Lycians, and proving Apollonia's antiquity. Isolated from the other tombs, at the west end of the hill facing Boğazcık, stands an unusual **carved tomb** on two levels. But there is more to see in the acropolis, at its east end effectively double: a much older stockade inside a Byzantine citadel. Particularly on the southwest flank, the **city walls** – made of unusually large quadrangular and pentagonal blocks – are pierced by windows and a gate. From atop the inner fort, you look west over a well-preserved **Byzantine church**, possibly of the sixth or seventh century; just west of this, overgrown but in a fair state of preservation, is a lovely little **theatre**. The views from the hill, whether inland to the Lycian mountains or out to sea, are the icing on the experience.

between Myra and Antiphellos (modern Kaş), and linked by a direct road to Teimiussa port, 12km away.

From Yavu village centre there's a signposted, two-kilometre **path to the site** – 45 minutes' extremely steep hiking. Rather easier is an unmarked four-kilometre **dirt road** that takes off from the north side of Highway 400, precisely 1km west of the side road to Yavu; the last stretch is rough, but negotiable with care in an ordinary car. It's possible to take a **local guide** along (from the so-called "tourist office" in the village, maximum €15 per party), but not strictly necessary; it is they who've had a hand in misleadingly signposting the slip road to Yavu as "Kyaneai 4". The only other facility, on Highway 400 about 500m in the direction of Demre, is the *Çeşme* **restaurant** (open in season only).

The site

Along the path up from Yavu are some of the oldest, most interesting **tombs**, flanking what may have been part of the ancient road. The most impressive – a sarcophagus carved completely from the rock on which it stands – lies south of the road. The Gothic-arch "lid", cut from the same piece of rock, has two lions' heads projecting each side. Near the top of the path, there's a subterranean shrine or tomb with six columns.

Below the city, fairly inaccessible on the south face of the hill, stands an impressive **temple-tomb** whose porch has a single freestanding column and, unusually, a recess above the pediment with a sarcophagus. An inscription states this was reserved for the heads of the household, while the rest of the family were buried in the tomb.

The **acropolis** is surrounded on three sides by a wall, the south side too precipitous to need protection. The buildings inside are ruined and vegetation-cloaked, but a library, baths and two Byzantine churches (one with a lengthy inscription) have been identified. Near the summit is a tomb with a relief of a charioteer driving a team of four horses. The city had no natural spring nearby, so vaulted cisterns and reservoirs square-cut into the rock are ubiquitous.

West of the summit beyond the parking area, a **theatre** retains 23 rows of seats. Those above the diazoma make ideal vantage points over the acropolis walls, Kekova inlet, and sarcophagi flanking an ancient path linking the theatre and the acropolis. Mainly Roman, these are mostly simple, with rounded lids and crests, but some have lion-head bosses.

Demre and around

East of Yavu, Highway 400 swoops down in a well-graded arc towards **DEMRE**, a rather scruffy, river-delta place, too far from the coast to be a beach resort. The main local businesses are citrus fruit and tomatoes, whose greenhouses – spread below as you descend the escarpment to the west – make Demre seem bigger than it really is. Unlike other nondescript towns on the coast nearby who juggle sun-and-wave motifs in their municipal logos, Demre is unequivocal about its priorities and self-image: a giant tomato occupies most of its coat of arms.

Lately, however, a silhouette-bust of Father Christmas has also crept in, and the town centre is absolutely overrun with **Santa kitsch**, as well as considerable midday parties of Russian pilgrims, for whom a huge number of icon stalls cater; Demre, once ancient Myra, was the adult home of **Saint Nicholas**, a major Orthodox saint, and the **central church** honours him. Nearby attractions include the site of **Myra** just north, the ancient harbour of **Andriake** and the Apollo oracle at **Sura**, a little way south (you pass close to both approaching from the west), plus beaches at **Çayağzı** and **Sülüklü**.

Some history

Myra was one of the chief members of the Lycian Federation, and retained importance during Byzantine times through association with Bishop, later, Saint **Nicholas** (aka Santa Claus; see box, p.366). Some have derived the city's name from the Greek for myrrh, a plant resin used in the production of incense, though there's no evidence it was made here and Myra is probably a corrupted Lycian place-name. Yet when the bishop's tomb was opened by eleventh-century grave robbers, they were supposedly overwhelmed by the smell of myrrh emanating from it.

Despite its later fame, Myra wasn't heard from before 42 BC, when the city displayed typical Lycian defiance by refusing to pay tribute money to Brutus; Brutus's lieutenant had to break the chain closing off the mouth of Andriake harbour – Myra's port – and force his way in. Subsequently, Myra had an uneventful if prosperous history until abandonment in the fourteenth century, treated well by its imperial overlords and becoming capital of Byzantine Lycia in the fifth century.

The Church of St Nicholas

The **Church of St Nicholas** (daily: May–Oct 9am–7pm; Nov–April 8.30am–5/6pm; 10TL) dominates central Demre, on the right of pedestrianized Müze Caddesi as you head west. Despite the erection of an unsightly synthetic protective canopy to one side, the building remains evocative of its patron saint. Nicholas was beatified after visitors to his purported tomb reported miracles, and Myra soon became a popular focus of pilgrimage; even after the Bari raiders stole his bones, the pilgrimages continued. Monks from a nearby monastery simply designated another tomb as the saint's, pouring oil through openings in the top and collecting it at the bottom, to sell to pilgrims as holy secretions.

The contemporary church, basically a three-aisled basilica, with a fourth added later, has little in common with the fourth-century original, having been rebuilt in 1043 after its destruction by occupying Saracens, and again in 1862 by Russian Tsar Nicholas I, who installed a vaulted ceiling instead of a cupola in the central nave, along with a belfry. Turkish archeologists have carried out more recent protective modifications, such as the extra small stone domes in the narthex.

The most typically Byzantine feature is the **synthronon** (bishop's throne) in the apse, rarely found *in situ* since most were removed when Anatolian churches were converted into mosques. Among various patchy interior **frescoes**, the best and clearest – in the dome of the north transept – is a *Communion of the Apostles*. **Mosaic floor**-panels, mainly comprising geometric designs, adorn the nave and south aisle, while masonry fragments near the entrance include one carved with an anchor – either symbolic of Christian faith, or Nicholas as protector of sailors. His purported **sarcophagus**, in the southernmost aisle as you face the synthronon, is not considered genuine. The saint's bones were reputedly stolen from a tomb under a pavement – and, more significantly, on this one there's a relief representation of a married couple on the lid.

Practicalities

All buses and dolmuşes drop you at the fairly central **otogar**. There's a single surviving **pansiyon** 2km out of town on the way to ancient Myra – the *Kent* (☎0242/871 2042; ❷) – though this is more of use to trekkers on the Lycian Way; central hotels are not recommendable. Among a half-dozen **restaurants** downtown clustered on Müze Caddesi, the unlicensed *İpek*, on the same side as the church, is popular with locals for its good, inexpensive *pide*, grills and *hazır yemek*.

St Nicholas

Myra's prestige was greatly enhanced by the reputation of one of its citizens, namely St Nicholas, born in Patara in 270 AD and later appointed local bishop. The Orthodox **patron saint** of sailors, merchants, students, prisoners, virgins and children, his Western identity as a genial old present-giver is perhaps more familiar, based on the story of the three daughters of a poor man who were left without dowries. Nicholas is credited with throwing three purses of gold coins into the house by night, enabling them to find husbands instead of prostituting themselves. Many posthumous miracles were attributed to the saint, but little is actually known about the man. However, after his death he was probably buried in the **church** in Demre now dedicated to him, and it is also widely believed that in 1087 his bones were carried off to Italy by a group of devout raiders from Bari. Demre still banks heavily on its connection with St Nicholas (**Noel Baba** or "Father Christmas" in Turkish); every December 6 (the saint's main feast day) a special mass is held here, attracting Orthodox and Catholic pilgrims, though these also take place on random Sundays throughout the year.

Myra

Ancient **Myra** (daily: April–Oct 8.30am–7.30pm; Nov–March 8.30am–5pm; 10TL) lies 2km north of Demre's town centre, one of the most easily visited Lycian sites. Accordingly it's packed with tours even in off season, let alone summer, when it's best visited early or late in the day. You will still run a gauntlet of overwhelming tourist tat lining the approaches, plus kids selling oregano and unneeded guide services.

Apart from a large theatre and some of the best house-style rock tombs to be seen in Lycia, most of the city is still buried. The **theatre** was destroyed by a 141 AD earthquake but rebuilt shortly afterwards; two concentric galleries cover the stairs (still intact) by which spectators entered the auditorium. Lying around the orchestra and just outside are substantial chunks of carving that once decorated the stage building, including several theatrical masks, a bust of a woman and a Medusa head.

The main concentration of **tombs** (currently off-limits) stands west of the theatre. Most are of the house type, in imitation of Lycian dwelling-places, even down to the wooden roof-beams. Some are decorated with reliefs, including warriors at the climax of a battle, a naked page handing a helmet to a warrior and a funerary scene. The second group of tombs, called the **river necropolis**, is around the side of the second long ridge on the right as you stand with your back to the theatre stage. To get there, leave the main site, turn left off the final access drive onto the main approach road, and continue inland for 1.5km. Here the **"painted" tomb** (though it is no longer pigmented) features the reclining figure of a bearded man and his family in the porch, and outside on the rock face what's presumed to be the same family, in outdoor apparel.

Andriake

Ancient Myra's port, **Andriake**, lies 2.5 km southwest of Demre, and nearly 5km from Myra itself. To get there (no public transport), head west out of Demre towards Kaş, and then bear left, following black-on-yellow signs, when the main highway begins tackling the grade on the right bank of the stream leading down to the sea.

Ancient **Andriake**, built astride the Androkos River, was the site of **Hadrian's granary**, vital to the whole Roman world, since its contents were sent to Rome to be distributed around the empire. The substantial remains of this building can still be seen south of today's river, which runs parallel to the road between Demre and the beach. The granary – built at Hadrian's behest in 119–139 AD, and very similar to Patara's – consists of eight rooms constructed of well-fitting square blocks, the outer walls still standing to their original height. Above the main central gate are busts of Hadrian and possibly his wife, the empress Sabina. Another decorative relief on the front wall, near the second door from the west, depicts two deities of disputed identity, one flanked by a snake and a griffin, the other reclining on a couch.

Çayağzı and Sülüklü

Another kilometre past Andriake lies modern **Çayağzı** ("Rivermouth") anchorage, a possible start-point for boat trips to the Kekova region. **Çayağzı** comprises perhaps a half-dozen snack-shacks opposite the main quay, though the shacks operate fitfully, as does the lone full-service restaurant on the far side of the pedestrian bridge. This is still a working fishing-port, with an active boatyard, and it's possible to get a **boat** from here to the Kekova area, a 45-minute journey, followed by the standard tour of the underwater ruins at Kekova island. You'll need a boatload (10–15 people) – although some owners (who tout aggressively on your arrival) will take individuals or couples for around 25TL.

The only other reason to come here is for a swim. The adjacent beach is fairly short, if broad and duney – though also trash-strewn and prone to algae slicks, which, together with the Kaş–Demre highway passing just overhead and the area's status as an archeological zone, accounts for the minimal development here. However, the beauty of the skyline to the west cannot be underestimated, where parallel ridges – as in a Japanese print – march down to Kekova. There's a far better beach at **Sülüklü**, however, 3km east of Andriake, reached via the narrow, initially uphill road beginning near Hadrian's granary. Although it's a more exposed bay than Çayağzı, the water and 700m of sand are cleaner, with a few simple restaurants just behind.

Sura

The little-visited Apollo oracle at **Sura** (unrestricted access) is accessible either from the direct Üçağız–Kapaklı–Andriake road, just before it joins the new Yuva–Demre highway, or via the Lycian Way. Don't try reaching it from Çayağzı; you will founder in the local marsh, and there is no usable trail along the rocky hillsides bracketing it either side.

Sura was never a city, just a sacred precinct with only priests resident. The modestly elevated **acropolis** had a square outer perimeter wall, and on the west side a peculiar twelve-chambered keep, possibly a pilgrims' hostel. Just southeast was a **priestly residence**, today only discernible as a large rock-cut terrace; a few paces west of this, a **stairway** (partly preserved) descended the sheer cliff to the vicinity of a still-flowing **sacred spring**. Close to this, across the mud flats, is the well-preserved **Temple of Apollo Surios**, focus of the peculiar oracle. Suppliants arrived bearing roasted meat, which they presented to the shrine's priests; though the temple is now 1.5km inland, back then the sea came almost up to its door. The priests would toss the meat into a sandy spot where freshwater springs welled up in the stream mouth; every surge of the sea would bring numerous fish, attracted by the meat. The pilgrims' fortunes were pronounced upon according to whether or not the fish accepted the meal, or by the fish species. The springs still ripple the surface of the stream in front of the temple. After the suppression of pagan oracles in 393 AD, two **Byzantine churches** appeared behind the temple and up in the acropolis.

Finike

A twisty half-hour drive beyond Demre, the harbour town of **FINIKE**, formerly Phoinike, preserves little of its past. Highway 400 has proven a double-edged sword: opening up the port, but also cutting off Finike's centre from the coast and precluding major touristic development.

The town used to empty out in summer when residents headed up to Elmalı's *ova*, but now concrete high-rises – vastly outnumbering the few remaining Ottoman houses – obscure the view of the bay. Finike's busy **marina** attracts *gulet*s and private yachts put off by Antalya's high docking fees and distance from the best cruising coasts. But otherwise the only reason to stay is for easy access to ancient Arykanda or Elmalı.

Finike's main **beach**, extending 4km east of town, has little to recommend it other than sandiness and length: not terribly scenic, clean or protected, and backed by **Sahilkent suburb** with its apartment blocks and lodging pitched at weekending Turks. Two prettier pebble coves are **Gökliman** (4km west) and **Çağıllı** (8km west).

Finike's central **otogar** is 300m along the road to Arykanda and Elmalı; the adjacent **hamam** is modern and well maintained. As at Demre, there's little central **accommodation**. Best budget option, up a long flight of steps 150m south of the *otogar*, is the hillside *Paris Hotel-Pansiyon* (℗0242/855 1488; ➋), with some plumbed rooms and a view terrace. The friendly managing family speaks French and English, and operates a rooftop restaurant in summer. For slightly more comfort, the *Bahar Otel* (℗0242/856 2020; ➌) is right in the town centre.

Eating venues in Finike are similarly limited, if mostly licensed. The best central all-rounder is *Birlik* (24hr; near the *Bahar Otel* across from the Ziraat Bankası), with good grilled fish plus a few *mezes* and soups. A more pleasant environment is provided by *Amfora*, 150m up the road from the yacht drydock, with an ample menu and surprisingly ordinary prices considering its likely clientele.

Arykanda

It's well worth breaking the ninety-minute uphill journey **from Finike to Elmalı along** Highway 635 at ancient Arykanda 34km north, not least to have a respite from the numerous trucks hurtling cavalierly along it with timber or loads of local orchard fruit. Coming directly from Kaş or Bezirgan, use the very scenic, short-cutting D751 between Kasaba and Çatallar, 4km below the ruins, entirely paved and fairly broad despite pessimistic depictions on old touring maps. Travelling by minibus, ask to be dropped off at **Arif** village, from whose gushing spring at the top end a signposted motorable side lane leads 1km to the ruins, on the east side of the road; at the site entrance you'll find water taps and parking, but as yet no fencing (though 4TL admission charged when ticket-booth-staffed). Individual monuments are scattered, often part-excavated and often unlabelled, though there are good site plans by the entrance and the acropolis. Finds here date to the fifth century BC, but the typically Lycian "-anda" suffix suggests foundation of the city a millennium earlier. Arykanda was a member of the Lycian Federation from the second century BC, and remained inhabited until the eleventh century, mainly confined to the area just to either side of today's main through-path.

The site

Arykanda's setting – a steep, south-facing hillside overlooking the main valley between the Akdağ and Bey mountain ranges – is breathtaking, comparable to Delphi in Greece. A pronounced ravine and power pylons divide the site roughly in half. Beside the parking area is a complex structure dubbed "**Naltepesi**"; entered by a right-angled stairway, its function is not yet completely understood, but you can make out a small bath-house and presumed shops. North of the parking area sprawls a large **basilica** with extensive mosaic flooring under tin-roof shelters posed over each aisle, and a semicircular row of benches (probably a synthronon) in the outer apse; there's a more colourful mosaic just below featuring two birds. Another, smaller basilica just inside suggests eighth-century destruction and more modest rebuilding. But the most impressive sight, looming on the east, is the ten-metre-high facade of the **main baths**, with numerous windows on two levels, and apsidal halls at each end – the westerly one with a still-intact plunge pool, the easterly one with stacked hypocausts.

Other constructions worth seeking out include a small **temple** or tomb above the baths complex (one of three "monumental tombs" on the site plan), adapted for Christian worship; there are more Roman or Byzantine mosaics in the tombs or temples immediately east of the Christianized one. West of the ravine and power lines, and above the **agora** – whose engaging odeion has been defaced by horrible new marble cladding – an impressive, six-aisled **theatre** retains twenty rows of seats plus a well-preserved stage building. Above this sprawls a short but attractive **stadium**, with several rows of seats exposed.

Elmalı

The 1100-metre-high plain around Elmalı is upland Lycia's biggest stretch of arable land, noted for its apples, potatoes, sugar beets and chickpeas – and, until modern conservation edicts, timber from the Beydağları cedars too. **ELMALİ** (literally, "apple-ish"; population 15,000), dominated by Elmalı Dağı (2296m), is notable for its domestic architecture: some houses in the hillside old quarter are beautiful Ottoman timber-framed *konak*s, though many are in precarious condition, and all are greatly outnumbered by the straggly sprawl of the new town. The air is fresh even in summer, with a faint smell of wood smoke, and Gömbe (see p.359) is even easier to reach from here than from Kaş.

Elmalı's fine Ottoman mosque, the 1610-vintage **Ömerpaşa Camii** (open prayer times), is decorated outside with beautiful faïence panels and inscriptions; the interior is disappointing, while the mosque *medrese* now serves as a library. The town comes alive for its Monday **market**, the best and least touristy in the region, and its **wrestling competition**, held for three days in a purpose-built stadium during early September. You may stay – though there's no need to – at the one central **hotel**, the *Arzu* (T0242/618 6604; ❷) just uphill beyond the mosque. There are no full-service **restaurants** in the centre, only a few *pastane*s.

With transport, head northwest beyond Elmalı to **Güğübeli**, an 1830-metre pass at the north end of the Akdağ massif. The pass allows a worthwhile short cut west to the Fethiye area, with fine views east to the Beydağları and west to the mountains behind Fethiye. It's a forty-minute drive through a river canyon, past tufts of juniper and the odd pastoral pen, while the descent southwest to Highway 350 via Seki passes the turning for Oenoanda (see p.338). Though well paved, this is considered a minor road, and not kept snow-ploughed from late December to mid-April, when chains will usually be needed.

The coast to Olympos

East of Finike, Highway 400 runs dead straight before turning ninety degrees to enter the high-rise market town of Kumluca. Beyond here, it curls up through the **Beydağları National Park**, comprising a spectacular sequence of densely pine-forested ridges and precipitous bare cliffs. Hidden at the mouths of canyons plunging to the sea are two relatively unspoiled beach resorts: **Adrasan** and **Olympos/Çıralı**. If you're heading towards either by your own transport, leave the main highway for the narrow but paved side road that veers off east of Kumluca, signposted "Beykonak, Mavikent". This short cut rollercoasters through forested valleys and along dramatic coastline to **Gelidonya Burnu**, with its lighthouse and scenic sections of the Lycian Way, before emerging at Çavuş, the nearest proper village to Adrasan and Olympos. The only trick en route involves turning left (north) at a signposted junction near the outskirts of Karaöz, the last bay and village before Gelidonya Burnu.

The Lycian Way at Gelidonya Burnu

From Karaöz, an obvious dirt road beginning at the small pebbly beach heads south along the coast towards the cape. About 6.5km from Karaöz, leave the track in favour of the marked **Lycian Way**, now a steadily rising path through oaks and pines; from the trailhead it's just under an hour with a daypack (round-trip) to the picturesque **lighthouse** just above Taşlık Burnu (as **Gelidonya Burnu**, "Swallow Cape", has been officially renamed). The photogenic lighthouse, French-built in 1936, is not currently inhabited, though the keeper bikes out from Karaöz at dusk to light the lamp. Beyond the cape straggle the treacherous **Beş Adalar** (Five Islands), shipping hazards that have caused many a wreck, including an ancient one which yielded a huge amount of treasure to archeological divers during the 1960s.

North of the lighthouse, the Lycian Way threads deserted hillside between the sea and a high ridge on its six-hour course to Adrasan (path or cross-country except for the last hour). This dramatic bit has become a popular organized group target, so you'll probably have company.

Adrasan

About 12km beyond Kumluca on Highway 400, a steep if paved side road descends to Çavuş village and the bay of Adrasan. Whether you arrive from this direction, or from Mavikent, turn east in the village centre (bank **ATM**) onto the seaward road (marked "Sahil"), following hotel placards for 4km to emerge under the shadow of pointy Musa Dağı at **ADRASAN**, an attractive beach resort, more mainstream and less hip than Çıralı (see p.374). Though falling within national park boundaries, development (including second-home building) is proceeding slowly. You can arrive directly by 9am & 3.30pm high-season **buses from Antalya** (returns 7.30am & 5pm).

About two dozen *pansiyons* and hotels are scattered inland from the long beach, or along the stream meeting the sea at its north end. The fancier **hotels** (though the term is only relative) overlook the south end of the bay, near the jetty. The very last one, with a pool and its own phalanx of beach sunbeds, is the *Ford* (☎0242/883 1098, ⓦwww.fordhotel.net; April–Oct; ⑤), with rooms (including three family suites) in two wings, with hillside or sea views. At the far north end of the beach, where the road turns inland to become the northerly access drive following the stream (joining the main road in at the Çakmak Camii), are two other worthwhile choices: *River Hotel* (☎0242/883 1325, ⓦwww.riveradrasan.com; April–Nov; ❹ B&B), with large if basic, air-conditioned white-tiled rooms, and (better) the newer ⌖ *Hotel Aybars* (☎0242/883 1133 or 0532/314 1887, ⓦwww.aybarshotel.com; April–Nov ⑤ half board only), with large, air-conditioned, balconied rooms overlooking lush grounds and an in-river restaurant. Aysın, on the mobile number given, speaks good English.

The *River* and *Aybars* hotels, plus several independent **restaurants** on the east bank of the watercourse, are reached by wobbly suspension bridges; diners are seated on platforms in the stream, where hundreds of ducks come to cadge your spare bread. The eateries are very anglicized in menu, clientele and price and none are really worth singling out. Back on the paved esplanade at the beach's south end, *İrfan Korkmazer'in Yeri* is popular with locals, and open in spring and autumn.

A popular **boat-trip** destination is **Ceneviz Limanı**, a cliff-girt bay beyond Musa Dağı inaccessible on foot. There's also a German/Turkish-run **scuba centre** at mid-beach, Diving Center Adrasan (☎0242/883 1353, ⓦwww.diving-adrasan .com; closed Feb to late March), which arranges local accommodation as part of its dive packages (CMAS/PADI certification from €300; 10 dives €220), though Ceneviz Limanı itself is off-limits to divers for archeological/military reasons.

Olympos and Çıralı

From Highway 400, two marked side roads provide access to the ruins of the ancient Lycian city of **Olympos**. After 8km, the southerly road (marked "Olympos 11, Adrasan (Çavuşköy) 15") ends at a fee car park and inland ticket booth for the ruins (see "The site of Olympos", below). Just upstream from here in the **Olympos valley** are a dozen-plus *pansiyon*s or "treehouse" lodges – a legendarily popular base with Anglophone backpackers. The northerly turning off Highway 400, 800m north of the southerly one and signposted "Çıralı 7, Yanartaş, Chimaera", leads down to coastal **Çıralı** hamlet, which also has food and accommodation, and equally easy access to the ruins. Inland from Çıralı burns a perpetual flame, fed by natural gases emanating from the ground. Since antiquity this has been called the **Chimaera**, after a mythical fire-breathing monster supposed to have inhabited these mountains.

There's a single daily direct minibus **from Antalya** to Çıralı, running Monday to Saturday in the late afternoon, returning the next day at 6.30am. Otherwise, between May and October, a **connecting minibus** runs from the respective main-road turn-offs to Çıralı (6 daily) and the Olympos site entrance (almost hourly), from 8am–7pm. At other times of the year the minibus only departs from either end of its run when full. Alternatively, most Olympos-valley lodges (and quite a few of the Çıralı *pansiyon*s) lie on a complimentary **shuttle-bus service** two or three times daily.

Some history

Nothing is known about the origins of Olympos, but the city presumably took its name from Mount Olympos, present-day Tahtalı Dağ, 16km north – one of over twenty mountains with the name Olympos in the ancient world. The city made its historical debut during the second century BC, minting its own coins; within a few decades Olympos was one of six cities in the Lycian Federation having three votes, confirming its importance.

The principal deity of Olympos was Hephaestos (the Roman Vulcan), god of fire and of blacksmiths. He was considered native to this region, and traces of a temple dedicated to him exist near the Chimaera. During the first century BC, the importance of his cult diminished when pirates led by Zeniketes overran both Olympos and nearby Phaselis, introducing the worship of the Indo-European god Mithras. Zeniketes made Olympos his headquarters, but in 78 BC he was defeated by the local Roman governor, and again in 67 BC by Pompey, after which Olympos became public property. The city's fortunes revived after absorption into the Roman Empire in 43 AD, and Christianity became prominent. Olympos was later used as a trading base by the Venetians and Genoese – thus Ceneviz Limanı (Genoese Harbour) just south – but was abandoned after the Ottomans dominated the Mediterranean.

The site of Olympos

Olympos (daily: April–Oct 8am–7pm; Nov–March 9am–5.30pm; 3TL 1-day ticket, 5TL for a week – must register and be date-stamped) has two entrances: one inland, at the end of the southerly approach road, and another (where the guards are reportedly not so vigilant) about fifteen minutes' walk south along the beach from Çıralı's river mouth. As at Patara, nocturnal "raids" of the ruins are expressly forbidden. It's potentially an idyllic site on the banks of an oleander- and fig-shaded stream running between high cliffs. Alas, years of littering or sleeping rough in the site (despite notices forbidding both) has seen the water muddied or

Bellerophon and Pegasus

In legend, Bellerophon was ordered by Iobates, king of Xanthos, to kill the Chimaera in atonement for the supposed rape of his daughter Stheneboea. Astride the winged horse Pegasus, Bellerophon succeeded, dispatching the beast from the air by dropping lead into its mouth. Later, Bellerophon was found to have been falsely accused, and avenged himself on Stheneboea by persuading her to fly away with him on Pegasus and flinging her into the sea. Retribution came when he attempted to ascend to heaven on Pegasus, was flung from the magical horse's back and, lamed and blinded, wandered the earth as a beggar until his death.

worse, and the turtles, ducks and frogs that may still live here now make themselves scarce. The scanty ruins line the banks of the stream, which rarely dries up completely in summer, owing to three freshwater springs welling up on the north bank, close to the ocean.

Extensive **Byzantine-Genoese fortifications** overlook the beach from each creek bank, just 25 metres up the crags. At the base of the north-bank fort are two **"harbour tombs"**, with a touching epigraph on a ship captain translated for viewers. Further along the south bank stands part of a quay and an arcaded **warehouse**; to the east on the same side lies a Byzantine **church**; while in the river itself is a pillar from a vanished **bridge**. In the undergrowth there's a **theatre**, its seats mostly gone.

The stream's north bank has the most striking ruins. East of the path to the beach looms a well-preserved marble **doorframe** built into a wall of ashlar masonry. At the foot of the carved doorway is an inscribed statue base dedicated to Marcus Aurelius, dated 172–175 AD. East of the portal hide a Byzantine **villa** with mosaic floors, a mausoleum-style **tomb** and a Byzantine **aqueduct** that carried water to the heart of the city. The aqueduct overlaps the outflow of one of the aforementioned springs; follow it upstream, past the mausoleum-tomb, to the villa.

The Chimaera

North of Olympos, the eternal flames of the **Chimaera** (alias Yanartaş; 3TL admission) are about an hour's stroll from Çıralı village; it's also possible to drive to the bottom of the ascent and walk from the car park (about 20min). The trailhead is well signposted, though the path up (part of the inland alternate Lycian Way) consists of garishly field-stoned steps with odd heights, on its way to a Byzantine chapel and tholos of Hephaestos as well as the flame. The climb is most rewarding (and coolest) at dusk, since the fire is best seen after dark; most Olympos-valley treehouse-lodges organize nocturnal visits for a nominal fee.

It's not certain what causes the phenomenon of clustered flames sprouting from cracks on the bare hillside; analysis reveals traces of methane in the gas but otherwise its make-up is unique. The flames can be extinguished temporarily if covered, when a gaseous smell is noticeable, but will spontaneously re-ignite. They have been burning since antiquity, and inspired local worship of Hephaestos (Vulcan), generally revered wherever fire or lava issued forth. The region was also home to a fire-breathing monster with a lion's head and forelegs, a goat's rear end, and a snake tail: the Chimaera. Its silhouette, incidentally, has long been the logo of the Petrol Ofisi chain of Turkish filling stations.

Olympos valley

The main drawback to basing yourself at the various *pansiyons* in the **Olympos valley** (plus more near the crossroads for Adrasan) is that you're quite some way from the beach. What's more, the valley is effectively a monochrome backpackers' ghetto, despite any pretensions to superiority over conventional package tourists. As a sign of the times, young patrons no longer amble about with beer in hand to reverberating soundtracks, but stroll around searching out a wi-fi signal (universally present) for their MacBook. During the week before or after Anzac Day, when any self-respecting Aussie or Kiwi will be paying homage at Gallipoli, don't expect many vacancies. The biggest, popular establishments listed below offer a full spectrum of adventure activities, the most worthwhile being sea-kayaking around the local coast (€20 for the day). Per-person prices at all listed establishments are 25–30TL for a shared-bath treehouse, 40–45 TL for en-suite bungalows (on a half-board basis); dorms (where available) usually cost 20–25TL.

Treehouse lodges

Bayram's In an orange grove, closest to the ruins ☎0242/892 1243, ⓦwww.bayrams.com. Somewhat stuffy, close-packed, all-wood treehouse-bungalows, with a youthful clientele lolling about the cushioned outdoor lounge.
Kadir's Top Tree Houses Furthest from the ruins ☎0242/892 1250, ⓦwww.kadir streehouses.com. The original backpacker's lodge here, its stilt-bungalows *objets trouvés* works of art in themselves, with the liveliest bar hereabouts.
Türkmen Between *Kadir's* and *Bayram's*, near the stream ford ☎0242/892 1249,

ⓦwww.olymposturkmentreehouses.com. The largest and most overtly commercial outfit, with "bloks" (sic) of standard, 2006-built hotel rooms at ❹ (HB) as well as densely sown cabins. It attracts a substantial Turkish clientele and serves some of the best food in the valley.
Şaban Opposite the *Türkmen* ☎0242/892 1265, ⓦwww.sabanpension.com. One of the more upmarket and (relatively) quiet establishments, this doesn't play constant music, but does have better-than-average food, more low-density treehouses (en suite and not), and more personable manage-ment in Ali and Meral.

Çıralı

In recent decades tourist development, albeit of a vaguely alternative sort, has taken off at **ÇIRALI**. Six hotels and about sixty *pansiyon*s have sprung up along the approach road and on two parallel lanes behind the superb three-kilometre **beach**, between the Ulupınar stream which meets the sea here, and the low hills to the north. Loggerhead and green sea **turtles** still lay their eggs here, so you shouldn't dig up, litter or nocturnally illuminate the beach during the summer nesting season. Çıralı barely counts as a hamlet, but just over the river-bridge, on the inland lane, is a short parade of basic shops and even scooter/bicycle/car rental (the latter pricey); many *pansiyon*s loan bikes for free.

The best **accommodation** is listed below; there's no formal **campsite**, and as rough camping is actively discouraged (because of the turtles), some *pansiyon*s offer space for tents. After ongoing disputes between the forestry and archeological services on the one hand, and local proprietors on the other, beachfront **restau-rants** have been moved back a token few metres from the sand, and seven survivors – in a line north of the river mouth – seem here to stay. Of these, *Oleander* is the most polished, though menu selection and prices (high) are much the same at equally popular *Orange Home* and *Azur*. You'll often get better value inland at *pansiyon* diners; the *Jasmin* (see below) and *Cemil* near the shopping parade can be recommended for normally priced Turkish grub.

Accommodation

Arcadia ☎0242/825 7340, ⓦwww.arcadia holiday.com. Towards the north end of the beach, and one of the few establishments actually abutting it, this Canadian-Turkish-managed

establishment consists of two clusters of all-wood chalet-suites well spaced on its lawn, with recessed lighting and modern baths. Good breakfast served any reasonable hour. Cash discounts available. ❻

▲ Çıralı beach

Barış Pansiyon ☎0242/825 7080. Just behind the beach near the restaurants, this has ample parking and a choice of spartan, older en-suite rooms, a new wing of part-balconied upper-floor units and 3 wooden chalets. ❸

Emin Pansiyon ☎0242/825 7320, ⓦwww .eminpansiyon.com. On the beach road, 80m past *Odile Hotel*. A mix of stone-and wood-built chalets, with plenty of orchard and/or lawn between the rows. Superior breakfasts include omelettes, quince jam and *pekmez* made from *tahin* or *harubu* (carob syrup). Friendly family management, ample parking. ❹ B&B

Güneş Pansiyon ☎0242/825 7161, ⓦwww .gunespansiyon.com. Start of beach road, inland from restaurants. Well-decorated, solid-build units with good bathrooms, fridges and (shock horror) TVs, reflecting part-Turkish clientele, set in lush premises edging onto the river. On-site restaurant, ample parking. All year. ❹ B&B

Jasmin Pansiyon ☎0242/825 7247, ⓦwww .cirali.de. Opposite Güneş, a bit further along. Characterful rooms with en-suite bathrooms in the main building, plus two more rooms in a modern annexe. There's a pleasant, wood-floor and dirt-terrace bar/restaurant/lounge area offering *mantı* and *pide* plus grills; flat bread and home-made apricot jam at breakfast. ❸

🏃 **Myland Nature Pansiyon** ☎0242/825 7044, ⓦwww.mylandnature.com. North

end of beach strip, between *Odile* and *Arcadia*. Better-than-average wooden chalets set in six hectares of orchard. Pınar and Engin, refugees from the urban rat-race, are your fluent English-speaking hosts. The upscale restaurant, open to all, features organic food, evening slide shows (photo courses on demand) and good breakfasts (even more satisfying after one of Pınar's free 8am yoga sessions). Open late March to early Nov. Credit cards accepted; cash and long-stay discounts from ❻

🏃 **Odile Hotel** Just past mid-beach. ☎0242/825 7163, ⓦwww.hotelodile.com. Set in lush gardens around a large pool, this 2008-rebuilt hotel has 36 large, decently equipped (fridges, top-drawer baths) rooms and suites. Keen management, a mixed clientele and yoga/massage teaching area complete the picture. Credit cards accepted; closed Nov–Feb. ❺ B&B

Olympia Tree House ☎0242/825 7351, ⓦhttp://olympiatreehouse.freeservers.com. If you want the treehouse experience without the juvenalia prevalent in the Olympos canyon, come instead to this friendly spot just north of the Ulupınar stream-mouth. Of the twelve units-on-stilts, three (all year, 25TL per person) are relatively luxurious, with sea-view balconies, the others (April–Nov) basic; all are plumbing-less. Tent space in summer only.

Beycik and Ulupınar

The village of **BEYCİK**, about 17km inland, up a side road from Highway 400 just past the Ulupınar turning, has been transformed by wealthy Turks and Russians buying property here to enjoy superb views over forest and mountain. Best of three **accommodation** options is the comfortable 𝒜 *Villa il Castello* (☎0242/816 1013, ⓦwww.villa-castello.com; ❹), uphill from the mosque, with a pool, fitness centre and stylish bar-restaurant, where you can get a decent cappuccino among other things. The nine large, well-appointed suites fit two kids and two adults and, at 1000m elevation, are heated but not air-conditioned.

Elsewhere, meals can be had in Beycik at more restaurants than are strictly necessary, or close to the northerly turning for Çıralı from Highway 400, at six trout farms in the tiny, wooded hill-hamlet of **ULUPINAR**. Many are outrageously priced; the least rapacious, downhill by the gushing spring, is *Botanik* – no stranger to coach tours, but acceptable value, with decent *mezes* and meat dishes besides trout.

The inland variant of the Lycian Way links Çıralı with Beycik, making the village a logical staging point on the traverse to Yayla Kuzdere and Gedelme along the Lycian Way, via the saddle just west of 2366-metre **Tahtalı Dağ**. There are good campsites just over the pass, at **Çukur Yayla**. Sadly, the peak itself is no longer worth a detour: a bunker-like restaurant adorns the flattened-down summit, and a cable car with unsightly pylons ascends from Tekirova for the convenience of Turkish and Russian mafiosi.

Phaselis

Heading north from Olympos, there's scant pretext to stop before Antalya. The overdeveloped, overpriced package resorts along this coast – Tekirova, Kemer, Göynük and Beldibi – leave much to be desired, and only ancient **Phaselis** will tempt you off the main road. With regular buses out of Antalya, the only reason to **stay** locally is the *Sundance Nature Village*, behind Phaselis's southwest beach, on the coastal variant of the Lycian Way (☎0242/821 4165, ⓦwww.sundancecamp .com; ❸). This complex of bungalows and treehouses, set amid 120 partly forested acres, also offers a respected restaurant using own-grown produce, horseback riding and tent space.

Some history

Founded in 690 BC by Rhodian colonists, Phaselis, almost in Pamphylia, was not always Lycian. The Phaselitans were great traders, sailing as far as Egypt, and their coins were decorated with ships. Along with most of Asia Minor, Phaselis was overrun by the Persians in the sixth century, and not freed until 469 BC, when Athenian general Kimon "liberated" them with some difficulty, enrolling the reluctant city in the Athenian maritime confederacy along with Olympos. A century later, Phaselis helped Mausolus, satrap of Caria, attempt to subdue Lycia, while in 333 BC Phaselitan sycophancy continued: not content with just surrendering to Alexander the Great, the city also proffered a golden crown.

Phaselis finally became part of the Lycian Federation during the second century BC, but was soon, like Olympos, occupied by Zeniketes' pirates. Although it rejoined the federation afterwards, the pirates had devastated the city. Under imperial Rome, Phaselis distinguished itself with yet more obsequiousness: when touring Emperor Hadrian visited in 129 AD, statues were erected, and a gateway dedicated to him.

The site

The **ruins** (daily: summer 8.30am–7pm; winter 9am–5.30pm; 8TL, plus parking fee), 1km off Highway 400, 3km north of Tekirova, flank three small bays, providing ample opportunity to contemplate antique monuments while lying on the beach. While it can't compare to some sites east of Antalya, or to nearby Arykanda, there's certainly enough to see at Phaselis, where *Jason and the Argonauts* was filmed in 1999. The natural beauty and clear sea make for a rewarding half-day outing – though bring a picnic if you don't fancy the car-park snack-caravans.

The access road passes under a bluff with a **fortified settlement** enclosed by a Hellenistic wall, including a tower and three archery slits. The most obvious landmark, behind a helpful map placard and the first car park, is the substantial, elegant Roman **aqueduct**. Supposed to have been one of the longest in the ancient world, it carried water from a spring inside the northern fortifications almost as far as the south harbour.

Arrayed around a promontory behind which most of the fan-shaped city is located, Phaselis's three **harbours** are obvious, and ideal for orientation. The **north harbour** was too exposed to be used except in very favourable conditions, but traces of the ancient south quay remain. It made an easy landing-point for aggressors, however, so was fortified with a three-metre-wide wall – now submerged, but still intact. The middle **harbour** also had a strong sea wall, and the eighteen-metre-wide entrance could be closed off; today it's a shallow cove with a small beach. The largest, **southwest port** (with its own parking and ticket booth for boat arrivals) was protected by a 180-metre-long breakwater, now mostly submerged. It sheltered the largest trading vessels, and now sees numerous pleasure craft calling for the sake of its fine, large beach.

Between the harbours the promontory **acropolis** is covered in overgrown ruins of dwellings and round cisterns. The city's main axis is the **paved avenue**, which crosses the neck of the promontory, linking the south and middle harbours; partway along a rectangular plaza is thought to be the heart of the **agora**. At the southern-harbour end, only the foundations and tumbled marble masonry survive of the monumental **gateway** constructed to honour Hadrian's visit.

The well-preserved, second-century AD **theatre**, looking towards Tahtalı Dağ from between the acropolis and the main street, held around 1500 people. Three large doors above present ground level probably led to the stage; below these five smaller doors would have opened into the orchestra, and were possibly used to admit wild animals.

Travel details

Buses and minibuses

The schedules below are greatly enhanced in season by the 24-seat minibus service of the Patara Ko-op, which plies the coast between Fethiye and Finike, and of the Batı Antalya Ko-op, which shuttles almost constantly between Kaş and Antalya.

Dalaman to: Antalya (2 daily in summer; 6hr inland route); Bodrum (5 daily; 3hr 30min); Denizli (2 daily; 4hr 30min); Fethiye (twice hourly; 1hr); İstanbul (2 daily; 14hr); İzmir (14 daily; 5hr); Kaş (4 daily; 3hr); Marmaris (12 daily; 2hr); Muğla (18 daily; 2hr); Ortaca (twice hourly; 20min).

Dalyan to: Fethiye (2 daily; 1hr); Göcek (2 daily; 30min); Marmaris (2 daily; 2hr). NB: All these services depart before noon – for more choice take a local minibus to Ortaca.

Demre to: Elmalı (5 daily; 2hr); Fethiye (6 daily; 4hr); Finike (hourly; 30min); Kaş (hourly; 1hr); Üçağız (1 daily; 45min).

Elmalı to: Antalya (9 daily; 2hr); Demre (6 daily; 1hr 30min); Kaş (3 daily; 2hr 30min).

Fethiye to: Antalya (8 daily; 4hr by inland route, 7hr by coast); Bodrum (6 daily; 4hr 30min); Denizli (5 daily; 4hr "express", 6hr normal); İstanbul (3 daily; 14hr); İzmir (twice hourly; 7hr); Kaş (15 daily; 1hr 45min); Marmaris (hourly; 3hr); Pamukkale (several daily; 5hr); Patara (15 daily; 1hr).

Finike to: Antalya (twice hourly; 2hr 15min); Demre (hourly; 30min); Elmalı (twice hourly; 1hr 30min); Fethiye (13 daily; 4hr); Kalkan (2 daily; 2hr); Kaş (7 daily; 1hr 15min).

Kalkan to: Antalya (7 daily; 4hr 30min); Bodrum (1 daily; 6hr); Fethiye (every 30min; 1hr 20min); İstanbul (1 daily; 15hr); İzmir (2 daily; 8hr); Kaş (every 30min; 30min); Marmaris (2 daily; 4hr 30min).

Kaş to: Antalya (6 daily; 3hr 30min); Bodrum (3 daily; 6hr); Fethiye (15 daily; 2hr); Gömbe (3 daily; 1hr 30min); İstanbul (2 daily; 14hr); Marmaris (4 daily; 5hr).

Ortaca to: Antalya (2 daily; 7hr coastal route); Bodrum (5 daily; 4hr); Dalaman (twice hourly; 20min); Dalyan (25 daily; 20min); İzmir (10 daily; 5hr 30min); Kaş (5 daily; 3hr 30min).

Patara to: Antalya (8 daily; 5hr); Fethiye (8 daily; 1hr 15min); Kalkan (10 daily; 30min); Kaş (10 daily; 1hr). NB: Most services depart from the main road, not the village centre.

International hydrofoils/ferries

Fethiye to: Rhodes (June–Sept, daily except Wed & Sun at 9am; late May & Oct Tues, Thurs, Fri; 1hr 30min). Ticket price approximately €60 one-way taxes inclusive, €90 return.

Kaş to: Kastellórizo (Mon–Fri April–Oct, minimum 10am out 3pm back, extra departures by demand; winter guaranteed Tues & Thurs 10.30am, returning 1.30pm; 20min). Tickets €20 day return, €15 one-way.

Flights

Dalaman to: İstanbul-Atatürk (THY June–Sept 3–5 daily, April, May & Oct 2 daily, Nov–March 1 daily; 1hr 15min); İstanbul-Sahiba Gökçen (Pegasus June–Sept 2 daily; otherwise 3–4 weekly). Other airline routes to points within Turkey, mostly charter, come and go.

The Mediterranean
coast and the Hatay

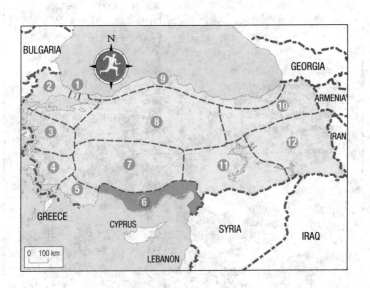

CHAPTER 6   # Highlights

✳ **Kaleiçi** Antalya's old quarter, clustered around a charming harbour, is great for nightlife and shopping. **See p.386**

✳ **Köprülü Kanyon** Spanned by a graceful Roman bridge, the Köprülü river gorge is ideal for novice whitewater-rafters. **See p.392**

✳ **Termessos** Arguably the most dramatically situated of all Turkey's ancient sites, perched on the edge of a precipitous gorge. **See p.393**

✳ **Aspendos** Stunningly preserved Roman theatre, the impressive venue for an annual opera and ballet festival. **See p.396**

✳ **Uzuncaburç** Wander along the streets and through the temples of the ruined city, now a sleepy mountain village. **See p.413**

✳ **Kızkalesi** Recline on the sandy Mediterranean shore and ponder the serenity of the offshore Maiden's Castle. **See p.415**

✳ **Antakya's Archeological Museum** Don't miss the immaculately preserved collection of Roman mosaics. **See p.429**

✳ **Regional cuisine** For a taste of the Hatay try the unique fiery *muhammara*, served with flat bread and a chilled beer. **See p.430**

▲ The theatre at Termessos

6

The Mediterranean coast and the Hatay

The **Mediterranean coast** of Turkey, where the Toros (Taurus) mountain range sweeps down to meet the sea, broadly divides into three parts. The stretch from Antalya to Alanya is the most accessible although intensive agriculture, particularly cotton growing, and package tourism have taken a toll on the environment. East of Alanya, the mountains meet the sea head-on, making for some of Turkey's most rugged stretches of coastline and some of its most hair-raising roads. As a result, this is the least developed and unspoiled section of Mediterranean coastline. Further east the mountains finally recede, giving way to the flat, monotonous landscape of the Ceyhan river delta. South and east of here, turning the corner towards Syria, the landscape becomes more interesting, as the Amanus mountain range dominates the fertile coastal plain, with citrus crops and olives the mainstay of the economy.

The bustling, modern city of **Antalya** is the region's prime arrival and junction point. East of here, in the ancient region of Pamphylia, the ruins of three cities – **Perge**, **Aspendos** and **Side** – testify to the sophisticated civilization that flourished during the Hellenistic period. Perge and Aspendos, in particular, are both well-established day-trip destinations from Antalya, while the modern town of Side has become a package-tour resort. The more isolated **Termessos**, a Pisidian city north of Antalya, is the most spectacularly sited one, and its rugged terrain peppered with stone ruins makes this a more than worthwhile excursion.

Seventy kilometres east along the coast, the former pirate refuge of **Alanya** – now a bustling package-tour destination – is set on and around a spectacular headland topped by a Selçuk citadel. Continuing east, the best places to break your journey are **Anamur**, where a ruined Hellenistic city abuts some of this coast's best beaches, and **Kızkalesi**, whose huge Byzantine castle sits 200m from the shore of a sandy bay. Kızkalesi also makes a good base from which to explore the ancient city of **Uzuncaburç**, a lonely ruin high in the Toros mountains.

Beyond Kızkalesi is the fertile alluvial delta known as the **Çukurova**, where the Ceyhan River spills down from the mountains and meanders sluggishly into the eastern Mediterranean. This end of the coast – characterized by concentrations of industry and low-lying cotton plantations – has very little to recommend it. **Mersin** has regular ferry connections to northern Cyprus; **Tarsus**, the birthplace of St Paul, has a few surviving reminders of its long history; while **Adana**, one of the country's largest urban centres, is a hectic staging-post for journeys further east.

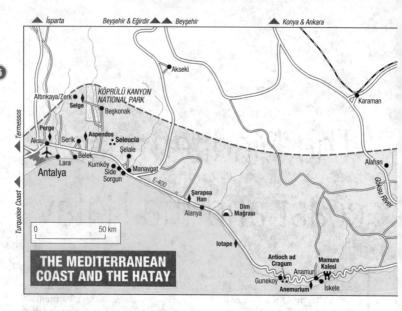

THE MEDITERRANEAN
COAST AND THE HATAY

From Adana, routes head north to the central Anatolian plateau (see Chapter 7) or east to the Euphrates and Tigris basins (Chapter 11), though this chapter turns its attention south, towards the area formed by the curve of the coast down towards Syria. This is the **Hatay**, a fertile, hilly region where different cultures have met – and often clashed – in their efforts to dominate the important Silk Route trade. **Antakya** is the Hatay's main centre and the best starting point for exploring the region, though cosmopolitan **İskenderun** makes for a surprisingly agreeable base. From Antakya there are frequent dolmuş connections to **Harbiye**, site of the Roman resort of Daphne, and to the town of **Samandağ**, from where you can visit Armenian **Vakıflı** and what's left of the ancient Roman port of **Seleucia ad Piera**.

Antalya to Alanya

The stretch of coast between **Antalya and Alanya** is one of the most developed in Turkey. With a four-lane highway running right behind many beaches, all-inclusive hotels and holiday-village complexes in various stages of completion, it is hard to imagine this was once ancient **Pamphylia**, a loose federation of Hellenistic cities established by incomers from northern Anatolia. With its busy international airport, the booming city of **Antalya** is the gateway to the region. Now a fully fledged resort, it is worth visiting for its restored old town and marvellous archeological museum. The nearest (and most fascinating) ruined city is **Termessos**, perched on the saddle of Mount Solymos overlooking the Antalya gulf. East of Antalya, the surviving ruined cities of Pamphylia also rival the

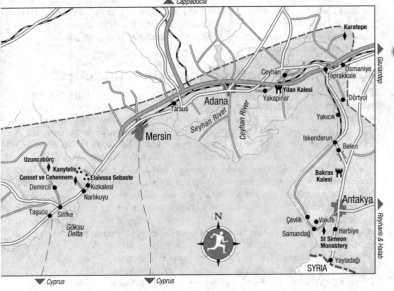

beaches as tourist magnets, with **Perge** and **Aspendos** the best preserved and most evocative sites. Further along the coast, **Side** is one of the region's major resorts, though the striking ruins of its ancient city have been sadly overshadowed by budget package tourist facilities. It warrants a brief stop, however, ideally en route to another destination.

Alanya, the next sizable centre, has also seen an explosion of hotel building and tourism-related commerce over the last few years, but has retained an attractive old quarter. Away from the coast, the **Köprülü Kanyon** national park and the ruins of ancient **Selge**, easily accessible from Antalya, Side and Alanya make a delightful day's excursion.

Antalya

One of Turkey's fastest growing cities, **ANTALYA** is blessed with an ideal climate (except during the searing heat of July and August) and a stunning setting atop a limestone plateau, with the formidable Beydağları looming to the west. In the heart of town, the pretty yacht harbour huddles below the Roman walls, while behind the new buildings the crescent of Konyaaltı bay curves to the industrial harbour 10km west of town. The main area of interest for tourists is confined to the relatively tiny and central old quarter within the Roman walls, known as the Kaleiçi (or "within the castle"). Three or four days in town – including half-day excursions to the nearby ruins of Termessos, Perge and Aspendos – should be sufficient.

Antalya was founded as late as the second century BC by Attalus II of Pergamon, and named **Attaleia** in his honour. The Romans did not consolidate their hold on the city and its hinterland until the imperial period, at the conclusion of successful campaigns against local pirates. Christianity and the Byzantines got a similarly slow start, though because of its strategic location and good anchorage Antalya was an important halt for the Crusaders. The Selçuks supplanted the Byzantines for good early in the thirteenth century, and to them are owed most of the medieval monuments visible today (albeit some built on Byzantine foundations). Ottoman Antalya figured little in world events until 1918, when the Italians made it the focus of their short-lived Turkish colony.

Arrival, information and city transport

Both **buses** and intertown **dolmuşes** use the *otogar*, about 7km north of town on the Ankara road; bus companies have their own *servis* buses, which will deliver you to the town centre, and there is also a blue-and-white municipal bus marked "Terminal Otobusu" linking the *otogar* with the centre. Whichever you use, alight either near the Atatürk statue on Cumhuriyet Caddesi for accommodation on the west of the old city, or at the *Belediye* (Town Hall) corner for the east side.

West of Konyaaltı Beach is the main harbour and dock where **ferries** arrive from Venice – it's 10km from the centre of town and **there is no dolmuş service**, so you'll have to take a taxi to the centre. Antalya's lushly landscaped **airport** stands at the centre of a maze of motorways some 12km east of the city. Taxis into town cost about €20 per car during the day and €30 between midnight and 6am. Be aware that taxi drivers often tell you that the hotel of your choice has closed and offer to take you to another where, predictably, they earn a commission. If this occurs, be insistent. There is a new municipal bus from the airport that goes to the *otogar* (1.5TL; departures every two hours) and the hourly Havaş airport bus (11TL), which drops off next to Yakuz Özcan Parkı on Konyaaltı Caddesi, 500m west of Kaleiçi.

The **tourist office** is located on Güllük Caddesi, 100m north of the PTT (Mon–Fri 8.30am–6.30pm, Sat & Sun 8.30am–5.30pm; ☏0242/247 7660). General information is available on Antalya and southern Turkey and city maps are available, but for in-depth information, enquire at your hotel or pension or a travel agency.

A tramway circles the old quarter and runs along the seafront; **tram services** are every half-hour (1.20TL) and departure times are posted at the tram stops. South from Kalekapısı, the Kaleiçi's labyrinthine alleys lead to the most desirable pensions and downhill to the harbour.

Accommodation

Most travellers stay in the walled quarter of **Kaleiçi**, in old houses restored as *pansiyons* or hotels, often set around attractive courtyard gardens. There is accommodation to suit all budgets, and prices are often heavily discounted out of season. Note that the accommodation here, particularly around the harbour-walls area, can be subject to late-night noise from nearby clubs.

Camping is not an option within the city limits. *Camping Bambus*, 3km along the road to Lara (☏0242/321 5263), is oriented towards caravanners, but does have its own beach and decent facilities.

Inside the walls

Abad Otel Hesapçı Sok 54 ☏0242/247 4466, ⓦwww.abadotelturkey.com. This well-converted old house has a family atmosphere, friendly staff and fish tanks in the breakfast room. Simple rooms have tiled floors, both ceiling fans and a/c, wi-fi and basic en-suite bathrooms. Drinks and dinner are served in the courtyard and half-board is available. ❸

Alp Paşa Hotel Hesapçı Sok 30 ☏0242/247 5676, ⓦwww.alppasa.com. Lush conversion of an Ottoman mansion, set around a cramped garden

with a tiny pool. The cheapest rooms are nicely furnished; pay more and you'll get antique fittings and marble bathrooms. Excellent buffet meals attract nonguests in the evenings. The staff is not exceedingly helpful. ❻

Atelya Pansiyon Civelek Sok 21 ☏0242/241 6416, ⓦwww.atelyahotel.com. Excellent restoration of two connected Ottoman houses set around a delightful courtyard – complete with a stir-crazy tortoise and a bar. The hotel boasts two annexes, the most recently restored of which has individually furnished rooms,

6

RESTAURANTS, CAFÉS & BARS

Akdeniz Çiçek Pasaji	5
Ayyaş	8
Can Can	7
Castle Restaurant	10
Dönerci Çarşısı	2
Gönlübol	4
Güneyliler	1
Hasanağa	6
Salman	11
Son Çare	3
St Paul's Place	9
Villa Perla	D

0 ——— 200 m

Ankara, Termessos & Otogar (7km)

FAHRETTIN ALTAY CAD

MILLI EGEMENLIK CAD

SARAMPOL (KAZIM OZALP CAD)

SUBAŞI CADDESE

ISMET PAŞA CAD

ALI ÇETINKAYA CAD

Friday Market

Murat Paşa Camii

AKM, Aqualand, Cine Bonus &

Airport

HÜKÜMET CAD

TAHIL PAZARI SOK

Iki Kapılar Hanı

BAZAAR

CUMHURIYET–CAD

THY

Atatürk Statue

Main PTT, (i) Güllük Cad, Alanya Museum, Konyaaltı Beach & Atatürk Parkı

Yivli Minare Complex

Saat Kulesi

Mehmet Paşa Camii

ESKI SEBZECILER SOK

Dönerci Çarşısı

Antalya 2000 Shopping Center

Plaza Cinema

UZUN ÇARŞI SOK

PAŞA CAMII SOK

HIDIRLIK SOK

IMRET SOK

Hadrian's Gate

ATATÜRK–CAD

KALEKAPISI

Old Harbour

MERMERLI BANYO SOK

CIVELEK SOK

HESAPÇI SOK

Mermerli Beach

Kesik Minare

YENIKAPI SOK

Medieval Walls

N

Hıdırlık Kulesi

Nexus

Lara & Düden Waterfalls, Aquapark &

Belediye

Mermerli & Karaalioğlu Parks

Adalar Swimming Platform

ISIKLAR CAD

FEVZI ÇAKMAK CAD

Car rental outlets

Antalyaspor stadium

ACCOMMODATION

Abad Otel	G
Alp Paşa Hotel	F
Atelya Pansiyon	B
Dantel Pansiyon	J
Marina Residence	E
Özmen Pansiyon	I
Sabah Pansiyon	H
Safran Sari	L
Senem Family Pansiyon	K
Tütav Türk Evi Otel	C
Tuvana Hotel	A
Villa Perla	D

ANTALYA

MEDITERRANEAN SEA

each named after a sultan – rooms here are a little more expensive. ❷

Dantel Pansiyon Zeytin Geçidi 4 ☎0242/247 3486, ⓦwww.dantelpansiyon.net. Immaculate conversion buried under overgrown bougainvillea. Rooms are simply but tastefully furnished, with nostalgic pictures of old İstanbul on the walls, have TV, wi-fi and a/c, and the bathrooms are spotless. Tasty evening meals (including shrimp casserole) are good value and served on the rooftop terrace. ❷

Marina Residence Mermerli Sok 15 ☎0242/247 5490, ⓦwww.marinaresidence.net. A charming luxury hotel embellished with murals and marble. It's a tasteful place with excellent views over the harbour, a raised glass-walled pool alongside the garden bar and appetizing food. ❹

🏃 Özmen Pansiyon Zeytin Çıkmazı 5 ☎0242/241 6505, ⓦwww.ozmenpension .com. Extremely well run by the energetic Aziz, it boasts airy, spotless, a/c rooms and a lovely breakfast terrace with views over the bay. Aziz will collect you from the airport for €20 (€26 after midnight) or the otogar for €12. All rooms and the terrace are wired with wi-fi. ❶

🏃 Sabah Pansiyon Hesapçı Sok 60 ☎0242/247 5345, ⓦwww.sabah pansiyon.8m.com. Run by three friendly brothers, this backpacker-oriented joint offers an informal information service (in English), good-value car rental, tours, fine food, cheap beer, paid email access, free wi-fi and satellite TV. All rooms now boast a/c, most have TV and a CD player, and the white walls and curtains set off the kilim-strewn tiled floors. Great value. ❶

Safran Sari Yenikapı Sok 10 ☎0242/2474682, ⓦwww.safranantalya.info. An exceedingly friendly family runs this new pansiyon, set in a restored konak. Four of the eight rooms have kitchens and all have parquet, antiques, a/c and wi-fi. ❷

Senem Family Pansiyon Zeytin Geçidi Sok 9, near Hıdırlık Kulesi ☎0242/247 1752, ⓦwww.senem pansiyon.com. Run by a lively and charming Turkish couple, this pension has clean rooms with white-washed walls and flowery curtains, and simple en-suite facilities. The rooftop breakfast bar affords wonderful views of the sea and mountains. ❷

🏃 Tütav Türk Evi Otel Mermerli Sok 2 ☎0242/248 6591, ⓦwww.turkeviotelleri .com. A good-value option, set in the old walls above the harbour, with superb views from the attached restaurant. It's tastefully restored, though some find its mock-Ottoman interior decor a little stuffy. The lovely pool is a real bonus. ❸

Tuvana Hotel Karanlık Sok 18 ☎0242/247 6015, ⓦwww.tuvanahotel.com. Top-notch hotel fashioned from a beautifully restored series of old houses. The characterful rooms, with intricately carved wooden ceilings, marble bathrooms, and parquet floors are individually furnished in a modern style and come with satellite TV, wi-fi, minibar and a/c. ❺

🏃 Villa Perla Hesapçı Sok 26 ☎0242/248 9793, ⓦwww.villaperla.com. Very authentic Ottoman building, with antique furnishings in ten individually styled rooms, plus an atmospheric courtyard garden with small pool. The attached restaurant has a very good reputation. There is free wi-fi in the courtyard and all rooms. ❷

The City

The best place to start exploring the old town, **Kaleiçi**, is from the old harbour, where the once-crumbling quays have been rebuilt, gardens laid out and the harbour walls and a mosque restored. Most attractions are within walking distance of each other, but jump on the tram or a dolmuş to visit the excellent archeological museum.

Kaleiçi

Inevitably, the authentic atmosphere of the **old harbour** has been sacrificed to the redevelopment – the harbour is now mainly home to day-trip boats, some charter *gulets* and a very few fishing boats, but on balance, the venture seems to have been a success, and the area is popular with tourists and locals alike, who frequent the quayside restaurants, cafés and clubs.

From the harbour, head uphill along Uzun Çarşi Sokak, past souvenir and carpet shops and the eighteenth-century **Mehmet Paşa Camii**. Along the way, you might want to stop off at the tiny garden of the local arts society, known as **ANSAN**, for a cool drink or to check notice boards advertising concerts, slide shows and even Sunday treks. At the northern end of Uzun Çarşi Sokak is **Kalekapısı** (Castle Gate), the main entrance to the old town. Nearby the **Saat Kulesi**, a Selçuk tower with inset Roman column drums, is built into a section of

▲ The Yivli Minare (Fluted Minaret)

the old walls. Kalekapısı is overlooked by the **Yivli Minare** or "Fluted Minaret", erected during the thirteenth-century reign of the Selçuk sultan, Alâeddin Keykubad, and today something of a symbol of the city. Facing the Yivli Minare is an early, plain **Selçuk han** whose crumbling walls have been "restored", a rather grand term for encasing the ruins in glass and filling the interior with souvenier shops. Above this area, but accessed from Cumhuriyet Caddesi, is an old baths, and a pyramidal **mausoleum** from 1377.

From Kalekapısı, bear right and right again onto Atatürk Caddesi, and you'll soon draw even with the triple-arched **Hadrian's Gate** (Üç Kapılar), recalling a visit by that emperor in 130 AD. Hesapçı Sokak, the quietest entry to Kaleiçi, also begins at Hadrian's Gate and if you follow it through the old town, you'll pass its restored Ottoman houses, many of which have been turned into pensions, trinket shops or restaurants and bars. Left off Hesapçı Sokak, on Kocatepe Sok 25, is the **Kaleiçi Museum** (Tues–Thurs 9am–noon & 1–6pm; 2TL; ⓦ www.kaleicimuzesi .org), set in two restored Ottoman houses built around courtyard gardens. Behind one house is the restored garden church of St George, which is used for exhibitions often made up of items from the private collection of the Koç family, Turkey's richest, who sponsor the institute. The second house contains a marvellous library (hours as above); treasures include original editions of the engravings made by the archeologist-cum-explorer Texier when he investigated Asia Minor for the French government in the 1840s.

About halfway along Hesapçı Sokak stands a tower and attendant buildings known collectively as the **Kesik Minare** (Broken Minaret), an architectural anomaly that's done successive duty as temple, church and mosque: compare the reused Roman capitals with later Byzantine ones.

Beyond the Kesik Minare, you emerge above the sea and turn left to reach the adjoining **Mermerli** and **Karaalioğlu** parks, which contain a number of pleasant tea gardens as well as the **Hıdırlık Kulesi** in the northwestern corner. This round Roman tower is the best place in town to watch the frequently spectacular sunsets over the snow-capped mountains across the gulf of Antalya. Return to the harbour past the *Mermerli* restaurant, which has a private staircase down to the only city-centre beach, **Mermerli** (8TL buys you a day pass). Alternatively try the **Adalar** swimming area (7.5TL), reached via steep steps from Karaalioğlu park, with decking on the rocks and ladders into the sea. The staff are friendly, drinks and snacks reasonably priced, and the views across the bay magnificent.

Antalya's **Pazar**, at the southeast corner of Şarampol, sells mainly gold, clothes and shoes. There are also daily bazaars throughout the city, the most interesting of which is the **Cuma Pazarı** (Friday Bazaar), with local produce stalls and clothing vendors packed into the streets west of Murat Paşa Camii.

The Archeological Museum

The one thing you shouldn't miss while in Antalya is the city's **Archeological Museum** (Arkeoloji Müzesi; Tues–Sun April–Oct 9am–7.30pm and Nov–March 8.30am–5pm; 15TL), situated on the western edge of town at the far end of Konyaaltı Caddesi. It's one of the top five archeological collections in the country, and it's well worth spending a few hours there. To reach it from the city centre, take any dolmuş labelled "Müze" or "Liman" – departing from one of the "D" signs along Cumhuriyet Caddesi – or take the westbound tramway to its last stop, Müze (1.2 TL).

The galleries are arranged both chronologically and thematically. Standing out among the early items are a cache of **Bronze Age** urn burials from near Elmalı, including several silver and ivory Phrygian figurines sporting droll yet dignified expressions and silver *paterae* (plates for wine libations). All date from the seventh and sixth centuries BC and are among the museum's worthiest treasures.

It's quite a jump in time to the next galleries, which contain many second-century AD **statues from Perge**: a complete pantheon in unusually good condition has been assembled. Best exhibits of the adjoining sarcophagus-wing are two almost undamaged coffers depicting the **labours of Hercules**. The corner hall leads into a gallery dedicated to **friezes** and statues from Perge's theatre. The all-over marble tiling doesn't show them off to their best advantage, but the display, which includes statues of gods and emperors and a frieze showing battles between heroes and giants, is marvellous.

The galleries upstairs are devoted to coinage and **icons** recovered after 1922 from various churches in the Antalya area. At the centre of the collection is a reliquary containing what are purported to be the bones of **St Nicholas of Myra** (see p.366).

Back on the ground floor, the collection is rounded out by an **ethnography** section, a hotchpotch of İznik ceramics, household goods and weapons.

Besides the collections, there's a bookshop, a **café** and a pleasant shady garden scattered with some fine overspill sculptures and tombs. Crossing the road from the museum reveals wide views of Konyaaltı bay and a sloping road that leads downhill to Konyaaltı beach (see below).

Beaches and activities

Antalya's lengthy western beach, **Konyaaltı**, now spruced up, is finally beginning to live up to its dramatic situation between Antalya's cliffs and the Beydağları mountains. It's shingle, rather than sand, but it's clean and well maintained. Entry to the beach is free, though to use the beach clubs' loungers and umbrellas, expect to pay from 5TL. Those with children should be aware that the beach shelves quite steeply and there is a slight tow from west to east. A pleasant **promenade** lined with palm trees and cafés backs the beach. Konyaaltı is easiest reached by the westbound tram – get off at the terminus (just past the archeological museum) and follow the road down the steep hill (five minutes' walk).

Lara beach, 10km southeast of town and reached by buses and dolmuşes running along Atatürk Caddesi, has fine sand. As at Konyaaltı Beach, there is a combination of free and pay beaches. Note that the municipal bus service is air-conditioned and tends to be quicker than taking a dolmuş.

Boats by the harbour in Kaleiçi offer a variety of tours ranging from 45 minutes to full-day local tours, the longer of which take in the best views of the **Düden waterfalls**, cascades that end at Lara Beach, plus a combination of local beaches, swimming, cruising the gulf and a barbecue lunch. Some also offer evening entertainment in the shape of moonlit buffets and belly dancing. Prices vary according to the number of people, season and itinerary, but you can expect a two-hour trip to cost from around €10 per person, from €25 for evening cruises with entertainment. For other tours see "Listings", p.392.

Antalya also has two water-parks with numerous slides, chutes and wave pools. **Aqualand** (May–Oct 10am–6pm; €20, €18 children), on the southwestern edge of the Kültür Parkı, is reached by the same dolmuşes. At the attached **Dolphinland** it's possible to swim with a dolphin for €60. The original **Aqua Park** (daily May–Oct 9am–dusk; 40TL adults, 30TL children), behind the *Dedeman* hotel, east of the centre, is reached by Lara-bound dolmuşes.

Eating

Antalya is full of cafés and **restaurants** and good places can be found all over town, but especially in Kaleiçi, Atatürk Parkı and along Atatürk and Işıklar caddesis. We've picked out some of the best choices, across all budgets, below. For the local speciality – *tandir kebap*, clay-roasted mutton – visit Eski Serbetçiler İçi Sokak, a narrow street running down the west side of the Dönerci Çarşısı (see "Atatürk Bulvarı and İşıklar Caddesi", below), crammed with restaurants, many with pavement tables.

Local street markets are open nearly every day in some part of the city and have a staggering array of fresh local produce at knockdown prices. The biggest is the Cuma Pazarı – **Friday market** off Milli Egemenlik Caddesi, west of Murat Paşa Camii, while on Sundays, head northwest of the main PTT and ask for the Pazar Pazarı – **Sunday market**.

Kaleiçi

Castle Restaurant Beside the Hıdırlık Kulesi, on the cliff top. A café-bar with the best views in Antalya and cooling updraughts for the very popular clutch of tables set right on the cliff edge. It serves *mezes*, kebabs and cold beer and is much favoured by Antalya's young lovers. A meal with beer will set you back around 15TL. Recommended.

Gönlübol İmaret Sok 30. Kaleiçi's best kebabs are grilled over charcoal and served by weight (from 3TL for 100g) at this alcohol-free *ocakbaşı*. The Urfa and Adana kebabs are especially good.

Hasanağa East of Paşa Camii Sok, near Hadrian's Gate. With tables set out under a canopy of citrus trees in a charming courtyard garden, and very popular with the locals, this is a good choice for an intimate evening meal. Black Sea dishes form an excellent addition to the Mediterranean cuisine on offer – try the spicy red-cabbage soup followed by fresh *hamsi* (sardines). A decent meal with a beer or the house wine shouldn't cost more than 20TL. Traditional live music sessions at weekends.

Son Çare Under the Saat Kulesi, at the entrance to Kaleiçi. Once a mobile stall owner, Mustafa has branched out to two proper locations. The specialty is *köfte*; help yourself to the array of tomatoes, onions, parsley, lettuce and rocket. With an *ayran* a full meal for two should set you back 10TL. The other location is on the south side of the Dönerci Çarşısı.

St Paul's Place Yenikapi Sok 24. Attached to the American-run evangelical church, a fine café serving delicious coffees (3TL), breakfasts, light meals, cookies and cakes. You can also check out the extensive library (not all of it religious). Closed Sun.

Villa Perla Hesapçi Sok 26. Kaleçi's best restaurant, serving Ottoman *mezes* and mains in the candlelit garden of the *Villa Perla* hotel. The *dolma* and *güveç* (lamb casserole) are especially good. Mains from around 15TL.

Atatürk Caddesi and İşıklar Caddesi

🏃 **Can Can** Corner of Ali Fuat Cebesoy and Recep Peker cads. Located 50m from the

Antalya 2000 shopping centre, this kebab and *pide* house is a favourite for locals who come for delicious *pide* from 3TL and has an assortment of grills for around 6TL. No alcohol.

Dönerci Çarşısı Corner of Atatürk and Cumhuriyet cads. "*Döner*-sellers' market" – fast-food joints under one roof, devoted to kebabs, *köfte* and *kokoreç*. Some sell *midye* (mussels) in season. A meal here should cost less than 5TL but select carefully; not all places are clean.

Güneyliler West of Şarampol on Elmali Mah 4 Sok 12/A. This bustling, spotlessly clean restaurant serves excellent *lahmacun* and kebabs (preceded by a complimentary helping of flat bread) and is always packed with locals. A substantial meal can be had for around 6TL.

Salman Işıklar Cad. Air-conditioned coffee bar–patisserie at the Atatürk Bul end of the street, with a good range of *poğça* (plain and filled savoury breads), *baklava*, continental-style cakes and tarts – plus a salad bar.

Drinking and nightlife

Much of Antalya's **nightlife** is concentrated around the harbour area, with its myriad bars, clubs and discos. Bars are often open all day and keep going until 4 or 5am, discos from around 8pm to 4am. There are also plenty of places to listen to live **Turkish music** in Antalya, particularly *halk*, *türkü* and *özgün*. Keep an eye out for fly posters advertising the concerts of the bigger stars of the Turkish music scene, who often play the **Açık Hava Tiyatro** (open-air theatre) situated at the eastern end of Konyaaltı beach. Tickets can be bought from an open-air stall at the northeast end of Atatürk Bulvarı, priced from 15TL and upwards depending on the popularity of the act.

Bars and clubs

Ayyaş Corner of Hamam and Zafer Sok. Music wafts into the square from this chilled-out bar with a bohemian atmosphere. In summer, wooden tables and chairs are set out front on the quiet square. Beers for 4TL and a good cheese plate with local products.

The Bar (aka *Rock Bar*) Uzun Carşışı Sok. Favoured by students from the local university and Antalya's grunge contingent. Surprisingly passable live rock acts play in a crowded, upstairs room most weekends. The downstairs bar is set in a pleasant courtyard garden.

Club Arma Kaleiçi Yat Limanı. Affluent restaurant-cum-dance club on the west side of the harbour. A spacious, colonnaded dining area in an old, stone-built warehouse serves expensive fish dishes. The dance area is on a terrace perched right at the sea's edge. Come here to watch Antalya's rich set enjoy an evening out.

Gizli Bahçe Kaleiçi, off Paşa Sok. Well-hidden student-oriented bar (ask for the Karatay Medresesi to locate it), beers at 4TL (served with a free helping of salted popcorn), a limited fast-food type menu, rock music and shady garden.

Olympos *Falez Hotel*, 100 Yıl Bul. The huge club in the hotel basement has a superb laser show and trilingual DJs playing mostly Eurodisco to a smart Turkish clientele.

Turkish music

Akdeniz Çiçek Pasajı Uzun Çarşısı Sok 24–26. Recently revamped, with tiered seating areas surrounding a central well where the musicians play. It is the best place in town to catch live Turkish music, situated a couple of hundred metres down from the clocktower. There's a small terrace with views over Kaleiçi and the bay.

Entertainment and festivals

The Hasan Subaşı Kültür Parkı – also known as AKM or **Atatürk Kültür Merkezi** – is a complex of two theatres and a pyramid-shaped glass exhibition centre set in a cliff-top park, 3km west of the centre; dolmuşes from the town centre marked "Adliye" or "AKM" pass the gates. With its tea gardens and children's playgrounds, the park is a favourite spot for joggers, roller-bladers and Sunday strollers, while the theatre complex stages the occasional classical concert and shows Hollywood films. Below the park, backing Konyaaltı Plajı, is the **Beach Park**, a landscaped complex of restaurants, cafés, bars and clubs and a seasonal open-air cinema.

The most convenient **cinema** is the Plaza, in the Antalya 2000 building, 100m northeast of Hadrian's Gate, which has three air-conditioned screens though for the best sound and seats try the eight-screen Cine Bonus in the Migros centre. Antalya plays host to a major international **film festival** in autumn (see box below). The town is also crowded during the **Aspendos Opera and Ballet Festival** (see box, p.397 for details).

Listings

Airlines THY, Konyaaltı Cad 24, Antmarın İş Merkezi ☎0242/243 4383, reservations ☎0212/444 0849; Onur Air, Çağlayan Mah, 2055 Sok 20, Barınaklar ☎0242/324 1335; reservations ☎0212/444 6687; Atlas Jet, Antalya Airport ☎0242/330 3900, reservations ☎444 3387.

Airport General information ☎0242/330 3030, flight enquiries ☎0242/330 3600; ⊛www.aytport.com.

Banks and exchange There are banks with ATMs and *döviz* offices throughout the city, and some *döviz* offices on Şarampol even open on Sundays (though most operate Mon–Sat 9am–7pm). You can also exchange currency at the PTT.

Books The Owl Bookshop, Kocatepe Sok 9 in the old town, has an excellent selection of mainly English-language secondhand books. Ardic, in the Seleker shopping mall on Güllük Cad, is the best place to buy English-language guides and novels.

Buses You can reach almost all provincial capitals in Turkey direct from Antalya *otogar*. Major companies such as Kamil Koç, Akdeniz and Metro, have ticket offices in town, especially on Subaşı

Cad, and their own shuttles servicing the *otogar*. Minor companies such as Göreme Tur (for Cappadocia) are "minded" by the majors; see the destinations and company logos on the bus office windows. Some pensions in the old town sell or book bus tickets.

Car rental There are numerous car rental agencies in Kaleiçi, and many more on Fevzi Çakmak Cad, near Antalyaspor's stadium. In July and August, book your car well in advance; at other times, bargain hard. Try the *Sabah Pansiyon* (see "Accommodation"), Mithra Travel (see "Tours", below), or Hertz out at the airport on ☎0242/330 3848.

Consulate UK, Gençlik Mahallesi, 1314 Sok, Elif apt 6/8 (☎0242/244 5313), to the right of and behind the *Talya Hotel*, off Fevzi Çakmak Cad.

Ferries The Turkish Maritime Lines office, for tickets for the fortnightly ferry to Venice, is at Konyaaltı Cad 40/19 (☎0242/241 1120).

Hamams In Kaleiçi, try the mixed Nazır on Hamam Aralığı Sok, behind the Mehmet Paşa mosque – built in 1611 and still going (daily: women 8am–noon; mixed 10am–12.30am; admission is a steep 40TL).

The Golden Orange

Antalya plays host to a major film international **film festival**, the Altın Portakal or Golden Orange, for a week each autumn, usually around the beginning of October. Overall, around 150 films are screened throughout the week, culminating at an award ceremony at the Atatürk Kültür Merkezi where golden statuettes of Venus carrying an orange are handed out. Throughout the week, directors, screenwriters and producers of Turkish and Eurasian cinema hold panel discussions and workshops and parties are held across the city. All films are subtitled in English as well as in Turkish. For the festival programme visit ⊛www.altinportakal.org.tr.

Hospital State Hospital (Devlet Hastane) and outpatients' clinic, Soğuksu Cad ☏ 0242/241 2010; University Teaching Hospital (Tip Fakultesi), Dumlupınar Bul ☏ 0242/227 4480.

Laundry Several places around the Kesik Minare offer laundry services, as do many *pansiyons*.

Left luggage There's a 24-hour office marked "Emanet" at the *otogar*; items priced by size.

Police Tourist Police, Emniyet Müdürlüğü, Yat Limanı, Kaleiçi ☏ 0242/527 4503.

Post office The main PTT is at Güllük Cad 9 (daily 9am–5pm for exchange and letter service; 24hr for phones).

Shopping Although traditional take-home items are rugs, minerals and leather, you'll find that jeans, gold and designer-label clothes and shoes are a better bet these days. Check out the boutiques along Atatürk and Işıklar *cad* and in the new Migros centre for the real

thing; and Cumhuriyet Cad (past Güllük Cad) for fakes.

Tours Whitewater-rafting on the Köprülü iver is a full-day excursion from Antalya. The most reliable company is Medraft (🖳 www.medraft.com, ☏ 0242/312 5770). A day's rafting, including transfers and meal, costs around €40. Many Antalya travel agents will book rafting trips for you – try Akay on Cumhuriyet Cad, Maki on Uzun Carşi Sok, as well as many Kaleiçi *pansiyons*. Mithra Travel, Hesapçı Sok (☏ 0242/248 7747, 🖳 www .mithratravel.com), in the old city, organizes one- or two-day treks (from about €20 per person per day) in the limestone massifs overlooking Antalya, and can also arrange self-guided walks.

Yachting Some yachts are open to charter for groups of four to twelve. Ask around at the harbour during the slow spring season and you could get a bargain cruise for the same price as hotel bed and board.

Around Antalya: Köprülü Kanyon and Selge

The **Köprülü Kanyon national park** (Köprülü Kanyon Milli Parkı) makes a good full-day outing from Antalya. There is little public transport to Selge (the ruins of which are scattered amongst the modern village of Zerk, also referred to as Altınkaya) or to the national park – one elusive afternoon dolmuş (ostensibly in the late afternoon) passes by each day between Serik, on the coastal highway, to Selge/Zerk, returning early the next morning. However, many companies operate half-day **rafting trips** down the Köprülü River, allowing time for a stop en route for a swim and lunch. Be warned that in peak season up to 45,000 rafters a day are bussed into this area, making both the road and river very crowded places – serious rafters should look elsewhere (see "Tours" above for operators).

Selge

The road up to **Selge** (always open; 4TL) is now paved. As you climb to an eventual altitude of 900m, the panoramas become more sweeping, the thickly wooded countryside more savage, and the 2500m Kuyucak range ahead more forbidding. The site itself is scattered around the hamlet of **ZERK** (also known as Altınkaya). Little is known for certain of the origins of Selge; it only left the realm of mythological ancestry and anecdote to enter history – and the Roman Empire – in the first century AD. The city was inhabited until early Byzantine times and must have been abandoned when the aqueduct supplying it with water collapsed.

The 10,000-spectator-capacity theatre that dominates **ancient Selge** is impressive despite the stage building having been pulverized by lightning some decades ago. Three of the five doors giving access backstage still remain. Close by are the ancient **agora** with its part-visible paving, jumbled masonry and chunks of unexcavated inscriptions and two hilltop temples. The foundations of a **Byzantine church** sit up on a hill to the southeast and enjoy panoramic views down the valley and up to the snow-streaked peak of Bozburun, while the jumbled remains of a temple of Zeus and a large water cistern lie to the northwest along the ridge. From here you can catch views to the ruined temple of Artemis and old city wall to the northwest and to the stoa in the valley below. Returning to the main track via some village farmyards, you'll pass the **stadium**, of which only the western ranks of seats are left; the sporting area itself is now a wheat field.

Termessos

Situated over a thousand metres above sea level 30km northwest of Antalya, the ancient site of **Termessos** is one of Turkey's prime attractions. Indeed, its dramatic setting and well-preserved ruins, tumbling from the summit of the mountain and enclosed within the boundaries of a national park – the Güllük Dağ Milli Parkı – merit a journey.

Despite its close proximity to Lycia, Termessos was actually a Pisidian city, inhabited by the same warlike tribe of people who settled in the Anatolian Lakeland, around Isparta and Eğirdir, during the first millennium BC. The city's position, commanding the road from the Mediterranean to the Aegean, gave Termessians the opportunity to extract customs dues from traders; a wall across the valley is believed to be the site of their customs post. Later, in 70 BC, Termessos signed a treaty with Rome, under which their independence was preserved – a fact the Termessians proudly expressed by never including the face or name of a Roman emperor on their coinage. The city must have been abandoned quite early, probably after earthquake damage in 243 AD, and has only been surveyed, never excavated.

The site

A thorough exploration of the **ancient site** (daily April–Oct 9am–7pm & Nov–March 8.30am–5pm; 5TL entry to the forest park, another 8TL to the site itself) can be quite strenuous. Sturdy footwear and a supply of water are advisable, and you should use summer visits to avoid the midday sun. After checking the site map at the car park you'll need to climb a good fifteen minutes before you reach the first remains of any interest, although on the way you'll pass a number of well-labelled, though mainly inaccessible, ruins, including the aqueduct and cistern high on the cliff face to the left of the path.

The second-century AD **King's Road** was the main road up to the city, close to which the massive lower and upper **city walls** testify to a substantial defence system. The central part of the city is beyond the second wall, to the left of the path. Its surviving buildings, formed of square-cut grey stone, are in an excellent state of repair, their walls standing high and retaining their original mouldings. In part, this is due to the inaccessibility of the site; it's difficult to imagine even the most desperate forager coming up here to pillage stone.

The first building you reach is the well-preserved **gymnasium**, with a baths complex alongside. This, however, is far overshadowed by the nearby **theatre**, one of the most magnificently situated in Turkey, with the mountain climbing behind and a steep gorge dropping to its right. Greek in style, it had seating space for 4200 spectators. Some of the seats are missing, but otherwise it's in a good state of preservation.

To the west of the theatre is the open grassy space of the **agora**, at the far end of which is a **Corinthian temple**, approached up a broad flight of steps, with a six-metre-square platform – at the back of which a pit sunk into the rock, claimed by some to be the tomb of Alcatus, the pretender to the governorship of Pisidia – though the tomb on the hill above (see p.394) is generally accepted as more likely. On the far side of the agora from the theatre stands a smaller theatre or **odeon**, which, according to inscriptions, was used for horse and foot races, races in armour, and – by far the most frequently held – wrestling. The walls of the building stand to almost ten metres. Surrounding the odeion are four **temples**, only one of which – that of Zeus Solymeus, god of war and guardian of the city of Termessos – is in a decent state of repair.

Following the trail up the hill from here brings you to a fork, the left-hand path of which continues on to the **necropolis**, where you'll see an incredible number of sarcophagi dating from the first to the third centuries AD. Most are simple structures on a base, though there are some more elaborate ones carved from the living rock, with inscriptions and reliefs.

Returning downhill, take the left-hand fork for several hundred metres to the so-called **Tomb of Alcatus** – widely accepted as the mausoleum of the general. The tomb itself is cave-like and undistinguished, but the carvings on its facade are remarkable, particularly one depicting a mounted soldier, with a suit of armour, a helmet, a shield and a sword – the armour of a foot soldier – depicted lower down to the right of the figure. Continuing along the path downhill will lead back to the car park.

Practicalities

Antalya, 30km southeast, is the most obvious base for visiting Termessos. To get there **by car**, take the Burdur road out of Antalya, turning left after 11km towards Korkuteli. The left turning to Termessos is marked off the Korkuteli road after about 14km, from where a track leads 9km up through the forested national park to the site. Using **public transport**, you need to take a bus (hourly) from the *otogar* headed for Korkuteli as far as the beginning of the forest track, from where you can take one of the taxis (around 40–50TL including waiting time and return to main road) that tout for business here. If you choose to stay the night, there is the *Yeşil Vadi* restaurant-pension just off the main road near the park entrance with quaint, comfortable rooms set among olive groves (☎0242/423/7555, ⓦwww .yesil-vadi.com; ➋).

The Pamphylian cities

The twelfth century BC saw a large wave of Greek migration from northern Anatolia to the Mediterranean coast. Many of the incomers moved into the area immediately to the east of Antalya, which came to be called **Pamphylia**, meaning "the land of the tribes", reflecting the mixed origins of the new arrivals. Pamphylia was a remote area, cut off from the main Anatolian trade routes by mountains on all sides; nevertheless three great cities grew up here – Perge, Aspendos and Side.

Most of Pamphylia fell to Alexander the Great in the fourth century BC. After his death the region became effectively independent, though nominally claimed by the various successor kingdoms that inherited Alexander's realm. During the first century BC the Romans, annoyed by the activities of the Cilician pirates operating from further along the Mediterranean, took control of the coast. Their rule ushered in three centuries of stability and prosperity, during which the Pamphylian cities flourished as never before. In later years, Mark Antony was sent to take charge of the region, treating it as his personal domain until defeated by Octavius at the battle of Actium in 31 BC, after which Pamphylia was formally absorbed into the Roman Empire under the Pax Romana.

If you want to visit the main Pamphylian sites in a single day a **taxi** is the best option, and should cost around €80 for the day (check out the rank at the southern end of Atatürk Bulvarı in Antalya, which lists prices for various destinations on a wooden board). The bus tours (from €25) organized by various agents in Antalya's Kaleiçi district seldom include Selge (see p.392), but do include tedious stops at out-of-town gold and carpet shops.

Perge

About 15km east of Antalya, the ruins of **Perge** can be reached by taking one of the frequent dolmuşes or *Belediye* buses (every 20min or so) to the village of Aksu on the main eastbound road; these leave from the otogar and can also be boarded closer to town at the roundabout at the north end of Dr Burhanetin Onat Caddesi, a fifteen-minute walk from Hadrian's Gate. From the village it's a fifteen-minute walk to the site itself, though you may be able to flag down a dolmuş from the village if you don't want to walk.

The **site entrance** (daily April–Oct 9am–7pm & Nov–March 8.30am–5pm; 15TL) and car park are marked by a cluster of souvenir stalls and soft-drinks stands. It's an enticing spot, the ruins expansive and impressive, and you could easily spend a long afternoon looking around.

Some history

Perge was founded around 1000 BC and ranked as one of the great Pamphylian trading cities, despite the fact that it's nearly 20km inland – a deliberate defensive siting so as to avoid the unwanted attentions of the pirate bands that terrorized this stretch of the Mediterranean. Later, when Alexander the Great arrived in 333 BC, the citizens of Perge sent out guides to lead his army into the city. Alexander was followed by the Seleucids, under whom Perge's most celebrated ancient inhabitant, the mathematician Apollonius, lived and worked. Most of the city's surviving buildings date from the period of Roman rule, which began in 188 BC. After the collapse of the Roman Empire, Perge remained inhabited until Selçuk times, before being gradually abandoned.

The site

Just before the site entrance, the **theatre** has been closed for repairs for some time. It was originally constructed by the Greeks, but substantially altered by the Romans in the second century AD. Built into the side of a hill, it could accommodate 14,000 people on 42 seating levels and was the venue for theatrical entertainment, poetry contests and musical concerts. To the northeast of the theatre is Perge's massive horseshoe-shaped **stadium**, the largest in Asia Minor at 234m by 34m, with a seating capacity of 12,000. It was the venue not only for chariot races, but also wild beast hunts, public executions and gladiator spectacle.

Past the site entrance, stretches of the Seleucid walls have survived, giving some indication of the extent and ground plan of the original city. Just in front of the outer gates is the **Tomb of Plancia Magna**, a benefactress of the city, whose name appears later on a number of inscriptions. Passing through the first **city gate**, you'll see a ruined **Byzantine basilica** on the right, beyond which lies the

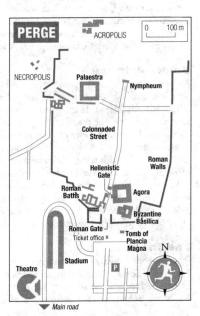

fourth-century AD **agora**, centred on a ruined temple. To the southwest of the agora are the excavated **Roman baths**, where a couple of the pools have been exposed. Across the cracked surface of the inlaid marble floor, the original layout of frigidarium, tepidarium and caldarium can – with the help of a few signs – still be discerned. Also visible in places are the brick piles that once supported the hypocaust floor of the baths, enabling warm air to circulate underneath.

At the northwest corner of the agora is Perge's **Hellenistic Gate**, with its two mighty circular towers, the only building to have survived from the Hellenistic period. Behind, the horseshoe-shaped court and ornamental archway were both erected at the behest of Plancia Magna, the former once adorned with statues – the bases of a number of which were found during excavations carried out during the mid-1950s. Beyond is the start of a 300-metre-long **colonnaded street**, with a water channel running down the middle and the shells of shops to either side. Walking along it, you'll be able to pick out the ruts made by carts and chariots in the stone slabs of the roadway. Also visible are a number of reliefs near the tops of the columns, just beneath the capitals, one of which depicts Apollo, while another shows a man in a toga, offering a libation at an altar. At the end of the street is the **nymphaeum**, an ornamental water outlet from where a stream splashes down into the water channel below. Above here is the **acropolis** – probably the site of the original defensive settlement, of which little has survived. To the west of a cross-roads just before the nymphaeum is a **palestra**, dating from 50 AD, according to an inscription found on its south wall. West of here, archeologists have found a **necropolis** leading from one of the city gates, sarcophagi from which can now be seen in the Antalya archeological museum.

Aspendos

Returning to the main road, head east for **Aspendos**, whose theatre is among the best preserved in Asia Minor – it's still used to stage the annual Aspendos Opera and Ballet Festival. From Antalya's *otogar*, there are regular **buses** to the village of Serik (around 40km, every 2hr), from which an intermittent dolmuş service drops at Aspendos, around 6km northeast. Just before Aspendos, the village of **Belkis** has several eating places. About a kilometre northeast of the village lie the car park and Aspendos **site entrance** (daily April–Oct 9am–7pm & Nov–March 8.30am–5pm; 15TL).

Some history

Aspendos changed hands regularly in ancient times between the Persians, Greeks and Spartans, finally coming under the control of Alexander the Great around 333 BC. After his death a decade later, Aspendos became part of the Seleucid kingdom and was later absorbed into the realm of the kings of Pergamon. In 133 BC, the city became part of the Roman province of Asia. Roman rule consisted mainly of a succession of consuls and governors demanding protection money and carting off the city's treasures. Only with the establishment of the Roman Empire did the city prosper, growing into an important trade centre, its wealth based on salt from a nearby lake.

Aspendos remained important throughout the Byzantine era, although it suffered badly from the Arab raids of the seventh century. During the thirteenth century the Selçuks arrived, followed a couple of hundred years later by the Ottomans, who ruled here until the eighteenth century, when the settlement was abandoned.

The theatre

The Aspendos **theatre** was built in the second century AD by the architect Zeno. He used a Roman design, with an elaborate stage behind which the scenery could be lowered, instead of allowing the natural landscape behind the stage to act as a backdrop, as had been the custom in Hellenistic times.

Aspendos Opera and Ballet Festival

The **Aspendos Opera and Ballet Festival** is staged in the theatre every year, from mid-June, over a three- to four-week period. Both Turkish and foreign companies perform, and the programme consists of popular and experimental opera, ballet and classical concerts. With an inflow of choreographers and musicians from the ex-Soviet Union, Turkish opera and ballet companies have improved out of all recognition, and stage design and costumes match the standard of the performers.

Tickets (30TL for foreigners, less for Turks) are available both in advance and on the night from the theatre, and you can also buy them in Antalya and Side, though the booking office seems to switch venues each year – ask at the tourist office. Check ⓦ www.aspendosfestival.org for programmes. Cheap city buses run here from Antalya and Side centre. Most festival-goers bring along supper to while away the time before the start of the 9.30pm performance, as well as cushions to sit on, and an umbrella or waterproof in case of a thunderstorm.

The stage, auditorium and arcade above are all intact, as is the several-storey-high stage building, and what you see today is pretty much what the spectators saw during the theatre's heyday, a state of preservation due in part to Atatürk, who, after a visit, declared that it should be preserved and used for performances rather than as a museum. A dubious legend relates that the theatre was built after the king of Aspendos announced he would give the hand of his beautiful daughter to a man who built some great work for the benefit of the city. Two men rose to the challenge, one building the theatre, the other an aqueduct, both finishing work simultaneously, with the result that the king offered to cut his daughter in two, giving a half to each man. The builder of the theatre declared that he would rather renounce his claim than see the princess dismembered and he was, of course, immediately rewarded with the hand of the girl for his unselfishness. Later, the theatre was used as a Selçuk *kervansaray*, and restoration work from that period – plasterwork decorated with red zigzags – is visible over the stage.

The acropolis and aqueduct

To the right of the theatre entrance, a path leads up to the **acropolis**, built on a flat-topped hill. The site is a little overgrown, but a number of substantial buildings are still in place, foremost among them being the **nymphaeum** and **basilica**, both 16m in height, as well as sections of the main street and a drainage system in good condition.

To the north of the acropolis, on the plain below, stretches a Roman **aqueduct**. Originally 15km long, it brought water to Aspendos from the mountains above and incorporates an ingenious siphonic system that allowed the water to cross the plain at low level; you can still (with care) climb the towers. The aqueduct and towers can also be reached by taking a left turn down a paved path just outside Belkis, skirting around the western side of the hill.

Side

About 25km east of Aspendos, **SIDE**, one-time trysting place of Antony and Cleopatra, was perhaps the foremost of the Pamphylian cities. The ruins of the ancient port survive, but over the last few years Side has become dominated by packaged tourism development. Constant restoration work is necessary to combat the deterioration brought on by thousands of visitors trekking through the ancient city day and night, but they are hardly able to keep up and many areas, particularly the theatre and colonnaded street are subjected to an accelerated rate of destruction. Given that accommodation and restaurant prices here are often double what you would pay in nearby Antalya, Side makes a decent stopover en route to another destination, but is hardly worth using as a base for exploring the region.

Some history

Side (meaning "pomegranate" in an ancient Anatolian dialect) was founded in the seventh century BC, its colonists attracted by the defensive potential of the rocky cape. It grew into a rich port with an estimated 60,000 inhabitants during its peak in the second century AD. Initially a significant proportion of Side's wealth rested on the slave trade, with the city authorities allowing pirates to run an illegal slave market inside the city walls. This trade was later outlawed, and after the collapse of the western Roman Empire, Side survived only until the Arab invasion during the seventh century AD. The Arabs put the place to the torch, driving out the last inhabitants, and Side was abandoned until the beginning of the twentieth century, when it was resettled by Muslim fishermen from Crete. Despite later attempts by the Turkish government and various archeological agencies to evict them, these villagers stayed, and by the 1980s their descendants were starting to reap the rewards of Side's tourist boom.

Arrival, information and services

Intercity buses drop passengers at the *otogar* in Sorgun (sometimes named as Manavgat on intercity bus tickets), from where there are dolmuşes every twenty minutes to Manavgat centre where you must switch to another dolmuş for Side's small bus station. From here it's a ten-minute walk into town, though in season tractors drag wagons full of tourists to the entrance to town at the top of the main street.

Side is effectively **pedestrianized** and cars can only enter the town between 7 and 10am, 3 to 6pm, and again after midnight (though if you have your own vehicle and are making your way to your hotel with luggage, the attendants will let you through). The **car park** is just outside the barrier and a modest daily fee is charged – don't make the mistake of parking anywhere along the approach road as towing is vigorously carried out.

Side's **tourist office** (Mon–Fri 8am–5pm, Sat–Sun 9am–5pm; ℡0242/753 1265) is on the main road into town, on the left just before the *otogar*, though it won't overburden you with information and carries no maps of the town or pamphlets on the ruins. **Banks** and a **PTT** can be found on the square at the southern tip of the promontory. **Car rental** places are ubiquitous, with outfits on the road approaching the main town entrance: Europcar (℡0242/753 1764; ⓦwww.europcar.com) is next to the *Asteria Hotel*; Avis is on Atatürk Bulvarı (℡0242/753 1348; ⓦwww.avis.com). There are several **internet** cafés, among them, Chips near the *Pettino Otel* on Camii Sokak. **Tours** from Side include outings to Manavgat (€15 boat tour), rafting on the Köprülü River (€20), the Pamphilian cities (€25), and Alanya (€8).

Accommodation

Side's best and most atmospheric **accommodation** lies within the town's ancient city walls, where you are surrounded by ruins, restaurants and bars, and the beach is never more than a few minutes' walk away. Bear in mind, though, that while the western section within the walls affords sunset views, it's noisier and hotter than the east, which is cooled by onshore breezes. Booking is essential in high season.

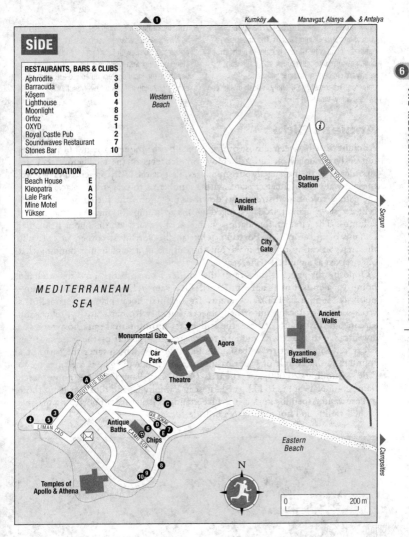

SİDE

RESTAURANTS, BARS & CLUBS

Aphrodite	3
Barracuda	9
Köşem	6
Lighthouse	4
Moonlight	8
Orfoz	5
OXYD	1
Royal Castle Pub	2
Soundwaves Restaurant	7
Stones Bar	10

ACCOMMODATION

Beach House	E
Kleopatra	A
Lale Park	C
Mine Motel	D
Yükser	B

MEDITERRANEAN
SEA

Western
Beach

Kumköy ▲   Manavgat, Alanya ▲ & Antalya

Dolmuş
Station

Ancient
Walls

City
Gate

Ancient
Walls

Monumental Gate

Car
Park

Agora

Byzantine
Basilica

Theatre

Antique
Baths

Chips

Temples of
Apollo & Athena

Eastern
Beach

Sargun

Campsites

N

0   200 m

Beach House Hotel Barbaros Cad
☎0242/753 1607, ⓦwww.beachhouse
-hotel.com. Highly recommended seafront hotel.
Most of the 25 comfortable rooms have pretty
wooden balconies overlooking the beach, and the
charming rear garden boasts the remains of a
Byzantine villa, a dovecote and a trampoline. It is
immaculately run by a Turkish/Australian couple,
and the food is wonderful. Incidentally, this was
Side's first hotel, and Simone de Beauvoir stayed
here back in the 1960s. ❸

Kleopatra Hotel Turgut Reis Cad ☎0242/753
1033. Situated on the western seafront, this

large hotel, with a funky concrete facade, has
comfortable a/c rooms, some with sea view, digital
TV and dated but clean furniture. ❸

Lale Park Lale Sok 5 ☎0242/753 1131,
ⓦwww.hotellalepark.com. A traditional stone-
built hotel, set back from the beach though some
rooms have sea views. Muted pastel walls and
white linen curtains give the rooms a soothing
atmosphere. There's a shady garden, a small
pool, darts and a pool table. Two apartments
have recently been added, one sleeping four,
the other five, for €95 – good value for
families. ❹

Mine Motel Gül Sok 61 ☎0242/753 2358, ©ceyhunbaldan@hotmail.com. The cheapest option in town, with 14 rooms painted a cheerful blue, new en-suite bathrooms, and a pleasant courtyard shaded by orange, plum and pomegranate trees. The friendly Turkish owner only speaks a few words of English. ❷

Yükser Pansiyon Sümbül Sok ☎0242/753 2010, ⓦwww.yukser-pansiyon.com. Small but well-appointed rooms with fans in a very attractive stone building with wooden shutters. The garden is beautiful, the location very quiet and the owners quietly hospitable. Closed Nov–March. ❸

Ancient Side

Ancient Side has been almost overwhelmed by the modern town, but if you set out early enough, you can still enjoy some corners of the city before they are smothered by the packaged tourism masses. East of the badly preserved **city gate**, the old walls are in a better state, with a number of towers still in place. Back at the gate, a colonnaded street runs down to the **agora**, the site of Side's second-century slave market, today fringed with the stumps of many of the agora's columns. The circular foundation visible at the centre of the agora is all that remains of a **Temple of Fortuna**, while in the northwest corner, next to the theatre, you can just about make out the outline of a semicircular building that once served as a public latrine, seating 24 people.

Opposite the agora is the site of the former Roman baths, now restored and home to a **museum** (Tues–Sun April–Oct 9am–7.15pm; Nov–March 9am–noon & 1–5pm; 10TL). It retains its original floor plan and contains a cross-section of locally unearthed objects – mainly Roman statuary, reliefs and sarcophagi. Just south of here, the still-intact **monumental gate** now serves as an entrance to the town's modern resort area. To the left of the gateway is an excavated monument to Vespasian, built in 74 AD, which takes the form of a fountain with a couple of water basins in front. Inside the gate is the entrance to Side's stunning 20,000-seat **theatre** (April–Oct 9am–7.15pm; Nov–March 9am–noon & 1–5pm; 10TL), the largest in Pamphylia, and different from those at Perge and Aspendos in that it is a freestanding structure supported by massive arched vaults, and not built into a hillside.

▲ The temple of Apollo, Side

From the monumental gate, modern Side's main street leads down to the old harbour and turns left toward the **temples of Apollo and Athena** (always open; free). The Athena temple has been partly re-erected, and its white portico is becoming Side's trademark and a favourite place to take sunset photographs. Both temples were once partially enclosed in a huge Byzantine basilica, parts of which gradually disappeared under the shifting sand; the still-visible section now provides a home to birds and bats.

In the days when Side was an important port, the area to the west of the temples was a harbour. Even in Roman times it was necessary to dredge continuously to clear silt deposited by the Manavgat River, and it soon became clogged up after the city went into decline. Elsewhere, you'll find a number of other buildings, including the city agora, on the eastern side of the peninsula just a stone's throw from the sea, and, a little inland from here, a ruined **Byzantine church** that's gradually disappearing under the dunes. Off Camii Sokak, are the remains of **antique baths** where Cleopatra is supposed to have bathed, which include several separate rooms, baths, a garden and even a marble seat with a dolphin armrest.

The beaches

Given Side's fine sandy **beaches**, it's not surprising the resort has developed so rapidly. To the west, the ten-kilometre stretch of beach is lined with expensive hotels, beach clubs and watersports rental outfits. **Sorgun** beach, 3km to the east, is well maintained by the local authority and is quieter and less tacky than Side's beaches. A dolmuş runs there every half-hour from Side's *otogar*.

Ten kilometres from Side, beyond the western beach, is **Kumköy**, with nearly as much in the way of beachside development as Sorgun, but again, its beaches aren't as crowded as Side's. There are direct dolmuş connections from the *otogar* and some of the buses and dolmuşes that run between Antalya and Side now go via Kumköy.

Eating

There are plenty of places to **eat** in Side, most of them overpriced and of dubious quality. Another challenge is trying to walk past one of them without being dragged inside by the smooth-talking hustlers employed for just this purpose. Also watch out for the ten percent service charge virtually every establishment here levies.

Aphrodite İskele Cad. Set back from the harbour, a low wooden building with tables out front and a play area for kids. The fish fillets start at 26TL and the speciality Chateaubriand steak a steep 70TL for two.

Köşem Yasemin Sok. Almost certainly the cheapest take-out in town, aimed more at the local shopkeepers than at tourists. A tasty flat-bread *döner* costs 2TL and flaky *borek* 2.50TL.

Moonlight Barbaros Cad 49. A romantic venue, with tables laid out on gravelled terraces overlooking the sea. The food is decent too, with a good range of *mezes* and fish dishes (lambfish kebab is 20TL). Cheaper and more interesting is *filet papyan*, chicken breast stuffed

with cheese and pistachios and there is a good wine list.

Orfoz Liman Cad 58. Down by the harbour, with tables on a large paved terrace and a small play-area for kids. Steaks are the speciality here, starting from 25TL, and fish is priced per kilo. Good for watching the sun go down.

Soundwaves Restaurant Küçük Plaj Üstü Köyçi. A very popular place, decked out like a pirate ship with waiters to match, and fine nautical views over the eastern beach. It does a tasty mix of Turkish standards (including *testi kebap*, a casserole of meat and vegetables baked in a sealed clay pot) and European dishes such as spinach pancakes (11TL). The wine is good value at 15TL a bottle.

Drinking and nightlife

There are plenty of places to while away the evening hours in Side. Turn left at the harbour and you'll pass a line of seafront **bars**. From here, walk through the Apollo and Athena temples to the southeast corner of town, where music-led bars, such as the *Stones Bar* (which hosts a "ladies" night and has karaoke and video games) and *Barracuda*, offer **dancing** and fine views out onto the Mediterranean. The *Royal Castle Pub* nearby shows football matches and serves beers from 5TL. To save money, you can cruise the staggered happy hours that run in different bars between 6 and 9pm.

The *Lighthouse*, just west of the harbour, plays a variety of (mainly dance and techno) music, with Russian podium dancers as a diversion and beers at around 8TL. Some 3km out of town on the west beach is the popular *OXYD* (20TL fee), a huge, 3000-capacity laser-lit rave venue. It has its own pool, more podium dancers and 8TL beers.

Manavgat

Fifteen minutes east of Side by dolmuş, the small town of **MANAVGAT** is not especially alluring, its chief attractions the river-boat tour up to the rather overrated Şelale or Manavgat waterfalls nearby and the isolated ruins of Seleucia, 20km inland. The 8km round trip to the **waterfalls** will set you back €15, boats leaving from a landing upstream of the town bridge. However, a longer trip offered in Side to the falls and Manavgat costs around €25, and is far more interesting.

To reach **Seleucia**, take the dolmuş from the northwest corner of the Manavgat *otogar* (see below) by the bridge to the Oymapınar Baraj. Alight at a left-hand turn signposted for Seleucia, from where it's a walk of 5km to the ruins. You will probably be able to hitch the first 4km to the nearest village, from where it's an uphill walk along a tractor track through pretty farmland. Set on a slope in pine forest, Seleucia, a Macedonian foundation later incorporated into the Roman Empire, is very overgrown. The tractor path leads through a city gate to some baths and an agora, the most obvious surviving structures. In spring, a pretty little waterfall cascades past the baths to a stream in the valley below.

Dolmuşes and buses shuttle between Manavgat (the dolmuş stop is just west of the bridge in the town centre) and Side every fifteen to twenty minutes (1.75TL). It's worth bearing in mind that intercity buses now use the new *otogar* at Sorgun (though marked as Manavgat on intercity bus tickets), midway between Manavgat and Side, with *servis* buses and dolmuşes linking it with Manavgat's centre.

Alanya and around

ALANYA is one of the Mediterranean coast's major resorts, a booming and popular place that in the last twenty years has expanded beyond all recognition along its sandy beaches. In addition to the massive influx of tourists, locals reckon that some thirty percent of the population is made up of expat Germans and Russians, whose villas litter the hillsides behind the town. Most visitors enter the town from the west, an approach that shows Alanya at its best, the road passing through verdant banana plantations on the outskirts and suddenly revealing a rocky promontory, topped by a castle, rearing out of the Mediterranean.

Little is known about Alanya's early **history**, although it's thought that the town was founded by Greek colonists who named it Kalonoros, or "beautiful mountain".

Things were pretty quiet until the second century BC, when Cilician pirates began using the town, known by now as Coracesium, as a base to terrorize the Pamphylian coast. Eventually, the Romans decided to put an end to the activities of the pirates and sent in Pompey, who destroyed the pirate fleet in a sea battle off Alanya in 67 BC. In 44 BC, Mark Antony gave the city to Cleopatra as a gift. Romantic as this might sound, there was a practical reason for his choice: the area around the city was an important timber-producing centre, and Cleopatra needed its resources to build up her navy. In 1221, the Byzantine city fell to the Selçuk sultan Alâeddin Keykubad, who gave it its present name and made it his summer residence. It's from this period that most buildings of historical importance date.

Arrival, orientation and information

Most of **old Alanya** is set on the great rocky promontory that juts out into the sea, dominating the **modern town** below it. Apart from the hotels and restaurants, and the Alanya Museum, there's little to see in the modern town.

It's about a thirty-minute walk to the town centre from Alanya's **otogar**, but there are plenty of *servis* minibuses and municipal buses to shuttle bus passengers in. Dolmuşes operating from the central terminal will take you to many of the local beaches. There are hydrofoils to Girne in Turkish Cyprus (see "Listings", p.407, for details).

The **tourist office** is on Bostancpınarı Cad 1 next to the Kuyularonü Camii (summer Mon–Tues & Thurs–Sat 9am–2am, Wed & Sun 9am–6pm; winter Mon–Tues & Thurs–Sat 9am–9pm & Wed & Sun 9am–6pm; ☎0242/513 1240).

Accommodation

Despite the boom in package tourism, rooms are easy to find in Alanya, even in high season, and competition has kept the prices manageable. If you've come primarily for the beach scene, then you might want to choose from one of the hotels on Meteorologi Sokak, near the *otogar*, from where it's an easy walk to the west beach. Keykubat Caddesi, the extension of Atatürk Caddesi, leading off to Mersin and backing the eastern beach, is Alanya's out-of-town resort strip, lined with more upmarket hotels.

Around İskele Caddesi

Pension Best Alaaddinoğlu Sok 23 ☎0532/485 7384, ✉bestapart@hotmail.com. Two-, four- and six-person apartments with bathroom, living room and kitchen are rented by friendly owners who speak excellent English. Very good value. ❷–❸

Çınar Otel Damlataş Cad ☎0242/512 0063. Near where the street becomes İskele Cad – a real oddity in this tourist mecca, a traditional Turkish town-centre hotel, basic but clean rooms (with fans) and passable bathrooms. The front rooms are a little noisy, the 1950s-style cube-effect tiles in the halls and rooms are fun. Great value and very central. No breakfast. ❺

Hotel Kaptan İskele Cad 70 ☎0242/513 4900, ✇www.kaptanhotels.com. Comfortable, central and reasonably classy, with its own pool and two restaurants, one overlooking the harbour. The rooms are blandly done out in white and pastel yellow, but have satellite TV, wi-fi and minibar. ❻

Temiz Otel İskele Cad ☎0242/513 1016, ✇www.temizotel.com.tr. Lives up to its name (*temiz* means clean) and has a very impressive reception and modern, minimalist rooms. Rooms at the back are quiet, the breakfast terrace has a lovely view. ❸

Meteoroloji Sokak

Hotel Hermes Meteoroloji Sok 2 ☎0242/513 2135, ✇www.hermesotel.com. Closest to the beach, with a small pool and forty-one appealingly white rooms with en-suite bathrooms. It's well run, and the manager speaks good English, though the clientele is largely Scandinavian. Full board only. ❽

Üstün Aile Pansiyon Meteoroloji Sok 4 ☎0242/513 2262, ✇www.ustunpansiyon.com. Run by a charming retired bank manager – spacious rooms painted a dubious but cheerful mustard yellow, with balconies (some with sea views) and a communal kitchen. Breakfast is an additional 10TL per person. ❹

ALANYA

ACCOMMODATION

Çınar	D
Hermes	B
Kaptan	F
Pension Best	C
Temiz	E
Üstün Aile Pansiyon	A

RESTAURANTS, CAFÉS & BARS

Bizim Ocakbaşı	2
Gaziantep Başpınar	4
Hancı Patisserie	3
Janus	5
Ottoman House	1

The Town

Guarding the harbour on the east side of the promontory stands the **Kızılkule** – the "Red Tower" – a 35-metre-high defensive tower of red stone built by Alâeddin Keykubad in 1226 and restored in 1951. Today it houses a pedestrian **ethnographic museum** (Etnografya Müzesi; Tues–Sun 9am–7.30pm; 3TL), and has a roof terrace that overlooks the town's eastern harbour. Old wooden houses cling to the slopes above the tower, and you can follow the old coastal defensive wall along the water's edge to the **Tersane**, an Ottoman shipyard, consisting of five workshops linked by an arched roof. Beyond here is a small defensive tower, the **Tophane**.

Alanya castle

It's a long, winding climb up to **Alanya castle**, and takes about an hour – in summer set off early to avoid the heat or, better, late afternoon and catch the sunset from the top. There are lots of restaurants and little cafés to stop off at on the way up. Alternatively, there's an hourly bus (on the hour) from the junction of İskele and Damlataş *caddesi*s or taxis will make the trip for 8TL.

The castle itself is a huge fortification system, with walls snaking right around the upper reaches of the promontory. A huge archway (bearing an inscription in Persian) leads into an area that demarcated the original limits of Alanya back in Selçuk times. In among the foliage off the road is an area known as **Ehmediye**, a small village with a few old Ottoman houses clustered around the dilapidated sixteenth-century **Süleymaniye Camii**, a *kervansaray* and the **Aksebe Türbesi**, a distinctive thirteenth-century tomb.

At the end of the road is the **İç Kale**, or Inner Fortress (daily 9am–7.30pm; 10TL), built by Keykubad in 1226. Inside the gates, local women sell tablecloths and lace and the smell of lavender hangs in the air. The fortress is pretty much intact, with the shell of a **Byzantine church**, decorated with fading frescoes, in the centre. Look out for the **cisterns** that supplied the fortress with water and to which it owed much of its apparent impregnability. In the northwestern corner of the fortress, a platform gives fine views of the western beaches and the mountains, though it originally served as a point from which prisoners were thrown to their deaths on the rocks below. These days tour guides assure their wards that it's customary to throw a rock from the platform, attempting to hit the sea rather than the rock below – an impossible feat supposed to have been set for prisoners as a chance to save their necks.

Alanya Museum

On the western side of the promontory, the **Alanya Museum** (Alanya Müzesi; Tues–Sun 8am–noon & 1–5pm; 3TL) is filled with local archeological and ethnological ephemera, including finds from (and photographs of) several small Pamphylian sites in the region. Most unusual is an inscription in sixth-century BC Phoenician, a sort of halfway house between cuneiform writing and the alphabet as the Greeks developed it. There's also a mock-up Ottoman living room complete with a beautiful carved ceiling, shutters and cupboards, and a model of a village wedding. The best thing about the museum, though, is the garden, a former Ottoman graveyard in which you can take refuge from the heat in summer; re-creations of grape presses and other farm implements share space with a gaggle of peacocks and chickens.

The beaches

Alanya's **beaches** are extensive, stretching from the town centre for a good 3km west and 8km east, and they are the reason most vistors come here. The resort offers a range of **watersports**, and the outlets along the west beach offer jet-ski rental (€30 for 15min), parasailing (€30 for 15min), waterskiing (€20 for 30min) and banana-boat rides (€8). If you fancy some scuba-diving, head to Dolphin Dive, on İskele Cad 23 by the harbour, offering dives with lunch from €62.

The caves and boat tours

Not far away from the museum, accessible from behind the *Damlataş Restaurant*, you'll find the **Damlataş**, or "Cave of Dripping Stones" (daily 10am–sunset; 3 TL), a stalactite- and stalagmite-filled underground cavern with a moist, warm atmosphere said to benefit asthma sufferers. There are other caves, dotted around the waterline at the base of the promontory, and various local entrepreneurs offer **boat trips** around them, charging about €15 per person for a four-hour trip, or €25 for a longer excursion that includes dolphin-watching. Boats leave from the harbour near Kızılkule, usually departing around 10am.

The first stop is usually the **Fosforlu** (Phosphorus Cave), where the water shimmers green; then it's on round the **Cilyarda Burnu**, a long spit of land that is home to a ruined monastery and former mint. It's not actually possible to go ashore, but on the other side of the skinny peninsula is the **Aşıklar Mağarası** (Lovers' Cave), in which, according to a bizarre local story, a German woman and her Turkish boyfriend were stranded for three months in 1965 while the police and army mounted searches for them. A little further round is the **Korsanlar Mağarası**, which, according to more believable stories, is where the pirates of yesteryear used to hide out. You will also be taken to **Cleopatra's Beach**, where the legends claim the queen used to descend to bathe while staying here with Mark Antony.

Eating

There are countless restaurants in Alanya, but most of them are overpriced (and invariably add on a ten percent service charge), so be prepared for take-outs if you're on a tight budget. The more expensive establishments line the harbour area; cheaper options can be found in the backstreets between Atatürk and Gazipaşa caddesis, and along Damlataş Caddesi. The weekly **market**, with masses of fresh provisions, is held every Friday, next to the dolmuş station, north of İsim Tokuş Bulvarı.

Bizim Ocakbaşı Müftüler Cad, Kalgıdım Sok. Bustling first-floor place on a side street behind the police station. Starters cost a reasonable 2TL, kebabs a heftier 13TL and up, beer 3.5TL. Well frequented by locals.

Gaziantep Başpınar Kebap ve Lahmacun Salonu Hükümet Cad, Kapalı Otopark Üstü. The huge red-awning-fronted restaurant serving small portions of stews, *lahmacun* and kebabs; a filling meal will set you back 15TL.

Janus İskele Cad. Rather flashy waterfront joint, with high prices (expect to pay from 40TL for a full meal), but it's been around since 1954 and has a good reputation for fish and steaks. It has an attached bar and disco.

Hancı Patisserie Hasan Akçalıoğlu Cad 12, fronting Atatürk Cad. A continental-style patisserie chain, with decent filter, espresso and cappuccino coffees for 2.5TL, and delicious cherry tarts for the same price. There are a few tables set out on the street.

Ottoman House Damlataş Cad 23. A characterful Ottoman-era building, with high wooden ceilings, bare boards, antique kilims and a vine-shaded veranda set back from the street. The food is only average and prices a little high (expect to pay around 35TL for a full meal with a beer, a little more for fish), but the ambience is good.

Drinking and nightlife

Alanya has a large number of bars, discos and clubs, but they are very much geared towards package tourists, and often centre on the complexes out of the town centre. One long-standing dance establishment is *Auditorium*, out on the west side of town, an open-air disco complete with its own pool. There are a couple of options close to the harbour. If you want to drink expensive beers (8TL) to a pumping MOR rock soundtrack, head for *The Doors Rock Bar*, a *Hard Rock* derivative just behind the waterfront, with mock palms, a cherry-red 1950s Chevy suspended from the ceiling and a tank of gormless-looking fish behind the bar. The adjacent *James Dean Bar* is equally overpriced, but plays a wider variety of music and has a choice of bars.

Listings

Banks and exchange There are several banks with ATMs on Atatürk and Hükümet cads.

Bicycle and motorbike rental Bikes cost from €5 per day, mopeds €12 and motorbikes

€30, available from numerous outlets around town.

Boats Fergün Denizcilik (ⓦ www.fergün.net) and Akgungler (ⓣ 0242/512 8889, ⓦ www.akgunler .com.tr) run hydrofoils to and from Girne-Kyrenia in Turkish Cyprus in the summer season only; services leave Mondays and Thursdays at noon, returning from Girne on Sundays and Wednesdays at 11am (78TL one way; 3hr 30min).

Buses Regular buses link Alanya with destinations east and west, including Antalya, Mersin and Adana, as well as north to Ankara, İstanbul and Konya. Most of the buses, however, start their journeys elsewhere, so make sure you book your departure seat well in advance.

Car rental There are numerous operators in Alanya; try several places and bargain hard as prices are higher than Antalya. Main agencies include Avis, just off the western end of Damlataş (ⓣ 0242/513 3513), and Europcar, Hasan Akcalioglu Cad 34 (ⓣ 0242/513 1929). Cheaper is Force Rental, Damlataş Cad 68/A (ⓣ 0242/511 4243).

Hospital The State Hospital (Devlet Hastane) is on the bypass, east of the centre.

Internet Casper Internet Café, behind the Yeni Cami on the waterfront.

Post office The PTT, Atatürk Cad, opposite Kültür Cad (daily 24 hours), sells phonecards. There are also PTT caravans scattered about the town during the summer.

Shopping Touristy silverware and carpets are on sale in İskele Cad, and there are yet more shops on the side streets between Gazipaşa and Hükümet cads. Fake designer-label clothes are ubiquitous, and if you are looking to add to your collection of soccer replica shirts, Alanya is the place to do it.

Tours and travel agents FAM Tour, Damlataş Cad 21 (ⓣ 0242/5120539, ⓦ www.famtours.com), and Classical Tourism, Atatürk Cad 65/5 (ⓣ 0242 511 1100), offer trips to Cappadocia, Pamukkale or the Pamphylian cities (from €25), as well as jeep safaris and boat tours; often they'll pick you up at your hotel.

Around Alanya

Alanya's tourist office distinguishes itself by its dearth of information about sites in the region, and even archeological sites are not signposted from the road, so haphazard is tourism development here. Private tour operators are helping to fill the gap, with trips to Alanya's nearby mountain villages and to the Dimçay River, but otherwise you'll need a good map and a car to get the most out of the town's surroundings.

The Dimçay River and the Dim Mağrası

The **Dimçay River**, 6km from the centre of Alanya, has become horribly disfigured by development along its lower reaches, and upward of thirty trout restaurants litter its banks higher up. You can reach the river area by dolmuş (take an hourly "Dimçay" or "Banana" dolmuş out of town from along Keykubut Caddesi to the bridge signposted "Dimçay"), but there are far more beautiful and peaceful valleys in the Toros mountains.

A more rewarding day out from Alanya is the **Dim Mağrası** (daily summer 9am–7.30pm, winter 9am–5.30pm; 8TL), a spectacular cavern set in the mountains high above the river, 11km from the town centre. A 360m-long walkway has been built through the well-lit cavern, with a series of limestone formations providing interest en route to the prime attraction, a lovely crystal-clear pool. There's a small café-cum-restaurant at the entrance, with great views over the heavily wooded mountains.

The cavern is served by the "Kestel" dolmuş from Alanya, which departs (and returns) hourly in season. With your own transport, continue past the Dimçay bridge for a few hundred metres, do a U-turn through a gap in the central reservation, head back to the bridge and take the right turn just before it. Follow this road for 3km before turning right and following a track for a further 5km through increasingly attractive scenery.

Alanya to Adana

The region between Alanya and Adana formed ancient **Cilicia**, and was settled by refugees from Troy at the same time as Pamphylia further west. Its remoteness meant that it was never as developed and its rugged, densely wooded coastline was a haven for pirates. This eventually spurred the Romans into absorbing Cilicia into the empire in the first century BC. Today, it retains a wild appearance, and travel through it involves some frighteningly daring drives along winding mountain roads that hug the craggy coastline. All this is to the good if you're trying to escape the crowds further west, since far fewer people make it along here.

There are some decent stretches of beach around **Anamur**, overlooked by an Armenian castle and a partially excavated Greek site, while in the mountains above **Silifke** – the next major town – the abandoned city of **Uzuncaburç** is perhaps the most extensive of the region's ancient remains. After **Kızkalesi**, where two huge castles break up the shoreline, there are more good beaches and weird ruins, running through flatter land into the outskirts of **Mersin**. This marks the end of the area's real touristic interest, with ferries to Northern Cyprus but nothing else to stop for. Similarly, **Tarsus**, a little further on, has little to betray its former historical importance; while **Adana**, Turkey's fourth largest city, contains few remains of any era despite a venerable history, but does have excellent market shopping.

Alanya to Silifke

Heading east from Alanya, the road starts to cut through the mountains, traversing occasional valleys planted with bananas but rarely losing sight of the sea. On the way, you'll pass little wayside restaurants, sheltered but difficult to reach sandy bays, and the odd camping ground.

To make the most of this stretch of coastline you really need your own transport, as only the beaches around the tiny resort of **İskele** (Anamur) merit a longer stay, and the few sights are difficult to reach by public transport. **Taşucu**, near to Silifke, is the best place to cross to Northern Cyprus.

Iotape and Antioch Ad Cragum

The first place of interest after leaving Alanya's hotel sprawl behind is **Iotape**, around 45km away. Oddly situated on a rocky promontory between the road and the sea, this ancient site was named after the wife of the Commagenian king Antiochus IV (38–72 AD), and struck its own coins from the reign of Emperor Trajan until that of Emperor Valerian.

The ruins are mainly very tumbledown apart from a fairly impressive triple-arched bath-house, which can be clearly seen from the road. Closer inspection uncovers drainage and heating systems. The acropolis is on the promontory out to sea and a colonnaded street runs east–west along the valley linking the promontory to the mainland. Also visible from the road are statue bases giving information about successful athletes and philanthropists of the city, and there are frescoes to be seen inside the niches of a small, single-aisled church. The **beach** below Iotape is idyllic: if you're lucky you might get it to yourself.

Around 30km further east, near the village of Guneykoy, a sign points south off the main road to the site of **Antioch Ad Cragum** (always open; free), 5km along a road that, for its last 2km, is unsurfaced and very steep and narrow – be warned. The setting of this remote site, founded by the Seleucid king Antiochus IV, is stupendous, perched on a rocky promontory jutting out into a deep-blue sea, edged in white where the waves crash onto the rocks. There's not a lot to be seen in the way of remains, but when you are here you can understand how the Cilician pirates held out against the might of Rome for so long.

Anamur, İskele and around

There's little of interest in **ANAMUR**, but its small harbour suburb, **İSKELE** (*İskele* means quay), 4km away, is slowly developing as a fully fledged, but unpretentious resort, packed in summer with holidaying Turks. It's reached via an unmarked road south from Anamur's *otogar*, which is at the junction of the main street and the coast road. Dolmuşes and city buses run from here to İskele from 7am until midnight in season, until 8pm in winter. Otherwise you can take a taxi from the *otogar* for around 10TL. İskele's small **museum** (Tues–Sun 8am–noon & 1.30–5pm; 2TL), just west of the town centre, contains some fine *Yörük* kilims and saddlebags, and finds from nearby classical sites, best of which is a Hellenistic-era cylindrical pottery burial-cask.

If you arrive in the early hours at Anamur *otogar* and are stranded in the centre, the *Dedehan Hotel* (☎0324/814 7522; ❶), just 50m away, is an undeniably cheap option, though not particularly clean or inviting. You are better off booking accommodation in advance and arrange for a pick-up with a pension in İskele. By far the best budget choice is the ✻ *Eser Pansiyon*, a block back from the sea (☎0324/816 4751, ⓦwww.eserpansiyon.com; ❷), which offers clean air-conditioned rooms, either en suite or shared bathroom, a vine-shaded rooftop restaurant, communal kitchen and bbq and free wi-fi. The owner and his son, Tayfun, both speak very good English and can help arrange visits to nearby Anemurium and Mamure Kalesi (for both see below), or even a jaunt into the mountains. Tayfun also runs the great-value *Bella Hotel* (☎0536/217 9878, ⓦwww.mybellahotel.com; ❷) just down the road, where the simply decorated but quality rooms all have balconies and TVs. To the west, on the seafront, the *Yan Hotel* (☎0324 8142123; ⓦwww.yanhotel.com; ❸) is built around an atrium, with dark but comfortable rooms and a roof terrace with wonderful sea views; breakfast and dinner are included in the price. The *Ünlüselek* (☎0324/814 1973, ⓦwww.hotelunluselek.com; ❸), 1.5km west of İskele, has large air-conditioned rooms with balconies and wi-fi, its own stretch of beach and a seaside restaurant.

İskele has several simple **restaurants**, all of which seem incredibly cheap after the overpricing so prevalent further west. The *Kap Anamur*, west of the main square, has a good reputation for fish, from 12TL a serving, and *mezes* are great value at 3TL. The interior is a vibrant blue and white, with funky "naïve"-style fish tiles. The *Elele*, right on the beach, dishes up *gözleme* and *mantı* at low prices. It's best at night when tables are laid out on the sand right to the water's edge.

Anemurium

Six kilometres southwest of modern Anamur, but without a local dolmuş service, is the ancient settlement of **Anemurium** (April–Oct Tues–Sun 9am–7pm & Nov–March 8.30am–5pm; 3TL), on the eastern side of a headland formed where the Toros mountains jut out into the sea. An access road leads down to the site from the main road (look out for the yellow sign). Anemurium was at its peak during the third century AD, and most of what remains dates from this period. As you approach you'll see two parallel **aqueducts** running north to south along the hillside to the right. Below these, a sun-baked **necropolis** contains numerous freestanding tombs whose cool interiors harbour murals of mythological scenes on the walls; however, the most notable tombs have been barred off with locked gates. To the right of the road are the hollow ruins of three **Byzantine churches**, set starkly against the blue backdrop of the Mediterranean.

Further down towards the beach you'll see the crumbling remains of a **bath complex** and a desolate **palaestra** or parade ground. Southwest of here is a ruined but still identifiable **theatre** set into the hillside of the headland. Above the theatre on the slope, between the lower and upper aqueducts, are the remains of a number of houses, some of which have intact vaulted roofs; and east of here is the shell of a building containing sixteen curved rows of seating and a mosaic floor, thought to have been either a **council chamber** or **concert hall** (possibly both). Returning towards the theatre and heading south, you'll come across another **baths complex**, a two-storey vaulted structure with discernible traces of decoration and tile-work on the interior walls.

With time, you might want to clamber up the scrubby slopes of the headland to what was once Anemurium's **acropolis**. There isn't a lot to see here, but the promontory is **Turkey's southernmost point**, and on a clear day gives views of the mountains of Cyprus, 80km to the south.

Mamure Kalesi

In the opposite direction from Anamur, a couple of kilometres east of İskele, is **Mamure Kalesi** (daily April–Oct 9am–7pm & Nov–March 8.30am–5pm; 3TL), a forbidding castle built by the rulers of the Cilician kingdom of Armenia on the site of a Byzantine fort. It was later occupied by Crusaders, who had established a short-lived kingdom in Cyprus and used Mamure Kalesi as a kind of bridgehead in Asia. Used by successive rulers of the area to protect the coastal strip, it was most recently garrisoned by the Ottomans, who reinforced it after the British occupied Cyprus in 1878, maintaining a strong presence here during World War I. Constructed directly above the sea, its stark facade of crenellated outer walls and watchtowers are certainly impressive. The interior, of languorously decaying buildings, has formed a backdrop to many Turkish films.

From İskele it is possible to walk the 2.5km along the seashore to the castle, though this requires being ferried across the Dragon River by boat for around 4TL. Alternatively, take a dolmuş from İskele to the BP garage on the main road, then another east along the coastal highway to the castle.

Opposite the castle are a couple of small fish **restaurants** and a few noisy pensions, while a couple of kilometres east there's a good forested **campsite**, the *Pullu-Mocamp*, which has a beach and an excellent restaurant.

Taşucu

Moving on, there are a couple of quiet bays with sandy beaches, but most people push straight on to the scruffy port of **TAŞUCU**, from where there are frequent ferry and hydrofoil services to Cyprus. Crossing the next day is the only reason you would choose to stay the night here, though the **Amphora Museum** (daily 9am–5.30pm; 2TL), set in a restored *han* behind the quay, has a fascinating collection of amphorae of Hellenistic, Roman and Byzantine origin, mostly from locally salvaged wrecks. Of **accommodation** options, on the east of town near the harbour, try the *Tuğran Pension* (☎0324/741 4493, ⓦwww.tugranpansiyon .com; ❷), a single-storey building in a garden set back from the beach. Just down from the *Tuğran*, the German-Turkish-run *Holmi Pansiyon* (☎0324/741 5378, ⓦwww.holmipansiyon.com; ❷) has spotless and cheerful rooms with fans, large en suites, and a pleasant breakfast area. Best in town is the *Lades Motel*, Inonu

Cad 45 (℡0324/7414008, Ⓦwww.ladesmotel.com; ❹), west of the centre. Painted in cooling blues and whites, it is heavily booked with birdwatchers in spring and autumn. A retro-style bar houses a collection of 1960s-vintage German-made roulette machines, and it has a swimming pool and fine sea view.

There are several **restaurants** backing the port area. Best is the *Baba*, on Atatürk Caddesi, next to the *Lades*, which offers a good range of *meze*, grilled meats and fish at competitive prices (a meal with beer for around 15TL).

Ferries and hydrofoils to Cyprus

The cheapest way to the Turkish Republic of North Cyprus (TRNC) is by ferry (Sun–Thurs at midnight; 5hr; 60TL one way, from 150TL for a car) to Girne/ Kyrenia, though as these are packed with heavy lorries and their drivers, women travellers may feel uncomfortable. A more pleasant alternative (assuming the sea is calm) is to take the hydrofoil (*denizotobüsü*; daily at 11.30am daily; 2hr; 69TL one way). **Tickets** for both services are available from Fergün (℡0324/741 2323, Ⓦwww.Fergün.net.) and Akgungler (℡0324/741 4033, Ⓦwww.akgunler.com .tr), on the waterfront. At present, EU, US, Canadian and Australian citizens require only a valid passport, on which your Turkish entry visa has not expired, for entry into the TRNC. It's not possible to enter southern (Greek-speaking) Cyprus from the TRNC.

Silifke and around

About 10km east of Taşucu, **SILIFKE** was once ancient Seleucia, founded by Seleucus, one of Alexander the Great's generals, in the third century BC. Nowadays, it's a quiet, fairly undistinguished town. Only the occasional tourist, en route to the ruins at Uzuncaburç, passes through.

Silifke Kalesi, a Byzantine castle, dominates the local skyline though it looks a lot less spectacular close up. It's about a twenty-minute walk southwest of town and at the top there's a café and a great view. On the way up you'll pass an old

Wildlife in the Göksu delta

The **Göksu delta** and its **Kuşcenneti bird reservation** are of outstanding environmental importance, boasting a tremendous variety of flora and fauna. The best place to start an exploration of the area is Akgöl, the westerly lagoon, where pygmy cormorants, Dalmatian pelicans, marbled and white-headed ducks and even the practically extinct black francolin and purple gallinule feed. The sand spit is a nesting ground for loggerhead and green turtles as well as a home to sea daffodils and Audouin's gulls. East of this, reached by an access road halfway between Taşucu and Silifke, are extensive ditches where you'll see kingfishers (including the rare chestnut brown and white Smyrna variety), coots, wagtails, spoonbills, egrets and grey, purple and squacco herons. Still further east, the huge natural fishpond of Paradeniz lagoon and the flats beyond it harbour waders, ospreys and terns. **Nesting and migration seasons** are in the spring (with a peak between late March and early April), and in October. Information leaflets on the delta are available from the Özel Çevre Koruma Kurumu (Special Environmental Areas Protection Agency; ℡0324/714 9508), 5km west of Silifke, near the church of Aya Tekla, in the grounds of the DSİ waterworks complex; if you contact them in advance you can also arrange an English-speaking guide for group trips. If you want to go independently, you'll need your own car or a taxi.

cistern – the so-called *tekir ambarı* or "striped depot" – which kept Byzantine Silifke supplied with water. Other sights include the second-century AD **Jupiter Tapınağı** (Temple of Jupiter) on İnönü Caddesi, which comprises little more than a pile of stones and one standing pillar with a stork's nest on top. On the main road to Taşucu and Antalya, about half a kilometre from the turn-off to Silifke, there's an **archeological museum** (Arkeoloji Müzesi; Tues–Sun 8am–noon & 1–5pm; 3TL) containing the finds from excavations at Meydancıkale, a fourth-century BC temple site in the mountains above the coast. Relics include two enormous caryatids; huge, shapeless stone blocks with human-looking feet carved into the bases; and a hoard of 5200 silver coins dating from the reigns of Alexander and his generals in Egypt, Syria and the province of Pergamon.

Incidentally, it was near Silifke that **Frederick Barbarossa**, the Holy Roman Emperor, met his end: he drowned while fording the Calycadnus (now Göksu) River about 9km north of town, en route to Palestine with the Third Crusade; today a plaque marks the spot. Otherwise, heading 4km west of Silifke and then 1km north takes you to Meyemlik and the early Christian site of **Aya Tekla** (open daily, assuming the warden is around; 3TL). There's little to see except the underground chapel (bring a torch) used by the early Christians, including Tecla, the first female Christian teacher.

Practicalities

The centre of town is Menderes Caddesi, around fifteen minutes' walk from the **otogar** along İnönü Caddesi. Silifke's helpful **tourist office** is at Veli Gürten Bozbey Cad 6 (Mon–Fri 8am–noon & 1.30–5pm; ☎0324/714 1151), reached by way of the Roman bridge spanning the Göksu River.

Hotel possibilities are limited. The *Arısan Pansiyon* on İnönü Caddesi (☎0324/714 3331; ❶) is not far from the *otogar*. Its rooms are bright and come with a fan, though some smell quite smokey; you pay 5TL more for an en-suite bathroom. Best-positioned hotel in town is the *Göksu Hotel*, Atatürk Cad 16 (☎0324/712 1021, ✉goksuotel@windowslive.com; ❸), on the north riverbank, with large, well-furnished rooms with air conditioning and TV, and wonderful views over the river, bridge and castle. The two-star *Otel Ayatekla*, opposite the *otogar* (☎0324/715 1081; ❸), is comparable to the *Göksu*, with an excellent restaurant and bar.

There are lots of basic places to **eat and drink**, but most close after dark, leaving you with only a few options for an evening meal. The *Göksu Hotel* serves excellent food and beer in its waterside garden, though you'll need to book in advance, as they cook to order. The *Gözde Lokantası*, on a quiet alley off Menderes Caddesi, a couple of hundred metres from the river, has decent *sulu yemek* and grills for around 7–10TL for a full meal. For a dessert, cross the river and head for the popular *Özkaymak Pastanesi*, just down from the *Göksu Hotel* on Atatürk Caddesi. The *şübiyet*, a kind of *baklava* with cream, is particularly good; it also does a range of savouries, including decent burgers.

Inland: Uzuncaburç and Alahan

Dolmuşes bound for the ancient city of **Uzuncaburç** leave from 50m west of the tourist office every two hours from 9am to 7pm weekdays (last departure back at 5pm), but there are just 3 departures weekends (though the last one back departs at 2pm); the ride costs 5TL each way. The 30km ride to Uzuncaburç is spectacular, taking you through a jagged gorge and a couple of villages that time seems to have forgotten. Beyond Uzuncaburç, with your own vehicle, it's possible to loop back to the main highway to Konya, calling in at the Byzantine site of **Alahan** en route.

Uzuncaburç

From Demırcılı, the road continues uphill and then turns off to the right towards the ruins at **Uzuncaburç**, originally a Hittite settlement that was known to the Greeks as Olba and to the Romans as Diocaesarea. A small, rural village has grown up in haphazard fashion around the ruins, but few concessions have been made to tourism. Uzuncaburç is famous for leather bags and handmade rugs known as *çul*; examples are often sold at makeshift stalls. Local culinary specialities include *kenger kahvesi* (coffee made from acanthus) and *pekmez* (grape molasses).

The ruins

The main **site of Uzuncaburç** (always open; 2TL when the site guardian is around) lacks the size and scale of Perge and Aspendos, but is atmospheric enough in its own way, if only because of its relatively neglected state. Although the area was first settled by the Hittites, they left little behind and the most impressive ruins that survive date from Hellenistic times.

Start your explorations at the overgrown Roman **theatre**, overlooked by a couple of beautiful houses whose walls are chock-a-block with Classical masonry. From here, pass through an enormous five-columned **monumental gateway**, beyond which is a colonnaded street, once the city's main thoroughfare: keep your eyes open for what look like small stone shelves on the columns, which once supported statues and busts. On the northern side of the street is a **nymphaeum**, now dried up, which once formed part of the city's water-supply system. This was part of a large network of pipes and tunnels, built by the Romans nearly two thousand years ago, that still supplies water to the modern village and others around.

To the south, the columns of the **Temple of Zeus Olbios** feature one of the earliest examples of the Corinthian order, erected during the third century BC by Seleucus I, of which only the fluted columns now remain intact. Look out for the fine sarcophagus carved with three Medusa heads and a sarcophagus lid depicting three reclining figures. At the western end of the colonnaded street is the **Temple of Tyche**, dedicated to the goddess of fortune, reckoned to date from the second half of the first century AD. Five Egyptian granite columns still stand, joined by an architrave bearing an inscription stating that the temple was the gift of a certain Oppius and his wife Kyria. From here a right turn leads to a large three-arched **city gate**, which, according to an inscription, dates from the fifth century AD and is home to nesting birds.

To the north of the main ruins (turn right at the Ak Parti office) is a 22-metre-high, five-storey Hellenistic **tower** that once formed part of the city wall and which today gives its name to the modern town (*Uzuncaburç* means "high tower"). It is believed that in addition to playing a defensive role this tower was also part of an ancient signalling network, whereby messages were relayed by flashing sunlight off polished shields.

Just outside the modern village, past the Atatürk statue (heed the signs for the "Antik Mezarlar" and follow the curve to the right), is a **necropolis** set among orchards used by Greek, Roman and Byzantine inhabitants of the area. It has three basic types of resting place: sarcophagi, graves carved into the rock and cave-tombs housing whole families or funeral clubs. Most of these are clearly visible, and it's even possible to enter some of the cave-tombs, though they have long since been cleaned out by grave robbers.

Alahan: the road to Konya

Some 110km northwest of Silifke, and reached by a spectacular road cutting through the Toros mountains en route for Konya, lies **Alahan** (daily 8am–sunset; 2TL), a well-preserved monastic complex in a beautiful mountain setting. The site is well signposted, 2km to the east of the main road (Highway 715). Intact buildings at the site include two late fifth- and sixth-century basilicas, one sporting elaborate relief sculptures of the Evangelists and the two archangels, and a baptistry. Alahan is best reached using your own transport, though the buses plying between the coast and Konya will drop you at the turn. Following your explorations you'll have to chance your luck on flagging down a Karaman/Konya bus.

East from Silifke

East of Silifke the coast road winds above the ocean to Kızkalesi, but a rash of development is rapidly despoiling this stretch of coastline. There are some interesting sites, particularly the Roman baths at **Narlıkuyu** and the caves of **Cehennem** and **Cennet**, but you need your own transport to make the most of them. Anyone with a special interest in exploring more ruins off the beaten track should buy Celal Taşkiran's *Silifke and Environs*, an exhaustive guide to all the sites between Anamur and Mersin, best bought at Silifke's tourist office for €10.

Narlıkuyu

Some 20km from Silifke, **NARLİKUYU** lies on the fringes of a rapidly developing bay with several restaurants. There's a small car park in the centre of the village, next to which are the remains of a Roman bath-house, known after its founder as the **Bath of Poimenius**. The museum on the town square (Tues–Sun 9am–noon & 1.30–5pm; 2TL) houses a dusty mosaic depiction of the well-rounded nude forms of the Three Graces, the daughters of Zeus and companions of the Muses. Poimenius' bath was fed from the limestone caves above by an ancient Roman spring that supplied a celebrated fountain, the waters of which were supposed to confer wisdom on those who drank from them.

Cennet ve Cehennem

From Narlıkuyu, a narrow paved road winds 3km northwards into the hills through groves of olive trees to **Cennet ve Cehennem**, or the "Caves of Heaven and Hell" (open in daylight hours; 3TL) – some of the most impressive of the many limestone caverns scattered along this coast.

The site consists of a series of three caves, the largest and most impressive of which is **Cennet Deresi** (Cave of Heaven), a seventy-metre-deep gorge entered via 452 steps cut into the rock. On reaching the bottom, head south towards the entrance to the **Tayfun Mağrası** (Cave of Typhon), reputed to be one of the gateways to Hades. Typhon, was an immense hundred-headed fire-breathing lizard, the father of Cerberus – the three-headed dog who guarded the entrance to Hades. At the entrance to the cave is the **chapel of the Virgin Mary**, a well-preserved Byzantine church built over the former temple of Zeus and still containing a few frescoes.

About 100m to the north of "Heaven", the **Cehennem Deresi** (Cave of Hell) is impossible to enter, as its sides are practically vertical. About 500m west of "Heaven" is a fourth cave, the **Dilek Mağarası** (Wishing Cave), the opening of which has been specially widened and a spiral staircase provided for ease of access. Down below, solid pathways connect a number of subterranean halls, with a total length of about 200m. The main chamber is filled with stalactites and stalagmites, and the air down below is supposed to be beneficial for asthma sufferers.

Kızkalesi and around

A few kilometres east of Narlıkuyu, and about halfway between Silifke and Mersin, **KIZKALESİ** ("Maiden's Castle") is the longest established resort along this stretch of coastline. It has scores of hotels, *pansiyon*s and restaurants, and the fine sandy beach slopes gently into the sea, making it ideal for kids (camels provide an alternative to donkey rides). The more active can parasail and jet-ski from the pier in front of the *Albatros Restaurant Café Bar*.

Known as Corycus in ancient times, Kızkalesi changed hands frequently until the arrival of the **Romans** in 72 BC, after which it prospered, becoming one of the most important ports along the coast. Roman-period relics still survive in the area, notably a series of mysterious rock reliefs north of town and the carvings at the chasm at Kanlıdivane to the east. Kızkalesi continued to thrive during the Byzantine era despite occasional Arab attacks – against which the town's defences were strengthened with two **castles** constructed during the twelfth and thirteenth centuries – before falling to the Ottomans in 1482.

The Town

The town's most compelling feature is the thirteenth-century **sea castle**, the *Kızkalesi* or Maiden's Castle (daily dawn–dusk), on an island lying about 300m offshore. The story (examples of which are found all over Turkey) goes that one of the Armenian kings who ruled the region in medieval times had a beautiful daughter. After it was prophesied that she would die as the result of a poisonous snakebite, the king had the castle built and moved the girl out to it, imagining that she would be safe there. One day one of the king's advisers sent a basket of fruit out to the island for her, out of which slid a snake that killed the girl. According to local stories, the snake still lives on the island, and the only people who venture out to it are tourists, for whose benefit boat services operate (7.5TL return trip) from the western end of the beachfront. The unadorned walls and sturdy towers still stand, but apart from masonry fragments and weeds there's little to see within.

Opposite the sea castle, the overgrown ruins of the mighty **land castle** (Korkyos Kalesi) at the eastern end of the beach (daily April–Oct 9am–7pm & Nov–March 8.30am–5pm; 3TL) are easily explored and its battlements make a good venue for some sunset-watching. The main gate, constructed from ancient stones, bears various Greek inscriptions. The western gate was originally a Roman structure, built during the third century AD and later incorporated into the castle.

Immediately northeast of the town, across the main road from the land castle, is a **necropolis**, dating from the fourth century AD and containing hundreds of tombs and sarcophagi, some of them beautifully carved. Many of the epitaphs give the jobs of the occupants – weavers, cobblers, goldsmiths, vintners, olive-oil manufacturers, shipowners and midwives, who all had their last resting places here. Also scattered around this area are the remains of a number of Byzantine churches and cisterns. Explore these out of town areas at your own risk, as they are scattered throughout overgrown fields and farmers' plots.

Practicalities

Buses plying the coastal road to and from Mersin will drop you on the main road in the town centre. Nearly all the **accommodation** is found between the main road and the beach to the south. It is possible to find somewhere to stay here, even in the very crowded months of July and August, while out of season you'll be able to negotiate a substantial discount. It's worth noting that all the hotels may be subject to thudding music coming from beachfront bars.

Running from east to west along the beachfront, furthest east is the German package-oriented *Hotel Peyda* (℡0324/523 2607, Ⓦwww.hotel-peyda.com; ❺), with clean, spacious air-conditioned rooms and breakfast tables set out on the path running parallel to the beach. Next one along, the *Hantur* (℡0324/523 2367, Ⓦwww.hotelhantur.com; ❹), stands on its own right on the beach, less noisy than many of its neighbours and with great views across to Maiden's Castle from its spotless, bright-white rooms; guests have use of beach umbrellas and loungers. North of the *Hantur*, set back from the beach, is the *Yaka Hotel* (℡0324/523 2444, Ⓦwww.yakahotel.com.tr; ❹), where the rooms are comfy, well proportioned and have balconies and tea kettles, the garden is delightful, and the helpful owner speaks English, French and German. The westernmost hotel on this strip is the swanky *Club Barbarossa* (℡0324/523 2364, Ⓦwww.barbarrossahotel.com; ❻) lying still further west, its lawn sloping down to the beach and littered with classical capitals. The air-conditioned rooms here have satellite TV, and the price is for half-board accommodation.

There are plenty of places to **eat and drink** and, generally speaking, the further away from the beach they are the better the value. The grills, *mezes* and fast-food places offer better value than those serving seafood. There are also a few beach-front bars and a couple of discos.

Around Kızkalesi

Really only practicable with your own transport, or by taxi, are two nearby sites: the **Adamkayalar rock reliefs**, and the ancient city of **Kanytelis**. A third antique settlement, **Elaiussa Sebaste**, is a 3km walk east along the coastal road or a short minibus ride away. You could see them all in a day away from the beach.

Adamkayalar rock reliefs

A most intriguing side trip from the town is to the series of **rock reliefs** in a valley about 6km to the north (the turning is near the PTT), marked by a sign bearing the legend "Adamkayalar" (Man's Rocks). Follow the path indicated from here for about a kilometre until it starts to dip down into a valley, where steps cut into the rock lead down to a platform from which you can view a series of Roman men, women and children carved into niches in the wall. There are seventeen human figures and a mountain goat. Unfortunately, extensive damage has been caused to one of the figures by treasure hunters who used dynamite in the hope of finding booty supposedly secreted inside the statue. It's not clear who the figures are, or why they might have been constructed, and the fragmentary inscriptions below most of them offer few clues.

Elaiussa Sebaste

East of Kızkalesi, on both sides of the road, various ancient ruins stretch as far as the village of **Ayaş**, 3km away. This was the site of the settlement of **Elaiussa Sebaste** (ruins north of coastal road always open, those to the south currently closed for excavation), which in the time of Augustus was important enough to coin its own money. Below the village is a theatre, and below that baths, a city gate and a nymphaeum. An aqueduct leads to an underground cistern near the baths, although villagers are still ploughing on top of this area. Above the site is a prominent house-tomb in remarkably good condition, dedicated by a mother to her husband and two sons. On the south side of the road is a Byzantine church, almost on the beach, while scattered around the area are numerous tombs, many of them richly decorated with reliefs. You can bathe by the southernmost ruins in the cove set around a sandy beach.

Kanytelis

About 7km east of Kızkalesi, a signposted turn-off leads 3km north to the village of **Kanlıdıvane**, literally "place of blood". This, the site of the ancient city of **Kanytelis**, is where locals used to believe condemned criminals were executed by being thrown into a huge chasm and devoured by wild animals. A car park and ticket-seller's hut mark the entrance to the **chasm** (daily 8am–1 hour before sunset; 3TL), which is certainly large and frightening enough to have given rise to the legends – at 90m long by 70m wide and 60m deep, it forms the core of the ancient city. Visitors descend into it by way of an eroded staircase. On the sides of the chasm there are a number of carvings in niches, one a portrait of a family of six and one of a Roman soldier. On its southwestern edge near the car park, a 17m Hellenistic tower bears an inscription on the southwestern corner next to a three-pronged triskele, a symbol that links the region to the nearby state of Olba. Near the tower are a number of large Byzantine basilicas in various states of collapse, of which the best preserved is the Papylas church. There's another big cluster of tombs northeast of the chasm, with numerous ancient sarcophagi and a few modern graves.

Mersin

The largest Mediterranean port in Turkey, with a population of 1.5 million, **MERSIN** is the first of the three large cities that gird the Ceyhan delta. It's a modern harbour city that – aside from its regular ferry connections to Cyprus – is almost entirely without interest, despite being inhabited since Hittite times. Until the beginning of the twentieth century the settlement was little more than a squalid fishing hamlet. However, over the last century rapid growth and industrialization, coupled with Mersin's role as an international free-trade zone, have turned it into a model, if soulless, example of contemporary Turkish urban planning.

The only real diversion is the local **museum** on Atatürk Caddesi (Tues–Sun 8am–noon & 1–5pm; 3TL). Housing a small but well-presented collection of local archeological finds from Neolithic times to the Byzantine era, especially notable are some Roman clay sarcophagi, some with lift-off, and others with sliding, lids. Adjacent to the museum is a substantial **Greek Orthodox church**, in a walled compound which is also home to a family of caretakers who, if not too busy, will show you the interior.

Practicalities

The city's **otogar** is just northeast of the centre, just off Gazi Mustafa Kemal Bulvarı. A few hundred metres southwest, the **train station** (services to and from Adana) is very central and convenient for the listed hotels. The **tourist office** is by the harbour just off İsmet İnönü Bulvarı (Mon–Fri 9am–5pm; ☏0324/238 3271). **Car rental** companies include Hertz, at Adnan Menderes Bulvarı, in the *Hilton Hotel* (☏0322/458 5062).

As an important port, Mersin has plenty of **accommodation**, but all of it is aimed at business travellers. Most of the hotels are on İstiklâl and Soğuksu caddesis, which run parallel to the seafront. Mid-range possibilities include the *Mersin Hotel*, in the centre of town on Gümrük Meydanı (℡0324/238 1040, Ⓦwww.mersinoteli.com.tr; ❸). Swisher, and only marginally dearer, is the *Nobel Oteli*, İstiklâl Cad 73 (℡0324/237 7700, Ⓦwww.nobelotel.com; ❹), where the foreign-language channels on the satellite TV may attract you more than the ballroom.

There are plenty of places to **eat** in Mersin. One of the best, opposite the *Nobel Oteli* on İstiklâl Caddesi, is the *Hacıbaba Et Lokantası* – clean, cheerful, with excellent service – dishing up normal grills from 5TL and southeastern Turkish specialities such as *kuburga* (lamb ribs). Another fine choice is the *Konak*, in a converted mansion building on Silifke Caddesi on the edge of the **Balık Pazarı** (fish market). There's a *şatk köşesi* laid out with cushions and low tables in one room, and all types of grills. The *lahmacun* are large rounds, hotly spiced with red pepper.

Ferries to Cyprus

Ferries depart from Mersin to Mağosa (Famagusta) in Northern Cyprus on Mondays, Wednesdays and Fridays at 8pm. You can also buy tickets in Mersin for the **Taşucu–Girne ferry and hydrofoil** (see p.410) – a much faster crossing. Buy tickets from Fergün on İsmet İnönü Bulvarı, Guvec Is Merkez (℡0324/238 2881, Ⓦwww.fergun.net). In Mersin, the **TRNC consulate** is at Atatürk Cad 71/3 (℡0324/237 2482).

Tarsus

About 30km east of Mersin, across the factory-dotted cotton fields of the Çukurova, lies **TARSUS**, birthplace of St Paul and the city where Cleopatra met Mark Antony and turned him into a "strumpet's fool". St Paul was born as Saul in Tarsus about 46 years after the meeting between Cleopatra and Antony. He returned after his conversion on the road to Damascus, fleeing persecution in Palestine. He seems to have been proud of his roots and is described as having told the Roman commandant of Jerusalem: "I am a Jew, a Tarsian from Cilicia, a citizen of no mean city." Nowadays, however, only a few reminders of the town's illustrious past remain, located nearby to the Kancık Kapısı.

Near the main bus drop-off point, the **Kancık Kapısı** ("the gate of the bitch") is a Roman construction, also known as Cleopatra's Gate. Although it doesn't actually have any known connection with the Egyptian queen, she is thought to have come ashore for her first meeting with Mark Antony somewhere in the vicinity (at that time Tarsus was linked to the sea by a lagoon which has since silted up).

From Cleopatra's Gate, go south to a roundabout flowing with fountains and turn right; a hundred metres west, the **Cultural Centre** (Kültür Merkezi) houses **Tarsus museum** (Tues–Sat 9am–5pm; 3TL), with an unexplained mummified lower arm of a woman and the odd case of jewellery. On Adana Caddesi nearby, the **Antik Şehir** or "old city" has been exposed by excavations. A good section of black-basalt main street and associated stoas and temples lie well beneath present-day ground level.

Make your way through the backstreets to **St Paul's well**; you'll have to ask for "Sen Pol Kuyusu". It may be something of a disappointment, since it's just a borehole in the ground covered by a removable lid. However, as it's said to be on the site of St Paul's house, the steady stream of visitors gladly pay 2TL for a sip of water from a bucket hauled up from the depths. North of the well, past the Hükümet Konağı (law courts), is a large mosque and local landmark known as **Makam Cami**. Opposite is the **Eski Cami**, a mosque that started life as a church, and, next door, the Roman baths.

Practicalities

Tarsus's **otogar** is 2km east of town, but minibuses to and from Mersin and Adana stop near Cleopatra's Gate, right in the town centre. **Accommodation** possibilities are limited, with the best budget option the *Cihan Palas Oteli* (☎0324/624 1623; ❷), 400m to the south, almost opposite the *otogar*; it has been decorated and modernized, and the air-conditioned rooms have fridges. Out of town, the monstrous *Tarsus Mersin Oteli* (☎0324/614 0600, ✉selaleotel@hotmail .com; ❼) overlooks the Şelale waterfall just north of town. It has its own pool and large air-conditioned rooms, and is often virtually empty, so you may be able to negotiate a substantial discount. While visiting Tarsus, refuel on Antep *baklava* at *Develiler* at Atatürk Cad 2 near the Antik Şehir site.

Adana

Forty kilometres east of Tarsus sprawls **ADANA**, Turkey's fifth largest city with over 1.5 million inhabitants – a modern place, which has grown rapidly since the 1990s. Today, as in the past, Adana owes much of its wealth to the surrounding fertile countryside of the Çukurova, with a textiles industry that has grown up on the back of the local cotton fields. It is also an important centre for the trade in gold.

Despite its contemporary, metropolitan feel, Adana has historical roots going back to 1000 BC. The arrival of the Greeks precipitated an on-off power struggle between them and the powerful Persian Empire to the east that was to last for a thousand years, ending only with the arrival of the Romans during the first century BC. Under the Romans the city became an important trading centre, afterwards passing through various hands before falling to the Ottomans during the sixteenth century. Despite all this, Adana has few sites of real interest, but if you are here between buses (it is an important communication hub) there is sufficient to keep you occupied for a few hours.

Arrival and information

Adana's **otogar** is located about 5km west of town on the E5 (referred to by many sources as Cemal Beriker Bulvarı). Frequent dolmuşes run from here to the town centre, and your bus company will probably lay on a *servis* minibus to and from their office in the centre (see "Listings", p.422). The city's **train station** is at the northern end of Atatürk Caddesi, about twenty minutes' walk north of the town centre, though there are dolmuşes from town. To get into town from the **airport**, 4km from the centre, don't take a cab from outside the door unless you want to pay double; instead, walk another 50m to the street and either catch a dolmuş into the centre or a normal cab. A THY shuttle bus leaves the city-centre THY office an hour and a half before departure, and there is (theoretically) a THY bus awaiting arrivals.

The local **tourist office** is at Atatürk Cad 11, near the roundabout junction with the E5 highway (Mon–Fri 8am–5pm; ☎0322/363 1448).

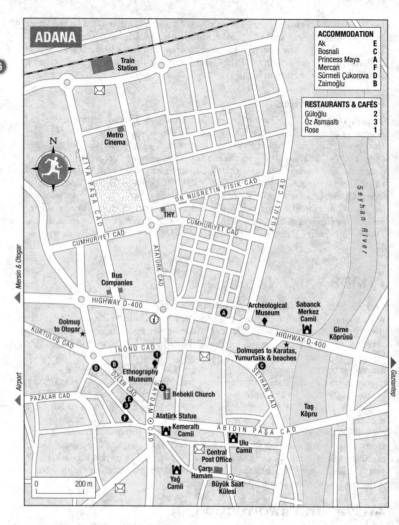

Accommodation

With a few exceptions, Adana's accommodation is uninspiring and tourists are a rare sight in the city's hotels. On and around Saydam and Özler caddesis, you'll find some cheap hotels, with mid-range places on İnönü Caddesi. The best options are listed below.

Ak Özler Cad 19 ☎ 0322/351 4208. Very basic rooms, some waterless, and carpets and curtains of dubious cleanliness, but undeniably cheap. Free wi-fi in the lobby is a perk. ❷

Otel Mercan Melek Girmez Çarşısı ☎ 0322/351 2603, ⊛ www.otelmercan.com. Very central and recently refurbished to an extremely

high standard, soothing decor, a/c and pristine en-suite bathrooms. The owner is very affable, speaks good English (learned while at Manchester University) and can help point you in the right direction for places to eat. Highly recommended. ❸

Princess Maya Cemal Beriker Bul 16 ☎ 0322/459 0966, ⊛ www.princessmayahotel.com. Only two minutes' walk from the museum, recently renovated, with a Neoclassical facade and rooms with all mod cons; rooms at the rear are much quieter. Will bargain out of season. ❹

Hotel Bosnali Seyhan Cad 29 ☎0322/359 8000, ⓦwww.hotelbosnali.com. A boutique hotel on the Seyhan River set in a 110-year-old wooden mansion. Its four-star, traditionally furnished rooms offer views over the river and to the Sabanci mosque nearby. ❼

Sürmeli Çukorova Özler Cad 49 ☎0322/352 3600, ⓦwww.surmeli.com. Comfortable rooms with a/c, TV and nice bathrooms in a modern building. Luxuries include a decent sauna and well-stocked bar. ❻

Zaimoğlu Özler Cad 22 ☎0322/363 5353, ⓦwww.zaimoglu.com.tr. Large, elegant rooms with a/c, TV, wi-fi and minibar. Friendly staff help make it a recommended option. ❺

The City

The city is divided, by the E5 Highway, into the swanky north, with its cinemas and designer malls, and the more traditional bustling south, with the markets, mosques and hotels of the old town. Traffic is uniformly helter-skelter and, as there are no pedestrian bridges or underpasses, you have to negotiate the traffic to reach many of Adana's sights.

Start off with the **Archeological Museum** (Arkeolji Müzesi; Tues–Sun 8am–noon & 1–4.30pm; 5TL) on the north side of the E5 Highway, containing predominantly Hellenistic and Roman statuary, plus some fine sarcophagi and Hittite statues. The **Sabancı Merkez Camii** next door – with a 28,500 capacity and the highest dome in Turkey – is a testament to the continued strength of Islam in the southeast. It was built mainly by subscription, but finished with the aid of the Sabancı family, local boys made good and now the second richest family in Turkey.

One hundred metres southeast, the city's most substantial ancient monument is the **Taş Köprü**, an impressive sixteen-arched Roman bridge built by Hadrian to span the Seyhan river and still carrying heavy traffic. Not far from the bridge in the centre, the **Ulu Cami**, on Abidin Paşa Caddesi, was built in the Syrian style out of white and black marble in 1507, the sole legacy of Halil Bey, Emir of the Ramazanoğlu Turks, who ruled Adana before the Ottoman conquest. Inside the mosque, Halil Bey's tomb has some fine tile-work and beautiful mosaics.

South of Ulu Cami, the large clocktower, **Büyük Saat Kulesi**, is at the edge of a bazaar area, where the sound of metalworking echoes through the air. Nearby, **Çarşı Hamam** (see "Listings" overleaf), with a beautiful doorway, is reputed to date back to the time of Piri, son of Emir Halil Bey. Walking west towards the Atatürk statue, you'll see the **Yağ Cami**, accessed across a courtyard; unusually, one bay of the mosque was a church until it was incorporated into the main structure in 1502. A peculiar square building in the courtyard has an interesting domed roof supported by a line of slabs with Selçuk decoration; its original purpose is unknown. Another old building just off İnönü Caddesi, first a church, then a mosque, now houses the **Ethnography Museum** (Etnografya Müzesi; closed for restoration), full of carpets and weaponry, with a nomad tent and its contents as an added attraction.

Eating and drinking

The local specialty is the spicy *Adana kebap* – minced lamb and pepper wrapped around a skewer and grilled – but frankly, you can eat better ones outside Adana. Pavement **food stalls** selling sandwiches and pastries abound, as do hole-in-the-wall *börek* and kebab places near the bazaar and central PTT. The *Öz Asmaaltı*, on a side street near the *Mercan* hotel, is a basic but clean, friendly kebab-oriented restaurant. The *Güloğlu* on Saydam Caddesi serves up tasty *börek* and *kır pide* at rock-bottom prices. The *Rose* **café**, next to the Ethnographic Museum, is also recommended, with beer and light food served in a friendly, homely atmosphere at reasonable prices.

Listings

Airlines THY, Prof Dr Nuşret Fişik Cad 22 (☎0322/457 0222), for flights to Ankara, İstanbul and İzmir; KTHY, Atatürk Cad 5 (☎0322/363 1224), near the tourist office, has five direct flights to Cyprus per week. For flights to İstanbul Onur Air's office is at the airport (☎0322/436 6766), while Atlas Jet tickets are sold at Adana Turizm at Toros Cad, Cemal Paşa Mah. Özlem apt 13/A, Seyhan (☎0322/458 7612).

Banks and exchange Most banks are located near the tourist office. There are also several *döviz* offices around Saydam and Özler cads.

Buses Most of the major bus-company offices are concentrated on Ziya Paşa Cad, just north of the E5. When you want to leave town, buy a ticket from one of these and a *servis* bus will take you to the *otogar*, from where you can reach virtually every city in the country.

Car rental Avis, Ziyapaşa Bul, Nakipoglu Apt 9/A ☎0322/453 3045; Europcar, at the airport ☎0322/433 2957; and Talay Turizm, Resatpasa Mah Bul 46/B ☎0322/459 6448.

Cinemas Try the Metro, a couple of blocks south of the train station.

Hamams Çarşı Hamam, Büyük Saat Civari (daily: women 9am–3pm, men 4–9.30pm; 8–15TL depending on level of service).

Hospital State Hospital (Adana Devlet Hastane) is on Riza Cad ☎0322/321 5752.

Post office The main PTT office (8.30am–9pm) is on Ulu Cami, the street running parallel to Abdin Paşa Cad, sells phonecards and *jetons*.

Shopping For foodstuffs, clothing and toiletries etc, head for Çetinkaya shopping arcade at the round-about at the western end of İnönü Cad. Also try the huge Galeria Shopping Mall, nearby on Fuzuli Cad.

East of Adana

Heading east from Adana, towards İskenderun and Antakya (referred to as "Hatay" at the *otogar*), the first town you reach, after 20km, is **YAKAPİNAR** (also known as Misis), just south of the main road. This has a small **mosaic museum** (Tues–Sun 8am–noon; 2TL), worth a quick look for its examples of locally unearthed Roman mosaics. Beyond here you'll see an Armenian castle on top of a mountain, 3km to the south of the main road – the **Yılan Kalesi**, or "Snake Castle" (always open; 2TL). If you're travelling with your own car, you can drive up to the top to admire the view of the meandering Ceyhan River.

About 12km further on is **CEYHAN**, which, despite the colourful-looking old houses in the town centre, doesn't rate more than a cursory look. About 40km east of Ceyhan the main road forks. Due east leads to Gaziantep and beyond, while the southern fork heads towards Antakya. The black basalt castle you can see towering above the road junction is **Toprakkale**, much fought over by the Armenians and Crusaders during medieval times, but abandoned since about 1337. You can visit Toprakkale, but be careful – much of it is very unstable and there are numerous concealed rooms and cisterns waiting for unwary people to fall into them.

Karatepe Arslantaş National Park

If you have your own transport you might want to consider a 70km detour to the **Karatepe Arslantaş National Park** (Karatepe Arslantaş Milli Parkı), with its fine neo-Hittite stone-carvings. The route is via Osmaniye on the main highway, where you turn north, crossing the Ceyhan River and passing the columned Hellenistic ruins of Hierapolis Castabala, before following signs up to the green pines and turquoise waters of the park – the **Arslantaş dam** that surrounds

Karatepe's stranded site provides the perfect venue for a picnic or a barbecue. Park your car at the entrance (2TL) and walk up to the gatehouse where you will be sold a ticket (Tues–Sun 8.30am–noon & 2–5.30pm; 3TL) and escorted on a tour of the site. **Karatepe** is thought to have been a frontier castle or summer palace of the ninth-century BC neo-Hittite king Asitawanda. Little of the building complex remains, but the eloquent stone-carvings arranged around the two entrance gates of the former palace are exquisite.

The Hatay

The **Hatay**, which extends like a stumpy finger into Syria, has closer cultural links with the Arab world than with the Turkish hinterland, and its multi-ethnic, multi-faith identity gives it an extra edge of interest. **Antakya** (ancient Antioch), the largest town, is set in the valley of the Asi River separating the Nur and Ziyaret mountain ranges. Its cosmopolitan atmosphere, excellent archeological museum, busy bazaars and great food make it worth a day or two on anyone's itinerary. The Hatay's other main centre is **İskenderun**, a heavily industrialized port that has more to offer than might appear at first sight.

The region only became part of modern Turkey in 1939, having been apportioned to the French Protectorate of Syria following the dismemberment of the Ottoman Empire. Following the brief-lived independent **Hatay Republic** of 1938 it was handed over to Turkey after a plebiscite. This move, calculated to buy Turkish support, or at least neutrality, in the imminent world war, was successful. It was Atatürk, in a move to "Turkify" the region, who dreamt up the name "Hatay", supposedly based on that of a medieval Turkic tribe. The majority of people here speak Arabic as well as Turkish and there's some backing for union with Syria though it for its part seems to have recognized de facto Turkish sovereignty. Relations between the two countries have improved significantly in recent years with new border crossings being opened and a relaxation in visa requirements.

Arab influence in the Hatay goes back to the seventh century AD, when Arab raiders began hacking at the edges of the collapsing Byzantine Empire. Although they were never able to secure long-lasting political control over the region, the Arabs were able to establish themselves as permanent settlers, remaining even when the Hatay passed into Ottoman hands. Prior to the arrival of the Arabs, the area had been held by the Romans and before that the Seleucids, who prized its position straddling trading routes into Syria.

İskenderun and around

İSKENDERUN was founded by Alexander the Great to commemorate his victory over the Persians at the nearby battle of Issus and, as Alexandria ad Issum, it became a major trade nexus during Roman times. Under the Ottomans, İskenderun became the main port for Halab (Aleppo), now in Syria, from where trade routes fanned out to Persia and the Arabian peninsula. The town was known as Alexandretta during the French-mandate era and is now essentially an industrial, military and commercial centre. Although there is little of historical interest left to see in İskenderun, the town centre is visually appealing, with its broad promenade and the magnificent backdrop of the Amanus mountains. A group of churches provides the main focus of a visit, while a trip to the nearby hill-town of Belen is rewarding for birdwatchers, lying as it does on a major migration route.

Arrival and information

Buses to all major towns, including Adana and Mersin, drop you at the *otogar*, a fifteen-minute walk north of the seafront. **Trains** also run daily to Adana and Mersin. The station is 1km east of the town centre, reached by following 5 Temmuz Caddesi and then Bahçeli Sahil Evler Caddesi. Buses to Antakya (en route from other destinations) leave regularly from the *otogar* and there are frequent minibus departures (5TL) from near the junction of Şehit Pamir and Prof Muammer Askoy caddesis, and take an hour.

The helpful local **tourist office**, at Atatürk Bul 49/B near the Adidas shop (Mon–Fri 8.30am–noon & 1–5pm; ☎0326/614 1620), is on the waterfront, a couple of hundred metres west of the junction of Şehit Pamir Caddesi and Atatürk Bulvarı. The manager speaks good English and will furnish you with a reasonable city guide, including a street plan locating the churches and train station.

Accommodation

Most of the town's cheaper **pansiyons and hotels** are centrally located. The best of the inexpensive places is the *Hotel Açıkalan*, Şehit Pamir Cad 13 (☎0326/617 3732; ❷), with clean and airy rooms including some good-value singles. Ask for one of the en-suite rooms to avoid a rather dismal shared bathroom situation. Practically next door at number 11 is the *Altındişler Oteli* (☎0326/617 1011, ⓦwww.iskenderunotel.net; ❸) – slightly more upmarket, with wi-fi and air conditioning in its plain but spacious rooms. Those facing Şehit Pamir Caddesi are particularly noisy. The traditional rooms of the *Hotel Cabir* at Ulu Cami Cad 16 (☎0326/612 3391, ⓦwww.hotelcabir.com; ❸) are rather worn, but the service is good, the atmosphere friendly, and there's an American-style bar and a disco.

The Town

Traces of the town's cosmopolitan Levantine trading past survive amongst the new apartment buildings. The offices of the Catoni shipping line are housed in a crumbling nineteenth-century building just behind the seafront – the upstairs suite once housed the British vice-consulate and, though now abandoned, is still filled with 1930s furniture and a forlorn framed print of a young Queen Elizabeth II. The **Adliye Sarayı** (courtroom) at the junction of Şehit Pamir Caddesi and Atatürk Bulvarı is an imposing French-mandate-era building, neo-Oriental in style but sporting Lyon-made clocks in its twin towers.

İskenderun, like the rest of the Hatay, prides itself on its tolerance, a virtue that can be seen most clearly by visiting the town's churches. Smallest of these is the **Surp Karasun Manuk Ermeni Kilisesi**, situated on a side street off Şehit Pamir Caddesi, more or less opposite the *Açıkalın Hotel*. Built in 1872, but recently restored, this small, plainly decorated church serves an Armenian community of around eighty families. It's usually locked, though the key is held at an Armenian accounting business whose office is reached via a flight of steps to the right of the church – look for the sign *Serbest Musabeci*. A member of the family will be only too pleased to show you around.

Further away from the seafront, on the opposite side of Şehit Pamir Caddesi, is the pastel-coloured Greek Orthodox church of **St Nicholas**, built in 1876, while a little more difficult to find is the older, but smaller, whitewashed **St George's**, opposite the *jandarma* post on Denizciler Caddesi. This is the most atmospheric of the town's churches, with a walled garden of palm and cypress trees, in which gravestones bear inscriptions in Greek, Arabic and even French. Families live in houses adjoining both the Orthodox churches and they are usually willing to let you look around. The largest of İskenderun's churches is Catholic **St Mary's**, a substantial nineteenth-century building behind the tourist office.

Don't leave town without a stroll along the newly renovated seafront park, where kiosks, canals and gardens partially shield the industrial landscape across the bay and provide a lovely atmosphere for a picnic or a stroll.

Eating and drinking

The best **restaurant** is the *Saray*, on Ataturk Bulvarı near the tourist office, with tables set out on the broad pavement. The *mezes* include *cevizli biber* (or *muhammara* in Arabic, a paste of walnuts, chilli peppers and wheat), tender grills for the main course and, of course, cold beer. The *Hasan Baba* at Ulu Cami Cad 43/E has excellent İskender *kebap* (which originates in Bursa, not here), while round the corner towards the *Hotel Açıkalan*, more *lokanta*s – such as the *Şehir* – serve cheap but tasty meals.

Café Körfez on Şehit Pamir Caddesi is good for **breakfasts**, including *menemen* (scrambled omelette with tomatoes). And head to *Kral Antakyalılar Künefe Salonu* Temmus Cad 5 near the Adliye Sarayı for a memorable *künefe* with ice cream for 4TL. The promenade area is home to several *gazino*s where you can enjoy a beer overlooking the sea.

Belen

The road southeast from İskenderun rises up into the mountains, passing through the small hill-town of **BELEN**, 13km away. From here, the road strains and curves through the **Belen pass** (Belen Geçidi) – of great strategic importance during Roman times, when it was known as the *Pylae Syriae* or "Gates of Syria". For a week or two in early October (if the winds are right), Belen becomes the most important **migration route** on the western Palearctic corridor for birds of prey.

About 5km beyond the Belen pass you'll come to a major road junction, from where a right turn leads towards Antakya. After a few kilometres a sign marks the road to **Bakras Kalesi**, an imposing medieval castle about 4km off the main road and a fifteen-minute climb from the village below. The first castle to be built on this site was erected by the Arabs during the seventh century and destroyed during the First Crusade. Later the Knights Templar built a new fortress, which became an important link in their defensive system, and which forms the basis of the impressive remains you see today. It was much fought over, and in 1156 a bloody battle took place here between the Templars and the soldiers of Thoros, ruler of Cilician Armenia. In 1188 the castle fell to Arabs but possession was fiercely contested until the Ottomans took over during the sixteenth century. There are dolmuşes from Antakya to Belen (4.50TL), Antakya to Bakras (2.50TL) and İskenderun to Bakras (4TL).

Antakya

ANTAKYA, 45km south of İskenderun, stands on the site of ancient Antioch and, although there's little sense of historical continuity, the city's laid-back pace, cosmopolitan outlook and subtly Arab atmosphere make it unique in Turkey. Flanked by mountains to the north and south, it sits in the bed of a broad river valley planted with olive trees, providing a welcome visual relief after travelling from the drab flatlands surrounding Adana. Although little survives from the city's Seleucid and Roman past, it has enough attractions to merit at least an overnight stop, including an excellent archeological museum and an unusual cave-church from which St Peter is said to have preached. The food in Antakya is some of the most varied and best in Turkey, thanks to the city's Arab heritage.

Some history

The city was founded as Antioch in the fourth century BC by Seleucus Nicator, one of the four generals among whom the empire of Alexander the Great was divided. It soon grew and by the second century BC it had developed into a multiethnic metropolis of half a million – one of the largest cities in the ancient world and a major staging-post on the newly opened Silk Road. It also acquired a reputation as a centre for all kinds of moral excess, causing **St Peter** to choose it as the location of one of the world's first Christian communities in the hope that the new religion would exercise a restraining influence. Indeed, the patriarchy of Antioch became one of the five senior official positions in the early Christian Church's organization.

Despite being razed by a series of earthquakes during the sixth century AD, Antioch was able to maintain its prosperity after the Roman era, and only with the rise of Constantinople did the city begin to decline. In 1098 the Crusader kings Bohemond and Raymond took the city in the name of Christianity after a vicious eight-month siege and a savage massacre of Turks, imposing a Christian rule in Antioch that lasted until the city fell to the Mamluks of Egypt, who sacked it in 1268. By the time the Ottomans, under Selim the Grim, took over in 1516, Antioch had long since vanished from the main stage of world history, and by the turn of the last century the city was little more than a village, squatting amid the ruins of the ancient metropolis. After World War I, Antakya, along with most of the rest of the Hatay, passed into the hands of the French, who laid the foundations of the modern city.

Arrival and information

From the new **otogar**, it's a 4km municipal bus ride (1TL) to the town centre. Some companies offer free service buses direct to central hotels. As well as domestic services, there are regular daily departures to towns in Syria (see box, p.430), while buses also travel several times a week direct to Amman in Jordan. Closer to town, a 15-minute walk from the centre and just past the intersection of Yavuz Sultan Selim and Şehit Ozman Durmaz caddesis, the *köy garajı* (village garage) has minibus departures to İskenderun, Harbiye, Samandağ, and Yayladağ. The Havaş (airport shuttle) delivers passengers at Inonu and Atatürk caddesis in the centre of town (8TL; at least 3 daily). Antakya's **tourist office** (Mon–Fri 8am–noon & 1.30–5pm; ☏0326/216 6098) is rather inconveniently sited on a roundabout at the end of Ataturk Bulvarı ten minutes' walk northwest of the museum.

Accommodation

Antakya has a good range of hotels across every price range, including some uninspiring cheapies on and around İstiklâl Caddesi.

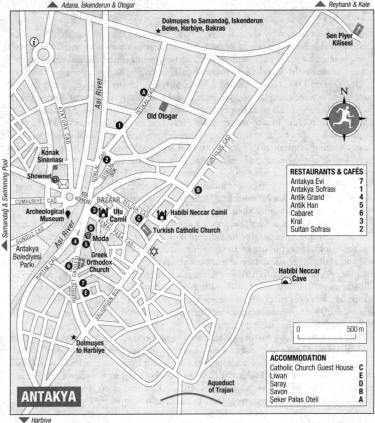

Adana, İskenderun & Otogar

Reyhanlı & Kale

RESTAURANTS & CAFÉS

Antakya Evi	7
Antakya Sofrası	1
Antik Grand	4
Antik Han	5
Cabaret	6
Kral	3
Sultan Sofrası	2

ACCOMMODATION

Catholic Church Guest House	C
Liwan	E
Saray	D
Savon	B
Şeker Palas Oteli	A

ANTAKYA

Harbiye

Catholic Church Guest House Kurtuluş Cad, Ataman Demir Sok 6 ☎0326/215 6703, ⓦwww .anadolukatolikkilisesi.org/antakya. Peaceful guesthouse aimed at Catholic pilgrims. The rooms (with shared kitchen) are high-ceilinged, comfortably furnished, and ranged around a shady courtyard. Very good value. The welcoming Italian *padre* has written a worthy history of Antakya. ❶

Hotel Saray Hürriyet Cad 3 ☎0326/214 9001, ⓕ214 9002. This first-floor hotel offers decent value with clean rooms with TV and fans. Good views from the rear rooms over the old quarter and the hillside beyond. They have had some problems with damp so ask to check rooms before committing. ❷

Liwan Hotel Silahli Kuvvetler Cad 5 ☎0326/215 7777, ⓦwww.theliwanhotel.com. This 1920s residence for Syria's first head of state has recently been transformed into boutique accommodation.

French, Armenian and Italian antiques accent the 24 individually designed rooms. There is a well-stocked bar and music club playing jazz, blues and traditional Arabic and Turkish music just off the lobby. ❻

Savon Hotel Kurtuluş Cad 192 ☎0326/214 6355, ⓦwww.savonhotel.com. An elegant boutique hotel set in a renovated soap and olive oil factory. The posh rooms, complete with marble bathrooms, are set around a quiet stone courtyard. The service is friendly and efficient, though the breakfast leaves something to be desired. ❹

Şeker Palas Oteli İstiklâl Cad 79 ☎0326/215 1603. A convenient choice just outside the *otogar*. Despite the spartan rooms and basic shared bathrooms, the hotel has a homely feel, with glass cabinets on each floor bursting with kitsch ornaments, and lovely old tiled floors. It is also very clean. Try to bag a rear room as they are much quieter. ❶

6

THE MEDITERRANEAN COAST AND THE HATAY | Antakya

427

The City

Antakya is cut in two by the **Asi River**, known in ancient times as the Orontes. Once a sizable river, it's now a brown and sluggish shadow of its former self, its flow depleted by water backed up in dams and drawn off for irrigation. The eastern bank is home to **old Antakya** – a maze of narrow streets, backed by the rocky cliffs of the Ziyaret Dağı range (ancient Mount Sipylus). It's well worth spending an hour or two wandering around the bazaar and market areas north of Kemal Paşa Caddesi (running from west to east just north of the main bridge, Ata Köprüsü). The **Kurşunlu Han**, incorporated in the bazaar, offers a shady courtyard for a tea stop. At the edge of the bazaar close to the bridge, the **Ulu Cami** mosque is an early Ottoman construction with a squat minaret. Far more recent is the **Gunduz** building, at the western end of the Ata Köprüsü. Resembling a typical 1930s suburban cinema (and now used as a porn cinema), with its graceful curves, geometric friezes and porthole windows, it was actually the Parliament building of the short-lived **Hatay Republic**. There are plans to turn it into a cultural centre and house the tourist office there.

At the junction of Kemal Paşa and Kurtuluş caddesis is the **Habibi Naccar Camii**, a mosque incorporated into the shell of a former Byzantine church, which was in turn built on the site of an ancient temple. The distinctive pointed minaret was added during the seventeenth century and is not – as you might be tempted to imagine – a former church tower. Over a kilometre to the east of here, in the hillside above the town, is the **Habibi Neccar cave** (Habibi Neccar Mağrası), a minor Muslim holy place that was once home to a solitary prophet. Habibi Naccar was violently put to death by the Christians; his head is said to be entombed under the mosque, his body in the cave.

The Hatay has a long history of tolerance, and some 4000 Christians live in the region, 1500 of them in Antakya itself. The majority are **Greek Orthodox** (twice daily masses Mon–Sat, once on Sunday), and their substantial nineteenth-century church in Antakya is on Hükümet Caddesi, and contains some beautiful Russian icons. The **Catholic church**, just off Kurtuluş Caddesi, is built around a pretty courtyard filled with orange trees and the resident Italian Padre Domenico is very

▲ Section of mosaic from Antakya Museum

friendly. Not far from here, on Kurtuluş Caddesi, is a small **synagogue** much visited by Israeli tourists, but identifiable only by the Star of David above its inconspicuous doorway.

The Archeological Museum

From the Ata Köprüsü, it's a quick hop across to the western side of the river and the **Archeological Museum** (Arkeoloji Müzesi; Tues–Sun summer 9am–6pm; winter 8.30am–noon & 1.30–4.30pm; 8TL), whose collection of locally unearthed Roman mosaics ranks among the best of its kind in the world. Laid out in the first four rooms of the museum, they are in a state of near immaculate preservation and mostly depict scenes from Greco-Roman mythology.

The majority were unearthed at the suburb of Daphne (now Harbiye), which was Antioch's main holiday resort in Roman times, and this is reflected in the sense of leisured decadence that pervades many of the scenes. A good example is the so-called **Buffet Mosaic** (no. 4), a vivid depiction of the rape of Ganymede, abducted by Zeus in the form of an eagle, and a banquet scene showing different courses of fish, ham, eggs and artichokes. Memorable images in room 3 include a fine portrait of **Thetis and Oceanus** (no. 1), the latter recognizable by the lobster claws protruding from his wet hair, and a fascinating depiction of the **Evil Eye** – a superstition that still has remarkable resonance in modern Turkey – being attacked by a raven, dog, scorpion, snake, centipede, panther, sword and trident as a horned goblin looks away (no. 6). Room 4 continues with an inebriated Dionysos, too drunk to stand (no. 12) and Orpheus surrounded by animals entranced by the beauty of his music (no. 23). Climb the spiral staircase in the corner of the room for a bird's-eye view of the floor mosaic showing hunters and dogs slaying lions, tigers and cheetahs.

After the mosaics, the rest of the museum seems a little mundane, though there are some stand-out pieces like the two stone lions, which were used as column bases during the eighth century BC, and the Antakya sarcophagus in a small chamber near the ticket office where the remains of two women and a man as well as the fine gold jewellery with which they were buried are displayed.

Sen Piyer Kilisesi

At the northeastern edge of Antakya is the **Sen Piyer Kilisesi** (Tues–Sun summer 9am–6.30pm; winter 8.30am–12.30pm & 1.30–5.30pm; 8TL), the famous cave-church of St Peter, from which it's said that the apostle preached to the Christian population of Antioch. It's reached by following Kurtuluş Caddesi in a northeasterly direction for about 2km until you come to a signposted right turn. After about five minutes' drive you come to the church, set into the hillside just above. It's about a forty-minute walk, or you can catch a dolmuş on Kurtuluş Caddesi, which will take you as far as the turn-off.

Whether St Peter really did preach from the Sen Piyer Kilisesi is – like the exact dates of his stay in the city – open to question. All that theologians seem to be able to agree on is that he spent some time in Antioch between AD 47 and 54, founding one of the world's first Christian communities with Paul and Barnabas. Inside, water drips down the cave walls and the cool atmosphere provides a welcome break from the heat of summer. Beneath your feet you'll be able to discern traces of fragmentary **mosaic** thought to date from the fifth century AD, while to the right of the altar is a kind of font set in the floor and fed by a spring with reputed curative properties. A special **service** is held here on June 29 to mark the feast of Sts Peter and Paul, attended by members of Antakya's small Christian community, while Sunday afternoon Mass is held every week at the tiny Catholic church on Kurtuluş Caddesi.

Carved into the mountainside above the church (ask for directions at ticket office), you'll find a relief thought by some to be of Charon, ferryman of the River Styx at the entrance to the underworld – though the portrait is more likely the face of a veiled woman, with a tiny man (probably the second-century BC Seleucid emperor Antiochus Epiphanes IV) perched on her shoulder.

With your own transport it's possible to drive the 15km – along Kurtuluş Caddesi and around the back of Mount Sipylus – up to the ruined *kale* (castle), from where there are fine views over the city.

Eating and drinking

Antakya's food is wonderful and shows its Arab influence with many **regional specialities**. Starters include *muhammara*, a fiery purée of walnuts, hot pepper and wheat; *bakla*, a purée of broad beans, garlic, tahini and parsley; and *tarator*, a tasty mix of tahini, walnuts and yoghurt. Main courses include *İspanak Borani*, a soup-like stew of spinach, chickpeas, shredded meat, yoghurt and lemon juice; *serimsek börek*, a sort of chicken-filled samosa; and *kağıt kebap*, kebabs cooked in greased-paper packages. Sweets include *künefe*, a shredded wheat and soft, mild cheese concoction, and *Haleb Burmasi* (Aleppo roll), a sweet confection stuffed with pistachios, which makes a welcome change from *baklava*.

Antakya Evi Silhali Kuvvetler Cad. Set in a series of intimate, upstairs rooms of a nineteenth-century townhouse. The food is traditional and a full meal with beer should cost no more than 16TL. A speciality is the Antioch *kebap*, a *köfte* of minced lamb stuffed with cheese, walnuts and olives.

Antakya Sofrası İstiklâl Cad 6, Ada Çarşışı. Tucked away amongst backstreets specializing in furniture retailing, this hole-in-the-wall serves home-cooked food from bubbling pots near the entrance. Specialties include unusual dishes such as *biberli ekmek*, a kind of spicy chapati spread with garlic, chilli and

Crossing into Syria

A number of bus companies operating out of Antakya offer services to cities in **Syria**; the best operator is Has, whose buses for Halab (Aleppo) depart from the *otogar* at 9am daily (11TL) and take three hours, while those for Şam (Damascus) depart at noon (15TL) and take seven hours. Another reputable company is Güney. Buses cross the border to the east of Antakya at Cilvegözü/Baba al Hawa, and delays can be considerable. Given massively improved relations between Turkey and Syria, far more people are crossing the border, and Turks are beginning to take day-trips from Antakya to Halab. A quicker option to Halab might be to get a dolmuş to Reyhanlı and then make your own way by shared taxi to the border, 5km away, from where you can pick up an onward Syrian microbus. It's also possible to take a bus from Antakya's Köy Garajı (village bus-garage) to the customs post 5km beyond Yayladağ (5TL) and from there cross into Syria. Another option is to hire a taxi; drivers tout around the old *otogar* and ask around 600 Syrian pounds to deliver you to Halab.

There are several other border crossings between Turkey and Syria, and the following departure points are all covered in Chapter 11. From Gaziantep, take a dolmuş to Kilis (1hr), from where you can take a shared taxi (around €25 for the vehicle) to Aleppo. It is also possible, to take a dolmuş from Urfa to Akçakale (1hr), walk across the frontier, and take a taxi to Abiyat, and then onto Halab. From Nusaybin (near to Mardin) it is again possible to walk across the border, to Kamışlı, and then on to other Syrian destinations.

For some nationalities it may be possible to obtain the **Syrian visa** on the border, but this is not always possible and you would be well advised to enquire at the Syrian embassy in your home country well before departure. Obtaining a visa from the Syrian embassy in Ankara can be time-consuming and expensive. You may also have to name the border you intend to use in advance and the hotel you intend to stay in.

other spices, and *doyme*, a stew of meat and soaked whole grains of wheat spiced with cumin. A full meal won't set you back more than a bargain 4TL, but the place closes early evening.

Antik Grand Hürriyet Cad 18. Smart first-floor place and good value, with hummus and *muhammara* at 2.5TL a portion, the usual range of kebabs at 5TL, and pizzas for the same price. Can be soulless when not busy.

Antik Han Hürriyet Cad. The unprepossessing exterior hides a walled garden courtyard and rooftop terrace. The *meze*s are particularly good (the hummus is a meal in itself, or try the *muhammara*) and the *ızgara* (grills) better than average. Check the cost before ordering, though, as the menu lacks a price list. No alcohol.

Cabaret Hürriyet Cad 26. Across from the Orthodox church, and with views into its courtyard from its first-floor rooms, this friendly pub set in a renovated Ottoman house caters to students and off-duty businessmen alike. A cold pint of Efes costs 3.5TL and light meals start at 5TL.

Kral Just down from the Ulu Cami. A long-established pudding shop, this is one of the best places to try the ubiquitous *künefe*.

Sultan Sofrası İstiklâl Cad 20/A. Serves all the regional dishes, including delicious *ıspanaklı katıklı ekmek* (like an Indian paratha) and *aşur*, a stringy stew of chickpeas, meat and wheat. Prices are a little higher than the competition (main courses from 5–9TL), and it's much favoured by tour groups, but the food and service are outstanding.

Listings

Banks and exchange There are several banks on İstiklâl and Atatürk cads, and you can change money at the weekends at the *döviz* on Kurtuluş Cad.

Car rental From Titus Turizm, under the *Büyük Antakya Oteli*, Atatürk Cad 8 Ⓣ 0326/213 9141.

Hospital The Devlet Hastane (State Hospital) is a couple of kilometres southeast of the centre.

Internet Modanet, on Hürriyet Cad, and Shownet, between the PTT and the Konak Sineması, on the west bank of the river.

Police Selçuk Cad; emergency number for foreigners is ⓉⓉ 0326/213 5953.

Post office The PTT is northwest of the round-about at the western end of the Ata Köprüs, across the square from the archeological museum (daily 9am–8pm).

Swimming There's an open-air pool on Gunduz Cad next to the municipal park (summer daily 10am–3pm (last entrance at 2pm); 5TL) with lockers where you can leave your gear if you are heading out on an evening bus.

West of Antakya

There are a number of interesting places to visit in the fertile, hilly countryside to the west of Antakya. The **Saint Simeon monastery** is the most renowned destination, while other local sights can be visited from the nearby resort of **Samandağ**. If you want to see all of the places in a day from Antakya, it's worth renting a car or taking a taxi and driver, as public transport is limited. The cost of a taxi for a full day runs 80–100TL.

Saint Simeon monastery

One of the more bizarre aspects of early Christianity was the craze for pillar sitting, which developed in Antioch during the fourth century. The trend was perfected by **Simeon Stylites the Younger**, whose **monastery** perches on a high ridge southwest of Antakya, 7km south of the road to Samandağ.

Simeon the Younger first chained himself to a rock in the wilderness in an act of ascetic retreat and then ascended progressively higher pillars before reaching a final height of some thirteen metres. He lived chained to the top of this pillar for 25 years, meditating and making sporadic pronouncements castigating the citizens of Antioch for their moral turpitude. The base of the pillar still remains, surrounded by the complex octagonal layout of the monastery that grew up around Simeon as he began to attract growing numbers of curious pilgrims eager to share in his enlightenment. It's possible to climb on top of the diminutive pillar, which is just wide enough to lie down on and reap the same views of the Orontes valley and of Mount Cassius looming out of the Mediterranean that Simeon must have enjoyed over fifteen centuries ago.

To reach the monastery, turn south off the main Antakya–Samandağ road at **Uzunbağ**, just past Karaçay. Continue uphill along a good road for about 4km, before branching off to the right, by a white Muslim shrine, and following a bad dirt track for another couple of kilometres. There is no public transport at all to the monastery, but you should be able to find a taxi in Karaçay willing to take you.

Samandağ

About 25km southwest of Antakya, **SAMANDAĞ** is an Arabic-speaking resort town of about 30,000 people. The town is currently undergoing something of a building boom, financed in part by local boys made good in the Gulf, displaying their newfound wealth with gaudy villas and four-wheel-drive utility vehicles. It is served by regular dolmuşes from Antakya's *köy garajı*, which will deposit you in the town's unprepossessing centre, a couple of kilometres inland. Here you'll find a few shops and restaurants and a couple of banks. To get to the **beach**, take any dolmuş heading for "Deniz" (the sea) – although swimming here is not really recommended because of pollution from İskenderun, 50km or so up the coast.

Vakıflı

The tiny village of **VAKIFLİ**, with its apparently unremarkable mix of dilapidated mudbrick and timber houses and modern concrete villas, is in fact unique. For this is Turkey's sole surviving **Armenian village**, set amidst orange groves on the lush lower slopes of Musa Dağı. During the Turkish deportations and massacres of the Armenians in 1915 the inhabitants of Vakıflı held out against the Turkish forces until they were evacuated to Port Said by French and British warships. Most of the villagers returned in 1919 when the Hatay became part of French-mandated Syria. When the Hatay joined the Turkish Republic in 1939, most of the area's Armenians, bar the inhabitants of Vakıflı, decided to leave. At the heart of the village is the recently restored and extended **Surp Asdvadzadzin Kilisesi**, to which the village *muhtar* (headman) has the key, though the church is not always locked.

Dolmuşes from Samandağ travelling the 6km or so to the village don't tend to leave till mid-afternoon (after the villagers have travelled into Samandağ and completed their shopping and errands), so it is best reached with your own transport or by taxi. If you do choose to visit the village, remember that it is a living community and not a mere curiosity.

Çevlik

A few kilometres north of Samandağ is the village of **ÇEVLIK**, easily reached by dolmuş from Samandağ town centre. In ancient times, Çevlik was the port of **Seleucia ad Piera**, serving Antioch, and it is from here that Paul and Barnabas are thought to have set off on their first evangelical mission to Cyprus. There are still a few ruins scattered around, including the 130-metre-long **Titus ve Vespasiyanus Tüneli** (open dawn–dusk; 3TL), a huge channel carved out of the hillside to prevent flooding and silting of the harbour. It's usually easy to find someone who will assist you to scramble around the huge gorge-like site (expect to leave a tip); two inscriptions at the upper end give details of its construction. Also scattered around you'll see foundations, sections of ruined wall and Roman tombs. Swimming is probably unwise, although the village beach is popular with local fishermen.

Çevlik has a few *pansiyon*s and a campsite, and you can also camp on the beach, although strictly speaking this is illegal and you might get moved on.

South: Harbiye and the road to Syria

About 10km south of Antakya is **HARBIYE**, the ancient and celebrated suburb of Daphne, a beautiful gorge to which revellers and holiday-makers flocked in Roman times, drawn by shady cypress and laurel groves dotted with waterfalls and pools. The Romans built a temple to Apollo here, since it was generally held to be the setting for the god's pursuit of Daphne. According to the myth, Daphne, when seized by amorous Apollo, prayed for deliverance; in answer to her prayers, Peneus transformed her into a laurel tree. Another legend relates that the resort was the venue of Paris's gift of the golden apple to Aphrodite, indirectly precipitating the Trojan War. Later, and with possibly more basis in fact, Mark Antony and Cleopatra are said to have been married here. With the departure of the Romans the place went into decline, a process compounded by the destructive attacks of the Persians and Arabs during the sixth and seventh centuries. Now Harbiye is famous for Daphne (Defne) soap, made from the fruit of the laurel tree and doubling as shampoo. You will see cubes of it for sale in the region's bazaars.

To get there, head to Antakya's *köy garajı* or flag down a dolmuş travelling southwest along Kurtuluş Caddesi. From the dolmuş drop-off point follow a road past modern houses until you come to a waterfall. From here, a litter-strewn path runs down into the gorge, where a number of shady and shabby tea gardens and trout **restaurants** (but not much else) await amid a landscape that has been constantly eroded by the river since Roman times. But note that the gorge is really not worth visiting unless the heat in Antakya is absolutely unbearable or you have been invited by the locals to join in a picnic.

About 8km south of Harbiye lies Qalat az Zaw, a ruined fortress originally built to defend the southern approaches to Antioch and much fought over by Crusaders, Arabs and Mamluks. Twenty-odd kilometres further on, close to the Syrian border, is the village of **YAYLADAĞI**, a quiet spot that has a pleasant picnic area, set in mountain woods down towards the frontier – a good point for a break if you're en route to the border itself.

Travel details

Trains

Adana to: Ankara (1 daily, overnight; 14hr); İskenderun (3 daily; 2hr 30min); Kayseri (daily; 6hr); Mersin (6 daily; 1hr 15min).
İskenderun to: Adana (3 daily; 2hr 30min); Mersin (3 daily; 3hr 30min).
Mersin to: Adana (6 daily; 1hr 15min).

Buses and dolmuşes

Adana to: Adıyaman (10 daily; 6hr); Afyon (4 daily; 7hr); Alanya (2 daily; 9hr); Ankara (hourly; 10hr); Antalya (13 daily; 12hr); Diyarbakır (10 daily; 10hr); Gaziantep (12 daily; 4hr); İstanbul (hourly; 12 hr); Kayseri (14 daily; 7hr); Konya (5 daily; 7hr); Malatya (8 daily; 8hr); Şanlıurfa (4 daily; 6hr); Van (1 daily; 18hr).

Alanya to: Adana (2 daily; 9hr); Ankara (7 daily; 9hr); Antalya (every 30min; 2hr); Diyarbakır (1 daily; 19hr); İstanbul (4 daily; 18hr); Konya (6 daily; 5hr); Mersin (8 daily; 8hr); Samsun (3 daily; 15hr); Silifke via Taşucu (5 daily; 6hr).

Antakya to: Adana (hourly; 3hr); Aleppo, Syria (3 daily; 3hr); Amman, Jordan (3 weekly; 12hr); Ankara (9 daily, 13hr); Antalya (14 daily; 14hr); Damascus, Syria (2 daily; 7hr); Gaziantep (half-hourly; 4hr); İskenderun (every 20min; 1hr); İstanbul (5 daily; 22hr); Konya (5 daily; 15hr); Riyadh, Saudi Arabia (3 weekly; 24hr); Samandağ (hourly; 1hr).

Antalya otogar to: Adana (13 daily; 12hr); Afyon (hourly, 5hr); Alanya (every 30 minutes; 2hr); Ankara (half-hourly; 10hr); Antakya (14 daily; 14hr); Denizli (5 daily; 5hr 30min); Diyarbakır (5 daily; 16hr); Eğirdir (8 daily; 3hr); Fethiye, by inland route (6 daily; 4hr); Isparta (hourly; 2hr 30min); İstanbul (half-hourly service; 12hr); İzmir (hourly; 9hr 30min); Konya (15 daily; 5hr 30min).

Antalya to destinations southwest (leaves from *otogar* minibus terminal then stops at Devlet Hastane roundabout): Fethiye by coastal route (8 daily; 8hr); Finike (8 daily; 2hr); Kalkan (8 daily; 5hr); Kaş (8 daily; 4hr 30min); Kemer/Beldibi/Göynük (every 30min; 1hr).

İskenderun to: Adana (hourly; 2hr 30min); Antakya (every 20min; 40min); Antalya (2 daily; 13hr).

Silifke to: Adana (every 15–20min; 2hr); Alanya (8 daily; 7hr); Antalya (8 daily; 9hr); Konya (8 daily; 5hr); Mersin (every 20min; 2hr).

Ferries

Mersin to: Mağosa/Famagusta, North Cyprus (3 weekly; 10hr). Tickets cost 60TL one way for foot passengers, cars €115.

Taşucu to: Girne/Kyrenia, North Cyprus (daily except Fri & Sat; 5hr). One-way tickets cost 59TL, cars 150TL.

Hydrofoils

Alanya to: Girne/Kyrenia, North Cyprus (twice weekly; 3hr 30min).

Taşucu to: Girne/Kyrenia, North Cyprus (daily; 2hr).

Flights

Adana to: Ankara (2 daily; 1hr); Antalya (daily; 1hr); Ercan (1 daily; 50min); İstanbul (15 daily; 1hr 20min); İzmir (2 daily; 1hr 30min); Lefkosa (daily; 45min).

Antalya to: Ankara (2 daily; 1hr); Bodrum via İstanbul (5 weekly; 6hr); İstanbul (15 daily; 1hr–1hr 20min); İzmir via İstanbul (1 or 2 daily; 3hr 40min).

Antalya (Hatay) to: Ankara (5 weekly; 1hr 5min); İstanbul (4 daily; 1hr 45min).

South Central Anatolia

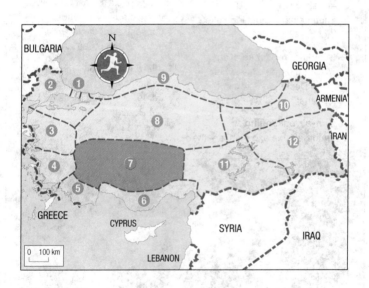

CHAPTER 7

Highlights

* **Sagalossos** Perched high above the lakes region, these remote ruins are among the most beautifully sited in Central Anatolia. **See p.444**

* **Eğirdir** Eat fillets of crisply fried lake fish as the sun sets over Lake Eğirdir. **See p.447**

* **St Paul Trail** Follow in the footsteps of the renowned missionary over the Toros mountains to stunning Lake Eğirdir. **See p.450**

* **Whirling dervishes, Konya** Watch the dervishes whirl each December in their spiritual home. **See p.457**

* **Hot-air ballooning** An unforgettable experience – the interplay of light and shadow over Cappadocia's geological fairy-tale landscape, seen from the basket of a balloon. **See p.468**

* **Göreme Open-Air Museum** The frescoes inside Göreme's cave churches are a vibrant reminder of the region's Christian past. **See p.473**

* **Mustafapaşa** One of Cappadocia's most attractive villages sports a wonderful concentration of old Greek houses. **See p.480**

* **Ihlara valley** Don't miss the natural beauty of this fertile gorge, enhanced by its rock-cut Byzantine churches. **See p.486**

▲ Fairy chimney rock formations, Cappadocia

South Central Anatolia

he **central Anatolian plateau** seems at first sight to be an unpromising
prospect. A large area is virtual desert, while much of the central plateau
is steppe, blitzed by cold and heavy snowfall in winter and suffering water
shortages in summer. Yet within this region are two landscapes any
traveller to the country should visit – the azure **lakes** west of Konya and north of
Antalya, and, fruther east, the unique rock formations of **Cappadocia**. The
region's **cities**, particularly Afyon, Konya and Kayseri are also well worth
exploring, each with a story to tell and a series of dramatic monuments from
towering fortresses and venerated tombs to exquisite mosques.

Turkey's **Lakeland** has been largely ignored by the Turkish tourist industry.
Stretches of silver waters stand out against the grey plateau, or appear suddenly
between mountains to startling effect. Accessible from **Afyon** to the north or
Antalya from the south, the lakes have supported small settlements of reed-cutters
and fishermen for thousands of years. Today their villages, for example Beyşehir,
Burdur and particularly **Eğirdir**, earn an income running simple *pansiyon*s for an
ever increasing number of visitors. Eğirdir also provides access to the **St Paul
Trail**, a fabulous trek through the Toros mountains, following in the footsteps of
the famous evangelist. Also accessible from here are the ski slopes of Mount
Davraz set in the highlands north of the lakes.

East of the lakes area, the city of **Konya** is the focus of Sufic mystical
practice and teaching throughout the Middle East. Once the capital of the
Selçuk Empire, it is today famous as the home of the **whirling dervish** sect,
the Mevlevî.

Further east, the area between the extinct volcanoes of Erciyes Dağ and the
Melendiz range is **Cappadocia**. Here, water and wind have created a land of
fantastic forms from the soft rock known as tuff, including forests of cones, table
mountains, canyon-like valleys and castle-rocks. From the seventh to the eleventh
centuries AD, it was a place of refuge for Christians during Arab and Turkish
invasions into the steppe and its churches and dwellings carved from the rock,
particularly by monastic communities, and its unearthly landscapes make an
irresistible tourist draw. At the northwest fringes of this region, the modern city
of **Kayseri** hides a wealth of Islamic monuments set below the imposing volcanic
peak of Mount Erciyes.

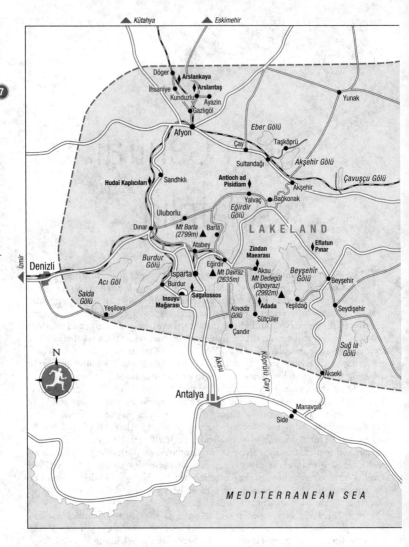

Lakeland

After years of isolation, Turkish **Lakeland** is just beginning to be discovered by birdwatchers, trekkers and skiers. Other tourists, meanwhile, stop off here at **Eğirdir** on the route from Cappadocia and Konya to the south coast around Antalya or Fethiye. At present, facilities are unevenly spread and not luxurious, but the various Lakeland attractions make it ideal for quiet, unhurried holidays away from the seething coastal resorts. As well as the eye-catching **lakes** themselves, there are the remains of Pisidian cities to see (most impressively at

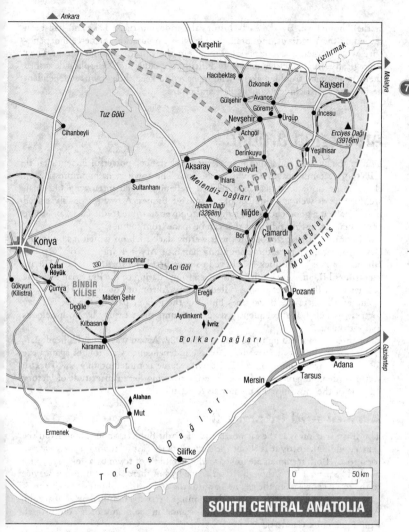

SOUTH CENTRAL ANATOLIA

Sagalassos and **Antioch ad Pisidiam** near Yalvaç), and largely unspoilt provincial towns, notably **Ayfon**, to explore.

Access to the lakes is from Antalya in the south, over the Taurus range to Isparta; from the plains of Konya in the east, over the Sultan Dağları to Eğirdir; and from Eskişehir or Kütahya in the north via the main north–south road to Afyon and Isparta. All routes are well served by buses.

Some history

Despite the inhospitable nature of this region, it has been populated as long as anywhere in Anatolia. From the early Paleolithic age man was drawn to the lakes, which provided a livelihood for primitive hunters and fishermen, and during the Bronze Age the **Hittites**, a race who once rivalled the Egyptians, chose the plateau as their homeland. By the early historical period, northern Lakeland had been settled by the **Pisidians**, mountain people with a reputation for fierce independence who worked as mercenaries throughout the eastern Mediterranean. Their strategically situated settlements were difficult to subdue, and Xenophon described them as obstinate troublemakers, who managed to keep their towns independent despite the encroachments of the Persian Empire.

Afyon and around

Dominated by a tall and imposing rock on which stands a powerful ancient citadel, **AFYON** certainly leaves a vivid impression. The town remains impressive on closer inspection: it is clean and relaxed, retaining much interesting Ottoman architecture as well as a number of attractive mosques. A few reasonably priced hotels make it a good choice for a night's stopover en route to the lakes, and there are several interesting side trips that can be made from town.

In honour of the fortress, and the towering dark rock on which it's built, the city until recently bore the resounding name of Afyon Karahisar, or "**Opium Black Fortress**". The rock is believed to have first been fortified by the Hittite king Mursil II, and remains have also been found dating to the Phrygian era. The Romans and Byzantines – who called the city Akronium or "High Hill" – also occupied the city, the Byzantines building the greater part of the present-day fortress, which was subsequently used as an imperial treasury by both Selçuks and Ottomans.

For three weeks leading up to August 26, 1922, Afyon was Atatürk's headquarters, prior to the last, decisive battle of the independence war, fought against the Greeks at nearby Dumlupınar. The town's statue commemorating the Turkish victory – depicting one naked man towering over another in an attitude of victory – is one of the most moving memorials to Atatürk.

Arrival and information

The **train station** is at the far north end of Ordu Bulvarı, about 500m from the centre, while the **otogar** is about the same distance east of town on the *çevre yolu* (ring road). Both terminals are linked with the middle of town by a dolmuş service marked "Sanayi/PTT", though if you arrive by bus there should be a free service to the town centre from the *otogar*. Towards the end of the dolmuş service's run, it passes close by all the city's best hotels, coming to rest at a terminal on Ambaryolu, two blocks behind the main **PTT** (which stands on the main north–south street, Milli Egemenlik Caddesi).

There is a **tourist booth** (Mon–Fri 8.30am–noon & 1.30–5.30pm; ☎0272/215 7600) in Hükümet Meydanı, which dishes out town maps and a brochure to the "Afyon Tourism Route" (see p.442) to the north of the city. The tourism official speaks good English and is very helpful. The major **banks and ATMs** are on Banklar Caddesi.

Accommodation

The cheapest **hotel** is the *Otel Lale* on Milli Gençlik Cad 23 (☎0272/215 1580; ●). The rooms are basic but adequate, with en-suite bathrooms, and it is very central. Also centrally located is the *Hotel Soydan* at Turizm Emeksiz Cad 2 (☎0272/215 6070, ℉212 2111; ●), a friendly place with small, prettily furnished rooms with bathrooms and TVs. It has a restaurant serving traditional dishes. A considerable step up is the *Cakmak Marble Hotel* at Süleyman Gonçer Cad 2 (☎0272/214 3300,

Ⓦwww.cakmakmarblehotel.com; Ⓢ) just east of Hükümet Meydanı, with airy rooms, satellite TV, a pool and hamam.

The Town

The best way of establishing what's where on arrival is to head for the highest point in town: the **fortress** (220m) scaled via some 700 steps on the southern face of the rock (a twenty-minute hike best avoided in the heat of the day). On the way up look out for hoopoes among the varied birdlife, and at the top for votive rags, representing wishes, tied to trees. At prayer time as many as eighty minarets resound and echo off the rock to dramatic effect. The fortress itself is thought to stand on the site of the Hittite fortress of Khapanouwa, built around the middle of the second millennium BC. The rock was subsequently fortified by the Phrygians, the Byzantines and the Turks, but all that remain are a few crenellated walls and towers.

Immediately surrounding the fortress rock is the **old town**, a warren of tiny streets. There are a number of impressively well-preserved mosques near here, with many more somewhat less distinguished ones in the bazaar proper. Opposite the base of the steps leading up the side of the rock stands the **Ulu Cami** (outside of prayer time wait for the caretaker to let you in; small donation). This typically square Selçuk construction, built between 1272 and 1277, has been restored, so its originally flat roof is now pitched, but it retains forty original carved wooden columns with stalactite capitals and beams supporting a fine geometric ceiling.

Slightly downhill from the Ulu Cami, the **Mevlevî Camii** is a double-domed mosque noticeable for its pyramid-roofed *son cemaat yeri*, a porch in which latecomers pray – literally the "place of last congregation". The adjoining *semahane*, or ceremonial hall, has a walnut-wood floor on which Mevlevî dervishes once performed their whirling ceremony. This building has now been converted into the **Mevlevî Museum** (Mevlevî Müzesi; open at prayer times or on request to the *imam*), with exhibits of musical instruments and the ceremonial costumes of the dervishes. Afyon became the second largest centre of the Mevlevî order after the branch of Islamic mysticism was introduced to the city from Konya by the son of the Mevlâna, Sultan Veled.

The Archeological museum and around

The **Archeological Museum** (Arkeoloji Müzesi; Tues–Sun 8am–noon & 1.30– 5.30pm; 3TL), 1km east of the centre on Kurtuluş Caddesi, warrants a visit. Despite rather dimly lit display cabinets, the objects are attractively set out and the explanatory signboards well written. The most interesting finds are Roman, excavated at nearby Çardalı and Kovalık Höyük, dating from the third and fourth centuries AD. The museum garden is full of impressive (and unlabelled) marble work and statuary from the Roman, Phrygian, Byzantine and Ottoman eras. It is

---

Opium

A quarter of the world's legal production of **opium** is harvested from the poppy fields surrounding Afyon. While the authorities are reluctant to tout the city's eponymous enterprise as a tourist attraction, there are still telltale signs of civic pride in the traditional industry: a close look at the fountain in the town square reveals that it is a graceful bronze sculpture of poppy seed-pods.

If you want to take a look at the crop, in May/June head out of town for around 5km on the Sandıklı road, and the open fields of poppies are clearly visible from the road. Much more grows around Yalvaç and in the Toros mountains. The fields are regularly patrolled by officials, who check if the seed heads have been illegally "bled" for heroin.

unsurprising that there are so many marble remains here, as the region was (and remains) the heart of the marble-quarrying industry in Anatolia.

Also on Kurtuluş Caddesi, but nearer the centre in its own patch of parkland, the **Gedik Ahmet Paşa Külliyesi** was built for one of the viziers of Mehmet the Conqueror in 1477. Adjoining it are a stone *medrese* and a functioning hamam – the original marble floors are in good condition, but it's otherwise in a bad state of repair. The complex's mosque, identified as the **İmaret Camii**, has a fluted minaret dashed with zigzagging blue İznik tiles.

Atatürk's brief stay in Afyon is commemorated in a museum, the **Zafer Müzesi** (daily 8.30am–noon & 1.30–5.30pm; 1TL), next to the tourist office on Milli Egemenlik Caddesi. This is the building in which he planned his victory at Dumlupınar: his office has been preserved, and weapons and other paraphernalia from the war, as well as old photos of Atatürk and Afyon, are on show.

Eating and drinking

Afyon is noted for its production of *sucuk* (sausage), *pastırma* (pastrami) and *kaymak* (clotted cream); look out for all of these products in the shops and bazaars. Established in 1922, the old-fashioned 🍴 *İkbal Lokantası*, close to Hükümet Meydanı on Uzun Çarşı, is the most famous **restaurant** in town. It exudes a period charm rare in Turkey, with a snaking Art Deco staircase leading up to the grand family dining area. It's not cheap (a full meal will set you back up to 15–20TL) but the grills are excellent and the famed puddings, all served with a generous slice of thick Afyon cream, delicious. On Ambaryolu 48, is the *Kuru Fasuliyeci*, an unusual place specializing in dried-bean dishes. Try them plain (in a tomato sauce), with meat or with *pastırma* for 3TL, best accompanied by a bowl of *cacık*. For a different feel, the *YKM Café* (on the top floor of the YKM department store, off Hükümet Meydanı) dishes up decent pizzas to the town's youth.

Around Afyon

The most interesting side trip from Afyon is to see a series of sixth-century **Phrygian sites**, notable for their stone-carvings, in the vicinity of İhsanıye. There are also several areas of rock formations here similar to those in Cappadocia, and even some rock-cut churches. This whole area is being promoted by the local tourism authorities, but as yet the *Afyon Turizm Kuşağı* (Afyon Tourism Route) exists largely in a brochure rather than on the ground. Village roads are badly signed and the locals unused to giving directions to the sites. You are probably better off forming a group and hiring a taxi for the day (around €80).

The Afyon region is also well known for its **hot springs**, whose waters bubble up at temperatures between 50 and 80°C and have a high content of fluoride, bromide and calcium salts. Mineral water from this region is bottled and sold all over Turkey.

Ayazın, Kaya and Döğer

Best of the remains are those of a Phrygian town located in the modern-day village of **AYAZİN**, reached via a right turn off the minor Afyon–Eskişehir road at Kunduzlu. **Cave houses** and a well-preserved ninth-century **Byzantine church** are visible across fields of opium poppies on the road to the village. Closer observation reveals lion reliefs and the scars from excavations by locals and archeologists, who have found coins and other objects in the rooms.

The rock-cut tomb of **Arslantaş** (Lion Stone), near the village of **KAYA** (formerly Hayranveli), is flanked by another relief of lions, two enormous beasts snarling at each other with bared teeth. This should not be confused with another Phrygian cult monument called **Arslankaya** (Lion Rock), featuring a high relief of the goddess Cybele flanked by two more enormous lions. Arslankaya is near Lake Emre in the village of **DÖĞER**, where the remains of a fifteenth-century Ottoman *kervansaray* can also be found.

Local spas

Fourteen kilometres north of town on the Kütahya road, is the massive *Termal Resort Oruçoğlu* (℡0272/251 5050, Ⓦwww.orucoglu.com.tr; ⑥), a **spa hotel** offering B&B, half- and full-board accommodation in luxurious rooms with air conditioning and balconies, and thermal water on tap. The price also includes use of the hamam, sauna, indoor and outdoor pools and a jolly water-slide; various massages and treatments are extra. This hotel is one of several in the Ömer/Gecek Kaplıcıları **hot springs** complex, with treatments accessible to less privileged customers, who usually stay in simple chalets. The tourist office should be able to help you find accommodation, and there are several dolmuşes a day from Afyon.

Hudai Kaplıcıları 48km south of Ayfon, beyond Sandıklı off the Denizli road, is worth a visit if only for a wallow in its deep **mud baths**. Dolmuşes run there every half-hour from Sandıklı. The place is like a large village, with a mass of basic chalets for cure-seekers, and public treatment centres, including mud baths (entry 4TL). The *Hüdai Termal Otel* (℡0272/535 7300, Ⓦwww.hudai.sandikli.bel.tr; ⑤ half-board, discounts for longer stays) has comfortable rooms and its own attached treatment centre, with mud baths that range up to 50°C and a small, naturally heated thermal pool. The spring waters of the thermal pools all have their own specific properties, which are used as curatives for a variety of ailments.

Isparta and around

Set on a flat plain dominated by 2635-metre Mount Davraz to the south, **ISPARTA** is a mostly modern town whose only suggestion of romantic appeal lies in its chief industries: rosewater, distilled here for over a century, and carpets, manufactured in industrial quantities. You're most likely to come through Isparta on your way to **Eğirdir**, 12km east.

There are a few things to see and do in town. On Kaymakkapı Meydanı, the **Ulu (Kutlubey) Cami** dates from 1417, its size and grandeur attesting to the importance of the town in Ottoman times; but the interior is badly restored. Up until the 1923 exchange of populations many **Greeks** lived in Isparta, and their old residential quarter is a fifteen-minute walk from the town centre, near the Devlet Hastanesi (State Hospital). The once handsome lath-and-plaster houses are now crumbling, but there are a couple of restored nineteenth-century churches to admire.

The town's **Archeological Museum** (Arkeoloji Müzesi; closed for restoration) is on Kenan Evren Caddesi, 500m northeast of the *Belediye* building. It has a reasonable collection of local finds, including some fine Roman grave stelae, plus assorted items from a nearby Bronze Age burial site. The ethnonography section includes a wonderful felt and reed *yurt*, which, along with the fine old carpets and kilims also on show, attests to a nomadic culture once an integral part of this region. Isparta's **market** day is Wednesday, when people come in from the surrounding rural areas to sell agricultural produce and stock up on necessities. It is located around the minibus terminal.

Practicalities

The **train station** is at the far northeastern end of Istasyon Caddesi, a 500-metre walk, from the town centre and the *otogar* is a few kilometres northwest of town on Süleyman Demirel Bulvarı – free service buses run in to the centre and to the **minibus terminal** (known as the *köy garajı*) in the middle of town, about 500m southwest of Kaymakkapı Meydanı, from where you can take a dolmuş to Burdur, Eğirdir, Ağlasun or Atabey, all around forty minutes away. There have been tales of travellers being ticketed to Eğirdir, but then left stranded in Isparta's *otogar*. If this happens to you, head for the *köy garajı* and thence onto Eğirdir by dolmuş, a twenty-minute journey costing 2.5TL (last bus at around 7.30pm).

Isparta's **tourist office** is on the third floor of the Valikonağı, or governor's building (Turizm Müdürlüğü; ℡0248/232 2210; Mon–Fri 8am–noon & 1.30–5pm), next to the main square, the Kaymakkapı Meydanı. The **PTT** (Mon–Sat 8.30am–7pm) is near the Valikonağı on Hükümet Caddesi.

Accommodation-wise, a recommended place, popular with the French, is the *Hotel Artan*, in a quiet side street at Cengiz Topel Cad 12/B (℡0246/232 5700, ⓦwww.hotelartan.com; ❸). The well-furnished rooms have central heating and satellite TV, and they serve a good buffet breakfast. The larger *Otel Bolat*, off Kaymakkapı Meydanı at Süleyman Demirel Bul 67 (℡0246/223 9001, ⓦwww.otelbolat.com; ❸), has both air conditioning and heating, a decent top-floor restaurant with great views towards Mount Davraz, and an American-style bar. The two best **restaurants** are virtually side by side on Kaymakkapı Meydanı: the *Hacı Benlioğlu* and the *Kebabçı Kadir*. Both serve excellent grills and fine desserts. *Ferah* serves outstanding *pide* and kebabs overlooking the same square.

Sagalassos

Although nearer Isparta, the Pisidian site of **Sagalossos** is a popular organized trip from Eğirdir, 55km to the northeast. By far the most impressive Pisidian site, it is undergoing extensive excavations. It was first discovered in 1806 when it was identified as the first city in Pisidia though most of what you see today dates from Roman imperial times. The population of Termessos (see p.393) probably moved to Sagalassos in 244 AD after an earthquake, though the site was abandoned soon after, when the population moved downhill to the present town.

The **site** (daily 7.30am–6pm, 5TL ⓦwww.sagalossos.be;) is well labelled with illustrations of the buildings in their original state. To the right of the entrance is the 96-metre-wide **theatre**, just as the earthquake left it, with seating mostly in place, but the stage building rather more wrecked. Two restored **nymphaea** (fountain-houses) are here: the smaller shows both early and Byzantine phases; the floor mosaic is almost intact, as are the alcoves and a major inscription. Walking west you come to the **upper agora**, of which the second, huge nymphaeum formed one side, two ceremonial arches opened off and there was a pagoda-like monument in the centre.

Just above, north of the upper agora, is one of the oldest parts of the site, a Doric **temple** of the second century BC, built of massive blocks still standing on two sides; it was later incorporated into the city walls and you can spot the joins. Walking down from the upper agora you'll see fragments of beautiful Roman friezes laid out like a giant jigsaw. Turn right on the level track through the site for **graves** cut into the rock face; they contained cremations. Below the main track is the **lower agora** with adjacent baths. Earthenware pipes and hypocausts reveal how water was distributed and heated. Beyond this area is a temple with Corinthian columns dedicated to Antonius Pius, now in rubble, but an informative contrast to the Doric one.

Straight ahead down the steps is the **necropolis** containing many graves, and a hill which locals say is the site of an Alexander monument – they believe that a gold statue dedicated to Alexander is waiting to be discovered.

To reach Sagalossos with public transport, take one of the five daily dolmuşes from Isparta to Ağlasun, then hire a taxi (15TL return, including wait time) the 7km uphill to the site. Beware that the last dolmuş back to Isparta leaves Ağlasun at 5.30pm. Wear sturdy shoes as Sagalassos is quite rugged and vertical.

Burdur

Lying 50km southwest of Isparta, and connected by regular dolmuşes, **BURDUR** town is situated some way from its lake. The only real reason to visit is the excellent **museum** (Burdur Müzesi; Tues–Sun 8.30am–noon & 1.30–5.30pm; 4TL). Housing finds from nearby Sagalassos (see p.444) and Kremna, it is well laid out and informative. To get there, either take a west-bound bus from Eğirdir or a dolmuş from Isparta. It's a twenty-minute walk into town from the *otogar*.

Eğirdir and around

EĞIRDIR is the natural focus of Turkey's Lakeland, boasting an astonishingly beautiful setting, clinging to a strip of flat land between the Toros (Taurus) mountains and Turkey's second largest freshwater lake (488 square kilometres). Lying around 900m above sea level, air temperatures are tolerable in summer (around 30°C), while the clear waters usually remain swimmable until the end of September (though sudden storms can cool things off at any time of year). In April the lake basin's numerous apple orchards bloom and in August/September the apples are harvested.

The town tends to suffer from its convenience as a stopover between the coast and Cappadocia, and most travellers stay only a night or two. This is a pity as **Yeşilada**, a tiny island connected to mainland Eğirdir by a kilometre-long causeway, is a wonderfully relaxing place to stay. It has many excellent *pansiyons* and makes a useful base from which to explore the region's natural and historic sights. **Watersports** are in their infancy in Eğirdir, though it is possible to rent small sailing dinghies and windsurfing is beginning to take off. Tandem paragliding is on offer for the more adventurous, but Eğirdir is best suited to its role as the Lakeland's **trekking** centre and major stop on the long-distance walking route, the **St Paul Trail** (see box, p.450).

Some history

Founded by the Hittites, Eğirdir was taken by the Phrygians in 1200 BC, but it was not until Lydian times, when it straddled the so-called King's Way from Ephesus to Babylon, that the town became famous for its recreational and accommodation facilities.

Early in the thirteenth century the town came under the control of the Konya-based Selçuks, who refortified it in its role as a gateway to Pisidia. Shortly thereafter the city reached the height of its fortunes as capital of the **emirate of Felekeddin Dündar**, remaining prominent during the reign of the Hamidoğlu clan. The Byzantines knew the place as **Akrotiri** ("promontory" in Greek) after its obvious geographical feature; this name was originally corrupted in Ottoman times to **Eğridir** (meaning "it's bent"), but was changed again in the mid-1980s to **Eğirdir**, meaning "s/he's spinning", which officialdom thought more dignified.

Arrival, information and services

The **otogar** is right in the town centre, south of the Hızırbey Camii, from where there are eight daily buses (five in low season) to Yeşilada, the last one at 9pm;

▲ The lakeshore at Eğirdir

alternatively it is only a fifteen-minute walk across the causeway – head east, passing the **harbour** (with its fishing boats, day-trip cruisers and dinghies) on your right and the ruins of the castle on your left. Note that east-bound buses stop opposite the Hızırbey Camii, not in front of the *otogar*.

The **tourist office** is at 2 Sahil Yolu 13 (Mon–Fri 8.30am–noon & 1.30–5pm; ⊕0246/311 4388) by the lakeside, a five-minute walk out of town on the Isparta road. Staff can suggest hotels or *pansiyons* and give limited advice on trekking. **Getting around** this compact market town is easy on foot as everything lies within five minutes' walk of everything else. There are a couple of **ATMs** in the town centre, and several **banks** where you can change money. All of the pensions on the Kale and Yesilada have **internet**. Galeri Nomad, opposite the main harbour on the peninsula, rents out good-quality **mountain bikes** (including helmets, spare tubes and a repair kit) for €12 for 9 hours and €15 for 24 hours, and also kayaks and windsurfers (€12 and €25 respectively per half-day).

Accommodation

Stiff competition keeps room prices low. It's best to stay on **Yeşilada** in order to take full advantage of the lake's charms, though the **Kale** district on the tip of the peninsula is nearer the town proper and has good budget accommodation.

The Kale

Charley's Pansiyon Kale ⊕0246/311 4611, ⓦwww.charleyspension.com. This small, friendly place is the cheapest option in town with 18TL dorm rooms and even cheaper tent space on the patio. The wooden terrace behind the *pansiyon* overlooks the lake and Mount Barla and there is free wi-fi. ❶

Lale Pension Kale ⊕0246/311 2406, ⓦwww.lalehostel.com. Another great budget option, with dorms (18TL per person) and en-suite doubles. There's a top-floor terrace restaurant with harbour views and a wide choice of breakfasts including pancakes, plus internet access, beer and bike rental. İbrahim, the friendly proprietor, rents out bikes and kayaks, and organizes all kinds of trips – from trekking around Kovada lake to night-time beach barbecues and excursions to Sagalassos. ❶

Yeşilada

Ali's Pension East side ☎0246/311 2547, ⓦwww.alispension.com.tr. The most hospitable place in town, located on the sunrise-facing shore. The newly decorated rooms are spotlessly clean, have hot water, central heating and bare wooden floors. The home cooking is wonderful and it's a thirty-metre stroll to a pleasant stony beach/swimming area, or you can rent a car for €35 a day and go exploring. ❸

Big Fish West side ☎0246/311 4413. Restaurant-pension facing the sunset, with newly refurbished rooms with small balconies affording lake views. There are a couple of big family rooms on the top floor, which sleep up to six. ❷

Göl Pension South side ☎0246/311 2370, ⓔgolpension@hotmail.com. Run by four siblings and their mother, this pension serves breakfast beside the lake and has extremely well-kept rooms with balconies; pricier rooms on the terrace offer the best views. ❸

Paris Pension South side ☎0246/311 5509, ⓦwww.parispansiyon.com. The owners of this tiny pension are extremely friendly. Mehmet still works as a fisherman, his wife cooks fine evening meals, and the atmosphere is intimate. The three rooms are a little small but prettily painted yellow. Open all year. ❷

Sehsuvar Peace Pension East ☎0543/811 4210, ⓦpeacepension.com. Up on the hill just behind *Ali's*, with large, clean, simple rooms with white walls and wood floors. The location is peaceful, looking onto the island's mulberry-shaded *meydan*, and the family very friendly. Open year-round. ❷

The town and Yeşilada

Eğirdir's secular architecture was largely damaged by Byzantine–Selçuk conflict, but the religious edifices survived and have been incorporated in the modern town centre. On a preliminary wander the most obvious remains are of the **Dündar Bey Medresi**, which began life in 1218 as an inn, was converted into a *medrese* by Felekeddin Dündar in 1281 and now serves as a shopping precinct. The adjoining **Hızırbey Camii** has also been nicely restored; the roof is supported by Selçuk wooden pillars and it has an ornately carved door, wooden porch and İznik-tiled *mihrab*. The earliest building in the *medrese* complex is Eğirdir's six-domed **bath-house** (1202) which retains its sixteen original washing basins. It provides six rooms for men and a large separate room for women (daily 8am–10pm). Nearby, overlooking the approach to the island, are the ramparts of the Byzantine and Selçuk **citadel** (*kale*), on which an imposing cannon is still perched as a reminder of the importance of the trading interests that were once protected.

Across the causeway, **Yeşilada** itself boasts the twelfth-century Byzantine church of **Ayios Stefanos**, now re-roofed but still awaiting internal restoration. The remaining Greek houses are mainly set in the centre of the island in walled gardens dominated by mulberries and grapes, accessed by tiny cobbled lanes. The small pebble **beaches** that border the island are hard on the feet, but the convenience of being able to take a dip from your pension before breakfast compensates.

Back on the mainland the **Belediye Plajı**, 750m from the town centre in the Yazla district, is the least attractive of the town's beaches. Much better is **Altınkum**, out by the train station, a sandy beach, great for children because of the shallow waters and offering umbrellas, pedal-boats and camping. However, its charm is diminished by a holiday-camp ambience and the modern housing development that backs it. Some 11km up the road on the way to Barla, **Bedre** beach is another option for those with their own transport.

Eating and drinking

Not surprisingly, **lake fish** – especially carp (*sazan*), zander and crayfish – figure prominently on local restaurant menus. On the island, many *pansiyon* owners double as fishermen and offer fresh-caught lake fish presented either as batter-fried fillets, grilled or poached in tomato sauce (*buğulama*). Most restaurants serve alcohol.

Big Apple West side of the island. Offers a choice of indoor or outdoor dining and a wide range of *meze*s. Main courses are substantial, the beer is cheap and there's a good (by local standards) choice of wine. A full meal, excluding alcoholic drinks, should cost no more than 15TL.

Big Fish Next door to the *Big Apple*, this bright-white building is decked out with house plants and an incongruous Swiss Alpine scene. The food and service are good, with the oven-baked trout both very tender and reasonably priced at 7.5TL. The specialty, *sazan dolma* (stuffed carp), must be ordered three hours in advance but is worth the wait. Tables are also set out on the lake's edge in summer.

Felakabad Northeastern tip of the island. A good lunchtime choice, with simple meals including delicious *gözleme* and a decent range of desserts.

Kebab 49 Opposite the Hızırbey Camii. A bustling place offering everything from *döner* sandwiches to *sulu yemek* and home-made rice pudding. Good value, but no alcohol.

Meşir Köftecisi Uzun Çarşı. Local chef Güngör Gül serves up home-made tahini from a secret recipe and delicious grilled *köfte* (meatballs) at this Eğirdir institution. The food is served by weight (5TL per 100g) and a full meal will set you back around 7TL.

Melodi Southeastern tip of the island. A deservedly popular establishment serving up better-than-average lake fish and a wide range of *meze*s. Expect to pay around 15TL for a full meal, but a bottle of wine will set you back the same amount. The tables set out under plane trees right on the foreshore are wonderful on a warm summer's evening.

Özcan Pastanesi Belediye Cad Sok 15. Eğirdir's longest established *pastane* dishes up decent *porça*, *simit* and cakes. It's also the cheapest (though not the smartest) in town.

Excursions from Eğirdir

Many of the *pansiyon*s in Eğirdir offer half- and full-day **boat trips** out on the lake (from about €8 per person) and the fishermen who take you usually know the best swimming and barbecue spots. There's also a range of minibus and taxi **excursions** to points of interest within a few hours' journey of the town. Unless you have a car, it's worth signing up for these, as you'd otherwise never get to many of the places described below. Prices vary between €8 and €15 per person for a typical day-trip, depending on whether it is a taxi or minibus, the distance and the number of people sharing.

Davraz Ski Centre

From December through to the end of March, the northern slopes of 2635-metre Mount Davraz, a half-hour (30km) drive from Eğirdir, offer decent downhill skiing and snowboarding – and the views from the slopes down to Lake Eğirdir are superb. Conditions are fairly reliable, though the limited runs won't satisfy everyone. Ski rental weekdays is 30TL, snowboards 35TL, and a weekday lift pass costs 30TL. Prices for both rental and lift passes rise by fifty percent at weekends.

If you have your own transport, the cheapest and best option is to stay in Eğirdir itself. There are, however, a couple of hotels virtually on the slopes at an altitude of 1800m. The *Davraz Selene* (☎0246/233 0176, ⊛www.davraz.com.tr; ❺) has comfortable, if rather spartan rooms, and the cavernous dining hall offers à la carte lunch and evening meals, with main courses around 10TL. The much grander *Sirene Davraz* (☎0246/267 2002, ⊛sirene.com.tr/sirenedavras.asp; ❽) has a bowling alley, satellite TV and pool tables.

Barla

Virtually the only settlement of any size near the lakeshore (other than Eğirdir itself) is the old village of **BARLA**, 25km northwest of Eğirdir. It makes an excellent starting point for day-walks, and you can see the roofless remains of the church of **Ayios Georgios** (dated 1805 but perhaps earlier) and a far older rock-cut tomb and cyclopean walls in the valley above the village. Barla has a reputation for religious conservatism, as it was the home for a short time of the controversial religious figure **Sait Nursi**. The wooden house where he lived and preached is something of a shrine for the *Nurculuk* ("followers of light") who admire his interpretations of the Koran.

Antioch ad Pisidiam

Around 75km northeast of Eğirdir, and 2km from the modern town of Yalvaç lies the ancient city of **Antioch ad Pisidiam** (Tues–Sun 8.30am–5.30pm; 3TL), where the apostle **St Paul** first attempted to convert pagans to Christianity. The city was originally a Hellenistic foundation of the late third century BC, but peaked in importance as the capital of the Roman province of Pisidia. The city remained important well into Byzantine times, but was abandoned and lost to history in the eleventh century AD.

The most unusual extant remains are of the sizable **temple**, at the highest point of the city, built in a semicircular colonnaded precinct in honour of the Emperor Augustus. Situated just below the temple is the toppled three-arched **propylon** (gateway) dedicated to Augustus, where the Tiberius and Augustus squares meet; most of the blocks lie scattered along the line of the road. Even more substantial are the remains of the **baths** fed by an **aqueduct**. There are also surviving sections of flagged Roman **street**, which once linked the various parts of this walled city and was once spanned by a wing of the **theatre**.

At the lower end of the site, a few courses of monumental stone blocks belonging to the fourth-century **Church of St Paul** (on the site of the synagogue) still stand, but little else can be seen except for the ground plan and some small areas of mosaic floor.

Back in town, the small but fine **Yalvaç Museum** (Yalvaç Müzesi; Tues–Sun 8am–5pm; 2TL), houses finds from the site. You can reach Yalvaç by minibus from Isparta (via) Eğirdir (12 daily in summer); the journey takes an hour and a half. From Yalvaç you'll have to walk or take a taxi the 2km on to the site.

Kovada Gölü and the Kral Yolu

The lake, marshland and forests of **Kovada Gölü**, 35km south of Eğirdir, form a carefully tended and hardly visited national park. Animals found here include wolves, bears and wild boars. The lake itself, teeming with fish, receives the outflow of Eğirdir Gölü. The limestone shore is harsh and the lake itself weedy so it is not particularly good for swimming. However, there's a picnic place with drinking water and seating.

Most tours continue another 30km south on the main road through a gorge towards **Çandır** (signed Yazılı Kanyonu), passing a series of icy but scenic pools and waterfalls, crisscrossed by bridges and best sampled at the height of summer. Here, too, are identifiable, well-preserved stretches of the road locally known as the **Kral Yolu**, or "King's Way", an ancient road that threaded through Pisidia. Just outside the park, and reached by a footbridge, is a **trout restaurant**, the *Baysallar Dinleme Tesisleri*.

Adada

Signposted off the Aksu road, 65km from Eğirdir, **Adada** is another ancient town cut from grey stone. Although there is a warden, no admission is charged and, as the site lies along both sides of a minor road, it is permanently open to visitors. It has never been excavated and history books are strangely silent on the place, but judging from coins found in the area, the place was thriving during imperial Roman times. Visible remains include a particularly well-preserved Corinthian temple, plus two other small temples, a forum with unusual seating along one side, a badly preserved theatre, a church and various Hellenistic buildings. If you follow the stream-bed between the acropolis hill and the adjacent hill, heading southwest behind the forum, it's possible to trace the original Greco-Roman road from the south. This is almost certainly the original road that St Paul walked on his first missionary journey from Perge to Antioch in Pisidia.

Beyşehir and its lake

Leaving Eğirdir in the direction of Konya the next major lake you come to is Beyşehir Gölü. The town of **BEYŞEHİR** – on its eastern shore – sees a lot of through traffic heading in this direction, and its attractive lakeside position and historical legacy make it a good prospect for at least a day-trip.

Judging by the Neolithic remains found in the region, there has been human settlement here since the sixth or seventh millennium BC. There is also extensive evidence of Hittite settlement around the lake. The town itself was originally Byzantine, known as Karallia, and in Selçuk times was surrounded by walls, as well as acquiring a citadel, mosques and hamams. The local golden age, though, came under the Eşrefoğlu dynasty (1277–1326), and its best building dates from that time.

There are a number of attractive monuments in the town, and a lovely weir-bridge, built by German workers in 1902, across the lake's outlet. From here you can watch locals throwing their nets out for the evening catch of *sazan* (carp) in defiance of the "No Fishing" signs.

The Town

The most important monuments in Beyşehir are situated right on the lakeshore to the northwest of the modern town. Finest of these is the **Eşrefoğlu Camii** (most reliably open at prayer time), built by Eşrefoğlu Seyfeddin Süleyman between 1297 and 1299. This large, flat-roofed stone building surmounted by a typical Selçuk flat-sided cone, is an exceptional example of a medieval wooden *beylik* mosque – the *beyliks* being the minor Turkish principalities that ruled Anatolia before the Ottomans gained supremacy. Restoration carried out in the 1950s explains the ugly concrete blocks at the base of the minaret, but otherwise the mosque is in a remarkable state of preservation.

The effect inside is incredibly forest-like: not only are the columns and capitals wooden, but also the rafters, the galleries, the furniture and the balustrades. Adding to the sylvan effect, light plays on the columns from a central aperture, now glassed over, and from high-set windows. Below this is a deep pit, which (according to the *imam*) once held ice for preserving food and cooling the mosque. The *mihrab* is decorated in typical Selçuk style, its turquoise, black and white tiles being almost the last surviving of their type, and the *mimber* is also a lovely period-piece of woodcarving, echoing the star motif apparent throughout the mosque.

The **Eşrefoğlu Türbesi**, the conically roofed building attached to the east side of the mosque, dates from 1302, and was also built for Eşrefoğlu Seyfeddin Süleyman who died in that year. It's worth asking the *imam* if he'll open it up for a look at its beautifully tiled interior, one of the most ornate surviving examples of its type.

To the north of the mosque is the late thirteenth-century **Dokumacılar Hanı** (Cloth Hall), also originally built during the Eşrefoğlu period, with six domes recently restored in brick; again, you'll need to ask permission to see it. To the northwest of the hall there's a double **hamam**, dating from 1260, usually open, but in poor and dilapidated condition. Outside, at the door, there's a pipe that is said to have supplied milk for bathing purposes.

Practicalities

The **otogar** (regular services from Eğirdir, Konya, Antalya and elsewhere) is 2km out of town, but a regular service bus links it with the centre, dropping you near the weir-bridge.

Beyşehir's only decent central **hotel** is the *Beyaz Park* (☏0332/512 4535, ⓦwww.beyazpark.net; ❷), an imposing stone building overlooking the weir at Atatürk Cad 1. Built in the early twentieth century, it has pleasantly furnished rooms; for period atmosphere and coolness, ask for the old building (as opposed to the modern extension), preferably overlooking the river as the roadside is noisy.

The best **restaurant** in town is at the *Beyaz Park*, with reasonable food (including lake fish) and drinks, served in the riverside garden, weather permitting. Opposite the *Beyaz Park* is a **carpet and antique dealer's** called Ceylanlar Sarraf, which sells a good selection of kilims, copperware, Ottoman handguns and old jewellery.

Around the lake

Religious and civic architecture aside, the most obvious local lure is the shallow, freshwater **Beyşehir Gölü**; although Turkey's largest lake in surface area, its 650 square kilometres average a mere 10m in depth. The number of its islands is a hotly disputed topic among the locals, which may be explained by the fact that smaller ones appear and disappear according to the water level (presently very low), but the named ones – many with ruined Byzantine monasteries upon them – number about twenty. The best beach on the lake is **Karaburnu**, 18km from Beyşehir on the Yeşildağ road, then signposted 500m off to the right. It's possible to rent a boat here and explore the islands and the lakeshore.

You can **circumnavigate the lake** by car (rental can be arranged through the *Beyaz Park* hotel) and the little-visited west shore is beautiful. Alternatively, rent a **boat** from Gedikli Köy, on the northwest shore, and visit the once magnificent Selçuk island palace of **Kubadabad**, whose unique tiles can be seen in the Karatay museum in Konya.

More easily accessible on the main, east-shore road towards Eğirdir is the **Eflatun Pınar** (Violet Spring), a thirteenth-century BC Hittite shrine initially signposted 15km northwest of town, just before a petrol station. Turn right, following a paved side road for 5km, then bear left for 2km more along a dirt track to the eponymous village.

At the outskirts, a large, walled pond filling a natural depression receives the flow of vigorous springs. At one corner stand huge carved blocks bearing four relief figures with winged sun discs (symbols of royalty) carried by semi-human monsters. To either side at water level are statues of seated divinities. Excavations by the Konya museum have revealed a row of mountain gods with holes in their skirts which once gushed water, and a large stone block with bull reliefs.

Konya

KONYA is a place of pilgrimage for the whole of the Muslim world. At its heart is the medieval Selçuk capital, which tugs at the hearts of all pious Turks and is often spoken of with more pride than the better-known tourist resorts. This was the adopted home of Celaleddin Rumi, better known as the Mevlâna (Our Master), the Sufic mystic who founded the **whirling dervish** sect, the Mevlevî; his writings helped reshape Islamic thought and modified the popular Islamic culture of Turkey.

In western Turkey, Konya has a reputation as one of the country's most religious and conservative cities, while simultaneously holding the title as the single greatest consumer of *raki* in the nation. At first, it can appear underdeveloped, with poorly equipped schools and people more dour and less sophisticated than those nearer the Aegean, but this perceived "backwardness" in fact goes some way to creating what for many visitors is Konya's charm.

Turkey's seventh largest city is surrounded by some of Turkey's most fertile countryside (the region is known locally as "the breadbasket of Turkey"), and its parks add a splash of greenery to the ubiquitous light-coloured stone. However, Konya can seem bleak in winter and sun-bleached in summer, and you'll find this contrast the rule rather than the exception for Turkish inland towns.

Some history

Konya boasts a history as long and spectacular as that of any Turkish city. The earliest remains discovered date from the seventh millennium BC, and the acropolis was inhabited successively by Hittites, Phrygians, Romans and Greeks. **St Paul** and **St Barnabas** both delivered sermons here after they had been expelled from Antioch and, in 235 AD, one of the earliest Church councils was convened in the city – known then, under the Byzantines, as Iconium.

It also took a central role during the era of the western Selçuks, becoming the seat of the **Sultanate of Rum**. After they had defeated the Byzantine army at the Battle of Manzikert in 1071, the Selçuks attempted to set up a court in İznik, just across the Sea of Marmara from İstanbul. They were expelled from there by the

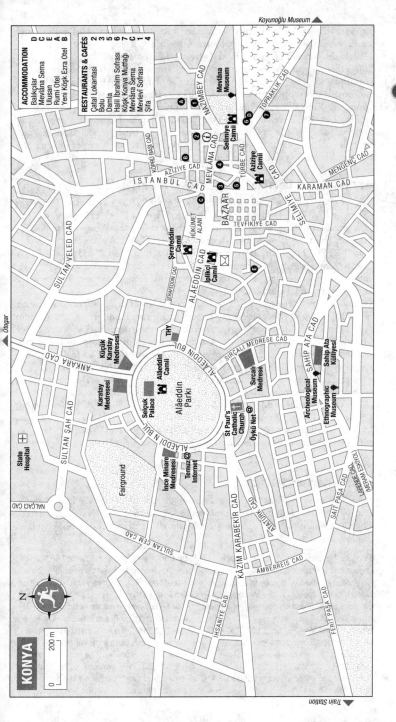

7

453

KONYA

0 ————— 200 m

N

Koyunoğlu Museum ▲

▲ Otogar

Train Station ▲

ACCOMMODATION
Balıkçılar   D
Mevlâna Sema   C
Ulusan   E
Rumi Otel   A
Yeni Köşk Ezra Otel   B

RESTAURANTS & CAFÉS
Çatal Lokantası   2
Bolu   3
Damla   5
Halil İbrahim Sofrası   6
Köşk Konya Mutfağı   7
Mevlâna Sema   C
Mevlevi Sofrası   1
Şifa   4

Mevlâna Museum

NÂZIMBEY CAD

TOPRAKLIK CAD

6 D

7

Selimiye Camii

MEVLÂNA CAD

Aziziye Camii

TÜRBE CAD

SELİMİYE CAD

MENGENÇ CAD

KARAMAN CAD

AZİZİYE CAD

İSTANBUL CAD

KÖPRÜ BAŞI CAD

BAZAAR

TEVFİKİYE CAD

HÜKÜMET ALANI

Şerafeddin Camii

ALÂEDDİN CAD

ŞERAFEDDİN CAD

İplikçi Camii

SULTAN VELED CAD

ANKARA CAD

THY

ALÂEDDİN BUL

SIRÇALI MEDRESE CAD

SAHİP ATA CAD

Küçük Karatay Medresesi

Karatay Medresesi

Alâeddin Camii

Selçuk Palace

Alâeddin Parkı

Sırçalı Medrese

Archeological Museum

Sahip Ata Külliyesi

Ethnographic Museum

St Paul's Catholic Church

Öykü Net

SULTAN ŞAH CAD

State Hospital

İnce Minare Medresesi

Temuz Internet

NALÇACI CAD

Fairground

SULTAN CEM CAD

ALÂEDDİN BUL

KÂZIM KARABEKİR CAD

ATATÜRK CAD

İHSANİYE CAD

AMBERREİS CAD

SAİT PAŞA CAD

LABERİE CAD (MERAM ESKİYOL)

FERİT PAŞA CAD

combined Byzantine and Crusader armies, but still ruled most of eastern and central Asia Minor until the early fourteenth century.

While the concept of a fixed capital was initially somewhat alien to the Selçuks, Konya became the home of their sultans from the time of Süleyman Ibn Kutulmuz, successor to Alparslan, the victor at Manzikert. **Alâeddin Keykubad**, the most distinguished of all Selçuk sultans, established a court of artists and scholars in Konya early in the thirteenth century, and his patronage was highly beneficial to the development of the arts and philosophy during the Selçuk dynasty. Many of the buildings constructed at this time are still standing, and examples of their highly distinctive tile-work, woodcarving, carpet making and masonry are on display in Konya's museums.

Arrival, orientation and information

Konya's **otogar** is a very inconvenient 15km north of the city centre. Take tram #2 marked "Alâeddin" to the end of the line, Alâeddin Parkı. From here you can walk or take a dolmuş to the main street, Mevlâna Caddesi. There is also dolmuş transport from the *otogar* to the Mevlâna Museum (1.40TL). Expect taxis to cost around 25TL. The **train station** is slightly closer, at the far end of Ferit Paşa Caddesi, connected to the centre by dolmuş or by taxi (around 5TL). A THY shuttle bus links the city centre (state theater) with Konya's **airport** 3 times a day for departures to İstanbul only.

Konya has its share of carpet-shop hustlers and self-styled guides, many having only a hazy idea of the location and history of Konya's monuments. Ignore them if you can, as finding your own way around in the compact city centre is not difficult. The town centre consists of a large roundabout – encircling the hillock of **Alâeddin Parkı** – and one main street, called **Alâeddin Caddesi** and, later, **Mevlâna Caddesi**, leading southeast from the hill to the Mevlâna museum. The city's preferred hotels and restaurants are all situated in this central area, and all of the monuments and other attractions are within walking distance.

The **tourist office** (May–Oct Mon–Sat 8.30am–12.30pm & 1.30–5.30pm; Nov–April Mon–Fri 8am–noon & 1–5pm; ☎0332/353 4021) is at Mevlâna Cad 73. This handles bookings for the December **dervish festival** (see box, p.457), for which you should contact them well in advance, as seats for the ceremonies always sell out.

Accommodation

Most of Konya's **hotels** are located on or just off Alâeddin/Mevlâna Caddesi. Finding a room shouldn't be a problem, except during the December festival, when Konya fills up, room prices rise substantially, and an advance booking is an absolute necessity.

Balıkçılar Mevlâna Karşısı ☎0332/350 9470, ⓦwww.balikcilar.com. If money's no object and you want an excellent location, try this flashy three-star hotel opposite the Mevlâna complex, with a/c, satellite TV and balconies with views over the museum. ❺

Mevlâna Sema Mevlâna Cad ☎0332/350 4623, ⓦwww.semaotel.com. Centrally heated, with a/c and minibar – the smallish rooms have been tastelessly refurbished, with garish bedspreads and wallpaper, but are at least comfortable. ❹

Ulusan Çarşı PTT Arkası ☎0332/351 5004. A cosy, spotless hotel behind the post office. The shared bathrooms, which serve the rooms on the first floor, are immaculate and the fittings brand new. Second-floor rooms are en suite, prettily decorated and have TV and fans. Extremely good value, but breakfast is not included. They offer a free laundry service, free internet and wi-fi. ❷

Rumi Otel Derafakıh Sok 5, opposite the Mevlâna, ☎0332/353 1121, ⓦwww.rumiotel.com. Posh digs a stone's throw from the Mevlâna with modern rooms, a rooftop restaurant, hamam and fitness centre. ❺

Yeni Köşk Ezra Otel Esra Kadalar Sok 28, off Aziziye Cad ☎0332/352 0671, ✆www .sevgiseliturizm.com. Small, quiet and well maintained, receiving uniformly positive reviews for its clean, a/c rooms with TVs and bright-blue-tiled bathrooms. The breakfast room is cheerful, and the management very welcoming. ❸

The Mevlâna Museum

A visit to the **Mevlâna Museum** (Mevlâna Müzesi; May–Oct Mon 10am–6pm, Tues–Sun 9am–6pm; Nov–April Tues–Sun 9am–5.30pm; tickets sold until 30min before closing time; 2TL) is among Turkey's most rewarding experiences. It's housed in a former *tekke*, the first lodge of the Mevlevî dervish sect, at the eastern end of Mevlâna Caddesi, and can most easily be found by locating the distinctive fluted turquoise spire that rises directly above Celaleddin Rumi's tomb. The *tekke* served as a place of mystical teaching, meditation and ceremonial dance (*sema*), from shortly after Rumi's death until 1925, when Atatürk banned all Sufic orders. Over the centuries the various dervish orders had become highly influential in political life and thus could pose a threat to his secular reforms.

Most of the **buildings** in the compound, including the *tekke* and *semahane*, were built late in the fifteenth and early in the sixteenth centuries by the sultans Beyazit II and Selim I. Along the south and east sides of the courtyard are the **cells** where the dervishes prayed and meditated, today containing waxwork figures dressed in the costume worn during the whirling ceremony. Next to the quarters of the *şeyh* (head of the dervish order), now the museum office, is a **library** of five thousand volumes on the Mevlevî and Sufic mysticism.

Across the courtyard in the main building of the museum is the **mausoleum** containing the tombs of the Mevlâna, his father and other notables of the order. Slip the plastic bags provided at the entrance over your shoes and shuffle along in a queue of pilgrims, for whom this is the primary purpose of their visit. Women must cover their heads, and if you're wearing shorts you'll be given a skirt-like

---

The life and teachings of the Mevlâna

Celaleddin Rumi, later known as the **Mevlâna**, was born in Balkh, a central Asian city, in 1207. At the age of 20, having received a warning vision, the young man convinced his father to flee Balkh with him for western Asia, which they did just in time to avoid being massacred with the rest of the town by marauding Mongols. They settled in Konya, where the reigning sultan Alâeddin Keykubad received them cordially. The city had a cosmopolitan population, whose beliefs were not lost on the young man and it was here that he emerged as a leading heterodox mystic or Sufi.

During the 1250s he completed a masterpiece of Persian devotional poetry, the *Mathnawi*. A massive work covering several volumes, it concerns the soul's separation from God – characterized as the Friend – as a consequence of earthly existence, and the power of a mutual yearning to bring about a reunion, either before or after bodily death. The Mevlâna – as Rumi was by now widely known – himself died on December 17, 1273.

On a practical level, the Mevlâna instructed his disciples to pursue all manifestations of truth and beauty, while avoiding ostentation, and to practise infinite tolerance, love and charity. He condemned slavery, and advocated monogamy and a higher prominence for women in religious and public life. The Mevlâna did not advocate complete monastic seclusion – the Mevlevîs held jobs in normal society and could marry – but believed that the contemplative and mystical practices of the dervish would free them from worldly anxieties. Although his ideas have never been fully accepted as Islamic orthodoxy they're still one of the most attractive aspects of the religion to Westerners and liberal Muslims alike.

455

▲ The Mevlâna Museum and mausoleum

affair to cover your legs, regardless of sex. The measure of devotion still felt toward the Mevlâna is evident in the weeping and impassioned prayer that takes place in front of his tomb, but non-Muslim visitors are treated with respect and even welcomed. This is in strict accordance with Rumi's own dictates on religious tolerance. If you're a lone *gavur* (infidel) in a centre of Islamic pilgrimage this sentiment is surely one to be cherished.

The semahane

The adjoining room is the original **semahane** (the circular hall in which the *sema* was performed), considered the finest in Turkey. Exhibits include some of the musical instruments of the original dervishes, including the *ney* (reed flute). Other exhibits include the original illuminated *Mathnawi* – the long devotional poem of the Mevlâna now translated into twelve languages – and silk and woollen carpets. One 500-year-old silk carpet from Selçuk Persia is supposed to be the finest ever woven, with 144 knots to the square centimetre; it took five years to complete.

The dervish festival and dances

Since Konya is the spiritual and temporal home of the whirling dervishes, the city plays host to the annual **dervish festival** every December 10–17, during the week prior to the anniversary of the Mevlâna's death. Unfortunately this is not the best time to witness a dervish rite with sub-zero temperatures, doubled hotel rates and shops full of whirling dervish kitsch. In fact the most authentic place to watch a ceremony is in the restored *semahane* in İstanbul, the Galata Mevlevîhane (see p.122). Unlike the dancers in Konya, its members are also practising dervishes who live according to the teachings of the Mevlâna. Alternatively, in July and August, there are official *sema* performances in the gardens of Konya's Mevlâna complex, priced at €20.

The **whirling ceremony** – more properly the *sema* – for which the Mevlevî dervishes are renowned is a means of freedom from earthly bondage and abandonment to God's love. The **clothes** worn by the Mevlevîs during the observance have symbolic significance. The camel-hair hat represents a tombstone, the black cloak is the tomb itself, and the white skirt the funerary shroud. During the ceremony the cloak is cast aside, denoting that the dervishes have escaped from their tombs and from all other earthly ties. The **music** reproduces that of the spheres, and the turning dervishes represent the heavenly bodies themselves. Every movement and sound made during the ceremony has an additional significance – as an example, the right arms of the dancers are extended up to heaven and the left are pointing to the floor, denoting that grace is received from God and distributed to humanity.

The latticed gallery above the *semahane* was for women spectators, a modification introduced by the followers of the Mevlâna after his death. The heavy chain suspended from the ceiling and the concentric balls hanging from it have been carved from a single piece of marble. In the adjoining room, a casket containing hairs from the beard of the Prophet Mohammed is displayed alongside some finely illuminated medieval Korans.

The rest of the city

The modern city radiates out from the **Alâeddin Parkı**, at the end of Mevlâna/Alâeddin Caddesi. As traffic islands go, it's a lovely, wooded place for a stroll and there are also many outdoor cafés to sit at. The site of the original acropolis, the *tepe*, has yielded finds dating back to 7000 BC as well as evidence of Hittite, Phrygian, Roman and Greek settlers, most of which are now in the museum in Ankara. At the foot of the hill to the north are the scant remains of a **Selçuk palace**: two pieces of stone wall, incongruously surmounted by an ugly concrete canopy.

The only other surviving building to bear witness to any of the long history of this mound is the imposing **Alâeddin Camii** (daily 8.30am–5.30pm), begun by Sultan Mesut I in 1130 and completed by Alâeddin Keykubad in 1221. Its typical plain Selçuk interior contains 42 ancient columns with Roman capitals supporting a flat roof, with a small domed area over the *mihrab*. The beautiful carved ebony *mimber*, dated 1155, is the oldest inscribed and dated Selçuk work of art in existence.

The Karatay Medresesi

The recently restored **Karatay Medresesi** on Ankara Caddesi (Tues–Sun 8.30am–noon & 1–5.30pm; 3TL) is another important Selçuk monument. Built in 1251, the *medrese*, or school of Islamic studies, now houses a museum of ceramics, but the building itself provides greater interest. The main **portal** is a fine example of Islamic art at its most decorative, combining elements such as Arabic striped stonework and Greek Corinthian columns with a structure that is distinctly Selçuk: a tall doorway surmounted by a pointed, stalactite arch, reminiscent of the entrance of a tent.

Inside the *medrese* the most attractive exhibit is again part of the building itself. Excavations beneath the floors reveal the building's terracotta hydraulic system, uncovered in 2008. The symmetrical tiling of the famed **dome of stars** is a stylized representation of the heavens in gold, blue and black monochrome tiles. Painted Ottoman tiles from İznik and Kütahya appear clumsy in contrast with those of this delicate mosaic. Selçuk **ceramics** on display in the galleries bear witness to the fact that pious concerns were overruled by secular taste – not to mention the contributions of conquered Christian and pagan subjects – even in medieval times. The striking images of birds, animals and even angels would have been strictly forbidden in more orthodox Islamic societies.

The İnce Minare Medresesi

Behind its fine Selçuk portal the **İnce Minare Medresesi**, or "Academy of the Slender Minaret" (daily: May–Oct 8.30am–12.30pm & 1.30–5.30pm; Nov–April 8am–noon & 1–5pm; 3TL), on the west side of Alâeddin Parkı by the tramway stop, is now being used as a lapidary (stone) and woodcarving museum. The minaret from which it takes its name was severely truncated by lightning in 1901; today the most exquisite feature is the **portal**, even more ornate than that at the Karatay Medresesi.

Most of the exhibits in the museum, like the ceramics in the Karatay Medresesi, came from the ruined Selçuk palace across the way. The finest individual items on display are Selçuk stone reliefs, explicitly showing the influence of Byzantium. Most prominent are winged angels, bestiary pediments and a two-headed eagle relief, said to be from the vanished walls of the medieval city and now the official logo of the modern town.

The Sırcalı Medrese and the archeological museum

A short walk southeast of Alâeddin Parkı along Ressam Sami Sokak, the thirteenth-century **Sırcalı Medrese** (daily: May–Oct 8.30am–12.30pm & 1.30–5.30pm; Nov–April 8am–noon & 1–5pm; free) now houses government offices. Highlights of the building, mostly restored in harsh brick, are the fine blue-glazed tile-work in the rear porch, all that remains of what was once a completely ornamented interior, the handsome portal, and a collection of tombstones – all visible even if the gate is locked.

Continuing in the same direction, you'll reach the small **Archeological Museum** (Arkeoloji Müzesi; Tues–Sun May–Oct 8.30am–12.30pm & 1.30–5.30pm; Nov–April 8am–noon & 1–5pm; 3TL), containing the only pre-Selçuk remains in the city. These include the few Hittite artefacts from the nearby site of Çatal Höyük (see p.460) that have not been relocated to Ankara, and six well-preserved Roman sarcophagi from Pamphylia, one of which depicts Hercules at his twelve labours. Note how the hero's beard grows as his labours progress. Just northeast of the museum, the thirteenth-century **Sahip Ata Külliyesi** is semi-ruined but retains its beautiful brick and stone entrance portal, plus a tiled minaret.

Around the bazaar

On Hükümet Alanı, 100m from the Mevlâna Museum, the north edge of Konya's workaday **bazaar** is marked by the brick **İplikçi Camii**, Konya's oldest (1202) mosque to survive intact and still be in use; legend claims that the Mevlâna preached and meditated here. It is also worth looking out for the **Aziziye Camii** in the bazaar, an Ottoman mosque easily recognized by its unusual (for Turkey) Moghul-style minarets. The bazaar, like the city itself, is very traditional and surprisingly relaxed. Look out for the alternative healing remedies on sale, from daisy water to leeches.

Eating and drinking

Konya's innate religious conservatism has hampered the development of a real "eating out" culture and, although this has begun to change recently, **restaurants** serving alcohol are few and far between, while decor and service are usually strictly functional. The better restaurants are listed below, but if you are after **fast food** check out the numerous places on Atatürk Bulvarı.

Çatal Lokantasi Naci Fikret Sok, off Mevlâna Cad. Small, homely restaurant that serves a decent, tender version of the local speciality, *fırın kebap* (a small portion of lamb or mutton oven-roasted in a clay dish) for around 3YTL.

Bolu İstanbul Cad. Located between Mevlâna Cad and Damla (see below), this Konya institution serves an excellent *etli ekmek* (the city's signature thin crust *pide* topped with ground meat and finely diced peppers) and *ayran* for 5TL.

Damla Türbe Cad. This bustling kebab *salonu* just a few blocks west of the Mevlâna complex turns out delicious *bamya* (okra soup), tender kebabs, and crispy *etli ekmek*. Full meals from 7TL. No alcohol.

Halil İbrahim Sofrası Opposite the Mevlâna complex. Housed in an old building to the right of the *Balıkçılar Hotel*, and recommended for decent kebabs and crispy *pide*.

Köşk Konya Mutfağı Topraklık Cad 66. A five-minute stroll south of the Mevlâna complex, this unusual restaurant serves a wide range of kebabs and grills, and specializes in a variety of *börek* dishes – at around 4TL per portion. In summer tables are set out along a veranda fronted by a pretty garden/allotment area, while in winter a converted 1930s mansion houses the dining room.

Mevlâna Sema Mevlâna Cad. Rooftop terrace-restaurant of the hotel, offering a standard range of grills and kebabs, but also a delicious okra stew. A full meal with beer should cost 12–15TL.

Mevlevî Sofrası Nazimbey Cad; north side of the Mevlâna complex. A restaurant contained within a series of beautifully restored houses, where prices for a wide range of well-prepared Turkish *meze*s, grills and kebabs are fairly reasonable, around 12TL a head. Serves typical dishes like okra soup and the local semolina-based sweet, *hoşmeriim*. In summer, tables on the terrace look over the Mevlâna complex's rose garden.

Şifa Mevlâna Cad, opposite the *Şifa Otel*. Convenient and well patronized by locals and pilgrims, with a wide variety of hot and cold *meze*s, plus the standard grills and a *pide* oven. A full meal with *ayran* should cost around 6TL.

Listings

Airport THY office, Konya Havalimanı ☎0332/239 /1177; airport buses are scheduled to leave from Alâeddin Cad before İstanbul-bound flights.

Banks and exchange There are several *döviz* offices and ATMs on Hükümet Alanı.

Car rental Available from Avis, Nalçacı Cad, Acentacılar Sitesi, B-Blok 87 (☎0332/237 3750); Rüya Turizm, Zafer Meydanı (☎0332/352 7228); and Selen, Aziziye Cad (☎0332/353 6745).

Hamam Behind Şerafeddin Camii on Hükümet Alanı. It's everything you could ask of a Turkish bath: white stone and marble with traditional tiny round skylights striping the steam with rays of sunlight. It has separate wings for men and women, and the masseurs are skilled and thorough. They charge tourists 16–20TL for a scrub and massage.

Internet access Öykü Net, opposite the front entrance of the Catholic church, just off Alâeddin Bul, and another couple of internet cafés near *McDonald's* on Alâeddin Bul.

Police Ferit Paşa Cad ☎0332/353 8141.

Post office PTT on Hükümet Alanı (daily 8.30am–midnight).

Tours Selene, Ayanbey Sok (☎0332/353 6745, ⓦwww.selene.com.tr), offers city tours, and trekking and hunting trips around Beyşehir.

Around Konya

There's little to see in the immediate environs of Konya, though enthusiasts might be persuaded to spend a day or so touring the area's more remote archeological and historical remnants – namely **Çatal Höyük**, possibly Anatolia's earliest settlement; and the ruined Byzantine churches and monasteries of the **Binbir Kilise** region.

Everything else to see from Konya is firmly **en route to Cappadocia**, a couple of hundred kilometres to the east. Depending on your available time, and your inclination, the journey can either take in the **Sultanhanı Kervansaray** (on the most direct route east) or, much more roundabout, the crater lake of **Acı Göl** and the isolated ancient site of **İvriz**.

Apart from Çatal Höyük, which can be visited by public transport, it goes without saying that you'll need your own transport to tour any of the sites scattered across the flat, fertile and relentless Konya plain.

Çatal Höyük

Excavations of prehistoric tumuli at the important Neolithic site of **Çatal Höyük** continue under an international team resident on site during the summer. This is the best time to visit, bearing in mind that there's little to see so you need a lively imagination. There are dolmuşes from Konya to the town of **Çumra**, 48km southeast, from where you will need to take a taxi to the site itself, 10km north of Çumra. With your own transport, leave Konya on the Karaman/Silifke road, Highway 715, and take a left to Çumra 2km before İçeri Çumra. The road to the site is marked in the town. Alternatively hire a taxi for around 60TL for a return trip.

Discovered by the British archeologist James Mellaart in 1958, **the site** (daily 8.30am–5.30pm; free) consists of twin, flattened hills that are supposed to resemble the shape of a fork, hence the name Çatal Höyük, or "Fork Tumulus". A number of exciting discoveries made here gave significant clues about one of the world's oldest civilizations, dating from 6800 BC. Evidence pointed to entire complexes of houses, crammed together without streets to separate them, and entered through holes in the roof. Also found were murals of men being eaten by vultures, animal-head trophies stuffed with squeezed clay, and human bones wrapped in straw matting and placed under the seats in a burial chamber. There is also the world's first landscape painting, a mural depicting the eruption of a volcano, presumably nearby Hasan Dağa.

Most famous of all the discoveries are statuettes of the **mother goddess**, supposed to be related to the Phrygian goddess Cybele and her successor Artemis. The baked earthenware or stone figures are 5–10cm tall and show a large-breasted, broad-hipped woman crouching to give birth. The most interesting pieces are now in Ankara's Museum of Anatolian Civilizations (see p.507), though a small **museum** near the site entrance houses some of the less fascinating finds.

Binbir Kilise

Binbir Kilise, or "A Thousand and One Churches", is the name given to a remote region directly north of Karaman, itself 107km southeast of Konya. Scattered across the base of the extinct volcano Kara Dağ are indeed close to that number of ruined churches and monasteries, mostly dating from the ninth to the eleventh centuries, when the region was a refuge for persecuted Christians.

To get there, travel on the paved road 21km north from Karaman via Kılbasan, and then turn left (northwest) on a rougher dirt track for 10km more towards the village of **MADEN ŞEHIR**, in the middle of one of the main concentrations of basalt-built chapels. These, many in good condition, are all that's left of a substantial, unidentified town that flourished from Hellenistic to Byzantine times.

Acı Göl

Ninety kilometres east of Konya, just off Highway 330, there's a very beautiful crater lake, **Acı Göl**. It lies just east of Karapınar, hidden from the road – the turn-off is a narrow, unsignposted, white-dirt track a little way east of a Türkpetrol truckstop on a knoll, about 11km after the Karapınar turn-off. You can camp, and perhaps even swim here, as you're far enough from the road to ensure some privacy, but as the name (Bitter Lake) implies, the water is undrinkable.

Cappadocia

The unique landscape of **Cappadocia** is now one of the star attractions of Turkey, yet on first impression it can seem a disturbing place. The still dryness and omnipresent dust give an impression of barrenness, and the light changes with dramatic effect to further startle the observer. Only with time comes the realization that the volcanic tuff that forms the land is exceedingly fertile, and that these weird formations of soft, dusty rock have been lived in over millennia by many varying cultures. The most fascinating aspect of a visit here is the impression of continuity: **rock caves** are still inhabited and pottery is still made from the clay of the main river, the Kızılırmak. **Wine** is produced locally as it has been since Hittite times, and the **horses** from which the region takes its name (Cappadocia translates from the Hittite as "land of well-bred horses") are still to some extent used in the region, along with mules and donkeys.

The peaks of three **volcanoes** – Erciyes, Hasan and Melendiz Dağları – dominate Cappadocia. It was their eruptions some thirty million years ago, covering the former plateau of Ürgüp in ash and mud, that provided the region's raw material: **tuff**. This soft stone, formed by compressed volcanic ash, has been worked on ever since, by processes of erosion, to form the valleys and curious fairy chimney rock formations for which the region is so famous.

The original eruptions created a vast erosion basin, dipping slightly towards the Kızılırmak River, which marks an abrupt division between the fantasy landscape of rocky Cappadocia and the green farmland around Kayseri. Where the tuff is mixed with rock, usually basalt, the erosion process can result in the famous cone-shape chimneys: the tuff surrounding the basalt is worn away, until it stands at the top of a large cone. Eventually the underpart is eaten away to such an extent that it can no longer hold its capital: the whole thing collapses and the process starts again.

In the Cemil valley, near Mustafapaşa, the cones give way to tabular formations – table mountains – caused by the deep grooves made by rivers in the harder geological layers. Another important region lies to the northwest of the Melendiz mountain range, the valley of the Melendiz Suyu, or Ihlara valley. The most individual feature of this region is the red canyon through which the river flows, probably the most beautiful of all the Cappadocian landscapes.

The best-known sites, are located within the triangle delineated by the roads connecting Nevşehir, Avanos and Ürgüp. Within this region are the greater part of the valleys of **fairy chimneys**, the **rock-cut churches** of the Göreme Open-Air Museum, with their beautiful frescoes, and the **Zelve monastery**, a fascinating warren of troglodyte dwellings and churches. **Nevşehir**, largest of the towns, is dull, but is an important centre for travel in the region, while **Ürgüp** and its neighbouring villages, **Göreme**, **Çavuşin**, **Üçhisar** and **Ortahisar**, all make attractive bases from which to tour the surrounding valleys, but aren't well served by public transport. **Avanos**, beautifully situated on the Kızılırmak River, is a centre of the local pottery industry.

Outside the triangle heading south, but still fairly well frequented by tour groups, are the underground cities of **Derinkuyu** and **Kaymaklı**, fascinating warrens attesting to the ingenuity of the ancient inhabitants. Less well-known sites are located further to the south, to the east and west. The **Ihlara** valley near **Aksaray**, a red canyon riddled with churches cut into its sides, is the most spectacular sight yet to feel the full force of tourism. **Kayseri** has long been a quiet provincial capital, recommended for its Selçuk architecture and bazaars, and side trips out to the ski resort on Erciyes Dağı and the Sultansazlığı bird sanctuary. To the south, attractions around the town of **Niğde** include the **Eski Gümüşler** monastery, whose frescoes rival the more famous examples in Göreme.

Some history

The earliest known settlers in the Cappadocia region were the **Hatti**, whose capital, Hattuşaş, was located to the north of Nevşehir. The growth of the Hattic civilization was interrupted by the arrival of large groups of Indo-European immigrants from Western Europe, the **Hittites** (see p.526). After the fall of the Hittite Empire around 1200 BC, the region was controlled to varying degrees and at different times by its neighbouring kingdoms, Lydia and Phrygia in the west, and Urartu in the east. This situation continued until the middle of the sixth century BC, when the Lydian king Croesus was defeated by the Persians under Cyrus the Great.

Cappadocia was saved from Persian rule by the arrival of **Alexander the Great** in 333 BC, and subsequently enjoyed independence for 350 years, until it became a Roman province with Kayseri (Caesarea) as its capital. Despite this nominal annexation, effective **independence** was ensured in the following centuries by the relative disinterest of the Roman and Byzantine rulers, whose only real concerns were to control the roads (and thereby keep open eastern trading routes) and to extort tributes of local produce. Meanwhile the locals existed in much the same way as they do now, living in rock-hewn dwellings or building houses out of local stone, and relying on agriculture, viniculture and livestock breeding.

This neglect, combined with the influence of an important east–west trading route, meant that a number of faiths, creeds and philosophies were allowed to flourish here. One of these was **Christianity**, introduced in the first century by St Paul. Taking refuge from increasingly frequent attacks by Arab raiders, the new Christian communities took to the hills, and there they literally carved out dwelling places, churches and monasteries for entire communities.

In the eleventh century the **Selçuk Turks** arrived, quickly establishing good relations with the local communities. They, too, were interested primarily in trading routes and their energies went into improving road systems and building the *kervansarays* that are strung along these roads to this day. In the middle of the thirteenth century the Selçuk Empire was defeated by the **Mongols** and Cappadocia was controlled by the Karaman dynasty, based in Konya, before being incorporated into the Ottoman Empire in the fourteenth century. The last of the Christian Greeks left the area in the 1920s during the exchange of populations by the Greek and Turkish governments.

Nevşehir and around

NEVŞEHIR is an important transportation node, but hardly a place to linger: the town consists of a couple of scruffy streets, with no real centre or monumental architecture. But since Nevşehir's *otogar* lies just 1km north of the centre of town on the Aksaray road, a quick trip downtown is easy if you have a layover between bus or dolmuş departures. If you do stay, however, you'll find that it's easy to make side trips by dolmuş to the monastic complex at Açıksaray.

The Town

The long walk up to the remains of the Ottoman **kale** is pleasant enough, but once you get there, there's little left apart from a few crenellated walls. Much more interesting is the **Damat İbrahim Paşa Camii** (1726), still the most imposing building in Nevşehir, situated on the side of the citadel hill with its *medrese* and library above it and a tea garden directly below. The stone of the building is a pleasant, unadorned yellow, and its internal painting, especially under the sultan's loge and around the casements, is delightful.

Nevşehir Museum, (Nevşehir Müzesi; Tues–Sun 8am–5pm; 3TL) on Yeni Kayseri Caddesi, is well worth the fifteen-minute walk out from the tourist office. Its comprehensively labelled exhibits include three terracotta sarcophagi, dating from the third to fourth centuries AD, which resemble abstract mummy cases with little doors inserted at face and knee level. Finds from the Phrygian and Byzantine periods include mirrors, pins, spoons, terracotta pots and the like; upstairs is an exhibition of Turkish carpets and kilims and the looms on which they were made, as well as lovely, old, heavy silver Ottoman jewellery.

Practicalities

From the **otogar** it's a short dolmuş or city-bus ride to the town centre. Orientation is a simple matter: the **kale** (castle), which stands at the heart of the old city – to the southwest of the modern centre – is a constant landmark. The new city below is divided by two main streets: **Atatürk Bulvarı**, on which are situated most of the hotels and restaurants, and **Lale Caddesi**, turning into Gülşehir Caddesi to the north.

The **tourist office** is on Atatürk Bulvarı (daily 8am–5.30pm; ☎0384/213 3659), on the right as you head downhill towards Ürgüp. The **PTT** is on Yeni Kayseri Caddesi, on the way out to the museum.

Accommodation in Nevşehir tends to be less good value than elsewhere in Cappadocia, and the nearby towns are so much more attractive that an overnight stop here is by necessity only. If you are absolutely stuck, the lowest rates are at the comfortable and friendly *Hotel Şems* (☎0384/213 3597; ❸), on Atatürk Bul 29 above the *Aspava Restaurant*. Rooms have en-suite bathrooms and guaranteed hot water, but are dingily furnished; ask for a room at the back, for quiet and views. The best **places to eat** are a string of kiosks at the end of Atatürk Caddesi which sell good, cheap kebabs, *kokorec* and *pide*. Near the *Belediye*, a restored Ottoman teahouse is far and away the most attractive place to linger.

Nevşehir's **market** is important to the region and consequently runs from Sunday morning to Monday night, taking over a large area below Eski Sanayı Meydanı.

Açıksaray

About 19km north of Nevşehir, the **Açıksaray** – reached by half-hourly Gülşehir dolmuşes from Nevşehir's *otogar* – is a sixth- to seventh-century monastic complex, carved out of fairy chimneys and tuff cliffs. Two kilometres further on the same road towards Gülşehir is the far more rewarding **church of St John** (daily 8.30am–5.30pm; 8TL). The Gülşehir dolmuşes, which depart half-hourly from the *otogar* in Nevşehir, will drop you on the main road. From here it's a five-minute walk to the church, signposted Karşı Kilise/St Jean Church. The **frescoes**, rescued from beneath the soot in 1995, are amongst the most vibrant in Cappadocia. As it is so rarely visited, you have time and space to appreciate the poignant biblical scenes, including the *Last Supper* and the *Betrayal by Judas*.

Hacıbektaş

The small town of **HACİBEKTAŞ**, 45km north of Nevşehir, was chosen by one of the greatest medieval Sufic philosophers, Hacı Bektaş Veli, as the location of a centre of scientific study. The town was renamed in his honour after his death. The tomb of Hacı Bektaş Veli is located within the monastery complex, but the main part of the complex dates from the Ottoman period, when it was the headquarters of a large community of Bektaşi dervishes. The teachings of Hacı Bektaş Veli (see box opposite) had reverberations throughout the Muslim world, and different sects, including the Bektaşi, the Alevî and the Tahtacı, still follow traditions that originated in his doctrines. These sects are now the main counterbalancing force to Islamic fundamentalism in Turkey.

Four daily Ankara-bound **buses** from Nevşehir run to the town (1hr), and there are frequent dolmuşes from Gülşehir, 20km north of Nevşehir, itself linked to Nevşehir by regular dolmuşes. The town of Hacıbektaş is also well known for its **onyx**, which is by far the cheapest in the region – the shops are found in the street

The life and teachings of Hacı Bektaş Veli

Little is known about the life of **Hacı Bektaş Veli**, but he is believed to have lived from 1208 to 1270. Like other Turkish intellectuals of the time he was educated in Khorasan, where he became well versed in religion and mysticism. After journeying with his brother, he returned to Anatolia and lived in Kayseri, Kırşehir and Sivas. Eventually he settled in a hamlet of seven houses, Suluca Karahöyük, the present location of the monastery.

In comparison to his life, his teachings are well known, especially his great work, the *Makalat*, which gives an account of a four-stage path to enlightenment or *Marifet* – a level of constant contemplation and prayer. The faults that grieved Hacı Bektaş most were those of ostentation, hypocrisy and inconsistency: "It is of no avail to be clean outside if there is evil within your soul." This could be the origin of the unorthodox customs of later followers of the **Bektaşi sect**, which included drinking wine, smoking hashish, eating during Ramadan and – for women – uncovering the head outside the home. Hacı Bektaş's own dictum on women was unequivocal, and it is one of the most popularly quoted of all his sayings: "A nation which does not educate its women cannot progress."

leading up to the Hacıbektaş monastery complex. August 16–18 annually there is a festival celebrating the philosopher's life.

The monastery complex

Construction of the **monastery complex** was begun during the reign of Sultan Orhan in the fourteenth century, and it was opened to the public as a **museum** (Tues–Sun 8am–5pm; 3TL) in 1964, after extensive restoration. It comprises three courtyards, the second of which contains the attractive Aslanlı Çeşmesi, the **lion fountain**, named after a lion statue that was brought from Egypt in 1853. The sacred *karakazan* or **black kettle** (actually a cauldron) can be seen in the kitchen to the right of the courtyard. Important to both the Bektaşi sect and the janissaries, the black kettle originally symbolized communality, with possible reference to the Last Supper of the Christian faith.

To the left of the courtyard is the **Meydan Evi**, bearing the earliest inscription in the complex, dated 1367. The timber roof of the Meydan Evi – where formal initiation ceremonies and acts of confession took place – has been beautifully restored, showing an ancient construction technique still in use in rural houses in central and eastern Anatolia. It's now an exhibition hall containing objects of significance to the order, including musical instruments and a late portrait of Hacı Bektaş, apparently deep in mystical reverie, with a hart in his lap and a lion by his side.

The third courtyard is the location of a **rose garden** and a well-kept **graveyard**, where the tombs bear the distinctive headware of the Bektaşi order. The **tomb of the sage** is also located in the third courtyard, entered through the Akkapı, a white-marble entranceway decorated with typical Selçuk motifs including a double-headed eagle. Off the corridor leading to the tomb is a small room that is said to have been the cell of Hacı Bektaş himself.

Derinkuyu and Kaymaklı

Among the most extraordinary phenomena of the Cappadocia region are the remains of **underground settlements**, some of them large enough to have accommodated up to thirty thousand people. A total of forty such settlements, from villages to vast cities, have been discovered, but only a few have so far been opened to the public. The best known are **Derinkuyu** and **Kaymaklı**, on the road from Nevşehir to Niğde. There are no fairy chimneys here, but the ground consists of the same volcanic tuff, out of which the beleaguered, ever-resourceful Cappadocians created vast cities that are almost completely unnoticeable from ground level.

In origin, the cities are thought to date back to **Hittite** times at least (1900–1200 BC). Hittite-style seals have been found during excavations and other Hittite remains, such as a lion statue, have turned up in the area. It is possible that the underground rooms were used as shelters during the attacks of 1200 BC, when the Hittite Empire was destroyed by invaders from Thrace. Later the complexes were enlarged by other civilizations, and the presence of missionary schools, churches and wine cellars would seem to indicate that they were used by **Christian communities**.

Derinkuyu

The most thoroughly excavated of the underground cities is located in the village of Derinkuyu, 29km south of Nevşehir. There are half-hourly dolmuşes here from Nevşehir *otogar*, and a daily bus from Aksaray.

The underground city of **Derinkuyu** (daily: May & June 8am–6pm; July–Sept 8am–7pm; Oct–April 8am–5pm; 15TL) is signposted off to the left as you approach from Nevşehir. It's advisable to get there before 10am, when the tour groups arrive. The city is well lit and the original ventilation system still functions remarkably well, but some of the passages are small and cramped, and can get overcrowded.

The area cleared to date occupies 1500 square metres and consists of a total of eight floors reaching to a depth of 55 metres. What you'll see includes: on the first two floors, stables, winepresses and a dining hall or school with two long, rock-cut tables; living quarters, churches, armouries and tunnels on the third and fourth floors; and a crucifix-shaped church, a meeting hall with three supporting columns, a dungeon and a grave on the lower levels. In a room off the meeting hall is a circular passageway, which is believed to have been a confessional.

Dropping between 70 and 85 metres to far below the lowest floor level were 52 large **ventilation shafts** and the **deep wells**, from which the city takes its name. There are a number of escape routes from one floor to another, and passages leading beyond the city, one of which is thought to have gone all the way to Kaymaklı (see below), 9km away. The walls of the rooms are completely undecorated, but chisel marks are clearly visible and give some idea of the work that must have gone into the creation of this extraordinary place. Most evocative are the huge **circular doors** that could be used to seal one level from another. The doors, which were virtually impregnable from the outside, would have been closed with a pole through the circular hole in their centre, and through this hole arrows could have been shot once the door was secure.

Kaymaklı

North of Derinkuyu, the Nevşehir–Niğde highway passes **Kaymaklı** (daily: March–Sept 8am–7pm; Oct–Feb 8am–5pm; 15TL). Smaller and consequently less popular than Derinkuyu, only five of this city's levels have been excavated to date. The layout is very similar: networks of streets with small living spaces leading off them open into underground plazas with various functions, the more obvious of which are stables, smoke-blackened kitchens, storage space and winepresses.

Üçhisar

ÜÇHISAR, 7km east of Nevşehir on the Nevşehir–Ürgüp and Nevşehir–Göreme dolmuş runs, is the first truly Cappadocian village en route to the centre of the region from Nevşehir. It's an attractive place, with some of the best accommodation options in the region, dominated by a central, sixty-metre-high **rock/castle** (daily 7am–8.15pm; 3TL) riddled with caves and tunnels which once housed the entire village, but are now abandoned. The best time for a visit is at sunset, when the views of the surrounding countryside, including Erciyes Dağı to the east and Melendiz and Hasan Dağları to the southwest, are particularly alluring. It's an excellent place to get a first impression of Cappadocia's extraordinary geology.

Arrival

Dolmuşes from Nevşehir, Göreme and Ürgüp drop you just west of the centre of the upper village. The **PTT** is just east of the main square. ATMs are located in the main square, but there are no banks here, so you'll have to drop into Göreme if you need to change money. The Üçhisar **internet** café is just off the main square.

Accommodation

Much quieter than neighbouring Göreme, Üçhisar is extremely popular with French visitors, who have been coming here for decades. The most atmospheric places are in the old village on the hillside below the rock, many of which are at least partially carved into the hillside.

1001 Nuits On the new Göreme road as you leave the village ☎0384/219 2293, ⒲www.1001 gecehotel.com. Occupying a series of caves cut into fairy chimneys, some with en-suite bathrooms and with magnificent views from its balconies, this place combines the quirkiness of a rock-cut *pansiyon* with the facilities of a hotel. ❹

Kale Konak Kale Sok 9 ☎0384/219 2828, ⒲www.kalekonak.com. Built from three stone houses facing onto the Göreme valley, this new guesthouse offers cave rooms decked out in antiques and artwork from the Middle and Far East. Common areas are set in terraced pergolas and stone courtyards and there is a wine cellar and hamam. ❻

Kaya Pansiyon Below the rock/castle ☎0384/219 2441, ⒲www.kayapension.com. The pleasant terrace restaurant affords fantastic views, an excellent buffet-style breakfast is included in the price and evening meals are a reasonable 20TL. Standard rooms ❹, cave rooms ❺

Lale Saray Tekelli Mah ☎0384/219 2333, ⒲www.lalesaray.com. In the old town under the rock/castle, a very attractive pale-stone building, with bands of carved black stonework framing doors and windows. Rooms are a mix of barrel-vaulted cellars and caves, all fitted with the usual mod cons, and immaculate bathrooms with hydro-massage baths or showers and five have views over the valley to Göreme. ❻

Les Maisons de Cappadoce Belediye Meydanı ☎0384/219 2782, ⒲www.cappadoce.com. A group of self-catering stone houses lovingly and stylishly restored by a French architect. Breakfast is delivered by basket to your door, otherwise you're left to your own devices. The fanciest house costs €1000 a night and sleeps six. ❺–❾

Les Terrasses D'Üçhisar ☎0384/219 2792, ⒲www.terrassespension.com. Run by a charmingly extrovert French couple, with well-furnished cave rooms, great views from the top floor and excellent Turkish food with French flair. Marco, the owner, leads visitors on local walks. Closed Dec–Feb ❸

Museum Hotel Tekhelli Mah ☎0384/219 2220, ⒲www.museum-hotel.com. In the lower village, a warren of thirty beautifully restored cave and vaulted cellar rooms, many with superb views. Rooms are individually furnished with fine antiques; some have wine taps, and even wine cellars. The restaurant serves creative Ottoman fare. The most expensive Imperial Suite will set you back a staggering €2250 in summer. ❻–❾

Eating

In spite of its wide range of accommodation, Üçhisar has relatively few **restaurants** to write home about. Many hotels offer half-board and average food. An exception, *Les Terrasses D'Üçhisar* is open to nonresidents, and serves fine Turkish food with a French touch for around 25TL a head. The smart *Lil'a*, in the *Museum Hotel*, is recommended for its magnificent views, and creative organic Turkish cuisine. A full meal will set you back around 60TL, but it's well worth it for a treat. The best place in town is the open-air ⚔ *Centre*, on the village square, which serves quality traditional Turkish *meze*s and grills at a good price.

Wine tasting is possible in many of Cappadocia's wineries, but Kocabağ Kav Butik in Üçhisar is among the best venues for sampling the finest products the region has to offer. It's worth remembering that Cappadocian whites are generally more elegant than reds, which tend to be a mixture of the acidic local varietals. Kocabağ winery's shop is located on the main road heading west out of town from Belediye Meydanı.

Göreme

The large village of **GÖREME** – just 3km northeast of Üçhisar – is of central importance to Cappadocian tourism, partly because of its open-air museum, located a couple of kilometres away on the Ürgüp road, but mostly because it is the most famous of the few remaining Cappadocian settlements whose rock-cut

---

Outdoor and adventure tourism in Cappadocia

Cappadocia's rugged terrain lends itself to outdoor and adventure tourism, from the relative effortlessness of hot-air ballooning to arduous ascents of towering volcanic peaks.

Hot-air ballooning

The region's canyons and fairy chimneys take on a whole new aspect when viewed from above, and **hot-air-balloon** trips are now incredibly popular. The original operator, with twenty year's experience, is Kapadokya Balloons (☎0384/271 2442, ⓦwww.kapadokyaballoons.com), based in Göreme. Its highly professional pilots ensure clients get the most out of their flight by manoeuvring the balloon between treetops and fairy chimneys. "Exclusive" flights (1hr 45min) begin around dawn, when the conditions are best, and cost €250 per person, including transfers, insurance and a champagne breakfast. Göreme Balloons (☎0384/341 5662, ⓦwww.goreme balloons.com) and Ez-Air of Çavuşin, (☎0384/341 7096 ⓦwww.ezairballoons.com) are other reliable companies offering daily flight departures. Whichever you choose, be sure to pick a reputable company; ballooning is an adventure but it is an activity that should be taken seriously.

Mountain biking and horseriding

Cappadocia is tailor-made for **mountain biking**, with a network of dirt tracks connecting villages to each other and to their fields, hilly terrain and plunging valleys. The annual Cappadocia Mountain Bike Festival attracts top bikers from around the world. The first local agency on the mountain-biking scene was Ürgüp-based Argeus (☎0384/341 4688, ⓦwww.capadocciaexclusive.com) which offer one- to eight-day guided tours. Trips are almost entirely off-road, and start at US$1180 per person, with accommodation in B&B. Argeus will rent customers its own bikes, but riders usually bring their own. Another good bike-trip operator is Kirkit Voyage of Avanos

houses and fairy chimneys are still inhabited. Still an institution on the Turkish backpacker circuit, its accommodation in the past few years has shifted towards well-heeled visitors while its main street is given over almost entirely to servicing tourists – there are carpet shops, *pansiyons*, tour companies and restaurants everywhere, and you don't even need to wander out of your cave room to connect to the wireless internet.

Whilst the influx of visitors has enabled the local economy to boom, the fragile environment is being put under increasing pressure. Already scarce water resources are dwindling and illegal building is rarely controlled by the local authorities. Yet despite the commercialization, the place has managed to hold onto a degree of authentic charm, and a short stroll off the main street or into the nearby valleys will still take you up into tuff landscapes, vineyards that the locals cultivate for the production of *pekmez* (grape molasses), and the occasional rock-cut church, unknown to the hordes who frequent the nearby museum.

Local public transport around the region is adequate, bicycle, motorbike and car rental outlets are plentiful, and daily tours are competitively priced, so it's not a bad base from which to make your explorations.

Arrival, information and tours

Orientation is quite straightforward in Göreme, as the **otogar** is right in the centre of the town. The unofficial **tourist office** (daily 5am–8pm) is also here, offering a list of accommodation, maps and books for sale, but little in the way of help, while several **ATM**s are nearby. The **PTT** is a five-minute walk away – head northeast

(see below). Both companies, and many other outlets in Göreme and Ürgüp, rent out bikes for half- and full days.

With its wide-open spaces, big skies, canyons and mesas, Cappadocia is reminiscent of the American West, and **horseriding** is a natural way to explore. There are several ranches in the region. Kirkit Voyage (℡0384/511 3259, ⊛www.kirkit.com; see p.652) has a well-regarded stable in Avanos, with 45 well-groomed horses. Sunset rides cost €25, half-day tours from €35, while a seven-day, all-inclusive camping expedition is €600. Also at Avanos, with similar standards and prices, is the Akhal-Teke (℡0384/511 5171, ⊛www.akhal-tekehorsecenter.com).

Hiking and skiing
There are plenty of **hiking trails** through the valleys, though so far only basic sketch maps are widely available, and signposts sparse. The trail from Göreme to Üçhisar through Pigeon Valley (see p.472), and the Ihlara Gorge are just two routes popular with independent walkers, though there are many more. "Walking Mehmet" (℡0532/382 2069, ⊛www.walkingmehmet.com), based at the *Café Roma* in Göreme, knows the area inside out, and leads groups for €50 per day. Middle Earth Travel (℡0384/271 2559, ⊛www.middleearthtravel.com) of Göreme charges from €40 per person for hikes in the Ihlara valley, from €175 for two-day climbs up Erciyes Dağı or Hasan Dağı, and around €560 for a one-week trek of the region, including accommodation.

From Christmas to early March, winter snows give the Cappadocian landscape an ethereal, hauntingly beautiful appearance, and **snowshoeing** is growing in popularity. Kirkit (see above) rents out equipment for €30 per day, and one-week guide-tours around Hasan Dağı cost from €480 all-inclusive. For downhill skiing the resort on the flank of Erciyes Dağı (see p.494) has reliable snow and reasonable facilities. Both Kirkit and Argeus can help organize **ski-touring/mountaineering** in the region.

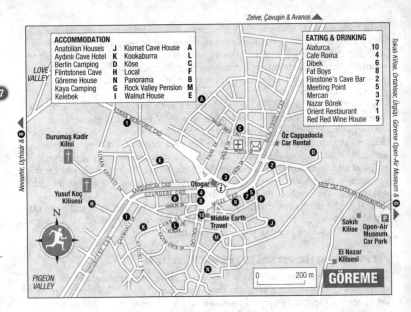

ACCOMMODATION			
Anatolian Houses	J	Kismet Cave House	A
Aydınlı Cave Hotel	K	Kookaburra	L
Berlin Camping	D	Köse	C
Flintstones Cave	H	Local	F
Göreme House	N	Panorama	B
Kaya Camping	G	Rock Valley Pension	M
Kelebek	I	Walnut House	E

EATING & DRINKING	
Alaturca	10
Cafe Roma	4
Dibek	6
Fat Boys	8
Flinstone's Cave Bar	2
Meeting Point	5
Mercan	3
Nazar Börek	7
Orient Restaurant	1
Red Red Wine House	9

on the main road to Avanos and turn left more or less opposite the right turn signposted "Göreme Open-Air Museum". It's a small town and the locals are more than happy to point you in the direction of your target accommodation, which may be necessary if it is one of those tucked away in the narrow backstreets.

Reputable **tour companies** include Middle Earth Travel (see box, p.469) on Cevizler Sok 20, Neşe (℡0384/271 2525, ⓦwww.nesetour), on the main street, and Matiana (℡0384/271 2902, ⓦwww.matiana.com) on Uzundere Sokak. All offer a variety of daily tours of the region starting at €40 per person (standard itineraries include Ihlara and the underground cities, and Mustafapaşa and Soğanlı). The more costly usually stick to the sites, hence the higher tour prices as there is no commission to be made.

If you want to do it yourself, arrange **car rental** with Öz Cappadocia (℡0384/271 2159, ⓦwww.ozcappadocia.com), near the *otogar*: cars from €40 per day, mountain bikes (€22 a day) and 100cc mopeds (€25 a day) available. Several other companies around the *otogar* also rent out cars, mountain bikes and scooters. Look around for the best deal, but make sure you check for any dents or scratches, as some agencies have been known to charge for damage caused by previous customers.

Accommodation

Göreme's *pansiyons* have long been a favourite with backpackers though accommodation can now be found in all price ranges. The tourist office at the bus station has information about most of the town's *pansiyons*, including photographs, prices and so on. Many of the hotels and *pansiyons* are now run by Turkish–European/Australian partnerships, and those that aren't will have fluent English-speakers at hand.

Backpacker/pansiyons

Flintstones Cave Karşıbucak Cad 3 ℡0384/271 2555, ⓦwww.theflinstonesvacehotel.com. A mix of cave and vaulted cellar rooms, and spotless en suites. The bed linen is a little tasteless, but the real draw here is the decent-sized pool, and the bar with free use of the pool table, ADSL internet connection and English-language films. Dorm rooms are 14TL including breakfast. ②

Kookaburra Konak Sok 10 ☎0384/271 2549, ⓦwww.kookaburramotel.com. Eclectically furnished rooms in an old Ottoman house with great views from the terraces – some rooms en suite, others waterless, plus dormitory accommodation. There is satellite TV, free internet, laundry service and a pleasant terrace bar. With a free beer or glass of wine thrown in on arrival, it's great value. Dorm beds 15TL (excluding breakfast); ❷

Köse ☎0384/271 2294, ⓦwww.kosepension .com. Run by the hospitable Mehmet and Dawn, this travellers' favourite just off the Avanos road offers a pleasant garden with an excellent swimming pool, and a choice of dorm beds, doubles with and without bathrooms, and simple singles. The food is well regarded, too, mixing local fare with backpacker staples. Free wi-fi for laptop users. Dorm beds 12TL; ❸

Rock Valley Pension Isali Mah, Iceri Dere Sok ☎0384/271 2153, ⓦwww.rockvalleycappadocia .com. Popular among budget travellers who use its dorm beds and with a reputation for kind and accommodating staff, the pension boasts a pool, café, free internet and summer bbqs. You can stay in a private en-suite room if a dorm bed doesn't suit you. Dorm beds from 12.5TL; ❸

Hotels

Göreme House Eselli Mah 47 ☎0384/271 2060, ⓦwww.goremehouse.com. A good example of how traditional stonecutting skills have survived; natural woodwork and local soft furnishings re-create an elegant period-style mansion. Immaculately run by a Turkish/Australian partnership, all thirteen rooms are good value. ❺

Kelebek Aydınlı Mah Yavuz Sok 1 ☎0384/271 2531, ⓦwww.kelebekhotel.com. Deservedly popular place above the town, with a range of rooms and suites all finished to a very high standard and furnished with locally sought antiques. The owners also own a couple of luxurious new suite-hotels nearby – check ⓦwww.sultancavesuites.com and www .cappadociataskonak.com for details. ❹

Kismet Cave House Kagnı Yolu 9 ☎0384/271 2416, ⓦwww.kelebekhotel.com. Kitsch Byzantine inspired frescoes decorate the common areas of this eight-room cave hotel where kilim-strewn hallways give way to small but comfortable rooms, some with fireplaces and jacuzzi baths. Free wi-fi. ❹

Local Cevizler Sok 11 ☎0384/271 2171, ⓦwww .localcavehouse.com. Well-restored cave and cellar rooms with central heating and a/c, set around a courtyard with a tempting pool, antique furniture and kilims. ❹

Walnut House Zeybek Sok ☎0384/271 2564, ⓦwww.walnuthouse.cjb.net. Right in the village centre, long established, with luxuriously furnished rooms in Ottoman style; excellent value, and with a pleasant lounge-restaurant area. ❷

Campsites

Berlin Camping Ürgüp road, opposite *Flintstones Cave Bar* ☎0384/271 2249. Good facilities and lots of shade. ❶

Kaya Camping Ortahisar road, 2.5km out ☎0384/343 3100. Excellent views over Göreme, Zelve and Çavuşin, with shade provided by apricot and cherry trees, and a pool. ❶

Panorama Üçhisar road, 1km out ☎0384/271 2352, ⓦwww.goremepanoramacamping.com. Hot water and good facilities, including a pool, plus panoramic views of the fairy chimneys, but it's a bit exposed to the road and has no trees to speak of. ❶

The village and nearby churches

The village's long history and the variety of its cultures are clear from the fact that Göreme is the fourth known name bestowed upon it. The Byzantines called it Matiana, the Armenian Christians Macan, and the Turks originally called it Avcılar, only giving it the name Göreme ("unseen") much later, in honour of its valley of churches of the same name.

There are two churches located in the hills above Göreme, both off Uzundere Caddesi and signposted from the road. The **Kadir Durmuş Kilisesi** (named after the man who owns the neighbouring fields) has a cave house with rock-cut steps next door to it, clearly visible from the path across a vineyard. It's not painted, but it has an impressive and unusual upstairs gallery, and cradle-shaped tombs outside. Thought to date from the seventh century, it could have been a parish church. The second church, the eleventh-century **Yusuf Koç Kilisesi**, is also known as "the church with five pillars"; its sixth was never carved. There are two domes, one of which has been damaged in the past to accommodate a pigeon coop, and frescoes in very good condition. Among them are the Annunciation, to the left; Sts George and Theodore slaying the dragon, to the right; and Helena and Constantine depicted with the True Cross beside the door. In the dome above the altar are the Madonna and Child, and below, beside the altar, are the four Evangelists, the only paintings in the church to have suffered substantial damage.

The walk to Üçhisar

The best-known, most rewarding **walk** in the Göreme region is to **Üçhisar** (4km; 2hr), along a path starting from just above the *Ataman Hotel*, through the Uzundere valley, passing through rock-cut tunnels into the heart of the Cappadocian countryside. Good shoes are a necessity, and the final descent into Üçhisar is precipitous, with fairly narrow stretches of path. It's better to go in a group from a *pansiyon* (the *Köşe* owner knows the route well), or with a local guide (see box, p.469) so you are sure not to miss Karşi Bucak or Yusuf Koç churches.

Eating

Catering for large numbers of travellers has not significantly affected the quality, variety or value of **restaurant** food here. It's still possible to find plenty of places serving traditional Turkish food, while local attempts at "backpacker" dishes, such as burgers, French fries, pizza and spaghetti are, on the whole, successful.

Alaturca Müze Cad. One of the town's finer dining options, its savoury pastries are among the best in the region and unusual mains like Ottoman chicken and beef *sarma* are skilfully prepared. The dining terrace is atmospheric, service excellent and the local wines well chosen. A full meal will set you back around 25TL without wine. For a less expensive taste, head to the café or indulge in a tea while lounging in the overstuffed cushions on the downstairs lawn.

Dibek Hakkı Paşa Meydanı. A good lunchtime choice: sit at *sofra* tables in a cool, vaulted cellar room and eat delicious home-cooked food including *gözleme*, *mantı* and *guveç* at bargain prices. No alcohol.

Meeting Point Müze Cad. Lively café dishing up good burgers, salads, juices and *gözleme* made from fresh ingredients. Their cakes are among the best in town. No alcohol.

Mercan Bilal Eroğlu Cad. Boasts an atmospheric terrace and good-value food. The hummus, served with flat *lavaş* bread, is tasty, and the *pirzola* (lamb chops) are tender.

Orient Restaurant Adnan Menderes Cad. Excellent *menemen* (Turkish-style scrambled egg) breakfasts, and a varied, reasonably priced daytime and evening menu, including excellent steak and a tasty rack of lamb, served in a pleasant garden. A full meal will set you back around 45TL. There is a reasonable backpacker's menu for 15TL.

Nazar Börek Müze Cad. Serving food from breakfast into the wee hours, the highlights are the *meze* plate, an assortment of delectable starters for 7TL and the reasonably priced *sigara böreği* filled with chicken, cheese or lamb for 5TL. The in *gözleme* make for a filling and affordable meal.

Drinking and nightlife

There is a very lively **bar scene**, particularly on Fridays and Saturdays, when the locals descend in force, mixing with the backpackers and expats down from Ankara for the weekend.

Fat Boys Run by Yilmaz and Angela, a Turkish-Australian couple, this pub is the best bar in town, serving local and imported beers from 4TL and good bar food.

Flintstones Cave Bar At the beginning of the road to the Open-Air Museum. Offers films, music, a disco, Aussie food and local beers at 4TL a pop. The stand-by spot for late-night drinking.

Paşa Bar Müze Cad, near the *otogar*. Has the town's biggest dancefloor and is more disco than

bar, usually heaving at the weekend. There's an electronic dartboard and a billiard table for quieter week nights, and beers run a reasonable 4TL, accompanied by a free dish of salted nuts.

Red Red Wine House Müze Cad. Lovely old barrel-vaulted cellar bar, with a wide range of Cappadocian wines. It also serves beer and you can have a puff at a *nargile* while watching one of the free films (get there early and choose your own). Wine from 5TL a glass.

Göreme Open-Air Museum

The **Göreme Open-Air Museum** (daily: summer 8am–7pm, last entrance 6.15pm; winter 8am–5pm, last entrance 4.15pm; 15TL) – easily reached by walking the 1.5km from the village along the road to Ürgüp – is the best known and most visited of all the monastic settlements in the Cappadocia region. It's also the largest of the religious complexes, and its **churches**, of which there are over thirty, contain some of the most fascinating of all the frescoes in Cappadocia. Virtually all date from the period after the Iconoclastic controversy, and mainly from the second half of the ninth to the end of the eleventh century.

The best known of the churches in the main complex of Göreme are the three columned churches: the **Elmalı Kilise** ("Church of the Apple"), the **Karanlık Kilise** ("Dark Church", restored but with a separate entrance fee of 8TL) and the **Çarıklı Kilise** ("Church of the Sandals"). These eleventh-century churches were heavily influenced by Byzantine forms: constructed to an inscribed cross plan, the central dome, supported on columns, contains the Pantocrator above head-and-shoulders depictions of the archangels and seraphim. The painting of the churches, particularly of Elmalı Kilise, is notable for the skill with which the form and movement of the figures correspond to the surfaces they cover. They are clad in drapery, which closely follows the contours of their bodies, and their features are smoothly modelled, with carefully outlined eyes. The facade of the Karanlık Kilise is intricately carved to give more of an impression of a freestanding building than elsewhere in Göreme. The expensive blue colour obtained from the mineral azurite is everywhere in the church, whereas in the Elmalı Kilise grey is the predominant tone.

A number of other late eleventh-century single-aisle churches in the museum are covered in much cruder geometric patterns and linear pictures, painted straight onto the rock. In this style is the **Barbara Kilise** (Church of St Barbara), named after a depiction of the saint on the north wall. Christ is represented on a throne in the apse. The strange insect-figure for which the church is also known must have had a symbolic or magical significance that is now lost. The **Yılanlı Kilise** ("Church of the

Christianity in Cappadocia

Today, the number of churches in the Cappadocia region is estimated at more than 1000, dating from the earliest days of Christianity to the thirteenth century. For many centuries the religious authority of the capital of Cappadocia, Caesarea (present-day Kayseri) extended over the whole of southeast Anatolia, and it was where Gregory the Illuminator, the evangelizer of Armenia, was raised. The region also produced some of the greatest early ecclesiastical writers. These included the fourth-century **Cappadocian Fathers**: Basil the Great, Gregory of Nazianzen and Gregory of Nyssa.

By the beginning of the eighth century the political power of Cappadocia's monks, whose numbers had increased considerably during the seventh century, began to cause concern. This led to the closure of monasteries and confiscation of their property. The worst period of repressive activity occurred during the reign of Constantine V, marked by the **Iconoclastic Council** of 754. All sacred images, except the cross, were forbidden, a ruling which had a profound affect on the creative life of the region's churches.

After the restoration of the cult of images in 843, there was a renewed vigour in the religious activity of Cappadocia. During this period, the wealth of the Church increased to such an extent that in 964 monastery building was prohibited, an edict only withdrawn in 1003. Meanwhile, the religious communities were brought to heel, controlled to a greater extent by the ecclesiastical hierarchy. Even though Cappadocia continued to be a centre of religious activity well into the Ottoman period, it had lost the artistic momentum that had produced the most extraordinary works of earlier centuries.

Snake"), also in this group, is most famous for the depiction of St Onophrius on the west wall of the nave. St Onophrius was a hermit who lived in the Egyptian desert in the fourth and fifth centuries, eating only dates, with a foliage loincloth for cover. Opposite St Onophrius, Constantine the Great and his mother St Helena are depicted holding the True Cross. Between the Yılanlı and the Karanlık churches is a **refectory** with a rock-cut table designed to take about fifty diners.

There are a couple of churches worth visiting on the road back to Göreme village from the open-air museum. The best preserved and most fascinating is the **Tokalı Kilise** ("Church with the Buckle"; keep ticket from main site), located away from the others on the opposite side of the road, about 50m before the ticket office. The church is different in plan to others in the area, having a transverse nave and an atrium hewn out of an earlier church, known as the "Old Church". The **frescoes** here, dating from the second decade of the tenth century, are classic examples of the archaic period of Cappadocian painting: the style is linear, but like the mosaics of Aya Sofya in İstanbul, the faces are modelled by the use of different intensities of colour and by the depiction of shadow. The paintings in the **New Church** are some of the finest examples of tenth-century Byzantine art. The semicircular wall is used for the four scenes of the Passion and Resurrection: the Descent from the Cross, the Entombment, the Holy Women at the Sepulchre and the Resurrection.

The **El Nazar Kilisesi** or "Evil Eye Church" (daily: summer 8am–7pm & winter 8am–5pm; 8TL), carved from a tuff pinnacle (follow signs from the road between the village and the Open-Air Museum), has been over-restored but contains some fine frescoes. The **Saklı Kilise** ("Hidden Church"), about halfway between the museum and the village, uses Cappadocian landscapes complete with fairy chimneys as a background for biblical scenes. It lives up to its name, and you're advised to ask the church's keyholder (who's also the proprietor of the shop Hikmet's Place, which is where you'll find him) to show you the way.

Çavuşin

Six kilometres from Göreme, off the road to Avanos, **ÇAVUŞIN** is a small village with a good hotel and a few nice *pansiyons*, as well as a really beautiful church located in the hills nearby. The best approach to the village is to **walk from Göreme** through the fabulous tuff landscapes of the Rose Valley. The path begins just beside the onyx vendors and *Kaya Camping*, 2.5km from Göreme, on the road to Ürgüp/Ortahisar. Follow the path for about forty minutes, and where it takes a helter-skelter bend through a tuff tunnel to the left, follow the precipitous path to the right, heading down into the Kızılçukur valley: this will lead you to Çavuşin in another half-hour or so. Alternatively, the Avanos dolmuş will drop you at the village.

The villagers have gradually moved out of their cave dwellings as a result of rock falls, but the old **caves** (daily: summer 8am–7pm; winter 8am–5pm; 8TL), in the hills above the village, can be explored if some care is taken; it's best to take a guide from the *Panorama Café* in Çavuşin. In their midst is the **church of St John the Baptist**, a large basilica thought to have been a centre of pilgrimage. Its position up on the cliff-face, combined with the imposing aspect of its colonnaded and moulded facade, gives it prominence over the whole valley. The church, most probably constructed in the fifth century, contains a votive pit, the only one in Cappadocia, that is thought to have contained the hand of St Hieron, a local saint born a few kilometres away. A short distance away, located in a tower of rock in the same valley, the church known as the **"Pigeon House"** has frescoes commemorating the passage of Nicephoras Phocas through Cappadocia in 964–965, during his military campaign in Cilicia. The frescoes probably commemorate a pilgrimage to the church of St John the Baptist by the Byzantine emperor, who is known to have hankered after the monastic life.

Practicalities

For **accommodation** in the village itself, there's the *İn* (℡0384/532 7070, Ⓦwww .mephistotravel.com; ❷), on the left as you descend to the main road, a simple but comfortable restaurant-*pansiyon* with fourteen rooms with shared bathrooms set around a quiet courtyard. Set back from the road, just out of town, *Panorama Pansiyon* (℡0384/532 7002, Ⓔpanorama@cavusin.net; ❷) has slightly better facilities, a pleasant attached restaurant with *saç tava* (lamb, tomatoes and onions cooked in a wok) for 8TL on the menu, and a sunken Ottoman-style seating-area-cum-bar and a *prix fixe* dinner menu for 15TL. Behind the *Panorama*, the *Turbel Hotel* (℡0384/532 7084, Ⓦwww.turbelhotel.com; ❸) has well-furnished rooms, some with jacuzzis, with superb views over the dramatic rock containing the Pigeon House church. A full meal in the restaurant will cost around 20TL. An upmarket option is *The Village Cave Hotel* (℡0384/532 7197, Ⓦwww.thevillagecave.com; ❺), nestling beneath a cliff at the head of a small valley, and with wonderful views across to the cliff church and abandoned houses. It offers a range of tasteful vaulted cellar and cave rooms, delicious home-cooked food and a very warm welcome.

Zelve

The deserted **monastery complex** spread across the three valleys of **Zelve**, 3km off the Avanos–Çavuşin road, is one of the most fascinating remnants of Cappadocia's troglodyte past. The site (daily: May–Oct 8am–7pm, last entrance at 6.15pm; Nov–April 8am–5pm, last entrance at 4.15pm; 8TL) is accessible by the circular dolmuşes, which run between Avanos, Göreme and Ürgüp, and drop off here every two hours. The valley was inhabited by Turkish Muslims until 1952, when rock falls, which still occur, made the area too dangerous to inhabit.

An exploration of the complex really requires a torch and old clothes, along with a considerable sense of adventure. At the top of the right-hand valley, on the right as you go up, a honeycomb of rooms is approached up metal staircases. Some are entered by means of precarious steps, others by swinging up through large holes in their floors (look out for ancient hand and foot holes). Another daunting challenge is the walk through the tunnel that leads between the two valleys on the right (as you face them from the car park) – impossible without a torch and nerves of steel. None of this is recommended for the infirm or claustrophobic, but it's good fun if you're reasonably energetic.

A large number of chapels and medieval oratories are scattered up and down the valleys, many of them decorated with carved **crosses**. This, combined with the relatively small number of frescoes in the valleys, is thought to date them to the pre-Iconoclastic age (ninth century). The few **painted images** found in Zelve are in the churches of the third valley, on the far left. The twin-aisled **Üzümlü Kilise** has grapevines painted in red and green on the walls, and a cross carved into the ceiling.

The most picturesque of all the Cappadocian valleys, **Paşabağı**, located 2km north of the Zelve turn-off on the Avanos road, is possibly also the most photographed. Previously the area was known as "Valley of the Monks", because it was a favourite place of retreat for stylite hermits who lodged in the fairy chimneys – which, with their black basalt caps, are double- or even triple-coned here. In one of the triple-coned chimneys is a **chapel** dedicated to St Simeon Stylites, hollowed out at three levels, with a monk's cell at the top. A hundred metres east of the chapel is a **cell**, bearing the inscription "Receive me, O grave, as you received the Stylite."

Ortahisar and around

A friendly little village located a little off the road between Göreme and Ürgüp, **ORTAHISAR** retains a degree of charm and innocence absent from many of the more touristed areas of Cappadocia. After a few hours here you feel as if you know the whole population – and they will certainly know you.

The chief attraction here is the staggering, fortress-like 86-metre-high **rock** (daily 7.30am–8.30pm; free) that, as at Üçhisar, once housed the entire village. It is now in precarious shape and should be explored only with extreme caution. The only other sight in town is the **Culture Museum**, in an atmospheric, restored *konak* building on Cumhuriyet Meydanı in the town centre (daily 9am–9pm; 2TL). It comprises a series of rooms with tableaux depicting Cappadocian life as it was lived until very recently (and indeed still is in remoter areas).

There are a few good **antique shops** (though no longer as affordable as they once were), at the foot of the rock, selling old light fittings, door knockers, silver- and copperware.

Practicalities

Regular *Belediye* buses run from Avanos direct to the village, otherwise board an Üçhisar–Ürgüp **dolmuş**, which will drop you on the main Nevşehir–Kayseri road, from where it's a twenty-minute walk down the hill.

There's plenty to explore in the valleys around Ortahisar, so if you don't have your own transport and you want to spend time in the area it makes sense to **stay** the night. The *Hotel Gümüş* (☏0384/343 3127, ⓦwww.gumushotel.com; ❸), next to the PTT on the road into town, has twenty plain but comfortable rooms

▲ Ortahisar

with bathrooms, and fabulous views from the terrace, at the back of which there are more attic-style rooms with sloping roofs. For a bit more style try the ⚹ *Alkabris* (☎0384/343 3433, Ⓦwww.alkabris.com; ❻) on Ali Reis Sok 23, signposted from the main road into town. It is tucked away in a peaceful warren of old dwellings behind the village rock, and has incomparable views of both it and distant Mount Erciyes. Inside, the immaculate white en-suite rooms are a model of restraint. The only drawback is the limited English of the friendly and knowledgeable Turkish owners. More humble accommodation worth trying includes the homey *Lusi Evi* (☎0384/343 3957, Ⓦwww.lusievi.com; ❷) on Bahçe Sokak and *Hariye House* (☎0536/429 3995; ❷) beside the rock, with simply furnished cave rooms.

The best **restaurant** is attached to the Culture Museum on Cumhuriyet Meydanı in the town centre, with excellent *testi kebabı* and attentive service. The *Park* on Cumhuriyet Meydanı has a shady garden area much frequented by the locals, serving soup, *pide*, *sulu yemek*, *izgara* and cold beer.

Churches around Ortahisar

Taking the road marked "Pancarlık Kilise" off the second square, you'll come to the valley of the Üzenge Çay, the opposite side of which is covered in pigeon coops. If you walked down this valley to the left for a little over 2km you'd arrive in Ürgüp, but straight ahead a rough track leads across the valley to the **Pancarlık church and monastery complex** (daily: summer 8am–7pm & winter 8am–5pm; 3TL), 3km from Ortahisar. Hardly visited because of the difficulty of access, the church has some excellent frescoes in good condition – even their faces are intact. They include the Baptism of Christ and the Annunciation, and to the left of the altar is the Nativity.

Ürgüp

ÜRGÜP now rivals Göreme in terms of accommodation and outdoes it in the breadth and quality of its nightlife and shopping. Yet unlike many resorts of this size, the place has also had the resilience and composure to accommodate its visitors without too many compromises. Before the exchange of populations in 1923, Ürgüp had a largely Greek population and there are still many distinctive and beautiful houses of Greek (and Ottoman) origin scattered around the town. The tuff cliffs above the town in the Esbelli district are riddled with man-made cave dwellings, now put to use as boutique hotels, shops and restaurants. Viticulture and apple farming provide an income for some, but tourism is the mainstay of the economy.

Arrival and information

The **otogar** is right in the centre of town, from where it's possible to get dolmuşes and *Belediye* buses to nearby villages such as Mustafapaşa, Göreme and Avanos, as well as more distant cities. The tourist office, PTT, museum, shops and banks are all close by. The best hotels are, at most, a cheap taxi ride away.

Kayseri Caddesi, the street leading downhill to the tourist office and museum, is also the main shopping street. The **tourist office** (daily: May–Sept 8am–6pm; Oct–April 8am–5pm; ☎0384/341 4059) is at Kayseri Cad 37, located next to the museum in a park complete with tea garden, where you can peruse their maps and hotel price list. They also have a home-made hiking map; ask for it.

ACCOMMODATION

4 Oda	A
Elkep Evi	C
Elvan	I
Esbelli Evi	D
Hitit	H
Kemerli Ev	K
Sacred House	J
Selçuklu Evi	E
Şerinn House	B
Ürgüp Inn Cave Hotel	G
Surban	F

OLD ÜRGÜP

AHMET REFİK CAD

Kebir Camii **G**

Kiliç Arslan Türbe

TEMMENİ

El Sanatlar Çarşısı

KAYSERİ CAD

Belediye

Hamam

CUMHURİYET MEYD.

Ötogar

Dolmuş garage

Duayeri Camii

Mustafa Ağa Camii

SARAÇOĞLU SOK

RESTAURANTS, BARS & CLUBS

68	2
Angel Café	4
Asim'in Yeri	1
Güleç Cihan	8
Han Çirağan	3
Kardeşler Pizza	7
Merkez Pastane	5
Şömine	6
Ziggy's	1

Damsa River

0   100 m

Sanayı Çarşısı

ÜRGÜP

▼ Market Place & Mustafapaşa

Accommodation

Ürgüp has a wide range of hotels. Those on the outskirts cater largely to tour groups, but there are plenty of good-value pensions and wonderfully restored old houses (now serving as upmarket "boutique" hotels) in the town centre and the Esbelli district.

Central Ürgüp

Elvan Barbaros Hayrettin Sok 11 ☏ 0384/341 4191, ⓦ www.hotelelvan.com. This old house is set around two characterful courtyards. The proprietors, Fatma and Ahmet, are extremely friendly and keep the place spotless. Some rooms have vaulted stone ceilings, and there's a cool, semi-underground lounge area. ➏

Hitit İstiklâl Cad 46 ☏ 0384/341 4481, ⓦ www .hitithotel.com. A 600-year-old house owned by a charming family. The rooms, looking onto a pleasant courtyard, have attractive vaulted ceilings, Kayseri rugs, minibars and TVs, but otherwise furniture and fittings, which include central heating, are everyday and practical. ➍

Kemerli Ev Dutlu Camii Cikmaz Sok ☏ 0384/341 5445, ⓦ www.kemerliev.com. Eight rooms with oriental decoration and fine linens in a beautifully

restored stone-built block in a quiet part of town. The lodge next door sleeps eight, can be rented by the week and looks onto a small pool. ➏

Sacred House Barbaros Hayrettin Sok 25 ☏ 0384/341 7102, ⓦ www.sacred-house.com. Twelve individually furnished rooms in a beautifully restored mansion. Genuine antiques mix well with reproduction pieces; dinners are candlelit, as are the jacuzzi-focused bathrooms. The rooms may be a little dark and fussy for some tastes, but they've been done with flair and certainly promote relaxation. ➐

Ürgüp Inn Cave Hotel Mescit Sok ☏ 0384/341 4147, ⓦ www.urgupinncavehotel.com. An excellent-value option in the centre of town run by the friendly and accommodating Omer. The six rooms have mod cons and spotless bathrooms and breakfast is served beneath a flower-filled pergola. ➌

Esbelli area

4 Oda Esbelli Sok 46 Cad ☎0384/341 6080, ⓦwww.4oda.com. Five, rather than four (*dort*) cave rooms as the name claims, each tastefully decorated in sombre tones and with its own southwest-facing terrace. Owners Elvan, a professional guide, and her husband Sermet are exceedingly helpful and will prepare dinner on the terrace on request. All rooms have free wi-fi. ❻

Elkep Evi Eski Turban Oteli Arkası 26 ☎0384/341 6000, ⓦwww.elkepevi.com. A handsomely restored pair of cave houses, with extremely comfortable cave or cellar rooms decorated with local handicrafts and antiques. ❻

Esbelli Evi Esbelli Sok 8 ☎0384/341 3395, ⓦwww.esbelli.com. The rock-cut rooms here are tastefully furnished with period furniture, though some are looking a bit worse for the wear. The place has a homey feel and you're invited to help yourself from the fridge in the kitchen, cook a meal and relax in the communal sitting room. Breakfast is excellent and the views from the rooftop terrace delightful. Closed Nov–April. ❻

Selçuklu Evi Yunak Mah ☎0384/341 7460, ⓦwww.selcukluevi.com. A well-run restored house-complex has a series of antique-furnished double and suite-rooms with opulent bathrooms. ❼

Serinn House Esbelli Sok 36 ☎0384/341 6076, ⓦwww.serinnhouse.com. Five ultra-modern rooms decked out in sleek industrial design pieces whose clean lines create a beautiful contrast with the soft curves of the cave rooms. The eclectic breakfast is the brainchild of acclaimed Turkish chef Defne Koryürek and is served on the panoramic terrace. ❻

Surban Yunak Mah ☎0384/341 4761, ⓦwww.hotelsurban.com. Well-decorated, modern and comfortable, with neat bathrooms. The rooms all have arched ceilings, and there's a satellite TV room. Reasonable value. ❹

The Town

Despite its rather incongruous modern central square, Ürgüp retains some of its rural village charm. Men and women in traditional working clothes, leading horse-drawn vehicles and donkeys out to the surrounding vineyards, orchards and vegetable gardens, are not an unusual early-morning sight. This is the time to explore the **old village**, whose buildings appear to be slowly emerging from the rocky hills into which they have been carved. Some feature stylish pillared and decorated facades of the same stone, others are simple caves with doors and windows cut into the cliffs themselves.

The walk up to the Temmeni "wishpoint" begins with a flight of steps opposite the thirteenth-century **Kebir Camii** and includes a 700-metre-long tunnel, which leads through the hill to a door and "balcony" on the other side, furnishing panoramic views of the town and surrounding countryside. Continuing uphill, past the former troglodyte town dwellings (now mainly used for storage or abandoned altogether), brings you to a park known as **Temmeni** ("Hill of Wishes"; daily 8.30am–6pm; free), where a Selçuk tomb, the **Kılıç Arslan Türbe**, dating from 1268, is open to visitors. A small renovated *medrese* from the same period is now used as a café.

The town's **museum** (Tues–Sun 8am–12.30pm & 2.30–5.30pm; free) on Kayseri Caddesi is tiny and not particularly well labelled, but the helpful staff are prepared to explain the exhibits. These include a selection of prehistoric ceramics, figurines, lamps, stelae, statues and ornaments found during excavations in the area.

Wine tasting is possible at any of Ürgüp's six wineries, but the best local wines are widely acknowledged to be those produced by the Turasan house in Esbelli, a kilometre northwest of the town centre, and by the welcoming and cheap Taskobirlik co-operative in a former *kervansaray* (also out of town, though they have a town-centre shop). It's worth remembering that white Cappadocian wines are much better than red; the reds are mixed with wines from other regions, and dyes are added.

Eating, drinking and nightlife

There's a decent selection of **restaurants**, from simple places serving traditional dishes to more tasteful places suitable for a night out. For snacks, there are several decent *pastane*s around Cumhuriyet Meydanı. Ürgüp's **nightlife** is also excellent when you consider that this is central Anatolia and there's not a beach in sight.

Restaurants

Han Çirağan Cumhuriyet Meyd. Atmospheric old house with a vine-shaded garden. Serves simple regional food, such as *düğün çorbası* (wedding soup), *saç tava* (wok-fried lamb in tomato sauce) and *manti* (Turkish ravioli). A full meal costs around 20TL. Inquire about the live musical performances.

Kardeşler Pizza Restaurant Dumlupınar Cad 9. Serves excellent crusty *pide* and beer, at around 10TL for two people. Its sister *Kardeşler* restaurant on Cumhuriyet Meyd is famous for *guveç*, a stew cooked in a clay pot sealed with bread (5TL).

Merkez Pastane Opposite the *otogar*. Small patisserie with tables inside and out. They serve healthy portions of *baklava* and good coffee and tea.

Güleç Cihan Next to the *otogar*. Excellent crispy *pide* and quality breads are served piping hot, fresh from the wood-burning oven at this popular *fırın*. Open daytime only.

Şömine Cumhuriyet Meyd ☎0384/341 8442. Ürgüp's best restaurant, recently revamped, and situated on the main square. The service is friendly

and the well-prepared food good value (allow 20–25TL for a complete meal). Local specialities include *osbar* (haricot beans with pastrami) and *testi kebap* (a lamb and vegetable stew cooked slowly in the oven).

Ziggy's Tevfik Fikret Cad. A foodie haven in the Esbelli district serving Turkish *meze*s and meat dishes with a twist. Their *meze* menu for two is 30TL and includes their signature *pastırmalı börek* (pastry filled with spiced beef and cheese) and *sarımsaklı tavuk çöp şiş* (skewered garlic chicken), as well as home-made dessert.

Bars

68 İstiklâl Cad 68. A bar and pub serving creative food and drink. Especially popular among İstanbul transplants to Cappadocia.

Angel Café Cumhuriyet Meyd. With its well-stocked bar and romantic red lighting, this sleek new café is popular with couples.

Asim'in Yeri Dolay Sok 24. "Asim's Place" is a wine bar and disco in the Esbelli district serving the best Cappadocian wines and featuring live music nightly beginning at 9.30pm.

Listings

Banks and exchange Garanti Bank on Kazım Karabekir Cad 7 has an English-speaking manager and the Ziraat Bankası on Atatürk Bul has a 24hr currency exchange machine.
Bike rental Alpin, on Cumhuriyet Meyd for scooters (€25 a day). Argeus (see "Tours", below) is good for mountain bikes (€20 a day).
Car rental Avis, İstiklâl Cad 19, Belediye Pasajı ☎0384/341 2177; Alpin, Cumhuriyet Meyd 32 ☎0384/341 7522.
Hamam Yeni Camii Mah 22, mixed men and women (daily 7am–11pm, 20TL including massage).
Hospital Posthane Cad ☎0384/341 4031.

Pharmacy Elif Eczanesi, Kayseri Cad, across from the main tourist office, is friendly, with some English spoken.
Police Opposite the PTT, in the centre.
Post office The PTT is on Posthane Cad (daily 8.30am–11pm for phone tokens and cards, 9am–5pm for ordinary business).
Tours Argeus, İstiklâl Cad 7 (☎0384/341 4688, ⓦwww.cappadociaexclusive.com), is the best local agent, and has comprehensive tours to the Ihlara valley and Soğanlı (€85), plus trips to the Kaçkar mountains and winter skiing tours to Erciyes – all its guides speak English.

Mustafapaşa and around

The small village of **MUSTAFAPAŞA**, 6km south of Ürgüp, makes for a pleasant excursion or, with your own transport, a good base from which to explore the region. The charm of the place lies in the concentration of attractive *konaks* with carved house-facades dating back a century or so, when it was known as Sinasos and home to a thriving Greek community; it is also central to a cluster of little-visited churches. Unfortunately, a paucity of public transport (regular dolmuş service to Ürgüp only) makes Mustafapaşa an awkward base unless you have your own transport.

The church of **Ayios Vasilios** (daily: summer 8am–7pm & winter 8am–5pm; 8TL) is located to the north of the village, and is well signposted from the centre of town; pick up the key from the makeshift **tourist office** (daily: summer 8am–7pm & winter 8am–5pm) on the main square. The church has well-preserved frescoes, although the faces are damaged, and four rock-cut pillars. Another church, below Ayios Vasilios in the Üzengı Dere ravine, is the **Holy Cross**, partly rock-cut and partly masonry-built, with pre-Iconoclastic and tenth-century paintings including a most attractive Christ of the Second Coming.

Back on the main square is the **Aios Konstantine Eleni Kilisesi** (daily: summer 8am–7pm & winter 8am–5pm; 8TL), a church dedicated to Constantine and his mother St Helena with nineteenth-century frescoes. On the other side of the village, passing through streets of houses cut by former Greek occupants into the tuff cliffs, is a monastery complex including the churches of **Aya Nicolas** and **Aya Stefanos**.

Practicalities

There are several good **places to stay**. The *Monastery* (℡0384/353 5005, ⓦwww .voyage-en-cappadoce.com; ❸) has a lovely, vine-shaded courtyard and thirteen smallish rooms, with wooden floors and spotless bathrooms. Slightly more expensive is the *Upper Greek House* (℡0384/353 5352, ⓦwww.uppergreekhouse .com; ❺), with six homely rooms around a fine terrace, perched high above town at the end of a steep cobbled street with fine views. Close by is the *Ukabeyn* (℡0384/353 5533, ⓦwww.ukabeyn.com; ❼), a small but atmospheric place with six well-restored rooms and delightful terraces for relaxing. A real plus is the small pool, situated on the lip of a cliff overhanging the valley below. The best-known place in town is the wonderfully preserved *Old Greek House* (℡0384/353 5141, ⓦwww.oldgreek house.com; ❺), also known as *Asmali Konak*. More than 200 years old, it was until 1923 the residence of the Greek mayor; several of the rooms have original murals and painted ceilings, and a tiny old chapel off the shady courtyard is now a Turkish bath. The hotel also has its own highly recommended **restaurant** serving Turkish specialities for around 20TL a head, eaten whilst sprawled on cushions around *sofra* tables.

South of Mustafapaşa

Along the Soğanlı road south from Mustafapaşa – there's no public transport – the fairy chimneys give way to a table-mountain formation that is no less fantastic and surreal than preceding landscapes: the red canyon ridge that the road follows could be a backdrop for *Roadrunner*.

About 3km from Mustafapaşa the **Keşlik Kilesi monastery complex** (April–Oct daily 9am–7.30pm; Nov–March by appointment only; contact the watchman at ℡0536/8875517; 3TL) – three churches, a winepress and a refectory – are signposted on the right. This is believed to be one of the earliest communal monastic establishments in the region. The watchman, Cabir, who speaks some English, gives a brief introduction of the complex in his garden before turning you loose in the churches: the first, named after a prominent picture of the archangel Gabriel, includes depictions of the Last Supper, the Annunciation and the Flight to Egypt, all badly damaged and soot-blackened (a torch is essential); the church of St Michael has a wine cellar downstairs; while the church of St Stephen (seventh-or eighth-century) is the most beautiful of all, and unusually decorated with stylized foliage and interlaced patterns reminiscent of Turkish kilims.

The Soğanlı valleys

One of the most spectacular sights this side of Ürgüp are the **Soğanlı valleys** (daily: summer 8am–6pm; winter 8.30am–5pm; 3TL), 5km off the road from Taşkınpaşa to Yeşilhisar, and less than 20km from either. **SOĞANLİ** itself is an attractive village in two parts, Yukarı (upper) and Aşağı (lower) Soğanlı, set into the side of a table-top mountain. Part of the place's charm derives from its inaccessibility; it's off the tour route of all but small local companies. There are just a couple of simple **restaurants**, like *Cappadocia Restaurant* (open April–Oct) serving simple meals in an apple orchard near the park entrance-gate ticket office, a few stalls selling the village-made rag dolls, and one **hotel**: the tiny, basic and friendly *Emek Pansiyon* (☏0352/653 1029; ❸), with five rooms and delicious home-cooked food. There's no public transport to the village, and in winter it is often completely cut off by snowdrifts.

The most interesting of the valley's churches and monasteries are located in the right-hand valley (as you face Yukarı Soğanlı). To reach the two-storeyed **Kubbeli Kilise** ("Church with the Dome"), follow the footpath across a stream-bed from the village square, and proceed uphill through the village and along the side of the valley. This has perhaps the most striking exterior of all the Cappadocian rock churches, its form – a conical dome that is the tip of a fairy chimney resting on a circular drum – being an imitation of a masonry structure. The **Saklı** (Hidden) **Kilise**, with frescoes of the Apostles, is 100m before the Kubbeli Kilise, its door facing into the valley.

Descend to the road and then head up the other side of the valley to reach the **Meryem Ana Kilisesi** ("Church of the Virgin"), which has four apsidal chapels with frescoes and Iconoclastic decoration. The **Yılanlı Kilise** ("Church of the Snake") is best seen using a torch, as it is blackened and damaged by Greek and Armenian graffiti. It derives its name from an eleventh-century painting of St George slaying the dragon, to the left of the entrance. Returning towards the village, the **Karabaş Kilise** ("Church of the Black Head") has two adjoining apsidal chapels, the first of which has well-preserved tenth- and eleventh-century frescoes depicting scenes from the life of Christ.

Avanos and around

The old city of **AVANOS** clambers up hills overlooking the longest river in Turkey, the Kızılırmak, a magnificently red river which after a good rainfall appears to be on the verge of bursting its banks. Avanos itself is a town of some character and famous for the distinctive earthenware pottery made here. The same red clay that colours the river has been worked for many centuries, and techniques dating right back to Hittite times are still in use. Strolling through the cobbled backstreets of the old town you'll find superb views out across the river – only slightly marred by the new housing development all too evident on the south bank. Exploration of the fields and hills around the town reveals further attractions: a tiny *kervansaray*, and even an underground city, 14km away at Özkonak.

Arrival, information and tours

There are hourly **dolmuşes** to Avanos from Üçhisar, Göreme and Nevşehir and every two hours from Ürgüp. From the **otogar**, head 250m north to the river and cross the bridge into town. The **tourist office** (summer Mon–Fri 8.30am–noon & 1.30–7pm; winter Mon–Fri 8.30am–noon & 1.30–5pm; ☏0384/511 2298) is more or less immediately on your right. The **PTT** is located just beyond the pottery monument on the main street, Atatürk Caddesi, next to the public toilets. Uğur Mumcu Caddesi runs parallel to the river.

Kirkit Voyage, Atatürk Cad 52 (☎0384/511 3259, ⓦwww.kirkit.com), is an excellent **tour operator** that runs horseback trips, as well as bike and snowshoe tours all over Cappadocia (see box, p.469).

Accommodation

It's easy enough to find **accommodation**, with a selection of hotels and *pansiyons* catering to most tastes and requirements. The *Venessa Pansiyon*, just off Atatürk Bulvarı on Hafızağa Sok 20 (☎0384/511 3840, ⓦwww.avanosum.org; ❹), is a rambling building with a bohemian atmosphere and wonderful views over the town and river. The friendly owner is in the process of opening an art gallery in the premises. *Kirkit Pension*, off Atatürk Caddesi (☎0384/511 3148, ⓦwww .kirkit pension.com; ❹), belonging to the tour company of the same name, is a series of beautifully converted sandstone houses, decorated with kilims and antiques; rooms have either full bathrooms or just a shower and all are equipped with wi-fi connections. In the evening, traditional food is served and music is played for 15TL per person. The *Sofa Hotel* (☎0384/511 5186, ⓦwww.sofa-hotel.com; ❸) is just next to the Hacı Nuri Bey Konağı (an imposing neo-Ottoman mansion highly visible as you cross the bridge). The hotel has been put together from twenty redesigned Ottoman houses, with immaculate rooms, a garden courtyard and a restaurant. If you want to **camp**, head to *Ada Camping* (☎0384/511 2429, ⓦwww.adacampingavanos .com; ❶), on the south bank of the Kızılırmak, which has its own pool.

The Town

Avanos' main tourist attraction is **pottery**, but the real charm of the town is in the quaint, cobbled backstreets and rustic, tumbledown Ottoman, Armenian and Greek buildings that climb the hill north of Atatürk Caddesi.

Most of the potter shops in town are located just off the main street, a few minutes, walk east of the potter's monument – a clay sculpture depicting a potter and, beneath it, a mother and daughter working a loom. The potters' square and the streets that surround it contain numerous tiny workshops where the local techniques can still be observed or even attempted.

Eating, drinking and nightlife

Sofra, on the main street near the PTT, is a reasonably priced **restaurant**, serving *döner* and steam-tray food in a friendly atmosphere. The *Tafana Pide Salonu*, on Atatürk Caddesi, is also cheap, and serves a local speciality called *kiremit kebap* (lamb cooked on a pottery dish), as well as excellent *pide*, but the pavement tables can be noisy. *Dayının Yeri* on Atatürk Caddesi next to the bridge is good value for all the standard kebabs and grills, though they do not serve alcohol.

The *Kervanhan Karmina Café* off the main square has nightly *saz* and *özgün* music and attracts the younger residents and visitors. During the day, it is a coffee shop offering free wi-fi connection. The *Labirent*, set in the crumbling old houses above the town, occasionally sees sets from Erkin Koray, one of Turkey's most famous guitarists, and local rock groups.

Around Avanos

There are several worthwhile trips to be made from Avanos. The most interesting is to **Özkonak** (daily: summer 8am–7pm; winter 8am–5pm; 8TL), 14km north of Avanos off the Kayseri road, one of the least-known and least-excavated underground cities in the Cappadocia region. Dolmuşes from Avanos leave hourly from beside the PTT.

In its present state it's not as interesting as Derinkuyu or Kaymaklı, but by the same token it's not as crowded. The city was discovered in 1972 by a muezzin, Latif Acar, who was trying to find out where the water disappeared to when he watered his crops. He discovered an underground room, which, later excavation revealed, belonged to a city with a capacity for sixty thousand people to exist underground for three months. Ten floors descend to a depth of 40m, though at present only four are open (to 15m). These first two levels were used for food storage and wine fermentation, and a press and reservoir are labelled, as are mangers for stabled animals. Another typical feature is the stone doors, moved by wooden levers; above them was a small hole, through which boiling oil would have been poured on an enemy trying to break the soft sandstone door.

Six kilometres east of Avanos, on the new Kayseri road, the Selçuk-era **Saruhan Kervansary** is well worth a visit. It is beautifully restored, and offers evocative evening performances by a troupe of **whirling dervishes** (25TL). Enquire at local agencies or your hotel/pension; schedules of performaces vary.

Southern Cappadocia

The majority of Cappadocia's visitors never get beyond the well-worn Nevşehir–Avanos–Ürgüp triangle, leaving **southern Cappadocia** far less charted and trampled. There is a reason for its obscurity – the two major towns, **Aksaray** and **Niğde** leave a lot to be desired as tourist centres and much of the scenery is a depressing mixture of scrub or barren steppe. That said, the area does have its fascinations, and these are worth a degree of discomfort to experience.

On the way to Niğde you can stop off at the underground cities of Derinkuyu and Kaymaklı (see p.465), located in a rain-washed basin between the central Anatolian plateau and the valleys of cones. Southwest of here is the **Ihlara valley**, where the Melendiz River, running between Aksaray and Niğde alongside the Melendiz mountain range, has created a spectacular narrow ravine with almost vertical walls. Also easily accessible from Niğde is a small enclave of beautifully painted rock-cut churches belonging to the **Eski Gümüşler** monastery. South and east of Niğde the spectacular limestone spires of the **Aladağlar mountains** rear up from the plateau, affording excellent trekking and climbing.

Niğde and around

Despite a long history spent guarding the important mountain pass from Cappadocia to Cilicia, the small provincial town of **NIĞDE** has few remaining monuments of any great interest. Apart from a Selçuk fortress perched above the main street on a hill of tuff, and a couple of medieval mosques, the town looks as if it has been thrown together by people who were more interested in nomadic wandering than town planning. Nearby, however, is the Eski Gümüşler monastery complex, with its impressive, well-preserved frescoes – the only real reason for coming here unless you are en route to the Aladağlar mountains.

Practicalities

The **otogar** is 1km from the centre, off the Nevşehir–Adana highway, on Emin Eşirgil Caddesi, and there are frequent dolmuşes from here into town. The **train station** is right on the highway, within sight of the citadel's clocktower, aconvenient marker for the centre. To get into town from here, cross the highway and take İstasyon Caddesi into the centre, a walk of ten minutes or so. The **tourist office** (Mon–Sat 8.30am–noon & 1.30–5.30pm is at Atatürk Meydanı 16, right in the town centre. To book a **trek in the Aladağlar mountains** (see below) go to Sobek Travel on Bor Cad 70/16 (℡0388/232 1507, Ⓦwww.sobekculture.com), a well-established, reputable company, mainly dealing with package groups, so pre-booking would be sensible.

Niğde's choice of **hotels** is uninspiring. The *Yeni Otel Evim* on Hükümet Meydanı (℡0388/232 3536, Ⓕ232 1526; ❸) has reasonable rooms with showers, and offers substantial discounts if you're prepared to bargain. A welcome addition to the scene is the *Grand Hotel Niğde* on Hükümet Meydanı (℡0388/232 7000, Ⓦwww.grandhotelnigde.com; ❺) with soothingly decorated and furnished rooms, immaculate bathrooms, satellite TV and a rooftop restaurant/terrace with views over the Melendiz mountains.

Niğde's **restaurants** are mainly very basic, concentrating on kebabs, *pide* and soups. Best of a bad bunch is the *Saruhan* on Bor Caddesi, a five-minute walk south of the central square, Hükümet Meydanı. Located inside a restored *han*, the kebabs are reliable.

Eski Gümüşler monastery

The **Eski Gümüşler monastery** (daily: summer 9am–6pm; winter 9am–12.30pm & 1.30–5pm; 3TL) lies 9km east of town, off the Kayseri road. Rediscovered in 1963, it has a deserved reputation for the excellent state of preservation of its paintings, which seem to have escaped Iconoclastic and other vandalism through the ages. To get there, take the white *Belediye* bus that leaves the Niğde *otogar* every hour or so for the village of Gümüşler. Gümüşler itself is attractively set in a valley surrounded by cherry orchards, but for the monastery you stay on the bus past it.

The **main church**, with its tall, elegant pillars, is entered through an almost circular arched doorway opposite the entrance to the courtyard. Decorated with black-and-white geometric designs, the church contains beautiful frescoes in the most delicate greens, browns and blues. They include a Nativity scene complete with tiny animal heads peering in at the swaddled Jesus and the Magi, off to the left, and a tall, serene Madonna, framed in a rock-cut niche. The upstairs **sleeping quarters** have rock-cut beds and the walls are decorated with a wolf, a deer, a lion, and a flamingo, being hunted by men with bows and arrows; there's also a depiction of a Roman soldier.

Outside in the central courtyard there's a skeleton in its grave, protected under glass. Next to the graves are round holes in which precious belongings would have been buried. Other rooms excavated to date include a kitchen and underground baths reached down a set of steps, while below ground level are various chambers and a water reservoir.

The Aladağlar mountains

The **Aladağlar mountains** are part of the Toros range at the point where it swings north of the Mesopotamian plain. The isolated gorges and lakes of the Aladağlar are a birdwatcher's paradise, best during the autumn migration – when the snow has melted and access is (relatively) easy. *Yayla*s (mountain pastures) are used after snowmelt by nomad families and their flocks; black tents dot the upper valleys from June to September.

Access is by **minibus from Niğde** to Çamardı; there are four daily services from the *otogar* in summer, taking about an hour. Ask for the Demirkazık road or the driver will automatically put you off at the *Şafak Pansiyon*. The best **trekking season** is May to June followed by September, when the weather is at its most dependable.

By far the most popular way up to the peaks is via the **Emler valley**, where, in season, there are permanent base camps run by Sobek Travel (see "Niğde: Practicalities" on p.485). From here you can take day-walks up many of the peaks, and also cross into the **Kokorot valley** on the east, or walk the north–south section of the range, emerging on the **Acıman plateau**. At the end of both these routes you have to hitchhike or catch a rare dolmuş to Adana.

For trekking inquire at your *pansiyon* or the tourist office in Niğde for maps and a guide. You may also be able to pick up the out-of-print **guidebook** *Aladağlar: An Introduction* by Haldun Aydıngün (Redhouse Books).

Accommodation close to the trailhead, just off the Niğde road, is provided by *Şafak Pansiyon* (☎0388/724 7039; ❸), in the hamlet of Çukurbağ, 4km east of Çamardı, which provides half-board in small rooms without bathrooms and with unreliable hot water but with excellent cooking. It's also possible to camp here. The state-owned *Demirkazık Dağ Evi* (☎0388/724 7200; ❷), a ski lodge at Demirkazık, is a few kilometres nearer the mountains (ask the dolmuş to drop you at the signed turn, from where it's a 3km walk) and provides large, en-suite double rooms, and a camping area (12TL).

Aksaray

Huddled in an oasis on the Melendiz River, on the far side of the Melendiz mountain range from Niğde, **AKSARAY** is a market town with no real interest except as a base for reaching the Ihlara valley. It is perhaps best known for its namesake suburb in İstanbul, founded by people from here after the fall of Constantinople in 1453.

Of marginal interest are the thirteenth-century **Eğri Minare**, the **Ulu Camii** on Banklar Caddesi, and the main square, with its Atatürk statue and restored public buildings. **Aksaray Museum** (Aksaray Müzesi; daily 9am–noon & 1.30–5.30pm; free) is housed in an architecturally interesting fourteenth-century *medrese*.

Practicalities

Aksaray is linked by regular bus with Niğde, 110km southeast (2hr), and Nevşehir, 85km north (1hr 30min). The **otogar** is some 6km west of the town centre, linked by service bus or the blue *Belediye* bus. If you arrive late, you may have to take a taxi into town. The **tourist office** (Mon–Fri 8am–noon & 1.30–5.30pm; ☎0382/213 2474), at Kadıoğlu Sok 1, is in a nicely restored Ottoman building a couple of minutes' signed walk from the main square.

Accommodation is limited, but you might need to stay over before making the onward trip to Ihlara. Best bet is the *Otel Yuvam* (☎0382/212 0024; ❹) which occupies a renovated old townhouse next to the Kurşunlu Camii at Eski Sanayı Caddesi; rooms are attractively furnished and clean, with modern bathrooms. A little cheaper, the *Otel Erdem* (☎0382/214 1500; ❷) on Banklar Caddesi, is a useful fall-back. There is nowhere exciting to eat in Aksaray; try the basic **kebab places** around Hükümet Meydanı.

The Ihlara valley

A fertile gorge cut by a deep green river between red cliffs, the **Ihlara valley** is as beautiful a place as you could conceive. If you add some of the most attractive and interesting churches and rock-carved villages in the Cappadocia region, it's easy to see why the valley is an increasingly popular destination. Most come only as part of a day-excursion from Ürgüp or Göreme, but to appreciate the valley at its best (early morning and early evening) try to spend a night in either Selime or Ihlara villages.

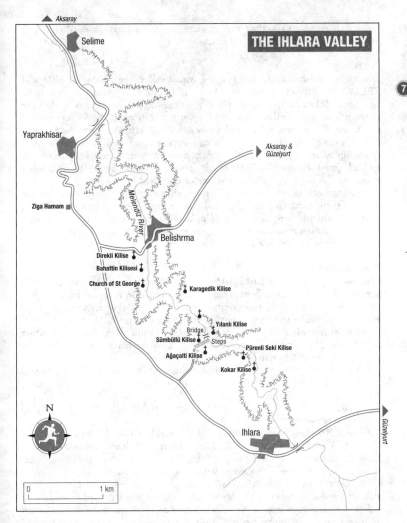

THE IHLARA VALLEY

Aksaray

Selime

Yaprakhisar

Aksaray &
Güzelyurt

Ziga Hamam

Melendiz River

Belishrma

Direkli Kilise
Bahattin Kilisesi
Church of St George

Karagedik Kilise

Yılanlı Kilise
Bridge
Sümbüllü Kilise   Steps
Ağaçalti Kilise   Pürenli Seki Kilise

Kokar Kilise

N

Ihlara

Güzelyurt

0   1 km

Minibuses to Ihlara village leave from Aksaray *otogar* three times daily, passing Selime and the turn-off to Belisırma, and returning the same day. A **taxi** from Aksaray to Ihlara costs €25 – you can also arrange to be picked up in Belisırma or Selime after you have completed your walk. In addition, there are six dolmuşes daily from Aksaray to Güzelyurt, and frequent dolmuş connections between Güzelyurt and Ihlara. A large enough group could rent a whole minibus either from the drivers in Aksaray *otogar* or from Ürgüp (you'll need about ten people to make it viable). There are three **entry points to the valley**, at Ihlara village, Belisırma and Selime (each open daily 8am–1 hour before sunset; 5TL).

If you have time, it's satisfying to do the trip **independently**. The six-kilometre walk from Selime to Belisırma takes around three hours, and a further three hours to complete the ten-kilometre walk to Ihlara village. There are places to eat en route, in Belisırma, and one or two river-pools to swim in if it's hot. Of course it is perfectly possible to do the walk in reverse, and there is accommodation in both Selime and, more plentifully, in Ihlara.

Selime

One of the most beautiful parts of the whole valley, the troglodyte village of **SELIME** has previously been passed over in favour of the better-known, more frequented Ihlara village area. It's the first village you pass on the way to Ihlara or to the official entry to the valley, and it's worth at least a couple of hours' visit, if not a stopover in one of the valley's best **hotels**. The *Piri Motel and Camping* (☎0382/454 5114; ❸) offers spotless, comfortable rooms, and its owner Mustafa is willing to act as a guide to the surrounding churches. The less conveniently located *Çatlak Pension* (☎0382/454 5065; ❸) has reasonable rooms and offers **camping**, but is a long walk from Selime's attractions.

A number of massive, rather squat **fairy chimneys** dot the valley at Selime, many of them containing churches, and there's even a rock-cut cathedral, divided into three aisles by irregularly shaped pillars. The village takes its name from a Selçuk **mausoleum** in the village cemetery, with a pyramidal roof inscribed "Selime Sultan", a dedication of unknown origin.

Belisırma

The troglodyte village of **BELİSIRMA** blends in with the tawny rock face from which it was carved to such an extent that in a bad light it can all but disappear from view. Its tranquil riverside location provides the opportunity to enjoy a meal at one of the simple tree-shaded restaurants on the west bank.

The most rewarding way to reach Belisırma is to **walk along the valley**, either from Selime (3hr) or from Ihlara village (3hr) – from the latter, you can take in the majority of the valley churches.

Belisırma village is home to three primitive **campsites**: *Valley Anatolia* (☎0382/457 3040; tents 10TL) has tents for rent and an excellent **restaurant** where you can eat trout or *saç kavurma* very cheaply, while the *Aslan* (☎0382/457 3033) also has a riverside restaurant. The *Tandırcı* (☎0382/457 3110; tents 10TL) is also a restaurant/campsite, and has a good reputation.

Around Belisırma, the eleventh-century **Direkli Kilise** ("Church with the Columns") has fine examples of Byzantine frescoes, including a beautiful long-fingered Madonna and Child on one of the columns from which the church takes its name, and a picture of St George fighting a three-headed dragon.

The **church of St George**, 50m up the cliffside, a half-kilometre south of Belisırma and 3km from the stairs at the main entrance, was dedicated to the saint by a thirteenth-century Christian emir, Basil Giagoupes, who was in the army of Mesut II. It bears an inscription expressing Christian gratitude for the religious tolerance of the Selçuk Turks. St George is depicted in armour and cloak, holding a triangular shield and flanked by the donor and his wife Tamara, who is handing a model of the church to the saint. To the right, St George can be seen in action, killing a three-headed serpent, with an inscription above that reads "Cleanse my soul of sins."

Ihlara village

Best known of the quaint villages in the valley bottom, **IHLARA** is slightly more developed than its rivals. Set by the river in the centre of the village, the *Star* (☎0382/453 7676; ❹) is overpriced for its clean, but waterless, rooms. To compensate, its location is the best in Ihlara. Above the old village, set on the lip of the valley, are several more **pensions**. The modern, well-built *Akar Pansiyon* (☎0382/453 7018, ℹ453 7511; ❸), just off the road to the main valley entrance, is the best – clean and quiet, with comfortable doubles and a basic restaurant attached.

The owner speaks good English and will arrange for you to be picked up from the Selime exit of the valley for a reasonable €6. *Akar* also offers **camping** in its garden.

The main churches

The monastic occupation of the Ihlara valley, or **Peristrema** as it was originally known, seems to have been continuous from early medieval times until the fourteenth century. It would seem from the decoration of the churches, whose development can be traced through pre- and post-Iconoclastic periods, that the valley was little affected by the religious disputes of the period. Paintings show both Eastern and Western influence, so that some figures wear Arab striped robes, whereas others resemble those in Byzantine frescoes in Europe.

Descending from the **main entrance**, midway between Ihlara and Belisırma, down several hundred **steps** to the valley floor 150m below, is precipitous, but manageable. The most interesting of the churches are located near the small wooden **bridge** at the bottom of the flight of steps. It's also possible to walk from Ihlara village along the southwest bank of the river to the bridge, or from Belisırma to the northwest keeping to the same side of the river. Walking from either village to this point takes about an hour and a half, a fairly straightforward hike that's well worthwhile for the tremendous sense of solitude.

At the bottom of the steps is a plan showing all the accessible churches, most of which are easy enough to find. To the right of the bridge, on the same side as the steps, is the **Ağaçaltı Kilise** ("Church under the Tree"). Cross-shaped with a central dome, the church originally had three levels, but two of them have collapsed, as has the entrance hall. The most impressive of the frescoes inside depict the Magi presenting gifts at the Nativity, Daniel with the lions (opposite the entrance in the west arm) and, in the central dome, the Ascension. The colours are red, blue and grey, and the pictures, naive in their execution, suggest influence from Sassanid Iran, particularly in the frieze of winged griffins. Unfortunately, in recent years these frescoes have suffered serious damage.

The **Pürenli Seki Kilise** lies 500m beyond this, also on the south bank, and can be seen clearly from the river, 30m up the cliffside. The badly damaged frescoes here mainly depict scenes from the life of Christ. Another 50m towards Ihlara, the **Kokar Kilise** is relatively easy to reach up a set of steps. Scenes from the Bible in the main hall include the Annunciation, the Nativity, the Flight into Egypt and the Last Supper. In the centre of the dome, a picture of a hand represents the Trinity and the sanctification.

One of the most fascinating of all the churches in the valley is located across the wooden footbridge, about 100m from the stairs. The **Yılanlı Kilise** ("Church of the Snakes") contains strikingly unusual depictions of sinners suffering in hell. Four female sinners are being bitten by snakes: one of them on the nipples as a punishment for not breast-feeding her young; another is covered in eight snakes; and the other two are being punished for slander and for not heeding good advice. At the centre of the scene a three-headed snake is positioned behind one of the few Cappadocian depictions of Satan; in each of the snake's mouths is a soul destined for hell.

Another church worth exploring is **Sümbüllü Kilise** ("Church of the Hyacinths"), just 200m from the entrance steps. The church shows Greek influence in its badly damaged frescoes and has an attractive facade decorated with horseshoe niches.

Güzelyurt

GÜZELYURT, the nearest small town to the Ihlara valley, 13km northeast of Ihlara village, provides an opportunity to catch a glimpse of the old, untouched Cappadocia, and to stay in the best hotel in the region. If that isn't enough incentive, there are good dolmuş connections with Aksaray and Ihlara, and plenty of sights worth visiting in the town and within easy walking distance.

The beautiful *Karballa* **hotel** on the main square (☎0382/451 2103, ⓦwww .karballahotel.com; ❺) occupies a nineteenth-century Greek monastery. The monks' cells are now bedrooms, with central heating and individual bathrooms now added, the refectory has become an excellent **restaurant**, with superb evening meals for 16TL, and there's a small pool. The *Hotel Karvallı* (☎0382/451 2736, ⓦwww.karvalli.com; ❹), on the southern outskirts of the town, has comfortable rooms in a new, but traditionally styled, building that has stunning views over a small lake, Yüksek Kilise (see below) and Hasan Dağı. Near the *jandarma* post in the town *Halil's Family Pension* (☎0382/451 2707; ❹) has a couple of spotless rooms in a genuine Turkish home, where you eat from a *sofra* table with the welcoming family. It's great value as the price includes breakfast and an evening meal.

The religious community of Güzelyurt was established by St Gregory of Nazianzen in the fourth century, and a newly renovated church dedicated to him, called **Kilise Camii** by locals, is located a short walk from the main street, past the PTT and mosque, on Kör Sokak. A golden bell given to the church by a Russian Orthodox community in Odessa is now in Afyon museum, but other items of interior decor, such as a carved wooden iconostasis and chair, gifts from Tsar Nicholas I in the eighteenth century, can still be seen *in situ*. Elsewhere on Kör Sokak and in the **old town** around it are still-inhabited troglodyte dwellings and old Greek houses with beautifully carved facades.

The most impressive sight in the Güzelyurt area, however, has to be "**Monastery Valley**", below the town to the northeast, approached by taking a right turn out of the village after the Cami Kilise. The valley is riddled with over fifty rock-cut churches and monastery complexes – some dating from the Byzantine era – of which the most attractive is the nineteenth-century **Yüksek Kilise** ("High Church"), dramatically located on a high rock. A walk up the entire 4.5-kilometre-long valley takes about two and a half hours, and brings you to the village of **Sivrihisar**. From there, a signposted fifteen-minute walk south leads to a freestanding church of note, the sixth- or seventh-century **Kızıl Kilise** ("Red Church"), one of the few remaining churches containing masonry in the whole of Cappadocia.

Kayseri and around

Green fields, wooded hills and a snow-capped volcano surround the modern-looking concrete that is today's **KAYSERI**, encircling an old Selçuk settlement of black volcanic stone. The city has a reputation for religious conservatism and ultra-nationalism; it's the heartland of the Milli Hareket Partisi, the nearest thing there is to a fascist party in the country. In spite of this, there's a gentle acceptance of the waywardness of foreigners. It's also a thriving business centre, where traditional commerce, particularly raw textiles and carpets, still flourishes in the medieval *han*s. The long history and strategic importance of the town have left it with a littering of impressive monuments, while two nearby attractions, Sultansazlığı bird sanctuary and Mount Erciyes are ideal for picnics in summer and skiing in winter.

Some history

The site of present-day Kayseri was originally called Mazaka. Its origins are unknown, but the city gained importance under the rule of the Phrygians. In 17–18 AD it was named **Caesarea** in honour of Emperor Tiberius, and at the same time it became the capital of the Roman province of Cappadocia. As part of the Byzantine Empire,

Caesarea was relocated 2km to the north of the ancient acropolis, allegedly around a church and monastery that had been built by St Basil, the founder of eastern monasticism and a bishop of Caesarea in the fourth century. The position was strategic in terms of both trade and defence, and it soon became a leading cultural and artistic centre, though always vulnerable to attack from the east. The Arab invasions of the seventh and eighth centuries were particularly threatening, and in 1067 it finally fell to the great Selçuk leader Kılıç Arslan II. In 1097 the Crusaders were in brief possession and it was ruled equally briefly by the Mongols in 1243 before finally becoming part of the Ottoman Empire in 1515, under Selim the Grim.

Arrival and information

To get into town from the **otogar**, take the "Terminal" dolmuş from the minibus station or from the opposite side of Osman Kavuncu Caddesi (the road that passes in front of the *otogar*). It will drop you in front of the hospital (*hastane*) 200m northwest of of the Hunat Hatun complex. Minibuses to and from Ürgüp, Aksaray and Nevşehir use the new minbus station next door instead. The **train station** is 1km north of town at the end of Atatürk Bulvarı: "Terminal" dolmuşes into town – and to the *otogar* in the other direction – pass frequently. THY (Turkish Airlines) has an office at Istasyon Cad 48 (☎0352/222 3858). An Argeus tour agency minibus (see "Ürgüp: Listings", p.649) also meets Turkish Airlines flights at the airport if requested and will deposit you in the village of your choice in Cappadocia. This costs 15TL per person to Ürgüp, for example. Göreme-based Neşe (see p.636) performs the same service for Turkish Airlines

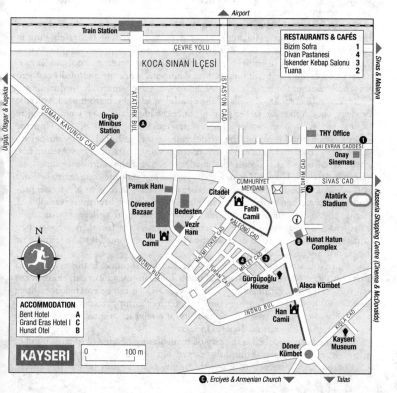

flights, (℡0384/271 2525, ⓦ www.nesetour.com). There is currently no shuttle bus between the airport and Kayseri.

The central **tourist office** (daily: summer 8am–6pm; winter Tues–Sun 8am–noon & 1–5pm; ℡0452/222 3903) is next to the Hunat Hatun complex. It has train, plane and bus timetables, hotel and restaurant lists, and the latest on the Mount Erciyes ski resort. For **internet** access, try the Hollywood Internet Café on Sivas Cad 15.

Accommodation

The *Hunat Otel*, behind the Hunat Hatun complex (℡0352/232 4319; ❶), is the best budget option. Quiet, convenient and clean, its en-suite rooms have pleasant views of the mosque and the management is very friendly. Alternatively, the *Bent Hotel*, on Atatürk Bul 40 (℡0352/2224364, ⓦ www.benthotel.com; ❹), has clean, comfortable rooms with all mod cons, wi-fi connections and is very central.

A decent choice, a little way out of the town centre en route to the Armenian church, is the *Grand Eras Hotel* (℡0352/330 5111, ⓦ www.granderashotel .com; ❻), with all the four-star facilities you'd expect, if rather more glitz than perhaps you'd want.

The City

Part of the delight of Kayseri is that its beautiful old buildings still play an important part in the everyday life of the place, their very existence witness to the social conscience of the Selçuks. Koranic teaching forbade excessive concern with private houses, so public figures poured money into buildings for public welfare and communal activities.

Other buildings still integral to Kayseri's life are the covered markets; there are three in the town centre, all dating from different periods. The **Bedesten**, built in 1497, was originally used by cloth-sellers but is now a carpet market; the **Vezir Hanı**, built by Damat İbrahim Paşa in 1727, is where raw cotton, wool and Kayseri carpets are sold, and leather is prepared for wholesale; while the beautifully restored **covered bazaar** in the same area, built in 1859, has five hundred individual shops.

The towering crenellated walls of the **citadel** (*iç kale*), built from black volcanic rock, are a good place to start exploring, since the life of the town seems to centre on this point. A sixth-century fortress erected in the reign of the Emperor Justinian once stood here, but the citadel you see was built in 1224 by the Selçuk Sultan Keykubad, and has been much restored since, particularly by Mehmet II, who also built the **Fatih Camii**, the small mosque near the southwest gate.

Near the citadel, **Hunat Hatun** *külliye* was the first mosque complex to be built by the Selçuks in Anatolia (construction began in 1239). It consists of a thirteenth-century mosque and *medrese*, the latter one of the most beautiful examples of Selçuk architecture in Turkey. This former theological college has an open courtyard and two *eyvan*s (vaulted chambers open at the front). A wooden box containing a hair reputed to be from the Prophet Mohammed is to be found near the beautifully decorated *mihrab*.

Beyond the market area is the first of several ancient mosques in the city, the **Ulu Cami**, or Great Mosque. Constructed under the Danişmend Turkish emirs in the first half of the thirteenth century, the mosque, which can be entered from three sides, is still in remarkably good condition. Its roof is supported by four rows of stone pillars with varied marble capitals, and it retains its original carved wooden *mimber*, although the central dome is modern.

Kayseri has been described as the **city of mausoleums** because of its large number of tombs: curious, squat, beautifully carved bits of masonry known as *kümbet*s, dating from the thirteenth to fifteenth centuries, which can be found scattered about in the most unlikely places – a couple of them are on traffic islands on the main highway to Mount Erciyes. The best known of them in Kayseri is the **Döner Kümbet**, "turning tomb", a typical example probably dating to the mid-thirteenth century, built for Shah Cihan Hatun. The tomb is decorated with arabesques and palmettes, and a tree of life with twin-headed eagles and lions beneath.

The Gürgüpoğlu House

The **Gürgüpoğlu House** (Gürgüpoğlu Konağı; Tues–Sun 8am–5pm; 3TL), just inside the city walls off Turan Caddesi, is a restored, half-timbered fifteenth-century Ottoman family home used as a museum of ethnography, complete with tableaux of wax dummies. The first room is a typical Turkish salon, its walls intricately painted using natural dyes, with models seated on low divans, holding musical instruments. Upstairs, the restored rooms have beautifully carved and painted wooden ceilings and display ethnographic exhibits featuring wedding objects: headdresses, make-up applicators, and masterfully crafted silver belts. One room houses beautiful Selçuk tiles from the Hunat Hatun and glass *nargiles*, while the landing has a *topak ev*, or nomad's tent.

Kayseri Museum

Kayseri Museum (Kayseri Müzesi; Tues–Sun 8am–5pm; 3TL) on Kışla Caddesi contains important finds from Kültepe (see p.667) and is extremely well labelled in English. The first room deals with the Hittites, their cuneiform writing and hiero-glyphics, and includes a fascinating Hittite rock-relief from Develi and the head of a sphinx. Items from Kültepe include early Bronze Age depictions of the mother goddess, Assyrian bowls and jugs in the shape of animals, dating from the second millennium BC, and a collection of clay tablets in their clay envelopes – essentially small cheques – from the same period.

In the second room are finds from around Kayseri itself, including Hellenistic and Roman jewellery, and grave gifts from a Roman tumulus, among them highly worked pieces in gold and silver. In the garden is a pair of lovely seventh-century BC Hittite lions, with all their own teeth, from Göllüdağ near Niğde.

Surp Krikor Lusuvoriç

The domed Armenian church of **Surp Krikor Lusuvoriç**, a half-hour walk out of town on the Hacılar/Erciyes road (ask the tourist office for directions), is the last architectural reminder of just how important Kayseri was in the Byzantine Christian world. Dating from around 700 AD, it is among Turkey's largest conse-crated churches, and can hold a congregation of a thousand, though at present services are held just twice a year, on March 16 and June 16. The worshippers are largely diaspora Armenians from İstanbul and elsewhere (only around fifty Armenians still live in Kayseri), who hold this church in high regard as Surp Krikor (St Gregory), the first bishop and official founder of the Armenian Church, spent much of his early life here. To gain entry, ring the bell and the caretakers, a friendly Armenian family from İstanbul, will be happy to let you look around.

Eating, drinking and entertainment

Although more famous for its spicy, garlicky *pastırma* (cured meat), *sucuk* (a kind of sausage-like salami) and *mantı* (Turkish ravioli) than for its actual **restaurants**, Kayseri does have some decent places to eat.

First stop should be the famous ⚭ *Bizim Sofra* on Ahı Evran Caddesi, opposite the Onay Sinemasi (from Sivas Caddesi, turn left opposite the Atatürk stadium and cut down an alley past the Melikgazi Hastanesi). *Yaprak sarması* (grape leaves stuffed with spicy rice, served in a rich tomato sauce) is their speciality, and a full meal won't cost more than 6–7TL. The immaculately clean, air-conditioned *Tuana Restaurant* near the PTT on Sivas Caddesi, serves reasonably priced kebabs, *mantı* and desserts, and has good views across to Mount Erciyes. An old favourite is the *İskender Kebap Salonu* at Millet Cad 5, across from the Hunat Hatun complex, with main grills around 9TL. The air-conditioned *Divan Pastanesi* on Millet Caddesi is the place to eat ice cream and cakes. If you are stuck at the *otogar* and can't get into town, head 200m west of the station to the Toyota Plaza. Above the dealership, the owner's wife runs *Kaşıkla*, known for its *mantı* and grills.

Erciyes Dağı

Erciyes Dağı, the 3916-metre-high extinct volcano dominating the city to the southwest, is one of the greatest pleasures the area offers. If you have transport, take a packed lunch and head for its foothills, a twenty-minute drive out of town. Otherwise, the Develi-bound dolmuş, which you can catch from near the Han Camii on Talas Caddesi, will take you to Tekir Yaylası, at an altitude of 2150m. Here you'll find *Kayak Evi*, a **ski lodge** run by Kayseri council (☏0352/342 2032, ⓦwww.erciyeskayak.com; €10 per person in summer, including breakfast; €15 during ski season). The *Bülent Otel* has simple rooms and dorms on the mountain (☏0352/342 2012, ⓦwww.bulenthotel.com; ❸) with a sauna, bar, restaurant and disco. The **ski season** runs from December to May, and there are five lifts and some 12km of piste; **ski rental** is around €12 per day (ski clothes also available). It's a little barren, but snow conditions are often very good.

Sultansazlığı

Beyond Erciyes Dağı the countryside around the Kayseri–Niğde road becomes flat, dull steppe, which you might assume was barren of bird or plant life. Consequently, the oasis of the **Sultansazlığı** bird sanctuary is easy to miss, but it's worth the effort of hunting out. Its two thousand hectares of freshwater marshes are positioned right at the crossroads of two migration routes, makeing it an extremely important wetland for breeding migrant and wintering birds. Visiting species include flamingos, pelicans, storks, golden eagles, herons, spoonbills and cranes.

The marshes, also known as Kuş Cenneti (Bird Paradise), are easily accessible **from Kayseri**: take the Yahyalı bus (6 daily from 8am until 5pm from the *otogar*) and get off at Ovaçiftlik (1hr), from where it's a one-kilometre walk to the water. The best time to **birdwatch** is at dawn, so it's worth staying in one of Ovaçiftlik's two **pansiyons** with camping facilities. *Sultan Pansiyon and Camping Restaurant* (☏0352/658 5549, ⓦwww.sultanpansionbirding.com; ❹) has fourteen en-suite rooms, and plates of *saç tava* (wok-fried lamb). It runs expensive **boat trips** in a flat-bottomed punt (be prepared to haggle) and organizes tours around Yay Gölü. *Atilla Pansiyon* next door (☏0352/658 5576; ❷) has similar accommodation, as well as a place to camp, and a boat for rent.

Kültepe

Twenty-two kilometres northeast of Kayseri lies the important archeological site at what is now known as **Kültepe** (Tues–Sun 8am–noon & 1–5pm; 3TL), the ancient city of Kanesh. To get there by **public transport** you'll have to take a bus, from Sivas Caddesi in Kayseri, along the main eastern highway headed for Bünyan. After some 20km the site is signposted, near a petrol station, but it's a 2km hike from the bus drop-off.

Some 15,000 clay tablets and a well-preserved selection of household furnishings, including human and animal statuettes, were discovered here – the best of which are housed in Kayseri and Ankara museums. The site itself has been well excavated and gives some idea of building plans and street layouts, as well as construction techniques that are still prevalent in Anatolia.

Some history

The city's golden age was in the second millennium BC. At that time, the nearby Karum of Kanesh – the most important of nine Assyrian *karums* (trade centres) in Anatolia, importing tin and textiles in exchange for cattle, silver, copper and skins – was inhabited by the Assyrian trading colony and the lower classes, while Kanesh itself was reserved for royalty of Anatolian stock. The thin layer of ash covering the site dates from two massive conflagrations, the first in around 1850 BC, and the second around 1200 BC. The city lost its importance during the Hittite age, but was still settled during the Hellenistic and Roman periods.

The sites

Excavations labelled "level II", from the second millennium BC, dominate the upper site of Kanesh, especially the Large Palace, which covered an area of 3000 square metres and included a paved central courtyard, and the **Palace of Warsana**, king of Kanesh. Walls were generally of large mud bricks with stone foundations, though the Large Palace had long storage rooms with stone walls.

The **Karum** is a five-minute walk further down the country lane that leads past the entrance to Kanesh. Here, excavations have revealed the foundations of shops, offices, archives and storerooms, all packed closely together inside a defensive wall. The dead were buried together with precious gifts under the floors of their own houses in stone cist graves, some of which can be seen on site.

Travel details

Trains

Afyon to: Adana (1 daily; 11hr); İstanbul (1 daily; 8hr 30min); Konya (2 daily; 6hr).
Kayseri to: Adana (2 daily; 7hr); Ankara (hourly; 9hr); Diyarbakır (4 weekly; 20hr); İstanbul (2 daily; 12hr); Malatya (2 daily; 6hr); Kars (1 daily; 24hr); Van (1 daily; 22hr).
Konya to: Adana (3 weekly; 8hr); Afyon (2 daily; 6hr); Gaziantep (3 weekly; 13hr); İstanbul (2 daily; 14hr).
Niğde to: Adana (2 daily, 4hr); Kayseri (2 daily; 3hr).

Buses

Afyon to: Adana (10 daily; 7hr); Alanya (5 daily; 6hr 30min); Ankara (21 daily; 4hr); Antalya (hourly; 5hr); Aydın (4 daily; 5hr); Bursa (6 daily; 4hr); Fethiye (2 daily; 7hr); Isparta (6 daily; 2hr); İstanbul (20 daily; 8hr); İzmir (4 daily; 6hr); Konya (14 daily; 3hr); Kuşadası (2 daily; 7hr); Kütahya (6 daily; 1hr 30min); Marmaris (2 daily; 9hr).
Aksaray to: Ankara (3 daily; 4hr 30min); Konya (6 daily; 1hr 45min); Niğde (6 daily; 2hr).

Avanos to: Göreme (hourly; 30min); Nevşehir (hourly; 40min); Özkonak (half-hourly; 30min); Ürgüp (every 2hr; 30min).
Beyşehir to: Alanya (6 daily; 4hr); Ankara (4 daily; 5hr); Antalya (5 daily; 4hr); Eğirdir (12 daily; 1hr 30min); Isparta (6 daily; 2hr 30min); İstanbul (4 daily; 10hr); İzmir (2 daily; 8hr); Konya (hourly; 1hr 15min).
Eğirdir to: Ankara (4 daily; 7hr); Antalya (8 daily; 3hr); Beyşehir (12 daily; 1hr 30min); Denizli (4 daily; 3hr); Göreme (2 daily; 8hr); İstanbul (1 daily; 10hr); Konya (4 daily; 4hr).
Göreme to: Alanya (2 daily; 12hr); Ankara (5 daily; 4hr); Antalya (2 daily; 10hr); Denizli (2 daily; 10hr); Eğirdir (2 daily; 8hr); İstanbul (3 daily; 11hr); İzmir (1 daily; 11hr 30min); Kayseri (hourly; 1hr 30min); Konya (4 daily; 3hr); Marmaris (2 daily; 15hr); Nevşehir (hourly; 30min); Ürgüp (hourly; 20min).
Isparta to: Afyon (6 daily; 2hr); Antalya (hourly; 2hr 30 min); Beyşehir (6 daily; 2hr 30min); Kayseri (5 daily; 9hr); Konya (4 daily; 4hr).
Kayseri to: Adana (22 daily; 7hr); Adıyaman (2 daily; 8hr); Afyon (6 daily; 9hr); Ankara (hourly; 4hr 30min); Antalya (8 daily; 11hr);

Bursa (4 daily; 11hr); Isparta (5 daily; 9hr); İstanbul (12 daily; 12hr); İzmir (3 daily; 12hr); Konya (8 daily; 4hr); Niğde (hourly; 1hr 30min); Ürgüp (hourly; 1hr 30min).

Konya to: Afyon (14 daily; 3hr); Alanya (6 daily; 5hr); Ankara (hourly; 3hr); Antalya (8 daily; 5hr); Beyşehir (hourly; 1hr 15min); Bursa (8 daily; 10hr); Göreme (6 daily; 3hr); Isparta (4 daily; 4hr); Kayseri (8 daily; 4hr); Silifke (8 daily; 5hr).

Nevşehir to: Adana (3 daily; 5hr); Ankara (7 daily; 4hr 30min); Antalya (3 daily; 11hr); Fethiye (1 daily; 11hr 30min); Göreme (every 30min; 15min); İstanbul (3 daily; 10hr); Kayseri (8 daily; 2hr); Konya (6 daily; 3hr); Mersin (3 daily; 5hr); Ürgüp (every 30min; 30min).

Niğde to: Aksaray (8 daily; 1hr 30min); Alanya (1 daily; 12hr); Ankara (10 daily; 4hr 30min); Antalya (2 daily; 12hr); Çamardı (summer 4 daily; 1hr); Derinkuyu (hourly; 45min); İstanbul (3 daily; 12hr); Kayseri (hourly; 1hr 30min); Konya (8 daily; 3hr 30min); Mersin (5 daily; 4hr); Nevşehir (hourly; 1hr 30min); Samsun (1 daily; 8hr); Sivas (1 daily; 6hr).

Ürgüp to: Adana (4 daily; 5hr); Ankara (6 daily; 5hr); Antalya (2 daily; 10hr); Denizli (2 daily; 12hr); Göreme (hourly; 20min); İstanbul (3 daily; 13hr); Kayseri (hourly; 1hr 30min); Konya (8 daily; 3hr); Marmaris (2 daily; 15hr); Mersin (3 daily; 5hr); Nevşehir (hourly; 30min).

Flights

Kayseri to: İstanbul (6 daily; 1hr 30min); İzmir (1 daily; 1hr 35min).
Konya to: İstanbul (6 daily; 1hr 10min); Van via İstanbul (1 daily; 4hr 5min).
Nevşehir to: İstanbul (1 daily; 1hr 20min).

North Central Anatolia

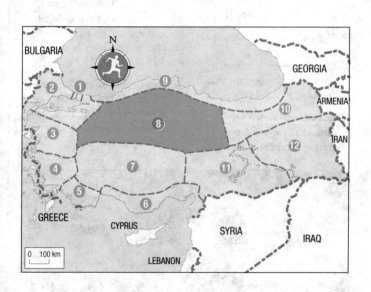

CHAPTER 8 # Highlights

✳ **Museum of Anatolian Civilizations, Ankara** A treasure-hoard of artefacts contained in one of the most prestigious museums in Turkey. See p.507

✳ **Safranbolu** A somewhat disarming place whose laid-back nature will almost compel you to prolong your stay - come on a day-trip from Ankara and you may well be here all week. See p.520

✳ **Hattuşa** Former Hittite capital set in a magnificently bucolic setting – even more reason for a six-kilometre trek around the old city walls. See p.527

✳ **Stay the Ottoman way in Amaysa** Low-slung beds, creaky floorboards and authentic antiques – the restored Ottoman houses of Amasya make for some of Turkey's most appealing accommodation. See p.532

✳ **Rock tombs of Amasya** Massive rock tombs of the Pontic kings carved into a cliff-face and lit up at night to great effect. See p.534

✳ **Tokat kebap** Julius Caesar uttered his famous "I came, I saw, I conquered" in Tokat, and you can do the same after sampling the huge local *kebap*. See p.537

✳ **Sivas's Selçuk monuments** Mongol-inspired architecture with highly decorative facades and beautiful mosaic work. See p.539

▲ Hittite carvings, Hattuşa

North Central Anatolia

W hen the first Turkish nomads arrived in Anatolia during the tenth and eleventh centuries, the landscape – rolling grassland dotted with rocky outcrops – must have been strongly reminiscent of their Central Asian homeland. Those who choose to trek through the region today are an equally hardy bunch, braving long journey times, occasionally tricky journeys and seasonal temperature extremes to visit towns, cities and sights far less heralded than their counterparts in South Central Anatolia. However, those willing to do a little digging will find it one of Turkey's most rewarding and undiscovered quarters.

It seems appropriate that the heart of original Turkish settlement should be home to **Ankara**, the political and social centre of modern Turkey. This European-style capital rises out of a stark landscape, a symbol of Atatürk's dream of a secular Turkish republic. Though it's a far less exciting city than İstanbul, Ankara does make a good base for travels through Anatolia. And while it has comparatively little in the way of architectural or aesthetic merit, a visit to the **Museum of Anatolian Civilizations** is an essential way of gaining some impression of how Anatolia has developed since it was first settled during Neolithic times.

Those not heading straight to Ankara can take in a number of sights on their way from İstanbul to the capital. The large cities of **Kütahya** and **Eskişehir** are easy enough to get to, and the former provides access to the Roman temple site of **Aezani**, and the latter – for those with their own transport – to the sacred site at **Midaş Şehri**. The delightful Phrygian treasures of **Gordion** can be visited on the way to Ankara, or on a day-trip from the capital, while way up north on the way to the coast you'll find enchanting **Safranbolu**, an almost completely intact Ottoman town, whose wooden houses are tucked into a narrow gorge.

Those heading east of Ankara will be able to make use of a fairly logical route. First up are the remains of **Hattuşa**, once the capital of the Hittite Empire and one of the earliest known cities in Turkey. Heading east again, you'll find that several later cultures and civilizations have left their successive marks: at **Amasya**, the rock-cut tombs of the pre-Roman Pontic kings tower over a haphazard riverside settlement of Ottoman wooden houses; **Tokat** has a fine Selçuk seminary; while **Sivas** displays some of the best Selçuk architecture found in Turkey.

Ankara

Those who have spent time in other Turkish cities may find **ANKARA** something of a culture shock. Atatürk declared it capital of the Turkish Republic in 1923, and

NORTH CENTRAL ANATOLIA

High Speed Train

BLACK SEA

BLACK SEA

Erzurum Erzurum

Divriği

Malatya

Kangal

Sivas

Kayseri

Giresun

Ordu

Tokat

Ezinepazarı

Pazar

Samsun

Amasya

Çorum

Alacahöyük Alaca Yazılıkaya

Boğazkale Hattuşaş

Yozgat

Kırşehir

Sungurlu

Kızılırmak

Kızılırmak

Akseray

Sinop

Kastamonu

ANKARA

Esenboğa

Polatlı

Konya

Adana

Safranbolu

Karabük

Amasra

Zonguldak

Bolu

Gordion

Sivrihisar

Adapazarı

İzmit

İstanbul İstanbul İstanbul

Eskişehir

Seyitgazi

Midas Şehri

Kütahya

Afyon

Yoncalı

Aezani

100 km

0

N

it has spent the intervening years moving forward at a breakneck pace, performing an ever more accurate impression of a modern European city. This was, of course, Atatürk's vision all along; before becoming capital Ankara (formerly known as Angora) was a small provincial city, almost lost in the midst of the steppelands and known chiefly for its production of angora, soft goat's wool. This older city still exists in and around the citadel, which was the site of the original settlement, but has been surrounded and almost swamped by the "other" Ankara, a carefully planned attempt to create a seat of government worthy of a modern, Westernized state.

For visitors, Ankara is never going to be as attractive a destination as İstanbul, and the couple of excellent museums and handful of other sights that it can offer are unlikely to detain you for more than a day or two. Even so it's worth the trip just to find somewhere as refreshingly forward-looking as Turkey's administrative and diplomatic centre.

Some history

It was the **Hittites** who founded Ankara around 1200 BC, naming it Ankuwash. Under them the town prospered due to its position on the royal road running from Sardis to their capital at Hattuşa. The Hittites were succeeded by the **Phrygians**, who called the city Ankyra (and left a significant reminder of their presence in the shape of a huge necropolis uncovered near the train station in 1925), and they, in turn, by the **Lydians** and the **Persians**. Alexander the Great passed through on his way east, while in the third century BC invading **Galatians** (Gauls) held sway for a while, renaming the city Galatia.

By the beginning of the first century BC the **Romans** had made substantial inroads into Asia Minor. In 24 BC Ankara was officially absorbed into the empire under Augustus and renamed Sebaste (Greek for Augustus). The city thrived under the Romans, but the later Byzantine era ushered in a period of decline. Arabs, Persians, Crusaders and Mongols stormed the city en route to greater prizes, but only the **Selçuks** were to settle, taking control of the city in 1071. By 1361 Ankara had been incorporated into the burgeoning **Ottoman state** and went into something of a decline, with only its famous wool to prevent it from disappearing altogether.

After Atatürk's final victory, Ankara was made the official **capital of the Turkish Republic**. However, at this time the city was little more than a backward provincial centre; Turkey's vociferous pro-İstanbul lobby was dismayed by the choice of Ankara as capital and many foreign governments also baulked at the idea of establishing embassies here. Gradually, however, the lure of free land for the building of embassies lured in the diplomatic corps. People were drawn to Ankara from the Anatolian countryside in search of work and a higher standard of living, the city's **population** soon swelled from 30,000 to around four million.

Orientation

The city is neatly bisected along its north–south axis by the five-kilometre **Atatürk Bulvarı**, and everything you need is in easy reach of this broad and busy street. At the northern end is **Ulus Meydanı** – usually known simply as **Ulus** ("Nation") – a large square and that has lent its name to the surrounding area. It's not a particularly attractive one, but the point to which you'll probably gravitate on arrival as it's the home of cheap hotels and well positioned for both sightseeing and city transportation.

Heading south down Atatürk Bulvarı from Ulus brings you to the main west–east rail line, beyond which lies **Sıhhıye Meydanı**, an important junction marking the beginning of **Yenişehir** ("New City"). A ten-minute walk south of Sıhhıye brings you to **Kızılay**, the busy square that is the main transport hub of the modern city. At the bottom of Atatürk Bulvarı is **Çankaya**, Ankara's most exclusive suburb and location of the **Presidential Palace**.

Arrival and information

Ankara's **Esenboğa airport** is 33km north of the city. Green, yellow and white Havaş buses from the airport into the centre (12TL; 45 min) tend to depart every half-hour. These will drop you off at the Havaş bus stop by the 19 Mayis Stadium. A taxi into the centre of Ankara from the airport will set you back about 50TL, though you're likely to pay far more than this between midnight and 6am.

If you **arrive** at the **city otogar**, Aşti, in the western suburbs, there will be a free *servis* minibus into the centre from the car park out front. Some run through to the plush hotels in Kavaklıdere, and others to Ulus station; alternatively, catch the Ankaray (LRT light railway; see below).

The **train station** (☎0312/311 0602) is close to the heart of things at the bottom of Cumhuriyet Bulvarı, with frequent buses from outside the main entrance to Ulus and Kızılay. Or you can walk through the tunnel under the railway line to Maltepe Ankaray (LRT) station.

Surprisingly, Ankara lacks a central **tourist office**. Those arriving by plane will be able to make use of the one at Esenboğa **airport** (daily 9.30am–6pm, sometimes later depending on the time of flight arrivals; ☎0312/398 0348), which is pretty helpful. The more upmarket hotels will be pleased to provide you with city maps and the like.

City transport

Ankara's public transport is pretty good, but **tickets** can be confusing for first-time arrivals. Standard EGO tickets are available at metro stations and street booths; they cost 3.40TL and are valid for 45 minutes on both metro lines and most buses, including transfers. If you're staying in Ankara for a few days you may wish to purchase a block of ten tickets (14TL).

Buses run the length of Atatürk Bulvarı from Ulus to Kızılay, and then either branch off to Maltepe under a tunnel or continue to Çankaya via Kavaklıdere; check the destinations on the front of the bus. Most common are blue and white EGO municipality buses, for which you'll need to buy a ticket in advance (see above). Sometimes you may board a privately run bus (usually older and shabbier looking) where you pay the conductor in cash.

There are two modern **metro lines** with efficient trains running at regular intervals throughout the day until around 10.30pm. One line is called the **Ankaray** or LRT (light railway), which joins the second line – simply called the **metro** – at Kızılay. This is also your best option for getting back out to the **otogar**.

Taxis are plentiful and can be flagged down just about anywhere, with 1.70TL (more between midnight and 6am) as the minimum fare. A trip such as Ulus to Kavaklıdere works out at about 12TL.

Accommodation

Accommodation covers the full price and quality spectrum, and finding a room is rarely a problem, given the relative absence of tourists. Most of the cheaper hotels are in **Ulus**, though lone women may not feel so comfortable in the very cheapest places. A couple of hotels have opened up in and around the **citadel**, great places to soak up a quiet night-time atmosphere totally at odds with the rest of the city.

Moving down into **Sıhhıye** and **Kızılay** will take you up another notch or two, and then prices and standards steadily increase as you move further south and into **Kavaklıdere**, home to top-of-the-range places.

Around Ulus

Otel Akman Opera Meyd, Tavus Sok 6
☎0312/324 4140, ✉akmanotel@ttnet.net.tr.
Clean and bright rooms with spacious wall-to-ceiling tiled bathrooms and a convenient and inexpensive *pide* restaurant attached. Breakfast 5TL extra. **❶**

Otel Buhara Sanayi Cad 13 ☎0312/310 7999,
📠324 3327. A good mid-range choice: clean rooms, attentive service and centrally located, though far enough off the main road to block out most noise. Also one of the few places in the area to provide parking. **❸**

Otel Çevikoğlu Çankırı Cad, Orta Sok 2
☎0312/310 4535, 📠311 1940. Clean option whose backstreet setting cuts out most of the local noise. Curved furnishings provide a bit of retro chic in the clean, simple rooms, which also feature TVs and a minibar, and this is also perhaps the cheapest safe option for lone females – single rooms can usually be haggled down to 30TL, including a tasty buffet breakfast. **❷**

Hisar Oteli Hisarparkı Cad 6 ☎0312/311 9889. A popular budget option with presentably clean rooms. You can save 10TL by opting for a shared bathroom – not a bad idea since those inside the en suites are somewhat visible from the rest of the room. There's a male-only hamam in the basement (15TL). **❶**

Hitit Otel Hisarparkı Cad 12 ☎0312/310 8617,
🌐www.otelhitit.com. A little dearer than most Ulus options, but you'll notice the step up in quality. Rooms are large and well appointed, though note that some back onto other rooms' balconies. **❹**

🏃 **Otel Örnek** Gülseren Sok 4 ☎0312/231 8170, 🌐www.ornekhotel.com. Friendly, intimate hotel in a boxy bright-blue building down a side street off Gazi Mustafa Kemal Bul. Neat rooms with TV, hairdryers, minibars and 24hr room service. Handily, it's also close to Maltepe LRT station. **❼**

Hotel Selvi Çankırı Cad 16 ☎0312/310 3500,
✉selvihotel@yahoo.com. Presentable possibility with a large ornate lobby with a barber's shop. Some attempt has been made at updating the old-fashioned rooms, and extras include a/c, a phone in the bathroom and hairdryer. Rooms at the front can get noisy, though there is a swimming pool, so all in all, not bad value. **❹**

The citadel

🏃 **Angora House** Kalekapısı Sok 11 ☎0312/309 8380, 📠309 8381. It's well worth splashing out for a stay at this boutique hotel, set inside a 200-year-old house. The citadel location is perfect and the service first-class, but best of all are the individually styled rooms – think carved wooden ceilings, quality linen, large bathrooms and arty flourishes. Only six rooms, so book ahead if at all possible. **❺**

And Ankara Kalesı Opposite Alâeddin Camii ☎0312/310 2304. Modern, super-clean rooms with flat-screen TV, in an excellent location just outside the citadel. One senses that the management got their sums wrong when figuring out prices, as they simply shouldn't be this cheap: singles are 40TL, and even the suite will only set you back 85TL, so take advantage before they finally find their calculator. Doubles **❸**

Kızılay and Kavaklıdere

Otel Aldino Tunalı Hilmi Cad, Bülten Sok 22 ☎0312/468 6510, 🌐www.hotelaldino.com. Prime location for dedicated shoppers, with a Turkish bath, two restaurant/bars, and garage parking. A/c rooms are bright and spacious with satellite TV, minibars and hairdryers. Friendly for a high-end place and rates are negotiable as low as €80 for a double. **❽**

Elit Otel Olgunlar Sok 10 ☎0312/417 4695,
✉elitotel@superonline.com. Nicely decorated with bright duvets and curtains, and equipped with heating and a/c, minibar and TV. There's a simple restaurant/bar in the lobby and it even has a garden out back – a rare find. **❹**

Gordion Hotel Büklüm Sok 59 ☎0312/427 8080,
🌐www.gordionhotel.com. Expensive and rather exclusive hotel with large, comfortable rooms all done in a tasteful, classical style. There's also a pool, and candlelit massages on offer in the health club. **❾**

Hilton International Hotel Tahran Cad 12 ☎0312/468 2888, 🌐www.hilton.com. Luxury rooms on sixteen floors, decorated in Anatolian stone and lots of plants, with individual a/c/heating systems and laptop connections. For those on a generous expense account – the cheapest rack rates are €245 for a double – though discounted weekend packages (Fri–Sun) can bring prices down to a very reasonable level. **❾**

Sheraton Noktalı Sok ☎0312/468 5454, 🌐www.sheraton.com. Enjoy a pampered existence in this cylindrical concrete monolith. There's a friendly atmosphere for a five-star hotel, a great view of the city from the top, plus various restaurants, a pool and two cinemas. Doubles from €285 and no shortage of people prepared to pay. **❾**

Sürmeli Hotel Cihan Sok 6 ☎0312/231 7660,
🌐www.surmelihotels.com. The works, including a lovely outdoor pool surrounded by sunloungers, a fabulous kidney-shaped indoor pool, gym, Turkish

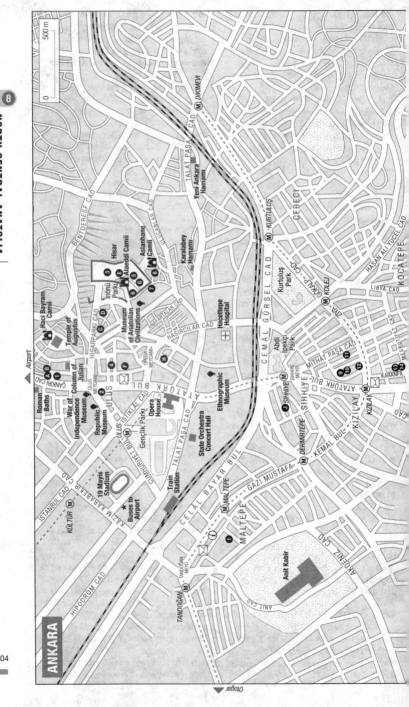

ANKARA

CAFÉS, BARS & CLUBS	
Bedesten	8
Cafemiz	20
Copper Club	10
Eski Yeni	18
Gitanes	22
Ivy	19
Kuğulu Park Café	11
Lost Bar	12
My Way	26
The Pub	24
Salata Bistro	27
Ufo	16
Yerfıstığı	

RESTAURANTS	
Bulvar İşkembecisi ve Lokantası	1
Büyük Pastane	2
Boyacızade Konağı	6
Cengelhan Museum	7
Gado	23
Hayyami	15
Kale Washington	3
Kınacızade Konağı	5
Köşk	9
Kubbe	25
Le Man Kültür	13
Pizzeria Tempo	14
Tapa Tapa Tapas	17
Tapi Tavuk	4
Yosun	21

Kocatepe Camii

RESIT GALIP CAD

Küçükesat Hamamı

Canadian Embassy

Iranian Embassy

BOĞAZ SOK

Australian Embassy

New Zealand Embassy

Kavaklıdere Cinema

United Nations

GÜNIZ SOK

Seğmenler Parkı

Karum Shopping Centre

Kuğulu Park

ATATÜRK BUL

THY Head Office

KAVAKLIDERE

PARIS CAD

GÜNEŞ SOK

GÜVENLİK CAD

Presidential Palace

CINNAH CAD

British Embassy

Russian Embassy

US Embassy

Parliament

BAKANLIKLAR

MUDAFAA

İSMET İNÖNÜ BUL

DIKMEN CAD

AŞAĞAYRANCI

Otogar (5km)

Simon Bolívar Cad, Atakule Mall & Tower & Çankya Hospital

GAZIOSMANPAŞA

ÇANKAYA

ÇANKAYA CAD

ACCOMMODATION	
Akman	H
Aldino	M
And Ankara Kalesi	E
Angora House	G
Buhara	F
Çevikoğlu	B
Efit	K
Gordion	L
Hilton International	P
Hisar	C
Hitit	D
Örnek	I
Selvi	A
Sheraton	O
Sürmeli	J
Tunalı	N

bath and assortment of restaurants and bars. The huge rooms are modern, if somewhat frilly, with cable TV and minibar. If booked online, doubles can go below €100: around a third of the rack rate. ❾ **Otel Tunalı** Tunalı Hilmi Cad 119 ☎0312/467 4440, ⓦwww.hoteltunali.com.tr. A good upper-mid-range

option run by the same family for thirty years; it's cheaper than most places in Kavaklıdere and close to all the nightlife. Rooms are ordinary but functional with fridge, satellite TV and huge windows overlooking busy Tunalı Hilmi Cad. Coffee shop and formal dining room attached. ❻

The City

For most visitors, the first taste of Ankara is **Ulus**, an unenticing area that once marked the westernmost limits of pre-Republican Ankara, which occupied the area between here and the citadel. Today, its streets are lined with drab, concrete stacks, but the area does hide a couple of **Roman monuments**, offering a hint at the depth of history beneath the prevailing modernity. East of Ulus Meydanı, the **Hisar** is the oldest part of the city: a Byzantine citadel whose walls enclose an Ottoman-era village of cobbled streets, below which lies the excellent **Museum of Anatolian Civilizations**.

Around Ulus Meydanı

At Ulus Meydanı, a towering equestrian **statue of Atatürk** – flanked by threatening bronze soldiers in German-style coal-scuttle helmets – gazes out over the busy intersection of Cumhuriyet and Atatürk bulvarıs. The former president faces the building that housed the Turkish Grand National Assembly, the provisional parliament convened by Atatürk and his Nationalist supporters on April 23, 1920. This modest, late-Ottoman schoolhouse building is also where the Turkish Republic was declared in 1923, and it served as the parliament building until 1925. Today it's home to the **Museum of the War of Independence** (Kürtülüş Savaş Müzesi; Tues–Sun 8.45am–12.15pm & 1.30–5pm; 3TL), devoted to the military struggle that preceded the foundation of the modern republic. An extensive collection of photographs, documents and ephemera covers every detail of the various campaigns and, though captions are all in Turkish, much of the material speaks for itself. Visitors can also view the chamber where delegates sat in small school desks, illuminated by candle- and oil-light, with Atatürk overseeing from the vantage point of a raised platform.

Further down the road is the **Republic Museum** (Cumhuriyet Müzesi; same times; 3TL). Housed in the post-1925 headquarters of the Grand National Assembly, it concentrates on the achievements of the Turkish Republic, and is worth a snoop around.

Roman Ankara

What's left of Roman Ankara lies just north of Hisarparkı Caddesi. Following Hükümet Caddesi and taking the first right fork leads to the remains of the **Temple of Augustus and Rome**, Ankara's most important ancient monument. Built in honour of Augustus between 25 and 20 BC, after Ankara was made the provincial capital of Galatia, its main claim to fame is an inscription on the outer wall. Detailing the *Res Gestae Divi Augusti* (Deeds of the Divine Augustus), this was the emperor's political testament, which was carved on every temple of Augustus in the Roman world after his death. The Ankara version is the only one that survives in its entirety. The temple, whose walls alone have endured, was converted into a Christian church around the fifth century AD, and during the fifteenth century it became the *medrese* of the **Hacı Bayram Camii**, named after Bayram Veli, founder of the Bayrami order of dervishes and Ankara's most celebrated Muslim saint. His body is buried in the tomb in front of the building.

A couple of hundred metres to the southwest on Hükümet Meydanı is the **Jülyanüs Sütunu** (Column of Julian), commemorating a visit to Ankara by the Byzantine emperor Julian the Apostate, chiefly remembered for his short-lived attempt to revive worship of the old Roman gods in the fourth century. The column's stonework is characterized by a strange, layered effect rather like a long, cylindrical kebab.

Ankara's other main Roman remains, the **Roma Hamamları**, or Roman Baths (daily 8.30am–noon & 1–5.30pm; 3TL), are about ten minutes' walk north of here on the western side of Çankırı Caddesi. The baths are set in a large *palaestra* (exercise field) scattered with overgrown truncated columns and fragments of cracked masonry. Of the baths themselves, which date back to the third century AD, only the brick pillars that supported the floors – and allowed warm air to circulate and heat the rooms above – survive.

Museum of Anatolian Civilizations

From İnönü Parkı, at the eastern end of Hisarparkı Caddesi, a sharp right turn leads to the **Museum of Anatolian Civilizations** (Anadolu Medeniyetleri Müzesi; daily 8.30am–5pm; 15TL), an outstanding archeological collection documenting the peoples and cultures of Anatolia from the late Stone Age through to Classical times. When you see a replica artefact at an archeological site elsewhere in Turkey, you can bet the original is here. Housed in a restored fifteenth-century *bedesten*, this unmissable museum is, for most visitors, the high point of a visit to Ankara.

Its vast cache of artefacts is laid out in chronological order, clockwise from the entrance, with large stone reliefs dating from the Hittite and Phrygian periods in the central chamber. Most exhibits are clearly labelled in English and German. As you enter, you may be approached by an **official guide** offering to accompany you on your tour (usually around 40TL).

From the Paleolithic to the Bronze Age

The museum's first four sections move visitors through Turkey-time from the Old Stone Age to 2000 BC. The **Paleolithic** section features an assortment of bone fragments and primitive stone tools and weapons from a cave site at Karain, 30km northwest of Antalya, while objects found at Çatal Höyük, a settlement of New Stone Age mud-brick houses 52km north of Konya, have yielded significant evidence about the **Neolithic** period (7000–5500 BC). The importance of agriculture in this era may account for the

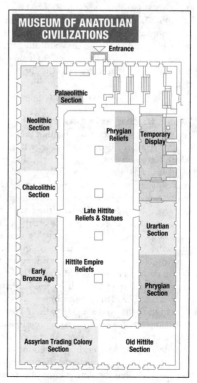

MUSEUM OF ANATOLIAN CIVILIZATIONS

Entrance

Palaeolithic Section

Neolithic Section

Phrygian Reliefs

Temporary Display

Chalcolithic Section

Late Hittite Reliefs & Statues

Urartian Section

Hittite Empire Reliefs

Early Bronze Age

Phrygian Section

Assyrian Trading Colony Section

Old Hittite Section

abundance of fertility goddess figures – represented by baked-clay female forms of ample proportions – that reappear in various forms throughout the museum.

Most of the objects in the **Bronze Age** section (3000–2000 BC) come from Alacahöyük; among the most striking exhibits are the pieces of gold jewellery unearthed in the royal tombs. There then follows a small **Assyrian Trading Colony** section (1950–1750 BC), with the most notable exhibits being well-preserved cuneiform tablets that rank among Anatolia's earliest written records.

The Hittite sections

The Hittites (1700–700 BC) left behind spectacular sites at Boğazkale and nearby Yazılıkaya, east of Ankara (see p.525). Most of the objects on display are from Boğazkale and Alacahöyük, with the most sophisticated example here being a vase with a relief depicting a lively wedding procession. Also included are a number of stelae carved with hieroglyphics that have proved a valuable source of information about the **Old Hittite kingdom** (1700–1450 BC).

There's even more to see from the **Hittite Empire** (1450–1200 BC) itself – elaborate reliefs from Alacahöyük indicate the sophistication of Hittite culture during this time, and if you're planning to visit Hattuşa, look out for the lion and sphinx figures from the city gates. The originals are here, replaced with replicas at the site itself.

Phrygian and Urartian sections

Most of the Phrygian objects (1200–700 BC) were recovered from the royal tumulus at Gordion (see p.518), capital of Phrygian Anatolia after the fall of the Hittites. The timber-framed chamber at the heart of the tumulus has been re-created and objects from it are on display nearby. Most impressive are a wooden table of intricate design and skilfully wrought bronze vessels. Most of what is known about the Urartians derives from clay tablets listing military successes. On the evidence of those artefacts on display here their culture was less sophisticated than that of the Phrygians, though the large bronze cauldron resting on a tripod with cloven bronze feet is austerely beautiful.

The citadel and old town

A pathway leads steeply up through İnönü Parkı between the inner and outer walls of the **Hisar**, the Byzantine citadel whose walls enclose the oldest part of the city. It's an Ottoman-era village of cobbled streets and ramshackle wooden houses that of all Ankara's districts most fully rewards a relaxed and aimless stroll. Most of the area is defiantly unrestored, but a number of grand Ottoman mansions have been renovated, decked out with carpets and antiques, and transformed into restaurants or carpet shops geared towards the tourist trade. Some succeed in recapturing the atmosphere of times past, while others are just hopelessly kitsch.

Ankara's **city walls** were probably first constructed by the Hittites over three thousand years ago when they recognized the defensive potential of the citadel outcrop. The walls that are seen today are much more recent, built on the orders of the Byzantine emperor Michael III (remembered as "Michael the Sot") in 859, who updated defences built by the Roman Emperor Heraclius (who in turn had used earlier Galatian fortifications as a foundation).

Just inside the western gate is the **Alâeddin Camii**, a twelfth-century mosque, much restored in later years, whose unexceptional exterior conceals a painstakingly carved Selçuk *mimber*. At the northern end of the citadel is the **Ak Kale** (White Fortress), presenting tremendous views. The northeastern edge of the city, just about visible from here, is the approximate site of the battlefield where Pompey defeated the Pontic king Mithridates the Great in 74 BC. **Şark Kulesi**, a ruined tower rising out of the eastern walls, also has a panoramic outlook, as well as being a favourite kite-flying spot for local children.

At the southern end of the citadel is the **Güney Kapı** (South Gate), with two vast towers flanking a twin portal. Embedded in the wall connecting the towers are various fragments of Roman masonry, including altars supported by recumbent statues of Priapus.

An unadulterated example of Selçuk architecture can be found a few streets to the southeast in the shape of the **Aslanhane Camii** (Lion-House Mosque), Ankara's oldest and most impressive mosque. The Aslanhane Camii is a "forest mosque", so called because of the 24 wooden columns (arranged in four rows of six) that support the intricately carved wooden ceiling. The astonishingly detailed walnut *mimber* dates back to 1209 and is one of the last examples of Selçuk decorative carving.

Near the mosque is the **Pirinç Han**, built beneath the walls of the citadel in the eighteenth century as an inn for travellers to provide protection from bandits. It has now been fully restored since as a shopping centre, and you can stop by for a glass of tea in the cool courtyard, where you'll hear the gentle sound of craftsmen tapping hammers on copper drifting from the inner rooms.

South to Kızılay

Just south of Ulus, **Gençlik Parkı** (Youth Park) was built on the orders of Atatürk to provide a worthy recreational spot for the hard-toiling citizens of his model metropolis. The park is often packed with families strolling around the artificial lake, and occasional outdoor concerts are held here. The **State Opera House** (Devlet Opera; see p.513), looking like a dark pink, Art Deco underground station, stands near the eastern entrance and was built at Atatürk's behest – he developed a taste for opera while serving as military attaché in Sofia in 1905.

Heading on down Atatürk Bulvarı you pass the **Ethnographic Museum** on Talat Paşa Caddesi (Etnografya Müzesi; Tues–Sun 9am–noon & 1–5pm; 3TL), a grandiose white-marble building that was the original resting place of Atatürk before the construction of the Anıt Kabir mausoleum (see p.510). The museum contains an extensive collection of folk costumes and artefacts from Selçuk times onwards, and some fine examples of Selçuk woodcarving.

Real-estate values increase exponentially as you move south of Kızılay towards Çankaya. A few blocks east of the main thoroughfare, the minarets of the massive **Kocatepe Camii** tower above the surrounding streets. This neo-Ottoman structure, finished in 1987 after twenty years of building, and complete with shopping centre and car park underneath, is Ankara's largest mosque and, indeed, one of the biggest in the world.

The Presidential Palace

At the end of Atatürk Bulvarı is Çankaya Caddesi, beyond which lies the **Presidential Palace** (Çankaya Köşkü; open Sun and national holidays only 1.30–5pm; free), Atatürk's Ankara residence, to which he moved in 1921. A visit here is something of a reverential pilgrimage for Turks, but if you want to go you must arrange a visit in advance with the tourist office, which will fax ahead a day or two beforehand – on arrival, check in at the guardhouse and surrender your passport before joining a group tour. The ground floor is furnished in the Ottoman Baroque style, with much heavily carved and inlaid dark-wood furniture in evidence. Upstairs in Atatürk's living quarters the decor is a little more relaxed, with personal touches, such as a billiard table, on display.

Back on Çankaya Caddesi, at the junction with Atatürk Bulvarı is the unmissable **Atakule Mall and Tower**, a vast mushroom of a tower in reinforced concrete and mirror glass, with a smart shopping centre at its foot. It's worth shelling out 2TL for the lift ride (daily 10am–10pm) up the 125-metre-high structure to enjoy an unbeatable view of the city and an expensive drink in the revolving bar (see p.512).

Anıt Kabir

The mausoleum of **Anıt Kabir** (Mon 1.30–5pm, Tues–Sat 9am–5pm; winter closes 4pm; free) is a national shrine to **Mustafa Kemal Atatürk**, the man who shaped modern Turkey (see Contexts, pp.695–700). The main entrance to the mausoleum is reached by travelling up Anıt Caddesi from Tandoğan Meydanı (at the northwestern end of Gazi Mustafa Kemal Bulvarı), and it's this approach that reveals the place at its most impressive (though you can also enter the grounds of the mausoleum from a rear entrance on Akdeniz Caddesi). Bus #265 runs from Ulus Meydanı, dropping you at Tandoğan Meydanı, or alternatively catch an Ankaray (LRT) train to Tandoğan.

At the head of the central courtyard lies the **mausoleum** itself, a squared-off Neoclassical temple with huge bronze doors. Visitors wearing hats must remove them as they enter and soldiers stand guard to ensure that everyone evinces the appropriate degree of respect. The mausoleum interior is almost completely bare – the only decoration is some discreet mosaic work – so that all attention is focused on the plain sarcophagus. Atatürk's body was brought here in 1953 from its original resting place in what is now the Ethnographic Museum.

Three large halls are positioned around the courtyard. The largest houses the **Atatürk Museum** in which you'll find everything from Atatürk's evening dress to the rowing machine he used for exercise. Among the most eye-catching exhibits are a gun disguised as a walking stick, of which Ian Fleming would have been proud, and the gifts of a diamond-encrusted sword from the shah of Iran and an elegant toilet set from the king of Afghanistan. An adjacent hall contains Atatürk's cars, namely a couple of Lincoln limousines used for official business and an imposing black Cadillac (reputedly still in working order) for personal use.

▲ Anıt Kabir (Atatürk Shrine)

Eating

Ulus is your best bet for cheap eats, **Kızılay** has most of the mid-range places (particularly on and around Karanfil and Selanik *sokak*s), and the classier restaurants can be found in **Kavaklıdere** and **Çankaya**. The exceptions to this general rule are the restaurants that have opened up in restored Ottoman houses in the **Hisar** (citadel) over the last few years.

Around Ulus

Bulvar İşkembecisi ve Lokantası Çankırı Cad 11. Excellent *İskender kebap*, *fırın sutlaç* (baked rice pudding) and other trusty favourites in a round-the-clock dining operation. It's next to the *Hotel Selvi*.

Büyük Pastane Atatürk Bul. In the shopping centre opposite the Museum of the War of Independence. Milk puddings, *baklava* and chocolate pastries served in a shady courtyard adorned with pot plants and a fountain.

Tapi Tavuk Posta Cad 23. Presentable canteen-style cafeteria where what you see is what you get. A wide selection of vegetable side dishes combine well for a filling meal; you can fill up for well under 10TL. Closed Sun.

Around the citadel

Boyacızade Konağı aka *Kale Restaurant*, Berrak Sok 9. Spread across several floors of a rambling mansion-house, decorated with carpets and bric-a-brac, and specializing in traditional cuisine. There's a good wine list and prices are surprisingly reasonable, from around 25TL a head. The separate fish restaurant on the second floor lacks atmosphere, though the dishes are tasty.

Çengelhan Museum Sutepe Mahallesi, Depo Sok 1. Classy restaurant set in the courtyard of a restored sixteenth-century *kervansaray*. Ideal for a coffee stop or a full-blown meal. There's an interesting museum arranged around the courtyard, charting the history of trade in Ankara.

Kale Washington Kale Sok 1. Atmospheric restaurant with a view-laden terrace perched on top of the old city walls. A good place for a cool beer, a dinner of the usual Turkish staples or something a little different, such as beef stroganoff or chicken Kiev.

Kınacızade Konağı Kalekapısı Sok 28. Set in a wonderful Ottoman house, and one of the cheapest places to eat in the citadel. Kebab dishes start at 8TL, and *mezes* from 5–7TL – try the *şakşuka*, a mix of tomato, yoghurt and fried aubergine.

Kızılay, Kavaklıdere and Çankaya

Gado Filistin Cad 4. Vaguely bizarre Dalí-inspired restaurant, done out in an Indonesian style but with dishes from all over the world on its excellent and varied menu. Meals are prepared in the open kitchen at the back, and you should make an effort to visit the outrageous toilets.

Hayyami Bestekar Sok 82. Cosy, laid-back wine-bar-cum-restaurant. Tasty local dishes and an enormous wine list to choose from, all served to a background of cool jazzy sounds. You'll pay around 30TL per head.

Köşk Tuna Cad, İnkılap Sok 2. The best *İskender kebap* and *inegöl köfte* in Ankara, and despite its well-earned reputation prices are still low – 6TL for a plate of succulent *köfte*. Eat on the lovely terrace from crisp white tablecloths, or inside the spotless two-storey restaurant decorated with chandeliers and gleaming brass.

Kubbe Atakule Tower ☎0312/440 7412. Highly romantic revolving restaurant right at the top of the tower complete with star-studded ceiling, live music and fantastic views.

Le Man Kültür Konur Sok 8. A prime example of Ankara's recent swing towards the trendy and hip – cartoon strips line the tables and walls, and dishes come with interesting names such as "Atom Boy" and "Selfish Chicken". Salads, sandwiches and pasta dishes go for around 7TL, Latino food for a little more.

Pizzeria Tempo Corner of Meşrütiyet Cad and Karanfil Sok. Very popular pizza-and-pasta place, with a reasonably authentic Italian atmosphere and moderate prices. Pizzas are generally a safer bet than the pasta dishes, which can miss the mark slightly, but service is quick and lone travellers – particularly women – will feel comfortable here.

Tapa Tapa Tapas Tunalı Hilmi Cad 87. Large, popular tapas restaurant, complete with well-stocked horseshoe bar. Live music on Tuesdays, and frequent salsa nights held on the dancefloor at the back.

Yosun Iran Cad 27 ☎0312/467 5464. Customers return again and again for an authentic Turkish night out – start with *mezes*, then move on to fish (red mullet, sea bass or bream), while Tolon, the aged owner, provides the entertainment by singing and playing the piano and accordion. Expect to pay around 35TL with a half-bottle of wine or *rakı* thrown in.

Drinking and nightlife

Cafés are strewn all over town, but for drinking you'll have to head south from Ulus. The *meyhanes* in **Kızılay** make a good starting point, and although these are largely male-dominated haunts, female visitors shouldn't attract too much unwelcome attention. For something more trendy head for the bars of **Kavaklıdere**.

Most **cafés** open during the day to offer food, tea and obligatory backgammon boards, some seguing into **bars** as the evening progresses. The **clubbing** scene is improving but don't expect too much; there are some studenty late-night venues hidden away in the backstreets of the university district, Cebeci, but you really need to find a local to guide you to them.

Cafés

Bedesten Opposite Aslanhane Camii, Hisar. Rickety teahouse meets oversized treehouse: have a good clamber around before settling on a place to sit, squat, lie or lounge. The coffee's good too (3.5TL), but best of all you can buy anything you see hanging around the place, with the likely exception of other customers.

Cafemiz Arjantin Cad 19, Kavaklıdere. Frilly, flowery café that's a place to be seen in, with a good range of sandwiches, light meals and cocktails which you can also enjoy in the conservatory out back.

Kuğulu Park Café Kuğulu Parkı, Kavaklıdere. Pleasant open-air retreat from the traffic, serving pastries, snacks and nonalcoholic drinks by the fountain until around 10pm.

Salata Bistro Reşit Galip Cad 57, Gaziosmanpaşa. Café-bar popular with the student crowd, serving snacks. There's outside seating in the garden during summer, and in winter they warm things up inside with a log fire.

Bars

Gitanes Tunalı Hilmi Cad, Bilir Sok 4/3, Kavaklıdere. An intimate candlelit bar with regular live music performances – often attracting the better-known Turkish jazz bands. As good a starting point as any for your in-depth exploration of the Tunalı Hilmi scene.

Ivy Arjantin Cad, Kavaklıdere. Large, very chic brasserie with a tempting though expensive food and drink menu; order a frozen margarita, accompanied perhaps by something from the vast home-made cheesecake menu. It's a perfect spot for a sundowner, and there's a good selection of English-language magazines.

Lost Bar Bayındır Sok 17, Kızılay. Grungy yet somehow homely, this sixth-floor bar is a friendly place with frequent live music and karaoke sessions – they'd be more than pleased to see a foreigner grabbing the mic.

The Pub Ahmet Efendi Sok 4, Çankaya. Beery, verging on studenty pub, with draught beer, good bar snacks and crêpes, a large screen for sporting events, an open-air terrace with nice views of the city, and the occasional darts night.

Ufo Atakule Tower, Çankaya. Fantastic bar just below the restaurant at the top of the Atakule Tower, with fabulous views over Ankara. Good for pricey cocktails, or tasty cakes and coffee, and open daily until 3am.

Yerfıstığı Bestekar Sok 88, Kızılay. Strange concept-bar serving monkey nuts (hence the name), the shells of which smother the floor. Good selection of beers and drinks, and the music pulls a large crowd at weekends. Not a place for those with nut allergies.

Clubs

Copper Club *Sheraton Hotel*, Noktali Sok, Kavaklıdere. Large club frequented by expats and diplomats. One of the few places in Ankara where you can successfully order a gin & tonic, but except to pay through the nose for it. Live music nightly from 10pm to 2am, closed Sun.

Eski Yeni İnkılap Sok 6, Kızılay. With draught beer for 4TL and a heaving dancefloor, this is a great place to have a drink and throw some shapes on a weekend evening. The bar's name translates as "Old New", which is rather apt: the happy, easy-to-please crowd squeals in delight when the latest "Ankara house" hit comes on, then does exactly the same thing for Annie Lennox or Simply Red.

My Way Corner of Selanik Sok and Ziya Gökalp Cad, Kızılay. Average fish restaurant on a balcony with *fasıl* music and plenty of *rakı*, with a downstairs disco playing Turkish pop daily until 4am, attracting die-hard clubbers still hanging around Kızılay after other places have closed.

Entertainment

With Ankara's designation as capital of the new republic, the city then had the responsibility of becoming the cultural capital of Turkey, supported by the opera-loving Atatürk. Concerts, and in particular the opera, are well worth attending here if you can. The atmosphere is refreshingly informal and as concerts are subsidized by the government, tickets are cheap. Otherwise, there are plenty of **cinemas** (*sineması*) found all over Ankara.

Classical music and opera

A visit to Ankara's Opera House is a unique experience if you are in town at the right time of year. Otherwise, there are classical music performances by the State Orchestra at the State Concert Hall and at various venues across the city. The main season starts in earnest in October and runs through to March, and monthly programmes are listed in the Sunday edition of the *Turkish Daily News*. The city hosts the **International Ankara Music Festival** during May (information on ⓦwww.ankarafestival.com).

State Opera (Devlet Opera). Atatürk Bul, just south of the entrance to Gençlik Parkı ☏0312/324 2210. Performances of classics such as *Tosca, La Bohème* and *Madame Butterfly*, as well as occasional piano recitals and classical concerts. Tickets (10–20TL) are available from the box office in season (9.30am–5.30pm, 8pm on performance days), up to a month in advance and from the Dost bookshop in Kızılay (see "Listings", below).

State Orchestra (Devlet Orkestrasi). Talat Paşa Cad 38, just south of the Opera House and Gençlik Parkı ☏0312/309 1343. The Presidential Symphony Orchestra performs here twice weekly at 8pm on Fri, and 11am on Sat during season, showcasing classical music by Turkish and foreign composers. Tickets (5–8TL) are available from the State Opera box office (see above).

Film

Recent international releases are usually shown in their original language with Turkish subtitles, and tickets cost around 10TL, with discounts before 6pm and for students. The tourist office can supply details of Ankara's **film festivals** – the International Film Festival in March, and the International Cartoon Film Festival in May.

Megapol Konur Sok 33, Kızılay ☏0312/419 4493. More arty than the Metropol, which it backs onto, screening anything from Japanese to Eastern European films. Look out for the occasional English-speaking classic.
Metropol Selanik Cad 76, Kızılay ☏0312/425 7479. Hugely popular multi-screen cinema showing new releases and special screenings of classic

movies and foreign films. There's a coffee shop inside, a beer garden outside and any number of cafés and bars along this street.
Sheraton Cinema Noktalı Sok, Kavaklıdere ☏0312/468 5454. Two small, cosy cinemas, open to non-guests, with some of the comfiest seats you could find.

Listings

Airlines Most airline offices are in Kavaklıdere or Çankaya. THY (ⓦwww.turkishairlines.com) has offices at the airport ☏0312/398 0100; at Atatürk Bul 154, Kızılay ☏0312/428 0200; and Atatürk Bul 231, Kavaklıdere ☏0312/468 7300. Others include: Air France ☏0312/467 4400; Atlasjet, airport only ☏0312/398 0201; Austrian Airlines ☏0312/433 2533; Delta ☏0312/468 7805; Lufthansa ☏0312/398 0374;

Singapore Airlines ☏0312/468 4670; and Swiss ☏0312/468 1144.
Airport Esenboğa airport, general enquiries and flight information ☏0312/398 0100.
Banks and exchange Banks and ATMs are all over the city, especially south of Ulus along Atatürk Bul. The airport also has several places to change money.
Books Tuhran, corner of Konur Sok and Yüksel Cad, Kızılay, has a good selection of books. Dost,

Karanfil Sok 11, Kızılay, has English novels and a good selection of pricier coffee-table books.

Car rental Avis, airport ☎0312/398 0315, and Tunus Cad 68, Kavaklıdere ☎0312/467 2313; Best, Büklüm Sok 89/9, Kavaklıdere ☎0312/467 0008; Budget, Tunus Cad 39, Kavaklıdere ☎0312/417 5952; Europcar, airport ☎0312/395 0506, and Koza Sok 154, Gaziosmanpaşa ☎0312/398 0503; Hertz, airport ☎0312/398 0535, and Atatürk Bul 138, Kavaklıdere ☎0312/468 1029.

Embassies Australia, Nenehatun Cad 83, Gaziosmanpaşa ☎0312/459 9500; Canada, Cinnah Cad 58 ☎0312/409 2712; Iran, Tehran Cad 10, Kavaklıdere ☎0312/468 2820; New Zealand, Iran Cad 13, Kavaklıdere ☎0312/467 9054; Russian Federation, Karyağdi Sok 5, Çankaya ☎0312/439 2122; USA, Atatürk Bul 110, Kavaklıdere ☎0312/455 5555; UK, Şehit Ersan Cad 46/A, Çankaya ☎0312/455 3344.

Emergencies Ambulance ☎112; Fire ☎110; Police ☎155.

Hamams Karacabey Hamamı, Talat Paşa Cad 101, Ulus, is the oldest in town, built in 1445 (daily 10am–10pm; 20TL). A little cheaper are the baths at the *Sürmeli Hotel*, Cihan Sok 6, Sıhhıye ☎0312/231 7660 (daily 10am–10pm).

Hospitals Hacettepe Hastanesi, just west of Hasırcılar Cad in Sıhhıye (☎0312/466 5858 or 5859), should have an English-speaking doctor available at all times. You may be treated more quickly at one of Ankara's private hospitals: Çankaya, Bülten Sok 44, Çankaya (☎0312/426 1450), is the most central.

Laundry All but the cheapest of hotels offer a reasonably priced laundry service, but if you get stuck try the Yimpaş department store on Sanayı Cad in Ulus – on the second floor is a laundry and dry cleaners.

Pharmacies In each neighbourhood pharmacies take turn in providing a 24hr service called *Nöbetçi*, the information posted on the window of the other pharmacy shops. Most central is Ülkü, Meşrütiyet Cad 23, Kızılay.

Police The tourist police (☎0312/384 0606) are located in Ankara's main police station (Emniyet Sarayı) in the district of Akköprü, a short walk south of the Akköprü metro station.

Post office Ankara's main PTT is on Atatürk Bul in Ulus (open 24hr) for international calls and to buy stamps, phonecards, *jetons* etc. You can also place transfer-charge calls here. There's also a PTT at the train station (7am–11pm), and one on Gazi Mustafa Kemal Bul (8.30am–7pm) near the tourist office.

Kütahya and around

Halfway between İzmir and Ankara is the large, forward-looking city of **KÜTAHYA**, whose location between capital and coast makes it a good place to kick off a tour of Northern Anatolia. The city has few draws of its own – note the near-total absence of tourists – but serves as a jumping-off point for the splendidly isolated Roman ruins of **Aezani** (see p.516). Dominated by an Ottoman fortress, Kütahya is famous above all for its fine **tiles**, which are used throughout Turkey, especially in restoration work on Ottoman mosques, replacing the İznik originals (just as Kütahya has replaced İznik as the country's leading tile-producing centre). Many modern local buildings, including the *otogar*, are swathed in tiles; and there are ceramic shops on virtually every street, selling tiles, dinner services and vases – not to mention toilets, of which Kütahya is the nation's largest producer.

Some history

It was under the Ottomans that Kütahya enjoyed its golden age as a **tile-making centre**, after Sultan Selim I forcibly resettled tile-workers from Tabriz here after defeating the Persians at Çaldıran in 1514. Contemporary Kütahya tiles look a little garish and crude in comparison with Ottoman-era examples – the secret of the pigment blends that gave the original Kütahya tiles their subtle and delicate lustre has been lost with the centuries.

During the War of Independence, the Greek army were defeated twice in battles at the defile of İnönü, northeast of Kütahya, in January and April 1921. They managed to break out in the summer of the same year, capturing Eskişehir and

Afyon and launching an offensive that took them to within striking distance of Ankara. The following year the Turkish offensive that was to throw the Greeks out of Anatolia once and for all began at Dumlupınar, midway between Kütahya and Afyon.

Arrival and information

If you're arriving by bus you'll be dropped off at Kütahya's **otogar** (known as Çinigar, or "Tile Station") on Atatürk Bulvarı, just to the northeast of the centre. Turn right out of the *otogar* and it's a short walk up the main road, Atatürk Bulvarı, to reach Belediye Meydanı, the town's main square, distinguished by a fountain with a huge ceramic vase as its centrepiece. There's a **tourist information** booth (May–Nov Tues–Sun 8am–5.30pm; ☎0274/223 6213) right on the main square.

Accommodation

Pick of the budget hotel options is the *Hotel Yüksel*, Belediye Meyd 1 (☎0274/212 0111, ✉otelyuksel@hotmail.com; ❶), which is plain but clean and about as central as you could hope for. The *Otel Kösk 1*, Lise Cad 1, just north of the square towards the bazaar district (☎0274/216 2024, ✉otelkosk1@hotmail.com; ❶), has spacious doubles, though is not as clean as the *Yüksel* (if arriving from the bus station, ignore signs off the main street to *Kösk 2* – a less than salubrious hotel).

For considerably more you can enjoy the tiled comfort of the *Hotel Gül Palas*, on Belediye Meydanı (☎0274/216 1233, ℻216 2135; ❹), or the *Hotel Erbaylar*, Afyon Cad 14 (☎0274/223 6960, ✉erbaylar@superonline.com; ❹); the latter, although faded, has a pleasant terrace-bar and restaurant, just off the main square.

The Town

A number of well-preserved Ottoman-era houses in the immediate vicinity of the main square, **Belediye Meydanı**, set the tone for Kütahya. The rest of the city's attractions, however, lie at the end of Cumhuriyet Bulvarı, which runs west from Belediye Meydanı. After about 500m, at the point where the road splits off in several directions, you'll find the **Ulu Cami**, an attractive but unexceptional fifteenth-century mosque that stands in the midst of Kütahya's lively **bazaar** area, which extends over several streets in the vicinity.

Just next to the Ulu Cami is the town **museum** (Tues–Sun 8.30am–noon & 1–5.30pm; 3TL), with a collection of archeological finds from the area, including a beautiful sarcophogus found at Aezani depicting a heroic battle between the Greeks and Amazons. The contents of the museum are considerably less interesting than the building that houses them, the **Vacidiye Medresesi**, a fourteenth-century *medrese* built by the Germiyanid emir Bey Bin Savcı as an astronomical observatory and school of science and mathematics. The high point of the interior is the central marble pool beneath a dome with glass skylights.

Beyond the Ulu Cami and museum, signs point out the way to the **Kossuth Evi** (Tues–Sun 8.30am–noon & 1.30–5.30pm; 3TL), a few minutes' walk to the west. This was home to Lajos Kossuth (1802–1894), the Hungarian patriot who fled to Turkey after the failure of the 1848 uprising against Habsburg rule. The immaculate house has been preserved much as it must have been when he lived there in 1850–51, although it's the nineteenth-century Ottoman ambience of the rooms, rather than the Kossuth connection, which will be of interest to most visitors.

Kütahya's **kale** towers above the Kossuth house and signposts point you in the right direction should you wish to wander up to the summit, from where there are predictably impressive views of the city below. The fortress was originally built by the Byzantines and extended by their successors, but these days only the western walls survive in anything like their original state.

⑧ Eating and drinking

Kütahya's culinary scene is underwhelming, but you'll find great grilled meat and super-friendly service at the attractive *Mülayimoğulları* on Atatürk Bul 11 (mains from 4TL). Across the road at no. 12 is the popular *Karavan Gözleme*, which serves a variety of simple staples, as well as more modern additions such as chocolate *gözleme*; you can also try a cappuccino *nargileh* in which the smoke is drawn through milk, rather than water. There's a sister branch – *Karavan Döner* – up by the fortress, focusing on grilled meats; prices are a little higher but still reasonable considering the views. Back on Atatürk Bulvarı there's *Gül*, a stylish café serving shakes, waffles, ice cream and the like; and a few good drinking options, of which the best is probably *Voodoo*, just downhill from *Karavan Gözleme*.

Aezani

Easily reachable, 60km or so southwest of Kütahya, is the site of Roman **Aezani**, famed for its atmospheric Temple of Zeus, one of Anatolia's best-preserved Roman buildings. To get there, take a Gediz-, Samav- or Emet-bound **bus** from Kütahya *otogar*, and ask to be let out at **Çavdarhisar** (journey time approximately 1hr) – the site lies just 1km north of this tranquil village. Getting a ride back may involve a long wait on the main road, but a dolmuş leaves **Çavdarhisar** for Kütahya at 1pm.

The site

The **Temple of Zeus** (tickets 3TL), built by Hadrian in 125 AD, occupies a commanding position on top of a large, rectangular terrace. To reach it walk up the side road that leads from the main road in Çavdarhisar in the direction of Emet, and cross the Koca Çay over the Roman bridge. On the north and west sides of the main temple building, double rows of columns topped by a pediment survive, but elsewhere the columns have largely collapsed and their broken fragments are scattered on the ground nearby.

At the heart of the temple is the **inner sanctum**, once dominated by a magnificent statue of Zeus. Its walls, made of rectangular stone blocks, are largely intact, but the roof has long since caved in. Beneath there's a subterranean **sanctuary** dedicated to Cybele, which the affable site attendant will open up on request. Back outside just northeast of the building, a fallen but well-preserved bust of Cybele – not, as locals will tell you, Medusa – surveys the landscape.

From the temple, you can walk north past the baths to the remains of the uniquely combined **stadium–theatre**. Paths lead up from the fine inscriptions of the southern gate between ruined stadium seats to the backdrop wall of the theatre and the fallen remains of its marble facade. East of the temple stand the arches of the ruined **agora**, and from here the old ceremonial road leads south over a second Roman bridge to the enigmatic **macellum** (marketplace), whose walls carry a fourth-century decree from Emperor Diocletian fixing market prices in an attempt to stop rampant inflation. Complete your circular tour by heading back to the first Roman bridge and ask the site guardian to open up the nearby second set of **baths**, with their satyr mosaic and statue of Hygeia, goddess of the baths.

Eskişehir and around

The modern university city of **ESKİŞEHİR** is handily positioned on the new high-speed train line from Ankara, and therefore makes a potential stopover on the way from İstanbul, especially to those seeking to purchase trinkets made from **meerschaum** (see box below), or on their way to the charming village of **Seyitgazi**.

Eskişehir's energetic mayor, Yılmaz Büyükerşen, recently implemented pleasing reforms such as pedestrianization of swathes of the centre, gentrification of the canal area, implementation of a flashy new tram system and restoration of an appealing district of **Ottoman houses**. Said buildings, located just west of the centre in a district named Eski Eskişehir, should be your focus if you choose to visit the city – imagine a miniature, pastel-painted version of Amasya or Safranbolu. Adjoining this area is the **Kurşunlu Külliye**, a recently renovated complex featuring a mosque and a meerschaum museum.

Practicalities

Eskişehir's **train station** is on the northwestern edge of the city centre (it's an easy walk into town along the nearby canal), while the colossal **otogar**, 3km east of town, is linked to the centre by a brand-new tramline (tickets bought from the booth next to the stop). **Hotels** tend to be expensive, catering mostly to business travellers; the best option by far is the *Sale Oteli*, by the tram stop at İnönü Cad 9 (℡0222/220 7320; ❸), or you could try the *Termal Otel Sultan* at Hamamyolu Cad 1 (℡0222/231 8371; ❷), which features thermal baths, as well as rooms nicer than the lobby might suggest. You might also care to sample **nuga helvası**, the nougat-like local delicacy available at every self-respecting *pastane* in town. Sadly only one reliable **restaurant** has opened in the Ottoman district, but it's a gem: imagine eating Turkish home-cooking at a quirky artist's place, and that's what you'll get at *Kolektif*, Fırın Sok 7.

Seyitgazi

Little **SEYİTGAZİ** sits in a fertile valley set incongruously amid the rolling Anatolian steppe. Despite the beautiful location and historical draws, visitors are rare and your arrival may take the tractor-driving farmers by surprise. It's some 45km south of Eskişehir, from which it's accessible by direct bus, or on some of those heading for Afyon.

Seyitgazi takes its name from Şehit Battal Gazi, the commander of one of the Arab armies that forayed into Anatolia during the eighth century, around whom an unlikely legend has grown up. The story has it that he was killed during the siege of Afyon and buried with a Byzantine princess who had pined away through love for him. The site of their resting place was revealed to the mother of the

---

Meerschaum

Literally "sea foam" in German, **meerschaum** is a porous white stone, large deposits of which are mined in the surrounding villages. While wet, the soft stone is carved into all manner of ornaments, but it's the smoke-cooling properties of a meerschaum pipe that make it the most highly prized item. The mineral is worked in a number of shops around Eskişehir and with a little haggling it should be possible to pick up some bargains. The largest concentration of pipe shops is located under the Büyük Otel on İnönü Caddesi.

Selçuk sultan Alâeddin Keykubad, who promptly built a *türbe* (tomb) for the *gazi*. It became a popular place of pilgrimage and during the thirteenth century Hacı Bektaş Veli, founder of the Bektaşi dervish order, established a *tekke*, or monastery, here.

The **türbe-tekke complex** (tickets 3TL), on the slopes of the valley above the town, seems nothing more than an agglomeration of sandy walls topped by grey-white domes when seen from the distance. The ground plan is roughly horseshoe-shaped, open towards the valley slope with a Byzantine church and a Selçuk mosque by the entrance. The former is a reminder that a Christian convent originally stood on the site, while the latter contains the outsize sarcophagus of Şehit Battal, which measures just under seven metres in length. Next to it is the more modest sarcophagus of his princess.

Midas Şehri

Stretching between Seyitgazi and Afyon is a wonderful valley full of eerie rock formations, and dotted with Phrygian tombs, temples and fortifications. **Midas Şehri** is by far the most accessible and substantial Phrygian sight; its name means "City of Midas" in Turkish, but though there's no specific Midas connection, for a while it was supposed that one of the Phrygian kings of that name was buried here.

The **site** itself (tickets 3TL) comprises the sketchy ruins of a Phrygian city set on top of a thirty-metre-high plateau whose steep rock sides have been carved with elaborate decorative facades. The one on the northwestern face of the plateau has come to be known as the **Midas tomb**; following around to the west from here leads to more niches carved in the rock, a number of rock tombs and an incomplete relief.

Access to the upper part of the plateau and the remains of the Phrygian **citadel** is via a flight of steps on the eastern side. Near the top of the steps are a number of altars and tombs, some of which bear inscriptions and decorative reliefs. In the southwestern part of the citadel is a **rock throne**, a kind of stepped altar on which the figure of a deity would have been placed. The upper part of this throne has a clear **inscription** and crude decorative scratchings. Elsewhere a few fragments of the citadel's defensive wall survive.

Gordion

After the collapse of the Hittite Empire the Phrygians briefly dominated Anatolia, and their capital, **Gordion**, is one of western Anatolia's most important archeological sites. It's a name of much resonance, associated not only with the eponymous knot, but also with King Midas and his golden touch (see box opposite). The first things you'll see as you approach are the immense royal tumuli scattered across the drab, steppe-like landscape. Inside these, archeologists found a wealth of stunning artefacts indicating the sophisticated nature of Phrygian culture. Nearby, the foundations of the Gordion acropolis have been uncovered.

There are **buses** every half-hour from Ankara's *otogar* to the town of **Polatlı**, 18km southwest of Gordion. From Polatlı *otogar*, take a *servis* minibus into town and seek out one of the dolmuşes (every couple of hours depending on demand) to the village of **Yassıhüyük**, just short of the site itself. A taxi to and from the site from Polatlı will cost around 45TL.

The myths and legends of Gordion

The name **Midas** is inextricably associated with Gordion. A number of Phrygian kings bore this name, and over the centuries a kind of composite mythical figure has emerged around whom a number of legends have grown up. The best known of these is that of Midas and the golden touch. According to the story Midas captured the water demon, Silenus, after making him drunk by pouring wine into his spring. In ransom for Silenus, Midas demanded of Dionysos the ability to turn all he touched into gold. Dionysos granted this wish but Midas was dismayed to find he had been taken quite literally, and his food and even his own daughter were transformed. He begged Dionysos for release from the curse and was ordered to wash his hands in the River Pactolus. The cure worked and thereafter the river ran with gold.

Another tale tells of how Midas was called upon to judge a musical contest between Apollo and the satyr Marsyas. Midas decided in favour of Marsyas and in revenge Apollo caused him to grow the ears of an ass. (Marsyas came off even worse – the god skinned him alive.) To hide his new appendages, Midas wore a special hat, revealing them only to his barber who was sworn to secrecy on pain of death. Desperate to tell someone the king's secret, the barber passed it on to the reeds of the river who ever after whispered, "Midas has ass's ears."

Another story may have some basis in reality. It tells how, during the reign of Gordius, an oracle foretold that a poor man who would enter Gordion by ox-cart would, one day, rule over the Phrygians. As the king and nobles were discussing this prediction, a farmer named Midas arrived at the city in his cart. Gordius, who had no heirs, saw this as the fulfilment of the prophecy and named Midas his successor. Subsequently, Midas had his cart placed in the temple of Cybele on the Gordion acropolis, where it was to stand for half a millennium. Somehow the belief arose that whoever untied the knot that fixed the cart to its yoke would become master of Asia. During his stay in the city Alexander the Great took it upon himself to undo the **Gordian Knot**, severing it with his sword; today the phrase "cutting the Gordian knot" is used to describe solving any intractable problem in one swift move.

Some history

The original settlement at Gordion dates back to the Bronze Age and the site was certainly occupied during the Hittite period. The Phrygians probably took up residence during the middle of the ninth century BC and a hundred years later the settlement became capital of the empire founded by the Phrygian king **Gordius**. The history of Gordion under the Phrygians mirrors the history of the Phrygian Empire itself – a brief flowering followed by destruction and protracted decline.

There's little left in the records, save for the myths and legends associated with the empire (see box above), though some concrete information survives about the final king of the Phrygian Empire, Mitas (Midas) of Mushki, who is thought to have reigned from 725 BC to 696 BC.

Ironically it was another set of invaders, the **Cimmerians**, who laid waste to the Phrygian Empire, destroying Gordion, and though the Phrygians made a comeback and rebuilt their capital, their power had been irreversibly reduced. The city was occupied in 650 BC by the **Lydians**, fell in turn to the **Persians** just over a century later, and in 333 BC welcomed **Alexander the Great** for wintertime during his great march east. The arrival of the **Galatians** (Gauls) in Asia Minor in 278 BC was the final chapter in the long decline of Gordion, precipitating the flight of the city's population.

The acropolis

From the dolmuş drop-off point in Yassıhüyük village it makes sense to head first for the eighth-century BC **acropolis**. This raised area was the heart of the city, location of the royal palace, temples and administrative buildings, the foundations of which have been revealed by excavations. Substantial remains of the huge Phrygian-era **town gate** survive on the southeastern side of the acropolis. This must have been a formidable structure in its day: even in its present truncated state it's over ten metres high, making it one of the largest surviving pre-Classical buildings in Anatolia. The outer portal was flanked by twin towers, from which defenders would have been able to inflict heavy casualties on attackers in front of the gate.

The **palace** at the heart of the acropolis consisted of four megara, or large halls with vestibules. The second of these is the most impressive, with the remains of red, white and blue mosaics forming geometrical patterns still visible on the floor. When it was excavated, charred fragments of wooden furniture inlaid with ivory were found in the rubble, suggesting that this could have been the central hall of the palace. The fourth megaron was probably a temple to Cybele, the Phrygian incarnation of the mother goddess. If this is the case, then it's here that Alexander the Great **cut the Gordian Knot** (see box above). Behind the palace are the foundations of eight more large megara, thought to have been the quarters of palace servants.

The royal tombs and museum

The main concentration of the huge and inscrutable tumulus tombs of the Phrygian kings is at the eastern end of Yassıhüyük, but only the **Midas Tümülüsü** (Royal Tomb) near the museum (Tues–Sun 8am–noon & 1.30–5pm; combined ticket with museum 3TL) is likely to attract your attention. At 300m in diameter and over 50m high (reduced by erosion from its original height of around 80m), the Royal Tomb dominates the vicinity, and is thought to be the burial chamber of a Phrygian king, his identity unknown, curiously buried without weapons or ornaments. The tumulus was excavated during the early 1950s, when American archeologists bored a sixty-metre excavation tunnel through to its centre and discovered the intact wooden chamber. Inside they found the skeleton of a man in his 60s on a wooden couch surrounded by grave objects. Among these were three exquisitely crafted wooden tables, inlaid wooden screens, large numbers of bronze clasps for garments and 178 bronze vessels of various sizes, including three large cauldrons.

Across the road, the worthwhile **museum** (hours and price as above) contains some of the items recovered from the tombs and some attractive mosaics, though inevitably the best of the finds are in Ankara's Museum of Anatolian Civilizations.

Safranbolu

Whitewashed, half-timbered houses are one of the most distinctive and enduring legacies of Ottoman rule, but little **SAFRANBOLU** has by far the greatest concentration – essentially an entire village where architectural time seems to be standing still. Many Turkish towns feature a smattering of these **Ottoman buildings**, and sizable clutches can be found as far afield as Albania and Bosnia, but the constant stream of domestic tourists – and a growing number of foreign

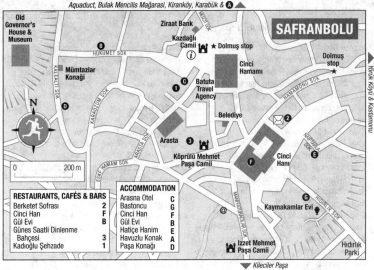

Map labels:

Aquaduct, Bulak Mencilis Mağarasi, Kiranköy, Karabük & **A**

SAFRANBOLU

Old Governor's House & Museum

Ziraat Bank

Kazdağlı Camii ★ Dolmuş stop (i)

Dolmuş stop ★

Cinci Hamamı

Mümtazlar Konağı

Batuta Travel Agency

Yörük Köyü & Kastamonu

Belediye

N

Arasta

Köprülü Mehmet Paşa Camii

Cinci Hanı

0   200 m

Kaymakamlar Evi

Izzet Mehmet Paşa Camii

Hıdırlık Parkı

Kileciler Paşa

RESTAURANTS, CAFÉS & BARS	
Berketet Sofrası	2
Cinci Han	F
Gül Evi	B
Güneş Saatli Dinlenme Bahçesi	3
Kadıoğlu Şehzade	1

ACCOMMODATION	
Arasna Otel	C
Bastoncu	G
Cinci Han	F
Gül Evi	B
Hatiçe Hanim	E
Havuzlu Konak	A
Paşa Konağı	D

adventurers – is proof of just how unique this place is. Despite the town's popularity, the old way of life stays remarkably intact, and apart from a bazaar of souvenir shops, few concessions have been made to the twenty-first century: various restoration projects are underway, but most of the town remains slightly run-down and it is all the better for it.

Safranbolu is also famed for the growing of **saffron**, but despite taking its name from the precious herb, production fell to almost nothing before a recent revival. It's now quite possible to buy some to take home, or sample its taste in locally made sweets.

Arrival and information

Some travellers are initially disappointed with Safranbolu, before realizing that they're not yet in the right place: **Eski Safranbolu**, the old town area downhill and totally disconnected from its newer brother, is the place to head for. The confusion arises from the different arrival routes: your **bus** may stop at Karabük, though most companies now continue the quarter-hour further to Kıranköy, near Safranbolu's new town. From here you can take a dolmuş, one of the half-hourly buses (both 1TL) or a taxi (10TL) to Eski Safranbolu, or even plod the delightful forty-minute walk down into the valley.

The helpful **tourist office** (daily 9am–5.30pm, summer to 7pm; ☏0370/712 3863) is next to the Kazdağlı Camii in the main square. It hands out brochures and maps, and can provide you with bus times, although tickets must be bought at the *otogar*. At the rear of the Cinci Hamamı you'll find Batuta (☏0370/725 4533), a **travel agency** which arranges golf-buggy **tours** of Safranbolu (8.5–22.5TL per person, depending on the length of tour), with taped information delivered in squawky and rather annoying English. They also conduct half-day tours of sights around Safranbolu.

Accommodation

Safranbolu's old **Ottoman houses** make for some of the most atmospheric accommodation in the whole country. While prices may be a little higher than you may be used to (and bathroom sizes necessarily smaller), they're still quite affordable, and there are suitable options for all budgets.

Arasna Otel Arasta Sok ☎0370/712 4170, ☏712 4811. Creaky floorboards, dim corridors and pleasingly wonky rooms – this is the place to go for a little old-time atmosphere, though it occasionally suffers from noise from the downstairs bar. 10TL discount if you forego breakfast. ❷

Bastoncu Kaymakamlar Müzesi Yanı 4 ☎0370/712 3411, ⊛www.bastoncupension .com. Guesthouse with affable, English-speaking owners and dormitory accommodation (20TL). Those unlucky enough to miss out on a berth in this refurbished Ottoman-era house will be taken to an overflow building down the road. Doubles ❷

Cinci Han ☎0370/712 0680, ⊛www.cincihan .com. Pricey hotel housed in a seventeenth-century *kervansaray* in the heart of the town. Rooms are arranged around an open courtyard; one senses that they could try harder with the standard doubles, though the top-floor suites (from 400TL) are nothing short of fantastic. ❺

🏃 **Gül Evi** Hükümet Sok 46 ☎0370/725 4645, ⊛www.canbulat.com.tr. This boutique hotel, refurbished by an amiable local architect, is now

the best place to stay in town. Rooms are traditionally styled but feature modern tweaks such as large bathrooms – a rarity in Safranbolu's space-conscious old buildings – and comfy beds. Be sure to pay a visit to the bar (see p.524). ❸

Hatiçe Hanim Naiptarla Sok 4, ☎0370/712 7545. Large, authentic Ottoman house with rooms named after their traditional functions. Comes complete with creaking floorboards and closet bathrooms. 95TL

Havuzlu Konak Çelik Gülersoy 18 ☎0370/725 2883, ⊛www.safranbolukonak.com. One of Safranbolu's most appealing options, set in a splendid 1820s building just outside the centre of the Old Town. The four corner-rooms are best, but all are immaculate and well laid out with brass fittings and thin rugs. The eponymous indoor pool (*havuz*) provides a superb setting for breakfast or coffee. 140TL

Paşa Konağı Kalealtı Sok ☎0370/725 3572. Charming old house on a quiet backstreet, with nice views of the town, and authentic touches such as bathrooms hidden in cupboards. Ignore the ridiculous rack rates – you'll usually be able to score a double for 120TL. ❼

The Town

Ottoman buildings line the slopes of the ravine on the descent into the old town, presenting a smudge of dirty pastel-coloured timber and red-tiled roofs. It's quite possible to see everything by foot, though it's also possible to get a guided tour (see "Arrival" p.521).

Three mansions have been restored for visitors to peek at (all daily 9am–6pm; 2–2.5TL). Built in 1727, the **Kaymakamlar Evi**, or "Lieutenant Colonel's House", is most popular, and serves as a fine example of the time; the ground floor, devoid of external windows, would have been used as a stable, while on the upper floors the *selâmlık*, overlooking the street, would have been divided from harem quarters, with a separate entrance and lattice windows looking onto interior courtyards. Each room has a distinctively carved wooden ceiling and furniture would have been sparse, with personal items stored in decorative wall-niches, and bedding in cupboards doubling as bathrooms. On the other side of town, **Mümtazlar Konağı** needs a little more love; its exhibits seem like modern-day castoffs, and dusty rugs make it look like a house under construction. Coffee-coloured **Kileciler Paşa Evi** is more worthy of a visit, and you'll receive an information sheet detailing the various facilities therein.

Cinci Hamamı and the mosques

Adjoining the town square, the seventeenth-century Ottoman baths of the **Cinci Hamam**ı (separate men's and women's sections; daily 6am–10pm; 20TL) have been fully restored so that you can relax in comfort surrounded by their marble splendour. Past the hamam, old streets lead towards the restored **Cinci Han**, a huge seventeenth-century *kervansaray*, now a hotel-cum-restaurant (see p.524) dominating the town centre.

▲ Safranbolu cityscape

Roughly northwest of the *Cinci Han* is the unexceptional seventeenth-century **Köprülü Mehmet Paşa Camii**, whose courtyard leads to its restored **arasta** (bazaar). This is where the day-trippers are brought to browse at the well-stocked souvenir and antique shops. The bazaar is completely covered by a magnificent vine with bunches of grapes hanging so close above your head you will be tempted to pick them – there are notices telling you not to. South of the *arasta* lies the old bazaar district, where traditional stalls of blacksmiths, cobblers, leatherworkers, tanners and saddlemakers still work away, much as they would have when they serviced the needs of Black Sea traders, and beyond which lies the **İzzet Mehmet Paşa Camii**, an elaborate, late eighteenth-century mosque. Past here, the town slides into dilapidation, with a ravine now used as a household dump and, further downstream, women washing clothes in the stream. If you walk down here, though, there's a stunning view back towards the mosque, whose domes and minarets seem to hover above the surrounding houses.

Above town

Superb views of Safranbolu can be had from the hilltop **Hıdırlık Parkı** (2.5TL), which looks out over town from the east. The buildings appears at their best in the late afternoon light, a view that can be enjoyed with the free tea or coffee thrown in with the price of your ticket.

The palatial-looking edifice on the opposite side of the ravine is the old Governor's House, which replaced what was once a castle and is now a so-so **museum** (daily 9am–6.30pm; 3TL). There are a few interesting exhibits but next to no

Ottoman houses

So well preserved is Safranbolu's Old Town that almost every building is an Ottoman original. Many of these houses were masterful pieces of design, exhibiting a flair for function and a use of space that prompts some to draw comparisons with Japanese design of the time – think built-in cupboards, carved ceilings and central heating, as well as plumbing systems able to draw cooking, cleansing and waste-disposal processes from a single stream of water.

The larger Ottoman mansions would have three or more levels and over a dozen rooms. The ground floor was often used as stable-space, though thanks to ingenious design the smell would not waft through to the upper floors, which were themselves split into male (*selâmlik*) and female (*haremlik*) quarters. Other features to look out for are interior courtyards, revolving cupboards and conical safe-rooms, as well as one innovation found in many Safranbolu hotels: tiny bathrooms located inside what appears to be a cupboard.

English-language signage, and the general layout is pretty slapdash: the modern-day mannequins, all too apparently lifted straight from some high street clothing store, may give you a laugh.

Eating and drinking

The nicest places to **eat** are all found in the old town, though prices are a little high. *Lokantas* in the new town are far cheaper, but getting there necessitates a taxi ride or long walk. Safranbolu is famed for its *lokum* and *helva* **sweets**, some of which contain the saffron that gave the town its name. You can purchase them – or just munch free samples if you're feeling cheeky – in the ubiquitous *pastanes*. Such is the nature of Safranbolu that it's arguably best to buy **drink** from a shop and hunt down a quiet ledge with a view over town.

Berketet Sofrası Pazar Yerı. One of the cheapest places to eat in town, with kebab meals going for around 5TL, breakfasts for about the same, and soups for 2TL.

Cinci Han Located inside an upmarket hotel (see p.522), this restaurant is the doyen of the tour-bus crowds, and deservedly so given the high-quality food and reasonable prices – simple mains cost from 6–15TL.

Gül Evi Hükümet Sok 46. The old safe-room at this hotel (see p.522) has been hauled into the modern day with the addition of a miniature bar. A few primary-colour spotlights poke up out of the

darkness – highly atmospheric, and nightmarish in the best possible way.

Güneş Saatli Dinlenme Bahçesi Köprülü Mehmet Paşa Camii. Just adjacent to the Köprülü Mehmet Paşa mosque you'll find this pleasant outdoor courtyard, an ideal place to relax over tea (1TL) or a *nargileh* (7.5TL).

Kadıoğlu Şehzade Sofrası Arasta Sok 8. In a secluded niche just off the main square, featuring fairly priced local staples such as grilled meats (7–13TL) and *pide* (from 6TL). Service can be grumpy, but it's usually efficient.

Around Safranbolu

Another reason to stay for more than a night in Safranbolu is the small, but appealing, clutch of sights in its vicinity. Public transport is non-existent so most get around in the company of a **tour**. Batuta travel agency (see "Arrival", p.521) arranges half-day tours of the following sights from 40TL per person, but if a large enough group can be found, you'll pay less for the same thing with *Bastoncu* guesthouse (p.522) – it's 140TL for a minivan seating seven.

Try to imagine a smaller, more remote version of Safranbolu, minus the tourists and polished Ottoman renovations, and you're already halfway to the the tiny village of **Yörük Köyü**, around 16km to the east of its more illustrious brother. Its one concession to the tourist trade is the **Sipahioğlu Evi**, a restored mansion that feels even more authentic than its counterparts in Safranbolu. Owned by the same family for almost three centuries, it's now split in two by feuding sons. It's a bit of a slog to the *kule* on top, though the views are superb and you'll even find a handy stand on which to pop your fez. Those that feel like staying the night in such isolated splendour should hunt down signs for the *Yörük Evi* (0370/737 2153; 60TL), whose rooms are rustic but comfortable enough.

On their way back to Safranbolu, most tours will loop around to visit the Byzantine-era **aqueduct** in İncekaya, which is also set amidst idyllic pastoral scenery. It's set in a tranquil gorge that's best viewed from the top of the aqueduct itself. On the other side of Safranbolu is the cave network of **Bulak Mencilis Mağarasi**, of which over half a kilometre is open for viewing. As with cave systems across Asia, your guide will compare some of the more distinctive formations to animals or religious figures.

The Hittite sites

The **Hittite sites** centred on the village of **Boğazkale** are the most impressive and significant in the whole of Anatolia, and are appropriately located amidst rolling countryside that has changed little through the centuries. This area was once the heart of the Hittite Empire and **Hattuşa**, spread over several square kilometres to the south of the modern village, was its capital. A few kilometres to the east is the temple site of **Yazılıkaya**, while **Alacahöyük**, a smaller Hittite settlement dating back to 4000 BC, 25km north of Boğazkale, is further off the beaten track, but worth the trip if you have your own transport. Excavation here began in earnest in 1905 and many of the objects unearthed are now housed at the Museum of Anatolian Civilizations in the capital. If you've already seen the museum, a visit to the original excavations is doubly interesting; if not, a quick visit to the new archeological museum in nearby Çorum is definitely worthwhile.

Note that despite the undoubted tourist appeal of the Hittite sites, **public transport** to Boğazkale is far from straightforward and can be incredibly frustrating – if you don't have your own wheels, be sure to read the advice below. Most visit on their way between Ankara and Amasya.

Arrival and getting around

Boğazkale is the best accommodation hub for the Hittite sights, but to head there by public transport you'll first have to get to the small town of **Sungurlu**, lying just off the main Ankara–Samsun road 24km north. After being dropped off at the *otogar*, your search for the lesser-spotted **Boğazkale-bound dolmuş** (30min; 5TL) can begin in earnest; some are lucky enough to find one waiting at the *otogar*, but you're likely to have to head a kilometre or so into Sungurlu where it will leave from a spot alongside the park – taxis will take you there from the *otogar* for 3–5TL – but times are frustratingly irregular, and on weekends there may even be none at all. Most depart in the morning, so the best advice is to get to Sungurlu as early as possible. The easiest option is to take a **taxi** all the way to Boğazkale – prices from 30–50TL, depending on your powers of persuasion – and if you get stuck in Sungurlu, there are plenty of cheap hotels to choose from.

Hattuşa and Yazılıkaya can be covered on foot **from Boğazkale** if you're reasonably fit, though on a hot summer's day you may prefer to take a **taxi** to the latter, and you'll certainly need one – or your own transport – to get to **Alacahöyük**. Drivers are available in Boğazkale. If you don't want to spend the night in either Boğazkale or Sungurlu, then it's also possible to get a **taxi from Sungurlu** around all three sites in a few hours, arriving back in time for an onward bus. This will set you back about €50, though you may have to haggle.

The Hittites

The **Hittites** appear to have been an Indo-European people who moved into Anatolia around 2000 BC. Where exactly they came from remains unclear, though the Caucasus and the Balkans have been suggested. They entered the territories of the Hatti, an indigenous people, and though no records survive of how the Hittite rise to dominance came about, archeologists have found layers of burned material in most Hatti settlements indicating that there was at least some degree of violence involved. However, the fact that the Hittites also absorbed important elements of Hatti culture suggests that a more complex interaction may have taken place.

Initially the Hittites set up a number of **city-states**, drawn together during the mid-eighteenth century BC under King Anitta who transferred his capital from the city of Kushara (possibly modern Alişar) to Nesha (Kültepe), and destroyed Hattuşa, cursing any Hittite king who might attempt to rebuild the place. A century or so later his successor Labarna returned to Hattuşa and did just that. The Hittites came to regard Labarna and his wife Tawannanna as founders of the Hittite kingdom and their names were adopted as titles by subsequent monarchs.

In 1595 BC, Mursili I succeeded in capturing distant Babylon, but his successor (and assassin) Hantili lost many previous gains. Stability was restored under Tudhaliyas II around 1430 BC, and he re-established the Hittite state as an empire. An important period of expansion followed under King Suppiluliuma (1380–1315 BC), who secured the northern borders and conquered the Hurrian kingdom of Mitanni. This achievement raised the Hittites to superpower status, equal with Egypt, Assyria and Babylon. The Egyptians even asked Suppiluliuma to send one of his sons to marry the widow of Tutankhamun (the union never took place as the boy was murdered en route). After Suppiluliuma's death, Hittite expansion continued and in 1286 BC, during the reign of Muwatalli II, a Hittite army defeated the Egyptians, commanded by Ramses II, at the Battle of Kadesh. Events from the battle can be seen carved into the columns at Luxor.

Following the conflict, peace between the two empires was established, cemented by the marriage of one of the daughters of Ramses II to Hattuşiliş III. However, the Hittite Empire had less than a century left. The arrival of the Sea Peoples in Anatolia ushered in a period of instability that was to erode Hittite power, culminating in the **destruction of Hattuşa** around 1200 BC, roughly the same time as the fall of Troy. The Phrygians replaced the Hittites as the dominant power in central Anatolia, taking over the ruins of Hattuşa and other Hittite cities.

Hittite civilization was highly advanced with a complex **social system**. The Hittite kings were absolute rulers, but there was an assembly called the *panku*, which at times appears to have wielded considerable influence. The major division in Hittite society was between free citizens and slaves: the former included farmers, artisans and bureaucrats, while the latter, although they could be bought and sold, probably had the right to own property and marry.

Hittite **religion** seems to have been adopted from the Hatti, with the weather god Teshuba and the sun goddess Hebut as the two most important deities. Up to a thousand lesser gods also played a role in the beliefs of the Hittites, who were in the habit of incorporating the gods of conquered peoples into their own pantheon.

Boğazkale

BOĞAZKALE is a modern village, with the ancient Hittite capital of Hattuşa fanning out from its southern rim. Finding your way around is fairly straightforward, as it basically consists of one street, running up a hill to the main square. The only attraction in the village itself is a small **museum** (daily 8am–5pm but ask around if it looks closed; 2TL) on the left-hand side of the street on the way up to the village square, which has a small collection of cuneiform tablets, pottery and other objects from the Hattuşa site.

Accommodation

The listed **hotels** are often block-booked by tour groups, so it's worth making an advance reservation; these are also the only options in the village for **eating and drinking**. If you're here in winter, note that heating and hot water is far from reliable in the village, so come prepared.

Aşıkoğlu Motel At the entrance to the village ☎0364/452 2004, ⓦwww.hattusas.com. Slightly overpriced modern rooms but with immaculate bathrooms and superb buffet breakfast. A cheaper extension has smaller rooms with older bathrooms, and there's a rarely used campsite at the back (it's better to go to the *Başkent*). A regular tour group watering hole, the busy restaurant has tables in an Ottoman salon and excellent food. Closed Nov–Feb. ❸

Başkent Tourist Motel ve Camping Yazılıkaya Yolu Üzeri ☎0364/452 2037, ⓦwww.baskent hattusa.com. The better of the two options perched on a hill on the outskirts, with large sunny rooms, new plumbing in the bathrooms, and a serene campsite for €4 per person per night. The restaurant, although lacking in atmosphere, has a view of the ruins of the Great Temple, and is good value. ❶

Hotel Baykal Next to the PTT on the village square ☎0364/452 2013, ⓦwww.hattusha .com. Also known as the *Hattuşaş Pension*, it offers two types of accommodation: clean and spacious pension rooms, mostly with showers (discounts for those without), and comfortable double/triple rooms in the hotel at the back, with cool granite floors and smart bathrooms. The downstairs restaurant serves up tasty and economical dishes of the day. Breakfast €2 extra. Pension ❶, hotel ❷.

Kale Otel Yazılıkaya Yolu Üzeri ☎0364/452 3126, ⓦwww.bogazkoyhattusa.com. Family-run hotel in a pretty location, with simple whitewashed rooms and adequate bathrooms, but lacking atmosphere. There's no real restaurant – though you may get a meal if the hotel is already catering for a tour group – otherwise walk down the hill to the *Başkent*. Closed Nov–March. ❷

Hattuşa

Enclosed by 6km walls, **Hattuşa** was, by the standards of the time, an immense city, and its scale is still awe-inspiring today. The site was originally occupied by the Hatti, who established a settlement here around 2500 BC. The Hittites moved in after their conquest of central Anatolia, making it their capital from about 1375 BC onwards, during the period when their empire reached its greatest extent.

The Hittite city was unearthed by archeologists during the first half of the nineteenth century. It occupies a steeply sloping expanse dotted with rocky outcrops, to the southwest of modern Boğazkale. Of the numerous buildings once scattered over a wide area, only the limestone foundation blocks survive. The vulnerable upper parts, originally consisting of timber frames supporting clay brick walls, have long since vanished.

Approaching the site from the village square takes you past a freshly reconstructed section of the old city wall (paid for with Japanese money) and leads to a **ticket office** (daily 8am–5pm, to 7pm in summer; 5TL joint ticket for Hattuşa and Yazılıkaya). This office is left unmanned at night, which some find the most atmospheric time to visit Hattuşa – there are no touts or tour buses, and Boğazkale's sleepy constellation provides just about enough light to get around without a torch.

The Büyük Mabet

Beyond the ticket office is the **Büyük Mabet**, or "Great Temple", one of an original seventy on the site. The largest and best-preserved Hittite temple in existence, it was built around the fourteenth or thirteenth century BC and dedicated to the storm god Teshuba and the sun goddess Hebut. It consisted of a central temple building surrounded by 78 storage rooms laid out in an irregular plan.

After running a gauntlet of would-be guides, you pass between two large stone blocks, remnants of the **ceremonial gateway**. Nearby is a stone lion that originally formed part of a cistern and, a little further on, a large, green cubic stone, which was reputedly a wedding present from Ramses II of Egypt. In Hittite times the king and queen, in their roles as high priest and priestess, would have led processions through here on holy days. Today most visitors end up following the route they took,

BOĞAZKALE AND HATTUŞA

Sungurlu

Yazılıkaya

Yozgat

Boğazkale

Ticket Office

Büyük Mabet

Büyük Kale

Nişantepe

Sarıkale

Aslanlıkapı (Lion Gate)

Yenicekale

Kralkapı (King's Gate)

Tunnel

Yerkapı (Sphinx Gate)

0   100 m

Yeşil Stream

MAIN SQUARE

N

ACCOMMODATION
Aşıkoğlu   C
Başkent   A
Baykal   D
Kale   B

Old City Walls
Restored City Walls

along a clearly defined processional way of uneven slabs.

The **temple** consisted of about twelve small chambers around a central courtyard, with the rooms that would have contained the cult statues of Teshuba and Hebut at the northeastern end – the god on the left and the goddess on the right. Just below the Büyük Mabet, archeologists have identified an early Assyrian **merchant quarter**, which held the Hittite equivalent of the Rosetta Stone, a parallel Hittite hieroglyphic and Akkadian inscription instrumental in the final cracking of the hieroglyphic code, and now visible in Ankara's Museum of Anatolian Civilizations.

The Yenicekale and the Aslanlıkapı

About 350m beyond the Great Temple, on the site of the original Hattic city, the road forks. Taking the right-hand branch leads you up a steep hill. After about 800m (this is the worst foot-slogging section), the **Yenicekale**, a ruined fortress, is visible about 50m to the left of the road. Although little remains, its construction was some achievement as Hittite engineers had to create an artificial platform out of the uneven and rocky terrain before they could even start building.

A little higher up is the **Aslanlıkapı** or "Lion Gate", one of the three gateways that studded the southern section of the city wall. It takes its name from the two stone lions that flank the outer entrance, symbolically guarding Hattuşa from attackers and evil spirits. The Aslanlıkapı marks the beginning of the surviving section of dry-stone **city wall**, which runs along the top of a massive sloping embankment ten metres in height and surfaced with irregular limestone slabs.

The Yerkapı

The road follows the embankment to the **Yerkapı**, or "Earth Gate", more popularly known as the Sphinx Gate after the two huge sphinxes that once guarded its inner portal, but which now live in museums in İstanbul and Berlin. The most striking feature of the Sphinx Gate is the seventy-metre **tunnel** that cuts through from the city side of the walls to the exterior. The tunnel was built using the corbel arch technique, a series of flat stones leaning towards each other creating its triangular profile. One theory about its purpose is that it served to let the defenders of the city make surprise attacks on besieging enemies. However, its obvious visibility from the outside and the presence of two sets of monumental steps leading up the embankment on either side of the outer portal cast doubt on this, and a more ceremonial function has been suggested.

The Kralkapı, the Nişantepe and the Sarıkale

Following the road east from the Sphinx Gate leads to the **Kralkapı**, or "King's Gate", named after the regal-looking figure carved in relief on the left-hand pillar of the inner gateway. This actually represents the god Teshuba and shows him sporting a conical hat while raising his left fist in the air as though holding an invisible sword. What you see is a copy – the original is in Ankara's Museum of Anatolian Civilizations.

Further down the hill lies the **Nişantepe**, a rocky outcrop with a ten-line Hittite inscription carved into its eastern face. The thirty-centimetre hieroglyphs are badly weathered but enough has been deciphered to suggest that it's a memorial to Suppiluliuma II, last of the Hittite kings. To the immediate southwest is the Sarıkale, the foundation of a Phrygian fort built on the site of an earlier Hittite structure.

The Büyük Kale

From the Nişantepe the road leads down to the **Büyük Kale**, or "Great Fortress", which served the Hittite monarchs as a fortified palace during the fourteenth and thirteenth centuries BC. The palace consisted of three courtyards, each higher than the previous one, meaning that any attacker would have had to capture it piecemeal. The lower and middle courtyards are thought to have been given over to servants and aides of the royal family, while the upper courtyard was the palace proper. It's easy to see why they chose to reside at this wild and windswept location on the very eastern edge of Hattuşa. In effect, it was a citadel within the city, protected on all flanks by steep drops.

On the site of a building near the southeastern entrance archeologists found three thousand **cuneiform tablets**, which, when deciphered, yielded important clues about the nature of Hittite society. Among them was the Treaty of Kadesh, signed in around 1270 BC by the Hittite king Hattuşiliş II and Ramses II of Egypt, the earliest surviving written treaty between two nations. The lower parts of walls and some masonry fragments are all that survive of the Büyük Kale, but it's worth coming up here to wander among the weather-battered remnants and take in the stunning view of the Great Temple.

Yazılıkaya

From the Hattuşa ticket office, signs point to the temple site of **Yazılıkaya** with its famous reliefs, about 3km (under an hour's walk) to the east. The route there more or less follows the Hittite processional course from city to temple, and is well signed.

Archeological evidence suggests that a temple of some sort existed on the site as early as 1500 BC, but it wasn't until the thirteenth century BC that the two small ravines cutting into a rocky outcrop at the rear of the site were decorated with reliefs (hence Yazılıkaya, Turkish for "inscribed rock"). At roughly the same time a **gateway** and the **temple buildings** were constructed. Today, a few sketchy foundations are all that remain of these ancient structures and attention is focused on the two "galleries" of reliefs depicting nearly a hundred figures, mostly gods from the vast array of Hittite deities.

The reliefs

The entrance to the **larger ravine** of the two is on the left behind the temple foundations. The left-hand wall is lined with images of gods moving from left to right, and the right-hand one with images of goddesses wearing identical long, pleated dresses and conical headgear. A number of the figures on the male side of the ravine stand out, in particular the group of twelve war gods bringing up the rear of the procession. Further along are two figures with human bodies and bulls' heads. The deities seem to rise in rank as the procession progresses, and towards the front are the conspicuous figures of the moon god Kusuh, with a crescent moon, and the sun god, seemingly balancing a winged sun symbol on his head. The two lines of deities meet on the far wall of the ravine. The scene carved here depicts Teshuba astride a couple of mountain peaks facing Hebut, who is standing on a panther.

The **smaller ravine** lies over to the right and can be reached via the short flight of steps that leads up to a cleft in the rock. The entrance to the ravine is guarded by two sphinx reliefs, which can be hard to spot, while a group of twelve figures armed with swords lines the left-hand wall. These are similar to the warrior-god figures seen in the first ravine but are much better preserved. Opposite this group are two separate reliefs. One shows an unusual figure that has come to be known as the "Sword God", a blade with a human torso and head where the handle should be. To add to the already strange effect, lions' heads, instead of arms, sprout from the torso shoulders. This vaguely disturbing image is thought to represent Neargal, the Hittite god of the underworld.

Alacahöyük

After Hattuşa, **Alacahöyük** 25km north of Boğazkale, is the most important Hittite site in existence. Originally a major Hattic settlement, it was taken over by the Hittites during the early stages of the second millennium BC and, as at Hattuşa, the Phrygians seem to have taken over the site for a while after the demise of the Hittites. The ruins that remain are mainly Hittite, but a number of extensive archeological digs have unearthed a vast array of Hattic artefacts, including standards featuring stags, bulls, sun-discs and statues of the earth goddess, from a number of tombs on the site.

From Boğazkale head back in the direction of Sungurlu and turn right at the road signposted for Alacahöyük. After about 11km take a signposted left turn for the remaining 12km to the site. By public transport, you should be able to pick up a **dolmuş** from Boğazkale or Sungurlu to the village of Alaca, about 10km southeast of the site, but from there you'll have to hitch. The only other alternative is to take a **taxi from Boğazkale or Sungurlu**, which will set you back at least 50TL.

The site

Next to the **site** (daily 8am–noon & 1.30–5.30pm; 3TL) is a small **museum** (same hours, but closed Mon), which, for once, is well worth investigating, as it includes some striking Hattic standards and pottery with elegant designs.

The site is entered via the southern **Sphinx Gate**, named after the large sphinxes that guard it. These eerily impressive figures, stained ochre by lichen, have blunted faces with empty eye sockets, and sweeping headdresses. Either side of the gate are **reliefs** (copies of originals now in Ankara), depicting religious ceremonies. The left-hand section is the more lively of the two, showing a procession moving towards the god Teshuba – shown here as a slightly comical-looking bull with outsized sex organs. Approaching him are a king and queen, followed by sacrificial animals and priests, with a group of what look like acrobats bringing up the rear.

The Sphinx Gate opens onto a pathway with excavated areas on either side, all well signposted in English. Immediately behind the gate are vast irregular blocks, the remnants of the city walls, followed by the foundations of storage buildings. Beyond the storage areas, a few metres below ground level to the left of the path, are thirteen **tombs**. These date from the Hattic period and yielded much of the vast hoard of archeological treasure now in the Bronze Age section of the Museum of Anatolian Civilizations in Ankara. Judging by the opulence of the grave goods found in them, these were the tombs of Hatti monarchs.

Amasya

Blessed with a super-abundant historical legacy, and occupying a river valley so narrow that it's almost a gorge, **AMASYA** is one of the high points of the region. Most people come here to see the **rock tombs** hewn into the cliffs above the town by the kings of Pontus over two thousand years ago, but Amasya also harbours some truly beautiful Selçuk and Ottoman architecture, and a multitude of colourful, restored nineteenth-century **wooden houses**. A great number of these have been superbly restored with funding from the Ministry of Culture, many reopening as authentic and atmospheric antique shops, *pansiyons* and restaurants, in keeping with the general Ottoman theme.

Some history

Amasya was once part of **Pontus**, one of several small kingdoms to spring up following the death of Alexander the Great; indeed, the cliffside tombs of the Pontic kings remain the number one attraction for visitors today. Pontus survived for two hundred years before being absorbed into the Roman sphere of influence around 70 BC; its downfall began when Mithridates VI Eupator reputedly ordered the massacre of eighty thousand Romans in one day and plunged his kingdom into a series of wars, which culminated in its being absorbed by Pompey into the Roman sphere of influence around 70 BC.

Under the Romans, and through the succeeding centuries of Byzantine rule, the town prospered, and it continued to do so after falling to the **Selçuks** in 1071. In the late thirteenth century, the **Ottomans** emerged as a force to be reckoned with in Anatolia, and Amasya soon became part of their burgeoning state. It became a training ground for crown princes, who would serve as governors of the province to prepare them for the rigours of statesmanship at the Sublime Porte. Amasya then became a vital staging post en route to the creation of modern Turkey: it was here that, on June 21, 1919, Atatürk delivered a speech that was in effect a call to arms for the coming **War of Independence**.

Arrival and information

Amasya's **otogar** lies to the east of the town proper and you'll need to take a dolmuş into the centre (though buses passing through the centre on their way to the *otogar* can drop you off). When leaving town you can buy your ticket from the

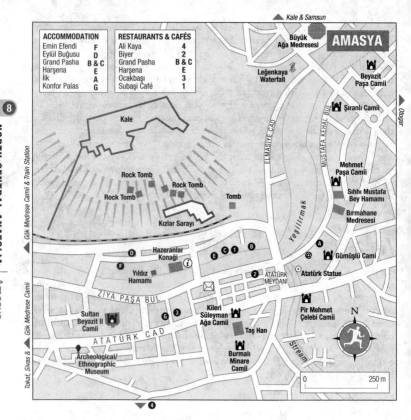

▲ Kale & Samsun

AMASYA

ACCOMMODATION		RESTAURANTS & CAFÉS	
Emin Efendi	F	Ali Kaya	4
Eylül Buğusu	D	Biyer	2
Grand Pasha	B & C	Grand Pasha	B & C
Harşena	E	Harşena	E
İlk	A	Ocakbaşı	3
Konfor Palas	G	Subaşı Café	1

Büyük Ağa Medresesi

Leğenkaya Waterfall

Beyazit Paşa Camii

Şiranlı Camii

Kale

Mehmet Paşa Camii

Sıhhı Mustafa Bey Hamamı

Rock Tomb

Rock Tomb

Rock Tomb

Tomb

Bırmahane Medresesi

Kızlar Sarayı

Hazeranlar Konağı

Gümüşlü Cami

Yıldız Hamamı

ATATÜRK MEYDANI

Atatürk Statue

ZIYA PAŞA BUL

Sultan Beyazit II Camii

Kileri Süleyman Ağa Camii

Pir Mehmet Çelebi Camii

N

ATATÜRK CAD

Taş Han

Archeological/ Ethnographic Museum

Burmalı Minare Camii

Stream

0   250 m

◀ Tokat, Sivas & Gök Medrese Camii   ◀ Gök Medrese Camii & Train Station   Otogar ▶

Yeşilırmak

ELMASİYE CAD

MUSTAFA KEHAL BUL

▼ 4

bus offices on Atatürk Caddesi, which might well provide transport to the *otogar*. The **train station** (services from Samsun and Sivas) is about 1km to the west, also connected to the centre by regular dolmuşes.

There's a new **tourist information office** inside the uninteresting Ottoman **Selçuk** museum (9am–5pm, closed Mon; ☏0358/212 4059), but don't expect any more than a cheery "You want map?".

Accommodation

Amasya's most appealing accommodation options are the clutch of antique-decorated, kilim-strewn *pansiyon*s in restored Ottoman houses. Rates are reasonable so it's well worth splashing out, particularly given that the city's budget options are less than salubrious.

Emin Efendi Pansiyon Hazeranlar Sok 73 ☏0358/212 0852, ☏212 2552. Friendly *pansiyon* with a few simple rooms, some overlooking the river, and with bathrooms in cupboards in the corridor. There's also an attractive vine-shaded courtyard where, if you're lucky, you may be treated to a little evening music. ❸

Eylül Buğusu Figani Sok 1 ☏0385/212 1405, ☏www.eylulbugusu.com. Rooms in this restored

Ottoman house are impressively large and well decorated, with many of the bathrooms tucked into what initially appear to be cupboards; unfortunately there are no river views. Try to score one of the two rooms with traditional carved ceilings. ❹

Grand Pasha Across the Alçak footbridge ☏0385/212 4158, ☏www.grandpashaotel.com. Beautiful Ottoman house on the river, arranged around a leafy courtyard. Small, with only eight vast, traditionally decorated rooms with cabinet bathrooms and river views. Rooms in the new building down the road are less appealing, but still perfectly comfortable. ❹

Harşena Otel Across the Alçak footbridge ☎0358/218 3979. Stunning former Ottoman residence with creaky floorboards and rooms furnished with period antiques, lace and linen curtains, and low-slung Ottoman beds. Some overlook the river, where you can breakfast on the balcony, but the best rooms are at the back under the floodlit rock tombs where you can sleep to the sounds of gentle guitar music from the garden below. ❹

İlk Pansiyon Hittit Sok 1 ☎0358/218 1689, ✉ilkpansion@hotmail.com. Faultlessly restored eighteenth-century Armenian mansion, retaining much of the original decor and period antiques. Reservations advisable as there are just six rooms, some of which are priced a category higher. Breakfast is not included in the price – it'll be €3 extra. ❸

Konfor Palas Ziyapşa Bul 2 ☎0358/218 1260, 🌐www.konforpalas.com. The only decent budget option in Amasya. Large, impersonal hotel in a nice location south of the river, and not too noisy despite the bustling square below. All rooms are en suite, with TV but no breakfast, and it may be worth haggling. ❷

The Town

At the centre of Amasya, the riverfront Atatürk Meydanı commemorates Atatürk's 1919 visit with an equestrian statue of the hero surrounded by admirers. At the eastern end of the square, the creamy yellow **Gümüşlü Cami**, or "Silvery Mosque", was originally built in 1326 but has been reconstructed at various intervals since. Its almost pavilion-like oriental exterior and carved wooden porch overlook the river, and there's an unusual tall brick minaret.

There's another architectural oddity on the south side of the square in the shape of the **Pir Mehmet Çelebi Camii**, which dates from 1507. It's an extremely small *mescit*, or mosque without a minaret, the Islamic equivalent of a Christian chapel. The carved facade of this particular example has been decorated with ochre paint, and it's improbably tiny, almost as though it were a play mosque built for children.

West to the Gök Medrese Camii

West of the square, Atatürk Caddesi runs off through the town. Two hundred metres or so along, on the southern side, is the **Kileri Süleyman Ağa Camii**, an imposing but conventionally designed Ottoman mosque, built in 1489. Behind it lies the eighteenth-century **Taş Han**, a crumbling old brick and stone structure that is now home to a metal workshop. To the rear of the Taş Han is the **Burmalı Minare Camii** (Twisted Minaret Mosque), named after the spiral effect of the stonework of its minaret. The compact building was erected in 1242 but heavily restored in the eighteenth century following a fire.

Back on Atatürk Caddesi, a twin-domed **bedesten** in grey stone stands opposite the Kileri Süleyman Ağa Camii, still home to various shops and businesses. Continuing west brings you to the **Sultan Beyazit II Camii**, set in a spacious rose garden on the northern side of the street. Built in 1486, this is Amasya's largest mosque, laid out on a symmetrical plan with two large central domes flanked by four smaller cupolas and two slightly mismatched minarets. Though some of Amasya's other mosques beat it for sheer whimsicality, none of them can quite match it for structural harmony. The front of the mosque faces the river, flanked by two plane trees thought to be as old as the mosque itself, and it's from this side that the whole is best appreciated.

Continue west along Atatürk Caddesi, past the museum (see below), and it's a five-minute walk to the **Gök Medrese Camii**, the thirteenth-century Selçuk "Mosque of the Blue Seminary", with a particularly intricate carved doorway (the actual door is in the museum). This doorway was once covered in blue tiles – hence the name – but time seems to have taken its toll and today there's little trace of them.

The Archeological and Ethnographic museum

Amasya's **Archeological/Ethnographic Museum** (Arkeoloji/Etnografya Müzesi; Tues–Sun 8.30am–noon & 1–5pm; 3TL) is a gem among Turkish municipal museums, well worth an hour or so of your time. Archeological finds dating back as far as the Bronze Age are represented by some practical-looking pottery and a caseful of rather unwieldy tools. Hittite relics include beak-spouted jugs, some with what look like built-in filters, and there's also a bronze statue of the storm god Teshuba – though this tends to get loaned out to other European museums. Centre of attraction, however, is the door of the Selçuk Gök Medrese Camii, on the second floor, a riot of arabesque geometrical patterns enclosing lattice reliefs.

North of Atatürk Meydanı

The **Bırmahane Medresesi** was built by the Mongols in 1308 as a lunatic asylum. The popular image of the Mongols as a brutal, destructive people makes the presence of this abiding monument to their occupation of Amasya something of a surprise. The Mongols used music therapy to pacify the lunatics in the asylum and throughout the centuries the *medrese* has been used as a music school. There's a lovely atmosphere in the courtyard and it's well worth asking if you can step inside – you may be offered tea – to listen to the impromptu practice sessions.

Further on is the **Sıhhı Mustafa Bey Hamamı** (daily: men 7–10am & 5–11pm; women 10am–5pm; 10TL for bath, 10TL extra for massage), very old but very much in use, as the wreaths of vapour emerging from its chimneys testify. Next comes the **Mehmet Paşa Camii**, constructed in 1486 by Mehmet Paşa, who was the tutor of Prince Ahmet, son of Sultan Beyazit. It's a sizable place, with a guesthouse, soup kitchen and *medrese*, and boasts a finely decorated marble pulpit.

A little further along is the **Şıranlı Camii**, built a little over a hundred years ago though it looks far older. According to a sign outside, it was constructed using money that had been raised by Azeri Turks, although it's not at all clear why they should have paid to build a mosque in Amasya. The final mosque of any importance is the early fifteenth-century **Beyazit Paşa Camii**, whose leafy riverbank location enhances the quiet beauty of its architecture.

From here a bridge crosses the Yeşilırmak river to the **Büyük Ağa Medresesi**, a seminary/university founded in 1488 by the chief white eunuch of Beyazit II. This roughly octagonal structure of stone and brick is nowadays a Koran school. Although it's not officially open to the public, no one seems to mind if you take a look inside the courtyard where the boys who study here play football between lessons.

The rock tombs

The massive **rock tombs** (daily 8am–5pm; 3TL) of the Pontic kings are carved into the cliff-face on the northern bank of the Yeşilırmak. There are two main clusters of tombs, and bearing right from the Kızlar Sarayı will bring you to the most accessible group, as well as to a café and toilet. You may want to clamber up inside some of the tombs through the raised stone doorways, but if you find the doorways padlocked you will need to rouse the site guardian to open them. Passages cut out of the rock run behind two of the tombs and you can only marvel at the work that must have been involved in excavating them. Bearing left will bring you to two larger tombs; beside the entrance to one of them is the mouth of a tunnel, thought to lead to the river. More tombs can be found with a bit of effort – there are a total of eighteen throughout the valley.

The Ottoman houses

Amasya's half-timbered **Ottoman houses** contribute so much to the atmosphere of the town; see p.524 for more information about their design. A good starting point for explorations is the nineteenth-century **Hazeranlar Konağı** (Tues–Sun 9am–noon & 1.30–5pm; 2TL), an imposing mansion at the river's edge. The heavily restored interior has been turned into a convincing re-creation of a nineteenth-century family home, liberally decked out with carpets, period furniture and domestic artefacts. It incorporates typical features of the time: wall niches for oil lamps, bathrooms secreted away behind cupboard doors, and *sedir*s or divan seating running along the walls. In the basement of the house, accessed by a separate entrance, there's a small **art gallery** (same hours as above; free). Paintings by local artists are displayed and it's often possible to watch artists at work. Follow the street west from the Hazeranlar Konağı as far as the footbridge leading across to the Sultan Beyazit Camii and it'll take you through the heart of the old house district.

The kale

In the crags high above the rock tombs is Amasya's sprawling citadel, or **kale**, a structure that dates back to Pontic times, though the surviving ruins are of Ottoman vintage. The *kale* is difficult to reach, but well worth the effort for the stupendous views of the town below. The most straightforward way to get there is to follow the Samsun road out of town from near the Büyük Ağa Medresesi until you spot the "Kale" sign hidden in a backstreet to the left. From here a steep dirt road winds its way up to the summit for about 2km. It's quite a climb on foot (reckon on an hour or two), so if you're not up to the trek, consider taking a taxi – 12TL for the journey there and back.

At the top, the outer walls of the *kale* have been rebuilt in bright, modern stone, but beyond you'll find the crumbling remains of the Ottoman-era fortress. Nothing is signposted and there are no clear paths through the ruins, so much of the time you'll find yourself scrambling over rocks and rubble and through undergrowth.

Eating and drinking

With a riverside setting and the rock tombs above lit up at night, dining out in Amasya provides unbeatable ambience. Classical music is a feature here, too, with many of the **cafés** catering to the students from the town's music *medresesi* who meet to practise their instruments. Cheap eats can be found at a number of *lokanta*-style joints around Atatürk Caddesi on the south side of the river, or you can enjoy a traditional meal in one of the Ottoman-house **restaurants** on the north side.

Ali Kaya On the hill on the south side of town; look up and you'll see the sign. Magnificent views, attentive service and tables under shady pine trees, with meals clocking in at around 30TL including drinks. Best of all, they provide a free transport service from your hotel – just ask at reception.

Biyer Ziyapaşa Bul. Great studenty place, entered through a small door at street level, playing rock music, and serving cheap and cheerful Turkish and Western fare. Aim for one of the tables on the small balcony overlooking the river.

Grand Pasha Across the bridge from the main square ☏0358/218 6269. Stylish venue with bare wooden floors, rustic furniture, exquisite antiques and kilims, a pretty walled garden with wishing well, and a riverside balcony. À la carte menu is typically Turkish, and there's an atmospheric basement bar, with tiny wooden tables and cushions set into stone walls, that stays open until 5am if the demand is there.

Harşena Otel Across the Alçak footbridge. The café-bar here is a fine Ottoman restoration overlooking the Roman bridge, offering cold beer on tap, *nargile*s and backgammon boards to while away hours in the kilim-covered booths. More of Amasya's formidable musicians play in the garden every evening.

Ocakbaşı Restaurant Ziya Paşa Bul 5. Popular place with outdoor seating area but surly waiters. Inexpensive and piping hot selection of stews, soups, *pide*s, and more Westernized dishes such as pizzas and lamb burgers. Also *the* place to head for breakfast – laid out buffet style, and therefore all you can eat, for just 4TL.

Subaşı Café Across the bridge from the main square. Ottoman-inspired teahouse with stone floors, wooden beams and a terrace over the river, attracting earnest-looking university students. No alcohol.

Tokat

TOKAT clusters at the foot of a jagged crag with a ruined Pontic fortress on top. Despite its undeniably dramatic setting, it comes as something of an anticlimax after Amasya, with none of the soothing riverside atmosphere and much less to see – the local claim to fame is the Gök Medrese, another Selçuk "Blue Seminary", now used as a museum. Nonetheless, Tokat makes a good stopoff when travelling between Amasya and Sivas.

The bus journey from Amasya – 103km away – takes a couple of hours, but those with their own wheels can take in a couple of ruined *kervansaray*s en route. The first – after about half an hour – is at **Ezinepazarı**; in the days of the great caravans, this was a day's ride by camel from Amasya. The second is at the signposted village of Pazar, about 26km short of Tokat, where you'll find the well-preserved Selçuk **Hatun Hanı**.

Some history

Tokat first came to prominence as a **staging post** on the Persian trans-Anatolian royal road, running from Sardis to Persepolis. Later it fell to Alexander the Great and then to Mithridates and his successors. In 47 BC, **Julius Caesar** defeated Pharnaces, son of the Pontic king Mithridates VI earlier Eupator, who had taken advantage of a period of civil war in Rome to attempt to re-establish the Pontic kingdom as an independent state. Caesar's victory in a five-hour battle at Zile, just outside Tokat, prompted his immortal line "*Veni, vidi, vici*" (I came, I saw, I conquered).

Under **Byzantine rule**, Tokat became a frontline city in perpetual danger of Arab attack, a state of affairs that continued until the Danişmend Turks took control of the city after the battle of Manzikert in 1071. Less than one hundred years later the İlhanid Mongols arrived, then Tokat was briefly transferred to the Ottoman Empire before a second great Mongol wave under **Tamerlane**.

With the departure of the Mongols and return of the **Ottomans**, life returned to normal and a period of prosperity ensued. In time, though, trade patterns shifted, the east–west routes to Persia lost their importance and Tokat became the backwater it remains today.

Arrival and information

Tokat's **otogar** is a little way outside town on the main road. It takes about fifteen minutes to walk to the centre from here – head for the roundabout near a bridge flanked by cannons and turn left down Gazi Osman Paşa Bulvarı. Pressing on straight down the main street eventually brings you to busy **Cumhuriyet Alanı**, the town's central square, location of the **PTT** and an underground shopping mall.

There's a tiny **tourist office** in Taş Han (daily 8am–6pm), but you'll need a phrasebook to extract any information and there are no maps or leaflets to collect.

Outdoor adventure

Turkey boasts one of the world's most exciting and diverse topographies. Spectacular alpine mountain ranges parallel both the azure waters of the Mediterranean and the storm-tossed Black Sea. Inland the vast uplands of ancient Anatolia are studded with volcanic peaks and sliced through by surging rivers culminating in the 5000m bulk of legendary Mount Ararat. In Cappadocia, weirdly sculpted pinnacles stand like sentinels in a landscape reminiscent of the old Wild West. To make the most of these fabulous land- and seascapes, get off that sunbed and get active.

Crossing the Çandır gorge, St Paul Trail ▲

Climbing Mount Resko ▼

Hiking

Turkey's wild mountain ranges such as the Kaçkar are a treat for experienced hikers prepared to carry their own tents and food and cope with few facilities, not least the lack of accurate maps. Far more accessible are two magnificent **long-distance walking routes** in southwest Mediterranean Turkey, both some 500km long. The **Lycian Way** (see p.325) winds through pine-forested mountains, dips to secluded coves and charming fishing villages and leads the lucky walker to a succession of wonderfully situated ancient sites. The **St Paul Trail** follows in the footsteps of the apostle from the wonderfully preserved Greco-Roman site of Perge, just shy of the Mediterranean east of Antalya, over the lofty Toros mountains and past stunning Lake Eğirdir, to ancient Antioch in Pisidia. Both trails are waymarked using red and white paint flashes, and each has an accompanying guidebook and map (see ⓦwww.trekkinginturkey.com for more information). Apart from being exhilarating hikes they also give walkers a unique insight into rural Turkish life.

Hot rocks

With cheap flights, countless rock faces and ample winter sun, it's only a matter of time before Turkey begins to rival Spain on the itineraries of **climbers**. The best place to start is Geyikbayırı, conveniently located just 25km from the gateway Mediterranean resort of Antalya. Five hundred bolted routes track their way up an imposing limestone cliff, and there's a pleasant campsite amongst the orange trees below. There's more climbing from beach level at the beautiful resort of nearby Olympos. For more information check out ⓦwww.climb-europe.com.

The wet stuff

Whitewater rafting has taken off in a big way in southwest Turkey. The Köprülü river near Antalya, and the Dalaman river close to Fethiye, both plunge down from the Toros mountains and offer novice rafters a thrilling introduction to the sport. The dam-threatened Çoruh, in the northeast of the country, is world-class, with grade five rapids and rafting operators offering multi-day itineraries through remote country.

▲ Rafting the Köprülü canyon

▼ Wreck diving near Kaş

The clear, warm waters of the southwest Mediterranean are perfect for **scuba-diving**, with reefs alive with colourful fish and underwater caves and sunken wrecks to explore. Best bases are the charming former Greek fishing villages of Kaş and Kalkan and, further west, Bodrum, Marmaris and Fethiye. More experienced divers may prefer the chillier north Aegean, diving amongst the wrecks of World War I ships off Gallipoli.

Sea-kayaking is gaining in popularity, and is a great way to explore the indented coastline, islets and shallow, clear waters east of Kaş. Alaçatı, on the Aegean coast west of İzmir, is the place to head for **kitesurfing**, while waterskiing, windsurfing and sailing are possible at most medium to large resorts.

▼ Cayoning in Lycia

Cool canyons

Ideal for the congenitally active in the hot summer months, **canyoning** involves abseiling down cascading falls, leaping into pools and exploring the shady depths of spectacular gorges such as Saklıkent, Kaputaş or Kıbrıs in the Lycian mountains. Many resorts, for eample Kaş, now offer one-day (or more) expeditions which make a perfect break from the beach.

The white stuff

Turkey has a number of small but rapidly developing **ski resorts** that seem only to be known to a select few foreigners. The best conditions (three metres or more of crisp, powder-snow) and longest season (Oct–May) are to be found at Palandöken, near the far northeastern city of Erzurum, while the volcanic cone of Mount Erciyes (3916m) just east of Cappadocia, offers good skiing from December through April. Overlooking the Sea of Marmara is Uludağ, Turkey's longest-established resort. It's very popular with people from Bursa and İstanbul, as is newer Kartalkaya to the east. Those enjoying some winter sun on the southwest Mediterranean coast usually head to either the small resort of Saklıkent, a little over an hour's drive above Antalya or, for more reliable snow, Davraz. For more information on Turkey's ski-scene see "Basics" (p.64).

Fresh powder at Kartalkaya ▲

Paragliding above Ölüdeniz ▼

That floating feeling

Cappadocia's bizarrely sculpted rock pinnacles, plunging valleys and rock-cut churches, are one of the world's most striking landscapes. The best way to see this geological wonder is drifting over it in an expertly piloted **hot-air balloon** (see p.468). A dramatic dawn lift-off and a champagne breakfast on touchdown make this as indulgent as it gets – make sure you've got your credit card handy. For more of an adrenaline rush, try leaping from the mountains behind the bustling resorts of Kaş or Ölüdeniz hanging from a **paraglider** (don't worry, unless you are an expert you'll be flying tandem with a professional pilot). Enjoy clear air, fabulous views, soaring thermals and spectacular landings on either Ölüdeniz beach or Kaş harbour.

Accommodation

Finding a **place to stay** should present few problems, with a clutch of establishments on Gazi Osman Paşa Bulvarı.

Büyük Tokat Oteli Demirköprü Mevkii ⊕0356/229 1700, ⓦwww.buyuktokatoteli.com.tr. A couple of kilometres northwest of the town centre. The magnificent reception hides rather less impressive rooms, but a swimming pool goes some way to compensate. ❺

🏃 **Hotel Çağrı** Gazi Osman Paşa Bul 92 ⊕0356/212 1028. A pretty decent budget option: modern, clean and offering a spread of presentable en suites. ❷

Çavuşoğlu Otel Gazi Osman Paşa Bul 168 ⊕0356/212 2829, ⓕ212 8568. An interesting, boutique-style establishment, whose colourful rooms have been individually decorated. ❹

Yeni Çinar Otel Gazi Osman Paşa Bul 167 ⊕0356/214 0066, ⓦwww.yenicinar.com. Has businesslike en suites and a good buffet breakfast. ❹

🏃 **Yücel Hotel** Meydan Cad 22 ⊕0356/212 5235, ⓦwww.yucelotel.com. Located on a pleasant side street, this cheery hotel has fresh-looking rooms, some with mosque views. There's also a hamam in the basement. ❷

The Town

The real reason to stop is to visit the **Gök Medrese** on the main Gazi Osman Paşa Bulvarı, a squat, rectangular building with a portal whose recessed arch resembles a picturesque cluster of stalactites. Built in 1275 by the Selçuk emir Mu'in al-Din Süleyman (also known as Pervane, or "butterfly", an epithet given to advisers of the Selçuk sultans), the *medrese* was named for the turquoise tiles that once covered its entire exterior. Most of these have unfortunately vanished, but a few still tenaciously grip the walls of the inner courtyard.

Today the Gök Medrese is home to the town's **museum** (Tues–Sun 8am–noon & 1–5pm; 3TL), a repository for local archeological finds and various unusual relics collected from the churches that served the town's sizable Greek and Armenian communities before World War I. Typical of these is a wax effigy of Christina, a Christian martyred during the rule of the Roman Emperor Diocletian. The ethnographic section features examples of local *yazma*-making – printing on cloth by means of wooden blocks to produce colourful patterned handkerchiefs, scarves and tablecloths.

Keep walking down Gazi Osman Paşa Bulvarı towards the main square and you'll come to the **Taş Han**, originally called the Voyvoda Han, built in 1631 by Armenian merchants. A large, rectangular building of two storeys, it houses a collection of shabby shops centred on a weed-infested courtyard.

A number of Ottoman-era half-timbered houses survive in the side streets of Tokat, but most are in states of advanced decrepitude. One exception is the **Latifoğlu Konağı** (Tues–Sun 9am–noon & 1.30–5pm; 2TL) on Gazi Osman Paşa Bulvarı, a couple of hundred metres past Cumhuriyet Alanı. Heavily restored, it stands out a mile from the surrounding modern buildings with its plain white walls, brown-stained woodwork and low-pitched roof. The interior is opulent almost to the point of tastelessness, but gives a good impression of how a wealthy nineteenth-century family would have lived.

Eating

There are cheap **restaurants** on virtually every street in town. If the weather's good, head for the tea garden in the Dudayev Parki, next to the Vilayet building on Cumhuriyet Alanı. To sample the local speciality, *Tokat kebap*, a mouthwatering and very filling combination of roast lamb, potatoes, aubergine, tomato and peppers head for the *Sofra* restaurant at Gazi Osman Paşa Bul 8.

Karadeniz Gazi Osman Paşa Bul 142. Swish café-cum-*pastanesı* that's immensely popular with locals; the upper floor boasts a balcony, though Tokat's teeming traffic makes it a less appealing proposition. Turkish coffee (3TL), Turkish tea (1.5TL) and a fine range of Turkish sweets are available, as are simple pasta dishes. Just up the road from the Taş Han.

Konak Café Pleasant café in the garden of the Latifoğlu Konağı, and an ideal place to recharge your batteries after touring the Ottoman houses.

Şanlıurfa Plevne Modern *kebap* house in town. It's quite unfortunate that the best *kebap* house in town does not dish out the famed local variety, but for all others, this friendly restaurant is the place to go. Opposite the Ali Paşa Camii.

Taş Han Divan Gazi Osman Paşa Bul. The large courtyard of this old merchant building is a good place to drain a glass of tea (1TL) or suck on a *nargileh* (12TL), though the Turkish pop is usually too loud and gloriously inappropriate for such surroundings.

Yeşil Köşe Gazi Osman Paşa Bul 1. One of the only restaurants in town to dish out the delicious *Tokat kebap*. At 13TL it may seem a little dear, but when you see the size of the dish and take your first bite, you'll know that you've got yourself a deal. Across the main road from the Ali Paşa Camii.

Sivas

As much as any other city in Turkey, **SİVAS** has been a battleground for the successive empires struggling to rule central Anatolia. Now this well-planned city of 200,000 people wouldn't figure on anybody's itinerary were it not for a concentration of Selçuk buildings – among the finest in Turkey – conveniently located in a town-centre park. The 113km journey southeast from Tokat is uninspiring, over barren hills that rise to 1600m metres, with the presence of snow poles giving some indication of what this region looks like in winter.

Sivas has been settled since Hittite times and according to local sources was later a key centre of the Sivas Frig Empire (1200 BC), which seems to have been consigned to historical oblivion. The town's real flowering came during **Selçuk** times, after the Battle of Manzikert (1071), and Sivas intermittently served as

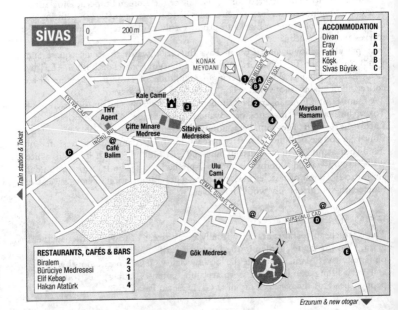

▲ Çifte Minare Medrese

the Selçuk capital during the Sultanate of Rum in the mid-twelfth century, before passing into the hands of İlhanid Mongols during the late thirteenth century. The Ottomans took over in 1396 only to be ousted by the Mongols four years later under Tamerlane, who razed much of the city after an eighteen-day siege and put its Christian inhabitants to the sword. The Ottomans returned in 1408 and Sivas pretty much faded out of history until a nineteenth-century reawakening.

Arrival

Buses from Ankara and beyond arrive at the **otogar**, 1.5km south of town. From here *servis* buses (1.5TL) run to the centre of town, along İnönü Bulvarı. The **train station** is 2.5km west of town, but municipal buses and dolmuşes run down İstasiyon Caddesi (later İnönü Bulvarı) to Konak Meydanı.

Accommodation

Otel Divan Atatürk Cad ☎ 0346/221 7878, ℱ 221 1407. Best budget option in Sivas. Friendly, newly renovated hotel with spotless rooms and reliable hot water. You'll also get a large buffet breakfast thrown in. ❸

Eray Pansiyon Eski Belediye Sok 12 ☎ 0346/223 1647. A few apartment rooms trying their best to function as a youth hostel. Dormitory beds go for 25TL and are comfy enough, but aside from an

excellent location there's not too much to recommend. Dorm beds 25TL.

Otel Fatih Kurşunlu Cad 22 ☎ 0346/223 4313. The rooms don't quite match the promise of an ornate lobby, but all are kept clean and some have balconies. Unfortunately it's in one of the uglier quarters of town. ❸

Hotel Köşk Atatürk Cad 7 ☎ 0346/255 1724, ⓦ www.koskotel.com. Beautifully decked-out contemporary hotel, complete with fitness centre. All rooms are spacious and spotless, with excellent showers, and breakfast is included in the price. **❻** **Sivas Büyük Oteli** İstasyon Cad ☎0346/225 4763, ⓦwww.sivasbuyukotel.com. Monolith of a

hotel trying desperately to cling onto its class. Bedrooms are large and soulless, but it's useful to know that the dining room is one of the few places in town that serves alcohol. **❼**

The Town

Most of Sivas's Selçuk monuments were built during the Sultanate of Rum and in the period of Mongol sovereignty that followed under the İlhanids. With their highly decorative facades and elaborately carved portals, the buildings epitomize Selçuk architectural styles, and nearly all are conveniently grouped together in and around a small area just off **Konak Meydanı**. Closest to the *meydan* is the **Bürüciye Medresesi**, founded in 1271 by the İlhanid emir Muzaffer Bürücirdi. The building consists of a series of square rooms laid out to a symmetrical ground plan around a central courtyard. As you pass through the entrance, the *türbe* of the emir and his children is to the left. The *medrese* now contains a few uninteresting pieces of stonework, as well as a popular courtyard café (see below). Nearby is the **Kale Camii**, dating from 1580 and an oddity in this area since it's a straightforward Ottoman mosque.

South of here is the stunning **Çifte Minare Medrese** (Twin Minaret Seminary), also built in 1271. The facade alone survives, adorned with tightly curled relief filigrees, topped by two brick minarets, which are adorned here and there with pale blue tiles. Behind, only the well-defined foundations of student cells and lecture halls survive. Directly opposite is the **Şifaiye Medresesi** (1217), a hospital and medical school built on the orders of the Selçuk sultan Keykavus I. At the time of writing it was the subject of heavy renovation, but it's likely to revert to its previous function as a bazaar.

The rest of the town's Selçuk monuments lie outside the park. If you turn onto Cemal Gürsel Caddesi (just south of the park), you'll find the **Ulu Cami**, the oldest mosque in Sivas, built in 1197. If you step inside the northern entrance you will enter the subterranean cool of an interior supported by fifty wooden pillars. The peaceful silence is broken only by the murmur of boys reading from the Koran.

A right turn from Cemal Gürsel Caddesi will take you onto Cumhuriyet Caddesi where, on the left after a couple of hundred metres, you'll find the **Gök Medrese**, with its ornate tile-studded minarets. Like the **Şifaiye Medresesi**, the stunning "Blue Seminary" was undertaking substantial renovation at the time of writing. It was built in 1271 by the Selçuk grand vizier Sahip Ata Fahrettin Ali, who was also responsible for buildings in Kayseri and Konya.

Eating and drinking

There are a number of cheap **kebab places** lining the road behind the PTT, and some **teahouses** in the park serving up snacks. Up a side street leading off Atatürk Caddesi stands the **Meydan Hamamı** (daily 7am–10.30pm; 10TL for bath), which has been hissing and steaming for over four centuries and is still going strong.

Biralem Atatürk Cad 26. This bar can be a lifesaver in a city where it's even tough to find shops selling alcohol, though women may not feel entirely comfortable as it's entirely male-dominated. A half-litre of draught Efes will set you back 3.5TL.

Bürüciye Medresesi Gulp down a tea in the superb setting of this *medrese* courtyard (see above), which also functions as a swallow's playground of some sort – come evening the air is also filled with the haunting sounds of folk music.

Elif Kebap Atatürk Cad 2. Clean, friendly and popular, this two-level restaurant doles out round after round of excellent *kebap* from 6TL, and some very lengthy *pide* for a little less.

Hakan Atatürk Atatürk Cad 22. Presentable place whose upper floor is a great place for breakfast (5.5TL) and Turkish coffee (2.5TL); they also dish out some of the best *baklava* and desserts in town.

Divriği

Stuck in the middle of a mountainous nowhere, on a hill overlooking a tributary of the young Euphrates, 162km southeast of Sivas, sleepy **DIVRIĞI** merits a visit for the sake of a single monument, the whimsical and unique Ulu Cami and its dependency, the Darüşşifa (Sanitorium). These date from early in the thirteenth century, when the town was the seat of the tiny Mengüçeh emirate; the Mengüçehs were evicted by the Mongols in 1252, who demolished the castle here but left the religious foundations alone, and the place was not incorporated into the Ottoman Empire until 1516.

The Town

Divriği retains a ramshackle bazaar area, crisscrossed by cobbled lanes and grape-vines. Architecturally the town sports distinctive wooden **minarets** and old houses with inverted-keyhole windows, neither of which are seen elsewhere in Anatolia. The conspicuous **mosque** and **sanitorium**, joined in one complex at the top of a slope 250m east of town, command a fine view.

The **Ulu Cami**, dedicated in 1228 by a certain Ahmet Şah, is remarkable for its outrageous external **portals**, most un-Islamic with their wealth of floral and faunal detail. Rather far-fetched comparisons have been made to Indian Moghul art, but a simpler, more likely explanation is that Armenian or Selçuk craftsmen had a hand in the decoration. The north door, festooned with vegetal designs, is the most celebrated, although the northwestern one is more intricately worked – note the pair of double-headed eagles, not necessarily copied from the Byzantines since it's a very old Anatolian motif. Inside, sixteen columns and the ceiling they support are more suggestive of a Gothic cloister or a Byzantine cistern. There's rope-vaulting in one dome, while the northeastern one sports a peanut-brittle surface, in terms of both the relief work and variegated colouring; the central dome has been rather tastelessly restored. The *mihrab* is plain, flanked by an extravagant, carved wooden *mimber*.

The adjoining **Darüşşifa** was also begun in 1228 by Adaletli Melike Turan Melek, Ahmet Şah's wife. Its portal is restrained in comparison to the mosque's, but still bears medallions lifted almost free from their background. The sanitorium complex is theoretically open daily 8.30am to 5pm, but in these lean tourist times the gate is usually locked, so you must find the caretaker to gain admission – easiest just after prayers next door. A small donation is requested after signing the guest register at the conclusion of the tour.

The caretaker proudly points out some of the more arcane features of the interior, which is asymmetrical in both ground plan and ornamentation, and even more eclectic than the mosque. Overhead, the dome has collapsed and been crudely replaced in the same manner as the mosque's, but four-pointed **vaulting** graces the entry hall, with even more elaborate ribbing over a raised platform in the *eyvan*, or domed side-chamber, at the rear of the nave. The fan-reliefs on the wall behind this once formed an elaborate **sundial**, catching rays through the second-floor window of the facade.

Practicalities

The **train station** is down by the river, a twenty-minute walk from the bazaar; taxis meet most arrivals and don't cost more than a couple of dollars. The **otogar**, essentially a dirt car park, is 400m south of town on the road to Elazığ.

Accommodation in Divriği is pretty poor, with the scruffy *Otel Ninni* (no phone) one of the only options (25TL), so it's best to avoid staying the night if you can. **Eating** options are a little better, especially at *Konak* on the way up to the mosque, which has citadel views and dishes out the best *kahvaltı* for miles around (6TL), as well as succulent kebabs.

Travel details

Buses and dolmuşes

Amasya to: Ankara (hourly; 6hr); İstanbul (12 daily; 12hr); Kayseri (3 daily; 8hr); Malatya (5 daily; 9hr); Samsun (10 daily; 3hr); Sivas (10 daily; 3hr 30min); Tokat (10 daily; 1hr 30min).

Ankara to: Adana (10 daily; 7hr); Amasya (hourly; 6hr); Antalya (12 daily; 7hr); Bodrum (10 daily; 12hr); Bursa (hourly; 5hr 30min); Diyarbakır (6 daily; 14hr); Erzurum (4 daily; 13hr); Eskişehir (6 daily; 3hr); Gaziantep (12 daily; 10hr); İstanbul (every 30min; 4hr 45min–6hr); İzmir (hourly; 7–8hr); Kayseri (14 daily; 5hr); Konya (hourly; 3hr); Kütahya (7 daily; 6hr); Mardin (3 daily; 16hr); Nevşehir (12 daily; 4hr 30min); Polatlı (every 30min; 1hr); Safranbolu (16 daily; 3hr 30min); Samsun (10 daily; 6hr 30min); Sivas (hourly; 6hr 30min); Sungurlu (hourly; 2hr 30min); Şanlıurfa (4 daily; 12hr); Tokat (12 daily; 6hr 30min); Trabzon (5 daily; 12hr).

Eskişehir to: Ankara (6 daily; 3hr); Bursa (6 daily; 2hr 30min); İstanbul (4 daily; 5hr); Kütahya (11 daily; 1hr 20min).

Kütahya to: Afyon (14 daily; 1hr 45min); Ankara (7 daily; 6hr); Antalya (5 daily; 5hr); Bursa (12 daily; 3hr); Eskişehir (11 daily; 1hr 20min); İstanbul (14 daily; 6hr); İzmir (12 daily; 6hr).

Safranbolu to: Ankara (16 daily; 3hr 30min); Göreme (daily, 8hr); İstanbul (15 daily; 6hr 30min); İzmir (daily; 12hr).

Sivas to: Amasya (10 daily; 3hr 30min); Ankara (hourly; 6hr 30min); Divriği (4 daily; 3hr); Diyarbakır (12 daily; 8hr); Erzurum (12 daily; 7hr 30min); Kayseri (10 daily; 3hr); Malatya (12 daily; 4hr 30min); Tokat (10 daily; 1hr 30min).

Tokat to: Amasya (12 daily; 2hr); Ankara (12 daily; 6hr 30min); Erzurum (2 daily; 9hr); Sivas (10 daily; 1hr 30min).

Trains

Ankara to: Adana (1 daily; 11hr 20min); Divriği (2 daily; 15hr); Diyarbakır (daily; 23hr); Erzurum (2 daily; 21hr); Eskişehir (13 daily; 1hr 30min–3hr 30min); İstanbul (10 daily; 5–9hr); İzmir (3 daily; 13–15hr); Kars (2 daily; 26hr–28hr); Kütahya (3 daily; 4hr 30min); Malatya (2 daily; 15–17hr); Sivas (4 daily; 11hr); Tatvan (2 weekly; 40hr); Tehran, Iran (Thursdays at 7.40am; 60hr); Zonguldak (3 weekly; 10hr).

Divriği to: Erzurum (2 daily; 7hr); Sivas (3 daily; 4–7hr).

Sivas to: Ankara (4 daily; 11hr); Divriği (3 daily; 4–7hr); Diyarbakır (4 weekly; 12hr); Erzurum (2 daily; 10hr); Kars (2 daily; 16hr).

Flights

Ankara to: Adana (at least 1 daily; 1hr); Antalya (at least 2 daily; 1hr); Batman (4 daily; 1hr 30min); Bodrum (at least 2 daily; 1hr 20min); Dalaman (daily; 1hr 15min); Diyarbakır (at least 3 daily; 1hr 20min); Elazığ (daily; 1hr 15min); Erzincan (4 weekly; 1hr 20min); Erzurum (at least 1 daily; 1hr 25min); Gaziantep (daily; 1hr 10min); İstanbul (hourly; 1hr); İzmir (at least 5 daily; 1hr 20min); Kars (daily; 1hr 35min); Malatya (daily; 1hr 10min); Mardin (daily; 1hr 35min); Muş (4 weekly; 1hr 35min); Şanlıurfa (daily; 1hr 20min); Trabzon (3 daily; 1hr 20min); Van (3 daily; 1hr 35min).

The Black Sea coast

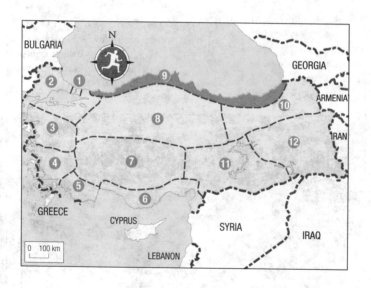

CHAPTER 9 # Highlights

* **A coastal drive** Cruise the little-used coast road from Sinop to Amasra, where sharp switchbacks lead to peaceful bays and long beaches. **See p.552**

* **Amasra** Enjoy the small-town charm and historical pedigree of Amasra, with its old cobbled streets, Byzantine gateways and Genoese castle walls. **See p.553**

* **Aya Sofya** Thirteenth-century frescoes in this Byzantine monastery at the edge of Trabzon are among the most vivid sacred art in Anatolia. **See p.561**

* **Sumela** Cliff-clinging thirteenth-century monastery in a superb forested setting. **See p.565**

* **Uzungöl** Large natural lake in the foothills of the Pontic range, the focus of a popular resort. **See p.568**

* **Hemşin valleys** This lushly forested district is home to a colourful, outgoing people with their own tenaciously preserved culture. **See p.569**

* **Tea** Learn the skills of making the nation's favourite drink and watch the leaves being picked from the hillsides surrounding Rize. **See p.574**

▲ Boats lining the harbour, Amasra

The Black Sea coast

xtending from just east of İstanbul to the frontier with Georgia, the **Black Sea** region is an anomaly, guaranteed to smash any stereotypes held about Turkey. The combined action of damp northerly and westerly winds, and an almost uninterrupted wall of mountains south of the shore, has created a relentlessly rainy and riotously green realm. It's not unlike North America's, or Spain's, northwest coast. The peaks force the clouds to disgorge themselves on the seaward side of the watershed, leaving central Anatolia beyond the passes in a permanent rain shadow.

The short summer season means there is little in the way of organized foreign tourism and backpackers, archeology groups and trekkers form the bulk of visitors. Yet, in those months when the semi-tropical heat is on (July and August), you'll certainly want to swim. The sea here has its own peculiarities, just like the weather. It is fed huge volumes of fresh water by the Don, Dnieper and Danube rivers to the north, and diminished not by evaporation but by strong currents through the Bosphorus and the Dardanelles. The resulting upper layer is of such low salinity that you could almost drink it, were it not for the pollution of recent decades.

The coastal ranges begin as mere humps north of Ankara but attain world-class grandeur by the time the Georgian border is reached. Until recently they made land access all but impossible, and provided refuge for a complex quilt of tribes and ethnic subgroups which still exist among the **Hemşin valleys** and the **Kaçkar mountains** making the eastern end of the Black Sea one of Turkey's most anthropologically interesting regions. Even so, travelling around largely consists of soaking up the atmosphere and you rarely need worry about missing important sights. Aside from the old mercantile towns of **Ünye** and **Giresun** there really aren't any major attractions outside the ancient port city of **Trabzon** (Trebizond) with its nearby **monastery of Sumela**.

By comparison the region's middle portion is dominated by the hulking port of Samsun and consequently lacks character. However, head further west from the evocatively located town of **Sinop** to the Byzantine/Genoese harbour of **Amasra** and the area is full of attractive coastal villages and deserted beaches, as the infrequency of bus and dolmuş links shelters the area from mass tourism.

Some history

The ancient Greeks ventured onto the Pontos Euxine (as they called the Black Sea) at the start of the first millennium BC. They fought with the local "barbarians" and occasionally, as in the semi-legendary tale of Jason and the Argonauts, got the better of them. Between the seventh and fourth centuries BC numerous colonies of the Aegean cities were founded and these became the ancestors of virtually

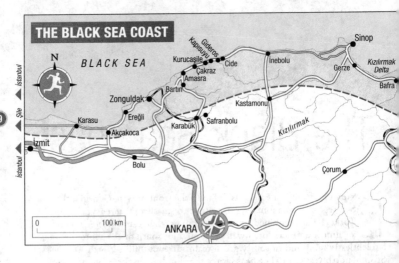

every modern Black Sea town, whose name often as not is a Turkification of the ancient moniker. The region had its first brief appearance on the world stage when one of the local Pontic kings, **Mithridates IV Eupator**, came close to expelling the Romans from Anatolia.

With the arrival of Christianity, relations between natives and imperial overlords hardly changed at all. Only the Byzantine urban centres by the sea became thoroughly Hellenized. The Byzantine defeat at Manzikert in 1071 (see p.688) initially meant little to the Black Sea, safe behind its wall of mountains; the fall of Constantinople to the Fourth Crusade in 1204 had far greater immediate effects, prompting the Black Sea's second spell of historical prominence. The empire-in-exile of the Komnenos dynasty centred on **Trebizond** (today's Trabzon) exercised influence grossly disproportionate to its size for two and a half cultured (and ultimately decadent) centuries.

After Manzikert, Turkish chieftains had begun to encroach on the coast, especially at the gap in the barrier ranges near Sinop and Samsun; the Trapezuntine dynasty even concluded alliances with them, doubtless to act as a counter to the power of the Genoese and Venetians who also set up shop hereabouts. Most of this factionalism was brought to an end under the **Ottomans**, though even they entrusted semi-autonomous administration of the Pontic foothills to feudal *derebeys* (literally "valley lords") until the early nineteenth century.

The equilibrium was upset when the Black Sea area entered the history books for the third time as a theatre of war between imperial Turkey and **Russia**. These two clashed four times between 1828 and 1915, with the Tsarist regime giving active aid and comfort to various separatist movements in the region after 1877. Between 1918 and 1922, Greeks attempting to create a Pontic state fought with guerillas loyal to Atatürk's Nationalists. Following the victory of the **Republic**, the Greek merchant class was expelled along with the rest of Turkey's Greek Orthodox population, and the Black Sea experienced temporary economic disarray, verging on famine during the 1930s.

Most of the credit for the last few decades of **recovery** must go to the *hamsi*s, as the locals are nicknamed (after the Black Sea anchovy formerly caught here in large numbers during winter). Enterprising, voluble and occasionally

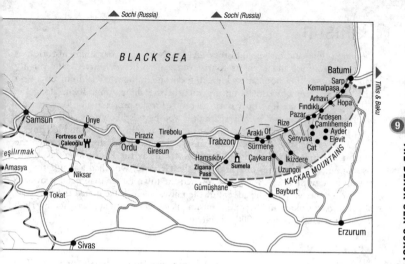

scandalous, they have set up mafias in the shipping, property and construction industries throughout the country, much of which is funded by industrious *hamsi*s overseas. The opening of Turkey's eastern border in the early 1990s brought a new supply of goods to the region's doorstep, most visible in the form of thousands of prostitutes, or *natashas* as they're colloquially known. Most of the latter have now departed, due in part to Turkey's economic woes, and a new coastal road and bout of urbanization is the most visible sign of the post-Soviet era. A recent discovery of vast beds of oil and gas reserves may give the Black Sea region a further boost.

The western Black Sea

The coast from Samsun west to Amasra is perhaps the least visited part of the entire Turkish shoreline. This neglect is a joint result of poor communications and the relative lack of tourist facilities and specific attractions. **Samsun** makes a dreary and discouraging gateway to the region, but matters improve as you head northwest to **Sinop**, a more interesting place than any other Black Sea town except Trabzon. Beyond Sinop the coast road west is tortuous and slow, but spectacular scenery, scattered, unspoiled beaches and small ports do something to compensate. The only place that sees many tourists is **Amasra**, an old medieval stronghold at the western end of this beautiful stretch.

As a rule, the **beaches** are cleaner and the weather drier along this section of the Black Sea than further east. Figs and olives attest to the mild climate, and if you just want to laze on the sand without any other stimulation, then you'll find plenty of opportunity. Sparse **bus** and **dolmuş** schedules are the only drawbacks; check frequencies to avoid getting stranded.

Samsun

Despite its long and turbulent history **SAMSUN** has scant remaining historical or scenic attractions, and even its tourist office now lies defunct. A thoroughly modern city with a population knocking on one million, it's laid out on a grid plan, with seemingly endless unruly suburbs stretching some 30km along the east–west coast road. It's a busy port and centre for the processing of local agricultural produce and tobacco. Any spare time you have is likely to weigh heavy on your hands – though it has a fair amount to offer in terms of food and lodgings.

Because of its strategic location, Samsun changed hands frequently over the centuries; besieged, captured (and usually sacked) by the Pontic kings, Romans, Byzantines, several tribes of Turks and the Genoese, who had a major trading station here until 1425, when they torched the town rather than hand it over to Ottoman control. With the advent of the railway, which facilitated the transport of tobacco to Ankara and beyond, Samsun's flagging fortunes revived and by 1910 it was a thriving city of 40,000 inhabitants.

The City

The main coastal road separates Samsun's museums from its hotels and shops. The city centre's main square, **Cumhuriyet Meydanı** boasts a statue of Atatürk on horseback. **İstiklâl Caddesi** runs parallel with the main highway and is the heart of the new city, in marked contrast to the profusion of narrow and twisting side streets to be found clustered around the **Saat Külesi Meydanı**.

Samsun's **Archeological Museum** (Arkeoloji Müzesi; Tues–Sun 8.30am–noon & 1–5pm; 3TL) is poorly laid out but worth visiting for its main exhibit, a Roman mosaic found in Karasamsun, site of an ancient acropolis which juts out to sea, 3km west of town. The museum's grounds are also beautifully landscaped. A life-sized installation marks the spot where Atatürk arrived on May 19, 1919 to take control of the local anti-Greek forces. His visit is detailed in the **Gazi Museum** on İstiklâl Caddesi (Gazi Müzesi; Tues–Sun 8am–noon & 1–5pm; 3TL) in the former *Mintika Hotel*, which has been preserved as a memory to Atatürk's trip with scores of photos, letters and even clothing from the great man on display.

Practicalities

The **otogar** lies 4km south of the city centre on the main Trabzon road, but just about all the bus companies have ticket offices on the east side of Cumhuriyet Meydanı, from where service buses run to and from the *otogar*. The **train station** is halfway towards the centre; buses #2 and #10, as well as dolmuşes marked "Garaj", link both with Cumhuriyet Meydanı, the town's hub. The **airport** is 19km out of town on the coastal road to Trabzon and linked to the town centre by a service bus.

A number of well-priced, respectable hotels lie on, or just off, Cumhuriyet Meydanı. You're advised to book ahead in July, when Samsun hosts an international trade fair lasting the whole month. The *Otel Yafeya*, Cumhuriyet Meydanı (☎0362/435 1131, ⓦwww.yafeyaotel.com; ❻) is housed in an imposing building on the corner of the square and boasts large, comfortable rooms, bar and restaurant, and a spacious air-conditioned lobby. Around the corner at the junction of Cumhuriyet Meydanı and Kazımpaşa Caddesi is the shiny business option *Otel Vidinli* (☎0362/431 6050, ⓦwww.otelvidinli.com.tr; ❺) with satellite TV, stylish rooms and a terrace-bar. Further along Kazımpaşa Caddesi – look out for the signs – is the super-friendly ⚑ *Otel Necmi* Kale Mah 6, Bedesten Sokak (☎0362/432 7164 ⓦwww.otelnecmi.com.tr; ❸).

Equidistant between the latter two hotels on Cumhuriyet Meydanı is the aptly named 𝔄 *Samsun Balik Restaurant*, where diners select their fish downstairs and have it brought to them in the refined upstairs dining room. Alcohol is available. Aside from the other *kebap* and *pastane* joints around town, *Oskar Restaurant* Şeyhhamza Sok 3, off Belediye Meydanı is recommended for its surroundings, service and food, offering *meze*s a variety of meat and fish dishes and sweets to follow.

West to Gerze

Head west out of Samsun along the coast road and it soon cuts inland through extensive tobacco fields to the market town of **BAFRA**, an ugly, grimy town of around 80,000 who mostly work in the tobacco industry. There's no reason to stop, though the surrounding countryside encompasses the **Kızılırmak delta**, also called Bafra Balık Gölleri ("Bafra fish lakes"), a 56,000-hectare birdwatchers' paradise of wetlands, lakes, flooded forests, reedbeds and sand dunes formed by the Kızılırmak River as it falls into the Black Sea.

Continuing west from Bafra, the road returns to the sea, passing some stunning sandy beaches and pastoral scenery a few kilometres before **GERZE**, a pretty village with many handsome old buildings in a reasonable state of repair. Its handful of hotels – the pick of which is the *Otel Ermiş* (℡0368/718 1540; ❷) overlooking the harbour – and restaurants are flanked by stony, not too crowded beaches.

Sinop

Blessed with the finest natural harbour on the Black Sea, sleepy **SINOP** straddles a beach-studded isthmus and is renowned as one of the prettiest towns along the coast. The town's clutch of monuments bestows a real authority on the place although most visitors are content to relax along the café-lined harbourfront where bobbing boats supply the day's catch to the line of restaurants behind: nowadays it's both fishing and tourism that provide most of the local income for the 35,000 inhabitants. Sinop also used to be the location of a NATO listening post: the peninsula is just about the northernmost point of Anatolia, less than two hundred nautical miles from the Crimea, and this formerly US-run base played a front-line role in the Cold War. A more contemporary battle is now raging locally, as residents fight proposals for Turkey's first nuclear power station, which threatens to blight the local landscape.

Some history

Sinop takes its name from the mythical **Sinope**, an Amazon queen and daughter of a minor river-god. She attracted the attention of Zeus, who promised her anything she desired in return for her favours. Her request was for eternal virginity; Zeus played the gentleman and complied.

After a wealthy period of Roman rule, Sinop declined during the Byzantine period, and sixth- and seventh-century attempts to revive the town's fortunes were thwarted by Persian and Arab raids. The Selçuks took the town in October 1214, converting a number of churches into mosques and erecting a *medrese*, but after the Mongols smashed the short-lived Selçuk state, Sinop passed into the hands of the İsfendiyaroğlu emirs of Kastamonu until Ottoman annexation in 1458. Thereafter the town was rarely heard of, except on November 30, 1853, when the Russians destroyed both Sinop and an Ottoman fleet anchored here, thus triggering the Crimean War, and again on May 18, 1919, when Atatürk passed through en route to Samsun.

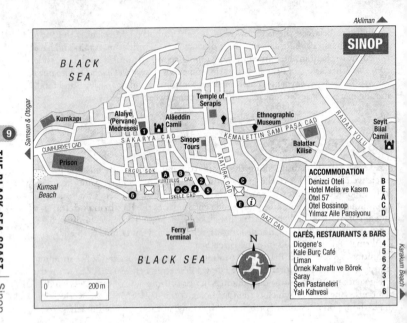

ACCOMMODATION

Denizci Oteli	B
Hotel Melia ve Kasım	E
Otel 57	A
Otel Bossinop	C
Yılmaz Aile Pansiyonu	D

CAFÉS, RESTAURANTS & BARS

Diogene's	4
Kale Burç Café	5
Liman	6
Örnek Kahvaltı ve Börek	2
Saray	3
Şen Pastaneleri	1
Yalı Kahvesi	6

Arrival and information

Sinop's **otogar** is 3km south of town on the way to the tiny shed of an **airport**, which is a further 2km west. Service buses laid on by the bus companies connect the former, while a 20TL taxi ride is recommended for the latter. An irregular airport bus also leaves from beside the taxi rank outside the main PTT on Atatürk Caddesi (open daily 8am–7pm): it should depart every half–hour but seldom does. Most dolmuşes from either the peninsula or around town arrive and depart from the stop behind the *Hotel Melia ve Kasım*. Next door, just to the north of the hotel, you'll find the friendly **tourist office** (June–Aug daily 9am–11pm; ☎0368/261 5298).

Accommodation

Sinop has a great selection of town-centre **hotels**, mostly in the streets behind the harbour. They tend to fill up in summer when an advanced booking becomes a necessity. Unusually for this part of Turkey, the majority have free wi-fi. In recent years many small *pansiyon*s have sprung up at Karakum beach near the large *Holiday Village*, a couple of kilometres east of the centre, though these are mostly private homes offering their spare bedroom to rent for the night and you will have to look carefully for the signs.

Otel 57 Kurtuluş Cad 29 ☎0368/261 5462, ⊛www .otel57.com. Good-value place with very comfortable a/c rooms with balconies. ❹

Otel Bossinop Uğurmumcu Mey 37 ☎0368/260 5700, ⊛www.bossinopotel.com. The newest and coolest hotel in town with slickly designed double rooms. Breakfast is served on the roof terrace. ❺

Denizci Otel Kurtuluş Cad 13 ☎0368/260 5934, ⊛www.denizciotel.com. One of the town's plushest and best-value options with tasteful doubles with stylish en suites and satellite TV. ❺

Hotel Melia ve Kasım Gazi Cad 49 ☎0368/261 4210, ⓕ261 1625. The rather standard rooms in Sinop's best-located hotel boast en-suite baths and cracking views over the sea and harbour. However, it suffers from dated decor and the summer hum of the *gazino* (nightclub) downstairs. ❹

Yılmaz Aile Pansiyonu Tersane Çarşısı 11 ☎0368/261 5752. The best-value budget option close to the water's edge with small but clean doubles with TV, basic shared bathrooms, and a kitchen for guest use. ❷

The Town

Sinop's **city walls** are still highly prominent and, although time has inevitably taken its toll, they remain by far the most atmospheric thing about the town. Down near the harbour, a hefty square tower offers good views out to sea and you can stroll along nearby sections of wall. The first thing you'll notice on entering the town is a ruined **prison** on Sakarya Caddesi. The building was put to this use in 1882; before that it was a dockyard and a bastion of the citadel. Visitors are free to poke around both the prison and the bulky **Kumkapı**, which lies almost opposite and juts out bastion-like into the sea on the northern shore.

Heading east from Kumkapı, Sakarya Caddesi leads to the **Alâeddin Camii**, a mid-thirteenth-century Selçuk mosque that's the oldest in town. Entry is via the tree-shaded courtyard with a central *şadırvan*, where a blue-painted porch lets onto a plain interior enlivened by a fine *mimber*. Behind the mosque is the **Alaiye Medresesi**, which also dates from the 1260s. The most notable feature is a marble-decorated entrance portal, relatively restrained by Selçuk standards. It's also known as the Pervane Medresesi after its founder, Mu'in al-Din Süleyman.

Heading north down one of the side streets at the end of Sakarya Caddesi leads to Sinop's newly renovated **museum** (Tues–Sun 9am–noon & 1–5.30pm; 3TL), which has an array of objects from the Bronze Age onwards. Many of its oldest exhibits were unearthed at Kocagöz, an archeological site a few kilometres southwest of Sinop. In the museum grounds are the sparse remains of the Hellenistic **Temple of Serapis**, excavated in 1951.

Following Kemalettin Sami Paşa Caddesi onto the headland will lead you past the small **ethnography museum** (Tues–Sun 8am–5pm; 3TL) housed in an old wooden mansion. Further along this road is the well-signposted **Balatlar Kilise**, a large ruined seventh-century Byzantine church with traces of frescoes inside.

The town beaches

Sinop's main beaches are **Kumsal**, less than a kilometre southwest of the bus station, and a pay beach at **Karakum** (meaning "black sand", which is a fairly honest description). They are connected with each other, via the *otogar* and the town centre, by twice-hourly dolmuşes. Kumsal beach is smaller, but the sand is lighter and the sea rather more enticing than at Karakum. The best beach on the northern side of the peninsula is **Akliman**, a twenty-minute *dolmuş* ride from town, where a fine stretch of white sand is backed by pine forests and picnic areas, but it's less frequented than the other beaches, as unpredictable currents make swimming here dangerous.

Eating and drinking

For food and drink, there are plenty of options down by the enchanting harbour on İskele Caddesi. The picturesque wooden *Yalı Kahvesi* and the *Liman*, in a restored stone house next door, are the most popular of the many **teahouses**, with chairs on the waterfront and a fine view of the boats in the harbour. Further along there are several fish **restaurants** in a tightly packed row: the *Saray* is the most popular with fresh mackerel or sea bass for 10–15TL served out on little floating piers. *Örnek Kahvaltı ve Börek*, at İskele Cad 1/A, serves light and delicious breakfast pastries which you may take away to enjoy in any of the local teahouses. The *Şen Pastaneleri* at Sakarya Cad 34 sells a wide variety of Sinop's famed gooey desserts in air-conditioned comfort.

For a taste of local **bar** life, head for the popular *Diogene's Disco-Bar* next to the Ayhan boat shop off İskele Caddesi which has live Black Sea folk music most nights, or to the *Kale Burç Café* on top of the massive stone tower by the waterfront, which plays folk tunes well into the evening.

West of Sinop: the coast to Amasra

Most public transport from Sinop heads either east towards Samsun or inland to Kastamonu. There are dolmuşes plying the little-travelled coast **west to Amasra**, but none provides a direct service. Expect to travel from village to village and change frequently. If you plan to stop anywhere along the way, the nine hours' total driving time will have to be spread over two days due to infrequent departures. However, with your own vehicle, the smooth roads enable you to explore the coastline's empty coves and sleepy villages at your leisure.

İNEBOLU, the biggest place between Sinop and Amasra, is still a sleepy harbour town and resort mustering only ten thousand inhabitants. A few isolated Ottoman houses grace the web of narrow streets, which is bisected by a river and wedged between the hills and the sea, with a long, empty shingle beach. Between the coast road and the sea, on the western approach to the centre via İsmet Paşa Caddesi, are a couple of recommended **resorts,** both with rambling beachside tea gardens where women holiday-makers sit and knit while their husbands throw pebbles into the sea: the *Huzur Motel* (☏0366/811 4502; ❸) is more basic than the *Yakamoz Tatil Köyü* (☏0366/811 4305, ⓦwww.yakamoztatilkoyu.com; ❹), which boasts cosy bungalows and beachside apartments.

The constant curves mean that it takes a good two hours to drive to **CIDE**, whose town centre is actually a couple of kilometres inland: it's a basic grid of shops with a PTT, a range of banks and tiny *otogar*, served by one daily direct bus to İstanbul. The **beach** near here is pebbly but extends for nearly ten uncrowded kilometres to the west of the harbour.

GİDEROS, 15km west of Cide, is a small cluster of houses surrounded by green cliffs and makes a serene, beautiful spot to swim and take a break. The next popular stop is **KAPISUYU**, an idyllic village where a bucolic mountain stream enters the Black Sea. Just a few kilometres ahead lies **KURUCAŞİLE**, long renowned as a boat-building centre – craftsment can still be seen making them on the eastbound road. The town's *Kalyon Hotel*, at İskele Cad 18, is pleasantly located on the harbour (☏&ⓕ0378/518 1463; ❷), with adequately furnished rooms.

Amasra

AMASRA brazenly flaunts its charms to new arrivals. Approached from any direction, the town suddenly appears below you, swarming up onto a rocky headland sheltering two bays. Amasra's historical pedigree and colourful atmosphere make it worth at least an overnight stop. During the day it is a quiet place, full of shady corners to sit and contemplate; by night it's much livelier and the old walls are lit up attractively, though it doesn't lose its small-town charm.

Originally called Sesamus – mentioned in Homer's *Iliad* – it was colonized by Miletus in the sixth century BC. The name Amasra derived from Queen Amastris, a lady of the court of Alexander the Great, who, after the death of her husband, acted as regent for her young son, only to be repaid with murder at his hands. The city then passed rapidly through the grip of a succession of rulers, until avid letter-writer Pliny the Younger was appointed Rome's special commissioner of the region in 110 AD. From the ninth century, after a barbarian attack, the town declined in importance, though the Byzantines maintained a garrison here. The Genoese took over when Byzantine strength began to decline, and held the city until the Ottomans assumed control in 1460.

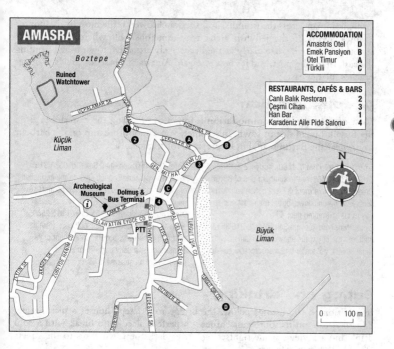

Arrival and information

The **dolmuş and bus terminal** is near the **PTT** on the small Atatürk Meydanı, near the middle of the main part of the headland. From here everything is in easy reach, including a small **tourist information kiosk** (Ⓦ www.amasra.net) just behind the museum, which is open whenever they can find someone to staff it.

The Town

The modern town occupies a headland; a narrow stone bridge links the main town to the island of Boztepe further out. The headland shelters the west-facing Küçük Liman (Little Harbour) on one side and the east-facing Büyük Liman (Big Harbour) on the other. Both the main town and island are scattered with stretches of ancient fortifications from two Byzantine/Genoese **castles** near the tip of the peninsula. One of these is situated in the modern town above Büyük Liman, and a short walk in this area, above the *Otel Timur*, reveals old cobbled streets straddled by Byzantine gateways. The other castle is reached by following Küçük Liman Caddesi across the bridge to **Boztepe**, where a ruined watchtower on a piece of land jutting out into the harbour is still visible. Boztepe's heavy-duty walls, pierced by several gates, are still largely intact. The **inner citadel** is studded with towers and the Genoese coat of arms; of the two **Byzantine churches** that you can hunt down in the maze of alleys on Boztepe, the larger was converted to a mosque after the Ottoman conquest, while the ruined smaller one was in use until 1923.

Amasra also boasts a good **museum**, located at the western inland extremity of Küçük Liman (Tues–Sun 8.30am–5.30pm; 3TL). It contains locally unearthed archeological finds, including a beautiful selection of Roman sculptures discovered in Bartın. Pride of place is given to the torso of an emperor, with Romulus and Remus carved on his tunic, discovered in the citadel area in 1995.

Küçük Liman across the isthmus, near the watchtower, is the most likely spot for a quick **swim** (if the jellyfish aren't too numerous). Elsewhere, the water is seriously polluted, particularly at the deceptively attractive town beach fronting the eastern fishing port, and it's best to regard Amasra as a base for forays to better beaches further east.

Accommodation

Most of the town's **accommodation** is found overlooking the eastern beach on the Büyük Liman side of town. In summer, you can opt to **camp** on the harbour front, near the Bartın road, but be prepared for traffic noise.

Amastris Otel Kum Mah Cumhuriyet Meydanı ⊕0378/315 2465. At the southern end of Büyük Liman, the town's most opulent option with luxury doubles and bungalows, buffet breakfast and an enormous swimming pool. ⑥

Emek Pansiyon Topyanı Sok ⊕0378/315 3548. Built into the city walls above Büyük Liman, with clean sheets, hot water and a spectacular cliff-top view. ②

Hotel Türkili Özdemirhan Sok 6 ⊕0378/315 3750, ⓦwww.turkili.com.tr. Just to the northeast of the main square modern with a/c comfort but no views. ④

Otel Timur Çekiciler Cad 53 ⊕378/315 2589, ⓦwww.timurotel.com. One block back from the seafront; deservedly popular on account of its comfortable – mostly pink – rooms and professional management. ④

Eating and drinking

In addition to the listings below, the bridge to Boztepe houses a picturesque, unnamed café on its southwest corner – a perfect place for a break with a cool drink and sea views while sightseeing. After dark the town takes to the streets along both harbour fronts.

Canlı Balık Restoran Küçük Liman 8 ⊕0378/315 2606. Also known as *Mustafa Amca'nin Lokantasi, Canlı*, this 60-year-old fish restaurant has terraces on the water overlooking the Black Sea. A plate of *ıstavrit* (Black Sea mackerel) and a beer will set you back 20TL.

Çeşmi Cihan Büyük Liman Cad 21 ⊕0378/315 1062. On the eastern beach, a three-storey affair at the harbour entrance with wraparound balconies

and commanding views (around 25TL for fish, salad and a beer).

Han Bar Küçük Liman Cad 17. Posters all around town point to this season's late-night bar of choice, with plenty of drinking, dancing and live music.

Karadeniz Aile Pide Salonu Eyiceoğlu Cad 25 ⊕0378/315 1543. Piping-hot *pide* (from 7TL) served up at shady tables just off the town's main drag. Deservedly popular.

The eastern Black Sea

The eastern coast of the Black Sea sees far more visitors than the western half, partly because there's more of interest here, partly because it's easier to get to. **Trabzon**, with its romantic associations and medieval monuments, is very much the main event and, with good air and bus services, it makes a logical introduction to the region. It's also the usual base for visits to **Sumela monastery**, the only place in this chapter that you could describe as being overwhelmed by tourists. Other forays inland, however, are just as rewarding – particularly the superlatively scenic **Hemşin valleys**, home to a welcoming, unusual people, and the northern gateway to the lofty Kaçkar Dağları, covered fully in Chapter 10.

Other than Trabzon, the coast itself between the Georgian frontier and Samsun offers little apart from fine scenery and increasingly restricted swimming opportunities – **Giresun** and **Ünye** being the most attractive and feasible bases for exploration. It's best appreciated with your own transport, but even without this you'll face few problems. The towns are close together, served by seemingly endless relays of dolmuşes, and as just about every journey is covered, you can safely ask to be set down at an isolated beach in the near certainty that another minibus will be along to pick you up when necessary.

East of Samsun: the coast to Trabzon

Just east of Samsun, the Black Sea coastal plain, watered by the **Yeşilırmak delta**, widens to its broadest extent. The area was once thought to be the land of the **Amazons**, a mythical tribe of men-hating women who cauterized their right breasts to facilitate spear-throwing and arrow-shooting, and who only coupled with men – their neighbours the Gagarians – during two months of the year, sending male babies to the Gagarians to rear. Nowadays the delta is home to rather more conventional Black Sea Muslims, who are welcoming enough to members of either sex.

The main highway, slightly elevated to avoid flooding, heads well inland thanks to a new series of tunnels, thereby avoiding the deathly slow coastal road. This section of Turkey's interior is one of the region's most fertile stretches.

Ünye and around

ÜNYE, the ancient Oinaion, is a small, friendly place just over 100km east of Samsun that makes for a thoroughly pleasant overnight stay. The town has a few grand buildings dating from Byzantine times and its eighteenth-century heyday as a regional port, including a former Byzantine church that now serves as a **hamam** (open 5am–midnight daily: women-only 11am–5pm Tues, Fri & Sat; men only all other times), on the main square, Cumhuriyet Meydanı. On the seafront is a leafy park, a pedalo hire station and a pier which was built with leisure in mind rather than commerce or fishing, a rarity in these climes. It's worth timing your visit for the burgeoning **Wednesday market**, where you'll see gold-toothed farm women selling hazelnuts (harvested in August) and unusual edible plants (described under the catch-all term of *salata*), alongside churns full of milk and cheese.

Ünye also profits from its status as a **beach resort**. You see the best strands approaching from the west, where the highway is lined by ranks of motels and *pansiyons* reminiscent of the Aegean or the Marmara regions. The best of these give onto aptly named **Uzunkum** (Long Sand) beach, though signs warn you not to bathe when the sea is rough, and there's no consistent lifeguard presence.

The only specific local sight is the medieval **fortress of Çaleoğlu**, just off the minor 850 road to Niksar and Tokat. Inland 5km from the coast, these hulking ruins are signposted as "Ünye Kalesi" to the left and lead another 2km all the way up to the base of a natural pinnacle crowned by the fortifications. Those arriving on a Niksar- or Tokat- bound minibus will probably have to hike this last stretch themselves, as only infrequent dolmuşes run all the way to the ruins. The Byzantine ramparts around the south-facing gateway have been restored, but the adjacent rock-cut tomb, of Roman or Pontic-kingdom vintage, suggests that one or the other originally fortified the site. Beyond the gate little remains intact, though you can follow a slippery, usually damp path almost to the summit. The final approach to the very top of the fort is for competent climbers only. Your reward close to the summit is the view south over an exceptionally lush valley, and north to the Ünye coast.

Practicalities

Ünye's minuscule **otogar** is at the eastern edge of town, by the road to Niksar; there's a separate stop for minibuses to Tokat. The tourist **office** consists of a locked room on the ground floor of the *kaymakamlık* (county administrative offices) building at the rear of central Cumhuriyet Meydanı. Wait around and an English-speaking member of staff should materialize, although the information they can dispense is sketchy at best.

For central **accommodation**, one of the best options is the *Hotel Grand Kuşçalı*, at Şehir Merkezi 42 (☏0452/324 5200; ⓦwww.hotelgrandkuscali.com ⑤), with modern en-suite bathrooms and an on-site hamam. For beachside accommodation, continue 2km further west to Uzunkum, where the three-star *Park Hotel* (☏0452/323 2738, ⓕ323 7032; ⑤) has well-equipped en-suite rooms with TVs, a bar and breakfast on the lawn garden. **Campers** should head for the well-equipped *Uzunkum Restaurant Plaj and Camping* (☏0452/323 2022; ❷), one of several campsites along the coast, sheltering in the pines west of the *Belediye Çamlık Motel*. The accommodation mentioned above all have **restaurants** of some sort, while in town, *Sofra* at Belediye Cad 25 is a cut above the vast array of eateries with grills, *mezes*, patisseries and some Western dishes in rather trendy surroundings.

Ordu

Called Kotorya by the ancients, **ORDU** is now an undistinguished city of 117,000, with just a few older houses scaling the green slopes of Boztepe to the west, above the recently restored nineteenth-century Greek Orthodox cathedral. The only other historic remnants are in the local **museum** in the Paşaoğlu Konağı (Mon–Sat 8am–noon, 1–5pm; 3TL), signposted off Hükümet Caddesi, past the main PTT. There are few really appealing or decent-value **hotels** in or around Ordu. The outstanding exception, just uphill from the Greek cathedral, is the *Karlıbel İkizevler Hotel* (☏0452/225 0081, ⓦwww.karlibelhotel.com.tr; ⑤), occupying two surviving old mansions. Both the smaller doubles and larger suites (sleeping three) offer wooden floors and good bathrooms with shower cubicles.

Giresun

The town of **GIRESUN**, founded in the second century BC by the Pontic king Pharnaces, is one of the most pleasant stops between Samsun and Trabzon. Its main square is backed up by Alparsan Caddesi with its host of banks and travel agencies. This road turns into Osmanağa Caddesi the eastern end of town, home to a strip of decent hotels including the *Otel Çarikçi* with its sea-view rooms and *objet-d'art* stuffed lobby at no. 6 (☏0454/216 1026; ❸). *Pide* and kebab houses abound, although pick of the lot is friendly *Yetimoğullari* on Eski Yagcilar Sokak, which boasts menus – a rarity in Giresun – detailing a range of soups, appetizers and meats cooked over hot coals. Buses run towards Samsun and Trabzon from along the main road every 15 to 30 minutes.

About 2km offshore lies **Giresun Adası**, the only major island in the Black Sea. In pre-Christian times it was called Aretias, and was sacred to the Amazons who dedicated a temple to the war god Ares on it. Jason and his Argonauts supposedly stopped here to offer sacrifice, but were attacked by vicious birds. The island is also associated with ancient fertility rites and still attracts women who wish to conceive during a festival each May. Travel agents in Giresun offer trips to the island.

East to Trabzon

Curled above a bay enclosed by two headlands 41km east of Giresun, **TİREBOLU**, home to a Greek Orthodox community until 1923, is an attractive spot. On the easterly promontory stands the intact **castle of St John**, built for a fourteenth-century Genoese garrison: your only chance to see the fort's interior is by visiting the nocturnal tea garden that operates on the lawn inside the castle – pleasant except for the blaring pop music. As well as Tırebolu's central *Belediye* **beach**, there's a much larger if more exposed sandy stretch to the east, plus more decent beaches towards Espıye, 12km west.

Tırebolu lies at the heart of the *fındık*- or **hazelnut-growing** area, which extends roughly from Samsun east to the Georgian frontier. During late July and August you'll see vast mats of them, still in their husks, raked out to dry. Impatient locals perversely insist on eating them slightly green, when the taste resembles that of acorns.

Trabzon

No other Turkish city except İstanbul has exercised such a hold on the Western imagination as **TRABZON** (ancient Trebizond). Travel writers from Marco Polo to Rose Macaulay have been enthralled by the fabulous image of this quasi-mythical metropolis, long synonymous with intrigue, luxury, exotic customs and fairy-tale architecture. Today the celebrated gilded roofs and cosmopolitan texture of Trebizond are long gone, replaced by the blunt reality of an initially disappointing Turkish provincial capital of over 400,000 people. But a little poke around the cobbled alleyways will unearth tangible evidence of its former splendour – not least the monastic church of **Aya Sofya**, home to some of the most outstanding Byzantine frescoes in Anatolia.

Some history

The city was founded during the eighth century BC by colonists from Sinope and Miletus attracted by its easily defendable high plateau or *trapeza* ("table" in ancient Greek) after which it was first named "Trapezus". Under the Romans and Byzantines the city continued to prosper but Trabzon's romantic allure is derived almost totally from a brief, though resplendent, golden age during the thirteenth and fourteenth centuries when it became the capital of the breakaway **Trapezuntine Empire** after the sacking of Constantinople. Its wealth grew as the main Silk Route was diverted through the town owing to Mongol raiders controlling territory further south.

Someone had to transport all the goods accumulated at Trebizond's docks and this turned out to be the **Genoese**, followed soon after by the Venetians as well. Each demanded and got the same maritime trading privileges from the Trapezuntine Empire as they did from the re-established empire at Constantinople. Western ideas and personalities arrived continually with the Latins' boats, making Trebizond an unexpected island of art and erudition in a sea of Turkish nomadism, and a cultural rival to the Italian Renaissance city-states of the same era.

Unfortunately, the empire's factional politicking was excessive even by the standards of the age. One civil war in 1341 completely destroyed the city and sent the empire into its final decline. It was Mehmet the Conqueror, in a campaign along the Black Sea shore, who finally put paid to the self-styled empire; in 1461 the last emperor, David, true to Trapezuntine form, negotiated a more or less bloodless surrender to the sultan.

In late Ottoman times the city's Christian element enjoyed a resurgence of both population and influence. The presence of a rich merchant class ushered in a spate of sumptuous civic and domestic building. But it was a mere echo of a distant past, soon ended by a decade of world war, the foundation of the Republic and the steady transference of trade from ship to rails.

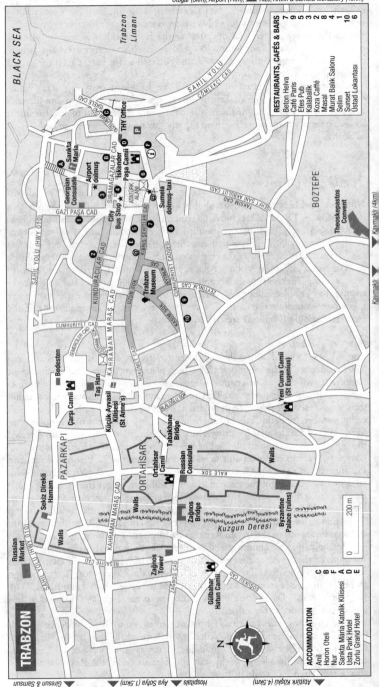

TRABZON

BLACK SEA

Trabzon Limanı

Otogar (3km), Airport (7km), ▲ Rize, Artvin & Sumela Monastery (43km)

BOZTEPE

Theoskepastos Convent

► Kavmaklı (4km)

► Kavmaklı

► Kavmaklı

RESTAURANTS, CAFÉS & BARS

Beton Helva	7
Café Paris	9
Efes Pub	5
Kalabalık	3
Koza Caffé	2
Masal	8
Murat Balık Salonu	4
Selim	1
Sunset	10
Üstad Lokantası	6

Sankta Maria

Georgian Consulate
Airport dolmuş
İskender Paşa Camii
THY Office
Sumela dolmuş-taxi

City Bus Stop
ATATÜRK ALANI

SAHIL YOLU (HWY OTO)
GAZİ PAŞA CAD
SIRAMAGAZALAR CAD
İSKELE CAD
KALE CAD
GAZALAR CAD
SAHIL YOLU
ÇÖMLEKÇİ CAD

KUNDURACILAR CAD
KIBRIS ŞEHİTLER CAD
UZUN SOK
CUMHURİYET CAD
KAHRAMAN MARAŞ CAD
SEMERCİLER SOK

Trabzon Museum

ZEYTİNLİK CAD
CUMHURİYET CADDESİ
KAZIK SOK
HÜKÜMET CAD

TAKSİM CAD
ŞEHİT SANİ AKBULUT CAD

Bedesten
Taş Han
Çarşı Camii
Küçük Ayvasıl Kilisesi (St Anne's)

Sekiz Direkli Hamam
Russian Market

PAZARKAPI

Ortahisar Camii
ORTAHİSAR
Russian Consulate

Tabakhane Bridge

Zağnos Bridge
Zağnos Tower

Byzantine Palace (ruins)

Walls
Walls
Walls

Yeni Cuma Camii (St Eugenius)

Kuzgun Deresi

Gülbahar Hatun Camii

KALE SOK
BİLALOĞLU SOK
KEMERKAYA SOK
SOĞUKSU CAD
ZAĞNOS CAD
REŞADİYE CAD
KAHRAMAN MARAŞ CAD

0   200 m

N

ACCOMMODATION

Anıl	C
Horon Oteli	B
Nur	F
Sankta Maria Katolik Kilisesi	A
Usta Park Hotel	D
Zorlu Grand Hotel	E

◄ Giresun & Samsun   ◄ Aya Sofya (1.5km)   ◄ Hospitals   ◄ Atatürk Köşkü (4.5km)

Today the outlook is still uncertain: both port and town have been overtaken by Samsun to the west although Trabzon now makes much from the transhipment of goods to the Caucasian republics and onwards to Russia.

Arrival and information

Trabzon's **airport** is 7km away at the eastern edge of town, connected by frequent dolmuşes to a town-centre stop near the *Horon Oteli*; confusingly these do not stop at the terminal building, but on the main road up the ramp to the right, heading westwards towards town. However, buses to Samsun and Rize are frequently parked outside the terminal to meet incoming flights. Trabzon's **otogar** is closer to town, 3km out, near the junction of Highway 010 with Route E97/885 (heading towards Sumela and Erzurum) and served by dolumşes marked "Meydanı". All long-distance coaches and most short-hop minibuses use this terminal, with some local lines heading west towards Görele leaving from a small terminal opposite the Russian bazaar. **Parking** is a trial anywhere in congested Trabzon – the closest legal car park to the centre is by the tourist office, next to the İskender Paşa Camii.

The **tourist office** (officially Mon–Fri 9am–5pm) has rather erratic opening hours and is located on a side street just east of Atatürk Alanı, opposite the İskender Paşa Camii. Visitors will find a broad range of moderately useful brochures. The excellent fold-up map of Trabzon – which contains the phone numbers of every travel agent, campsite and mountain hut in the region – is probably more helpful than the staff themselves.

Accommodation

Atatürk Alanı is the heart of the city, home to many of its hotels, nightclubs, restaurants and tourist sights, as well as being the main transport hub for attractions further afield such as Sumela; staying near here will help make Trabzon a surprisingly straightforward and hassle-free base. That said, if you have transport, you might consider more peaceful stopovers on the way to Sumela, at Uzungöl. In midsummer it's advisable to book ahead, as the more comfortable lodgings in Trabzon are often jam-packed with tour groups.

The traditional red-light district lies along İskele Caddesi and the streets immediately off it, right down to the port along Çömlekçi Caddesi. Although teaming in post-Soviet days just a handful of "pay-by-the-hour" hotels remain, and only the very naïve would confuse one with an honest lodging.

Anil Güzelhisar Cad 12 ☏ 0462/326 7282. Best of the cheapies with clean, plain rooms with TV and a/c. Attractive foyer and breakfast salon is a vision of chrome and steel. ❸

Horon Oteli Sıramağazalar Cad 125 ☏ 0462/326 6455, ⓦ www.otelhoron.com. Don't be scared off by the plush lobby and rack rates aimed at business customers – staff readily offer big reductions, even in summer. Rooms are furnished in style, with superior new bathrooms, a/c and double glazing. There's also a large if rather spartan rooftop sea-view bar/restaurant. ❼

Nur Cami Sok 15 ☏ 0462/323 0445, ⓕ 323 0447. Small, decently equipped and fresh from a recent makeover. Rooms boast a fridge, TV and double glazing, some have cracking sea views. Good-natured management, used to foreign guests. ❹

Sankta Maria Katolik Kilisesi Sümer Sok 28 ☏ 0462/321 2192. The most characterful and cheapest place to stay in Trabzon is this French Capuchin church and monastery, built around two courtyards just north of Atatürk Alanı. The welcoming voluntary staff offer spacious double rooms and hot showers down the hall to guests of any religion in return for a reasonable donation (say 20–40TL) at the end of a visit; kitchen, washing machine and garden are all available, free of charge.

Usta Park Hotel İskenderpaşa Mah 3 ☏ 0462/326 5700, ⓦ www.ustaparkhotel.com. Large, plush hotel with impressive plasma-screened lobby and 120 luxury en-suite rooms with all the trimmings you'd expect. Pricey (rooms start at €115), but discounts of up to 50 percent are easily negotiable. Free parking and wi-fi. ❼

Zorlu Grand Hotel Maraş Cad 9 ☏ 0462/326
8400, 🕸 www.zorlugrand.com. Rooms are plush,
with marble-clad bathrooms, but you're really
paying for the facilities – especially the grand,
opulent atrium, two restaurants, "English pub",
nightclub, gym and indoor pool. Rack rates (€150 a
room) are massively overpriced, but advance
booking/bargaining may produce discounts. ❼

The City

Most of Trabzon's sights are within walking distance of Atatürk Alanı, usually
called "Meydanı" or "Parkı". You'll need a dolmuş (here often a saloon car rather
than a minibus) to get to Aya Sofya, and a bus or taxi to reach the Kaymaklı
monastery behind Boztepe.

Around Atatürk Alanı and Uzun Sokak

An east-to-west walk along the seaward portion of town begins with the Genoese
bastion: a tea garden and small park on the west flank of the castle. This seems to
be Trabzon's sole acknowledgement of its seaside location, since – apart from the
busy Russian market on Sahil Yolu – the shoreline in general is quiet, with the city
introverted up on its plateau. The **Catholic church of Sankta Maria** (Tues–Sun
2–3pm), a few alleys west of the ramparts, is the last surviving reminder of the
Western powers' former pivotal role here.

Things brighten up northwest of Atatürk Alanı on pedestrianized **Kunduracılar
Caddesi** (Shoemakers' Street), the usual entry to Trabzon's **bazaar**. Ironically just
about everything *except* shoes can be found on this avenue, with a special emphasis
first on pharmacies and doctors, then gold jewellery. Once past Cumhuriyet
Caddesi, Kunduracılar veers right to become **Semerciler Caddesi** (Saddlers'
Street), devoted to a mix of factory-made clothing and the vibrantly coloured,
striped *keşans* (shawls) and *peştemals* (waistbands) that are standard issue for so many
Trabzon-province women. Copper merchants and tin-platers cluster on and just
off Alacahan Sokak, which leads downhill from Semerciler to the water.

Sooner or later you'll stumble upon the monumental heart of the bazaar, and the
Çarşı Camii, Trabzon's largest mosque, with a handsome exterior and late-
Ottoman interior. Just behind it, the sixteenth-century **Taş Han** is a rather
standard tradesmen's hall, still the location of retail outlets and (inside the
courtyard) tailors' workshops. The **Bedesten**, below the mosque, was built by the
Genoese in the fourteenth century, and revamped by the Ottomans. After decades
of dereliction, and use as a lumber mill, the *bedesten* has been restored as a
somewhat touristy crafts bazaar, with a small café-restaurant on the top floor.

Leave the bazaar going uphill, cross Kahraman Maraş Caddesi, and you can't miss
the ninth-century Byzantine **Küçük Ayvasil Kilisesi** just the other side. Also
known as St Anne's, the diminutive shrine is permanently locked – little matter as
its frescoes have been obliterated since 1923. A stroll along Uzun Sokak, lying to
the southeast and dotted with imposing *belle époque* mansions, may be more satisfying. There's no real concentration of old houses in Trabzon; the appeal of
leisurely strolling lies partly in the unexpected confrontation with a creaking
masterpiece.

One of the best examples of this is the Italian-designed Kostaki Theophylaktos
Konağı, just south of Uzun Sokak on Zeytinlik Caddesi, now housing the
Trabzon Museum (Trabzon Müzesi; Tues–Sun 9.30am–noon & 1–5pm; 3TL).
The ground-floor and first-floor rooms, with their parquet floors, painted ceilings,
fancy drapes and plush armchairs give a wonderful idea of life amongst the *belle
époque* Ottoman bourgeoisie with displays of glitzy furniture, silverware and
antiques. The basement is devoted to the archeological collection, where pride of
place is given to a complete but slightly crushed bronze, life-sized statue of
Hermes found during excavations in 1997.

The old town

Following Uzun Sokak further west soon brings you to the **Tabakhane Deresi** (Tannery Ravine) and the namesake bridge spanning the gorge. On the other side sprawls the fortified old town on its "table", but before crossing you should make a detour left along the east bank of the ravine, being careful to bear onto **Bilaloğlu Sokak** (there is a street sign but it's hard to spot so ask a local if you get lost). After about 350m you'll come to the thirteenth-century **Yeni Cuma Camii**, formerly the church of St Eugenius, patron saint of Trabzon. Mehmet the Conqueror offered up his first Friday prayers here after capturing Trabzon in 1461, and immediately reconsecrated the church and added its minaret.

Crossing the Tabakhane bridge you arrive in the **Ortahisar** (Middle Castle) district of the old town. The walls are in variable condition but at their crenellated and vine-shrouded best give some idea of Trabzon's skyline in its heyday. The highlight here is the former church of Panayia Khrysokefalos, now the **Ortahisar Camii** (usually open) and also referred to as the Fatih Camii. As in the case of the Yeni Cuma Camii, there was almost certainly a church on this site from the third century, but the present building dates mostly from the thirteenth, with massive renovation after a fire during the 1341 civil war. This was the main cathedral of the Trapezuntine Empire, and most royal weddings, funerals and coronations took place here. Some fine Byzantine *opus sectile* stonework remains visible in the apse although it's the volume of the soaring basilica, with its massive interior columns, that impresses.

Heading west the **Zağnos bridge**, built by a Greek convert who was one of Mehmet the Conqueror's chief generals, leaves Ortahisar over the Kuzgun ravine where dilapidated Greek mansions are steadily losing ground to contemporary tenements. Down below the municipality has laid out a park and amphitheatre. On the far side, the **Zağnos tower**, the southernmost dungeon in the outer boundary walls, sports the ornate, late-Ottoman, Abdullah Paşa fountain at its base.

Across a busy boulevard and a swathe of parkland from the tower squats the **Gülbahar Hatun Camii**, the most important Ottoman monument in Trabzon. This alluring scene includes a huddle of teahouses and a lake filled with swans, although the picture is often sullied by Trabzon's raw climate. From just in front of the Gülbahar Hatun complex, Soğuksu Caddesi heads up toward the finest surviving example of the palatial bourgeois follies that sprouted locally at the end of the nineteenth century.

The Atatürk Köşkü

Set in immaculately maintained gardens, the **Atatürk Köşkü**, or Atatürk Villa (daily 8am–5pm; 3TL), began life in 1903 as the property of the Greek banker Karayannidhis, who was obliged to abandon it two decades later. Atatürk stayed here on the first of three occasions in 1924, and the city formally presented it to him a year before his death. As another example of patrician Black Sea architecture, the mansion is more compelling than the contents – which include a bevy of photos of Atatürk, plus a map bearing his strategic scribbles during the Kurdish Dersim revolt of 1937.

Both dolmuşes to the "Köşk" stop and red-and-white city buses marked "Park-Köşk" serve the villa – which is 6.5km southwest of Atatürk Alanı. You can also catch the bus as it passes Gülbahar Hatun.

Aya Sofya

Overlooking the Black Sea west of the city, the monastery **church of Aya Sofya** (Haghia Sophia) is one of the most romantic set of Byzantine remains in Turkey. It seems certain that there was a pagan temple here, and then an early Byzantine chapel, long before Manuel I Komnenos commissioned the present structure

▲ Frescoes at Aya Sofya

between 1238 and 1263. The ground plan and overall conception were revolutionary at the time, successfully assimilating most of the architectural trends, Christian and Muslim, prevalent in contemporary Anatolia. Converted to a mosque after 1461, Aya Sofya subsequently endured some even leaner and more ignominious times as an ammunition store and then as a hospital.

From Atatürk Alanı numerous **dolmuşes** labelled "BLK Sigorta/Aya Sofya" cover most of the 3km to the monument, dropping you 300m south of Aya Sofya, with the way onwards fairly well signed.

The site

The **church** (April–Oct daily 9am–6pm; Nov–Feb Tues–Sun 8am–4pm; March Tues–Sun 8am–5pm; 3TL) is laid out along a greatly modified cross-in-square scheme, with a dome supported by four columns and three apses at the east end of the triple nave. Before rushing inside to view the famous frescoes, take a moment to study the finely sculpted, albeit weatherworn, **frieze** illustrating *Adam and Eve in the Garden of Eden*, which surrounds the south portal, the only one of the three not tampered with by the Ottomans when they reconsecrated the church.

In their fluidity, warmth and expressiveness, Aya Sofya's original **frescoes** represented a drastic break with the rigidity of prior painting, and compare well with the best work of their century, and the next, in Serbia and Macedonia as well as in Constantinople itself. Of the frescoes in the central **apse** a serene *Ascension* hovers over *The Virgin Enthroned* between the two Archangels; on the north wall of the same apse appears *The Miraculous Draught of Fishes*. The southeast apse is thought to have once been the location of Manuel I's tomb. The Pantocrator in the **dome** was unhappily beyond repair, but a host of angels swirls around him, just above the Apostles.

The **narthex**, whose ceiling is divided into three sections by stone ribs, is almost wholly devoted to scenes from the life of Christ. The central zone exploits its complicated quadruple vaulting by depicting each of the Tetramorphs, symbols of the Evangelists, accompanied by seraphim. Alongside, such miraculous episodes as *The Wedding at Cana*, a decidedly adolescent *Child Jesus Teaching in the Temple*, *Healing the Blind Man at Siloam* and *Healing the Canaanite's Daughter* (complete with vomited demon) fill the south vault, while *Feeding the Five Thousand* and *Calming* *the Storm on the Lake of Galilee* grace the north vault. The north portico is taken up mostly by Old Testament scenes, including *The Sufferings of Job* and *Jacob's Dream*. Between 1957 and 1964, technicians restored dozens of these frescoes to their former glory. Well lit and accurately labelled in English, these are compulsory viewing even if you've only a passing interest in religious art.

Just north of the church an ensemble of sunken masonry was once the baptismal font; the square belfry to the west is a 1443 afterthought, indicative of the strong Italianate flavour of the waning empire. If the tower is open – a rare event – you'll find that the frescoes within are not nearly of the same quality as those in the church proper.

In the garden opposite the ticket office is a small **museum** consisting of a village house built and furnished in typical Black Sea style, and a 1920s-vintage *serender* or grain crib on stilts, with wooden discs at the top of the stilts, to prevent mice attacking the stored grain. The setting of the adjacent café, covered in wisteria and offering tea and snacks, is bucolic.

Boztepe

Boztepe, the hill dominating Trabzon to the southeast, has always been held in religious esteem. In the past it was the site of the amalgamated cults of the Persian sun god Mithra and the Hellenic deity Apollo, an ironic dedication when you consider how little unfiltered sun this coast receives. This reverence persisted into Christian times, when the hill was studded with churches and monasteries. Two of the latter still stand – after a fashion – and one at least is well worth the effort to visit.

Theoskepastos Convent

The ruined former **Convent of the Panayia Theoskepastos** or "God-protected Virgin" (in Turkish, Kızlar Manastırı or "girl's monastery") backs into the rocky slope 1.5km from Atatürk Alanı, reached by following Taksim Caddesi south and then bearing left when you see the shell of the building on the hillside. Dolmuşes marked "Boztepe" leave from Atatürk Alanı.

Though founded in the fourteenth century, and in continuous use by the Greek Orthodox Church until 1923, few internal frescoes or other artistic details remain, and in any case the place has been securely locked since the early 1990s while the Ministry of Culture deliberates how or whether to restore it. Just above the convent an appealing **picnic park**, a **tea garden** and restaurant share the view over the city with a military base and the locked **mosque and tomb of Ahi Evren Dede**, a target of pilgrimage for Trabzon's faithful.

Kaymaklı monastery

The former Armenian **Kaymaklı monastery**, reached by a 900m side track 3.5km beyond the turn-off for Theoskepastos, is in an altogether different league, containing as it does the finest frescoes in the region after those of Aya Sofya and Sumela. It's too far to walk, so take a taxi, or a bus marked "Çukurçayır" from Atatürk Alanı. The bus will drop you at the Mısırlı Cami, out by the local prison on the flat summit of Boztepe; 100m past the mosque, turn left (east) and down onto an unsigned but paved lane. Bear right at a fork 250m along, then keep right again a similar distance along, soon reaching concrete's end next to an ugly green and cream house with a garage underneath. When the ground is dry you can continue by vehicle another 150m along a dirt track to the proper "car park" in the centre of a farmyard.

What's left of Kaymaklı studs a green plateau overlooking the highway to Erzurum; today the monastery grounds are a farm, and the resident family is used to showing visitors around. Much of the place dates from the mid-fifteenth century, though more recent tenants have wedged a concrete dwelling into the former cells on the east edge of the courtyard. The **west wall** bears a Bosch-like conception of *The Last Judgement*, complete with a *Four-Headed Cerberus*, *The Whore of Babylon Riding the Beast of the Apocalypse* and *The River of Fire* draining into Hell. In the badly damaged **apse**, you can still make out a *Dormition* and *The Entry of Christ into Jerusalem*, with the Saviour riding a horse rather than an ass.

Eating

There are plenty of places to eat in central Trabzon, most are good value but few of them are really outstanding. Apart from the establishments listed, booze in this conservative town is hard to come by, as is – surprisingly for a port – fish. The almost uninterrupted line of **restaurants** on the north side of Atatürk Alanı gets most of the tourist custom, although scores more lie along Uzun Sokak and around. Most restaurants offer at least some **desserts** – the confectioners of Hemşin (see box, p.569) aren't far away – but some exclusively sweet-dedicated venues are worth seeking out.

Restaurants

Kalabalık Siramanğazalar Cad 14. Slightly trendy – for Trabzon – with fine fish *meze*s including pickled sea bass and *hamsi* (anchovy), with grilled and fried local seafood for mains.

Koza Caffé Kunduracılar Cad, Sanat Sok 1. First-floor café serving a surprising array of coffees and teas from around the globe. Despite the ersatz castle interior it's a warm and welcoming place to while away a few hours.

Murat Balık Salonu Atatürk Meyd, north side. Tiny hole-in-the-wall joint doing inexpensive grilled *hamsi* in winter, otherwise *mezgit* or *uskumru* (mackerel), accompanied by salad and soft drinks. Closes 9.30pm.

Üstad Lokantası Atatürk Alanı 18. Always packed with a solid selection of the usual Turkish suspects – meatballs, kebab, bean stew – from 2TL per dish.

Sweets and desserts

Beton Helva Uzun Sok. Huge blocks of *helva* on display – thus the somewhat off-putting name, "Concrete Helva" – but also good *dondurma* (ice cream) and *sıra* (half-fermented grape must), in wonderfully retro-1950s surroundings, next to Seyitoğlu Lahmacun.

Selim Gazipaşa Cad 11/A. A wide range of *dondurma*, milk-based sweets, pastry and *boza* (a millet-based drink), served in airy surroundings; open from 7am until nearly midnight.

Drinking and entertainment

Trabzon has a few buzzing **bars** backed up by something of a café culture. The *birahane*s on and off İskele Caddesi contain a handful of late-night pick-up joints for prostitutes and their clients. The Saray Sineması, about 400m west of Atatürk Alanı, then south of Uzun Sokak, on Kasımoğlu Çıkmazı, shows slightly dated Hollywood **films**, often with the original soundtrack.

Café Paris Cumhuriyet Cad 151. Red wine, vodka tonics and an intelligent 30-somethings crowd. Live acoustic sets at weekend.

Efes Pub Maraş Cad 5. A surprisingly accurate, not to mention pleasant, rendition of an English pub where music takes a backseat to conversation. The right-hand room is for couples and women only.

Masai Cumhuriyet Cad 89. Artsy first-floor hangout serving Trabzon's best coffee. Boasts board games from Monopoly to Scrabble and a *National Geographic* back catalogue.

Sunset Cumhuriyet Cad 145. Rooftop bar hideaway pumping out Black Sea folk tunes – live at the weekend – to a very local crowd. Soft drinks only.

Listings

Airlines Ticketing agencies selling tickets for all carriers are dotted around Atatürk Alanı: or try Onur Air, Gazipaş Cad 18 ☎0462/325 6292; Pegasus, Atatürk Alanı ☎0462/3257 713;

THY, in front of the *Usta Park Hotel* ☎0462/325 7536.

Airport There are frequent dolmuşes marked "Havalimanı" from a small plaza one block north of

At present, all non-Turkish travellers need to buy a **visa for Russia** in order to go from Turkey into Russia. The local consulate (see "Listings" below) is unlikely to prove too helpful in this matter, and it is easier to obtain a visa in your home country than in either İstanbul or Ankara. Citizens of Australia and New Zealand still need a visa from the Georgian consulate to visit Georgia (see "Listings" above) although most other nationals, including those from the EU, US and Switzerland, may enter visa free.

In the wake of severe economic conditions affecting all countries concerned, **trans-Black Sea services** to Russia (Sochi) have been drastically reduced; contact one of the ferry agencies in Trabzon (see "Listings" below) for the most current information. Azerbaijan Airlines offers regular **flights to Baku** in Azerbaijan.

Overland **bus services** have been less affected with several services a day running over the border to Batumi. The Georgian frontier is crossed either at Sarp, or (for onward connections to Armenia and Azerbaijan) Posof which only opened in 2001 for non-local traffic. It's easy enough to do the trip to Georgia in smaller chunks, taking a dolmuş or taxi from Sarp to the border and then arranging local transport on to Batumi on the Georgian side, from where several daily buses run to Armenia.

Atatürk Alanı, just off Sıramağazalar Cad near the Horon Oteli.

Car rental In summer, when Trabzon swarms with locals returned from northern Europe, an advance rental booking is advisable. Companies with both in-town offices and airport booths include: Avis, Gazipaşa Cad 20/A ℡0462/322 3740; Cande, Atatürk Alanı, southwest corner ℡0462/321 6200; and De Car/Thrifty, airport ℡0462/323 0927.

Consulates Georgia, Ortahisar Mah Pertev Paşa Sok 10 ℡0462/323 1343 or 326 2226; Russia, opposite Ortahisar Camii, Refik Cesur Cad 6 ℡0462/326 2600.

Ferries Ticketing agencies dot İskele Cad. including Karden Tur (℡0462/321 3479). The offices for the Princess Victoria Trabzon–Sochi line (℡0462/326 6674) and the Asya Ro-Ro line (℡0462/321 6035) are also here; see "Travel details" at the end of the chapter for schedules and ticket prices to Russia.

Hamams Much the best on offer is Sekiz Direkli Hamam, Pazarkapı 8, Direkli Hamam Sok 1 (daily 7am–11pm; women-only on Wed, men-only all other days; 9TL).

Hospitals The Özel Karadeniz (private), Reşadiye Cad (℡0462/229 7070), and SSK (Social Security), Trabzonspr Bul (℡0462/230 2285), are both out near Aya Sofya. However the biggest hospital in the region is the KTÜ's medical-school teaching hospital, or Tip Fakültesi Hastanesi (℡0462/325 3011 or 377 5000) – buses and dolmuşes marked "KTÜ" run from the centre.

Police Tourism Police, at the harbour customs-zone gate, and on the east side of Atatürk Alanı (daily 9am–7pm; ℡0462/326 3077).

Post office PTT at Posthane Sok, corner of Kahraman Maraş Cad (post and exchange daily 8am–7pm); also a booth at southeast corner of Atatürk Alanı. Payphones and card sales on the south side of Atatürk Alanı.

Travel agencies The most reputable agency in town is Eyce Tours, run by Volkan Kantarci and his team, İskenderpaşa Cad 36, first floor (℡0462/326 5177). Both offer day tours to Sumela, Ayder and assorted caves in the mountains, plus air tickets, car hire and independent drivers.

The monastery of Sumela

At the beginning of the Byzantine era a large number of monasteries sprang up in the mountains behind Trabzon. The most important and prestigious – and today the best preserved – was **Sumela** (increasingly signposted as Sümela), clinging to a cliff-face nearly a thousand feet above the Altındere valley, the sort of setting that has always appealed to Greek Orthodox monasticism. Despite the habitual crowds, often rainy or misty weather – and rather battered condition of the frescoes – Sumela still rates as one of the mandatory excursions along the Black Sea.

The name *Sumela* is a Pontic Greek shortening and corruption of *Panayia tou Melas* or "Virgin of the Black (Rock)". She has been venerated on this site since at least the year 385 AD, when the Athenian monk Barnabas, acting on a revelation from the Mother of God, discovered an **icon** here said to have been painted by St Luke. He and his nephew Sophronios found the holy relic on a site that matched the one in his vision – a cave on a narrow ledge part of the way up the nearly sheer palisade – and installed the icon in a shrine inside.

A **monastery** supposedly grew around the image as early as the sixth century, but most of what's visible today dates from the thirteenth and fourteenth centuries. Over the centuries the icon was held responsible for numerous miracles, and the institution housing it shared its reputation, prompting even Turkish sultans to make pilgrimages and leave offerings.

Sumela was hastily evacuated in 1923 along with all other Greek Orthodox foundations in the Pontus; six years later it was gutted by fire, possibly started by careless squatters. In 1931 one of the monks returned secretly and exhumed a number of treasures, including the revered icon of the Virgin, now housed in the new monastery of Sumela, in northern Greece. Since 1996, the monastery has been undergoing **restoration**. The work done thus far is in reasonable taste, even extending to proper ceramic canal-tiles for the roof. Most important of all, the surviving frescoes have been consolidated and cleaned.

Arrival and information

Without your own transport, you have two ways of making the hour-long journey to Sumela from Trabzon: **taxis** from a rank signposted "Sumela Manastırı'na" on the south side of Atatürk Alanı, which charge 120TL return for a carload of four people; or an **organized tour**, run at 10am daily by the Eyce travel agency (see "Listings", p.565) bookable in person or through your hotel and costing 25TL per person for a return minibus seat (you pay the admission fee). However you arrive, aim to spend at least three hours at the site, allowing for a good look around and a spot of lunch by the rapids which flow through the valley below.

Driving, it's 43km in all from the coastal junction of highways 010 and E97/885, 3.5km east of central Trabzon, to the main car park lot for Sumela; after 26km you turn off Highway E97/885 at Maçka to follow the Altındere valley upstream. This side road provides a stunning approach to the monastery; as you climb, the habitual cloud ceiling of these parts drifts down from the equally dense fir forest to meet you. In exceptional circumstances you may catch an advance glimpse of the monastery's faded, whitewashed flank soaring above the trees at the top of the valley, at an altitude of 1200m. A few kilometres before you reach the site is a toll booth signifying the start of the national park (admission 8TL per private car).

The monastery proper is linked to the valley bottom where the accommodation and eating options are located by a commonly used, often slippery woodland **trail** (30min). At the time of writing a paved road was due to open, allowing buses and cars to park a few hundred metres away from the monastery itself.

Accommodation

The road up to Sumela is littered with trout farms and campsites, including the rustic *Verizana* and *Sumelas* campsite-cum-restaurants, 2km and 7km past Maçka respectively.

A hundred metres below the monastery where the buses arrive is a shop, snack bar and picnic area, all scattered around the teaming rapids that mark the valley floor. The only accommodation option belongs to *Hotel Büyük Sümela* (☎0462/512 3540; ❻) who rent seven Swiss-style chalets with cosy interiors and a wood-burning stove, a necessity almost year-round at these altitudes. Service in the restaurant over the bridge can be abrupt but the fish, *meze* and meat dishes are both reasonable and tasty, perhaps surprisingly so given the captive clientele. Alcohol is available.

The site

However you arrive, all paths converge at the **ticket booth** by the monastery gate (daily: May–Sept 9am–6pm; Oct–April 9am–5pm; 8TL).

Sumela actually occupies a far smaller patch of level ground than its five-storeyed facade would suggest. A climb up the original entry stairs, and an equal drop on the far side of the gate, deposits you in the central courtyard, with the monks' cells and guest hostel on your right overlooking the brink, and the chapel and cave sanctuary to the left. Reconstruction of most of the former living areas is complete, though there are still a number of off-limits areas and unsightly scaffolding. The degree of vandalism and decay is appalling: sophisticated art thieves were caught levering away large slabs of the famous frescoes in 1983, and any within arm's reach have been obliterated by graffiti-scrawlers – much of the graffiti is pre-1923 vintage Greek, with some even as old as 1875, but Turkish, European and North American visitors have also left their marks.

The main grotto-shrine is closed off on the courtyard side by a wall, from which protrudes the apse of a smaller chapel. A myriad of **frescoes** in varying styles cover every surface, the earliest and best ones dating from the fourteenth or fifteenth century, with progressively less worthwhile additions and retouchings done in 1710, 1740 and 1860. The highest cave paintings are in good condition – ceilings being harder to vandalize – though the irregular surface makes for some odd departures from Orthodox iconographic conventions. The Pantocrator, the Mother of God and various apostles seem to float overhead in space; on the south (left) wall is an archangel and various scenes from the Virgin's life (culminating in *The Virgin Enthroned*), while *Jonah in the Whale* can be seen at the top right.

Outside on the divider wall, most of the scenes from the life of Christ are hopelessly scarred. Among the more distinct is a fine *Transfiguration* about ten feet up on the right; just above sits *Christ in Glory*, with two versions of the *Ascension* nearby. At the top left is *Christ Redeeming Adam and Eve*. On the apse of the tiny chapel the *Raising of Lazarus* is the most intact image. Next to it is the *Entry into Jerusalem*, with the *Deposition from the Cross* just right of this. On the natural rock face north of all this appears the *Communion of Saints in Paradise*. When craning your neck to ogle the surviving art gets too tiring, there is (mist permitting) always the spectacular view over the valley – and the process of imagining what monastic life, or a stay in the wayfarers' quarters, must have been like here in Sumela's prime.

Inland: the foothills from Trabzon to Rize

While Sumela is a hard act to follow, there are a number of other possible destinations in the hills southeast of Trabzon. The valleys leading to and past them are also useful alternative routes toward Erzurum, avoiding some or all of the often congested E97/885 Highway.

Of, Çaykara and around

The coastal starting point for excursions up the valley of the Solaklı Çayı is the unprepossessing **OF** (pronounced "oaf", the ancient Ophis). Both Of and **ÇAYKARA**, around 7km south, the unexciting main town of the lower valley, are renowned for their devoutness, with the highest ratio of *kuran kursu*s (Koran schools for children) per capita in the country, and phalanxes of bearded and skull-capped *hoca*s and *hacı*s striding about in the shadow of huge, ever-multiplying mosques. It should come as no surprise, then, that you haven't a prayer of anything stronger than a fruit juice between Of and Uzungöl.

Sixteen kilometres inland stands the covered wooden bridge of **Hapsiyaş** (Kiremitli), photogenic despite its prosaic setting. The present structure dates from only 1935, and was badly damaged to the point of collapse by floods in 1998, but it seems likely there's been a span here for several centuries. Common are the cross-river *teleferikler*, rope bridges that whizz shopping, sheep and the occasional person across the raging river to the other side.

Uzungöl Lake

From Çaykara, it's 45km on a paved road up to **Uzungöl** (Long Lake), the main attraction of this area. After Sumela, it's the second most popular excursion out of Trabzon, and could be Switzerland were it not for the mosques. Frequent dolmuşes make the hour and a half trip up from Of, and tours (about 20TL a head, transport only) are laid on daily according to demand by Trabzon travel agencies (see p.565). The scenic lake, at just under 1100m, has a bazaar district around its outlet and is best seen by hiring a mountain bike from one of the teashops. Parascending from the surrounding hills is also popular.

Uzungöl makes an ideal base for rambles southeast up to the nearby peaks of **Ziyaret** (3111m) and **Halizden** (3376m), with a chain of glacier lakes at the base of the latter. It's a very long day's hike there and back – though you can go part-way by car to save time – so take a tent and food for two days if at all possible.

Practicalities

In line with its mushrooming popularity as a destination, **accommodation** here is plentiful, with fifteen or so licensed hotels, all similar in both style and value, plus a handful of *pansiyon*s; it's a popular overnight stop for foreign travellers en route to or from Trabzon airport. The pretty *İnan Kardeşler Tesisleri* (T0462/656 6260, Wwww.inankardeslerotel.com; ❺), at the high south end of the lake is the oldest hotel in town, a combination trout farm/restaurant/bungalow complex whose menu consists of trout, salad and pudding, but no alcohol. Opposite, the *Ensar Motel* (T0462/656 6321, Wwww.ensarotel.com; ❹) has a welcoming feel, friendly management and good traditional cuisine, with wooden cabins and en-suite doubles arranged around small gurgling fountains.

The İkizdere Valley

The next major valley east of Uzungöl, the **İkizdere Valley**, holds no special attraction to stop for, but the scenery along the way is memorable and the road eventually winds up to the highest drivable pass in the Pontic ranges – one of the three loftiest in all Turkey. The place is mostly worth knowing about as an alternative route to Erzurum, or as an approach to the Kaçkar range (see Chapter 10).

İKİZDERE, with frequent minibuses from Rize, is the main town; just before the town, the *Hancı'nın yeri* **restaurant** has tables set next to the raging river and serves *köfte* cooked over hazelnut shells. İkizdere is also the transfer point for the 27km trip up the Yetimhoca valley to Başköy, the westernmost trailhead for the Kaçkar Dağları. Watch out though: there are at least three other Başköys or Başyaylas in a 30km radius, so don't let yourself or your driver get confused. A better alternative, if possible, is to arrange transfer to Saler, the highest village in the valley with road access.

Beyond İkizdere, the main road soon finds itself between jagged peaks and the *yayla*s gathered at the 2640-metre **Ovitdağı pass** (only negotiable May–Oct), marking the edge of Rize province and far more alpine than the overrated Zigana Pass to the west. On the way up you'll pass various grill and trout **restaurants**, and the large, incongruously placed concrete-block **hotel** in the middle of nowhere, the *Genesis* (℡0462/476 8090; ❸).

The Hemşin valleys

The most scenic and interesting of the foothill regions east of Trabzon are the valleys of the **Fırtına Çayı** and its tributaries, which tumble off the steepest slopes of the Pontic ranges, here known as the Kaçkar Dağları. Between the mountains and the sea lie a few hundred square kilometres of rugged, isolated territory known simply as **Hemşin**.

Çamlıhemşin

ÇAMLİHEMŞIN, 21km upstream from the mouth of the Fırtına Çayi, is still too low at 300m to give you a real feel for the Hemşin country, but offers a hint of what's to come. It's the last proper town before the mountains, utilitarian and busy, with a constant chaos of minibuses (mid-June to mid-Sept hourly from Pazar until 7pm) and shoppers clogging its single high street.

There's a **bank** with an ATM, a **PTT**, stores for last-minute hiking supplies, and a recommended **travel agency** at no. 47 on the main street, Türkü Tourism (℡0464/651 7230 or 651/7787, Ⓦwww.turkutour.com). Proprietor Mehmet Demirci is among the most genial and knowledgeable of local mountain guides, and offers a variety of five- to seven-day treks (early June to late Oct), starting at €300 per person, either tent-based (camping equipment provided), farmhouse-based or *pansiyon*-based. To either side of Çamlıhemşin, along both the main stream and the tributary flowing down from Ayder, you begin to see some of the two dozen or so graceful **bridges** that are a regional speciality.

A short trek: Pokut and Amlakit

If your level of commitment isn't up to multi-day treks involving camping out in the high mountains, consider the track that heads southeast from Şenyuva, a typically dispersed community of occasionally impressive farmstead dwellings 6–8km above Çamlıhemşin. Currently the only **accommodation** here is at the charming *Fırtına Pansiyon* (℡0464/653 3111 or 0532/783 2708, Ⓦwww.firtinavadisi.com; ❷), opened in 2000 and housed in the former schoolhouse. As with all high Hemşin country accommodation, call to check they're open outside of July and August.

The route continues from Şenyuva via Sal to Pokut *yayla* and is only advisable during high summer as snow blocks the route for much of the year. **POKUT**, three hours' walk from Şenyuva, is fairly representative of the more substantial Black Sea *yayla*s, with handsome woodwork capped by mixed tin-and-timber roofs rising from stone foundations. For the first night's **lodging**, the wooden huts of *Poket Yaylasi* (℡0464/651 7530 or 530 228 6620; ❸ half-board) are a homely option.

The following day you hike east to **Hazindag** (Hazıntak), a handsomely clustered settlement just above the tree line, and then briefly follow a majestic river canyon on a corniche route south before veering up and southeast to the primitive rock-and-sod cottages of **Samistal**. From the ridge above Samistal, weather permitting, you'll have spectacular views of the main Kaçkar summit ridge. You then double back west to **AMLAKIT**, with its *Amlakit Pansiyon* (book through Türkü Tourism in Çamlıhemşin, see above; ❸), or drop in stiff zigzags from Samistal to Aşağı Kavron from where minibus services link to Ayder (see p.572).

If you stay in Amlakit, a final day of walking would see you use a direct trail north to Hazindag and thence back to Pokut and Sal (a steep path northeast through cloudforest direct to Ayder exists, but it's presently in bad condition). Alternatively, keener trekkers can carry on south from Amlakit for 45 minutes on a rough road to Palovit (2300m), and thence to Apevanak Yayla (2500m) en route to the true alpine zone. For details on the rest of the Kaçkar, refer to Chapter 10.

The upper Fırtına valley

Above Şenyuva, along the main branch of the Fırtına Çayı, the road steadily worsens while the scenery just as relentlessly becomes more spectacular. Below, the water roils in chasms and whirlpools that are irresistible to the lunatic fringe of the rubber-rafting fraternity – as well as the central government which, in the face of local opposition, plans to divert most of the river's flow into assorted hydroelectric projects. Some 12.5km from Çamlıhemşin, the single-towered castle of **Zilkale**, improbably sited by either the Byzantines or the Genoese to control a decidedly minor trade route, appears at a bend in the track. The tree-tufted ruin, more often than not garnished with wisps of mist, today dominates nothing more than one of the most evocative settings in the Pontus.

▲ Hemşinli women, Ayder

Çat and around

After another 16km of violent abuse to your vehicle's suspension you'll arrive at **ÇAT**, 1250m up. Despite the horrid road in, there is a fairly regular – at least daily – dolmuş service from Çamlıhemşin, but it's more comfortable to use your own transport, whether mountain bike or 4WD. This is another classic base for rambles in the western Kaçkar, though there's not much to the village beyond a few scattered buildings and a final, exquisite bridge leading upstream.

The most conspicuous building is a surprisingly good combination **hotel/ restaurant** (and general store/souvenir shop), the *Cancık* (☏0464/654 4120; ❹ half-board), with six clean wood-trim rooms upstairs, several bungalows and a simple trout and grilled meat restaurant. If the *Cancık* is full, your fallback is the concrete *Toşi Pension*, 1km downstream (☏0464/654 4002 or 0535/621 5215; ❹), again with a riverside terrace and restaurant, though the double, triple, quads and bungalows can get packed out by organized trek groups.

At Çat the upper reaches of the Fırtına divide. A road running parallel to the main fork heads 30km due south to Ortayayla or Başhemşin, passing Zilkale's sister fort of **Varoş** (Kale-i-Bala) at Kaleköy, where yet another side road winds up to an alternative trailhead for the western Kaçkar mountains at Kale Yayla. Don't try to walk any more of these tracks than you have to – between Kale Yayla and Çat, for example, you've a very boring three- to four-hour slog in either direction.

The other turning above Çat bears almost due east, still on a poor surface; minibuses ply the 7km up to **ELEVIT** (1800m), a surprisingly substantial place. This is as far as ordinary cars will prudently go. Only daily minibuses and 4WD vehicles continue east to Karunç, Tirovit and Palovit. Elevit, like its nearest neighbour Tirovit, an hour and a half's walk east, is a Laz *yayla*, an enclave of sorts in Hemşin territory. It's also high enough to be a good trek from your doorstep base, though the only **accommodation** is the exceedingly basic *Otel Kartal* (no phone, no sign – look for the eagle statue; ❸ half-board), and a slightly seedy independent **restaurant**, *Aruçoğlu/Naci'nin Yeri*.

For the lightly equipped, there are several possible day-hikes from Tirovit, most rewardingly the three-hour walk up to **Yıldızlı Göl** (Starry Lake) at the top of the vale opening to the south of Elevit. You won't appreciate the name unless you camp overnight there, for just after sunrise little scintillating points of light flash briefly – for perhaps twenty minutes – on the surface of the water. The properly outfitted can continue along a superb **three-day traverse** southwest across the western Kaçkar, taking in Başyayla, Çiçekliyayla, the 2800-metre-high lakes at the base of Tatos and Verçenik peaks – all potential campsites – and finishing at Başhemşin at the head of the Fırtına valley. If necessary you can "bail out" at Çiçekliyayla, which has a road leading out.

Ayder

The busiest, road above Çamlıhemşin ends after 17km at **AYDER**, the highest permanently inhabited settlement in the Hemşin valley system. (At Km13, all cars pay a toll of 8TL.) Ayder has long since given up the struggle to be a genuine village or *yayla* and now revels in its role as a mountain-ringed spa resort packed with river-terrace restaurants and charming wooden bungalows. It's also a showcase for Hemşinli culture (see box, p.569) with displays of ethnic pride during August featuring spontaneous outbreaks of *horon* (dancing) both on the central meadow and in many of the restaurants.

The surrounding scenery – a narrow, sharply inclined valley with waterfalls pouring off the sides – has always been the main attraction, but with roads being pushed ever higher, Ayder can no longer rate as a genuine trekking trailhead. Every walk necessitates a minibus transfer: the two notables are the day-jaunt to the Çengovit lakes above the Laz *yayla* of Yukarı Avusor, and the three lakes above Kavron.

Arrival and information

In season (mid-June to mid-Sept), hourly **minibuses** depart from Pazar (between 10am and 6pm) for the one-hour-plus trip to Ayder; you may have to change vehicles in Çamlıhemşin, and out of season you may have to stump up 60TL or so for a taxi beyond. Back down to the coast from Ayder, departures to Rize and Trabzon are much more frequent from Çamlıhemşin. You can descend from Ayder to pick up the single daily minibus going up the Fırtına valley toward Çat and Elevit without having to return all the way to Pazar, but you'll need to be in Çamlıhemşin by noon or so.

Ayder is divided into two *mahalles* or districts: **Birinci** (Lower) Ayder at about 1250m, and İkinci (Upper), better known as **Yukarı Ambarlık**, at about 1350m elevation. Birinci has the spas, **dolmuş stop**, a **PTT** booth – although there are no banking facilities, so get any money you need in Pazar or Çamlıhemşin – and most of the considerable high-season noise and congestion; Yukarı Ambarlık is loads calmer and has most (but not all) of the more desirable accommodation.

Accommodation
Most establishments are open April to October only, though a bare few trade all year round; showing up on an August weekend without a reservation is not recommended.

Kalegon Butik Otel Near the top of Yukarı Ambarlık ☎ 0464/657 2135, ⓦ www .ayderkalegon.com. Swiss-style wooden-panelled rooms complement a cosy communal area with open fire in winter and an outdoor summer dining terrace. The restaurant serves up a top-notch spread of trout, salads and lamb to guests and non-guests alike. ❺

🏃 **Kuşpuni** Downhill from *Koru* ☎ 0464/657 2052, ⓦ www.kuspuni.com. Ayder's cutest establishment, open all year, is popular with city professionals and expat Turks. Centrally heated rooms vary from doubles to family suites. The regional food – river trout, salads, *muhlama* and

home-made desserts – is abundant and deftly executed. ❼ half-board

🏃 **Haşimoğlu Otel** Birinci Ayder ☎ 0464/657 2037, ⓦ www.hasimoglu otel.com. Large, well-run, luxurious hotel with cosy communal areas with fireplaces. The wood-lined rooms come in all sizes and shapes. ❼ half-board.

Serender Pansiyon Near top of Yukarı Ambarlık ☎ 0464/657 2201, ⓦ www.serenderpansiyon.net. Decent wood-trim rooms (with wooden cubicle bathrooms) in varying formats: it's in a peaceful location, with lots of common sitting areas and a self-catering kitchen. ❺

The spas
Ayder boasts an old *kaplıcalar* or sulphurous modern **hot-spring complex** (separate sections for men and women; daily 7am–7pm; 7TL), a big crowd-puller for the town. It's fed by a communal *havuz* (pool) from which scalding water (close to 60°C) is piped into rectangular tiled pools. More expensive private family tub rooms are available (25TL) as well as safe-boxes for your valuables.

Eating and drinking
Most people arrange half-board with their *pansiyon*s and local **cuisine** tends to be repetitive, although that's no bad thing as it's based largely on trout, salad and *muhlama* (a fondue-like dish of cheese, butter and cornflour), the last scooped up with corn bread.

The best-placed **restaurant**, and one of the few licensed ones, is the *Ayder Sofrası* between Birinci and Yukarı Ambarlık, with outdoor seating overlooking the river. Highly recommended is *Ayde Çise* with its stews, sweets, grills and the odd traditional band.

The coast east of Trabzon

The coast **east of Trabzon** gets progressively more extreme as you approach the Georgian border – if the Black Sea coast as a whole is wet, here it's positively soggy. The mountains, shaggy with tea plants and hazelnut trees begin to drop directly into the ocean – imposing natural defences which have led to the development of distinct ethnic groups such as the Laz. Sadly, the coast route has remarkably little to offer travellers. The first decent, unpolluted beaches east of Trabzon are found between **Arakli** and **Sürmene**. The towns themselves are nothing to write home about. The same goes for the boatyards with their colourful, top-heavy *taka* fishing boats at **Çamburnu**, 3km east. A much-touted pay beach is tucked at the base of the cliff just beyond the port, but equally good or better free beaches line the road to Of.

Rize

A modern Turkish city of over 70,000 in a grand setting, **RIZE**'s name at least will be familiar to every traveller who's bought a souvenir box of "Rize Turist Çay" to brew back home. Of its ancient history as Rhizos nothing survives, and of its role as the easternmost outpost of the Trapezuntine Empire hardly more than a tiny, eighth-century castle. If you do pause it would be to visit the **Tea Institute** (Mon–Fri 7am–noon; ℡0464/213 0241), a combined botanical garden, tasting (9am–10pm) and sales outlet on a hill overlooking the town; follow the signs to the "Çay Araştırma Enstitüsü".

There are two main streets, Atatürk Caddesi (inland) and Cumhuriyet Caddesi which runs parallel to the sea; the town square, **Belediye Parkı**, lies between them. The PTT here has been smartened up with wooden trimmings, complementing the two nineteenth-century restored **wooden houses** and the archeological museum (daily 9am–noon, 1–4pm, 8TL) on the hill behind. East of the square lies Rize's major **tea garden**, which, not surprisingly, is the focus of the town's social whirl. Surrounding shops sell Rize tea in every conceivable packaging, plus the unlikely spin-off product of tea cologne.

Practicalities

The **otogar** is 800m to the west of town, with service buses bringing you into the centre. However, minibuses heading east and west also leave from the main highway, the shore road. There are several buses daily to Batumi and Tbilisi in Georgia. On the north side of the park, near the mosque, there's a helpful summer-only **tourist office** usually staffed by eager local English students (daily 9am–5pm; ℡0464/213 1716).

Most **hotels** stand on or near Atatürk Caddesi and Cumhuriyet Caddesi running east of Belediye Parkı. A few shady looking ones double as brothels, though a good exception is the *Otel Efes* at Atatürk Cad 402, 100m east of the square (℡0464/214 1111; ❸): it's a friendly wood-panelled place, bedecked with kilims. The two-star *Otel Milano*, at Cumhuriyet Cad 169 (℡0464/217 4612, ⓦwww .hotelmilanorize.com; ❸), is a vision of pink with clean bathrooms and comfortable, though faded, rooms with fridges and TVs. For the full works, head for the

Tea

East of Trabzon, thanks to a climate ideal for its cultivation, **tea** is king. The tightly trimmed bushes are planted everywhere between sea level and about 600m, to the exclusion of almost all other crops. Picking the tender leaves is considered women's work, and during the six warmer months of the year they can be seen humping enormous loads of leaves in back-strap baskets to the nearest consolidation station. The tea, nearly a million raw tonnes of it annually, is sent more or less immediately to the cutting, fermenting and drying plants whose stacks are recurring landmarks in the region.

Oddly, tea is a very recent introduction to the Black Sea, the pet project of one Asim Zihni Derin, who imported the first plants just before World War II to a region badly depressed in the wake of the departure of its substantial Christian population in 1923. Within a decade or so tea became the mainstay of the local economy, overseen by Çaykur, the state tea monopoly. Despite the emergence of private competitors since 1985, and the Chernobyl accident, which spread radiation over the 1986 crop, Çaykur is still a major player in the domestic market. Export, however, seems unlikely since supply can barely keep pace with domestic demand.

luxurious, four-star *Rize Dedeman* (℡0464/223 4444, ⓦwww.dedeman hotel.com; ❽) on Alipaşa Koyu, at the western outskirts of town which also serves as the local outlet for Decar/Thrifty **car rental**; it's pricey, though bartering can often bring the rack rate down.

For **food**, there are several simple but hearty *pide ve kebap salonları* along Cumhuriyet Caddesi. *Konak*, at Cumhuriyet Cad 97 midway between the *otogar* and Belediye Parkı has a leafy garden and roof terrace, ideal for a pre-bus *pide* or pizza. The *Müze Kafeteriya*, a restored Ottoman house behind the PTT, is a little more atmospheric and features regional dishes such as *muhlama* (similar to fondue). The centrally located *Merkez Bar*, Deniz Cad 26, is the best of the limited **drinking** options in town, with downstairs being the better of the two floors.

Hopa

HOPA, which used to be the end of the road until the nearby frontier was opened and the route to it was militarily declassified, is a grim industrial port, devoted to shipment of the copper mined slightly inland. The **otogar** is just on the east bank of the Sundura Çayı, which laps the west side of Hopa.

If you have to stay here – and this would only happen if you were en route to Georgia and arrived too late to get an onward connection – head for one of several reasonable, relatively *natasha*-free **hotels** within walking distance of the *otogar*, almost all of them on the coast road, Ortahopa Caddesi. Just on the far side of what passes for the central square and tiny adjacent park stands the helpful, clean

---

Lazland

Thirty to forty kilometres beyond Rize you pass the invisible former eastern limit of the Trapezuntine Empire and enter the territory of the **Laz**, the Black Sea's most celebrated minority group. Strictly speaking, the Laz are a Caucasian people speaking a language related to Georgian, 150,000 of whom inhabit Pazar, Ardeşen, Fındıklı, Arhavi and Hopa, plus certain inland enclaves. The men, with their aquiline features and often reddish hair, particularly stand out; they also distinguish themselves by an extroversion unusual even for the Black Sea and an extraordinary business acumen. A fair chunk of Turkey's shipping is owned and operated by Laz and the wealth so generated makes them relatively progressive in outlook; the women are out and about in Western garb from Fındıklı east, and the men, too, seem better dressed in the latest styles, though "progress" has also been translated into making the towns around here some of the ugliest on the Black Sea – which is saying a lot.

It seems most likely that the Laz are descendants of the ancient Colchians (from whom Jason supposedly stole the Golden Fleece). The Laz accepted Christianity in the sixth century and almost immediately got embroiled in a series of protracted wars with the Byzantines, whose governors had managed to offend them. No power managed fully to subdue them until the Ottomans induced conversion to Islam in the early sixteenth century. Like their neighbours the Hemşinli (see box, p.569), they don't lose too much sleep over their religious affiliation, though they are now well integrated into the national fabric.

Perhaps too well integrated – **Lazuri**, the spoken language, is under threat, as until recently no systematic transcription system existed. The Turkish authorities have strongly discouraged any attempts to study the language *in situ*. Having been declared persona non grata, German linguist Wolfgang Feurstein finally compiled the first Turkish–Lazuri dictionary, complete with a specially devised alphabet, in 1999.

one-star *Cihan* (℡0466/351 2333; ❺). Top billing, however, goes to the recently built *Sarp Hotel*, just out of town at Uzunyalı Atatürk Bul 69 (℡0466/361 3900, Ⓦwww.sarphotel.com; ❼), which has a sauna, restaurant, disco-bar and bargain-able rates.

On to the Georgian border

Ten cliff-hemmed, twisty kilometres northeast of Hopa, **KEMALPAŞA** is the next-to-last Turkish village on the Black Sea, with a huge pebble beach, still known by its pre-1923 name of **Makriyalı**, on the seaward side of the four-lane highway. Minibuses cover the 20km from Hopa to the **Turkish–Georgian frontier**, set by the Turkish and Soviet revolutionary governments in 1921 at the stream dividing the previously insignificant village of **SARP** (rather than more logically at the Çoruh river by Batumi). The crossing was virtually inactive between 1935 and 1988, a casualty of Stalinist, then Cold War, paranoia, but since the gates have opened, Turkish Sarp has become a busy 24-hour way-station. If you intend to do more than just ogle the colourful spectacle, bring your passport (see p.565 for visa requirements); minibuses to Batumi in Georgia leave early evenings from Sarp.

Travel details

Trains

Samsun to: Amasya (1 daily; 4hr 30min); Kayseri (4 weekly; 19hr); Sivas (1 daily; 12hr).

Buses and dolmuşes

Amasra to: Ankara (5 daily; 7hr); Bartın (every 30min; 25min); İstanbul (8 daily; 11hr); İzmir (2 daily; 25hr); Sinop (6 daily; 6hr).
Ayder to Pazar (hourly; 1hr); Rize (2 daily; 2hr).
Giresun to: Ordu (every 30min; 1hr); Tirebolu (every 30min; 45min); Trabzon (hourly; 2hr 15min).
Hopa to: Artvin (hourly 7am–5pm;. 1hr 30min); Rize (hourly; 1hr 15min).
Ordu to: Giresun (every 30min; 1hr); Samsun (hourly; 2hr 15min); Ünye (hourly; 1hr).
Rize to: Ankara (6 daily; 14hr); Ayder (2 daily; 2hr); Bursa (5 daily; 18hr); Erzurum via İspir (5 daily; 7hr); Hopa (hourly; 1hr 15min); İkizdere (hourly; 1hr); İstanbul (7 daily; 18hr); Samsun (every 30min; 8hr); Trabzon (every 30min; 1hr).
Samsun to: Afyon (4 daily; 10hr); Amasya (hourly; 2hr 30min); Ankara (hourly; 7hr); Artvin (4 daily; 10hr); Balıkesir (2 daily; 14hr); Erzurum (2 daily; 10hr); Giresun (10 daily; 3hr 30min); İstanbul (15 daily; 11hr); Rize (every 30min; 8hr); Sinop (every 30min; 3hr); Sivas (5 daily; 6hr 30min); Trabzon (hourly; 7hr); Van (2 daily; 18hr).
Sinop to: Ankara (5 daily; 9hr); İstanbul (5 daily; 11hr); Kastamonu (hourly; 2hr); Samsun (every 30min; 3hr).

Trabzon to: Ankara (10 daily; 12hr); Artvin (5 daily, may have to change at Hopa; 4hr); Bayburt (5 daily; 4hr 30min); Erzurum (6 daily; 6hr); Giresun (every 30min; 2hr 15min); Hopa (every 30min; 2hr 30min); İstanbul (12 daily; 17hr); İzmir (5 daily; 22hr); Of (every 30min; 45min); Rize (every 30min; 1hr); Samsun (hourly; 7hr).

International buses

Rize to: Batumi, Georgia (5 daily; 2hr); Tbilisi, Georgia (1 daily; 11hr).
Samsun to: Tbilisi, Georgia (1 daily; 16hr).
Trabzon to: Baku, Azerbaijan (1 daily via Georgia; 20hr); Batumi, Georgia (3 daily; 3hr); Posof, Georgian border (2 daily); Tbilisi, Georgia (1 daily; 12hr).

International ferries/catamarans

Trabzon to: Sochi, Russia (twice-weekly ferries; 14hr; €60 one way for a cabin berth).

Flights

Samsun to: İstanbul (6 daily; 1hr 20min); İzmir (1 daily; 1hr 40min).
Sinop to: İstanbul (1 daily; 1hr 10min).
Trabzon to: Adana (2 daily; 1hr 30min); Ankara (4 daily; 1hr 30min); İstanbul (9 daily; 1hr 50min); İzmir (2 daily; 1hr 30min).

Northeastern Anatolia

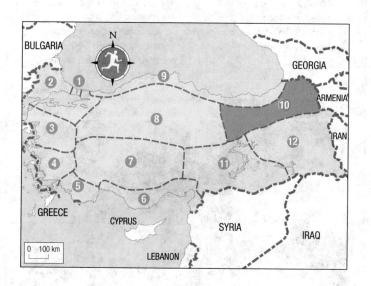

CHAPTER 10   # Highlights

* **Skiing at Palandöken** The peaks just south of Erzurum boast the finest skiing in the land. **See p.587**

* **Georgian churches** These isolated reminders of Georgian rule are still remarkably intact and framed by stunning scenery. **See p.589**

* **Whitewater rafting on the Çoruh River** Yusufeli is the base for a sport that draws hundreds of enthusiasts during May and June. **See p.592**

* **Kaçkar Dağları** The glacially sculpted, wildflower-carpeted Kaçkar mountains rank as the most versatile and popular alpine trekking area of Turkey. **See p.595**

* **Kafkasör festival** One of the most authentic folkloric expressions in the country can be witnessed every June outside Artvin. **See p.601**

* **Ani** Don't miss the ruined medieval capital at Ani, site of the region's densest concentration of Armenian churches and castles. **See p.608**

▲ Georgian church of Öşk Vank

Northeastern Anatolia

F ew travellers make it to Turkey's **northeast**, but many of those who do find it the most stimulating part of the country – imagine rafting down a raging whitewater river, hiking along a bucolic valley, or peering at distant horizons from a snow-covered mountaintop. Yet this outdoor appeal is far from the full story, since you'll also find a fair amount of history sprinkled into the mix – the area now borders the modern states of **Georgia** and **Armenia**, but was once actually part of their two predecessor kingdoms. A tremendous number of ruins survived the Ottoman era, and eagle-eyed travellers will spy castle after castle crumbling away on inaccessible peaks.

Much of northeastern Anatolia is a high, windswept plateau segmented by ranks of eroded mountains. Four great rivers – the Çoruh, Kura, Aras and Euphrates – rise here, beginning courses that take them to scattered ends in the Black, Caspian and Persian seas. Despite ambitious development projects, much of the area remains poor – horse-drawn ploughs are still a common sight, as are stacks of cow-dung used for fuel; indeed, some of the more remote farm communities, and even whole villages, live partly underground in burrow-houses. In comparison, the relatively prosperous and forested valleys around Yusufeli and Artvin have a lighter atmosphere and quasi-Mediterranean climate, as a tangible Caucasian influence begins to be felt.

However you approach – from central Anatolia, the extreme southeast of Turkey, or the Black Sea – your first stop is likely to be **Erzurum**, long a goal of armies and merchants and the only real urban centre. Today it's the main jumping-off point to just about anywhere else in the region, with a clutch of post-Selçuk Turkish monuments to distract you. North of Erzurum lie the **valleys of early medieval Georgia**, now part of Turkey, which hide dozens of churches and enchantingly set castles, all little visited and arguably the most rewarding targets in this area. The provincial capital of **Artvin** and the small town of **Yusufeli** are the logical overnight stops while in search of Georgian monuments, and Yusufeli also sits astride the most popular southern approach to the magnificent **Kaçkar Dağları**, a trekker's paradise that separates northeast Anatolia from the Black Sea. Northeast of Erzurum, **Kars** is the last major town before the Armenian frontier, and serves as the base for visits to the former Armenian capital of **Ani** and less heralded, isolated **Armenian churches** and **castles** in the province, together comprising the biggest tourist attraction in the region. There's also good skiing in the area, at **Palandöken** near Erzurum, and **Cibiltepe** near Kars.

Some history

Perhaps because of the discouraging climate and meagre resources, this corner of the country was thinly settled until the second millennium BC. The **Urartians** had their northernmost city at today's Altıntepe, near Erzincan, between the ninth

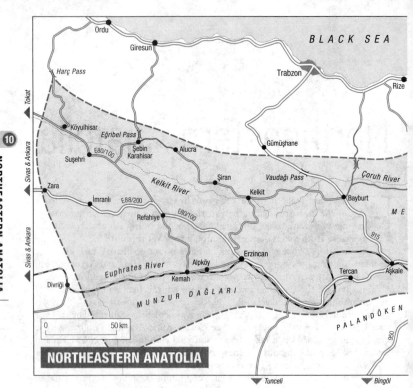

NORTHEASTERN ANATOLIA

and sixth centuries, but the next real imperial power to make an appearance was the **Roman** Empire, succeeded by the Byzantines and **Armenians**. The eleventh-century undermining of the Armenian state and the Byzantine defeat at Manzikert marked the start of a pattern of invasion and counterattack, which was to continue until 1920. The **Selçuks**, their minor successor emirates and the newly ascendant **Georgian** kingdom jockeyed for position in the territory until swept aside by **Mongol** raids in the early thirteenth century and Tamerlane's juggernaut in the early 1400s; the **Ottomans** finally reasserted some semblance of centralized control early in the sixteenth century.

Just as the northeast had been a remote frontier of the Byzantines, so it became the border of this new Anatolian empire, confronting an expansionist Tsarist Russia, which effectively ended what remained of Georgia's autonomy in 1783. As the Ottomans declined, **Russia** grew bolder, advancing out of its Caucasian fortresses to lop off slices of the region on several occasions during the nineteenth century, though they got to keep their conquests only in 1829 and 1878. Until 1914 nearly half of the sites described in this chapter were under Russian rule, with additional conquests up to 1917 nullified by the Bolshevik Revolution and the collapse of the Caucasian front. Between 1915 and 1921 the area was the scene of almost uninterrupted **warfare** between White Russian, Armenian Dashnakist and Turkish Nationalist armies, and of massacres among the mixed civilian population that had historically been over a third Armenian and Georgian-Christian.

By 1923 the northeast was all but prostrate, with ninety percent of its former population dead or dispersed. The present international boundaries between

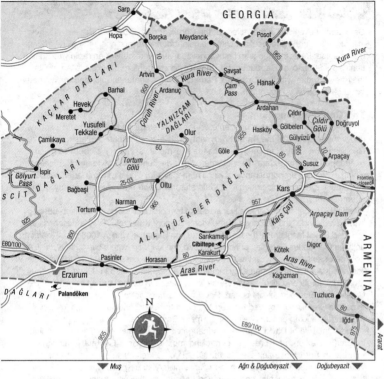

Turkey and Georgia or Armenia are the result of treaties between Atatürk and the **Soviet Union** in March and October 1921, and don't necessarily reflect historical divisions (indeed as late as 1945 Stalin was still demanding that Kars and Ardahan be returned to the "Russian motherland").

The Georgian valleys and Kaçkar mountains

Turkey's far northeast was once under the command of the **Georgian kingdom**, and despite centuries of Ottoman rule, evidence of this historical legacy remains tangible – ruined castles and churches abound, dotting a valley-chiselled landscape more redolent of modern Georgia than "regular" Turkey. The years of Georgian rule are also reflected in some place names, most commonly in the form of the

The Georgians

Georgians have lived in the valleys of the Çoruh, Tortum, Kura and Berta rivers, now in Turkey, since the Bronze Age. Like the neighbouring Armenians, they were among the first Near Eastern nations to be evangelized, and were converted rapidly to Christianity by St Nino of Cappadocia in the mid-fourth century. Unlike the Armenians, they never broke with the Orthodox Patriarchate in Constantinople, and maintained good relations with Byzantium.

The Georgian kingdoms

An effective Georgian state only entered the local stage early in the ninth century, under the auspices of the **Bagratid** dynasty. This clan contributed rulers to both the Georgian and Armenian lines, and hence the medieval history of both kingdoms overlapped to some extent. They claimed direct descent from **David** and Bathsheba, which explains a preponderance of kings named David, a coat of arms laden with Old Testament symbols and curiously Judaic stars of David embossed on many of the churches they built.

Ashot I Kuropalates began the first stages of territorial expansion and church-building in the area, under the guidance of the monk Gregory Khantzeli. Ashot's descendants included David Magistros ("the Great") of Oltu and Bagrat III, who in 1008 succeeded in unifying the various Georgian principalities into one kingdom with a capital at Kutaisi. A decade or so later the Byzantines compelled Bagrat's successor, Georgi I, to evacuate Tao and Klarjeti, making it an easy matter for the Selçuks to step in during 1064. They ravaged Georgia and all of eastern Anatolia, but as soon as they turned to confront the Crusaders a Bagratid revival began. David the Restorer not only managed by 1125 to expel the Selçuks, but moved the Bagratid court to newly captured Tblisi, and reunited the various feuding principalities ruled by minor Bagratid warlords.

Under the rule of David's great-granddaughter **Tamara**, medieval Georgia acquired its greatest extent and prestige, controlling most of modern Georgia, Armenia and Azerbaijan from the Black Sea to the Caspian, as well as the ancestral Georgian valleys. The queen was not only a formidable military strategist and shrewd diplomat, but displayed a humanity and tolerance unusual for the era. Many churches and monasteries were repaired or re-endowed by Tamara, and despite being a woman and a non-Muslim, her name still elicits respectful compliments from local Turks.

Following Tamara's death the Georgian kingdom began a slow but steady decline, effectively partitioned between the Ottoman and Persian empires. The rise of imperial Russia signalled the end of any viable Georgian state, and the last semi-independent king effectively surrendered to Catherine the Great in 1783.

Georgian monuments

The Bagratids were a prolific bunch, and they erected **castles** on just about every height; generally a passing glance is what you'll have to be satisfied with, since access to many of these eyries has long been impossible except for technical climbers. The most remarkable examples are the early Bagratid monastic **churches**, all dating from before the move northeast to the Caucasus proper, and most sited amid oases at the heads of remote valleys. The Georgians borrowed many of the architectural features of Armenian churches and it takes a trained eye to distinguish the two styles, though in general the Georgians rarely attempted the rotundas or multi-lobed domed squares beloved of the Armenians.

There's not been nearly the degree of official stonewalling about Georgian Christians as there is concerning Armenians, and the churches have become recognized as tourist attractions. Almost all have suffered some damage from dynamite- and pickaxe-wielding **treasure-hunters**: the locals have an unshakeable conviction that all of the Christians who left the area in 1923 secreted precious items in or under their churches in the mistaken belief that they'd eventually be able to return.

common prefix "Ar-" (as in Ardahan, Artvin, Ardanuç and so forth), equivalent to "-ville" or to "-burg".

Erzurum is the area's largest urban base, and the most common gateway for the few intrepid travellers that choose to pop by. To the north lie the southern valleys, the highlights of which are the churches of Haho and Öşk Vank. Those without their own transport will find it easier to tour the western valleys: the area's main town, Yusufeli, has reasonable transport links and accommodation options, and also provides a good base from which to organize a tour of the **Kaçkar Dağları**, one of Turkey's most stunning mountain ranges. Artvin is the best base for those touring the churches and castles of the northern valleys, or continuing on to Georgia proper; it's also possible to hit the border from Ardahan, the main base of the eastern valleys.

You'll need your own vehicle, or a lot of time for walking and hitching, to visit most of the sights. Bus services, where they exist, usually arrive near the sights in the afternoon and depart for the nearest town in the morning – exactly the opposite of tourist schedules. Some of the roads are bad, but if you can assemble a group and find a willing taxi driver, this can end up being far cheaper than renting a vehicle in Erzurum or Trabzon. Even with a car or taxi, at least three days will be required to see all of the monuments detailed in this text.

Erzurum

Nearly 2000m up, its horizons defined by mountains a further 1000m above, and rocked by frequent earthquakes, **ERZURUM** is Turkey's highest and most exposed city, and one of its most devout; some women wear sack-like *çarşafs* (full-length robes with hoods and veils) tinted the same dun colour as the surrounding steppe, whilst others wear the black chador, a cultural import from nearby Iran. Because of a strategic location astride the main trade routes to Persia, the Caucausus and western Anatolia, its sovereignty has always been contested, and today it's still a major garrison town of over 400,000 people. All told, the combination of history, climate and earthquakes has resulted in a bleak, much-rebuilt place where sunlight can seem pale even in midsummer, and where the landscaped, broad modern boulevards often end abruptly in literally the middle of nowhere.

While it spent the 1960s and 1970s as a transit stop for overlanders on the way to Iran, Afghanistan and India, Erzurum never really made the transition from hippy hub to mass tourism, though it gets some trade in winter thanks to the excellent skiing facilities at **Palandöken** just to the south (see p.587). During summer, the city serves as an occasional base and staging point for mountaineering and rafting expeditions bound for the Kaçkar Dağları, but it also deserves a full day in itself to see a compact group of very early Turkish monuments.

Some history

Although the site had been occupied for centuries before, a city only rose to prominence here towards the end of the fourth century AD, when the Byzantine emperor Theodosius II fortified the place and renamed it **Theodosiopolis**. Over the next five hundred years the town changed hands frequently between Constantinople and assorted Arab dynasties, with a short period of Armenian rule.

After the decisive battle of Manzikert in 1071, Erzurum – a corruption of Arz-er-Rum, or "Domain of the Byzantines" in Arabic – fell into the hands of first the Selçuks and then the Saltuk clan of Turks. These were in turn displaced by the İlhanid Mongols during the fourteenth century, forerunners of Tamerlane himself, who used the city as a springboard for his brief blitzkrieg into western Anatolia. Erzurum was incorporated into the Ottoman Empire by Selim I in 1515, where it remained securely until 1828, after which the Russians occupied it on three occasions.

Arrival, information and transport

Erzurum has two main bus terminals: the long-distance **otogar**, located almost 3km northwest of the city centre (taxis around 8TL), and the **Gölbaşı Semt Garajı**, for Yusufeli and Artvin, conveniently situated just over 1km northeast of downtown. Many, though by no means all, long-distance buses stop at both of these stations – when it's time to move on from Erzurum, make sure you know exactly which one your vehicle starts from.

The **train station** is around 1km north of the centre, close to a concentration of inexpensive accommodation. If you fly into the **airport**, 10km northwest of town at the end of the same road serving the *otogar*, try and catch the THY bus (3TL) into town – a taxi will set you back 25TL. The **tourist office**, at Ömer Nasuhi Bilmen (ex-Cemal Gürsel) Cad 9, 500m west of the centre, is not much use but may be able to hand out a town map.

Aside from walking, **taxis** are really the way to get around Erzurum, since the town is rather spread out and working out bus routes is a chore best avoided.

Accommodation

The supply of **accommodation** in Erzurum usually exceeds demand, and you should have no trouble finding a decent room to suit any budget, although many hotels are still used by prostitutes. With your own vehicle, it makes most sense to stay south of town at the base of **Palandöken** ski resort (see p.587) about 5km south.

City centre

Dilaver Hotel Aşağı Mumçu Cad 59 ⓣ0442/235 0068. Despite a rooftop-view restaurant, tubs in the bathrooms and BBC/CNN on the telly, this three-star has one star too many. Breakfast served in the mezzanine bar. Rack-rates for doubles are high at 120TL, but they'll generally take 75TL. ❹

Kral Otel Erzincankapı 18 ⓣ0442/234 6400, ⓔkralhotel@gmail.com. Under renovation at the time of research, and if a few minor flaws are ironed out this may once again offer good value. Some rooms have been intriguingly designed – the most striking feature mock İlhanid-Mongol decor in their mosaic-tiled baths. ❺

Oral Otel Terminal Cad 3 ⓣ0442/235 2500, ⓕ235 2600. On a quiet, almost leafy (for Erzurum) street, this worthy three-star is a 1970s period piece (albeit a well-kept one), from the lobby with its white-leather armchairs to the individual room decor, though bathrooms have been updated and fridges added. Convenient for the *otogar*. ❶

Polat Otel Kâzım Karabekir Cad 2 ⓣ0442/235 0364, ⓕ234 4598. Central hotel whose rooms are far more plush than the drab lobby might suggest, though it pays to check a few out before committing. The rooftop breakfast room is another bonus. ❸

Yeni Çinar Ayazpaşa Cad 18 ⓣ0442/213 6690, ⓕ213 8456. Friendly, comfortable and cheap, this is about as far downmarket as you'll want to go in Erzurum. The establishment itself is fine for single females, though the dark alley it's located on does not encourage wandering around at night. ❶

Palandöken

Dedeman Palandöken 8.5km from Erzurum ⓣ0442/316 2414, ⓦwww.dedeman.com. Four-star hotel in an alpine bowl at 2450m, pitched at doorstep skiers who want to be right at the heart of the action. Large, if spartan, rooms and wooden mock-chalet common areas. Closed mid-May to Nov. They also run the smaller *Ski Lodge* down the way, which some may find more likeable. ❽

Kardelen Oteli 5km from Erzurum ⓣ0442/316 6851, ⓕ316 6070. Definitely the runt of the litter of the Palandöken hotels, this three-star is the least expensive up here but fairly basic, barely functioning in summer and with a management somewhat suspicious of foreigners. ❹

Palan Otel 6.5km from town ⓣ0442/317 0707, ⓦwww.palanotel.com. Located at about 2250m, and a decent choice. Rooms are on the large side, with tubs in the bathrooms, though try not to get

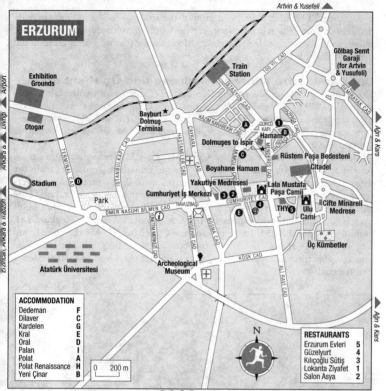

ERZURUM

Artvin & Yusefeli ▲

Train Station

Gölbaş Semt Garaji (for Artvin & Yusufeli)

Exhibition Grounds

Otogar

Bayburt Dolmuş Terminal

Dolmuşes to İspir

Gürcü Kapı Hamamı

Rüstem Paşa Bedesteni
Citadel

Boyahane Hamam

Stadium

Yakutiye Medresesi
Cumhuriyet İş Merkezi

Lala Mustafa Paşa Camii

Park

Çifte Minareli Medrese

THY

Ulu Cami

Üç Kümbetler

Atatürk Üniversitesi

Archeological Museum

ACCOMMODATION

Dedeman	F
Dilaver	C
Kardelen	G
Kral	E
Oral	D
Palan	I
Polat	A
Polat Renaissance	H
Yeni Çinar	B

0   200 m

N

RESTAURANTS

Erzurum Evleri	5
Güzelyurt	4
Kılıçoğlu Sütiş	3
Lokanta Ziyafet	1
Salon Asya	2

▼ Elâzığ, Bingöl & Palandöken ▼ Palandöken, Iranian Consulate & Research Hospital

one facing the car park. There's also an indoor pool, gym and sauna. ⑦

Polat Renaissance Erzurum Oteli 5km from Erzurum ☏0442/232 0010, ⓦwww.polat renaissance.com. Turkey's most comfortable hotel

east of Cappadocia, this five-star at 2200m is a bit remote from most of the ski slopes – a private chairlift bridges the gap – but compensates with cheerful, fair-sized rooms. Palatial common areas include a pleasant indoor pool, hamam and gym. ⑧

The City

All features of interest in Erzurum lie along – or just off – Cumhuriyet Caddesi, and a leisurely tour shouldn't take much more than half a day. Start at what is the de facto city centre – the Yakutiye Parkı – a landscaped area with benches and a tea garden around the Yakutiye Medresesi.

Yakutiye Medresesi and around

The **Yakutiye Medresesi** was begun in 1310 by Cemaleddin Hoca Yakut, a local governor of the İlhanid Mongols, and with its intricately worked portal, and truncated minaret featuring a knotted lattice of tile-work, it's easily the most fanciful building in town. The minaret in particular seems displaced from somewhere in Central Asia or Persia – not such a far-fetched notion when you learn that the İlhanids had their seat in Tabriz. The beautiful interior of the *medrese* now holds an excellent **Museum of Islamic and Turkish Arts** (Türk-İslam Eserleri ve Etnografya Müzesi; Tues, Thurs, Fri & Sat 8am–noon &

1.30–5pm; 3TL), nicely arranged around the students' cells. Exhibits include displays of local *oltu taşı* jewellery (see opposite), various dervish accessories, *ehram* (woven waistcoats for pilgrims to Mecca) and a selection of interesting old prints of Erzurum.

Ulu Cami, Çifte Minareli Medrese and Üç Kümbetler

Continuing east about 300m along Cumhuriyet Caddesi you pass the **Ulu Cami**, erected in 1179 by Nasirüddin Muhammed, third in the line of Saltuk emirs. Like most mosques of that age, it's a big square hall, with dozens of columns supporting bare vaults; the one note of fancy is a wedding cake of stalactite vaulting culminating in the central skylight.

Immediately adjacent stands the **Çifte Minareli Medrese**, Erzurum's main tourist attraction. Its name – meaning "double-minareted" – derives from the most conspicuous feature of the seminary, two thirty-metre-high towers curiously devoid of a balcony for the muezzin to sound the call to prayer. There is some dispute about the structure's vintage, but the majority opinion holds that Hüdavend Hatun, daughter of the Selçuk sultan Alâeddin Keykubad II, commissioned it in 1253. In conception the Çifte Minareli was the boldest and largest theological academy of its time, but was never finished. The courtyard reguarly functions as a marketplace, and on Fridays plays host to a cute sweeties and tea stall.

▲ The Çifte Minareli Medrese with mountain backdrop

A cluster of less enigmatic mausoleums, the **Üç Kümbetler**, graces another small park about 250m directly south. The oldest of the three tombs, and the most interesting, is probably that of the first Saltuk emir and dates from the early twelfth century, its octagonal base of alternating light and dark stone breached by half-oval windows demonstrating the mutual influence of Georgian, Armenian and early Turkish architecture.

The citadel and Rüstem Paşa Bedesteni

On the opposite side of Cumhuriyet Caddesi from the Çifte Minareli Medrese, a narrow lane leads past some of the oldest houses in town and a handful of carpet/ antique shops to the **citadel** or *kale* (daily 8am–5pm; 3TL), whose vast rectangular bulk was originally laid out by Emperor Theodosius II. The adjacent freestanding **Tepsi Minare** now doubles as a clocktower; like the mosque it's mostly twelfth-century, though the superstructure (which can be climbed) was added by the Russians during one of their occupations. Stairs on the east side lead up to the ramparts, and while the citadel is no longer the highest point in town, it still lends the best view over the city – and the great, intimidating vastness of the plateau beyond.

Just northwest of the castle stands the **Rüstem Paşa Bedesteni**, the covered bazaar, endowed by Süleyman the Magnificent's mid-sixteenth-century grand vizier. Erzurum owed much of its wealth to transcontinental trade routes, and even in the nineteenth century some forty thousand laden camels were passing through the city every year. Today trade is almost totally monopolized by **oltu taşı**, an obsidian-like material mined near Oltu, 150km northeast, and most frequently made into *tespih* (prayer beads), *kolye* (necklaces) and *küpe* (earrings).

Eating and drinking

Restaurants in Erzurum tend to offer good value, with a concentration of sorts on or around Cumhuriyet Caddesi and the central park. Licensed places are rare in this devout town.

Erzurum Evleri Yüzbaşı Sok 18, south of Cumhuriyet Cad. Eight old dwellings knocked together to make an institution that's equal parts funhouse maze, folklore museum and restaurant. Antique displays comprise everything from Ottoman houseware to 1950s portable gramophones. The food's merely OK, but the cushion-seats in secluded alcoves are highly atmospheric.

Güzelyurt Restaurant Cumhuriyet Cad 54/C. One of the oldest (founded 1928) restaurants in town, and one of the few licensed ones. Erzurum's *beau monde* retire behind curtained windows for a nip of *rakı* (in small-measure pitchers), wine or beer to accompany good vegetable *mezes* and less-exalted grilled mains. Budget 30TL depending on how much booze you have.

Skiing at Palandöken

Palandöken, stretching 5–6.5km south of town, offers far and away the best skiing in Turkey, more than adequate compensation for being stuck in Erzurum during its habitually arctic winters. With largely north-facing slopes ranging from 2300m near the *Palan Hotel* up to Point 3125 on Mount Ejder, excellent conditions (essentially nice dry powder on a two-metre base) are just about guaranteed. Pistes total 35km at present, with 10km more projected; currently seven chairlifts, two drag-lifts and a telecabin give access to eight easy, six intermediate and two advanced runs, as well as four recognized off-piste routes.

Palandöken is easily reached by taxi from Erzurum – the fare will be around 15TL, depending on where you get on and off – and there's decent accommodation in the area (see p.584). The hotels are your best bets for equipment rental, which will set you back about 40TL per day.

Kılıçoğlu Sütiş Cumhuriyet Cad 20. The main branch of three in town for this premier pudding-shop and nemesis of dieters: two dozen flavours of *dondurma*, plus profiteroles, biscuits and every imaginable sort of oriental sticky cake.

Lokanta Ziyafet Gürcükapı Akbank 93. Working man's den, specializing in *pide* and soups.

Particularly popular in the mornings, when they can whip up a decent breakfast for 4TL.

Salon Asya Cumhuriyet Cad 27. Ace for kebabs and a full soup menu, with willing service, dazzling (read migraine-inducing) lighting and contemporary decor; you can fill up for under 8TL.

Listings

Airport bus Departs 2hr before flight time from in front of the THY office, Cumhuriyet Cad, Eren İş Merkezi 88/3 ⓣ0442/218 1904.

Car rental Avis, Terminal Cad, Mavi Site, Birinci Blok ⓣ0442/233 8088; Evis, Terminal Cad 13/A ⓣ0442/234 4400, airport ⓣ0442/327 1377; Decar/Thrifty, airport only ⓣ0442/233 3560.

Cirit This is a sort of cross between polo and a jousting tournament, with the players on horseback eliminating opponents from the field by thrusts of a blunted javelin. Ask at the tourist office during spring and summer if a match is scheduled nearby.

Consulate Iran, Ülçer Apartments, Atatürk Bul, Yeni Şehir Girişi, on the minor road to Palandöken ⓣ0442/316 2285, ⓕ315 9983. Read the box on p.678 for details on crossing into Iran before you leave Erzurum.

Hamam Most historic and salubrious is probably the Boyahane Hamamı, in the warren of lanes west of the Rüstem Paşa Bedesteni.

Hospitals Best is the research and teaching hospital, south of the Ağrı- and Kars-bound highway in Yenişehir itself.

Supermarket There's a Migros, by the train station – good for stocking up with trek-suitable food.

Bayburt

Worth mentioning is **BAYBURT**, a town that makes an acceptable stopover between Erzurum and the coast. Bayburt is dwarfed by the largest **fortress** in Turkey, its history virtually synonymous with the town. Thought to have been erected in the sixth century during Byzantine emperor Justinian's skirmishes with the Laz tribe from the Black Sea, it was later appropriated by the Bagratids, until being taken and renovated by the Saltuk Turks early in the thirteenth century. Little else redeems Bayburt other than its position astride the young Çoruh River, best enjoyed at one of several riverside **restaurants** or **cafés** with wonderful views of the castle.

Bayburt's small **otogar** is 500m south of the centre on the main highway, but buses to and from Erzurum often begin and end in the bazaar. If you need to stay, your best bets are two **hotels** on Cumhuriyet Caddesi, the main drag aiming right for the castle. The budget *Saracoğlu* at no. 13 (ⓣ0458/211 7217; ❶) has rooms overlooking the river; across the road, a little way towards the *otogar*, the two-star *Hotel Adıbeş* (ⓣ0458/211 5813; ❹) is clean and comfortable. For **eating out**, the enclosed *Yeni Zafer*, next to the central vehicle bridge over the Çoruh, is more appealing in winter, but the *Çoruh Lokantası* upstream, with riverbank seating under willow trees, has the edge during the warm months.

The southern Georgian valleys

Highway 950 heads north out of Erzurum across the steppe, aiming for a nearly imperceptible gap, too trivial to call a pass, in the surrounding mountains. Almost without noticing it you're across the watershed, and as you begin a slow descent the landscape becomes more interesting, with the Tortum Çayı alongside and trees appearing for the first time in a long while. Just over 70k

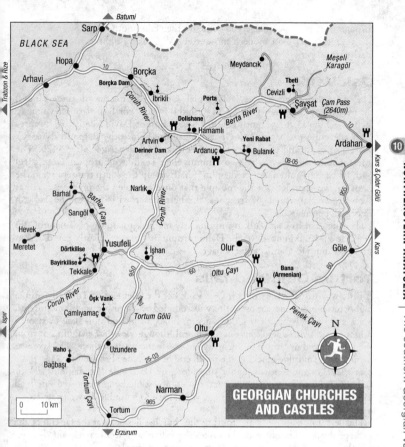

Batumi

Sarp

BLACK SEA

Hopa

Arhavi

Trabzon & Rize

Borçka

Borçka Dam

İbrikli

Çoruh River

Meydancık

Meşeli Karagöl

Tbeti

Cevizli

Porta

Şavşat

Çam Pass (2640m)

Berta River

Dolishane

Hamamlı

Artvin

Deriner Dam

Ardanuç

Yeni Rabat

Bulanık

Ardahan

Kars & Çıldır Gölü

Narlık

Barhal

Barhal Çayı

Sarıgöl

Çoruh River

Hevek

Meretet

Dörtkilise

Bayirkilise

Tekkale

Yusufeli

İşhan

Olur

Oltu Çayı

Bana (Armenian)

Göle

Kars

Öşk Vank

Çamlıyamaç

Tortum Gölü

Oltu

Penek Çayı

Haho

Bağbaşı

Uzundere

Tortum Çayı

Narman

Tortum

GEORGIAN CHURCHES AND CASTLES

0   10 km

N

Erzurum

from Erzurum, a pair of **castles** to left and right, crumbling away atop dramatic pinnacles, announce more effectively than any signpost that you've now reached the southern limits of **medieval Georgia** (see box, p.582). Highlights of the area are the churches of Öşk Vank, İşhan and Bana, though access is tricky without your own transport.

Haho

The tenth-century church of **Haho** owes its excellent state of repair to its continual use as a mosque since the eighteenth century. Entry is only possible on Friday around prayer time, or by tracking down the key-keeper in the village. Most of the monastery complex – the boundary wall and gate, and three satellite chapels – is in good condition, the effect spoiled only by aluminium corrugated sheets on the roof, though the conical-topped dome is still covered in multicoloured tiles.

To get to Haho you'll first need to head to Bağbaşı, a large village 8km west of Highway 950, dispersed in a fertile valley. Two minibuses a day make the trip from Erzurum's Gölbaşı Semt Garajı (see p.584) out to the village – a lot of toing and froing just to see Haho. If you're heading there with your own wheels, take the signed turn west from the highway over the Taş Köprü humpback bridge, keep left through the first large village you come to, then take another left towards İspir, a few minutes later by a modern mosque. Finally, take a right at the next, well-marked junction.

Öşk Vank

The most elaborate example of Georgian Gothic architecture in these valleys, the monastery church of **Öşk Vank** (Oshkhi) is well worth the trouble you may incur reaching it. A late tenth-century foundation of David Magistros, it represents the culmination of Tao Georgian culture before the Bagratid dynasty's move northeast and the start of the Georgian "Golden Age" after 1125. The interior colonnade – with no two columns alike – exudes a European Gothic feel with its barrel-vaulted, coffered ceiling; halfway up the south transept wall, the vanished wooden floor of the mosque that once occupied the premises acted as protection for a stretch of **frescoes**, the best preserved in any of the Turkish Georgian churches.

The side road to Öşk Vank is prominently marked just south of Tortum Gölü (see below), 15.4km north of the Haho turning. It's an easy, mostly paved 7.2km straight run up to **Çamlıyamaç** village.

Tortum Gölü and falls

A little way past the turn-off for Öşk Vank lies the inlet end of **Tortum Gölü**, a highly picturesque lake almost entirely surrounded by chunky, unspoilt mountains. Since the water is by turns muddy green, milky beige and dull slate even on a bright day, a swim doesn't necessarily appeal, though views are magnificent from the road, forced up onto a corniche bypass above the western shore. The lake was formed by a landslide blocking the north end of the valley between two and three centuries ago, and is now roughly 10km long by 1km wide. The famous *şelale* or **falls of Tortum** are today its natural outlet, accessible by a signposted side road 12km north of the Öşk Vank turning; you'll have to scramble down a path to get a good look of the 48-metre cascade.

The best **lunch** option while touring the churches lies here, at the far end of the little peninsula 8km north of the Öşk Vank side road: the *İskele Alabalık Tesisleri*, simple but salubrious, serving salad, trout and nothing else.

İşhan

Fifteen kilometres below the falls there's an important intersection in the steadily descending highway; banking left will lead you to Yusufeli. Bear right instead towards Olur and after 6km you'll reach a sign pointing to **İŞHAN** (Ishkani), a bluff-top oasis village 5.7km up a partly paved road; the crumpled hills of a heavily eroded, lifeless moonscape contrast sharply with the apple, mulberry and walnut groves in the village.

The imposing **church**, originally dedicated to the Virgin, was constructed in stages between the eighth and eleventh centuries, ranking it among the oldest extant sacred Georgian architecture. The semicircular colonnade lining the apse, with superb carved capitals, is the earliest surviving portion of the building, and was modelled consciously after the church at Bana (see opposite); great chunks of the roof are now missing, meaning that the 42-metre-high dome, built in a similar fashion to Öşk Vank's, rests in isolation on four columns. The acoustics, however, remain superb, as you can hear for yourself if you stand directly beneath the dome, and there are some patches of fresco to be seen high up on the surviving walls of the south transept.

Oltu and Bana

A detour from Tortum via Narman and Oltu on Highway 965 is time well spent, especially if you have your own vehicle. Stands of poplars and green fields are juxtaposed against a cobalt sky and reddish bluffs, often crowned with crumbling Georgian castles.

Beside the river at **Oltu** stands the first of the citadels – well restored by the Ottomans and again in 2002. A further 18km north brings you to the junction with Highway 80; continue left for 4km to the confluence of valleys as the Penek Çayı joins the Narman Suyu to become the Black Sea-bound Oltu Çayı. Here on either side of the strategic Y-fork rise two castles – one backed into the cliff, the other freestanding and flanked by a small church. Continuing towards İşhan takes you past yet another redoubt, atop a rock spur by the minor road to Olur.

Bearing right (east) instead onto Highway 80 leads towards Göle and Kars; 28km beyond Oltu (or 37km southwest of Göle) you'll see the seventh-century Armenian **church of Bana** on the north bank of the Penek (Irlağaç) Çayı. Carry on 4km further east from your first glimpse of it to take the side track that hairpins off left just before the gorge, just past where the main road crosses the river. Continue through the village of **Penek**, branching left after 2.8km to approach the church – in sight much of the way – from the northeast; depending on ruts and mud an ordinary car can drive with care almost up to Bana.

Perched on a knoll surveying water meadows, and dominated in turn by tawny crags, the church enjoys a commanding position. A century after local Christians abandoned it, the Ottomans accordingly fortified Bana during the Crimean War, adding the crude bulwark still visible on the south side. The Russians blasted the upper levels off during the 1877–78 war, and later carted away much of the masonry to build a turn-of-the-nineteenth-century church in Oltu. Of an originally three-storeyed, vast rotunda, one floor remains, half-submerged in its own ruins.

The western Georgian valleys

The **western Georgian valleys**, forming the area around the confluence of the Barhal and Çoruh rivers, are scenically and climatically some of the most favoured corners of the northeast. During the balmy summers, all sorts of fruits ripen and you're treated to the incongruous spectacle of rice paddies (and further downstream, olive groves) by the Çoruh, within sight of parched cliffs overhead. Functional **Yusufeli** is gateway to these river valleys, which in their lower reaches can offer **Georgian churches** near **Tekkale** and **Barhal**, plus trekkers' trailheads higher up at **Hevek** and **Meretet**, as well as Barhal.

The rivers themselves are a magnet for visitors, making Yusufeli a popular base for **whitewater rafters** finishing the challenging runs from İspir or Barhal upstream. Highest water is between early May and late June, when the overseas adventure companies (listed in the "Getting there" section of Basics) run their trips, but there is always at least one local outfitter arranging days out on the spot from May to September.

General tourism has never really taken off in the area, and the stark simplicity of local facilities will appeal mostly to the hardier breed of traveller: you'll need a steady hand at the wheel – or a strong stomach if you're a minibus passenger – for the often bumpy, steep rides out to the local Georgian churches.

Yusufeli

Straddling the Barhal Çayı just above its junction with the Çoruh, **YUSUFELI** is a gritty, rather time-warped town living under a death sentence; if funds ever permit construction, it will disappear under the waters of the highest Çoruh dam, and accordingly nothing new has been built here since the 1970s. Traveller opinion on the place is sharply divided: some can't wait to see the back of it, hitching out at dusk to avoid staying the night, while others, en route to or from the Kaçkar mountains, end up spending a few nights here and making a day-trip up one of the nearby river valleys.

Arrival, onward transport and services

If you're unable to get a direct **bus** service to Yusufeli from Erzurum, ask to be set down at Su Kavuşumu junction, 10km below the town centre; **taxi** shuttles up to Yusufeli from the junction are available for about 10TL per car. Heading in the other direction, the junction is also a good place to pick up transport to Ardahan and Kars, and the aforementioned sights along the way.

Yusufeli marks the start of **dolmuş routes** to various villages further upriver, including Barhal (see p.594) and Hevek (p.595). Service to these two high settlements is available daily all year, since both are inhabited in winter, but adheres to a somewhat informal schedule. The Barhal vehicles usually leave Yusufeli from the **otogar** between 2 and 5pm, the first and last departures going all the way to Hevek. If there is a group of you, and you want to guarantee your connection into the mountains, try calling local guide and dolmuş owner Osman (℡0466/826 2026), who will ferry you up to Barhal. There's a small **tourist office** just up the road from the *otogar* (℡0466/811 4008); **banks** with ATMs, a **PTT** and **shops** with basic trekking staples round out the list of essential services.

Accommodation

Few of Yusufeli's **accommodation** options can be recommended with much enthusiasm, but there are a few good picks. The *Barhal* is in town next to the footbridge, but for *Barcelona* and *Greenpeace* you'll have to cross and walk around 500m upstream.

Hotel Barcelona ℡0466/811 2627, ⓦwww .hotelbarcelona.com.tr. The comfiest accommodation in town, though prices are a little steep for what you get; you can usually get them down to 120TL for a double. Rooms are airy and bright, there's a swimming pool out front, and a passable on-site restaurant. ❺

Hotel Barhal ℡0466/811 3403, Ⓔselimabcd @hotmail.com. Near the pedestrian suspension bridge, this has small, cleanish, en-suite rooms that are deservedly popular with backpackers.

Also able to help with the organization of rafting trips. ❶

Greenpeace ℡0466/811 3620, ⓦwww .birolrafting.com. Ideally located just out of Yusufeli – easy to access, yet far away enough to foster a feeling of remoteness. Rooms are clean, if a bit small, and some are so close to the roaring river that you may have trouble sleeping. Camping is also available for 7.5TL per person, and the in-house restaurant can knock up a tasty fish supper. ❶

Eating and drinking

The *Çınar Restoran* under the *Barhal Hotel* is a good place to eat, with a terrace overhanging the river, and good *mezes* and grills. Runner-up is the *Mavi Köşk*, just off İnönü Caddesi (the main drag), opposite Halkbank, while just over the road-bridge *Çoruh Pide ve Lahmacun Salonu* is the best spot to load up on its namesake flat breads.

Rafting and trekking in Yusufeli

A number of professional **rafters** have put the Çoruh River at the top of their global list – when the river is at its fullest in May and June, it thumps along at a quite incredible speed, emitting a roar audible all across Yusufeli. A number of rafting outlets operate here, though since tourist numbers can be low even during peak season, many opt instead to organize trips from abroad (see "Basics", p.32) or agencies in İstanbul (see p.596). A wide range of itineraries available, from quick three-hour trips to three-day beasts starting in İspir. The most popular of Yusufeli's outfits are Çoruh Rafting (Ⓣ0466/811 3151, Ⓦwww.coruhrafting.com), who operate from an office just across the pedestrian bridge, and Birol Rafting (Ⓣ0466/811 3620, Ⓦwww.birolrafting.com), run by *Greenpeace* guesthouse (see opposite). Both charge around 50TL per person for the short trips.

Trekking around the wonderful **Kaçkar Dağları** (see p.596) can be just as exciting. Çoruh Rafting rent out equipment and arrange expeditions, as does local guide Sirali Aydın (Ⓣ0466/811 3893, Ⓔsirraft@hotmail.com). It's also possible to hit the peaks from Tekkale; Cemil, he of the eponymous *pansiyon* (see below), gets good reviews for his trips and general advice.

Tekkale and its churches

Sleepy **TEKKALE** lies 7km southwest of Yusufeli on the same bank of the Çoruh, connected by dolmuşes heading to either Kılıçkaya or the remoter Köprügören, 27km further upriver and the last point served by public transport. The road to Tekkale passes two ruined chapels (one perched above the Çoruh in Yusufeli town, the second on the far side of the river 2km upstream) and a vertiginous castle guarding the valley road, before curving the last 2km into the village.

The only **accommodation** is *Cemil's Pansiyon* (Ⓣ0466/811 2908, mobile 0536/988 5829; ❶ half board), a ramshackle guesthouse that would be quite at home in Thailand. As well as basic doubles, there's sleeping-bag space on the wooden terrace, tent-space out back, a single communal hot shower, and a tank full of trout that you may well be eating come suppertime – meals are included in the price, which is a good thing since there are no restaurants for miles around.

Dörtkilise

From Tekkale, just a few paces upstream from *Cemil's Pansiyon*, a dirt side road heading uphill and away from the Çoruh allows you to walk or drive the 6.3km further to **Dörtkilise** (Otkhta Eklesia; the road sign says "7"). En route, ignore the first two bridges spanning the stream to the right, and find the church a bit uphill to the left on a grassy hillside at 1140m, just beyond the third bridge over a tributary. Despite the name – meaning "Four Churches" – only one is found intact, but it's very fine and unlike most other Georgian places of worship. Domeless, with a steep gabled roof and relatively plain exterior, Dörtkilise is a twin of the church at nearby Barhal, though built several decades earlier and later renovated by David Magistros (see box, p.582). Since the closest *yayla* is about 3km away, Dörtkilise was never reconsecrated as a mosque, and is now home only to bats, swallows and occasionally livestock. Inside, a double line of four columns supports the barrel ceiling hiding under the pitched roof; some traces of fresco persist in the apse, while an unusual choir takes up much of the west end. The large half-ruined building to the northeast, arcaded and double-vaulted, was the monastery refectory, joined to the main body of the church by an equally decrepit gallery that served as a narthex.

Bayırkilise

The adventurous – equipped with anti-bug spray – can continue west on foot to the remote chapel of **Bayırkilise** (elevation 1680m); it's a tough ascent, with a proper path for only about two-thirds of the way. The route begins at a jeep "ramp" and culvert by a power pylon, 150m north of Dörtkilise; an initially broad path dwindles as it climbs, changing banks of the adjacent stream and fizzling out completely about 45 minutes along, just after recrossing the stream. Thereafter you face an increasingly steep, trackless half-hour scramble on an unstable surface, though the church – outrageously perched on a seemingly inaccessible pinnacle rearing above the canyon – is in distant view just long enough to give you bearings. In fair to middling condition, Bayırkilise has a gabled roof like its lower neighbour, with a single barrel vault and traces of frescoes inside; the views, and the sense of accomplishment in arriving, are the main rewards. The downhill return takes just under an hour, for a two-hour-plus round trip; pick up a sketch map of the route from *Cemil's*.

Barhal

The most popular route out of Yusufeli follows the valley of the Barhal Çayı north through a landscape straight out of a Romantic engraving, complete with ruined Georgian castles on assorted crags overlooking the raging river. After 18km of one-lane asphalt, the road surface changes to dirt at river-straddling Sarıgöl; **BARHAL** (1300m), officially renamed Altıparmak after the mountains behind, is reached 11km beyond, an hour and a half's drive in total from Yusufeli. With its scattered wooden buildings peeking out from lush pre-alpine vegetation, Barhal conforms well to most people's notions of a mountain village.

The tenth-century **church of Barhal** (Parkhali), the final legacy of David Magistros, is a twenty-minute walk up the secondary track toward the Altıparmak mountains (not the main one headed towards Hevek and the central Kaçkar); follow signs for the path to the *Karahan Pansiyon*, which climbs a lushly vegetated slope. Set in a hillside pasture next to the *mahalle's* school, it's virtually identical to Dörtkilise (see p.593), except for being somewhat smaller – and in near-perfect condition owing to long use as the village mosque. It's now only used for Friday prayers, but it's worth securing admission (try the school next door for keys) to appreciate the sense of soaring height in the barrel-vaulted nave – and the debt European Gothic owed to Georgian and Armenian architects.

Accommodation

There are several **accommodation** options, for which advance booking is strongly advisable in July or August. Village **facilities** are completed by a bakery, a few well-stocked shops, a restaurant and a well-attended teahouse.

Barhal Pansiyon ☎ 0466/826 2031. An acceptable choice at the entrance to Barhal, with pine-clad rooms and a homely atmosphere. You'll eat well here, too. ❸

Karahan Pansiyon ☎ 0446/826 2071. The most characterful option: choose between treehouse-type double chalets or mattresses on the airy terrace-dorm. It's located 1.2km out of the centre on the Altıparmak-bound turning and then uphill. ❸

Marsis Village House ☎ 0466/826 2026, ⓦ www.marsisotel.com. Three-storey building with clean double/triple/quad rooms (sharing bathrooms). A *teleferik* winch hoists your bags up the slope from the roadside. Suppers are large and strictly vegetarian, with beer available. You'll wake early here, as every footfall reverberates from the upper floors to the lower ones. ❸

Hevek

HEVEK (Yaylalar) lies another ninety-minute drive from Barhal along a scenic 21km dirt road. At an elevation of over 2000m, you'd expect the setting to be spectacular, and it doesn't disappoint – jagged peaks muscle their way into the distance, and life dawdles by at a pedestrian pace. There are a choice of places to stay in the village – all run by the same owner (℡0466/832 2001). The 25-bed *Altunay Pansiyon* (€15 per person) is the cheapest option, whilst across the road, the brand-new *Çamyuva Pansiyon* (❹ half board) is a deluxe version with an open kitchen and a sitting room. There are also some four-person chalets to rent (€50 per chalet) which work out pretty reasonably. The manager also runs a large food shop and the village **bakery** downstairs, hires out mules and generally arranges **trekking expeditions**. Architecturally the village varies from new concrete to century-old houses, though the only specific sight is an Ottoman **bridge** just downstream at the mouth of the Körahmet valley. If you're leaving by dolmuş, rather than on foot, there's usually one departure a day at dawn for the spectacular ride to Yusufeli.

Meretet

MERETET (officially Olgunlar), currently the road's end and the highest trailhead for the Kaçkar at 2200m, is a three-kilometre hike southwest of Hevek, though private cars regularly make the journey in dry conditions, and the dolmuş calls once daily in summer. The spartan but clean *Deniz Gölü Pansiyon* (℡0466/832 2105; ❸) with its communal balcony, self-catering kitchen and reliable hot water provides an even more scenic alternative to a night in Hevek. Backing onto this is the newer *Kaçkar Pansiyon* (℡0466/824 4432, ⓦwww.kackar.net; ❹) with large en-suite rooms, a communal TV area and shared kitchen. You can rent trekking equipment here, including tents, for around €10 per day, and the owner is able to help you with your trekking plans.

The Kaçkar Dağları

A formidable barrier between the northeastern Anatolian plateau and the Black Sea, the **Kaçkar Dağları** are the high end of the Pontic coastal ranges – and Turkey's most rewarding and popular trekking area. Occupying a rough rectangle some 70km by 20km, the Kaçkars extend from the Rize–İspir road to the Hopa–Artvin highway, with the more abrupt southeast flank lapped by the Çoruh River, and the gentler northwest folds dropping more gradually to misty foothills. At 3932m, their summit ranks only fourth highest in Turkey after Ararat, Gelyaşin peak in the Cilo mountains and Süphan Dağı, but in scenic and human interest they fully earn their aliases "the Little Caucasus" and "the Pontic Alps".

In addition to the principal summit area, several other major massifs are recognized: the Altıparmak and Marsis groups of about 3300m, at the north end of the Bulut ridge, which links them with Point 3932; and the adjacent Tatos and Verçenik systems of about 3700m, at the extreme southwest of the chain.

Partly because of intensive human habitation, the high Kaçkars support relatively few large **mammals**; bear and boar prefer the forested mid-altitude zones, while wolves and ibex are ruthlessly hunted in the treeless heights. **Birds** of prey and snow cocks are more easily seen and heard, while the summer months witness an explosion of **wildflowers**, butterflies – and vicious deer flies.

▲ Kaçkar mountain scenery

Practicalities

The six most popular **trailhead villages** are – on the Black Sea slopes – Çat and Ayder (see Chapter 9), and on the Çoruh side Barhal, Hevek, Meretet and Tekkale (see "The western Georgian valleys" starting on p.591). The approach from the Black Sea hills is gentler, with clearer trails, but the paths and villages can be crowded, and the almost daily mist rising up to 2900m is a problem. Hiking grades are tougher on the Çoruh flank, but the weather is more dependable. The main **season** is June to September, with the mists less of a hazard as autumn approaches; if you show up earlier than late July, you may need crampons and an ice axe to negotiate some of the higher passes. Note that it gets warm enough in midsummer for a quick swim in most of the lakes.

In terms of **itineraries**, the Kaçkars are infinitely versatile. The manic and the pressed-for-time cross from Hevek to Ayder via certain passes in two gruelling days, but there's little pleasure in this, and a more reasonable minimum time to switch sides of the mountains would be three or four days, and most people are happy to spend a week or even ten days trekking around.

Guides

If you'd rather go with a **guide**, there are a number of helpful individuals in Ayder and Şenyuva, as well as in Yusufeli, Hevek and Meretet. Otherwise try the İstanbul agents listed below or the adventure travel companies listed in the Basics section of this book (see p.32) who often run Kaçkar group itineraries.

Bukla Seyahat Yeniçarşi Cad, Gür Han 28/1–2, Galatasaray, İstanbul ℡ 0212/245 0635, ⊛ www .bukla.com. Offer regular one-week trips from June to September, usually under the supervision of local mountaineers.

Ogzala Turizm İstiklâl Cad, Bekar Sok 16/4, Beyoğlu, İstanbul ℡ 0212/293 9195, ⊛ www .ogzala.com. Also worth contacting for fully outfitted treks.

Equipment and local conditions

You'll need a **full trekking kit** appropriate to similar conditions in the Scottish Highlands, the Pacific Northwest or the Pyrenees: high-quality walking boots, wool socks, waterproof jacket and trousers or gaiters, a backpack cover and a proper, freestanding tent. You'll need to bring much of this from home, or at least a larger Turkish city, since there are few suppliers in the area. A camp stove and ample backpacking food are also essential – and you should bring ten to twenty percent more **supplies** than you think you'll need for the projected length of the trek, to allow for being stuck for an extra day by thick mist. Pure **water**, available everywhere from springs, is never scarce.

The lack of good-quality, large-scale **maps** is a major drawback, but some thorough route descriptions are available in mountaineering books (see p.736). Even though no compatible maps exist, a GPS device is still very useful: the integral altimeter function will be a godsend in the typically unstable weather conditions where conventional barometric altimeters are useless.

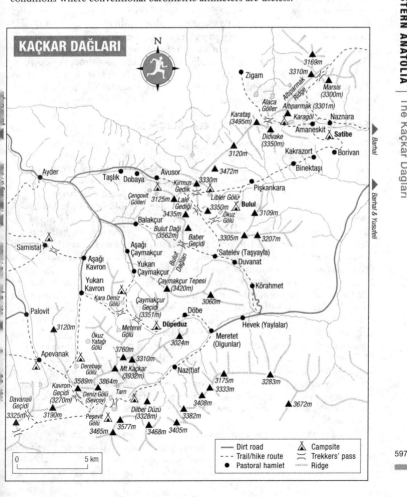

Paths are not waymarked or signposted, but cairns may be present at ambiguous points. Otherwise, there are few specific **dangers**, besides the absolute necessity of crossing all tricky passes early in the day – certainly by noon – before they're shrouded in mist or storm cloud. Territorial domestic bulls are also a nuisance, far more likely to charge a tent than any wild beast.

Routes in the northern Kaçkar

Starting from **Barhal** (1300m), most trekkers head west to the top of the valley walled off by the Altıparmak chain, finishing a tough first day either near **Karagöl** (2800m) or the nearby **Satibe** meadow (2450m). The following day usually involves a drop down to the Kışla/Önbolat valley just south, threading through the *yaylas* of Borivan, Binektaşı and Pişkankara before making camp higher up. If you pitch tent at **Libler Gölü** (2700m), near the top of the main valley, the next day will see you over the tricky Kırmızı Gedik saddle for an easy descent to **Avusor**, end of the road up from Ayder.

Alternatively, you can bear south from Pişkankara up to a camp in the Bulul valley, at the head of which is the wonderful **Öküz Gölü** (Ox Lake; 2800m) and an initially easy – but later steep – pass giving on to the **Körahmet valley**, still on the Çoruh side of the range. From an overnight next to **Satelev** *yayla*, you can choose between crossing the Bulul ridge via the Baber pass, dropping down to **Balakçur** just above Ayder; or rolling down-valley to **Hevek** via Körahmet (now served by a dirt road), with the option of ending your hike or stocking up to continue through the central Kaçkar.

Routes in the central Kaçkar

Above Hevek, two more valleys lead up to the base of the highest Kaçkar peaks; at **Meretet** (2200m) the split occurs. Bearing right (northwest) takes you within three and a half hours to camping spots near spectacular wildflowers high up in the Düpedüz valley, just below the **Çaymakcur pass** (3230m), the easiest in the entire Kaçkar range. You should leave for the pass (1hr 30min further) early the following morning, when you'd camp at **Kara Deniz Gölü** an hour beyond, with plenty of time for a day-hike south up to a group of three lakes at the top of the Cennakçur valley (see opposite) – and from a nearby overlook, your first, spectacular nose-to-nose view of Point 3932's north face. From Kara Deniz Gölü you can reach **Ayder** in another long walking day north, via the upper and lower **Çaymakçur** *yaylas*, which may have minibus service.

The path through the other valley follows the Büyük Çay southwest and upstream to the apparent cul-de-sac of the meadows at **Dilber Düzü** (3050m; 3hr from Meretet), a popular (and oversubscribed) camping venue at the formidable base of Point 3932 itself. Despite appearances there is a way up and out: first to the lake of **Sevcov** (Deniz Gölü; 3400m; 1hr 45min more), with just two or three cramped sites for tents, and then over the low crest just south to **Peşevit** (Soğanlı; 3377m; 2hr 15min from Dilber Düzü) lake with much better camping. Try to get an early enough start out of Meretet to make one of the lakes before dark, in preference to Dilber Düzü. Sevcov, where ice floes last into August during many summers, is the veering-off point for the moderately difficult, five- to six-hour return climb north to the **summit**, where the climbers' register is hidden underneath a rubble cairn.

From Peşevit lake you've a pathless scree-scramble west up to a false pass, then an even more miserable scree descent, another climb and a final drop to some water meadows near the top of the **Davali valley**, where a faint cairned path takes you up to the **Kavron pass** (3310m; 2hr 45min from Peşevit). Because of the rough terrain, no organized expeditions or pack animals come this way, and you'll need walking poles to save your knees – and yourself from a nasty fall.

Once on the Black Sea side of the pass, the most popular choice involves following the distinct path north an hour to another col (3200m) overlooking the **Kavron valley** – and allowing superb afternoon views of Point 3932's west flank. The trail, fainter now, drops within 45 minutes to **Derebaşı lake** (2885m) where it's advisiable to camp. There are limited sites at the inflow, and a few better ones by the lake's exit, where you scout around for the easiest cross-country route down to the floor of the U-shaped, glacial Kavron Deresi. After two hour's walk along a clear, right-bank trail, you'll reach a roadhead at the busy, electrified *yayla* of **YUKARI KAVRON** (2350m), a quite substantial place with daily minibus service down to Ayder, a central teahouse where you can get basic supplies and the more trekker-friendly *Şahin Pansiyon/Kamping/Kafeterya* (no phone; 20TL) at the outskirts, with double chalets.

From just past the *Şahin Pansiyon* on the access road, a sporadically cairned route leads west-southwest up the **Çennakcur valley** to the lakes at its head (2hr 30min; c.2900m). There are at least three lakes here – **Kavron Gölü**, right by the path with emergency camping, and **Büyük Deniz** and **Meterel** off to one side – Meterel is the highest and, in summer, often the driest. Another hour over a saddle behind Kavron Gölü will take you to Kara Deniz Gölü, and usually a lot of company. From here it's simple enough to reverse the directions given above for traversing the Düpedüz valley and Çaymakcur pass from Meretet, and complete a three-day, three-night circuit around Point 3932 – an excellent plan if you've left a vehicle or stored extra gear in Meretet or Hevek.

Another possibility from the ridge above Derebaşı lake is to veer west, initially cross-country, to Apevanak *yayla*, which is linked by path or track to the *yaylas* of Palovit and Tirovit; the latter gives access to the western Kaçkar.

Routes in the western Kaçkar

Elevit *yayla* (mountain hut) is roughly midway between Tirovit and Çat, and is the starting point for the march up to **Yıldızlı Gölü** (Star Lake; good camping), just across the top of the valley from Haçevanag *yayla*. The nearby, gentle Capug pass allows access to the headwaters of the Fırtına Çayı, though the onward route is briefly confused by the maze of bulldozer tracks around Başyayla (2600m) and Kaleyayla. At the latter, bear south up toward campsites by a lake at the foot of Tatos peak; the following day you'd cross a saddle to another lake, Adalı, at the base of 3711-metre Verçenik.

From this point you'd either descend to Çat via Ortaköy and Varoş, using a morning bus if possible part of the way, or continue walking west for another day, past other lakes just below the ridge joining Verçenik to Germaniman peak. A final 3100-metre pass just north of Germaniman leads to the valley containing Saler and Başköy *yayla*s, linked by daily bus to **İkizdere**.

Routes in the southern Kaçkar

Starting from Tekkale, the same dirt road that serves Dörtkilise continues another 3km to Bölükbaşı *yayla* and the start of a two to three-day traverse finishing in the Hevek valley. The weather is more reliable (and also hotter) than elsewhere in the Kaçkar, but this route is thus far relatively unspoilt; sketch map and arrangements are available from Cemil at his *pansiyon* in Tekkale (see p.593).

From **Bölükbaşı** (1400m), a path heads west via the *yaylas* of **Kusana** (1630m) and **Salent** (2400m), before reaching a pair of **lakes** (imaginatively dubbed Küçük – "little" – and Büyük – "big"), below a 3300-metre pass. You'd prudently overnight east of the pass, possibly beside **Büyük Gölü** (2900m), before descending a valley northwest to **Modut** *yayla* (2300m) and then **Mikeles** (1700m), on the side of the Hevek Deresi, about 5km downstream from Hevek itself.

The northern Georgian valleys

The northerly Georgian valleys form the heart of the **province of Artvin**, lying within a fifty-kilometre radius of the town of the same name. Nowhere else in Turkey, except for the Kaçkars, do you feel so close to the Caucasus: ornate wooden domestic and religious architecture, with lushly green slopes or naked crags for a backdrop, clinch the impression of exoticism. Here, too, you may actually encounter native **Georgian-speakers**, though they're mostly confined to the remote valleys around the towns of Camili, Meydancık and Posof, and the immediate surroundings of Şavşat.

The region, with its wet, alpine climate on the heights, formerly had potential as a winter-sports playground, but global warming – and the fact that, in Turkey's current economic straits, existing ski resorts can barely cope – scotched such hopes. For the moment most tourists come in summer to see the local **Georgian churches**; individually these are not as impressive as their southern relatives, but their situations are almost always more picturesque.

Artvin

Arrayed in sweeping tiers across a steep, east-facing slope, the lofty town of **ARTVIN** should possess one of the finest views in Turkey but successive road-building schemes have etched unsightly scars across the valley it calls home. In addition, the town itself is gritty and unappealing, but it makes by far the most comfortable base for explorations of the surrounding area, and becomes a destination in its own right when the **Kafkasör festival** comes to town (see box opposite).

The **otogar** is just down the hill from the main street – head straight on past the non-functioning hut pretending to be a tourist office. All the bus companies have ticket offices along **İnönü Caddesi**, the single high street running past the Hükümet Konağı (Government Hall), where you'll also find the **PTT**, various **banks** with ATMs, and a handful of **internet cafés**.

Accommodation

Things have improved slightly since the 1990s when nearly every **hotel** featured hot and cold running *natashas* as standard and Artvin ranked as the hooker capital of Turkey, but it's still pays to be vigilant when selecting a place to stay.

Kafkasör Tatil Köyü Dağ Evleri ☎0466/212 5013. During the festival it may be more convenient to stay at this establishment, which offers en-suite bungalow rooms up on the Kafkasör meadow, 10km out of town – though you must book months in advance to secure a vacancy. ❷

Karahan İnönü Cad 16 ☎0466/212 1800. The one passably comfortable place in town. Access from İnönü Cad is up a concrete stairwell in a grim shopping centre just downhill from the hotel sign; if you're driving, swing around behind to the tiny, controlled-access car park. The rooms, mostly en suite, are clean and comfortable, with a/c and satellite TV. ❸

Otel Kaçkar Hamam Sok 5 ☎0446/212 9909, ℱ212 8315. Excellent budget option with decent sized and cheerful en-suites with TV and central heating. Sign visible from İnönü Cad but is in an alley parallel and downhill from the main road. ❶

The Kafkasör festival

June is the best month in which to visit Artvin province, since it's possible to take in the fantastic **Kafkasör festival**, a multi-day event taking place at a *yayla* above town. The highlight has traditionally been the pitting of bulls in rut against each other, but since the opening of the nearby frontier the event has taken on a genuinely international character, with wrestlers, vendors, jugglers, musicians and dancers from both Turkey and Georgia appearing among crowds of over 50,000. It's one of the last genuine folk fairs in the country so be there if you can. It usually takes place for several days over the third or fourth weekend in June, but in recent years has occasionally been brought forward as far as late May.

Eating and drinking

Food in the *Karahan*'s licensed **restaurant** is good and not too overpriced, while at the bottom of İnönü Caddesi there's the *Nazar Restorant*, which has good *mezes* and *meyhane*-format food, and by far the best valley views. Breakfast-time *börek* and the usual range of **puddings** are on offer at *Sedir*, a cake-shop near the top of the road.

Ardanuç and Yeni Rabat

The river valleys east of Artvin are no less spectacular than their counterparts around Yusufeli. The approach to **ARDANUÇ**, once the capital of Klarjeti Georgia, is through the spectacular, high-walled gorge of the Köprüler Çayı, defended by the **Ferhatlı Kale**, 5km along. It's easily accessible by **dolmuş** from Artvin, a 45-minute ride away; since there's no accommodation in Ardanuç, be aware that the last one returns to Artvin at 5pm. The dwindling, slightly shabby old quarter of Ardanuç, 10.5km from the main highway, crouches at the foot of a giant wedding cake of crumbling orange rock, on top of which sits the giant Bagratid **castle of Gevhernik**. With an early start to beat the heat, you can climb it on foot or (partway) by car, but to do that and see the church up the valley in one day you'll need your own transport.

The newer bazaar cantonment, a kilometre or so further, is arrayed around a pleasant, plane-tree-studded "village green" – a legacy of the Russian occupation – with teahouse tables in the middle and a few *döner/pide salonları* at which to stop for a **snack**.

Yeni Rabat

The tenth-century monastery church of **Yeni Rabat** (Shatberdi), nestled in the vegetable gardens of its four-house hamlet, has an idyllic setting up the slopes of one of the loveliest Georgian valleys. The long-vanished monastery, founded a century earlier by Gregory Khantzeli, was renowned as a school for manuscript illuminators. The dome, nave and transept are still virtually intact, with extensive relief carving on the south and east facade, but the exterior has been stripped of most of its dressed stone.

Yeni Rabat is accessible from Bulankık (also known by its Georgian name, Lengetev), a village just east of Ardanuç, to which it's connected by an inconvenient daily dolmuş. From the *meydan* in "downtown" **Bulanık**, 1km along and distinguished by fine vernacular log cabins, an onward dirt track leads off slightly down and left (east-northeast) for the remaining 2.5km (best done in a 4WD) to the church.

Georgian vernacular architecture reaches its apotheosis along the upper reaches of the **Berta River** and its tributaries, most notably in the intricately carved chestnut-wood balustrades of the houses' wraparound balconies. The saturated greens of the lower hillsides rival those around Bulanık, while higher up dense forest cover evokes the alps of central Europe. Having your own wheels is a near necessity in this area, since public transport is both sparse and unreliable.

Drawing a lazy parallel with the Berta (Imerhevi in Georgian), Highway 10 links Artvin (p.600) and Şavşat. Other than these towns, and Ardahan further east, the only real tourist facility in the area is found at **Meşeli Karagöl**, 20km beyond Ciritdüzu via Veliköy and Meşeli villages. Open in the summer only, the *Karagöl Pansiyon* (℡0466/537 2137 or 537 2300; ❷) is a simple four-room lodge by a lake; reservations are suggested unless you don't mind camping, though note that bears, wild boar and deer roam hereabouts at night.

Dolishane

The dome of the tenth-century church of **Dolishane** peeks above the lush vegetation of the oasis village of Hamalı, easily accessible from Artvin. The interior is now being used as an agricultural tool shed, but the exterior is rewarding, the south facade window surrounded by such reliefs as the Bagratid builder-king Smbat I (954–958) offering the church to Christ, a Star of David and an archangel. Easily accessible by dolmuş from Artvin.

Porta

The ninth-century monastery of Khantza is now known as **Porta**. Its main church is still impressive despite gaping holes in the dome and walls, but the walk up is of greater reward: from the sign on Highway 10, it's an enjoyable but steep 45-minute climb up to the Bağcılar district of Pırnallı village, though the slippery track makes good footwear an absolute necessity.

Tbeti

The tenth-century monastic **church of Tbeti** peeks out of the trees at the head of a beautiful valley. Its remains are visible at a distance to the sharp-eyed, though up close the building has suffered extensive damage from local treasure-hunters. It lies 10.5km off the Artvin–Şavşat road, starting from the compact fortress of **Söğütlü Kale**. Turn up the paved but one-lane side road marked for Veliköy, and follow the Kaleboyu stream valley for 7km to the village of Ciritdüzü, then another couple of clicks to Cevizli village.

The eastern Georgian valleys

Bridging the overland trail between Artvin and Kars, the eastern Georgian valleys ripple their way across one of Turkey's most pristine and least visited corners. Here it's unspoilt countryside, rather than ancient ruins, that provide the main draw - some mountain passes edge towards 3000m in altitude, and you'll see patches of ice through to June. From Artvin most travellers will want to move southeast towards Kars without making the lengthy detour through Erzurum. There are basically three routes to consider, all heading via the area's main base, Ardahan: first via **Çıldır Gölü**, second via Susuz, and third via Göle. The first, most north-easterly route is the scenically superior, though public transport is sparse; there are a couple of daily **dolmuşes** between Kars and Posof via Çıldır town, especially useful for those seeking an adventurous route into Georgia proper.

Ardahan

Faintly reminiscent of Kars with its Russian grid-plan and *fin-de-siècle* architecture, **ARDAHAN** is one of the smallest Turkish provincial capitals. There's nothing in particular to see here, except a fine old **bridge** over the Kura River, just opposite the massive **citadel**, originally Georgian but restored by Selim the Grim early in the sixteenth century. It's still an army camp, so no photography is allowed.

Ardahan isn't somewhere you'd want to stay for long, and its hotels are less than inviting, many of them occupied by prostitutes. If you need to **stay**, try the *Kera Oteli*, Atatürk Cad 21 (☎0478/211 3458; ❸). Moving on is pretty simple: from town, regular buses run to Erzurum and Yusufeli, departing from the **otogar** near the citadel; for Kars, Artvin or Çıldır you'll have to seek out the **dolmuş depot** in the centre.

Çıldır Gölü

The slate-like expanse of **Çıldır Gölü**, nearly 2000m up, is the primary source of the Arpa Çayı/Ahuryan River, and the highest sizable lake in Turkey; only during the summer – when hay and grain are growing by the shore – is there a hint of colour. Men on horseback, wielding scythes, rakes and other farming implements, canter splendidly across the steppe against the backdrop of 3197-metre Kısır Dağı, but their families live like moles, with houses burrowed even deeper than the norm for this province. Abundant birdlife, fishing boats and changeable weather give the shallow lake an air redolent of a Scottish highland loch. It's frozen over for six months of the year, but becomes an important **bird habitat** during the warmer months, when handsome falcons and hawks swoop over your vehicle, while migrating waterfowl include pelicans and more mundane gulls.

The town of **ÇİLDİR** is an unprepossessing place north of the lake, out of sight of the water; the single commercial street is hard-pressed to muster a proper restaurant, and the only grubby "hotel" is best left unpatronized. Çıldır serves as the theoretical jumping-off point for **Şeytan Kalesi** (Satan's Castle) a brooding medieval keep and watchtower perched on a gorge but local taxis are pricey and it's best visited on a group tour from Kars.

More appealing is **DOĞRUYOL** (Djala in Georgian), the only substantial town on the lake's eastern shore; the thirteenth-century hilltop church masqueraded until recently as a mosque, and there are other eleventh- to- thirteenth-century churches on the lake's southwest shore at the villages of **GÜLYÜZÜ** (Pekreşin; badly ruined) and **GÖLBELEN** (Urta; in a better state, still used as a mosque).

On to Georgia

While most travellers cross from Turkey to Georgia through the Black Sea ports of Sarp and Batumi (see p.565), the adventurous may choose to make use of an inland border post linking Posof and Akhaltsikhe. At the time of writing, citizens of most countries were able to get a free visa on arrival, though double-check with your nearest Georgian embassy.

There are buses to the Turkish border town of Posof from Kars, Ardahan and even İstanbul. While there's nothing of note to see, this cute town's lofty views may even entice you to stay the night; the *Dönmez Otel* (☎0478/511 2659; ❶) is the best of a motley crew around the *otogar*. The border is 12km away and accessible by taxi (20TL); you'll pay just a little more for the remaining run to Akhaltsikhe (drivers will accept euros and Turkish lira), a pleasant Georgian town with banks, hotels and good links to Tbilisi and Batumi.

The Armenian ruins

Centuries of Armenian rule have bequeathed eastern Turkey with a series of superb ruins, whose remains – many made from a peach-coloured local stone known as "Duf" in Armenian – pepper the modern-day border. Many find this area even more scenic than that housing the Georgian ruins: think lofty, rolling fields instead of crinkle-cut valleys. You're almost certain to pass through **Kars**, the area's main city and transport hub, especially if you're on your way to Ani, justifiably the best-known complex in the area. Once the Armenian capital, it now possesses an isolated, decaying grandeur carrying subtle echoes of former glories. Also in the area are the complexes of **Karmir Vank and Horomos**, though the latter is closed to tourists for the time being. Futher afield, but well worth the trouble you'll incur getting there, are the churches at Khtskonk and Mren, both accessible from the small town of Digor.

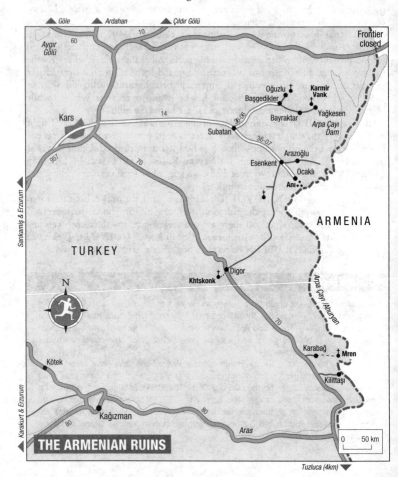

The Armenian issue

The Turkish-Armenian border has been closed since 1993, when politicians in Ankara chose to side with their Turkic brethren in Azerbaijan over the conflict in Nagorno-Karabakh, a majority-Armenian area that lies in Azeri territory, and now forms a de facto independent state. Complicating matters were decades of ill feeling surrounding the fate of the Ottoman Empire's ethnic Armenians in the years following the World War I: a hugely contentious issue on both sides of the border. The events are viewed by Armenia – and most international historians – as the world's first orchestrated genocide, a term that the Turkish government has repeatedly refused to accept (see p.668).

Matters have improved in recent years, with Turkish Prime Minister Recep Erdoğan's 2009 visit to Baku the high point of a political thaw. The above issues remain major obstacles to a possible opening of the border; there may one day be a reopening of the Kars–Yerevan rail line, but for now the fastest overland route from Turkey to Armenia is through Georgia, via the border crossing near Posof (see p.603).

Kars

Hidden in a natural basin on the banks of the Kars Çayı, **KARS** is an oddly attractive town, unusual in Turkey thanks to a few incongruous terraces of Russian *belle époque* buildings. Although a couple of hundred metres lower than Erzurum, the climate is even more severe; the potholed streets never quite recover from the fierce winters and when it rains, which it often does, the outskirts become a treacherous swamp. There are a few sites in town worth dallying for, but most visitors have made the long trek out here for the sole purpose of visiting the former Armenian capital of Ani (see p.608).

Kars was once one of Turkey's ugliest cities but things continue to improve – central streets are clean and have been repaved with cobbles or bricks, with even a designated pedestrian zone or two. Unfortunately the area leading up to the citadel remains something of an eyesore, though this too is slated for substantial redevelopment. Perhaps most visually appealing is the stretch of Ordu Caddesi north of Faikbey Caddesi, studded with several relics of Russian architecture.

Some history

Originally founded by the Armenians who knew it as Kari, Kars became the capital of their Bagratid dynasty early in the tenth century when the citadel, which still dominates the town, was substantially improved. Later in that century the main seat of Armenian rule was transferred to nearby Ani, and Kars lost some of its importance. The Selçuks took it along with almost everything else in the area during the mid-eleventh century, but devastating Mongol raids made a mockery of any plans the new overlords had for Kars. In 1205 the Georgians, profiting from the wane of both Selçuk and Byzantine power in the area, seized the town and held it for three centuries until displaced by the Ottomans.

As the key to Anatolia, the Russians tried repeatedly during the nineteenth century to capture the place. Sieges in 1828 and 1855 were successful – the latter during the Crimean War, when a British and Turkish garrison was starved out of the citadel after five months – but on both occasions Kars reverted to the Ottomans by terms of peace treaties. Not so in 1878, when, after a bloody eight-month war between the two powers, Kars was finally awarded to the Tsar. It remained in Russian or Armenian hands until 1920, a period that bequeathed both the unusual grid layout of the city centre and the incongruous *belle époque* buildings found here.

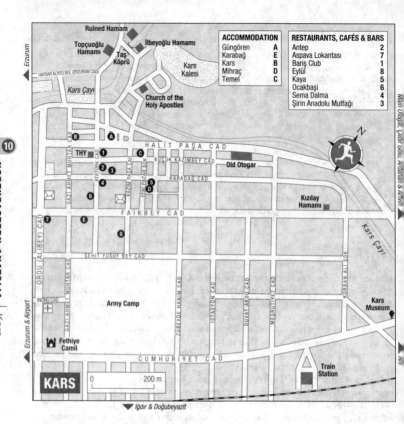

On the map:

ACCOMMODATION

Güngören	A
Karabağ	E
Kars	B
Mihraç	D
Temel	C

RESTAURANTS, CAFÉS & BARS

Antep	2
Aspava Lokantası	7
Barış Club	1
Eylül	8
Kaya	5
Ocakbaşı	6
Sema Dalma	4
Şirin Anadolu Mutfağı	3

Map labels: Ruined Hamam, Topçuoğlu Hamamı, İlbeyoğlu Hamamı, Taş Köprü, Kars Kalesi, HAYDAR ALİYEU BUL (ERZURUM CAD), Kars Çayı, Church of the Holy Apostles, HALİT PAŞA CAD, THY, KÜÇÜK KÂZIMBEY CAD, Old Otogar, ATATÜRK CAD, GAZİ AHMET MUHTAR CAD, KÂZIM PAŞA SOK, YENİ PAZAR SOK, KARADAĞ CAD, Kızılay Hamamı, FAİKBEY CAD, ORDU (ALİBEY) CAD, GAZİ AHMET MUHTAR CAD, ŞEHİT YUSUF BEY CAD, Kars Çayı, İNÖNÜ CAD, Army Camp, ZÜBEYDE HANIM CAD, İSTASYON CAD, DUVAR AKSU CAD, MESRUTİYET CAD, KURBAN ALİ SOK, Kars Museum, Fethiye Camii, CUMHURİYET CAD, Train Station, **KARS**, 0 — 200 m

Arrival and information

In the northeast of the town and within walking distance of most points of interest, the **old otogar**, on Küçük Kâzımbey Caddesi, now houses only dolmuşes to nearby Yusufeli, Ardahan, Posof (for Georgia) and Iğdır (change there for Doğubeyazit). For major towns such as Erzurum and beyond, you'll need the **long-distance otogar**, 5km east of the town centre – *servis* buses link it with bus company ticket offices in the town centre. Daily flights from Ankara land at the **airport**, 6km south of town beyond the bypass highway; a shuttle-bus service runs you into the centre, stopping at the THY office (see "Listings" p.608). The **train station** lies 1km southeast of the centre, off Cumhuriyet Caddesi, on the way to the museum.

The **tourist office**, on the corner of Atatürk and Karadağ *caddesi* (daily 8.30am–5.30pm; ℡0474/212 6817) is only worth visiting for its maps. They may refer you to local English-speaking **guide** Celil Ersözoğlu (℡0532/226 3966, ℮celilani @hotmail.com), who arranges reliable group taxi and minibus tours to Ani and remoter monuments – though he will probably find you first.

Accommodation

Accommodation options in Kars have improved immeasurably through the years, although some cheaper establishments remain beyond the pale.

Güngören Oteli Millet Sok 4, just off Halitpaşa Cad ⓉO474/212 5630, ⒻO223 4821. Large, rambling hotel whose rooms have shocking colour schemes but modernized furniture and bathrooms. On site you'll also find a decent ground-floor restaurant, as well as a hamam. ❷

Hotel Karabağ Faikbey Cad 142 ⓉO474/212 3480, ⓌWwww.hotel-karabag.com. A mid-1990s, overpriced three-star whose decor and furnishings are already ageing. Rear rooms are the largest and quietest, with tubs in large bathrooms, and there's heating throughout. There's a naff bar with disco-ball just off the lobby, but the mezzanine breakfast salon/restaurant is OK. ❺

Kars Otel Halitpaşa Cad 79 ⓉO474/212 1616, ⒻO212 5588. The only decent higher-end option in town, whose eight muted-grey rooms feature flat-screen TVs, super-comfy beds and powerful showers. There's also an excellent restaurant downstairs, though staff speak little English. ❻

Hotel Mihraç Cengiztopel Cad 19 ⓉO474/212 3768. Good mid-range choice, located just behind the *Kent* and beating rivals in its price category for service and room cleanliness; single rooms are also a bargain at 25TL. Breakfast is served on a terrace that provides pleasant castle views. ❷

Otel Temel Yeni Pazar Cad 9 ⓉO474/223 1376. Comfortable rooms in a good location just off Halitpaşa Cad, though the management can be somewhat grumpy. They have a second, slightly cheaper hotel a little further down the same road. ❷

The Town

Just the other side of the Kars Çayı on the way to the castle, the **Church of the Holy Apostles** was erected between 930 and 937 by the Armenian king Abbas I. Crude reliefs of the twelve Apostles adorn the twelve arches of the dome, but otherwise it's a squat, functional bulk of dark basalt; the belfry and portico are relatively recent additions. A church when Christians held Kars, a mosque when Muslims ruled, it briefly housed the town museum before being reconsecrated in 1998 as the Kümbet Camii. Just before or after prayer times, you can slip inside to view the elaborately carved altar-screen.

After decades as an off-limits military reserve, **Kars Kalesi**, as it's officially known (daily 9am–7pm; free), is now open as a park. Locals come to enjoy the panoramic view, but there's little else to see other than the black-masoned military engineering. There has been a fortress of some kind on the hill overlooking the river confluence for well on two millennia. The Armeno-Byzantine structure was maintained by the Selçuks but levelled by the Mongols; the Ottomans rebuilt it as part of their late sixteenth-century urban overhaul, only to have the Russians blast it to bits, then put it back together again during the nineteenth century. On October 30, 1920, an Armenian Dashnakist army besieged in the castle surrendered to Turkish general Halitpaşa, and with that went any hopes of an Armenian state straddling both banks of the Ahuryan River.

At the time of writing, the only other compelling attraction in Kars is the excellent **Kars Museum** (Kars Müzesi; daily 8.30am–5pm; 3TL), a fifteen-minute walk out to the east end of town. The downstairs is given over to ancient pottery, and ecclesiastical artefacts of the departed Russians and Armenians, particularly a huge church bell inscribed "This Tolls for the Love of God".

Eating and drinking

Fortunately the **restaurant** scene in Kars is excellent; much better, in any case, than its accommodation prospects. It's also easier than in Erzurum to get alcohol with your meal; best of a number of youth-oriented **bars** is the Barış Club on Atatürk Cad 33, a stylish place that pumps out freezing-cold beer, and often puts on traditional music in the evening (usually an extra 10TL per table).

Antep Pide ve Lahmacun Atatürk Cad. Ordinary-looking restaurant doling out extraordinarily good *pide* for 4TL and up. Simply delectable.

Aspava Lokantası Faikbey Cad 74, corner of Ordu Cad. Never mind the lurid lighting and kitsch decor, this is the best of a handful of 24hr soup and *sulu*

Skiing at Cibiltepe

Just 55km west of Kars, conifer-surrounded **Sarikamiş** is the coldest town in the country; accordingly, thick seasonal snow supports the very good **Cibiltepe ski resort**, 3km back east towards the main highway. Facilities comprise just two chairlifts from 2150m up to 2700m, serving two advanced runs, two intermediate ones and one novice piste threading the trees. Equipment rental is cheap at around 20TL per day.

At the foot of the lifts, the ostensibly three-star *Çamkar* (☎0474/413 5259, ⓦwww.camkar.com; ❹ half board) offers medium-sized standard units in a chalet-style structure with a sauna and licensed restaurant. The newer *Toprak Hotel* (☎0474/413 4111, ⓔsalessarikamishotel@toprak.com.tr; ❹), nearby, is a deal more comfortable. If you intend to ski here it's cheapest to arrange rental of equipment, lift passes and instruction at the lift offices and stay instead at the *Sarıkamış Turistik Otel* at Halk Cad 64 in **Sarikamiş** (☎0474/413 4176; ❶), with its funky rustic-style lobby and spacious rooms.

yemek kitchens in town – a godsend if you've arrived on a late bus.

Eylül Kâzımpaşa Cad, just south of Faikbey Cad. The most appealing and quietly set of a handful of *pastanes*, with milk-based sweets, wood-panelled decor and an upstairs gallery. Try the famous local honey (*bal*) with a continental breakfast.

Kaya Hapan Mevkii. Quite possibly the best *kahvaltı* in east Turkey. Filling breakfasts (4.5TL) feature plates of cream and local honey to dip your bread in—resistance is futile. Opposite *Otel Kent*.

Ocak Başı Atatürk Cad 156. The more appealing of two identically named

restaurants on Atatürk Cad, notable for its mock-troglodytic style. Prices are surprisingly reasonable, and portions large – try the superb *patlıcan kebap* for 7TL.

Sema Dalma Atatürk Cad. A terrific escape from Kars' grimy streets, this relaxed courtyard café provides a bit of modern-day style to go with its teas and coffees. Food and *nargileh* also available.

Şirin Anadolu Mutfağı Karadağ Cad 5. Offers well-done *pide* and *kebap*. Features ground-floor seating in a contemporary environment and a pleasant, nocturnal café section upstairs for dessert and nonalcoholic drinks.

Listings

Airport bus Shuttle bus (3TL), departing 1hr 45min before flight time from the THY agent, which is Sınır Turizm, Atatürk Cad 86 (☎0474/212 3838), or from Atlas Jet on Faikbey Cad 66 (☎0474/212 4747), also 1hr 45min before take-off.

Banks and exchange There are several ATMs dotted around the town centre. Otherwise use several efficient *döviz* on Kazımpaşa Cad.

Hamams The *Güngören* hotel has an attached hamam for men only. The newer Kızılay Hamamı (men 6.30am–11pm; women noon–5pm) is about 500m northeast of the town centre on Faikbey Cad.

Hospital On the way to the airport, a few kilometres from the centre.

Post office Main PTT branch (open late into evenings) is a bit out of the way on Ordu Cad; there's also a useful *çarşı* branch on Kâzımpaşa Cad.

Ani and around

Once the capital of Bagratid Armenia, **ANI** is today a melancholy, almost vacant triangular plateau, divided from Armenia by the stunning Arpa Çayı (Ahuryan river) gorge and very nearly separated from the rest of Turkey by two deep tributaries. The site is mainly an expanse of rubble, but from it rise some of the finest examples of ecclesiastical and military architecture of its time. The Armenians were master stoneworkers, and the fortifications that defend the northern, exposed side of the plateau, and the handful of churches behind, are

Map labels:
- ▲ Kars
- P
- Aslan Kapısı (Lion Gate)
- TURKEY
- Selçuk Palace
- Church of St Gregory (of Gagik)
- Georgian Church (ruined)
- Path
- Path
- Stream
- Church of the Holy Apostles (Arak Elots)
- Oil or Wine Press
- Church of St Gregory (Abighamrets)
- Shops
- Cathedral
- Church of the Redeemer (Prkitch)
- Church of St Gregory (Tigran Honents)
- Alaca Çayı (dry)
- Menüçehir Camii
- "Palace"
- Convent of the Virgins (Kusanats)
- TURKEY
- Ruined Bridge
- Apra Çayı or Ahuryan River
- Citadel or İç Kale (off limits)
- ARMENIA
- Alaca Çayı (dry)
- Apra Çayı or Ahuryan River
- Monastery Kız Kilisesi (off limits)
- N
- 0   200 m
- ANI

exquisite compositions in a blend of ruddy sandstone and darker volcanic rock. Mining of the same materials has resulted in a few unsightly scars on the Armenian side of the border – surely a matter of spite, given their positioning. However, the gently undulating landscape remains as evocative as the ruins: it's inconceivable that you'd venture east of Erzurum or Artvin without fitting Ani into your plans.

Some history

The city first came to prominence after the local instalment of the Armenian Gamsarkan clan during the fifth century. Situated astride a major east–west caravan route, Ani prospered, receiving fresh impetus when Ashot III, fifth in the line of the Bagratid kings of Armenia, transferred his capital here from Kars in 961. For three generations the kingdom and its capital enjoyed a golden age. Beautified and strengthened militarily, with a population exceeding a hundred thousand, Ani rivalled Baghdad and Constantinople themselves.

By the middle of the eleventh century, however, wars of succession took their toll. The Byzantine Empire annexed the city in 1045, but in the process dissolved an effective bulwark against the approaching Selçuks, who took Ani with little resistance in 1064. After the collapse of the Selçuks, the Armenians returned in less than a century. The Pahlavuni and Zakhariad clans ruled over a reduced but still semi-independent Armenia for two more centuries, continuing to endow Ani with churches and monasteries. The Mongol raids of the thirteenth century, a devasting earthquake in 1319 and realigned trade routes proved mortal blows to both Ani and its hinterland; thereafter the city was gradually abandoned, and forgotten until noticed by European travellers of the nineteenth century.

The site

The vast **boundary walls** of Ani, dating from the late tenth century and studded with countless towers, are visible from several kilometres as you approach past villages teeming with sheep, buffalo, horses, donkeys and geese. The **ticket office** (daily 7am–8pm; 5TL) is at the **Aslan Kapısı**, so named because of a sculpted Selçuk lion on the wall just inside, and sole survivor of the four original gates.

Once beyond the inner wall you're confronted with the sight of the vast forlorn, weed-tufted plateau, dotted with only the sturdiest bits of masonry that have outlasted the ages. A system of **signposted paths**, many of them remnants of the former main streets of Ani, lead to or past all of the principal remains.

Church of the Redeemer

Bear slightly left and head first about 500m southeast to the **Church of the Redeemer** (Prkitch), built between 1034 and 1036. In 1957, half of the building was sheared away by lightning, so that the remainder, seen from the side, looks uncannily like a stage set, albeit one with carved filigree crosses and Armenian inscriptions. Three metres up on the exterior wall you can see a

---

Visiting Ani

Ani lies 45km southeast of Kars, just beyond the village of Ocaklı. Without your own transport, the most common way of getting there is to take a **taxi tour**, which will set you back around 120TL per car after haggling. Those travelling alone or in a pair should make use of the minibus drivers who do the rounds of hotels in Kars (see p.606), typically charging 30TL per person. The ruins are scattered, and many monuments are absorbing, so allow a good two and a half to three hours at Ani, plus two hours for going there and back – make sure your driver agrees to a **five-hour** stint. Midsummer is usually very **hot**, so you're advised to bring a hat, sun cream and water to tour the site – as well as some snack food. The site still nudges up against the highly sensitive Armenian border, and whole areas remain out of bounds. The *jandarma*, who patrol the site continuously, will let you know which areas these are.

frieze of a cross on an ornate rectangular background; this is a fine example of the typically Armenian *khatchkar* (literally "cross-stone") carvings that gave their name to the Kaçkar mountains.

Church of St Gregory

Some 200m east, tucked down a stair-path by a course of wall overlooking the Arpa Çayı, the charming monastic **Church of St Gregory the Illuminator** (Tigran Honents) is the best preserved of Ani's monuments, and somewhat confusingly one of three dedicated to the saint who brought Christianity to Armenia at the start of the fourth century. The pious foundation of a merchant nobleman in 1215, it's unusually laid out in a rectangle divided width-wise into three (though a colonnaded narthex and small baptistry have mostly collapsed). The ground plan reflects the prominent Georgian influence in thirteenth-century Ani, and the fact that the Orthodox, not the Armenian Apostolic, rite was celebrated here. The church still sports delicate exterior relief-work, including extensive avian designs.

The church is most rewarding for its **frescoes**, the only ones surviving at Ani, which cover most of the interior and spill out around the current entrance onto what was once the narthex wall, giving the church its Turkish name *Resimli Kilise* or "Painted Church". They are remarkable both for their high degree of realism and fluidity – especially compared to the static iconography of the contemporaneous Byzantines – and for the subject matter, depicting episodes in early Armenian Christianity as well as the doings of ordinary people.

The Convent of the Virgins

From Tigran Honents, a narrow trail leads past the Selçuk baths and skims the tops of the cliffs above the Arpa Çayı before finding a steep way down to the thirteenth-century **Convent of the Virgins** (Kusanats), perched on a ledge even closer to the river. A minuscule, rocket-like rotunda church, contemporary with Tigran Honents, is flanked by a smaller chapel or baptistry, and the whole enclosed by a perimeter wall. Just downstream are the evocative stubs of the ruined medieval **bridge** over the Arpa, though it's unwise (if not actually forbidden) to approach it – the Turkish bank of the river is stoutly fenced and probably mined as well.

The cathedral and around

Rejoining the main plateau trail heading west from Tigran Honents, you reach the elegantly proportioned **cathedral**, completed between 989 and 1010. The architect, one Trdat Mendet, could present rather impressive credentials, having very recently completed restoration of the earthquake-damaged dome of Aya Sofya in Constantinople. However, this is a surprisingly plain, rectangular building, with just the generic blind arcades of Armenian churches and no external apse; the dome, once supported by four massive pillars, has long since vanished. The main entrance was – unusually – not to the west, opposite the apse, but on the side of the nave, through the south wall. A **replica** of this church was in the early stages of being built at the time of writing – across on the Armenian side of the river, and clearly visible (and audible) from Ani itself.

Menüçehir Camii

A little to the west, within sight of the cathedral, is an excavated area, apparently a medieval **street lined with shops**. Just beyond stands what's known as the **Menüçehir Camii**, billed as the earliest Selçuk mosque in Anatolia, though its lack of *mihrab*, its alternating red and black stonework and its inlaid mosaic ceiling, invite suspicions of mixed antecedents. Certainly the view from the ornate gallery over the frontier river fits more with use as a small palace. The truncated minaret was briefly off-limits for a while after a tourist committed suicide by leaping off, though the daring may now clamber up the eroded steps for an unrivalled aerial view of the site. Slightly southwest, the foundations of a purportedly verified "**palace**" have been exposed.

The citadel and Kız Kilisesi

After the mosque, you'll probably meet the friendly *jandarma*, who will prevent you from wandering any further, and, presumably, from climbing up the minaret. The inner **citadel**, or İç Kale, has long languished in a forbidden zone and is likely to remain so, but a few travellers—and occasionally entire groups—are lucky enough to sneak through.

Beyond the fortress at the far south end of the city, also off-limits but visible from many points of the riverbank escarpment, perches the fairy-tale monastery of **Kız Kilisesi**, spectacularly sited above a sharp curve in the river gorge, and originally accessed by a tunnel carved into the rock that has long since eroded.

The northerly churches

North of the Menüçehir Camii stands the second **Church of St Gregory** (Abighamrets), begun in 1040 by the same individual responsible for the Church of the Redeemer. This rotunda is like no other at Ani – instead of just merely blind arcades in a flat surface, the twelve-sided exterior is pierced by functional recessed vaults, which alternate with the six rounded interior niches to lend extra structural stability.

The nearby, so-called "Kervansaray" began life as the eleventh-century **Church of the Holy Apostles** (Arak Elots), and despite ruinous first impressions proves a rewarding hybrid Selçuk–Christian monument. At first the church seems to have an odd south to north orientation, with a rounded apse at the north end – then you realize that this is the *kervansaray* bit added at a later date, and that the western half of the church nave is three-quarters crumbled but still discernible. Copious Armenian inscriptions confirm the building's original use, while overhead in the nave, superb four-way ribbing arcs cross an intricate ceiling in a two-colour mosaic pattern, culminating in a stalactite-vaulted dome.

The main circuit continues north to the sparse ruins of a third **Church of St Gregory of Gagik**, begun in 998 by Trdat, architect of the cathedral. Intact, it would have been one of the largest rotundas in medieval Armenia proper, but the design, based on the three-storey, seventh-century rotunda at Zvartnots in Armenia, collapsed almost immediately, so that today only man-high outer walls, bases of the dome piers and giant column-stumps remain.

Before completing your tour at the Aslan Kapısı, you can stop in at the **Selçuk Palace**, the only indisputably Islamic item at Ani, tucked into the northwest extremity of the ramparts. Since 1988, this has been meticulously rebuilt – the only structure to receive any degree of archeological investigation and mainte-nance, and a striking example of ultranationalist archeology in action.

Monuments around Ani

There are numerous local **churches and castles** – mostly Armenian – besides those at Ani, and a few can be visited with your own transport or a cooperative taxi. Be warned that there are absolutely no formal tourist facilities near any of those remote sites – bring picnic fare or trust in village hospitality. It's also worth enquiring about the status of Horomos, a monastic complex rivalling Ani for beauty and location, but currently off-limits to tourists.

Oğuzlu and Karmir Vank

The massive, tenth-century hilltop church of **Oğuzlu** is visible from some distance away; roofless and half-collapsed, it's devoid of ornament other than some blind niches on the exterior, flanking the apse. To reach it, head first to Subatan, itself 27km from Kars, then 11km northeast along the minor 36-06 road to Başgedikler; bear left at the T-junction.

Much more intact and interesting is the thirteenth-century **church of Karmir Vank** (in Turkish *Kızıl Kilise* – both mean "Red Monastery"). It's a beauty, despite being currently used as a barn, with hay and *tezek* patties stacked to one side and the land sloping gently down to a stream on the other. To get here from **Oğuzlu, return** to the junction at Başgedikler and proceed 4.5km east to the hamlet of **Bayraktar**. Loop around the right of the village, fork left and continue for 3.2km more to **Yağkesen**.

Monuments around Digor

The two currently visitable churches covered below are even more architecturally and historically significant than those around Ani, but require fairly long walks to reach and together will occupy nearly a full day in themselves, even with your own transport. **Digor** (Tekor in Armenian), 40km southeast of Kars, is the closest large village but has few amenities other than fairly frequent dolmuşes to and from Kars.

Khtskonk

The closest monument to Digor is a dramatically set church at **Khtskonk**, a few kilometres upstream along the Digor Çayı. There were originally five churches (hence the Turish name, *Beşkilise*) perched on the rim of the narrow canyon, but the rotunda of **St Sergius**, founded in 1029, is the sole survivor. All five were restored in 1878, but at some time between 1920 and 1965 the other four were destroyed either by rolling boulders onto them or with explosives. St Sergius's side-walls are rent by fissures, but the dome is still intact and the west wall is covered in intricate Armenian inscriptions, making it the equal of any single monument at Ani.

If you don't want to walk a fairly taxing hour up the gorge from the village, have the bus set you down, or drive, 4.5km north of town along Highway 70, near the top of the pass. Leave the vehicle here and turn onto a dirt track veering southwest from the asphalt, heading some 600m towards the gorge of the Digor Çayı. Walk behind the quarry and uphill for 200m, then turn left down a dry ravine. The path follows the right-hand bank downhill and then curves northwest to enter the gorge. Continue along the path, midway between the valley floor and cliff top above, for twenty minutes to reach the church.

Mren

Once the focus of a fair-sized town, the seventh-century Cathedral of **Mren** (Mirini) stands atop a very slight rise, near the confluence of the Digor and Arpa streams. The town was abandoned at some point in the fourteenth century amidst İlhanid Mongol raids, but its rubble still litters the immediate surroundings. The cathedral was completed in 640 by David Saharuni, Prince of Armenia, and is one of Turkey's earliest examples of Armenian architecture. Built of alternating red and dark basalt blocks, it weathered the centuries remarkably well before 1920, though the southwest corner and south transept vault have collapsed since then. The most outstanding **decorative features** include numerous, extravagant *khatchkars* on the inner and outer south wall; the outer apse and north wall are by contrast featureless except for a somewhat defaced lintel relief over the north door, showing the *Restoration of the Cross* at Jerusalem in 630, following its removal by the Persians in 614.

To reach Mren from Digor, head southeast for 21km on Highway 70. Keep an eye peeled for a dirt road heading east, rustily signposted for the village of **Karabağ**. After 2km along the proper detour, Mren appears on the horizon beyond the village. Vehicles must be left just after Karabağ, from where it's a fifty-minute walk (4.5km) to the church.

Travel details

Trains

Erzurum to: Ankara (2 daily; 21hr); Divriği (2 daily; 7hr); İstanbul (daily; 32hr); Kars (2 daily; 5hr); Sivas (2 daily; 10hr).
Kars to: Ankara (2 daily; 26–28hr); Erzurum (2 daily; 5hr); İstanbul (daily; 37hr); Sivas (2 daily; 16hr).

Buses and dolmuşes

Artvin to: Ardahan via Şavşat (10 daily; 3hr); Ardanuç (6 daily; 45min); Erzurum (4 daily; 4hr 30min); Hopa (hourly until 3pm; 1hr 30min); Kars (1 daily; 6hr); Rize (hourly until 3pm; 2hr 15min); Şavşat (7 daily; 2hr); Trabzon (5 daily; 4hr); Yusufeli (4 daily; 1hr 45min).
Erzurum to: Ankara (4 daily; 13hr); Artvin (5 daily; 4hr 15min); Bayburt (hourly; 2hr); Doğubeyazıt (4 daily; 4hr); İspir (3 daily; 2hr); Kars (6 daily; 3hr); Rize (2 daily; 6hr); Sivas (12 daily; 7hr 30min); Trabzon (3 daily; 5hr); Van (1–2 daily; 6hr); Yusufeli (3 daily; 3hr).
Kars to: Ardahan (hourly; 1hr 30min); Artvin via Göle (daily; 5hr); Çıldır (2 daily; 1hr 30min); Digor (hourly; 45min); Erzurum (6 daily; 3hr); Iğdır (hourly; 3hr); Trabzon (daily; 7hr).
Yusufeli to: Artvin (5 daily; 1hr 45min); Barhal (4 daily; 1hr 30min); Erzurum (2 daily in the morning before 1pm; 3hr); Hevek (2 daily; 3hr); Tekkale (1–3 daily; 15min).

Flights

Erzurum to: Ankara (1 or 2 daily; 1hr 30min); İstanbul (2 or 3 daily; 2hr).
Kars to: Ankara (1 daily; 1hr 50min); İstanbul (2 or 3 daily; 2hr 30min).

11

The Euphrates and Tigris basin

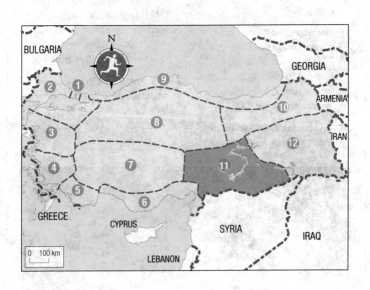

CHAPTER 11 # Highlights

* **Gaziantep Archeology Museum** A magnificent collection of Roman-era mosaics, rescued from the drowned site of Zeugma and displayed in a state-of-the-art museum. **See p.621**

* **Göbekli Tepe** This spectacular hilltop Neolithic site, still under excavation, is offering new insights into hunter-gatherer societies. **See p.628**

* **Nemrut Dağı** One of the classic images of Turkey – massive stone heads of Hellenistic deities glare out from a remote mountain-top sanctuary. **See p.633**

* **Diyarbakır** Walk around the mighty basalt walls of this predominately Kurdish city, high above medieval alleys teeming with street kids. **See p.638**

* **Mardin** A hilltop town of beautiful Arab-style houses interspersed with graceful mosques affording stunning views over the Mesopotamian plain. **See p.645**

* **Syrian Orthodox Church** Catch a service in Diyarbakır, Mardin or Midyat, and experience a liturgy that has remained virtually unchanged for 1500 years. **See p.648**

* **Hasankeyf** A dam-threatened medieval city, spectacularly situated on a soaring cliff overlooking the green Tigris. **See p.652**

▲ Sultan İsa Medresesi, Mardin

The Euphrates and Tigris basin

The **basin of the Euphrates and Tigris rivers**, a broad plain ringed on three sides by the mountains is the most exotic part of Turkey, offering travellers a heady mix of atmospheric ancient sites and bustling Middle East-style towns. The region forms the northern rim of ancient Mesopotamia (literally "between two rivers") and has been fought over for thousands of years. Having formed the boundaries of the Roman and Byzantine empires, the Euphrates and Tigris were crossed by Muslim invaders from the south and east after the birth of Islam in 632 AD. Thereafter, almost everybody of any import in Middle Eastern affairs seems to have passed through the region: Arabs, Crusaders, Armenians, Selçuks, Turcomans, Mongols and finally the French, who invaded southeastern Turkey as part of a wider attempt by the victorious World War I Allies to break up the defeated Ottoman Empire.

Traditionally, smallholding farmers and herdsmen scratched a living from this unrewarding land. Today, the new dams of the **Southeastern Anatolia Project** (see boxes, p.619 & p.652) have dramatically improved fertility in the west of the area, but population drift to the big cities continues. Ethnic Turks are in the minority here. Close to the Syrian border, Arab influence is strong, but **Kurds** predominate the further east or north you go. The potential volatility of this racial mix has been exacerbated by the separatist sympathies of some Kurds, and there is often a security presence in the area – particularly around Diyarbakır and the frontier zone south and east of Mardin (see p.67 for more information).

First stop coming from the west is **Gaziantep**, a city booming on its new-found industrial wealth. East of here, the road shoots across the plain to cross the River Euphrates at bleached **Birecik** before cutting through rocky uplands to the venerable town of **Şanlıurfa** – more commonly known as Urfa – well worth a couple of days' sightseeing and a good base for exploring **Harran**, an evocative village of beehive-shaped houses, and Neolithic **Göbekli Tepe**.

North of Gaziantep, the spectacular mountain-top funerary sanctuary of **Nemrut Dağı** fully justifies a pilgrimage, though neither of the two bases for reaching it from the south – small, scruffy **Kahta**, and larger, tidier **Adıyaman** – are particularly enticing towns. Malataya, to the north, makes for a more attractive gateway to Nemrut, and boasts the nearby attractions of **Eski Malatya** and **Aslantepe**.

From either Şanlıurfa or Malatya, it's a journey of half a day or less to **Diyarbakır**, a rapidly expanding, predominantly Kurdish city on the banks of the River Tigris.

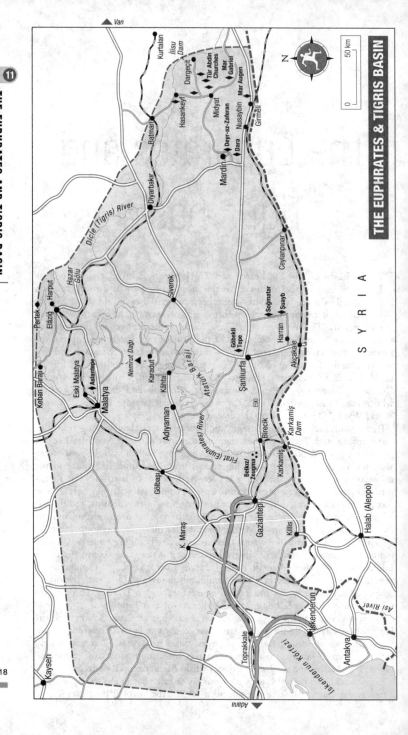

THE EUPHRATES & TIGRIS BASIN

The Southeastern Anatolia Project (GAP)

The colossally expensive Güneydoğu Anadolu Projesi (GAP), or **Southeastern Anatolia Project** was begun in 1974 with the aim of improving economic conditions in Turkey's impoverished southeast. Centred on the massive Atatürk Dam, the fourth largest in the world, the US$32 billion scheme has diverted waters from the Euphrates and Tigris to irrigate vast swathes of previously barren land and generate much needed hydroelectric power. The scheme also has a clear political aim in reducing support for the separatist Kurdistan Workers Party (PKK) who have long been active in this region and vehemently oppose the project.

In terms of the local benefits of GAP, the improvement to agriculture is apparent from the main road. Eastwards from Gaziantep new pistachio and olive plantations flourish and cotton is being grown around Harran. Yet, while this has benefited large landowners able to secure state bank loans to buy fertilizer and machinery, smaller farmers have seen few improvements. Many have given up agriculture altogether and migrated to the cities to work as unskilled labourers.

Environmentalists point out the scheme's other pitfalls, from local climate change caused by evaporation from the reservoirs, to depletion of the soil from the overuse of artificial fertilizers and severe loss of habitat for local wildlife. The region's archeological heritage has been hit, too. While some artefacts have been painstakingly excavated and relocated (note especially the wonderful finds from Zeugma now on display in Gaziantep, much has vanished forever beneath the waters.

Famed for its 6km black basalt city walls, Diyarbakır is also peppered with some fine mosques and churches. To the south lies **Mardin**, with its atmospheric collection of vernacular houses set on a crag overlooking the Syrian plain. East of here, the **Tür Abdin** plateau, scattered with monasteries and churches, is home to the remnants of Turkey's Syrian Orthodox Christian population. At its heart lies **Midyat**, a town of elegant mansions and working churches. The monastery of **Mar Gabriel** to the south, supported largely by émigrés, keeps the faith alive. Between Midyat and Diyarbakır, are the evocative ruins of **Hasankeyf**, breathtakingly sited on the Tigris, yet soon set to disappear beneath the waters of the İlisu Dam (see box, p.652).

Travelling around is easy, with good bus links between all the major towns – though road-improvement works are prevalent in many places, increasing journey times. Hotel facilities have improved steadily and you will have little trouble finding a reasonable hotel. Summers are scorching; try to visit during spring or autumn.

Bear in mind that the main point for **crossing to Syria** is not in this region, but Antakya in the Hatay (see p.430).

Gaziantep and around

Rapidly expanding **GAZIANTEP**, with a population in excess of a million, is the wealthiest city in the region. One of the main beneficiaries of the GAP project, its income derives largely from textile production, agriculture (it's famed for its **pistachio nuts**) and trade with Syria (Aleppo, Syria's second city, is just 100km away). Under its go-ahead AKP mayor, many of the city's beautiful, pale-stone historic buildings have been restored, including its impressive castle. The **archeological museum**, which houses the best collection of **mosaics** in the country, is simply stunning and it alone makes a trip here worthwhile.

Known by local people as "Antep", a corruption of the Arab *ayn teb* ("good spring"); the prefix "Gazi" ("warrior for Islam") was only added in 1920 after Turkish Nationalist forces withstood a ten-month siege by the French.

Arrival, information and services

Gaziantep's old Christian/Jewish quarter is built on a hill above the prominent Atatürk statue in front of the *Adliye* (court) building. From here, Hürriyet Caddesi/İstasyon Caddesi runs 1.5km down past a large park flanking the river to the museum. The old Muslim quarter, centred on the castle, lies a short walk northeast of the Atatürk statue.

The **otogar**, 5km northwest of the centre, has free service buses, minibuses (1.25TL) or taxis (12TL) into town. Get off at Hükümet Konağı, near the junction of Suburcu and Hürriyet *caddesi*s, close to most of the city's hotels and restaurants. The **train station** stands at the north end of İstasyon Caddesi, 2km from the centre; with dolmuşes (1.25TL) into town. **Sazgan airport** is 10km to the southeast; taxi (35TL) or Havaş buses (8YTL) run to a spot just west of the *Büyükşehir Belediyesi* (Municipality Building), some 500m northwest of the city centre. The THY office is at the airport (☎0342/582 1045). Onur Air has a ticket office in İncirli Pınar Mah, Kazaz İş Merkezi 26 (☎0342/221 0304), though most travel agencies sell tickets for all domestic carriers – try Fırsat Turizm on Suburcu Cad 16/A (☎0342/232 8825).

Gaziantep's **tourist office** occupies a colonial-style building in Yüzüncü Yıl Parkı (Mon–Fri 9am–noon & 1–5pm; ☎0342/230 5969) and provides good maps of the town. The main **PTT** is just west of the *Adliye* building. **Car rental** outfits abound, with rates from 70TL per day: try Şimsek, Değirmiçem Mah, Dr Kemal Ahi Cad, Barış Apt 16 (☎0342/215 1770), Avis, Ordu Cad 15/A (☎0342/336 1194) or Hertz, Ordu Cad 92/C (☎0342/336 7718). The Sev Amerikan Hastanesi (☎0342/220 0211) on Yuksek Sok 3, Tepebaşı Mah, housed in old American mission buildings, is the city's best **hospital**.

Accommodation

The city has a healthy mix of business-orientated and boutique-style hotels, though there's less choice at the budget end of the market. The boutique hotels, all housed in period Ottoman or Armenian dwellings, are either in the old Christian/Jewish quarter or the bazaar.

A Butik Otel Eyüpoğlu Mah, Baymahli Sok 1 ☎0342/230 1013, ⊛www.butikaotel.com. Beautifully converted Armenian house dating back to 1886. There's all mod cons including wi-fi, a/c and spacious bathrooms with tubs. Very well run by the lively manager, Leyla. ⑤

Anadolu Evleri Köroğlu Sok 6 ☎0342/220 9525, ⊛www.anadoluevleri.com. The most authentic of the boutique hotel conversions, the high-ceilinged rooms are lined with period fitted cupboards. There's a cosy bar off the courtyard, there's bags of atmosphere and the castle is just a few minutes' walk. ⑥

Belkiz Suburcu Cad, Çamurcu Sok 4 ☎0342/220 2020. Dowdy but quiet and comfortable a/c rooms, it is convenient for the bazaar and castle. It's also very good value for a two-star establishment. ②

Belkis Han Kayacık Ara Sok 16 ☎0342/231 1084, ⊛www.belkishan.com. A carefully restored old townhouse built around a courtyard in the old Christian/Jewish quarter, it offers individually decorated and furnished rooms, a reading room, cellar bar and wonderful breakfasts. ⑤

Evin Kayacak Sok 11 ☎0342/231 3492. Small but passable rooms, the *Evin* is handily situated between the modern centre and the old Christian/Jewish quarter. Unfortunately its unventilated bathrooms are showing some mould. Bargaining should produce a discount. ②

Katan İstasyon Cad 58 ☎0342/230 6969, ⒻAX 220 8454. It's much better than it looks from the outside and the well-tended rooms are air-conditioned, with mini-bar and TV. Back rooms are quieter and have great views to the castle, plus there's a cosy lobby bar and wi-fi. ③

Met Gold Suburcu Caddesi, Çamurcu Sok 1 ☎0342/231 4242, ⊛www.gaziantepmetgold.com. Flashy, centrally located joint which may appeal if boutique hotels are not your thing. Bathrooms boast big tubs, there's an impressive open-buffet breakfast, plus a fitness centre, sauna and all the usual 4-star trimmings, including wi-fi. ④

Tudyalı Konak Tepebaşı Mah, Hastahane Cad 13 ☎0342/232 7060, ⊛www.tudyalikonak.com. With an excellent location on a hill behind the

Armenian Church of St Mary's, this newly opened boutique hotel has great potential. It's superbly appointed (wi-fi, a/c etc), very tasteful and has smart, attentive staff; the only letdown is its exposed courtyard. ⑤

The City

Gaziantep has been successively occupied by the Hittites, Assyrians, Persians, Alexandrines, Romans, Selçuks, Crusaders, Byzantines and Arabs. Its prize asset is the **archeological museum** on İstasyon Caddesi (Arkeoloji Müzesi; Tues–Sun 8.00am–noon & 1–5pm; 3TL). Pick of the exhibits is a superb collection of some 800 square metres of mosaic rescued from the once-luxurious Hellenistic/Roman border-city of Zeugma (see p.623), now virtually submerged by the Birecik dam on the Euphrates. Particularly impressive are the re-creations of Roman peristyle villas, complete with their original mosaic flooring. The mosaics are complemented by some fine frescoes, salvaged from Zeugma, and a magnificent bronze statue of the god of war, Mars. The original part of the museum also houses a collection of Hittite reliefs from Yesenek, 100km west of Gaziantep.

Gaziantep's imposing **kale** (under restoration at the time of writing) dominates the town from the eastern hill – a partly artificial mound comprising the accumulated debris of millennia of occupation. The present structure, with its 36 towers, is largely Mamluk, though there has been a castle here at least since Roman times. A ramp leads to the interior, where there are the remains of an excavated Ottoman hamam and a couple of nineteenth-century Russian-made cannon. The views over the city are splendid.

The **bazaar quarter** to the south of the *kale* is home to several *han*s, as well as a number of attractive mosques, with Syrian-style enclosed balconies atop the minarets. Look out in particularly for the nineteenth-century **Alauddevle Camii**, with its bands of contrasting black and white stone, designed by an Armenian architect. The Ottoman-era **Tahtani** and **Şirvani** mosques, to the south and west of the *kale* respectively, are also worth seeking out. Many of these fine buildings

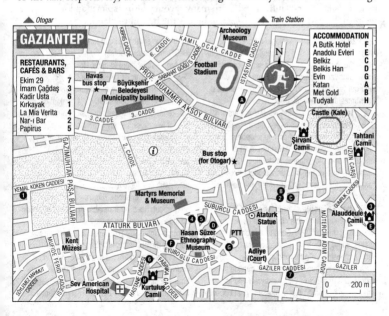

have been restored recently, with handy explanatory signboards in Turkish, Arabic and English. Craftsmen still manufacture furniture inlaid with *sedef* (mother-of-pearl) and beat tin and copper in the bazaar.

Built on a hill west of the Atatürk statue the former **Christian/Jewish quarter** boasts a large number of old courtyard houses. In readiness against attack, every dwelling had its own well, food cellars and stabling, as can be seen at the **Hasan Süzer Ethnography Museum** (Hasan Süzer Etnografi Müzesi; daily 8am–noon & 1–5pm; 3TL). The museum freeze-frames the life of an upper-class Antep family in the 1930s, with a series of traditionally laid-out rooms slightly let down by the incongruous mannequins. Under the courtyard is a basement used originally for food storage, above it a German-made motorcycle said to have belonged to Lawrence of Arabia. Perched near the top of the hill is the monumental **Kurtuluş Camii** (Independence Mosque), with black and white stone trim and restrained carvings around the windows. Built in 1892 as the Church of the Virgin Mary, it is claimed to be the largest Armenian church in the Middle East.

Another nineteenth-century church, the Catholic **Kendirli Kilisesi**, on Atatürk Bulvarı, is now an exhibition hall, but its imposing black and white banded exterior still bears bullet and shrapnel scars from the War of Independence. Nearby is the **Martyrs Memorial and Museum**, remembering the 6317 Turks who lost their lives between April 1920 and February 1921, defending their city against a vastly superior French force. For more on the city's fight for independence, visit the state-of-the-art **Gaziantep Kent Müzesi** (9.00am–6.30pm daily except Mondays; free). A mixture of exhibits, mock-ups and video presentations give fascinating background information on the city's history, culture and economy (headsets with English-language commentary are available).

Eating and drinking

Gaziantep is unrivalled in Turkey for sweets, particularly pistachio-based pastries like *baklava* and *fıstık sarma*. Not surprisingly given the proximity of Syria, much of its cuisine is Arab-influenced, with many savoury dishes spicier and sourer than western Turkish dishes – the *lahmacun* here is the best in the land.

Ekim 29 Gaziler Cad, Cekemoğlu Çıkmaz. Attracting a mainly young clientele, this café/bar in a beautiful old Armenian house is set around a shady courtyard. It serves simple snacks or will send out for kebabs and there is live Turkish music lunchtimes and evenings. Beer 6TL.

İmam Çağdaş Kale Cıvarı Uzun Çarşısı 49. Best at lunchtimes (when it's thronging with local shopkeepers, craftsmen and shoppers) is this long-established traditional restaurant. The *lahmacun* are spicy, huge and delicious (2.5TL) and the *ayran* is served up in a tinned copper bowl. Its *baklava* is famed even in Gaziantep, the home of the stuff.

Kadir Usta Eyüpoğlu Mah Eblehan Cad 25. Close to the Kurtuluş Camii, this cheap and cheerful place was established in 1966. Despite its humble origins, some of Turkey's top celebrities have eaten here – choosing from *lahmacun*, kebabs – or trying the local meaty soup, *beyran*. Some outside tables.

Kırkayak Kemal Köker Cad, Kırkayak Parkı İçi, Palatial, faux-Ottoman place, pleasantly set opposite a park. The emphasis is on families and local fare (6–9TL for a main course). Try the tiny, sour *köfte* or the tender mushroom kebabs. No alcohol.

La Mia Verita Hanifioğlu Sok 15 Gaziantep's only rock/blues/rap bar doesn't come cheap, with beers 8TL (first drink at weekends 10TL includes admission) but there's decent live music nightly in an old courtyard house with a cool, open-air terrace at one end. Also dishes up local Gaziantep food.

Nar-ı Bar Çamurcu Sok, off Suburcu Cad. A dark, atmospheric basement bar next to the *Met Gold* hotel, with live *Türkü* music every night – it's a far cry from the other seedy *Türkü* bars and *birahane*s roundabout. Beers a reasonable 6TL, kebabs cooked up in the *Met Gold*'s restaurant are 12TL.

Papirus Noter Sok 10 There's a rash of *nargile* cafés in the old Jewish/Christian quarter – this was one of the first and has a great vine-shaded courtyard and cheap (nonalcoholic) drinks. In the empty upstairs rooms are some peeling, over-the-top nineteenth-century European-style murals.

East of Gaziantep: towards Şanlıurfa

Summer temperatures edge into the mid-40s centigrade east of Gaziantep. When buying a bus ticket, try and get a seat on the shady side.

Karkamış and Zeugma

Karkamış, the ancient Hittite city of Carchemish, 25km south of the highway, lies in a military zone right on the Syrian frontier and is off-limits at present. Many of the reliefs unearthed here by British archeologist Leonard Woolley, along with T.E. Lawrence, in the early twentieth century, can be seen in the Museum of Anatolian Civilizations in Ankara.

From Nizip, on the same highway, it's 9km north to the waterside excavations at Hellenisitic/Roman **Zeugma**. The once-rich city was strategically founded on a major crossing point of the Euphrates by one of Alexander the Great's generals. The Birecik Dam waters submerged most of the ancient villas here but an international archeological rescue mission in 2000 recovered many mosaics, now on display in Gaziantep. Set to become an open-air museum, the site was off-limits at the time of writing due to ongoing excavations. For the latest on both sites ask at Gaziantep's archeological museum.

Birecik

The highway crosses the Euphrates River at scruffy **BIRECIK**, 40km from Gaziantep. The endangered **bald ibis**, a relative of the stork, once nested wild here but is now confined to a **breeding station** (April–Oct daily during daylight hours), 1km north of town on the east riverbank. Birds are released into the wild every year, but so far none has migrated back. **Storks** themselves are ubiquitous both here and elsewhere in this region, best seen in spring and summer occupying their nests atop electricity pylons, telegraph poles and minarets.

Birecik's **castle**, founded during the eleventh century, was a frontier outpost for the Crusader state of Edessa. In ruins now, both it and its entourage of old houses backed into the cliff-face are best seen from the west bank of the Euphrates, where the pleasant *Kıyı Restaurant* stands in shady grounds right on the water's edge.

Şanlıurfa

The name of **ŞANLIURFA**, or "Glorious Urfa" (most of the locals just say Urfa) commemorates resistance to the French invasion and occupation of 1918–1920. A place of pilgrimage for many religions and the reputed birthplace of the prophet Abraham, its chief attraction is a beautiful mosque complex, reflected in the limpid waters of a sacred pool. Just as compelling is the town's distinctly Middle Eastern atmosphere. Much of the population is Kurdish, a significant minority Arab, and you'll find the bazaars full of veiled, henna-tattooed women and men wearing baggy trousers and traditional headdresses. In Turkey this "city of the prophets" has gained a reputation as a focus for Islamic fundamentalism – alcohol has almost disappeared from restaurants (though not bars) and the good citizens retire early to bed. Visiting female pilgrims are often fully veiled and clad in black from top to toe.

Urfa is currently Turkey's second fastest-growing city, thanks largely to the money generated by the GAP project, though it still ranks very low (68 out of 81) in terms of socio-economic development, a fact clear from a walk around its impoverished backstreets.

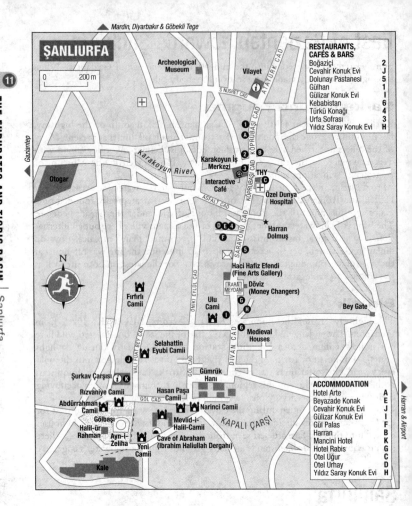

Mardin, Diyarbakır & Göbekli Tege

ŞANLIURFA

0   200 m

Archeological Museum

Vilayet

Otogar

Karakoyun River

Karakoyun İş Merkezi

Interactive Café

Özel Dunya Hospital

Harran Dolmuş

Hacı Hafız Efendi (Fine Arts Gallery)

KARA MEYDANI

Döviz (Money Changers)

Ulu Camii

Medieval Houses

Bey Gate

Fırfırlı Camii

Selahattin Eyubi Camii

Gümrük Hanı

Şurkav Çarşısı

Rızvaniye Camii

Hasan Paşa Camii

Narinci Camii

KAPALI ÇARŞI

Abdürrahman Camii

Gölbaşı

Mevlid-i-Halil-Camii

Halil-ür Rahman

Ayn-i-Zeliha

Yeni Camii

Cave of Abraham (Ibrahim Haliullah Dergahı)

Kale

Gaziantep

Harran & Airport

RESTAURANTS, CAFÉS & BARS

Boğaziçi	2
Cevahir Konuk Evi	J
Dolunay Pastanesi	5
Gülhan	1
Gülizar Konuk Evi	I
Kebabistan	6
Türkü Konağı	4
Urfa Sofrası	3
Yıldız Saray Konuk Evi	H

ACCOMMODATION

Hotel Arte	A
Beyazade Konak	E
Cevahir Konuk Evi	J
Gülizar Konuk Evi	I
Gül Palas	F
Harran	B
Mancini Hotel	K
Hotel Rabis	G
Otel Uğur	C
Otel Urhay	D
Yıldız Saray Konuk Evi	H

Some history

The first settlers were the Hurri, members of one of Anatolia's earliest civilizations, who built a fortress on the site of the present citadel around 3500 BC. Later came the Hittites and Assyrians, but only after it was re-founded as Edessa by Seleucus Nicator in 300 BC did the city eclipse nearby Harran. It later became an important eastern outpost for the Romans against Persia.

From the second century AD, Edessa was a thriving centre of Christianity, and Abgar IV (176–213) made it the world's first Christian kingdom. The city changed hands between Byzantine and Arab several times; according to Syrian Orthodox legend it was once ransomed for the "*mandalyon*", a hankerchief bearing the imprint of Christ. As Byzantine control ebbed, the Arabs moved in, staying until the eleventh century. During the First Crusade, a French count, Baldwin of Boulogne, stopped off en route to Tripoli and the Holy Land to establish the county of Edessa, a short-lived Christian state. In 1144 the Arabs recaptured Edessa, giving the rulers of Europe a pretext to launch the Second Crusade. In

1260 it was sacked by the Mongols and never recovered, declining into obscurity before being absorbed (as Urfa) into the Ottoman Empire in 1637.

Arrival and information

Urfa's current **otogar** is a kilometre west of the centre, but a new one is under construction further out. Adjoining it is the provincial dolmuş garage for transport onto Kahta/Adiyaman for Nemrut Dağı. Buses into town are (1TL), taxis a steep 10TL. The well-known *Hotel Harran* on Köprübaşı Caddesi, makes a good orientation point, as most of the hotels and other tourist facilities are found around here. The **airport** is about 6km south of town, on the road to Harran, with a Havaş bus (8TL) into the centre.

The **tourist office**, located in the *Vilayet* building (Provincial Governor's headquarters), out of town on Atatürk Caddesi, is next to useless.

Accommodation

Accommodation at all levels is plentiful, from simple backpacker joints to plush chains. A fairly recent addition to the scene are "boutique" hotels fashioned from some of Urfa's fine old stone houses. Be warned, though, that the quality of some of these is variable (always ask to see a room first) – and others host noisy traditional music evenings (see box, p.627) until the early hours.

Hotel Arte Atatürk Bul/Sinema Sok 7, ☏ 0414/314 7060, ⊛ www.otel-arte.com. Good-value designer hotel with simple but stylish rooms boasting laminate parquet floors, a/c, flat-screen TVs et al, and is very well located in the central business/tourist area around Köprübaşı. There's wi-fi and beer in the minibar. ❸

Beyazade Konak Sarayönü Cad, Yusufpaşa Camii Yanı ☏ 0414/216 3535, ⊛ www.beyzadekonak .com. First of the new wave of budget boutique hotels, this authentic old mansion building is good value and, despite the disappointingly modern furnishings, has character. Particularly impressive are the vaulted-ceiling dining room and shady courtyard. Occasionally hosts *sıra gecesi* (traditional music nights). ❷

Cevahir Konuk Evi Selahhattin Eyyub Camii Karşısı, ☏ 0414/215 9377. Best of the city's boutique hotels, it's set in a quiet street in a beautiful building (once part of an Armenian monastery) set around a courtyard. It has been very expertly restored and oozes good taste and boasts all the requisite luxury features. The only potential drawback is the noise from the *sıra gecesi*. ❺

Harran Atatürk Cad ☏ 0414/313 2860, ⊛ www .hotelharran.com. Good-value four-star place, the *Harran* is equipped with a pleasant and private

outdoor swimming pool, hamam and bar. The rooms are comfortable and bathrooms spotless – ask for one in the newer B block, which is quieter. ❹

Mancini Hotel Şurkavi Alışveriş Merkezi 68, ☏ 0414/215, ⊛ www.mancini.com.tr. Successor to the now defunct *Edessa*, this opulent (some might say over-the-top) hotel is well located right opposite Balıklı Göl. Rooms feature elaborately hand-painted furniture and chintzy soft-furnishings as well as standard features like a/c, wi-fi, TV and en-suite bathrooms with tubs. ❺

Hotel Rabis Sarayönü Cad, PTT Karşısı, ☏ 0414/216 9595, ⊛ www.hotelrabis.com. New and spotlessly clean, comfortable hotel, with a/c, flat-screen TVs, wi-fi and minibar. It's not quite so stylish as the *Arte*, but just as comfy and boasts a terrace where you can breakfast overlooking the old city. Recommended. ❹

Otel Uğur Köprübaşı Cad 3 ☏ 0414/313 1340, ⓔ musma63@yahoo.com. Behind the Özel Dünya Hospital, the *Uğur* is much favoured by backpackers, with basic, garish but clean a/c rooms and comfy beds. The few rooms without bathrooms are even cheaper and the shared showers and loos are kept very clean. Also has wi-fi or free internet access. The helpful owner Mustafa can arrange Harran/Nemrut tours (see listings). ❶

Old Urfa

At the extreme south end of Sarayönü Caddesi is the restored **Hacı Hafiz Efendi** house, now a fine arts gallery. Adjacent is the **Kara Meydanı**, boasting a venerable-looking nineteenth-century mosque, the Yusuf Paşa Camii. Past Kara

Meydanı, Sarayönü Caddesi becomes Divan Caddesi, where you'll find the twelfth-century **Ulu Cami**, a typical Arab design based on the Grand Mosque in Aleppo in Syria. The courtyard boasts a massive octagonal minaret (originally the belfry of the fifth-century Church of St Stephen) and graves, though the interior is unexceptional. Old, stone-built houses, many of them once owned by the city's long-departed Armenian community, sprawl either side of the main drag.

The **Gümrük Hanı**, at the end of Divan Caddesi, is a magnificent late sixteenth-century *kervansaray*, whose shady courtyard is taken up by the tables of teahouses and watch repairers. Surrounding it is a warren of narrow, covered streets – the **Kapalı Çarşı**, or covered bazaar. Here there are stalls and hole-in-the-wall shops selling everything imaginable, from spices to guns. Green Diyarbakır tobacco is sold by the kilo out of plastic sacks, while the pungent stink of skins from freshly slaughtered sheep vies with the more pleasant odour of various powdered herbs.

Turning right out of the Gümrük Hanı brings you to the *bedesten* next door, beyond which lies the **Hacı Kamil Hanı** and the coppersmiths' bazaar. Further west lie the **Sipahi** and **Hüseyniye** bazaars, both left over from the time when camel caravans moved regularly between Urfa and Aleppo, Palmyra, Mari and Baghdad.

İbrahim Halilullah Dergahı

West of the bazaar, the **Hızır İbrahim Halilullah**, a colonnaded mosque and *medrese* complex named after the "Prophet Abraham and Friend of God", attracts numerous pilgrims. The **İbrahim Halilullah Dergahı** or "Cave of Abraham" (daily 8am–5.30pm; donations welcomed) is set in the wall of the far courtyard. According to local legend, the prophet Abraham was born here, spending the first ten years of his life in hiding because a local Assyrian tyrant, Nemrut (Nimrod), had decreed that all newborn children be killed.

As Abraham is recognized as a prophet by Muslims, his birth-cave is a place of worship and the majority of visitors are pilgrims from all over Turkey and the Muslim world. Inside is a pool where women throw a coin in the hope of having their wish (often to become pregnant) granted. The atmosphere is reverential; there are separate entrances for men and women, dress must be respectful and shoes removed. There is another holy cave nearby, reputed to hold a hair plucked from Mohammed's head, and a modern, Ottoman-style mosque, the Yeni Cami.

Gölbaşı and the kale

Gölbaşı – literally "at the lakeside" – is a beautifully green and shady park at the foot of the *kale*, centred on a pair of mosques and two pools filled with fat carp. According to a continuation of the local legend, Abraham, after he emerged from his cave, became an implacable opponent of King Nemrut and tried to smash the idols in the local temple. The displeased tyrant had Abraham hurled from the citadel battlements into a fire below. Abraham was saved when God turned the flames into water and the firewood into carp. The carp are considered sacred, and it's said that anyone who eats them will go blind.

Beside the first pool, the **Ayn-i-Zeliha** (named after the daughter of Nimrod), are shady teahouses and cafés. The elongated **Halil-ür Rahman** or Balıklı Göl is the pool that saved Abraham from a fiery end; it's surrounded by stone arches, its banks usually swarming with pilgrims and the water seething with fish (you can feed the carp with bait bought from poolside vendors).

The far western end of Balıklı Göl is closed off by the seventeenth-century **Abdür-rahman Camii**. The present mosque replaced an older twelfth-century building whose square minaret, possibly once a church belfry, has survived. The north side of the pool is flanked by the **Rizvaniye Camii**, built by an Ottoman governor in 1716, with some intricately carved wooden doors giving onto its peaceful courtyard.

Above Gölbaşı, and reachable via a signed path between the new mosque and the first pool, is Urfa's massive **kale** (Tues–Sun 9am–6pm; 3TL). Much of the castle's surviving structure is Mamluk. The interior has long-since vanished but it's worth clambering up (either by an external stairway or through a long, stepped tunnel) for the bird's-eye view over Urfa. At the top are a couple of massive, lone Corinthian columns, thought to be the remains of the palace of a second-century Christian king, Abgar. Look out for the crudely carved Syriac inscription near the bottom of one of the columns.

North to the archeological museum

The **Selahattin Eyubi Camii**, on Vali Fuat Bey Caddesi, was built in 1860 as the Armenian church of St John and only recently converted into a mosque. Head north again for a glimpse of the former Armenian church of the Twelve Apostles, now the **Fırfırlı Camii**. Further north is the **Karakoyun River**, spanned by a Byzantine aqueduct, built in 525 and now squeezed between two Ottoman bridges. Some of the ruined old houses above the river bear the pockmarks of French rifle bullets fired during the assault on the city in 1920.

The city's excellent **archeological museum** (Arkeoloji Müzesi; Tues–Sun 8am–noon & 1.30–5.30pm; 3TL) is just north of the town centre. Inside, there's jewellery and pottery from funerary tumuli on the Euphrates flood plain, and from the sites of ancient Harran and Lidar. Look out for the stunning anthropomorphic statue, found in central Urfa and dating back 11,000 years, and the animal carvings (only marginally more recent) from the unique Neolithic site of Göbekli Tepe (see p.628). The garden contains more statuary and relief-carvings, and there's a very pleasant tea garden in the adjacent park.

Eating and drinking

This is the home of the **Urfa kebap** (spiced minced meat on a skewer) and **lahmacun** (a thin, chapati-like bread topped with spicy lamb). Numerous simple eateries offer other local specialities based on bulgur (cracked wheat), notably *çiğ köfte*). *Ciğer* (liver) kebabs are big business too, eaten accompanied by lashings of raw onion and hot pepper; **şıllık**, a local *baklava*, is made with walnuts and cream. Be warned that travellers seem to suffer more from **stomach bugs** and food

---

Sira Geceleri – a night out in Urfa

Originally **sira geceleri** (literally "nights by turn") were informal gatherings of male friends at one of their homes, where a meal and conversation was accompanied by traditional live music. The idea was picked up by several Urfa restaurants (invariably sited in an old courtyard house) and now "guests" pay for the experience, sitting cross-legged at a low *sofra* table and tucking into a banquet of speciality local dishes whilst being serenaded by a traditional band. Three of the best venues are listed below:

Cevahir Konak Evi Selahhattin Eyyub Camii Karşısı ☎0414/215 9377; ⓦwww .gulizarkonukevi.net. Probably the best, and certainly the dearest (35TL for the set menu of eight different dishes).

Gülizar Konuk Evi Sarayönü Caddesi, İrfaniye Sokak ☎0414/215 0505. Part of a boutique hotel, this place has a courtyard set below the towering Ulu Cami minaret, 30TL set menu.

Yıldız Saray Konuk Evi, Yorgancı Sokak ☎0414/216 9494, ⓦwww.yildizsaraykonukevi .com. Another old courtyard mansion with a good reputation, 30TL for the set menu and also houses a boutique hotel.

poisoning in Urfa than elsewhere in Turkey so be extra-careful, especially during the hottest months.

Dotted along a terrace opposite the *Harran* hotel on Atatürk Caddesi, a line of **bars** serves beer or *rakı* (but not during Ramadan) and snacks such as fruit and nuts. The only alternatives for alcoholic drinks are the upmarket bars at the *Harran* and the *Dedeman* hotels, or the *Türkü* bar (see below).

Boğazıçı Off Atatürk Cad. Set in an old stone building with a vaulted ceiling, it's the best of the bars on this strip, recommended for its attentive service and cheap beer (4TL).

Dolunay Pastanesi Sarayönü Cad PTT Karşısı 2. A flashy patisserie serving delicious chocolate puddings, *baklava* and ice cream. There are numerous other appetizing *pastane*s on this street.

 Gülhan Atatürk Bul Akbank Bitişiği. Highly recommended, particularly for the lunchtime *sulu yemek* (vegetable dishes 5TL, meat-based ones 7TL) and the evening grills (9TL for a delicious kebab). Well frequented by the local middle classes, its bustling nature ensures a fast turnover and fresh food.

Kebabistan Yıldız Meydanı 23. Often packed with locals, this place serves excellent kebabs and the *lahmacun* are large, hot and spicy. The upstairs *aile salonu* has low tables where you sit cross-legged on kilim cushions.

Türkü Konağı Sarayönü Cad, Vatan Sok 7. Atmospheric bar with live *Türkü* music nightly. Set in the old camel stables of a *kervansaray*, it is very atmospheric on the right evening. Beers are a reasonable 5TL, wine 7TL a glass – but watch out for the price of *çerez*.

Urfa Sofrası Karakoyun ış Merkezi, Kat 1 No 226. Just off Köprübaşı Cad, this roof-terrace restaurant is spotlessly clean and a/c, though a bit on the pricey side. Tender kebabs from 10TL, *pide* and pizzas are a little less. Also does *kaburga dolması* (lamb ribs stuffed with *pilaf* rice) for four people (80TL). No alcohol.

Listings

Airport The Turkish Airlines (and Sunexpress) ticketing office is in Kaliru Turizm, on the ground floor of the Özel Dünya hospital on Sarayönü Cad. Airport shuttles (15TL) depart from the office 1hr 30min before check-in.

Banks and exchange There are a couple of convenient *döviz* offices and many ATMs on Sarayönü Cad.

Buses The usual eastern bus companies have offices all around town, especially on Sarayönü Cad, and provide service buses to the *otogar*. Harran Nemrut Tur (see "Tours", below) and some hotels will also book tickets for you.

Car rental Harran Nemrut Tur, and one or two other places, rent cars for €35 daily upwards.

Hospital Özel Dünya Hastanesi (Dünya private hospital), Köprübaşı Cad ☏ 0414/216 3616 or 215 4348; Devlet Hastane ve Polikliniği (State Hospital), Hastane Cad ☏ 0414/313 1928 or 313 1220.

Police Police station is on Sarayönü Cad.

Post office The PTT is on Sarayönü Cad (Mon–Sat 9am–noon & 1–5pm for money exchange and mail; 24hr for telephones).

Tours Harran Nemrut Tur (☏ 0414/215 1575), just behind the Özel Dünya hospital, runs half- and full-day trips to Harran (€10 half-day, €35 full day including Şuayb and Soğmatar), as well as to Nemrut Dağı (€45). Mustafa at the *Uğur* hotel (see accommodation on p.625) has his own a/c minibus and arranges one-day trips to Nemrut for 90TL, including all subsidiary sites, and trips including Harran, Şuayb, Soğmatar and Göbekli Tepe for 50TL.

Göbekli Tepe

Around 15km northeast of Urfa, where the southern foothills of the Toros Mountains fade into the scorching flatlands of upper Mesopotamia, lies **Göbekli Tepe** (Hill of the Navel), one of Turkey's most intriguing archeological sites. Here, on a hilltop 870m above sea level, is an artificial mound some 300m in diameter and 15m high, containing a series of circular chambers, carbon-dated to a period between 9500 and 7500 BC. The chambers have burnt-lime floors and are lined with stone benches, but most remarkably contain a series of T-shaped monoliths, the tallest of which are 5m high. Clearly anthropomorphic, many of the monoliths are liberally covered with incredible relief-carvings of wild animals, from scorpions and snakes to lions and wild boar.

This site appears to disprove the theory that only settled societies were capable of producing monumental buildings and sophisticated art, as much of the work at Göbekli Tepe was done when man was still in the hunter-gatherer stage of development. Visit between May and October and there's a chance you'll see archeologists at work excavating the site; in winter the monoliths are protected from the elements by metal covers. To reach the site with your own transport, head out of town on the Mardin road. After around 10km turn left (it's now signed Göbekli Tepe) and head some 9km north to Örencik village. Turn right here and follow a track a further 2km to the gated site – a taxi from Urfa should cost around 50TL return, including waiting time. As yet there are no opening hours or admission fees, only a *bekçi* (watchman).

Harran

Some 45km southeast of Urfa, the beehive-style houses of **HARRAN** (Altınbaşak) are an established tourist attraction. The village has grown up within the crumbling remnants of the old, four-kilometre circumference walls of a settlement once much more important than Urfa. Harran has strong biblical links, too: according to Genesis 11:31 and 12:4, the patriarch Abraham dwelt here before moving onto Canaan.

These days, Arabs and a few Kurds live amid the ruins of old Harran, surviving by farming the newly irrigated fields and smuggling goods across the Syrian border, 10km to the south. The stone-built, mud-covered beehive-shaped buildings owe their distinctive shape to the fact that no wood is used as support. Virtually all are now used for storage or animal – not human – habitation.

Some history

Harran is thought to have been continuously inhabited for at least 6000 years. It became a prosperous trading town under the Assyrians, who turned it into a centre for the worship of Sin, god of the moon; there was a large temple here, later also used by the Sabians. Planet worshippers, they stand accused of holding lurid orgies and carrying out human sacrifice in some accounts, and with the arrival of the Arabs were given the choice of conversion to Islam or death. In 53 BC the Roman general Crassus was defeated here, crucified and had molten gold poured into his mouth by the Parthians. Despite this, the Romans later converted Harran into an important centre of learning, a role it continued to play under the Byzantines, then the Arabs, first under the Umayyad dynasty, then the Ayyubid. However, the arrival of the Mongols during the thirteenth century meant devastation.

Arrival and accommodation

Dolmuşes to Harran (4TL) also run hourly from Şanlıurfa *otogar*; the last returning dolmuş is at 7pm. Alternatively, a taxi for the two-way trip with waiting time should be around 50TL.

The group-orientated *Bazda Motel* (☎0414/441 2001; ❷) on the village bypass road offers clean, en-suite but overpriced **accommodation** in a mock-beehive-style concrete building, breakfast 10TL extra. It is also possible to stay in the more atmospheric *Harran Kültür Evi* (☎0414/441 2477; €15 per person half-board), a complex of restored beehive dwellings right amongst the ruins. You'll sleep on mattresses on the floor, but the place is scrupulously clean, the food good and owner Reşat (the village headman) friendly and resplendent in his flowing Bedouin robes.

The site

Harran's enigmatic ruins exude tragic grandeur, dwarfing the beehive dwellings. Near the *jandarma* an artificial tumulus marks the site of the original settlement. Excavations are currently underway here by a team from Ankara University, revealing the remains of an Umayyad palace. North of the mound, and most impressive of the ruins, is the **Ulu Cami**, the first mosque ever built on what is now Turkish soil. Its substantial square minaret, originally built in the eighth century, was mistaken for a cathedral belfry by T.E. Lawrence when he passed through in 1909. The layout of the mosque, much re-built under the Ayyubid dynasty in the twelfth century, can be made out clearly, though only fragments of its structure survive relatively intact.

Village kids accost visitors, selling curious wall-hangings made from dried chickpeas and cloth, the more vociferous beg for money, pens or sweets. If you want to take pictures of the traditionally dressed girls, expect to part with some money for the privilege. Most speak Arabic (their first language), Turkish (learned in school) and often Kurdish.

The eleventh-century **citadel**, in the southeast corner of the old walled city, is possibly built on the site of the ancient temple of the moon god Sin. Three of its four polygonal towers have survived reasonably well, but take care scrambling around as there are several holes in the upper part of the structure.

Only practicable with your own transport (or as part of a tour organized in Urfa) are the sites of ancient **Şuayb**, northeast of Harran, a partially subterranean settlement dating back to Roman times, and **Soğmatar**, 65km from Harran. The centre of the Sabian religion (a development of the moon cult of Sin at Harran), the village here is ringed by seven circular hilltop ruins which once formed the Sabians' temple and observatory complex.

Adıyaman

ADIYAMAN, 60km northeast of Gaziantep, is the least-used base for the trip to Nemrut Dağı, but it's a prosperous place with a few things worth exploring. The **copper bazaar**, south of the bus station at the far end of town, and, behind it, a *kervansaray*, used for tethering animals. Between the main traffic lights and the bus station, the sleepy **museum** (Tues–Sun 8am–noon & 2–5pm; 3TL) houses artefacts from local tumuli, which were excavated prior to submersion under the Atatürk Dam waters. The small, late nineteenth-century **Syrian Orthodox Church of St Peter and St Paul** in the old quarter, is now home to one of the four metropolitan bishops of this ancient church in Turkey, and there are services Sundays from 9.30am–noon.

Practicalities

The **bus station**, where Nemrut tours are booked, is east of the main traffic lights on Atatürk Bulvarı. As for **hotels**, the central *Hotel Yolaç*, Harıkçı Cad 26 (☎0416/216 1301; ❸), has been refurbished, with laminate parquet floors, small but spotless bathrooms and a funky, kitsch breakfast. The four-star *Grand İsias*, Atatürk Bul 180 (☎0416/214 8800, ⓦwww.grandisias.com; ❼), is Adıyaman's best hotel, with plush rooms and decent facilities, including wi-fi, and a bar, sauna, *hamam* and car-hire.

Standard grill and kebab joints abound, but the female-run *Hanimeli Sofrası*, Eskisaray Mah, Hügem Karşısı, en route to the church, has a pleasant roof terrace and home-cooked specialities.

Excursions to Nemrut Dağı

Organized minibus trips to Nemrut Dağı run in the summer season (May–Oct) from Kahta, Adıyaman, Malatya, Şanlıurfa and Cappadocia and, given the distances involved, these are about the only way of getting there unless you have your own transport. Note that the summit road is only open from April 15 until the first snowfall of winter, but outside the peak summer months (July & Aug) there may well be insufficient demand to make up groups each day. For more on the best time of day to visit the site, see p.633.

From Kahta and Karadut

In season, there are sunrise or sunset tours from **Kahta** (see p.632) – sunset trips leave at 1pm and return at 9pm; sunrise tours leave at 3am, returning at 10am. The trips, best arranged by the transport co-operative (see Bayram Çınar at the Karadut market, opposite the dolmuş garage) cost 100TL for the dolmuş (entrance fee extra) irrespective of numbers, and should include the subsidiary sites of the Karakuş tumulus, Cendere bridge and the ancient Commagene capital of Arsameia. Don't be bludgeoned into booking a tour before you have checked various options – indeed assuming you arrive in time to catch the last dolmuş (6pm), it's far better to head straight up to the nicer village of **Karadut** (see p.633). All the accommodation options here arrange summit tours at similar prices to Kahta – a minibus to the summit is around 50TL regardless of numbers, entrance extra.

From Adıyaman

Adıyaman (see opposite) has more facilities than Kahta; the only disadvantage is the additional half-hour journey time. Adıyaman Unal bus company, represented by the ebullient Ali Bey, is based in the *otogar*. It costs around 20TL per person assuming there are a minimum of 8 people. (8–9hr, early-morning departures). Tours take in the subsidiary sites – Karakuş tumulus, Cendere bridge and Arsameia – and the Pirinç prehistoric caves.

From Malatya

Tours from **Malatya** (p.635), on the north side of the range, may look more expensive, but if you count in the night's stay at the *Guneş Hotel* virtually at the summit, the difference is negligible. The main disadvantage is that you miss out on Nemrut's subsidiary sites, but on the other hand you view both sets of heads at sunrise and sunset, and you get to stay at the welcoming stone-built *Guneş Hotel*, a well-built hotel with clean and cheerful en-suite rooms and good food. A Kurdish *yayla* (summer tent encampment) lies but a few minutes' walk away.

Bookings are best made the day before, either at the tourist office or the tea garden to one side of it. Departures are usually at noon, reaching the summit in good time for sunset; the return trip starts at about 7am, allowing time to admire the sunrise, reaching Malatya at about 11am. The 80TL fee per person includes transport, lodging and two meals and trips run even if there's only one taker; the entrance fee is extra. If it suits your onward travel plans, you could walk over to the south side of Nemrut and find a lift to Kahta. This way, you get to see the subsidiary sites.

From Şanlıurfa

Visiting Nemrut from **Şanlıurfa** (p.623) has the advantage of cutting out Adıyaman and Kahta, and can include a trip to see the Atatürk Dam, but the 420-kilometre (14-hour) round trip takes in lots of uninteresting scenery – for details see "Listings" on p.628.

Kahta

From Adıyaman, it's a half-hour dolmuş journey (5TL) to dull **KAHTA**, 25km to the east. Although it is only about a kilometre from the Atatürk Baraji, you can't see the lake from Kahta.

The obvious budget **accommodation** choice is the *Hotel Kommagene* (☎0416/725 9726, ✉kommagenem@hotmail.com; ❶), at the junction of the town's main street with the road up to Nemrut, which attracts (or even grabs) backpackers and relieves them of their money; it also has rudimentary camping facilities. Rooms with air conditioning will put it into a higher price bracket. Kahta's best hotel is the *Zeus Hotel* (☎0416/725 5694, ⓦwww.zeushotel.com.tr; ❹), with prettily landscaped swimming pool, bar-restaurant, and rooms with air-conditioning, flat-screen TVs and wi-fi.

There are a few cheap and basic **restaurants** on Kahta's broad main street, though none stand out. A couple of kilometres east of town, overlooking the Atatürk lake is the *Neşetin Yeri* **fish restaurant** which serves excellent-value lake fish and grills on terraces with a view of the mountain and lake, but you need your own transport or a taxi to reach it.

The road to Nemrut Dağı

The 75km, recently re-paved road from Kahta to the sanctuary atop Nemrut Dağı (Mount Nemrut) is easily done in your own transport, but make sure you fill up with fuel in Kahta. Visitors heading for the summit sanctuary for dawn go up the quick way (via Narince) and return via the subsidiary site route, those aiming for a sunset visit to the top usually take in the lesser sites en route.

Karakuş tumulus and Cendere Köprüsü

Some 9km north of Kahta, the huge **Karakuş tumulus**, said to be the funeral mound of Antiochus's wife, rises up dramatically by the roadside, just past a small oil-drilling field. It's adorned by three separate groups of three columns, surmounted by either an animal statue or a relief-carving. The best preserved is an eagle that gives the site its name – "black bird".

Another 9km along, the **Cendere Köprüsü** is a monumental Roman bridge built between 193 and 211 AD during the reign of Emperor Septimius Severus. Its graceful, single-arch spans the mouth of a spectacular gorge. Originally there was a pair of columns at either end of the bridge, of which three survive. The fourth, dedicated to Severus' younger son Geta, was removed when his eldest son, Caracalla, had his brother put to death in a successful bid to become sole emperor.

Eski Kahta and Arsameia

After another 6km or so you come to the left turn for **ESKI KAHTA**, a traditional village layered onto the hills behind and dominated by the **Mamluk Yeni Kale**. The castle is spectacular when viewed from a distance, but few people have the time or nerve to explore its precipitous heights.

Not far to the south is the ancient site of **Arsameia** (daily 8am–7pm; 6TL; includes summit entrance), the summer capital of the ancient Commagene kingdom, excavated in the 1950s. There's a right turn for the site about a kilometre along the main road. From the shop/café/toilet block area take the lower path to a truncated relief-stele of the god Mithras. Head up the steps to join the main path and continue to a man-made cave with a tunnel running down to what is thought to be a Mithraic cult chamber. Below the cave entrance is a damaged stele depicting Mithridates I Callinicus, and his son, Antiochus I.

Head back a short way and take the path up the hillside to the highlight of the site, a fabulous, perfectly preserved **relief depicting Hercules and Antiochus I** shaking hands – as impressive, if not more so, than anything you'll see on the top of Nemrut Dağı itself. Next to it is a tunnel leading down to another cult chamber. Above the tunnel entrance a huge, 25-line Greek inscription tells you that Mithridates I Callinicus, father of Antiochus (founder of the complex at Nemrut Dağı), is buried in the vicinity, and that the site is consecrated to him.

Continuing a short way up and beyond the relief of Hercules and Antiochus is a plateau with the remnants of a funerary/cult sanctuary complex that once must have rivalled that on Nemrut. Little remains, but the views across the mountains and down over Yeni Kale are spectacular. A road cuts across the mountains to join the major sumit road just above Karadut.

Karadut

The last village served by local dolmuş from Kahta (departing at 8am, 10am, 11am, 12pm, 2pm, 4pm and 6pm), **KARADUT** probably makes for the most relaxing approach to Nemrut. Some 800m above sea level, with grand views over terraced fields, a plunging valley and limestone peaks, it's a lovely cool place named after the black mulberry trees that grow here amongst apricot groves.

Just above the village is the *Karadut Motel Pansiyon* (℡0416/737 2169; Ⓦwww .karadutpansiyon.net; ❷) with basic but comfortable en-suite rooms, a very friendly atmosphere, good home-cooked food (8TL extra for dinner) and wi-fi. A couple of kilometres higher up the mountain is the sparer *Çeşme* restaurant and *pansiyon* (℡0416/737 2032; ❷), also offering tasty meals, expansive views but basic rooms. Between these two pensions are a couple of dearer alternatives: the group-orientated *Hotel Euphrat* (℡0416/737 2175; ❻), with a pool and reasonable rooms, and – the cheaper and better choice – *Otel Kervansaray Nemrut* (℡0416/737 2190; ❺), which has good bathrooms and a shady pool. Both rates include half-board, both have great views and offer hikes up to Nemrut (3hr).

Nemrut Dağı

The remote, grandiose mountain-top sanctuary at **Nemrut Dağı** is unforgettable, and the mighty stone heads adorning the temple and tomb of King Antiochus have become one of the best-known images of Eastern Turkey.

The majority of people visit at dawn, to watch the sunrise, and most of the minibus tours are geared up to this timescale. The downside of a dawn visit is a very early start (between 2 and 4am depending on season) and a crowded and oft chilly summit (it's 2150 metres above sea level). There's often snow on the ground from late October until April. Minibus tours also target sunset, when it is less cold and the setting sun illuminates the western terrace in a warm glow. A daytime visit, however, means there are fewer visitors and you can explore the sanctuary at leisure and in the warmth.

Some history

The result of one man's delusions of grandeur, the great tomb and temple complex of Nemrut Dağı was built by **Antiochus I Epiphanes** (64–38 BC), son of Mithridates I Callinicus, the founder of the Commagene kingdom. The

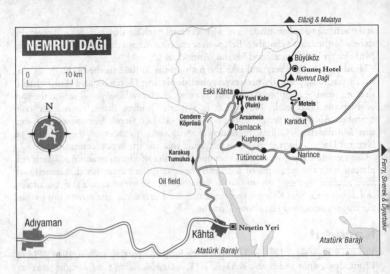

NEMRUT DAĞI

0   10 km

N

Elâziğ & Malatya

Büyüköz
Guneş Hotel
Nemrut Dağı

Eski Kâhta
Yeni Kale (Ruin)
Arsameia
Cendere Köprüsü
Damlacık
Karadut
Motels

Karakuş Tumulus
Kuştepe
Tütünocak
Narince

Oil field

Adıyaman

Kâhta
Neşetin Yeri

Ататürk Barajı

Ататürk Barajı

Ferry, Siverek & Diyarbakir

Commagene dynasty was a breakaway from the Seleucid Empire, covering only a small territory from modern Adıyaman to Gaziantep, and it wouldn't rate much more than a passing mention in histories of the region were it not for the fact that Antiochus chose to build this temple as a colossal monument to himself. Having decided he was divine in nature, or at the very least an equal of the gods, he declared: "I, the great King Antiochus have ordered the construction of these temples…on a foundation which will never be demolished…to prove my faith in the gods. At the conclusion of my life I will enter my eternal repose here, and my spirit will ascend to join that of Zeus in heaven."

Antiochus's vanity knew no bounds – he claimed descent from Darius the Great of Persia and Alexander the Great – but eventually he went too far, siding with the Parthians against Rome, and was deposed. This was effectively the end of the Commagene kingdom, which afterwards passed into Roman hands

The sanctuary lay undiscovered until the late nineteenth century, when Karl Puchstein, a German engineer, located it while making a survey in 1881. In 1883 he returned with Karl Humann (the man who removed the Pergamon altar to Berlin) to carry out a more thorough investigation, but it wasn't until 1953 that a comprehensive archeological survey of the site began, under the direction of an American team.

Arrival and accommodation

Below the summit of Nemrut Dağı is a parking/café/souvenir stall/toilet area – which at dawn and sunset can be full of milling crowds. There's an eight-bed **dormitory** here too (15TL), but bring your own sleeping bag. Better suited to those ascending from Malatya is **accommodation** at the comfortable *Guneş Hotel* (☎0422/323 9378; ❷), a half-hour walk below the summit site on the north and reachable from the south only on foot. If you are determined, it is possible to visit the site from the Kahta side, walk down and overnight at the *Guneş*, and then head down to Malatya.

The site

Behind the car-park buildings is the entrance to the **site** (6TL), beyond which is a fifty-metre-high tumulus of small rocks (rated by the *Guinness Book of Records* as the world's largest man-made mound, some 60m high and covering an area of

7.5 acres), thought to cover the tomb of Antiochus. It's forbidden to climb the mound but the views from its base are spectacular enough.

A paved path leads along the south side of the tumulus, coming to a terrace area after fifteen to twenty minutes' walk, on which stands the **eastern temple** with six decapitated seated statues, each several metres in height. Lined up in front of these truncated figures are the much-photographed **detached heads**, each measuring a couple of metres in height. From left to right they represent: Antiochus I, Fortuna (symbol of the Commagene kingdom), Zeus, Apollo and Hercules. Scattered around them are the remains of massive stone eagles and lions – one of each creature originally stood, as symbolic guardian, at either end of the royal line-up.

They were meant to incorporate several similar deities drawn from different cultures, according to the principle of syncretism, which Alexander the Great had promoted to try and foster a sense of unity among the disparate peoples of his empire. On the date of Antiochus's birthday and the anniversary of his coronation, the Commagene people would file up to the mountain-top to witness the dawn sacrifice and make offerings, carried out in strict accordance with the Greek inscriptions carved onto the back of the royal statues. The stepped, sandstone sacrificial **altar** still stands in front of the statues.

A path leads around the northern base of the tumulus to the **western terrace**, lined by slabs once decorated with reliefs. None of the western statues is even partially intact, although the dispersed **heads** here are much less weathered than those on the east, and there are more statues – a complete set of five, plus two eagle-heads to flank them. The alignment of statues was originally the same as the east side, but the heads here have not been lined up in front of their "bodies".

The best of the **relief-stelae** that once adorned the sanctuary, including the so-called Zodiac Lion, thought to be an astrological chart referring to the date of Antiochus's conception, are currently being stored in a metal shed just below the funerary complex.

Malatya and around

Famed for its apricots, **MALATYA**, around 60km north of Nemrut Dağı, is a lively city of around 600,000 people. Scratch beneath the surface, though, and a sometimes uneasy mix of Turkish nationalists, devout Sunni Muslims, Alevîs and Kurds soon becomes apparent. Despite a long history going back to 3000 BC, there's little left to see within the city, but it's a pleasant place for an overnight stop before tackling Nemrut Dağı, and the old town of Eski Malatya and the site of ancient Aslantepe are nearby.

Always a political town, Malatya is the home of two former presidents of the Republic, General İsmet İnönü (who gets a statue in his honour) and part-Kurdish Turgut Özal (who has a road named after him). There's also a huge army base here as well as a university of around 25,000 students.

Arrival, information and services

The tree-lined, modern centre is compact and most of the hotels and restaurants are within walking distance of each other.

The **otogar** and **train station** (both served by the Maşti bus from opposite the *Vilayet*; 0.90TL, buy ticket from booth before boarding) are 7km and 2km respectively west of the centre on the Çevre Yolu (ring road). Service buses run into town from the *otogar*, dropping you at the Çevre Yolu junction closest to the centre. From Malatya's **airport**, 28km northwest of the city, a shuttle bus (8TL) meets THY

MALATYA

RESTAURANTS, CAFÉS & BARS
Beyaz Sarayı	2
Destina	1
Melita	4
Nostalji	5
Sevinç Pastanesi	3

ACCOMMODATION
Altın Kayısı	A
Malatya Büyük Hotel	C
Otel Park	D
Yeni Hotel	B

0   500 m

flights and ferries passengers to Sivas Caddesi, a ten-minute walk northeast of the town centre. Tickets for domestic flights from Bertaş, ☎0422/326 0037, Sivas Caddesi, Semercioğlu Apt Alt; Onur Air is on İnönü Cad 17 (☎0422/325 6060), Pegasus at Atatürk Cad 38 (☎0422/325 2121), the THY office is at the airport.

There's a helpful **tourist office** (Mon–Sat 9am–noon & 1–5pm; ☎0422/323 3025) in the *Vilayet* (governor's office) building, behind the statue of İnönü in the main square, İnönü Meydanı. The office's main function is to sign you up for a **trip to Nemrut Dağı** (see box, p.631). See either Bülent at the tourist office, or the ebullient freelancer and all-round character İngiliz (English) Kemal, who hangs out in the tea garden adjacent to the *Vilayet* building in season. The **PTT** is near the square at the very start of İnönü Caddesi and there are **banks and exchange facilities** on Fuzili Caddesi.

Accommodation

Accommodation in Malatya is plentiful, but aimed squarely at businessmen rather than tourists, so is invariably rather bland.

Altın Kayısı İstasyon Cad ☎0422/211 4444, ⓦwww.otelaltinkayisi.com. A very comfortable base, but inconveniently located out of town near the train station. Boasts an array of top-notch facilities, including smart restaurant, gardens and a pool. ❹

Malatya Büyük Hotel Yeni Cami Karşısı ☎0422/321 1400, ⓕ321 5367. Offering good views of the pretty, early twentieth-century Yeni Camii, this is a friendly hotel with comfy en-suite rooms, all with TV, double-glazing, central heating and a/c. Serves up an excellent buffet breakfast. ❹

Otel Park Atatürk Cad 17 ☎0422/321 169, ⓔparkotel@malatya.com. The city's best budget option, with tidy, pastel-hued rooms, some with en-suite showers, but shared (squat) toilets down the hall. No breakfast; and some noise from the mosque behind and major street out front. ❶

Yeni Otel Yeni Cami Karşısı ☎0422/323 1423, ⓔyenihotel@turk.net. A good mid-range option, the two-star *Yeni Hotel* has all mod cons – a/c, TV, minibar etc – and a decent buffet breakfast. The room's soft-furnishings are a little garish, though. ❷

The City

The old **Şire Pazarı**, in the centre between Atatürk Bulvarı and the ring road, is devoted to local agricultural produce, namely cherries, mulberries, apples, walnuts and, especially, apricots. There's an **apricot festival** (second week in July) at Mişmiş Parkı, 5km east of the centre. Next to the Şire bazaar is Malatya's **copper bazaar**, where craftsmen hammer away or tin-plate surfaces intended for use with food.

On the south side of Malatya, at the end of Fuzuli Caddesi and much favoured by local families, is Kanalboyu. Here a strip of ice-cream parlours and fast-food places line twin cobbled streets running either side of a watercourse. Close by is the excellent **Malatya museum** (Malatya Müzesi; Tues–Sun 8am–noon & 1–5pm; 3TL). Small but extremely well laid out, it concentrates on finds from nearby Aslantepe (see below). The room to the left as you enter has fine examples of pottery and copper swords, plus reconstructions of graves from Aslantepe. Upstairs is a glass case devoted to decorative seals (used to guarantee the integrity of goods in containers), the most common motifs in evidence being deer and antelope.

A ten-minute walk northwest of the town is the neglected seventeenth-century **Taşhoran Armenian church**. Its doors and windows have been bricked up (the central dome has collapsed, rendering it unsafe) prior to a planned restoration.

Eating and drinking

There are plenty of **cafés and restaurants** in Malatya, though none are outstanding. The *Sevinç Pastanesi* at Atatürk Cad 46 does a decent Turkish breakfast and delicious, flaky *börek*, and has a retro-1970s-style eating area at the back and an *aile salonu* upstairs. The *Beyaz Sarayi*, next to the Otel Park at Atatürk Cad 8, is good value for *pide*, kebabs and soups – it also serves comb honey and creamy yoghurt for breakfast. More unusual is the *Nostalji*, on Mucelli Caddesi, more or less opposite the five-screen Yeşil Sineması. The wooden house in which it is set dates back to 1840, and it's a great place to sample local specialities such as *analı kızlı köfte*, or laze over a Turkish coffee and a *nargile*.

For a little more in the way of (alcohol-free) entertainment try the rooftop *Destina* bar on Atatürk Cad 1. It's as trendy as it gets in conservative Malatya, and there's live music (rock and traditional) most evenings. For beer, try the posh-looking *Melita* opposite, a first-floor diner (kebab and grills) with decent live *Türkü* music.

Aslantepe

A few kilometres northeast of the centre, **Aslantepe** (Tues–Sun 8am–5pm; 3TL), is reached by *belediye* buses and dolmuşes marked "Orduzu" or "Aslantepe", from the Doğu Garaj (see Eski Malatya on p.638).

This artificial, 16,000-square-metre settlement mound, dating back to the fourth millennium BC, has been meticulously excavated by Italian archeologists from Rome University since 1962. Work on turning the site into an open-air museum was approaching completion in the summer of 2009, and it's possible the pair of Hittite stone lions found here (now in Ankara's Anatolian Civilizations Museum) will be returned – as will the finds currently housed in Malatya's archeological museum.

The best of the remains are a vast, fourth-millennium BC **palace complex**, built of mud bricks on a stone foundation. Also unusual are a pair of **wall-paintings** from approximately 3200 BC, and a mosaic-style section of Hittite-era flooring from a palace on the northeast side of the mound. The site is attractively surrounded by a veritable sea of apricot trees.

Eski Malatya

About 12km north of the modern city is **Eski Malatya**, or "Old Malatya", a ruined Roman/Byzantine town now engulfed by the modern settlement of Battalgazi. Buses and dolmuşes marked "Battalgazi" depart from the Doğu Garaj (East Garage) a ten-minute walk northeast of the city centre.

Buses arrive at the main square. From here it's a 200-metre walk southwest to a lovely seventeenth-century *kervansaray*, restoration of which was approaching completion at the time of writing. A five-minute walk south of here is the wonderful Selçuk **Ulu Cami**, a huge mosque complex commissioned by Selçuk sultan, Alâeddin Keykubad. Built around a central courtyard, it consists of summer and winter mosques. The latter is of plain stonework with massive pillars, the former consists of a central bay with a soaring domed roof flanked by two wings, the whole surrounding the *eyvan*. The brickwork of the dome reveals complicated herringbone patterning relieved by pretty blue-glazed tiles.

Diyarbakır

Superbly positioned on a bluff above the coiling loops of the Tigris, the old city of **DİYARBAKIR** shelters behind massive medieval walls of black basalt, enclosing a maze of cobbled streets and alleys. Many of the city's finest mosques and churches have been restored, in part thanks to EU grants, and there's plenty of decent accommodation right in the heart of the walled city. Given these attractions Diyarbakır is starting to market itself successfully as a tourist destination and with no real industry to speak of (unemployment reaches 60 percent) this income is badly needed.

The city struggled to cope with an influx of Kurdish refugees fleeing the state–PKK war in the 1990s, many of whom now occupy old houses in the very heart of the walled city. Now the most overtly Kurdish city in Turkey, it has a definite "edge" to it. Violent street demonstrations break out from time to time, with pickpockets and the odd stone-throwing youngster other potential hazards. Indeed an old Arab saying runs "Black the walls, black the dogs and black the hearts in black Diyarbakır". Having said this, if you keep your wits about you and avoid the backstreets around and after dusk you'll have no problem – the vast majority of the population are justly proud of their fascinating city and very welcoming to visitors.

In the summer vacation, local students anxious to try out their English may offer you a guided tour of the town. Talking to them is a good way to learn about Diyarbakır and pick up a basic **Kurdish** vocabulary – try *sipas* (pronounced "spaas" – thank you) and *rojbaş* (pronounced "rojebosh" – good day). They may point out the finer points of Kurdish dress, the predominance of Kurdish music for sale and the nuances of the local dialects, Zaza and Kurmancı.

Some history

Diyarbakır's existence dates back at least to the Hurrian period, some 5000 years ago. Subsequently subject to successive periods of Urartian, Assyrian and Persian hegemony, it fell to Alexander the Great and his successors, the Seleucids, in the late fourth century BC.

The Romans appeared on the scene in 115 AD and over the next few centuries they and their successors, the Byzantines, struggled violently over the town with the Sassanid Persians. The Romans, who above love Diyarbakır as **Amida** built the first substantial walls around the city in 297 – the ones visible today are the result of Byzantine and Arab rebuilds. The threatening, basalt bulwarks gave the place its popular ancient name – Amid the Black – still used in the Kurdish language. The

▲ Pilgrims at Diyarbakır

modern name comes from the Arabs: in 638 the Bakr tribe of Arabs arrived and renamed the city Diyar Bakr or "Place of the Bakr". With the decline of Arab influence in the region, Diyarbakır became a Selçuk, then a Turcoman, and finally an Ottoman stronghold.

The city's position on the banks of the fertile Tigris encouraged fruit growing, particularly **watermelons** which continue to be grown here. In the old days they are said to have weighed 100kg and had to be transported by camel.

Arrival, orientation and information

There's little need to stray beyond the confines of old, walled Diyarbakır. The **train station** lies a kilometre west of town at the end of İstasyon Caddesi, the new **otogar** (Yeni Otogar) is inconveniently located 10km west of the centre. Buses into town run 7am–11pm (1.25TL) and will drop you at **Dağ Kapısı**, (the northern gate to the old city) otherwise a taxi will set you back 15TL. Dolmuşes from Mardin, Batman and other provincial towns arrive at a new **dolmuş terminal** (İlçe Otogar), from where it's a 1.25TL, fifteen-minute bus ride into **Dağ Kapısı**. Kaplaner **airport** is 3km southwest of town, a taxi to the centre costs 10TL.

The state **tourist office** (Mon–Sat 9am–5pm; ☎0412/221 2173), in the tower at Dağ Kapısı, has limited information. Far better is the **Buyükşehir Belediyesi Turiszm Burosu**, (Tues–Sat 9am–noon, 1–6pm) run by the local municipality and staffed by a charming and knowledgeable Armenian woman. It hands out attractively presented information on the city (some of it in Armenian and Syriac as well as English and Turkish) and good street plans. The grid plan of the major streets in the old city makes route-finding easy, though the backstreets are a maze of narrow alleys.

Accommodation

Most of the desirable accommodation in Diyarbakır lies within a short walk of the Dağ Kapısı – the further away from here, the quieter it's likely to be.

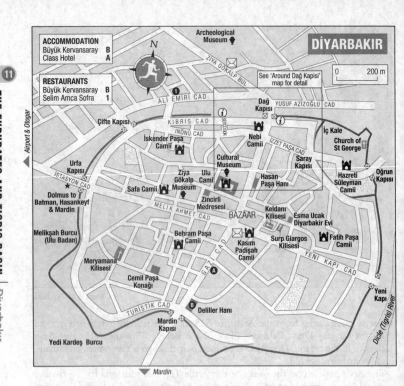

Accommodation is marked on the "Around Dağ Kapısı" map, except for a couple of places towards Mardin Kapısı and outside the walls, which are shown on the main Diyarbakır map.

Around Dağ Kapısı

Aslan Palas Oteli Kıbrıs Cad 21 ☎ 0412/228 9224, ☏ 223 6810. A good budget choice with small but newly renovated rooms (with a/c and TVs), crisp white sheets and firm beds. The only downside are the tiny bathrooms which, although clean, have no shower curtains. No breakfast. ➊

Balkar Hotel İnönü Cad 26 ☎ 0412/228 7131, ☏ 228 7145. Beautifully fitted out with nice textiles and paintwork, with a terrace restaurant for breakfast. Homelier than average but with all that you'd expect by way of wi-fi, a/c, fridge, TV etc. The attractive breakfast room overlooks a section of old city wall. ➌

Hotel Birkent İnönü Cad ☎ 0412/228 7131, ☏ 228 7145. Good-value two-star place with very friendly staff. It's kept spotlessly clean and TV, wi-fi and minibar are standard. With bright (and very blue) rooms, it's a good option and slightly quieter than similar establishments fronting Kıbrıs Cad. ➋

Hotel Kaplan Kıbrıs Cad, Yoğurtçü Sok 14 ☎ 0412/229 3300, ☏ 224 0187. Friendly and in a

quiet location on a side street to the north of İnönü Cad. All rooms have a TV, fridge and a/c, bathrooms are spotless and breakfasts (served in a room shared with the adjoining *Kristal Hotel*) are filling. Note that it can often be block-booked by Turkish tour groups. ➋

Hotel Surkent Hz Süleyman Cad 19, Saraykapı ☎ 04142/228 1014, ⓦ www .hotelsurkent.com. Immaculately run hotel on a quiet(ish) street running down to the İç Kale. All mod-cons include wi-fi, minibar, a/c – plus it's spotlessly clean with small but tidy en-suite bathrooms. Excellent value and highly recommended. No breakfast. ➊

Towards Mardin Kapısı

Büyük Kervansaray Gazı Cad, Deliller Hanı ☎ 0412/228 9606, ⓔ kervansarayas @superonline.com. Smallish a/c rooms, nicely decorated and with new bathrooms, set in a converted *kervansaray* with a large swimming pool and hamam. The central courtyard is an oasis of

peace, and wonderful for a relaxing breakfast or evening meal. Non-guests are welcome to drink and/or dine here. ❹
Class Hotel Gazı Cad 101 ☎ 0412/229 5000, ⓦ www.diyarbakirclasshotel.com. An incongruously

modern hotel in the heart of the old city, with good facilities and value-for-money prices. Behind the flashy facade is the restored courtyard of a medieval mansion, with swimming pool, bar and restaurant. ❻

The walls

Diyarbakır's six-kilometre-long **city wall**, breached by four huge main gateways plus several smaller ones, is dotted with 72 defensive towers. Much of what can be seen today dates from the eleventh-century Artukid kingdom of Malık Salih Şah. When exploring the walls in hot weather make sure you've got water and a head-covering. A torch is handy for the darkened interiors of the gate-towers. Be warned that some sections lack either an external or internal parapet wall or rail and it is only a couple of metres wide in places. Especially at dusk watch out for stone-throwing youngsters.

Most visitors start at the **Saray Kapısı** which marks the entrance to the **İç Kale**, Diyarbakır's citadel. The section from Saray Kapısı to Oğrun Kapısı is navigable, but take care while ascending the steps. The crumbling tower just south of **Oğrum Kapısı** gives fine views over the Tigris valley and the alluvial plain on which Diyarbakır's famous melons grow in special holes dug in the sandy riverbanks.

The citadel, until recently a military zone, is now open and under restoration. Inside is the substantial **Church of St George**, probably dating back to the early Byzantine period. It once had twin domes, but later structural changes suggest it was subsequently used as a palace by Muslim rulers of the city. The black stone **Hazreti Süleyman Camii** boasting a huge square minaret, built in 1160 by the Artukids, comes alive on a Thursday, when hundreds of female pilgrims arrive to pray for their wishes to be granted. Diyarbakır's **archeological museum**, which lay outside Dağ Kapası, is closed, though there are plans to re-open it in one of the empty buildings here within the next two years.

The best stretch of wall to walk is that between Mardin Kapısı and Urfa Kapısı. From **Mardin Kapısı**, turn right and follow the inside of the wall for four hundred metres, at which point some steps lead up to the battlement walkway. Turn left and head back to Mardin Kapısı, threading through a vaulted passageway en route to an excellent viewpoint, then retrace your steps west along the ramparts. First up is the **Yedi Kardeş Burcu** (Seven Brothers Tower), a huge circular bastion decorated with Selçuk lions and a double-headed eagle. Beyond this is the **Melikşah Burcu** (also known as the Ulu Badan), also decorated with Selçuk motifs.

The views from the walls and towers over the Tigris are superb. Allow around thirty minutes to reach **Urfa Kapısı**. Follow the steps down into the gate-tower (hold your nose as there is a pungent stench of human excrement) and take care as finding the next set of steps down to street level is not easy in the semi-darkness.

The City

Dağ Kapısı makes a good starting point for an exploration of the city proper – two days are necessary to do justice to the city's sights. Just south of Dağ Kapısı the **Nebi Camii**, or Mosque of the Prophet, is a late fifteenth-century foundation Akkoyun Turcoman building. This attractive mosque is built of contrasting bands of black basalt and white limestone. This banded effect is common in Diyarbakır, as both stones are quarried locally and their combination is considerably less threatening than the unrelenting black of the walls.

Further down Gazı Caddesi is the late sixteenth-century **Hasan Paşa Hanı** on the eastern side of the street, now home to a few decent café/restaurants (see listings on p.644) and carpet, jewellery and souvenir shops. The city's **main bazaar** area occupies the narrow, twisting streets around it.

The Ulu Cami and around

Opposite the *han* stands the gatehouse of the **Ulu Cami**, Diyarbakır's most important mosque. The first of Anatolia's great Selçuk mosques, it was probably extended in 1091 by Melik Şah, the Selçuk conqueror of the city, though it was likely built on the site of, and with masonry from, the Byzantine church of St Thomas at the time of the Arab conquest in 639. Gutted by fire in 1155, it was extensively refurbished, but has been little altered since.

Beyond the entrance portal, decorated with bull and lion motifs, is a large and singularly impressive **courtyard**, occupied by two *şadırvan*s (ritual fountains). The north and south sides of the courtyard sport arcades, constructed using pillars salvaged from ornate late-Roman and Byzantine buildings. The wing to the east and above the arch is a library, incorporating a much earlier stoa beneath it. At the northeast corner of the courtyard is the locked entrance to the **Mesudiye Medresesi**. Built in 1198 by the Artukids, this became the first university of Anatolia and is still in use as a Koranic school.

The prayer hall is a triumph of Islamic restraint, its simple white interior and supporting arches enlivened by a superbly decorated carved-wood roof and a white *mimber*. The banded minaret is tall and angular, like many such structures in Diyarbakır.

The **Ziya Gökalp museum** (Tues–Sun 8.30am–noon, 1–4.30pm; free), west of the Ulu Cami was, ironically given the predominantly Kurdish nature of the city today, the former home of the architect of Turkish nationalism. Over two hundred years old, it houses sections devoted to the man's life and work. Another restored mansion, opposite the Surp Giragos church, is the **Esma Ocak Diyarbakır Evi**, a typical black-and-white stone construction around a courtyard. The rooms have been refurbished as they would have appeared in 1899. Officially it's only open at weekends, but the caretaker may open up for you in return for a small tip.

Diyarbakır's other mosques

West of the Ziya Gökalp museum is the stunning fifteenth-century **Safa Camii**, a mosque of notably graceful design and construction. Its tall, cylindrical minaret, a departure from the city norm, still bears traces of blue tile-work on its white, relief-worked surface. Archway masonry in the courtyard alternates between black and white in the local fashion, while the interior ceiling is accented by blue and green tile-work.

Some way southeast across Melik Ahmet Caddesi stands the **Behram Paşa Camii**, Diyarbakır's largest mosque, built in 1572 by Behram Paşa, the then Ottoman governor. It's been well restored and is one of the most important Ottoman-era mosques in southeastern Anatolia.

Also worth seeking out, east of Gazı Caddesi on Yenikapı Caddesi in the Balıkçılarbaşı bazaar, is the early sixteenth-century **Kasım Padişah Camii**, virtually the last Akkoyun monument built before the Ottomans took over. Its tall, square detached minaret, set on four two-metre basalt pillars, is known colloquially as the *Dört Ayaklı Minare* ("Four-Legged Minaret"). According to legend, if you walk around the minaret seven times and make a wish, it will be granted.

Diyarbakır's churches

Despite the fact virtually the entire non-Muslim population of the city (who numbered around a third in the early years of the twentieth century) has gone, the city is now promoting itself as a multicultural, multi-faith destination. To reach the **Keldanı Kilisesi**, walk past the Kasım Padişah Camii and turn left down an alley, then immediately right. The church is about 100m down the alley on the right; ring the bell for entry. The church and bell tower date from 1602; the spacious, arched interior contains a rather garish altar with a crucifix and icons. It's a Chaldean foundation (a Catholic schism of the Nestorian church), but unfortunately the last remnants of the community left in 2008.

Continuing past the Chaldean church the alley takes a sharp left. Follow it round, and in the wall on the right is a door marked "4". Knock and the friendly Kurdish family who live here will probably let you through their courtyard into the grounds of the late nineteenth-century **Surp Giragos Kilisesi**, a once-thriving church in the days when the population of Diyarbakır was one-quarter Armenian. The roofless shell still contains the gold-painted woodwork of the altar. The church is still owned by the Armenian church, and there are plans to restore it and re-open it as a place of worship soon – despite the fact only three Armenians now remain in the city.

The Syrian Orthodox compound, the **Meryamana Kilisesi** (Church of the Virgin Mary), lies southwest of the Behram Paşa Camii. A small door leads onto a paved courtyard surrounded by buildings that were once part of a seventh-century monastery. The church itself dates from the third century, making it one of the oldest in the world. It was reconstructed after a fire a couple of centuries ago, and has been much renovated recently, the funding coming from the sizable Syrian Orthodox diaspora. Visitors may be allowed to attend the services, which are conducted in either Syriac (a form of Aramaic) or Turkish at 8am each Sunday morning, though official opening times are Sunday 2–5pm and other days 9am–noon & 2–5pm. Contributions welcomed, as there are only five Syrian Orthodox families left here.

Eating and drinking

The **local speciality** is lamb *kaburga* (ribs stuffed with fragrant *pilaf* rice), *bumbar* (stuffed intestines) and succulent *içli köfte* (meatballs in a bulgur-wheat casing) available at various restaurants in town, and the syrup-soaked shredded wheat dessert, *kadayif*. Only the *Büyük Kervansaray* listed below is licensed.

Aslan Yemek Salonu Kıbrıs Cad. Welcoming a/c restaurant – try the *yufkalı incik*, lamb on the bone with peas, pepper and tomato, wrapped in pastry. It also does a decent breakfast, with clotted cream, honey, bread and tea a bargain 4TL.

Büyük Kervansaray Gazi Cad, Deliller Hanı (see map, p.640). The courtyard of the hotel hosts the closest thing in the city centre to a nightclub; dinner is served around the pool, and there's live music and dancing most nights. Expect to pay around 13TL for a meal.

Çarşı Konağı Gazi Cad, Çarşı Karakolu Çarşısı. Set in an old Armenian courtyard house, this pleasant café/restaurant dishes up delicious *menemen* and grills. You can admire the terrapins sculling around the courtyard's pool while you eat. To find it head down the narrow alley running west of the Akbank on Gazi Cad.

Kamer'in Avlusu Gazi Cad, Hasan Paşa Hanı. Home-cooking dished up in the atmospheric vaulted basement of this historic *han*. There's fresh green beans or a spinach dish for vegetarians, aubergine stuffed with mince or meat and veg fried up in a mini-wok for omnivores – and much else besides. Profits go to victims of domestic violence.

Kıvırcığın Gazi Cad, Eğilli İs Hanı 6. Better than average grill/*pide* place, with old photos of the city adorning the walls and a friendly atmosphere. Local dishes include *bumbar* and *lahmacun* as well as the standard kebabs. Also does a full Turkish breakfast for 5TL.

Şafak Kahvalti Salonu Kıbrıs Cad 34. Open 24 hours a day, this makes a good choice for breakfast, serving comb honey with butter and fresh bread for breakfast, as well as the usual soups or Turkish breakfasts. They also dish up *pide*, *lahmacun* and kebabs later in the day, and there's a comfortable *aile salonu* upstairs.

Selim Amca Sofra Salonu Ali Emiri Cad. A Diyarbakır institution, a 5min walk west of Dağ Kapısı, serving both chicken and lamb *kaburga* mains, *içli köfte* starters and *İrmik helvası* desserts. A fixed menu will set you back 23TL, good value considering the opulence of the surroundings and the quality of the food, but there's no alcohol.

Şanlıurfa Kebap Evi İzzet Paşa Cad 4. Very popular with the locals for its fast service, tasty food and keen prices. Watch your *lahmacun* (1.5TL) or *pide* (4TL) being prepared in the wood-burning downstairs oven, or retire upstairs to the cooler *aile salonu*. Also does a good range of kebabs.

Listings

Airlines The THY office is in the Bağlar district (☎0412/236 8960), the Onur Air office is at İnönü Cad 28/B (☎0412/223 5312). City buses to the airport run from a stop on Kibris Cad, just west of the Büyükşehir Belediyesi Turizm Burosu.

Banks and exchange Most of the banks and *döviz* offices are on Gazi Cad; Akbank takes most credit cards and travellers' cheques.

Buses The usual eastern bus companies have booths near Dağ Kapısı on Kıbrıs Cad. Service buses to the *otogar* have been discontinued, but it's worth asking. City buses to both the Yeni Otogar and İlçe Otogar run from a stop on Kibris Cad, just west of the Büyükşehir Belediyesi Turizm Burosu.

Car rental Class, next to the *Class Hotel* on Gazı Cad 101 (☎0535/921 5572), or Avis, İnönü Cad (☎0412/229 0275).

Hospital The Devlet Hastanesi (State Hospital) is north of Dağ Kapısı, or try the private Özel Veni Vidi Hastanesi (☎0412/229 2025) at Al Emiri Cad 1 (near Dağ Kapısı).

Police Police station on Gazı Cad, just north of the main crossroads.

Post office There is a small PTT on Yeni Kapı Cad, near the junction with Gazı Cad (Mon–Sat 9am–noon and 1–5pm for mail; 24hr for telephones). For money exchange, go to the larger PTT on Ziya Gökalp Bul, 300m north of Dağ Kapısı (same hours).

Trains The *Güney Ekspresi* departs for İstanbul every Mon, Wed, Fri & Sun. Tickets from the station at the end of İstasyon Cad.

Travel agencies Diyarbakır has several reputable agencies, best of them being Bat-Air, İnönü Cad 9 (☎0412/223 5373).

Mardin and around

Seen from the south, **MARDIN** looks spectacular, its tiered layers of vernacular houses, mansions, mosques and churches clinging to a huge citadel-topped rock rising out of the north Mesopotamian plain. Sunset here is particularly striking, with locals flying kites, a deep-blue sky filled with wheeling swifts, and shadows swallowing up the patchwork of fields on the endless plain.

Mardin's position has always made it a strategic military outpost – the higher of the two castellated bluffs today sports golf-ball radar domes. The population is a mix of Kurds, Arabs, Turks and Syrian Orthodox Christians (known in Turkey as Süriyani). Like Diyarbakır, the city has had to cope with an influx of people from surrounding villages forced from their homes by the state/PKK conflict. Now the political situation is reasonably stable, Mardin has become the centre of the region's tourism industry. Several boutique hotels, fashioned from the charming old buildings, have opened in recent years, and it has become a popular (and thus overpriced) spot for well-off İstanbul Turks in search of the "quaint east". Handmade soaps are big business here, as is silver jewellery and, more prosaically, dried fruits and nuts. Mardin also boasts a small film festival, Sinemardin, held towards the end of June, with the accent on Middle Eastern cinema.

Some history

Mardin's probable Roman origins are lost in the welter of war and conquest that forms this region's historical backdrop, while the town's later history is tied up with the development of early Christianity. The first Christians to settle here were Syrian Orthodox, who arrived during the third century AD. The Christians survived the period of Arab occupation from 640 to 1104, and were left alone by the Selçuk and Turcoman rulers. Today, eleven churches are hidden away in the backstreets.

From the twelfth to the fourteenth centuries, the citadel was the capital of the Artukid Turcoman tribe. They were able to beat off Arab attacks and endure an eight-month siege during the first Mongol onslaught, falling only to the second Mongol wave under Tamerlane in 1394. The Mongols doled out death and misery in equal measures to Christian and Muslim alike, before, in 1408, handing Mardin

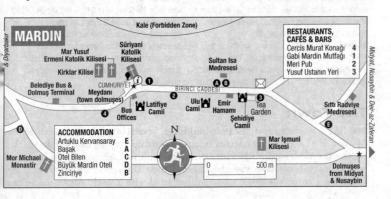

over to the Karakoyun Turcoman tribe, who built the (now ruined) palace and mosque inside the citadel walls. In 1517 it became an Ottoman possession.

Before and during Turkey's War of Independence, Mardin's Christian population was drastically reduced by massacre and emigration. There were renewed emigrations in the early 1990s and today only a few hundred practising Syrian Orthodox, Catholic and Armenian Christians remain. Local émigrés made good in Europe and the USA are now pouring money into the local Syrian Orthodox communities in Mardin and the Tür Abdin.

Arrival, orientation and information

The old town lies on the steep southern slopes below the citadel. The principal street, **Birinci Caddesi**, branches off the main road at the western end of town, and rejoins it at the eastern end.

There's no *otogar* as such. Dolmuşes for Diyarbakır and other destinations usually depart from the **Belediye bus terminal** at the western end of Birinci Caddesi. You can buy coach tickets from a couple of companies on Birinci Caddesi (near the *meydan*) but need to take the blue Şehir İçi (inside the city) bus (1TL) down to Yenşehir (New City), a kilometre or so to the west, to board the coach. There is a **dolmuş terminal** at the eastern end of town on the main Syria-bound road, with services to Midyat and Nusaybin. Blue Şehir İçi buses go from Cumhuriyet Meydanı or anywhere along Birinci Caddesi to either of these terminals. There's a small **tourist office** in Cumhuriyet Meydanı.

Accommodation

Artuklu Kervansaray Birinci Cad 70 ☎0482/213 7353, ⍟www.artuklu.com. Fashioned from a restored *kervansaray* dating back to the thirteenth century, this hotel has comfortable rooms and a wonderful roof terrace, but the service can be eccentric at best. ⑤

Otel Başak Birinci Cad ☎0482/212 6246. Small rooms, cleanish squat toilets in the corridor and separate, grimy showers with no hot water. But the sheets are clean, there's a fan in the room, it's very central and the only budget hotel in the old town. ①

Otel Bilen ☎0482/212 5568. Bland but better value than the old town hotels, the *Bilen* has a/c, spotless en-suite bathrooms and wi-fi – and there are regular municipal buses up to the old town from a stop opposite the hotel. ④

Büyük Mardin Oteli Yeni Yol Cad ☎0482/213 1047, ⍟www.buyuknardinoteli.com. This monumental block at the foot of the old town (and spoiling the view across the Syrian plain from it) is aimed squarely at the coach-tour trade, and offers attractively furnished rooms (with kilims for curtains) boasting a/c and satellite TV. May bargain if slack. ⑤

Erdoba Konakları Hotel Birinci Cad ☎0482/212 7677, ⍟www.erdoba.com.tr. Built in "period style" around a courtyard, the main building has an upmarket restaurant attached. A separate building lower down the hill offers rooms in a converted merchant's mansion, and there are a further two annexes to the east. All rooms have a/c and are very comfortable, but make sure you have a look before making your choice – they vary markedly. ⑤

Zinciriye Medrese Mah 243, Sok 13 ☎0482/212 4866, ⍟www.zinciriye.com. Well placed in the old town just below the Sultan İsa Medresesi, is the newest of the boutique hotels. Rooms have exposed stone walls, vaulted ceilings and tasteful furnishings – and the view from the terrace is great. ⑤

The Town

Mardin boasts some superb **Islamic buildings**. Several hundred metres east of the Meydan, the easterly of two sets of stone steps lead up from Birinici Caddesi to the **Sultan İsa Medresesi** (daily 9am–6pm; free) built in 1385, a striking, structure with a magnificent doorway and fluted domes; the semi-translucent volcanic stones used in the *mihrab* glow when illuminated with a torch. Above the Sultan

İsa Medresesi is the **kale**, or citadel, originally built by the Romans and extended by the Byzantines. It's possible to climb part wayup the *kale* hill to a cemetery and get views down over the town and plain beyond, though the castle itself is a forbidden military zone. The **Ulu Cami** is an eleventh-century Selçuk mosque with a striking minaret, below Birinci Caddesi. Further east on Birinci Caddesi is the prominent **Şehidiye Camii**, also with a very ornate minaret. Also worth a look, above the *Selçuklu Kervansay Hotel*, is the **Sıttı Radviye Medresesi**, a newly restored theological school containing a footprint in stone believed to be of the Prophet Mohammed.

To the south of Cumhuriyet Meydanı is the **Latifiye Camii**, dating from the fourteenth century. It has a carved Selçuk-style portal, and a courtyard with a shady garden. Around here lies a maze of streets, forming part of the **bazaar**. At the western end of town, south of the main road, is the fifteenth-century **Kasım Paşa Medresesi**, similar in design to the Sultan İsa Medresesi.

Mardin has a vibrant **Christian heritage**, and adherents of the two faiths have always intermingled rather than living in separate quarters. The Syrian Orthodox **Kirklar Kilise** (Arbin Söhad in Syriac) or Church of the Forty Martyrs, is the most welcoming to visitors and dates back, in part, to the sixth century. Best time to attend is Sunday morning (around 9am) when the local Süriyani population comes to pray, though you must dress respectfully and photography is forbidden. Next door **Mar Yusuf** (St Joseph's), serves the town's tiny Armenian Catholic population. Lacking a priest, it's usually locked, and the congregation attends services at the Kirklar Kilise. Adjoining the museum (see below), is the town's largest church, the **Süriyani Katolik Kilisesi** (Church of the Virgin Mary), used by five families of Syrian Catholics. At the bottom of the hill in the southeastern part of the old town, with a typical Syrian Orthodox walled courtyard, is the **Mar İşmuni Kilisesi**.

Mardin is famed for its **domestic architecture** too – its soft, pale honey-coloured stone is easy to work, allowing for the intricate relief-carvings which embellish most old houses here. Look out for the wonderfully ornate post office building on Birinici Caddesi (designed in the nineteenth century by the Armenian architect, Lole). Also of note are the *abarra*, arched passageways covering the street, formed from the two houses either side. They give much-neacled shade and act as cooling wind tunnels.

Immediately above the two car parks at Cumhuriyet Meydanı is Mardin's **museum** (Tues–Sun 8.30am–4.30pm; 3TL), housed in a restored nineteenth century mansion, once the residence of the Syrian Catholic patriarch. It contains impressive finds from nearby sites, from the Chalcolithic period onwards. Most impressive are some burnished red Urartian pots, a large kneeling Assyrian figure carved from black basalt, and a terracotta toy chariot dating back some 5000 years.

Eating and drinking

The best restaurant in town is the upmarket ⅍ *Cercis Murat Konağı* to the west of the Meydan on Birinci Caddesi. Set in a restored Süriyani house, with great views from the terrace, it specializes in local dishes such as *incassıye*, lamb flavoured with sweet *pekmez*, plums, chilli and tomato; alcohol is available, including a passable local wine. Apart from that, options are rather limited. *Yusuf Ustanın Yeri*, a simple family-orientated place opposite the PTT, is an *ocakbaşı* (charcoal grill) garden **restaurant** serving delicious kebabs and *köfte*, but no alcohol. For beer the only real choice is the *Meri Pub*, a couple of hundred metres west of Cumhuriyet Meydanı on Birinici Caddesi. It's far better than its gloomy entrance suggests. Grab a window table and admire the sunset over the Syrian plain with a cool (but expensive, 7.5TL) beer. The nearby *Gabi Mardin Mutfağı*, owned by a local

Süriyani, has a nice terrace above the street action (but no views over the plain) and does a decent shredded meat *kaburga*, served on a bed of *pilaf* rice.

Opposite the PTT is a small and leafy terrace **tea garden**, where you can watch the sun set over Syria.

Deyr-az-Zaferan

Six kilometres southeast of Mardin is the Syrian Orthodox monastery of **Deyr-az-Zaferan** (9am–noon, 1.30–4.30pm; 3TL) or the "Saffron Monastery", so named for the yellowish rock from which it's built). Founded in 493 AD, it was, from 1160 until the 1920s, the seat of the Syrian Orthodox patriarch – though he has since relocated to Damascus. It has become the showpiece of the Syrian Orthodox church in Turkey, and has been lovingly restored – largely with funds from the diaspora.

To visit, take a Şehir İçi bus from Birinci Caddesi to its easternmost stop, then walk southeast down the Nusaybin road. The monastery is signed off to the left (east) from the main road – it's a little over an hour's walk. A taxi from old Mardin should cost around 30TL for a return trip with waiting time.

There's a posh gift shop and cafeteria at the entrance, and young Süriyani men are on hand to give you a quick guided tour of the main parts of the monastery complex. Most impressive are the domed **Church of Beth Kadishe**, with elaborately carved Corinthian capitals and a late-Roman-style frieze, and the patriarch's or metropolitan's **throne**, on which are carved the names of all the patriarchs since 792 AD. The nearby underground vault, topped by a stone ceiling constructed without mortar, is believed to have been a sun-worshipper's

The Syrian Orthodox Church

The Mardin region has been a stronghold of the **Syrian Orthodox or Jacobite Church** since 543 AD, when Jacobus Baradaeus was appointed bishop of Edessa. A native of Mesopotamia, Baradaeus was – like most of the Christians in the eastern and southern reaches of the Byzantine Empire – a Monophysite, and was locked in a century-old theological dispute with the patriarchate in Constantinople about the divine nature of Christ. The ecclesiastical Council of Chalcedon (451 AD) ruled that Christ had both a human and a divine nature, but dissenting bishops throughout the Middle East held that Christ had only a divine nature – a creed known as Monophysitism, whose adherents risked condemnation as heretics and excommunication.

Baradaeus was an energetic proselytizer throughout what is now the Hatay and Syria, helping to revive his Church as it suffered determined attack by the agents of Constantinopolitan orthodoxy. Under Arab dominion in the seventh century, Syrian Orthodox Christians enjoyed considerable religious freedom. By the time of the First Crusade at the end of the eleventh century, the Tür Abdin in particular encompassed four bishoprics and eighty monasteries, the ruins of which are dotted across the plateau. Ironically, the Christian Crusaders persecuted the "heretical" Syrian Orthodox church, the Mongols later massacred its adherents and pillaged its properties.

The Syrian Orthodox community enjoyed a long period of tolerance and stability under Ottoman rule. During World War I, though, they were tainted by association with Allied plans to dismember the Ottoman Empire and suffered widespread persecution and massacre, a fate they shared with the Armenian and Greek minorities. Of today's global population of seven million Syrian Christians there are now just a few thousand left in Turkey served by the bishoprics of Tür Abdin (Midyat/Mor Gabriel), Mardin (Deyr-az-Zaferan), Adiyaman and İstanbul. Many have emigrated to Europe (notably Sweden) and North America, but the seat of the patriarchy is in Damascus.

temple in pagan times. This is a working church, with one of the four metropolitan bishops of the Syrian Orthodox church in Turkey still in residence, plus a few monks and nuns.

Nusaybin, Mar Augen and Dara

About 50km southeast of Mardin is **NUSAYBIN**, on the frontier with Syria. Nusaybin was the site of the **Roman town of Nisibis** and has a triumphal arch. The sporadically functioning Syrian Orthodox church, **Mar Yakoub** (officially open only on Sundays) has a crypt containing the bones of St Jacob. From here it's a fifty-metre walk southeast to the border-crossing point with Syria. The town's ornate **train station**, built by the Germans just before World War I and the last stop in Turkey on the Berlin–Baghdad railway lies out to the east.

Nestorian **Mar Augen** is the most poignant of all the abandoned monasteries in the area, though only the fifth-century monastery church is intact. With your own car, drive 25km towards Cizre and turn left to the village of Girmeli, 1km away; just past the village take a right turn and follow it 3km to the foot of the cliffs below the monastery. From a parking point it's a twenty-minute climb up to the monastery. A taxi from Nusaybin is around 50TL, with waiting time. On the main road to the monastery from Nusaybin, just before the Girmeli turn, is the *Nezirhan Motel* (T 0482/446 3416, W www.nezirhan.com; ❹). The modern concrete equivalent of a *kervansaray*, established in 1976, has become something of an institution on this godforsaken border-road, and has comfortable rooms with air conditioning and an Olympic-sized pool out back.

Like Mar Augen, the evocative ruins of Byzantine **Dara**, (ancient Anastopolis) picturesquely set amidst the houses of the traditional Kurdish village of Oğuz, is difficult to access without your own wheels. From Nusaybin take a Kızıltepe-bound dolmuş (3TL) and the driver will drop you at the turn (due north) to the village, a 6km walk or hitch away. There are three dolmuşes a day from Mardin (40km to the north) or take a Nusaybin-bound dolmuş (5TL) and get out at the turn for the village, 10km east of the main road, and hitch. The remains are very extensive, with stretches of paved road, bridges, rock-cut and cave dwellings and, most impressive of all, a massive underground (and well-lit) storage depot some thirty metres high. These are the most extensive remains in the region, testament to a time (mid-sixth century AD) when this area formed the eastern bastion of the Byzantine Christian world against the Persian Empire.

The Tür Abdin plateau

The undulating plateau of the **Tür Abdin**, traditional heartland of the Syrian Orthodox Church (see box opposite) – begins just east of Mardin. It is still home to a few Christians, who coexist uneasily with the local Kurds. Aside from a traditional livelihood of grape growing, the rocky, parched plateau is a poor region even by the standards of eastern Turkey, but the Christian villages are partly supported by émigrés.

Midyat is the western gateway to the Tür Abdin proper, which still has several villages either wholly, or partially, inhabited by Syrian Orthodox Christians, plus 46 **monasteries and churches**, some recently restored. Most are tricky to reach by public transport so either arrange a taxi or hire car.

Mıdyat

From Mardin, the "double" town of **MIDYAT** is an uneventful journey of just under an hour. The westerly portion is the unremarkable, Kurd-inhabited business district of **Estel**. Two kilometres east is the originally Christian portion of half-abandoned medieval mansions, known as **Eski** (Old) **Mıdyat**. Tourism is beginning to take off in the town, though facilities are still limited.

As recently as 1974 there were nearly 5000 Syrian Orthodox Christians in residence here, the men mostly engaged in gold- or silversmithing, but following PKK extortion and death threats, the population has dwindled to eighty families and one priest. However, because of the changed political climate a few Syrian Orthodox families are beginning to return.

The town's **churches** are easily spotted by virtue of their graceful belfries. **Mor Barsaumo**, close to the main road and reached by an alleyway opposite the *Cihan* restaurant, was built as early as the fifth century, destroyed in 1793 and rebuilt in 1910. This is the best church to visit as it is the most active, and has a small schoolroom where the kids of the remaining Syrian Orthodox families come to learn Syriac, a language closely related to that used by Christ.

Practicalities

The dolmuş *garaj* in old Mıdyat is a couple of hundred metres south of town on the İdil/Mor Gabriel road. Dolmuşes for Mardin (8TL), Hasankeyf (5TL) and Nusaybin (8TL) run more or less hourly from 7.30am to 6pm. Above a small **bazaar** the residential quarter climbs up a low hill, with mysterious gateways opening onto the courtyards of imposing mansions, inhabited by extended families of Kurds and Syrian Orthodox Christians.

The *Metro* hotel, on the fringes of old Mıdyat (℡0482/464 2317; ❶), just northeast of the central roundabout on the Hasankeyf–Batman road, offers basic rooms with metal-framed beds and shared bathrooms but it is friendly enough and reasonably clean. Alternatively, on a hilltop in the centre of the old quarter, is the *Konak Evi* (℡0452/464 0719; ❸, no breakfast) a beautiful two-hundred-year-old mansion converted into a boutique hotel. The rooftop gives wonderful views over the entire town and surroundings, especially appealing towards sunset. As for eating try 🍴 *Cihan Lokantası*, just south of the junction roundabout on the Mar Gabriel road. It is spotlessly clean and packed at lunchtimes for the superb *sulu yemek*, which includes tender *kaburga* (rib of lamb) and *perde pilaf* (delicately spiced rice with shredded chicken). The creamy *ayran* served here comes in copper bowls and is drunk from a ladle. More touristy is the *Tarihi Mıdyat Café & Restaurant*, set in the restored Gelüşke Hanı, a two minute walk up into the old town from the silversmiths' quarter, with a (too) wide selection of Turkish and regional dishes.

Assyriska – a national team without a nation

While they lack a country of their own, Turkey's Süriyani or Assyrian population have found an unlikely rallying point – a football club in Sweden. **Assyriska**, a second-division team based near Stockholm is made up entirely of immigrants (two-thirds of them Syrian Orthodox Christians who have emigrated from Turkey). In 2006, Mıdyat-born journalist **Nuri Kino** brought their story to life in an award-winning documentary, *Assyriska*, charting the side's progress to a brief spell at the top of the Swedish premiership. The team are a symbol of pride for the Assyrian diaspora throughout the world, who have often been persecuted in their traditional heartlands (modern Turkey, Iraq, Iran and Syria). The documentary is controversial in Turkey, as it alleges that the massacres suffered by Assyrians at the hands of the Ottomans in World War I amount to genocide. See ⊛www.nurikino.com for more information.

Mar Gabriel

Situated some 22km southeast of Midyat, a couple of kilometres east of the İdil/Cizre road, the monastery of **Mar Gabriel** (Deyrulumur) is the geographical and spiritual centre of the plateau. A **taxi** from Midyat costs around 30TL, including waiting time. Alternatively, catch an İdil-bound dolmuş (2TL) from old Midyat's dolmuş garage. It will drop you at the signed Mar Gabriel junction, a twenty-minute ride, from where it's a half-hour, 2km walk on a surfaced road cutting across the undulating, scrub-oak-blanketed plateau.

Founded in 397 AD, Mar Gabriel is the oldest and most vital surviving Syrian Orthodox monastery in Turkey. It's the seat of the metropolitan bishop of Tür Abdin, who is aided by thirteen resident nuns and three monks, as well as a fluctuating number of local lay workers, guests and students. A working community, set among gardens and orchards, its primary purpose is to keep Syrian Orthodox Christianity alive in the land of its birth by providing schooling and ordination of native-born monks. Visiting hours are 9–11.30am & 1–4.30pm, with a lay person giving visitors a guided tour of the monastery. The glittering, mosaic-covered ceiling of the apse of the main Anastasius (512 AD) church is particularly memorable, though Tamerlane stripped the gold ceiling of the nave. The tour also takes in the circular dining room, surmounted by a dome donated by the Byzantine empress Theodora early in the sixth century AD, and the Church of the Mother of God, dating back some fourteen hundred years.

Recent restoration work has given the monastery a new lease of life, and there's a tangible aura of prosperity, a sign that securer times have returned again to the Tür Abdin. Unfortunately, local Kurdish villagers and the Turkish State have contested the ownership of some of the monastery's land, and the ongoing court case is seen as a litmus test of Turkey's commitment to minority rights by some European bodies.

The Church of the Mother of God

The most beautiful Syrian Orthodox building in Turkey is undoubtedly the remote, monastic **Church of the Mother of God** (İndath Aloho in Syriac, Meryemanna in Turkish). To reach it follow the Hasankeyf road for 3km, then turn right for Dargeçit. After 17km turn right (signed Meryemanna/Hah) and follow the road for 6km to Hesterek village, turn left here for Anıtlı – also known as Hah – a further 7km away. The church, on your right as you enter the village, is justifiably regarded by the local Süriyanis as the jewel in the Tür Abdin crown. This fifth-century foundation sports a two-storey wedding-cake-like turret with blind arches topped by a pyramidal roof; the archways and lintels are also heavily ornamented. The church has a virtually square ground plan, with a transverse nave, but what's striking about the domed interior are the gorgeously ornate Corinthian capitals and an elaborate, relief-carved frieze. The village itself is fascinating. Once the centre of a community of several thousand, with over 44 churches in the vicinity, there are now just sixteen families remaining. At the centre of the village, atop a small rise, are a group of fortified houses where some five thousand Christians held out for months against a vastly superior Ottoman force in 1915 – with no Christian lives lost. Downhill from here are the remains of the church of **Mor Bacchus**, dating back to the second century, and en route back to the Church of the Mother of God, is the sixth-century church of **Mor Sovo**, destroyed by Tamerlane.

Heading back towards Midyat, and just to the left of the road by the main right turn for Anıtlı, is the prominent hilltop village of **Zaz**. What from the main road looks to be a castle turns out on closer inspection to be the Syrian Orthodox church of **Mor Dimet** (fourth century AD). It's a striking place, inhabited by Jacob, a Süriyani returned from six years' exile in Sweden and Germany, a nun, and a few Kurdish families. Further back towards Midyat, 10km along the Dargeçit road and then 3km north on a dirt track, the important **Mar Yakoub** monastic church in Baraztepe (Salah) village is substantial, but lacks the grace of the Church of the Mother of God at Anıtlı. Returning to the Dargeçit road, continuing east for 2km and then turning south for a further couple of kilometres, you reach the slightly later church of newly renovated **Mor Kyriakos**, with its small courtyard, in the mixed Christian/Kurdish village of Bağlarbaşı (Arnas). Its architect also built the **Mar Azazael** church on a knoll at the edge of Altıntaş (Keferzeh) village, about 7km east of Mor Kyriakos.

Hasankeyf

The spectacular ruined settlement of **HASANKEYF** is one of the most evocative in Turkey. Here the swift-flowing waters of the Tigris have carved a sheer cliff from the mountainside, and poised on its very lip are a remarkable series of remains of Selçuk, Arabic and Kurdish origin. Below the ruins the Tigris is spanned by the arches of a vintage 1950s concrete bridge, itself overlooking the mighty piers of its medieval precursor. It's a photographer's dream, especially at sunset and sunrise, and a meal at one of the many simple fish restaurants lining the bank beneath the cliff is unforgettable.

In the surrounding hills, are over 4000 caves many inhabited in prehistoric times, but the original settlement was founded by the Romans as an eastern bastion of the empire, and later became the Byzantine bishopric of Cephe. In 640, the conquering Arabs changed the town's name to Hisn Kayfa. During the twelfth century the Artukid Turcoman tribe made it the capital of their realm, which it remained until the Mongols arrived in 1260. Hasankeyf then served as the stronghold of the Ayyubids, a clan of Kurdish chieftains supplanted by the Ottomans early in the fifteenth century.

The town and site

The modern town is strung out either side of the road leading to the concrete bridge across the river. Reach the **site** (always open; 3TL) by heading west then south from the southern end of the modern bridge. The one-kilometre-long road

---

That sinking feeling

In 2008 Hasankeyf was put on the World Monuments Fund Watch List as one of the hundred most endangered heritage sites in the world. Despite this, and a domestic and international outcry, much of the ancient city looks certain to be drowned by the waters of the **İlisu dam** across the Tigris, part of the GAP project (see p.619). Pledges to save key elements of the site, (for example the brick-built Zeyn El-Abdin Türbesi) and remove them to a reservoir-side open-air museum are decried by critics, who say the remains are far too delicate to move. The most vociferous critics of the scheme are the eighty thousand or so locals likely to be displaced by the floodwaters though several other groups oppose it including those living downstream in Iraq (who fear their already scant water resources will be wiped out by the dam), Kurdish nationalists (who view the dam as a deliberate attempt to wipe out their cultural heritage) and assorted environmental groups.

▲ Hasankeyf's ruins above the Tigris

is lined by rows of souvenir stalls, selling everything from tasteful, locally woven goat-hair blankets to garish wall-hangings. The **ascent to the cliff-top ruins**, up a time-polished stone pathway is demanding in the heat of the day. The path cuts back from the cliff-edge and weaves up to the **Ulu Camii**, an evocatively ruined Ayyubid (built in 1305) mosque with a long, narrow prayer hall, finely carved *mihrab* and truncated minaret. Scattered roundabout are the remains of abandoned houses, exposed cisterns (take care) and Muslim cemeteries and mausoleums. Below it, the twelfth-century building conjectured to be the **palace of the Artukid kings**, is perched right on the cliff-edge above the Tigris.

En route to the citadel area you pass the **El Rizk Camii**, built under the Ayyubids in 1409 AD. It has a beautiful minaret decorated with *kufic* inscriptions and teardrop patterns, and is topped by a stork's nest. The river is below and just west of the mosque, lined by dozens of simple, shady fish restaurants and backed by a sheer cliff-face. The stepped tunnel, which once gave secret access to the Artukid city above, has been closed on grounds of safety. Just downstream are the four pillars of the old **Artukid bridge**, once the largest in Anatolia. The central span is thought to have been constructed from wood.

The conspicuous fifteenth-century **Zeyn El-Abdin Türbesi**, a beautiful, onion-domed cylindrical building clad in glazed turquoise tiles and red brick, is a ten-minute walk west from the northern end of the bridge. Constructed in 1475, it was made for Zeynel Bey, the son of an Akkoyunlu sultan, Uzun (Tall) Hasan. Recent excavations around the tomb have revealed an extensive complex of buildings including a couple of *medreses* (theological schools).

Practicalities

From Midyat the hour-long dolmuş trip to Hasankeyf takes an hour (5TL). Appoaching **from Diyarbakır** you first need to get to Batman (regular dolmuşes run from Diyarbakır's İlçe Otogar taking 1hr 30min; 7TL). From Batman, half-hourly dolmuşes (3TL; last one around 6pm) take an hour to reach Hasankeyf. **Leaving Hasankeyf** the first Midyat-bound dolmuş passes through at 8am. There's also a direct coach onto Van at 9.30am daily.

An **overnight stay** is recommended to fully appreciate the wonderful setting and subtle early-morning and sunset light. The *Oğretmen Evi* just south of the bridge is open to tourists between June and August (the rest of the year it houses teachers working in the local villages). This provides basic rooms (shared bathroom) with bunk beds for 15TL but is often full at weekends. Just below and opposite the *Oğretmen Evi* is the *Hasankeyf Motel* (❶), with dirty carpets, no hot water and no en-suite rooms, but great views over the river. The *Nehir Et Lokantası* on the main street is good for soup, grills and *lahmacun*, whilst just west of the bridge the *Elit Lokantası*, with similar food but boasting a rear terrace overlooking the Tigris. Of the numerous fish and meat grills right on the water's edge try the *Şahmaran Çardak*, with platforms set in the river. Grills come to around 10TL per head including a salad, the catfish caught from the river is dressed in a slightly spicy sauce. There's a small PTT, ATM and internet café on the main drag south of the bridge.

Travel details

Buses and dolmuşes

Adıyaman to: Adana (4 daily; 6hr); Ankara (5 daily; 13hr); Diyarbakır (2 daily; 3hr 30min); Kahta (hourly; 45min); Kayseri (1 daily; 8hr); Malatya (hourly; 3hr); Şanlıurfa (hourly; 2hr 30min).
Batman to: Hasankeyf (6 daily; 1hr); Diyarbakır (hourly; 1hr 30min).
Diyarbakır to: Adana (6 daily; 8hr); Ankara (6 daily; 13hr); Batman (hourly; 1hr 30min); Bitlis (5 daily; 3hr 30min); Gaziantep (5 daily; 5hr); Malatya (6 daily; 4hr); Mardin (6 daily; 1hr 45min); Şanlıurfa (8 daily; 3hr); Siirt (hourly; 3hr); Sivas (4 daily; 10hr); Siverek (hourly; 2hr); Tatvan (4 daily; 4hr); Van (4 daily; 7hr).
Gaziantep to: Adana via Mersin (10 daily; 3hr 30min); Ankara (12 daily; 10hr); Antakya (8 daily; 4hr); Diyarbakır (5 daily; 5hr); Malatya (3 daily; 4hr); Mardin (5 daily; 5hr); Şanlıurfa (10 daily; 2hr).
Hasankeyf to: Batman (6 daily; 45min); Cizre (1 daily; 2hr); Midyat (6 daily; 45min); Van (1 daily; 7hr) .
Kahta to: Adıyaman (hourly; 45min), Karadüt (7 daily in season; 30min); Siverek (several daily; 2hr).
Malatya to: Adana (5 daily; 7hr 30min); Adıyaman (hourly; 3hr); Ankara (8 daily; 10hr); Diyarbakır (6 daily; 4hr); Erzurum (1 daily; 7hr); Gaziantep (6 daily; 4hr); İstanbul (5 daily; 15hr).
Mardin to: Cizre via Nusaybin (3 daily; 3hr); Diyarbakır (6 daily; 1hr 45min); Midyat (frequently on demand; 1hr); Şanlıurfa (5 daily; 3hr).
Midyat to: Batman (6 daily; 1hr 30min); Hasankeyf (6 daily; 45min).

Şanlıurfa to: Adana (6 daily; 6hr); Adıyaman (6 daily; 2hr 30min); Ankara (5 daily; 13hr); Diyarbakır (8 daily; 3hr); Gaziantep (8 daily; 2hr); Harran (hourly 7am–7pm; 1hr); Mardin (5 daily; 3hr).

Trains

Diyarbakır to: Ankara (4 weekly; 26hr 15min); İstanbul (4 weekly; 32hr); Kayseri (4 weekly; 18hr); Malatya (4 weekly; 6hr); Sivas (4 weekly; 13hr).
Gaziantep to: Nusaybin (3 weekly; 11hr).
Malatya to: Adana (daily; 8hr 30min); Ankara (daily; 20hr); Diyarbakır (4 weekly; 6hr 30min); İstanbul (4 weekly; 26hr); Tatvan (3 weekly; 10hr 30min).

Flights

Adıyaman to: İstanbul (5 weekly; 1hr 55min).
Batman to: Ankara (daily; 1hr 35min); İstanbul (daily; 2hr 10min).
Diyarbakır to: Ankara (3 daily; 1hr 30min); Antalya (at least 2 weekly); İstanbul (5 daily; 2hr).
Gaziantep to: Ankara (2 daily; 1hr 10min); Antalya via İstanbul (6 daily; 3hr 20min; direct; 1 weekly); İstanbul (6 daily; 1hr 40min).
Malatya to: Ankara (daily; 1hr 20min); Antalya via İstanbul (1 daily; 4hr 10min; direct; 1 weekly; 1hr 30min); İstanbul (at least 3 daily; 1hr 45min), İzmir (2 weekly).
Mardin to: Ankara (daily; 1hr 35min); İstanbul (daily 2hr 5min).
Şanlıurfa to: Ankara (1 daily; 1hr 20min); İstanbul (1 daily; 1hr 55min).

12

Lake Van and the southeast

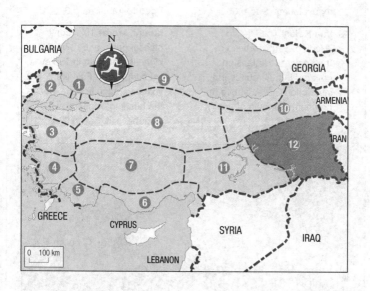

CHAPTER 12 Highlights

* **Nemrut Dağı** The massive crater of this towering volcano shelters migrating birds in May and September, and in between offers the possibility of a dip in the crater lakes. See p.661

* **Ahlat** The eerie cemeteries of lakeshore Ahlat are home to beautifully carved, improbably angled tombstones and striking cylindrical mausoleums. See p.662

* **Van Kalesi** The lakeside "Rock of Van", fortified by the ancient Urartians and covered in their cuneiform inscriptions, rises above the poignant old town of Van. See p.665

* **Akdamar Kilisesi** Superbly restored tenth-century Armenian church, liberally decorated with relief-carved biblical scenes, picturesquely set on a tiny island in Lake Van. See p.669

* **İshak Paşa Sarayı** An architectural folly of richly carved golden limestone, nestling beneath a dramatic rocky spur above the Silk Road to Iran. See p.678

* **Mount Ararat** This iconic biblical peak, at 5137m the highest mountain in Turkey rises, in Mount Fuji-like volcanic magnificence, above the bustling frontier town of Doğubeyazit. See p.679

▲ Mount Ararat, Turkey's highest peak

Lake Van and the southeast

T urkey's remote **southeast**, bordered by Iran to the east and Iraq to the south, is a land dominated by soaring peaks, rugged plateaux and plunging valleys. Its austere natural beauty makes the perfect backdrop for some of Turkey's most impressive and intriguing sights, whilst the predominantly ethnically Kurdish population makes the region feel distinctively different to the rest of the country. At its heart lies **Lake Van**, a vast inland sea ringed by snow-capped peaks. The Armenians who once lived around the lake were so enamoured with its beauty and fertility they had a saying "Van in this, paradise in the next". North of the lake is the graceful 5137-metre volcanic cone of Ağrı Dağ – better known as **Mount Ararat** – the highest peak in Turkey, whilst the wild, alpine range south of the lake contains mighty Reşko (4135m), second highest peak in the land. Winters, starting in early November, are severe, with roads often blocked by heavy snow, but in July and August, whilst much of the rest of Turkey is sweltering, these highlands are relatively cool and humidity free.

The once-poor road system has been improved significantly, often due to military requirements during the PKK troubles (see box, p.712), but ongoing roadworks are a minor nuisance. Food out here is plainer than in the west of Turkey, but it's worth trying some of the local Kurdish specialities such as the matured herb cheese, *otlu peynir*. Until quite recently the economy of the region was largely based on nomadic pastoralism, but the lure of the big cities and the forced evacuation of hundred and hundreds of villages during the struggle with the PKK has decimated the rural population.

There are daily flights from various cities in western Turkey to the regional capital, **Van** (1642km from İstanbul), on the eastern shore of the lake. Van has an ancient citadel set atop a dramatic limestone outcrop, overlooking the atmospheric but scant remains of the tragically destroyed old town. Rapidly expanding and modernizing, Van is a remarkably civilized and welcoming centre for exploration. Overland, the conventional approach is by bus from Diyarbakır (see Chapter 11), via the old trade route through the stark hill-town of **Bitlis** and dull **Tatvan**, itself a base for exploring the northwestern shore of Lake Van. Alternatively, from Erzurum (Chapter 10), travellers can head due east to **Doğubeyazıt** and its fanciful palace below the impressive bulk of Mount Ararat. From Van it's a four-hour journey through spectacular mountains to **Hakkari**. From here, the truly adventurous can exit the region by following the road along the Iraqi Kurdish border to **Şırnak**.

LAKE VAN AND THE SOUTHEAST

50 km
0

N

▲ Tehran

ARMENIA

I R A N

I R A Q

Ağrı Dağı
(Mount Ararat
5165m)

Iğdır

Gürbalak

Esendere

Şemdinli

Surb Bartolomeos

Soradir

Albayrak

Yüksekova

Reşko
(4136m)

CILO-SAT DAĞLARI

Çukurca

Doğubeyazıt

Işhak Paşa Sarayı

Tendirek Pass
(2644m)

Çaldıran

Muradiye

Güzelsu

Hoşap

Başkale

Karadağ
(3752m)

Kochanes

Hakkari

Yeni Köprü

Gürpınar

Çavuştepe

Diyadin

Balık
Gölü

Ulu Pamir

Erciş

Alaköy

Yedi
Kilise

Edremit

Van

Çarpanak

Ayanis

Akdamar

Gevaş

Aşağı
Narlıca

Çatak

Beytüşşebap

Uludere

Andzghonts

Ağrı

HWY E-23

Patnos

Malazgirt

Süphan Dağı
(4058m)

Kefkalesi

Adilcevaz

Ahlat

Nemrut Dağı
(3050m)

Tatvan

Altınsaç

St Thomas

Göründu

Bahçesaray

El-Aman
Kervansarayı

Bitlis

Siirt

Kurtalan

Şırnak

Cudi Dağı
(2134m)

Cizre

Midyat

Erzurum

Muş

Malabadi
Köprüsü

Silvan

Batman

Mardin

Bingöl

Murat River

Murat River

Diyarbakır

L a k e   V a n

Şanlıurfa

Bitlis

En route to Lake Van from Diyarbakır (and just a short diversion back west if you're coming up from Mardin/Hasankeyf) is the **Malabadi Köprüsü**, one of the most impressive bridges in Anatolia, built in 1146 by an Artukid ruler. Next up is the historic town of **BITLIS** (1545m altitude), reached along an attractive winding gorge dotted with *hans* and old bridges.

Most people pass straight through this atmospheric, if impoverished, town in the headlong rush to Lake Van. This is a shame, as there is much to be seen here, and assuming you get here early enough in the day it's easy to alight and explore the town before catching one of the very frequent dolmuşes on to Tatvan. With its dark stone houses and steep valley setting, Bitlis has the feel of an isolated nineteenth-century English mill-town, though it once controlled the pass from Syria to the Van region and Persia and Armenia beyond. Before World War I about half the inhabitants were Armenian, now it is predominantly Kurdish and famed for its tobacco.

The Town

Bitlis' lifeblood, the main west–east transit road linking the Tigris and Euphrates basins with that of Lake Van, is also a curse, with the town straggling along either side of this noisy, polluted main drag. Most of the important monuments, however, lay to the north of the road, in narrow streets busy with people rather than vehicles. The most notable monument is the sixteenth-century **Şerefiye Külliyesi**, a fine mosque/*medrese*/hamam complex. Built from dark sandstone, the mosque has a finely carved Selçuk-style portal, enlivened by a band of black and white stone. As impressive is the turreted **İhlasiye Medresesi**, built in 1569 by the Kurdish emir Şerefxan. The **Ulu Cami**, an unusual-looking mosque built in 1126 by the Artukids, and the **Saraf Han** *kervansaray*, are also worth seeking out.

Reached by the steps above the Tatvan dolmuş stop on the main street is a walled complex containing the **Küfrevi Türbesi**, dating from 1316, and a much more modern *türbe* built by Greek craftsmen under the orders of Sultan Abdülhamid in 1898. Together they house the tombs of six Sunni saints, who draw pilgrims from all over the Muslim world, but to gain entry you'll need to find the caretaker.

The huge **citadel**, originally built by one of Alexander the Great's generals (though the walls now visible date back only to 1530 AD), is built on a rock outcrop looming over the town. Reach it by following a road that snakes around its base to the far side, from where steps continue to the top, with great views over the town.

Practicalities

Tatvan **dolmuşes** depart from the foot of the steps below the Küfrevi Türbesi, on the main road just south of the *Dideban* hotel. They run regularly from 8am to 6pm (4TL). Intercity buses heading west from Van pass through Bitlis, but may be full.

If you decide to stay, Bitlis has the notionally three-star *Dideban* on Nur Cad 1 (T 0434/226 2821; ❸). Functional, clean en-suite rooms boast wi-fi, hairdryers and a fridge, and the attached restaurant is plush by Bitlis standards, with some good local dishes. The *Hanedan* (no phone; ❶) is cheaper but set in a dingy building, opposite a seedy bar, and is not recommended unless economy is all.

Local speciality, *büryan kebap*, leg of goat steamed in a *tandır* oven for four hours and served on the bone, is served up at numerous simple eateries tucked beneath the *kale*, try the *Büryancı Azmi Ustanin Yeri* on Balıkçılar Caddesi.

The El-Aman Kervansaray

Between Bitlis and Tatvan, on the right as the road reaches the plain, just after the turning to Muş, is the **El-Aman Kervansaray**. A classical Ottoman *kervansaray* built of dark volvcanic stone by Hüşref Paşa in 1502, it is one of the largest of the period, 90m long and with 160 rooms, and a vivid reminder of the volume of trade through the Bitlis gap. Recently restored, it is well worth visiting; and afterwards you can hail a passing dolmuş (2TL) to continue your journey to Tatvan, twenty minutes away.

Tatvan and around

Some 25km northeast of Bitlis, **TATVAN**, a functional town stranded between the mountains and lakeshore, makes a good base for exploring the surrounding sights. It has smartened up considerably in the last few years, with a new shopping centre and cinema wowing the bemused citizens. To the north is the massif of **Nemrut Dağı** with its crater lakes; further east around the lake are the impressive Selçuk remains at Ahlat (see p.662).

Arrival and information

Tatvan's streets follow the grid layout common in new developments in Turkey with the main street, **Cumhuriyet Caddesi**, running east to west 100m south of the lake. The otogar is 1km along the Bitlis road, but buses invariably drop passengers near the PTT on Cumhuriyet Caddesi. You can pick up onward **dolmuşes** from in front of the various companies' ticket offices around here. The dolmuş to Van costs 5TL and takes around three hours, following the main road along the beautiful south shore of the lake; Ahlat dolmuşes leave approximately every 45 minutes from the corner of the PTT, near Cumhuriyet Caddesi, and run along the north shore of the lake, taking some 45 minutes.

The **train station** is a kilometre northwest of the town centre. *Van Gölü Express* trains arrive from İstanbul at 2pm on Wednesdays and Saturdays, *Transasya Ekspresi* trains at 11.30am on Fridays. All trains theoretically link-up with the ferry that crosses the lake to Van, but only carriages from the *Transasya* are actually shipped. **Ferries** usually make at least two daily crossings (morning and afternoon) between Tatvan and Van. The 5TL foot passenger fee makes for a bargain five-hour cruise, but timings are unpredictable and you may wait hours to depart.

The **tourist office** is inconveniently located in the new Kültür Merkezi, 1km out of town on the Bitlis road, the **PTT** in the town centre.

Accommodation

All of Tatvan's accommodation is right in the centre, so it's easy to check out the options before making your choice.

Hotel Altılar ⊕0434/827 4096. Friendly place just behind the main drag, with worn carpets but spotless bed linen, soap and towels provided, clean loos (squat) and showers down the hall. Rooms at the back are quieter and the strip-light at least gives enough light to read by. **❶**

Hotel Dilek Yeni Çarşı ⊕0434/827 1516. This friendly and well-run hotel just off Cumhuriyet Cad has compact but spotless rooms, tidy bathrooms and a breakfast room with stunning views over the lake and Mount Nemrut. **❷**

Hotel Kardelen Belediye Yanı, Cumhuriyet Cad ⊕0434/827 9500, ⓔotelkardelen@turkei.net. The town's top-rated accommodation (accessed from a narrow lane from the PTT). En-suite rooms have satellite TV, fridges, central heating and bathrooms with tubs. The list price is outrageous, offer half. **❻**

Üstün Otel Hal Cad 23 ⊕0434/827 9014. A couple of blocks east of Cumhuriyet Cad, the *Üstün* is a little dearer than the *Altılar*, but family-run and some of the simple but adequate rooms have their own bathroom. **❶**

Lake Van and its wildlife

Lake Van, virtually an inland sea of almost 4000 square kilometres, at an elevation of 1750m, is one of the most unusual features of eastern Turkey. Along with Lake Sevan in Armenia and Lake Urumiya in Iran, it is one of a trio of huge upland lakes without outlets in the region. Surrounded on all sides by a narrow but fertile plain, and then mountains, the lake – nearly 200m deep in spots – occupies what was once a lowland basin that was later dammed by lava flowing from Nemrut Dağı. Owing to rapid evaporation in this desert climate, the lake water is highly alkaline, rendering it slightly soapy and slimy to the touch; local people can sometimes be seen washing clothes at the shoreline.

You can swim from the stony beaches on and opposite Akdamar Island, and along the more sparsely populated stretches of shoreline, but it's inadvisable to bathe near Tatvan or Van because of **pollution**. In places the shoreline is littered with plastic detritus washed up from the lake – it's a major eyesore and a public awareness campaign launched in 2009 has had little appreciable effect. Two species of fish – one called *dareka* – live in the lake though only where fresh water enters. They are caught for food during spring when, salmon-like, they migrate up incoming streams to spawn.

The lake is on the main bird migration route to Africa and is a magnet for serious bird watchers. Pelican and flamingo can be seen as well as the rare white-headed duck, velvet scoter and paddyfield warbler. The Van cat, a fluffy white beast endowed naturally with one blue and one gold eye, is now rare, but a few specimens are still kept at local hotels and carpet shops as tourist bait, and there is a breeding station (open to visitors) on the campus of Van's Yüzüncü Yıl university. Reports of a bus-sized Van Canavarı (Van Monster) have been made since the 1960s.

Eating and drinking

Restaurants

Eyvan Birinci Sok (tucked away behind the Şimşek (see review below). This basic but clean restaurant provides tasty *pide* (5TL) and different types of the egg dish *menemen*, served up sizzling hot in a small wok-style pan – try the one dripping with *kaşar* cheese.

Gökte Ada Cumhuriyet Cad. On the top floor of the Cinemed shopping centre, this shiny, spacious place dishes up a wide range of kebabs, *lahmacun, pide* etc from 5TL. Much favoured by the local middle classes, it's also handy for the cinema opposite.

Şimşek Cumhuriyet Cad. Long-established place offering a range of *sulu yemek* and kebabs from 5TL a head.

Per 10 Cumhuriyet Cad. Near the stop for the Ahlat dolmuş, this small café does a decent breakfast with flat bread, butter, honey and a large tea for 5TL.

Bars

Altın Kup/Deniz Kızı Just off the main drag, behind the *Hotel Dilek*. This small, male-oriented bar plays *Türkü* music and doles out cheap beer (3.5TL). It also serves up decent grills, with *pirzola* (lamb chops) and *alabalık* (trout) both 10TL.

Nemrut Dağı

Immediately north of Tatvan, the extinct volcano of **Nemrut Dağı** (no relation to the mountain with the statues), rises to 3050m. Six thousand years ago Nemrut is believed to have been 4450m high; as a result of a huge volcanic explosion, the whole upper section of the peak was deposited in the Van basin, thus blocking the natural outlet and creating the lake. The present-day volcanic cone contains two crater lakes, one of which is pleasantly warm.

After snowmelt in May/June, the crater is accessible by car or dolmuş. Dolmuşes cost around 120TL for a three- to four-hour excursion to the crater, try Ekrem Kaplan (☎0535/544 9901) at the Ahlat dolmuş stop on Cumhuriyet Caddesi. With your own car, take the Bitlis road out of Tatvan and almost immediately take the signed right (13km), or head for Ahlat and look for the signpost.

From the rim, an asphalt road drops down and right towards the warm lake; bear left on a dirt track to the cold crater lake. The 7km-diameter **crater** is lushly vegetated (beech, aspen and juniper), contrasting sharply with the bare landscape outside. In summer Kurds graze their flocks on slopes. The crescent-shaped **Soğukgöl** (cold lake) occupies the western half of the crater, and on its east shore there are some swimmable hot springs. Better for a dip is smaller **Sıcakgöl** (warm lake), connected to its partner by a narrow path leading east or a left branch off the asphalt road and heated to 60°C by ongoing volcanic activity.

Ahlat and the northern shore

Lake Van's northern shore, a sometimes austere volcanic landscape relieved intermittently by charming pastoral valleys and a lush foreshore, is well worth exploring. First up, a picturesque 42km drive from Tatvan is the shabby town of **AHLAT**, known chiefly for its Selçuk cemetery, with hundreds of medieval stone graves, and for its monumental tombs.

First an Urartian, then Armenian settlement, Ahlat fell to the Arabs during the seventh century, was retaken by the Byzantines two hundred years later, and passed to the Selçuks after the nearby Battle of Manzikert in 1071. The Mongols arrived in 1244, succeeded by the İlhanids a century later; by the 1400s Ahlat was the main base of the Akkoyun Turcomans. Even after the local Ottoman conquest of 1548, real power in this remote region remained in the hands of the Kurdish emirs of Bitlis. Ahlat was a populous, polyglot city until World War I.

Today Ahlat's famous *kümbet* **tombs** are scattered about some 2km southwest of the modern settlement's centre. In a typical local *kümbet* (which accommodated one to four persons), the deceased was interred in an underground chamber, beneath a prayer room reached by steps from the outside. It's thought that the traditional nomadic tent inspired the distinctive conical design, executed in deep brown basalt, often by Armenian stonemasons.

The **Ulu Kümbet** (Great Tomb), built for a late thirteenth-century Mongol chieftain and set in a field just south of the main road as you approach the town, is the largest in the Van region On the opposite side of the road is a small **museum** (Tues–Sat 8am–noon & 1–5pm; 3TL). It contains much useful information about, and finds from, the medieval city that once spread all around here. There are also some fine examples of Urartian bronze-work.

The **Selçuk cemetery** covers almost two square kilometres, crammed with tilted, lichen-encrusted headstones dating from the eleventh to the sixteenth centuries. Most are covered with floral, geometric and calligraphic (Persian and Arabic scripts) decoration.

Walk north across the cemetery to the **Bayındır Türbesi**, with its colonnaded upper storey and distinctive *mescit* (prayer room); built in 1492 to house the remains of the Turcoman chief Bayındır. Left and downhill from this tomb, signed Harabe Şehir (City Ruins) is an idyllic valley alive with colourful birds such as hoopoes and bee-eaters as well as the odd tortoise. Here there are rock-cut houses and the pretty fifteenth-century humpbacked bridge of Emir Bayındır. On a bluff above stands the prominent **Hasan Padişah Türbesi**, built in 1275. Almost twenty metres high its cylindrical body is topped by a pyramidal roof.

Closer to the modern town centre is the **Çifte Kümbet** (Twin Tomb), dating from 1281. One of the pair of tombs was built for a Mongol emir and his wife, the other for their son and daughter-in-law. The **fortress** to the northeast of town was built during the sixteenth century by sultans Süleyman the Magnificent and his son Selim. Once grand, it is now a crumbling ruin with good views of the lake.

Practicalities

Frequent dolmuşes from Tatvan take 45 minutes (4TL), starting at 7.30am, last one back at 6pm. Ask to be dropped by the museum. After your explorations regular dolmuşes run into the town centre (0.80TL), from where you catch a dolmuş back to Tatvan or on to Adilcevaz (4TL), or a bus on to Ercis/Van/Doğubeyazıt.

Regarding **accommodation**, the dark-stone *Selçuklu* on Zübeyde Hanım Caddesi (T0434/412 5697, F412 5699; ❹), right on the shore at the extreme east end of town has been given a makeover and rooms are comfy, if eclectically and garishly furnished. Two kilometres east, again on the shore, is the better-value *Metropol* (T0434/412 4572; ❷), with cheerful rooms (upstairs ones have better views) and a good grill restaurant. For the impecunious, the basic *Göktaş* (T0434/412 5050; ❶), just east of the *Selçuklu*, has clean, waterless rooms and a decent restaurant below.

The *Vangölü*, opposite the PTT in the lower town, is excellent; scrupulously clean and always full of local teachers, women and families. Döner kebab and *sulu yemek* take precedence in the day, grills and *pide* in the evenings.

Around Ahlat

The attractive modern village of **ADILCEVAZ**, 25km north of Ahlat, is huddled in a fertile valley surrounded by poplars, walnut and apricot trees. It is dominated by the shattered shell of a Selçuk fortress, which is in turn overshadowed by the 4058-metre volcanic peak of **Süphan Dağı**, Turkey's fourth highest. Not technically difficult to climb, its remoteness and unreliable water supply make it a serious undertaking (temperatures which can drop to -50°C in winter). Below Adilcevaz, near the shore and constructed using the dark brown volcanic stone typical of the area, is the distinctive thirteenth-century **Tuğrul Bey Camii**. The lakefront near here now has an attractive promenade area and a pleasant café.

High on the bare mountainside above a small dam on the town's upper slopes is the **Armenian monastery church of Skantselorgivank**. A rocky trail leads to the church, which boasts a startlingly evocative shattered shell, with bands of red and black stonework, *khatckars* (stones inscribed with crosses) and a black basalt font. Above it is the Urartian citadel of **Kefkalesi**, separated from the church by a steep, scree-strewn valley which can only be negotiated with difficulty. To reach Kefkalesi from Adilcevaz take a taxi direct to the site (around 30TL).

Charming Adilcevaz is a more pleasant place to stay than either Tatvan or Ahlat. As for **hotels**, best bet is the *Otel Kent* (no phone; 30TL) with waterless but immaculately clean rooms (you have to take off your shoes before entering your room; slippers are provided), spotless shared bathrooms, and fruit trees out back. Just south of the main square is a most unexpected and welcoming *birahane*, serving beer and delicious salads and grills at bargain prices. The last of the five daily buses to Van departs at 2pm (12TL).

Van

Once drab, **VAN** is rapidly transforming itself into a modern, buzzing city and makes a great base to explore Lake Van's numerous attractions. Set 4km back from the lake against the backdrop of volcanic, 2750-metre Erek Dağı, its prime attraction, ancient **Van Kalesi**, is spectacularly situated 3km to the west by the lake, where it overlooks the poignant remains of the old city destroyed by the Ottomans during World War I.

Although it remains a very conservative town, this is mitigated by the presence of the large student population attending Yüzüncü Yıl university, and it's possible to have a drink here in mixed company. Van is also a good place to shop with a

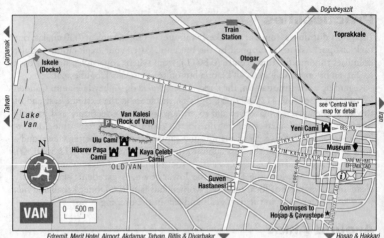

see 'Central Van' map for detail

Edremit, Merit Hotel, Airport, Akdamar, Tatvan, Bitlis & Diyarbakır ▼   ▼ Hoşap & Hakkari

wide selection of local (Kurdish) tribal rugs, as well as largely cheaper ones from nearby Iran, though you need to bargain hard to get a good price. Following the winding down of the war with the PKK, the locals are increasingly beginning to assert their **Kurdish identity** and in 2009 the pro-Kurdish DTP party won 60 percent of the vote in the local elections.

Arrival, information and services

Most visitors arrive via the scenic **southern-shore route** from Tatvan. This initially follows a pretty willow-fringed valley to the pass of Kuskunkıran (2234m) then a descent through a checkpoint and along the lakeshore with vistas of Akdamar and Süphan Dağı reflected in the still waters. If you fly in or out, the lake and mountain views are spectacular, as they are from the erratic ferries that arrive from Tatvan.

The **airport** is 6km south of town, linked to the centre by shuttle bus and taxis (20TL). The **otogar** is a little way northwest of the centre: dolmuşes and *servis* buses run from here to the busy junction of **Beş Yol**, at the northern end of Cumhuriyet Caddesi. Dolmuşes to Douğbeyazit (15TL) run from the otogar at 7.30am, 9am, noon, 2pm and 3.30pm. **Trains** arrive at the station 3km northwest of the centre, where you can find a dolmuş or taxi into town. If you arrive by **ferry**, a dolmuş runs the 5km into town (1.30TL). The **tourist office** at Cumhuriyet Cad 127 (☏0432/216 2018) has little to offer apart from a sightseeing brochure worth picking up for its photos of some obscure sights.

Accommodation

Van has plenty of **hotels**, in all price ranges; and for women travelling alone staying in Van is more comfortable and safer than other towns in the area.

Ada Palas Cumhuriyet Cad ☏0432/216 2716. Gleaming new, contemporary-styled hotel with top-notch beds and bathroom fittings, plus a very cheerful breakfast room. Spotlessly clean (and with female staff on reception), this is a great choice for women travellers. Wi-fi and foreign-channel TV too. ❹

Akdamar Hotel Kazım Karabekir Cad 56 ☏0432/214 9923, ⓦwww.otelakdamar.com. Very friendly, efficient old place with restaurant, bar and wi-fi. The rooms are a little plain but the service more than makes up for it. ❹

Hotel Aslan Cumhuriyet Cad, Sok 3 ☏0432/216 2469. A real backpackers' favourite, largely because English-speaking Harun Toprak, who works with the

Ayanis travel agency (see listings, p.669) hangs out here and dishes out advice to travellers. Rooms are small and basic, but the shared squat loos and showers in the corridor are clean. No breakfast. ❶

Büyük Asur Hotel Cumhuriyet Cad, Turizm Sok 5 ☎0432/216 8792, ⓦwww.buyukasur.com. Overpriced (but spotless) accommodation. Rooms are painted a plain white and are pleasantly simple and well kept. The management speaks good English and offers day-trips taking in Hoşap, Çavuştepe and Akdamar, and there's a well-stocked bar. ❹

Büyük Urartu Oteli Hastane Cad 60 ☎0432/212 0660, ⓦwww.buyukurartuotel.com. Well-run, safe choice with an indoor pool, sauna, wi-fi access and rooftop breakfast room. At the time of writing the old-fashioned but comfortable rooms were in the process of being updated. ❺

Merit Edremit Yolu ☎0432/312 3060, ⓦwww.merithotels.com. If you're after some peace and quiet try this friendly group-orientated place on the lakeshore 12km out of town, beyond the airport. The spacious rooms are tastefully decorated and the en suites all have large baths. The buffet breakfast is excellent. ❺

Hotel Şahin İrfan Baştuğ Cad ☎0432/216 3062, ⓦwww.otelsahin.com. Reliable choice. Back rooms are claustrophobically close to the next building, but front rooms are spacious and, together with the rooftop breakfast room, offer views over the city. Firm beds, very clean and well kept. ❷

Tamara Otel Yüzbaşıoğlu Sok 1 ☎0432/214 3296, ⓦwww.tamaraotel.com. Van's first attempt at a boutique-style hotel works pretty well. Crisp white linen on firm beds, light-wood furniture, sparkling bathrooms complete with spacious tubs, wi-fi access, foreign-channel TV as well as a/c. There's even an in-house grill-your-own-meat restaurant – and a bar. ❺

Modern Van

Modern Van is laid out on a user-friendly grid plan. The main thing to see is the **Van museum** (Van Müzesi; Tues–Sun 8am–noon & 1.30–5.30pm; 3TL) on Cengiz Caddesi. Small but newly renovated, it houses exhibits (with English explanations) on the major archeological excavations in the region and makes an excellent primer for visiting the **Urartian** sites such as Çavuştepe or Ayanis.

Downstairs finds from Çavuştepe include some intricately decorated bronze belts and jewelled breastplates, as well as daggers, spear-heads and bone implements. Particularly fascinating are the finds from Ayanis, notably the shield from a large statue of the chief god Haldi. A small courtyard off the main hall houses the mysterious Hakkari stelae, a collection of large, eerie relief-carved figures of naked warriors dating back to between 1450 and 1000 BC, unique in Turkey.

Upstairs there's an **ethnographic** section displaying some fine kilims from Van and Hakkari provinces, and finds from Tilki Tepe, a settlement mound in the grounds of Van's airport. Pride of place in the newly modelled garden is given to the black basalt relief-carving of an Urartian god, possibly Shivini, astride a bull, but there are a number of fine stelae liberally covered in cuneiform Urartian inscriptions as well.

Van Kalesi: the Rock of Van

Van Kalesi, 3km to the west, is the nearest visitable Urartian fortification to Van. A narrow outcrop 1.5km long, over 100m tall and perhaps 300m wide at the base; equipped with its own spring, it was once an eminently suitable Urartian stronghold. Frequent dolmuşes (1TL) run to it from the Beş Yol junction in town. You'll be dropped at the eastern end of the Rock; follow the road for 500m towards the lake to the entrance. Passing the northern face, note the arched niches, part of an **Urartian temple**, set in the base of the cliff, behind an Ottoman-era mosque and *türbe*. These once held statues, and cuneiform inscriptions on the base of one of them document the life and works of the powerful Urartian king.

Entry is from the car park and **ticket booth** (3TL) on the northwest side, where there's also a decent restaurant/café and a replica of an old Van house, built of mud-brick and home to one of the famous Van cats. Just west of the tea gardens is a large stone platform (possibly a jetty) made of limestone blocks, some of which are over five metres long. Two inscriptions adorn the structure, both in the

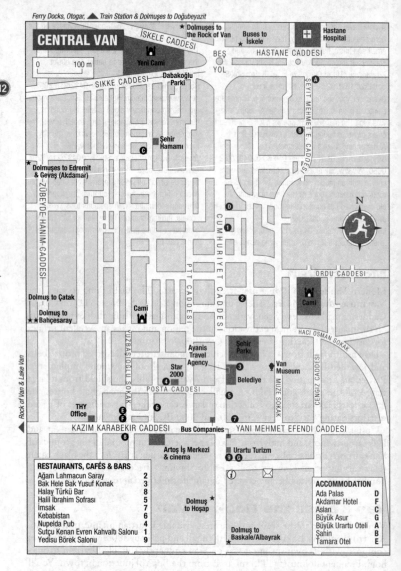

CENTRAL VAN

İSKELE CADDESI
★ Dolmuşes to
the Rock of Van

Buses to
★ İskele

✚ Hastane
Hospital

0   100 m

Yeni Cami

BEŞ
YOL

HASTANE CADDESI

SIKKE CADDESI

Dabakoğlu
Parkı

★ Dolmuşes to Edremit
& Gevaş (Akdamar)

Şehir
Hamamı

Ⓒ

Ⓐ

Ⓑ

SEYIT MEHMET E. CADDESI

Ⓓ
❶

Dolmuş to Çatak

Dolmuş to
★★ Bahçesaray

Cami

ORDU CADDESI

❷

Cami

HACI OSMAN SOKAK

Ayanis
Travel
Agency

Şehir
Parkı

Van
Museum

Star
2000
❹

❸

Belediye

POSTA CADDESI

❻

❺

CENGIZ CADDESI

THY
Office

Ⓔ
Ⓕ

❼

KAZIM KARABEKIR CADDESI

Bus Companies

YANI MEHMET EFENDI CADDESI

❽

Artoş İş Merkezi
& cinema

Urartu Turizm

❾ Ⓖ

Dolmuş ★
to Hoşap

ⓘ

✉

Dolmuş to
★ Başkale/Albayrak

RESTAURANTS, CAFÉS & BARS

Ağam Lahmacun Saray	2
Bak Hele Bak Yusuf Konak	3
Halay Türkü Bar	8
Halil İbrahim Sofrası	5
İmsak	7
Kebabistan	6
Nupelda Pub	4
Sütçu Kenan Evren Kahvaltı Salonu	1
Yedisu Börek Salonu	9

ACCOMMODATION

Ada Palas	D
Akdamar Hotel	F
Aslan	C
Büyük Asur	G
Büyük Urartu Oteli	A
Şahin	B
Tamara Otel	E

Assyrian, rather than the Urartian, language, praising the Urartian king Sarduri I
(844–838 BC).

From the "jetty" or ticket booth a path ascends the gentler north face of the
Rock leading, eventually, to the citadel on top. The single most impressive part of
Van Kalesi is the rock **tomb of Argishti 1** (785–760 BC). It's set in the sheer cliff-
face on the south side of the Rock, west of the summit area. It's reached by a set
of worn steps, fortunately protected by metal railings. The carved rock face above
the stairs is covered in well-preserved cuneiform inscriptions relating Argishti's
conquests. Take a torch to explore the interior, where the fixing holes for votive

plaques can still be seen. There are several more anonymous rock-cut tombs on the south face of the Rock, east of the summit area, but take care when exploring as the path is badly worn and the drops deadly.

The most prominent building on the top today is a **ruined mosque**, the arch-roofed building is a *medrese* and, close by, are the barracks of the Ottoman garrisons once billeted here. The curious steps cut into the limestone are actually the foundation bases for cyclopean Urartian walls, the mud-brick ones visible today are much later.

Old Van

The destruction of **Old Van** in 1915 (see box, p.668) was so thorough that today only four mosques and fragments of an Armenian church remain. The rest is a sea of overgrown, rubble-strewn mounds where once was an attractive settlement inhabited by some 80,000 people. Within the walls lay bazaars, churches, mosques and government offices. Nearby orchards give an indication of the once-extensive "garden suburbs" of Aygestan, where the bulk of the population lived in the nineteenth and early twentieth centuries. To walk through Old Van, head around the western (lake) end of the Rock to skirt the southern face of the Rock.

The first structure from the west is the badly ruined **Topçuoğlu Camii**, of more interest is the fifteenth-century **Ulu Cami** with an attractive brick minaret still bearing traces of faïence tiles. Look due north from the mosque to see the massive fifth-century BC **cuneiform inscription** of Xerxes. Inscribed in Persian, Medean and Babylonian, celebrating the might of the famous Persian king, it was first recorded in 1827 by the traveller/archeologist Schulz (later murdered by Kurdish tribesmen), dangling on a rope from the summit.

Huddled right under the Rock towards its southeastern corner are the remains of an Armenian church, still bearing traces of frescoes; behind it are some *khatchkar*s inscribed onto the rock face. Close to the crumbled south town wall are a pair of well-restored, sixteenth-century Ottoman-era mosques. The easterly one is the **Kaya Çelebi Camii** (1586), the western mosque, rather more intact, with attractive banded stonework and an attached tomb, is the **Hüsrev Paşa Camii** (1567). The only other significant remnants are some stretches of the medieval wall that once girded the town, a couple of tombs and a ruined hamam.

Eating and drinking

Van's famous **breakfast salons**, most on or just off Cumhuriyet Caddesi, serve a selection of cheeses (including the mature, herb-studded *otlu peynir*), olives, honey and cream (*kaymak*) with fresh hot bread and gallons of tea.

Cafés and restaurants

Ağam Lahmacun Saray Ordu Cad 8. Just east of Cumhuriyet Cad, this bustling place dishes up tasty and cheap *cevizli* (walnut) and *isot* (hot pepper) *lahmacun* (2TL), kebabs (7TL) and *pide* (5TL).

Bak Hele Bak Yusuf Konak Van Belediye Sarayı. Just off Cumhuriyet Cad, this folksy place is run by local character Yusuf, who greets every customer as if they are his long-lost friend. A slap-up local breakfast with spiced-sausage omlette, cucumber, tomato, various cheeses, honey, clotted cream and tea will set you back 15TL.

Halil İbrahim Sofrası Cumhuriyet Cad, Ziraat Bankası Yanı 62. Spotlessly clean, prettily

decorated but cavernous place, with a pleasant rear terrace. All the standard grills, *sulu yemek* dishes, *pide*s etc, plus more unusual offerings (for this type of restaurant) like grilled trout and *hamsi* (anchovies). İskender kebab 8TL, trout the same.

İmsak Mareşal Fevzi Çakmak Cad. Small, unpretentious breakfast place, with quality cream and honey and a wide range of egg dishes. Interesting old photographs of Van adorn the walls and the staff are friendly – enjoy.

Kebabistan Off Kazım Karabekir Cad. A three-storey affair specializing in large, hearty kebabs (around 7TL and up), their twin restaurant on the

⑫

Van and the Armenians

Van is at the very heart of the **propaganda struggle** between Turkey and Armenia over the terrible events of World War I (see also Contexts, p.696). The city became a battleground in April 1915 when Armenian civilians, considered Russian collaborators by the Turkish authorities, barricaded themselves in a quarter of the old town and mounted a resistance against Turkish forces. Much of the city was destroyed when the Turkish garrison up on the Rock pulverized it with heavy artillery during which around 6000 Armenians were killed. During the rest of the war the town changed hands a couple of times; but following the Tsarist collapse in late 1917 the Russians and remaining Armenians left for the last time.

Armenian history and Christianity

The Armenians had first appeared in the region in the late seventh century, following the collapse of the Urartian Empire. Although usually the vassals of more powerful states, they gradually developed their own identity, a process which began to crystal-lize with the advent of **Christianity**, which they fervently embraced. Towards the end of the third century Armenia became the first nation to officially adopt the new faith, thanks mainly to the efforts of St Gregory "the Illuminator". The invention of the Armenian alphabet in 404 by Mesrop Mashtots furthered the Armenians' view of themselves as a distinct race.

This separate identity was further strengthened when the Armenian Apostolic Church refused to accept the ruling of the Byzantine Council of Chalcedon in 451, which declared that Christ had two equal and co-existent natures. The Armenians, in retaining their monophysite views (ie that Christ had a single, divine nature), cut themselves off from the mainstream Byzantine Orthodox Christian world, which held that Christ combined both human and divine natures.

Armenian culture, particularly in the Van basin under the Artsruni dynasty, flowered in the ninth and tenth centuries, but the arrival of the Selçuk Turks and other Turcoman groups in the eleventh century heralded the start of a decline in their fortunes.

The Ottomans finally took control of Armenia during the fifteenth and sixteenth centuries. Ottoman rule benefited the Armenians who, like the other non-Muslim minorities, were conceded substantial control over education and family law, and even earned for themselves the epithet of *sadık millet* (loyal nation). During the nineteenth century, however, as the Ottoman Empire declined, some Armenians (along with other Christian groups in Anatolia) developed nationalist aspirations – often encouraged by the **Russians**, who were intent on fragmenting the Ottoman Empire.

The Genocide issue

In 1915 the Turkish authorities ordered the deportation of all Anatolian Armenians to Syria. All across Anatolia Armenian women, children and the elderly were rounded up for transportation, men of fighting age were executed. Between 700,000 and one and a half million Armenian civilians were killed between 1915 and 1920. Today Armenians, both in the modern Republic of Armenia and the diaspora, claim these events constituted genocide. The Turkish state vehemently refutes the charge, arguing that up to 600,000 Turks and Kurds were killed by Armenians in their attempts to wrest their own state from the hands of the dying Ottoman Empire.

This dispute still poisons relations between Turks and Armenians. Diplomatic relations were broken off in the 1990s and the land border between the two countries remains closed. Efforts at rapprochement have been tentative, the Turkish govern-ment's restoration of the long-negelcted Armenian church on Akdamar island (see opposite is at least at start. The issue is a PR nightmare for Turkey, which constantly lobbies other countries not to officially acknowledge the "genocide" (twenty-one have done so).

opposite side of this narrow side street serves up good *pide* and *lahmacun*.

Saçı Beyaz King of Van's patisseries, occupying a prime place at the junction of Cumhuriyet and Kazım Karabekir *caddesis*. Delicious *baklava*, gateaux or ice cream.

Sutçu Kenan Evren Kahvaltı Salonu Kahvaltıcılar Sok 7/A. On a small street devoted to breakfast places, this is the best. All the usual fare and tables out on the street in the warmer months.

Yedisu Café Börek Cumhuriyet Cad, Büyük Asur Oteli Altı 69. A great alternative breakfast choice serving flaky, melt-in-your-mouth cheese-filled pastries. It's tiny, so a takeaway is the best bet.

HalayTürkü Bar Kazım Ärtabekir Cad, Artoş İş Merkezi Karşısı. Trendy top-floor *Türkü* bar with live music 8pm–2am nightly, an open-air terrace and *ocakbaşı* (charcoal grill) restaurant. Beers are 5TL, grills 8TL. British film director Ben Hopkins shot some of his 2008 film *Pazar* here.

Nupelda Pub & Club Sanat Sok, Emek Sineması Üstü. Club and rock music venue popular with the city's uni students. Open 8pm–2am, there's no entrance fee and beers are a reasonable 5TL, chips and other snacks available. Not sure about the mock-stalactite ceiling, though.

Listings

Airline tickets, car rental and tours Try Ayanis, Cumhuriyet Cad, Belediye Saray Altı. Urartu Turism (☎0432/214 2020) on Cumhuriyet Cad, agents for Avis and Sunexpress, Pegasus and THY.

Banks and exchange Cumhuriyet Cad is home to several banks with ATMs.

Books and newspapers Star 2000, Sanat Sok 2. Student-orientated book and music store, with a trendy interrnet café upstairs. Best place to find *Today's Zaman*.

Buses The major companies have offices clustered around the junction of Cumhuriyet/Kazım Karabekir/Fevzi Çakmak cads.

Carpets and kilims Galeri Van Gölü at the Kartal İşhanı Altı 25, on Cumhuriyet Cad, has a wide range of carpets and kilims at decent prices.

Hamam The Şehir on Zübeyde Hanım Cad is modern, clean and friendly; it's a bargain 8TL for the standard works.

Hospital The Devlet Hastanesi is on Hastane Cad, just east of Beş Yol (☎0432/216 4740), or try Güven Hastanesi (☎0432/217 5900) near the Van cat statue on İpek Yolu.

Police West of town on İpek Yolu.

Post office Behind the tourism office.

Around Van

The main attraction near Van is the Armenian island church of **Akdamar**, but nearby **St Thomas** and the splendidly isolated church on the island of **Çarpanak** are almost equally worthwhile. The ancient Urartian settlements at **Çavuştepe** to the south and **Ayanis** to the north also make excellent day-trips from Van. In the rocky foothills to the east there are more church remains at **Yedi Kilise**, whilst the area to the south of Van is the most physically impressive in Turkey, featuring rugged mountains dotted with isolated settlements such as **Çatak** and **Bahçe-saray**. En route for the wild mountain town of Hakkari is the imposing castle at **Hoşap** and, beyond it, the remote but substantial Armenian churches of **Surb Bartolomeos** and **Soradir**.

Akdamar island

On the tiny island of **Akdamar** (daily 8.30am–7.30pm, 3TL) just off Lake Van's southern shore, stands the exquisite tenth-century Armenian **Akdamar Kilisesi**, the church of the Holy Cross. Recently restored to the tune of US$1.5 million by the Turkish government, it stands as a glimmer of hope of reconciliation between Turks and Armenians.

The church was erected between 915 and 921 AD, at the behest of Gagik Artsruni, ruler of the Armenian kingdom of Vaspurakan. The small building is gracefully proportioned, but what makes it so special are the **relief carvings**,

▲ The Armenian church on Akdamar island

which run in a series of five bands around the exterior. As well as animal scenes there are several depictions of Bible stories including Jonah appearing to dive from a boat into the jaws of a most unlikely looking whale (south facade) and David taking on Goliath, sling in hand (south facade). King Gagik himself is carved in bold relief on the west facade, presenting a model of Surb Khach to Jesus. A number of **khatchkars** – the Celtic-looking, obsessively detailed carved crosses that the Armenians used both as celebratory or commemorative offerings and as grave markers – are also set into the facade.

Inside the **frescoes**, formerly in a shocking state, have been sensitively restored and it's easy to make out New Testament scenes such as the Baptism of Christ, the raising of Lazarus and the Crucifixion.

Practicalities

Dolmuşes (5TL) from Van run from Zübeyde Hanım Caddesi, near the junction of Sikke Caddesi, from 6am to 7pm in summer. Unless they are full of people who want to visit the island, they run only to the town of Gevaş, 5km short. From here it's a 15TL taxi ride. From the roadside **quay** it's a twenty-minute, 5TL boat journey, with a further 3TL for admission to the island. *Akdamar Camping Restaurant* (☏0432/216 1515), at the quay offers free camping providing you eat at the (reasonable) restaurant, which serves fish from the lake.

The church of St Thomas

The monastic **church of St Thomas** (Kamrak Vank), situated on an isolated promontory in the lake can be reached with your own vehicle or by taxi; it's about thirty minutes' drive from the main road and two hours from Van, followed by an hour's walk. The church overlooks the bay of Varış from a plateau 5km from the modern village of Altınsaç (formerly Ganjak); alternatively, a zigzag path (2hr) starts from Göründü village, which is quite close to the main road. It's also possible to visit **by boat from Akdamar** (3hr), though you would have to make arrangements at the Akdamar quay (see above) at an off-peak time of the day/week.

Built to a cruciform plan, the sparsely decorated walls of this fourteenth-century church uphold a twelve-sided, capped drum; on the west is an extensive covered courtyard added late in the seventeenth century.

Çavuştepe

ÇAVUŞTEPE (always open, 3TL) 28km from Van on the Hakkari road and accessible by the Başkale, Hakkari or Güzelsu dolmuş, is a **Urartian royal palace**, built between 764 and 735 BC by King Sardur II. It is built in classic Urartian style, at the end of a rocky spur running down onto a plain. The quality of the masonry here is incredible, with expertly cut andesite blocks joining so perfectly no mortar was necessary. Pick of the hilltop remains are some massive sunken *pithoi* (storage urns), a temple with a remarkably well-preserved cuneiform inscription, some sunken cisterns and what is quite clearly a squat toilet. Below the ridge the line of the so-called Semiramis Canal can be seen, a Urartian irrigation channel used to take water to Van, and which still functions.

Former warden Mehmet Kuşman is one of the few people in the world who can read, write and speak Urartian, and now lectures in the language at Van University. Despite his retirement, Mehmet is often on site, ready to read out the temple inscription for you and sell you attractive, if pricey, Urartian-style carvings made from basalt.

Hoşap Kalesi

Beyond Çavuştepe and some 55km from Van on the Hakkari road, is the photogenic medieval Kurdish fortress of **Hoşap Kalesi** (daily 8.30am–noon & 1.30–5pm; 3TL), closed for restoration at the time of writing. Dolmuşes heading for Güzelsu (5TL) depart from the Başkale or Yüksekova dolmuş garages on Cumhuriyet Caddesi. An extraordinary flight of fancy, the fortress was constructed

A forgotten civilization – Urartu

From the ninth to the seventh centuries BC, the **Urartian Empire**, centred on Van (then known as Tushpa), encompassed most of the territory described in this chapter, plus parts of present-day Iran, Iraq and Syria. Around a dozen Urartian citadels have been unearthed in modern Turkey and Armenia, always sited on naturally defensible rocky spurs or outcrops. More than a castle, they incorporated a palace, workshops, storage depots and temples. Great engineers, the Urartians built numerous dams and irrigation channels, and their bronze-work was legendary – examples of it have been found in the Etruscan cities of Italy. They planted many vineyards and have been credited with the discovery of wine-making; curiously their biggest rivals, the Assyrians from the flatlands of Mesopotamia to the south, were beer drinkers. Eventually centuries of fighting with the Assyrians and later the Scythians took their toll, and the Urartian Empire went into decline at the start of the seventh century.

at the behest of Sarı Süleyman Mahmudı, a local Kurdish strongman, in the 1640s. Take a look at the pretty bridge, dating to 1671, at the foot of the castle before wending your way up. The main entrance boasts lion **reliefs**, a symbolic chain of power and a Persian inscription. Little is left of the mosques, three hamams and *medrese* inside. Best preserved is the **keep** – reached by a path from the outer fortress. Looking east from the fortress you can see a skeletal line of mud defensive walls that once encircled the village.

Yedi Kilise

About 10km east-southeast of Van, in the village of Yukarı Bakraşlı, are the remains of the once-grand monastery of the Holy Cross, founded in the seventh century and beautifully situated in the foothills of Erek Dağı. The locals know the village as **Yedi Kilise** (Seven Churches), or "Varaga Vank" in Armenian, as seven Armenian churches and the monastery once stood here. Most of the structures have been destroyed by earthquakes, but the once-domed **church of St George** survives. The church is kept locked, and there's a small fee for access. Dating from the thirteenth century the church has retained traces of seventeenth-century frescoes and crosses carved into the walls. A trip here will also give you a glimpse of contemporary Kurdish village life.

The best way to reach Yedi Kilise is by **taxi from Van**. The taxi drivers outside the *Akdamar* hotel will take you there, find the key to the locked church, wait and bring you back, for around 40TL.

Çarpanak

The well-preserved remains of the **monastery church of St John** are set on the pear-shaped island of **Çarpanak** (Ktuts in Armenian), just offshore from a promontory some 25km northwest of Van. You can rent a boat for the hour-and-a-half trip there from Van İskelesi (docks), but you'll need a Turkish speaker to bargain – expect to pay upwards of 200TL. Alternatively, you could chance your luck at Van İskelesi on a Sunday morning, when locals cross by boat to picnic. There is a huge Armenian gull colony on the island.

A monastery grew up here around a twelfth-century church at least as early as 1414, but a disaster befell it during the next century and the present church was heavily restored during the early 1700s. Despite this late date it's a handsome, rectangular compound, with a shallow dome sporting a pyramidal roof, though graffiti mars some of the walls. After Akdamar's Surb Khach, this is the best-preserved Armenian church around Van.

Ayanış Kalesi

Ayanış Kalesi, a hilltop Urartian fortification still under excavation, perches above the beautiful lakeside north of Çarpanak. Access is by private car or taxi (70TL with waiting time); drive 20km north of Van on the main road, turn left at the signpost and, some 8km further on, turn right in the village of **Alaköy**; from here the unsurfaced road rises over hills and approaches the lake before veering right through a small settlement.

Dating to the reign of Rusa II (685–645 BC) **excavations** have revealed the perimeter walls and an impressive central **temple** compound, whose doorway bears a long cuneiform inscription. Remarkably, the interior of the temple (only visitable when the archeologists are on site in July and early August) is decorated with stone-inlay (intaglio) designs including lion and griffin, unique in the Urartian world. The **beaches** below the site are great for a dip.

Bahçesaray and Çatak

The rural town of **BAHÇESARAY**, a long windy 110km southwest of Van, hits the headlines every year on the occasion of the reopening of the road over the Karabel Geçiti that links it to the outside world. At 2985m, this is the highest road pass in Turkey and usually the last to open after the winter snow (May/June). Bahçesaray was once far more important than its present-day size would suggest, with a population of 12,000 over a century ago (three times today's size). If you have two days to spare, the long (up to 6hr) dolmuş journey here from Van is better than the trip to Hakkari (see below) for the variety of scenery, vegetation and birdlife on display. On the east slopes of the pass are seasonally scattered **encampments** (*zoma*) of Kurdish shepherds and their flocks, forming a colourful complement to the spectacular mountain views.

Entering the town, you pass attractive tea gardens at the start of the single main street, which ends at a mosque and a welcoming restaurant by the stream. Bahçesaray, still known to most of the locals by the Armenian name of Müküs, has the remains of a small Armenian church, called **Andzghonts**. Much damaged by fire in 1805, it still has *khatckars* (stones inscribed with crosses) visible in the exterior walls. Other pleasant diversions are an upstream walk to the underground source of the **Botan Çay**, a tributary of the Tigris, and, a few kilometres downstream, a single-arched brick Selçuk bridge, the **Kızıl Köprü**.

Practicalities

A daily **dolmuş** (18TL) from Van leaves any time after 9am from the *Bahçesaray Çay Evi*, a small teahouse off Zübeyde Hanım Caddesi. There's a local council **visitors' house** (*misafir evi*), which contains a couple of rooms with beds and blankets, and a small washroom; enquire at the **restaurant** by the stream.

The **drive to Bahçesaray** is superb (and considerably quicker than taking a dolmuş), but make sure you fill up with fuel, and be prepared to show your papers at the major **checkpoint** and barracks at Yukarı Narlıça – there is a small chance you'll be turned back.

The large mountain village of **ÇATAK**, 40km south of Van, makes a an alternative, one-day outing. Dolmuşes (5TL) depart from a garage just below the Bahçesaray teahouse, hourly from 8am, taking one and a half hours; last return to Van at 5pm. The road from Van heads south into the mountains, passing the village of **Emlacı** with the remains of the Armenian church of Surb Tikin, and (5km short of Çatak), the popular picnic spot of **Kanispi**, where a cascade of white water spurts out of the mountainside. The village has the remnants of the once sizable Armenian church of St John the Baptist (the roofless interior now serves as a "walled" garden for local villagers) and the gushing headwaters of the Botan Çayı.

The route to Hakkari

The three- to four-hour bus or dolmuş trip to **Hakkari**, along the gorge of the Zab River, has spectacular mountain scenery, especially beyond the town of **Başkale**. With your own transport Çavuştepe and Hoşap Kalesi could be visited en route.

Nondescript **Başkale**, 113km south of Van is, at 2500m, the highest town in Turkey. Some 14km before town, however, a road leads northeast to the village of Albayrak. Here is the once-important Armenian monastery **church of Surb Bartolomeos**, founded in the sixth century. The west entrance has some beautiful relief carvings, but unfortunately the hilltop building is surrounded by razor-wire (it is part of an army camp) and is off-limits unless you gain permission from the military, best done through Remzi Bozkurt at the *Büyük Asur Hotel* in Van, or Harun at the *Hotel Aslan* (see p.664). Although you can at least look at the exterior of the church from the road it's only worth coming here if you head a further 20km on to the village of Yanal. Here is a fine sixth/seventh-century church, **Surb Echmiadzin in Soradir**, which some architectural historians believe was the inspiration for the later Surb Khach on Akdamar. Near Yavuzlar village are some rock formations similar to the fairy chimneys in Cappadocia.

Hakkari and around

HAKKARI, 200km south of Van, is dramatically situated high above the surging Zap River and ringed by soaring peaks. The people of this wild, impoverished mountain town wear their Kurdish identity more openly than anywhere else in Turkey apart from Diyarbakır, and many women, particularly those from the surrounding villages, still wear flamboyant traditional dress. The relatively few visitors who do make it down to Hakkari come mainly to enjoy the spectacular mountain and gorge scenery en route. After spending a night it's back to Van for the majority, though a few adventurous souls take the checkpoint-littered road south then west, along the mountainous Iraqi border to Şırnak.

The only historic monument is the newly restored, austere **Meydan Medresesi** in the lower town, just south of the petrol stations, but it's usually kept locked – and the fabulous Hakkari stelae which it once housed are now in Van's archeological museum. Of most interest are the striking views (admittedly often across jerry-built apartment blocks and assorted telegraph poles and electricity pylons) to the surrounding peaks, including Sumbul Dağı and, looming behind it, the 4135-metre Cilo range.

Practicalities

Buses and dolmuşes arrive outside the bus offices on the main street. The **PTT** is in another side street, opposite the Atatürk statue. For **accommodation**, the overpriced *Ümit Otel* (☎0438/211 2469; ➋) on Altay Caddesi, has a restaurant (though no breakfast) and clean rooms with patched-up bathrooms. On Bulvar Caddesi is the better *Şenler Hotel* (☎0544/211 3808, ℻211 5512; ➍), a three-star place with spacious, rooms with wi-fi, TVs and (alcohol-free) minibars. Bathrooms have mosaic tiles and small tubs. There's a hamam, sauna and a new rooftop terrace (bizarrely funded by the EU) with stunning views over Mount Sümbül.

The best restaurant is the *Özdamak Ocakbaşı Et Lokantası* on Bulvar Caddesi. This lively first-floor place serves up grills (including trout) from 8TL, and *pide* from

---

Kurdish weddings

Hakkari is one of the best places in Turkey to see, hear and, with luck, be invited to, a proper **Kurdish wedding**. These celebrations involve much dancing, usually with a paid band of musicians setting up their screeching electrical amplifiers on any suitable piece of level ground. In contrast to Turkish custom, women and men dance together to traditional music played on the fiddle, *demblik* (drums) and electric keyboard. Dancers link little fingers in a line, before advancing in step with much shaking of the shoulders and intricate footwork (a dance known in Kurdish as *govend*). Married women may wear a headscarf, but younger women let their hair fall free; both men and women wear as much gold as they can possibly muster.

5TL. For snacks such as toasted sandwiches and (soft) drinks head for the *Valilik Parkı* at the end of Bulvar Caddesi. Here, a steep hillside has been terraced to create a very pleasant chill-out spot above the bustle of the main street, with sweeping views across the Zap valley to the Cilo range.

Around Hakkari

Some 20km north of Hakkari is **Koçhanes** (Quodshanes on some maps), once the patriarchal seat of the Nestorian Christians. Small and plain, save for some inscribed geometric designs around the doorway, the church is beautifully situated on a grassy spur high above the Zab valley. The church is best found with the help of a taxi driver from Hakkari. It is not officially off-limits, but the security forces may discourage you from visiting. The village around the church was ruined when the army forcibly evacuated it during the 1990s, but a couple of elderly watchmen and former residents still tend vegetable plots here in the summer.

Above Koçhanes lies **Berçelan** *zoma*, a huge, lush summer pasture. A big festival takes place there each year towards the end of June but foreigners may be discouraged from going there because of possible PKK activity.

Close to the pastures, studded with the black goat-hair tents of Kurdish pastoralists from late June to early September, is a small glacial lake and the 3752m peak of **Karadağ**, suitable for a day-hike and giving superb views across the Zab valley to the spectacular **Cilo-Sat** range of mountains.

West from Hakkari to Şırnak and Cizre

From Çukurca, southwest of Hakkari, a **road** runs west, mainly just south of the mountainous massif, to Şırnak. As this road runs parallel to the Kurdish enclave in northern Iraq (and was built in order to patrol it) expect a heavy military presence and up to ten checkpoints, where your bags may be searched. One **bus** from Hakkari (departing from near the Atatürk statue) runs every other day at 7am (but make sure you enquire the night before), and takes about six hours (20TL). You

Nestorian Christians

The Nestorian Church traces its existence back to Nestorius, bishop of Constantinople who formulated a doctrine that Christ was predominantly human in nature. This was declared a **heresy** by the Council of Ephesus in 431, but the faith flourished and Edessa (Şanlıurfa), Antioch (Antakya) and Nusaybin near Mardin became important Nestorian centres. After Mongol attacks the Nestorians fled to the Zagros mountains of western Iran and the wild mountains around present-day Hakkari. Isolated in the inaccessible mountains, the Nestorians developed their own ethnic as well as religious identity, with half the population organized into tribes little different from their Kurdish neighbours.

During the nineteenth century serious rivalries developed between the Nestorians and the Kurds, exacerbated by the efforts of British and American missionaries who were proselytizing in the region. Local Kurdish leaders massacred many Nestorian men around Hakkari and sold the women and children into slavery. In 1915 the Nestorian patriarch sided with the World War I Allies. After the war the Nestorians, now seen as traitors, fled to Iran and Iraq, though half their number perished in the exodus. A short-lived attempt to resettle their mountain fastnesses was crushed by Atatürk in the early years of the Turkish Republic. Today just a few tens of thousands survive in Iraq, Iran and Syria, with the patriarchate now in Chicago.

may be refused permission to make this journey if there have been any recent incidents involving the PKK, who cross the border here from their bases in the Kandil mountains, in what now amounts to an autonomous Iraqi Kurdistan.

The border road runs parallel to the rapid-strewn Zab River for about 50km; at a major checkpoint the bus turns right instead of continuing to Çukurca, down on the border with Iraqi Kurdistan. From here, it rises over the Konaklı mountains to a beautiful pass at 2350m, and descends to a junction with the Beytüşşebap road in a gorge. The climate is noticeably warmer here than around Hakkari, with walnuts, poplars and even rice paddies in the valleys. The Egyptian vulture abounds, as do rolls of discarded razor-wire in the bushes.

Şırnak

An hour past Uludere is **ŞİRNAK**, perched on a hillside with views over Cudi Dağı. Best **hotel** is the central *Murat* (☎0486/216 2857; ❷), a modest place with air conditioning, wi-fi and passable bathrooms. Around Cumhuriyet Caddesi are various **restaurants**, including the *Sinan 2 Kafeterya*, which serves some local dishes including *perde pilaf*. More standard fare (ie kebabs) is available at the *Diyarbakir Faysal Ustanin Evi*. The *Atatürk Park* **tea garden** in the town centre has extensive views of the vast cemetery and its blue irises, which dominates the southern slopes of the town. From the corner opposite the tea garden, **buses** leave to Cizre (5TL) every hour until mid-afternoon. The Hakkari bus leaves from the near the *Hotel Murat* at around 8.30am (20TL). A couple of dolmuşes depart for Siirt (15TL) for onward travel to Bitlis/Tatvan and Van.

Cizre

In Kurdish tradition, the resting place of Noah's Ark is **Cudi Dağ**, a modest 2134m peak above the River Tigris and the town of **CIZRE**, near the point where the modern Turkish, Syrian and Iraqi frontiers meet. The main reasons to go to Cizre are to catch a bus to westward destinations such as Mardin and Diyarbakır, eastwards to Şırnak (for the border road to Hakkari), or to cross the Habur border-gate into the Kurdish enclave in northern Iraq.

The road to Doğubeyazıt

Heading **northeast from Van**, the road skirts the lake before heading up into the volcanic peaks bordering Iran. The drive, over a bizarrely contorted laval landscape, is spectacular in places, especially on the 2644m Tendurek Pass. The first views of Mount Ararat from the far side of the pass are stunning.

It's three hours from Van to Doğubeyazıt direct, but it is possible to break your journey at the **roadside waterfalls** at **Muradiye**. Dolmuşes depart hourly from a side street leading north off İskele Caddesi, 500m west of Beş Yol in Van, and from the northbound side of the main road in Tatvan. As long as you don't tarry until late afternoon, it's pretty easy to pick up another northbound dolmuş to resume your journey; there are regular services between Muradiye and Çaldıran, a major bus garage, 26km further northeast and from Çaldıran to Doğubeyazıt.

The **falls** (2TL) are signed on the west side of the main Doğubeyazıt road, some 20km north of the junction with the road from Tatvan and past the village of Muradiye. From the café opposite the viewpoint there are **riverside walks** along the stream and through cool poplar woods. One kilometre south of the falls is an old bridge known as **Şeytan Köprüsü** (Devil's Bridge), spanning the deep gorge.

Doğubeyazıt and around

About 130km northeast of Van and just half an hour from Iran, impoverished **DOĞUBEYAZIT** is the base for ascents of Mount Ararat and for visits to the fine old fortress of İshak Paşa Sarayı, set on a hill above. Thanks to its border position and largely Kurdish population, Doğubeyazıt is heavily militarized, with a huge army camp just outside town on the road to İshak Paşa Sarayı. In response the truculent locals boldly elected a (female) DTP mayor in 2009 and have named the main street after dissident pro-Kurdish intellectual İsmail Beşikçi.

Arrival, information and tours

Dolmuşes from Van drop you on the eastern side of town on Küçük Ağrı Caddesi, buses stop at the **otogar**, on the western side of the town centre. Note that dolmuşes to Van are cheaper (10TL) than travelling the other way because of higher taxes at Van's *otogar*. Departures at 6.30am, 9am, noon, 2pm and 3.30pm daily. Dolmuşes to the Iranian border depart regularly until 5pm (5TL).

There is no official tourist office, but the various **travel agents** and **bus companies** – mainly on Belediye Caddesi (south of the Atatürk statue) – will be able to help. Armount Travel (☎0535/616 0267) and Tamzara Travel (☎0472/312 2189, ⓦwww.letsgotomtararat.com), both on Dr İsmail Beşikçi Caddesi, offer reliable Ararat ascents and daily tours to Diaydin hot springs, the supposed "Ark" and a meteor crater near the Iranian border, around €50.

Doğubeyazıt is well supplied with **banks**, there's a **PTT** (Mon–Sat 8.30am–12.30pm & 1–5.30pm) on the main İsmail Beşikçi (Çarşı) Caddesi, and the **Yeni Hamam** near the *İsfahan Hotel* (men and women; from 8TL).

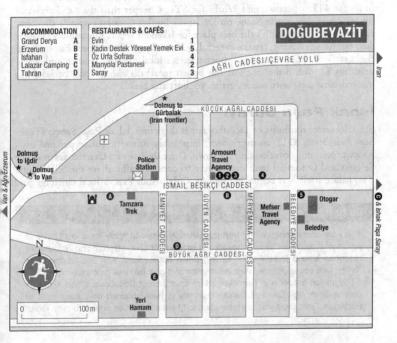

ACCOMMODATION
Grand Derya	A
Erzerum	B
İsfahan	E
Lalazar Camping	C
Tahran	D

RESTAURANTS & CAFÉS
Evin	1
Kadın Destek Yöresel Yemek Evi	5
Öz Urfa Sofrası	4
Manyola Pastanesi	2
Saray	3

DOĞUBEYAZIT

Accommodation

Accommodation in Doğubeyazıt is plentiful, catering largely to border traders, but several hotels are well used to hosting foreigners.

Hotels

Grand Derya Çarşı Cad ☎0472/312 7531, ℻312 7833. Central, friendly place, almost next door to the mosque, popular with trekking groups. Rooms are cheerful, not to say garish, but there's a bar and wi-fi. Overpriced for independent travellers, so bargain. ❹

Hotel Erzerum Dr İsmail Beşikçi Cad 79 ☎0472/312 5080. Ultra-basic, old-school backpackers' joint. Rooms are cheerfully painted, carpets scruffy. The shared bathrooms are ridiculously big, water lukewarm, but the squat toilets are clean. ❶

Isfahan Hotel İsageçit Cad 26 ☎0472/312 4363, ⓦwww.hotelisfahan.com Rooms are spacious, beds firm and English-speaking management can advise about Ararat and local tours. Good value. ❷

🏃 **Hotel Tahran** Büyük Ağrı Cad 124 ☎0472/312 0195, ⓦwww.hoteltahran.com.

Despite the cramped toilets and scruffy carpets, this is a good-value budget option, with free internet (or wi-fi) access and comfortable beds. Some rear rooms have Ararat views, as does the breakfast terrace. Best thing is friendly, fluent English-speaking manager Bilal, a fount of knowledge about the local area and getting to Iran. ❶

Campsite

Lalazer Camping İshak Paşa Saray Yolu Üzeri ☎0544/2691960, ⓔlalazercamping@hotmail.com. A couple of kilometres from town on the road to the palace is this curious place run by Kurdish Mecit and Dutchman Bertil. Very popular with the camper-van contingent, it has clean loos and showers and decent tent pitches. It's not cheap (10TL per person) but there's a decent on-site café and Mecit plays a mean *bağlama*.

Eating and drinking

For **breakfasts and desserts**, try the *Manyola Pastanesi*, Dr İsmail Beşikçi Cad 78, with a large selection of sweets and savouries, and a swish *aile salonu* upstairs. The *Öz Urfa Sofrası* at Dr İsmail Beşikçi Cad 64, dishes up decent *sulu yemek* at lunchtimes for 4TL a portion, and kebabs for 8TL. Cheaper than the *Öz Sofrası* and longer established is the *Saray*, on Dr İsmail Beşikçi Caddesi opposite the *Hotel Erzerum*. Very friendly, it's the best place for İskender kebab, but also does tender *pide*. For home cooking, try the cheerful 🏃 *Kadın Destek Yöresel Yemek Evıı* on Rifki Başkaya Caddesi; a women's co-operative, it's ideal for solo women and serves delicious Kurdish dishes such as the boiled meatballs *abdigor köfte*, or *keledoş*, a minced-meat stew with onion, garlic, yoghurt and bread.

İshak Paşa Sarayı

Six kilometres southeast of Doğubeyazıt is the iconic **İshak Paşa Sarayı** (Tues–Sun 8am–5pm; 3TL), an overblown, impossibly romantic palace perched on a rocky promontory overlooking the town. Once the site of a Urartian fortress, the Selçuks and Ottomans built castles here to control traffic along the Silk Route. The palace itself was begun in 1685 by Çolak Abdı Paşa, a local chieftain, and

On to Iran

If you are considering visiting **Iran** it's generally better to apply for a tourist visa in your home country. Iranian consulates in İstanbul, Ankara, Erzurum and Trabzon are notorious among travellers for turning down applications. Ask Bilal at the *Hotel Tahran* (see above) for the latest information and possible visa procurement.

The Iranian border is at Gürbulak, 34km southeast of Doğubeyazıt, accessible by dolmuş from Ağrı Caddesi. Iranian currency is best obtained over the border at Bazargan. From there you can take a taxi to Maku and then an onward bus to Tabriz.

completed by his son, İshak Paşa, in 1784. By 1877 the complex was already in decline, being used by the Turkish army as a barracks; subsequent periods of Russian occupation set the seal on its decay.

Especially at weekends **dolmuşes** (1TL) ply the route from the main road outside the *otogar* – mainly for locals visiting the shrine above the palace. Otherwise a **taxi** from Doğubeyazıt's Atatürk statue costs around 25TL return including waiting time. At the time of writing an odd curved wood and glass structure was being placed over the roofless sections of the palace, which was closed to visitors.

The palace

The grandiose **gateway** once boasted gold-plated doors but the Russians removed these in 1917 during their retreat from Anatolia, and they're now on show at the Hermitage Museum in St Petersburg. From the outer courtyard, an ornately carved portal leads to a smaller, inner courtyard. Straight ahead is the harem entrance, while to the right is the entrance to the *selâmlık* or men's quarters. The **tombs** of İshak Paşa and his favourite wife stand in a *türbe* in one corner of the inner court.

The **harem** contains fourteen fireplace-equipped bedrooms (in which four hundred soldiers were quartered in 1877) overlooking the valley below, a kitchen and two circular bathrooms. At its centre is a colonnaded dining hall. The *selâmlık* also contains a library, bedrooms and a fine **mosque**, retaining much of its original relief decoration and ceiling painting.

Behind the palace is the picturesque, recently restored Ottoman mosque. It's possible to scramble up behind the mosque to a rock-cut **Urartian tomb** flanked by two carved relief figures. Above this, reachable only by a scramble, is a narrow niche in the dramatic ridge-top fortress wall. Squeeze through this and you can descend to the much-visited tomb of the Kurdish poet and philosopher Ehmede Xani. His **Mem u Zin** (1692), a tale of star-crossed lovers, is *the* epic work of Kurdish literature. There are drinks and souvenir stalls here to serve the pilgrims.

The foundations on the plain below the palace are all that's left of **Eski Beyazıt** (Old Beyazit), a city founded by the Urartians. It was inhabited until 1930, when – in the wake of an unsuccessful local Kurdish rebellion – it was forcibly depopulated and the new Doğu (East) Beyazıt founded in its present location.

Mount Ararat

Few mountains west of the Himalayas have as compelling a hold on Western imagination as **Mount Ararat** (Ağrı Dağı in Turkish). And for once this huge volcano – where Noah's Ark supposedly came to rest – manages to deliver that promise in reality. Traditionally, Armenian monks considered Mount Ararat holy and nobody was allowed to climb it; it was not until 1829 that Dr Johann Jacob Parrot, a German academic, conquered the peak. Numerous other ascents have followed, but even today some villagers believe that it's not possible to climb the mountain, and Turkish officials did not allow it until the 1950s.

Despite the efforts of American astronaut James Irwin and others, no reliable trace of Noah's Ark has been found. Locals, however, insist that the oval mound of earth spotted by a Turkish airforce pilot on a routine flight is the "Ark", which now boasts a visitor centre and is routinely included in tours of the area. Ararat, of course, may simply be the wrong place to look. Genesis 8:4 reports the Ark as coming to rest on the "mountains of Ararat". This is prone to misinterpretation, as Ararat was the Assyrian rendition of Urartu, the ancient empire centred on Lake Van, meaning the Ark could have come to rest anywhere within the empire's bounds. According to the Koran, the Ark was deposited on Mount Cudi, hundreds of kilometres to the south near Cizre (see p.676).

Access to Mount Ararat

The mountain lies in a sensitive military zone, adjoining both the Armenian and Iranian frontiers and was also a focal point for PKK activity – in 2008 the group kidnapped three German climbers, though they were later released unharmed. Access is strictly by **permit** only, best obtained through a reputable, registered travel/trekking agency (see p.677). They require a photocopy of your passport, at least two months in advance of the mooted climb. Permits are then processed by the Tourism Ministry and local military (applicants with Armenian surnames will be denied permission to climb). Qualified guides are mandatory and trips cost around €470 per head.

Local **touts** in Doğubeyazıt may offer to obtain a permit for you immediately, or even take you up the peak without one; you risk loss of your deposit at best and at worst arrest if you take their advice – that said, quite a few people risk it.

The ascent

Ararat is a serious mountain (two Italians died in a blizzard descending the peak in August 2006) and you will need proper **equipment**, including an ice axe and crampons. The main climbing season is June to September.

Treks are normally of three to four days' duration, and are supported up to Camp 2 by mules. The starting point is **Eli** (2150m), some 10km north of Doğubeyazıt, from where it's a half-day walk to **Camp 1** (3200m). **Camp 2**, at 4200m, is a strenuous six-hour march higher. From Camp 2, a 1am start is needed to reach the summit (five hours) before cloud cover becomes too thick. At around 4900m the stones give way to permanent snowpack and then glacier. The views on a clear day are stupendous, compensating for the hard slog of the ascent. Most groups head straight back to Eli from the summit, and return to Doğubeyazit the same day.

Travel details

Trains

Tatvan to: İstanbul (Tues & Thurs at 9.45am; 36hr; Saturday 5.05am; 38hr); Tehran (Fri at 1am; 31hr).
Van to: Tehran (Fri at 6.25pm; 25hr).

Buses and dolmuşes

Doğubeyazıt to: Ankara (1 daily at 1pm; 16hr); Erzurum (10 daily; 4hr); Iğdır (hourly; 45min); Van (5 daily; 3hr).
Hakkari to: Şırnak (daily; 6hr); Van (hourly in daylight hours; 3–4hr).
Şırnak to: Hakkari (1daily; 6hr); Cizre (hourly; 30min).
Tatvan to: Ahlat (every 45min; 30min); Bitlis (hourly; 30min); Erciş (2 daily; 2hr), Diyarbakır (5 daily; 4hr); Van (5 daily; 3hr).

Van to: Ankara (8 daily; 22hr); Bahçesaray (1 daily; 5hr), Diyarbakır (5 daily; 7hr); Doğubeyazıt (5 daily; 3hr); Erzurum (4 daily; 7hr); Hakkari (hourly in daylight hours; 3–4hr); Şanlıurfa (5 daily; 9hr); Tatvan (5 daily; 3hr); Trabzon (2 daily; 15hr).

Ferries

Tatvan to: Van and vice versa (up to 3 daily; 5hr).

Flights

Van to: Ankara (2 daily; 1hr 35min); Antalya (2 weekly; 2hr 5min); İstanbul (3 daily; 2hr 15min); İzmir (daily; 2hr 20min).

Contexts

Contexts

History

The present Turkish Republic is just the remnant of a vast medieval empire, which at its zenith extended from the Indian Ocean almost to the Atlantic – and all of its territories contributed personalities and events. The following covers the key events of a complex subject.

The earliest cultures

Discoveries in the heart of modern Turkey – the region known historically as Anatolia or Asia Minor – indicate settled habitation since the eighth millennium BC Paleolithic age, among the oldest on earth. More extensive Neolithic discoveries include entire farming communities, notably Çatal Höyük near Konya (c.6500–5650 BC), demonstrating that early settlers lived in sizable, walled villages. Their tools were made from local obsidian and flint; pottery included stylized figures representing the Mother Goddess.

Influence from Upper Mesopotamia and northern Syria brought southeast Anatolia into the **Chalcolithic Age**. Sites of this period were more like fortified towns, and evidence of violent destruction suggests that they regularly waged war. More independent cultures of central Anatolia and the west Anatolian lakeland produced burnished pottery and idols of local deities.

The third-millennium BC **Bronze Age** witnessed the emergence of local dynasties ruling from fortified settlements. Sophisticated equipment found in Alacahöyük's royal cemetery suggests metallurgy enabled early Anatolian kings. Religious art included standards crowned with stylized deer and bulls; hoards of gold jewellery plus musical instruments were also common.

Meanwhile, on the south and west coasts, trade was increasingly important. **Troy** had links with Aegean islands and mainland Greece, and with other Anatolian populations in the southeast. Anatolian metals, jewellery, weapons and tableware were traded for lapis lazuli, rock crystal and ivory and great wealth was amassed, for example the so-called "Treasure of Priam", a third-millennium hoard of jewellery and tableware discovered in the late nineteenth century.

The Middle and Late Bronze Ages, during the second millennium BC, began with violent destruction and turbulence, out of which the **Hatti** emerged in central Anatolia, whose culture was later to be assimilated by the Hittites. Commerce took place along fixed trade routes, and many Anatolian cities were colonized by Assyrian merchants. Their meticulous records show that textiles and tin were traded for copper and ornamental pottery.

The Hittites

The first truly major civilization to emerge in Anatolia was that of the **Hittites**, who first appeared around 2000 BC, though their so-called "Old Kingdom" was founded around 1650 BC. The capital at Hattuşaş, created by Hattusilis I, was a huge city for its time, with a citadel overlooking a gorge. Hittite artistic style was a direct outgrowth of Anatolian predecessors and, unlike Syrian art, was never overwhelmed by Mesopotamian and Egyptian conventions. The principal examples are enormous rock-cut reliefs of warrior gods and stylized sphinx-like beings.

Besides their imperialist nature, the Hittite kingdoms are known for their relatively humane constitution and religion, and highly developed sense of ethics. Diplomacy was preferred to warfare, and often cemented by royal marriages. Libraries, archives and bureaucracy were central to Hittite society, and rulers were not despotic but tied to a constitution like their subjects. The Old Kingdom dynasty lasted several generations before being riven by succession struggles; the empire was re-established by Tudhaliyas II in about 1430 BC, just as a rival power arose in Upper Mesopotamia. These Mitanni or Hurrians, ruled by an Indo-European dynasty, were defeated in battle by Hittite king Suppiluliumas (1385–1345 BC).

Under Muwatallis, the Hittites confirmed their military strength at the battle of Kadesh (1290 BC) where they defeated the Egyptians under Ramses II. Subsequently the two dynasties became allied through the division of Syria and the marriage of Ramses II to a daughter of another Hittite ruler. The Hittites' landlocked empire was not completely secure, however, and in the southeast Mediterranean, the Kizzuwadna region, later Cilicia, was taken by the Hurrians, who also married into the Hittite royal line.

The west coast was not well documented in Hittite records, but excavations show that Troy was rebuilt by a new dynasty, and vast supplies were amassed inside its citadel. The second-millennium Trojans were rivals to the Greeks, who eventually sacked Troy in the **Trojan War** around 1200 BC, when the Hittite Empire also collapsed.

The post-Hittite era

As more Indo-European tribes, especially the "Sea Peoples", early Iron Age migrants from the Aegean and Balkan mainland, invaded, Hittite cities were destroyed as Anatolia entered a long cultural Dark Age. Small city-states were founded in the southeast by surviving Hittites and their Anatolian allies, preserving elements of the old culture and forming a bridge between the Bronze and **Iron ages**. At these lively Neo-Hittite entrepôts, early Greek art encountered Hittite reliefs and statuary, and knowledge of oriental mythology and religion passed to Greece. The Neo-Hittite city-states finally fell to the Arameans and the Assyrians in the eighth century BC.

To the east, the kingdom of **Urartu** was founded by descendants of the Hurrians. Their cities, including Tushpa near Lake Van, were elaborately engineered, with citadels and tunnel systems for escape or survival under attack. The Urartians expanded into central Anatolia and northern Syria before being checked, in the latter eighth century BC, by the Assyrians. The Urartians specialized in metalwork, and bronzeware was traded as far away as Greece.

To the west, a new immigrant tribe, the **Phrygians**, attained prominence; their capital was Gordion, on a strategic trading route by the River Sangarius (today Sakarya), and this kingdom peaked around 725 BC under King Midas, but when Cimmerian horsemen sacked Gordion, he committed suicide in despair. The southwest coast was settled during the Iron Age by Lycians, possibly the "Lukka" of Bronze Age records.

The **Lydians** occupied the Hermus valley, with their capital at Sardis. They survived the Bronze Age with an indigenous Anatolian language, emerging from the eighth century BC to dominate western Anatolia, including former Phrygian zones. Lydian luxury goods were widely exported, and their elegant art forms influenced those of Greek Ionia and even Persia.

The Persians and Alexander

Lydian power endured until 546 BC, when their king, **Croesus**, was defeated by Cyrus's ascendant **Persian Empire**. Over the next half-century, the Persians subdued the Greek coastal cities and the interior, ending Anatolian self-rule. Satraps (compliant local puppets) were enthroned but obliged to pay tribute to the Persian "Great King"; Persian allies like the Phoenicians were favoured at the expense of Greek cities as commercial intermediaries with the West. In 499 BC, western Anatolia, led by Miletus, revolted, but lacking massive aid from mainland Greece, the rebellion failed.

Enraged by even token Athenian support for the rebels, **Darius** I and his successor **Xerxes** crossed into Greece and were soundly beaten at the land battles of Marathon and Plataea, and the sea engagements of Salamis and Mykale, the latter in the straits between Samos and Anatolia. This thwarting of Persia initially availed the cities of Asia Minor little, though they soon exploited growing rivalry between Athens and Sparta to negotiate more autonomy. By the mid-fourth century BC, some quasi-independent dynasties had arisen in western Anatolia, the most notable being the Hecatomnids at Halikarnassos, whose illustrious rulers included **Mausolus** (377–353 BC), and his wife and successor Artemisia II.

In spring 334 BC, a new power swept out of Macedonia: **Alexander**, later "the Great", equipped merely with a guiding vision and some Corinthian volunteers to supplement his small Macedonian army. Having crossed the Dardanelles, he defeated the Persians and proceeded down the Asia Minor coast via the major cities, treating them with lenience or harshness depending on whether or not they rallied to his standard. Having wintered in Lycia, Alexander and his juggernaut rolled on across Pamphylia, inland to Gordion, then over the Toros range into coastal Cilicia, intent on attacking the Persian heartland beyond Syria. **Darius III** awaited Alexander at Issos (modern Dörtyol), but was crushed by the Macedonians, despite outnumbering them two to one. This rapid conquest of Anatolia was indicative as much of Persian dynastic rottenness as it was of Alexander's military genius.

The prodigy swept through Persia proper as far as the Indus valley, but died of malaria – or possibly poisoning – on the return trip, in 323 BC. Following his death, Alexander's generals **divided Anatolia**: Lysimakhos took the west, while Seleukos – succeeded by Antiokhos – received most of the southeast; much of the centre and north remained independent. Lysimakhos's successor Philetaros made Pergamon the greatest Hellenistic city of Asia Minor; by the late second century BC, however, his heir Attalos III bequeathed it to the Romans.

Roman rule

Almost immediately Roman power in Asia Minor was challenged by **Mithridates** of Pontus (ruled 110–63 BC), a brilliant, resourceful polymath; from 89 BC on, his rebellious campaigns kept assorted Roman generals occupied. In 72 BC, Mithridates sought refuge at the court of Tigranes the Great in regional power Armenia, promptly invaded by the Romans. But it suited them to maintain Armenia as a buffer principality between themselves and the Parthians on the east, successors to the Persians.

First Emperor Augustus's reign marked the start of fairly durable peace and prosperity in Anatolia, as witness the numerous ruined cities dating from Roman imperial rule, many endowed by **Hadrian** (117–138 AD). Politically, however, it remained a backwater, with only the texts of Strabo and Pliny to flesh out life here – as well as the first-century AD biblical writings of St Paul during his evangelical tours of Asia Minor.

In 284 AD, **Diocletian** divided the empire into two administrative units, each ruled by an emperor (Augustus) co-operating with a designated successor (Caesar), the so-called tetrarchy. Within forty years, however, this system collapsed into civil war. The victor, **Constantine**, moved the headquarters of the eastern portion from Salonica to the minor, but strategically located, town of Byzantium, on the western shores of the Bosphorus straits linking the Black Sea and the Sea of Marmara. This new capital, renamed **Constantinople**, was a conscious imitation of Rome. Soon afterwards Constantine began to favour **Christianity**, which by the end of the fourth century became the state religion of an empire that had long persecuted Christians.

A unified empire, too unwieldy to be governed from a single centre, did not survive much beyond Constantine's forceful reign. Theodosius the Great (ruled 379–395), who officially proscribed paganism in 391, was the last sovereign of a united empire, which upon his death formally split into two realms: the western one Latin-speaking and Rome-based, the eastern part Greek-speaking and focused on Constantinople.

The Byzantine Empire

The western provinces had always depended financially on the east, and the badly governed west could not easily survive this revenue loss – or "barbarian" invasions from the north. The wealthier, more densely populated eastern **Byzantine Empire** had abler rulers and more defensible frontiers, but internal religious disputes severely weakened it. Constantinople's writ was resented in the south-eastern provinces of Egypt, Palestine, Syria and Armenia with their non-Classical indigenous cultures; moreover their churches embraced the **Monophysite doctrine**, which maintained that Christ had a single divine nature. Until the thirteenth century clerics in the capital persecuted the provincial "heretics", at the same time resenting claims to papal supremacy and quarrelling over dogma with Rome. This culminated in the formal separation of the eastern **Orthodox** and western **Roman Catholic** churches in 1054.

Following Justinian's death the empire's character changed radically. All his peripheral conquests were lost: the western realms to the Lombards and Goths, the southeastern provinces to Persians and Arabs. By 711, the Byzantine Empire consisted only of the Balkan coasts, parts of Italy, and Asia Minor. Equally significantly, it had acquired a strongly Greek character, both linguistically and philosophically, and Latin influence faded as relations with Rome worsened.

After 867, the **Macedonian dynasty**, founded by Basil I, a former stable-boy who rendered Justinian's law code into Greek, reversed Byzantium's fortunes. Under Basil II (976–1025), nicknamed "Bulgar-Slayer" for his ruthless campaigns against the Slavs, the empire again extended its frontiers into eastern Anatolia and up the Balkan peninsula, while Constantinople enjoyed unparalleled prosperity at the crossroads of new Eurasian trade routes. Literature and the arts flourished; missionaries converted Balkan Slavs to Orthodoxy.

After Basil II, however, the empire began its final decline, slow but relentless over four centuries. For much of the eleventh century, Anatolia was wracked by civil war, with bureaucrats in Constantinople pitted against landed generals in the countryside. Each promoted their own candidates for the throne, resulting in successive nonentities as emperors. Simultaneously the patriarchate renewed its

Emperor Justinian

Byzantium's response to the West's collapse after the fifth century was expansionist – or rather, nostalgic. Energetic emperor **Justinian** (527–565) attempted to recapture the glory and territory of ancient Rome in campaigns across the Mediterranean. Imperial generals Belisarius and Narses reabsorbed Italy, North Africa and southern Spain into the empire, though the Byzantines were unable to stem the flow of Slavs into the Balkans, and concluded an uneasy truce with the Persians after a long, inconclusive war.

Justinian also pursued an ambitious domestic agenda. He inaugurated a programme of public works, resulting in such masterpieces as **Aya Sofya** in Constantinople and San Vitale in Ravenna. Justinian's streamlining of the huge, often contradictory body of Roman **law** was perhaps his most enduring achievement: the new code became the basis for the medieval legal systems of France, Germany and Italy.

Justinian's reign marked the definitive emergence of a strictly Byzantine – as opposed to Roman – identity, with institutions that sustained the empire for the rest of its life. Having widened its boundaries to their maximum extent and established the theocratic nature of Byzantium, he can be reckoned as one of the greatest Byzantine emperors. Ultimately, though, many of his achievements proved ephemeral, and so exhausted the empire that it had difficulty withstanding subsequent attacks.

vendetta against the Monophysite churches, whose members were concentrated in the critical eastern borderlands. The warlords reduced the free peasantry to serfdom, eliminating sources of revenue and recruitment; the bureaucrats, usually in control at Constantinople, matched their own extravagance with stinginess toward the army – increasingly staffed by unreliable mercenaries.

The first major threats came from the West. The **Normans**, their greed excited by Byzantine craftsmanship and splendour, invaded the Balkans late in the eleventh century, and were only repulsed with Venetian help, who in return demanded trading concessions – as did the **Genoese**. Government tolls and taxes plummeted as imperial monopolies were broken by the new Latin maritime powers, and western covetousness – which culminated in the sacking of Constantinople by the Fourth Crusade in 1204 – knew no bounds. Though able emperors emerged from the twelfth-century Komnenos dynasty and the later Paleologos clan, without consistent western aid the Byzantines were doomed to fight a long, rearguard action against enemies from the east and north. Imperial twilight was marked by a final flourishing of sacred art and architecture, as Anatolia and the Balkans were adorned with numerous beautiful churches – this period's main legacy.

The arrival of the Turks

Early in the 1000s a new people began raiding Byzantium from the east. They had first appeared in seventh-century Mongolia, a shamanistic, nomadic bunch whom the Chinese called "Tu-kueh" or Dürkö – **Turks** to the west. These tribes began migrating westward, encountering the Arabs by the ninth century. The latter, recognizing their martial virtues, recruited them and began converting them to Islam, a process completed by the late 900s.

One branch of the Turkish tribes, followers of the chieftain **Selçuk**, adopted **Sunni Islam** and a settled life in Baghdad. The majority, however, the so-called Turcomans, remained nomadic and heterodox, drawing on **Shi'ite** and pagan beliefs, and unamenable to state control. Selçuk rulers took advantage of their warrior zeal by diverting them into Byzantine territory.

These raiders penetrated Byzantine Armenia, and it was more to restrain them than to confront the Byzantines that Selçuk ruler Alparslan marched north from Baghdad in 1071. Meeting, almost accidentally, the demoralized armies of Byzantine emperor Romanus IV Diogenes, he defeated them easily at Manzikert. The Selçuks didn't follow up this victory, but it led to redoubled rampages by the Turcomans. The Byzantines, alternately menaced and assisted by Latin crusaders, managed to re-occupy western Anatolia, plus the Black Sea and Mediterranean coasts, by the mid-twelfth century. The Selçuk **Sultanate of Rum**, based at Konya (Iconium), consolidated the Turcoman-ravaged areas; after winning the battle of Myriokephalo in 1176, the Selçuks came to terms with the Byzantines.

Following the occupation of Constantinople by the Fourth Crusade in 1204, the Selçuks continued their good relations with the provisional Byzantine Empire of Nicaea; with peace assured, the Sultanate of Rum evolved into a highly cultured mini-empire, reaching its zenith in the first half of the thirteenth century as imposing *kervansarays*, *medreses* and other monuments adorned central Anatolia. The Selçuks also excelled in tile- and relief-work, and in the spiritual field the sultanate, despite Sunni orientation, gave refuge to many heterodox religious figures, including Celaleddin Rumi, founder of the Mevlevî dervish order.

The **Mongols** crushed the Selçuks at the battle of Köse Dağ in 1243, and although the sultanate lingered on until about 1300, the Turcoman tribes, never fully pacified, swarmed over the lands of both Selçuks and the Byzantines, who had abandoned Asia Minor after returning to Constantinople in 1261. For two centuries there was no single authority in Anatolia, but the process of Turkification and Islamization, begun in 1071, continued meanwhile.

The rise of the Ottomans

Following the Selçuk collapse, Anatolia fragmented into mostly Turcoman **emirates**. That centred on Söğüt was not initially important; its chieftain Ertuğrul was a typical *gazi*, a convert to Islam, and carried the faith ever westward. His son Osman, however, head of the clan from the 1290s, would give his name to a dynasty: Osmanlı in Turkish, "**Ottoman**" to the West. This emirate began to expand under Osman's son Orhan, who by the 1330s captured Byzantine Bursa and İznik.

Anatolian culture had long been hybrid, with frequent intermarriage between Muslims and Christians, and descendants or converts bilingual in Greek and Turkish. The Bektaşi dervish order effected a synthesis between Islam and numerically dwindling Christianity. As Byzantine authority diminished, the assets and facilities of Christian monasteries were appropriated by the **vakıfs**, or Islamic pious foundations; the demoralized Christian priesthood and population often converted to Islam simultaneously.

Complementing this was the *devşirme*, a fourteenth-century innovation whereby boys from conquered Christian districts were levied by the Ottomans to serve as an elite force, the janissaries. Slaves of the sultan, they were admitted to the eclectic Bektaşi order, and trained meticulously to become not only warriors but administrators. Free-born Muslims were ineligible for this corps, and promotion was by merit, so that the Ottoman state, up to the office of grand vizier, was run by converts. The only chance of advancement for free-born Muslims was within the *ulema*, the Koranic sages who decreed on religious matters, or as a member of the *defterdar* (accountant) bureaucracy overseeing the empire's revenues.

While the janissaries formed a powerful praetorian guard, they were supplemented by a standing army, paid indirectly by *timar* (land grant), an adopted Byzantine practice. Conquered territory remained the sultan's property, with such grants dispensed on the understanding that the man's "salary" was the proceeds of his estate – and that he remained liable for armed service at any time. *Timars* reverted to the crown upon the holder's death, with his sons having to re-earn their portion by service.

Despite tolerance shown to Christians, Ottoman society was hierarchical, with distinctions between Muslims and infidels preserved in every particular from dress code to unequal status before the law. Christians were not conscripted for campaigns, and hence could not qualify for *timars*; instead they paid a tax in lieu of military service, and congregated in towns as tradesmen.

To continue the *timar* system, more land had to be seized, and the *gazi* ethos continued. By the mid-fourteenth century the Ottomans had entered Thrace, and in 1362 **Sultan Murat** I took Adrianopolis (Edirne). Constantinople was surrounded, and the almost-vanished Byzantine Empire existed on Ottoman sufferance. With Latin and Orthodox Christians at each other's throats, Ottoman ascendancy was assured, and Murat further isolated Constantinople with new acquisitions in the lower Balkans, routing a Serbian-led coalition at Kosovo in 1389. Murdered on the battlefield by a Serbian infiltrator, his elder son and successor **Beyazit** I established an unfortunate precedent by promptly strangling his brother Yakub to assure untroubled rule. Beyazit, nicknamed Yıldırım (Lightning) for his swift battle deployments, bested a Hungarian/Crusader army at Bulgarian Nicopolis in 1396, and the fall of Constantinople seemed imminent.

However, in expanding eastwards, Beyazit – more impulsive and less methodical than Murat – provoked the great Mongol warrior **Tamerlane**. Tamerlane routed Beyazit's armies at the **Battle of Ankara** in 1402, trundling the captive sultan about in a cage for a year before his demise, while laying waste to much of Anatolia. Even though the Mongols soon vanished, the remnant Byzantine Empire was granted a fifty-year reprieve, and for a decade the fate of the Ottoman line hung in the balance as Beyazit's four sons fought it out. The victor, Mehmet I, and his successor the mystically inclined Murat II, restored Ottoman fortunes.

The fall of Constantinople

The greatest prize – **Constantinople** – still eluded the Ottomans. Both symbolically, as the seat of two previous empires, and practically – as the throttle between the Black Sea and the Mediterranean – its capture was imperative. **Mehmet II**, who became sultan in 1451, immediately began preparations, studding the sea approaches to the severely depopulated capital with fortresses, engaging artillery experts from Europe with an eye to breaching the city walls, and for the first time outfitting a substantial Ottoman fleet. The final siege of Constantinople, during spring 1453, lasted seven weeks, ending on May 29 when the sultan's armies finally entered the city while the last Byzantine emperor died unnoticed in the melee. Mehmet's epithet was henceforth Fatih, "the Conqueror", and there was no longer any doubt that the Ottoman Empire was the legitimate successor of the Roman and Byzantine ones.

The Ottoman Golden Age

Mehmet refurbished the city, renamed **İstanbul**, as a worthy imperial capital, repopulating it with Muslims and Christians from rural areas, establishing public amenities and constructing a fine palace at Topkapı. The non-Muslim communities were organized into *millets* (nations), headed by a patriarch or rabbi, answerable for his flock's good behaviour (plus tax remittances) and under whom Greek or Slavic Orthodox, Armenian and Jew were subject to their own communal laws. This system, which guaranteed more freedom of worship than in contemporary Europe, lasted until 1926.

Mop-up campaigns during 1458–60 in the Peloponnese and along the Black Sea eliminated satellite Byzantine and Genoese states. Mehmet then returned to the upper Balkans, adding Wallachia, most of Greece, Bosnia-Herzegovina and part of Albania to his domains, while expanding his navy to counter the Venetians.

Mehmet was succeeded in 1481 by **Beyazit II**, "the Pious", who despite that disposition relegated Venice to secondary maritime status by enlisting pirates into the Ottoman navy. The skills of Greek renegades and Italian mercenaries were supplemented in 1493 by those of Iberian Jews, the ancestors of most contemporary Turkish Jewry, fetched by "mercy ships" sent by Beyazit upon their expulsion from Spain and Portugal.

In 1512 Beyazit was forced to abdicate by his son **Selim I**, vigorous like his grandfather but with an added streak of cruelty and bigotry, hence his moniker Yavuz ("the Fierce" – "the Grim" to the West). Both of Selim's predecessors had entertained Sufic and heterodox doctrines, but now religious orthodoxy was seen as vital, since neighbour Shah İsmail of Persia was promoting Shi'ism both within and without his frontiers. Selim massacred forty thousand Shi'ites in Anatolia, and then defeated the Shah at Çaldıran in 1514. Rather than continue into Persia, however, Selim turned his armies south against the Mamluks, overrunning Mesopotamia and Egypt by 1516 and occupying most of the holy cities of Islam. By capturing the caliph in Cairo and transporting him back to İstanbul, Selim became Defender of the (Sunni) Faith – and the caliphate was identified with the Ottoman sultanate.

Although the empire would reach its greatest extent after his death, **Süleyman the Magnificent** laid the foundations for this expansion during a long (1520–1566) reign. Early on, the strongholds of the Knights of St John at Rhodes and Bodrum – which controlled the sea lanes to Egypt – were taken, as was Belgrade, leaving lands further up the Danube unguarded; by 1526 Budapest was in Ottoman hands. Campaigns in Persia and the Arabian peninsula were successful, but the siege of Vienna in 1529 was not – nor was an attempt to drive the Portuguese from the Indian Ocean. Süleyman was better able to control the Mediterranean, with such admirals as Greek-born Barbaros Hayrettin (**Barbarossa**) and Turgut Reis besting Venetian/Habsburg fleets. But in 1565 the siege of Malta, where the Knights of St John had retreated, failed, marking the end of the Mediterranean as an Ottoman lake. Nonetheless, the Ottoman Empire, however unwieldy and heterogeneous, was the leading world power of the sixteenth century.

Süleyman the Magnificent and Roxelana

Domestically Süleyman distinguished himself as an administrator, builder and patron of the arts; in Turkey he is known as *Kanunî*, "the Lawgiver". In his personal life, however, his judgement had enduringly harmful consequences. He became so enamoured of his favourite concubine Roxelana that he broke with Ottoman precedent and married her. Scheming and ambitious, she used her influence to incite the sultan to murder his capable son and heir (by a previous liaison), Mustafa, and later her own son Beyazit – as well as his grand vizier İbrahim. Süleyman died a lonely, morose man on his last campaign on the Danube in 1566; with the two ablest princes gone, there were no obstacles to the succession of Roxelana's first-born son, the useless Selim.

It was accordingly regarded with both terror and fascination by Europe; only the **French**, under Francis I, saw possibilities of alliance and manipulation, concluding a treaty with Süleyman in 1536. In addition to granting France trading advantages in the empire, the treaty's clauses stipulated various privileges for French nationals, the so-called **Capitulations**: exemption from most Ottoman taxes and the right to be judged by their own consuls under foreign law. What began as a stimulus to commerce became, over time, a pernicious erosion of Ottoman sovereignty, as many European nations and overseas companies secured their own capitulations, extending immunity to local employees (usually Christian) provided with appropriate passports.

Centuries of Ottoman decline

The reign of bibulous **Selim II** ("the Sot" to the West) is the best era to assign as the start of Ottoman decline. He was succeeded by sixteen other, generally ineffectual sultans, of whom only bloodthirsty but resolute **Murat IV**, and peace-loving aesthete **Ahmet II**, did much to prevent the gradual deterioration. From Roxelana's time onwards the **harem** occupied Topkapı palace, so that the scheming of its tenants impinged directly on day-to-day government. Early in the seventeenth century the grisly custom of fratricide upon the enthronement of a new sultan was abandoned in favour of the debilitating confinement of other heirs-apparent to the so-called Kafes (Cage). Few sultans campaigned overseas any longer, or presided personally over councils of state, instead delegating most authority to their grand viziers.

Able and honest viziers halted or reversed the downward slide of the empire, but usually nepotism and corruption flourished in the decadent palace atmosphere. The early Ottoman principle of meritocracy was replaced by **hereditary aristocracy**; the *devşirme* was all but abandoned by the late seventeenth century, and the janissary corps was no longer celibate or religiously exclusive. Sinecure passed from father to son, and the corps expanded as free Muslims enrolled. Many were artisans who only appeared to collect pay, desire for more of which often prompted the janissaries to rebel, extorting money from hapless villagers and sultans alike, and on occasion deposing and murdering the sovereign. Similarly, land grants became hereditary, and their holders evolved into local warlords (the *derebeys*, "lords of the valley"). Revolts of idle, underpaid troops devastated Anatolia, already wracked by overpopulation and land shortage; thus began a steady rural depopulation which continues today.

More problems came from abroad. The influx into the Mediterranean of gold and silver from the New World set off a spiral of inflation, while the Age of Exploration forged new sea lanes around Africa to the East Indies, reducing the importance of overland caravan routes through Ottoman territories. Most importantly, Europe underwent the **Renaissance**, while the Ottomans remained stagnant. New, centralized nation-states in the West began to acquire well-trained standing armies and navies, equipped with new armaments, ships and navigation devices, outgrowths of the Renaissance's spur to scientific enquiry. To these manifestations of European superiority the Ottomans reacted disdainfully, seeing no reason to learn from the infidels.

External evidence of the rot took nearly a century to show: although the defeat of an Ottoman fleet at **Lepanto** (today Náfpaktos) in 1571 shattered the myth of Turkish invincibility, that victory was neutralized by their taking Cyprus from Venice the same year, and the reconquest of North Africa by 1578. The 1600s proceeded well, with the seizure of Crete and parts of Poland, but already the

Ottomans were drafting treaties with adversaries as equals rather than, as before, condescending to suppliant Christian kings. During the late seventeenth century, the most notorious of several defeats at the hands of the Austrians and allies was the bungled second siege of Vienna in 1683. Most of Hungary and other central European lands were ceded before the treaties of Carlowitz (1699) and Passarowitz (1718) stabilized the Balkan frontier for two centuries.

During the eighteenth century most Ottoman territorial loss was to **Russia**; Russo-Turkish enmity was a historical constant thereafter until the 1920s. Catherine the Great humiliated the Turks with the treaties of Küçük Kaynarca (1774) and Jassy (1792), which ceded extensive territory to the tsarina and gave Russia long-coveted access to the Black Sea – as well as the right to interfere, anywhere in the Ottoman Empire, to protect Orthodox Christians.

Reforms and Young Ottomans

The 1789 start of **Selim III**'s rule coincided with new revolutionary regimes in France and the US – thus the name of his proposed reforms, the Nizam-i-Cedid (**New Order**). With the Napoleonic wars as a background, he hired foreign experts to set up a Western-style army. This aroused the hostility of the janissaries and the *ulema*; Selim was deposed, then murdered, in 1808, despite having dissolved the new army as a sop to the conservatives.

The new sultan, **Mahmut II**, innovated more cautiously, before being confronted by the major crisis of his reign: full-scale Greek rebellion in 1821. This proved impossible to crush even after the army of Mehmet Ali, semi-autonomous ruler of Egypt, was sent to the scene. The destruction of an Ottoman fleet at Navarino by French, Russian and English ships in 1827, a 1829 overland attack by Russia on İstanbul and a treaty in 1830 created an **independent Greece** – the first major Ottoman loss in the south Balkans. The French simultaneously invaded Algeria, and Mehmet Ali attacked Anatolia, which went unchecked until the Russians, now supporting Mahmut, landed on the Bosphorus. In consideration for services rendered they imposed the Treaty of Hunkâr İskelesi, which gave the tsar unimpeded access to the Bosphorus straits.

Mahmut had notably more success at home. In 1826 the janissaries mutinied again, but the sultan liquidated them with loyal forces in the so-called "**Auspicious Incident**". The Bektaşi sect, the janissary "house religion", was suppressed until the 1860s, and a proper army created. During the 1830s Prussian and Austrian advisers came to train it, beginning a tradition of Teutonic involvement in Turkey's military which endured for nearly a century. A formal foreign service and civil service were also established. A version of Western dress for all except clerics became mandatory – including the replacement of the turban by the more "progressive" **fez**. These centralizing reforms widened the gap between the Ottoman masses and the new elite.

Mahmut's efforts bore more fruit when his son Sultan Abdülmecid and vizier Mustafa Reşid proclaimed the **Tanzimat** (Reorganization) in 1839, an Ottoman Magna Carta which delegated some sultanic authority to advisers, ended taxation irregularities, and stipulated equal legal treatment of Muslims and non-Muslims. While this permitted the founding of newspapers and secular schools, the proposal of infidel equality deeply offended many.

Foreign economic penetration of the Ottoman Empire increased sharply, with growing commerce in port cities, and massive imports of European products; the Greeks, Armenians and foreign-Christian merchants benefited disproportionately.

Inland centres and traditional bazaar crafts declined sharply, unable to compete with industrial products.

By mid-century the empire was thoroughly enmeshed in European power struggles, since England and France had determined that the Ottomans must be propped up as a counter to Russian expansionism. Thus the empire found itself among the winners of the 1853–56 **Crimean War**, which began as a dispute between Russia and France over the protection extended by each to Christians in Ottoman Palestine. The war ended with little significant territorial adjustment, but did bring twenty years of peace for the Ottomans.

Abdülmecid, well-meaning but weak and extravagant, was succeeded in 1861 by **Abdülaziz**, who combined his predecessor's defects with a despotic manner. From among the first graduates of the empire's secular schools arose the Society of **Young Ottomans**, which advocated a constitutional monarchy; its stellar figure was poet and essayist Namık Kemal, exiled (like others) by the sultan. Young Ottomans overseas penned reams of seditious literature, smuggled into the empire to good effect.

Faced with Abdülaziz's financial irresponsibility and his growing mental instability, together with new Russian mischief in İstanbul and brutally suppressed revolts in the Balkans, Young Ottomans among the bureaucratic elite deposed him on May 30, 1876. The sultanate was passed to his promising nephew Murat, but he too suffered a nervous breakdown and was declared unfit to rule. The next heir-apparent was his brother **Abdülhamid**, an unknown quantity, offered the throne on condition that he accept various Young Ottomans as advisers and rule constitutionally.

Abdülhamid and the Young Turks

The new sultan duly presided over the first Ottoman parliament and retained – briefly – his hapless brother's advisers. But implementation of reforms was interpreted by outsiders as a sign of weakness. Accordingly **Russia attacked** in 1877, in the Caucasus and in the Balkans, with an explicitly pan-Slavic agenda. The war went badly for the Ottomans, with extensive territorial losses confirmed by the harsh peace treaty of San Stefano (at the ceasefire line near İstanbul), later mitigated by the 1878 Conference of Berlin. This provided for an independent Romania, Montenegro and Serbia; an autonomous if truncated Bulgaria; the cession of Kars and Ardahan districts to Russia; and the occupation of Bosnia and Herzegovina by Austria. **Nationalism** had been unleashed – and rewarded – in the Balkans, and would be a theme for the next forty years. Britain, as compensation for fending off further Russian advances, was given Cyprus.

During all this the new **parliament** displayed too much independence for the sultan's taste, criticizing policy and summoning ministers to answer for their conduct. In early 1878, between the San Stefano and Berlin negotiations, Abdülhamid dropped any pretence of consultative government and dissolved the Chamber of Deputies; with all restraining influences gone, he ruled despotically and directly. Numerous spies and rigorous press censorship attended a police state and a new telegraph network helped surveillance.

After the disastrous wars early in his reign, Abdülhamid's foreign policy was xenophobic and Asia-oriented, espousing Islam as a unifying force and emphasizing his role as caliph. This didn't prevent the loss of Tunis and Egypt, along with worsening treatment of the Armenians of eastern Anatolia, who began to show the same nationalist sentiments as Balkan Christians. Abuses culminated in

The Young Turk Revolution

In 1889 the Ottoman Society for Union and Progress – later the **Committee for Union and Progress** (CUP) – arose among army doctors and the huge exile community in Europe. It took strong root in **Macedonia**, the most polyglot Ottoman province, completely infiltrating the Third Army at Salonica. Threats of intervention by European powers in Macedonia – where disorderly Greek and Bulgarian guerilla bands rampaged – coincided with arrears in army pay, sparking the revolt of the so-called **"Young Turks"**. Macedonian army units demanded by telegraph that Abdülhamid restore the 1876 constitution, or face unpleasant consequences; on **July 24, 1908**, the sultan assented. There was rejoicing in major imperial cities as mullahs fraternized with bishops, and Bulgarians walked arm in arm with Greeks.

Euphoria subsided as the **revolutionary government** fumbled for coherent policy. The coup had had as immediate goals the curbing of Abdülhamid's despotism and the physical preservation of the empire – but even these limited aims proved beyond it. By October Bulgaria declared full independence and absorbed eastern Rumelia, while Austria formally annexed Bosnia-Herzegovina. **Elections** for the reconvened parliament were reasonably fair, and the CUP, organized as a party, gained a majority. Opposition to its Westernization and autocracy simmered, however, and in spring 1909 a **counter-revolt** of low-ranking soldiers, anti-CUP politicians and religious elements seized İstanbul. Abdülhamid, overestimating the rebels' strength, unwisely supported them. The "Young Turks" fought back from Salonica, sending Third Army general Mahmut Şevket to crush the insurrection, and then **banished the sultan** to house arrest in Salonica. His younger brother ascended the throne as Mehmet V, promising to respect the "will of the nation".

organized **pogroms** of 1895–96, during which nearly 150,000 Armenians died. In 1897, war with Greece and a revolt on Crete coincided; although the Prussian-trained army defeated the Greeks, the Ottomans were forced to grant Crete autonomy.

Despite opposing political reform, Abdülhamid promoted technological Westernization – most famously German-built railways across Anatolia. Investment credits were extended, and a Public Debt Administration gathered revenues of state monopolies to service the enormous debt run up since the 1850s. Secular schooling and technical training were encouraged, as long as they remained apolitical – but the creation of an educated elite inevitably resulted in change.

Nationalism and the Balkan wars

The CUP revolution had been saved, but there was still no agreed programme as three notions contended for supremacy. **Ottomanism** asserted that a Eurasian federal empire, in which all ethnic and religious minorities had equal rights – in return for loyalty to the sultan – was both viable and desirable. **Pan-Islamism**, Abdülhamid's pet creed, stressed the Islamic nature of the Ottoman Empire and the ties between Muslim Albanians, Caucasians, Kurds, Arabs and Turks. **Pan-Turanism**, mainly promoted by Caucasian Muslims exiled by the Russians, was more blatantly racial, dwelling on the affinities of all Turkic peoples in central Asia and the Balkans; over time it morphed into a more realistic Turkism, protecting the interests of Anatolia's Turkish-speaking Muslims, and this eventually carried the day. But discussion of these alternatives – and cultural life in general – briefly flourished uninhibitedly. Between 1908 and 1912 the CUP was hardly monolithic, and parliamentary opposition was not completely quashed until 1912.

The CUP's growing authoritarianism coincided with renewed external threats. Italy invaded Tripolitania (Libya) in 1911, and the next year took all of the Dodecanese islands. In late 1912, Bulgaria, Serbia, Montenegro and Greece united, driving Turkey out of Europe in the **First Balkan War**, even approaching İstanbul by early 1913. Enraged at attempts to limit the army's, and the CUP's, involvement in government, and the poor terms of a pending peace treaty, key CUP officers staged a coup, murdering the minister of war; new grand vizier Mahmut Şevket's assassination soon after allowed the CUP to suppress all dissent and establish a **military junta**.

The unlikely Balkan alliance fell apart, with Bulgaria turning on Serbia and Greece in the **Second Balkan War**, and the Ottomans regaining eastern Thrace up to Edirne. This made temporary heroes of the triumvirate junta: **Enver Paşa**, dashing, courageous, abstemious, as well as vain, ambitious and megalomaniac; **Talat Paşa**, a brutal Thracian civilian who later ordered the 1915 deportation of the Armenians; and **Cemal Paşa**, a ruthless but competent professional soldier from an old family. They avenged the ethnic cleansing of Balkan Muslims by deporting or killing nearly half a million Greek Orthodox from Aegean Turkey in early 1914.

World War I

CUP ideology was now overtly Turkish-nationalist and secular, as well as antidemocratic – and increasingly pro-German. Public opinion, and sager CUP members, hoped that the Ottoman Empire would remain neutral in the pending conflict, but Germanophile Enver signed a secret agreement with the Kaiser on August 2, 1914. Britain committed a major blunder the same day, impounding two battleships paid for by public subscription in Turkey. In response the Germans sailed two replacement ships through an Allied blockade to İstanbul in October, presenting them to the Turkish navy – whose German commander promptly sent them to bombard Russian Black Sea ports. By November the Ottomans were at war with the Allies, though some CUP ministers resigned in protest.

The **Turkish war effort**, fought on five fronts simultaneously, was an almost unmitigated disaster. Within four years, the empire lost all Middle Eastern domains, as Arabs backed the British on the promise of subsequent autonomy, thus proving pan-Islamism as dead as Ottomanism. Enver Paşa lost an entire army on the Russian front during winter 1914–15; the subsequent Tsarist advance deep into Anatolia was only reversed after 1917. The sole Ottoman successes were bloodily defeating the British at Mesopotamian Kut, and the successful defence of **Gallipoli**, guarding the Dardanelles and the sea approaches to İstanbul. Credit for the seven-month Turkish resistance there belonged largely to a hitherto unknown Colonel **Mustafa Kemal**, later Atatürk. He had come of age just before the Young Turk agitation and, while an early CUP member, had opposed its autocratic tendencies and entry into the war with Germany. The Turkish public craved a hero, but jealous Enver denied them this satisfaction by shuttling Kemal between various backwoods commands, until war's end saw him overseeing a strategic retreat near Syria.

On October 30, 1918, Ottoman and British officers signed an **armistice** at Greek Límnos. Two weeks later an Allied fleet sailed into İstanbul, and occupied strategic points around the Sea of Marmara, though Turkish civil administration continued

The Armenian deportations

For the Ottoman Empire's **Armenians**, April 24, 1915 was a fateful day on which the CUP authorities – acting on plans finalized in March – disarmed all Armenians serving in the Turkish army, and rounded up Armenian civilians from Anatolian cities, towns and villages; only İstanbul and İzmir were exempted, for economic and public-relations reasons. Over ten months of deportations, Armenian men were usually shot immediately by gendarmes, Kurdish irregulars or bands of recruited thugs, while women and children were forced to march hundreds of kilometres towards concentration camps in the Mesopotamian desert. Estimating **total casualties** is controversial, but Ottoman and foreign censuses around 1900 counted nearly 1.5 million Armenians living in Anatolia. Allowing for about half a million refugees who managed to hide in Turkey or escape abroad, most of the difference can be assumed to have perished, making it the first deliberate, large-scale genocide of the twentieth century – in 1919 the Ottomans themselves admitted 800,000 killed.

The above scenario is hotly disputed by more recent Turkish governments, which deny that any officially approved, systematic expulsion or killing occurred, and allow a maximum of 300,000 Armenian fatalities – while implying most were combatants in treasonous alliance with Russia or France. While it is true that many Armenians, particularly in Van, Kars and Adana, sided with those two powers in the hopes of securing a postwar state for themselves, this happened after the deportation and massacre orders were issued, and could be construed as legitimate self-defence. The issue is still very much alive, with relatively clumsy Turkish propaganda developed since the 1980s to counter increasingly successful Armenian lobbying for international recognition of the tragedy.

providing no "disturbances" took place. Meanwhile the CUP triumvirate had fled on German ships, and all soon met violent deaths: Talat killed in revenge by an Armenian in Berlin; Cemal assassinated in Caucasian Georgia; and Enver dying flamboyantly as a self-styled emir fighting the Bolsheviks in central Asia.

The struggle for independence

The Allies could now carry out long-deferred designs on the Ottoman heartland. By early 1919 French troops occupied southeast Anatolia, the Italians landed on the coast between Bodrum and Antalya, and the Greeks disembarked at İzmir, where Greek Orthodox formed much of the population. The British concentrated their strength in İstanbul and Thrace, and along with the other victors garrisoned in the capital dictated policy to the defeated. New sultan **Mehmet VI** was interested mainly in retaining his throne, and ready to make any necessary territorial or administrative concessions – including dissolving the Ottoman parliament.

In Thrace and Anatolia, however, various Committees for the Defence of Rights – patriotic guerilla bands often led by ex-CUP personnel – had arisen, and a substantial Ottoman army survived at Erzurum, under Kâzım Karabekir. Together these would form the nucleus of resistance. Only visionary leadership, and further Allied provocations, were lacking; neither was long in coming.

Mustafa Kemal was the only undefeated Ottoman commander at war's end and was not compromised by association with the CUP leadership. Popular and outspoken, Kemal itched to cross over to Anatolia and begin organizing **resistance**, but not without a suitable pretext. In spring 1919, he wrangled a post as a military inspector empowered to wind up the CDRs. His first destination was the Black Sea, where **Turkish guerrillas** were battling local Greeks intent on setting up a Pontic republic. On May 19, 1919, he landed at Samsun, four days after the Greek landing at İzmir – the last straw for many hitherto apathetic Turks. Contrary to his brief, Kemal promptly began organizing and strengthening the Turkish guerrillas. The İstanbul government, realizing what he was up to, dismissed him, then ordered his arrest; he responded by resigning his commission. Kemal and Karabekir, plus other high-ranking Ottoman officers, planned resistance with support from Anatolian religious authorities. Two ideological congresses (at Erzurum in July, in Sivas in September) elected Kemal chairman, and ratified the so-called National Pact, which demanded Turkish borders approximating those of today, an end to the Capitulations and a guarantee of rights to all minorities. The pact also reaffirmed its loyalty to the institution of the caliphate, if not the sultan himself, deemed an Allied puppet.

The **Nationalists**, as they were soon called began to joust with the İstanbul regime. By late 1919, they forced the resignation of the grand vizier and elections for a new parliament dominated by Nationalists, which proclaimed the National Pact. Thefts from Allied arms depots, with the connivance of the French and Italians who opposed Greek aims, became common. At the instigation of the outraged Ottoman court, the British placed İstanbul under formal occupation on March 16, 1920, raiding parliament and bundling many deputies into exile on Malta. Luckier MPs escaped to Ankara, where on April 23 the Nationalists opened the first Grand National Assembly. The sultanate secured a **fetva** from Islamic authorities sanctioning holy war against the "rebels" and condemning Nationalist leaders to death in absentia. Kemal and friends secured a counter-fetva from sympathetic religious figures in Ankara, and shortly after the Bektaşi dervish *şeyh* ordered his followers to help the Nationalists.

Such moral support was vital to the beleaguered guerillas, now fighting a multiple-front war: against the French in the southeast, the Italians in the southwest, Armenians in the northeast, irregulars supporting the sultan in various locations and – most dangerously – the Greeks in western Anatolia. The only consistent aid came from the young Soviet Union, which sent gold and weapons, then partitioned the short-lived Armenian republic between itself and Turkey, thus closing that theatre of war by late 1920.

The Allied governments, oblivious to all this, presented the humiliating **Treaty of Sèvres** to the Ottoman government in May 1920. By its terms, an independent Armenia and an autonomous Kurdistan were created; the Dardanelles and Bosphorus straits were internationalized; Thrace plus İzmir and its hinterland were given to Greece; France and Italy were assigned spheres of influence in Anatolia; and Turkish finances were placed under Allied supervision, with a revival of the Capitulations. By signing this document, the demoralized sultanate sacrificed its last shred of credibility, convinced waverers to back the Nationalist movement – and sparked a predictable Greek response.

The Greco-Turkish War

Greek forces, authorized by British prime minister Lloyd George, pressed inland from İzmir to capture Edirne, İzmit and Bursa, seeking to realize a "Greater Greece" on both shores of the Aegean. Only French and Italian objections halted them short of the strategic Afyon–Eskişehir railway. In early 1921 the Greeks were on the move again, but Nationalist general İsmet Paşa stopped them twice at the **İnönü** gorge, from which he later took his surname. Since the replacement of the republican Venizelos government in Greece by royalists, the Greek armies had become more corrupt, incompetently led and brutal in their treatment of Muslim civilians. Kemal's forces, on the other hand, had gotten more cohesive and professional, with irregular bands suppressed or absorbed.

But when the Greeks advanced east once more in July 1921, they swiftly captured Afyon, Eskişehir and its vital linking railway; the Nationalists strategically retreated east of the Sakarya River, less than 100km from Ankara, to buy time and extend enemy lines. Panic and gloom reigned in Ankara, with Kemal appointed to command the defending army, and share its fate. The Greeks went for the bait, sensing an easy chance to finish off the Nationalists. But in the ferocious, three-week **Sakarya battle** beginning August 13, they failed to make further headway. Although most of the Greek army survived, anything but the capture of Ankara was a defeat. The jubilant GNA conferred on Kemal the title *Gazi*, or "Warrior for the Faith".

Sakarya greatly enhanced the Nationalists' position: both the French and Italians soon concluded peace treaties, and contributions from Muslims abroad poured in to finance the "holy war". With support for the Greek adventure evaporating, the British tried unsuccessfully to arrange an armistice. Both sides dug in until, on August 26, 1922, Kemal launched a **final offensive** to drive the Greeks out of Anatolia, at Dumlupınar near Afyon. The Greek lines crumbled, and those not taken prisoner or killed fled in a disorderly rout towards waiting boats in İzmir, committing atrocities against the Turkish population, destroying the harvest and abandoning Greek civilians to the inevitable Turkish reprisals. The latter included the **sacking and burning of İzmir** within four days of the triumphant entry of the Nationalists.

Despite this resounding triumph, ongoing conflict beckoned. A large Greek army remained in Thrace, disposed to fight on, and British contingents guarding the **Dardanelles** faced off against the Nationalist army sent to cross the straits. Some Nationalists even advocated re-taking western Thrace and Greek Macedonia, a sure path to renewed world war. Cooler heads prevailed, however, and at Mudanya on October 11, 1922, an armistice was signed, obliging the last Greek troops to quit eastern Thrace. A week later British premier Lloyd George, utterly discredited, resigned.

The fall of the sultanate and the population exchanges

There remained just one obstacle to full Nationalist control: Sultan Mehmet VI still presided over İstanbul. Few in Ankara had much time for the man himself, but many expressed reluctance to abolish his office, favouring a constitutional monarchy. The Allies helped decide the matter by extending a clumsy double invitation to a final peace conference – one to the sultanate, the other to the Grand National Assembly. The outrage this provoked in the GNA made it easy for Kemal to persuade them to **abolish the sultanate** which took place on November 1. Within two weeks Mehmet VI, last of the House of Osman, sneaked ignominiously out of the old imperial capital on a British warship, bound for Italian exile; his cousin Abdülmecid became caliph, but with no temporal powers.

At the 1923 Lausanne peace conference İsmet Paşa was the sole Turkish representative. The Allies, hoping to dictate terms as at Sèvres, were quickly disappointed; the dogged İsmet reduced seasoned diplomats to despair by feigning deafness and repetitive insistence on the tenets of the National Pact. The **Treaty of Lausanne**, signed on July 24, recognized the National Pact frontiers; abolished the Capitulations; demilitarized the Dardanelles; and postponed a decision on the status of oil-rich Mosul (now in Iraq).

More drastically, Greece and Turkey agreed to **exchange minority populations** to eliminate future communal conflict. Nearly half a million Muslims in Greece were sent to Turkey, and the remaining 1.2 million Greek Orthodox Christians in Turkey were officially despatched to Greece (many had already fled there). The only exceptions were the Turkish minority in western Thrace, and Greeks with Ottoman citizenship in İstanbul and on İmroz and Tenedos islands ouside the Dardanelles. The sole criterion was religion, so that many Turkish-speaking Christians and Greek-speaking Muslims suddenly found themselves in an alien linguistic (and cultural) environment.

Lausanne marked the true end of World War I, and saw Turkey, alone of the defeated, emerge in dignity, with modest demands made of her. Compared to the old empire, this was a compact state – 97 percent Anatolian and Muslim. A new political party, the **Republican People's Party**, was formed, as was a new GNA, its members drawn from RPP ranks.

The young republic

In October 1923 the GNA officially moved the capital to **Ankara** and proclaimed the **Republic**; Kemal was designated head of state and İsmet prime minister. Although the sultan was gone, Caliph Abdülmecid was still around and a conspicuous public personality – an intolerable situation for Kemal and other Westernizers; with the war over, they no longer needed the legitimizing function of Islam. In March 1924 the caliphate was abolished and all royal Osmalıs exiled, the *medreses* and religious courts closed, and **vakıf** assets assigned to a new Ministry of Religious Affairs.

Many were dismayed by Kemal's increasing autocracy, and some – including Kâzım Karabekir – resigned from the RPP in October to form the opposition **Progressive Republican Party** (PRP). At first Kemal tolerated it as a safety valve, but became alarmed when PRP speakers attracted large crowds and the less supervised İstanbul press sided with them. In February 1925 the first of several twentieth-century **Kurdish revolts** – both fundamentalist Muslim and separatist-nationalist in nature – erupted; it took Ankara two months to suppress. Kemal, demanding unity in crisis, secured the PRP's closure and established draconian Independence Tribunals; the revolt's leaders plus a few PRP members found themselves on the wrong end of a rope. By autumn 1925 all **dervish orders** had been prohibited (though they were never completely suppressed), and pilgrimage to Sufi saints' tombs was forbidden.

Kemal's reforms re-inflamed opposition, and in mid-1926 a plot to assassinate him was uncovered. Most of the former PRR leadership, including Karabekir, were charged and tried, plus the entire surviving CUP leadership, who were hanged; even those acquitted were barred henceforth from public life. This was the last purge, however, and the feared Independence Tribunals were disbanded, having served their purpose.

Belatedly Atatürk addressed the economy. Already weakened by ten years of constant warfare and the loss of Greek and Armenian industrial know-how, its problems were exacerbated by the 1929 crash. **"Kemalism"** stressed state-funded heavy industry with a goal of complete import substitution (except for factory equipment). Development banks had been set up in 1925, and the rail network extended, with mining, steel, cement and paper mills heavily subsidized in imitation of Italian fascism. This programme was, however, grossly inefficient, and relegated agriculture to penury until the 1950s. The east was condemned to a

Kemal Atatürk's Reforms

In tandem with the dervish clampdown, Kemal moved against **traditional headgear**: women's veils, the turban and the fez. Sartorial laws outlawing turbans and fezes, and requiring use of hated European hats, were met with stiff resistance; Ottoman dress had been a vital indicator of social rank. Not a few recidivists were hanged by the Independence Tribunals, but secularists have to this day not eliminated the cloaking of women in rural areas.

In 1926, the **Gregorian calendar** supplanted the Muslim lunar one for official use, and the *şeriat* (Islamic **law code**) was replaced by adaptations of European versions. The Jewish, Armenian and Greek minorities relinquished their communal laws; henceforth all citizens were judged by a uniform legal system. Along with a secular law code came relative **emancipation of women**: marriage and divorce became civil rather than religious or customary, polygamy was abolished, and by 1930 women were voting in local elections.

Kemal's next agenda item was **alphabet reform**. A special commission prepared a Roman script within six weeks in 1928, and by 1929 its universal use was law. The entire language was targeted over the next few years, with a language commission purging Turkish of Arabic and Persian accretions and reviving old Turkish words, coining new ones or adopting French words. Scholars now reckon the process was carried too far, with the language soon as top-heavy with borrowed Western terms as it had been with oriental ones, but with the script change the measures substantially increased literacy and comprehension. (A deliberate side effect of language reform was to isolate Turks from their imperial past by becoming unable to read Ottoman Turkish.)

Less successful, and ultimately embarrassing, were historical "revision" programmes, variously asserting that all other languages derived from Turkish; that the Turks were Aryan (and other racial nonsense mimicking Nazi theories), or that they descended from Hittites or Sumerians. Such hypotheses, springing from feelings of inferiority and a need for political legitimacy, remained in Turkish schoolbooks until the 1970s. A more constructive 1934 move was full **suffrage for women** in national elections and the mandatory adoption of **surnames**; previously this had been discretionary. Kemal chose for himself **Atatürk**, "Father-Turk", dropping his first name Mustafa.

subsistence existence – aggravating Kurdish feelings of punitive neglect – a situation unchanged until massive irrigation and hydroelectric projects of the 1970s–80s.

Foreign policy espoused non-interventionism and isolationism, though Turkey joined the League of Nations in 1934. Atatürk's slogan "Peace at home, peace in the world" bore unfortunate resemblance to Neville Chamberlain's utterances after Munich, but secured for Turkey years of badly needed calm. Though the RPP imitated aspects of contemporary totalitarian systems, Turkey had no wish to follow Germany, Italy and the USSR over a cliff. Atatürk removed the last irritant to Anglo-Turkish relations by renouncing claims to Mosul, but began in 1936 a campaign to annex the Hatay, part of French Syria with a large Turkish population.

Fortunately for Turkey, Atatürk had accomplished most of his intended life's work by 1938, since his health, after decades of heavy drinking, was steadily worsening. He died from liver cirrhosis in İstanbul's Dolmabahçe palace at 9.05am on November 10, 1938. Thousands of mourners bearing torches lined the route of his funeral cortege-train between İstanbul and Ankara. Fifteen years later he was interred in a mausoleum, the Anıt Kabir – designed by an Italian and a German, in monumental 1930s fascist style.

Atatürk's legacy is considerable: unlike totalitarian peers, he refrained from expansionism and overt racial/ethnic hatred, leaving behind a compact state and a guiding ideology, however uneven, expressly intended to outlive him. Personally he was a complex, even tragic figure: his charisma, energy and quick grasp of situations and people were unparalleled, but he had little inclination for methodical planning or systematic study. While revered, he was not particularly lovable – despite sponsoring women's rights, he was a compulsive womanizer, with one brief, unhappy marriage. He nursed grudges which had deadly consequences for those who might otherwise have lived to extricate Turkey from later dilemmas. Atatürk, like a huge tree allowing nothing to grow underneath, deprived Turkey of its next generation of leadership. His personality cult, obvious from the silhouettes and quotations on every hillside, is symptomatic of an inability to conceive of alternative ideologies or heroes, though since 1983 Kemalist economics has vanished completely.

World War II and after

Atatürk was succeeded as president by **İsmet İnönü**, and his Hatay policy was posthumously vindicated in 1939 with its annexation. France, eager for Turkish support in the imminent war with Germany, acquiesced in return for Turkey signing a vaguely worded treaty of alliance with France and Britain in 1939. But France was swiftly defeated, while German propaganda convinced Turkey that Britain was probably doomed too, and that the Axis would also dispatch Russia, the herditary Turkish enemy. Accordingly a "Treaty of Friendship" was signed with Nazi Germany in 1941, guaranteeing at least Turkish non-belligerence. Entry into the war on either side was always doubtful, since Turkey's armed forces had become desperately antiquated; memories of World War I defeat were strong as well. Turkey remained **neutral**, but despite this fence-sitting, the country was on a war footing with mobilization, and the economy stressed by black markets and huge budget deficits.

All these, and the infiltration of Nazi ideology, provoked the 1942 imposition of the **Varlık Vergisi** (Wealth Levy), a crippling, discriminatory tax applied against businessmen of Armenian, Greek, Jewish and Dönme descent. Non-payers had their property confiscated and/or were deported to labour camps in the interior, where many died. The measure, having raised very little money, was rescinded in 1944, but not before urban commerce had been set back a decade, and the Republic's reputation with non-Muslim minorities severely dented.

Even after Italy's collapse, Turkey still declined to enter the war, despite assurances of Allied support. Turkey only declared war on Germany early in 1945 to qualify for UN membership, not soon enough to prevent the USSR from demanding the return of Kars and Ardahan, and joint control of the Sea of Marmara straits. While demurring, Turkey badly needed a protective ally, and found one in the **United States**. The 1946 arrival in İstanbul of the American warship USS *Missouri* was greeted with such euphoria that the city fathers opened the local bordellos for free to the sailors.

The first results of this mutual wooing were Turkey's participation in the Korean War and admission to **NATO**. This new pro-Western stance had as other consequences the expulsion from Warsaw Pact Bulgaria into Turkey of numerous ethnic Turks, harbinger of an identical act four decades later, and consistently bad relations with neighbouring Arab states, particularly after Turkey recognized Israel.

At home, discontent with one-party rule, secularization and the stagnant, centralized economy coalesced when four MPs expelled from the RPP formed the **Democrat Party** in early 1946. Despite snap elections that summer and widespread balloting irregularities, the new opposition won fifteen percent of parliamentary seats. Amazingly, this result was not reversed by force or chicanery, but a definitive showdown could not be long postponed, and campaigning for May 14, 1950 polls was unimpeded. The DP promised an end to anti-business strictures, freer religious observance, and attention to neglected farmers. Although the Democrats were sure to win, the scale of their victory – 55 percent of votes, and over eighty percent of parliamentary seats – proved a surprise. **Celal Bayar** replaced İnönü as president, while **Adnan Menderes** became prime minister.

Populist government

Among the first acts of the new government was to permit, after a seventeen-year gap, calls to prayer in Arabic; simultaneously, outbreaks of fez- or turban-wearing, polygamy and the use of Arabic script erupted in the provinces (where Atatürk's reforms had barely penetrated). With sweeping **economic reforms** Menderes effectively opened up a country where for three decades little in the way of people, ideas, capital or goods had moved in or out. However, much of this relied on unsound investment in state enterprises or patronage to supporters. Farmer-lawyer Menderes had his colossal vanity aggravated by adoring peasants who sacrificed livestock in his honour and named boy-children after him.

Bumper harvests helped keep the electorate sweet through the mid-1950s, though by 1954 enormous **national debt** and trade deficits helped put the black-market value of the Turkish lira at one-fourth the official exchange rate. But the increasingly sensitive DP would not tolerate criticism: in 1953 both the RPP and the right-wing/religious **National Party**, with their handful of seats, were dissolved, while repressive press laws took effect just before May 1954 elections. These the Democrats won even more easily, but instead of giving them confidence, they took this as a mandate to continue crushing dissent and run the country even more shamelessly for their clientele's benefit. The economy kept deteriorating with rampant **inflation**, thereafter a constant of Turkish life. During 1955 the government, looking for a distraction from, and scapegoats for, domestic problems, found both in the Cyprus issue and minorities – especially İstanbul Greeks. DP-instigated street demonstrations escalated into destructive riots aimed at foreigners and the wealthy in all three major cities.

In the wake of all this, support for the government tumbled and although they won the 1957 elections these were heavily rigged with the tally never being announced. Turkey thus approached 1960 in a parlous state, with a huge gulf between the pro-DP peasantry and the urban elite – and, more dangerously, an alienated, antagonized military.

First military coup and the 1960s

Nowhere had dismay over DP policies been more keen than in the military, who considered themselves the guardians of Atatürk's heritage. The officer corps, barred from voting, the value of their fixed salaries eroded by inflation, watched rural nouveaux riches and Democrat apparatchiks surpass them economically and socially. On May 27, 1960, middle-ranking officers staged a **coup** – announced on the radio by a certain Colonel Alpaslan Türkeş.

The putsch was bloodless, swift and complete; DP MPs and ministers were jailed as the larger cities celebrated. For the next sixteen months, a **National Unity Committee** (NUC) under Cemal Gürsel governed Turkey, while preparing a new constitution to supersede the 1924 one. The NUC, however, was a marriage of convenience between idealistic top brass expecting resumed civilian rule and junior officers wishing for an indefinite period of authoritarian military government. The new constitution, which provided for a bicameral legislature and proportional representation in the lower house, was submitted to public referendum in July, with elections set for October.

The **referendum**, essentially a vote of confidence on the NUC, clocked just 62 percent in favour – evidence of lingering support for the Democrat Party. Leading DP members, including Menderes and Bayar, were being tried at bleak Yassıada in the Sea of Marmara, on charges of undermining the 1924 constitution, corruption and planning the 1955 riots. Upon the return of guilty verdicts and fifteen death sentences, the NUC hastily carried out three – against Menderes, foreign minister Zorlu and finance minister Polatkan. The three hangings just before the elections backfired badly, making Menderes a martyr and ensuring a long life for the Justice Party (JP), the Democrat Party reincarnated.

The elections again disappointed the NUC; neither the Justice Party nor a revitalized RPP gained a majority. The two front-runners formed a coalition, with Gürsel as president and İnönü prime minister for the first time since 1938. All this annoyed disaffected junior officers who mounted two subsequent coup attempts, one in February 1962 and another fourteen months later. Both were suppressed and the latter's leader executed.

Unstable coalitions continued as NUC reforms faltered; import-substitution policies were revived, while land reform and rural development were deferred. The first wave of **emigration to Europe** acted as a social safety-valve, and "guest workers" returned on holidays with consumer goods and – to a limited extent – European notions. Independent labour unions organized, with the right to strike conferred in 1963. The urban proletariat flocked to the Turkish Workers' Party (TWP), whose very existence nudged the RPP, now led by Bülent Ecevit, leftward. **Süleyman Demirel**, among the main political figures of the next three decades, became JP leader in 1964, pushing free enterprise and foreign investment. In October 1965 elections, Demirel's JP got a solid majority.

Cyprus, independent since 1960 with extensive constitutional concessions to its Turkish Cypriot minority, again intruded as the rickety setup there collapsed in December 1963. This cued civil strife on the island throughout 1964, abetted by smuggled-in Greek and Turkish troops; a full-scale Greco-Turkish war was only avoided by US pressure. The Turkish government had to confine itself to retaliations against the Greeks of Turkey's Aegean islands and İstanbul (including the expulsion of 12,000 resident Greek nationals).

The spirit of 1968 was manifest in increased **anti-Americanism** and leftist sentiments, particularly at universities. Many Turks felt betrayed by the US's lack of support on Cyprus, having studiously followed its foreign-policy lead since 1946. Even the government found obvious American tutelage offensive, and soon most US military installations passed to Turkish control or that of NATO. Demirel was returned to office in 1969 amidst increased political violence. Extreme left-wing groups like Dev Sol (Revolutionary Youth) clashed with right-wing and/or Islamist activists like the Grey Wolves, their paramilitary training camps set up by Alpaslan Türkeş, founder of the fascist **Nationalist Action Party** (MHP).

"Memorandum coup" and the 1970s

Faced with domestic unrest and sterile parliamentary manoeuvres, the generals acted again. Their March 12, 1971 proclamation forced Demirel out in favour of an "above-party" technocratic government. This **"memorandum coup"** kept parliament in session, but martial law was imposed, thousands were arrested and tried for inciting violence or class conflict, and much of the 1961 constitution was curtailed. The new government, stymied by JP MPs, resigned, though under threat of an overt coup, a facade of civilian rule was preserved. The army, mindful of the hash the colonels' junta had made of neighbouring Greece since 1967, decided to let politicians take the blame for any adverse outcome here. October 1973 elections produced a coalition of Ecevit's RPP with Necmettin Erbakan's Islamist National Salvation Party.

In July 1974, the Greek junta ousted Cypriot president Makarios, replacing him with extremists supporting union with Greece. Ecevit's appeal to Britain to intervene went unheeded, so he ordered an **invasion of Cyprus** on July 20. The illegal regime fell three days later, after Turkish forces had secured a bridgehead around Kyrenia. Negotiations continued until, on August 14, after the Greek Cypriots refused a Turkish ultimatum, its army advanced further to occupy the northern third of the island, which has since become the self-proclaimed Turkish Republic of Northern Cyprus. Ecevit – riding a "victory"-induced tide of popularity – resigned in September to seek early elections and a decisive majority. But opposition foot-dragging delayed polling until April 1975, when Demirel did a deal with the NSP and the MHP, clinging to power until 1977.

All this further polarized Turkey, which by 1980 saw escalating political violence ratchet annual death tolls up to 3000. While extremists initially confined activities to each other, deteriorated parliamentary decorum and politicized workplaces meant that incidents became widespread. İstanbul neighbourhoods were controlled by factions – having the wrong newspaper, or the wrong attire and moustache (each faction had a "dress code") ensured trouble.

Ecevit regained power in late 1977, but proved unequal to a dire situation. In December 1978, Türkeş's MHP orchestrated bloody street battles in Maraş between fundamentalist Sunnis and left-wing Alevîs; in Fatsa, an Alevî commune was smashed by army tanks. Demirel took office again in October 1979, but he too failed to halt the maelstrom despite declaring martial law.

The 1980 coup and after

The army soon decided that the Republic was facing its gravest crisis yet. Plans for a coup existed earlier, but public rumblings first surfaced as an open letter to civilian politicans at New Year's 1980. Economist-engineer **Turgut Özal** was appointed head of the State Planning Organization; he jettisoned import-substitution policies in favour of an export-orientated economy.

Turkey's importance had been underlined by the Iranian revolution and Soviet invasion of Afghanistan, and the US was keen to secure a stable Middle Eastern base. Following five years of cool relations after the Cyprus action, rapprochement feelers included signals of tacit assent to a coup. Given martial law, the continued swirl of domestic violence was improbable without military toleration – and/or agents provocateurs to furnish a pretext for a full-scale takeover.

Coup number three

It was soon obvious that this coup would not resemble the previous two. A junta of generals, not junior officers – the **National Security Council** (NSC) – controlled matters, and return to civilian rule would be long delayed. Bannings, indictments and purges proceeded apace, and while the radical Right was not immune, the Left bore the brunt of prosecutions. Nationalist right-wing beliefs, if not violent or fascist, were compatible with the NSC agenda – as were mildly Islamic views, as long as fundamentalists stayed out of the military.

The NSC's principal targets, relatively untouched in prior putsches, were labour unions, internationalist or separatist groups and the left-leaning intelligentsia, all crippled by show trials that dragged on so long that many defendants walked free based on time served on remand. NSP leader Necmettin Erbakan was acquitted on charges of attempting to create an Islamic state. The MHP was decimated by eight capital verdicts and dozens of prison-terms – though leader Türkeş was acquitted. The military purged university staff, and all campuses were supervised by a Higher Education Council (YÖK).

A committee of carefully vetted applicants drew up a new, highly restrictive constitution in 1982, countermanding most of its 1960 predecessor. This was ratified by ninety percent of the electorate in a coercive referendum, also an election for the presidency. No campaigning against was allowed; the only candidate was NSC chief **General Kenan Evren**, and it was an all-or-nothing package.

This occurred bloodlessly on September 12, 1980, to the initial relief of most Turks. The frenzied killing ceased; all political parties were disbanded, their leaders detained; all trade unions and NGOs were closed down. Turgut Özal was, however, left in charge of the economy, since his reforms were seen as both effective and essential for Western support.

Return to civilian rule: ANAP

Pre-coup parties and personalities remained banned at heavily supervised November 1983 elections, which only three new parties contested. But the generals' centrist slate came last, as Turgut Özal's centre-right Motherland Party (ANAP) won just under half the votes and just over half of parliamentary seats.

ANAP was a party of uneasy alliance incorporating a wide range of opinion from economic liberals to Islamists. Özal embodied these contradictions in his person: though a devout Muslim, ex-member of the NSP and adherent of the still-clandestine Nakşibendi order, he had strong appetites for booze, tobacco, food and *arabesk* tunes, while his charismatic speaking-manner belied a Texan engineering degree. He juggled ANAP's technocratic and traditionalist factions while introducing sweeping economic reforms, with record export levels and six percent growth rates. Inflation and foreign debt, however, soared, as budgets were swollen.

ANAP (and Özal) can be credited with ushering Turkey into the world economy but an ostentatious display of wealth created an ethical climate conducive to corruption. A provincial elite, sharing Özal's small-town, lower-middle-class background, earned an initial reputation of "getting things done". While trained abroad, they hadn't necessarily absorbed Western values, and when they had, their model was Texas, not Europe. English became their lingua franca, and of many universities, which under YÖK's watchful eye became apolitical polytechnics.

Pre-coup politicians were un-banned by referendum in mid-1987; November parliamentary elections gave just 36 percent to ANAP but, thanks to a skewed system, nearly two-thirds of the seats. The Social Democrat Party (SHP) emerged as the main opposition, despite perceptions of leader **Erdal İnönü**, professor-turned politician and son of İsmet, as a nice but ineffectual individual unkindly nicknamed "ET" after his resemblance to Spielberg's hero.

Özal's two prime-ministerial terms saw a dramatic, deliberate increase in Islamic activity, to offset Iranian-style fundamentalism and leftist ideology. The Department of Religious Affairs expanded, mandatory teaching of Islam in schools increased and *vakıfs* swelled with Saudi donations. **Kurdish separatism** resurfaced violently in the southeast, courtesy of the Kurdish Workers' Party (PKK), strengthened by over-zealous reaction of the authorities (see pp.712–713).

Ties with Greece were strained by Cyprus, plus disputes over Aegean airspace and territorial waters, and by the Greek government's harassment of ethnic Turks in Greek Thrace. Bulgarian-Turkish relations made headlines during summer 1989, as the Communist Bulgarian regime's policy of forced Slavification ultimately escalated into the largest European **mass emigration** since World War II. Over 300,000 ethnic Turks fled Bulgaria for Turkey, which initially welcomed them and tried to capitalize politically on the exodus. The numbers soon hit home, however, the border was shut by August, and in 1990 Sofia's new post-communist government renounced the heavy-handed assimilationist campaign, while many new arrivals returned to Bulgaria or emigrated to western Europe.

Much effort went to countering proposals in the United States Congress to designate April 24 as a day of "national remembrance" for the 1915 deportations of the Ottoman Armenian community. Finally, the dramatic 1989 changes in Eastern Europe further marginalized Turkey, as its post-Cold War importance became moot.

In contrast to Turkey's concern for Turkish minorities abroad, **human rights violations** continued at home with inhumane prison conditions, torture of suspects and increased prosecutions of journalists and publishers testing the limits of censorship. Özal in particular reacted to even mild criticism with dozens of libel suits.

Özal as president

ANAP's influence was waning due to hyperinflation and blatant nepotism benefiting Özal's cronies and extended family – including his flamboyant, cigar-smoking wife Semra. Under the circumstances most observers found his self-nomination for the **presidency** – and election in November 1989 by a half-empty parliament – presumptuous. Only the second civilian president, and officially "above-party", Özal still acted as the ANAP chief. He chose the next prime minister, Yıldırım Akbulut, a lacklustre yes-man, then repeatedly undermined him.

Iraq's August 1990 **invasion of Kuwait** reinforced Özal's position, and reiterated Turkey's strategic importance. Özal signed Turkey up as an enthusiastic adherent of sanctions, in anticipation of tangible benefits in return. He invited the US to use İncirlik and Diyarbakır airbases, incurred considerable financial loss by closing the pipeline shipping Iraqi oil through Turkey, and permitted coalition troops near the Iraqi Kurdish "safe haven". Özal perhaps entertained hopes that Turkey would be rewarded after the 1991 war by the annexation of oil-rich Mosul. All he got was Bush the Elder's promise that an independent Kurdistan would not emerge from a dismembered Iraq, and a July visit – the first of an American president to Turkey since the 1950s.

Domestic politics, meanwhile, featured a yawning policy vacuum and sterile feuding. The only political consensus concerned the posthumous rehabilitation of Menderes, an act of contrition involving numerous streets and public facilities being renamed after him, and – on the thirtieth anniversary of the hangings of the three ministers – their solemn reburial in a special İstanbul mausoleum.

Early October 1991 polls, the fairest ever, surprisingly had DYP finishing first, ANAP a strong second, İnönü's SHP third – and Erbakan's Islamist Welfare Party (Refah Partisi) a close fourth. A DYP–SHP coalition, with Demirel prime minister and İnönü deputy prime minister, began with both parties pledging to pull together in rescuing the economy. The task of curbing inflation was assigned to Tansu Çiller, the sole woman cabinet-member.

There were also promises to make Turkey a *konuşan* (talking) society, where opinions were freely aired without fear of retribution. This ideal ran aground immediately when some of the 22 Kurdish HEP MPs – compelled to run on the SHP national ticket – refused to recite the standard loyalty oath upon being sworn in. An un-banning of pre-1980 parties revived the Republican People's Party (CHP); the contest to assume its leadership between Ecevit, İnönü or SHP general secretary Deniz Baykal was won by Baykal (still the chair).

During 1992 Özal played an increasingly negative role, goaded by a hatred of Demirel; Özal also feuded with new ANAP premier Mesut Yılmaz, attempting to unseat his protégé. As president, Özal delayed signing many bills, prompting discussion of impeaching him. This proved unnecessary when Özal died suddenly of a heart attack on April 17, 1993.

Özal, despite his many faults, was the most eloquent and influential head of state since Atatürk. Respected by many for his energy, courage and vision, despised by an equal number for his overbearing manner and shameless self-aggrandizement, he remains an ambiguous figure who sometimes did the right thing (eg, advocating concessions to the Kurds) for opportunistic reasons.

After Özal, chaos

Demirel eventually emerged as president, while **Tansu Çiller** became prime minister in June 1993. Like many centre-right politicians, she was a US-educated technocrat recruited by Demirel. With her assertive style and telegenic manner, her rise to power was initially viewed positively, though she soon proved woefully inadequate. Hopes of a fresh take on Kurdish issues vanished as Çiller deferred to military hardliners, the death toll in east Anatolia rocketed and the latest Kurdish-interests party (DEP) was proscribed. Inflation shot up to a staggering 120 percent, before dipping to "only" 80 percent. Substantive privatization and tax reform failed to materialize, while industrial disasters with large loss of life made headlines. Major **corruption scandals** erupted regularly; no party escaped guilt, as all had governed recently. In 1996 an Associated Press article listed Tansu Çiller among the world's ten most corrupt politicians, so unsurprisingly sleaze remained endemic in public life.

The only significant – if controversial – foreign-policy success was the March 1995 customs union with the EU. Overseas, there was stiff opposition because of Turkey's poor human rights record; domestic opponents noted that considerable import duties were being forfeited, while Turks would still not have freedom of movement in Europe. Though falling well short of EU membership, the agreement, applied incrementally between 1996 and 2000, was brandished as a triumph by the beleaguered coalition.

Turkey's **human rights record** has been a perennial irritant in foreign relations. Notwithstanding Demirel's 1991 pledge that police stations would have "walls of glass", there was little significant change for years, with torture and suspicious deaths in custody frequent, and Turkish jails holding over a hundred nonviolent political prisoners well into the new millennium. Civilian governments deferred to the internal security forces, which, together with elements of the State Security Tribunals, the police and the gendarmerie, formed a para-state – the so-called **"deep state"** (*derin devlet*) – accountable to no one.

Urban terrorism re-emerged in the 1990s, with political assassinations perpetrated by Islamists, far-leftists and rogue operatives of the Special Warfare Department, with police mysteriously unable to identify suspects. Targets included army officers; secularist professors; prominent lawyers; and the Jewish community. The murder of prominent journalist **Uğur Mumcu** in a 1993 Ankara car-bombing caused widespread revulsion. His funeral, attended by hundreds of thousands, included mass demonstrations of support for his secularist, democratic ideals. As ever, nobody significant was apprehended, prompting allegations of a cover-up and/or involvement of the "deep state". Another feature of the era was numerous **"disappeared" persons** – usually left-wing or Kurdish activists who vanished after being detained by police or unidentified civilians.

Following his January 1995 article in *Der Spiegel* describing the Turkish state as a "system of unbearable repression and atrocity" and deeming the Kurdish rebellion a justifiable response to official repression, prominent novelist **Yaşar Kemal** was charged with promulgating "separatist propaganda" and fomenting "hatred between races". With the European customs-union ratification at stake, he was given a suspended sentence in March 1996 after a year-long trial, but not before 99 other prosecutions against artists and intellectuals who supported him. Similar court cases and violent incidents [including the attempted assassination of the İHD (Turkey's Human Rights Association chief)] continued until the unprecedented liberalization laws of summer 2002.

But there was another upsurge in 2005, occasioned by penal code Article 301's making it a crime to "denigrate Turkishness" and by **Orhan Pamuk**'s attempted prosecution under it for comments to a Swiss newspaper asserting the killing of a million Armenians and 40,000 Kurds. Worse was to come, when – after also being prosecuted under Article 301 – **Hrant Dink**, proprietor of Armenian-Turkish newspaper *Agos*, was assassinated on January 19, 2007 by a young nationalist acting at the behest of Trabzon "deep state"-ers. Dink's funeral, attended by 100,000, became a protest with chants of "We are all Armenians!".

Even before Çiller's term began, the coalition was becoming unpopular, with a bare majority of three, while her many enemies – including Demirel and Yılmaz – fuelled intrigues. Racked by dissension, the SHP dissolved in February 1995, the remnants merging with the CHP. In September Baykal and Çiller dissolved the coalition; elections were set for December.

The rise and fall of Refah

The results furnished a rude shock for established parties, with Islamist **Refah** the top vote-getter, supported by the urban underclass, devout Kurds and disparate individuals fed up with the discredited mainstream parties. The establishment attempted to bar Refah from office, but a patchwork coalition of second-bests

The source of Islamist politics

In post-1923 Turkey, "secularism" means the state controlling religious affairs and suppressing public expressions of Islam. An official ban on **traditional Islamic dress** in state facilities effectively bars many young people of conservative social background from a public career, or even admittance to university. But for most Turks, Islam remains a much stronger values-source than assertive Westernizing, and a more homespun expression of national spirit than the quasi-colonial arrogance associated with the Kemalist elite, which offers little spiritual succour.

soon fell apart. DYP leader Çiller, under investigation for corruption, negotiated a coalition with Refah provided all proceedings against her ceased. Erbakan became prime minister, with Çiller as his deputy; the NSC, at this point with mixed civilian-military membership, geared up to safeguard secularism. In June 1997, Erbakan was forced out in the so-called "**soft coup**", replaced by an unlikely ANAP-DSP coalition.

Seven months later, Refah was closed down (for "acting against the principles of the secular Republic"); the Islamists regrouped as the Fazilet party, but in September 1998 the popular Fazilet mayor of İstanbul (and future prime minister), **Recep Tayyip Erdoğan**, was jailed for four months for a speech the prosecution claimed "incited armed fundamentalist rebellion". He had in fact quoted from a poem by Ziya Gökalp, main architect of secular Turkish nationalism. Erdoğan was respected for both literally and figuratively cleaning up İstanbul, and his imprisonment was widely regarded as a hollow victory by a suspect establishment over an honest (if "Islamist") politician. In November, the coalition collapsed as Prime Minister Yılmaz was accused of corruption.

April 1999 elections had the MHP under new chief Devlet Bahçeli finishing second, not far behind Bulent Ecevit's DSP. Fourth-placed ANAP, together with the two front-running parties, formed yet another unwieldy coalition, excluding third-placed Fazilet.

Earthquake – and meltdown

On August 17, 1999 a catastrophic **earthquake** struck the eastern Marmara region, killing almost 40,000. Many died trapped in shoddily built tower-blocks, exposing the corruption of local authorities who had allowed building and zoning codes to be flouted. Both the shambolic emergency response and the army were criticized, with soldiers tending to their own rather than joining the rescue effort. Ironically, the earthquake had lasting positive consequences. Substantial material aid and sympathy from Greece – whose aid teams were first on the scene – heralded a sustained thaw in bilateral relations. In December 1999 Greece dropped its objections to Turkish accession and Turkey became an official candidate for eventual **EU membership**.

A wave of private bank failures preceded a definitive economic crash in February 2001. The Turkish lira – formerly tied to the dollar in an IMF-backed plan – was free-floated; the exchange rate (and domestic inflation) soared as the value of lira investments and wages plummeted. The crisis forced sweeping monetary reforms under the aegis of veteran World Bank supremo Kemal Derviş.

In June, Fazilet was banned for "anti-secular activities", specifically inciting protests against the prohibition of headscarf-donning by women in schools and government offices. The closure proved futile as the **AK** (*Adalet ve Kalkınma*, Justice and Development) Party, led by former İstanbul mayor Erdoğan, replaced it immediately.

By mid-2002, PM Ecevit was an invalid, the DSP had imploded, the economy had contracted eight percent and Turkey had become the IMF's single biggest debtor. More positively, despite the imminent end of the coalition, legislators passed several **EU-required reforms** touching on human rights and freedom of expression. The death penalty was abolished, press freedom increased and education and broadcasting in several minority languages was now theoretically permissible.

Start of the AK era

Given the preceding stasis, the **AK swept to power** easily on November 3, 2002, on 34 percent of the vote. For the first time since 1987 Turkey had a majority government, and if it failed in the job ahead it would not be able to blame coalition bickering. The only other parliamentary party was the CHP; all others failed to clear the ten percent nationwide minimum. By European standards, this is exceptionally high, but other parties, having benefited handsomely from this bar (introduced by the 1982 constitution to exclude "minority or regional" – ie Kurdish – parties) weren't in a position to complain.

Turkey's secularist establishment suspected that AK would soon drag the nation into an **Islamic theocracy**; instead, given stable government, Turkey's economy revived. More remarkable was the new government's commitment to compliance with EU directives by introducing 36 reforms meeting the "Copenhagen criteria" of acceptable civic practice. Both foreign and domestic observers appreciated the irony of Turkey's EU membership quest – and meaningful reform – being pursued more fervently by an "Islamic" government than by any of the country's previous secularist governments.

In early 2003, Turkey declined to be used as a springboard for the **US-led invasion of Iraq**. Eventually Parliament voted (on March 20, invasion day) to allow US planes to overfly Turkish airspace, but Turkish–American relations had already hit an all-time low. Turkey's reluctance to be involved stemmed from fears that the war would lead to a Kurdish state, and that the country might suffer a terrorist backlash. On November 15, 2003 car bombs exploded outside İstanbul synagogues, killing 25 and injuring 300. Five days later, suicide car-bombers targeted the British consulate and the HSBC bank, killing 30 and injuring 450. Although the perpetrators were linked to al-Qaeda, they proved to be ethnic Kurds from the southeast.

The long-running **Cyprus problem** continued to bedevil foreign affairs and Turkey's EU quest. A UN-devised reunification scheme backed by (and rather favourable to) Turkey seemed to offer hope that the long-divided island would unify under the EU umbrella. But on April 24, 2004, despite a solid majority (65 percent) of Turkish Cypriots voting in favour, 75 percent of Greek Cypriots rejected it in the necessary referendum. A week later southern (Greek) Cyprus joined the EU on behalf of the whole island. Turks – unaccustomed to occupying the moral high ground on Cyprus – were understandably annoyed.

On October 3, 2005, **accession talks** for Turkey's joining the EU formally began. A November EU report criticized human rights issues, military–civilian relations and inequality but, more positively, praised the "functioning market economy." The AK government had proven a competent manager under IMF guidelines, with inflation down to single figures for the first time in decades.

AK's second term

After a relatively quiet 2006, 2007 began tumultuously with the **assassination of Hrant Dink** (see p.708). For many, the enduring power of the "deep state" was demonstrated by photographs showing the underage assassin posing with a Turkish flag in front of a poster of Atatürk, flanked by smiling police. This fundamental rift in Turkish society was evident as liberal Turks marched in solidarity with İstanbul's Armenian community, while ultra-nationalists viewed the deed as a heroic defence of the homeland.

In spring 2007, AK nominated foreign minister **Abdullah Gül** as president over military objections, particularly as Gül's wife publicly wore a headscarf. In what became known as the **"e-coup"** the military posted an online warning, hinting they might act if Gül were appointed. Millions of secular Turks took to the streets in orchestrated rallies against Gül's candidacy and what they saw as creeping Islamicization. The threat of a coup forced an early election in July 2007, in which the AK party captured 47 percent of the vote, the first time in fifty years that a party had won a second term in office with an increased majority. Ominously the CHP lost seats to the MHP, now back in parliament along with Kurdish independents. Gül was duly elected president and attention focused on the **headscarf issue** once again, as the AK party attempted to repeal a 1998 law forbidding its wearing in universities. In response the state prosecutor filed a case against the party early in 2008 for "anti-secular activities". In July, the constitutional court by a one-vote margin declined to wind up AK, but deprived the party of state funding as a warning. Legislation introduced by the party allowing the headscarf to be worn in universities was overturned, the guardians of the state having deemed it "an expression of Islamic sympathies in a state institution".

With France and Germany openly hostile to Turkish EU membership, and Erdoğan failing to implement more reforms, the **accession process** stalled. The 2008 global slump hit the economy badly, and despite a banking system annealed by the 2001 crisis, the TL tumbled against other currencies and by mid 2009 unemployment stood at over 16 percent. Erdoğan's feistyness won him admirers and critics in equal measure when he stormed out of a February Davos summit after an altercation with Israeli president Shimon Peres over Gaza. The Arab world (and domestic supporters) applauded, but Israelis, who normally visit Turkey in droves, responded by cancelling their holidays there.

The Ergenekon Conspiracy

The alleged **Ergenekon conspiracy** was revealed in June 2007, with defendants finally sent to trial in late 2008. The plot, a variation on the usual methods of the "deep state", had long been hinted at in the media. But the sight of high-ranking generals (albeit retired ones), a *jandarma* commander, a lawyer, a nationalist politician, journalists, academics and mafiosi charged with membership in an armed terrorist group, attempted overthrow of the (AK) government, and treason, was one the Turkish public never thought they'd witness. The group is accused of carrying out high-profile provocateur assassinations (including Dink's) and bombings of secularist entities such as the *Cumhuriyet* newspaper, to create the impression that Kemalism was under threat from Islamic extremists and thus justify a coup. The case drags on as of writing, with ever more suspects being arrested and arms and explosives caches uncovered in unlikely places. Advocates say that the "deep state" is finally being decisively confronted; detractors dismiss the proceedings as a frame-up concocted by a vindictive AK regime.

March 2009 local elections gave only 39 percent of the vote to AK, and many municipalities (especially on the south and west coasts) were recaptured by the CHP. Declining support – despite an attempt to buy votes by issuing slum-dwellers with titles to their illegal shacks – may be why AK has been reluctant to enact new EU-orientated reform, though cynics say their initial policies were just window-dressing to attract swing voters. They did manage, however, to pass legislation enabling military figures to be tried in civilian courts, thus reducing chances of a future coup. Europe approved, while the supposedly progressive CHP objected, referring the measure to the Constitutional Court.

The Kurdish question

The **Kurds** inhabit several Middle Eastern countries, including Iran, Iraq and Syria, but the largest population is in southeastern Turkey. Present in Anatolia long before the Turks, they are of Indo-European origin and language, and until the twentieth century were largely a tribal, nomadic people. Their dominant faiths are the same as the Turks – Sunni Islam, with significant numbers of Alevî. As Kurds are not recognized as a minority by Turkey, accurate figures are debatable, but at least twelve million (and up to twenty) of the country's seventy-million-plus population is ethnically Kurdish.

A history of rebellion

Relations between the Ottomans and the Kurds were generally good, and successive sultans let the Kurds, split into semi-autonomous federations, act as a buffer between the Ottoman Empire and Russia or Persia. After the collapse of the Ottoman Empire, most Kurds supported Kemal's Nationalists in the independence struggle; following the Republican victory, however, relations began to sour. Many Kurds had backed the Turkish nationalists as co-religionists, but when Atatürk abolished the caliphate in 1924 they were outraged, especially as all institutions of a specifically Kurdish nature were also closed down.

The initial response was a revolt under Nakşibendi dervish şeyh Said; then a more overtly nationalist insurrection broke out near Mount Ararat, not quelled until 1929. A 1936 rebellion further west in the Alevî Kurdish heartland of Dersim (modern Tunceli) lasted two years. The Turkish state crushed each uprising with executions, expulsions to western Anatolia, and supression of all expressions of ethnic identity. The entire southeast became a military zone, closed to foreigners until the 1960s, with a backward, stagnant economy.

The PKK and its guerilla war

Inevitably, an extremist organization – the **PKK** (Kurdish Workers' Party) – emerged in 1978 in reaction to such forced-assimilation policies. Its founder, political-science student Abdullah Öcalan, set up a nominally Marxist guerrilla group intent on independence for Turkey's Kurds. The PKK's appeal lay in cutting across traditional tribal loyalties, offering something to those at the very bottom of the clan hierarchies, and it thrived in the repressive atmosphere after the 1980 coup. In 1984, from Syrian bases, the PKK began launching attacks against the *jandarma* and army; later it began to target civil servants, especially teachers.

PKK power peaked in the mid-1990s, with over 15,000 guerillas in the field. The state barely controlled some parts of the southeast as the PKK encouraged mass civil disobedience, schools closed as teachers refused to operate in the danger zone, and the army forcibly evacuated thousands of settlements to stop villagers (willingly or unwillingly) aiding the PKK. Successive pro-Kurdish political parties, accused by the state (sometimes correctly) of being fronts for the PKK, were closed down and their leaders imprisoned. By 1998, however, the army's superior tactics and weaponry began to tell, and in 1999 Öcalan, having been expelled from his base in

Trends for the future

Thus far AK has successfully challenged the so-called "**White Turks**" – mostly of Balkan descent – comprising the army, academia, civil service, big business and much of the media, who have run the republic since 1923. AK and its supporters, despite being mostly devout and lower-middle-class, ostensibly view EU entry as the best way to raise their voters' standard of living and promote reform. The burning question is whether AK is genuinely liberal, or merely introducing Islamic theocracy by the back door, as their opponents assert.

Damascus, was captured in Kenya with CIA and Mossad aid. Convicted of treason and murder, Öcalan was imprisoned on İmrali island in the Sea of Marmara, where he still languishes.

Despite these setbacks, the PKK had succeeded in putting Turkey's Kurdish issue on both the domestic and world stages. In 2005, PM Erdoğan departed from official doctrine that there were no Kurds in Turkey – "mountain Turks" were historically the code words – by referring, in a speech at Diyarbakır, unofficial capital of Turkish Kurdistan, to the "Kurdish problem". Prohibitions on the public use of Kurdish were lifted, private courses in the language permitted and in 2008 a state-broadcast Kurdish channel opened to great fanfare (and controversy).

Prospects for the future

The bloody struggle between Turkish forces and the PKK has indisputably polarized Turkish society. Many Turkish families have lost sons, and the sight of them weeping as the Turkish-flag-draped coffin of their loved one is borne through the streets of their hometown is a familiar sight on TV. The less scrupulous media exploit this to stoke nationalist feelings, and most processions are accompanied by chants of "Martyrs don't die, the homeland can't be divided". But in fact the majority of the 45,000-plus estimated to have lost their lives in the conflict are of Kurdish origin.

The PKK, now down to perhaps 5,000 combatants based on Mount Kandil in Iraqi Kurdistan, continue attacks across remote stretches of the Turkish–Iraqi frontier, usually using remote-controlled mines to blow up military vehicles. Turkish Kurds have since 1986 been divided by the village-guard system, which exploits local rivalries with around 55,000 gun-toting, state-paid militiamen "protecting" their village against PKK attack. The southeast's economy is otherwise ruined, and millions of Kurds have emigrated westward in search of work. This has led to tension in some cities, as the often poorly educated new arrivals bring a different way of life (and language) with them – and compete on the local job and housing markets. Many Kurds are in turn resentful about having to leave their homes to face discrimination in the west.

There are grounds for cautious optimism, however. The ethnic genie is now out of the bottle, which at least means the Kurdish question can be openly discussed. The PKK have announced a new goal of cultural and linguistic rights rather than independence, and the Turkish state may be willing to compromise, by removing provocative Turkish nationalist slogans (such as "How happy is he who can say 'I am a Turk'") from the hillsides of the southeast, and permitting settlements to use their original Kurdish names rather than the Turkish ones imposed early in the Republic. Investigations are probing an illegal branch of the *jandarma* responsible for thousands of extra-judicial killings of Kurds during the 1980s and 1990s. If Turkey continues to implement EU-mandated reforms, there is hope that Turks and Kurds can heal the wounds of the past few decades and co-exist peaceably in a more inclusive, fully democratic Turkey.

Paradoxically, a secular elite of strange bedfellows apparently opposes EU accession of a truly democratic Turkey: nationalists loathing the prospect of increased minority rights, military brass who'd be denied the role of national guardians, old-style leftists who brand the EU as an imperialist plot. The **Ergenekon case** (see box, p.711) may be a litmus test of whether the country will turn out a truly democratic state with a conservative, Muslim majority, or one ruled by a military/bureaucratic elite intent on preserving its privileges at all costs. A solution to the interrelated **Kurdish problem** (see box, p.712) is also crucial.

A substantial body of European opinion views Turkey as a Third World country inherently unsuitable for membership in a "white, Christian" club which would be overwhelmed by Turkey's geographically lopsided development and demographic profile. This in turn has sparked a resentful attitude amongst many Turks, and support for accession has dropped noticeably.

Turkey's **economy** is far more resilient than formerly, with consumer spending steady and foreign investment flooding in – especially since 2002 – from the Gulf states (but also through the purchase of second homes by Europeans). Particularly important is the country's role as a oil and natural gas conduit, with pipelines from Russia, Azerbaijan and Kazakhstan all crossing Turkish territory. In 2009 a deal was signed to pipe gas from Iran to Western Europe. **Tourism** is also crucial, and increasing annual visitor numbers topped 23 million in 2008. But unemployment, exacerbated by rural depopulation, remains stubbornly high, while the poor educational system cannot produce sufficient well-trained workers. Despite lip service to the Islamic tenet of alms-giving, AK has done nothing to reduce the massive gap between rich and poor, second only to Brazil's.

Turkey is rapidly becoming a major regional power as the country, under moderate Islamist government, is viewed as a bulwark against Islamic extremism. As the US leaves Iraq, the Turks anxiously contemplate the de facto independent Kurdish entity on its southeastern frontier. Turkey's links with the Arab World have improved, including plans to de-mine the Syrian frontier, and many wealthy Arabs holiday and invest in the country. What could derail good relations is a "water war": the Euphrates and Tigris rivers, crucial to both Syria and Iraq, have their headwaters in Turkey, and the dams (some complete, others still projected) of the gigantic GAP project (see p.619) threaten these two countries' water supplies. Turkey's **relationship with Israel**, though currently frosty, remains solid, with the Israeli air force using Turkish airspace for training.

In the Caucasus, Turkey assiduously cultivates **Azerbaijan**, a nation not only ethnically Turkish (if Shi'ite), but also petroleum-rich. Until recently, this precluded links with **Armenia** following its occupation of the ethnically Armenian Azerbaijani enclave of Nagorno-Karabagh in 1992. But abruptly in autumn 2009, a blueprint for normalizing relations was announced jointly, to be ratified by each country – though nationalists on both sides denounced it, Armenian ones because it skirted the "genocide" issue (see box, p.696).

Turkey has also shown increased interest in its former Balkan territories, especially those retaining Muslim populations. Albania has received military training and civilian advisers, and Turkey was among the first countries to recognize Macedonia. But the biggest surprise is strong links with Greece in trade, banking and tourism.

Music

Overseas, Turkish music was long considered mere accompaniment to belly dancing or, more recently, to Mevlevî ("Whirling") dervish ritual. But beyond these stereotypes there's far more, from refined classical to camp *arabesk* by way of rural bards and fiery Gypsy ensembles. Turkish music is at best the millennial legacy of the many Anatolian civilizations, at worst globally marketed pop music with a bit of exotic color.

Music and politics

Music became a political battlefield early in republican years. The new state strove to construct a unitary national culture, emphasizing the ancestry of "true" Turks in central Asia, and anything that could distance contemporary Turks from neighbouring Middle Easterners. Atatürk declared "The capacity of a country to change is demonstrated by its ability to change its music" and his cadres set about doing so by banning lyrics in minority languages from the state radio as well as, briefly, Ottoman classical music which was considered tainted by Arab culture and Islam.

"Genuine" folk and Western classical music were decreed to be the oddly twinned musical destinies of Turkey. Accordingly, officially funded musicologists traversed Anatolia from the late 1920s onwards, archiving and recording the folk repertoire. While valuable material was rescued for posterity, distortions born of ideology and the inherent limitations of the collecting process crept in. Melodies were standardized, ensemble playing mandated, and improvisation or non-Turkish lyrics frowned on, on air as well as in the field.

A generation of musicians was trained in special schools to propagate orally transmitted folk music through written scores, performed in choral-orchestral settings; composer-researcher Muzaffer Sarısözen, founder of the Radio Ankara folk ensemble, and singer Neriman Altındağ, first female chief of its choir, were key in this. Their disciples dominated TRT (state radio and television) until the 1980s, faithful to the ideal of a hybrid Western/Anatolian music.

Such restrictive policies eventually ran aground. The *sanat* genre (see p.719), associated with cosmopolitan, Ottoman İstanbul, İzmir and Bursa, slowly recovered. After 1930 such a group reformed at the İstanbul municipal conservatory, and there were other, semi-tolerated Turkish classical music societies which provided musicians for the state radio. The process culminated in the 1976 foundation of a dedicated conservatory in İstanbul. Here Turkish classical musicians were given the same quality training as the previously privileged folk musicians and could teach unhindered, while *klasik* ensembles got steadily increasing broadcast air time.

A decade later, Prime Minister Özal began deregulating the media as part of his stealthy dismantling of Atatürkist values. Pop, rock and *arabesk* (see p.721) appeared on private FM radio stations, plus satellite and cable TV channels which burgeoned semi-legally. Faced with competition, TRT updated its formats while still retaining talented performers. More startlingly, music with minority-language lyrics could be heard either live in trendy İstanbul cafés or on recordings.

So too could **Sufi music**. Following the forcible suppression of all dervish orders in 1925, its music was driven deep underground. Individual Mevlevîs had been music patrons across the Ottoman Empire, but until the 1980s, the Mevlevî *âyin* (musical ritual) was performed in public only for tourists in Konya, historical base of the order – but where no living tradition now existed. The Mevlevîs were prime beneficiaries of Özal's reforms, which encouraged a public face for Islam; the order now performs in several locations. Archival and contemporary recordings are easily available, though this is primarily a reflection of Western interest in Sufi and Ottoman high culture. By contrast, **Alevî music** is a living tradition but the current government, despite lip service to religious freedom, seems distinctly uninterested in allowing it to flourish, enforcing Sunni religious education and building mosques in villages where the Alevîs' *cem* house is the real place of worship. Music is fundamental to the Alevî ceremony (*cem*) which includes prayers, singing and the *sema* (a circle dance). The **bağlama**, dubbed "the stringed koran", is a sacred object, a symbol of the İmam Ali. Special tuning results in a particularly sombre, intense sound, with complex chord patterns.

Folk music

Folk music is, despite (or because of) recent massive rural migration to towns, the most popular genre in Turkey. A generation of younger singers interpreting traditional material in new orchestrations, plus top performers bringing the music to prestigious concert halls, have made it commercially viable and respected. The spiritual current of Alevî mysticism is powerful and influential throughout.

Turkish folk music is dominated by the **saz**, a long-necked fretted lute with seven strings in three clusters, and its variant the *bağlama*. Played with or without a plectrum in regional styles and tunings, the *saz* in particular has a silvery tone, providing not just notes and rhythmic patterns, but an ambience. In Ali Ekber Çicek's dramatic *Haydar Haydar*, it's hard to say whether the instrument is accompanying the voice, or vice versa. Compare this to Talip Özkan's intricate solo style, embracing idiosyncratic tunings and plectrum techniques, with each phrase embellished and nuanced.

Regions and ethnicity

Various types of folk music now flourish, recognizable by associated instruments and dances. The quintessential **rural ceremonial music** of *zurna* (shawm) and *davul* (double-sided bass drum) is ubiquitous at weddings or circumcisions. Often played by Gypsies, their enormous unamplified volume is inevitably accompanied by **dancing**. In the east this will usually be the *halay* line-dance (hands linked or arms on shoulders); on the Aegean coast the odd-metered *zeybek*; and almost everywhere the couples' dances *çiftetelli* and *karşılama*. Along the Black Sea a small, upright, three-stringed fiddle (*kemençe*), bagpipe (*tulum*) and smaller versions of *davul* accompany the *horon* circle-dance. These are danced by university students, political protesters or football fans; a Black Sea step, the *kolbastı*, is currently enjoying enormous popularity. In provincial cities *elektrosaz* (amplified *saz*) with keyboards and *darbuka* (goblet drum) constitute the main musical fare for celebrations held in *düğünsalonları* (wedding salons for hire).

Contemporary musicians update and reinvent regional styles, creating universally accessible music. Especially active are artists from the eastern Black Sea coast, home to the ethnic Laz group, from *kemençe* and *tulum* player plus folkloric collector Birol Topaloğlu, to popular singer-songwriters Fuat Saka, Volkan Konak and the late Kazım Koyuncu. *Türkü* (folk song) bars, where young musicians play traditional material on rock instruments, have multiplied in larger towns.

Bozlak is free-rhythm, semi-improvised declamation of scorching intensity, somewhat akin to flamenco, associated with the Abdal sect. The singer sings, literally, at the top of his voice, and the *saz* is tuned in open fifths for dramatic melodic flourishes and a sparse, astringent sound. Neşet Ertaş from Kirşehir, son of Muharrem Ertaş, another *bozlak* singer of mythic reputation, enjoys cultic veneration amongst enthusiasts. Traditionally a male preserve, *bozlak* is now being attempted successfully by female singers.

Traditionally, **Kurdish** cultural identity was preserved by the *dengbey* (bard), the *stranbey* (popular singer) and the *cirokbey* (storyteller). A *dengbey* must have an exceptional memory to master hundreds of songs existing only in oral tradition. *Dengbeys* chronicle Kurdish legends, rebellions and successive rulers and occupiers, as well as interpreting love songs and lighter entertainment. Owing to recurrent strife in the southeastern Kurdish areas, some of the best *dengbeys*, like Şivan Perwer and Temo, live exiled in northern Europe, as did Kurdish left-wing militant Ahmet Kaya (died 2000 in Paris) whose first album *Ağlama Bebeğim* was also the first recording to be banned by the Supreme Court in the 1980s. Since the late 1990s, however, optional Kurdish-language schooling, and Kurdish-language radio/TV broadcasting have begun, along with incremental relaxation of bans on public Kurdish musical events and recordings.

The aşıks

Aşıks are the folk troubadours nurtured by the Alevî tradition. Originally Muslim communities allied to Shi'ism, especially in Sivas, Tunceli, Çorum and Erzincan provinces, Alevîs (some twenty percent of the population) are now settled across Turkey. *Aşıks* purportedly receive gifts of musical and spiritual knowledge imparted while in a trance by the prophet İlyas (Elijah); literally "the ones in love", they sing of mystical quest, plus invocations to the various Alevî saints as well as Ali, Muhammad's brother-in-law. At the core of their repertoire are the poems of Pir Sultan Abdal, a sixteenth-century *aşık* martyr, and of Şah Hatayi, nom de plume of Şah Ismail, founder of the Safavid state defeated at Çaldıran 1514.

The most celebrated *aşık* was Aşık Veysel (1894–1973), born in Sivas province. Blinded aged seven by smallpox, he was taught by local *saz* masters. His most famous songs, such as "Dostlar Beni Hatırlasın" (May My Friends Remember Me), "Kara Toprak" (Black Earth) and "Uzun İnce Bir Yoldayım" (I'm on a Long Difficult Journey), mystical contemplations on the human condition, are still sung. Like many Alevî he strongly endorsed the young republic, which seemed to promise the social change Alevîs had always favoured, and lent his talents to official efforts to explain the new regime.

An *aşık* revival was encouraged in the early 1970s by opera singer and *saz*-player Ruhi Su. Though not Alevî, he was uncompromisingly left-wing and thus lost his job at the state opera; later he was denied a passport to go abroad to treat the cancer which killed him. Musa Eroğlu began singing traditional songs of his hometown Mersin, and now he's considered the purest contemporary incarnation of the *aşık* tradition. Arif Sağ, Eroğlu, Yavuz Top, and the late Muhlis Akarsu (killed along with 37 other bards in a 1993 Sivas hotel fire set by Sunni fundamentalists) have made excellent recordings both as a group, Muhabbet, and individually. The best *aşık* music has always had a latent political content; songs by **Ali İzzet** and Mahsuni Şerif, popular with the 1960s urban left, ranged from passionate denunciations of social injustice to gentle satires on Turkish football, and have been revived by a new generation. Feyzullah Çınar is an impressive, recent representative of this tradition, "discovered" at the annual gathering of *aşık*s at the mausoleum of Hacı Bektaş Veli, founder of the Bektaşi order.

*Aşık*s traditionally make their living as café entertainers and storytellers, with audiences enjoying ritualized exchanges of insults between two rival performers.

No detail of appearance or character trait is spared, and the contest concludes when one musician fails to come up with a witty riposte. Even without understanding Turkish, tears of mirth rolling down the cheeks of listeners transmit the sense of occasion. Aşık Şeref Taşlıova and Murat Çobanoğlu are masters of such events.

Aşık music generally features solo voice and *saz*, but there have been experiments like Arif Sağ's orchestral "Concerto for Bağlama" and virtuoso Erol Parlak's *saz* chamber quintet. Younger performers include Gülay, Kubat, and Sabahat Akkiraz, steeped in Alevî culture but comfortable in contemporary music projects. Kardeş Türküler's repertoire is a well-researched choice of Alevî, Kurdish, Armenian, Greek, traditional and contemporary Turkish tunes in new arrangements, adding electric bass, classic guitar, violin and accordion to excellent *saz*- and *zurna*-playing.

Greek and Jewish traditions

Collaboration between Turkish and **Greek musicians** and Turkish covers of Greek songs are common. Even during the worst crises between the two countries this never completely stopped, but the once-flourishing ethnic Greek community of İstanbul has dwindled to under 3000. Yeni Türkü pioneered this reciprocity, while other groups now focus on different aspects of this shared heritage. Accordion player Muammer Ketencioğlu specializes in music from the Aegean areas and the Balkans; in a rare instance of voluntary emigration to (rather than from) İstanbul, Greek Nikiforos Metaxas created the Boğaziçi ensemble of Turkish musicians. Turkish singer Melihat Gülses favours melodies about İstanbul and Athens, while *Letter from İstanbul* (Golden Horn) by *kemençe* virtuosos Derya Türkan and Sokratis Sinopoulos is a delicate, acoustic dialogue.

The **Jewish presence** in İstanbul dates from 1493, when thousands of Sephardim expelled from Spain were given refuge by Sultan Beyazit II. The Ladino language (Judaeo-Spanish) is still spoken and Sephardic music, both secular songs (*romanzas*) and liturgical, still sung. Over time Jews adapted the Ottoman classical style, and many became important composers and performers. Key current exponents of secular songs are Janet and Jak Esim and Israeli researcher-singer Hadass-Pal Yarden, long resident in İstanbul, who has released *Yahudice* (Kalan).

Classical traditions

Based partly on theoretical treatises of the ancient Greeks and their Arab successors, **classical Ottoman** music has a history matching western European classical music, with a notational system introduced by composer Abdülkadir Merağı (died 1435). Over the next few centuries, the style evolved in cosmopolitan İstanbul under such figures as Hâfız Post (died 1694), Buhurizade Mustafa İtri (1640–1712), the Romanian prince Dimitri Cantemir and other Greek, Armenian, Jewish, Crimean and Azeri composers. Ottoman court music continued to flourish under Sultan Selim III (1789–1807), himself a composer, and Hamamizade İsmail Dede Efendi (1778–1846).

Turkish urban music constitutes three genres: **religious**, **classic** (*klasik* or *sanat*) and **nightclub** (*fasıl*), which share the compositional rules of *makam*. **Makam** are modes (with rules governing melodic flow and prominent notes) in which the musicians compose their pieces and weave the improvisations (*taksim*) central to classical music performance. The *taksim* usually precedes, but also punctuates, suites of vocal compositions (*kâr*, or *şarkı*) framed by instrumental pieces (*peşrev* and *saz semaisi*). Most *şarkı* sung today are by the great songwriter **Hacı Arif Bey** of the late nineteenth century.

These are essentially chamber genres, where soloists each take turns improvising. Typical **instruments** are the *ud* (fretless, 11-stringed lute), the *ney* (end-blown reed flute), the *tanbur* (3-stringed long-necked lute) and the *kanun* (finger-plucked zither). Rhythm (*usul*) is provided by the *def* (frame drum); later, in secular contexts, were added the *darbuka* drum and the *klarnet*. Some instruments – especially the *ney* and *küdüm* (paired kettle drums) – are effectively synonymous with spiritual music. Performers are extremely versatile, so stylistic distinctions made here and in the discography are not rigid. *Sanat* and *fasıl* practitioners largely overlapped, while classical musicians would even perform folk songs on demand.

Many virtuosi composer-performers are associated with particular instruments, their recordings still listened to as role models: Tanburi Cemil Bey (1871–1916) and Necdet Yaşar (born 1930) on *tanbur*, Yorgo Bacanos (1900–77), Marko Melkon Alemsherian and Udi Hrant Kenkulian (1901–78) on *ud*, Cüneyd Orhon on *kemençe*, Tatyos Efendi (1863–1913), Kemani Haydar Tatlıyay and Kemani Nubar Çömlekçiyan on violin, Şükrü Tunar (1907–62) on *klarnet* and Mesut Cemil Bey, Tanburi's son, on *tanbur* and cello.

Many Ottoman and Republican players and composers inhabited the world of professional, secular music-making, whose associations with drink and dance – outside bourgeois Muslim respectability – made it the preserve of İstanbul's and İzmir's Armenian, Greek, Jewish and Gypsy minorities. Despite no official encouragement (see above), these genres flourished in the private sector, with abundant recordings between the 1920s and 1950s. Non-Muslim musicians continued to dominate urban music until mid-century; an Armenian *kanun* player, Artaki Candan-Terzian, ran the Sahibinin Sesi (HMV-Turkey) recording studios from 1925 until 1948.

Contemporary, top-quality instrumentalists maintain traditions as well as producing original compositions. *Kemençe* player and conservatory teacher İhsan Özgen's ensemble Anatolia fostered a new generation of musicians, including daughters Neva and Yelda, *kanun* players Göksel Baktağir and Ruhi Ayangil, *ney* players Süleyman Erguner and Sadrettin Özçimi, and *ud* player Yurdal Tokcan. The improvisations of Yansımalar (Birol Yayla on guitar and *tanbur*, Aziz Şenol Filiz on *ney*) allude to Ottoman music; guitarist Çengiz Özdemir's acoustic group İnce Saz plays an elegant take on the Western-influenced repertoire of golden age İstanbul.

Sanat vocal artists

Influenced by Koranic recitation as well as the *ezan* (call to prayer), the **voice** is the core of classical genres. The late Kani Karaca's recording of *ezan*s, some suras from the Koran plus traditional *ilahi*s (hymns) are collected on the CD *Aşk İle/With Love*. *Gazel*, the art of vocal improvisation, was epitomized by Hafız Burhan Sesiyılmaz and Abdullah Yüce with their broad range of vocal hue.

First recording in the early 1920s, Münir Nurettin Selçuk (1901–81) is a key figure. He pioneered a more straightforward delivery, less influenced by Koranic recitation's guttural trills. A dashing figure, among the first to stand centre-stage and acquire the trappings of a "star", he was equally at home with Western-inflected bel canto or intense, brooding *gazel*.

Zeki Müren (1931–96), perhaps the top-rated vocalist of the latter twentieth century, first made his name in 1950s classical broadcasts, then with versions of Egyptian and Lebanese musicals, but attained stardom through passionate 1960s performances. Müren flirted with all popular genres – tango, chanson and *arabesk*

– but throughout his career produced austerely classical recordings. His refined diction is considered near perfect, and despite increasingly camp stage decor and costumes (he was a gay transvestite) there was little discernible drop in performance quality. He died dramatically onstage of heart failure while receiving an award in İzmir.

Female singers like Safiye Ayla (Atatürk's favourite), Hamiyet Yüceses and Müzeyyen Senar (1918–) also enjoyed considerable popularity and are still much listened to. Bülent Ersoy studied with Senar, and began as a male classical singer; in 1980 (s)he had a gender reassignment operation, following which she was prohibited from TV on moral grounds, but she successfully lobbied then-President Özal (a big fan) to lift the ban. She outraged devout Muslims with an *ezan* as the opening track of *Alaturka 95*, and indeed a fanatic shot at her during one concert. Ersoy supposedly knows more classical songs than any other active singer and now her artistry is frequently heard on air.

The Mevlevî dervish âyin

Ottoman religious music is based on that of the **Mevlevî ("Whirling")** **dervishes**. Mevlevî performances consist of long **âyin**, complex compositions unified by their identifying *makam*, eg "Saba Ayini". They include pieces with words by thirteenth-century Sufi poet **Celaleddin Rumi (Mevlâna)**, the order's founder, interspersed with *taksim*s. The best-known Mevlevî composers are Köçek Derviş Mustafa Dede (17th century), Dede Efendi (18–19th century) and Rauf Yekta (19–20th century). Public performances of *âyin* are staged, as they've been since Ottoman times, for foreigners; the Halveti-Cerrahi sect emphasizes more the practice of *zikr*, a trance-inducing repetition of some of the 99 names of God, and the collective singing of *ilahi*.

The Erguner family tradition of *ney*-playing started with Süleyman the elder (born 1902); his son Ulvi became director of Radio İstanbul. Since settling in Paris in 1975, musicologist grandson Kudsi has become one of the most visible exponents of Turkish music overseas, publishing his own field recordings; his labels Equinox and Imaj issue new CDs and re-release old recordings. Other grandson Süleyman the younger chose to stay in İstanbul, where he is a prominent *ney* soloist, and instructor at the İstanbul Conservatory, performing regularly in Turkey and abroad; his recent recordings are available on his Erguner label.

Gypsies and fasıl music

As so often in the Balkans, **Gypsies** (*Roman* or *Çingene*) are musically prominent, particularly in the semi-classical, urban-nightclub **fasıl** style, where vocal suites alternate with light ensemble pieces and solo *taksim*s; every short rest (*fasıl* means "interval") is filled with improvisations. *Fasıl* suffers somewhat from association with sleazy *gazino* or *paviyon* nightclubs around Laleli and Aksaray in İstanbul, and **belly dancing** for tourists, but it's also performed in more respectable restaurants. The style incorporates recent songs, and sticks less assiduously to classical formula – this is, after all, music to drink and dance to. Among the best places to hear Gypsy musicians is *Badehane*, General Yazgan Sok 5, Tünel.

Although much of its repertoire overlaps with classical, *fasıl* is very different. The classical values of precision and adherence to tradition are replaced by demonstrative, present-tense music sweeping all before it. The low-tuned G-*klarnet* with its throaty sound epitomizes *fasıl*, and with *darbuka* dominates the ensemble. Tunes are tossed around with exhilarating ease, notes held on the *klarnet* for extended yet exquisitely poised moments, the *kanun* interrupts and the violin spikes pieces with lightning-fast glissandos. The *ud* is often replaced by a *cümbüş*, a fretless type of banjo more easily be heard above the din.

The most famous clarinettist is Mustafa Kandıralı (born 1930). Other celebrated *fasıl* musicians, both living and deceased, include *kanun* player Ahmet Yatman, *oud*ist Kadri Şençalar, violinist Kemani Cemal, the Erköse brothers (clarinettist Barbaros still performs) and clarinettist Deli Selim. Younger clarinettist (born 1957) Selim Sesler stands out as an interpreter of wedding and dance tunes from his native Thrace. Burhan Öçal, from Kırklareli in Thrace, is a virtuoso, conservatory-trained *darbuka* player. Not from a Gypsy family, he nonetheless blended classical Turkish and Gypsy music with his Oriental Ensemble. Laço Tayfa, led by Hüsnü Şenlendirici, was a short-lived band combining Bergama Gypsy music with groovy electric bass and rock-drumming. Singer Kemal Gürses, with his unparalleled knowledge of the repertoire, became the best leader of *fasıl* recordings during the 1970s.

Arabesk

Arabesk has its roots in Egyptian "oriental dance" music – *raks şarkı* or *oriyental* – combined with folk, classical and fasıl; the name alludes to its predominantly Arabic rather than Turkish melodies. During the 1980s and early 1990s *arabesk* was the dominant Turkish music, a working-class and somewhat outsiders' sound which expressed the everyday realities of the urban underclass. *Arabesk* was as much a stance towards life – complete with windscreen ornaments, tacky postcards, dayglo stickers and associated melodramatic films – as a music.

Numerous classical Turkish musicians worked across the Middle East during the early twentieth century, as film composers, instrumentalists or singers. Violinist Haydar Tatlıyay (1890–1963), after returning to Turkey from Egypt in 1947, set up a dance orchestra as heard in Arab musical films, enormously popular in Turkey despite brief banning, while Turkey's recording and film industry produced versions of Middle Eastern hits. *Sanat* singers Zeki Müren and Münir Nurettin Selçuk first succeeded as film stars during the 1940s and 1950s, singing – backed by large string orchestras – abstract but intense lyrics of unrequited love. But from the late 1940s, the genre which would eventually become *arabesk* began to address specifically Turkish problems such as rural–urban migration. Diyarbakırlı Celal Güzelses and Malatyalı Fahri Kayahan were amongst the earliest to record folk-based songs for an urban audience, drawing on styles of southeastern Turkey. Ahmet Sezgin elaborated this by creatively mixing urban and rural elements during the mid-1960s; by the 1970s *arabesk* relied on strings (particularly *elektrosaz*), keyboards and percussion.

The heyday of arabesk

The first major *arabesk* star was Orhan Gencebay (born 1944), a disciple of Ahmet Sezgin. His first hit, *Bir Teselli Ver* (1969) relied on classical forms, but a sobbing vocal intensity owed much to *gazel*, and frank lyrics depicted the plight of the lonely lover. A more eclectic set of references, particularly rock and flamenco, appeared in his 1975 album *Batsın Bu Dünyayı* (A Curse on This World).

The voice defines *arabesk* aesthetics, and those of İbrahim Tatlıses, Müslüm Gürses and Ferdi Tayfur (all film actors like Gencebay) are the most significant. Their songs, thinly disguised autobiographies, tell of self-pity and humiliation in the big city, experiences familiar to Turkey's numerous internal migrants. Of

Kurdish background, Tatlıses himself migrated from Urfa; since the late 1970s, his albums have featured well-drilled orchestras, danceable tunes and electrifying vocals (plus occasional Kurdish lyrics). Ferdi Tayfur's voice also has strong resonances with southeastern styles, and his reputation, like that of Tatlıses, rests on his portrayal of a poor villager made good in the big city. Urfa-born Müslüm Gürses is still adored for his older hits: mournful, fate-obsessed numbers inviting listeners to light another cigarette ("Bir Sigara Yak") or to curse the world ("Yeter Allahım"). His audiences were long notorious for unruly behaviour at concerts, slicing themselves with razor blades during performances to demonstrate how the songs were expressing their deep pain and suffering. Lately Gürses has stretched to interpreting Dylan and Björk tunes, winning a new generation of admirers.

Despite (or because of) being a music with a chequered history and dubious origins, *arabesk* acquired powerful advocates and defenders during the 1980s, part of the general "revision" of republican cultural mores. Özal even used an *arabesk* theme song for his 1988 election campaign. Establishment apparatchiks were duly horrified, and the music was briefly banned from state airwaves in 1989; the tragic lyrics were claimed to encourage the retrograde oriental vices of despair, fatalism and even suicide. Private FM radio and TV gave the music a new lease of life, and younger stars began acting in TV soap-operas, the genre that has largely replaced the *arabesk* movie. Mahsun Kırmızıgül's style evolved in a more pop-influenced direction; others like Özcan Deniz turned folkish. Deniz (along with Gürses) acted in *Neredesin Firuze*, an exhilarating look at Turkish commercial music, while Kırmızıgül turned actor/director with the sentimental epic *Günese Gördüm* (2009).

Rock and özgün

Rock has a long history in Turkey – after all, brothers Ahmet and Nesui Ertegün founded the influential Atlantic jazz, rock and blues label in New York, just one example of the Turkish practice of producing local versions of international genres. During the 1970s an **Anadolu (Anatolian) Rock** movement melded Anatolian folk with Western rock; the new bands' growing identification with the international Left was reflected in increasingly politicized lyrics, so many groups disintegrated when the generals took over in 1980.

Cem Karaca (died 2004), who had worked with every significant Anadolu Rock band (Apaşlar, Kardaşlar, Moğollar, Dervişan), fled to Germany before the coup, returning only in 1987. His voice combined histrionics with cultivated bel canto, his songs a taste for highbrow literature with social realism; 1979's *Safinaz* was a rock opera about a poor girl's struggle with honour and blood feuds. He also superbly set to music the poetry of Nazım Hikmet and Orhan Veli Kanık, the two most influential Turkish republican poets. Moğollar, under Cahit Berkay, has reformed; politically edged lyrics are still present, though an up-tempo stadium-rock style has replaced chamber-ensemble lyricism. A few bands maintained the original impetus into the mid-1980s. Bulutsuzluk Özlemi (Longing for Unclouded Skies), one of the most radical, is still active, while Mozaik gave way to Ayşe Tütüncü's brand of jazz (see below). Yeni Türkü, inspired by Latin American "New Song", was among the first groups to play traditional Turkish acoustic instruments in good arrangements, as well as original, topical lyrics with a liberal to left stance.

Özgün (original) music was an intimate, mellow vocal style, combining rural melodies with guitar- or *saz*-based harmonies. Composer and *saz*-player Zülfü Livaneli – best known for his work with Greek composer Mikis Theodorakis and singer Maria Farandouri, and for the soundtrack to Yılmaz Güney's film *Yol* –

dominated the genre during the 1980s. Born in the eastern Black Sea region, as a leftist intellectual he spent the early 1970s exiled in Sweden, where he met like-minded Theodorakis.

Inspired by groups like Inti-Illimani and sharing their militant vision, Grup Yorum formed during the mid-1980s, their political commitment combined with serious, grass-roots folk research; they remain active and influential, with lead singers Ayşegül, Gülbahar, Yasemin Göksu and İlkay Akkaya embarking on successful solo careers.

Contemporary bands relying on indigenous styles and instruments as well as technological props and avant-gardeism include Zen, Replikas and Baba Zula. Popular mainstream acts include Mavi Sakal, Mor ve Ötesi (Turkish grunge), Duman, Athena (Turkish Ska) and Cargo. Turkish hip-hop, kick-started in Germany by Cartel and its debut *Cartel Cartel* – a witty commentary about Turkish-German street life with sampling of folk sounds – has gone mass-market with Ceza, Karargah, and Circassian rapper Sultana.

Pop, ethno-jazz and electronica

At the heart of **Turkish pop** stands Sezen Aksu, who began as a *sanat* singer in her native İzmir, but owes her standing to an early partnership with the late Onno Tunç, a jazz musician of Armenian descent who oversaw Turkey's 1980s Eurovision entries. Aksu's soulful voice, updating traditional Turkish urban musical aesthetics, and Tunç's elliptical arrangements and keyboard-based harmonics, made a winning combination. After the premature death of Onno his brother Arto, a well-known jazz percussionist, took over as Aksu's arranger. Sezen gave Turkish music one rare global hit with "Şımarık", which swept Europe covered as "Kiss Kiss". She's still noted for her love songs but has also been a canny political figure, embracing concerns and campaigns: Bosnia, feminism, ecology, human rights. Her CDs, almost thirty since 1975, often match the zeitgeist: 1997's *Düğün ve Cenaze/*"Wedding and Funeral", with Goran Bregovic, reworked popular Balkan tunes – and had considerable resonance in a Turkey contemplating the ruins of ethnically cleansed Yugoslavia, ancestral home to many modern Turks. Her voice continues developing in subtlety, range and control, the songwriting by turns playful and experimental, her stage presence magnetic.

Among those emerging from Sezen's "conservatory" were Levent Yüksel, a talented instrumentalist and singer, whose carefully crafted music connects explicitly with indigenous Turkish traditions and literature; 2003 Eurovision winner Sertab Erener; teen idol Tarkan who cracked the world market, and powerful Işın Karaca. Candan Erçetin has conspicuously continued the Aksu tradition, tapping a range of Anatolian, Balkan, Latin and Mediterranean influences. Serdar Ortaç and Mustafa Sandal produce danceable sounds in an extroverted, late-1990s genre with lyrics, driving rhythms and tunes pitched at youthful, cosmopolitan city-dwellers.

Turkish percussionist Okay Temiz first fused jazz and Turkish music with his Oriental Wind group, then created ad hoc ensembles for specific projects dedicated to Black Sea music, *mehter* music, and so on. A recent strain of electronica flavoured with ethnic elements and Sufi music is exemplified by Mercan Dede, who records acoustic solos from traditional instruments over a rich electronic base. Guitar player Erkan Oğur is most celebrated as a folk performer, but his improvisations on fretless electric guitar with jazz trio Telvin (Kalan) are unsurpassd. Idiosyncratic pianist and arranger Ayşe Tütüncü draws inspiration from folk music as well as from the Turkish fascination with tango.

Selected discography

The leading Turkish label is Kalan (ⓦ www.kalan.com), with recordings of historic performers, contemporary folk, popular singers and regional/minority music. Doublemoon specializes in fusion projects, while Ada features everything from fringe rock to ethno-jazz and folk. Outside Turkey, Traditional Crossroads (ⓦ www.traditionalcrossroads.com) has an excellent backlist of archival and contemporary recordings. Golden Horn Records (ⓦ www.goldenhorn.com) represents many different genres with immaculate productions. Pressings from US, German or French labels and increasingly Turkish labels can easily be obtained online – try NewYork-based specialist Tulumba (ⓦ www.tulumba.com). Good shops in İstanbul include Lale Plak, Tünel, Galipdede Cad 1, Beyoğlu; Ada, İstiklâl Cad 330; and the Municipal Bookstore, also on İstiklâl Caddesi. A trip to Blok 5 of IMC in Unkapanı, HQ for most labels, will get you wholesale prices. All CDs below are issued by Turkish labels, unless specified otherwise.

General compilations

Elveda Rumeli (Kalan) Best-selling soundtrack to the popular TV serial, with infectious Turkish songs and instrumentals from Macedonia; Yasemin Göksu features on several tracks.

Made in Turkey (8 CDs; Soulstar, Germany). Compiled by DJ Gülbahar Kültür, this collection complements the Rounder discs with the current İstanbul scene: classical and folk music, Anatolian rock, pop, rap, dance, electronica.

🏃 **Masters of Turkish Music, Volumes 1, 2, 3** (Rounder, US) Still the best single starting point for Turkish music, these compilations from restored vintage recordings feature artists from the 1910s to the 1960s. The stress is on *sanat*, *gazel*, *şarkı* and instrumental solos, with folk music not so well represented.

Folk and aşik: compilations

Ashiklar: Those Who Are In Love (Golden Horn, US). Recorded at the Hacı Bektaş festival and the houses of leading *aşık*s: a vibrant document.

Dost Kervani (ASC). One of many recommendable folk anthologies by this Ankara label, mostly famous songs by musicians like Musa Eroğlu and Oğuz Aksaç.

🏃 **Salkım Söğüt 1 & 2** (Metropol). Contemporary acoustic-folk samplers with İlkay Akkaya, Arzu Görücü, Birol Topaloğlu and Alaaddin Us. The first two performers make Disc 1; no. 2 features a reprise by Görücü, Laz singing by Kazım Koyuncu, and central Anatolian pieces by Mustafa Özarslan and Hakan Yeşilyurt.

Turquie Aşık: Chants d'Amour et de Sagesse d'Anatolie (Inedit/Auvidis, France). Excellent introduction to *aşık* music, featuring Nuray Hafiftaş, Ali Ekber Çiçek and Turan Engin, plus a spectacular *saz* solo by Arif Sağ.

Folk and aşik: individual artists

Ali Ekber Çiçek *Folk Lute from Anatolia* (2 CDs; Anadolu). Recent studio recordings, including a video documentary; not the same as an eponymous, earlier Canadian disc.

DEM Trio *The Fountain* (Felmay, Italy). Symbolic instruments of high culture (*tambur*) and folk (*bağlama*) in dialogue over a jazz-inflected *divan sazı* accompaniment. Unusual interpretations of dances on *tambur*, folk twists to pieces by Tamburi Cemil Bey and Cinucen Tanrıkorur.

Neşet Ertaş *Zülüf Dökülmüş Yüze* (Kalan). His enormous output has been organized into a complete series. This first volume contains popular songs, vocal improvisations, and astonishing *saz*-playing.

Erdal Erzincan *Anadolu* (Güvercin). An excursion through Anatolian folk, with intoxicating *bağlama* using both finger-picking and plectrum.

Erkan Oğur ✽ *Hiç* (Kalan) Superbly produced, instrumental-only versions of standard folk songs. His delicate, almost ascetic *Gülün Kokusu Vardı* (Kalan) has innovative vocals by İsmail Hakkı Demircioğlu on traditional songs from across Turkey.

Talip Özkan *Dark Fire* (Axiom, US). Intense recital encompassing various regional styles and instruments, the lower resonances of *saz* well in evidence. ✽ *L'art du Tanbur* (Ocora) is a wonderfully meditative foray into classical *tanbur*, varied by folk melodies and unexpectedly delicate singing.

Erol Parlak *Bağlama Beslisi* (Akkiraz). Elegant, complex chamber music for different-sized *bağlama*s.

Arif Sağ *Davullar Çalınırken* (Iber). Striking 2005 album with Sağ on percussion rather than the usual *saz*, featuring rhythms from different Anatolian regions.

Ruhi Su *Zeybekler/Ezgili Yürek* (Nepa-İmece Müzik). 1981's *Zeybekler* – west-Anatolian folk epics delivered in Ruhi Su's unmistakable, dramatically deep voice – rank among his most famous recordings.

✽ **Birol Topaloğlu** *Heyamo* (Kalan). Showcases vocalists from the Black Sea Laz population, with Topaloğlu on *kemençe* and *tulum*, and musicians from Grup Yorum.

✽ **Aşık Veysel** *Aşık Veysel* (2 CDs, Kalan). The "definitive" Veysel collection, with the best versions of his most-loved songs, fully annotated in English.

Classical and devotional music: compilations

The Bektashi Breathes (Cemre). Bektaşi rituals feature hymns called *nefesler*, or "breaths". An extraordinarily powerful disc with solemn melodies that sigh and droop.

✽ **Istanbul 1925** (Traditional Crossroads, US/Kalan). İstanbul music anthology played by Turkish, Armenian and Greek musicians during the early republic, including the odd urban *türkü* and *fasıl* instrumental.

Masters of Turkish Music: Ney (Kalan). Listening consecutively to various *ney* masters, one appreciates the diversity of styles. Similar Kalan collections feature *kemençe* and *ud*. Scholarly notes in English.

Women of Istanbul (Traditional Crossroads, US/Kalan) An all-singing companion to *Istanbul 1925*; great female vocalists of cabaret-nightclub style from the 1930s.

Tanburi Cemil Bey *Volumes 1, 2 & 3* (Traditional Crossroads, US/Kalan). Recorded 1910–14 in a spare, elegant style on various stringed instruments (including cello).

🏃 **Mesut Cemil** *Early Recordings* (*Volume 1*) and *Instrumental and Vocal Recordings* (*Volumes 2-3*) (Golden Horn Records, US). Recordings from a Cairo music congress of 1932, an extremely rare Cemil vocal, some definitive *taksim*s and a superb two-*tanbur* version of Cemil's famous *Nihavent Saz Semaisi*.

Kudsi Erguner *Les Passions d'Istanbul* (Imaj). Original suite for large ensemble, including vocalists stressing the multi-ethnic character of the city. On *Tatyos Efendi: Vocal Masterpieces* (Traditional Crossroads, US), a classical instrumental ensemble accompanies Melihat Gülses singing a selection of *şarkı* composed by this Armenian violinist.

Süleyman Erguner/İhsan Özgen *Tende Canım* (Sera). Extraordinary live recording of classical and religious compositions with Koray Safkan on vocals, and excellent English notes. *Şah Ney* (Mega Muzik) is a unique opportunity to hear the lower-register *ney*.

Bülent Ersoy *Alaturka 1995* (Raks). Popular classics from the 1880s to the 1960s, with some *gazels* of scorching intensity. *Seçmeler* (Raks) collects greatest hits from her prolific *arabesk* output.

Udi Hrant Kenkuliyan *The Early Recordings, Vols. 1 & 2* (Traditional Crossroads, US). Turkish recordings from the 1920s with heart-rending love lyrics, many *taksim*s and affecting ensemble work with violin, clarinet and piano. *Udi Hrant* (Traditional Crossroads, US/Kalan) has better sound from a 1950s tour of the US.

Mevlâna: Dede Efendi Saba Âyini (Kalan). Benchmark recording of a complete Mevlevî suite (*âyin*) in *makam Saba*. The performers, including Mesut Cemil and Niyazi Sayın, epitomize Turkish *sanat* music of the first half of the 1900s.

Zeki Müren *Kahir Mektubu* (Türküola). Composed by Zeki's long-time associate Muzaffer Özpınar, this 1979 *arabesk* landmark is simultaneously vast in scope and intimate in style. *Türk Sanat Müziği Konseri* (Coşkun Plak) is a near-perfect example of Zeki's mastery of the classical genre.

Muzaffer Özak This late *şeyh* of the Halveti order conducted ceremonies on *Derviches Tourneurs de Turquie* (Arion, France), plus *Garden of Paradise* and *Reunion* (Pir, US): *ilahi* hymns, Koranic recitation, and rarely heard prayers.

Münir Nurettin Selçuk *Bir Özlemdir* (Coşkun Plak). Some enduring hits: "Aziz İstanbul", "Kalamış", "Endülüste Raks" (Turkish flamenco) and an electrifying *gazel*, "Aheste Çek Kürekleri".

🏃 **Şükrü Tunar** *Şükrü Tunar* (Kalan). Great Gypsy clarinettist from the İzmir region, one of Zeki Müren's first accompanists, whose repertoire encompassed everything from *zeybek* to *fasıl*.

Vosporos *Zontani Ihografisi sto Irodio* (MBI, Greece). Vosporos is the Greek name of Boğaziçi; this documents a 1990 Athens concert. Greek composers of Ottoman music and songs of the Alevî *aşık*s, with stellar Turkish vocalists.

Hamiyet Yüceses *Makber* (Istanbul). Includes her magnificent "Bakmıyor Çeşm-i Siyah Feryade", a Hacı Arif Bey piece to which she added a long improvised *gazel*, and "Her Yer Karanlık", an intense interpretation of the famous Hafız Burhan composition.

Fasıl/Gypsy music

Barbaros Erköse Ensemble *Lingo Lingo* (Golden Horn Records, US). Urban folklore at its best, with superb *meyan* (improvisation over a rhythmic background). Liner notes by Sonia Seeman, an authority on Turkish Gypsy music.

Istanbul Oriental Ensemble *Gypsy Rum* (Network, Germany). Led by percussionist Burhan Öçal, this delivers fourteen tracks of tight instrumental playing.

Mustafa Kandıralı *Caz Roman* (Network, Germany). The epitome of instrumental *fasıl*, subtly iconoclastic in melodic invention; backing by Ahmet Meter (*kanun*), Metin Bükey (*ud*) and Ahmet Kulık (*darbuka*).

Karşılama *Karşılama* (Green Goat, Canada/Kalan). İstanbul Gypsy musicians led by Selim Sesler, plus locally trained Canadian vocalist Brenna MacCrimmon, interpret *Roman* music – including older songs

gleaned from archival recordings – of western Turkey and the Balkans with real panache.

Laço Tayfa *Çiftetelli* (Traditional Crossroads, US), also as *Bergama Gaydası* (Doublemoon). Mildly electrified Gypsy jazz funk; the musicianship of Hüsnü Şenlendirici (especially on "Harmandalı" and "İzmir'in Kavakları") and his band carries the day.

Ödemişli Mehmet *Avare* (Milhan). Until recently circulating only on cassette, with connoisseurs scouring street stalls for a copy, this is Aegean celebration music at its most inventive.

The Road to Keşan: Turkish Rom and Regional Music of Thrace (Traditional Crossroads, US/Kalan). Gypsy music featuring Selim Sesler gets a full, percussive hearing in its native setting on this superb production overseen and annotated by Sonia Seeman.

Arabesk

Orhan Gencebay *Yalnız Değilsin* (Kervan). Middle Eastern, European and American genres in one magisterial sweep, from the thunderous belly-dance number ("Gencebay Oriyentali") to a mock-Baroque overture ("Nihavent Üvertür").

Müslüm Gürses *Senden Vazgeçmem* (Elenor Plak). Lush violins, a *bağlama* section, and full "classical" instrumentation backs Müslüm "Baba" singing despairing lyrics with characteristically

intense vocals, paired with discernible European and even C&W influences; also an Azeri folk song and the Alevî evergreen "Haydar Haydar".

İbrahim Tatlıses *Fosforlu Cevriyem* (Emre). What *arabesk* sounded like in concert, and a sense of Tatlıses' phenomenal presence. Includes all-time favourites ("Beyaz Gül, Kırmızı Gül", "Fosforlu Cevriyem", "Beyoğlu", "Yeşil Yeşil"), plus superb *uzun hava* improvisations.

Rock, pop, özgün and fusion

Sezen Aksu *Işık Doğudan Yükselir/The Light Rises in the East* (Foneks). An overblown orchestral opening yields to intimate sparseness; some songs are studiously authentic ("Ben Annemi Isterim", and "Rakkas", in Black Sea

and urban styles respectively), others more abstract and allusive ("Halımımı Yaktılar", based on traditional laments). Aksu's best disc is arguably *Deli Veren* (Balet, Turkey), from the quiet intensity of "Hoş Geldin" to

"Gidiyorum bu Şehirden" with Greek star Haris Alexiou.

Cem Karaca *Cemaz ül-Evvel* (Kalan). A retrospective of early Karaca, tracing his experiments with Western genres, plus his emerging political radicalism. Essentially the history of Turkish highbrow rock on one disc.

🏃 **Ahmet Kaya** *An Gelir* (Taç). Plangent *saz*, up-tempo *halay* dances, deep, melancholy vocals. The title song is based on a poem by Attila İlhan.

Kirika *Kaba Saz* (Baykuş).The best surprise of 2008: *rebétiko* and *zeybek* styles meet raw acoustic rock by daring young musicians from İzmir.

Zülfü Livaneli *Maria Farandouri Söylüyor* (Raks). Landmark collaboration from the early 1980s: Greek star Farandouri singing Livaneli compositions in both Greek and Turkish. Beautiful, often dark, melodies, finely arranged.

Burhan Öçal *Groove alla Turca* (Doublemoon). Öçal joins forces with bassist Jamaladeen Tacuma and

trumpet supremo Jack Walrath for an exciting jazzy mix; Natasha Atlas guests.

Şivan Perwer *Kirive, Volumes 1 & 2* (SES Plak, Turkey) are among nearly twenty "Best Of..." Perwer CDs on this label with *duduk*, *bloor*, *ud* and *kanun* backing.

🏃 **Fuat Saka** *Lazutlar* II (Kalan) Dynamic session of Black Sea folk-rock, with participation by Georgians, and Pontic musicians from northern Greece, where the huge refugee community's music has changed little since they left the region.

Tarkan *Karma* (İstanbul Plak). Tarkan assembles an exotic team (Hossam Ramzy's ensemble, Ruben Harutunian on Armenian *duduk*, Jean-Louis Solon on *didj*, *sitar* and *sarod*) and then imposes his voice.

Okay Temiz *Zikir* (Ada). Successful fusion outing by a group including Akagündüz Kutbay (*ney*), D. D. Guirand (soprano sax), Onno Tunç (bass) and Tuna Ötenel (piano).

Francesco Martinelli, Martin Stokes and Marc Dubin

Books

T here are numerous books about every aspect of Turkey in English, many recently published or reissued. Books with Turkish publishers are rarely available outside Turkey. "o/p" means out of print, but almost every book so listed can be easily found through websites such as ⑩www.abe.com/.co.uk or www.bookfinder.com.

The classics

Herodotus *The Histories*. A fifth-century BC citizen of Halikarnassos (Bodrum), Herodotus – the first systematic historian/anthropologist – described the Persian Wars and assorted nations of Anatolia.

Strabo *Geography*. A native of the Pontus, Strabo travelled widely across the Mediterranean; our best (multi-volume) document of Roman Anatolia.

Xenophon *Anabasis*, or *The March Up-Country* (best as the abridged *The Persian Expedition*). The Athenian leader of the Ten Thousand, mercenaries for Persian king Cyrus the Younger, led the long retreat from Cunaxa to the Black Sea. An ancient travel classic still mined for titbits of of ethnology, archeology and geography.

Ancient history and archeology

Ian Hodder *On the Surface: Çatalhöyük 1993–1995*. Neolithic Çatal Höyük is the world's earliest city, thus crucial to the origins of Western civilization. This relates the first years of a projected 25-year excavation.

Seton Lloyd *Ancient Turkey – A Traveller's History of Anatolia*. Without sacrificing detail and research results, it's accessibly written by a former head of Ankara's British Archeological Institute.

J.G. Macqueen *The Hittites and Their Contemporaries in Asia Minor*. Well-illustrated general history of the first (c.1800–1200 BC) great Anatolian civilization.

David Traill *Schliemann of Troy: Treasure and Deceit* (o/p). The man versus his self-promulgated myth. This portrayal of the crumbling edifice of Schliemann's reputation, also helps bring the old walls of Troy to life.

Byzantine history

Roger Crowley *Constantinople*. Former İstanbul resident Crowley's 2005 account of the 1453 siege is more detailed than Runciman's (see below) but the pace never flags.

Cyril Mango *Byzantium: The Empire of the New Rome*. Survey of daily life, economic policy and taxation, scholarship, cosmology and superstition, among other topics. The newer, more

lavishly illustrated *Oxford History of Byzantium*, edited by Mango, will also appeal.

John Julius Norwich *Byzantium: The Early Centuries, Byzantium: The Apogee* and *Byzantium: The Decline*. Astonishingly detailed trilogy, well-informed and wittily readable account (there's a single-volume abridgement, *A Short History of Byzantium*).

Procopius *The Secret History*. Often raunchy demolition job of Justinian and his sluttish empress, Theodora, from the imperial general Belisarius's official chronicler. Belisarius, one of the greatest Byzantine generals, is (like Justinian) portrayed as spinelessly uxorious.

Michael Psellus *Fourteen Byzantine Rulers: The Chronographia*. Covers the turbulent period 976–1078, when the scholarly author was adviser to several of these emperors.

🏃 Steven Runciman *Byzantine Style and Civilisation* (o/p). Eleven centuries of Byzantine art, culture and monuments in one small paperback; still unsurpassed. His *The Fall of Constantinople, 1453* remains the classic account of the event, while *The Great Church in Captivity*, about Orthodoxy under the Ottomans, is readable if partisan.

Speros Vryonis *The Decline of Medieval Hellenism in Asia Minor and the Process of Islamization from the Eleventh through the Fifteenth Century*. The definitive study of how the Byzantine Empire culturally became the Ottoman Empire.

Ottoman history

Halil İnalcık *The Ottoman Empire 1300–1600*. The standard work since its 1973 appearance.

🏃 Caroline Finkel *Osman's Dream*. Meticulously researched yet engaging history of the Ottoman empire, from twelfth-century origins to collapse.

🏃 Patrick Balfour Kinross *The Ottoman Centuries*. Comprehensive, balanced summary of Ottoman history from the fourteenth to the twentieth century.

Metin Kunt and Christine Woodhead *Süleyman the Magnificent and His Age*. Concise summary of the greatest Ottoman sultan's reign and its cultural renaissance.

🏃 Philip Mansel *Constantinople: City of the World's Desire, 1453–1924*. Nostalgic, faintly anti-Republican popular history, organized topically as well as chronologically. Obscure, intriguing factoids abound – Boğaziçi University began life as a hotbed of Bulgarian nationalism; Russian floozies have previously (1920–22) held Turkish men in thrall. *Highlights of his Sultans in Splendour – Monarchs of the Middle East, 1869–1945* are rare photos of characters from the late Ottoman Empire.

Andrew Wheatcroft *The Ottomans: Dissolving Images* (o/p). An analysis of trends in Ottoman life, and its perception by the West, demonstrated by period art, cartoons and photos.

Modern histories

🏃 Feroz Ahmad *The Making of Modern Turkey*. Not the most orthodox history: lively, partisan and full of wonderful anecdotes and quotes you'll find nowhere else. His more recent *Turkey: The Quest for Identity* updates matters to 2003.

🏃 Marjorie Housepian Dobkin *Smyrna 1922: The Destruction of a City*. Partisan (ie rabidly anti-Turkish) but scholarly and harrowingly graphic account of the sack of İzmir, when about 150,000 of the 400,000 Armenians and Greeks trapped in the city were killed. Focuses on why the Allied powers failed to act and subsequently covered up the incident.

Michael Hickey *Gallipoli: A Study in Failure*. Currently the best history of the campaign.

Hugh Poulton *Top Hat, Grey Wolf and Crescent: Turkish Nationalism and the Turkish Republic*. Poulton dissects the "holy trinity" – secularism, ethnically based nationalism and Islam – which powers Turkey, and also summarizes antecedents such as Pan-Ottomanism. Plenty of asides on minorities (mostly Kurds), but stops short of the political-Islam period.

🏃 Barry Rubin *Istanbul Intrigues: A True-Life Casablanca* (o/p). Unputdownable account of Allied/Axis activities in neutral Turkey during World War II, and their attempts to drag it into the conflict. Surprising revelations about the extent of Turkish aid for Britain, the US and the Greek resistance.

🏃 Antonio Sagona *The Heritage of Eastern Turkey*. Copiously illustrated guide to the archeology and history of neglected eastern Turkey,

covering everything from the Neolithic to the Selçuk periods.

Richard Stoneman *A Traveller's History of Turkey*. Easy-reading volume, updated to 2009, which touches all bases from Paleolithic times to the AK government.

Speros Vryonis *The Mechanism of Catastrophe: The Turkish Pogrom Of September 6–7, 1955, And The Destruction Of The Greek Community Of Istanbul*. Remarkably impartial considering the author's Greek background; shows how the Menderes government and police actively aided the rampaging mobs.

🏃 Erik J. Zürcher *Turkey, A Modern History*. If you have time for only one book covering the post-1800 period, make it this one (revised up to 2004), which breathes revisionist fresh air over the received truths of the era.

Biographies

Saime Göksu and Edward Timms *Romantic Communist: The Life and Work of Nazım Hikmet*. Definitive biography of Turkey's most controversial modern poet, who once rubbed shoulders with Pablo Neruda, Jean-Paul Sartre and Paul Robeson. Banned and imprisoned for seventeen years at home, Hikmet spent much of his life in exile, dying in 1963 in Moscow.

Thea Halo *Not Even My Name*. Remarkable, moving story of a Pontic-Greek girl, caught up in the 1920s ethnic cleansing, who managed to escape to America. Aged 79 she returns, in the company of her daughter (the author) to her birthplace in the Black Sea mountains.

Patrick Balfour Kinross *Atatürk, the Rebirth of a Nation*. Long considered the definitive English biography – as opposed to hagiography – of the father of the Republic, and still preferred by some to the newer Mango text (see below).

Andrew Mango *Atatürk*. Does not supersede Kinross's more readable tome, but complements it. Authoritative, but also steeped in military and conspiratorial minutiae. Sympathetic to its subject, and the Turkish national project overall; the post-1922 population exchanges and the Armenian episodes rate hardly a mention.

Ethnic minorities and religion

🏃 Taner Akçam *From Empire to Republic: Turkish Nationalism and the Armenian Genocide*. Brilliant study by a Turkish academic resident in the

US, which shows how the ethnic cleansing of the Armenian population from 1895 to 1923, and subsequent suppression of any memory of these events, was essential for Turkish nationalism – and remains at the root of the Republic's modern problems. His more recent *A Shameful Act: The Armenian Genocide and the Question of Turkish Responsibility*, focuses more closely on how CUP nationalist ideology bred the massacres, and the failed attempt at reckoning in postwar parliament debates and trials.

Peter Balakian *The Burning Tigris: the Armenian Genocide and America's Response*. As partisan as you'd expect from an Armenian-American, but nonetheless compelling analysis of the background to, and execution of, the massacres. Strong evidence from American and European missionaries in the region; harrowing photographs.

Bruce Clark *Twice a Stranger: How Mass Expulsion Forged Modern Greece and Turkey*. The build-up to and execution of the 1923 population exchanges, and how both countries are still digesting the experience eight-plus decades on. Readable and compassionate, especially encounters with surviving elderly refugees.

William Dalrymple *From the Holy Mountain: A Journey in the Shadow of Byzantium*. Retraces a classic sixth-century monkish journey through the Near East. Section II is devoted to Turkey, and Dalrymple takes a suitably dim view of the sorry history and current poor treatment of Christians and their monuments in eastern Turkey.

John Freely *The Lost Messiah: In Search of the Mystical Rabbi Sabbatai Sevi*. Story of the millennial, Kabbalistic, seventeenth-century movement in İzmir and Salonica that engendered the Dönme, a crypto-Judaic sect

disproportionately prominent in modern Turkish history.

F.W. Hasluck *Christianity and Islam under the Sultans*. Ample documentation of shrines and festivals, their veneration and attendance by different sects at the turn of the last century, plus Christian and pagan contributions to Bektaşi and Alevî rites. Great for dipping into, though a bit repetitive since edited posthumously.

R.G.Hovannian, ed. *Armenian Van*. Essays on everything from the origins of the Armenians, through medieval church architecture and modern iterature, to the massacres.

Aliza Marcus *Blood and Belief: The PKK and the Kurdish Fight for Independence*. Definitive, if controversial, study on the organization; neither the Turkish state nor the PKK (especially its leader, Abdullah Ocalan) get an easy ride.

David McDowall *A Modern History of the Kurds*. About a third of this book is devoted to Turkey's Kurds, the balance to those in Iran and Iraq – few states getting high marks here for their treatment of Kurds, up to 2003.

Yaşar Nuri Öztürk *The Eye of the Heart: An Introduction to Sufism and the Tariqats of Anatolia and the Balkans* (Redhouse Press, İstanbul). Frustratingly brief description of mystical Islam and the main dervish orders; lavishly illustrated.

Jonathan Rugman and Roger Hutchings *Atatürk's Children: Turkey and the Kurds*. Excellent, even-handed handling of the topic up to 2001 by (in part) the Guardian's former Turkey correspondent.

Views of contemporary Turkey

Tim Kelsey *Dervish: The Invention of Modern Turkey* (o/p). The troubled soul of the 1990s country, sought amongst

minority communities, faith healers, bulging prisons, brothels and the transsexual underground, plus the mystics of the title; pitiless analysis of Turkish angst, with little optimism for the future.

🏃 **Stephen Kinzer** *Crescent and Star: Turkey Between Two Worlds*. Entertaining account from a former *New York Times* bureau chief in İstanbul. Whether *rakı*-drinking or *nargile*-toking with ordinary Turks, interviewing politicos, swimming across the Bosphorus or DJ-ing his own Turkish radio show, Kinzer brings the country to life.

Andrew Mango *The Turks Today: Turkey after Atatürk*. Current to 2004, this overview by a long-standing Turkish advocate is by no means rose-tinted, but he gives Turkey an easy "pass" in too many areas, and Chapter 10 on Kurdish issues is quite disposable.

Travel and Impressions

🏃 **Neal Ascherson** *Black Sea: The Birthplace of Civilisation and Barbarism*. Excellent historical, ethno-logical and ecological meditation, updated in 2007, explores these supposed antitheses around Turkey's northerly sea; only two chapters specifically on the Pontus and Bosphorus, but still recommended.

🏃 **John Ash** *A Byzantine Journey*. Historically inclined reflections of a poet taking in all the major, and some minor, Byzantine sites in Anatolia; a lot better than it sounds.

Anastasia Ashman and Jennifer Eaton Gökmen *Tales from the Expat Harem: Foreign Women in Modern Turkey*. Collected short memoirs of female experiences; light but insightful.

Frederick Burnaby *On Horseback through Asia Minor*. Victorian officer's thousand-mile ride to spy on the Russians in the run-up to the 1877 war. Prophetically observant and inadvert-ently humorous; anti-Armenian, condescendingly Turkophilic.

🏃 **Chris Morris** *The New Turkey: The Quiet Revolution on the Edge of Europe*. Morris (long Turkey's BBC correspondent) writes accessibly on the usual topics: political Islam, Greeks and Armenians, the Kurdish question, Turkey's EU quest. An ideal introduction to contemporary Turkey.

Nicole and Hugh Pope *Turkey Unveiled*. Interlinked essays, arranged topically and chronologically, by two foreign correspondents who over two decades got to understand Turkey pretty well. Good grasp of Kurdish- and Europe-related issues, and wonderful anecdotes (though too adulatory of Özal). Despite their affection for the country, unflinching description of its shortcomings, though the Armenian issue is botched.

Laurence Kelly (ed) *A Traveller's Companion to Istanbul*. Writing on various aspects of the city includes eyewitness accounts of historical events such as the Fourth Crusade's sack of Constantinople.

🏃 **Geert Mak** *The Bridge*. Quite brilliant travelogue weaving the compelling tales of the petty street-traders, hustlers, pickpockets, shoe-shiners, fishermen and other characters who frequent İstanbul's landmark Galata bridge with a marvellously succinct, yet evocative, history of one of the world's great cities.

Mary Wortley Montagu *Turkish Embassy Letters*. Impressions of an eccentric but perceptive traveller, resident in İstanbul during 1716–18, whose open-mindedness gave her the edge over contemporary historians.

Michael Pereira *East of Trebizond* (o/p). Late 1960s travels between the Black Sea and northeast Anatolia, interspersed with readable history of the area.

Brian Sewell *South from Ephesus:
An Escape from the Tyranny of
Western Art* (o/p). Pre-touristic coastal
Turkey and its ruins during the 1970s
and 1980s, when vile hotels,
domineering guides, patchy transport
and amorous, bisexual villagers were a
constant hazard (or attraction,
depending on point of view). As

erudite and curmudgeonly as you'd
expect from the former art critic of
London's *Evening Standard*.

Freya Stark *Ionia – a Quest, Alexander's Path, The Lycian Shore* and *Riding
to the Tigris* (all o/p). Among the most
evocative Turkish travel writing ever,
if now inevitably dated.

Memoirs

Aziz Nesin *İstanbul Boy* (o/p). Autobiography set in the same era as Orga's
first work; strong on local colour (eg
"Howling" dervish ceremonies), but
not as good a read.

İrfan Orga *Portrait of a Turkish
Family*. This heartbreaking story
follows Orga's family from idyllic
existence in late Ottoman İstanbul
through grim survival in the early
Republican era. His *The Caravan Moves
On: Three Weeks among Turkish Nomads*
is a fine snapshot of the Menderes era
– and a clear-eyed portrayal of a Toros
yörük community, who otherwise have
had reams of rose-tinted nonsense
written about them.

Orhan Pamuk *İstanbul: Memories
of a City*. Thoughtful, sometimes
moving memoir (translated by
Maureen Freely) by Turkey's 2007
Nobel laureate in literature, reflecting
on the author's troubled relationship

with himself, his parents, and the city
he was born and raised in – but is now
in self-imposed exile from. The
overriding theme is melancholy and
decline from imperial greatness –
reinforced through Ara Güler's
copious black-and-white photographs.

Mary Seacole *The Wonderful
Adventures of Mrs Seacole in Many
Lands*. This alternative Florence
Nightingale was a black Jamaican who
tended to Crimean War casualties in
İstanbul at her own expense. Subsequent history has not done Seacole
justice, but her autobiography has
remained in print uninterruptedly.

Daniel de Souza *Under a Crescent
Moon* (o/p). Turkish society seen from
the bottom looking up: prison
vignettes by a jailed foreigner, and in
its compassion and black humour the
antithesis of *Midnight Express*. Compel-
lingly written.

Architecture, art and monuments

Metin And *Turkish Miniature Painting –
the Ottoman Period* (Dost Yayınları,
İstanbul; o/p). Attractive coverage of
the most important Ottoman art form,
with well-produced colour plates.

**Diana Barillari and Ezio
Godoli** *Istanbul 1900: Art
Nouveau Architecture and Interiors*.
Superbly researched and illustrated
account of İstanbul's neglected Art
Nouveau legacy, in particular works
by Italian architect and resident

Raimondo D'Aronco. A nice correc-
tive to the axiom that the city consists
only of palaces, concrete tower-blocks
and wooden terrace-houses.

Godfrey Goodwin *A History of
Ottoman Architecture*. Definitive
guide covering the whole country and
providing a sound historical and
ethno-geographical context for every
important Ottoman construction. His
*Sinan: Ottoman Architecture and Its
Values Today* is also eminently readable.

Spiro Kostof *Caves of God – Cappadocia and Its Churches* (o/p). Dry rendering of a fascinating subject, but there's still no rival.

Richard Krautheimer *Early Christian and Byzantine Architecture* (o/p). Excellent survey from Pelican's "History of Art" series.

Raymond Lifchez (ed) *The Dervish Lodge: Architecture, Art and Sufism in Ottoman Turkey* (o/p). Lavishly illustrated essays on all aspects of dervish life, stressing the relation between *tekke* layout and function. While nineteenth-century İstanbul is disproportionately represented, as are the Mevlevî and Bektaşi orders, there's material on rural *zaviyes*, Nakşibendi practice, tomb veneration and pictorial calligraphy and poetry.

Cyril Mango *Byzantine Architecture* (o/p). A complete survey of the most significant Byzantine structures, around a quarter of which fall within modern Turkey.

Gülru Necipoğlu *The Age of Sinan: Architectural Culture in the Ottoman Empire*. As it says: the master in his social context, and the best, newest of several studies on the man.

T.A. Sinclair *Eastern Turkey: An Archaeological and Architectural Survey* (4 vols.). The standard, prohibitively priced reference, with copious plans and covering every monument east of Cappadocia. University libraries have copies.

David Talbot Rice *Islamic Art* (o/p). Vast geographical and chronological span gives useful perspectives on Ottoman and Selçuk art forms. His *Art of the Byzantine Era* (o/p), a lavishly illustrated study in the same "World of Art" series, is unlikely to be ever superseded. For specialists *The Church of Hagia Sophia in Trebizond* (o/p) remains the last word, from the Talbot Rice-headed team that restored its frescoes.

Stephane Yerasimos *Constantinople: Istanbul's Historical Heritage*. Good colour photos, with attention to mosaics and icons, plus coverage of Edirne and Bursa. The English translation of the French original via a German edition is stilted, though.

Stephane Yerasimos, Ara Güler and Samih Rifat *Living in Turkey* (Overseas, and by Dünya in Turkey). Views and interiors to drool over – a bit prettified and nouveau riche but still an alluring ideal.

Carpets

Alastair Hull and José Luczyc-Wykowska *Kilim: The Complete Guide: History – Pattern – Technique – Identification*. Comprehensive and thoroughly illustrated survey of Turkish kilims. Hull's *Living with Kilims* (with Nicholas Barnard) is an excellent use-and-care manual.

James Opie *Tribal Rugs: A Complete Guide to Nomadic and Village Carpets*. Contains examples of Turcoman and Kurdish rugs as part of a general Central Asian survey.

Yanni Petsopoulos and Belkis Balpınar *Kilims: Masterpieces from Turkey* (o/p). Less rigorous but more available than Petsopoulos' rare but definitive *Kilims: Flat-Woven Tapestry Rugs* (o/p).

Kurt Zipper and Claudia Fritzsche *Oriental Rugs: Turkish* (o/p). Volume 4 of this series. Coverage of weaving techniques, symbols and rug categories, plus regional surveys of distinctive patterns.

Specialist guidebooks

Arın Bayraktaroğlu *Turkey: Culture Shock! A Survival Guide to Customs and Etiquette.* Useful, especially for a prolonged stay or business trip.

George E. Bean *Turkey's Southern Shore, Turkey Beyond the Maeander, Lycian Turkey, Aegean Turkey* (all o/p). Scholarly guides to coastal archeological sites based on Professor Bean's original research, much of it never superseded.

Everett Blake and Anna Edmonds *Biblical Sites in Turkey* (o/p). If it's mentioned in the New Testament, it's fully described here. Edmonds' *Turkey's Religious Sites* (o/p) is better produced and includes Jewish and Muslim sites.

Hasan Dindi et al *Turkish Culture for Americans* (o/p). Hilarious problem/solution examples of cultural misunderstandings Americans may experience in Turkey.

Hilary Sumner-Boyd and John Freely *Strolling Through Istanbul.* First published in 1972 and indispensable. The authors' knowledge of, and love for, the city shine through; sketch-maps and monument plans complement informative text.

Jane Taylor *Imperial Istanbul.* Excellent, stone-by-stone guide, complete with site plans, of the major Ottoman monuments in Bursa and Edirne as well as the old capital.

Hiking and mountaineering

Kate Clow and Terry Richardson *The Lycian Way.* Hour-by-hour, west to east route guide for Turkey's first officially marked long-distance trail (see p.325); supplied with folding map.

Kate Clow and Terry Richardson *St Paul Trail.* Illustrated uide to Turkey's second long-distance, waymarked trail (see p.450), loosely following in the footsteps of St Paul from Perge to Antioch in Pisidia, taking in wonderful mountain and lakeland scenery en route. GPS data and map included.

Kate Clow and Terry Richardson *The Kaçkar: Trekking in Turkey's Black Sea Mountains.* Meticulously described routes in the centre of Turkey's most popular alpine range, plus ample background material and a large-scale, plastic map by György Zsiga.

Ömer B. Tözel *The Ala Dağ: Climbs and Treks in Turkey's Crimson Mountains.* More technical and less hike-orientated than the title implies, but the only volume in English.

Turkish fiction in translation

Selçuk Altun *Songs My Mother Never Taught Me.* A world apart from Barbara Nadel's works (see p.738), this cerebral İstanbul-set thriller is clinical yet strangely compelling.

Sait Faik *A Dot on the Map* (o/p). Short-story collection, translated by various scholars, from the acknowledged Turkish master of the genre; most are set around İstanbul during the early Republican years.

Moris Farhi *Young Turk.* Ankara-born Farhi conjures thirteen interwoven short stories in this delightful evocation of İstanbul either side of World War II. Characters, whether Armenian, Greek, Gypsy, Levantine or Turkish, are lovingly sketched; the "coming of age" tales are the most convincing.

Yaşar Kemal Besides Orhan Pamuk, this is the best-known Turkish novelist, thanks to English translations by his wife Thilda of most of his titles. His older books are folksy epics set in Anatolia for example *Mehmed My Hawk* and its sequel *They Burn the Thistles* (o/p). Better are the later novels, including ⚑ *The Sea-Crossed Fishermen* (o/p), contrasting an old man's struggle to save the dolphins in the Sea of Marmara with the fortunes of a desperate hoodlum in the city; and *The Birds Have Also Gone* (o/p), a symbolic, gentle story about bird-catchers. In the more recent *Salman the Solitary*, Kemal returns to his native Çukurova with a tale of a displaced Kurdish family.

Orhan Pamuk Nobel Prize-winning Turkish writer with the largest overseas (and domestic) audience. Pamuk's enduring concerns are Turkey's often corrosive encounter with the West and the irrepressibility of its Islamic heritage. His debut, ⚑ *The White Castle*, was an excellent historical meditation about a seventeenth-century Italian scholar enslaved by an Ottoman astronomer but he arrived on the world literature scene with 1998's *The New Life* which had foreign critics hailing the heir-apparent of Calvino and Borges, despite its unappealing narrator and slight tale. ⚑ *Snow*, Pamuk's most controversial and political novel, is arguably his best. Set in bleak, north-eastern Kars, it examines once-taboo topics such as political Islam and Kurdish nationalism. Since being threatened with prosecution for publically discussing the Armenian genocide, Pamuk lives mostly in New York, where he wrote his latest novel, *The Museum of Innocence*, a memoir of *amour fou* set in late-1970s İstanbul.

⚑ **Elif Shafak** *The Flea Palace*. Interwoven, tragicomic lives in a once-grand İstanbul apartment block. The author – born in Strasbourg, raised in Spain and currently residing in the US – found herself, like Pamuk, a target of establishment ire (including threatened prosecution), for her 2007 ⚑ *The Bastard of Istanbul*, where an exuberant, if dysfunctional, Turkish family host an Armenian-American girl in search of her identity. Well-drawn, strong female characters drive a narrative which inevitably delves into Ottoman Turkey's treatment of its Armenians.

Latife Tekin *Berji Kristin: Tales from the Garbage Hills*. The hard underbelly of Turkish life, in this surreal allegory set in a shantytown built on an İstanbul rubbish dump. By the same author, and similar in tone, is *Dear Shameless Death* which examines how rural families cope with the move to the big city.

Foreign literature set in Turkey

Louis de Bernières *Birds Without Wings*. This repeats, with mixed results, the formula of his blockbuster *Captain Corelli's Mandolin*, applied to Asia Minor of the 1910s and 1920s. Most of the action occurs in "Eskibahçe", a fictionalized version of Kaya Köyü near Fethiye, though the Gallipoli set-pieces are the best bits. Take it as epic entertainment, not gospel – his grip on Turkish language, ethnography and history can be shaky.

⚑ **Maureen Freely** *The Life of the Party* (o/p). Salacious cavortings of a Bosphorus University faculty and their families during the 1960s, including a fictionalized amalgam of the author's father John Freely and others.

Jason Goodwin *The Janissary Tree*. Historical thriller of skulduggery uncovered by eunuch detective Yashin. A palatable entry into nineteenth-century İstanbul on the eve of the Tanzimat reforms.

Pierre Loti *Aziyade*. For what's essentially romantic twaddle set in nineteenth-century İstanbul, this is surprisingly racy, with good insights into Ottoman life and Western attitudes to the Orient.

Rose Macaulay *The Towers of Trebizond*. Classic send-up of Low and High Church conflict, British eccentricity and naïvety amongst a group travelling from Istanbul to Trebizond in the 1950s.

Barbara Nadel *A Chemical Prison; Arabesque; Harem*. Some love Nadel's İstanbul-set thrillers, where doughty, chain-smoking Inspector İkrem and

associates trawl the city's underworld; others find them a tad unconvincing. But they do evoke a side of the city barely imaginable to the average visitor.

Edouard Roditi *The Delights of Turkey*. Twenty short stories, by turns touching or bawdy, of rural Turkey and İstanbul, by a Sephardic Jew of Turkish descent long resident in Paris and America.

Barry Unsworth *The Rage of the Vulture* (o/p). Paranoid Sultan Abdülhamid during the last year of his reign observed by a troubled British officer-with-a-past stationed in İstanbul.

Turkish poetry in translation

Coleman Barks (trans) *Like This; Open Secret; We are Three*. Three of various volumes of Rumi's poetry, in lively if not literal translations.

Yunus Emre (tr. Süha Faiz) *The City of the Heart: Verses of Wisdom and Love* (o/p). After Rumi, the most esteemed Turkish medieval Sufi poet. *The Drop That Became the Sea*, rendered by Kebir Helminski, will also appeal.

Talat S. Halman *Living Poets of Turkey* (Milet, İstanbul). A wide selection of modern Turkish poetry, with an introduction.

Nazım Hikmet *Poems of Nazım Hikmet* and *Beyond the Walls*. The most easily available, reasonably priced anthologies by the internationally renowned Turkish communist poet. *A Sad State of Freedom* (o/p) is an earlier collection also worth looking for.

Language

Language

Turkish

t's worth learning as much Turkish as you can; if you travel far from the tourist centres you may well need it, and Turks always appreciate foreigners who show enough interest and courtesy to learn at least basic greetings. The main advantages of the language for learners are that it's phonetically spelt and (98 percent of the time) grammatically regular. The disadvantages are that the vocabulary is unrelated to any language you're likely to have encountered (unless you know Arabic or Persian), and the grammar, relying heavily on suffixes, gets thornier the further you delve into it. Concepts like vowel harmony further complicate matters.

Pronunciation

Pronunciation in Turkish is worth mastering, since once you've got it, the phonetic spelling and regularity helps you progress fast. The following letters differ significantly from English pronunciation.

Aa	short a, similar to that in far	**Çç**	like ch in **ch**at
Ee	as in bet	**Gg**	hard g as in **g**et
İi	as in pin	**Ğğ**	generally silent, but lengthens the preceding vowel, and between two vowels approximates a y sound
Iı	vowel resembling the vestigial sound between the b and the l of probable		
Oo	as in note	**Hh**	as in **h**en, never silent
Öö	like ur in burn	**Jj**	like the s in plea**s**ure
Uu	as in blue	**Şş**	like sh in **sh**ape
Üü	like ew in few	**Vv**	soft sound, somewhere between a v and a w
Cc	like j in **j**elly		

Phrasebooks and dictionaries

For a straightforward **phrasebook**, look no further than Turkish: A Rough Guide Phrasebook with useful two-way glossaries and a brief and simple grammar section. For an **at-home course**, Geoffrey L. Lewis's Teach Yourself Turkish still probably has a slight edge over Yusuf Mardin's Colloquial Turkish (o/p). If you're serious about learning Turkish after you arrive in the country, the best series published there is a set of three textbooks and tapes, Türkçe Öğreniyoruz (Engin Yayınevi), available in good İstanbul and Ankara bookshops.

Among widely available Turkish **dictionaries**, the best are probably the Langenscheidt/Lilliput in miniature or coat-pocket sizes, or the Concise Oxford Turkish Dictionary (o/p but sold online), a hardback suitable for serious students. The Redhouse dictionaries produced in Turkey but marketed by Milet in the UK are the best value, despite eye-straining fine print.

The **circumflex** (^), found only over vowels a, u and i in loan words from Arabic or Persian, has two uses. It usually lengthens (and stresses) the vowel it crowns, eg Mevlâna sounds like "Mevl**aana**", Alevî is pronounced "Alev**ee**", but when used after the consonants g, k or l the affected vowel sounds like it's preceded by a faint y or h, and distinguishes homonyms: eg *kar* (snow) versus *kâr* (profit). Although its meticulous use over "i" is dwindling, news of the circumflex's demise has been greatly exaggerated, and it still features in media as diverse as airline schedules and newspaper headlines – while its use in academic texts remains universal.

Vowel harmony and loan words

Turkish usually exhibits **vowel harmony**, whereby words contain either so-called "back" vowels a, ı, o and u, or "front" vowels e, i, ö and ü, but rarely mix the two types. Back and front vowels are further subdivided into "unrounded" (a and ı, e and i) and "rounded" (o and u, ö and ü), and again rounded and unrounded vowels tend to keep exclusive company. A small number of native Turkish words (eg, *anne*, mother; *kardeş*, brother) violate the rules of vowel harmony, as do compound words, eg *bugün*, "today", formed from *bu* (this) and *gün* (day).

The main exceptions to vowel harmony, however, are foreign **loan words** from Arabic or Persian (plus Greek), and despite Atatürk's best efforts to substitute Turkish or French expressions (the latter again violating vowel harmony), they still make up a good third of modern Turkish vocabulary. Most words beginning with f, h, l, m, n, r, v and z are derived from Arabic and Persian.

Words and phrases

Basics

Good morning	Günaydın	I beg your pardon	Affedersiniz
Good afternoon	İyi günler	Excuse me (in a crowd)	Pardon
Good evening	İyi akşamlar		
Good night	İyi geceler	I'm sightseeing	Geziyorum or Dolaşıyorum
Hello	Merhaba		
Goodbye	Allahaısmarladık	I'm English/Scottish Irish/ American/ Austalian	İngilizim/Iskoçyalım/ Irlandalıyım/ Amerikalı/ Avustralyalım
Yes	Evet		
No	Hayır		
No (there isn't any)	Yok		
Please	Lütfen	I live in...	...'de/da oturuyorum
Thank you	Teşekkür ederim/ Mersi/Sağol	Today	Bugün
		Tomorrow	Yarın
You're welcome	Bir şey değil	Day after tomorrow	Öbür gün/Ertesi gün
How are you?	Nasılsınız? Nasılsın? Ne haber?		
		Yesterday	Dün
I'm fine	İyiyim/iyilik	Now	Şimdi
Do you speak English?	İngilizce biliyormusunuz?	Later	Sonra
		Wait a minute!	Bir dakika bekle!
I don't understand (Turkish)	Anlamadım/Türkçe anlamıyoru	In the morning	Sabahleyin
		In the afternoon	Öğle'den sonra
I don't know	Bilmiyorum	In the evening	Akşamleyin

Here/there/over there	Bur(a)da/Şur(a)da/ Or(a) da	Enough	Yeter
Good/bad	İyi/Kötü, Fena	Mr	Bey (follows first name)
Big/small	Büyük/Küçük	Miss	Bayan (precedes first name)
Cheap/expensive	Ucuz/Pahalı		
Early/late	Erken/Geç	Mrs	Hanım (polite Ottoman title follows first name)
Hot/cold	Sıcak/Soğuk		
Near/far	Yakın/Uzak		
Vacant/occupied	Boş/Dolu	Master craftsman	Usta (honorific title bestowed on any tradesman; follows first name)
Quickly/slowly	Hızlı/Yavaş		

Driving

Left	Sol	No entry	Araç giremez
Right	Sağ	No through road	Çıkmaz sokak
Straight ahead	Doğru, direk	Abrupt verge	Düşük banket
Turn left/right	Sola dön/Sağ'ta dön	Slow down	Yavaşla
No parking	Parkyapılmaz	Road closed	Yol kapalı
Your car will be towed	Aracınız Çekilir	Crossroads	Dörtyol, kavşak
One-way street	Tek yön	Pedestrian crossing	Yaya geçidi

Some common signs

Entrance/exit	Giriş/Çıkış	First aid	İlk yardım
Free/paid entrance	Giriş ücretsiz/ Ücretlidir	No smoking	Sigara içilmez
		Keep off the grass	Çimenlere basmayını
Gentlemen	Baylar	Stop, halt	Dur
Ladies	Bayanlar	Military Area	Askeri bölge
WC	WC/Tuvalet/Umumî	Entry Forbidden	Girmek yasaktır
Open/closed	Açık/Kapalı	No entry without a ticket	Biletsiz girmek yasaktır
Arrivals/departures	Varış/Kalkış		
Pull/push	Çekiniz/İtiniz	No entry without a woman	Damsız girilmez
Out of order	Arızalı		
Drinking water	İçilebilir su	Please take off your shoes	Lütfen ayakkabılarınızı çıkartınız
To let/for hire	Kiralık		
Foreign exchange	Kambiyo	No entry on foot	Yaya giremez
Beware	Dikkat		

Accommodation

Is there a hotel nearby?	Bir yakında otel var mı?	Single/double/triple	Tek/çift/üç kişilik
		Do you have a double room for one/two/three nights?	Bir/iki/üç gecelik çift yataklı odanızvar mı?
Pension, inn	Pansiyon		
Campsite	Kamping		
Tent	Çadır		
Do you have a room?	Boş odanız var mı?	For one/two weeks	Bir/iki haftalık
		With an extra bed	İlâve yataklı

743

With a double bed	Fransiz yataklı	I have a booking	Reservasyonum var
With a shower	Duşlu	Is there wifi?	Kablosuz var?
Hot water	Sıcak su	What's the	Şifre nedir?
Cold water	Soğuk su	password?	
Can I see it?	Bakabilirmiyim?		

Questions and directions

Where is the...?	...nerede?	How do I get to...?	...'a/e nasıl giderim?
When?	Ne zaman?	How far is it to...?	...'a/e ne kadar uzak?
What/What is it?	Ne/Ne dir?	Can you give me a	Beni...'a/e
How much (does	Ne kadar/Kaça?	lift to...?	götürebilirmisiniz?
it cost?)		When does it open?	Kaçta açılıcak?
How many?	Kaç tane?	When does it close?	Kaçta kapanacak?
Why?	Niye?	What's it called in	Türkcesi ne dir? or,
What time is it?	(polite) Saatınız var mı?	Turkish?	Turkçe nasıl
	(informal) Saat kaç?		söylersiniz?

Travelling

Aeroplane	Uçak	Can I book a seat?	Reservasyon
Bus	Otobus		yapabılırmıyım?
Train	Tren	When is the next	Bir sonraki otobus/
Car	Araba	bus/train/ferry?	tren/vapur kaçta
Taxi	Taksi		kalkıyor?
Bicycle	Bisiklet	Where does it	Nereden kalkıyor?
Ferry	Feribot, vapur	leave from?	
Catamaran, sea-bus	Deniz otobüsü	Must I change?	Aktarma var mı?
Hitch-hiking	Otostop	What platform does	Hangi perondan
On foot	Yaya	it leave from?	kalkıyor?
Bus station	Otogar	How many	Kaç kilometredir?
Railway station	Gar, tren ıstasyonu	kilometres is it?	
Ferry terminal/jetty	İskele	How long does	Ne kadar sürer?
Harbour	Liman	it take?	
A ticket to...	...'a bir bilet	Which bus	Hangi otobus... 'a
One-way	Gidiş sadece	goes to...?	gider?
Return	Gidiş-dönüş	Which road leads	Hangi yol...'a çıkar?
What time does	Kaçta kalkıyor?	to...?	
it leave?		Can I get out at a	Müsait bir yerde
		convenient place?	inebilirmiyim?

Days of the week, months and seasons

Sunday	Pazar	Saturday	Cumartesi
Monday	Pazartesi	January	Ocak
Tuesday	Salı	February	Subat
Wednesday	Çarşamba	March	Mart
Thursday	Perşembe	April	Nisan
Friday	Cuma	May	Mayıs

744

June	Haziran	December	Aralk
July	Temmuz	Spring	İlkbahar
August	Ağustos	Summer	Yaz
September	Eylül	Autumn	Sonbahar
October	Ekim	Winter	Kış
November	Kasım		

Numbers and ordinals

1	Bir	60	Altmış
2	İki	70	Yetmiş
3	Üç	80	Seksen
4	Dört	90	Doksan
5	Beş	100	Yüz
6	Altı	140	Yüz kırk
7	Yedi	200	İki yüz
8	Sekiz	700	Yedi yüz
9	Dokuz	1000	Bin
10	On	100,000	Yüz bin
11	On bir	500,000	Beşyüz bin
12	On iki	1,000,000	Bir milyon
13	On üç	Compound numbers tend to be run together in	
20	Yirmi	spelling: 50,784 Ellibinyediyüzseksendört	
30	Otuz	First	Birinci
40	Kırk	Second	İkinci
50	Elli	Third	Üçüncü

Time conventions

(At) 3 o'clock	Saat üç(ta)	It's 8.10	Sekizi on geçiyor
2 hours (duration)	İki saat	It's 10.45	On bire çeyrek var
Half hour (duration)	Yarım saat	At 8.10	Sekizi on geçe
5.30	Beş büçük	At 10.45	On bire çeyrek kala

Food and drink

Basics

Bal	Honey	Kekik	Oregano
Bulgur	Cracked wheat	Makarna	Pasta (noodles)
Buz	Ice	Nane	Mint
Ekmek	Bread, as:	Pilav, pirinç	Rice
Çavdar	Rye	Şeker	Sugar
Kepekli	Wholegrain	Sirke	Vinegar
Mısır	Corn	Su	Water
Karabiber	Black pepper	Süt	Milk

Tereyağı	Butter	Yoğurt	Yoghurt
Tuz	Salt	Yumurta	Eggs
(Zeytin) Yağ(ı)	(Olive) Oil	With/without (meat)	(Et)li/(Et)siz

Useful words

Bakarmısınız!	Polite way of getting waiter's attention	Çatal	Fork
Bardak	Glass	Kaşık	Spoon
Başka bir...	Another...	Peçete	Napkin
Tabak	Plate	Hesap	Bill, check
Bıçak	Knife	Servis ücreti	Service charge
		Garsoniye	"Waiter's" charge

Cooking terms

Acı	Hot, spicy	Kıymalı	With minced meat
Buğlama	Steamed	Peynirli, kaşarlı	With cheese
Çevirme	Spit-roasted	Pilaki	Vinaigrette, marinated
Etli	Containing meat		
Etli mi?	Does it contain meat?	Pişmemiş	Raw
Etsiz yemek var mı?	Do you have any meatless food?	Sıcak/soğuk	Hot/cold (*meze*)
		Soslu, salçalı	In red sauce
Ezme	Puréed/mashed dip	Sucuklu	With sausage
Fırında(n)	Baked	Tava, sahanda	Deep-fried, fried
Haşlama	Meat stew without oil, sometimes with vegetables	Yoğurtlu	In yoghurt sauce
		Yumurtalı	With egg (eg *pide*)
		Zeytinyağlılar	Vegetables cooked in their own juices, spices and olive oil (*zeytin yağı*), then allowed to cool
İyi pişmiş	Well-cooked		
Izgarada(n), Izgarası	Grilled		
Kızartma	Fried then chilled		

Soup (*çorba*)

Düğün	Egg-lemon	Tarhana	Yoghurt, grain and spice
Ezo gelin	Rice/vegetable broth	Tavuk	Chicken
İşkembe	Tripe	Yayla	Similar to *tarhana*, with mint
Mercimek	Lentil		
Paça	Trotters	Yoğurt	Yoghurt, rice and celery greens

Appetizers (*meze* or *zeytinyağlı*)

Amerikan salatası	Mayonnaise and vegetable salad	Börülce	Black-eyed peas, in the pod
Antep or acılı ezmesi	Hot chilli mash with garlic, parsley, onion	Cacık	Yoghurt, cucumber and herb dip
Barbunya	Red kidney beans	Cinter	Chanterelles
Beyin salatası	Lamb-brain salad	Çerkez tavuğu	Chicken in walnut sauce

Çoban salatası	Tomato, cucumber, parsley, pepper and onion salad	Piyaz	White haricots, onions and parsley vinaigrette
Deniz börülcesi	Glasswort, marsh samphire	Rus salatası	"Russian" salad – potatoes, peas, gherkins in mayonnaise
Deniz otu	Rock samphire		
Haydarı	Dense garlic dip		
Hibeş	Spicy sesame paste	Semizotu	Purslane, usually mixed into yoghurt
İçli köfte	Bulgur, nuts, vegetables and meat in a spicy crust	Sigara böreği	Cheese-filled pastry "cigarettes"
İmam bayıldı	Cold baked aubergine, onion and tomato	Tarama	Pink fish-roe
		Tere	Rocket greens
Mantar sote	Sautéed mushrooms	Turşu	Pickled vegetables
Mücver	Courgette frittata	Yaprak dolması	Stuffed vine leaves, with mince
Paçanga böreği	*Pastırma* containing, tomato and cheese	Yalancı dolması	Vegetarian stuffed vine leaves
Pancar	Beets, marinated	Yeşil salata	Green salad
Patlıcan ezmesi	Aubergine pâté	Zeytin	Olives

Meat (*et*) and poultry (*beyaz et*)

Adana kebap	Spicy Arab-style kebab	Karışık ızgara	Mixed grill
		Kiremit'te kebap	Meat served on a hot ceramic tray
Beyti	Minced kebab wrapped in pitta	Köfte	Meatballs
Bıldırcın	Quail	Koyun	Mutton
Billur, koç yumurtası	Sheep testicle	Kuzu	Lamb
		Keçi	Goat
Böbrek	Kidney	Orman kebap	Roast lamb refried with vegetables
Bonfile	Small steak		
Çiğ köfte	Raw meatballs	Pastırma	Cured beef
Ciğer	Liver	Piliç	Roasting chicken
Çöp kebap	Tiny chunks of offal	Pirzola	Chop, cutlet
Dana eti	Veal	Saray kebap	Rissoles baked with vegetables
Dil	Tongue		
Döner kebap	Rotisseried cone of fatty lamb slabs	Sığır	Beef
		Şiş kebap	Shish kebab
İnegöl köftesi	Mince rissoles laced with cheese	Tandır kebap	Tender, boneless lamb baked in outdoor oven
İskender or Bursa kebap	Döner drenched in yogurt and sauce		
		Tavuk	Boiling chicken
Kaburga	Spare ribs	Tekirdağ köftesi	Finger-shaped rissoles with cumin, onion, mint
Kağıt kebap	Meat and vegetables baked in wax paper		
Kanat	Chicken wing	Yürek	Heart

Fish (*balık*) and seafood (*deniz ürünleri*)

Ahtapod	Octopus	Kolyoz	Club mackerel
Akya	Leerfish; low-quality	Levrek	Bass; usually farmed
Alabalık	Trout	Lüfer	Bluefish
Barbunya/tekir	Red mullet, small/large	Melanurya	Saddled bream
Çinakop	Baby lüfer	Mendik	Type of bream
Çipura	Gilt-head bream	Mercan	Pandora or red bream
Hamsi	Anchovy (Black Sea)	Mezgit	Whitebait
İskaroz	Parrotfish	Midye	Mussel
İsparoz	Annular bream	Orfoz	Giant grouper
İstakoz	Aegean lobster	Orkinos	Tuna
İstavrit	Horse mackerel	Palamut/torik	Small/large bonito
Kalamar	Squid	Sarıgöz	Black bream
Kalkan	Turbot	Sarıkanat	Young lüfer
Karagöz	Two-banded bream	Sardalya	Sardine
Karides	Prawns	Uskumru	Atlantic mackerel
Kefal	Grey mullet (Aegean)	Yayın	Catfish
Kılıç	Swordfish	Yengeç	Crab

Vegetables (*sebze*)

Acı biber	Hot chillis	Mantar	Mushrooms
Bakla	Broad beans	Marul	Lettuce
Bamya	Okra, lady's fingers	Maydanoz	Parsley
Bezelye	Peas	Nohut	Chickpeas
Domates	Tomato	Patates	Potato
Enginar	Artichoke	Patlıcan	Aubergine, eggplant
Hardal	Mustard greens	Roka, tere	Rocket greens
Havuç	Carrot	Salatalık	Cucumber
Ispanak	Spinach	Sarımsak, sarmısak	Garlic
İstifno	Boiled wild greens	Sivri biber	Thin peppers, hot
Kabak	Courgette, zucchini		or mild
Karnabahar	Cauliflower	Soğan	Onion
Kuru fasulye	White haricots	Taze fasulye	French beans
Kuşkonmaz	Asparagus	Turp	Radish

Snacks

Badem	Almonds	Fındık	Hazelnuts
Börek	Rich layered pastry with varied fillings	Gözleme	Village crêpe with various fillings
Çerez	Nibbles, usually nuts	Kestane	Chestnuts
Cezer(i)ye	Carrot, honey-nut bar	Kokoreç	Mixed innard roulade
Çiğ börek	Hollow turnovers	Kuru üzüm	Raisins
Dürüm	Pitta-like dough roll used to wrap meat for takeaway	Lahmacun	Round Arabic-Armenian "pizza"
		Leblebi	Roasted chickpeas

Midye dolması	Mussels stuffed with rice and pine nuts	Şam fıstığı	Pistachios
Pestil	Sheet-pressed dried fruit	Simit	Bread rings studded with sesame seeds
Pide	Turkish "pizza"	Su börek	"Water börek" – runny cheese between filo
Poğaça	Soft round biscuit served with *börek*	Yer fıstığı	Peanuts

Typical dishes

Civil	Variant of *mihlama*, served on Çoruh side of Kaçkar	Otlu peynir	Herb-flavoured cheese, common around Van
Güveç	Meat and vegetable clay-pot casserole	Saç kavurma	"Wok"-fried medley
İç pilav	Spicy rice	Sebze turlu	Vegetable stew
Karnıyarık	Aubergine and meat dish, firmer than *mussaka*	Şakşuka	Aubergine, tomato, pepper and other vegetable fry-up
Lahana sarma	Black Sea dolma, with baby cabbage leaves	Tas kebap	Meat and vegetable stew especially in eastern Anatolia
Laz böreği	Meat-filled crêpes, topped with yoghurt	Tatar böreği	Similar to *mantı* but served with cheese and mint
Mantı	Mince-stuffed "ravioli" topped with yoghurt and chilli oil	Testi kebap	Stew in a sealed Avanos (Cappadocia) pot, broken at serration to serve
Menemen	Stir-fried omelette with tomatoes and peppers	Türlü sebze	Alias of *tas kebap*
Mıhlama, muhlama	Fondue-like Hemşin dish of cheese, butter and corn flour		

Cheese (*peynir*)

Beyaz	White; like Greek feta	Kaşar	Kasseri, variably aged
Çerkez	Like Edam	Tulum	Dry, crumbly, parmesan-like cheese
Dil	Like mozzarella		
Lor	Like ricotta		

Fruit (*meyve*)

Ahududu	Raspberry	(Kara)dut	(Red) mulberry
Armut	Pear	Karpuz	Watermelon
Ayva	Quince	Kavun	Persian melon
Böğürtlen	Blackberry	Kayısı	Apricot
Çilek	Strawberry	Kiraz	Sweet cherry
Elma	Apple	Limon	Lemon
Erik	Plum	Mandalin	Tangerine
Hurma	Persimmon or date	Muşmula	Medlar (northern Turkey)
İncir	Figs		

Muz	Banana	Şeftali	Peach (June)
Nar	Pomegranate	Üzüm	Grape
Papaz/hoca eriği	Green plum	Vişne	Sour cherry
Portakal	Orange	Yarma	August Bursa peach

Sweets (*tatlılar*) and pastries (*pastalar*)

Acı badem	Giant almond biscuit	Komposto	Stewed fruit
Aşure	Pulse, wheat, fruit and nut "soup"	Krem karamel	Créme caramel
		Kurabiye	Almond-nut biscuit dusted with powdered sugar
Baklava	Layered honey and nut pie		
Dondurma	Ice cream	Lokum	Turkish Delight
Kaymak	Clotted cream	Muhallebi	Milk pudding with rice flour and rosewater
Fırın sütlaç	Baked rice pudding		
İrmik helvası	Semolina and nut *helva*	Mustafakemalpaşa	Syrup-soaked dumpling
Kabak tatlısı	Baked orange-fleshed squash topped with nuts and *kaymak*	Sakızlı	Anything mastic-flavoured
		Süpangile	Ultra-rich chocolate pudding, with sponge or a biscuit embedded
Kadayıf	"Shredded wheat" in syrup		
Kadın göbeği	Doughnut in syrup	Sütlaç	Rice pudding
Kaymak	Clotted cream	Tahin helvası	Sesame paste *helva*
Kazandibi	Browned version of *tavukgöğsü*	Tavuk göğsü	Chicken-breast, milk, sugar and rice taffy
Keşkül	Vanilla-almond custard	Zerde	Saffron-laced jelly

Drinks

Ada çayı	Sage tea	Şarap	Wine
Ayran	Drinking yoghurt	Şıra	Grape must, lightly fermented
Bira	Beer		
Boza	Lightly fermented millet or wheat drink	Sütlü/Sütsüz	With/without milk
Çay	Tea		
Kahve	Coffee		
Maden suyu	Mineral water (fizzy)		
Memba suyu	Spring water (non-fizzy)		
Meyva suyu	Fruit juice		
Papatya çayı	Camomile tea		
Rakı	Aniseed-flavoured spirit distilled from grape pressings		
Sahlep	Orchid-root-powder drink		

Common toasts

The closest equivalents to "Cheers" are: **Şeref'e, şerefiniz'e** "to your honour" and **Neşe'ye** "to joy". Otherwise there's the more formal **Sağlığınız'a'** "to your health" or **Mutluluğ'a** "to happiness".

To a good cook one says: **Eliniz'e sağlık** "health to your hands". For a short grace after meals: **Allah bereket versin** ("may Allah bring blessings").

Glossary

Many of the Turkish terms below will change their form according to their grammatical declension (eg *ada*, island, but *Eşek Adası*, Donkey Island); the genitive suffix is appended in brackets, or the form written separately when appropriate.

General Turkish terms

Ada(sı) Island.

Ağa A minor rank of nobility in the Ottoman Empire, still a term of respect; follows the name (eg Ismail Ağa).

Ahi Medieval Turkish apprentice craftsmen's guild and religious brotherhood, predecessor of the more conventional dervish orders.

Ayazma Sacred spring.

Bahçe(si) Garden.

Bekçi Caretaker or warden at an archeological site or monument.

Belediye(si) Municipality – both the corporation and the actual town hall, for a community of over 2000 inhabitants.

Bey Another minor Ottoman title like *ağa*, still in use; follows the first name.

Cami(i) Mosque.

Çarşaf "Sheet" – the full-length, baggy dress-with-hood worn by religious Turkish women.

Çarşı(sı) Bazaar, market.

Çay(ı) 1) Tea, the national drink; 2) a stream or small river.

Çeşme(si) Street-corner fountain.

Çıkmaz(ı) Dead-end alley.

Dağ(ı) Mount.

Dağlar(ı) Mountains.

Dolmuş Shared taxi system operating in larger towns.

Eski Old (frequent modifier of place names).

Ezan The Muslim call to prayer; these days often taped or at the very least transmitted up to an elevated loudspeaker.

Ferace Similar to a *çarşaf*, but less all-enveloping.

Gazi Warrior for the (Islamic) faith; also a common epithet of Atatürk.

Gazino Open-air nightclub, usually featuring live or taped music.

Gecekondu A house built quickly without proper permission. Translates as "founded-by-night" – a reference to the Ottoman law whereby houses begun in darkness which had acquired a roof and four walls by dawn were inviolable.

Gişe Ticket window or booth.

Göl(ü) Lake.

Hamam(ı) Turkish bath.

Hamsi The Black Sea anchovy; by extension, nickname for any native of this area.

Han(ı) Traditionally a tradesmen's hall, or an urban inn; now also means an office block.

Harabe Ruin; *harabeler* in the plural, abbreviated "Hb" on old maps.

Harem Women's quarters in Ottoman houses.

Hastane(si) Hospital.

Hicrî The Muslim dating system, beginning with Mohammed's flight to Medina in 622 AD, and based on the thirteen-month lunar calendar; approximately six centuries behind the *Miladî* calendar. Abbreviated "H." on monuments and inscriptions.

Hisar Same as *kale*.

Hoca Teacher in charge of religious instruction.

Ilıca Hot spring.

İl(i) Province, subdivided into *ilçes* (counties or districts).

İmam Usually just the prayer leader at a mosque, though it can mean a more important spiritual authority.

Irmak River, eg Yeşilırmak (Green River).

İskele(si) Jetty, dock.

Janissary One of the sultan's elite corps of the fourteenth to eighteenth centuries; *yeniceri* in Turkish. Famous for their devotion to the Bektaşi order, outlandish headgear and marching music.

Kaplıca Developed hot springs, spa.

Kervansaray(ı) Strategically located "hotel", often Selçuk, for pack animals and men on Anatolian trade routes; some overlap with *han*.

Kilim Flat-weave rug without a pile.

Kilise(si) Church.

Konak Large private residence, also the main government building of a province or city; genitive form *konağı*.

Lokanta Restaurant; from Italian *locanda*.

Mağara(sı) Cave.

Mahalle(si) District or neighbourhood of a larger municipality, village or postal area.

Meydan(ı) Public square or plaza.

Meyhane Tavern where alcohol and *meze*-type (see below) food are served together.

Meze Often vegetable-based appetizer, typically fried, puréed and/or marinated.

Miladî The Christian year-numbering system; abbreviated "M." on inscriptions.

Muezzin Man who pronounces call to prayer (*ezan*) from the minaret of a mosque.

Muhtar Village headman.

Muhtarlık The office of the *muhtar*; also designates the status of any community of under 2000.

Namaz The Muslim rite of prayer, performed five times daily.

Nehir (Nehri) River.

Otogar Bus station.

Ova(sı) Plain, plateau.

Ören Alternative term for *harabe*, "ruin"; common village name.

Pansiyon Typical budget to mid-priced accommodation in Turkish resorts.

Ramadan The Muslim month of fasting and prayer; spelt *Ramazan* in Turkish.

Saz Long-necked, fretted stringed instrument central to Turkish folk ballads and Alevî/Bektaşi devotional music.

Selçuk Pertaining to the first Muslim Turkish state based in Anatolia, lasting from the eleventh to the thirteenth centuries.

Sema A dervish ceremony; thus *semahane*, a hall where such ceremonies are conducted.

Şehzade Prince, heir apparent.

Şeyh Head of a Sufi order.

Sufi or dervish an adherent of one of the heterodox mystical branches of Islam. In Turkey the most important sects were the Bektaşi, Mevlevî, Helveti, Nakşibendi, Cerrahi and Kadiri orders.

Sultan valide The Sultan's mother.

Tatil köyü or site(si) Holiday development, usually for Turkish civil servants – not meant for foreign tourists.

Tuğra Monogram or seal of a sultan.

Ulema The corps of Islamic scholars and authorities in Ottoman times.

Vakıf Islamic religious trust or foundation, responsible for social welfare and upkeep of religious buildings.

Vezir The principal Ottoman minister of state, responsible for managing the empire.

Vilayet(i) Formal word for province; also a common term for the provincial headquarters building itself.

Yalı Ornate wooden mansion on the Bosphorus.

Yayla(sı) Pastoral mountain hamlet occupied only in summer; in the Black Sea region, may have rustic accommodation.

Yeni New (common component of Turkish place names).

Architectural/artistic terms

Acropolis Ancient fortified hilltop.

Agora Marketplace and meeting area of an ancient Lycian, Greek or Roman city.

Apse Curved or polygonal recess at the altar end of a church.

Arasta Marketplace built into the foundations of a mosque, a portion of whose revenues goes to the upkeep of the latter.

Bedesten(i) Covered market hall for valuable goods, often lockable.

Bouleuterion Council hall of a Hellenistic or Roman city.

Camekân Changing rooms in a hamam.

Capital Top, often ornamented, of a column.

Cavea Seating curve of an ancient theatre.

Deesis or **Deisis** Portrayal of Christ between the Virgin and John the Baptist.

Diazoma A horizontal walkway dividing the two blocks of seats in an ancient theatre.

Exedra Semicircular niche.

Eyvan Domed side-chamber of an Ottoman religious building; also applies to three-sided alcoves in secular mansions.

Göbek taşı Literally "navel stone" – the hot central platform of a hamam.

Halvet Corner room in a hamam.

Hararet The hottest room of a hamam.

İmaret(i) Soup kitchen and hostel for dervishes and wayfarers, usually attached to a *medrese*.

Kale(si) Castle, fort.

Kapı(sı) Gate, door.

Katholikon Central shrine of a monastery.

Kemer Aqueduct, or a series of vaults/arches.

Khatchkar An ornate relief-carving centred around stylized crosses, on the walls of Armenian churches; also a freestanding cruciform gravestone so carved.

Köşk(ü) Kiosk, pavilion, gazebo, folly.

Kubbe Dome, cupola – as in *Kubbeli Kilise* (the Domed Church).

Kule(si) Tower, turret.

Kurna Hewn stone basin in a hamam.

Külliye(si) A mosque and dependent buildings taken as a whole.

Kümbet Vault, dome; by analogy the cylindrical "hatted" Selçuk tombs of central Anatolia.

Mabet Ancient temple; genitive *mabedi*.

Medrese(si) Islamic theological academy.

Mescit Small mosque with no *mimber*; Islamic equivalent of a chapel; genitive *mescidi*.

Mezar(i) Grave, tomb; thus *mezarlık*, cemetery.

Mihrab Niche in a mosque indicating the direction of Mecca, and prayer.

Mimber Pulpit in a mosque, from where the *imam* delivers homilies; often beautifully carved in wood or stone.

Minare(si) Turkish for "minaret", the tower from which the call to prayer is delivered.

Naos The inner sanctum of an ancient temple.

Narthex Vestibule or entrance hall of a church; also *exonarthex*, the outer vestibule when there is more than one.

Nave Principal lengthwise aisle of a church.

Necropolis Place of burial in an ancient Greek or Roman city.

Nymphaeum Ornate, multistoreyed facade, often with statue niches, surrounding a public fountain in an ancient city.

Odeion Small ancient theatre used for musical performances, minor dramatic productions or civic councils.

Pendentive Curved, triangular surface, by means of which a dome can be supported over a square ground plan.

Pier A mass of supportive masonry.

Porphyry Hard purplish-red volcanic rock containing crystals.

Revetment Facing of stone, marble or tile.

Saray(ı) Palace.

Sebil Public drinking fountain, freestanding or built into the wall of an Ottoman structure.

Selamlık Area where men receive guests in any sort of dwelling.

Serender Wooden, enclosed corn-crib on stilts, particular to the Black Sea; sometimes spelt *serander*.

Son cemaat yeri Literally "Place of the last congregation" – a mosque porch where latecomers pray.

Stoa Colonnaded walkway in an ancient Greek agora.

Synthronon Semicircular seating for clergy, usually in the apse of a Byzantine church.

Şadırvan Ritual ablutions fountain of a mosque.

Şerefe Balcony of a minaret.

Tabhane Hospice for travelling dervishes or *ahi*s, often housed in an *eyvan*.

Tapınak Alternative term for "temple" at archeological sites; genitive *tapınağı*.

Tekke(si) Gathering place of a Sufi order.

Tersane(si) Shipyard, dry-dock.

Transept The "wings" of a church, extending north and south perpendicular to the nave.

Tuff Soft rock formed from volcanic ash.

Türbe(si) Freestanding, usually domed, tomb.

Tympanum The surface, often adorned, enclosed by the top of an arch; found in churches or more ancient ruins.

Verd(e) antique Mottled or veined green serpentine.

Voussoir Stripes of wedge-shaped blocks at the edge of an arch.

Zaviye Mosque built specifically as a hospice for dervishes, usually along a T-plan.

Zhamatoun Chapter (council) hall of an Armenian church.

Acronyms and abbreviations

AK *Adalet ve Kalkınma Partisi* or Justice and Development Party; Islamist movement headed by Recep Tayyip Erdoğan, which has governed with a large majority from 2002 until the present.

Bul Standard abbreviation for *bulvar(ı)* (boulevard).

Cad Standard abbreviation for *cadde(si)* (avenue).

CHP *Cumhuriyetçi Halk Partisi* or Republican People's Party (RPP) – founded by Atatürk, disbanded in 1980, revived in 1992; the main opposition party at present, also controls many municipalities.

KDV Acronym of the Turkish VAT.

MHP *Milliyet Hareket Paritisi* (National Action Party); originally quasi-fascist group, later rebranded by new leader Devlet Bahçeli; now third party in parliament.

NSC National Security Council (*Milli Güvenlik Kurulu*); mixed military-civilian council established after the 1980 coup; despite being the target of AK reforms, still effectively runs Turkey.

PKK *Partia Karkaris Kurdistan* or Kurdish Workers' Party, actually an armed guerrilla movement, formed in 1978 and still present in the southeast.

PTT *Post Telefon ve Telegraf*, the joint postal, telegraph and (formerly) phone service in Turkey, and by extension its offices.

Sok Abbreviation for *sokak* (*sokağı*) or street.

THY *Türk Hava Yolları*, Turkish Airways.

TIR (pronounced "turr" locally) *Transport International Routière* – large, slow trucks, your greatest road hazard.

TL Standard symbol for the Turkish lira.

TRT Acronym of *Türk Radyo ve Televizyon*, the Turkish public broadcasting corporation.

Travel store

Travel

Andorra The Pyrenees, Pyrenees & Andorra Map, Spain

Antigua The Caribbean

Argentina Argentina, Argentina Map, Buenos Aires, South America on a Budget

Aruba The Caribbean

Australia Australia, Australia Map, East Coast Australia, Melbourne, Sydney, Tasmania

Austria Austria, Europe on a Budget, Vienna

Bahamas The Bahamas, The Caribbean

Barbados Barbados DIR, The Caribbean

Belgium Belgium & Luxembourg, Bruges DIR, Brussels, Brussels Map, Europe on a Budget

Belize Belize, Central America on a Budget, Guatemala & Belize Map

Benin West Africa

Bolivia Bolivia, South America on a Budget

Brazil Brazil, Rio, South America on a Budget

British Virgin Islands The Caribbean

Brunei Malaysia, Singapore & Brunei [1 title], Southeast Asia on a Budget

Bulgaria Bulgaria, Europe on a Budget

Burkina Faso West Africa

Cambodia Cambodia, Southeast Asia on a Budget, Vietnam, Laos & Cambodia Map [1 Map]

Cameroon West Africa

Canada Canada, Pacific Northwest, Toronto, Toronto Map, Vancouver

Cape Verde West Africa

Cayman Islands The Caribbean

Chile Chile, Chile Map, South America on a Budget

China Beijing, China, Hong Kong & Macau, Hong Kong & Macau DIR, Shanghai

Colombia South America on a Budget

Costa Rica Central America on a Budget, Costa Rica, Costa Rica & Panama Map

Croatia Croatia, Croatia Map, Europe on a Budget

Cuba Cuba, Cuba Map, The Caribbean, Havana

Cyprus Cyprus, Cyprus Map

Czech Republic The Czech Republic, Czech & Slovak Republics, Europe on a Budget, Prague, Prague DIR, Prague Map

Denmark Copenhagen, Denmark, Europe on a Budget, Scandinavia

Dominica The Caribbean

Dominican Republic Dominican Republic, The Caribbean

Ecuador Ecuador, South America on a Budget

Egypt Egypt, Egypt Map

El Salvador Central America on a Budget

England Britain, Camping in Britain, Devon & Cornwall, Dorset, Hampshire and The Isle of Wight [1 title], England, Europe on a Budget, The Lake District, London, London DIR, London Map, London Mini Guide, Walks In London & Southeast England

Estonia The Baltic States, Europe on a Budget

Fiji Fiji

Finland Europe on a Budget, Finland, Scandinavia

France Brittany & Normandy, Corsica, Corsica Map, The Dordogne & the Lot, Europe on a Budget, France, France Map, Languedoc & Roussillon, The Loire, Paris, Paris DIR, Paris Map, Paris Mini Guide, Provence & the Côte d'Azur, The Pyrenees, Pyrenees & Andorra Map

French Guiana South America on a Budget

Gambia The Gambia, West Africa

Germany Berlin, Berlin Map, Europe on a Budget, Germany, Germany Map

Ghana West Africa

Gibraltar Spain

Greece Athens Map, Crete, Crete Map, Europe on a Budget, Greece, Greece Map, Greek Islands, Ionian Islands

Guadeloupe The Caribbean

Guatemala Central America on a Budget, Guatemala, Guatemala & Belize Map

Guinea West Africa

Guinea-Bissau West Africa

Guyana South America on a Budget

Holland see The Netherlands

Honduras Central America on a Budget

Hungary Budapest, Europe on a Budget, Hungary

Iceland Iceland, Iceland Map

India Goa, India, India Map, Kerala, Rajasthan, Delhi & Agra [1 title], South India, South India Map

Indonesia Bali & Lombok, Southeast Asia on a Budget

Ireland Dublin DIR, Dublin Map, Europe on a Budget, Ireland, Ireland Map

Israel Jerusalem

Italy Europe on a Budget, Florence DIR, Florence & Siena Map, Florence & the best of Tuscany, Italy, The Italian Lakes, Naples & the Amalfi Coast, Rome, Rome DIR, Rome Map, Sardinia, Sicily, Sicily Map, Tuscany & Umbria, Tuscany Map,

Venice, Venice DIR, Venice Map

Jamaica Jamaica, The Caribbean

Japan Japan, Tokyo

Jordan Jordan

Kenya Kenya, Kenya Map

Korea Korea

Laos Laos, Southeast Asia on a Budget, Vietnam, Laos & Cambodia Map [1 Map]

Latvia The Baltic States, Europe on a Budget

Lithuania The Baltic States, Europe on a Budget

Luxembourg Belgium & Luxembourg, Europe on a Budget

Malaysia Malaysia Map, Malaysia, Singapore & Brunei [1 title], Southeast Asia on a Budget

Mali West Africa

Malta Malta & Gozo DIR

Martinique The Caribbean

Mauritania West Africa

Mexico Baja California, Baja California, Cancún & Cozumel DIR, Mexico, Mexico Map, Yucatán, Yucatán Peninsula Map

Monaco France, Provence & the Côte d'Azur

Montenegro Montenegro

Morocco Europe on a Budget, Marrakesh DIR, Marrakesh Map, Morocco, Morocco Map,

Nepal Nepal

Netherlands Amsterdam, Amsterdam DIR, Amsterdam Map, Europe on a Budget, The Netherlands

Netherlands Antilles The Caribbean

New Zealand New Zealand, New Zealand Map

DIR: Rough Guide **DIRECTIONS** for short breaks

Available from all good bookstores

For more information go to www.roughguides.com

When you are travelling,
there are small moments...

Like the first time you observe a wild Brown Bear or the golden bells
a rare Frittilaria Aurea. Like the moment of peace and quiet after a long d
when you are watching the glorious sunset and sipping your coffee ma
with snow-melt water. Or when you are exploring an ancient s
the words of your guide bring the ancient days vividly to life.

These are the moments which turn an ordinary touristic visit into a uniq
travelling experience. Our job is to make sure that you will be in the ri
place at the right time to capture these moments.

Our task is to create unique travelling experiences.

Middle Earth Travel Gaferli Mah. Cevizler Sok. No.20 Goreme / Nevsehi
Tel. +90384 271 25 59 Fax. +90384 271 25 62
www.middleearthtravel.com e-mail. info@middleearthtravel.com

Be inspired.
Turkey & Cephalonia

We're here to provide you with wonderful villas
and boutique hotels in beautiful places, all exclusive to us.
An exceptional service is supported by real attention to detail,
and on your escape we're here to help when you need us –
and leave you alone when you don't.

Exclusive Escapes

Discover so much more online: www.exclusiveescapes.co.uk

Reservations: +44 (0)20 8605 3500

Small print and Index

A Rough Guide to Rough Guides

Published in 1982, the first Rough Guide – to Greece – was a student scheme that became a publishing phenomenon. Mark Ellingham, a recent graduate in English from Bristol University, had been travelling in Greece the previous summer and couldn't find the right guidebook. With a small group of friends he wrote his own guide, combining a highly contemporary, journalistic style with a thoroughly practical approach to travellers' needs.

The immediate success of the book spawned a series that rapidly covered dozens of destinations. And, in addition to impecunious backpackers, Rough Guides soon acquired a much broader and older readership that relished the guides' wit and inquisitiveness as much as their enthusiastic, critical approach and value-for-money ethos.

These days, Rough Guides include recommendations from shoestring to luxury and cover more than 200 destinations around the globe, including almost every country in the Americas and Europe, more than half of Africa and most of Asia and Australasia. Our ever-growing team of authors and photographers is spread all over the world, particularly in Europe, the US and Australia.

In the early 1990s, Rough Guides branched out of travel, with the publication of Rough Guides to World Music, Classical Music and the Internet. All three have become benchmark titles in their fields, spearheading the publication of a wide range of books under the Rough Guide name.

Including the travel series, Rough Guides now number more than 350 titles, covering: phrasebooks, waterproof maps, music guides from Opera to Heavy Metal, reference works as diverse as Conspiracy Theories and Shakespeare, and popular culture books from iPods to Poker. Rough Guides also produce a series of more than 120 World Music CDs in partnership with World Music Network.

Visit www.roughguides.com to see our latest publications.

Rough Guide credits

Text editor: Andy Turner, Amanda Tomlin
Layout: Anita Singh
Cartography: Animesh Pathak
Picture editor: Chloë Roberts
Production: Rebecca Short
Proofreader: Karen Parker
Cover design: Dan May, Chloë Roberts
Photographer: Roger d'Olivere Mapp
Editorial: London Keith Drew, Edward Aves, Alice Park, Lucy White, Jo Kirby, James Smart, Natasha Foges, Róisín Cameron, James Rice, Lara Kavanagh, Emma Traynor, Emma Gibbs, Kathryn Lane, Monica Woods, Mani Ramaswamy, Harry Wilson, Lucy Cowie, Alison Roberts, Joe Staines, Peter Buckley, Matthew Milton, Tracy Hopkins, Ruth Tidball; Delhi Madhavi Singh, Lubna Shaheen
Design & Pictures: London Scott Stickland, Dan May, Diana Jarvis, Mark Thomas, Nicole Newman, Sarah Cummins, Emily Taylor; Delhi Umesh Aggarwal, Ajay Verma, Jessica Subramanian, Ankur Guha, Pradeep Thapliyal, Sachin Tanwar, Nikhil Agarwal, Sachin Gupta

Production: Liz Cherry
Cartography: London Ed Wright, Katie Lloyd-Jones; Delhi Rajesh Chhibber, Ashutosh Bharti, Rajesh Mishra, Jasbir Sandhu, Karobi Gogoi, Alakananda Roy, Swati Handoo, Deshpal Dabas
Online: London Faye Hellon, Jeanette Angell, Fergus Day, Justine Bright, Clare Bryson, Aine Fearon, Adrian Low, Ezgi Celebi; Delhi Amit Verma, Rahul Kumar, Narender Kumar, Ravi Yadav, Debojit Borah, Rakesh Kumar, Ganesh Sharma, Shisir Basumatari
Marketing & Publicity: London Liz Statham, Jess Carter, Vivienne Watton, Anna Paynton, Rachel Sprackett, Laura Vipond; New York Katy Ball, Judi Powers; Delhi Ragini Govind
Reference Director: Andrew Lockett
Operations Assistant: Becky Doyle
Operations Manager: Helen Atkinson
Publishing Director (Travel): Clare Currie
Commercial Manager: Gino Magnotta
Managing Director: John Duhigg

SMALL PRINT

Publishing information

This seventh edition published June 2010 by
Rough Guides Ltd,
80 Strand, London WC2R 0RL
11 Community Centre,
Panchsheel Park,
New Delhi 110017, India

Distributed by the Penguin Group
Penguin Books Ltd,
80 Strand, London WC2R 0RL
Penguin Group (USA)
375 Hudson Street, NY 10014, USA
Penguin Group (Australia)
250 Camberwell Road, Camberwell,
Victoria 3124, Australia
Penguin Group (Canada)
195 Harry Walker Parkway N, Newmarket, ON,
L3Y 7B3 Canada
Penguin Group (NZ)
67 Apollo Drive, Mairangi Bay, Auckland 1310,
New Zealand
Cover concept by Peter Dyer.

Typeset in Bembo and Helvetica to an original design by Henry Iles.

Printed in Europe

© Marc Dubin and Terry Richardson 2010

Maps © Rough Guides

No part of this book may be reproduced in any form without permission from the publisher except for the quotation of brief passages in reviews.

776pp includes index

A catalogue record for this book is available from the British Library

ISBN: 978-1-84836-484-4

The publishers and authors have done their best to ensure the accuracy and currency of all the information in **The Rough Guide to Turkey**, however, they can accept no responsibility for any loss, injury, or inconvenience sustained by any traveller as a result of information or advice contained in the guide.

1 3 5 7 9 8 6 4 2

Help us update

We've gone to a lot of effort to ensure that the seventh edition of **The Rough Guide to Turkey** is accurate and up-to-date. However, things change – places get "discovered", opening hours are notoriously fickle, restaurants and rooms raise prices or lower standards. If you feel we've got it wrong or left something out, we'd like to know, and if you can remember the address, the price, the hours, the phone number, so much the better.

Please send your comments with the subject line "Rough Guide Turkey Update" to @mail @roughguides.com. We'll credit all contributions and send a copy of the next edition (or any other Rough Guide if you prefer) for the very best emails.

Have your questions answered and tell others about your trip at @www.roughguides.com

Acknowledgements

Marc Dubin would like to thank: Andrew Lee and Joan Curgenven of Exclusive Escapes for travel facilities; Erol and Pauline Şalvarlı in Bezirgan; Muzaffer Otlu and Anne Louise Thomson (for 17 years now) at Patara; Pınar and Engin in Çıralı; Clare Baker in Dalyan; Phil Buckley, Tevfik Serin and staff at Bougainville in Kaş; Alison Hawkes for the lowdown on Göcek; Melahat in Tlos; Eric Goossens in Kocadere for encyclopedic knowledge of Gallipoli; and Sevan in Şirince for helpful pointers.

Terry Richardson would like to thank: Ismail, Zehra and family for their continued hospitality in Van; Ahmet and Aydin in Hakkari for the same; Pete and Darryl for the ride around Lake Van and an insight into the crazy world of twitching; the welcoming Firuze and family at Surp Giargos in Diyarbakır and Luca Belis for the lift to Nemrut; Ayhan at Mor Barsaumo church in Midyat; Nuri Kino for patiently answering all my queries; Bulent and the incorrigible Ingiliz Kemal in Malatya; Sufi-inspired Tony Smith for his views on

the same city; Klaus Schmidt for kindly showing me the incredible Göbekli Tepe; Hakan, Erkan, Tahsin and Middle Earth Travel for invaluable assistance in İstanbul. I also owe debts to my co-author Marc Dubin and to Andy Turner for his understanding editing. Finally, thanks to the lovely Lem for keeping me sane.

Katie Parla would like to thank: Susan Walsh, Ali Bey, Ibrahim Agartan, Aziz Ozmen, Elvan Ozbay, Ruth Lockwood, Cem Ural, Dervis Dural, Ismail Keremoglu and Geert Van Wolvelaer.

Tristan Rutherford and Kathryn Tomasetti would like to thank: Ilginay Göbüt, Mine Kasapoğlu and the indefatigable Jonathan Lewis in İstanbul; Dominic Whiting in Alaçatı; Liezel dela Isla Alemany, Jesús Alemany and Michael Furniss for the in-depth dining knowledge; and Jesús for the inside story on Fernando Alonso at İstanbul's F1 racetrack. Regards also to Jessica and Chris Wood, we'll make Beşiktaş fans of you yet!

Readers' letters

Thanks to all the readers who have taken the time to write in with comments and suggestions (and apologies if we've inadvertently omitted or misspelt anyone's name):

Phil Andre, Nils Bal, Louise Barbeau, Adam Berg, Richard Bloomsdale, Madelon Boeye, Archie Bowman, Patrick Breslin, Stephen Bugno, Serena Chong, Simon Cowper, Runa Gravensteen,

Geoff Kelsall, Kristian Kemp, Joanna Lyons, Heather Penstone, William Pollard, Paul Redman, Clifford & Maryke Roberts, Laura Slade, Dave Tootell, Nigel Watt.

Photo credits

All photos © Rough Guides except the following:

Introduction
Cappadocian landscape © Frank Krahmer/ Corbis
Temple of Apollo, Side © Slow Images/Getty
İznik tiles, Topkapı Palace © Frank van den Bergh/iStock
İstanbul sunrise © James Strachan/Corbis
Fairy chimneys, Cappadocia © svetico/iStock
Boy with Turkish flag © Fatih Saribas/Corbis
Stork's nest © blickwinkel/Alamy
Lycian ruins, Kekova © ZeynepOzturk/iStock
Summit of Mount Barla © Terry Richardson
Camel, Cappadocia © Richard Hamilton Smith/Corbis

Things not to miss
01 Roman theatre at Aspendos © Marco Simoni/ Corbis
02 Head of Zeus, Nemrut Dağı © Terry Richardson
03 Statue near Lone Pine Cemetery, Gallipoli © Marc Dubin
04 Museum of Anatolian Civilizations, Ankara © Adam Woolfitt/Corbis

05 Acropolis of ancient Pergamon © Marc Dubin
06 Hot-air ballooning, Cappadocia © George Steinmetz/Corbis
07 Ani Ruins © Marc Dubin
08 Byzantine frescoes, Karanlık Kilise, Göreme © Ivan Vdovin/Corbis
09 Selimiye Camii, Edirne © Gian Berto Vanni/ Corbis
10 Gulet boats, Gulf of Gökova © Camille Moirenc/Corbis
11 Sunrise over Aya Sofya, İstanbul © Travelpix Ltd/Getty
12 Lighthouse at Gelidonyu Burnu, Lycian Way © Jane Fownes/Alamy
13 Hittite ruins, Hattuşa © Oriol Alamany/Corbis
14 Orthodox monastery of Sumela © Jane Sweeney/Corbis
15 Oil wrestling at Kırkpınar Festival © Jeffrey L Rotman/Corbis
16 Patara beach © BMPix/iStock
17 Library of Celsus, Ephesus © Grafton Smith/ Corbis
20 Sultan Isa Medresesi, Mardin © Terry Richardson

21 Cağaloğlu Hamam © Gavin Hellier/Corbis
22 Trekking in the Kaçkar Dağları © Images & Stories/Alamy
23 Woman preparing Gözleme © David Lefranc/Corbis
24 Outdoor restaurant, Sultanahmet, İstanbul © Gavin Hellier/Corbis
25 Window with hanging corn, Safranbolou © ecevit /iStock
26 Lake Van © Terry Richardson
27 Whirling dervish performance in İstanbul © Massimo Borchi/Corbis
28 İşak Paşa Sarayı at sunset © Marc Dozier/Corbis
29 Georgian church of Yeni Rabat © Marc Dubin
30 Mosaic, Gaziantep Archeological Museum © Terry Richardson

Outdoor adventure colour section
Hot-air ballooning, Cappadocia © Scott Stulberg/Corbis
Trekkers in the Çandır Gorge, St Paul Trail © Terry Richardson
Climbing Mount Resko © Images&Stories/Alamy
Rafting the Köprülü canyon © Images&Stories/Alamy
Wreck diving near Kaş © WaterFrame/Alamy
Canyoning in Lycia © exodus.co.uk
Skiing in Kartalkaya © Images&Stories/Alamy
Paragliders above Ölüdeniz © Chris Rout/Alamy

Food and drink colour section
Fish seller at Galata bridge, İstanbul © Dave G. Houser/Corbis
Vineyards in Cappadocia © Simon Gurney/iStock
Helva © Photolibrary.com

Black and whites
p.165 Selimiye Camii, Erdine © Marc Dubin
p.185 Muradiye tomb, Bursa © Marc Dubin
p.194 Artemis Temple, Sardis © Marc Dubin
p.217 Ayvalık © Sumbul/iStock
p.234 Ruins of Heracleia at Lake Bafa © Images & Stories/Alamy
p.243 Alsancak quarter, İzmir © Danita Delimont/Alamy

p.260 Şirince village © syagci/iStock
p.279 Bodrum castle © Zeynep Mufti/iStock
p.303 Pamukkale terraces © Pferd/iStock
p.310 Lycian ruins near Kekova © Images & Stories/Alamy
p.321 Kaya Köyü abandoned village © Marc Dubin
p.333 Kaunos ruins near Dalyan © NBoyd/Alamy
p.356 Kaş harbour © BMPix/iStock
p.375 Çiralı beach © kaptnali/iStock
p.380 Theatre at Termessos © syagci/iStock
p.387 Yivli Minare, Antalya © Ozgurdonmaz/iStock
p.400 Temple of Apollo, Side © Bogdb/iStock
p.428 Antakya Mosaic Museum © Bayram TUNÇ/iStock
p.436 Fairy chimney rock formations, Cappadocia © PEDRE/iStock
p.446 Lake Eğirdir © Sean Burke/Alamy
p.456 Mevlana Museum and Mausoleum © syagci /iStock
p.476 Ortahisar, Cappadocia © EmmePi Travel/Alamy
p.498 Hittite carvings, Hattuşa © Alamy
p.510 Atatürk shrine © Ugur Demir/iStock
p.523 Safranbolu © Tulay Over/iStock
p.539 Çifte Minare Medrese, Sivas © Alamy
p.544 Boats at Amasra harbour © Images & Stories/Alamy
p.562 Christ fresco at Aya Sofya, Trabzon © Marc Dubin
p.570 Hemşinli women in Ayder village © Giuglio Gil/Hemis.fr
p.578 Georgian church of Öşk Vank © Marc Dubin
p.586 Çifte Minareli Medrese, Erzurum © Jon Arnold Images/Alamy
p.596 Kackar mountain scenery © Images&Stories/Alamy
p.616 Sultan Isa Medresesi, Mardin © klenger/iStock
p.639 Pilgrims in Diyarbakır © Terry Richardson
p.653 Hasankeyf ruins © 1001nights/iStock
p.656 Mount Ararat © Terry Richardson
p.670 Aktamar Church © Terry Richardson

Index

Map entries are in colour.

NOTES

Map symbols

maps are listed in the full index using coloured text

-----	International boundary		⚲	Skiing
----	Chapter boundary		♜	Castle
▬▬▬	Motorway		⚱	Church (regional maps)
▪ ▪ ▪	Motorway under construction		⚲	Monastery
══	Major road		✡	Synagogue
══	Minor road		☪	Mosque
▓▓▓	Pedestrianized road		🏛	Monument
──	Unpaved road		⊙	Statue
⊪⊪⊪	Steps		⚠	Campsite
⁚⁚⁚⁚	Tunnel		♦	Point of interest
------	Path		◉	Accommodation
▬·▬·	Railway		▣	Restaurant/café
⊪⊪⊪⊪	Funicular railway		♟	Museum
──	Tramway		(i)	Tourist office
-----	Metro line		✉	Post office
– – –	Ferry route		@	Internet access
──	Waterway		⊞	Hospital
────	Wall		🏊	Swimming pool
✈	Airport		⚓	Boat
⌃⌃	Mountain range		★	Bus stop
▲	Mountain peak		Ⓜ	Metro stop
⁓⁓⁓	Cliffs		Ⓣ	Tram stop
⁓⁓	Gorge		🄿	Parking
⁓⁓⁓	Hill shading		⊠	Gate
∴	Ruins		▬	Building
⌂	Cave		✚	Church (town maps)
⚶	Spa		⬭	Stadium
⚲	Waterfall		▦	Park
⚲	Lighthouse		▦ Ⓑ	Beach
⌣	Pass		▦	Muslim cemetery
⚲	Marshland		▦	Christian cemetery

775

So now we've told you about the things not to miss, the best places to stay, the top restaurants, the liveliest bars and the most spectacular sights, it only seems fair to tell you about the best travel insurance around

WorldNomads.com
keep travelling safely

Recommended by Rough Guides